S0-AET-710

Competency 7: Assess Individuals, Families, Groups, Organizations, and Communities. Social workers

- collect and organize data, and apply critical thinking to interpret information from clients and constituencies;
- apply knowledge of human behavior and the social environment, person-in-environment, and other multidisciplinary theoretical frameworks in the analysis of assessment data from clients and constituencies;
- develop mutually agreed-on intervention goals and objectives based on the critical assessment of strengths, needs, and challenges within clients and constituencies; and
- select appropriate intervention strategies based on the assessment, research knowledge, and values and preferences of clients and constituencies.

Competency 8: Intervene with Individuals, Families, Groups, Organizations, and Communities. Social workers

- critically choose and implement interventions to achieve practice goals and enhance capacities of clients and constituencies;
- apply knowledge of human behavior and the social environment, person-in-environment, and other multidisciplinary theoretical frameworks in interventions with clients and constituencies;
- use interprofessional collaboration as appropriate to achieve beneficial practice outcomes;
- negotiate, mediate, and advocate with and on behalf of diverse clients and constituencies; and
- facilitate effective transitions and endings that advance mutually agreed-on goals.

Competency 9: Evaluate Practice with Individuals, Families, Groups, Organizations, and Communities. Social workers

- select and use appropriate methods for evaluation of outcomes;
- apply knowledge of human behavior and the social environment, person-in-environment, and other multidisciplinary theoretical frameworks in the evaluation of outcomes;
- critically analyze, monitor, and evaluate intervention and program processes and outcomes; and
- apply evaluation findings to improve practice effectiveness at the micro, mezzo, and macro levels.

Dimensions of Human Behavior: The Changing Life Course and Social Work Core Competencies

Chapter	Ethical and Professional Behavior	Engage Diversity and Difference	Human Rights and Justice	Research and Practice	Policy Practice	Social Work Engagement	Assessment	Intervention	Evaluation
1	√	√	√	√	√	√	√	√	√
2	√	√	√	√	√	√	√	√	
3		√	√	√	√	√		√	√
4		√	√	√	√	√	√	√	
5	√	√		√	√	√	√	√	
6	√	√	√	√	√	√	√	√	
7		√	√	√	√		√	√	√
8		√	√	√		√	√	√	
9		√	√	√	√	√	√	√	√
10	√	√	√	√	√	√	√	√	√
Total Chapters	5	10	9	10	9	10	10	10	5

To all the teachers and students who have inspired me to think more critically about human behavior.
They are always in my head and heart as I continue to learn about the fascinating subject of human behavior.

Sara Miller McCune founded SAGE Publishing in 1965 to support the dissemination of usable knowledge and educate a global community. SAGE publishes more than 1000 journals and over 800 new books each year, spanning a wide range of subject areas. Our growing selection of library products includes archives, data, case studies and video. SAGE remains majority owned by our founder and after her lifetime will become owned by a charitable trust that secures the company's continued independence.

Los Angeles | London | New Delhi | Singapore | Washington DC | Melbourne

Dimensions of Human Behavior

The Changing Life Course

Sixth Edition

Elizabeth D. Hutchison
Virginia Commonwealth University, Emerita
and Contributors

Los Angeles | London | New Delhi
Singapore | Washington DC | Melbourne

FOR INFORMATION:

SAGE Publications, Inc.
2455 Teller Road
Thousand Oaks, California 91320
E-mail: order@sagepub.com

SAGE Publications Ltd.
1 Oliver's Yard
55 City Road
London EC1Y 1SP
United Kingdom

SAGE Publications India Pvt. Ltd.
B 1/I 1 Mohan Cooperative Industrial Area
Mathura Road, New Delhi 110 044
India

SAGE Publications Asia-Pacific Pte. Ltd.
3 Church Street
#10-04 Samsung Hub
Singapore 049483

Acquisitions Editor: Joshua Perigo
Editorial Assistant: Noelle Cumberbatch
Production Editor: Tracy Buyan
Copy Editor: Mark Bast
Typesetter: C&M Digitals (P) Ltd.
Proofreader: Rae-Ann Goodwin
Indexer: Molly Hall
Cover Designer: Scott Van Atta
Marketing Manager: Jenna Retana

Copyright © 2019 by SAGE Publications, Inc.

All rights reserved. No part of this book may be reproduced or utilized in any form or by any means, electronic or mechanical, including photocopying, recording, or by any information storage and retrieval system, without permission in writing from the publisher.

Printed in the United States of America

Library of Congress Cataloging-in-Publication Data

Names: Hutchison, Elizabeth D.

Title: Dimensions of human behavior : the changing life course / Elizabeth D. Hutchison, Virginia Commonwealth University, Emerita, and contributors.

Description: Sixth edition. | Thousand Oaks, California : SAGE, [2019] | Includes bibliographical references and index.

Identifiers: LCCN 2018021374 | ISBN 9781544339344 (pbk. : alk. paper)

Subjects: LCSH: Social psychology. | Human behavior. | Life cycle, Human. | Social service.

Classification: LCC HM1033 .D553 2019 | DDC 302—dc23
LC record available at https://lccn.loc.gov/2018021374

This book is printed on acid-free paper.

SUSTAINABLE FORESTRY INITIATIVE
Certified Chain of Custody
Promoting Sustainable Forestry
www.sfiprogram.org
SFI-01268

SFI label applies to the text stock

18 19 20 21 22 10 9 8 7 6 5 4 3 2 1

• Brief Contents •

• Detailed Contents •

• Case Studies •

• Preface •

like many people, my life has been full of change since the first edition of this book was published in 1999. After a merger/acquisition, my husband took a new position in Washington, DC, and we moved to the nation's capital from Richmond, Virginia, where we had lived for 13 years. I changed my teaching affiliation from the Richmond campus of the Virginia Commonwealth University School of Social Work to the satellite program in northern Virginia. While I worked on the second edition of the book in 2002, my mother-in-law, for whom my husband and I had served as primary caregivers, began a fast decline and died rather quickly. A year later, my mother had a stroke, and my father died a month after that. Shortly after, our son relocated from Pennsylvania to North Carolina, and our daughter entered graduate school. In 2005, we celebrated the marriage of our daughter. After the third edition was published, we welcomed a first grandchild, my husband started an encore career in California, and our son was married. In the year I worked on the fourth edition, I retired from teaching and joined my husband in California, we welcomed a second grandchild, and my mother's health went into steep decline and she died. That was a year of great change in our family. After the fourth edition, my son moved back to Massachusetts and now lives in the neighborhood where we lived when he was a toddler. He and his wife are raising their own young daughter there, and when we visit them, I am reminded that sometimes the life course takes us in circles. Just as the fifth edition went to press, my husband and I sold our home in California and moved to Reno, Nevada, where we live 5 minutes from my daughter's family and 40 minutes from beautiful Lake Tahoe. With this move, we have been able to participate actively in the lives of two of our grandchildren. These events and transitions have all had an impact on my life course as well as the life journeys of my extended family.

But change has not been confined to my multigenerational family. Since the first edition of the book was published, we had a presidential election for which the outcome stayed in limbo for weeks. The economy has peaked, declined, revitalized, and then gone into the deepest recession since the Great Depression in the 1930s. It is strong again, for now. Also since the first edition, terrorists hijacked airplanes and forced them to be flown into the twin towers of the World Trade Center in New York City and into the Pentagon near my school. The United States entered military conflicts in Afghanistan and Iraq, and the one in Afghanistan continues to be waged at this writing, the longest war in U.S. history. Thirty-three students at Virginia Tech died in a mass murder/suicide rampage that shook the campus on a beautiful spring day, and a number of school shootings have broken our collective hearts, including the recent shooting at Marjory Stoneham Douglas High School in Florida. Natural disasters have killed and traumatized millions around the world, and the climate is becoming increasingly unstable. New communication technologies continue to be developed at a fast clip, increasing our global interdependence and changing our behavior in ways both good and bad. The United States elected, and then reelected, its first African American president, but our government has been locked in an increasingly polarized philosophical division, made worse by foreign interference in a presidential election and increasingly hostile interactions on social media.

Since I was a child listening to my grandmother's stories about the challenges, joys, and dramatic as well as mundane events in her life, I have been captivated by people's stories. I have learned that a specific event can be understood only in the context of an ongoing life story. As social workers you will hear many life stories, and I encourage you to remember that each person you meet is on a journey that is much more than your encounters might suggest. I also encourage you to think about your own life story and how it helps and hinders your ability to really see and hear the stories of others.

Organized around life course time, this book tries to help you understand, among other things, the relationship between time and human behavior. The companion volume to this book, *Person and Environment*, analyzes relevant dimensions of person and environment and presents up-to-date reports on theory and research about each of these dimensions. This volume shows how these multiple dimensions of person and environment work together with dimensions of time to produce patterns in unique life course journeys.

Life Course Perspective

As in the second, third, fourth, and fifth editions, my colleagues and I have chosen a life course perspective to capture the dynamic, changing nature of person–environment transactions. In the life course perspective, human behavior is not a linear march through time, nor is it simply played out in recurring cycles. Rather, the life course journey is a moving spiral, with both continuity and change, marked by both predictable and unpredictable twists and turns. It is influenced by changes in the physical and social environment as well as by changes in the personal biological, psychological, and spiritual dimensions.

The life course perspective recognizes *patterns* in human behavior related to biological age, psychological age, and social age norms. In the first edition, we discussed theory and research about six age-graded periods of the life course, presenting both the continuity and the change in these patterns. Because mass longevity is leading to finer distinctions among life phases, nine age-graded periods were discussed in the second through fifth editions and are again covered in this sixth edition. The life course perspective also recognizes *diversity* in the life course related to historical time, gender and gender identity, race and ethnicity, social class, sexual orientation, ability/disability, and so forth, and we emphasize group-based diversity in our discussion of age-graded periods. Finally, the life course perspective recognizes the *unique life stories* of individuals—the unique configuration of specific life events and person–environment transactions over time.

General Knowledge and Unique Situations

The social and behavioral sciences help us to understand *general patterns* in person–environment transactions over time. The purpose of social work assessment is to understand *unique configurations* of person and environment dimensions at a given time. Those who practice social work must interweave what they know about unique situations with general knowledge that comes from theory and empirical research. To assist you in this process, as we did in the first five editions, we begin each chapter with three stories, which we then intertwine with contemporary theory and research. Most of the stories are composite cases and do not correspond to actual people known to the authors. In this sixth edition, we continue to expand on our efforts in the last five editions to call more attention to the successes and failures of theory and research to accommodate human diversity related to gender and gender identity, race and ethnicity, culture, sexual orientation, disability, and so on. We continue to extend our attention to diversity by being intentional in our effort to provide a global context to understand the human life course.

In this sixth edition, we continue to use some special features that we hope will aid your learning process. We have added learning objectives to each chapter. As in the first five editions, key terms are presented in bold type in the chapters and defined in the glossary. As in the fourth and fifth editions, critical thinking questions are used throughout the chapters to help you think critically about the material you are reading. Active learning exercises and web resources are presented at the end of each chapter.

The bulk of this sixth edition will be familiar to instructors who used the fifth edition of *Dimensions of Human Behavior: The Changing Life Course*. Many of the changes that do occur came at the suggestion of instructors and students who have been using the fifth edition. To respond to the rapidity of changes in complex societies, all chapters have been comprehensively updated. As the contributing authors and I worked to revise the book, we were once again surprised to learn how much the knowledge base had changed since we worked on the fifth edition. We did not experience such major change between the first four editions, and this led us to agree with the futurists who say we are at a point where the rate of cultural change will continue to accelerate rapidly. You will want to use the many wonders of the World Wide Web to update information you suspect is outdated.

Also New in This Edition

The more substantial revisions for this edition include the following:

- Learning objectives have been added to each chapter.
- Consistency with Council on Social Work Education (CSWE) curriculum guidelines is emphasized in Chapter 1.

- Coverage of advances in neuroscience continues to expand.

- More content on traumatic stress appears throughout the book.

- Content on the impact of information, communication, and medical technologies on human behavior in every phase of life is greatly expanded.

- Coverage of the global context of human behavior continues to expand.

- More content has been added on the effects of gender and gender identity, race and ethnicity, social class, sexual orientation, and disability on life course trajectories.

- New content on gender identity and expression was added to several chapters.

- New exhibits have been added and others updated.

- Some new case studies have been added to reflect contemporary issues.

- Web resources have been updated.

Digital Resources

⑤SAGE edge™

edge.sagepub.com/hutchisonclc6e

SAGE edge offers a robust online environment featuring an impressive array of tools and resources for review, study, and further exploration, keeping both instructors and students on the cutting edge of teaching and learning. SAGE edge content is open access and available on demand. Learning and teaching has never been easier!

Instructor Teaching Site

SAGE edge for instructors supports teaching by making it easy to integrate quality content and create a rich learning environment for students.

- **Test banks** provide a diverse range of prewritten options as well as the opportunity to edit any question and/or insert your own personalized questions to effectively assess students' progress and understanding.

- Editable chapter-specific **PowerPoint®** **slides** offer complete flexibility for creating a multimedia presentation for one's course.

- Exclusive access to full-text **SAGE journal articles** that have been carefully selected support and expand on the concepts presented in each chapter.

- **Multimedia content** including audio and video resources are available for use in independent or classroom-based explorations of key topics.

- **Class activities** for individual or group projects reinforce active learning.

- **Course cartridges** allow for easy LMS integration.

Student Study Site

SAGE edge for students provides a personalized approach to help students accomplish their coursework goals in an easy-to-use learning environment.

- Mobile-friendly **eFlashcards** strengthen understanding of key terms and concepts.

- Mobile-friendly **practice quizzes** allow for independent assessment by students of their mastery of course material.

- **Learning objectives** reinforce the most important material.

- Exclusive access to full-text **SAGE journal articles** that have been carefully selected support and expand on the concepts presented in each chapter.

One Last Word

I hope that reading this book helps you understand how people change from conception to death and why different people react to the same situations in different ways. I also hope that you will gain a greater appreciation for the ongoing life stories in which specific events are embedded. In addition, when you finish reading this book, I hope that you will have new ideas about how to reduce risk and increase protective factors during different age-graded periods and how to help clients find meaning and purpose in their own life stories. I also hope you will have new ideas about the implications of scientific knowledge about human behavior across the life course for social work engagement, assessment, intervention, and evaluation.

You can help me in my learning process by letting me know what you liked or didn't like about the book. Sometimes communications from student readers have led to additions to the book.

—Elizabeth D. Hutchison
Reno, Nevada
ehutch@vcu.edu

• Acknowledgments •

A project like this book is never completed without the support and assistance of many people. A sixth edition stands on the back of the first five editions, and over the years, a large number of people have helped me keep this project going. I am grateful to all of them, some of them known to me and others working behind the scenes in a way not visible to me.

Steve Rutter, former publisher and president of Pine Forge Press, shepherded every step of the first edition and provided ideas for many of the best features of the second edition that are carried forward in this book. Along with Paul O'Connell, Becky Smith, and Maria Zuniga, he helped to refine the outline for the second edition, and that outline continues to be used, in large part, in this sixth edition. I am especially grateful to Becky Smith, who worked with me as developmental editor for the first two editions. She taught me so much about writing and readers, and I often find myself thinking *How would Becky present this?* Kassie Graves provided disciplined and creative editorial assistance from 2006 to 2016, for the third, fourth, and fifth editions of this book, and she became a dear friend.

The contributing authors and I are grateful for the assistance Dr. Maria E. Zuniga offered during the drafting of the second edition. She provided many valuable suggestions on how to improve the coverage of cultural diversity in each chapter. Her suggestions improved the second edition immensely and have stayed with us as lasting lessons about human behavior in a multicultural society.

I am grateful once again to work with a fine group of contributing authors. They were gracious about timelines and incorporating feedback from reviewers. Most important, they were committed to providing a state-of-the-art knowledge base for understanding human behavior across the life course. I am also grateful to collaborators who have provided rich case studies for Chapters 5, 7, and 8.

We were lucky to be working again with the folks at SAGE. Joshua Perigo came aboard as I worked to turn months of research and writing into what you see in this book. He came with prior experience in working with professors who use the book and with an organized view of what is helpful to instructors and students. He has consistently been responsive to my questions and concerns. How lucky I am to be working with Mark Bast as copy editor again. He is a delight to work with, catches my errors, and makes the words flow better. I would work with him forever. I am grateful to have Tracy Buyan join the project as production editor; she is the person who turns words and ideas into a gorgeous book. Thanks also to Alexandra Randall who has provided editorial assistance with a number of tasks. Many more people have worked behind the scenes to help us complete this project. I wish I could thank them by name. I love the folks at SAGE.

I am grateful to my former faculty colleagues at Virginia Commonwealth University (VCU) who set a high standard for scientific inquiry and teaching excellence. They also provided love and encouragement through both good and hard times. My conversations about the human behavior curriculum with colleagues Rosemary Farmer, Stephen Gilson, Marcia Harrigan, Holly Matto, Mary Secret, and Joe Walsh over many years have stimulated much thinking and resulted in many ideas found in this book.

My students over 30 years also deserve a special note of gratitude. They taught me all the time, and many things I learned in interaction with them show up in the pages of this book. They also provided a great deal of joy to my life journey, and I continue to enjoy keeping up with many of them on social media. Those moments when I learn of former students doing informed, creative, and humane social work are special moments, indeed, and I am happy to say there are many such moments. Three former students are chapter authors, and two former students have contributed case studies for this edition. I have also enjoyed receiving e-mails from students from other universities who are using the book and have found their insights to be very helpful.

My deepest gratitude goes to my husband, Hutch. Since the first edition of this book was published, we have weathered several challenging years and experienced many celebratory moments. He is constantly patient and supportive and often technically useful.

But, more important, he makes sure that I take time for fun and celebration. What a joy it has been to travel over three fourths of my life journey with him.

Finally, I am enormously grateful to a host of reviewers who thoughtfully evaluated the fifth edition and provided very useful feedback about how to improve on it. Their ideas were very helpful in framing our work on this sixth edition:

Carla Mueller
Lindenwood University

Julie Altman
California State University, Monterey Bay

Roger Delgado
California State University, Los Angeles

Rose Perz
Fordham University

Tracy Marschall
University of Indianapolis

Abbie Frost
Simmons College

Alexandra Crampton
Marquette University

Curtis Proctor
Millersville University

Dan Knapp
Aurora University

Debra Norris
University of South Dakota

Gabriela Novotna
University of Regina

E. Gail Horton
Florida Atlantic University

Ilze Earner
Hunter College, City University of New York

John McTighe
Ramapo College of New Jersey

Marissa Happ
Aurora University

Rosalind Corbett
San Diego State University

Annalease Gibson
Albany State University

Terri Lewinson
Georgia State University

Sonja Harry
Winston-Salem State University

A Life Course Perspective

Elizabeth D. Hutchison

Learning Objectives

1.1 Compare one's own emotional and cognitive reactions to three case studies.

1.2 Summarize the relevance of the life course perspective for social work competencies.

1.3 Identify some of the theoretical roots of the life course perspective.

1.4 Summarize five basic concepts of the life course perspective (cohorts, transitions, trajectories, life events, and turning points).

1.5 Critique six major themes of the life course perspective (interplay of human lives and historical time, timing of lives, linked or interdependent lives, human agency in making choices, diversity in life course trajectories, and risk and protection).

1.6 Evaluate the strengths and limitations of the life course perspective.

1.7 Recognize where themes of the life course perspective are consistent with eight other major theoretical perspectives on human behavior.

1.8 Apply basic concepts and major themes of the life course perspective to recommend guidelines for social work engagement, assessment, intervention, and evaluation.

CASE STUDY 1.1

THE SUAREZ FAMILY AFTER SEPTEMBER 11, 2001

Maria is a busy, active 19-year-old whose life was changed by the events of September 11, 2001. Her mother, Emma Suarez, worked at the World Trade Center and did not survive the attack.

Emma was born in Puerto Rico and came to the mainland to live in the South Bronx when she was 5, along with her parents, a younger brother, two sisters, and an older brother. Emma's father, Carlos, worked hard to make a living for his family, sometimes working as many as three jobs at once. After the children were all in school, Emma's mother, Rosa, began to work as a domestic worker in the homes of a few wealthy families in Manhattan.

Emma was a strong student from her first days in public school and was often at the top of her class. Her younger brother, Juan, and the sister closest to her in age, Carmen, also were good students, but they were never the star pupils that Emma was. The elder brother, Jesus, and sister, Aida, struggled in school from the time they came to the South Bronx, and both dropped out before they finished high school. Jesus returned to Puerto Rico to live on the farm with his grandparents but has recently moved back to the South Bronx now that both grandparents have died.

During her summer vacations from high school, Emma often cared for the children of some of the families for whom her mother worked. One employer was particularly impressed with Emma's quickness and pleasant temperament and took a special interest in her. She encouraged Emma to apply to colleges during her senior year in high school. Emma was accepted at City College and was planning to begin as a full-time student after high school graduation.

A month before Emma was to start school, however, her father had a stroke and was unable to return to work. Rosa and Aida rearranged their work schedules so that they could share the care of Carlos. Carmen had a husband and two young children of her own. Emma realized that she was now needed as an income earner. She took a position doing data entry in an office in the World Trade Center and took evening courses part-time. She was studying to be a teacher, because she loved learning and wanted to pass on that love to other students.

And then Emma found herself pregnant. She knew that Alejandro Padilla, a young man in one of her classes at school, was the father. Alejandro said that he was not ready to marry, however. Emma returned to work a month after Maria was born, but she did not return to school. At first, Rosa and Aida were not happy that Emma was pregnant with no plans to marry, but once Maria was born, they fell hopelessly in love with her. They were

happy to share the care of Maria, along with Carlos, while Emma worked. Emma cared for Maria and Carlos in the evenings so that Rosa and Aida could work.

Maria was, indeed, an engaging baby, and she was thriving with the adoration of Rosa, Carlos, Aida, Juan, and Emma. Emma missed school, but she held on to her dreams to be a teacher someday.

On the morning of September 11, 2001, Emma left early for work at her job on the 84th floor of the south tower of the World Trade Center, because she was nearing a deadline on a big project. Aida was bathing Carlos when Carmen called about a plane hitting the World Trade Center. Aida called Emma's number but did not get through to her.

The next few days, even weeks, are a blur to the Suarez family. Juan, Carmen, and Aida took turns going to the Family Assistance Center, but there was no news about Emma. At one point, because Juan was worried about Rosa, he brought her to the Red Cross Disaster Counseling Center where they met with a social worker who was specially trained for working in disaster situations. Rosa seemed to be near collapse.

Juan, Rosa, and Aida all missed a lot of work for a number of weeks, and the cash flow sometimes became problematic. They were blessed with the generosity of their Catholic parish, employers, neighbors, and a large extended family, however, and financial worries were not their greatest concerns at that time. They struggled to understand the horrific thing that happened to Emma, and although she didn't understand what had happened, Maria was aware of a great sadness in the household for several years. Emma's remains were never identified, but the Catholic parish helped the family plan a memorial service.

Maria is lucky to have such a close, loving family, and they have tried to give her a good life. She continues to live with Aida and Rosa while she attends City College. Juan has married and has two young children now, living around the corner from Aida and Rosa. Carlos died in 2011, 10 days before the 10-year anniversary of the 9/11 attacks. Carmen and her family also live nearby, and Maria has become close friends with Carmen's two daughters. She also has a special relationship with Carmen, who reminds her of the pictures she has seen of her mother.

Maria is a good student and is meeting her dream of studying to be a teacher. She loves to hear stories about the mother she can't remember, and one of Rosa's favorite stories is about how smart Emma was and what a great teacher she would have been. On Maria's 13th birthday, Rosa gave her the necklace that had been Emma's 13th birthday gift, and Maria wears it every day. Growing up in the Bronx, Maria has seen many television images of those airplane attacks at the World Trade Center. She was disturbed, however, by all the media coverage at the time of the 10th anniversary of the attack. She began to think a lot about what her mother might have suffered before her death, and she had nightmares for several nights. She built a small memorial to her mother in the backyard and goes there to talk with her mother when she is feeling particularly sad or when good things happen.

After Hurricane Maria hit Puerto Rico in September 2017, Maria had a taste of what her family had gone through after the airplanes struck the World Trade Center. It was weeks before they learned the whereabouts of all their relatives still living in Puerto Rico, and Maria thought she saw a reactivation of traumatic stress in her grandmother and Aunt Aida. Some of their relatives lost their homes and moved in with other relatives, and the future is still uncertain for most of them. A social worker doing disaster relief must be aware of the large impact that disasters have on the multigenerational family, both in the present and for years to come.

CASE STUDY 1.2

MICHAEL BOWLING, SWALLOWING HIS PRIDE

Michael Bowling always thought that if you are willing to work hard, you will never need public assistance. He realizes now that he made judgments about other people's lives without really knowing much about them. And he is convinced that his very life depends on getting some public assistance. Here is his story.

Michael grew up in a small town in Missouri, the oldest of five children. His parents were White hardworking factory workers who had grown up in the midst of the Great Depression. His dad had to turn down a college scholarship to work odd jobs to help scrape together enough to feed the family. Michael's parents were determined to give their children an easier time, and though it was never easy, at least Michael and his siblings never went to bed hungry. They always felt loved, and their parents had high hopes for their children's futures.

Michael started working 20 hours a week when he was 16 to help his parents pay a hospital bill for one of his younger brothers. When he graduated from high school, he joined the U.S. Army, hoping that might provide some financial security for him and his family. He stayed in the U.S. Army for 4 years and then returned to his hometown. He soon found that there were no good jobs there for him, and he decided to move to a nearby college town to begin to study for a college degree. He found a low-paying job for 30 hours per week, so it took him 7 years to earn his engineering degree.

When he graduated from college, he married the woman he had been dating and found an engineering job in a larger city. The marriage lasted for 7 years, there were no children, and the divorce was friendly. The career went well, and Michael moved up the ranks in small and moderate-size firms. He was able to buy a small house. He never married again, but he has been very close to a younger sister who lives in the same city, and he became a kind of substitute dad to her son and daughter after her husband left the family. His parents lived long enough to see him doing well and took pride in his success. Both parents died at a relatively young age, however, his dad of a stroke at age 55 and his mother of breast cancer at age 58, after moving in with Michael and using hospice care during her final 5 months.

At the age of 50, Michael got his dream job in a very large engineering firm. Life was good! Then the firm hit hard times, and as one of the last hired, Michael was one of the first to be laid off. He had some savings, so he could make his mortgage payments and put food on the table. He cut where he could, things like his gym membership and cable television, but held on to the car and cell phone because he would need them for the job search. He put out 10 resumes a day and made two cold calls per day. He felt lucky when he found temporary jobs, but these projects never lasted long, and they never offered health insurance. For the first 2 years after he was laid off, he bought a very expensive individual health insurance policy, but as his savings diminished, he dropped the policy.

Then one morning, when he was only 55 years old, Michael awoke with a severe headache, numbness in the right side of his face, and weakness in his right arm and leg. Because of his earlier experience with his father's stroke, Michael recognized these symptoms as warning signs of a stroke. He also knew that it was imperative that he get immediate medical care; he called 911 and was taken to the comprehensive hospital a few blocks from his home. Over the next 2 years, Michael used all his savings and took a second mortgage on his house to pay his hospital and rehabilitation bills. He was lucky that his stroke was not as serious as the one that had killed his dad, that

(Continued)

(Continued)

he knew to get immediate help, and he has made a good recovery. The only remaining noticeable symptom is some left-sided weakness, particularly when he is tired. As he recovered from the stroke, he resumed the job search but, to date, has only found one very short-term project. His two brothers have helped him out a little, when they realized that he was choosing between buying food or his medication to prevent another stroke. But Michael knows that his brothers struggle financially, and he finally realized that he had to swallow his pride and apply for SNAP (food stamps) and energy assistance, which he did in early 2014. At the same time, he signed up for health insurance through the Affordable Care Act's federal marketplace.

He is sad that he is not able to help send his niece and nephew to college as he had expected to do, but he is still very involved in their lives. Michael is grateful to have survived his stroke, and he says that one bright spot is that he has begun a daily meditation practice, which he finds spiritually, emotionally, and physically beneficial. He credits this practice for helping him to stay calm in the midst of the stresses in his life, and he adds that it has helped him develop better understanding of himself and his life journey. It has also helped him to pay attention to what is happening in his body. He attends a stroke recovery support group at the rehabilitation center and has developed some close friendships in the group.

CASE STUDY 1.3
PHOUNG LE, SERVING FAMILY AND COMMUNITY

Le Thi Phoung, or Phoung Le as she is officially known in the United States, grew up in Saigon, South Vietnam, in the midst of war and upheaval. She has some fond memories of her first few years when Saigon was beautiful and peaceful. She loves to remember riding on her father's shoulders down the streets of Saigon on a warm day and shopping with her grandmother in the herb shops. But she also has chilling memories of the military presence on the streets, the devastation caused by war, and the persistent fear that pervaded her home.

Phoung was married when she was 17 to a man chosen by her father. She smiles when she recounts the story of her future groom and his family coming to visit with the lacquered boxes full of betrothal gifts of nuts, teas, cake, and fruit. She admits that, at the time, she was not eager to marry and wondered why her father was doing this to her. But she is quick to add that her father made a wise choice, and her husband Hien is her best friend and is, as his name suggests, "nice, kind, and gentle." Their first child, a son, was born just before Phoung's 20th birthday, and Phoung reveled in being a mother.

Unfortunately, on Phoung's 20th birthday, April 30, 1975, life in Saigon turned horrific; that is the day the North Vietnamese army overran Saigon. For Phoung and Hien, as well as for most people living in South Vietnam, just surviving became a daily struggle. Both Phoung's father and her father-in-law were in the South Vietnamese military, and both were imprisoned by the Viet Cong for a few years. Both managed to escape and moved their families around until they were able to plan an escape from Vietnam by boat. Family members got separated during the escape, and others were lost when pirates attacked their boats. Phoung's father and one brother have never been heard from since the pirate attack.

Phoung and Hien and their son spent more than 2 years in a refugee camp in Thailand before being resettled in Southern California. Their second child, a daughter, was born in the camp, and a second daughter was born 1 year after they resettled in California. Over time, other family members were able to join them in the large Vietnamese community where they live. Phoung's and Hien's opportunities for education were limited during the war years, but both came from families who valued education, and both managed to receive several years of schooling. Luckily, because they were living in a large Vietnamese community, language did not serve as a major barrier to employment in the United States. Phoung found a job working evenings as a waitress at a restaurant in Little Saigon, and Hien worked two jobs, by day as a dishwasher in a restaurant and by night cleaning office buildings in Little Saigon. Phoung's mother lived with Phoung and Hien and watched after the children while Phoung and Hien worked. Hien's parents lived a few blocks away, and several siblings and cousins of both Phoung and Hien were in the neighborhood. The Vietnamese community provided much social support and cultural connection. Phoung loved taking the children to visit the shops in Little Saigon and found special pleasure in visiting the herb shops where the old men sat around and spoke animatedly in Vietnamese.

Phoung grieved the loss of her beloved father and brother, but she wanted to create a positive life for her children. She was happy that she was able to stay connected to her cultural roots and happy that her children lived in a neighborhood where they did not feel like outsiders. But she also wanted her children to be able to be successful outside the Vietnamese community as well as a resource for the community. She was determined that her children would have the education that she and Hien had been denied. Although she could have gotten by well in her neighborhood without English, she studied English along with her children because she wanted to model for the children how to live a bilingual, bicultural life. She was pleased that the children did well in school and was not surprised at how quickly the older two adapted to life in their adopted country. Sometimes there was tension in the multigenerational family about how the children were acculturating, and Phoung often served as the mediator in these tensions. She understood the desire of the older generation to keep cultural traditions, and she herself loved traditions such as the celebration of the Chinese New Year, with the colorful dresses and the little red lai-see envelopes of good-luck money that were given to the children. She wanted her children to have these traditional experiences. But she also was tuned in to the children's desire to be connected with some aspects of the dominant culture, such as the music and other popular media. She was also aware of how hard it was for the family elders to enforce the traditional family hierarchy when they depended on younger family members to help them navigate life in the English-speaking world outside their cultural enclave.

When her children reached adolescence, Phoung herself was uncomfortable with the Western cultural ideal for adolescent independence from the family, but she found ways to give her children some space while also holding them close and keeping them connected to their cultural roots. Other mothers in the neighborhood began to seek her advice about how to handle the challenging adolescent years. When her own adolescent children began to be impatient with the pervasive sadness they saw in their grandparents, Phoung suggested that they do some oral history with their grandparents.

This turned out to be a therapeutic experience for all involved. The grandparents were able to sift through their lives in Vietnam and the years since, give voice to all that had been lost, but also begin to recognize the strength it took to survive and their good fortune to be able to live among family and a community where much was familiar. The grandchildren were able to hear a part of their family narrative that they did not know because the family had preferred not to talk about it. Phoung was so pleased with this outcome that she asked to start a program of intergenerational dialogue at the Vietnamese Community Service Center. She thought this might be one way to begin to heal the trauma in her community while also giving the younger generation a strong cultural identity as they struggled to live in a multicultural world. She continues to be an active force in that program, even though her own children are grown.

Their 40s and early 50s brought both great sorrow and great joy to Phoung and Hien. Within a 2-year period, Phoung's mother and Hien's mother and father died. Phoung and Hien became the family elders. They provided both economic and emotional support during times of family crisis, such as a sibling's cancer, a niece's untimely pregnancy, and a nephew's involvement with a neighborhood gang. But there was also great joy. Phoung was very good at her job and became the supervisor of the wait staff at the best restaurant in Little Saigon. Hien was able to buy his own herb shop. After attending the local community college, the children were all able to go on to university and do well. Their son became an engineer, the older daughter became a physician, and the younger daughter recently finished law school. Their son is now father to two young children, and Phoung finds great joy in being a grandmother. She is playing an important role in keeping the grandchildren connected to some Vietnamese traditions. Phoung finds this phase of life to be a time of balance in all areas of her life, and she is surprised and pleased to find renewed interest in spiritual growth through her Buddhist practices.

Social workers working with refugee families must be aware of the conditions that led these families to flee their home countries as well as the adjustments they have made upon resettlement.

THE LIFE COURSE PERSPECTIVE AND SOCIAL WORK PRACTICE

One thing the stories of the Suarez family, Michael Bowling, and Phoung Le have in common is that they unfolded over time, across multiple generations. We all have stories that unfold as we progress through life. A useful way to understand this relationship between time and human behavior is the **life course perspective**, which looks at how biological, psychological, and social factors act independently, cumulatively, and interactively to shape people's lives from conception to death, and across generations. It attempts to explain how humans change and stay the same as they make their journey from conception to death. It also examines how cultures and social institutions shape the patterns of individual and family lives. Time, as well as characteristics of the person and the environment in which the person lives, all play a large part in human behavior (see Exhibit 1.1). It is common and sensible to try to understand a person by looking at the way that person has developed throughout different periods of life and in different environments.

You could think of the life course as a path. But note that it is not a straight path; it is a path with both continuities and twists and turns. Certainly, we see twists and turns in the life stories of Emma Suarez, Michael Bowling, and Phoung Le. If you want to understand a person's life, you might begin with an **event history**, or the sequence of significant events, experiences, and transitions in a person's life from conception to death. For young Maria Suarez, the events of September 11, 2001, will become a permanent part of her life story, even though she has no memory of that day. She looks forward to the time when she will realize her mother's dream of becoming a teacher. Hurricane Maria has become another important part of the event history of her family. An event history for Michael Bowling might include joining the army, college graduation, wedding, divorce, buying a house, deaths of his mother and father, dream job at age 50, and stroke at age 55. Phoung Le's event history would

most likely include military presence in the streets, getting married, becoming a mother, escaping from Saigon, time spent in a refugee camp, resettlement in California, family loss, and promotion at work.

You might also try to understand a person in terms of how that person's life has been synchronized with family members' lives across time. Maria Suarez's, Michael Bowling's, and Phoung Le's stories are thoroughly entwined with those of their multigenerational families.

Finally, you might view the life course in terms of how culture and social institutions shape the pattern of individual lives. Maria Suarez's life course was changed forever by culture-related geopolitical conflict. The economic and health care institutions are playing a central role in Michael Bowling's life in late midlife. Phoung Le lives biculturally and has taught her children to do that as well.

This book and its companion volume *Dimensions of Human Behavior: Person and Environment* provide ways for you to think about the nature and complexities of the people and situations at the center of social work practice. To begin to do that, we must first clarify the purpose of social work and the approach it takes to individual and collective human behavior. This was laid out in the 2015 Educational Policy and Accreditation Standards of the Council on Social Work Education:

EXHIBIT 1.1 ● Person, Environment, and Time Dimensions

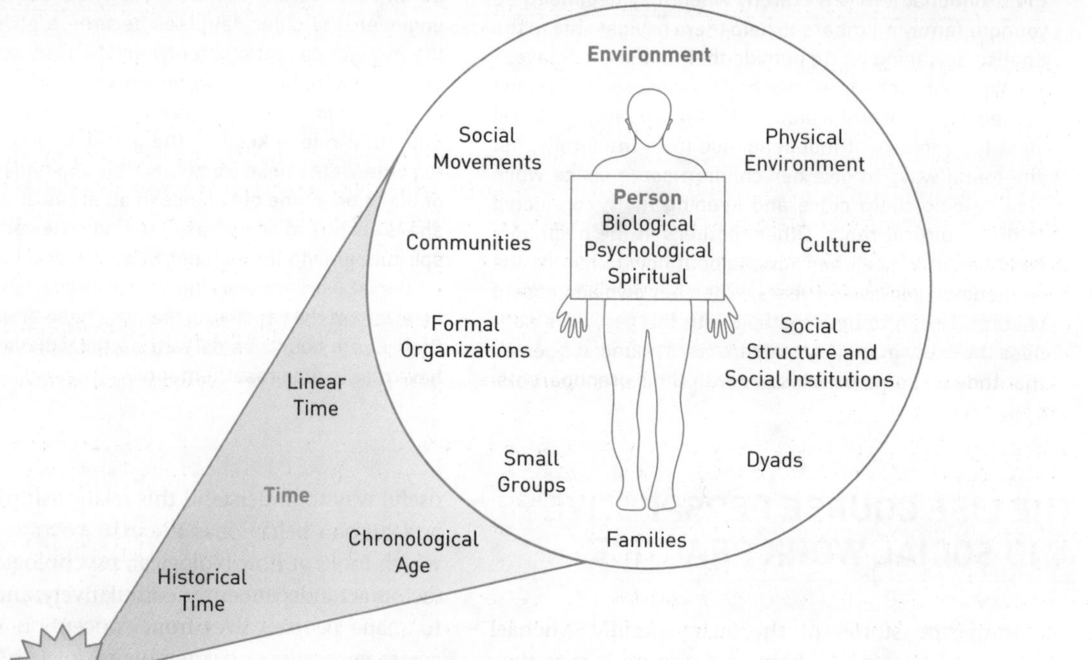

The purpose of the social work profession is to promote human and community well-being. Guided by a person and environment construct, a global perspective, respect for human diversity, and knowledge based on scientific inquiry, the purpose of social work is actualized through its quest for social and economic justice, the prevention of conditions that limit human rights, the elimination of poverty, and the enhancement of the quality of life for all persons. (Council on Social Work Education, 2015, p. 1)

Let's put that statement in some historical context. In 1952, at the annual meeting of the American Association of Schools of Social Work, a forerunner of the Council on Social Work Education, the presenters of a workshop titled "Who Should Teach What in Human Growth and Development" opened the workshop with this statement: "Knowledge and understanding of human behavior is considered an indispensable base for social work education and all of social work" (Social Welfare History Archives, 1952). That made sense in 1952, and it makes sense today. At the time of the workshop, human growth and behavior (HG&B) was identified as essential content

for the education of social workers. After the formation of the Council on Social Work Education (CSWE) in 1952 and the National Association of Social Workers (NASW) in 1955, the first working definition of social work was drafted in 1958. In that definition, Harriet Bartlett linked the person-in-environment perspective on human behavior to the definition of social work (Kondrat, 2008). As you can see in CSWE's 2015 Educational Policy and Accreditation Standards, six decades later social work professional organizations continue to use the person-in-environment—or person and environment—construct to describe the profession's approach to understanding human behavior. Different subjects and different theories have been considered essential to knowledge of person and environment at different times, but the person-in-environment perspective has been a signature feature of the social work profession. The life course perspective is a relatively recent attempt to understand how people and environments influence each other and change over time. It is an important theoretical perspective for developing several social work competencies as outlined in the 2015 CSWE Educational Policy Statement and presented in abbreviated form in Exhibit 1.2. One of the reasons it is such an important theoretical perspective is that it has

---

EXHIBIT 1.2 ● Summary of Social Work Competencies Supported by the Life Course Perspective

Competency 2: Engage Diversity and Difference in Practice

"Social workers understand how diversity and difference characterize and shape the human experience and are critical to the formation of identity."

Relevance of the life course perspective (LCP): Diversity of life course trajectories is one of the major themes of the LCP.

Competency 4: Engage in Practice-Informed Research and Research-Informed Practice

"Social workers understand that evidence that informs practice derives from multi-disciplinary sources and multiple ways of knowing."

Relevance of the LCP: The LCP has been supported by research across a large number of disciplines, using different research methodologies, including both quantitative and qualitative research.

Competency 5: Engage in Policy Practice

"Social workers recognize and understand the historical, social, cultural, economic, organizational, environmental, and global influences that affect social policy."

Relevance of the LCP: Interplay of human lives and historical time is one of the major themes of the LCP, and life course scholars engage in study of how policy varies across historical times. Linked lives is another major theme of the LCP, and some life course researchers examine the link between public policy and life course trajectories.

Competency 6: Engage with Individuals, Families, Groups, Organizations, and Communities

"Social workers understand theories of human behavior and the social environment, and critically evaluate and apply this knowledge to facilitate engagement with clients and constituencies, including individuals, families, groups, organizations, and communities."

Relevance of the LCP: The LCP incorporates other theories of human behavior, and life course researchers have applied life course concepts to the study of families and other social groups as well as to individuals. Three important themes of the life course perspective—timing of lives, diversity in life course trajectories, and human agency—are particularly useful for engaging diverse individuals and social groups.

(Continued)

EXHIBIT 1.2 ● (Continued)

Competency 7: Assess Individuals, Families, Groups, Organizations, and Communities

"Social workers understand theories of human behavior and the social environment, and critically evaluate and apply this knowledge in the assessment of diverse clients and constituencies, including individuals, families, groups, organizations, and communities."

Relevance of the LCP: The LCP, with its emphasis on timing of lives and developmental risk and protection, is particularly strong in guiding assessment with individuals and families. Its emphasis on linked lives provides guidance for assessing groups, organizations, and communities.

Competency 8: Intervene with Individuals, Families, Groups, Organizations, and Communities

"Social workers understand theories of human behavior and the social environment, and critically evaluate and apply this knowledge to effectively intervene with clients and constituencies."

Relevance of the LCP: Guidelines for social work intervention can be extrapolated from all six LCP themes: interplay of human lives and historical time, timing of lives, linked lives, human agency in making choices, diversity in life course trajectories, and developmental risk and protection.

Competency 9: Evaluate Practice with Individuals, Families, Groups, Organizations, and Communities

"Social workers understand theories of human behavior and the social environment, and critically evaluate and apply this knowledge in evaluating outcomes."

Relevance of the LCP: The LCP has strong research support that can be helpful in evaluating practice outcomes.

© Kristy-Anne Glubish/Design Pics/Corbis

PHOTO 1.1 The life course perspective emphasizes ways in which humans are interdependent and gives special emphasis to the family as the primary arena for experiencing the world.

been supported by a growing body of multidisciplinary research as you will see in the ensuing discussion in this and all other chapters of the book.

Social workers also have a well-defined value base to guide their efforts to promote individual and community well-being. Six core values of the profession have been set out in a preamble to the Code of Ethics established by the National Association for Social Workers (NASW) in 1996 and revised in 2017 (NASW, 2017). These values are service, social justice, dignity and worth of the person, importance of human relationships, integrity, and competence. Throughout the chapters of this book, the contributing authors and I provide suggestions about needed social work services and how to provide those services in an ethical and trustworthy manner. We take social work's commitment to social justice seriously, and social justice issues are highlighted in every chapter. The life course perspective that forms the basis of this book puts equal value on individual agency and human connectedness; therefore, it serves as a good framework for social work's commitments to both the dignity and worth of the person as well as the importance of human relationships. The contributing authors and I draw on the best available evidence about the life course to assist you to develop and enhance expertise in working with people of all life stages. The analysis of the life course perspective presented in this book supports the development of the remaining two social work competencies identified by the 2015 CSWE Educational Policy Statement:

- Competency 1: Demonstrate Ethical and Professional Behavior: "Social workers understand the value base of the profession and its ethical standards."

- Competency 3: Advance Human Rights and Social, and Economic, and Environmental Justice: "Social workers understand the global interconnections of oppression and human rights violations, and are knowledgeable about theories of human need."

THEORETICAL ROOTS OF THE LIFE COURSE PERSPECTIVE

The life course perspective (LCP) is a theoretical model that has emerged over the last 50 years, across several disciplines. Sociologists, anthropologists, social historians, demographers, epidemiologists, and psychologists—working independently and, more recently, collaboratively—have all helped to give it shape. The ideas have been developed from multidisciplinary theory and research.

Glen Elder Jr., a sociologist, was one of the early authors to write about a life course perspective, and his work is still foundational to the ongoing development of the perspective. In the early 1960s, he began to analyze data from three pioneering longitudinal studies of children that had been undertaken by the University of California, Berkeley. As he examined several decades of data, he was struck with the enormous impact of the Great Depression of the 1930s on individual and family pathways (Elder, 1974). He began to call for developmental theory and research that looked at the influence of historical forces on family, education, and work roles.

At about the same time, social history emerged as a serious field. Social historians were particularly interested in retrieving the experiences of ordinary people, from their own vantage point, rather than telling the historical story from the vantage point of wealthy and powerful persons. Tamara Hareven (1978, 1982a, 1996, 2000) played a key role in developing the subdiscipline of the history of the family.

As will become clearer later in the chapter, the life course perspective also draws on traditional theories of developmental psychology, which look at the events that typically occur in people's lives during different stages. The life course perspective differs from these psychological theories in one very important way, however. Developmental psychology looks for universal, predictable events and pathways, but the life course perspective calls attention to how historical time, social location, and culture affect the individual experience of each life stage. A primary contribution of the life course perspective is its focus on the life course as a whole, how what happens in one period of a person's life is connected to what happens in other periods of that person's life. For example, it calls attention to the ways in which what happens in adolescence is influenced by what happened in childhood and also influences the long period of adulthood (Johnson, Crosnoe, & Elder, 2011).

The life course perspective is still relatively young, but its popularity has grown across a broad range of disciplines (Alwin, 2012). In recent years, it has begun to be used to understand the pathways of families (Min, Silverstein, & Lendon, 2012), organizations (King, 2009), and social movements (Della Porta & Diani, 2006). I suggest that it has potential for understanding patterns of stability and change in all types of social systems. Gerontologists increasingly use the perspective to understand how old age is shaped by events experienced earlier in life (Seabrook & Avison, 2012), but it has also become an increasingly popular perspective for considering adolescent and young-adult transitions, such as the transition to high school (Benner, 2011) and the transition to motherhood

(Umberson, Pudrovska, & Reczek, 2010). The life course perspective has become a major theoretical framework in criminology (Chen, 2009; Prior, 2013) and the leading perspective driving longitudinal study of physical and mental health behaviors and outcomes (Bauldry, Shanahan, Boardman, Miech, & Macmillan, 2012; Evans, Crogan, Belyea, & Coon, 2009). It has also been proposed as a useful perspective for understanding patterns of lifetime drug use (Hser, Longshore, & Anglin, 2007; Lindström, Modén, & Rosvall, 2013).

CRITICAL THINKING QUESTIONS 1.1

Think of your own life path. How straight has your path been? What continuities can you identify? What, if any, twists and turns have been a part of your life journey?

BASIC CONCEPTS OF THE LIFE COURSE PERSPECTIVE

Scholars who write from a life course perspective and social workers who apply the life course perspective in their work rely on a handful of staple concepts: cohorts, transitions, trajectories, life events, and turning points (see Exhibit 1.3 for concise definitions). As you read about each concept, imagine how it applies to the lives of Maria Suarez, Michael Bowling, and Phoung Le as well as to your own life.

Cohorts

As noted, Glen Elder Jr.'s observation that historical, sociocultural forces have an impact on individual and family pathways was a major inspiration for development of the life course perspective. With their attention to the historical context of developmental pathways,

life course scholars have found the concept of cohort to be very useful. In the life course perspective, a **cohort** is a group of persons born during the same time period who experience particular social changes within a given culture in the same sequence and at approximately the same age. *Generation* is another term used to convey a similar meaning. Generation is usually used to refer to a period of about 20 years, but a cohort may be shorter than that, and life course scholars often make a distinction between the two terms, suggesting that a birth cohort becomes a generation only when it develops some shared sense of its social history and a shared identity (see Alwin, McCammon, & Hofer, 2006).

Cohorts differ in size, and these differences affect opportunities for education, work, and family life. For example, the baby boom that followed World War II (1946 to 1964) in the United States produced a large cohort. When this large cohort entered the labor force, surplus labor drove wages down and unemployment up (Pearlin & Skaff, 1996; Uhlenberg, 1996). Recently, researchers have been interested in the Millennial generation, born from 1980 to the late 1990s, a generation that has now surpassed baby boomers as the largest demographic group in the United States. They have been found to have more student loan debt, poverty, and unemployment when compared to the previous two generations at the same age, and it is not yet clear how these circumstances will affect the long-term trajectories of their lives (Drake, 2014).

Some observers suggest that cohorts develop strategies for the special circumstances they face (Newman, 2008). They suggest that "boomers"—the large cohort born from 1946 to 1964—responded to the economic challenges of their demographic bubble by delaying or avoiding marriage, postponing childbearing, having fewer children, and increasing the presence of mothers in the labor force. However, one study found that large cohorts in affluent countries have higher rates of suicide than smaller cohorts, suggesting that not all members of large cohorts can find

EXHIBIT 1.3 ● Basic Concepts of the Life Course Perspective

Cohort: Group of persons born during the same time period who experience particular social changes within a given culture in the same sequence and at the same age

Transition: Change in roles and statuses that represents a distinct departure from prior roles and statuses

Trajectory: Relatively stable long-term processes and patterns of events, involving multiple transitions

Life event: Significant occurrence in a person's life that may produce serious and long-lasting effects

Turning point: Life event or transition that produces a lasting shift in the life course trajectory

positive strategies for coping with competition for limited resources (Stockard & O'Brien, 2002). Other researchers have been interested in the adaptations of Generation X— born from 1965 to 1979—and the Millennial generation. Gen Xers grew up with fewer siblings and experienced higher rates of parental divorce than the boomers. They have been less likely than earlier generations to marry (Carlson, 2009). The Millennial generation is more ethnically diverse than previous cohorts and grew up in a time of great technological innovation. They have been found to be more tolerant of diversity and more media-connected than earlier cohorts (Fry, Igielnik, & Patten, 2018).

One way to visualize the configuration of cohorts in a given society is by using a **population pyramid**, a chart that depicts the proportion of the population in each age group. As Exhibit 1.4 demonstrates, different regions of the world have significantly different population pyramids. The first pyramid shows the age distribution in the United States, one of the Global North countries that has both low birth rates and low death rates. The populations are getting older in these societies, with a declining youthful population. These countries are becoming increasingly dependent on immigration (typically more attractive to young adults) for a workforce and taxpayers to support the aging population. It is predicted that 82% of the projected U.S. population increase from 2005 to 2050 will be

the result of immigration (Passel & Cohn, 2008). Despite the economic necessity of immigrants in societies with aging populations, in the United States, as in many other affluent countries, there are strong anti-immigrant sentiments and angry calls to close the borders.

The second pyramid in Exhibit 1.4 shows the age distribution for Uganda, one of the less affluent Global South countries that have high birth rates and shorter life expectancy, leading to a situation in which the majority of people are young. In these countries, young people tend to overwhelm labor markets and education systems, and national standards of living decline. Some of these countries, such as the Philippines, have developed policies that encourage out-migration, whereas other countries, such as China, have developed policies to limit fertility.

Exhibit 1.4 also shows the ratio of males to females in each population (women are represented on the left of each pyramid and men on the right). A cohort's **sex ratio** is the number of males per 100 females. Sex ratios affect a cohort's marriage rates, childbearing practices, crime rates, and family stability. Although there are many challenges to getting reliable sex ratio data, it is estimated that there are 105 males born for every 100 females in the world (Central Intelligence Agency, 2017). However, several countries have a sex ratio at birth of more than 110 males per 100 females. It is

EXHIBIT 1.4 ● Population Pyramids for United States and Uganda

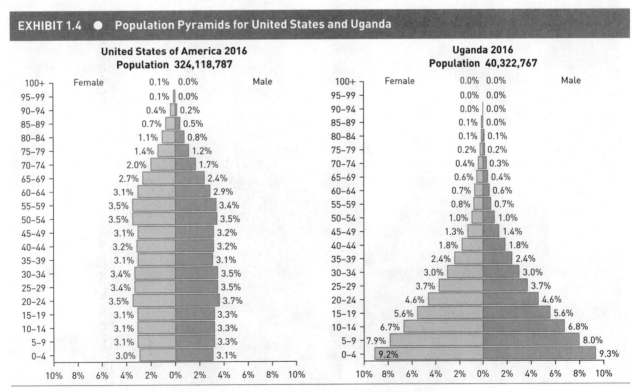

Source: United Nations, Department of Economic and Social Affairs Population Division (2016).

thought that high sex ratios at birth represent a kind of sex discrimination in some countries, where it might be attributed to sex-selected abortion and infanticide. As you can see in Exhibit 1.4, sex ratios decline across adulthood because males die at higher rates at every age. Sex ratios can be further unbalanced by war (which leads to greater male mortality) or death at childbirth (which leads to greater female mortality) or to high rates of either male or female out-migration or in-migration.

Transitions

A life course perspective is stagelike because it proposes that each person experiences a number of **transitions**, or changes in roles and statuses that represent a distinct departure from prior roles and statuses (Torres & Young, 2016). Life is full of such transitions: starting school, entering puberty, leaving school, getting a first job, leaving home, migrating, retiring, and so on. Leaving the military, marrying and divorcing, and rehabilitation from a stroke were important transitions for Michael Bowling. Phoung Le has experienced a number of transitions, including the beginning of war, becoming a mother, escaping, moving to a refugee camp,

and resettling in California. A transition is a process of gradual change that usually involves acquiring or relinquishing roles, but it can be any change in status, such as change in health status (Barban, 2013) or citizenship status (Torres & Young, 2016). A transition can produce both stress and opportunity (Benner, 2011).

Many transitions relate to family life: marriages, births, divorces, remarriages, deaths. Each transition changes family statuses and roles and generally is accompanied by family members' exits and entrances. We can see the dramatic effects of birth and death on the Suarez family as Maria entered and Emma exited the family circle. Health professionals have recently used the life course perspective, the concept of transitions in particular, to understand role changes that occur in family caregiving of older adults (Carpentier, Bernard, Grenier, & Guberman, 2010; Evans et al., 2009). The concept of transitions is also increasingly used to study the migration/immigration process (Gong, Xu, Fujishiro, & Takeuchi, 2011).

Transitions in collectivities other than the family, such as small groups, communities, and formal organizations, also involve exits and entrances of members as well as changes in statuses and roles. In college, for

PHOTO 1.2 The life course is full of transitions in roles and statuses; graduation from college or university is an important life transition that opens opportunities for future statuses and roles.

© ComStock/ThinkStock

example, students pass through in a steady stream. Some of them make the transition from undergraduate to graduate student, and in that new status they may take on the new role of teaching or research assistant.

Trajectories

Each life course transition is embedded in a trajectory that gives form to the life course (Alwin, 2012). They are entry points to a new life phase. In contrast with transitions, **trajectories** involve relatively stable long-term processes and patterns of life, involving multiple transitions (Ruark et al., 2016). For example, you may look forward to graduating from your program of social work study. Graduation is a transition, but it is a transition embedded in a career trajectory that will probably involve a number of other transitions along the way, such as a licensing exam, job changes, promotions, and perhaps periods of discontent or burnout. At some point, you may look back on your career path and see patterns that at the moment you can't anticipate. Trajectories are best understood in the rearview mirror. We do not necessarily expect trajectories to be a straight line, but we do expect them to have some continuity of direction. Hser et al. (2007) recommend the life course perspective for understanding drug use trajectories (or careers) that may include onset of use, acceleration of use, regular use, cessation of use, and relapse. Treatment may or may not be included in this trajectory.

Because individuals and families live in multiple spheres, their lives are made up of multiple, intertwined trajectories—such as educational trajectories, family life trajectories, health trajectories, and work trajectories (Leong, Eggerth, & Flynn, 2014). These strands are woven together to form a life story. The interlocking trajectories of a life course can be presented visually on separate lifeline charts or as a single lifeline. See Exhibit 1.5 for instructions on completing a lifeline of interlocking trajectories.

Life Events

Specific events predominate in the stories of Maria Suarez, Michael Bowling, and Phoung Le: terrorist attack, a stroke, escape from the homeland. A **life event** is a significant occurrence in a person's life that may produce serious and long-lasting effects. The term refers to the happening itself and not to the transitions that occur because of the happening. For example, loss of a spouse is a relatively common life event in all societies. The death of the spouse is the life event, but it precipitates a transition that involves changes in roles and statuses. When we reflect on our own lives, most of us can quickly recall one or more major life events that had long-lasting impact.

One common method for evaluating the effect of life events is the use of a life events rating scale such as Thomas Holmes and Richard Rahe's Schedule of Recent Events, also called the Social Readjustment Rating Scale (Holmes, 1978; Holmes & Rahe, 1967). The Schedule of Recent Events, along with the rating of the stress associated with each event, appears in Exhibit 1.6. Holmes and Rahe constructed their schedule of events by asking respondents to rate the relative degree of adjustment required for different life events.

Inventories like the Schedule of Recent Events can remind us of some of the life events that affect human behavior and life course trajectories, but they also have limitations:

> Life events inventories are not finely tuned. One suggestion is to classify life events along several dimensions: major versus minor, anticipated versus unanticipated, controllable versus uncontrollable, typical versus atypical, desirable versus undesirable, acute versus chronic. (Settersten & Mayer, 1997, p. 246)

Most existing inventories are biased toward undesirable, rather than desirable, events. Not all life events prompt harmful life changes. Indeed, researchers have begun to distinguish between positive and negative life events and to measure their different impacts on human behavior. For example, one research team explored the impact of recalled positive and negative life events on

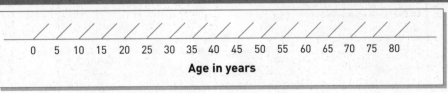

EXHIBIT 1.5 ● My Lifeline (Interlocking Trajectories)

0 5 10 15 20 25 30 35 40 45 50 55 60 65 70 75 80

Age in years

Assuming that you live until at least 80 years of age, chart how you think your life course trajectory will look. Write major events and transitions of your lifeline—you may want to write family events and transitions in one color, educational events and transitions in another, occupational events and transitions in another, and health events and transitions in another.

EXHIBIT 1.6 ● Life Change Events From the Holmes and Rahe Schedule of Recent Events

Life Event	Stress Rating	Life Event	Stress Rating
Death of a spouse	100	Wife beginning or ceasing work outside the home	26
Divorce	73	Taking out a mortgage or loan for a lesser purchase (e.g., a car, TV, freezer)	26
Marital separation from mate	65		
Detention in jail or other institution	63	Major change in sleeping habits (a lot more or a lot less sleep, or change in part of day when asleep)	25
Death of a close family member	63		
Major personal injury or illness	53	Major change in number of family get-togethers (e.g., a lot more or a lot less than usual)	24
Marriage	50		
Being fired at work	47	Major change in eating habits (a lot less food intake or very different meal hours or surroundings)	23
Marital reconciliation with mate	45		
Retirement from work	45		
Major change in the health or behavior of a family member	44	Vacation	20
		Christmas	20
Pregnancy	40	Minor violations of the law (e.g., traffic tickets, jaywalking, disturbing the peace)	20
Sexual difficulties	39		
Gaining a new family member (e.g., through birth, adoption, elder moving in)	39		
Major business readjustment (e.g., merger, reorganization, bankruptcy)	39	Beginning or ceasing formal schooling	19
Major change in financial state (a lot worse off or a lot better off than usual)	38	Major change in living conditions (e.g., building a new home, remodeling, deterioration of home or neighborhood)	19
Death of a close friend	37		
Changing to a different line of work	36	Revision of personal habits (e.g., dress, manners, associations)	18
Major change in the number of arguments with spouse (more or less)	35		
Taking out a mortgage or loan for a major purchase	31	Trouble with the boss	17
		Major change in working hours or conditions	16
Foreclosure on a mortgage or loan	30	Change in residence	15
Major change in responsibilities at work (e.g., promotion, demotion, lateral transfer)	29	Major change in usual type and/or amount of recreation	13
		Major change in church activities (e.g., a lot more or a lot less than usual)	12
Son or daughter leaving home	29		
Trouble with in-laws	29	Major change in social activities (e.g., clubs, dancing, movies, visiting)	11
Outstanding personal achievement	28	Change to a new school	5

Source: Holmes, T. H., & Rahe, R. H. (1967). The social readjustment rating scale. *Journal of Psychosomatic Research, 11*(2), 213–218.

the psychological well-being of adolescents and found that the impact of recalled events varies by personality type (Garcia & Siddiqui, 2009). Another research team investigated how positive and negative life events trigger weight loss and weight gain, finding that weight loss is more associated with positive life events and weight gain with negative life events (Ogden, Stavrinaki, & Stubbs, 2009). And another research team examined the impact of positive and negative life events on oral health, finding that negative life events are associated with poor oral health, but no association exists between oral health and positive life events (Brennan & Spencer, 2009).

However, the preponderance of research on the impact of life events on human behavior focuses on the negative impact of negative life events, and researchers still find life events scales to be useful tools, especially in light of evolving research on developmental risk and protection. Some researchers are trying to understand the mechanisms that link stressful life events with immune system pathology (Herberth et al., 2008). Other often researched topics include the role of negative life events in depressive symptoms (Miklowitz & Johnson, 2009) and high blood pressure (Feeney, Dooley, Finucane, & Kenny, 2015), and the impact of traumatic life events on mental health (Mongillo, Briggs-Gowan, Ford, & Carter, 2009). One research team found the Holmes-Rahe scale to be helpful in predicting suicide risk in a Madrid, Spain, sample (Blasco-Fontecilla et al., 2012). A Chinese research team used Zhang's life events scale and found death of a spouse and financial crisis to be associated with higher risk of cognitive impairment in older adults (Deng et al., 2012).

Psychologists have long studied the short- and long-term impact of stressful life events on child, adolescent, and adult functioning. More recently, they have also studied the relationships among stressful life events, biology, and personality. Here are three examples of that research. A Swiss research team (Orth & Luciano, 2015) studied the relationships among self-esteem (defined as one's evaluation of one's worth), narcissism (characterized by grandiose self-concept, feelings of superiority, and self-centeredness), and stressful life events. They found that people high in narcissism have an increased likelihood of experiencing a larger number of stressful life events. They also found that an increase in stressful life events was predictive of lower self-esteem. A team of international researchers (Salvatore et al., 2015) studied a U.S. sample to investigate the interaction of stressful life events and the GABRA2 gene in producing intergenerational continuity in parents' and adolescents' externalizing behavior (problem behavior directed toward the external environment). They found that parental externalizing behavior

predicts a greater number of stressful life events, which in turn predicts higher levels of adolescent externalizing behavior. However, they found that the pattern of parental externalizing → stressful life events → adolescent externalizing was stronger for those adolescents with a specific GABRA2 genotype. Another international research team (Hygen et al., 2015) studied longitudinal data from a sample of children living in Norway to investigate the relationships among child exposure to stressful life events, the COMT gene, and aggression. They found that children with the COMT gene were more likely to behave aggressively in reaction to stressful life events than children without the gene. Taken together these three studies suggest that both biological and personality factors play a role in how different people respond differently to the same stressful life events.

Turning Points

It would be interesting to ask Michael Bowling and Phoung Le whether they identify any turning points in their lives. We might be surprised by their answers. Even though Maria Suarez was too young to think of September 11, 2001, as a turning point in her life, there is no doubt that the events of that day changed the course of her life. A **turning point** is a time when major change occurs in the life course trajectory. We sometimes call these "defining moments." Turning points may occur in the individual life course, but social science researchers also study turning points in social systems such as families, cultures, organizations, economies, or governments.

At the individual level, the turning point may involve a transformation in how the person views the self in relation to the world and/or a transformation in how the person responds to risk and opportunity (Cappeliez, Beaupré, & Robitaille, 2008; Ferraro & Shippee, 2009). It serves as a lasting change and not just a temporary detour. As significant as they are to individuals' lives, turning points usually become obvious only as time passes (George, 2009). Yet in one Finnish study, 99% of respondents in their mid-30s reported that there had been at least one turning point in their lives; the average number of reported turning points was three (Rönkä, Oravala, & Pulkkinen, 2003).

The addition of the concept of turning point is an important way that the life course perspective departs from traditional developmental theory. According to traditional developmental theory, the developmental trajectory is more or less continuous, proceeding steadily from one phase to another. But life course trajectories are seldom so smooth and predictable. They involve many discontinuities, or sudden breaks, and some special life events become turning points that produce a lasting shift in the life course trajectory. Inertia tends to keep us on a particular trajectory, but turning points add twists and turns or even reversals to the life course. For example, we expect someone who is addicted to alcohol to continue to organize his or her life around that substance unless some event becomes a turning point for recovery (Hser et al., 2007).

Transitions and life events do not always produce the major change that would constitute a turning point. However, either a transition or life event may be perceived as a turning point as time passes. Longitudinal research indicates that three types of life events can serve as turning points (Rutter, 1996):

1. Life events that either close or open opportunities

2. Life events that make a lasting change on the person's environment

3. Life events that change a person's self-concept, beliefs, or expectations

Some events, such as migration to a new country, are momentous because they qualify as all three types of events (Gong et al., 2011). Migration, whether voluntary or involuntary, certainly makes a lasting change on the environment in which the person lives; it may also close and open opportunities and cause a change in self-concept and beliefs. Certainly, that seems to be the case for Phoung Le. Keep in mind, however, that individuals make subjective assessments of life events. The same type of life event may be a turning point for one individual, family, or other collectivity, but not for another. For example, one research team found that an HIV diagnosis was a turning point for 37% of their sample of HIV-positive people but was not reported as a turning point for 63% of the sample (Kremer, Ironson, & Kaplan, 2009). Another researcher found that myocardial infarction can be a turning point because it leads to reevaluation of attitudes about self, life, religion, and others (Baldacchino, 2011). It appears that Michael Bowling's stroke was a turning point in the same way.

We have been talking about life events as turning points, but slower-moving transitions can also serve as turning points depending on the individual's assessment of their importance. A transition can become a turning point under five conditions (Hareven, 2000):

1. When the transition occurs simultaneously with a crisis or is followed by a crisis

2. When the transition involves family conflict over the needs and wants of individuals and the greater good of the family unit

3. When the transition is "off-time," meaning that it does not occur at the typical stage in life

4. When the transition is followed by unforeseen negative consequences

5. When the transition requires exceptional social adjustments

One research team interviewed older adults aged 60 to 87 about perceived turning points in their lives and found that the most frequently reported turning points involved health and family. The perceived turning points occurred across the entire life course, but there was some clustering at midlife (ages 45–64), a period in which 32.2% of the reported turning points occurred (Cappeliez et al., 2008). Gender differences have been found in reported turning points in samples of young adults as well as samples of older adults, with women reporting more turning points in the family domain and men reporting more turning points in the work domain (Cappeliez et al., 2008; Rönkä et al., 2003). It is not clear whether this gender difference will be manifested in future cohorts if women's work trajectories continue to become more similar to men's. Researchers have studied the turning points that lead women to leave abusive relationships (Khaw & Hardesty, 2007) and the turning points in the caregiving careers of Mexican American women who care for older family members (Evans et al., 2009). This latter research identifies a "point of reckoning" turning point when the caregiver recognizes the need for extensive caregiving and reorganizes her life to accept responsibility for providing care.

Loss of a parent is not always a turning point, but when such a loss occurs off-time, as it did with Maria Suarez, it is often a turning point. Emma Suarez may not have thought of her decision to take a job in the World Trade Center as a turning point for her family, because she could not foresee the events of September 11, 2001.

Most life course pathways include multiple turning points, some that send life trajectories off track and others that bring life trajectories back on track. In fact, we could say that the intent of many social work interventions is to get life course trajectories back on track (Olsson, Strand, & Kristiansen, 2014). We do this when we plan interventions to precipitate a turning point toward recovery for a client with an addiction. Or we may plan an intervention to help a deteriorating community reclaim its lost sense of community and spirit of pride. It is interesting to note that many social service organizations have taken "Turning Point" for their name. Criminal justice researchers have been interested in learning what types of role transitions can become turning points in a criminal career, leading to desisting from criminal activities. They have found that for some offenders, marriage, military experience, employment, or becoming a parent can precipitate such a turning point (Michalsen, 2011; Schroeder, Giordano, & Cernkovitch, 2010). One researcher found that residential change can be a turning point for parolees leaving prison (Kirk, 2012). Researchers have also found that turning points can facilitate posttraumatic growth for men with histories of child sexual abuse, although the exact nature of these turning points is not clear (Easton, Coohey, Rhodes, & Moorthy, 2013).

CRITICAL THINKING QUESTIONS 1.2

Consider the life course story of either Michael Bowling or Phoung Le. Based on the information you have, what do you think would be the chapter titles if Michael Bowling wrote a book about his life? What would be the chapter titles if Phoung Le wrote about her life? How about a book about your own life to date: what would be the chapter titles of that book? Which show up more in the chapter titles, life transitions (changes in roles and statuses) or life events (significant happenings)?

MAJOR THEMES OF THE LIFE COURSE PERSPECTIVE

Two decades ago, Glen Elder Jr. (1994) identified four dominant, and interrelated, themes in the life course approach: interplay of human lives and historical time, timing of lives, linked or interdependent lives, and human agency in making choices. The meaning of these themes is discussed shortly, along with the meaning of two other related themes that Elder (1998) and Michael Shanahan (2000) have subsequently identified as important: diversity in life course trajectories and developmental risk and protection. These six themes continue to be the framework for life course researchers across a number of disciplines, although different researchers emphasize different themes. The meaning of these themes is summarized in Exhibit 1.7.

EXHIBIT 1.7 ● Major Themes of the Life Course Perspective
Interplay of human lives and historical time: Individual and family development must be understood in historical context.
Timing of lives: Particular roles and behaviors are associated with particular age groups, based on biological age, psychological age, social age, and spiritual age.
Linked or interdependent lives: Human lives are interdependent, and the family is the primary arena for experiencing and interpreting wider historical, cultural, and social phenomena.
Human agency in making choices: The individual life course is constructed by the choices and actions individuals take within the opportunities and constraints of history and social circumstances.
Diversity in life course trajectories: There is much diversity in life course pathways as a result of, for example, cohort variations, social class, culture, gender, and individual agency.
Developmental risk and protection: Experiences with one life transition or life event have an impact on subsequent transitions and events and may either protect the life course trajectory or put it at risk.

Interplay of Human Lives and Historical Time

As sociologists and social historians began to study individual and family life trajectories, they noted that persons born in different years face different historical worlds, with different options and constraints. They suggested that different social, political, and economic contexts of different historical eras may produce **cohort effects** when distinctive formative experiences are shared at the same point in the life course and have a lasting impact on a birth cohort. The same events of a particular historical era may affect different cohorts in different ways. For example, Elder's (1974) research on children and the Great Depression found that the life course trajectories of the cohort that were young children at the time of the economic downturn were more seriously affected by family hardship than the cohort that were in middle childhood and late adolescence at the time. He also notes, however, that these young children were adolescents when fathers were fighting in World War II and mothers were often in the workplace. More recently, Australian researchers (Page, Milner, Morrell, & Taylor, 2013) found that the cohort born after 1970–1974 was more prone to suicide across the young-adult period than earlier cohorts. The researchers also found that this cohort faced higher rates of unemployment and underemployment as they entered young adulthood than earlier cohorts and propose a relationship between these two factors.

Analysis of large data sets by a number of researchers provides forceful evidence that changes in other social institutions impinge on family and individual life course trajectories (Vikat, Speder, Beets, Billari, & Buhler, 2007). Researchers have examined the impact of globalization, declining labor market opportunities, and rising housing costs on young-adult transitions (see Newman, 2008; Scherger, 2009). These researchers are finding that transitions associated with young adulthood (leaving the parental home, marriage, first parenthood) are occurring later for the current cohort of young adults than for their parents in many countries, particularly in countries with weak welfare states. The popular media in the United States has described the relationship between some parents and their Millennial young adults as helicopter parents and landing pad kids, suggesting that the intense support offered by many parents to their adult offspring violates earlier norms of the young-adult transition. One research team found, however, that young adults who received such intense support reported better psychological adjustment and life satisfaction than young adults who did not receive such support. The parents were less satisfied with provision of intense support, however (Fingerman et al., 2013).

The social, political, and economic contexts of different historical eras have also been a focus of some attempts to understand the impact of military service and immigration on health. One research team (Landes, Wilder, & Williams, 2017) considered a finding from earlier research that military service is a protective factor for subsequent health and mortality. They found that veteran cohorts who served during nonwar eras had lower rates of mortality before the age of 85 than their nonveteran peers, but veteran cohorts who had served during war eras did not have a mortality advantage over their nonveteran peers. Researchers who study the impact of immigration on health point out that immigrants face different social, political, and economic contexts during different historical eras as conditions change in both their sending and receiving countries. In addition, shifting immigration policies and shifting attitudes toward particular immigrant groups change the landscape for immigrants over different historical eras (see Torres & Young, 2016).

Demographers analyze the myriad impacts on human functioning of what they describe as first and second demographic transitions. The first demographic transition occurred in the 19th century and involved declines in both mortality (death) and fertility (reproduction). The second demographic transition began in the 1960s in western Europe and North America and involved postponed marriage and parenthood, diversity in living arrangements, increased cohabitation, and increased births to unmarried women (Avison, 2010). Tamara Hareven's (2000) historical analysis of family life documents the lag between social change and the development of public policy to respond to the new circumstances and needs that arise with social change. One such lag today in the United States is between trends in employment among mothers and public policy regarding childcare during infancy and early childhood. Social work planners and administrators confront the results of such a lag in their work. Thus, they have some responsibility to keep the public informed about the impact of changing social conditions on individuals, families, communities, and formal organizations.

Timing of Lives

"How old are you?" You have probably been asked that question many times, and no doubt you find yourself curious about the age of new acquaintances. Every society appears to use age as an important variable, and many social institutions in advanced industrial societies are organized, in part, around age—the age for starting school, the age of majority (age at which one is legally recognized as an adult), retirement age, and so on. In the United States, our speech abounds with expressions related to age: "terrible 2s," "sweet 16," "20-something," "life begins at 40," "senior discounts," and lately "60 is the new 40."

Age is also a prominent attribute in efforts by social scientists to bring order and predictability to our understanding of human behavior. Life course scholars are interested in the age at which specific life events and transitions occur, which they refer to as the timing of lives. They may classify entrances and exits from particular statuses and roles as "off-time" or "on-time," based on social norms or shared expectations about the timing of such transitions (McFarland, Pudrovska, Schieman, Ellison, & Bierman, 2013). For example, child labor and childbearing in adolescence are considered off-time in late-industrial and postindustrial countries, but in much of the world such timing of roles is seen as a part of the natural order. One research team found that people diagnosed with cancer at earlier ages had a greater increase in religiosity than people diagnosed at later ages, suggesting that off-time transitions are more stressful than on-time transitions (McFarland et al., 2013). Further support for this idea is found in research on family trajectories that finds that nonnormative early entry into family formation and parenthood is associated with lower self-reported health (Barban, 2013). Survivors' grief is probably deeper in cases of "premature loss" (Pearlin & Skaff, 1996), which is perhaps why Emma Suarez's family continues to say, "She was so young; she had so much life left."

Dimensions of Age

Chronological age itself is not the only factor involved in timing of lives. Age-graded differences in roles and behaviors are the result of biological, psychological, social, and spiritual processes. Thus, age is often considered from each of the perspectives that make up the biopsychosocial framework (Solomon, Helvitz, & Zerach, 2009). Although life course scholars have not directly addressed the issue of spiritual age, it is an important perspective as well.

Biological age indicates a person's level of biological development and physical health, as measured by the functioning of the various organ systems. It is the present position of the biological person in relation to the potential life cycle. There is no simple, straightforward way to measure biological age, but there is an ongoing process to identify an optimal set of biomarkers for accurate measure of biological age (Jee & Park, 2017). One method is to compare an individual's physical condition with the conditions of others; for example, bone density scans are compared with the scans of a healthy 20-year-old.

Psychological age has both behavioral and perceptual components. Behaviorally, psychological age refers to the capacities that people have and the skills they use to adapt to changing biological and environmental demands. Skills in memory, learning, intelligence, motivation, emotions, and so forth are all involved. Perceptually, psychological age is based on how old people perceive themselves to be. Life course researchers have explored the perceptual aspect of psychological age since the 1960s; recent research has referred to this perceptual aspect of age as "subjective age" or "age identity."

The preponderance of research on subjective age has focused on older adults and found that older adults in Western societies feel younger than their chronological age (Stephan, Chalabaev, Kotter-Grühn, & Jaconelli, 2013). This has not been found to be the case among Chinese oldest old, but recent research finds that the percentage of China's oldest old reporting not feeling old has increased in the past decade (Liang, 2014). It is important to remember that, traditionally, Chinese culture has accorded high status to old age, but the traditions are weakening. A large majority of a Polish sample of older adults reported feeling younger than their chronological age, with an average discrepancy of about 12 years (Mirucka, Bielecka, & Kisielewska, 2016). Youthful subjective age was associated with high satisfaction with life and high self-esteem in this sample. A French research team (Stephan, Sutin, Caudroit, &

Terracciano, 2016) used a longitudinal design that asked about subjective age at Time 1 and 4 years later tested for memory performance. They found that younger subjective age at Time 1 was associated with better memory performance 4 years later. Another French research team found that a sample of older adults performed significantly better on a physical test when they were told that their earlier performance on the same test was better than 80% of the people their age; the improvement did not happen in the control group who did not receive this feedback (Stephan et al., 2013).

Other researchers have examined the subjective age of early adolescents, young adults, and middle-aged adults. One research team (Hubley & Arim, 2012) found that a sample of Canadian early adolescents reported slightly older subjective ages, on average, than their chronological ages. This tendency to feel older than one's chronological age began at 10.4 years of age and peaked at 14.1 years. Subjective age in this sample was influenced by pubertal timing, with late-maturing adolescents reporting a subjective age that was about the same as their chronological age in contrast to the older subjective age of earlier maturers. Young adults have been found to feel their same age or slightly older. Middle-aged and older adults' subjective age is related to their self-reported health, but that is not the case for younger adults (Stephan, Demulier, & Terracciano, 2012). In their study of 107 organizations, German researchers found that a workforce that, on average, feels younger than their chronological age is associated with an improvement in the overall performance of the organization (Kunze, Raes, & Bruch, 2015).

Social age refers to the age-graded roles and behaviors expected by society—in other words, the socially constructed meaning of various ages. The concept of **age norm** is used to indicate the behaviors expected of people of a specific age in a given society at a particular point in time. Age norms may be informal expectations, or they may be encoded as formal rules and laws. For example, cultures have an informal age norm about the appropriate age to leave the parental home. Conversely, many countries have developed formal rules about the appropriate age for driving, drinking alcohol, and voting. Life course scholars suggest that age norms vary not only across historical time and societies but also by gender, race, ethnicity, and social class within a given time and society. They have paid particular attention to recent changes in age norms for the transitions of young adulthood (Newman, 2008; Scherger, 2009).

Although biological age and psychological age are recognized in the life course perspective, social age receives special emphasis. For instance, life course scholars use life phases such as middle childhood and middle adult-hood, which are based in large part on social age, to con-ceptualize human lives from birth to death. In this book, we talk about nine phases, from conception to very late adulthood. Keep in mind, however, that the number and nature of these life phases are socially constructed and have changed over time, with modernization and mass longevity leading to finer gradations in life phases and consequently a greater number of them. Such fine gradations do not exist in most nonindustrial and newly industrializing countries (Dannefer, 2003a, 2003b).

Spiritual age indicates the current position of a person in the ongoing search for meaning, purpose, and moral relationships. Michael Bowling appears to be in a different position in his search for life's mean-ing than he was before his stroke. Although life course scholars have not paid much attention to spiritual age, it has been the subject of study by some developmental psychologists and other social scientists. In an explora-tion of the meaning of adulthood edited by Erik Erikson in 1978, several authors explored the markers of adult-hood from the viewpoint of a number of spiritual and religious traditions, including Christianity, Hinduism, Islam, Buddhism, and Confucianism. Several themes emerged across the various traditions: contemplation, moral action, reason, self-discipline, character improve-ment, loving actions, and close community with oth-ers. All the authors noted that spirituality is typically seen as a process of growth, a process with no end.

James Fowler (1981) has presented a theory of faith development, based on 359 in-depth interviews, that strongly links it with chronological age. Ken Wilber's (2000, 2001) integral theory of consciousness also pro-poses an association between age and spiritual devel-opment, but Wilber does not suggest that spiritual development is strictly linear. He notes, as do the con-tributors to the Erikson book, that there can be regres-sions, temporary leaps, and turning points in a person's spiritual development.

Standardization in the Timing of Lives

Life course scholars debate whether the trend is toward greater standardization in age-graded social roles and sta-tuses or toward greater diversification (Brückner & Mayer, 2005; Scherger, 2009). Simone Scherger (2009) examined the timing of young-adult transitions (moving out of parental home, marriage, becoming a parent) among 12 cohorts in West Germany. Cohorts of a 5-year range (e.g., born 1920–1924) were used for the analysis, beginning with the cohort born 1920–1924 and ending with the cohort born 1975–1979. This research indicated a trend toward destandardization. There was greater variability

in the timing of transitions (moving out of the paren-tal home, marriage, and becoming a parent) among the younger cohorts than among the older cohorts. Scherger also found the transitions were influenced by gender (men made the transitions later than women) and edu-cation level (higher education was associated with delay in the transitions). It is important to note, however, that another research team found that young-adult transi-tions have remained stable in the Nordic countries where strong welfare institutions provide generous supports for the young-adult transitions (Newman, 2008). The impli-cation for social workers is that we must pay attention to the uniqueness of each person's life course trajectory, but we can use research about regularities in the timing of lives to inform social policy.

Many societies engage in **age structuring**, or stan-dardizing of the ages at which social role transitions occur, by developing policies and laws that regulate the timing of these transitions. For example, in the United States there are laws and regulations about the ages for compulsory education, working (child labor), driving, drinking alcohol, being tried as an adult, marrying, hold-ing public office, and receiving pensions and social insur-ance. However, countries vary considerably in the degree to which age norms are formalized (Newman, 2008). It is often noted that formal age structuring becomes more prevalent as nations modernize. European life course scholars suggest that U.S.-based life course scholars have underplayed the role of government in age structuring, suggesting that, in Europe, strong centralized govern-ments play a larger role than in the United States in structuring the life course (Leisering, 2003; Marshall & Mueller, 2003). Indeed, there is evidence that life course pathways in Germany and Switzerland are more stan-dardized than in the United States and Britain (Perrig-Chiello & Perren, 2005). There is also evidence that events and transitions in childhood and adolescence are much more age-normed and structured than in adult-hood (Perrig-Chiello & Perren, 2005). Life course tra-jectories also vary in significant ways by gender, race, ethnicity, and social class (Scherger, 2009).

Linked or Interdependent Lives

The life course perspective emphasizes the interdepen-dence of human lives and the ways in which people are reciprocally connected on several levels (Djundeva, 2015). It calls attention to how relationships both sup-port and control an individual's behavior. **Social sup-port**, defined as help rendered by others that benefits an individual or collectivity, is an obvious element of interdependent lives. Relationships also control behav-ior through expectations, rewards, and punishments.

Social and behavioral scientists have paid particular attention to the family as a source of support and control. In addition, the lives of family members are linked across generations, with both opportunity and misfortune having an intergenerational impact. The cases of Maria Suarez, Michael Bowling, and Phoung Le are rich examples of lives linked across generations. But they are also rich examples of how people's lives are linked with those of people outside the family.

Links With Family Members

We are all linked genetically to our intergenerational families, and we may live with both genetic vulnerability and genetic advantage. Researchers have recently examined how women living with hereditary breast and ovarian cancer risk cope over the life course. One research team (Hamilton, Innella, & Bounds, 2016) studied a sample of women who had tested positive for a BRCA gene mutation associated with greater risk of breast and ovarian cancer and found that women cope in different ways at different stages of the adult life course. For the cohort in their 40s and 50s, linked lives was the overriding concern; women in this cohort were focused on their daughters' risk and how to talk with their daughters about this genetic vulnerability. The cohort in their 30s was also concerned about linked lives, but human agency was the dominant theme in their interviews, what they could do to manage the risk. Human agency and linked lives were important themes of the cohort in their 20s, but this group was more focused on the timing of events in the immediate future, with questions about what if any screening to pursue and whether or when to have prophylactic mastectomies and/or oophorectomies.

Shared genetics is not the only way that parents' and children's lives are linked. Elder's longitudinal research of children raised during the Great Depression found that as parents experienced greater economic pressures, they faced a greater risk of depressed feelings and marital discord. Consequently, their ability to nurture their children was compromised, and their children were more likely to exhibit emotional distress, academic trouble, and problem behavior (Elder, 1974). The connection among family hardship, family nurturance, and child behaviors and well-being is now well established (e.g., Barajas, Philipsen, & Brooks-Gunn, 2008; Conger & Conger, 2008). In addition to the economic connection between parents and children, racial discrimination has an intergenerational effect. It is generally reported that students do better in school when their parents are involved in the schooling process, but one research team (Rowley, Helaire, & Banerjee, 2010) found that parents who perceived racial discrimination from their own teachers were more

reluctant than other parents to be involved with their children's schooling. In recent years, we are also aware that deportation-related family separation impacts the relationships between children and parents. Yoshikawa (2011) reports that mothers' fear of deportation increases the likelihood of maternal depression, which in turn is associated with impaired cognitive skills among preschool age children. Parental hardship has a negative impact on child development, but parents also provide social capital for their children, in terms of role models and networks of social support (Szydlik, 2012).

It should also be noted that parents' lives are influenced by the trajectories of their children's lives. For example, parents may need to alter their work trajectories to respond to the needs of a terminally ill child. Or parents may forgo early retirement to assist their young-adult children with education expenses. Parents may be negatively affected by stressful situations their children face. Emma Suarez's tragedy was a source of great stress for her mother and her siblings, and Hurricane Maria has impacted the entire extended family. One research team found a relationship between the problems of adult children and the emotional and relational well-being of their parents. Research participants who reported having adult children with a greater accumulation of personal and social problems (e.g., chronic disease, mental health problems, substance abuse problems, work-related problems, relationship problems) also reported poorer levels of well-being than reported by participants whose children were reported to have fewer problems (Greenfield & Marks, 2006). Without longitudinal research, it is impossible to know which came first, reduced parental well-being or adult child problems, but this research does lend strong support for the idea that lives are linked across generations.

The pattern of mutual support between older adults and their adult children is formed by life events and transitions across the life course. It is also fundamentally changed when families go through historical disruptions such as wars or major economic downturns. For example, the traditional pattern of intergenerational support—parents supporting children—is often disrupted when one generation migrates and another generation stays behind. It is also disrupted in immigrant families when the children pick up the new language and cultural norms faster than the adults in the family and take on the role of interpreter for their parents and grandparents (Clark, Glick, & Bures, 2009).

What complicates matters is that family roles must often be synchronized across three or more generations at once. Sometimes this synchronization does not go smoothly. Divorce, remarriage, and discontinuities in parents' work and educational trajectories may conflict with the needs of children. Similarly, the timing of adult children's educational, family, and work transitions often conflicts with the needs of aging parents (Huinink & Feldhaus, 2009). The "generation in the middle" may have to make uncomfortable choices when allocating scarce economic and emotional resources. When a significant life event in one generation (such as death of a grandparent) is juxtaposed with a significant life event in another generation (such as birth of a child), families and individual family members are especially vulnerable.

Links With the Wider World

The life course perspective has its origins in Elder's (1974) research on the ways that families and individuals are linked to situations in the economic institution, and in recent years life course researchers have been documenting the ways that individual and family life course trajectories are linked to situations in the labor market, housing market, education system, and social welfare system (Newman, 2008; Scherger, 2009; Szydlik, 2012). This line of research is well illustrated by one research project that examined young-adult transitions in western Europe and Japan (Newman, 2008). Katherine

Newman (2008) reports two divergent trends in the timing of young-adult transitions in postindustrial societies. On the one hand, young adults are staying in the parental home for a prolonged period in Japan and the southern European countries. For example, in Japan, the age of marriage has been rising, and more than 60% of unmarried men and 70% of unmarried women aged 30 to 34 live with their parents. On the other hand, youth typically leave home at the age of 18 in the Nordic countries of northern Europe (Denmark, Finland, Norway, and Sweden). This raises a question about the structural arrangements in these countries that are producing such divergent trends in life course trajectories.

First, changes in the labor market are driving the delayed departure of young adults from the parental home in southern Europe and Japan (Newman, 2008). In the 1980s, when globalization began to produce higher unemployment, governments in southern Europe and Japan began to loosen their commitment to lifetime employment. As a result, companies began to hire part-time and temporary workers; such tenuous connection to the labor market is associated with continued co-residence of young adults with their parents.

© iStockphoto.com

PHOTO 1.3 Parents' and children's lives are linked—when parents experience stress or joy, so do children, and when children experience stress and joy, so do parents.

Unemployment has always been higher in southern Europe than in northern Europe, but the divergence in young-adult transitions in these two European regions is not fully explained by conditions in the labor market.

Second, timing of departure from the parental home is linked to situations in the housing market. In the United States, there are a number of housing options for marginally employed young adults, including pooling resources with a roommate or romantic partner or finding rental housing in a less desirable neighborhood. Such options depend on a strong rental housing market, however. In southern European countries, great emphasis is put on owner-occupied housing, and relatively little rental housing is available. For example, more than 85% of the population in Spain lives in homes they own. In addition, European banks typically are willing to lend only 50% of the cost of a house. In contrast, in the Nordic countries, there is a large rental sector in the housing market, with only 60% to 65% of the population living in homes they own. Katherine Newman (2008) builds the case that these conditions in the housing market influence the timing of departure from the parental home.

Third, it is often suggested that there is a linkage between the education system and timing of departure from the parental home. More specifically, it is argued that young adults who participate in higher education leave the parental home later than those who do not participate in higher education and that the trend toward greater participation in higher education is an important factor in the trend toward later departure from the parental home (see Scherger, 2009). This is not the whole story, however, because the Nordic countries have a higher proportion of emerging adults in higher education than countries in southern Europe, and yet young adults in the Nordic countries depart the parental home earlier than those in southern Europe (Newman, 2008).

And, finally, there is strong evidence of a linkage between the social welfare system and the timing of departure from the parental home (Newman, 2008). More specifically, the early departure from the parental home in Nordic countries is subsidized by a generous welfare system that provides generous housing and educational benefits. The Nordic governments provide much of what families are expected to provide in the weaker welfare systems in southern Europe and Japan.

Katherine Newman (2008) argues convincingly that it is a confluence of situations in different societal systems that impact individual and family life trajectories. In terms of linked lives, she found some evidence that young adults feel more closely linked to their families in Japan and southern Europe than in Nordic countries—a situation that carried both positive and negative consequences. Nordic young adults, conversely, feel more

closely linked to the government and the welfare institution than young adults in Japan and southern Europe.

Using data from 11 European countries, Marc Szydlik (2012) has taken a similar look at the influence of the social welfare system on family solidarity between older adults and their adult children. He found strong family solidarity across the 11 countries but some differences in how the state and family are linked across national lines. He found that adult children in countries with strong social welfare systems provided more practical household help (e.g., home repairs, gardening, transportation, shopping, household chores, and paperwork) to their aging parents than adult children in countries with weaker social welfare systems. On the other hand, adult children in countries with weak social welfare systems provided more personal care (e.g., dressing, bathing, eating, getting in and out of bed, using the toilet) to their aging parents than adult children in countries with stronger social welfare systems. Szydlik suggests that societies with an aging population need family-friendly policies to protect family members from excessive demands, noting that middle-aged adults may get overburdened from the need to care for aging adults while also supporting their young-adult offspring who are struggling in a labor market becoming increasingly less secure.

Here is another example from the research about how social policy affects individual and family lives. Researchers have documented a wage penalty for mothers compared to childless women, with childless women receiving higher wages than mothers. In a study of the motherhood penalty in 13 European countries, one research team (Abendroth, Huffman, & Treas, 2014) found that there is also an occupational status penalty to motherhood, with motherhood depressing the occupational status of women over time. They also found, however, that the motherhood penalty is lower in countries that provide higher public expenditures on childcare. This is a good example of how links with family members intersects with links with the wider world.

It is important for social workers to remember that lives are also linked in systems of institutionalized privilege and oppression. The life trajectories of members of minority groups in the United States are marked by discrimination and limited opportunity, which are experienced pervasively as daily insults and pressures. However, various cultural groups have devised unique systems of social support to cope with the oppressive environments in which they live. Examples include the extensive and intensive natural support systems of Hispanic families like the Suarez family (Price, Bush, & Price, 2017) and the special role of the church for African Americans (Billingsley, 1999). Others construct lives of desperation or resistance in response to limited opportunities.

Philip McMichael (2017) reminds us that, in the global economy, lives are linked around the world. The lifestyles of people in affluent countries depend on cheap labor and cheap raw products in Africa, South America, the Caribbean, parts of Asia, and other places. Children and women in impoverished countries labor long hours to make an increasing share of low-cost products consumed in affluent countries. Women migrate from impoverished countries to become the domestic laborers in affluent countries, allowing women in affluent countries to leave the home to take advantage of career opportunities and allowing the domestic workers to send the money they make back home to support their own families.

CRITICAL THINKING QUESTIONS 1.3

What, if any, historical event or events have had a large impact on your cohort? In your family of origin, what were the norms about when young adults should leave the parental home, complete formal education, establish a committed romantic relationship, or become a parent? How consistent are your own ideas about these young-adult transitions with the ideas of your family of origin? Cross-national research indicates that the social welfare system has an influence on intergenerational family relationships. Do you think that research supports a strong welfare system or a weak welfare system? Explain.

Human Agency in Making Choices

Phoung Le and her husband decided that they wanted to live a bilingual, bicultural life, and this decision had a momentous impact on their own life course as well as the life course trajectories of their children. In other words, they participated in constructing their life courses through the exercise of **human agency**, or the use of personal power to achieve one's goals. The emphasis on human agency may be one of the most positive contributions of the life course perspective. Steven Hitlin and Glen Elder Jr. (2007) note that the concept of human agency is used by different theorists in different ways, but when used by life course theorists it refers to "attempts to exert influence to shape one's life trajectory" (p. 182). It involves acting with an orientation toward the future, with an eye for "possible selves" (Markus & Nurius, 1986). Possible selves represent our ideas of what we might become, what we would like to become, and what we are afraid we will become. They serve as incentives for action.

A look at the discipline of social history might help to explain why considering human agency is so important to social workers. Social historians have attempted to correct the traditional focus on lives of elites by studying the lives of common people (Hareven, 2000). By doing so, they discovered that many groups once considered passive victims—for example, working-class people and slaves—actually took independent action to cope with the difficulties imposed by the rich and powerful. Historical research now shows that couples tried to limit the size of their families even in preindustrial societies (Wrigley, 1966), that slaves were often ingenious in their struggles to hold their families together (Gutman, 1976), and that factory workers used informal networks and kinship ties to manage, and sometimes resist, pressures for efficiency (Hareven, 1982b). These findings are consistent with social work approaches that focus on individual, family, and community strengths (Walsh, 2016a).

Emphasis on human agency in the life course perspective has been greatly aided by the work of psychologist Albert Bandura. Bandura (2002, 2006) proposes that humans are agentic, meaning they are capable of intentionally influencing their own functioning and life circumstances. In his early work, he introduced the two concepts of *self-efficacy*, or sense of personal competence, and *efficacy expectation*, or expectation that one can personally accomplish a goal. More recently (Bandura, 2006), he has presented a psychological theory of human agency. This theory proposes three modes of human agency:

1. *Personal agency* is exercised individually, using personal influence to shape environmental events or one's own behavior.

2. *Proxy agency* is exercised to influence others who have greater resources to act on one's behalf to meet needs and accomplish goals.

3. *Collective agency* is exercised on the group level when people act together to meet needs and accomplish goals.

Bandura argues that everyday life requires use of all three modes of agency. There are many circumstances, such as those just discussed, where individuals can exercise personal agency to shape situations. However, there are many situations over which individuals do not have direct control, and they must seek out others who have greater influence to act on their behalf. Other circumstances exist in which goals are only achievable or more easily and comprehensively achievable by working collectively with others.

Cultural psychology critics of the concept of human agency argue that it is a culture-bound concept that does not apply as well in collectivist societies as in individualistic societies (see Markus & Kitayama, 2003). They argue that individualistic societies operate on a model of *disjoint agency*, where agency resides in the independent self. In contrast, collectivist societies operate on a model of *conjoint agency*, where agency resides in relationships between interdependent selves. Markus and Kitayama (2003) provide empirical support for their proposal that agency is experienced differently by members of individualistic and collectivist societies. They cite several studies providing evidence that European American children perform better and are more confident if they are allowed to make choices (of tasks, objects, and so on), but Asian American children perform no better if allowed to make such choices. Markus and Kitayama do not deny that individuals from collectivist cultures sometimes think in terms of personal agency and individuals from individualistic cultures sometimes think in terms of collective agency. They argue, however, that there is a difference in the emphasis placed on these approaches to agency in different cultures. Gretchen Sisson (2012) suggests that in the United States, working-class individuals are more likely than middle-class individuals to follow a conjoint model of agency concerned with obligations to others. She notes that pregnancy prevention programs typically are based on a disjoint model, which may be inappropriate for the intended audience.

Bandura (2002, 2006) argues that although people in all cultures must use all three modes of agency (personal, proxy, and collective), there are cultural variations in the relative emphasis put on the different modes. He also argues that there are individual variations of preferences within cultures and that globalization is producing some cultural sharing.

Parsell, Eggins, and Marston (2017) argue that "human agency is core to social work" (p. 238), but social workers also recognize the barriers to expressing individual agency. Social work's person-in-environment approach recognizes how the environment influences the individual as well as how the individual influences the environment. Parsell et al. (2017) engaged in content analysis of 48 social work journals to examine how social work academic literature deals with the concept of human agency. They found that social work scholars think of human agency in two primary ways: first, they think of human agency as taking action in the context of particular supports and constraints, and, second, they think of human agency as actively making meaning of oneself and one's world and actively participating in identity development.

Clearly, human agency has limits. Individuals' choices are constrained by the structural and cultural arrangements of a given historical era. For example, Phoung Le and her family did not have the choice to continue to live peacefully in Saigon. Michael Bowling assumed that he had few economic choices but to enlist in the military after high school, and he now faces choices he never expected to face, choices such as applying for SNAP and energy assistance or forgoing the refill of his medications to prevent another stroke. Unequal opportunities also give some members of society more options than others have. For example, voluntary immigrants seeking better educational and economic opportunities can exercise more agency in the migration process than refugees like Phoung Le's family who are fleeing war or other dangers (Gong et al., 2011). Hitlin and Elder (2007) acknowledge both biological and social structural limits to agency. They note research indicating that greater perceptions of personal control contribute to better health among older adults but also propose that agency declines across the life course because of declining physical functioning.

The concepts of proxy agency and collective agency bring us back to linked and interdependent lives. These concepts add important dimensions to the discussion of human agency and can serve to counterbalance the extreme individualism of U.S. society. These modes of agency also raise important issues for social workers. When do we encourage clients to use personal individual agency, when do we use our own influence as proxy agents for clients, and when is collective agency called for?

Diversity in Life Course Trajectories

Life course researchers have long had strong evidence of diversity in individuals' life patterns. Early research emphasized differences between cohorts, but increasing attention is being paid to variability within cohort groups. Some sociologists have suggested that globalization is leading to less diversity in the world. In this vein, some have suggested that the Millennial generation is the first "global generation," for which generational consciousness overrides national culture (Pollak, 2013). However, in their comparative analysis of the work values of Greek Millennials, Papavasileiou and Lyons (2015) found that Millennials around the world are not homogeneous in their work values. Much diversity continues to exist in this generation and others.

We want to interject a word here about terminology and human diversity. As we attempted to uncover what is known about human diversity in life course trajectories, we struggled with terminology to define identity groups.

We searched for consistent language to describe different groups, and we were dedicated to using language that identity groups would use to describe themselves. However, we ran into challenges endemic to our time related to the language of diversity. First, not all members of a given identity group at any given time embrace the same terminology for their group. Second, as we reviewed literature from different historical moments, we recognized the shifting nature of terminology. In addition, even within a given era, we found that different researchers used different terms and had different decision rules about who comprises the membership of identity groups. So, in the end, you will find that we have not settled on fixed terminology used consistently to describe identity groups. Rather, we use the language of individual researchers when reporting their studies, because we want to avoid distorting their work. We hope you will recognize that the ever-changing language of diversity has both constructive potential to find creative ways to affirm diversity and destructive potential to dichotomize diversity into *the norm* and *the other*.

As we strive to provide a global context, we encounter current controversies about appropriate language to describe different sectors of the world. Following World War II, a distinction was made between First World, Second World, and Third World nations, with *First World* referring to the Western capitalist nations, *Second World* referring to the countries belonging to the socialist bloc led by the Soviet Union, and *Third World* referring to a set of countries that were primarily former colonies of the First World. More recently, many scholars have used the language of First World, Second World, and Third World to define global sectors in a slightly different way. *First World* has been used to describe the nations that were the first to industrialize, urbanize, and modernize. *Second World* has been used to describe nations that have industrialized but have not yet become central to the world economy. *Third World* has been used to refer to nonindustrialized nations that have few resources and are considered expendable in the global economy. This approach has lost favor in recent years because it is thought to suggest some ranking of the value of the world's societies. Immanuel Wallerstein (1974, 1979) uses different language but makes a similar distinction; he refers to wealthy *core* countries, newly industrialized *semiperiphery* countries, and the poorest *periphery* countries. Wallerstein is looking not to rank the value of societies but to emphasize the ways that some societies exploit other societies. Other writers divide the world into *developed* and *developing* countries (McMichael, 2017), referring to the level of industrialization, urbanization, and modernization. Although scholars who use those terms are not necessarily using them to rank

the value of different societies, the terms are sometimes used that way. Still other scholars divide the world into the *Global North* and the *Global South*, calling attention to a history in which the Global North colonized and exploited the resources of the Global South. This system of categorization focuses specifically on how some societies exploit other societies. And, finally, some writers talk about the *West* versus the *East*, where the distinctions are largely cultural. We recognize that such categories carry great symbolic meaning and can either mask or expose systems of power and exploitation. As with diversity, we attempted to find a respectful language that could be used consistently throughout the book. Again, we found that different researchers have used different language and different characteristics to describe categories of nations, and when reporting on their findings, we have used their own language to avoid misrepresenting their findings.

Life course researchers have recently begun to incorporate intersectionality theory to understand diversity in life course trajectories (see Raphael & Bryant, 2015; Warner & Brown, 2011). **Intersectionality theory** recognizes that all of us are jointly and simultaneously members of a number of socially constructed identity groups, such as gender, race, ethnicity, social class, sexual orientation, age, religion, geographical location, and disability/ability identity groups (Guittar & Guittar, 2015). The theory is rooted in the writings of U.S. Black feminists who challenged the idea of a universal gendered experience (see Collins, 2012). For any one of us, our *social location*, or place in society, is at the intersection of our multiple identity groups. Either advantage or disadvantage is associated with each identity group, and when considering the life journey of any one individual, it is important to consider the multiple identity groups of which he or she is a part (see Hankivsky, 2012; Seng, Lopez, Sperlich, Hamama, & Meldrum, 2012).

An important source of diversity in a country with considerable immigration is the individual experience leading to the decision to immigrate, the journey itself, and the resettlement period (Gong et al., 2011). The decision to immigrate may involve social, religious, or political persecution, and it increasingly involves a search for economic gain. Or, as in Phoung Le's case, it may involve war and a dangerous political environment. The transit experience is sometimes traumatic, as was the case for Phoung Le and her relatives, who were attacked by pirates and separated, never to see some family members again. The resettlement experience requires establishment of new social networks, may involve changes in socioeconomic status, and presents serious demands for acculturating to a new physical and social environment. Phoung Le and her family were lucky to be able to settle into a large community of Vietnamese immigrants, a situation that eased the process of acculturation. Gender, race, social class, and age all add layers of complexity to the migration experience. Family roles often have to be renegotiated as children outstrip older family members in learning the new language. Tensions can also develop over conflicting approaches to the acculturation process (Falicov, 2016). Just as they should investigate their clients' educational trajectories, work trajectories, and family trajectories, social workers should be interested in the migration trajectories of their immigrant clients.

Developmental Risk and Protection

As the life course perspective has continued to evolve, it has more clearly emphasized the links between the life events and transitions of childhood, adolescence, and adulthood (Gilman, 2012). Studies indicate that childhood events sometimes shape people's lives 40 or more years later (Ferraro & Shippee, 2009; Shonkoff, Garner, and the Committee on Psychosocial Aspects of Child and Family Health, 2012). Indeed, recent biomedical research has suggested we should look at factors that occur earlier than childhood, focusing on fetal undernutrition as a contributing factor in late-life cognition and late-life health conditions such as coronary heart disease, type 2 diabetes, and hypertension (see Joss-Moore & Lane, 2009; Rooij, Wouters, Yonker, Painter, & Roseboom, 2010).

It is quite an old idea that what happens at one point in the life journey influences what happens at later points. No doubt you have heard some version of this idea for most of your life. However, the idea of earlier life experience affecting later development has taken on new energy since the explosion of longitudinal research a few decades ago. In longitudinal research, researchers follow a group of people over a period of time, rather than comparing different groups at one point in time. This allows them to study individual lives over time, noting the factors that influence individual life trajectories.

Two different research traditions have examined how early life experiences affect later outcomes, one based in sociology and the other based in ecological developmental psychology. The sociological tradition is interested in cumulative advantage/cumulative disadvantage. The ecological developmental tradition is interested in risk, protection, and resilience. As you can see, we are borrowing language from the ecological developmental tradition. For a long time, there was little cross-flow of ideas between these two disciplinary traditions, but recently, there has been some attempt to integrate them.

Let's look first at research that focuses on **cumulative advantage/cumulative disadvantage**. Life course scholars have borrowed these concepts from sociologist Robert Merton to explain inequality within cohorts across the life course (Crystal, Shea, & Reyes, 2016). Merton (1968) found that in scientific careers, large inequalities in productivity and recognition had accumulated. Scholarly productivity brings recognition, and recognition brings resources for further productivity, which of course brings further recognition and so on. Merton proposed that, in this way, scientists who are productive early in their careers accumulate advantage over time whereas other scientists accumulate disadvantage. More recently, a similar process of accumulating advantage and disadvantage over time has been found for nongovernmental charitable organizations (Leek, 2015). Sociologists propose that cumulative advantage and cumulative disadvantage are socially constructed; social institutions and societal structures develop mechanisms that ensure increasing advantage for those who succeed early in life and increasing disadvantage for those who struggle (Ferraro & Shippee, 2009). Researchers have applied the concepts of cumulative advantage/cumulative disadvantage to study racial health disparities across the life trajectory (Pais, 2014), financial assistance from midlife parents to adult children (Padgett & Remle, 2016), and evolving patterns of inequality among late-life adults (Crystal et al., 2016). Leopold (2016) found that even in Sweden, a relatively egalitarian country, cumulative socioeconomic advantage produced health gaps, but the life course pattern of health disparity was different from the U.S. pattern. In the United States, the health gap continued to widen throughout late adulthood, but in Sweden the health gap widened throughout middle adulthood but came to a halt at the age of 55. Leopold suggests that one explanation for this difference in health disparity patterns between the United States and Sweden may be the more robust welfare system in Sweden.

Consider the effect of advantages in schooling. Young children with affluent parents attend enriched early childhood programs and well-resourced primary and secondary schools, which position them for successful college careers; which position them for occupations that pay well; which provide opportunities for good health maintenance; which position them for healthy, secure old age. This trajectory of unearned advantage is sometimes referred to as **privilege** (McIntosh, 1988). Children who do not come from affluent families are more likely to attend underequipped schools, experience school failure or dropout, begin work in low-paying sectors of the labor market, experience unemployment, and arrive at old age with compromised health and limited economic resources. **Oppression** is the intentional or unintentional act or process of placing restrictions on an individual, group, or institution; it may include observable actions but more typically refers to complex, covert, interconnected processes and practices (such as discriminating, devaluing, and exploiting a group of individuals) reflected in a perpetuation of exclusion and inequalities over time.

Now let's look at the other research tradition. Longitudinal research has also led researchers across several disciplines to study human lives through the lens of ecological developmental risk and protection. They have attempted, with much success, to identify multidimensional **risk factors**, or factors at one stage of development that increase the probability of developing and maintaining problem conditions at later stages. They have also been interested in individuals who have adapted successfully in the face of risk and have identified **protective factors**, or factors (resources) that decrease the probability of developing and maintaining problem conditions (see Hutchison, Matto, Harrigan, Charlesworth, & Viggiani, 2007; Jenson & Fraser, 2016). For example, recent longitudinal research of a sample of New Zealanders born in 1972 and 1973 found childhood lead exposure to be associated with lower cognitive functioning and socioeconomic status at the age of 38, with declines in IQ and status occurring over time (Reuben et al., 2017). In the same journal edition in which this research was reported, neuropsychologist David Bellinger (2017) reported that interventions to reduce lead exposure in the United States over the past 40 years have resulted in a mean increase in IQ of about 4.5 points. In this example, exposure to lead is a *risk factor*, and societal interventions to reduce lead exposure is a *protective factor*.

In the past decade or so, biomedical researchers have proposed an *ecobiodevelopmental* framework for studying health and disease across the life course, and their research has greatly enriched and expanded the ecological developmental risk and protection approach (see Shonkoff et al., 2012). They articulate the ways genetic predispositions interact with social and physical environments to drive development, referring to the human life course as "nature dancing with nurture over time" (Shonkoff et al., 2012, p. e234). They draw on neuroscience, molecular biology, geonomics, developmental psychology, epidemiology, sociology, and economics to consider how early life experiences and environmental circumstances can leave a lasting impact on brain architecture and long-term health.

The major focus of ecobiodevelopmental research is on the ways that early toxic stress disrupts brain development and development in other biological systems. One example of this research is the Adverse Childhood Experiences (ACE) Study initiated by the health maintenance organization Kaiser Permanente and the U.S. Centers for Disease Control and Prevention. The original study found that as the number of adverse childhood experiences increased so did the likelihood of risky health behaviors, chronic physical and mental health conditions, and early death (Felitti et al., 1998). Other researchers have found early life stress, such as economic deprivation, discrimination, and maltreatment, to be associated with reduced head circumference and height deficit, and impairments in learning and behavior, including problems in linguistic, cognitive, and social-emotional skills; decision making; working memory; self-regulation; and mood and impulse control (Abajobir, Kisely, Williams, Strathearn, & Najman, 2017; Shonkoff et al., 2012). Adversity may begin in the prenatal period, either in the form of undernutrition or as exposure to maternal stress.

Researchers have been identifying the biological mechanisms by which chronic and/or traumatic stress become a risk for subsequent disease and impairment (see Shonkoff et al., 2012). Here are some examples of what they are finding. The body responds to stress by a process that increases stress hormones that are protective in transitory situations. But chronic or traumatic stress creates an overexposure to stress hormones and produces inflammatory cytokines in the immune system (which pass to the brain), leading to vulnerability to disease, including mood disorders. The chemical processes involved in intensive or chronic stress response can disrupt the architecture of the developing brain. For example, chronic stress during early life has been found to produce enlargement and overactivity in the amygdala and orbitofrontal cortex and loss of neurons and neural connections in the hippocampus and medial prefrontal cortex. Impaired memory and emotion regulation are two of the consequences of these brain changes. Researchers are discovering how environmental conditions and early life experiences influence "when, how, and to what degree" specific genes are actually activated (Shonkoff et al., 2012, p. e234). Neuroscientist Richard Davidson puts it this way: "Genes load the gun but only the environment can pull the trigger" (Davidson & Begley, 2012, p. 63).

Recently, gerontologists in the life course tradition have tried to integrate the cumulative advantage/disadvantage and the ecological developmental risk and protection streams of inquiry. Kenneth Ferraro and Tetyana Shippee (2009) present a cumulative inequality (CI) theory. They propose that advantage and disadvantage are created across multiple levels of systems, an idea similar to the multidimensional aspect of the ecological risk and protection approach. They also propose that "disadvantage increases exposure to risk but advantage increases exposure to opportunity" (p. 335). They further submit that "life course trajectories are shaped by the accumulation of risk, available resources, and human agency" (p. 335).

It is important to note that neither cumulative advantage/disadvantage theory nor the ecological developmental risk and protection approach argue that early deprivations and traumas inevitably lead to a trajectory of failure. Research on cumulative advantage/disadvantage is finding that cumulative processes are reversible under some conditions, particularly when human agency is exercised, resources are mobilized, and environmental conditions open opportunities (Ferraro & Shippee, 2009; O'Rand, 2009). For example, it has been found that when resources are mobilized to create governmental safety nets for vulnerable families at key life transitions, the effects of deprivation and trauma on health are reduced (Gilman, 2012).

In the ecological developmental risk and protection stream of inquiry, protective factors provide the antidote to risk factors and minimize the inevitability of a trajectory of failure. Researchers in this tradition have begun to recognize the power of humans to use protective factors to assist in a self-righting process over the life course to fare well in the face of adversity, a process known as **resilience** (Jenson & Fraser, 2016). For example, researchers have found that disadvantaged children who participated in an enriched preschool program had higher levels of education, employment, and earnings and lower levels of crime in adulthood than a control group of similar children who did not participate in the program (Heckman, Moon, Pinto, Savelyev, & Yavitz, 2010). Werner and Smith (2001) found that a relationship with one supportive adult can be a strong protective factor across the life course for children with an accumulation of risk factors.

The life course perspective and the concept of cumulative disadvantage are beginning to influence community epidemiology, which studies the prevalence of disease across communities (e.g., Dupre, 2008; Mishra, Cooper, & Kuh, 2010). Researchers in this tradition are interested in social and geographical inequalities in the distribution of chronic disease. They suggest that risk for chronic disease gradually accumulates over a life course through episodes of illness, exposure to unfavorable environments, and unsafe behaviors, which they refer to as a *chain-of-risk model*. They are also interested in how some experiences in the life course can break the chain of risk.

CRITICAL THINKING QUESTIONS 1.4

Do you think Maria Suarez would endorse a disjoint or conjoint form of agency? What about Michael Bowling? Phoung Le? Explain. Of what identity groups are you a member? Which identities provide you with privilege? Which provide you with disadvantage? How might your social location affect your ability to provide social work services to someone like Maria Suarez, Michael Bowling, or Phoung Le? What risk factors do you see in the lives of Maria Suarez, Michael Bowling, and Phoung Le? What protective factors do you see?

STRENGTHS AND LIMITATIONS OF THE LIFE COURSE PERSPECTIVE

As a framework for thinking about the aspect of time in human behavior, the life course perspective has several advantages over traditional theories of human development. It encourages greater attention to the impact of historical and sociocultural change on human behavior, which seems particularly important in rapidly changing global societies. Its emphasis on linked lives shines a spotlight on intergenerational relationships and the interdependence of lives. At the same time, with its attention to human agency, the life course perspective is not as deterministic as some earlier theories and acknowledges people's strengths and capacity for change. Life course researchers are also finding strong evidence for the malleability of risk factors and the possibilities for preventive interventions. With attention to the diversity in life course trajectories, the life course perspective provides a good conceptual framework for culturally sensitive practice. And finally, the life course perspective lends itself well to research that looks at cumulative advantage and cumulative disadvantage, adding to our knowledge about the impact of power and privilege and subsequently suggesting strategies for social justice.

To answer questions about how people change and how they stay the same across a life course is no simple task, however. Take, for example, the question of whether there is an increased sense of generativity, or concern for others, in middle adulthood. Should the researcher study different groups of people at different ages (perhaps a group of 20-year-olds, a group of 30-year-olds, a group of 40-year-olds, a group of 50-year-olds, and a group of 60-year-olds) and compare their responses, in what is known as a cross-sectional design? Or should the researcher study the same people over time (perhaps at 10-year intervals from age 20 to age 60) and observe whether their responses stay the same or change over time, in what is known as a longitudinal design? I hope you are already raising this question: What happens to the cohort effect in a cross-sectional study? This question is, indeed, always a problem with studying change over time with a cross-sectional design. Suppose we find that 50-year-olds report a greater sense of generativity than those in younger age groups. Can we then say that generativity does, indeed, increase in middle adulthood? Or do we have to wonder if there was something in the social and historical contexts of this particular cohort of 50-year-olds that encouraged a greater sense of generativity? Because of the possibility of cohort effects, it is important to know whether research was based on a cross-sectional or longitudinal design.

Although attention to diversity may be the greatest strength of the life course perspective, heterogeneity may be its biggest challenge. I am using diversity to refer to group-based differences and heterogeneity to refer to individual differences. The life course perspective, like other behavioral science perspectives, searches for patterns of human behavior. But the current level of heterogeneity in countries such as the United States limits our capacity to discern patterns. Along with trying to understand patterns, social workers must try to understand the unique circumstances of every case situation. Another challenge related to diversity—perhaps a larger challenge—is that much of the research of the life course perspective has been done with samples from wealthy advanced industrial societies. This is true of all existing social and behavioral science research. I would suggest, however, that there is nothing inherent in either the basic conceptions or the major themes of the life course perspective that make it inappropriate for use to understand human behavior at a global level. This is particularly true if human agency is understood to include proxy agency and collective agency, conjoint as well as disjoint agency.

Another possible limitation of the life course perspective is a failure to adequately link the micro world of individual and family lives to the macro world of social institutions and formal organizations. Social and behavioral sciences have, historically, divided the social world up into micro and macro and studied them in isolation. The life course perspective was developed by scholars like Glen Elder Jr. and Tamara Hareven, who were trying to bring those worlds together; much progress has been made in this area, but there is still much work to be done (Mitchell & Wister, 2015). It can probably be said that the life course perspective does a better job than most other behavioral science theories in this regard.

INTEGRATION WITH A MULTIDIMENSIONAL, MULTITHEORETICAL APPROACH

The Council on Social Work Education (2015) notes that social work practice is guided by "knowledge based on scientific inquiry" (p. 5). It further states that "social workers understand that evidence that informs practice derives from multi-disciplinary sources and multiple ways of knowing" (p. 8) and that social workers understand theories of human behavior and the social environment" (pp. 8–9) and use that knowledge to engage with, assess, intervene with, and evaluate practice with individuals, families, groups, organizations, and communities. The life course perspective was derived from and is continually informed by multidisciplinary research, using both qualitative and quantitative methods as well as historical analysis. One of its greatest strengths is its ability to incorporate new research in disciplines that include anthropology, developmental psychology, demography, epidemiology, neurobiology, and sociology. Scientific knowledge about human behavior is an essential part of engaging in research-informed practice. Clearly both theory and empirical research are important to social work practice, and the life course theoretical perspective is strongly supported by ongoing empirical research. It has been used to suggest practice and policy interventions and to evaluate them.

A companion volume to this book, *Dimensions of Human Behavior: Person and Environment*, recommends a multidimensional, multitheoretical approach for understanding human behavior. This recommendation is completely compatible with the life course perspective presented in this volume. The life course perspective clearly recognizes the biological and psychological dimensions of the person and can accommodate the spiritual dimension. The life course emphasis on linked or interdependent lives is consistent with the idea of the unity of person and environment presented in *Dimensions of Human Behavior: Person and Environment*. It can also easily accommodate the multidimensional environment (physical environments, cultures, social structure and social institutions, families, small groups, formal organizations, communities, and social movements) discussed in the companion volume.

Likewise, the life course perspective is consistent with the multitheoretical approach presented in *Person and Environment*. The life course perspective has been developed by scholars across several disciplines, and they have increasingly engaged in cross-fertilization of ideas from a variety of theoretical perspectives. Because the life course can be approached from the perspective of the individual or from the perspective of the family or other collectivities, or seen as a property of cultures and social institutions that shape the pattern of individual lives, it builds on both psychological and sociological theories. In addition, throughout each chapter, you are introduced to a number of theories that are pertinent to particular developmental stages and can be enfolded into the life course perspective. To help you track the theories covered in this book, Exhibit 1.8 provides an overview of the theories introduced in Chapters 2 through 10.

CRITICAL THINKING QUESTIONS 1.5

Which concepts and themes of the life course perspective seem most useful to you? Explain. Which, if any, concepts and themes would you argue with? Explain.

EXHIBIT 1.8 ● Theories Introduced in Chapters 2 Through 10	
Chapter 2 Conception, Pregnancy, and Childbirth	Social constructionist perspective; developmental risk and protection theory
Chapter 3 Infancy and Toddlerhood	Classical conditioning theory; operant conditioning theory; Piaget's cognitive theory; information processing theory; Erikson's psychosocial theory; Davidson's theory of emotional styles; Bowlby's theory of attachment; Ainsworth's theory of attachment; developmental risk and protection theory
Chapter 4 Early Childhood	Piaget's cognitive theory; Vygotsky's sociocultural perspective on cognitive development; information processing theory; theory of mind; psychodynamic approach to moral development; social learning approach to moral development; Piaget's, Kohlberg's, and Gilligan's cognitive approaches to moral development; Erikson's psychosocial theory; developmental risk and protection theory
Chapter 5 Middle Childhood	Piaget's cognitive theory; nonlinear dynamic systems theory; Freud's psychosexual stage theory; Erikson's psychosocial theory; Kohlberg's and Gilligan's moral development; Selman's theory of perspective taking; Schwartz's value theory; intersectionality theory; social learning theory; social constructionist orientation; feminist psychodynamic theory; Gardner's theory of multiple intelligences; developmental risk and protection theory
Chapter 6 Adolescence	Positive psychology theory; Piaget's cognitive theory; intersectional perspective on identity; Freud's psychosexual stage theory; Erikson's psychosocial theory; Kegan's stage model of early adolescence; Marcia's theory of identity development; Kohlberg's theory of moral development; Rosenberg's model of identity development; Meed's theory of the generalized other; developmental risk and protection theory
Chapter 7 Young Adulthood	Erikson's psychosocial theory; Levinson's theory of life structure; Arnett's theory of emerging adulthood; Piaget's cognitive theory; Kohlberg's theory of moral development; Fowler's theory of faith development; Marcia's theory of identity development; developmental risk and protection theory
Chapter 8 Middle Adulthood	Erikson's psychosocial theory; Jung's and Levinson's theories of finding balance; life span theory; trait approach to personality; human agency approach to personality; life narrative approach to personality; Fowler's theory of faith development; socioemotional selectivity theory; social convoy theory; developmental risk and protection theory
Chapter 9 Late Adulthood	Theory of cumulative advantage/cumulative disadvantage; disengagement theory; activity theory; continuity theory; social construction theory; feminist theories; social exchange theory; life course capital perspective; age stratification theory; productive aging theory; environmental gerontology perspective; programmed aging theories; damage or error theories of aging; developmental biocultural co-constructivist theory; Erikson's psychosocial theory; developmental risk and protection theory
Chapter 10 Very Late Adulthood	Erikson's psychosocial theory; Kubler-Ross's stages of accepting impending death; Freud's theory of mourning; Lindeman's stage theory of grief work; John Bowlby's model of grief; Rando's stage model of grief; Worden's tasks of mourning; Martin and Doka's approach to adaptive grieving

IMPLICATIONS FOR SOCIAL WORK PRACTICE

The life course perspective has many implications for social work practice, including the following.

- Engage clients to make sense of their unique life journeys so they can use that understanding to improve their current situations. Where appropriate, help them to construct a lifeline of interlocking trajectories.

- Work with client systems to assess the historical contexts of their lives and the ways that important historical events and public policies have influenced their behavior.

- Where appropriate, use life event inventories to assess the level of stress in a client's life.

- Be aware of the potential to develop social work interventions that can serve as turning points that help individuals, families, small groups, communities, and organizations get back on track.

- Work with the media to keep the public informed about the impact of changing social conditions on individuals, families, communities, and formal organizations.

- Recognize the ways the lives of family members are linked across generations and the impact of circumstances in one generation on other generations.

- Recognize the ways lives are linked in the global economy.

- Use existing multidisciplinary research on risk, protection, and resilience to assess and intervene with individuals and families and to develop community-based prevention programs.

- When working with recent immigrant and refugee families, be aware of the age norms in their countries of origin.

- Be aware of the unique systems of support developed by members of various cultural groups and encourage the use of those supports in times of crisis.

- Support and help to develop clients' sense of personal competence for making life choices.

Key Terms

age norm 19	intersectionality theory 26	risk factors 28
age structuring 20	life course perspective 5	sex ratio 11
biological age 19	life event 13	social age 19
cohort 10	oppression 27	social support 20
cohort effects 17	population pyramid 11	spiritual age 20
cumulative advantage 27	privilege 27	trajectories 13
cumulative disadvantage 27	protective factors 28	transitions 12
event history 6	psychological age 19	turning point 15
human agency 24	resilience 29	

Active Learning

1. Prepare your own lifeline of interlocking trajectories (see Exhibit 1.5 for instructions). What patterns do you see? What shifts? How important are the different sectors of your life—for example, family, education, work, health?

2. One research team found that 99% of young-adult respondents to a survey on turning points reported that there had been turning points in their lives. Interview five adults and ask whether there have been turning points in their lives. If they answer no, ask about whether they see

their life as a straight path or a path with twists and turns. If they answer yes, ask about the nature of the turning point(s). Compare the events of your interviewees as well as the events in the lives of Maria Suarez, Michael Bowling, and Phoung Le with Rutter's three types of life events that can serve as turning points and Hareven's five conditions under which a transition can become a turning point.

3. Think of someone whom you think of as resilient, someone who has been successful against the odds. This may be you, a friend, a coworker, a family member, or a character from a book or movie. If the person is someone you know and to whom you have access, ask them to what they owe their success. If it is you or someone to whom you do not have access, speculate about the reasons for the success.

Web Resources

No doubt you use the Internet in many ways and know your way around it. I hope that when you find something in this book that confuses or intrigues you, you will use the incredibly rich resources of the Internet to do further exploration. To help you get started with this process, each chapter of this textbook contains a list of Internet resources and websites that may be useful in your search for further information. Each site listing includes the address and a brief description of the contents of the site. Readers should be aware that the information contained in websites may not be truthful or reliable and should be confirmed before being used as a reference. Readers should also be aware that Internet addresses, or URLs, are constantly changing; therefore, the addresses listed may no longer be active or accurate. Many of the Internet sites listed in each chapter contain links to other Internet sites containing more information on the topic. Readers may use these links for further investigation.

Information not included in the Web Resources sections of each chapter can be found by using one of the many free Internet search engines. These search engines enable you to search using keywords or phrases, or you can use the search engines' topical listings. You should use several search engines when researching a topic, for each will retrieve different Internet sites.

AOL Search: http://search.aol.com

Ask: www.ask.com

Bing: www.bing.com

Google: www.google.com

YAHOO!: http://search.yahoo.com

A number of Internet sites provide information on theory, research, and statistics on the life course.

Bronfenbrenner Center for Translational Research (BCTR): www.bctr.cornell.edu

Site presented by the Bronfenbrenner Center for Translational Research at Cornell University contains information on the center, publications, and news and resources.

Institute for Lifecourse and Society: www .nuigalway.ie/ilas

Site presented by the Institute for Lifecourse and Society at the National University of Ireland, a specially designated research institute in applied social science specializing in research on human flourishing, well-being, and intergenerational connections.

Maternal and Child Health Life Course Research Network: www.lcrn.net

Site maintained by Maternal and Child Health of the Health Resources and Services Administration contains information on the life course approach to conceptualizing health care needs and services and a bibliography.

Project Resilience: www.projectresilience.com

Site presented by Project Resilience, a private organization based in Washington, DC, contains information on teaching materials, products, and training for professionals working in education, treatment, and prevention.

U.S. Census Bureau: www.census.gov

Site presented by the U.S. Census Bureau provides current and historical population data related to diversity and the life course.

Conception, Pregnancy, and Childbirth

Marcia P. Harrigan and Suzanne M. Baldwin

Learning Objectives

2.1 Compare one's own emotional and cognitive reactions to three case studies.

2.2 Summarize some themes in the sociocultural context of conception, pregnancy, and childbirth.

2.3 Recognize important mechanisms of reproductive genetics.

2.4 Analyze the ways that humans try to get control over conception and pregnancy.

2.5 Summarize the major stages of fetal development.

2.6 Describe the special challenges faced by premature and low-birth-weight newborns and newborns with congenital anomalies.

2.7 Give examples of different circumstances under which people become parents.

2.8 Give examples of risk factors and protective factors in conception, pregnancy, and childbirth.

2.9 Apply knowledge of conception, pregnancy, and childbirth to recommend guidelines for social work engagement, assessment, intervention, and evaluation.

CASE STUDY 2.1
JENNIFER BRADSHAW'S EXPERIENCE WITH INFERTILITY

Jennifer Bradshaw always knew she would be a mom. She remembers being a little girl and wrapping up her favorite doll in her baby blanket. She would rock the doll and dream about the day when she would have a real baby of her own. Now, at 36, the dream of having her own baby is still just a dream as she struggles with infertility.

Like many women in her age group, Jennifer spent her late teens and 20s trying not to get pregnant. She focused on education, finding the right relationship, finances, and a career. As an African American woman, and the first person in her family to earn a graduate degree, she wanted to prove that she could be a successful clinical social worker. She thought that when she wanted to get pregnant, it would just happen; that it would be as easy as scheduling anything else on her calendar. When the time finally was right and she and her husband, Allan, decided to get pregnant, they couldn't.

With every passing month and every negative pregnancy test, Jennifer's frustration grew. First, she was frustrated with herself and had thoughts like *What is wrong with me? Why is this happening to us?* and *We don't deserve this.* She would look around and see pregnant teens and think, *Why them and not me?* She also was frustrated with her husband for not understanding how devastating this was to her and wondered to herself,

Could it be him with the problem? In addition, she was frustrated with her family and friends and started avoiding them to escape their comments and the next baby shower. Now, she is baby-less and lonely. It has also been hard for Allan. For many men, masculinity is connected to virility; Allan would not even consider that he might be the one with the fertility problem, even though it is a male-factor issue in about 50% of infertility cases.

After months of struggling to get pregnant, multiple visits to the obstetrician/gynecologist, a laparoscopic surgery, a semen analysis, and timed intercourse (which began to feel like a chore), and after taking Clomid, a fertility drug that made her feel horrible, she and Allan finally accepted that they might need to see a specialist. She will never forget the first visit with the reproductive endocrinologist (RE). She was expecting a "quick fix," thinking that the RE would give her some special pills and then she would get pregnant. But, instead, he casually said to her, "I think your only option is in vitro fertilization [IVF], which runs about $16,000 per cycle, including medications." The RE also told her that for someone in her age range the success rate would be about 35% to 40%.

From her clinical practice and her friendship circle, Jennifer knows that many women think of in vitro as

(Continued)

(Continued)

a backup plan when they delay pregnancy. But she is learning that in vitro is a big deal. First, it is expensive. The $16,000 per cycle does not include the preliminary diagnostic testing, and in Jennifer's age group, the majority of women pursuing IVF will need at least two IVF cycles, $32,000 for two tries; three tries brings the bill up to $48,000. Jennifer has heard of couples spending close to $100,000 for infertility treatments.

Although about 15 states mandate insurance companies to cover fertility treatments, in the state where Jennifer lives, there is no fertility coverage mandate; consequently, her insurance company does not cover any infertility treatments. So at the very least, Jennifer and Allan would need to come up with $16,000 to give one IVF cycle a try. It's heartbreaking for them because they don't have $16,000, and their parents can't help them out. So to give IVF even one try, they need to borrow the money. They are considering taking out a home equity loan to pay for the needed IVF cycles and know they are lucky to be in a position to do that. They have heard of people packing up and moving to states with mandated fertility coverage and/or quitting their jobs and finding jobs that carry specific insurance that will cover fertility treatments. Some couples are even traveling abroad for fertility treatments that can be had for much less than in the United States.

Jennifer has heard that IVF is physically and emotionally exhausting. First, the in vitro patient is forced into menopause, and then the ovaries are hyperstimulated to release numerous eggs (up to 15 to 17 instead of 1), which can be painful. The eggs are surgically extracted, and finally the fertilized embryos are introduced to the IVF patient's body. Throughout this process, various hormone treatments are given via daily injections, multiple blood tests are taken, and at any point during the procedure something could go wrong and the IVF cycle could be called off. If all goes well, the IVF patient is left to keep her fingers crossed for the next 2 weeks waiting for a positive pregnancy test. If the test is negative, the treatment starts over again. Jennifer has heard that most women are an emotional wreck during the entire process because of the high stakes and the artificial hormones.

Jennifer and Allan decided to go the IVF route 7 months after visiting the RE. Before they made this decision, however, Jennifer carefully tracked her BBT (basal body temperature), purchased a high-tech electronic fertility monitor, used an ovulation microscope, took multiple fertility supplements, and used sperm-friendly lubricant during intercourse. Still nothing helped. When she heard that acupuncture has been found to increase the success rate of IVF, she started seeing a fertility acupuncturist on a weekly basis for both herbal formulas and acupuncture treatments. The acupuncture treatments and herbs are averaging about $100 per week, also not covered by insurance in her state.

Jennifer and Allan have decided to give IVF three tries, and after that they will move on to the next plan, adoption. They adore each other and want more than anything to have their own biological little one, but if they cannot have that, they will adopt, and Jennifer will realize her dream of being a mom.

—Nicole Footen Bromfield

CASE STUDY 2.2
CECELIA KIN'S STRUGGLE WITH THE OPTIONS

June 9th: Maybe we just were not meant to have another baby!!! What we have been through is all too amazing: three miscarriages before we had our darling 18-month-old Meridy, plus two more miscarriages since then. Well, at least I know I can get pregnant and we did have a healthy kid, so why not again?

August 20th: YEH! This pregnancy is going sooo well: 10 weeks along ALREADY! I am tired, but I've thrown up only once and feel sooo much different from the pregnancies I lost!!! Looking back, I knew that each one was not right!!! I felt AWFUL ALL the time!!! But not this time!!! What a relief!!! Or is it a reward?

September 1st: It's been more than a week since I wrote!!! Today we went for the ultrasound, both of us thinking it would be so perfect. It wasn't. How could this happen to us? What have we done or not done? Haven't I done everything I could possibly do? I eat right, steered clear of drugs, and hate any kind of alcohol!!! I exercise regularly!!! I am in perfect health!!! Wham! I can't believe what we were told. I can't cry like this any longer. Writing about it may help; it usually does. So, here's how it went. We just sat there staring at each other after hearing, "A 1:25 chance of a baby with Down syndrome." And they told us, "Don't worry"! You have to be kidding! We both insisted that the next step be done right away, so in 3 (LONG) days, we go back again, this time for something called chorionic villus testing!!! Never heard of it.

September 16th: I can't believe this is happening; I feel so angry, so out of control. Then I think of Meridy and that we should just be thankful we have her and believe that our lives can be full, totally complete with just one kid. But this is not what we want! How can I hold it all together? I don't want to cry all the time, especially at work!!! I feel like such a wuss, and I can't really tell anyone, just my husband!!! Worse yet, I don't think that we agree that we will terminate the pregnancy. I feel so guilty, so alone, so empty. How can HE say, "Oh, we can handle that"? I'M the one who arranges childcare, I'M the one who stays home if Meridy is sick, takes her to the doctor, buys her clothes, her food. He comes home to dinner and a smiling kid racing to jump in his arms. What would a child with Down syndrome be like? I can't bear to think of standing there holding this child while HE plays with Meridy. Bills!!! I haven't even thought about that! Our life is great now, but I work to provide extras!!! I love my job. I love my kid. I love my husband. I HATE what is happening. If I don't work, our lives are drastically changed!!! Not an option: I carry the health insurance; he is self-employed. Perhaps this is all a mistake, you know, one of those "false positives" where I will get a call that all is just fine or they reported someone else's test!!! Right! Wishful thinking!!! Who could begin to understand where I AM COMING FROM? I know my family!!! They would never "get it"; I would be SOOOO judged if the word "abort" passed my lips, even by my mom, and we are sooo close!!! But not on this!!! And in this small, small town EVEERYONE would know what I DID!!! Who can possibly help me—help us—with this mess?

CASE STUDY 2.3
THE THOMPSONS' PREMATURE BIRTH

Within days of discovering she was pregnant, Felicia Thompson's husband, Will, suddenly deployed to a combat zone. Through e-mails, occasional cell phone calls, and Skype, Felicia told Will details about the changes she experienced with the pregnancy, but his world was filled with smoke, dirt, bombs, and danger, punctuated with periods of boredom. Six months into the pregnancy, Felicia's changing figure was eliciting comments from her coworkers in the office where she worked part time as an office administrator. With weeks of nausea and fatigue behind her, she was experiencing a general sense of well-being. She avoided all news media as well as "war talk" at the office to protect herself from worry and anxiety. Yet even the sound of an unexpected car pulling up to the front of her home produced chills of panic. Was this the time when the officers would come to tell her that Will had been killed or wounded in combat? Her best friend only recently had experienced what every military wife fears may happen.

Then, with dawn hours away, Felicia woke to cramping and blood. With 14 more weeks before her delivery date, Felicia was seized with fear. Wishing that Will were there, Felicia fervently prayed for herself and her fetus. The ambulance ride to the hospital became a blur of pain mixed with feelings of unreality. When she arrived in the labor and delivery suite, masked individuals in scrubs took control of her body while demanding answers to a seemingly endless number of questions. Felicia knew everything would be fine if only she could feel her son kick. Why didn't he kick? The pediatrician spoke of the risks of early delivery, and suddenly the doctors were telling her to push her son into the world.

In the newborn intensive care unit (NICU), a flurry of activity revolved around baby boy Thompson. Born weighing only 1 pound 3 ounces, this tiny red baby's immature systems were unprepared for the demands of the extra-uterine world. He was immediately connected to a ventilator, intravenous lines were placed in his umbilicus and arm, and monitor leads were placed on all available surfaces. Nameless to his caregivers, the baby, whom his parents had already named Paul, was now the recipient of some of the most advanced technological interventions available in modern medicine. About an hour after giving birth, Felicia saw Paul for the first time. Lying on a stretcher, she tried to find resemblance to Will, who is of Anglo heritage, or herself, a light-skinned Latina, in this tiny form. Felicia's breathing synchronized to Paul's as she willed him to keep fighting.

Later, alone in her room, she was flooded with fear, grief, and guilt. What had she done wrong? Could Paul's premature birth have been caused by paint fumes from decorating his room? From her anxiety and worry about Will?

The Red Cross sent the standard message to Will. Was he in the field? Was he at headquarters? It mattered because Paul may not even be alive by the time Will found out he was born. How would he receive the news? Who would be nearby to comfort him? Would the command

(Continued)

(Continued)

allow him to come home on emergency leave? If he were granted permission for emergency leave, it could be days of arduous travel, waiting for space on any military plane, before he landed somewhere in the United States. Felicia knew that Will would be given priority on any plane available; even admirals and generals step aside for men and women returning home to meet a family crisis. But, then again, the command may consider his mission so essential that only official notification of Paul's death would allow him to return home.

Thirteen days after his arrival, Paul took his first breath by himself. His hoarse, faint cry provoked both ecstasy and terror in his mother. A few days earlier Felicia had been notified by the Red Cross that her husband was on his way home, but information was not available regarding his arrival date. Now that her baby was off the ventilator, she watched Paul periodically miss a breath, which would lead to a decreased heart rate followed by monitors flashing and beeping. She longed for Will's physical presence and support.

Will arrived home 2 days later. He walked into the NICU having spent the last 72 hours flying. He started the trip being delivered to the airport in an armed convoy and landed stateside to find the world seemingly unchanged from his departure months before. Although Paul would spend the next 10 weeks in the hospital, Will had 14 days before starting the journey back to his job.

Paul's struggle to survive was the most exhilarating yet terrifying roller-coaster ride of his parents' lives. Shattered hopes were mended, only to be reshattered with the next telephone call from the NICU. Now Felicia dreaded the phone as well as the sound of an unfamiliar car. For Felicia, each visit to Paul was followed by the long trip home to the empty nursery. For Will, stationed thousands of miles away, there was uncertainty, guilt, helplessness, and sometimes an overwhelming sense of inadequacy. Felicia feared the arrival of a car with officers in it, and Will dreaded a Red Cross message that his son had died.

Great joy and equally intense anxiety pervaded Paul's homecoming day. After spending 53 days in the NICU and still weighing only 4 pounds, 13 ounces, Paul was handed to his mother. She made sure that a video was made so that Will could share in this moment. With more questions than answers about her son's future and her ability to take care of him, Felicia took their baby to his new home.

For the NICU social worker at the military hospital, the major goal is to support the family as they face this challenging transition to parenthood. In the past 53 days, the social worker has helped Felicia answer her questions, understand the unfamiliar medical language of the health care providers, and understand and cope with the strong emotions she is experiencing. The social worker also helped during the transition of Will's arrival from war and his departure back to war. Understanding the dynamics of the NICU, families in crisis, and the needs of the military family separated by an international conflict is critical to providing this family the level of support they need to manage their multifaceted role transitions.

SOCIOCULTURAL ORGANIZATION OF CHILDBEARING

These three stories tell us that conception, pregnancy, and childbirth are experienced in different ways by different people. The biological processes vary little for the vast majority of women and their families, but researchers continue to study the psychological, social, and spiritual dimensions of childbearing. This chapter presents a multidimensional overview of current knowledge about conception, pregnancy, and childbirth gleaned from the literatures of anthropology, genetics, medicine, nursing, psychology, social work, and sociology.

As you read, keep in mind that all elements of childbearing have deep meaning for a society. We can draw on the social constructionist perspective to think about this. This perspective proposes that social reality is created when people, in social interaction, develop shared meaning, a common understanding of their world (you

can read more about this in the chapter Theoretical Perspectives on Human Behavior in *Dimensions of Human Behavior: Person and Environment*). Meanings about and expectations for human behavior vary across time, place, and culture. Cultural groups develop common understandings about all aspects of procreation: the conditions under which it should happen; whether, and if so how, to control it; proper behavior of the pregnant woman and her family system; and the where and how of childbirth. Pregnancy and childbearing practices are changing with advances in technology and increased diversity in the population of childbearing age. We in the United States are in the midst of an ongoing national debate about health care policy, and social workers will need to monitor the impact of proposed policies on the well-being of women and their families during the childbearing years.

In the United States, the social meaning of childbearing has changed rather dramatically in several ways over the past several decades:

- Various options for controlling reproduction are more available and accessible but oftentimes only to the economically advantaged.

- Childbirth is more commonly delayed, and more people are seeking fertility treatment and remaining involuntarily childless.

- The marriage rate has declined, and more children are born to unmarried mothers.

- The birth rate has declined, resulting in smaller families.

- Teen pregnancy is at a historic low.

- There are greater variations in family values and sexual mores than in previous generations.

- Parents are less subject to traditional gender-role stereotyping.

- It is becoming much more common for gay and lesbian individuals and couples to become parents.

These trends have prompted considerable debate over how our society should define *family*. The family operates at the intersection of society and the individual. For most people it serves as a safe haven and cradle of emotional relationships. It is both the stage and partial script for the unfolding of the individual life course.

Conception and Pregnancy in Context

The three case studies at the beginning of this chapter remind us that emotional reactions to conception may vary widely. The Thompsons' conception brought anxiety and then joy, in contrast to Jennifer Bradshaw's frustration and lost dreams followed by her rising hopefulness; Cecelia Kin feels caught between her own values and wishes and those of important people in her life. The conception experience is influenced by expectations the parents learned growing up in their own families of birth as well as by many other factors, including the parents' ages, health, marital status, and social status; cultural expectations; peer expectations; school or employment circumstances; the social-political-economic context; and prior experiences with conception and childbearing, as well as the interplay of these factors with those of other people significant to the mother and father.

The conception experience may also be influenced by organized religion. The policies of religious groups reflect different views about the purpose of human sexual expression, whether for pleasure, procreation, or perhaps both. Many mainstream religions, in their policy statements, specify acceptable sexual behaviors (Kurtz, 2016). Unwanted conception may be seen as an act of carelessness, promiscuity, or merely God's will—perhaps even punishment for wrongdoing. These beliefs are usually strongly held and have become powerful fodder for numerous social, political, economic, and religious debates related to conception, such as the continued debates about abortion legislation in the United States and around the globe.

Just as the experience of conception has varied over time and across cultures, so has the experience of pregnancy. It too is influenced by religious orientations, social customs, changing values, economics, and even political ideologies. For example, societal expectations of pregnant women in the United States have changed, from simply waiting for birth to actively seeking to maintain the mother's—and hence the baby's—health, preparing for the birth process, and sometimes even trying to influence the baby's cognitive and emotional development while the baby is in the uterus.

Childbirth in Context

Throughout history, families—and particularly women—have passed on to young girls the traditions of childbirth practices. These traditions are increasingly shaped by cultural, institutional, and technological changes. The multiple influences on and changing nature of childbirth practices are exemplified in three related issues: childbirth education, place of childbirth, and who assists childbirth.

Childbirth Education

It is probably accurate to say that education to prepare women for childbirth has been evolving for a very long time, but a formal structure of childbirth education is a relatively new invention. In the United States, the early

PHOTO 2.1 Societal views of pregnancy in the United States have changed from simply waiting to being actively involved in nurturing the mother's and baby's health.

© iStockphoto.com/Rawpixel

roots of formal childbirth education were established during the Progressive Era when the Red Cross set up hygiene and health care classes for women as a public health initiative. In 1912, the U.S. Children's Bureau, created as a new federal agency to inform women about personal hygiene and birth, published a handbook titled *Prenatal Care*, emphasizing the need for medical supervision during pregnancy (Barker, 1998).

Childbirth education, as a formal structure, took hold in the United States and other wealthy countries in the 1960s, fueled by the women's and grassroots consumer movements. Pioneers in the childbirth education movement were reacting against the increasing medicalization of childbirth, and they encouraged women to regain control over the childbirth process. Early childbirth education classes were based on books by Grantly Dick-Read (1944), *Childbirth Without Fear*, and French obstetrician Dr. Fernand Lamaze (1958), *Painless Childbirth*. Lamaze proposed that women could use their intellect to control pain while giving birth if they were informed about their bodies and used relaxation and breathing techniques. Early classes involved small groups meeting outside the hospital during late pregnancy and emphasized unmedicated vaginal birth. Pioneers in the childbirth education movement believed that such childbirth classes would provide the knowledge and skills women needed to change maternity practices, and indeed, the movement had an impact on the development of family-centered maternity practices such as the presence of fathers in labor and delivery and babies rooming with mothers after birth. Over time, childbirth education became institutionalized and was taught in large classes based in hospitals (Lothian, 2008).

There have been many societal changes in the 50 years since childbirth education was formalized, and in 2007, DeVries and DeVries suggested that childbirth education as it currently exists fits the ethos of the 1960s but is out of step with current societal trends. Here are some examples of how the experience of pregnancy and childbirth has changed since the early days of the childbirth education movement.

- Pregnant women had few sources of information about pregnancy and birth in the 1960s, but women today are overloaded with information from multiple sources. A 2013 U.S. survey of women's childbearing experiences found that besides maternity care providers and childbirth education classes, women reported getting information from online resources by using a number of devices, including smartphone and tablet. Two out of three women received weekly educational e-mail messages, and one quarter received regular text messages about pregnancy and childbirth (Declercq, Sakala, Corry, Applebaum, & Herrlich, 2014). Other researchers have found that women rely heavily on the Internet (Lagan, Sinclair, & Kernohan, 2010) and reality television shows with a birth theme (Morris & McInerney, 2010) for this information. Women also make use of a plethora of books on pregnancy-based topics and learn from friends and family. Unfortunately, women may need help in sorting out inaccurate and out-of-date information from any of these sources. One study found that pregnant women sought information more often from commercial Internet sites than from not-for-profit organizational or professional sites, and misinformation may be a problem at some of these sites (Lima-Pereira, Bermudez-Tamayo, & Jasienska, 2012).

- The current generation of pregnant women is more likely than the earlier cohort of pregnant women to be involved in a variety of health promotion activities that will help them manage childbirth. For example, they may be involved in alternative modalities for relaxation and fitness, such as mindfulness meditation, yoga, Pilates, or massage (Fisher, Hauck, Bayes, & Byme, 2012; Morton & Hsu, 2007).

- Pregnant women are much more likely to be employed today than in the 1960s and 1970s. The multisession formats of most models of childbirth education often seem like an extra burden for contemporary pregnant women. One trend in maternity care is to provide group appointments for prenatal care, incorporating education and group support along with maternity checkups. Research shows that some women prefer group care and have better pregnancy and birth outcomes when participating in group care (Walker & Worrell, 2008).

- The current cohort of pregnant women are more likely to be unmarried than was true 50 years ago. The emphasis on husband involvement in traditional models of childbirth education may not resonate with many of these women.

- The current population of pregnant women is much more culturally diverse than the White, middle-class women for whom childbirth education was designed. Research indicates that childbirth education classes are still made up largely of White, middle-class women (Lothian, 2008).

- Many new technological and pharmaceutical childbirth interventions have been introduced in the past 15 years, and many contemporary pregnant women prefer high-tech, pain-free, and scheduled (if possible) birth. This is not a good fit with models of childbirth education from the earlier era that discourage medical intervention. There is some evidence, however, that today's women are given little choice in whether to use medical interventions (Declercq et al., 2014).

A number of government initiatives promote access to childbirth resources, initiated by the Maternity Care Access Act of 1989, which provided support for low-income women (Rabkin, Balassone, & Bell, 1995). Healthy People 2000, 2010, and 2020, an effort by the federal government to enhance the nation's health, supports prenatal education (Healthy People, 2016).

The research is inconclusive about whether childbirth education classes in the traditional model produce better pregnancy and childbirth outcomes (Koehn, 2008; Lothian, 2008), and there are mixed results as to whether the father's role is enhanced through childbirth education (Premberg, 2006; Premberg, Hellström, & Berg, 2008). In a recent review of randomized trials of childbirth education, one research team found that the evidence indicates that expectant fathers who participated in childbirth education reported lower parenting stress 3 months after birth than expectant fathers who did not participate in childbirth education. They also reported lower postnatal anxiety 2 hours after birth, were more likely to participate in the delivery room, and reported more satisfaction with the birth experience (Suto, Takehara, Yamane, & Ota, 2017). As childbirth education branches from the traditional classroom model to home-based services and interactive media presentations, it is important for social workers to help parents negotiate the changing landscape to make the choice that fits them the best (Lothian, 2008) while ensuring that the educational needs of parents of all racial and ethnic groups, economic circumstances, disabilities, and localities are met (Linn, Wilson, & Fako, 2015).

Place of Childbirth

Large changes in the place of childbirth have occurred in many parts of the world in the past century. In 1900, almost all births in the United States and other countries occurred outside of hospitals, usually at home (MacDorman, Mathews, & Declercq, 2012). Today, in high- and moderate-income countries, labor wards in hospitals are the usual settings for childbirth (Hodnett, Downe, & Walsh, 2012). In the United States, the percentage of births occurring outside the hospital dropped to 44% in 1940 and 1% in 1969 (MacDorman et al., 2012). As formalized medical training developed, so did the medicalization of childbirth, and the current childbirth experience commonly includes such medical interventions as intravenous lines, electronic fetal monitors, and epidural anesthesiology (Lothian, 2008). Induced labor and cesarean delivery are becoming increasingly common.

In the early part of the 20th century, the feminist movement advocated for hospital childbirth because it was considered to be safer than home birth, but beginning in the 1960s, feminists began to advocate for less invasive deliveries in more friendly environments that give women more choices over their care (DeVries & DeVries, 2007). In the past few decades, in the United States and other wealthy countries, a variety of institutional care settings have been developed, ranging from freestanding birth centers located near a hospital to more home-like birthing rooms within hospital labor departments (Hodnett et al., 2012). In 2012, the Centers for Medicare and Medicaid Services (2012) included birthing center care as one of three options for enhanced prenatal care under the Strong Start Initiative. A very small minority of pregnant women, less than 1% in the United States, give birth at home (MacDorman et al., 2012; Wyckoff, 2013). The same is true for most European countries, with the exception of the Netherlands, where home birth has been seen as the first option for uncomplicated pregnancies; even so, the percentage of home births in the Netherlands decreased from 38.2% to 23.4% from 1990 to 2010 (Chervenak, McCullough, Brent, Leven, & Arabin, 2013). It is important to remember that in many low-income countries, high maternal mortality rates are due, in great part, to poor women in remote rural areas having no option but to give birth at home without access to emergency health care (Kristof & WuDunn, 2009). In some of these countries, birthing shelters provide dormitory rooms near hospitals so that women can receive emergency care during childbirth if the need arises (Brzeski, 2013).

Although alternatives to conventional hospital settings, such as birthing centers and home-like birthing rooms, have been somewhat slow to develop in the United States, they are not considered controversial, and available research indicates some benefits and no drawbacks to them. Women giving birth in such settings have reduced likelihood of medical interventions, increased likelihood of spontaneous vaginal birth, and increased satisfaction (Hodnett et al., 2012; Stapleton,

Osborne, & Illuzzi, 2013). Home birth has been very controversial, however. In 1975, the American College of Obstetricians and Gynecologists (ACOG) issued a policy statement that protested in-home births and asserted that acceptable levels of safety were only available in the hospital. This policy statement was reaffirmed in 2013; it was supported that same year by the American Academy of Pediatrics, who noted that babies born during a planned home birth have a two- to threefold increased risk of death (Wyckoff, 2013). In response, in 2012, three major midwifery groups (the American College of Nurse-Midwives, Midwives Alliance of North America, and National Association of Certified Professional Midwives) strongly endorsed the practice of home delivery and challenged the medical profession to consider the advantages of a woman delivering her **neonate** (newborn) in the sanctity of her home. One research team recently analyzed birth data for the years 2009–2013 and recommended five contraindications for a planned home birth: fetal malpresentation such as breech birth, multiple gestations, a history of cesarean delivery, first-time birth, and a gestation age of 41 weeks or more (Grünebaum, McCullough, Sapra, Arabin, & Chervenak, 2017).

Who Assists Childbirth

In most countries of the world, childbirth was assisted exclusively by women until the middle of the 19th century when physicians, who were almost exclusively male, began delivering babies (Gardiner, 2018). Before childbirth became medicalized, midwives, trained birthing specialists, assisted most births. Midwifery went into decline in the United States for a few decades, but today 1 in 8 vaginal deliveries are attended by a nurse midwife; most of these are in hospitals (Declercq, 2012). In 2014, most midwives worked in a hospital setting (94.2%), 3% worked in birthing centers, and 2.7% attended home deliveries (American College of Nurse-Midwives, 2015). Most birthing centers have midwives as the primary care provider (Stapleton et al., 2013).

In most times and places, fathers have been excluded from participation in childbirth. This began to change in the United States and other countries in the 1970s, and worldwide there is an increasing trend for fathers to be present at the birth of their babies (Steen, Downe, Bamford, & Edozien, 2012). In some cultures, however, there is still a taboo about fathers witnessing childbirth (Sengane, 2009). In the past 40 years of having fathers involved in

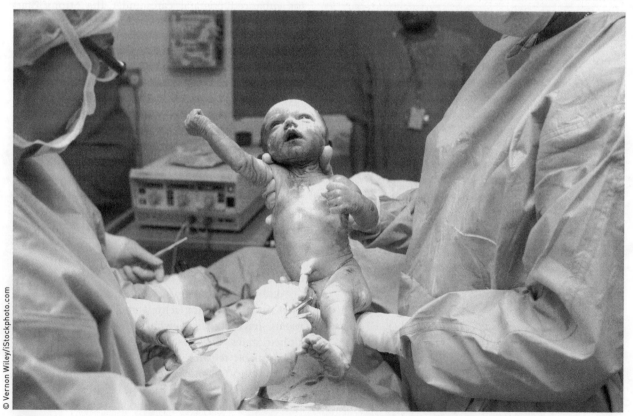

© Vernon Wiley/iStockphoto.com

PHOTO 2.2 A typical delivery—here a newborn baby is delivered by medical professionals in a hospital delivery room.

the birthing process, research has indicated a number of benefits of this involvement, including improved maternal well-being, improved father–infant attachment, and paternal satisfaction (Alio, Lewis, Scarborough, Harris, & Fiscella, 2013; Premberg, Carlsson, Hellström, & Berg, 2011). In recent years, however, several pieces of qualitative research have reported that fathers are struggling with their role in the birthing process. One research team (Steen et al., 2012) examined the qualitative research on fathers' involvement with childbirth published from 1999 to 2009. They found that most fathers saw themselves as partner, had a strong desire to support their partner, and wanted to be fully engaged. They also found that fathers often felt uncertain, excluded, and fearful. They felt frustrated about their helplessness to relieve their partner's pain, they felt good when they could support their partner but bad when they did not feel supported by the childbirth team, and they found the transition to fatherhood to be profoundly life changing. Another research team (Bäckström & Hertfelt Wahn, 2011) found that fathers perceived themselves as receiving support when they were allowed to ask questions, when they had an opportunity to interact with the midwife and their partner, and when they could choose when to be involved and when to step back from involvement. They want to be recognized as part of the laboring couple.

In the past 3 decades, birth doulas have become a part of the childbirth experience for increasing numbers of women. *Doulas* are laywomen who are employed to stay with the woman through the entire labor, assisting with the nonmedical aspects of labor and delivery, encouraging her, and providing comfort measures. A Cochrane systematic review of the research on the effects of continuous labor support found that women receiving such support had higher rates of spontaneous vaginal birth, lower rates of cesarean delivery, lower rates of epidural anesthesia, lower rates of instrument-assisted delivery, shorter labors, and higher levels of maternal satisfaction. They also found that labor support was most effective when provided by someone with special training, not on the hospital staff and not a family member or close friend (Hodnett, Gates, Hofmeyr, Sakala, & Weston, 2012). Given this latter finding, it is important that the doula support the role of the father when he is present. Some policy analysts have pointed out that neither private nor public health insurance covers the cost of doulas but should consider doing so given the cost savings from reduced cesarean delivery, epidurals, and instrument-assisted delivery (Kozhimannil, Hardeman, Attanasio, Blauer-Peterson, & O'Brien, 2013). The Patient Protection and Affordable Care Act (often referred to as the Affordable Care Act

or Obamacare), passed by Congress in 2010, allocated $1.5 million for community-based doula programs, following the success of a model program for disadvantaged and teen mothers (Sonfield, 2010). Think about the Thompsons' situation with Will in Afghanistan, unaware of the pending birth of his first child, and Felicia in premature labor without any family present. Perhaps a doula would have been a great benefit in that situation, as well as situations of other military wives.

CRITICAL THINKING QUESTIONS 2.1

What were your reactions to the situations of the people in the three case studies at the beginning of this chapter? How would your reactions be helpful if you were to encounter each person in your social work practice? How would your reactions complicate your ability to be helpful to each one of them?

REPRODUCTIVE GENETICS

The life course perspective reminds us that we are linked back in time with our ancestry, as well as with our culture. Genetic factors are one important way we are linked to our ancestry. Recognition of the need for genetics knowledge is not new to social work. In fact, Mary Richmond (1917) advocated that a social worker "get the facts of heredity," in the face of marriage between close relatives, miscarriage, tuberculosis, alcoholism, mental disorder, nervousness, epilepsy, cancer, deformities or abnormalities, or an exceptional ability. Very little was known about genetic mechanisms at the time, however.

Almost 40 years later, James Watson and Francis Crick (1953) first described the mechanisms of genetic inheritance. In 1990, the Human Genome Project (HGP) was funded by the U.S. Department of Energy and the National Institutes of Health as an international effort to map all the human genes, and that project was completed by 2003. As genetic knowledge continued to grow, the National Association of Social Workers established Standards for Integrating Genetics Into Social Work Practice in 2003. These standards cover ethics and values, genetics knowledge, practice skills, a client–practitioner collaborative practice model, interdisciplinary practice, self-awareness, genetics and cross-cultural knowledge, research, and advocacy (National Association of Social Workers, 2003). Genetic research continues around the world, with future findings that will impact social work practice.

Genetic Mechanisms

Chromosomes and genes are the essential components of the hereditary process. Genetic instructions are coded in **chromosomes** found in each cell; each chromosome carries **genes**, or segments of deoxyribonucleic acid (DNA), that contain the codes producing particular traits and dispositions. Each mature **germ cell**—ovum or sperm—contains 23 chromosomes, half of the set of 46 present in each parent's cells. As you can see in Exhibit 2.1, when the sperm penetrates the ovum (**fertilization**), the parents' chromosomes combine to make a total of 46 chromosomes arrayed in 23 pairs. The genes constitute a "map" that guides the protein and enzyme reactions for every subsequent cell in the developing person and across the life course. Thus, almost every physical trait and many behavioral traits are influenced by the combined genes from the ovum and sperm.

The Human Genome Project (1990–2003) researchers estimated that there are 20,000 to 25,000 genes in human DNA, with a broad range of total genes (449–2,400) across all chromosomes (National Human Genome Research Institute, 2010). Ongoing research has reduced the number of genes to 19,000 to 20,000, instead of the 20,000 to 25,000 originally identified (Ezkurdia et al., 2014). Research continues to articulate the complete sequencing of the 3 billion subunits of the human genome, an effort of global proportions involving both public and privately funded projects in more than 18 countries, including some developing countries (National Human Genome Research Institute, 2010).

Every person has a unique **genotype**, or array of genes, unless the person is an identical twin. Yet the environment may influence how each gene pilots the growth of cells. The result is a **phenotype** (observable trait) that differs somewhat from the genotype. Thus, even a person who is an identical twin has some unique characteristics. On initial observation, you may not be able to distinguish between identical twins, but if you look closely enough, you will probably find some variation, such as differences in the size of an ear, hair thickness, or temperament.

A chromosome and its pair have the same types of genes at the same location. The exception is the last pair of chromosomes, the **sex chromosomes**, which, among other things, determine sex. The ovum can contribute only an X chromosome to the 23rd pair, but the sperm can contribute either an X or a Y and therefore determines the sex of the developing person. A person with XX sex chromosomes is female; a person with XY sex chromosomes is male (refer to Exhibit 2.1).

A gene on one sex chromosome that does not have a counterpart on the other sex chromosome creates a **sex-linked trait**. A gene for red/green color blindness, for example, is carried only on the X chromosome. When an X chromosome that carries this gene is paired with a Y chromosome, which could not carry the gene, red/green color blindness

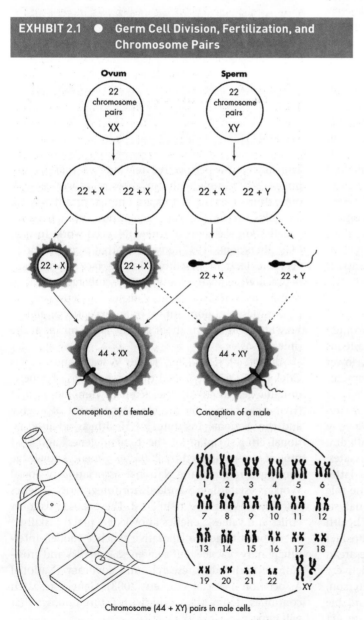

EXHIBIT 2.1 ● Germ Cell Division, Fertilization, and Chromosome Pairs

Ovum

22 chromosome pairs XX

22 + X   22 + X

22 + X   22 + X

44 + XX

Conception of a female

Sperm

22 chromosome pairs XY

22 + X   22 + Y

22 + X   22 + Y

44 + XY

Conception of a male

13 14 15 16 17 18
19 20 21 22   XY

Chromosome (44 + XY) pairs in male cells

is manifested. So, almost all red/green color blindness is found in males. This gene for color blindness does not manifest if paired with an X chromosome unless the gene is inherited from both parents, which is rare. However, if a woman inherits the gene from either parent, she can unknowingly pass it on to her sons.

Whether genes express certain traits depends on their being either dominant or recessive. Traits governed by **recessive genes** (e.g., hemophilia, baldness, thin lips) will only be expressed if the responsible gene is present on each chromosome of the relevant pair. In contrast, traits governed by **dominant genes** (e.g., normal blood clotting, curly hair, thick lips) will be expressed even if only one chromosome has the gene. When the genes on a chromosome pair give competing yet controlling messages, they are called **interactive genes**, meaning that both messages may be followed to varying degrees. Hair, eye, and skin color often depend on such interactivity. For example, a light-skinned person with red hair and hazel eyes may mate with a person having dark skin, brown hair, and blue eyes and produce a child with a dark complexion, red hair, and blue eyes. Anomalies may occur in genetic transmission, an issue discussed later.

Genetic Counseling

Recent research has identified many genes that govern some of the physical traits and mental/medical problems that Mary Richmond noted in 1917. Today the goal is to develop genetic interventions to prevent, ameliorate, or cure various diseases or disorders as well as inform decisions about conception, pregnancy, and childbirth. One example is the Preimplantation Genetic Diagnosis (PGD) test for more than 100 genetic conditions used for in vitro fertilization to ensure that the embryo has no mutations (American Pregnancy Association, 2017a). Almost 54,000 genetic tests for over 10,000 conditions are listed through the Centers for Disease Control and Prevention Genetic Test Registry. Many tests are marketed prematurely to the public (Centers for Disease Control and Prevention [CDC], 2017a). Of special note are the 2008 Genetic Information and Nondiscrimination Act (GINA) that prohibits discrimination by U.S. insurance companies based on genetic test results and the June 2013 unanimous Supreme Court decision to prohibit patenting of genes (Liptak, 2013).

Our rapidly increasing ability to read a person's genetic code and understand the impact it could have on the person's life oftentimes demands the expertise of a genetic counselor to provide information and advice to guide decisions for persons concerned about hereditary abnormalities. Social workers, with their biopsychosocial perspective, are well positioned to assess the need and in some circumstances provide such services, and the interdisciplinary field of genetic counseling acknowledges social work as one of its essential disciplines (National Association of Social Workers, 2003; Price, 2008a, 2008b). Social workers need to understand the rising bioethical concerns that genetic research fosters and to use such knowledge to help clients faced with genetically related reproductive decisions. The U.S. government has the largest bioethics program in the world to address questions such as the following: Who should have access to genetic information? Do adoptive parents have the right to know the genetic background of an adoptee? Will genetic maps be used to make decisions about a pregnancy? Which genes should be selected for reproduction? Will persons who are poor be economically disadvantaged in the use of genetic information? Should all genetic information be shared with a client?

Recent advances in genetic research allow for earlier in utero diagnosis, which reduces or prevents the effects of some rare diseases and may provide more options for action. Today, for example, a late-life pregnancy can be evaluated genetically using amniocentesis in the third trimester, or earlier in the first trimester using chorionic villus sampling, which allowed Cecelia Kin to know that her unborn child had Down syndrome. Such evaluation could lead to difficult decisions ranging from abortion to preparation for parenting a child with a disability. However, these options typically are laced with economic, political, legal, ethical, moral, and religious considerations.

Ethical issues related to genetic engineering have an impact not only at the individual and family levels but also at the societal level. For example, when we are able to manipulate genes at will, we must be on guard against genetic elitism. It is one thing to use genetic engineering to eliminate such inherited diseases as sickle-cell anemia but quite another to use it to select the sex, body type, or coloring of a child. We are living in a time of tremendous ethical complexity, involving the interplay of new reproductive technologies; changing family structures, values, and mores; political and religious debate; and economic considerations. As increasing numbers of persons gain the ability to control conception, plan pregnancy, and control pregnancy outcomes, social workers need to protect the interests of those who lack the knowledge and other resources to do so.

CONTROL OVER CONCEPTION AND PREGNANCY

One way that humans exercise human agency is to attempt to get control over conception and pregnancy.

The desire to plan the timing of childbearing is an ancient one, as is the desire to stimulate pregnancy in the event of infertility. Contraception and induced abortion have probably always existed in every culture but continue to generate much controversy. Effective solutions for infertility are more recent. It is important to remember that not all methods of controlling conception and pregnancy are equally acceptable to all people. Cultural and religious beliefs, as well as personal circumstances, make some people more accepting of certain methods than others. Social workers must be aware of this diversity of attitudes and preferences related to the control of conception and pregnancy. Cultural and religious beliefs also drive social policy in this area. Under the U.S. Patient Information and Affordable Care Act passed in 2010, employers were required to provide insurance to cover women's birth control at no charge. With the urging of religious leaders, President Donald Trump announced plans to overturn that requirement in October 2017.

Although there is evidence that many women of the world want to control conception and pregnancy, unintended pregnancy is a global problem, estimated to be 40% of all pregnancies worldwide (Sedgh, Singh, & Hussaine, 2014). About 45% of all pregnancies in the United States are unintended (Finer & Zolna, 2016). The unintended pregnancy rate is significantly higher in the United States than in many other wealthy nations. A greater percentage of unintended pregnancies are reported by teenagers, women aged 18 to 24, cohabiting women, low-income and less educated women, and minority women (Finer & Zolna, 2016; Guttmacher Institute, 2016). For those pregnancies resulting in birth, unintended births (vs. intended births) are associated with delayed or no prenatal care (19% of unintended vs. 8.2% intended births), smoking during pregnancy (16% vs. 10%), low birth weight (12% vs. 7.2%), and no breastfeeding (39% vs. 25%) (Mosher, Jones, & Abma, 2012). Unintended pregnancy and birth are also associated with increased likelihood of perinatal depression, psychological aggression, and neglect in mothers and physical aggression in fathers (Abajobir, Maravilla, Alati, & Najman, 2016; Guterman, 2015).

Contraception

The range of birth control options available today provides women and men in many parts of the world with the ability to plan pregnancy and childbirth more than ever before. Currently 62% of U.S. women of reproductive age use some form of contraception, and 99.1% of sexually active women use a contraceptive during their lifetime (Jones, Mosher, & Daniels, 2012). However, it is estimated that 214 million women in low-income countries who don't want to get pregnant have no access to contraceptives (World Health Organization [WHO], 2017a). Forms of birth control are varied, in both effectiveness and costs. Complete sexual abstinence is the only form of contraception that has no financial cost and is completely effective. It is important for social workers to be familiar with the choices women have. Each birth control option needs to be considered in light of its cost, failure rate, potential health risks, and probability of use, given the user's sociocultural circumstances. Exhibit 2.2 summarizes the types of currently available female and male contraception, including model of delivery, failure rate, advantages, and complications and side effects.

Induced Abortion

Induced abortion may be the most politicized, hotly debated social issue related to pregnancy today in the United States and elsewhere. Researchers have found that highly restrictive abortion laws do not lead to fewer abortions. Global data indicate that the abortion rate is lowest in regions of the world that have liberal abortion laws (Sedgh et al., 2016). Abortion laws do make a difference, however, in whether abortion is safe or unsafe.

In 1973, in *Roe v. Wade*, the U.S. Supreme Court legalized abortion in the first trimester and left it to the discretion of the woman and her physician. Three years later, in 1976, the Hyde Amendment limited federal funding for abortion, and the Supreme Court ruled in 1989, in *Webster v. Reproductive Health Services*, that Medicaid could no longer fund abortions, except in cases of rape, incest, or life endangerment (Guttmacher Institute, 2018). Renewed annually, this ban on the use of federal funds for abortion has now extended to all federal employees and women in the military and the Indian Health Service. With much of the decision making related to abortion left to the states, there is wide variation in who has access to abortion, when, how, and at what cost. In some states, new rules effectively decrease access, particularly for poor and minority populations and others who are educationally disadvantaged. Seventeen states and the District of Columbia use state-only funds to cover abortions for women on Medicaid and four other states ban abortion coverage by private insurers. In 2014, 90% of U.S. counties did not have a clinic provider, and 37% of women aged 15 to 44 live in these counties (Guttmacher Institute, 2016), resulting in rural disparities in access to abortion.

EXHIBIT 2.2 ● Types of Male and Female Contraception

Type	Mode of Delivery	Failure Rate	Advantages	Complications/ Side Effects	Reference
Breastfeeding (lactational amenorrhea method)		2% with perfect use	Free, 98% effective with perfect use	17.2% to 26% of U.S. women have perfect use (still experiencing amenorrhea, breastfeeding exclusively, nursing at least 6 times every 24-hour period); no protection from sexually transmitted infections (STI)	CDC, 2014a; Garad, McNamee, Bateson, & Harvey, 2012; Warboys, 2015
Coitus interruptus		18%	Free, can be used during breastfeeding	No protection from STI; hard to predict when to withdraw penis; some sperm may enter vagina; may be harder for woman to have an orgasm	CDC, 2015a; Jones, Lindberg, & Higgins, 2014; Mayo Clinic, 2015; Reproductive Health Access Project, 2014
Fertility awareness–based methods (FABMs) (periodic abstinence; rhythm method). Six subcategories: (1) basal body temperature, (2) cervical mucus or ovulation, (3) symptothermal method, (4) calendar method, (5) standard days method, (6) 2-day method		24%	Minimal costs; no health risks	Requires careful record keeping; no protection from STI; abstinence required several days every month	CDC, 2015b; Garad et al., 2012; Smoley & Robinson, 2012
Barrier methods: male condom	Personal application	18%	Easily obtained; low cost; most effective protection from STI	Can break or slip off; decreases sensation	CDC, 2015b; Garad et al., 2012
Barrier methods: female condom	Can be inserted in vagina up to 8 hours before intercourse	21%; failure rate decreases with use over time	Inexpensive; can help prevent STI	Can decrease sensation; can be noisy; can be hard to insert; may slip out of place during sex	Beksinska, Smit, Greener, Piaggio, & Joanis, 2015; Reproductive Health Access Project, 2014

(Continued)

EXHIBIT 2.2 ● (Continued)

Type	Mode of Delivery	Failure Rate	Advantages	Complications/ Side Effects	Reference
Implant (only Nexplanon approved in the United States)	Insertion by MD under skin of upper arm; effective for up to 3 years	0.05% (highest effectiveness of any contraceptive)	Simple office procedure; dysmenorrhea will improve	Obese women have increased chance of bleeding; acne flairs; amenorrhea; no STI protection	CDC, 2015b; Jacobstein & Polis, 2014; Kolman, Hadley, & Jordahllafrato, 2015
Contraceptive patch	Applied to skin (lower abdomen, buttocks, upper body) and changed once weekly for 3 weeks; removed for 1 week	9%; increased failure for women who weigh more than 198 pounds	Periods can be less painful and more regular	Possible increase in blood clots compared to combined oral contraceptive pill; can irritate skin; no STI protection	Garad et al., 2012; M. Perry, 2015
Injectables	Injection by health professional, usually every 12 weeks (note: a new form has been developed that is subcutaneous and could be self-administered	0.40%	Can be used up to age 50; immediate effectiveness; no drug interactions	Decreased bone density; irregular bleeding	CDC, 2015a; Garad et al., 2012; Kolman et al., 2015
Intrauterine devices (IUD). Four devices approved by U.S. FDA (3 hormonal and 1 copper)	Insertion by health professional; 86% required two or more visits for insertion	<.01%	May be left in place 3–12 years (depending on type); can be used when breastfeeding	Possible uterine perforation at insertion or removal; increased bleeding and pain (primarily with copper IUD); expulsion of devise; increased or decreased bleeding at menses; no STI protection	Berry-Bibee et al., 2016; Branum & Jones, 2015; Luchowski et al., 2014; Reproductive Health Access Project, 2014
Oral contraceptives: progesterone only pill	Oral	.01%–.08%	May reduce arterial disease; good option for women who cannot have estrogen; safe for breastfeeding women	Poor efficacy in younger women; can cause depression, hair/skin changes, changed sex drive, changes in bleeding patterns; no STI protection	Angioni et al., 2015; Jacobstein & Polis, 2014; Reproductive Health Access Project, 2014

Type	Mode of Delivery	Failure Rate	Advantages	Complications/ Side Effects	Reference
Combined oral contraceptives: estrogen & progesterone	Oral	.01%–.08%	Periods more regular, less painful; improves acne; prevents ovarian cancer	Nausea; weight gain; higher risks if woman has migraines; arterial cardiovascular disease; hypertension; no STD protection	Daniels, Daugherty, & Jones, 2014; Dragoman, 2014; Reproductive Health Access Project, 2014; Xu, Eisenberg, Madden, Secura, & Peiper, 2014
Male oral contraceptive (in development; may take 10 years)	Oral		Only current contraceptives for men are condoms or vasectomy	Concern by women that men may not take it; possible change in blood pressure and heart rate; possible change in ejaculation volume	Anguita, 2014; National Library of Medicine, 2017; Roth, Page, & Bremner, 2016
Emergency contraception (EC)	Oral or vaginal insertion	0.1%–50% (most effective is insertion of copper IUD)	Some over the counter	No STI protection; time limitations to use; costs; need for medical care for some forms of EC	Cleland, Raymond, Westley, & Trussell, 2014; Jatlaoui & Curtis, 2016
Vaginal ring	Insertion; remains in place for 3 weeks and is removed for 1 week	9%	Less menstrual discomfort; ability to manipulate hormonal cycles; long-term dosing; ease of administration; reversibility	Contraindicated for obese women and those with migraines with auras; increased vaginal discharge; heavy bleeding; acne; no STI protection	Nappi, 2013; Reproductive Health Access Project, 2014
Surgical sterilization: female (tubal ligation)	Surgical	.002%–.01%, depending on procedure	Possible reversal; can prevent cancer	Surgical complications	CDC, 2015a; Daniels et al., 2014; Gariepy, Creinin, Smith, & Xiao, 2014; Malacova et al., 2015; van Seeter, Chua, Mol, & Koks, 2017
Surgical sterilization: male (vasectomy)	Surgical	0.10%	55% can be reversed in first 10 years, 25% after 10 years	Surgical complications	Guttmacher Institute, 2015; Herrel, Goodman, Goldstein, & Hsiao, 2015

During the first trimester and until **fetal viability** (the point at which the baby could survive outside the womb) in the second trimester, U.S. federal law allows for a pregnant woman to legally choose an abortion, although states can narrow this option. Data from 2013 indicate that 89% of abortions in the United States are performed during the first 12 weeks of pregnancy, 10% from 13 to 20 weeks, and 1.3% after 21 weeks (Guttmacher Institute, 2018). Recent controversy regarding procedures for terminating a pregnancy after fetal viability has called attention to ethical and legal dilemmas that are being addressed in the legal system, by most religions, and in other parts of U.S. culture. Opinion polls reveal, however, that the majority of Americans favor abortion as an option under specified conditions. A Pew Research Center (2017a) poll revealed that 57% of the U.S. population think abortion should be legal in all or most cases in comparison to 40% who believe it should be illegal in all or most cases. These attitudes have been relatively consistent since 1975. According to the Guttmacher Institute (2018), 12% of women obtaining an abortion in the United States are teenagers, and 61% are in their 20s. Non-Hispanic White women receive 39% of abortions, non-Hispanic Black women receive 28%, and Hispanic women receive 25%. Women who have never married and are not cohabiting receive 46% of abortions, and 59% are obtained by women who have one or more children. About half, 49%, of women obtaining abortions have incomes 100% below the federal poverty level.

Two types of abortion are available to women.

1. *Medication abortion.* Medication abortion is the term used to refer to an abortion brought about by medication taken to end pregnancy. Most commonly, the drugs mifepristone (also known as RU-486) and misoprostol are used in combination in the first 9 weeks after the woman's last period. In the United States, a few states limit the use to 49 days after the last period. In 2014, medication abortions made up 31% of all non-hospital abortions and 45% of abortions before 9 weeks' gestation (Guttmacher Institute, 2018). The number of medication abortions increased from 2001 to 2011 (growing from 6% to 23% of all abortions) while the overall number of abortions declined. Medication abortion works about 97% of the time.

2. *Surgical abortion.* Surgical abortions must be done in a health provider's office or clinic. There are several surgical options, depending on how far along a woman is in her pregnancy. The standard first-trimester vacuum aspiration, also called D&A (dilation and aspiration) is the type most frequently performed in the first 16 weeks after the woman's last period. A suction device is threaded through the cervix to remove the contents of the uterus. The use of this procedure decreased by 14% from 2005 to 2014. Sometimes, a spoon-shaped instrument called a curette is used to scrape the uterine lining, a procedure called a D&C. In the second trimester (13th to 24th week), dilation and evacuation (D&E) is typically performed. This involves instruments, such as forceps, to empty the uterus (Jatlaoui et al., 2017).

Regardless of the timing or type of abortion, most women should be carefully counseled before and after the procedure. One research team (Fergusson, Horwood, & Boden, 2009) found that more than 85% of women reported feeling at least one negative reaction, such as grief, guilt, sadness, or sorrow, after having an abortion. These negative reactions were offset by positive reactions, and over 85% of the women also reported feeling relief, happiness, and satisfaction. The researchers also found that looking back at the abortion decision later, nearly 90% reported that the decision to have an abortion was the correct decision, and only 2% reported that it was the wrong decision. Women who reported more negative reactions were more likely to have later mental health problems. Another research team (Steinberg & Finer, 2011) found that women who had risk factors such as physical or sexual abuse prior to abortion were more likely to have mental health issues after abortion. They also found that women with prior mood and anxiety disorders were more likely to have multiple abortions. It is important for social workers working with clients with unintended pregnancy to assess for prior traumatic experiences as well as know the current federal and state legalities and resources, especially when clients have limited income. They also need to be mindful of their personal views about abortion to help clients make informed decisions that reflect their own values, religious beliefs, and available options as well as agency/organization policy related to abortion.

Infertility Treatment

Infertility, the inability to create a viable embryo after 1 year of intercourse without contraception (Centers for Disease Control and Prevention, 2017b), is a major life stressor. Because both male and female factors are involved, determining infertility prevalence rates is challenging. It is estimated that one in four couples in low-income countries struggle with infertility (Mascarenhas, Flaxman, Boerma, Vanderpoel, & Stevens, 2012) and that 12.1% of women in the United States have reduced fertility and 6.7% are infertile (Centers for Disease Control and Prevention, 2016a). It is estimated that one third of the problems reside in the man and one third in the woman. Sometimes no cause can be found (MedlinePlus, 2015).

Jennifer Bradshaw poignantly conveys her emotional distress about infertility, but we don't know much about what her husband was experiencing. Although it is thought that infertility causes emotional distress to both women and men (Mascarenhas et al., 2012), little is known about the impact on men. Recent research indicates that men with the most infertility distress are likely to see infertility as an attack on their masculinity and perceived need to maintain emotional control (Dooley, Dineen, Sarma, & Nolan, 2014). Available research indicates that infertility places women at risk for depression, anxiety, substance abuse, social stress, isolation, and marital dissatisfaction (see, e.g., Baldur-Felskov et al., 2013; Rockwood & Pendergast, 2016). Women have traditionally sought informal support whereas men have

focused on the financial impact of infertility. Social support, specifically a positive marital relationship, has been found to be positively associated with increased coping skills, but the process of disclosing one's infertility to others can increase anxiety (Martins et al., 2013). Both the experience of infertility and the treatment of infertility can cause emotional distress (Greil, McQuillan, Lowry, & Shreffler, 2011). Narrative, existential, and cognitive behavioral approaches have been shown to be effective for this population (Ridenour, Yorgason, & Peterson, 2009; Stark, Keathley, & Nelson, 2011).

The causes of infertility are many and complex. Infertility, like other aspects of human behavior, is multidetermined. Exhibit 2.3, which draws on numerous sources to identify medical causes, environmental

---

EXHIBIT 2.3 ● Possible Causes of Male and Female Infertility

Male Causes	Female Causes
Medical Causes	*Medical Causes*
• Varicocele (swelling of the veins that drain the testicle) • Infection (sexually transmitted infections, inflamed testicles due to mumps) • Antibodies that attack sperm • Tumors and treatments for tumors (surgery, radiation, and chemotherapy) • Undescended testicles • Hormone imbalances • Sperm duct defects • Chromosome defects (e.g., Klinefelter's syndrome, cystic fibrosis) • Problems with sexual intercourse (erectile dysfunction, premature ejaculation) • Celiac disease • Medications (testosterone replacement therapy, anabolic steroids, antifungal medications, some ulcer drugs)	• Ovulation disorders (polycystic ovary syndrome [PCOS], hypothalamic dysfunction, premature ovarian insufficiency, too much prolactin) • Damage to fallopian tubes (caused by pelvic inflammatory disease, previous surgery in abdomen, or pelvic tuberculosis) • Endometriosis • Uterine or cervical causes (uterine polyps or tumors, abnormally shaped uterus, cervical stenosis, cervical mucus insufficiency) • Sexually transmitted infections
Environmental Causes	*Environmental Causes*
• Industrial chemicals (benzenes, toluene, xylene, pesticides, herbicides, painting material, lead) • Heavy metal exposure • Radiation or X-rays • Overheating the testicles (frequent use of saunas and hot tubs, sitting for long periods, wearing tight clothing, working on laptop computer for long stretches)	• Industrial chemicals • Radiation • Chemotherapy

(Continued)

EXHIBIT 2.3 ● (Continued)

Male Causes	Female Causes
Health, Lifestyle, and Other Causes	*Health, Lifestyle, and Other Causes*
• Illegal drug use (cocaine or marijuana)	• Illegal drug use
• Alcohol use	• Alcohol use
• Tobacco smoking	• Tobacco smoking
• Occupation (those involving extended use of computers, shift work, work-related stress)	• Physical and emotional stress
• Emotional stress	• Eating disorders, obesity
• Obesity	
• Prolonged bicycling	

causes, and health and lifestyle causes, demonstrates this complexity. New research also indicates that some men have a genetic factor that intersects with environmental factors to increase the risk of infertility (Hamada, Esteves, & Agarwai, 2011; Miyamoto et al., 2012). Medical causes have received more research attention than other causes; consequently, there is clearer evidence for medical causes. Fertility decreases as men and women age (Amudha, Rani, Kannan, & Manavalan, 2013). There are racial differences in infertility in the United States, with Black and Hispanic women having twice the rate but using infertility services significantly less than White women (Greil, McQuillan, Shreffler, Johnson, & Slauson-Blevins, 2011).

In the past, infertile couples could keep trying and hope for the best, but medical technology has given today's couples a variety of options, summarized in Exhibit 2.4. Women may be advised to lose or gain weight or to modify exercise habits to maximize the chances of ovulation and pregnancy. Medications may be used to help women ovulate, to treat infections in

EXHIBIT 2.4 ● Treatments for Infertility

Male Infertility		Female Infertility	
Problem	Treatment	Problem	Treatment
Low sperm count	Change of environment; antibiotics; surgery; hormonal therapy; artificial insemination	Vaginal structural problem	Surgery
		Abnormal cervical mucus	Hormonal therapy
Physical defect affecting transport of sperm	Microsurgery	Abnormal absence of ovulation	Antibiotics for infection; hormonal therapy
Genetic disorder	Artificial insemination	Blocked or scarred fallopian tubes	Surgery; IVF
Exposure to work environment substances	Early detection and changes in work environment	Uterine lining unfavorable to implantation	Hormone therapy; antibiotics; surgery
Alcohol and caffeine use and cigarette smoking	Reduction or abstinence preconception	Obesity	Weight reduction
Advancing age	Sperm banking at younger age; artificial insemination	Alcohol and caffeine use and cigarette smoking	Abstinence preconception (and postconception to maximize pregnancy outcome)

both men and women, and to treat ejaculation problems in men (Amudha et al., 2013). Surgeries may be used to correct structural problems in the reproductive systems of both men and women (Mayo Clinic, 2018). Today, a little over 1% of infants born in the United States are the result of **assisted reproductive technologies (ART)** (CDC, 2017b). ART is any fertility treatment in which both eggs and embryos are handled. As demonstrated by the Jennifer Bradshaw case, by the time a couple considers the use of ART, they have often struggled with infertility for some time, emotionally and physically, and may be desperate. But the high cost and limited success rates deter some prospective candidates. The most common types of ART include the following.

- *IVF.* In vitro fertilization (IVF) is the most common and most effective ART used today. The woman is treated with a drug that causes the ovaries to produce multiple eggs. Mature eggs are surgically removed from the woman and combined with sperm in a dish in the lab. Healthy embryos are then implanted in the woman's uterus (American Society for Reproductive Medicine, 2013). This method is often used when a woman's fallopian tubes are blocked or a man produces too few sperm. Treatment costs may vary widely among clinics and states, with one cycle of IVF averaging $12,000 with an additional $5,000 for drugs used in the process. Genetic testing, egg and embryo freezing, and other procedures, when desired, can add another $100,000 to the costs (McCarter, 2016). Some clinics allow partial or complete refunds if pregnancy does not occur with higher-priced multiple-cycle plans, a practice referred to as "shared risk" (Advanced Fertility Center of Chicago, 2014). Success rates vary, but most clinics suggest that with a single cycle of IVF, there is a 40% success rate for women age 34 and younger, 4% for women age 40, and 1% for women age 44 (Gordon et al., 2013; National Center for Chronic Disease Prevention and Health Promotion, 2014). Previously frozen eggs may also be used, but the rate of success decreases.

- *Intracytoplasmic sperm injection (ICSI).* ICSI is typically used for couples when there are serious problems with the sperm. In ICSI, rather than mixing egg and sperm in a dish, a single sperm is injected into a single mature egg (American Society for Reproductive Medicine, 2013).

- *Egg donors and gestational carriers.* A couple may use donor eggs to be fertilized with the sperm of the male partner and then have the fertilized egg placed in the uterus of the female partner. The resulting child will be genetically related to the egg donor and the male partner. Another option is to implant a gestational carrier with the couple's embryo produced through IVF. This option may be used when the woman can produce healthy eggs but is unable to carry a pregnancy to term. Donor eggs or sperm may also be used in IVF to produce the embryo, which is then placed in the gestational carrier. The resulting child has no genetic relationship to the gestational carrier (American Society for Reproductive Medicine, 2013). The costs of using a gestational carrier can easily reach $100,000 because insurance usually does not cover the medical costs of the pregnancy (Herron, 2013).

- *Intrauterine insemination (IUI).* Healthy sperm are collected, washed, and concentrated, then placed directly into the uterus through a fine tube inserted through the cervix around the time the ovary releases one or more eggs (American Society for Reproductive Medicine, 2013). It is the primary treatment for male infertility. It is also the treatment of choice for lesbian couples and single parents, using sperm of a male donor (De Brucker et al., 2009). The sperm of the male partner of a couple may also be placed in the uterus of a surrogate who gestates and carries the pregnancy for the couple. The resulting child will be biologically related to the male partner and the surrogate, but not to the female partner in the couple.

- *INVOcell (IVC), a new method.* Following the retrieval of the eggs (after mild stimulation of the ovaries with medication), they are combined with sperm and placed in a small plastic chamber. This is then inserted into the woman's vagina for 3 to 5 days. After retrieval, the most viable embryos are transferred to the uterus. The cost of IVC ($6,500) is significantly less than traditional IVF, bringing assistance to a larger population. Some centers continue to incubate the embryos in a laboratory setting because this method allows direct observation of the embryos. The birth rates for IVF and IVC are similar. Many women feel that this method is more natural and provides emotional bonding (Doody, Boome, & Doody, 2016).

- *Uterine transplantation* is another infertility treatment that is on the frontier. The first successful live birth after a uterine transplant was in Sweden in 2014, and by 2017, uterine transplants in Sweden had resulted in five pregnancies and four live births (Brown, 2014; Fayed, 2018).

Each ART procedure carries risks. These include multiple gestations, which carry higher risks of maternal and neonate complications. In 2009, almost half of ART births resulted in more than one neonate (CDC, 2016a, 2017b). IVF can be used by a parent or parents who know they have a genetic defect that can be passed to the child. The embryos are harvested and checked at the 8-cell growth level, and those with genetic defects are not implanted (Eckman, 2014).

The new technologies for assisting reproduction raise a number of ethical and legal issues. A major issue relates to the disparities in access to these technologies and the related question of whether some groups should be refused access (Brezina & Zhao, 2012). Another issue is what should happen to unused embryos created by IVF (Clark, 2009). There are also questions about whether embryos created by IVF should be allowed to be selected based on gender or specific physical traits. There are many questions about the roles, rights, and responsibilities of surrogates and gestational carriers (Frith & Blyth, 2013; James, Chilvers, Havermann, & Phelps, 2010). Uterine transplantation carries many questions about access, risks, and costs (Catsanos, Rogers, & Lotz, 2013). Questions are also raised about the costs of reproductive technologies in light of the need for adoptive families.

Adoption is another alternative for the infertile couple. In 2012, there were 119,514 adoptions in the United States, a 6% decrease from 2008 (U.S. Department of Health and Human Services, 2016). Recent data indicate that 25% of adopted children in the United States are international adoptions, 38% are private domestic adoptions, and 37% are foster care adoptions (Statistic Brain, 2017). On average, adoption is a highly successful solution to providing permanent family relationships to children whose biological parents are unavailable. The adoption process is almost as emotionally daunting as infertility treatment, however. A time-consuming multiphase evaluation, which includes a home study, is required before finalization of custody. The idea of parenting an infant with an unknown genetic heritage may be a challenge for some people, particularly because an increasing number of problems previously thought to be environmentally induced are being linked—at least in part—to genetics. On the positive side, however, some individuals and couples prefer adoption to the demands and uncertainties of ART, and some adoptive parents are also committed to giving a home to children in need of care. And, truthfully, most of us are not aware of all the genetic secrets in our lineage.

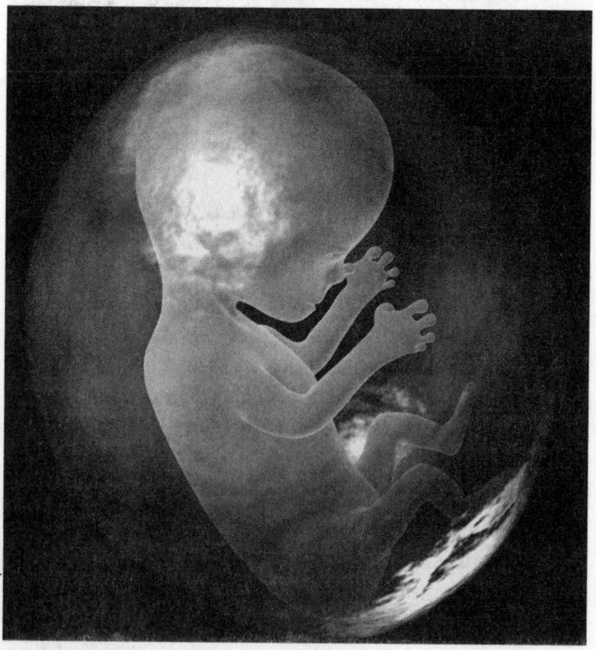

PHOTO 2.3 After week 8, the embryo is mature enough to be called a fetus.

© iStockphoto.com

CRITICAL THINKING QUESTIONS 2.2

In recent years, there has been much controversy about sex education in public schools. Some people argue that there should be no sex education in public schools. What is your opinion on this topic? If you think there should be sex education in public schools, at what age do you think it should start? If you think there should be sex education in public schools, what should it cover?

FETAL DEVELOPMENT

The 40 weeks of **gestation**, during which the fertilized ovum becomes a fully developed infant, are a remarkable time. **Gestational age** is calculated from the date of the beginning of the woman's last menstrual period, a fairly easy time for the woman to identify. In contrast, **fertilization age** is measured from the time of fertilization, approximately 14 days after the beginning of the last menstrual period. The average pregnancy lasts 280 days when calculated from gestational age and 266 days from the time of fertilization. Conventionally, the gestation period is organized by trimesters of about 3 months each. This is a convenient system, but note that these divisions are not supported by clearly demarcated events.

First Trimester

In some ways, the first 12 weeks of pregnancy are the most remarkable. In an amazingly short time, sperm and ovum unite and are transformed into a being with identifiable body parts. The mother's body also undergoes dramatic changes.

Fertilization and the Embryonic Period

Sexual intercourse results in the release of an average of 200 million to 300 million sperm. Their life span is relatively short, and their journey through the female reproductive tract is fraught with hazards. Thus, only about one or two in 1,000 of the original sperm reach the fallopian tubes, which lead from the ovaries to the uterus. Typically, only one sperm penetrates the ripened ovum, triggering a biochemical reaction that prevents entry of any other sperm. The **zygote** (fertilized egg) continues to divide and begins an approximately 7-day journey to the uterus.

Following implantation in the uterine wall, the zygote matures into an **embryo**. The placenta, which acts like a filter between the mother and the growing embryo, also forms. The umbilical cord connects the fetus to the placenta. Oxygen, water, and glucose, as well as many drugs, viruses, bacteria, vitamins, and hormones, pass through the placenta to the embryo. Amniotic fluid in the uterus protects the embryo throughout the pregnancy.

By the 3rd week, tissue begins differentiating into organs. During this period, the embryo is vulnerable to **teratogens**—substances that may harm the developing organism—but most women do not know they are pregnant. Exhibit 2.5 shows how some relatively common drugs may have a teratogenic effect in the earliest stage of fetal development. The importance of a healthy diet cannot be overestimated for the pregnant woman because her choices can have a lifelong impact on her baby (Stanford Children's Health, 2018). Studies have found that nutritional deficiency in the first trimester results in an increase in brain abnormalities and early death from natural causes (Ekamper, van Poppel, Stein, Bijwaard, & Lumey, 2015). High-fat diets negatively affect the development of the hippocampus, which helps control

EXHIBIT 2.5 ● **Potential Teratogens During the First Trimester**	
Substance	Effects on Fetal Development
Antacids	Increase in anomalies
Antianxiety medications	Cranial facial
Anticonvulsant medications	Facial defects, neural tube defects
Barbiturates	Increase in anomalies
Bisphenol A (BPA)	Mammary glands, immune system, brain, reproductive tract
Glucocorticoids (steroids)	Cleft palate, cardiac defects
Haloperidol	Limb malformations
Insulin	Skeletal malformations
Lithium	Goiter, eye anomalies, cleft palate
LSD	Chromosomal abnormalities
Podophyllin (in laxatives)	Multiple anomalies
Selective serotonin reuptake inhibitors (SSRIs)	May lead to neurobehavioral disturbances
Tetracycline (antibiotic)	Inhibition of bone growth, discoloration of teeth
Tricyclic antidepressants	Central nervous system and limb malformations

long-term memory and spatial navigation. Researchers have discovered that offspring of women who were either obese or pregnant during a famine were at significantly increased risk for developing schizophrenia (Khandaker, Dibben, & Jones, 2012; Roseboom, Painter, van Abeelen, Veenendall, & de Rooij, 2011). Isothiocyanate and cruciferous vegetables (such as broccoli, brussels sprouts, radishes, turnips), beta-carotenes (found in yellow, red, and orange fruits and vegetables and whole grains), and carotenoid lycopenes (found in tomatoes, guava, apricots, watermelons, and papaya) have been found to promote healthy cellular growth in the fetus (Kaur et al., 2013). The intake of folate and folic acid (found in cereal, spinach, beans, oranges, and peanuts) helps to prevent birth defects; calcium (found in cereal, milk, juice, yogurt, cheese, and salmon) strengthens the bones as does Vitamin D (found in fish, milk, juice, and eggs) (U.S. Department of Agriculture, 2015). The development of a healthy cellular structure promotes health throughout the life course, and the positive effects appear to extend into future generations because the change occurs at the cellular level (Kaur et al., 2013).

Ectopic pregnancy is one type of mishap that occurs during this period. An ectopic pregnancy occurs if the zygote implants outside the uterus, 93% of the time in the fallopian tubes (Murano & Cocuzza, 2009) and sometimes in the ovaries. Approximately 1% to 2% of pregnancies in the United States result in an ectopic pregnancy. Women older than 35 have a 3.5% greater chance of an ectopic pregnancy. Women who experience one ectopic pregnancy have higher rates of future ectopic pregnancies (5% to 20%) and infertility (ranging from 20% to 70%) (Healthline, 2018). Chlamydia, the most commonly occurring sexually transmitted disease, increases the risk for an ectopic pregnancy (Centers for Disease Control and Prevention, 2018a).

With advancements in ultrasound technology and microsurgery, the maternal mortality rates in cases of ectopic pregnancy have decreased (Creanga et al., 2011). The treatment for ectopic pregnancy is either medication to terminate the pregnancy or surgery (American College of Obstetricians and Gynecologists, 2017a).

The Fetal Period

By about the 8th week after fertilization, the embryo implanted in the uterine wall is mature enough to be called a **fetus**, or unborn baby, and the mother is experiencing signs of her pregnancy. Usually the mother has now missed one or two menstrual periods, but if her cycle was irregular, this may not be a reliable sign. A **multigravida**, or woman who has had a previous pregnancy, often recognizes the signs of excessive fatigue and soreness in her breasts as a sign of pregnancy. Approximately 80% of women experience nausea and vomiting (morning sickness) during the first trimester, as was the case for Felicia Thompson. It has been found that women are at a greater risk for morning sickness if there is a low protein intake. Some early studies have demonstrated that there may be positive benefits in stabilizing early fetal nutrition when a woman experiences morning sickness (Patil, Abrams, Steinmetz, & Young, 2012). Ginger, which has been used for more than 2,000 years to treat morning sickness, has been scientifically shown to reduce vomiting (Ozgoli, Goli, & Simbar, 2009). A few women experience vomiting so severe that it causes dehydration and metabolic changes requiring hospitalization. Hyperemesis gravidarum (HG) occurs in about 1% of all pregnant women

and is characterized by excessive and persistent nausea and vomiting (Stokke et al., 2015). It can last through all three trimesters and has been associated with prematurity, low birth weight, preeclampsia, placental abruption, and stillbirth (Bolin, Akerud, Cnattingius, Stephansson, & Wikstrom, 2013). Furthermore, mental health is negatively affected by HG at the time of pregnancy, and this situation may continue after childbirth (Senturk, Yildiz, Yorguner, & Cakmak, 2017). Researchers have also found that women with HG are significantly more likely to self-report physical and psychosocial issues both before and after pregnancy (Tian, MacGibbon, Martin, Mulin, Fejzo, 2017). Norwegian researchers have found enteral tube feeding to be a feasible treatment to produce sufficient maternal weight gain and favorable pregnancy outcomes (Stokke et al., 2015). Teaching the mother progressive muscle relaxation along with medication management has been shown to reduce HG (Gawande, Vaidya, Tadke, Kirpekar, & Bhave, 2011).

From the 7th to 12th week, the fetal heart rate can be heard using a Doppler fetal monitor (Merce, Barco, Alcazar, Sabatel, & Trojano, 2009). Early ultrasounds are used to predict prenatal complications (Parra-Cordeno et al., 2013). At 12 weeks, the sex of the fetus usually can be detected, and the face is fully formed. The fetus is moving within the mother, but it is still too early for her to feel the movement.

Newly pregnant women often feel ambivalence. Because of hormonal changes, they may experience mood swings and become less outgoing. Anxiety and depression have been found to be higher during the first trimester and in the postpartum period than the subsequent two trimesters and can affect attachment to the fetus (Fan et al., 2009; Figueiredo & Conde, 2011). Maternal depression, occurring in 10% of pregnant women, increases the rate of prematurity, low birth weight, intrauterine growth restriction, and postnatal complications (Eke, Saccone, & Berghella, 2016). Concerns about the changes in their bodies, finances, the impact on their life goals, lifestyle adjustments, and interpersonal interactions may cause anxiety. Often the father experiences similar ambivalence, and he may be distressed by his partner's mood swings. Parents who have previously miscarried may have a heightened concern for the well-being of this fetus.

Miscarriage, or **spontaneous abortion**, is a pregnancy loss prior to 20 weeks of gestation and is most prevalent in the first trimester. Approximately 17% of pregnancies end in miscarriage, 18% in medical abortion, and 65% in live birth (Oaklander, 2015). Recurrent miscarriage, three or more consecutive miscarriages, occurs in 1% of women and carries a higher risk for maternal and fetal complications (Fawzy, Saravelos, Li, & Metwally, 2016). Sometimes the causes of miscarriage are not clear, but researchers have identified a number of potential causes. It is estimated that about half of all miscarriages are caused by abnormalities in the genetic makeup of the fetus. Chronic conditions such as uncontrolled diabetes, thyroid disease, high BMI, and other underlying maternal health conditions increase the risk of miscarriage, as do smoking and alcohol use (Matijila, Hoffman, & van der Spuy, 2017). Other potential causes are problems in placental development, womb structure abnormalities, polycystic ovary syndrome, obesity and underweight, environmental toxins, and some medications.

The signs and symptoms of miscarriage include vaginal spotting or bleeding, cramping or pain in the abdomen or lower backache, fluid or tissue discharge from the vagina, and feeling faint or light-headed (American Pregnancy Association, 2017b). These symptoms do not always mean a woman is having a miscarriage, and sometimes miscarriage happens with no symptoms (American College of Nurse-Midwives, 2013). Miscarriage is most commonly diagnosed these days by ultrasound; blood tests may also be done (Al-Memar, Kirk, & Bourne, 2015). Some women choose to allow the miscarriage to pass naturally; this may take 2 weeks. Sometimes it is not possible to pass all of the pregnancy without further assistance. Women may take medication to help the body pass the miscarriage, and sometimes surgery is needed to complete the miscarriage (American College of Nurse-Midwives, 2013). Counseling of women who struggle with miscarriages focuses on genetics and the biopsychological needs of the woman and her family (Randolph, Hruby, & Sherif, 2015). Social workers need to understand the possibility of both short-term and long-term grief following a pregnancy loss and attachment issues that might arise during subsequent pregnancies (Chetu, 2017). They should be prepared to talk with women about whether a subsequent pregnancy is planned, the importance the mother attributes to motherhood, and fertility issues (Shreffler, Greil, & McQuillan, 2011; Wright, 2011).

Second Trimester

By the 16th week, the fetus is approximately 19 centimeters (7.5 inches) long and weighs 100 grams (3.3 ounces). The most rapid period of brain development is during the second trimester (Zhan et al., 2013). In recent years, there have been controversies about pregnant women eating fish, but recent evidence shows that eating fish during the second trimester may have a positive effect on fetal birthweight. Two fish meals per week are recommended, without the earlier worries about mercury levels (Taylor, Golding, & Emond, 2016). Insufficient weight gain by the pregnant woman during this trimester has been shown to be associated with a small-for-gestational-age (SGA) neonate (Drehmer, Duncan, Kac, & Schmidt, 2013). Excessive weight gain during this period can lead to hypertension and diabetes (Ruhstaller et al., 2016). The second trimester is generally a period of contentment and planning for most women, as it seems to have been for Felicia Thompson. For problem pregnancies, or in troubled environments, quite the opposite may occur. However, the fatigue, nausea and vomiting, and mood swings that often accompany the first few weeks usually disappear in the second trimester.

Hearing the heartbeat and seeing the fetus via ultrasound often bring the reality of the pregnancy home. As seen in the story of the Thompsons, *quickening*—the experience of feeling fetal movement—usually occurs around this time, further validating the personhood of the fetus. *Fetal differentiation*, whereby the mother separates the individuality of the fetus from her own personhood, is usually completed by the end of this trimester. Many fathers too begin to relate to the fetus as a developing offspring.

Some fathers enjoy the changing shape of the woman's body, but others may struggle with the changes. Unless there are specific contraindications, sexual relations may continue throughout the pregnancy, and some men find the second trimester a period of great sexual satisfaction. Often during the second trimester the pregnant woman also experiences a return of her prepregnancy level of sexual desire.

Third Trimester

The third trimester is critical for continued fetal development and preparation for birth. The mother must be able to effectively meet both her nutritional needs and those of the growing fetus. Women who have excessive weight gain are at risk for preterm delivery and higher rates of cesarean section (Drehmer et al., 2013). Maternal smoking decreases fetal circulation and has been correlated with lower birth weight; older mothers have increasingly negative effects from smoking while pregnant (Trojner-Bregar et al., 2018; Zheng, Suzuki, Tanaka, Kohama, & Yamagata, 2016). Spouses who smoke increase the nicotine level in the nonsmoking pregnant woman, even if the spouse smokes outside (Andriani & Hsien, 2014). The provision of in-home services early in the pregnancy to encourage smoking cessation has been shown to be effective in reducing the incidence of smoking during the third trimester (Windsor, Clark, Davis, Wedeles, & Abroms, 2017).

More than 30% of women are iron-deficient by the third trimester, placing the neonate at risk for anemia. Low iron levels can result in permanently altered developmental and metabolic processes and negatively impact brain development (Cao & O'Brien, 2013). In addition, maternal stress can reduce fetoplacental blood flow and fetal weight gain (Helbig, Kaasen, Mait, & Haugen, 2013). Today, a 3-D diffusion tensor image MRI can be used to visualize the movement in the fetal brain (Fogtmann et al., 2014). By 24 weeks, the fetus is considered viable in many hospitals. In spite of fetal viability, parents are not usually prepared for childbirth early in the third trimester. Felicia Thompson, for instance, was not prepared for the birth of her son, Paul, who at 26 weeks' gestation struggled to survive.

The tasks of the fetus during the third trimester are to gain weight and mature in preparation for delivery. As delivery nears, the increased weight of the fetus can cause discomfort for the mother, and often she looks forward to delivery with increasing anticipation. Completing preparations for the new baby consume much of her attention.

Labor and Delivery of the Neonate

Predicting when labor will begin is impossible. However, one indication of imminent labor is *lightening* (the descent of the fetus into the mother's pelvis). For a **primipara**— a first-time mother—lightening occurs approximately 2 weeks before delivery. For a **multipara**—a mother who has previously given birth—lightening typically occurs at the beginning of labor. Often the mother experiences Braxton Hicks contractions, brief contractions that prepare the mother and fetus for labor—what is often referred to as "false labor." Usually, true labor begins with a show or release of the mucous plug that covered the cervical opening.

Labor is divided into three stages.

1. In the first stage, the cervix thins and dilates. The amniotic fluid is usually released during this stage ("water breaking"), and the mother feels regular contractions that intensify in frequency and strength as labor progresses. Many factors determine the length of this stage, including the number of pregnancies the mother has experienced, the weight of the fetus, the anatomy of the mother, the strength of the contractions, and the relaxation of the mother in the process. Despite the stories that abound, most mothers have plenty of time to prepare for the upcoming birth. Near the end of this phase, "transition" occurs, marked by a significant increase in the intensity and frequency of the contractions and by heightened maternal emotionalism. The head crowns (is visible at the vulva) at the end of this stage.

2. The second stage is delivery, when the neonate is expelled from the mother. If the newborn is born breech (feet or buttocks first) or is transverse (positioned horizontally in the birth canal) and cannot be turned prior to birth, the mother may require a cesarean section.

3. Typically, within 1 hour after delivery, the placenta, the remaining amniotic fluid, and the membrane that separated the fetus from the uterine wall are delivered with a few contractions. If the newborn breastfeeds immediately, the hormone oxytocin is released to stimulate these contractions.

Following birth, the neonate undergoes rapid physiological changes, particularly in its respiratory and cardiac systems. Prior to birth, oxygen is delivered to the fetus through the umbilical vein, and carbon dioxide is eliminated by the two umbilical arteries. Although the fetus begins to breathe prior to birth, breathing serves no purpose until after delivery. The neonate's first breath, typically in the form of a cry, creates tremendous pressure within the lungs, which clears amniotic fluid and triggers the opening and closing of several shunts and vessels in the heart. The blood flow is rerouted to the lungs.

Many factors, such as maternal exposure to narcotics during pregnancy or labor, can adversely affect the neonate's attempts to breathe—as can prematurity, congenital anomalies, and neonatal infections. Drugs and other interventions may be administered to maintain adequate respiration. To measure the neonate's adjustment to extrauterine life, Apgar scores—simple measures of breathing, heart rate, muscle tone, reflexes, and skin color—are assessed at 1, 5, and 10 minutes after birth. Apgar scores determine the need for resuscitation and indicate whether there are heart problems. The other immediate challenge to the newborn is to establish a stable temperature. Inadequately maintained body temperature creates neonatal stress and thus increased respiratory and cardiac effort, which can result in respiratory failure. Close monitoring of the neonate during the first 4 hours after birth is critical to detect any such problems in adapting to extrauterine life.

Sometimes the baby is born showing no signs of life; this is known as stillbirth. The Centers for Disease Control and Prevention (2017c) define stillbirth as "the death of or loss of a baby before or during delivery" (para. 1). They further classify stillbirth as *early* (occurring from 20 to 27 completed weeks of pregnancy), *late* (occurring from 28 to 36 completed weeks), and *term* (occurring at 37 or more completed weeks). The World Health Organization (2016a) reports that in 2015, there were an estimated 2.6 million late or term stillbirths around the world, with

98% taking place in low-income and middle-income countries. In the United States 1% of pregnancies end in stillbirth. Advanced technology and improved prenatal care have reduced the number of late and term stillbirths in the past 30 years, but the rate of early stillbirth has remained about the same over time (Centers for Disease Control and Prevention, 2017c). The primary causes of stillbirth are well known: advanced maternal age, noncommunicable infections, nutrition deficits, obesity, smoking, poor prenatal care, and lifestyle issues (The Lancet, 2016). There is a greater chance of subsequent pregnancies ending in stillbirth once this has occurred (Barclay, 2009). In cases of fetal death, labor generally proceeds immediately and is allowed to occur naturally. But the pregnancy may continue for several days following cessation of movement. Although this wait can be distressing for the mother, cesarean sections are usually avoided because of the potentially high number of complications for the mother (Barclay, 2009). Stillbirths are often unexpected, resulting in great stress and anguish for parents, who blame themselves and struggle with unresolved guilt. Social workers can help parents understand and cope with the strong emotions they are experiencing due to such a significant loss (Navidian, Saravani, & Shakba, 2017).

CRITICAL THINKING QUESTIONS 2.3

How is ultrasound technology changing the process of fetal development for the mother? What are the benefits to these technologies? What ethical issues are raised by the use of these technologies?

PREGNANCY AND THE LIFE COURSE

The childbearing age for women is usually listed as 15 to 44, but physiologically, women are considered to be at the optimal age for pregnancy from the ages of 20 to 35. Pregnant women of every age need the support of caring family members, friends, and health providers, but women of different ages face pregnancy with different biological bodies and different psychological and social resources. The special circumstances and needs of pregnant adolescents are discussed in Chapter 6, and this section considers pregnancy during young adulthood as well as what is referred to as delayed pregnancy after age 35.

Pregnancy during young adulthood is a normative event in most cultures. Psychosocially, young adults are involved in establishing life goals, and both parenthood and employment are often a part of those goals. Women in young adulthood are trying to balance love and work, become more financially secure, and develop a career path or other positive work trajectory (Koert & Daniluk, 2017). Over the last 3 decades, pregnant women's employment patterns have seen major changes, with more women working overall and longer into the pregnancy cycle. From 2006 to 2008, two thirds of first-time mothers in the United States worked during their pregnancy, up from 44% from 1961 to 1965 (Martin, Hamilton, Osterman, Driscoll, & Matthews, 2017). There are legal, physical, and psychosocial considerations for maintaining employment during pregnancy. Salihu and colleagues (Salihu, Myers, & August, 2012) have done an in-depth review of research related to these considerations. The following three paragraphs summarize their important findings.

In terms of the legal considerations, a number of countries have laws to protect the rights of pregnant women in the workplace. In the United States, the Pregnancy Discrimination Act (PDA), passed in 1978, established that organizations cannot refuse to hire a woman because she is pregnant, cannot fire a woman or force her to leave because she is pregnant, cannot take away credit for previous years of work during maternity leave, and cannot fire or refuse to hire a woman because she had an abortion. It further states that a pregnant woman may be eligible for temporary job reassignment if she is unable to perform current duties during pregnancy. In 2015, the United States Supreme Court ruled that employers subject to the PDA may be required to make reasonable accommodations for pregnancy. This ruling was based on the Equal Employment Opportunity Commission's (EOOC) 2015 ruling that requires employers under the Americans with Disabilities Act to provide reasonable accommodations for pregnant women (Martin, Kitchen, & Wheeler, 2016; U.S. Equal Employment Opportunity Commission, 2015). Other countries have laws that provide additional financial and legal protections. In spite of these laws, researchers have found that pregnant women experience a large amount of discrimination. Pregnant women continue to be terminated and demoted when their employers learn they are pregnant.

In terms of physical considerations, most of the available studies have found little or no negative physical effects on either the fetus or the mother from typical job activity, and high levels of physical activity have a positive effect on some pregnancy outcomes (Spracklen,

Ryckman, Triche, & Saftlas, 2016). There is evidence, however that exposure to solvents and radiation in the workplace is hazardous to the fetus.

In terms of psychosocial considerations, research has found no differences in stress, depression, and anxiety between pregnant homemakers, part-time workers, and full-time workers. Some researchers have found, however, that some pregnant women face negative stereotypes about pregnant women from their work colleagues (Deardorf, 2016). They also found that pregnant women tend to respond by delaying informing the workplace that they are pregnant and by refusing special accommodations or time off.

An increasing number of women are delaying childbirth until their late 30s and 40s, even into their 50s and 60s. In the United States, the average age of first-time mothers has increased from 21.4 in 1970 to 25.8 in 2012. For all births in 2012, 14.9% were to women older than 34 (Martin et al., 2013). Many women struggle with infertility for years before becoming pregnant; others, like Jennifer Bradshaw, deliberately choose to wait until their careers are established. Other women choose to have children with a new partner. Some single women, driven by the ticking of the so-called biological clock, may decide to have a child on their own, often using artificial insemination or, more recently, banking their eggs for a future pregnancy.

At birth a woman has 6 to 7 million oocytes, but at menarche these decrease to 250,000, declining to only 25,000 at age 37 and declining again at age 38 to a few hundred to 1,000. Although there is no absolute fertility age for men, semen volume and sperm motility decrease with age, and there are some changes in sperm cell morphology (Balasch & Gratacos, 2011). Despite decreasing odds of conception as one ages, because of the increasing success rate of infertility treatment, there are reports of women bearing their own child or grandchild(ren) at an elderly age (Hale & Worden, 2009; Weingartner, 2008). However, waiting until later in the life course to reproduce increases pregnancy risks (Asgharpour et al., 2017; Bellieni, 2016).

In a national representative sample of U.S. women of reproductive age (25–45), Simoni, Lin, Collins, and Mu (2017) found that career-focused women are more likely than women who do not have a strong career focus to put a high value on family planning and planned pregnancies, to have increased optimism about ART's success, and to have increased ethical acceptance of the use of donor gametes in preference to IVF and IUI using partner sperm. Their optimism appears to far exceed the medical reality. Egg freezing has become socially acceptable, but the risks of delaying pregnancy must be considered

(Dunne & Roberts, 2016). As with Jennifer and Allan Bradshaw, couples may be faced with a rude awakening when they start the process of fertility treatment.

Women with delayed pregnancy have increased challenges but also some protective factors. Older mothers are more likely to seek early prenatal care, to be of a higher socioeconomic group, and to have private health insurance (Vaughan, Cleary, & Murphy, 2013). They are also more likely to be obese or to have medical conditions such as hypertension or diabetes. The likelihood of birth by cesarean section increases with the age of the mother, as do preterm birth and low birth weight. Neonates born to older mothers are more likely to require admission to the neonatal unit and to have fetal chromosomal abnormalities (Vaughan et al., 2013).

AT-RISK NEWBORNS

Not all pregnancies proceed smoothly and end in routine deliveries. Every year an estimated 15 million babies are born preterm (before 37 completed weeks of gestation) worldwide, and this rate is increasing (World Health Organization, 2017b). Preterm birth complications are the leading cause of death of children under age 5. Across the world, the rate of preterm birth ranges from 5% to 18% of babies born. One in ten births in the United States is premature, with prematurity the leading cause of neonatal illness and responsible for 17% of infant deaths (Centers for Disease Control and Prevention, 2017d). In low-income countries, half of the babies born at or below 32 weeks die, but most of these babies survive in high-income countries (World Health Organization, 2017b). More than 75% of the deaths of premature infants are preventable with low-cost interventions such as providing warmth, basic care, and breastfeeding (World Health Organization, 2017b). Compared with 34 high-income countries, the United States ranks 31st in infant mortality, despite having state-of-the-art medical services (Heisler, 2012). There are subcategories of preterm birth, based on gestational age: *extremely preterm* (less than 28 weeks), *very preterm* (28 to 32 weeks), and *moderate to late preterm* (32 to 37 weeks).

Prematurity and Low Birth Weight

Prematurity has a profound long-term effect on the family, including parental mental health problems related to parental stress (Mathews & MacDorman, 2013; Treyvaud et al., 2011). It is estimated that the cost associated with premature birth in the United States is $26.2 billion each year: $16.9 billion in medical and health care costs for the baby, $1.9 billion in labor and delivery costs for the mother, $611 million in early intervention services, $1.1 billion for special education services, and $5.7 billion in lost work and pay for people born prematurely (March of Dimes, 2015). The average cost of a premature neonate is 10 times greater than a full-term neonate.

Approximately 70% of premature births (6.8% of all births) occur from 34 to 36 weeks (40 weeks is full gestation), and the rate of these **late preterm births** has increased whereas the rate of preterm births before 34 weeks has decreased (Martin et al., 2017). Most of these late preterm births are precipitated by induced labor, an elective cesarean, or maternal medical complications (including incorrect gestational estimation) (Loftin, Habli, & DeFranco, 2010). These babies may weigh more than 2,500 grams (5.5 pounds) but are still premature. They are at risk for respiratory distress during the neonatal period as well as increased respiratory problems during the first year of life, feeding problems, hypoglycemia (low blood sugar), hypothermia (low body temperature), and hyperbilirubinemia (jaundice) (Cohen, McEvoy, & Castile, 2010; Loftin et al., 2010).

Low-birth-weight (LBW) neonates (weighing from 1,500 to 2,500 grams, 3.3 to 5.5 pounds) account for 8.07% of preterm births. Sometimes the LBW infant is **small for gestational age (SGA)**, generally weighing below the 10th percentile for sex and gestational age (Martin et al., 2017). In other situations, the LBW infant is premature. These neonates have an increased risk for death in the neonatal period when they need support in feeding, temperature maintenance, and respiration (Cohen et al., 2010). Later, they have a 5.2% increased risk for developing asthma, showing delayed growth patterns, developing eye problems, and experiencing cardiovascular and renal disorders (McCormick, Litt, Smith, & Zupancic, 2011; Simeoni, Ligi, Buffat, & Boubred, 2011). Additionally, they are at higher risk for depression, anxiety, and inattention/hyperactivity than are full-term infants (Hall, Jaekel, & Wolke, 2012; Serati, Barkin, Orsenigo, Altamure, & Buoli, 2017; Sullivan, Msall, & Miller, 2012). The risks continue into the next generation; it has been shown that women who themselves were premature or SGA had a higher risk for pregnancy complications (Boivin et al., 2012). Depression prior to pregnancy has been associated with the delivery of an LBW neonate, and the social worker needs to be aware of the multiple stressors these mothers face (Witt, Wisk, Cheng, Hampton, & Hagen, 2012).

The rate of **very-low-birth-weight (VLBW)** infants—infants weighing less than 1,500 grams (3 pounds, 3 ounces)—is approximately 1.5% (Martin et al., 2017). These neonates are at greater risk for poor physical growth, a lower IQ, learning problems, and dropping out of high school (Child Trends Data Bank, 2016; Tamaru et al., 2011). Some will develop cerebral palsy (2 to 3 per 1,000 live births) (Lie, Groholt, & Eskild, 2011) and experience a lower quality of life (McCormick et al., 2011). There is a higher incidence of anxiety disorder and attention deficit/hyperactivity disorder in VLBW and SGA children compared with their full-term counterparts (Lund et al., 2011). Although the cause(s) of all LBWs may not be known, maternal smoking, low prepregnancy weight, infection, increased maternal weight gain during pregnancy, and domestic violence have been shown to be contributors, as have multiple pregnancies. When a neonate is both premature and SGA, there are additive negative physiological and neurological effects (Boulet, Schieve, & Boyle, 2011).

Extremely low-birth-weight (ELBW) infants—infants weighing less than 1,000 grams (2.2 pounds)—add dramatically to the neonatal and infant mortality rates. Approximately 1.4% of all births are VLBW neonates, and the rate of survival of these neonates has been improving with neonatal technologies (Subramanian, 2014). The smallest survivors have a very high risk of lifelong neurological, psychological, and physical problems, including cerebral palsy, blindness, deafness, cognitive delays, feeding intolerance, chronic lung disease, failure to thrive, anxiety, and attention deficit/hyperactivity disorder (Boat, Sadhasivam, Loepke, & Kurth, 2011; Boyle et al., 2011; Dewey et al., 2011). One research team recently found mild impairments of motor ability, learning, and behavior in a sample of healthy 11- to-13-year-old ELBW children. They recommended that supporting motor competence in ELBW children can contribute to improved attention and social behaviors (Danks, Cherry, Burns, & Gray, 2017). Another research team found that a quarter of ELBW teenagers in Iceland have disabilities, mostly mild, and half (57%) have long-term health problems that require regular medical attention (Georgsdottir, Erlingsdottir, Hrafnkelsson, Haraldsson, & Dagbjartsson, 2012). We know that most ELBW births are due to obstetric complications (especially placental insufficiency due to hypertension) (Claas, de Vries, & Bruinse, 2011). Social workers have an essential role in helping the family because most parents are not aware of the long-term implications of an ELBW neonate and are often asked to make decisions regarding interventions that may involve ethical consideration during a time of crisis (Govande et al., 2013). Paul Thompson is considered an ELBW newborn, and at approximately 540 grams, he has a 50% chance of survival.

The social worker needs to be familiar with some of the key risk factors for prematurity and low birth weight. Smoking during pregnancy increases the risks of ectopic pregnancy, placental abruption, stillbirth, and LBW. Women who abuse substances, including alcohol, are among the heaviest cigarette smokers, compounding risks (Burns, Mattick, & Wallace, 2007). Advanced maternal age (greater than 30), high blood pressure (Laskov et al., 2012), and obesity also are associated with higher rates of prematurity (Aly et al., 2010). A variety of other factors have been shown to increase the risk of prematurity, including exposure to air pollution (DeFranco et al., 2014); male neonate (Society for Maternal and Fetal Medicine, 2015); feelings of unhappiness during the pregnancy (Eke et al., 2016); STIs, especially in adolescent pregnancy (Borges-Costa, Matos, & Pereira, 2012); and intrauterine infections (Claas et al., 2011). Mothers enrolled in Medicaid have increased rates of prematurity and infant death compared with mothers enrolled in nonpublic insurance plans (Eisenhauer, Uddin, Albert, Paton, & Stoughton, 2011), a factor no doubt related to economic status. The mother's adequate nutrition prior to conception, as well as during pregnancy, is another important factor in fetal health. Worldwide, more than one third of infant deaths are related to maternal and child malnutrition (Zerfu & Ayele, 2013).

Several policy initiatives in the United States address the issue of prematurity. Passage of the Prematurity Research Expansion and Education for Mothers who Deliver Infants Early (PREEMIE) Act in 2006 (Pub. L. No. 109-450) mandated interagency coordination, improved data collection, and education for health care professionals. In 2013, the PREEMIE Reauthorization Act (S-252, 113th Congress) was passed to promote further federal funding and awareness campaigns (Govtrack, 2013). The March of Dimes (2017) has promoted a National Prematurity Campaign since 2003 and has been at the forefront in bringing attention to this serious health problem. The Affordable Care Act of 2010 has a provision for in-home services for pregnant women and mothers, but states have the option to opt out of the block grants that fund this initiative (National Partnership for Women & Families, 2012).

Newborn Intensive Care

The survival rates of premature infants in high-income countries have improved largely because of explosive growth in the field of neonatal medicine and the establishment of regional neonatal intensive care units (NICUs). Studying the long-term effects of prematurity is difficult because today's 5-year-old who was born at LBW received significantly less sophisticated care than will the current patients in the NICU.

As the Thompsons know all too well, parents' expectations for a healthy newborn are shattered when their child is admitted to an NICU. Their fear and anxiety often make it hard for them to form a strong emotional bond with their newborn. About 90% of mothers and 80% of fathers report developing an attachment to the infant during the third trimester of pregnancy (Latva, Lehtonen, Salmelin, & Tamminen, 2007). But when an infant is premature, the parents have not had the same opportunity. With premature birth, maternal postnatal attachment has been found to be most related to the mother's own antenatal internal attachment to the fetus, whereas the father's postnatal attachment is associated with marital quality (Luz, George, Vieux, & Spitz, 2017). Fear that a sickly newborn may die inhibits some parents from risking attachment (Al Maghaireh, Abdullah, Chan, Piaw, & Al Kawafha, 2016). Some parents are consumed with guilt about their baby's condition and believe that they will only harm the newborn by their presence. Developmental outcomes have been linked to the level of maternal sensitivity during the NICU experience, especially for VLBW neonates (Neri et al., 2017). The NICU experience places both parents at high risk for anxiety and depression. Cognitive behavioral intervention has been shown to reduce the depressive symptoms but not to influence anxiety (Iono et al., 2016; Mendelson, Cluxton-Keller, Vullo, Tandon, & Noazin, 2017). Felicia and Will Thompson had to work hard to contain their anxiety about Paul's frailties.

With increased awareness of prematurity, parents often have more questions. The importance of effective communication and support from the NICU team is critical to short-term and long-term outcomes for both the neonate and the parents (Al Maghaireh et al., 2016; Barr, 2015). The response has been a movement toward family-centered NICU environments that are structured to promote interaction between the infant and the parents, siblings, and others in the family's support system. Mothers seem to more readily engage in caring for their infants in this environment than fathers (Enke, Hausmann, Miedaner, Roth, & Woopen, 2017; Noergaard, Johannessen, Fenger-Gron, Kofoed, & Ammentorp, 2016; Yaman & Atlay, 2015). Ample opportunity to interact with Paul facilitated Felicia and Will Thompson's attempts to bond with him.

Neuroscientists have recently called attention to the physical environment needs of prematurely born babies, noting the competing needs of these vulnerable babies and the medical staff that care for them in NICUs. The medical staff need lights, noisy equipment, and alarms to signal physiological distress. The vulnerable baby needs a physical environment that more nearly approximates the uterus, without bright lights and stressful noise stimulation, and the premature brain is negatively affected by the stressful neonatal environmental conditions (Xiong & Zhang, 2013). With this discrepancy in mind, NICUs are being modified to accommodate the neurological needs of the vulnerable newborns (Haumont, 2016; Ramm, Mannix, Parry, & Gaffney, 2017; Romeu, Cotrina, Perapoch, & Lines, 2016).

Neonatology, the care of critically ill newborns, has only recently been recognized as a medical specialty. It is a much-needed specialty, however. Since the advent of the NICU in the 1970s, the survival rate of critically ill neonates has continued to increase. It is highly unlikely that Paul Thompson would have survived in 1970. Social workers in an NICU must negotiate a complex technological environment requiring specialized skill and knowledge while attempting to respond with compassion, understanding, and appropriate advocacy. Research has clearly shown the need for social work intervention that enables parents to bond with their children and decreases stress. The National Association of Perinatal Social Workers (NAPSW, 2017) is taking the lead in this area. It helps to remember that the effort could affect a neonate's complete life course.

Major Congenital Anomalies

Overall, only 2% to 4% of all surviving newborns have a birth defect. However, the number of neonates born with anomalies caused by genetics, exposure to teratogens, or nonhereditary factors that affect development of the fetus does not reflect the number of abnormal embryos. Fewer than half of all fertilized ova result in a live birth; the rest are spontaneously aborted, oftentimes before a woman knows she is pregnant. Based on data from a 10-year study of placental tissue following pregnancy loss, 80.5% of these spontaneous abortions were caused by a genetic anomaly (Kliman & Milano, 2013). Social workers need to be mindful of the low probability that a child will be born with a genetic disorder or congenital anomaly when responding to parental fears.

The U.S. Health Resources and Services Administration (HRSA, 2016) provides a Recommended Uniform Screening Panel of 34 core and 26 secondary metabolic, endocrine, and hemoglobin disorders for newborns. The National Newborn Screening and Global Resource Center (NNSGRC) also provides genetic and newborn screening information, including resources for parents and providers to respond to positive testing results (NNSGRC, 2014). A *screening* test may not be definitive, however, and, if positive, is usually followed by a *diagnostic* test to confirm a genetic mishap. Some screening may be done before birth (Centers for Disease Control and Prevention, 2016b).

Preventing, diagnosing, and predicting the outcome of genetic disorders are very difficult because of the complexities of many genetic processes, including the following (National Human Genome Research Institute, 2017).

- *Variable expressivity.* Genes manifest differently in different people. For example, persons with cystic fibrosis, caused by a recessive gene, display wide variability in the severity of symptoms. The expression of the disorder appears to be influenced by the interplay of psychological, social, political, economic, and other environmental factors. The effects can be exacerbated by maternal substance abuse, inadequate maternal nutrition, birth trauma, and poverty.

- *Genetic heterogeneity.* The same characteristic may be a consequence of one of several genetic anomalies. For example, neural tube defects may result either from gene mutations or from exposure to specific teratogens.

- *Pleiotropy principle.* The same gene may influence seemingly unrelated systems. Hair color, for example, is typically linked to a particular skin color (such as blonde hair with light complexion, black hair with olive complexion).

- *Epigenetics.* Environmental factors may influence gene expression (phenotype) without changing the genetic makeup of a person (genotype). These factors influence the chemicals that trigger (methyl groups) or inhibit (acetyl groups) genetic expression. Furthermore, these chemicals appear to have a generational influence without genetic alterations. Examples of these epigenetic environmental influences include nutrition, trauma such as childhood abuse, and teratogens (Kubota & Hata, 2013). The epigenetic influences in many cases are preventable and treatable, especially if identified early in development.

Congenital anomalies fall into four categories, summarized in Exhibit 2.6, which includes examples of the most prevalent anomalies (Pierce, 2017).

1. *Inheritance of a single abnormal gene.* An inherited anomaly in a single gene may lead to a serious disorder. The gene may be recessive, meaning that both parents must pass it along, or it may be dominant, in which case only one parent needs to have the gene in

EXHIBIT 2.6 ● Four Categories of Congenital Anomalies

Inheritance of Single Abnormal Gene		
Recessive	**Dominant**	**Sex-Linked**
Sickle-cell anemia Tay-Sachs disease Cystic fibrosis	Neurofibromatosis Huntington's disease	Hemophilia Duchenne muscular dystrophy

Multifactorial Inheritance
Possible mental illness, alcoholism, heart disease, diabetes

Chromosomal Aberration
Down syndrome (additional 21st chromosome), Turner syndrome (X), Klinefelter syndrome (XXY)

Exposure to Teratogens			
Radiation	**Infections**	**Maternal Metabolic Imbalance**	**Drugs and Environmental Chemicals**
Neural tube defects	Rubella: deafness, glaucoma Syphilis: neurological, ocular, and skeletal defects Zika virus: microcephaly and ocular defects	Diabetes: neural tube defects Folic acid deficiency: brain and neural tube defects Hyperthermia (at 14–28 days): neural tube defects	Alcohol: intellectual disability Heroin: attention deficit disorder Amphetamine: congenital defects

order for it to be expressed in the child. A third possibility is that the disorder is sex-linked, meaning that it is passed along by either the father or the mother (National Human Genome Research Institute, 2017; Pierce, 2017).

2. *Multifactorial inheritance.* Some genetic traits, such as height and intelligence, are influenced by environmental factors such as nutrition. Their expression varies because of **multifactorial inheritance**, meaning they are controlled by multiple genes. Multifactorial inheritance is implicated in traits that predispose a person to mental illnesses, such as depression. However, these traits are merely predisposing factors, creating what is called **genetic liability**. Siblings born with the same genetic traits thus may vary in the likelihood of developing a specific genetically based disorder, such as alcoholism or mental illness (National Human Genome Research Institute, 2017).

3. *Chromosomal aberration.* Some genetic abnormalities are not hereditary but rather caused by a genetic mishap during development of the ovum or sperm cells. Sometimes the cells end up missing chromosomes or having too many. When the ovum or sperm cell has fewer than 23 chromosomes, the probability of conception and survival is minimal. But in the presence of too many chromosomes in the ovum or the sperm, various anomalies occur (National Human Genome Research Institute, 2017). Down syndrome, or trisomy 21, the most common chromosomal aberration, is the presence of 47 chromosomes—specifically, an extra chromosome in the 21st pair. Its prevalence is 1 in 691 live births overall, but it increases to 1 in 214 for women over age 35, and to 1 in 25 for women over the age of 45. Yet, although the prevalence increases with maternal age, 80% of children born with Down syndrome are to mothers under the age of 35 (National Down Syndrome Society [NDSS], 2018).

4. *Exposure to teratogens.* Teratogens can be divided into four categories: radiation, infections, maternal metabolic imbalance, and drugs and environmental

chemicals. In the Thompson story, Felicia wondered if Paul's premature birth was a result of prenatal exposure to paint fumes. It may have been, depending on what specific chemicals were involved, when exposure occurred, and to what degree. Parents who, like the Thompsons, are experiencing considerable guilt over their possible responsibility for their baby's problems may take comfort from the knowledge that the impact of exposure to teratogens can vary greatly. Much depends on the timing of exposure. The various organ systems have different critical or **sensitive periods**, summarized in Exhibit 2.7.

Today most pregnant women in the United States undergo a maternal blood screen and ultrasound from week 11 to week 13. Most recently recommended is the noninvasive prenatal screening, or NIPS (American College of Medical Genetics, 2016; Centers for Disease Control and Prevention, 2016b). Second trimester screening, weeks 15 to 20, includes a maternal serum screen and an anomaly ultrasound (18 to 20 weeks), which produces a visual image of the developing fetus. Based on these results, the doctor may offer diagnostic tests such as high-resolution ultrasound and chorionic villi sampling (CVS). CVS involves the insertion of a catheter through the cervix into the uterus to obtain a sample of the developing placenta and can be done as early as 10 to 12 weeks. *Amniocentesis* is the extraction of amniotic fluid for chromosomal analysis; it involves inserting a hollow needle through the abdominal wall during the second trimester. At greater risk of a genetic anomaly are women older than age 35, carriers of sex-linked genetic disorders and single gene defects, parents with chromosomal disorders, and women who have had previous and recurring pregnancy loss. When any of these risks is present, screening or diagnostic tests may be offered earlier in pregnancy (American Pregnancy Association, 2017a; Centers for Disease Control, 2016b).

If an anomaly is detected, the decisions that need to be made are not easy ones. The possibility of false readings on these tests makes the decisions even more complicated. Should the fetus be aborted? Should fetal surgery be undertaken? Could gene replacement therapy, implantation of genetic material to alter the genotype—still a costly experimental procedure—prevent an anomaly or limit its manifestation? Do the parents have the financial and psychological means to care for a neonate with a disability? What is the potential impact on the marriage and extended family system? What is the potential long-term impact of knowing one's genetic makeup? For example, the 2008 Genetic Information Nondiscrimination Act (GINA) prohibits insurance companies and employers from using genetic information

EXHIBIT 2.7 ● Critical Periods in Prenatal Development

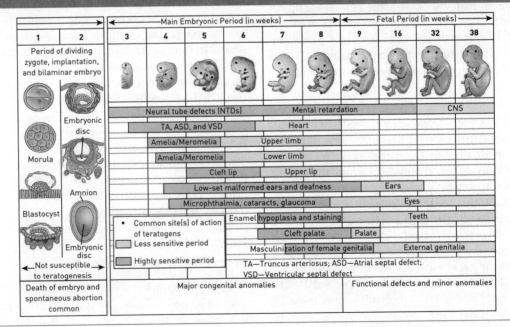

Source: Moore, K. L., Persaud, T. V. N., & Torchia, M. G. (2013). *Before we were born: Essentials of embryology and birth defects* (8th ed.). Philadelphia: Saunders/Elsevier, Figure 19-11.

in discriminatory ways (U.S. Equal Employment Opportunity Commission, 2008). However, as the U.S. health care system undergoes change and new knowledge about genetic engineering emerges, this is an issue that should be considered by social workers. We do know that nonurgent decisions should be postponed until parents have an opportunity to adjust to the crisis and acquire the necessary information (National Association of Social Workers, 2003).

CRITICAL THINKING QUESTIONS 2.4

Why do you think the rate of prematurity is higher in the United States than in most other industrialized countries? How could you learn more about the answer to this question?

CONCEPTION, PREGNANCY, AND CHILDBIRTH UNDER DIFFERENT CIRCUMSTANCES

Social workers should recognize the many different circumstances under which conception, pregnancy, and childbirth occur. Many prenatal groups have to contend with negative stereotypes and prejudice, by health care professionals as well as the general public. Some of them fear that other health issues will be exposed by their participation in maternity care. Some need assistance to manage other health problems in the context of maternity care. Six circumstances of becoming a parent are discussed here, but this discussion is not meant to be inclusive of all circumstances for becoming a parent.

Substance-Abusing Pregnant Women

Our knowledge of the developmental impact of maternal use of illegal and legal substances is rapidly increasing. The good news is that health care professionals are increasingly able to avoid prescribing legal drugs that might harm the developing fetus, once pregnancy is confirmed. The bad news is that too many pregnant women are still harming their babies through use of illegal drugs or abuse of legal substances. And, unfortunately, many women do not know they are pregnant during the first trimester, a period when the fetus is very vulnerable to teratogens.

The 2010 National Survey on Drug Use and Health (NSDUH) found that 4.4% of pregnant women aged 15 to 44 reported using illicit substances in the past month, an increase from 3% in 2002 (Wendell, 2013). These figures are considered to be a low estimate because drug use during pregnancy is underreported. The rate of illicit drug use by pregnant women was 16.2% among pregnant women aged 15 to 17, 7.4% aged 18 to 25, and 1.9% aged 26 to 44. There is also an epidemic of prescription drug abuse of such opioids as oxycodone and fentanyl, and this issue needs further attention (Centers for Disease Control and Prevention, 2016c; Sheehan & Sheehan, 2013).

From 2000 to 2009, opioid use among U.S. women who gave birth increased from 1.19 to 5.63 per 1,000 hospital births per year (Patrick et al., 2012). Data combined from 2007 to 2012 revealed that almost 1% of pregnant women ages 15 to 44 misused opioids within the past month. This misuse was more common among 15- to 17- and 18- to 25-year-olds than among 26- to 34-year-olds. Misuse also was more common among those living below the federal poverty level than among those living at or above it (Smith & Lipari, 2017). The impacts of prescription opioid misuse on the developing child include congenital heart, spine, brain, and abdominal wall defects. Three out of four heroin users start with the abuse of prescription medications, making this rising epidemic even more important to address (Tavernise, 2015).

Despite the opioid epidemic, marijuana (cannabis sativa) is the drug most commonly used by women who are pregnant, with self-reported prevalence rates from 2% to 5% in most studies (American College of Obstetricians and Gynecologists, 2017b, 2017c). This rate increases to 15% to 28% for young, urban, socioeconomically disadvantaged women in part due to the misbelief that marijuana is not harmful, and it can be less expensive than cigarettes. Because current research points to impaired neurodevelopment during fetal development, the American College of Obstetricians and Gynecologists recommends that women planning to become, or who are, pregnant should not use marijuana even when it is for medicinal purposes (American College of Obstetricians and Gynecologists, 2017b, 2017c).

Possible effects of commonly abused legal and illegal substances are presented in Exhibit 2.8. Social workers are collaborating with other professionals to provide public education to women and men in the childbearing years about the teratogenic effects of alcohol, tobacco, and other drugs.

Pregnant Women With Eating Disorders

Eating disorders, primarily anorexia nervosa (self-imposed starvation) and bulimia (binging and purging), among U.S. teenagers and women in the United States increased during the past century, but the rate has stabilized in the last 2 decades (Smink, vanHoeken, & Hoek, 2012). The

EXHIBIT 2.8 ● **Commonly Abused Drugs and Fetal Effects**

	Alcohol	Cocaine	Amphetamines	Cigarettes	Opioids
Abortion	X	X	X		X
Stillbirth	X	X	X		X
Prematurity	X	X	X	X	X
Low birth weight	X	X	X	X	X
Intrauterine growth restriction	X	X	X	X	X
Respiratory distress	X	X			X
Withdrawal	X	X	X		X
Fine motor problems	X				X
Malformations	X	X	X		X
Developmental delays	X	X	X		X

four most common eating disorders recognized by *DSM-5* are anorexia nervosa, bulimia nervosa, binge eating disorder, and other specified feeding or eating disorders (OSFED). Eating disorders are most commonly found in women of childbearing age and are estimated to be an issue for 7,000,000 women in the United States annually (American Pregnancy Association, 2017c), but incidence among pregnant women is reported to be lower than that (Broussard, 2012). Several researchers have found that women with eating disorders reduce or suspend symptoms while pregnant and return to disordered eating after giving birth (Broussard, 2012).

Restricting caloric intake, binge eating, purging, or any combination of these behaviors can lead to nutritional insufficiency for both the mother and the fetus. Maternal outcomes can include poor nutrition, dehydration, cardiac irregularities, gestational diabetes, preeclampsia, depression, labor complications, and nursing difficulties (American Pregnancy Association, 2017c; National Eating Disorders Association, 2016). Diets lacking in essential nutrients have been associated with infertility, spontaneous abortion, preterm birth, low birth weight, and SGA neonates. SGA neonates are at great risk for perinatal death, congenital anomalies, impaired postnatal growth, and neurological disabilities (Broussard, 2012). It is critical that maternity care providers screen for eating disorders.

Pregnant Women With Disabilities

More than 27 million women in the United States have a disability, and, due to longer life expectancy, that number

is growing, especially for those who reach childbearing age (Centers for Disease Control and Prevention, 2014b). For example, women with spina bifida are a population that, because of medical advances, only recently is living beyond sexual maturity (Jackson & Mott, 2007). People with physical or mental disabilities may be perceived as "asexual," and health care providers may not consider conception, pregnancy, and childbirth as relevant issues for them (Sawin, 1998). Health care providers may communicate unwarranted negative expectations about pregnancy outcomes or not take the woman's disability into consideration when providing contraceptive options. For example, women with spinal cord injury should not use IUDs due to an increased risk of bleeding, and barrier methods requiring manual dexterity may not be feasible. This is an issue worldwide and is perhaps even more pervasive in nonindustrialized countries (Emmett & Alant, 2006; Kristof & WuDunn, 2009).

Most women with disabilities can manage pregnancy and give birth to healthy babies if they have a health provider familiar with the disability and related risks, and they are monitored more closely than are women without disabilities (Center for Research on Women with Disabilities, 2017). Some risks include increased blood clots for women who use wheelchairs, risk of pneumonia when a respiratory impairment preexists, bladder infections that can lead to spontaneous abortion and miscarriage, and preterm labor and low-birth-weight babies. Women with spinal cord injury may have more spasticity, seizures, and a life-threatening sudden rise in blood pressure that is not related to pregnancy, per se. Some chronic problems such as multiple sclerosis and rheumatoid arthritis may improve during pregnancy (Center for Research on Women with Disabilities, 2017).

Despite public distaste for the practice, some persons with disabilities continue to be targets of forced or coerced sterilization (International Federation of Persons with Physical Disability, 2017). Professionals do not agree about how to handle the reproductive rights of individuals with severe inheritable disorders or with limited capacity to care for a child. Many do agree, however, that physical, environmental, interpersonal, informational, and policy barriers leave people with disabilities disenfranchised from both the reproductive health system and other reproductive options. As society continues to recognize persons with disabilities as full members, some of the negative implications of conception, pregnancy, and childbirth with this population may decline. Social workers can be partners in this quest.

Incarcerated Pregnant Women

Although women are still a minority in jails and prisons, the population of women incarcerated in the United States increased by 657% from 1980 to 2013, with approximately 213,000 women incarcerated on any given day (Goshin, Arditti, Dallaire, Shlafer, & Hollihan, 2016). This dramatic increase is largely due to mandatory drug sentencing laws, and most of the women are incarcerated for nonviolent offenses. Approximately one third of the world's incarcerated women are in U.S. correctional facilities (Goshin et al., 2016).

More than three quarters (76%) of incarcerated women are of childbearing age. Bureau of Justice statistics estimate that 3% to 4% of incarcerated women in the United States are pregnant at the time of admission, but other estimates suggest the pregnancy rates are much higher. For example, according to one study, nearly 30% of incarcerated women in New York were pregnant at the time of admission (Shlafer, Stang, Dallaire, Forestell, & Hellerstedt, 2017). Prior to entering the criminal justice system, these women are less likely than other pregnant women to receive prenatal care and more likely than both incarcerated men and other pregnant women to have experienced poverty, trauma, serious mental illness, and substance dependence (Goshin et al., 2016). For some women, pregnancy is a leading factor in their arrest, with three states (Alabama, Tennessee, and South Carolina) making prenatal drug abuse a crime and additional states introducing "chemical endangerment" laws in recent years (Goshin et al., 2016).

Guidelines developed by the National Commission on Correctional Health Care, the American College of Obstetricians and Gynecologists, and the American Public Health Association Task Force on Correctional Health Care Standards recommend that correctional facilities provide "pregnancy counseling, prenatal care, appropriate nutrition, and prenatal health education, as well as care for substance use and mental illness" for incarcerated pregnant women (Goshin et al., 2016, p. 56). The evidence is clear that correctional facilities are not adhering to these guidelines. In 2011, the National Women's Law Center reported that 43 U.S. states do not require medical examinations as a part of prenatal care for incarcerated pregnant women, 41 states do not require prenatal nutrition counseling or provide appropriate nutrition, 34 do not require screening and treatment for women with high-risk pregnancies, and 48 do not require screening for HIV. Advocacy organizations have protested the routine shackling of pregnant women that continues to go on in some state prisons. In addition, federal courts have ruled that restraint during active labor violates the Eighth Amendment's prohibition of inhumane treatment (Dignam & Adashi, 2014).

These mothers and babies are a particularly vulnerable group. Social workers working in prisons and jails can advocate for conditions to improve birth outcomes for the infants and pregnancy circumstances of the mothers and their extended families. We can begin with Shlafer and colleagues' (2017) six recommendations for securing the nutritional status of incarcerated pregnant women:

- Pregnancy testing upon intake
- Prenatal vitamins upon diagnosis of pregnancy
- Adherence to the nutrition recommendations outlined by the Academy of Nutrition and Dietetics for healthy pregnancy
- Additional food provided and modifications made to meet pregnancy needs
- Regular access to water
- Resources and education on healthy diet provided as well as nutrition information for food available in the cafeteria and the commissary

HIV-Infected Pregnant Women

Worldwide, women were more than half of all people living with HIV/AIDS in 2016, and new infections among young women aged 15 to 24 were 44% higher than among men of the same age (amfAR, the Foundation for AIDS Research, 2017). In the United States, women accounted for 24% of new HIV diagnoses in 2015, with 86% of these resulting from heterosexual contact and 13% attributable to injection drug use. Among White women, however,

32% of HIV diagnoses were attributed to injection drug use. Among all women diagnosed with HIV in 2015, 61% were African American, 19% were White, and 15% were Hispanic/Latina. Women accounted for 24% of all new AIDS diagnoses in 2015 and 20% of the cumulative AIDS diagnoses. The good news is that from 2010 to 2014, the annual HIV diagnosis rate in the United States declined 20% among all women (Centers for Disease Control and Prevention, 2017e).

Approximately 8,500 women living with HIV give birth annually, but the annual number of infections to newborn babies has declined by more than 90% since the 1990s. It is estimated that 21,956 cases of perinatally acquired HIV infections were prevented from 1994 to 2010 (Centers for Disease Control and Prevention, 2017e). Women with HIV who take antiretroviral (ARV) medications, refrain from breastfeeding, and provide HIV medicines to the baby for 4 to 6 weeks postpartum can reduce the risk of transmitting the disease to their babies to less than 1%. To avoid transmitting HIV to the partner while attempting to become pregnant, HIV-infected women and their partners can use assisted insemination at home or in a provider's office, using the partner's semen (National Institutes of Health, 2017). Women who are HIV negative but whose partner is HIV positive can reduce the risk of transmission to a baby by taking preexposure prophylaxis (PrEP) medicines. It should be noted, however, that in low-income countries without potable water, formula feeding may be more dangerous than breastfeeding with an HIV-infected mother (Centers for Disease Control and Prevention, 2017e).

In 2003 a coordinated response of multinational and U.S. agencies to the worldwide HIV/AIDS epidemic was launched, the President's Emergency Plan for AIDS Relief, or PEPFAR, with promising results. As of 2017, five of the 12 African countries with the highest rates of HIV and AIDS are approaching epidemic control. From 2000 to 2016, there was a 70% decrease globally in new HIV infections in children, and since 2014 there has been a 50% increase in the number of people accessing treatment worldwide (Centers for Disease Control and Prevention, 2017e). In 2016, 76% of pregnant women living with HIV received medicines to prevent the transmission of HIV to their children (amfAR, 2017). Currently the WHO recommends early HIV testing of all pregnant women. In spite of decreasing treatment costs, treatment barriers continue, including the stigma of HIV/AIDS paired with the low status of women in many countries (Gable, Gostin, & Hodge, 2008; Kristoff & WuDunn, 2009). Treatment barriers in the United States include the lack of financial resources and health insurance; limited transportation; and responsibilities to care for others, especially children (American College of Obstetrics and Gynecology, 2012a). Working to increase HIV awareness and promote clear notification of HIV status will continue to be important social work roles.

Pregnant Transmen

Population surveys rarely ask questions to identify transgender people, but the best available data indicate that about 0.6% of the adult population in the United States, about 1.4 million adults, identify as transgender. The data also indicate that younger adults are more likely than older adults to identify as transgender (Flores, Herman, Gates, & Brown, 2016). A *transman* is a person born biologically female with a male gender identity. Many transmen may desire to undergo surgical changes to their bodies, but most do not do so thereby retaining the biological ability (ovaries, uterus, and hormones) to become pregnant and give birth (Obedin-Maliver & Makadon, 2016). It is common, however, that transmen use hormone therapy to develop male characteristics such as facial hair and lower voice tone. The desire to parent may remain, however, and drive the decision to bear a genetically related child (Wierckx et al., 2012). To fulfill this desire transmen are advised to stop testosterone therapy before becoming pregnant, but a pregnancy still can occur even without resuming menses (Light, Obedin-Maliver, Sevelius, & Kerns, 2014). After stopping testosterone, the person's body acquires female characteristics such as enlarged breasts, loss of facial hair, and higher voice pitch. These changes then may result in gender dysphoria or psycho-emotional discomfort due to the pregnancy changes not aligning with male gender identity (Obedin-Maliver & Makadon, 2016).

In a study of 41 transmen who were pregnant, 61% reported having used testosterone before pregnancy. Of those who had used testosterone, 80% had resumed menstruation within 6 months after stopping testosterone. Five respondents conceived while still amenorrheic from testosterone. Most of the transmen in this study became pregnant within 4 months of trying. Two thirds of the pregnancies were planned, with most of the unplanned pregnancies occurring in transmen who had never used testosterone. Most respondents (88%) in this study used their own eggs fertilized by a partner's sperm. There were no differences in pregnancy, delivery, and birth outcomes between those who had previously used testosterone and those who had never used testosterone (Light et al., 2014). Another pregnancy option for transmen is oocyte cryopreservation, or the freezing of one's eggs for a future pregnancy of the transman or a surrogate (Practice Committees of American Society for Reproductive Medicine, 2013).

Obstacles exist, however. Transmen already face societal stigmatization and discrimination, and a gender-variant pregnancy can further these negative experiences. A qualitative study of eight transmen indicated that transmen pregnancies involved significant loneliness and a lack of role models to help navigate pregnancy (Ellis, Wojnar, & Pettinato, 2014). Transmen who are pregnant also can be burdened with ongoing management of the perceptions of others coupled with their own apprehension to disclose their thoughts and feelings related to the pregnancy. This can lead to inadequate access to, underuse of, and disparities within the health care system (Hoffkling, Obedin-Maliver, & Sevelius, 2017).

Although the psychosocial dimensions of the pregnancy experience are different for transmen compared to others, the biological course of pregnancy is the same. Another important decision faced by transmen is whether to chest (breast) feed the newborn (McDonald et al., 2016), a parental role that aligns with the desire to provide for a child but does not align with the role of being male.

Although the larger society may struggle with the idea of this variation of pregnancy, the medical community is embracing the need to provide appropriate care and support to transmen who want to be, or are, pregnant. Guidelines for the education of health care professionals and practice standards have been developed by several health care

groups to promote patient-centered perinatal health care services to transmen (American College of Nurse-Midwives, 2012; American College of Obstetricians and Gynecologists, 2012b). Research is ongoing to inform the medical community about the unique needs of transmen (Obedin-Maliver & Makadon, 2016; Redfern & Sinclair, 2014).

RISK AND PROTECTIVE FACTORS IN CONCEPTION, PREGNANCY, AND CHILDBIRTH

As the life course journey begins, human behavior is being shaped by risk factors and protective factors. Throughout this chapter, you have read about factors that either increase risk or offer protection for healthy processes of conception, pregnancy, and childbirth. Selected factors are summarized in Exhibit 2.9. A confluence of biological, psychological, and social factors determine whether a couple can conceive. Once the woman is pregnant, an interplay of biological, psychological, and social factors influence the growth and development of the fetus, the childbirth experience, and the health of the new baby. You also read about how the health of the new baby has long-term implications across the life course.

EXHIBIT 2.9 ● Selected Risk and Protective Factors for Conception, Pregnancy, and Birth

	Risk Factors	Protective Factors
Conception	Low sperm count	Father drug abstinence (marijuana)
	Fallopian tubal factors	Gynecological care
	Genetic abnormality	Genetic counseling
	Adolescent promiscuity	Family life education; contraception; abstinence
	Endometriosis	Hormone therapy; surgery
	Inadequate nutrition for sexually active women of childbearing age	Folic acid supplement
	Obesity	
Pregnancy	Obesity	Normal weight maintenance
	Sexually transmitted diseases	Barrier birth control methods
	Female age ($\leftarrow$18 or $\rightarrow$35)	Family life education; birth control
	Delivery before 38 weeks	Women, Infants, and Children program
	Gestation, toxemia, diabetes	Prenatal care
	Stress because of inadequate resources	Social and economic support
	Trauma	Accident prevention (falls, fire, car)
	Smoking	smoking cessation program
Birth	Venereal diseases such as gonorrhea and positive Group B strep	Prenatal care; antibiotic eye drops for neonate; maternal testing
	Meconium aspiration; anoxia	C-section delivery; drugs during pregnancy; well-managed labor and delivery
	Prolonged and painful labor	Birthing classes; social support; father's presence at birth; adequate pain control
	Obesity	Newborn screening tests

There is growing evidence from life course epidemiological research that experiences in these earliest days of a human life course have health impacts at every stage of the life course. This has led to a new developmental model for the origins of disease (for an overview of this model, see Barker & Thornburg, 2013). This model proposes that nutrition during fetal life is a key factor in later chronic disease. The fetal response to malnutrition is to slow growth and alter the metabolism in order to survive. It is not just the mother's diet during pregnancy that matters but also her nutrient stores at the time of conception. There is much research evidence that a range of chronic diseases have their origin in malnutrition during fetal life and infancy, including cardiovascular disease, type 2 diabetes, some cancers, and chronic infections. Research also indicates that a baby's birth weight is affected not only by maternal nutrition before and during pregnancy but also by the shape and size of the placenta at birth. And certain patterns of shape and size of the placenta have been found to be a risk factor for heart disease, hypertension, and some forms of cancer. How and why the placenta develops a particular shape and size is not well understood, but animal research has found that the placenta enlarges in response to malnutrition in midpregnancy. Barker and Thornburg (2013) conclude that this research on fetal nutrition indicates that "protecting the nutrition and health of girls and young women should be the corner stone of public health" (p. 518).

Seldom is one environmental, social, or biological risk factor solely responsible for an outcome. As you review the selected risk and protective factors in Exhibit 2.9, keep in mind that most outcomes are influenced by several factors, and ongoing research shows an ever-increasing complexity of interacting factors.

CRITICAL THINKING QUESTIONS 2.5

Pregnancy is a powerful experience for the pregnant woman as well as for her partner. What are the biological needs of the pregnant woman? The psychological needs? The social needs? Where there is an involved father, what are the biological needs of the father? The psychological needs? The social needs?

IMPLICATIONS FOR SOCIAL WORK PRACTICE

Social workers practicing with persons at the stage of life concerned with conception, pregnancy, and childbirth should follow these principles.

- Respond to the complex interplay of biopsychosocial and spiritual factors related to conception, pregnancy, and childbirth.

- When working with clients, both females and males, of childbearing age, always consider the possibility of conception, pregnancy, and childbirth; their potential outcomes; and their impact on the changing person–environment configuration.

- Identify the needs of vulnerable or at-risk groups and work to provide services for them. For example, structure birth education classes to include not only family but family-like persons and provide interpreters for the hearing impaired or use appropriate technology to deliver content.

- Actively pursue information about particular disabilities and their impact on conception, pregnancy, and childbirth and include this topic in client assessment.

- Acquire and apply skills in advocacy, education about reproductive options, consumer guidance in accessing services, and case management.

- Assume a proactive stance when working with at-risk populations to limit undesirable reproductive outcomes and to help meet their reproductive needs. At-risk groups include adolescents; low-income women; women involved with substance abuse; women with eating disorders; and women with disabilities who lack access to financial, physical, psychological, and social services.

- Assist parents faced with a potential genetic anomaly to gain access to genetic screenings, prenatal diagnosis, postnatal diagnosis, treatment, and genetic counseling.

- Involve parents in decision making to the greatest extent possible by delaying nonurgent decisions until parents have had a chance to adjust to any crisis and acquire the necessary information to make an informed decision.

- Establish collaborative relationships with other professionals to enhance and guide assessment and intervention.

- Identify and use existing programs that provide education and prenatal services to women, particularly for those most at risk of undesirable outcomes.

Key Terms

assisted reproductive
   technologies (ART) 53
chromosomes 44
dominant genes 45
embryo 55
extremely low birth weight
   (ELBW) 61
fertilization 44
fertilization age 54
fetal viability 50
fetus 56
genes 44
genetic liability 64

genotype 44
germ cell 44
gestation 54
gestational age 54
infertility 50
interactive genes 45
late preterm birth 61
low birth weight (LBW) 61
miscarriage 56
multifactorial inheritance 64
multigravida 56
multipara 58
neonate 42

phenotype 44
primipara 58
recessive genes 45
sensitive period 65
sex chromosomes 44
sex-linked trait 44
small for gestational age (SGA) 61
spontaneous abortion 56
teratogens 55
very low birth weight (VLBW) 61
zygote 55

Active Learning

1. Locate the National Association of Social Workers Code of Ethics on the organization's website at www.naswdc.org. Choose an ethical issue from the following list. Using the Code of Ethics as a guide, what values and principles can you identify to guide decision making related to the issue you have chosen?

   - Should all women and men, regardless of marital status or income, be provided with the most current technologies to conceive when they are unable to do so?

   - What are the potential issues of preservation and gestational surrogacy in terms of social justice and diversity?

   - Should pregnant women who abuse substances be incarcerated to protect the developing fetus?

   - Do adoptive parents have the right to know the genetic background of an adoptee?

   - Which genes, if any, should be selected for reproduction?

   - Will persons who are poor be economically disadvantaged in the use of genetic information?

2. Select one of the three life journeys that introduced this chapter: Jennifer Bradshaw's, Cecelia Kin's, or the Thompsons'. Identify the risk and protective factors related to their conception, pregnancy, and childbirth experience. Then change one factor in the story; for example, assume that Cecelia Kin's income was not needed. How might that alter her life course? Then try changing one factor in another story; for example, assume Jennifer had only a 10th-grade education. How does that change the trajectory of her story? Try again; for example, assume Felicia Thompson was being treated for depression when she became pregnant. Again, how does that factor alter her life course and that of her child?

3. In student groups of three or four, or working individually, review the list of contraception options presented in this chapter. With each group representing a different 3- to 5-year age range of the childbearing age spectrum (ages 15 to 44), discuss the potential access and use or misuse of each form of contraception. Also, consider the role of a social worker in various social welfare settings in helping women (who represent different age, religious, and ethnic groups) select a form of birth control.

Web Resources

American College of Obstetricians and Gynecologists (ACOG): www.acog.org

Site provides educational information and resources related to sexuality and women's health, including a section for patients, and offers materials in both Spanish and English.

American Pregnancy Association: americanpregnancy.org

Site presented by the American Pregnancy Association contains information on a number of pregnancy-related topics, including infertility, adopting, pregnancy options, multiples pregnancy, and the developing baby.

Center for Research on Women with Disabilities (CROWD): www.bcm.edu/research/centers/research-on-women-with-disabilities

Site presented by the Center for Research on Women with Disabilities contains reports on sexual and reproductive health for women with disabilities, educational materials, and links to other related research.

Centers for Disease Control and Prevention: www.cdc.gov

U.S. government site contains public health information, current research, and health census data that include diseases and conditions related to conception, pregnancy, and childbirth with a focus on prevention; materials in both Spanish and English.

Childbirth.org: www.childbirth.org

Award-winning site maintained by Robin Elise Weiss contains information on conception, pregnancy, and birth, including recommended pregnancy books and access to a free online childbirth class.

National Healthy Mothers, Healthy Babies Coalition (HMHB): www.hmhb.org

Site maintained by HMHB, an informal coalition dedicated to improving the quality and reach of public education about prenatal and infant care, contains a blog, newsroom, and virtual library.

The National Human Genome Research Institute (NHGRI): www.genome.gov

Site maintained by NHGRI, which oversaw the Human Genome Project completed in 2003, provides quick access to recent news, including legislation related to genetics for use by students, educators, researchers, and the general public; available in both Spanish and English.

Planned Parenthood: www.plannedparenthood.org

Official site of the Planned Parenthood Federation of America Inc. contains information about Planned Parenthood, health and pregnancy, birth control, abortion, STDs, prochoice advocacy, educational tools for parents and educators, and information for teens.

3

Infancy and Toddlerhood

Debra J. Woody and
Elizabeth D. Hutchison

The authors wish to thank Cara L. Wallace for assistance with an earlier edition of this chapter.

Learning Objectives

3.1 Compare one's own emotional and cognitive reactions to three case studies.

3.2 Identify aspects of the developmental niche that affect infant and toddler development.

3.3 Summarize typical physical, cognitive, and socioemotional development of infants and toddlers.

3.4 Analyze the role of play in infancy and toddlerhood.

3.5 Compare developmental delay and developmental disability as they apply to infancy and toddlerhood.

3.6 Compare the childcare arrangements in infancy and toddlerhood in the United States with the arrangements in other wealthy countries.

3.7 Identify issues that face multigenerational families with infants and toddlers.

3.8 Give examples of risk factors and protective factors during infancy and toddlerhood.

3.9 Apply knowledge of infancy and toddlerhood to recommend guidelines for social work engagement, assessment, intervention, and evaluation.

CASE STUDY 3.1

HOLLY'S EARLY ARRIVAL

Although Marilyn Hicks had been very careful with her diet, exercise, and prenatal care during pregnancy, Holly arrived at 26 weeks' gestation, around 6 months into the pregnancy. Initially she weighed 3 pounds, 11 ounces, but she quickly lost the 11 ounces. Immediately after birth, Holly was whisked away to the neonatal unit in the hospital, and her parents had just a quick peek at her. The assigned social worker's first contact with Marilyn and Martin Hicks, an African American couple, was in the neonatal unit. Although Marilyn Hicks began to cry when the social worker first spoke with her, overall both parents seemed to be coping well and had all their basic needs met at that time. The social worker left his business card with them and instructed them to call if they needed anything.

Despite her early arrival, Holly did not show any signs of medical problems, and after 6 weeks in the neonatal unit, her parents were able to take her home. The social worker wisely allowed the newly formed Hicks family time to adjust and, in keeping with the policy of the neonatal program, scheduled a follow-up home visit within a few weeks.

When the social worker arrives at the house, Marilyn Hicks is at the door in tears. She states that taking care of Holly is much more than she imagined. Holly cries "constantly" and does not seem to respond to Mrs. Hicks's attempts to comfort her. In fact, Mrs. Hicks thinks that Holly cries even louder when her mother picks her up or tries to cuddle with her. Mrs. Hicks is very disappointed, because she considers herself to be a nurturing person. She is unsure how to respond to Holly's "rejection of her." The only time Holly seems to respond positively is when Mrs. Hicks breastfeeds her.

Mrs. Hicks has taken Holly to the pediatrician on several occasions and has discussed her concerns. The doctor told her that nothing is physically wrong with Holly and that Mrs. Hicks has to be more patient.

Mrs. Hicks confides during this meeting that she read some horrifying material on the Internet about premature infants. According to the information she read,

(Continued)

(Continued)

premature infants often have difficulty bonding with their caretaker, which in some children may ultimately result in mental health and emotional problems. Mrs. Hicks is concerned that this is the case with Holly.

The social worker must take into consideration that in addition to her fears, Mrs. Hicks must be exhausted. Her husband returned to work shortly after the baby came home, and Mrs. Hicks has not left the house since then. She tried taking a break once when her aunt came for a visit, but Holly cried so intensely during this time that her aunt refused to be left alone with Holly again. The social worker must now help Mrs. Hicks cope with the powerful feelings that have been aroused by Holly's premature birth, get any needed clarification on Holly's medical condition, and find ways to get Mrs. Hicks a break from caregiving. He will also want to help her to begin to feel more confident about her ability to parent Holly.

CASE STUDY 3.2
SARAH'S TEEN DAD

Chris Johnson, an Anglo adolescent, is the only dad in the teen fathers group, facilitated by the social worker at a local high school, who has sole custody of his infant daughter. Initially Sarah, Chris's infant daughter, lived with her mom and maternal grandparents. Chris was contacted by the social worker from Child Protective Services (CPS), who informed him that Sarah was removed from the mom's care because of physical neglect. The referral to CPS was made when Sarah was seen in a pediatric clinic and the medical staff noticed that she had not gained weight since the last visit and was generally unresponsive in the examination. Further investigation by the CPS worker revealed that Sarah was left in her crib for most of the day, and few of Sarah's basic daily care needs were being fulfilled. Although Chris's contact with Sarah had been sporadic since her birth, he did not hesitate to pursue custody, especially given that the only other alternative was Sarah's placement in foster care. Chris's parents were also supportive of Chris's desire to have Sarah live with all of them. However, although they were willing to help, they were adamant that the responsibility for Sarah's care belonged to Chris, not them. They were unwilling to raise Sarah themselves and in fact required Chris to sign a written statement indicating that he, not they, would assume primary responsibility for Sarah's care. Chris's parents also insisted that he remain in school and earn his high school diploma.

Thus far the situation seems to be working well. At the last medical appointment, Sarah's weight had increased significantly, and she responded to the nurse's attempts to play and communicate with her. Chris is continuing his education at the alternative high school, which also has a day care for Sarah. Chris admits that it is much more difficult than he anticipated. He attends school for half the day, works a part-time job the other half, and then has to care for Sarah in the evenings. Chris has shared several times in the group that it is a lot for him to juggle. He still mourns the loss of his freedom and "carefree" lifestyle. Like most of the other teens in the group, whether they physically live with the child or not, Chris is concerned about doing the best he can for Sarah; he states that he just wants to be a good dad.

CASE STUDY 3.3
OVERPROTECTING HENRY

Irma Velasquez, a second-generation Hispanic American, is still mourning the death of her little girl Angel, who was 2 years old when she was killed by a stray bullet that came into their home through the living room window. Although it has been about a year since the incident, no one has been arrested. The police do know, however, that neither Ms. Velasquez's daughter nor her family was the intended victim. The stray bullet was the result of a shoot-out between two rival drug dealers in the family's neighborhood.

Ms. Velasquez is just glad that now 14-month-old Henry was in his crib in the back of the house instead of in the living room on that horrible evening. He had fallen asleep in her lap a few minutes before, but she had just returned from laying him in his crib when the shooting occurred. Irma Velasquez confides in her social worker at Victim Services that her family has not been the same since the incident. For one thing, she and her husband barely speak. His method of dealing with the tragedy is to stay away from home. She admits that she is angry with her husband because he does not make enough money for them to live in a safer neighborhood. She thinks that he blames her because she did not protect Angel in some way.

Ms. Velasquez admits that she is afraid that something bad will also happen to Henry. She has limited their area in the home to the back bedroom, and they seldom leave the house. She does not allow anyone, even her sister, to take care of him and confesses that she has not left his side since the shooting. Even with these restrictions, Ms. Velasquez worries. She is concerned that Henry will choke on a toy or food or become ill. She still does not allow him to feed himself, even dry cereal. He has just begun walking, and she severely limits his space for movement. Ms. Velasquez looks worn and exhausted. Although she knows these behaviors are somewhat irrational, she states that she is determined to protect Henry. She further states that she just could not live through losing another child.

DEVELOPMENTAL NICHE AND TYPICAL INFANT AND TODDLER DEVELOPMENT

What happens during the prenatal period and the earliest months and years of a child's life has a lasting impact on the life course journey. In the earliest moments, months, and years, interactions with parents, family members, and other adults and children influence the way the brain and the rest of the body develop, as do such factors as nutrition and environmental safety. Although it is never too late to improve health and well-being, what happens during infancy and toddlerhood sets the stage for the journey through childhood, adolescence, and adulthood. We were all infants and toddlers once, but sometimes, in our work as social workers, we may find it hard to understand the experience of someone 3 years old or younger. (Young children are typically referred to as **infants** in the first year, but as they enter the second year of life and become more mobile, they are usually called **toddlers**, from about 12 to 36 months of age.) As adults, we have become accustomed to communicating with words, and we are not always sure how to read the behaviors of the very young child. And we are not always sure how we are to behave with them. The best way to overcome these limitations, of course, is to learn what we can about the lives of infants and toddlers.

In all three of the case studies at the beginning of this chapter, factors can be identified that may adversely affect the children's development. However,

we must begin by understanding what is traditionally referred to as "normal" development. But because *normal* is a relative term with some judgmental overtones, we will use the term *typical* instead, meaning typical in a statistical sense.

Social workers employed in schools, hospitals, community mental health centers, and other public health settings are often approached by parents and teachers with questions about development in young children. To assess whether any of the children they bring to your attention require intervention, you must be able to distinguish between healthy and problematic development in three areas: physical, cognitive, and socioemotional development. As you will see, young children go through a multitude of changes in all three areas simultaneously. Inadequate development in any one of them—or in multiple areas—may have long-lasting consequences for the individual.

Keep in mind, however, that what is considered to be healthy is relative to environment and culture. Every newborn enters a world with distinctive features structured by the social setting that he or she encounters (Gardiner, 2018). Therefore, all aspects of development must be considered in cultural context. Each newborn enters a **developmental niche**, in which culture guides every aspect of the developmental process (Harkness & Super, 2003, 2006). Parents get their ideas about parenting and about the nature of children from the cultural milieu, and parents' ideas are the dominant force in how the infant and toddler develop. Harry Gardiner (2018) identifies three interrelated components of the developmental niche:

physical and social settings of daily life, child-rearing customs, and caregiver psychology. Exhibit 3.1 provides an overview of these three important components of the developmental niche encountered by every newborn. As you review this exhibit, think about the developmental niches encountered by Holly Hicks, Sarah Johnson, and Henry Velasquez as they begin their life journeys.

In the United States and other wealthy postindustrial societies, many newborns enter a developmental niche in which families have become smaller than in earlier eras. This results in a great deal of attention being paid to each child. Parents take courses and read books about how to provide the best possible care for their infants and toddlers. Infant safety is stressed, with laws about car seats, guidelines about the position in which the baby should sleep, and a "baby industry" that provides a broad range of safety equipment (baby monitors, baby gates, and so on) and toys, books, and electronics to provide sensory stimulation. Of course, this developmental niche requires considerable resources, and many families in wealthy nations cannot afford the regulation car seat or the baby monitor. Chris Johnson is attending school, working, and caring for Sarah; he probably would be hard-pressed to find time to read parenting books, but he does find time to attend a group for teen fathers. Irma Velasquez's concern for Henry's safety focuses on protecting him from stray bullets rather than on baby monitors and baby gates. And, of course, the developmental niches in nonindustrial and newly industrializing countries are very different from the niche described earlier. For example, anthropologists are studying how an increasingly migrating workforce is changing the nature of caregiving of infants and toddlers, as a developmental niche of multiple family caregivers gives way to a more isolated form of one primary caregiver (see Haviland, Prins, Walrath, & McBride, 2017). Unfortunately, many infants of the world live in developmental niches characterized by infection, malnutrition, and war. Please keep these variations in mind as you read about infant and toddler development.

To make the presentation of ideas about infancy and toddlerhood manageable, this chapter follows a traditional method of organizing the discussion by type of development: physical development, cognitive development, emotional development, and social development. In this chapter, emotional development and social development are combined under the heading Socioemotional Development. Of course, all these types of development and behavior are interdependent, and often the distinctions blur.

EXHIBIT 3.1 ● Components of Developmental Niche

Physical and Social Settings of Daily Life

Size, shape, and location of living space

Objects, toys, reading materials

Ecological setting and climate

Nutritional status of children

Family structure (e.g., nuclear, extended, single parent, blended)

Presence of multiple generations (e.g., parents, grandparents, other relatives)

Presence or absence of mother or father

Presence of multiple caregivers

Role of siblings as caregivers

Presence and influence of peer group members

Customs of Childcare and Child-Rearing

Sleeping patterns (e.g., co-sleeping vs. sleeping alone)

Dependence versus independence training

Feeding and eating schedules

Handling and carrying practices

Play and work patterns

Initiation rites

Formal versus informal learning

Psychology of the Caregivers

Parenting styles (e.g., authoritarian, authoritative, permissive)

Value systems (e.g., dependence, independence, interdependence)

Parental cultural belief systems or ethnotheories

Developmental expectations

Source: Gardiner, 2018. *Lives across cultures: Cross-cultural human development* (6th ed.),Table 2.1, p. 17.

PHOTO 3.1 Babies depend on others for basic physical and emotional needs. Family support and affection are important factors in healthy development.

PHYSICAL DEVELOPMENT

The infant's first test of physical development occurs about a minute after delivery. The APGAR test, developed by Virginia Apgar, assesses the newborn's color, heart rate, reflexes, muscle tone, and respiratory ability. Medical staff assess the newborn using a scale from 0 to 2 in each of the five areas. A perfect APGAR score of 10 is rare. A score of 7 or higher indicates only routine infant care is needed. Infants scored from 4 to 6 may need breathing assistance, and infants scored below 4 may require immediate medical attention, including lifesaving medical intervention. Most infants who receive a score below 7 are retested every 5 minutes for up to 20 minutes. (For more information about the APGAR test, see http://americanpregnancy.org/labor-and-birth/apgar-test.) Although a low APGAR score does not necessarily indicate long-term health problems or complications in physical development, social workers in child welfare and health care settings should be familiar with these types of standard assessment tools.

Newborns depend on others for basic physical needs. They must be fed, cleaned, and kept safe and comfortable until they develop the ability to do these things for themselves. At the same time, however, newborns have an amazing set of physical abilities and potentials right from the beginning.

Growth Patterns

In Case Study 3.2, the pediatrician and CPS social worker were concerned that Sarah Johnson was not gaining weight. With improved care in the home of her father and his parents, Sarah is making good weight gains and is more alert and responsive. With adequate nourishment and care, the physical growth of the infant is quite predictable. Infants grow very rapidly throughout the first 2 years of life, but the pace of growth slows a bit in toddlerhood. Both genetic and environmental factors can cause some children to grow faster than others. In the first few days after birth, newborns lose 5% to 10% of their body weight, but after this initial loss, they gain weight quickly.

Growth during the prenatal and infant periods follows particular patterns, which are called cephalocaudal development and proximodistal development. The *cephalocaudal development* principle of growth refers to the idea that growth proceeds from the head downward. The head and upper regions of the body develop before the lower regions. At birth the newborn's head is about one fourth the total body length, but the head becomes more proportionate to the body as the infant and toddler grows. The *proximodistal development* principle refers to the idea that growth occurs from the center of the body outward. During prenatal development, the internal organs develop before the arms and legs.

The World Health Organization (WHO) undertook a project, called the Multicentre Growth Reference Study (MGRS), to construct standards for evaluating children from birth through 5 years of age. One part of that project was to construct growth standards to propose how children *should* grow in *all* countries, of interest because of WHO's commitment to eliminate global health disparities. MGRS collected growth data from 8,440 affluent children from diverse geographical and cultural settings, including Brazil, Ghana, India, Norway, Oman, and the United States. To be eligible for the study, mothers needed to be breastfeeding and not smoking, and the environment needed to be adequate to support unconstrained growth.

The researchers found no differences in growth patterns across sites, even though there were some differences in parental stature. Given the striking similarity in growth patterns across sites, they concluded that the data could be used to develop an international standard. Across sites, the average length at birth was 19.5 inches (49.5 cm), 26.3 inches (66.7 cm) at 6 months, 29.5 inches (75.0 cm) at 12 months, and 34.4 inches (87.4 cm) at 24 months (WHO Multicentre Growth Reference Study Group, 2006a). By 1 year of age, infant height was about 1.5 times birth height, and by 2 years, the toddler had nearly doubled the birth height.

Most newborns weigh from 5 to 10 pounds at birth. Infants typically double their weight by age 5 months and triple their weight in the first year. The typical toddler gains 5 to 6 pounds during the second year and 4 to 5 pounds during the third year. The size of individual infants and toddlers can vary quite a bit. Some of the difference is the result of nutrition, exposure to disease, and other environmental factors; much of it is the result of genetics. Some ethnic differences in physical development have also been observed. For example, Asian American children tend to be smaller than average, and African American children tend to be larger than average (Tate, Dezateux, Cole, & the Millennium Cohort Study Child Health Group, 2006). In the past decade there has been a great deal of concern about rapid weight gain during the first 6 months, which has been connected to overweight by age 4 and to several chronic diseases in adulthood, but recent longitudinal research suggests that rapid weight gain in infancy is just as often associated with later height as with later obesity (Wright, Cox, & Couteur, 2011). The WHO child growth standards, calculated by different methods, can be found at www.who.int/childgrowth/standards.

The importance of nutrition in infancy cannot be overstated. Nutrition affects physical stature, motor skill development, brain development, and most every other aspect of development. A 2013 report by the Lancet Maternal and Child Nutrition series (2013) indicates that, globally, malnutrition contributes to 3.1 million deaths of children age 5 and younger each year. In 2011, 26% of children in low-income countries suffered from stunted growth because of chronic maternal and child undernutrition. This was down from 40% in 1990, but still a serious global public health problem. Eastern and western Africa and south-central Asia have the highest prevalence of stunting. Nutritional deficiencies during the first 1,000 days of the child's life can result in damage to the immune system and impair social and cognitive capacities.

Self-Regulation

Before birth, the bodily functions of the fetus are regulated by the mother's body. After birth, the infant must develop the capacity to engage in self-regulation (Davies, 2011). At first, the challenge is to regulate bodily functions, such as temperature control, sleeping, eating, and eliminating. That challenge is heightened for the premature or medically fragile infant, as Holly Hicks's mother is finding. Growing evidence indicates that some self-regulatory functions that allow self-calming and organize the wake-sleep cycles get integrated and coordinated during the third trimester, from 30 to 34 weeks' gestation (Institute of Medicine, 2006). Born at 26 weeks' gestation, Holly Hicks did not have the benefit of the uterine environment to support the development of these self-regulatory functions.

As any new parent will attest, however, infants are not born with regular patterns of sleeping, eating, and eliminating. With maturation of the central nervous system in the first 3 months, and with lots of help from parents or other caregivers, the infant's rhythms of sleeping, eating, and eliminating become much more regular (Davies, 2011). A newborn typically sleeps about 18 hours a day, dividing that time evenly between day and night. Of course, this is not a good fit with the way adults organize their sleep lives. By about 8 weeks, infants begin to show signs of day-night sleep rhythms. At the end of 3 months, most infants are sleeping 14 to 15 hours per day, primarily at night, with some well-defined nap times during the day. Parents also gradually shape infants' eating schedules so that they are eating mainly during the day.

There are cultural variations in, and controversies about, the way caregivers shape the sleeping behaviors of infants. The management of sleep is one of the earliest culturally influenced parenting behaviors. In some cultures, infants sleep with parents, and in other cultures, infants are put to sleep in their own beds and often in their own rooms. In some cultures, putting an infant to sleep alone in a room is considered to be neglectful (Gardiner, 2018). Co-sleeping, the child sleeping with the parents, is routine in most of the world's cultures (McKenna, 2002). Japanese and Chinese children often sleep with their parents throughout infancy and early childhood (Iwata, Iwata, & Matsuishi, 2013). Research indicates that sleeping with parents induces shorter bouts of sleep and less sound sleep (Blunden, Thompson, & Dawson, 2011). Some researchers have speculated that the infant's lighter and shorter sleep pattern may protect against sudden infant death syndrome (SIDS). The connection between co-sleeping and SIDS has been a controversial research issue. One research team conducted a meta-analysis of research of the issue published from 1970 to 2010; they found that co-sleeping increased the risk for SIDS, and the risk is highest for infants younger than 12 weeks and when parents smoke (Vennemann et al., 2012). A more recent study found an association between co-sleeping and somatic complaints for toddlers ages 18 months to 60 months (Peters, Lusher, Banbury, & Chandler, 2016). What is not always clear in these studies is whether the infant is sleeping in the same bed as the parents or whether he or she is sleeping in a type of bassinet attached to the parental bed. It would seem that the latter would overcome the risks found in the research. Proponents of co-sleeping argue that it does a better job of meeting the physiological, psychological, and developmental needs of newborns than sleeping separately (Willinger, Ko, Hoffman, Kessler, & Corwin, 2003).

Culture plays an important role in how parents manage the sleep patterns of infants (Owens, 2005). Parents in the United States look forward to the time when their infant will sleep through the night. In contrast, many European parents think of newborn sleep as part of normal development and do not intervene to shape newborn sleep patterns (Kuther, 2017). Many approaches to infant sleep training have been proposed, and researchers continue to debate the merits of different methods. A review of 52 sleep studies found that almost all of the interventions were effective if applied consistently, but different methods work with different infants (Sleep Center, 2016). A group of pediatric sleep experts from around the world (including Israel, China, India, Australia, Spain, Switzerland, Sweden, Italy, and Canada) held the first meeting of the International Pediatric Sleep Education (IPSE) Task Force in the spring of 2003 (Owens, 2005). Among the findings of this task force are these:

- Pediatric sleep problems are universal. Studies from diverse cultures find that about 25% of parents report sleep problems in their infants and toddlers.

- Many types of pediatric sleep problems are common in both Eastern and Western cultures, including bedtime resistance, night wakings, and inadequate sleep.

Feeding is another area in which parents must help infants and toddlers to begin to develop self-regulation, and there are cultural variations and controversies about breastfeeding versus formula feeding. Some cultures have historically supported feeding on demand in infancy whereas others have preferred early attempts to shape infant feeding schedules. Throughout history, most infants have been breastfed. However, alternatives to breastfeeding by the mother have always existed, sometimes in the form of a wet nurse (a woman employed to breastfeed someone else's infant) or in the form of animal milks. Following World War II, breastfeeding ceased to be the primary nutritional source for infants because of the promotion of manufactured formula in industrialized and nonindustrialized countries. Since the 1980s, cultural attitudes have shifted again in favor of breastfeeding. The American Academy of Pediatrics (AAP) argues that infant nutrition should be considered a public health issue, not a lifestyle choice (Eidelman & Schanler, 2012). The AAP recommends that infants be breastfed, or fed with human milk, exclusively for the first 6 months, followed by continued breastfeeding with some supplementary use of foods until the infant is at least 1 year old.

Research indicates that breastfeeding offers benefits for mothers and infants. Mothers who breastfeed have lower rates of diabetes, cardiovascular disease, and depression and are at lower risk for later ovarian and breast cancer and bone fractures (Godfrey & Lawrence, 2010). Breast milk has the right amount of fat, sugar, water, and protein for infant development. It contains immunizing agents that protect against infections (Hetzner, Razza, Malone, & Brooks-Gun, 2009). Breastfeeding is also associated with reduced risk of allergies, gastrointestinal symptoms, and SIDS (Schulze & Carlisle, 2010). Breastfeeding longer than 6 months is associated with reduced risk of obesity and childhood cancer (Schulze & Carlisle, 2010). Recent research indicates that breastfed children have significantly higher IQ scores and larger whole brain, gray matter, total cortical gray matter, and subcortical gray matter volumes than nonbreastfed children (Luby, Belden, Whalen, Harms, & Barch, 2016). Although this is a consistent finding, other researchers have found that the differences are small (Jenkins & Foster, 2014).

Breastfeeding continues to rise in the United States. In 2011, 79% of newborns started breastfeeding; 49% were breastfeeding at 6 months, and 27% were breastfeeding at 12 months (Centers for Disease Control and Prevention, 2014a). There are racial, ethnic, and social class differences in the rate of breastfeeding, suggesting that family, culture, and social policy play a role in the breastfeeding decision. Countries where women have paid maternity leave for much of the first year of life (for example, Australia, Denmark, Norway, and Sweden) have very high breastfeeding rates of 94% and more (Hauck, Fenwick, Dhaliwal, & Butt, 2011). In the United States and the United Kingdom, the lowest rates of breastfeeding are among low-income women, young mothers, and mothers with low levels of education. Research indicates that the employment settings of low-income mothers are less likely than other employment settings to provide places for women to use breast pumps (Racine, Frick, Guthrie, & Strobino, 2009). Societal customs can support or discourage breastfeeding. In Saudi Arabia, a woman may breastfeed her infant openly and receive no notice, although otherwise she is fully veiled. In France, topless swimming is culturally acceptable, but breastfeeding in public is not (Riordan & Auerbach, 1999).

Somewhere around 4 to 6 months, infants begin to eat solid food; the first solid food is usually iron-fortified cereal mixed with breast milk or formula. Then, pureed vegetables and fruits are introduced, followed by pureed meat (for meat eaters). Infants don't always like these new tastes and textures, and foods may have to be introduced over a dozen times before they are accepted. As infants become toddlers, their appetites decrease

and they begin to feed themselves. Feeding problems in infants and toddlers are discussed in a later section in this chapter.

Cultural variations exist in beliefs about how to respond when infants cry and fuss, whether to soothe them or leave them to learn to soothe themselves. When parents do attempt to soothe infants, interestingly, they seem to use the same methods across cultures: "They say something, touch, pick up, search for sources of discomfort, and then feed" (Shonkoff & Phillips, 2000, p. 100). Infants who have been consistently soothed usually begin to develop the ability to soothe themselves after 3 or 4 months. This ability is the precursor to struggles for self-control and mastery over powerful emotions that occur in toddlerhood. More is said about emotion self-regulation in a later section. In recent years, there has been an ongoing debate about how intensive parenting must be during infancy and toddlerhood (Moore & Abetz, 2016).

Parents become less anxious as the infant's rhythms become more regular and predictable. At the same time, if the caregiver is responsive and dependable, the infant becomes less anxious and begins to develop the ability to wait to have needs met.

Toilet training (potty training) is another area where caregivers assist infants and toddlers in their development of self-regulation. It is often a source of stress and uncertainty for new parents. Every human culture has mechanisms for disposing of human waste and socializes infants and toddlers to that method. One of the basic issues in this socialization is whether it should be in the hands of the child or the caregiver. In places in the world where there are no disposable diapers and no access to a washing machine, parents, even in the early months, become sensitive to signs that the infant is about to defecate or urinate and hold him or her over whatever type of toilet is available. This method, referred to as "assisted infant toilet training," is expected to work by about age 6 months. Although this method is not typically followed in the middle- to high-income countries, there is a current movement in the United States to raise diaper-free babies by using "elimination communication," based on timing, cues, and intuition (see the website www.diaperfreebaby.org). There is no clear consensus in the United States about the best method for toilet training (Howell, Wyosocki, & Steiner, 2010). The U.S. American Academy of Pediatrics recommends a child-oriented approach that emphasizes the child's interest in toilet training and tries to minimize the demands made by parents. Toddlers are introduced to a potty-chair and gradually encouraged to sit on it and over time actually use it, followed by positive rewards.

Reprimands or punishments are to be avoided. This can take weeks or months. In contrast, some parents use the train-in-a-day method developed by Azrin and Foxx (1989), which is recommended to start about the age of 20 months. Researchers have found that both the child-centered and the train-in-a-day method can lead to successful toilet training (Howell et al., 2010).

In the United States, the average age to complete toilet training has increased steadily over the past few decades, from 18 months in the 1940s to 27 months in 1980, and 37 months in 2003. There are subcultural variations, however. On average, girls achieve toilet training 2 to 3 months ahead of boys. Family stressors such as divorce, death, or birth of a new baby may lead to a delay in toilet training (Howell et al., 2010).

Sensory Abilities

Full-term infants are born with a functioning **sensory system**—the senses of hearing, sight, taste, smell, touch, and sensitivity to pain—and these abilities continue to develop rapidly in the first few months. Indeed, in the early months the sensory system seems to function at a higher level than the motor system, which allows movement. The sensory system allows infants, from the time of birth, to participate in and adapt to their environments. A lot of their learning happens through listening and watching. The sensory system is interconnected, with various sensory abilities working together to give the infant multiple sources of information about the world.

Developmental researchers make a distinction between sensation and perception. *Sensation* occurs when the senses detect a stimulus. *Perception* refers to the sense the brain makes of the stimulus and the awareness of the sensation. Although the infant is equipped with a full range of senses and ready to experience the world, perception develops over time. Researchers have examined how infants learn to change behavior in response to sensation and have identified four mechanisms of learning: habituation, classical conditioning, operant conditioning, and imitation (Kuther, 2017). *Habituation* occurs when the repeated exposure to a stimulus leads to a gradual decline in the intensity, frequency, or duration of response to the stimulus. Habituation starts before birth (Hepper, 2015). *Classical conditioning* involves the association between a conditioned stimulus and an unconditioned stimulus. For example, one researcher found that when stroking of an infant's forehead was paired with tasting sugar water, 2-hour-old infants were conditioned to suck in response to having their heads stroked (Blass, Ganchrow, & Steiner, 1984). Classical conditioning also begins before

birth (Herbert, Eckerman, Goldstein, & Stanton, 2004). In *operant conditioning* infants learn to behave in ways that are positively reinforced and avoid behaviors that are punished. For example, infants have been found to be conditioned to change the rate of sucking on a pacifier to receive a positive reinforcement such as a tape recording of the mother's voice or other voices they find pleasing (Floccia, Christophe, & Bertoncini, 1997). Third trimester fetuses can be operantly conditioned (Thoman & Ingersoll, 1993). All of us learn by *imitating* the behaviors of others, but so can infants. The mirror neuron system is thought to be an inborn capacity to respond to actions of others by mirroring their actions and is apparent in both newborn humans and monkeys (Cook, Bird, Catmur, Press, & Heyes, 2014).

Hearing is the earliest link to the environment; the fetus is sensitive to auditory stimulation in the uterus (Moraru et al., 2011). The fetus hears the mother's heartbeat, and this sound is soothing to the infant in the early days and weeks after birth. Newborns show a preference for their mother's voice over unfamiliar voices, but one research team found that this is not the case for newborns whose mothers were anxious or depressed during the third trimester (Figueiredo, Pacheco, Costa, Conde, & Teixeira, 2010). Early infants can also distinguish changes in loudness, pitch, and location of sounds, and they can use auditory information to differentiate one object from another and to track the location of an object (Bahrick, Lickliter, & Flom, 2006). These capacities grow increasingly sensitive across the first 6 months after birth. Infants appear to be particularly sensitive to language sounds, and the earliest infant smiles are evoked by the sound of the human voice (Benasich & Leevers, 2003). Unfortunately, research indicates that malnutrition during the infant's first 3 months increases the likelihood of early onset hearing loss (Olusanya, 2010).

At birth, vision is the least developed sense, but it improves rapidly during the first few months of life. From the ages of 6 months to 1 year, the infant begins to see objects the same way an adult does (Mercuri, Baranello, Romeo, Cesarini, & Ricci, 2007). Of course, infants do not have cognitive associations with objects as adults do. Infants respond to a number of visual dimensions, including depth, brightness, movement, color, and distance. Human faces have particular appeal for newborns. Although conflicting evidence exists, research suggests that several days after birth infants can discriminate between facial expressions (Farroni, Menon, Rigato, & Johnson, 2007). From 4 to 7 months, infants can recognize expressions, particularly happiness, fear, and anger (McClure, 2000). Infants show preference for faces, and by 3 months, most infants can distinguish a parent's face from the face of a stranger (Nelson, 2001). Ability to recognize familiar faces is enhanced through positive expression, suggesting an interaction between expression and infants' recognition of a familiar face (Turati, Montirosso, Brenna, Ferrara, & Borgatti, 2011). Some researchers have found that infants are distressed by a lack of facial movement in the people they look at, showing that they prefer caregivers to have expressive faces (Muir & Lee, 2003).

Taste and smell begin to function in the uterus, and newborns can differentiate sweet, bitter, sour, and salty tastes. A preference for sweet tastes is innately present for both preterm and full-term newborns (Pepino & Mennella, 2006). Research suggests that the first few minutes after birth is a particularly sensitive period for learning to distinguish smells (Delaunay-El Allam, Marlier, & Schaal, 2006). Breastfed babies are especially sensitive to their mother's body odors. One research team found that newborns undergoing a heel prick were soothed by the smell of breast milk, but only if the milk came from the mother's breast (Nishitani et al., 2009).

Both animal and human research tell us that touch plays a very important role in infant development. In many cultures, swaddling, or wrapping a baby snugly in a blanket, is used to soothe a fussy newborn. We also know that gentle handling, rocking, stroking, and cuddling are all soothing to an infant. Regular gentle rocking and stroking are very effective in soothing low-birth-weight (LBW) babies, who may have underdeveloped central nervous systems. Skin-to-skin contact between parents and their newborns has been found to have benefits for both infants and their parents. Preterm babies who have lots of skin contact with their parents, including gentle touching and massage, gain weight faster, have better temperature regulation, have better capacity for self-soothing, and are more alert compared with preterm babies who do not receive extensive skin contact (Feldman, 2004; Jean & Stack, 2012). Infants also use touch to learn about their world and their own bodies. Early infants use their mouths for exploring their worlds, but by 5 or 6 months of age, infants can make controlled use of their hands to explore objects in their environment. They learn about the world and keep themselves entertained by exploring small details, transferring objects from one hand to the other, and examining the differences in surfaces and other features of the object (Streri, 2005).

Clear evidence exists that from the first days of life, babies feel pain. Recently, pediatric researchers have been studying newborn reactions to medical procedures such as heel sticks, the sticks used to draw blood for lab analysis. One researcher found that newborns who undergo repeated heel sticks learn to anticipate pain and develop a stronger reaction to pain than other infants (Taddio, Shah, Gilbert-Macleod, & Katz, 2002). These findings are leading pediatricians to develop guidelines for managing pain in newborns (Spence et al., 2010). The findings are also influencing debates about male infant circumcision.

Reflexes

Although dependent on others, newborns are equipped from the start with tools for survival that are involuntary muscle responses to certain stimuli, called **reflexes**. Reflexes aid the infant in adapting to the environment outside the womb. The presence and strength of a reflex is an important sign of neurological development, and the absence of reflexes can indicate a serious developmental disorder (Health Encyclopedia, 2018). Given Holly Hicks's early arrival, it is likely her reflex responses were thoroughly evaluated.

Newborns have two critical reflexes:

1. *Rooting reflex.* When infants' cheeks or the corners of their mouths are gently stroked with a finger, they will turn their head in the direction of the touch and open their mouths in an attempt to suck the finger. This reflex aids in feeding, because it guides the infant to the nipple.

2. *Sucking reflex.* When a nipple or some other suckable object is presented to the infant, the infant sucks it. This reflex is another important tool for feeding.

Many infants would probably perish without the rooting and sucking reflexes. Imagine the time and effort it would require for one feeding if they did not have them. Instead, infants are born with the ability to take in nutriment.

A number of reflexes disappear at identified times during infancy (see Exhibit 3.2) but in some cases change into voluntary behavior; others persist throughout adulthood. Both the rooting reflex and sucking reflex disappear in the first few months. By this time, the infant has mastered the voluntary act of sucking and is therefore no longer in need of the reflexive response. Several other infant reflexes appear to have little use now but probably had some specific survival purposes in earlier times. The presence of an infant reflex after the age at which it typically disappears can be a sign of damage to the brain or nervous system (Kuther, 2017).

EXHIBIT 3.2 ● Infant Reflexes

Reflex	Description	Visible
Sucking	Sucking any object placed in the mouth	Birth to about 6 months
Rooting	Turning the head and tongue toward a stimulus when the cheek is touched	Birth to about 4 months
Moro/startle	Responding with a startle response to loud noise or sudden movement, throwing back the head, arching the back extending legs and arms, and then pulling arms and legs back in	Birth to 2 months
Swimming	Holding the breath and moving arms and legs in swimming motion when placed in water	Birth to about 4–6 months
Walking/stepping	Making stepping movements when held upright with feet touching a flat surface	Birth to about 2–3 months
Grasping	Grasping objects placed in the hand	Birth to about 4 months
Babinski	Fanning and curling the toes in response to having the bottom of the foot stroked	Birth to 8–12 months
Blinking	Blinking of eyes when touched or a sudden bright light appears	Lifetime
Cough	Coughing when airway is stimulated	Lifetime
Gag	Gagging when the throat or back of mouth is stimulated	Lifetime
Sneeze	Sneezing when the nasal passages are irritated	Lifetime
Yawn	Yawning when the body needs additional oxygen	Lifetime

Motor Skills

The infant gradually advances from reflex functioning to motor functioning. The development of **motor skills**—the ability to move and manipulate—occurs in a more or less orderly, logical sequence. It begins with simple actions such as lifting the chin and progresses to more complex acts such as walking, running, and throwing. Infants usually crawl before they walk.

Motor development is somewhat predictable, in that children tend to reach milestones at about the same age and in the same sequence. As a part of the MGRS, WHO undertook a project to construct standards for evaluating the motor development of children from birth through 5 years of age. MGRS collected longitudinal data on six gross motor milestones of children ages 4 to 24 months in Ghana, India, Norway, Oman, and the United States. The milestones studied were sitting without support, standing with assistance, hands-and-knees crawling, walking with assistance, standing alone, and walking alone. Because WHO was trying to

establish standards for evaluating child development, healthy children were studied in all five study sites. The researchers found that 90% of the children achieved five of the six milestones in the same sequence, but 4.3% of the sample never engaged in hands-and-knees crawling (WHO Multicentre Growth Reference Study Group, 2006b).

Based on the data collected, MGRS developed "windows of milestone achievement" for each of the six motor skills, with achievement at the 1st and 99th percentiles as the window boundaries. All motor achievement within the windows is considered normal variation in ages of achievement for healthy children. The windows of normal achievement for the six motor skills studied are reported in Exhibit 3.3. The results reveal that the range of the windows varies from 5.4 months for sitting without support (from 3.8 months at the 1st percentile to 9.2 months at the 99th percentile) to 10.0 months for standing alone (from 6.9 at the 1st percentile to 16.9 at the 99th percentile). This is quite

EXHIBIT 3.3 ● Windows of Milestone Achievement in Months	
Motor Milestone	Window of Milestone Achievement
Sitting without support	3.8–9.2 months
Standing with assistance	4.8–11.4 months
Hands-and-knees crawling	5.2–13.5 months
Walking with assistance	5.9–13.7 months
Standing alone	6.9–16.9 months
Walking alone	8.2–17.6 months

Source: WHO Multicentre Growth Reference Study Group, 2006b.

a wide range for normal development and should be reassuring to parents who become anxious if their child is not at the low end of the window. Many parents, for example, become concerned if their child has not attempted to walk unassisted by age 1. However, some children walk alone at age 9 months; others do not even attempt to walk until almost 18 months.

The physical environment as well as culture and ethnicity appear to have some influence on motor development in infants and toddlers. MGRS found that girls were slightly ahead of boys in gross motor development, but the differences were not statistically significant. The researchers did find small, but statistically significant, differences between sites of the study, however. They speculate that these differences probably reflect culture-based childcare behaviors, but the cause cannot be determined from the data, and a genetic component is possible. The earliest mean age of achievement for four

© iStockphoto.com

PHOTO 3.2 Fine motor skills, the ability to move and manipulate objects, develop in a logical sequence.

of the six milestones occurred in the Ghanaian sample, and the latest mean age of achievement for all six milestones occurred in the Norwegian sample (WHO Multicentre Growth Reference Study Group, 2006c). The U.S. sample mean was in the middle range on all milestones except for hands-and-knees crawling, where it had the lowest mean achievement.

A longitudinal study of almost 16,000 infants in the United Kingdom took up this issue of cultural differences in developmental motor milestones. In this study, Black Caribbean infants, Black African infants, and Indian infants were, on average, more advanced in motor development than White infants. Pakistani and Bangladeshi infants were more likely than White infants to show motor delays. Although the delays among Pakistani and Bangladeshi infants appear to be explained by factors associated with poverty, the earlier development of Black Caribbean, Black African, and Indian infants could not be explained by economic advantage. The researchers suggest that parental expectations and parenting practices play a role in cultural differences in motor development (Kelly, Sacker, Schoon, & Nazroo, 2006).

The development of motor skills (and most other types of skills, for that matter) is a continuous process. Children progress from broad capacities to more specific refined abilities. For example, toddlers progress from eating cereal with their fingers to eating with a spoon.

The Growing Brain

We are living in the midst of a neuroscientific revolution clarifying the important role of the brain in helping to shape human behavior (Matto, Strolin-Goltzman, & Ballan, 2014). At birth, the brain is about 25% of its adult weight and grows rapidly throughout infancy, reaching 80% of adult weight by the age of 2 (Nelson & Luciana, 2008). As the brain grows, it becomes not only larger but also more complex.

Like every other part of the human body, the brain is made up of billions of cells. Human brains and brains of other primates contain **neurons**, or specialized nerve cells that store and transmit information; they carry sensory information to the brain, and they carry out the processes involved in thought, emotion, and action. **Neurogenesis**, the creation of new neurons, begins before birth. We are born with more than 100 billion neurons, much more than we will ever need and more than we will ever have again. Some neurons die and new ones are created; neurogenesis continues throughout life but at a much slower pace than occurs prenatally (Stiles & Jernigan, 2010). Between the neurons are **synapses**, or gaps that function as the site of information exchange from one neuron to another. **Synaptogenesis**, the creation of synapses, begins to accelerate during the last trimester of pregnancy and peaks at 2 to 3 years of age, when the brain has about twice the synapses it will have in adulthood (Pierce, 2011; Urban Child Institute, 2018). This rapid synaptogenesis results in an overabundance of synapses and a tripling in brain weight during the first 3 years. The period of overproduction of synapses, or **synaptic blooming**, is followed by a period of **synaptic pruning**, or reduction, of the synapses to improve the efficiency of brain functioning. It is through this process of creating elaborate communication systems between the connecting neurons that more and more complex skills and abilities become possible. Thus, during these early years of life, children are capable of rapid new learning. The blooming and pruning of synapses process continues well into childhood and adolescence at different timetables in different regions of the brain. In addition to synaptogenesis, **myelination**, a process in which axons and neurons are coated with a fatty substance called myelin, begins during the first 2 years (Stiles & Jernigan, 2010). Myelination causes faster neural communication, which results in faster information processing. Myelination progresses most rapidly between birth and age 4 and continues through adolescence and young adulthood.

The available evidence suggests that both genetic processes and early experiences with the environment influence the timing of brain development. Brain plasticity has been a major finding of neuroscientific research of the past few decades. There are two elements of **brain plasticity**, also known as neuroplasticity; first, research indicates that the brain changes throughout life; and second, the brain changes in response to what it experiences—it is shaped by experience (Farmer, 2009). The human brain is genetically designed to accommodate an incredibly wide range of human experiences, and the environmental context helps to shape the brain for life in a particular developmental niche. What is used gets strengthened, and what is not used gets pruned. The infant and toddler contribute to their own brain development by repeating certain actions, attending to certain stimuli, and responding in particular ways to caregivers. Newer research supports a relationship between caregiver–infant interaction and brain structure. For example, results from one study indicate that the quality of interaction between the infant and caregiver may have a pronounced effect on the development of the infant brain (Bernier, Calkins, & Bell, 2016). The research hypothesis was that infants whose mothers demonstrate a higher quality of interaction at

5 months will have a higher-level brain development at 10 and 24 months, as measured by frontal resting EEG power. The researchers did find a relationship between quality of mother–infant interaction and frontal brain activity. The higher the quality of interaction, the higher the level of frontal brain functioning. Scientists continue to conduct new and innovative research in this area. See Harvard's Center on the Developing Child (https://developingchild.harvard.edu) for up-to-date research efforts in this area.

Exposure to speech in the first year expedites the discrimination of speech sounds; exposure to patterned visual information in the first few years of life is necessary for normal development of some aspects of vision. Some suggest that the entire infancy period is a crucial and sensitive time for brain development, given the quantity and speed at which the neurons develop and connect (Pierce, 2011). Positive physical experiences (feeding, safety, and so on) and positive psychological experiences (touching, cooing, and playing) activate and stimulate brain activity (Davies, 2011). Good nutrition and infant stimulation are essential for brain development, and exposure to environmental toxins, abuse, emotional trauma, and deprivation is hazardous. Persistent stress for the infant or toddler has been found to result in overdevelopment of areas of the brain that process anxiety and fear and underdevelopment of other brain areas, particularly the frontal cortex (Schore, 2002).

Certain risks to brain development are associated with prematurity. Premature infants like Holly Hicks, born at 24 to 28 weeks' gestation, have high rates of serious intracranial hemorrhage, which can lead to problems in cognitive and motor development, including cerebral palsy and intellectual disability. Less serious intracranial hemorrhage can lead to later behavioral, attentional, and memory problems (Tam et al., 2011). It is not yet clear whether Holly Hicks suffered any type of brain hemorrhage and what impact it will have on her development if she did.

Vaccinations

Vaccinations protect communities as well as individual children from diseases that once spread rapidly and killed many people. Over the past 50 years, the incidence of childhood illnesses such as measles, mumps, and whooping cough has dropped significantly because of widespread use of vaccines to immunize infants and young children. A *vaccine* is a small dose of a substance used to stimulate the production of antibodies to provide immunity against one or more diseases. Vaccines are provided early in life because many preventable diseases are common in infants and young children whose immune systems are not as well developed as they will be later. The Centers for Disease Control and Prevention (CDC) recommends that children be vaccinated against several diseases by the age of 2. Vaccine rates increased significantly from 1994 to 2004 in the United States but have stalled since then (Child Trends, 2014).

A major reason for the stalled vaccination rate is the misconception that vaccines are associated with autism and other developmental disorders as well as some chronic health problems, leading some parents to refuse to have their children vaccinated. Extensive research finds no association between vaccines and autism (see Taylor, Swerdfeger, & Eslick, 2014). One reason that some parents associate vaccines with autism, other developmental disorders, and some chronic illnesses is that these conditions tend to emerge during infancy and toddlerhood, the same age period for the vaccine administration. Research indicates that autism has a strong genetic component and is also associated with both maternal and paternal age (Idring et al., 2014; Waltes et al., 2014).

CRITICAL THINKING QUESTIONS 3.1

Revisit Exhibit 3.1, which lays out the components of the developmental niche. What do we know about the developmental niches involved in the three case studies at the beginning of the chapter, Holly, Sarah, and Henry? What strengths do you see in each of these developmental niches? What potential problems do you see?

COGNITIVE DEVELOPMENT

As the brain develops, so does its ability to process and store information and to solve problems. These abilities are known as cognition. When we talk about how fast a child is learning, we are talking about cognitive development. Researchers now describe the infant as "wired to learn" and agree that infants have an intrinsic drive to learn and to be in interaction with their environments. A central element of cognition is language, which facilitates both thinking and communicating.

Piaget's Stages of Cognitive Development

To assess children's cognitive progress, many people use the concepts developed by the best-known cognitive development theorist, Jean Piaget (1936/1952). Piaget proposed a cognitive-developmental theory that views

humans as active explorers who learn by interacting with the world. He believed that cognitive development occurs in successive stages, determined by the age of the child. His overall contention was that as a child grows and develops, cognition changes not only in quantity but also in quality.

Piaget used the metaphor of a slow-motion movie to explain his theory, which is summarized in Exhibit 3.4 as follows:

1. **Sensorimotor stage** (ages birth to 2 years). Infants at this stage of development can look at only one frame of the movie at a time. When the next picture appears on the screen, infants focus on it and cannot go back to the previous frame.

2. **Preoperational stage** (ages 2 to 7). Preschool children and children in early grades can remember (recall) the sequence of the pictures in the movie. They also develop **symbolic functioning**—the ability to use symbols to represent what is not present. However, they do not necessarily understand what has happened in the movie or how the pictures fit together.

3. **Concrete operations stage** (ages 7 to 11). Not until this stage can children run the pictures in the

EXHIBIT 3.4 ● Piaget's Stages of Cognitive Development	
Stage	**Characteristics**
Sensorimotor (birth–2 years)	Infant is egocentric; he or she gradually learns to coordinate sensory and motor activities and develops a beginning sense of objects existing apart from the self.
Preoperational (2–7 years)	The child remains primarily egocentric but discovers rules (regularities) that can be applied to new incoming information. The child tends to overgeneralize rules, however, and thus makes many cognitive errors.
Concrete operations (7–11 years)	The child can solve concrete problems through the application of logical problem-solving strategies.
Formal operations (11 years and beyond)	The person becomes able to solve real and hypothetical problems using abstract concepts.

movie backward and forward to better understand how they blend to form a specific meaning.

4. **Formal operations stage** (ages 11 and beyond). Children gain the capacity to apply logic to various situations and to use symbols to solve problems. Adding to Piaget's metaphor, one cognitive scientist describes formal operations as the ability of the adolescent not only to understand the observed movie but also to add or change characters and create an additional plot or staging plan (Edwards, 1992).

The first of Piaget's stages applies to infants and toddlers. During the sensorimotor period, they respond to immediate stimuli—what they see, hear, taste, touch, and smell—and learning takes place through the senses and motor activities. Piaget suggests that infant and toddler cognitive development occurs in six substages during the sensorimotor period.

Substage 1: Reflex activity (birth to 1 month). Because reflexes are what the infant can "do," they become the foundation to future learning. Reflexes are what infants build on.

Substage 2: Primary circular reactions (1 to 4 months). During this stage, infants repeat (thus the term *circular*) behaviors that bring them a positive response and pleasure. The infant's body is the focus of the response, thus the term *primary*. If, for example, infants by chance hold their head erect or lift their chest, they will continue to repeat these acts because they are pleasurable. Infants also have limited anticipation abilities.

Substage 3: Secondary circular reactions (4 to 8 months). As in the second substage, the focus is on performing acts and behaviors that bring about a response. In this stage, however, the infant reacts to responses from the environment. If, for example, 5-month-old infants cause the rattle to sound inadvertently as their arms move, they will continue attempts to repeat this occurrence.

Substage 4: Coordination of secondary circular reactions (8 to 12 months). The mastery of **object permanence** is a significant task during this stage. Piaget contended that around 9 months of age, infants develop the ability to understand that an object or a person exists even when they don't see it. Piaget demonstrated this ability by hiding a favored toy under a blanket. Infants are able to move the blanket and retrieve the toy. Object permanence is related to the rapid development of memory abilities

during this period and is necessary for mental representation to develop (Bruce & Vargas, 2013). Two other phenomena are related to this advance in memory. **Stranger anxiety**—also called stranger wariness or stranger fear—in which the infant reacts with fear and withdrawal to unfamiliar persons, has been found to occur at about 6 to 9 months across cultures. Many first-time parents comment, "I don't know what has gotten into her; she has always been so outgoing." Babies vary in how intensely they react to the strange situation and in how they express their anxiety (Rieser-Danner, 2003). Twin studies suggest that different patterns of stranger anxiety are influenced by genetics (Brooker et al., 2013). Culture also influences stranger anxiety, as do other factors such as experiences with strangers, and the mother's stress reactivity and anxiety, with infants whose mothers report greater stress reactivity showing higher rates of stranger anxiety (Brooker et al., 2013). Infants react more positively to strangers when the stranger approaches slowly and is sensitive to the infant's signals, and in the presence of caregivers. **Separation anxiety** also becomes prominent in this period. The infant is able to remember previous separations and becomes anxious at the signs of an impending separation from parents. With time, the infant also learns that the parent always returns.

Substage 5: Tertiary circular reactions (12 to 18 months). During this stage, toddlers begin to experiment with new behaviors to see the results. They become little scientists who engage in trial-and-error exploration. For example, if the first button on the talking telephone does not make it talk, they will continue to press other buttons on the phone until they find the correct one.

Substage 6: Mental representation (18 months to 2 years). Piaget described toddlers in this stage as actually able to use thinking skills in that they retain mental images of what is not immediately in front of them. For example, the toddler will look in a toybox for a desired toy and move other toys aside that prohibit recovery of the desired toy. Toddlers can also remember and imitate observed behavior, a skill called *deferred imitation*. For example, toddlers roll their toy lawn mower over the lawn, imitating their parents' lawn mowing.

As much as Piaget's work has been praised, it has also been questioned and criticized. Piaget constructed his theory based on his observations of his own three children. Thus, one question has been how objective he was and whether the concepts can really be generalized to all children. Also, Piaget has been criticized for not addressing the influence of environmental factors—such as culture, family, and significant relationships and friendships—on cognitive development. However, for the past 30 years, researchers around the world have put Piaget's theory to the test. This research literature is immense but has been summarized by several reviewers (see, for example, Bronfenbrenner, 1993; Rogoff & Chavajay, 1995; Segall, Dasen, Berry, & Poortinga, 1999). Piaget's sensorimotor stage has been studied less than his other cognitive stages, but the existing research tends to support Piaget's theory, even though some minor cultural differences are noted (Gardiner, 2018). For example, some research has found that African infants receive more social stimulation and emotional support than European and American infants, and European and American infants get more experience with handling objects. This leads to African infants and toddlers developing more social intelligence and European and American children developing more technological intelligence (cited in Gardiner, 2018). This supports the idea of the importance of the developmental niche but, overall, suggests much more similarity than difference in cognitive development across developmental niches during infancy and toddlerhood.

Research findings have called into question some aspects of Piaget's theory. For example, Piaget described young children as being incapable of object permanence until at least 9 months of age. However, infants as young as 3½ and 4½ months of age have been observed who are already proficient at object permanence (Ruffman, Slade, & Redman, 2005). Other researchers (Munakata, McClelland, Johnson, & Siegler, 1997) have found that although infants seem aware of hidden objects at 3½ months, they fail to retrieve those objects until about 8 months of age. These researchers suggest that cognitive skills such as object permanence may be multifaceted and gradually developed (Baillargeon, 2004). Cognitive researchers have been interested in the development of object permanence in children with very low birth weight and in children with a range of intellectual and physical disabilities. One research team found that toddlers born full-term were more than 6 times more likely to have developed object permanence than children born prematurely with very low birth weight (Lowe, Erickson, MacLean, & Duvall, 2009). Susan Bruce and Zayyad Muhammad (2009) reviewed the research on the development of object permanence in children with intellectual disability, physical disability, autism, and blindness. They concluded that this research indicates that children with these disabilities develop object permanence in a similar sequence as children without disabilities, but at a slower rate. They also found evidence that children with severe disability benefit from systematic instruction in object permanence. Bruce and Vargas (2013) provide a case example of a successful team effort to teach object permanence to a 4-year-old girl with severe multiple developmental delays and visual impairment. It is interesting to note that much of the recent research on object permanence studies nonhuman animals. For example, one research team who studied Piagetian object permanence in carrion crows found support for Piagetian stages of cognitive development in this avian species (Hoffman, Rüttler, & Nieder, 2011).

Information Processing Theory

Piaget's cognitive-developmental theory has been very influential, but it leaves many aspects of cognitive functioning unexplained. Piaget sought to explain the *stages* by which cognition develops, but **information processing theory** is interested in the *mechanisms* through which learning occurs, focusing specifically on memory encoding and retrieval (Oppenheimer & Kelso, 2015). It sees the mind as having distinct parts. Information processing theory can be thought of as a *sensory theory* because it depicts information as flowing passively from the external world through the senses to the mind. By contrast, Piaget's cognitive-developmental theory can be considered a *motor theory* because it sees the mind as playing an active role in processing information—not merely recording it but actively constructing the nature of the input it receives (Walsh, 2019). Both theories have merit and contribute to our understanding of human cognition.

Information processing theory sees the mind as composed of three mental states: sensory memory, working memory, and long-term memory. *Sensory memory* takes in sensory information and holds it in its original form. Because a great deal of information is taken in, much of it is discarded. *Working memory*, also called short-term memory, holds and processes information that is "worked on" in some way: considered, comprehended, encoded, or recalled. All conscious mental activity occurs in working memory. Research indicates that infants as young as 5 or 6 months can remember and manipulate information to ascertain the locations of hidden objects (Reznick, Morrow, Goldman, & Snyder, 2004). The typical infant makes great strides in the development of working memory from 6 to 8 months of age (Kwon, Luck, & Oakes, 2014). As information is manipulated in working memory, it becomes more likely to enter long-term memory. *Long-term memory* has unlimited storage and can hold information indefinitely. Information is not processed in long-term memory; it is simply stored until it is retrieved and returned to working memory (Oppenheimer & Kelso, 2015). Exhibit 3.5 provides a visual representation of the information processing system.

Categorization, a cognitive skill that begins to develop in the first year of life, is an important cognitive skill developed during infancy and toddlerhood in both Piaget's cognitive-developmental theory and information processing theory. Categorization, or recognizing similarities in groups of objects, is a fundamental element of information processing. There is evidence that by 6 months, infants begin to see patterns in and make distinctions about human faces (Ramsey, Langlois, Hoss, Rubenstein, & Griffin, 2004). There is also evidence that by 3 months of age, infants can make a distinction between people and inanimate objects. They have been observed to smile and vocalize more and become more active when they are interacting with people than when interacting with inanimate objects (Rakison & Poulin-Dubois, 2001). Research has also found that 4½-month-old babies indicate recognition when two objects are different from each other (Needham, 2001). As toddlers develop language skills, they use language as well as visual cues to categorize objects (Nazzi & Gopnik, 2001).

Language Development

Some of the developmental milestones for language development are listed in Exhibit 3.6. It is hypothesized that the left hemisphere of the human brain is the part poised to receive and produce language. There is some research evidence for this hypothesis and some evidence that, compared with other toddlers, the large majority of toddlers diagnosed with autism exhibit right-hemisphere dominance in responses to language (Pierce, 2011). Although babies seem to be born ready to begin processing language and infants communicate with their caretakers from the beginning (primarily by crying), language development truly begins around 2 months of age. The first sounds, cooing, are pleasing to most parents. By about age 4 to 6 months, infants babble. Initially, these babbles are unrecognizable. Eventually, at about 8 to 12 months, infants make gestures to indicate their desires. The babble sounds and gestures together, along with caretakers' growing familiarity with the infant's "vocabulary," make it easier for infants to communicate their

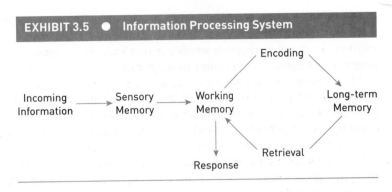

EXHIBIT 3.5 ● Information Processing System

desires. For example, 12-month-old infants may point to their bottle located on the kitchen cabinet and babble "baba." The caretaker soon learns that "baba" means "bottle."

The period from 16 to 24 months typically corresponds to a spurt in vocabulary development, with new words being learned rapidly. Piaget asserts that children develop language in direct correlation to their cognitive skills. Thus, most of the words spoken at this age relate to people and significant objects in the toddler's environment. These include words such as *mama, dada, cat,* and *sissy* (sister), for example. Across cultures, there is an overall bias in infancy to use nouns (Gardiner,

EXHIBIT 3.6 ● Selected Milestones in Language Development

Milestone	Age of Onset
Cries	From birth
Coos responsively	2–3 months
Laughs out loud	3–4 months
Babbles	4–6 months
Gestures to indicate desires	8–12 months
Understands simple commands	12 months
First word	1 year
Vocabulary spurt	16–24 months
Follows directions	2 years
Puts two words together to form sentence	About 21 months
Uses sentences of more than two words	2–3 years

2018). Toddlers' first words also include situational words such as *hot*, *no*, and *bye*. At about 21 months, toddlers begin to combine two words together to form simple sentences such as "Mommy milk." For example, children can say "all gone" as they develop an understanding of object permanence (Berk, 2012). Even with these skills, toddlers may be difficult to understand on occasion. From age 2 to 3, toddlers begin to put together sentences of more than two words.

Cindy, the mom of 24-month-old Steven, describes collecting her son from day care. During the trip home, Steven initiated conversation with Cindy by calling out "Mama." He began to "tell" her about something that Cindy assumes must have occurred during the day. Steven continued to babble to his mother with animation and laughs and giggles during the story. Although Cindy laughed at the appropriate moments, she was unable to understand most of what Steven was sharing with her.

The most important thing adults can do to assist with language development is to provide opportunity for interactions. Adults can answer questions, provide information, explain plans and actions, and offer feedback about behavior. Adults can also read to infants and toddlers and play language games. The opportunity for interaction is important for deaf children as well as hearing children, but deaf children need interaction that involves hand and eye, as with sign language (Shonkoff & Phillips, 2000). Researchers have found that when talking with infants and toddlers, adults and even older children will engage in behaviors that facilitate language development; they tend to speak in a high pitch, use shorter sentences, and speak slowly (Singh, Morgan, & Best, 2002). However, there appear to be cultural differences in how adults communicate with infants and toddlers, and it is not clear how these differences affect language acquisition (Sabbagh & Baldwin, 2001).

Although newborns show a preference for the language of the parents, research indicates that early infants are capable of recognizing and making sounds from a wide range of languages. However, as they have repeated interactions with caregivers and family members, they strengthen the neural connections for the sounds of the language(s) spoken in the home environment, and the neural connections for sounds from other languages are lost (Hoff, 2009). Miraculously, infants and toddlers who are bilingual from birth learn two languages as fast as monolingual infants learn one (Kovács & Mehler, 2009). Of course, ability in any language is not retained unless the environment provides an opportunity for using the language.

SOCIOEMOTIONAL DEVELOPMENT

Infants and toddlers face vital developmental tasks in the emotional arena (some of which are listed in Exhibit 3.7), as well as in the social arena. Development during these early ages may set the stage for socioemotional development during all other developmental ages. This section addresses these tasks.

Erikson's Theory of Psychosocial Development

Erik Erikson's (1950) theory explains socioemotional development in terms of eight consecutive, age-defined stages. Each stage requires the mastery of a developmental task. Mastery at each stage depends on mastery in the previous stages. If the "task facilitating factors" for a stage are absent, the individual will become stuck in that stage of development.

EXHIBIT 3.7 ● Selected Milestones in Emotional Development	
Milestone	**Age**
Emotional life centered on physical states. Exhibits distress, fear, and rage.	Newborn
Emotional life begins to be centered on relationships. Exhibits pleasure and delight and social smile.	3 months
Emotional life continues to be relational, but distinctions are made between those relationships, as in stranger anxiety and separation anxiety. Exhibits joy, fear, anxiety, and anger.	9 months
Emotional life becomes sensitive to emotional cues from other people. Exhibits a range of emotion from joy to rage.	End of first year
Emotional life becomes centered on regulation of emotional states.	Second and third year

Sources: Based on Davies, 2011, and Shonkoff & Phillips, 2000.

Each of Erikson's stages is overviewed in Exhibit 3.8 and discussed in the chapter regarding the part of the life course to which it applies. The following two stages are relevant to infants and toddlers.

1. *Trust versus mistrust* (ages birth–1½). The overall task of this stage is for infants to develop a sense that their needs will be met by the outside world and that the outside world is an okay place to be. In addition, the infant develops an emotional bond with an adult, which Erikson believes becomes the foundation for being able to form intimate, loving relationships in the future. Erikson argues the need for one consistent mother figure. The most important factor facilitating growth in this stage is consistency in having physical and emotional needs met: being fed when hungry, being kept warm and dry, and being allowed undisturbed sleep. In addition, the infant has to be protected from injury, disease, and so on and receive adequate stimulation. Infants who develop mistrust at this stage become suspicious of the world and withdraw, react with rage, and have deep-seated feelings of dependency. These infants lack drive, hope, and motivation for continued growth. They cannot trust their environment and are unable to form intimate relationships with others. Given Ms. Velasquez's view that the outside world is not a safe place, described at the beginning of the chapter, her young son, Henry, is at risk of developing feelings of mistrust.

2. *Autonomy versus shame and doubt* (ages 1½–3). A child with autonomy has a growing sense of self-awareness and begins to strive for independence and self-control. These children feel proud that they can perform tasks and exercise control over bodily functions. They relate well with close people in the environment and begin to exercise self-control in response to parental limits. To develop autonomy, children need firm limits for controlling impulses and managing anxieties but at the same time still need the freedom to explore their environment. Exhibit 3.9 summarizes possible sources of anxiety for toddlers (Davies, 2011). Toddlers also need an environment rich with stimulating and interesting objects and with opportunities for freedom of choice. Adults must accept the child's bodily functions as normal and good and offer praise and encouragement to enhance the child's mastery of self-control. At the other end of the spectrum are children

EXHIBIT 3.8 ● Erikson's Stages of Psychosocial Development

Life Stage	Psychosocial Challenge	Characteristic
Infancy (birth to about 1 year)	Basic trust versus basic mistrust	Infants must form trusting relationships with caregivers or they will learn to distrust the world.
Toddlerhood (about 1–3 years)	Autonomy versus shame and doubt	Toddlers must develop self-confidence and a sense of mastery over themselves and their worlds and they must use newly developed motor skills, or they will develop shame and doubt about their inability to develop control.
Early childhood (3–5 years)	Initiative versus guilt	Young children must develop a growing capacity to plan and initiate actions or they may feel guilt about their taking initiative.
Middle childhood (6–11 years)	Industry versus inferiority	School-aged children must develop a sense of competence to master and complete tasks or they learn to feel inferior or incompetent.
Adolescence (11–20 years)	Identity versus role diffusion	Adolescents must develop a sense of who they are and where they are going in life or they become confused about their identity.
Young adulthood (21–40 years)	Intimacy versus isolation	Young adults must develop the capacity to commit to deep associations with others or they feel a sense of isolation.
Middle adulthood (40–65 years)	Generativity versus stagnation	Midlife adults must develop the capacity to transcend self-interest to guide the next generation or they feel stagnated.
Late adulthood (over 65 years)	Ego integrity versus despair	Older adults must find integrity and contentment in their final years by accepting their life as it has been or they feel a sense of despair.

Source: Based on Erikson, 1950, 1978.

EXHIBIT 3.9 ● **Possible Sources of Anxiety for Toddlers**

Difficulty understanding what is happening

Difficulty communicating

Frustration over not being able to do what others can do or what they imagine others can do

Conflicts between wanting to be independent and wanting their parents' help

Separation or threat of separation from caregivers

Fears of losing parental approval and love

Reactions to losing self-control

Anxieties about the body

Source: Adapted from Davies, 2011.

who doubt themselves. They fear a loss of love and are overly concerned about their parents' approval. These children are ashamed of their abilities and develop an unhealthy kind of self-consciousness.

Erikson does not address whether tasks that should be mastered in one stage can be mastered later if the facilitating factors—such as a dependable, nurturing caregiver—are introduced. For example, we know that Sarah suffered neglect until Chris Johnson and his parents provided a dependable, nurturing environment for her. At what point is it too late to undo psychosocial damage? Critics also question Erikson's emphasis on the process of individualization, through which children develop a strong identity separate from that of their family. Many believe this to be a North American, Western value and therefore not applicable to collectivistic societies such as many African, Latin, and Asian societies or to collectivistic subcultures in the United States.

Emotion Regulation

Researchers have paid a lot of attention to the strategies infants develop to cope with intense emotions, both positive and negative. They have noted that infants use a range of techniques to cope with intense emotions, including turning the head away, sucking on hands or lips, and closing their eyes. By the middle of the second year, toddlers have built a repertoire of ways to manage strong emotions. They make active efforts to avoid or disregard situations that arouse strong emotions; they move away or they distract themselves with objects. They soothe themselves by thumb sucking, rocking, or stroking; they also engage in reassuring self-talk. In

addition, they develop substitute goals if they become thwarted in goal-directed behavior (Shonkoff & Phillips, 2000). However, researchers who do experimental infant research note that a number of infants must be discontinued from the research process because they cannot be calmed enough to participate (Newman & Newman, 2015). The ability to control the intensity of emotional states has important implications for early childhood school performance and social relationships (Davidson & Begley, 2012).

You may not be surprised to learn that researchers have found that one of the most important elements in how an infant learns to manage strong emotions is the assistance provided by the caregiver for emotion management (see, for example, Lowe et al., 2012). Caregivers may offer food or a pacifier, or they may swaddle, cuddle, hug, or rock the infant. By the time the infant is 6 months old, caregivers often provide distraction and use vocalization to soothe. One research team found that for all levels of infant distress, the most effective methods of soothing were holding, rocking, and vocalizing. Feeding and offering a pacifier were effective when the infant was moderately distressed but not at times of extreme distress (Jahromi, Putnam, & Stifter, 2004). Infants who demonstrate greater emotion regulation are much more likely to have parents who use higher levels of positive parenting behaviors, such as sensitivity, positive regard, stimulation, and animation (Ursache, Blair, Stifter, & Voegtline, 2013). Another important element that impacts an infant's ability to manage emotions is whether the infant receives adequate sleep (Kurcinka, 2006). The child's temperament also makes a difference, as you will see in the next section.

Finally, there are cultural differences in expectations for management of emotions in infants. For example, Japanese parents try to shield their infants from the frustrations that would invite anger. In other words, some emotions are regulated by protecting the child from situations that would arouse them (Kitayama, Karasaw, & Mesquita, 2004). Cultural differences also exist in how much independence infants and toddlers are expected to exercise in managing emotions. In one study comparing Anglo and Puerto Rican mothers, Harwood (1992) found that Anglo mothers expected their infants to manage their stranger anxiety and separation anxiety without clinging to the mother. The Puerto Rican mothers, conversely, expected their infants to rely on the mother for solace. Cultures also differ about the ways specific emotions should be managed, and babies are socialized to respond and display specific emotions in socially acceptable ways (Gardiner, 2018). Across cultures, however, infants who receive more responsive and immediate caregiving when they are distressed have lower rates of persistent crying, spend more time in happy and calm states, and cry less by age 1 (see Axia & Weisner, 2002).

Temperament

Another way to look at emotional development is by evaluating **temperament**—the characteristic way in which individuals approach and react to people and situations. The best-known study of temperament in infants and young children was the New York Longitudinal Study (NYLS), begun in 1956 (Thomas, Chess, & Birch, 1968, 1970). This study examined nine components of temperament: *activity level*, *rhythmicity* (regularity of biological functions), *approach-withdrawal* (initial reaction to any new stimulus), *adaptability* to new situations and experiences, *intensity of reactions*, *threshold of responsiveness* (level of stimulation needed to evoke a discernible response), *quality of mood* (happiness versus irritability), *distractibility*, and *attention span* or persistence. From their observations, the researchers identified three types of temperament: easy, slow to warm up, and difficult. The *easy* baby is characterized by good mood, being open and adaptable to new experiences, regular patterns of eating and sleeping, and general calmness. About 40% of study participants fell in this category. The *slow to warm up* baby tends to be low in activity level, moody, and slow to adapt to new situations and people. The researchers found that 15% of their study participants fell in this category. The *difficult* baby is active, irritable, irregular in biological rhythms, slow to change in routine or new situations, and not easily able to adjust to new routines. About 10% of infants fell in this category. About 35% of the NYLS sample did not fit neatly into any of these three categories, displaying instead a mix of characteristics. There is a tendency for recent researchers to focus on two clusters of temperamental traits, negative emotions (irritability, fear, sadness, shyness, frustration, and discomfort) and regulatory capacity (ability to self-regulate behavior and engage in self-soothing), as important to parent–infant relationships as well as to future personality and behavior development (see Bridgett et al., 2009).

For an idea of the differences in infant temperament, consider the range of reactions you might see at a baptism service. One infant might scream when passed from one person to the other and when water is placed on his or her forehead. The mother might have difficulty calming the infant for the remainder of the baptism service. At

PHOTO 3.3 Toddlers begin to build a repertoire of ways to manage strong emotions. The ability to control the intensity of emotional states has important implications for early childhood school performance and social relationships.

© Oleg Kozlov/iStockphoto.com

the other extreme, one infant might make cooing noises throughout the entire service and seem unbothered by the rituals. The slow-to-warm-up infant might cautiously check out the clergy administering the baptism and begin to relax by the time the ritual is completed.

Thomas and his colleagues believed that a child's temperament appears shortly after birth and is set, or remains unchanged, throughout life. Whether temperament is permanent or not is still unresolved. Recent research suggests that temperament is less stable in infancy than at any other time of life. Young infants' temperaments may be shaped by sensitive caregiving. By the second year of life, styles of responding to people and situations are more established, and in early childhood temperament is even more stable and predictive (Goodwin, Thompson, & Winer, 2015). Neurobiologists are suggesting that infants come into the world with preexisting temperaments or emotional styles (Davidson & Begley, 2012). They report strong evidence for a genetic basis of emotional styles, with the genetic contribution varying from 20% to 60% for different emotional style traits. But even traits with a strong genetic base can be modified by how parents, teachers, and other caregivers interact with the child. After several decades of study of the neuroscience of emotional style, Richard Davidson and colleagues (see Davidson & Begley, 2012) identify six dimensions of emotional style that have a strong neurobiological basis:

- *Resilience:* how quickly one recovers from adversity

- *Outlook:* how long one can sustain positive emotion

- *Social intuition:* how good one is at picking up social signals

- *Self-awareness:* how well one perceives bodily indications of emotions

- *Sensitivity to context:* how good one is at taking the context into account in regulating emotions

- *Attention:* how sharply and clearly one uses focused attention

Although most of these dimensions of emotional style will not become evident in the early months, there are early signs of a number of them.

Families like the Hicks family who have an infant with negative emotion and poor regulatory capacity may be in special need of interventions to prevent a troubling developmental trajectory for the infant and the relationship between the parents. Recent research provides some insight about what could happen between Holly and Mrs. Hicks, as well as between Mr. and Mrs. Hicks, over time. Researchers are finding that negative emotion in the first 3 months is related to decreases in regulatory capacity from 4 to 12 months. And decreases in regulatory capacity in the infant from 4 to 12 months predict poor parent–child relationships when the child is 18 months old (Bridgett et al., 2009). Another research team found a relationship between infant regulatory capacity and marital satisfaction. Following a group of infants and their families from the time the infants were 7 months old until they were 14 months, these researchers found that marital satisfaction increased as infants developed greater regulatory capacity and decreased when infants failed to gain in regulatory capacity (Mehall, Spinrad, Eisenberg, & Gaertner, 2009). The good news is that neuroscience research suggests that how easily a baby can be soothed has little or no genetic contribution (Davidson & Begley, 2012), so the important thing is for Mrs. Hicks to find the types of caregiving most soothing to Holly.

As parents discipline infants and toddlers to help them gain self-control, different methods of discipline are indicated for children of different temperaments. Infants and toddlers who are fearful and inhibited respond best to gentle, low-power discipline techniques, but these techniques do not work well with fearless infants and toddlers who do best when positive feelings between the caregiver and child are emphasized (Kochanska, Aksan, & Joy, 2007).

Researchers have also been interested in whether there are cultural and socioeconomic differences in infant temperament. Several studies have found small to moderate cross-cultural differences in infant temperament

and have attributed these differences mainly to genetics (see Gartstein, Knyazev, & Slobodskaya, 2005; Gartstein et al., 2006). To begin to examine the contributions of the role of genetics and environment to temperament, one research team compared three groups of Russian infants aged 3 to 12 months: infants living in Russia, infants of parents who immigrated to Israel, and infants of parents who immigrated to the United States. They found some differences in temperament across these three situations and concluded that the differences in temperament between the Russian Israeli infants and the Russian American infants probably reflect the different acculturation strategies used to adapt to different host societies (Gartstein, Peleg, Young, & Slobodskaya, 2009). Findings about the relationship between socioeconomic status and temperament are contradictory. Some researchers find no socioeconomic differences (Bridgett et al., 2009) whereas other researchers find that infants in more economically disadvantaged families have more difficult temperaments and conclude that this difference is largely explained by family stress (Jansen et al., 2009). The difference in findings about socioeconomic status and temperament could be caused by different samples, with socioeconomic variations in temperament more likely to show up when the sample includes greater income variability.

Attachment

Another key component of emotional development is **attachment**—the ability to form emotional bonds with other people. Attachment is a lasting emotional bond between two people who try to maintain closeness and ensure a continued relationship. Many child development scholars have suggested that attachment is one of the most important issues in infant development, mainly because attachment is the foundation for emotional development and a predictor of later functioning. Note that this view of attachment is similar to Erikson's first stage of psychosocial development. This perspective is similar to the one Mrs. Hicks found on the Internet, which raised issues of concern for her. The two most popular theories of attachment were developed by John Bowlby (1969) and Mary Ainsworth and colleagues (Ainsworth, Blehar, Waters, & Wall, 1978).

Bowlby's Theory of Attachment

Bowlby, who initially studied attachment in animals, concluded that attachment is natural, a result of the infant's instinct for survival and consequent need to be protected. Attachment between infant and mother ensures that the infant will be adequately nurtured and protected from attack or, in the case of human infants, from a harsh environment. The infant is innately programmed to emit stimuli (smiling, clinging, and so on) to which the mother responds. This exchange between infant and mother creates an emotional bond. The infant initiates the attachment process, but later the mother's behavior is what strengthens the bond.

Bowlby hypothesized that attachment advances through four stages: preattachment, attachment in the making, clear-cut attachment, and goal-corrected attachment (when the caregiver and toddler reach a balance between the toddler's urge for autonomy and the caregiver's need to protect and set limits). This process begins in the first month of life, with the infant's ability to discriminate the mother's voice. Attachment becomes fully developed during the second year of life, when the mother and toddler develop a goal-corrected partnership. During this later phase of attachment, the child is able to manipulate the mother into desired outcomes, but the child also has the capacity to understand the mother's point of view. The mother and the child reach a mutually acceptable compromise.

Bowlby contends that infants can demonstrate attachment behavior to others; however, attachment to the mother occurs earlier than attachment to others and is stronger and more consistent. It is thought that the earliest attachment becomes the child's **working model** for subsequent relationships (Bowlby, 1982).

Attachment explains the child's anxiety when the parents leave. However, children eventually learn to cope with separation. Toddlers often make use of a **transitional object**, or comfort object, to help them cope with separations from parents and to handle other stressful situations. During such times, they may cuddle with a blanket, teddy bear, or other stuffed animal. The transitional object is seen as a symbol of the relationship with the caregiver, but toddlers also see it as having magic powers to soothe and protect them (Davies, 2011).

Ainsworth's Theory of Attachment

One of the most widely used methods to investigate infant attachment, known as the strange situation procedure, was developed by Ainsworth and colleagues (Ainsworth et al., 1978). The Ainsworth group believed that the level of infant attachment to the mother could be assessed through the infant's response to a series of "strange" episodes. Basically, the child is exposed over a period of 25 minutes to eight constructed episodes involving separation and reunion with the mother. The type of child attachment to the mother is measured by how the child responds to the mother following the "distressing" separation.

Ainsworth and her colleagues identified three types of attachment.

1. *Secure attachment.* The infant uses the mother as a home base and feels comfortable leaving this base to explore the playroom. The infant returns to the mother every so often to ensure that she is still present. When the mother leaves the room (act of separation) and leaves the infant with a stranger, the securely attached infant responds with separation anxiety and stranger anxiety. The securely attached infant will cry and seek comfort from the mother when she returns and is easily reassured and soothed by the mother's return.

2. *Insecure anxious attachment.* The infant is reluctant to explore the playroom and clings to the mother. When the mother leaves the room, the infant cries for a long time. When the mother returns, this infant seeks solace from the mother but continues to cry and may swat at or pull away from the mother. Ainsworth and colleagues described these infants as somewhat insecure and doubted that their mothers would ever be able to provide the security and safety they need.

3. *Insecure avoidant attachment.* Some infants seem indifferent to the presence of their mother. This infant shows little distress during the strange situation and is not enthusiastic when reunited with the mother. Whether the mother is present or absent from the room, these infant's responses are the same.

More recent scholars have added a fourth response, known as the *insecure disorganized/disoriented* response (Belsky, Campbell, Cohn, & Moore, 1996; Main & Hesse, 1990). These children display inconsistent, contradictory behavior: They attempt physical closeness but retreat with acts of avoidance. These infants often have mothers who are depressed, have a history of being abused, or continue to struggle with a traumatic experience in their own lives. Observations of mothers of infants with disorganized attachment style reveal two patterns of parenting. Some mothers are negative and intrusive and frighten their babies with intense bursts of hostility. Other mothers are passive or helpless; they rarely comfort their babies and may actually appear afraid of their babies (Lyons-Ruth & Jacobvitz, 2008). As a result, the infants become confused in the strange situation. They fear the unknown figure and seek solace from the mother but retreat because they are also fearful of the mother (Abrams, Rifkin, & Hesse, 2006). Some authors have suggested that the behavior associated with the disorganized style is actually an adaptive response to harsh caregiving (Stovall & Dozier, 1998).

However, research suggests a link between disorganized attachment and serious mental health problems in later childhood and beyond (Lyons-Ruth & Jacobvitz, 2008; Wolke, Eryigit-Madzwamuse, & Gutbrod, 2014).

According to Ainsworth's attachment theory, children whose mothers are consistently present and responsive to their needs and whose mothers exhibit a warm, caring relationship develop an appropriate attachment. Findings from studies indicate that this is true, even when there are negative family issues such as alcoholism by the father (Edwards, Eiden, & Leonard, 2006). However, the implication is that only mother–infant attachment exists or is relevant to healthy infant development. This assumption probably seemed unquestionable when these theories were constructed. Research indicates that fathers in both Western and Eastern cultures interact with newborns in much the same way that mothers interact with them, cradling the infant and performing care tasks such as diaper changing, bathing, and feeding the infant when formula or bottled breastmilk are used (Combs-Orme & Renkert, 2009; Tamis-LeMonda, Kahana-Kalman, & Yoshikawa, 2009). As the infant develops, however, fathers and mothers develop different play and communicative styles with infants and toddlers, a subject discussed later in this chapter and in Chapter 4 under the heading Play as a Route to Attachment With Fathers. Today many fathers have prominent, equal, and/or primary responsibilities in child-rearing and childcare, sometimes by choice and other times by necessity. Sarah Johnson's dad, for example, became the primary caregiver for Sarah out of necessity. The gender of the parent is irrelevant in the development of secure infant attachment. Rather, it is the behavior of the primary caregiver, regardless of whether it is the mother or father, that has the most influence on infant attachment. When fathers who are the primary caregivers are able to provide infants with the warmth and affection they need, infants develop secure attachments to their fathers. In fact, under stress, fathers become a greater source of comfort to their infants than the mothers who are the secondary caregivers (Geiger, 1996). And, indeed, some infants and toddlers live in families with two fathers and demonstrate secure attachment to both fathers. Perhaps the best scenario is when infants develop secure attachments to both parents. In one study, infants with secure attachments to both parents demonstrated fewer behavioral difficulties as toddlers, even fewer problems than toddlers with only secure mother–infant attachment (Volling, Blandon, & Kolak, 2006).

In addition to a more prominent role by fathers over the past 20 to 30 years, more women have entered the workforce, and many more children experience alternative forms of childcare, including infant and toddler day care. The effect day care has on the development of attachment in infants and toddlers continues to be hotly debated. Some argue that day care has a negative effect on infant attachment and increases the risk of the infant developing insecure and avoidant forms of attachment (see, e.g., Belsky, 1987; Belsky & Braungart, 1991). The risks are thought to be especially high if the infant attends day care during the first year of life. Others argue that day care does not have a negative effect on infant and early childhood attachment (Shonkoff & Phillips, 2000). Friedman and Boyle (2008) reviewed 23 studies based on the National Institute of Child Health and Human Development (NICHD) data that tracked 1,000 children from birth through age 15. These studies found that the number of hours infants spend in nonmaternal care is not associated with the infants' security of attachment to the mother at age 15; they also found that working mothers interact with their infants almost as much as mothers who are not employed. The most robust finding was that mothers' sensitivity to their infants during interaction is a consistent predictor of secure attachment and positive child development. No main effects were found between the quality and type of childcare and mother–infant attachment. However, hours in alternative childcare was a risk factor for mother–infant attachment if combined with other risk factors such as maternal insensitivity and poor quality of childcare.

A study in the Netherlands found that professional caregivers may be alternative attachment figures for children when their parents are not available, but it is the professional caregivers' group-related sensitivity, rather than the child's individual relationship with one professional caregiver, that promotes a sense of security and safety in children. Girls were found to be more securely attached to their professional caregivers than boys, however (De Schipper, Tavecchio, & Van IJzendoorn, 2008). In one study in the United States, day care was found to mitigate the adverse effects of insecure mother–infant attachment (Spieker, Nelson, & Petras, 2003).

Recently, researchers have begun to study attachment among children in foster care. Most of these children come into foster care without secure attachments. Once in foster care, many children are subjected to frequent changes in their foster homes. Problems with attachment may contribute to foster home disruptions, but foster home disruptions also contribute to attachment problems. Two policy responses have been recommended to minimize the disruption of attachment in foster children: (1) matching the foster care strengths and capabilities with the needs of the child and (2) quick-as-possible family reunification. Existing research suggests that neither of these policy responses has sufficiently minimized attachment disruptions. Research by Tucker & MacKenzie (2012) suggests that the age of child, the nature of the circumstances leading to foster care placement, and the nature of the foster care situations and transitions must be understood to develop interventions to minimize attachment disruptions in specific children. Other researchers conclude that institutional care can also have the same devastating effects on attachment as repeated foster care disruptions (Johnson, Browne, & Hamilton-Giachritsis, 2006).

Let's look at one other issue concerning attachment. Most studies of attachment have used the Ainsworth group's strange situation method. However, this measure may not yield valid results with some groups or under certain conditions. For example, the insecure avoidant pattern of attachment some investigators have noted among children in day care may not indicate lack of attachment, as some have concluded. These children may be securely attached but seem indifferent to the exit and return of the mother simply because they have become accustomed to routine separations and reunions with their mother.

The appropriateness of using the strange situation method with certain ethnic groups has also been questioned. An early study found Japanese infants to demonstrate more insecure anxious attachment style than infants in other parts of the world and attributed this finding to the fact that Japanese mothers left their infants in the care of others much less often than mothers in a number of other cultures (Takahashi, 1990). A more recent study found that the distribution of attachment styles of Japanese infants was consistent with worldwide norms when the researchers controlled for the unfamiliarity of separation from the mother (Behrens, Hesse, & Main, 2007).

Conversely, in many cultures infants are cared for by a collective of mothers, older siblings, cousins, fathers, aunts, uncles, and grandparents. The level of sense of security in these infants depends on coordinated care of a number of caregivers. The strange situation does not capture the fluid nature of caregiving and the degree to which it supports infants' feelings of security and safety (Lewis, 2005). One study found that in Israeli kibbutz-reared children, one negative caregiving relationship could negatively affect other attachment relationships (Sagi, Koren-Karie, Gini, Ziv, & Joels, 2002). Some researchers are using methods other than the Ainsworth strange situation to measure attachment. For example, in a longitudinal study, a Chilean research group used an Attachment During Stress Scale (ADS) to measure attachment and found that day care, compared with maternal care, was not negatively associated with mother–child attachment, maternal sensitivity, or quality of the home environment (Cácamo, Vermeer, van der Veer, & van Ijzendoorn, 2016).

In spite of these concerns, findings from a large number of studies using the strange situation in Europe, Africa, Asia, and the Middle East as well as North America indicate that the attachment patterns identified by Ainsworth occur in many cultures (Gardiner, 2018). It is important to remember that attachment theory was developed by European American theorists who conceptualized attachment as the basis for developing subsequent independence. However, in more collectivist cultures, attachment is seen as the basis for developing obedience and harmony (Weisner, 2005).

Attachment and Brain Development

The attachment relationship is a major organizer of brain development and the facilitator of anxiety and stress management as well as emotion regulation (Cozolino, 2014; Newman, Sivaratnam, & Komiti, 2015). Attachment directly affects brain development. Gerhardt (2004) concludes that without emotional bonding with an adult, the orbitofrontal cortex in the brain of infants (the part of the brain that allows social relationships to develop) cannot develop well. During the first year of life, the infant must develop the capacity to tolerate higher and higher levels of emotional arousal. The caregiver helps the infant with this by managing the amount of stimulation the infant receives. As the right orbitofrontal cortex develops, the infant is able to tolerate higher levels of arousal and stimulation. However, when the caregiver is not attuned to the needs of the infant in regard to managing stimulation during the first year of life, negative emotions result, and growth of the right orbitofrontal cortex is inhibited (Farmer, 2009). This process has been called the *social brain*.

In addition, attachment with a sensitive caregiver appears to maximize the integration of neural circuitry in the right and left hemisphere systems, which promotes the development of emotion regulation, empathy, and motivation, as well as cognitive skills such as attention and decision making (Newman et al., 2015). It also helps to develop a "smart" vagus, the tenth and longest of the cranial nerves in the autonomic nervous system. Polyvagal theory identifies two distinct branches of the vagus: the *dorsal vagus*, the more evolutionary primitive branch, responds by freezing and conserving resources in all bodily systems when threatened. The *ventral vagus*, the more evolutionary advanced branch, works to regulate defensive reactions to stress by stimulating self-soothing and communication with others. Such vagal activity augments the ongoing interactions between the prefrontal cortex and the amygdala. It is thought that an attachment bond with a sensitive caregiver is crucial for development of the ventral vagus. Secure attachment relationships also stimulate growth of glucocorticoid receptors in the amygdala, hippocampus, and components of the hypothalamus-pituitary-adrenal (HPA) axis, and high stress during infancy and toddlerhood have been found to cause this system to be poorly regulated (Cozolino, 2014; Newman et al., 2015).

The emotion centers of the brain are softwired and heavily influenced by early relationships (Meyer, Wood, & Stanley, 2013). Some research has found that mild-to-moderate disruptions in early attachment relationships can interfere with right-hemisphere processing and lead to cell death (Newman et al., 2015). Among other things, the right hemisphere is associated with attachment, interpersonal relationships, nonverbal communication, and emotional awareness and memory (Meyer et al., 2013). An often-cited study is a brain imaging study that investigated brain activation in infants reared in orphanages in Romania. The infants had little contact with an adult, were left in their cots for most of the day, were fed with propped-up bottles, and were never smiled at or hugged. The study found that these infants had abnormally low metabolism in a network of areas involved in stress regulation, including the orbito-frontal cortex. Further studies have found decreased activation in other regions of the brain involved with emotion regulation and stress responses (Newman et al., 2015).

One concern is whether these deficiencies in brain development are permanent. Some suggest that the brain impairments can be reversed if changes in care and attachment occur early enough (Cozolino, 2014; Meyer et al., 2013; Newman et al., 2015). They highlight the strides in brain development made by the Romanian orphans who were adopted into caring homes before they were 6 months of age. Perhaps Sarah Johnson's improvement was the result of early intervention and moving her quickly to live with her dad. Others suggest that the brain impairments caused by lack of attachment with a primary caregiver are permanent (Perry, 2002). Regardless, the implication is that future brain growth is seriously jeopardized if brain development is not adequately nurtured in the first 2 to 3 years. We have clear evidence that the human brain is plastic and changes over time with new experiences, but we also know that it is not completely plastic; brain

vulnerabilities in early childhood predispose one to difficulties in managing social relationships, and social relationship problems affect ongoing brain development (Farmer, 2009). The existing literature suggests that early intervention should focus on helping the caregiver to be reflective about the inner world of the infant (Slade, 2005). The clinician can assist with this process by modeling such reflection—sharing with the caregiver the clinician-perceived mental states of the infant or toddler. Newman et al. (2015) note that many caregivers who have difficulty reflecting on the inner world of their infants had inadequate caregiving as infants and toddlers themselves. They may not be able to engage in such reflection without resolving issues related to their own inadequate caregiving through some form of psychotherapy. Cozolino (2014) suggests that although early experiences are powerful brain shapers, it is never too late to modify brain structure and functions through personal relationships, psychotherapy, and increased self-awareness. Neuroscience research is finding that many emotions and cognitions happen at the unconscious, automatic level and are not easily accessed for conscious exploration. This is especially true of traumatic memories. Given our commitment to evidence-based practice, social workers should be aware of empirical evidence of the benefits of adjunct nontalking, somatic interventions for traumatic memories and post-traumatic stress disorder (PTSD), including eye movement desensitization and reprocessing (EMDR) (van der Kolk, 2014), neurofeedback (van der Kolk et al., 2016), and yoga (Mitchell et al., 2014; van der Kolk et al., 2014). In exploratory study, music therapy has also been found to produce improvement in PTSD symptoms (Lightstone, Bailey, & Voros, 2015). Although the study of these methods has centered on adults with PTSD symptoms, they have also been found to be helpful to any adult with disrupted attachments. Polyvagal theory is being used to develop both biological and interpersonal interventions to stimulate and improve functioning in the vagus nerve, interventions that are considered promising for symptom improvement in treatment-resistant major depression. Such interventions include electrical stimulation of the vagus nerve (Tisi, Franzini, Messina, Savino, & Gambini, 2014), yoga (Tyagi & Cohen, 2016), and group therapy (Flores & Porges, 2017). Mindfulness meditation has been found to build better connections between the amygdala and prefrontal cortex (see Davidson & Begley, 2012) and to improve stress reactivity and anxiety symptoms associated with generalized anxiety disorder (Hoge et al., 2013).

- *6–12 months:* colorful picture books, stacking toys, nesting toys, sponges for water play, mirrors, toy telephones, toys that react to the child's activity
- *12–18 months:* push toys; pull toys; balls; plain and interlocking blocks; simple puzzles with

CRITICAL THINKING QUESTIONS 3.2

What have you seen the adults in your family, or other families you know, do to support language development in infants and toddlers? Do you know any bilingual infants and toddlers? If so, what have you observed about their language development? In your multigenerational family, what have you observed about the expectations parents have for how infants and toddlers should manage emotions?

THE ROLE OF PLAY

Play is crucial to child development. Play allows infants and toddlers to enhance motor, cognitive, language, emotional, social, and moral development. Because of their differences in development in all areas, infants and toddlers play in different ways. Exhibit 3.10 describes four types of infant play and three types of play observed in very young children. These later types of play begin in toddlerhood and develop in union with cognitive and motor development. For example, young toddlers will play with a mound of clay by hitting and perhaps squishing it. More developed toddlers will mold the clay into a ball, and older toddlers will try to roll or throw the molded ball.

One zealous mother describes joining the "toy of the month club" in which she received developmental toys through the mail each month for the first 2 years of her child's life. This mother wanted to be sure that her child had every opportunity to advance in terms of motor and cognitive skills. Although this mother's efforts are to be applauded, she admits that these toys were very costly and that perhaps she could have achieved the same outcome with other less costly objects. For example, there is no evidence that a store-bought infant mobile is any more effective than a homemade paper one hung on a clothes hanger. The objective is to provide stimulation and opportunities for play. Fergus Hughes (2010, p. 68) makes the following suggestions about the appropriate toys for infants and toddlers during the first 2 years of life:

- *Birth to 3 months:* toys for sensory stimulation, such as rattles, bells, colorful pictures and wallpaper, crib ornaments, mobiles, music boxes, and other musical toys
- *3–6 months:* toys for grasping, squeezing, feeling, and mouthing, such as cloth balls, soft blocks, and teething toys

EXHIBIT 3.10 ● Types of Play in Infancy and Toddlerhood

	Types of Infant Play
Vocal play	Playful vocalizing with grunts, squeals, trills, vowels, and so on to experiment with sound and have fun with it
Interactive play	Initiating interactions with caregivers (at about 4–5 months), by smiling and vocalizing, to communicate and make connection
Exploratory play with objects	Exploring objects with eyes, mouth, and hands to learn about their shape, color, texture, movement, and sounds and to experience pleasure
Baby games	Participating in parent-initiated ritualized, repetitive games, such as peek-a-boo, that contain humor, suspense, and excitement and build an emotional bond
	Types of Toddler Play
Functional play	Engaging in simple, repetitive motor movements
Constructive play	Creating and constructing objects
Make-believe play	Acting out everyday functions and tasks and playing with an imaginary friend

Source: **Based on Davies, 2011.**

large, easy-to-handle pieces; stacking toys; riding toys with wheels close to the ground

- *18–24 months:* toys for the sandbox and water play; spoons, shovels, and pails; storybooks; blocks; dolls, stuffed animals, and puppets

Researchers have become interested in the impact of new technologies and the effect they have on type of play, types of toys, and the amount of time spent in play (Bergen & Davis, 2011; Duch, Fisher, Ensari, & Harrington, 2013). It is not uncommon for children as young as several months old to be seen playing with technology-augmented toys or with apps on their parents' cell phones or tablets. The impact of this technology on young children and familial relationships is beginning to be addressed in research but needs much more attention (Lombardi, 2012). One research team found that mothers interact less with their toddlers while engaged in play with electronic toys than when engaged in other types of play (Woolridge & Shapka, 2012). How this technology-based play affects moral development is another area for further exploration (Bergen & Davis, 2011). The American Academy of Pediatrics and the government of Australia recommend that children under the age of 2 should not watch any television or video material (cited in Courage & Howe, 2010). Courage and Howe (2010) reviewed the empirical literature on the effects of screen time on infant and toddler development and found the evidence was not all bad. They found evidence for the following statements:

- Infants do not learn as readily from screen materials as do older children and adults.

- Infants learn more readily from people than from television and videos.

- Infants and toddlers are not passive when viewing television or videos; they engage more with screen material that is interesting to them.

- Excessive screen time can interfere with time spent on physical activities and creative play.

- Television and videos do not *cause* ADHD, but extremely high levels of viewing are associated with ADHD symptoms; parents may seek relief from constant interaction with a child with ADHD symptoms by encouraging screen time.

- Background television distracts the play of infants and toddlers.

- Infants spend more time looking at a video if a parent views it with them and talks with them about it.

- Television can provide a route to early language development in impoverished environments.

A later study systematically reviewed the results of 29 research reports on the correlates of amount of screen time in children under 3 years of age published between January 1999 and January 2013 (Duch et al., 2013). These researchers found that an average of 68% of infants and toddlers in the reviewed studies use screen media, such as television, DVDs, and video games daily. The demographic variables most commonly correlated with high screen time are the child's age (older) and race/ethnicity (minority). Child BMI, maternal distress/depression, media time of the mother, and cognitive stimulation in the home were also correlated with screen time of infants and times. Child BMI increased as screen time increased, screen time was greater if the mother was distressed or depressed, screen time of the child increased as the mother's screen time increased, and screen time increased as cognitive stimulation in the home decreased. Variables not associated with screen time include child sex, first-born status, paternal education, non–English speaking family, two-parent household, number of children in the home, and nonparental childcare. The associations were unclear for maternal age, maternal education, and household income.

Another important aspect of play is parent–child interaction. Parent–infant play may increase the likelihood of secure attachment between the parent and child (Davies, 2011; Hughes, 2010). The act of play at least provides the opportunity for infants and parents to feel good about themselves by enjoying each other and by being enjoyed. Even before infants can speak or understand language spoken to them, play provides a mechanism of communication between parents and infants. Infants receive messages about themselves through play, which promotes their sense of self (Scarlett, Naudeau, Salonius-Pasternak, & Ponte, 2005).

Many similarities exist in the way that mothers and fathers play with infants and toddlers but also some differences. Both mothers and fathers are teachers and sensitive communicators, and both enjoy rough-and-tumble play with their babies (Roggman, Boyce, Cook, Christiansen, & Jones, 2004). But research has also noted some differences in the ways that mothers and fathers play with infants and toddlers. Fathers tend to be more stimulating when they play with infants and toddlers and mothers tend to be more soothing (Feldman, 2003). Fathers engage in more rough-and-tumble play; they are more likely to lift their babies, bounce them, and move their legs and arms. Mothers are more likely to offer toys, play conventional games of peek-a-boo and pat-a-cake, and engage in constructive play. However, mothers have been found to play differently with infant sons than with infant daughters, engaging in more conversation with daughters and making more statements about the baby's feelings when talking with daughters; conversely, they engage in more direction with sons and make more comments to call the baby's attention to his surroundings (Clearfield & Nelson, 2006). Mothers have also been found to be more likely to follow the child's lead, whereas fathers are more likely to steer play activity according to their preferences. Some of these differences have been found in a number of cultures, but it is important to note that these mother/father differences have not been found in Sweden and Israel, both societies with more egalitarian gender roles than found in the United States (Hughes, 2010).

Play also is a vehicle for developing peer relations. A few decades ago, it was thought that babies really weren't interested in each other and could not form relationships with each other. Recent research challenges this view (Hughes, 2010). The peer group becomes more important at earlier ages as family size decreases and siblings are no longer available for daily social interaction. Researchers have found that very young infants, as young as 2 months, get excited by the sight of other infants; by 6 to 9 months, infants appear to try to get the attention of other infants; and by 9 to 12 months infants imitate each other (Hughes, 2010). Although toddlers are capable of establishing relationships, their social play is a struggle, and a toddler play session is quite a fragile experience. Toddlers need help in structuring their play with each other. And yet researchers have found that groups of toddlers in preschool settings develop play routines that they return to again and again over periods of months (Corsaro, 2018). These toddler play routines are primarily nonverbal, with a set of ritualized actions. For example, Corsaro (2018) notes a play routine in one Italian preschool in which a group of toddlers would rearrange the chairs in the room and work together to move them around in patterns. They returned to this routine fairly regularly over the course of a year, modifying it slightly over time. Peer relations are being built by "doing things together."

DEVELOPMENTAL DISRUPTIONS

Developmental delay is the name given to a situation in which an infant or toddler has a significant lag in development in any of the dimensions discussed earlier (Rosenberg, Ellison, Fast, Robinson, & Lazar, 2013). The delay may be temporary or may be a symptom of a lifelong condition. **Developmental disability** is the name given when a child has a lifelong impairment demonstrated in childhood that results in functional limitations in some dimension such as mobility, self-care, communication, or learning (Parish, Saville, Swaine, & Igdalsky, 2016). Part C of the Individuals with Disabilities Act (IDEA) is a nationwide program that provides services to infants and toddlers with developmental delays in cognitive, motor, communication, and social and emotional development, but there is no standard definition of what constitutes a developmental delay (Rosenberg et al., 2013). Premature infants like Holly Hicks, for example, often need time to catch up in terms of physical, cognitive, and emotional development. At what point does Holly's social worker decide that she is not developing fast enough and label her developmentally delayed? At what point would it be appropriate to decide that she has a lifelong developmental disability?

Because early interventions for infants and toddlers produce better outcomes in comparison with interventions for school-aged children (Matson, Fodstad, & Dempsey, 2009; McMahon, 2013), early detection and diagnosis is key. The Centers for Disease Control and Prevention (2018b), along with the American Academy of Pediatrics, recommends screening for all types of developmental delays and disabilities at 9, 18, and 24 or 30 months of age. Parents, grandparents, early childhood providers, and other caregivers can contribute to developmental monitoring. Doctors and nurses participate in developmental monitoring during well child visits. A brief checklist of developmental milestones for infants, toddlers, and young children ages 2 months through 5 years can be found at www.cdc.gov/ncbddd/actearly/milestones/index.html. This site also provides brief guidelines for how caregivers can assist infants, toddlers, and young children to achieve these developmental milestones.

In recent years, researchers have been studying the early impairments of developmental disabilities such as cerebral palsy, Down syndrome, and seizure disorder (Hattier, Matson, Sipes, & Turygin, 2011). A more aggressive research agenda has focused on early identification of autism spectrum disorders (ASD), because early intervention is seen as so critical for this developmental disability. Typical behaviors with these disorders include impairments in social and communication development and restricted and repetitive behaviors. Barbaro and Dissanayake (2012) investigated the early markers of ASD at the ages of 12, 18, and 24 months to understand how infants and toddlers with ASD could be distinguished from infants and toddlers with developmental delays that would disappear with time and early intervention. They found that infants with the most severe symptoms at 24 months had pervasive impairment on all social and communication items at 12 and 18 months. There was more variability in the impairments of 12- and 18-month-old infants who would later demonstrate less severe impairments at 24 months but were still on the autism spectrum. The infants and toddlers with developmental delays at 12 and 18 months had typical development in every area but language at 24 months. At 12 months the markers of later ASD were deficits in pointing, waving, imitation, eye contact, and response to name. At 18 months, the key markers were deficits in pointing, eye contact, and showing items to a communication partner. The same markers were present at 24 months, plus an added marker of deficits in pretend play. The children with developmental delay showed earlier deficits in pretend play but were performing at the typical level by age 24 months.

CRITICAL THINKING QUESTIONS 3.3

Why is play crucial to infant and toddler development? What do you think about infant and toddler use of television and videos? What do you think about toddler use of parents' cell phone and tablet apps? What have you observed about infant and toddler use of these technologies? Why do you think professionals and researchers recommend early intervention with infants and toddlers with developmental delays and disabilities?

CHILDCARE ARRANGEMENTS IN INFANCY AND TODDLERHOOD

Human infants start life in a remarkably dependent state, in need of constant care and protection. On their own, they would die. Toddlers are full of life and are making great strides in development in all areas. They are bubbling with energy and ideas that often seem improbable from an adult perspective. They are willful and pushing for mastery in many areas. Caregiving of toddlers has been compared to "paddling a canoe through the rapids" (Newman & Newman, 2015, p. 194). Societal health depends on finding good solutions to the question of who will care for infants and toddlers and do so in age-appropriate ways.

With large numbers of mothers of infants and toddlers in the paid workforce and not at home, this question becomes a challenging one. The United States seems to be responding to this challenge more reluctantly than other high-income capitalist countries. This difference becomes clear in comparative analysis of two solutions for early childcare: parental leave and paid childcare.

Parental Leave

Because of changes in the economic institution in the United States from 1975 to 1999, the proportion of children under the age of 3 who have mothers in paid employment increased from 24% to 54% and leveled off at about 58% by 2016 (Shonkoff & Phillips, 2000; U.S. Bureau of Labor Statistics, 2017). About one third of the employed mothers in 2016 were employed part-time, working less than 35 hours per week at all jobs. In 2016, the employment rate of mothers increased slightly across infancy and toddlerhood, with a 55% maternal employment rate for infants under 1 year of age, a 58% maternal employment rate for toddlers ages 1 to 2, and a 62% maternal employment rate for toddlers ages 2 to 3. A similar trend is occurring around the world.

In response, most wealthy industrialized countries have instituted social policies that provide for job-protected leave for parents to allow them to take off from work to care for their infants. Sweden was the first country to develop such a policy in 1974. The Swedish policy guaranteed paid leave. Other high-income capitalist nations followed suit over time and now offer paid leave on the birth or adoption of a child as part of their social care infrastructures (Rush & Seward, 2016).

By the early 1990s, the United States was the only high-income industrialized country without a federal family leave policy (Kamerman, 1996). But in 1993, the U.S. Congress passed the Family and Medical Leave Act (FMLA) of 1993 (Pub. L. No. 103-3). FMLA requires businesses with 50 or more employees to provide up to 12 weeks of unpaid job-protected leave during a 12-month period for workers to manage childbirth, adoption, or personal or family illness. Eligible workers are entitled to continued health insurance coverage during the leave period, if such coverage is a part of their compensation package.

Exhibit 3.11 highlights the maternal leave policies in selected wealthy countries in 2009, the last year for which good cross-national data are available. Most of the countries listed, including the United States, require that fathers are entitled to the same leave as mothers. That means, for example, that mother and father could each take a 12-week leave in the United States, or 24 weeks total. In 2011, the United States and Australia were the only affluent countries of the world that did not offer some paid parental leave at the time of birth and adoption, but Australia provided families with a universal, flat-rate maternity grant of $5,000 for each new child to assist with the costs of birth or adoption. In 2011, Australia initiated a paid maternal leave program of 18 weeks at the Australian minimum wage. Many Australian employers offered an additional paid maternal leave. Four years later, on Mother's Day 2015, the Australian government announced that mothers could no longer "double dip" to receive more weeks of paid leave. Mothers with no employer-provided leave will continue to receive the full Australian paid leave, but mothers who receive more employer-paid leave than the government provides will get nothing from the government. If the employer-provided leave is less than the government's benefit, the government will only make up the difference (Grose, 2015). This leaves the United States as the only high-income country without a federal *paid* parental leave plan. By 2016, some U.S. corporations had started their own programs of paid family leave, but these are typically jobs with high pay. In addition, in 2016, 14 states plus the District of Columbia had some version of paid family leave, and only 18 other states were complying with the federal minimum. In addition to paid parental leave, European countries also provide birth or maternity grants and family allowances.

Not only high-income countries provide paid family leave; many low- and middle-income countries also provide paid parental leave. Although most countries offer more leave for mothers than for fathers, at least 31 countries provide some leave for fathers. In most countries with paid parental leave, a social security–type system is used to fund the paid leave. Many countries reimburse nearly 100% of average earnings, but some only pay a portion of the missed earnings (Livingston, 2016).

The idea of *paid* parental leave is a highly contested political issue in the United States, and somewhat less so in Australia. Researchers who have studied why this policy is so controversial in the United States compared to countries in other regions of the world have

EXHIBIT 3.11 ● Family Leave Policies in Selected High-Income Countries in 2009		
Country	Paid	Unpaid
France	20	142
Austria	16	96
Sweden	40	45
United Kingdom	12	53
Australia	0	52
Canada	29	23
Denmark	19	31
Greece	34	13
Netherlands	16	13
Switzerland	11	3
United States	0	12

Source: Center for Economic and Policy Research, 2009.

identified three reasons: (1) a belief in American exceptionalism and hostility to the idea of following the social policy models of other countries; (2) a greater emphasis on individualism, with each family responsible for themselves; and (3) a more business-friendly political environment (Rush & Seward, 2016). U.S. employer hostility to paid parental leave policies was expressed by Randel Johnson, vice president of the U.S. Chamber of Commerce, in 2007, when he declared that the business community would wage "all-out war" against any extension of paid parental leave in the United States (cited in Rush & Seward, 2016, p. 4). During the 2016 U.S. presidential campaign, Hillary Clinton released a campaign video on Mother's Day, proposing a new paid Family and Medical Leave Act (FMLA), with the argument that "strong mothers build strong nations" (cited in Rush & Seward, 2016, p. 2). Clinton lost the election to Donald Trump, and although President Trump's daughter and adviser Ivanka Trump has supported the idea of paid family leave, it is not on the policy agenda of the administration. In addition to the benefits of paid parental leave for low-income families, a number of studies have underlined the public health outcomes of parental leave. For example, a major study by Heymann and McNeill (2013) found that 10 weeks of paid leave for new mothers was associated with a 9% to 10% drop in infant and child mortality rates. Other research has found that paid parental leave for both mothers and fathers improves family health and well-being and contributes to greater father involvement in parenting and more egalitarian parent–child relationships (Seward & Rush, 2016). Given what we are learning about the important role that early attachment plays throughout the life course, this is an area for social work advocacy in the United States.

Paid Childcare

Historically in the United States, mothers were expected to provide full-time care for infants and toddlers at home. If mothers were not available, it was expected that children would be cared for by domestic help or a close relative but still in the home setting. Even in the 1960s, with the development of Head Start programs, the focus was on preschool-age children; infants and toddlers were still expected to be cared for at home. Thus, historically there was very little provision of alternative childcare for most children younger than school age.

This phenomenon has changed dramatically, however, over the last 30 years. As noted earlier, in 2016, 58% of mothers with children under the age of 3 were employed, including 55% of mothers with children under the age of 1 (U.S. Bureau of Labor Statistics, 2017). Therefore, alternative childcare has become a necessity in the United States. In 2011, the last year for which comprehensive data are available, 61% of children in the United States younger than age 5 were involved in some type of regular childcare arrangement. About one third were not involved in any regular childcare arrangement, mostly children with unemployed mothers. Almost one quarter were cared for in organized facilities, 13% in day care centers and 6% in nursery or preschools. Another 11% were in home-based care with other nonrelative childcare providers, 5% of these in family day care. Another quarter of infants, toddlers, and young children were cared for by grandparents, 18% were cared for by the father, 7% were cared for by other relatives, 4% were cared for by the mother while she worked, and 3% were cared for by siblings. The numbers don't total 100% because some children are cared for in multiple arrangements (Laughlin, 2013).

Many advocates for early childcare and education refer to the European model as an ideal for the United States. Countries in Europe provide "universal" childcare for all children, regardless of the parents' income, employment status, race, age, and so forth. These programs are supported through national policy and funded through public funds. If they pay at all, parents pay no more than a quarter of the monies needed. Parents in Europe thus pay far less than parents in the United States typically pay. In 2012, only 1 in 6 eligible low-income families in the United States received federal childcare assistance (Lombardi, 2012). This is another issue in need of social work advocacy.

As suggested earlier, there are controversies about whether child day care centers are harmful to infants and toddlers, but there is growing consensus that nonparental childcare is not inherently harmful. The type of nonparental childcare must be put in ecological context and considered along with other variables such as the quality of the childcare, the amount of time spent in nonparental care, the sensitivity of both parental and nonparental care providers, and characteristics of the child.

INFANTS AND TODDLERS IN THE MULTIGENERATIONAL FAMILY

Maria, a new mom, describes the first visit her mother and father made to her home after the birth of Maria's new infant. "Mom and Dad walked right past me as if I was not there, even though we had not seen each other for 6 months. I quickly realized that my status as their 'princess' was now replaced with a new little princess. During their visit, my husband and I had to fight to see our own child. When she cried, they immediately ran to her. And my mother criticized everything I did—she didn't like the brand of diapers I used, she thought the color of the room was too dreary for an infant—and she even scolded my husband at one point for waking the baby when he went to check on her. I appreciated their visit, but I must admit that I was glad when it was time for them to leave." Maria's description is not unique. The involvement of grandparents and other extended family members in the care of infants and toddlers may be experienced either as a great source of support or as interference and intrusion (and sometimes as a little of each). And, of course, cultures of the world have different norms about who is involved, and in what ways, in the care of infants and toddlers.

Yet the specific roles of grandparents and other extended family members are rarely discussed within the family, which is why conflicts often occur (McGoldrick, Petkov, & Carter, 2016). When these roles are clearly articulated and agreed on, extended family members can provide support that enhances infant and toddler development. Family involvement as a form of social support is further discussed as a protective factor later in this chapter.

The birth of a child, especially of a first child, brings about a major transition not only for parents but also for the entire kin network. Partners become parents; sons and daughters become fathers and mothers; fathers and mothers become grandfathers and grandmothers; and brothers and sisters become aunts and uncles. The social status of the extended family serves as the basis of the social status of the child, and the values and beliefs of the extended family will shape the way they care for and socialize the child. In addition, many children's names and child-rearing rituals, decisions, and behaviors are passed from past generations to the next.

To illustrate this point, there is an old joke about a mother who prepared a roast beef for most Sunday family dinners. She would always cut the roast in half and place it in two pans before cooking it in the oven. Observing this behavior, her young daughter asked her why she cut the roast in half. After some thought she told her daughter that she did not know for sure; she remembered that her mother had always cut her roast in half. Later the mother asked her mother why she had cut her roast in half before cooking it. The senior mother explained that she did not have a pan large enough for the size roast she needed to feed her family. Thus, she would cut the roast in half to fit it into the two pans that she did own.

Here is another example. One mother reports giving her infant daughter herb tea in addition to an ointment provided by her physician for a skin rash. It seems that this skin rash was common among infant girls in each generation in this family. A specific herb tea was traditionally used to treat the rash. This mother confesses that she did not tell her mother or grandmother that she used the ointment prescribed by her doctor. It is interesting for us to note that although the mother did not have complete faith in the tea, she also did not have complete faith in the ointment. The mother states that she is not sure which one actually cured the rash.

Violation of family and cultural rituals and norms can be a source of conflict between new parents and other family members (McGoldrick et al., 2016). For example, differences of opinion about baptism, male circumcision, and even childcare arrangements can create family disharmony. There are many ways to grandparent, and grandparents often jump into the new role without prior planning or discussion with their children about expectations about the grandparent role. Complaints can arise about intrusive or indifferent grandparents or, on the other hand, about demanding or neglectful adult children. New parents inherit any unresolved family issues that should be dealt with at this time to avoid engulfing the new family in lasting emotional problems. McGoldrick et al. (2016) suggest that this is a good time to engage new parents in family-of-origin

work. It is also a good time for the grandparent generation to make renewed efforts to give up old grievances and accept their adult children and their partners as the adults that they are. They further suggest that grandparents may need reminding that in a society with high divorce rates, it is wise to keep good relationships with their in-laws to ensure ongoing access to grandchildren in the case of divorce.

CRITICAL THINKING QUESTIONS 3.4

Why do you think that the United States has been slower than other high-income capitalist countries to develop family leave policies? What have you heard people say about this? Why do you think the United States' policy does not include paid family leave as is the case in almost all other advanced industrial societies? Do you think the United States should have "universal" childcare for all children, regardless of parents' income, as they do in Europe? Why or why not?

RISKS TO HEALTHY INFANT AND TODDLER DEVELOPMENT

Unfortunately, not all infants and toddlers get the start they need in life. Millions of infants and toddlers around the world are impoverished, abandoned, neglected, and endangered. Collectively, the adults of the world have not ensured that every child has the opportunity for a good start in life. Not only do these adversities have consequences for the infant's or toddler's immediate development, but research indicates that adversities experienced in childhood can also have negative consequences throughout the individual's life span. In a large, well-known study referred to as the adverse childhood experience (ACE), study investigators examined the consequences of adverse childhood experiences—including abuse; family violence; and parental substance abuse, mental illness, or imprisonment—on the infant's later adult physical and mental health outcomes (Felitti et al., 1998). Not only did they find a relationship between the two, but they also concluded that exposure to adversities during childhood, especially abuse and household dysfunction, increased the likelihood of developing a potentially fatal disease in adulthood. As the number of adverse childhood experiences increased so did the likelihood of risky health behaviors, chronic physical and mental health conditions, and early death. You have probably already surmised what some of the environmental factors are that inhibit healthy growth and development in infants and toddlers. This section addresses a few of those factors that social workers are especially likely to encounter: poverty, inadequate care giving, and child maltreatment.

Poverty

Examining the social science evidence about the effects of family life on physical and mental health, Repetti, Taylor, and Seeman (2002, p. 359) made the following observation: "The adverse effects of low SES [socioeconomic status] on mental and physical health outcomes are as close to a universal truth as social science has offered." When a family is impoverished, the youngest are the most vulnerable, and, indeed, children birth to age 3 have the highest rates of impoverishment around the world (Koball & Jiang, 2018; UNICEF, 2012). Although there are many ways of measuring poverty, it is generally agreed that 1 billion children across the world live in poverty, representing 1 in 2 children (Global Issues, 2013). Although children living in the poorest countries are much more likely than children living in wealthy countries to be poor, the proportion of children living in poverty has been rising in many of the wealthiest nations (UNICEF, 2012). Using a relative measure of poverty as income below 50% of the national median income, the UNICEF researchers found that the percentage of children living in poverty in 35 economically advanced countries ranged from 4.7% in Iceland to 25.5% in Romania. The United States had the second highest rate, 23.1%. Fourteen countries, including most European countries, had child poverty rates of less than 10%.

In the United States, the National Center for Children in Poverty (NCCP) (Koball & Jiang, 2018) estimates that families need an income about 2 times the U.S. federal poverty level to meet basic needs, and they refer to families below this level as low income. NCCP (Koball & Jiang, 2018) reports that, in 2016, 5.0 million (44%) infants and toddlers lived in low-income families, 3.4 million (21%) lived in families below the poverty level, and 1.1 million (10%) lived in deep poverty. This is a slight improvement over the economic situation of infants and toddlers in 2010, when the country was still recovering from the deep recession of 2008, and is very similar to the prerecession rates. There are racial and ethnic differences in the rates of children under the age of 18 living in poverty: 61% of Black children live in low-income families, compared with 60% of American Indian children, 59% of Hispanic children, and 28% of White and Asian children. When looking at these overall rates for children under the age of 18, it is important to remember that low-income status is slightly more prevalent in the families of infants and

toddlers than in families with older children. Children with immigrant parents are more likely than children with native-born parents to live in low-income families, 51% compared with 38%. Geographical differences also exist in the rates of children in low-income families in the United States, with children in the South and West being more likely to live in low-income families than children in the Northeast. About half (53.5%) of low-income children under the age of 18 and 32% of children living under the poverty line live with at least one parent employed full time, year-round (Koball & Jiang, 2018).

Although some young children who live in poverty flourish, poverty presents considerable risks to children's growth and development. (That risk continues from infancy and toddlerhood into early and middle childhood, as Chapters 4 and 5 explain.) Children living in poverty often suffer the consequences of poor nutrition and inadequate health care. Undernutrition in infancy and toddlerhood is a major risk factor for serious health problems at later stages of life, especially if it is combined with prenatal undernutrition (Barker & Thornburg, 2013).

Negative associations between family poverty and children's cognitive development begin to emerge by the end of the second year of life. By age 2, poor toddlers score 4.4 points lower on IQ tests than nonpoor toddlers. In addition, poor infants and toddlers are more likely to demonstrate emotional and behavioral problems than nonpoor infants and toddlers. Three-year-olds who live in deep poverty have been found to display more internalizing behavior symptoms, such as anxiety, withdrawal, and depression, than other children of the same age (Barajas et al., 2008). Children are affected not only by the direct consequences of poverty but also by indirect factors such as family stress, parental depression, and inadequate or nonsupportive parenting (Davies, 2011). Irma Velasquez's depression and anxiety will affect her relationship with Henry. Poor children are also more likely to be exposed to environmental toxins (Hetherington & Boddy, 2013).

Most disturbing is the link between poverty and **infant mortality**—the death of a child before his or her first birthday. In general, infant mortality rates are highest in the poorest countries (Hug, Sharrow, & You, 2017). Infant mortality rates have been falling around the world, but there are huge regional disparities, and the infant mortality rate is not falling as rapidly as the mortality rate for older children. The infant mortality rate in the United States is high compared with other high-income nations, but Bosnia and Herzegovina, a country with less than one tenth of the average income of the United States, has achieved a slightly better infant mortality rate than the United States (Hug et al., 2017). Within the United States, mortality rates for infants are higher among those living in poor families and for infants in some racial and ethnic groups; the rate among non-Hispanic Black infants was 11.3 per 1,000 births in 2015, compared with 8.3 per 1,000 births among American Indian/Alaska Natives, 5.0 per 1,000 births among Hispanics, 4.9 per 1,000 births among non-Hispanic Whites, and 4.2 per 1,000 births among Asian/Pacific Islanders. As you can see, the infant mortality rate among non-Hispanic Blacks is more than twice the rate among Hispanic, non-Hispanic White, and Asian/Pacific Islander infants; the rates for American Indian/Alaska Native infants fall in the middle (Centers for Disease Control and Prevention, 2018c).

Inadequate Caregiving

Because they are so dependent on caregiver assistance in all areas of their lives, infants and toddlers' developmental risk is heightened when parents fail to carry out caregiving functions. There are many reasons why infants and toddlers may receive inadequate care. The care of some infants is compromised when their mothers suffer from depression. Research indicates that about 8% to 19% of women experience clinical depression following childbirth (Ko, Farr, Dietz, & Robbins, 2012; O'Hara & McCabe, 2013). Similar rates have been found around the world (Pearlstein, Howard, Salisbury, & Zlotnick, 2009; Wisner, Chambers, & Sit, 2006). Mothers are at greater risk of postpartum depression if they face chronic stressors during pregnancy (Liu & Tronick, 2013), and it is generally accepted that the precipitous hormonal changes at birth, to which some women seem especially sensitive, play a large role. Mothers who are depressed have been found to interact differently with their infants than nondepressed mothers. They are more likely to show negative emotions and behaviors such as withdrawal, hostility, intrusiveness, coerciveness, and insensitivity (Jennings et al., 2008). They are more likely to be less responsive to their babies, show less affection, and to touch their infants in more negative ways. They may fail to protect their infants from harm, and they rate their infants' behavior more negatively (Zajicek-Farber, 2009). Infants of depressed mothers have been found to show some negative outcomes, including overall distress, withdrawn behavior, deficits in social engagement, problems with sleep and feedings, and difficulty regulating emotions (Leventon & Bauer, 2013; Muscat, Obst, Cockshaw, & Thorpe, 2014). They are also more likely to show deficits in cognitive development, language development, and insecure attachment at 1 year and 18 months (Quevedo et al., 2012).

Postpartum depression often goes undiagnosed and untreated across cultural groups (Dennis & Chung-Lee, 2006), but it is more likely to receive attention in societies that have regular postpartum visits from midwives or nurses. Early intervention can help to improve the parent–child relationship and promote the health of both the mother and the infant. Antidepressive medications are often prescribed for the mother, and the entire family may benefit from psychotherapy, parent education, and parent support groups (Bobo & Yawn, 2014). Family dynamics are often altered when mothers are depressed following childbirth, and research indicates that infant relationships with fathers and other caregivers can buffer the negative effects of poor interactions with a depressed mother (Cabrera, Fitzgerald, Bradley, & Roggman, 2014).

Very little research exists on psychosocial and mental health issues for new fathers, but the Australian First Time Fathers Study attempted to address this gap in knowledge (Condon, 2006). This study found no evidence of male postnatal depression but did find that male partners of women with postpartum depression are at risk of depression, anxiety, and abusing alcohol. At first, most men are confused by their wives' depression but supportive. If the depression lasts for months, which it often does, support is usually gradually withdrawn. Men report that they find their wives' irritability and lack of physical affection more troubling than the sadness and tearfulness. This study also found that male partners and other family members of depressed mothers often take on more and more of the care of the infant over time, which reinforces the mother's sense of incompetence. Communication breakdowns are very common in these situations.

The most pervasive response to inadequate caregiving is *nonorganic* failure to thrive (NOFTT), a condition in which infants and toddlers have poor feeding habits and fail to make weight gains while having no underlying medical condition. Feeding disorders usually show up as food refusal or low food intake in relation to the infant or toddler age. Feeding problems have been found to be a concern of 10% to 25% of parents of healthy children under the age of 3, but only 1% to 5% of infants and toddlers suffer from the severe feeding problems that result in failure to thrive (Rybak, 2015). Infants and toddlers with feeding difficulties are a heterogeneous group that are challenging for both parents and health care providers. A basic medical evaluation involving a multidisciplinary team of dietician, speech pathologist, psychologist, and pediatrician is essential to rule out organic causes of the feeding problem. Feeding problems occur in 30% of preterm infants and in up to 80% of infants with neurological impairments or inborn metabolic dysfunctions (Rybak, 2015). When organic causes are ruled out, psychosocial deprivation and parental pathologies are often found to be involved. One recent longitudinal study produced findings consistent with an international scientific literature that infants and toddlers with feeding problems without organic origin tend to have mothers who are depressed or have a feeding disorder themselves (Cerniglia & Cimino, 2015). Cerniglia and Cimino (2015) also found that the fathers of infants and toddlers with nonorganic feeding problems are more likely than other fathers to have obsessive/compulsive behaviors and anxiety. Another research team has found that sensory processing problems involving an aversion or negative reaction to certain types of sensory stimuli are more common among toddlers with NOFFT (Yi, Joung, Choe, Kim, & Kwon, 2015). Research also indicates that around 18 months of age, many toddlers demonstrate a period of *neophobia* and begin to reduce the number and variety of accepted foods, with the consumption of meat, vegetables, and fruits being dramatically reduced (Rybak, 2015). With repeated exposure, this phase usually passes. As you can see, feeding problems and failure to make weight milestones can be tricky in infancy and toddlerhood. A thorough evaluation by a multidisciplinary team is critical, and parents must be approached with sensitivity and without prejudgement (Sipotz, 2015). A social worker can be an invaluable member of the diagnostic and treatment team.

Ongoing parental conflict, harsh parenting, and parental mental illness and substance abuse are also risk factors for infant and toddler development. When there is a high level of parental anger and conflict, parents typically become less available to the infant or toddler, creating an insecure home environment (Struge-Apple, Davies, & Cummings, 2006). Research indicates that infants and toddlers raised with high parental conflict have more active stress response systems. Parents who react to a toddler's assertive and limit-testing behavior with harsh discipline provide a model of aggression for solving relationship issues (Bayer et al., 2011). Serious parental mental illness, including chronic depression, bipolar disorder, post-traumatic stress disorder (PTSD), and schizophrenia, often compromise the ability of parents to meet the needs of infants and toddlers (Goodman & Brand, 2009; Natsuaki et al., 2010). Severe and chronic maternal depression has been associated with insecure attachment (Goodman & Brand, 2009).

Parents whose lives are organized around accessing and abusing legal and illegal substances are 4 times more likely than other parents to neglect their infants and toddlers (Street, Whitlingum, Gibson, Cairns, & Ellis, 2008). For example, opioid use during pregnancy increased in the United States from 1.19 per 1,000 births in 2000 to 5.63 per 1,000 births in 2009 (Patrick et al., 2012). Given these recent trends, it is not surprising that the incidence of neonatal abstinence syndrome (NAS) has increased by 300% since the 1980s (Sublett, 2013). NAS develops in infants exposed to opiates during pregnancy and often leads to infant withdrawal, with symptoms typically appearing 48 to 72 hours after birth. NAS often requires lengthy hospital stays, and symptoms can last up to 6 months after birth (Sublett, 2013). There is little rigorous research concerning outcomes for infants with NAS. The limited research available suggests that in general, opioid-exposed infants are more likely to have attention deficit disorders, disruptive behavior, and the need for psychiatric referrals (Ornoy & Yacobi, 2012). Also of concern is the effect of withdrawal on the infant's growth and development and the impact it has on maternal bonding. Infants with NAS often demonstrate excessive crying, irritability, poor sleep, rigid muscle tone, tremors, hyperthermia, excessive sucking with poor feeding, loose stools, yawning, sweating, nasal stuffiness, and sneezing, all of which can affect mother–child bonding and attachment. Social workers provide support to pregnant women and mothers attempting to remain free of opiates. Here is an example. Kim had been receiving treatment at a methadone clinic for 5 months for long-term heroin addiction when she found out she was pregnant. The staff at the clinic referred her to a substance abuse support program for pregnant women and new mothers staffed with social workers. Through individual and group counseling, along with case management, Kim was able to reduce the amount of methadone needed to remain heroin-free. She had difficulty finding prenatal care because many physicians in her area were reluctant to take patients who are on methadone during pregnancy. With some arm twisting from the social worker, the doctor agreed to provide prenatal care, and Kim had a successful delivery. About 4 or 5 days after the birth, Kim's infant demonstrated only mild symptoms of NAS. The hospital made a referral to child protective services who investigated but did not take custody of Kim's infant after learning from the social worker the consistent work Kim had demonstrated in remaining drug-free. Kim continued in the substance abuse support program and continued to remain drug-free and provide quality care for her new daughter.

Child Maltreatment and Trauma

National data indicate that in 2015, 683,000 children in the United States were assessed to be victims of abuse or neglect. (It is important to note that it is generally assumed that many abused and neglected children never come to the attention of government authorities.) Infants from birth to 1 year of age have the highest rate of victimization, at 24.2 per 1,000 (Child Welfare Information Gateway, 2017). The youngest children are the most vulnerable to child maltreatment. For all age groups, 75.3% of confirmed cases of child maltreatment involved neglect, 17.2% involved physical abuse, 8.4% involved sexual abuse, and 6.2% involved psychological abuse.

The effect of child maltreatment and other trauma on the brain during the first 3 years of life has been the subject of considerable study in recent years (Farmer, 2009; Fawley-King & Merz, 2014). Remember that neuroscientific research has clearly demonstrated that the brain is plastic throughout life, which means it is shaped by experiences across the life course. Research indicates that several brain parts involved in responses to stress are especially disrupted and changed by traumatic events during the first 3 years of life. They include the brain parts that regulate homeostasis (brain stem and locus coeruleus); form memory systems and regulate emotion (hippocampus, amygdala, and frontal cortex); and regulate the executive functions of planning, working memory, and impulse control (orbito-frontal cortex, cingulate and dorsolateral prefrontal cortex). In addition, the major neuroendocrine stress response system, the hypothalamic-pituitary-adrenal (HPA) axis, is also impacted by trauma. Research indicates that early life stress, such as child maltreatment, can lead to disruptions in HPA axis functioning and result in anxiety disorders and depression in adulthood (see Fawley-King & Merz, 2014).

The child who experiences maltreatment or other trauma at the age of 2, 3, or 4 is at risk of developing memory problems, difficulty regulating emotions, and problems integrating sensory experiences. Research shows that people who experience childhood trauma are more likely to develop decreased volume in the hippocampus, a brain characteristic also found with adults experiencing PTSD. Injuries to the hippocampus have been found to be associated with cognitive impairments, memory deficits, poor coping responses, and dissociation (Farmer, 2009). When a child is exposed to extreme stress or trauma, the autonomic nervous system is activated, resulting in increased heart rate, respiration, and blood pressure. The child may freeze in place before beginning to fight. In the case of child sexual abuse, the child may dissociate, or detach from what is happening, becoming compliant and emotionally numb (Fawley-King & Merz, 2014).

As noted, 75.3% of all confirmed cases of child maltreatment involve neglect. Child neglect is thought to occur when caregivers are ignorant of child development, overwhelmed by life stresses, or struggling with mental health or substance abuse problems. Children who experience neglect in the early years of life often do not thrive. Much of the early human research on child neglect focused on Romanian children who were placed in state-run institutions with few staff (staff–child ratio of 1:60) and very little sensory and emotional stimulation. At 3 years of age, these children were found to have delays in physical growth as well as in motor, cognitive, and language skills; they also had poor social skills. Preliminary research suggests that neglect leads to deficits in prefrontal cortex functioning (attention and social deficits) and executive functioning (planning, working memory, and impulse control). Working memory is key to learning. Early evidence suggests that these changes in brain functioning are related to difficulties in managing emotions, problem solving, and social relationships. Most troubling is the finding that children who are neglected early in life have smaller brains than other children; they have fewer neurons and fewer connections between neurons. Social workers need to keep abreast of the developing neuroscience research on the effects of child maltreatment and other forms of trauma on brain development, but we must also remember to put the brain in context. We must advocate for policies that ensure parents have the best available resources to provide the type of parenting infants and toddlers need. We must also encourage research that examines how to heal the disrupted brain.

An association has also been found between infant temperament and abuse (Grogan-Kaylor & Otis, 2007). Infants who have "difficult" temperament are more likely to be abused and neglected. The combination of difficult temperament and environmental stress increases the risk of child abuse. Infants and toddlers with mental, physical, or behavioral abnormalities are also at a higher risk for abuse (Guterman & Embry, 2004). Regardless, interventions with infants and toddlers who have experienced abuse and neglect should be administered as soon as possible with the infant and caregiver, and focus on the infant–caregiver relationship (Osofsky, Stepka, & King, 2017).

PROTECTIVE FACTORS IN INFANCY AND TODDLERHOOD

Many young children experience typical growth and development despite the presence of risk factors. They are said to have resilience. Several factors have been identified as mediating between the risks children experience and their growth and development. These factors are "protective" in the sense that they shield the child from the consequences of potential hazards. Following are some protective factors that help diminish the potential risks to infants and toddlers.

Maternal Education

International research indicates that the education of the mother directly affects the outcome for infants and toddlers. This effect has been found in very poor populations in low-income countries. Longitudinal research of families in the poorest parts of Ecuador found that maternal education was a strong predictor of children's cognitive development at 36 months (Schady, 2011). Longitudinal research of a birth cohort from one Brazilian city measured the social, motor, communication, and cognitive development of infants and toddlers at 3, 12, and 24 months of age and found the level of maternal schooling to be associated with developmental outcomes at all three ages (Barros, Matijasevich, Santos, & Halpern, 2010). Another research team investigated the risk and protective factors for child health in 42 developing countries and found that maternal education has a substantial influence on child health (Boyle et al., 2006). Given these findings, it is not surprising that all the researchers cited in this paragraph recommend education of girls and women as a protective factor for children.

Similar results have been found for another group of high-risk infants and toddlers—those born at very low birth weight (VLBW). One research team followed a group of VLBW infants in Taiwan during the first 2 years of life and found that maternal education and 6-month neurological status were the most significant predictors of the developmental trajectory from birth to age 2 (Wang, Wang, & Huang, 2008).

Social Support

Social support is often found in informal networks, such as friends and extended family members, or in formal support systems, such as the church, community agencies, day care centers, social workers, and other professionals. The availability of social support seems to buffer many risk factors, such as stress experienced by parents (Werner & Smith, 2001). For example, Mrs. Hicks could truly benefit from having the opportunity to take a break from the stresses of caring for Holly. Both formal and informal social support can fill this gap for her. One research team found that a combination of formal and informal social support, including both instrumental and emotional support, enhanced the ability of homeless mothers to provide consistent parenting (Marra et al., 2009).

Extended family members often serve as alternative caregivers when parents cannot provide care because of physical or mental illness or job demands. Reliance on an extended family is particularly important in some cultural and socioeconomic groups. In cultures where families live in multigenerational households, shared caregiving has been found to serve as a protective factor in situations where risk factors are involved (Feldman & Masalha, 2007). Sarah's dad, Chris Johnson, probably would not have been able to care for her without the support of his family. And it is through the support of his family that he has been able to continue his education.

Easy Temperament

There is evidence that infants with an easy temperament are less likely to be affected by risk factors. In a study of resilience in children exposed to domestic violence, one research team (Martinez-Torteya, Bogat, von Eye, & Levendosky, 2009) found that easy temperament was a significant predictor of resilience in 2-, 3-, and 4-year-old children. Another research team (Derauf et al., 2011) found that easy infant temperament was associated with better behavioral outcomes in 3-year-old toddlers who had been exposed prenatally to methamphetamine. The association between easy temperament and "protection" is both direct and indirect. Infants with a positive temperament may simply perceive their world more positively. Infants with a positive temperament may also induce more constructive and affirming responses from those in their environment. Researchers have found that mothers of infants with easy temperament are less likely than mothers of infants with difficult temperament to become depressed (Montirosso et al., 2012; Solmeyer & Feinberg, 2011).

National and State Policy

Many social workers and others advocate for better national and state policies that will enhance good health among infants and toddlers, build and support strong families, promote positive early learning experiences, and create systems that advance the development and well-being of infants and toddlers. This includes legislation and financial support to ensure things such as adequate health coverage for infants and toddlers, paid parental leave and childcare, improved policies and programs that prevent child abuse, and development of programs and policies that promote parental and infant mental health. Also, continued support of national programs like the Women, Infants, & Children (WIC) program and the Child and Adult Care Food Program (CACFP) are considered crucial to promoting healthy physical development in infants and toddlers. Other advocates promote improving existing social and educational programs. Knitzer (2007), for example, identifies what she wittingly refers to as legislation to improve the odds for young children. She suggests investing more federal and state financial resources to extend programs such as Early Head Start to incorporate home visiting, center-based instruction, and family support for all low-income babies and toddlers through (instead of up to) age 3. There is strong evidence that the tax and social welfare policies of other economically advanced countries are doing a better job of alleviating child poverty than the policies in the United States (UNICEF & World Bank Group, 2016). This has long-term consequences for the health of a society.

CRITICAL THINKING QUESTIONS 3.5

Why do you think that researchers consistently find a negative association between family poverty and children's cognitive development? What biological, psychological, and social factors might be involved in that association? There is growing evidence that child maltreatment has a negative impact on brain development. What role can social workers play in informing the public about the impact of the environment on brain development?

IMPLICATIONS FOR SOCIAL WORK PRACTICE

Knowledge about infants and toddlers has several implications for social work practice.

- Become well acquainted with theories and empirical research about growth and development among infants and toddlers.

- Assess infants and toddlers in the context of their environment, culture included.

- Promote continued use of formal and informal social support networks for parents with infants and toddlers.

- Continue to promote the elimination of poverty and the advancement of social justice.

- Advocate for compulsory health insurance and quality health care.

- Advocate for more affordable, quality childcare.

- Collaborate with news media and other organizations to educate the public about the impact of poverty and inequality on early child development.

- Learn intervention methods to prevent and reduce substance abuse.

- Help parents understand the potential effects of inadequate caregiving on their infants, including the effects on brain development.

- Help parents and others understand the association between child development and consequential outcomes during adulthood.

- Provide support and appropriate intervention to parents to facilitate effective caregiving for

Key Terms

attachment 96	motor skills 85	symbolic functioning 88
brain plasticity 87	myelination 87	synapses 86
cognition 88	neurogenesis 86	synaptic blooming 87
concrete operations stage 88	neurons 86	synaptic pruning 87
developmental delay 103	object permanence 89	synaptogenesis 87
developmental disability 103	preoperational stage 88	temperament 95
developmental niche 77	reflex 84	toddler 77
formal operations stage 89	sensorimotor stage 88	transitional object 97
infant 77	sensory system 83	working model 97
infant mortality 108	separation anxiety 89	
information processing theory 90	stranger anxiety 89	

Active Learning

1. Spend some time at a mall or other public place where parents and infants frequent. List behaviors you observe that indicate attachment between the infant and caretaker. Note any evidence you observe that may indicate a lack of attachment.

2. Ask to tour a day care facility. Describe the things you observe that may have a positive influence on cognitive development for the infants and toddlers who spend time there.
List those things you think are missing from that setting that are needed to create a more stimulating environment.

3. Social support is considered to be a protective factor for individuals throughout the life course. List the forms of social support available to Marilyn Hicks, Chris Johnson, and Irma Velasquez. How do they help them with their parenting? In what ways could they be more helpful? How do they add to the level of stress?

Web Resources

The Institute for Child and Family Policy: www.columbia.edu/cu/childpolicy

Site maintained at Columbia University contains international comparisons of child and family policies.

Jean Piaget Society: www.piaget.org

Site presented by the Jean Piaget Society, an international interdisciplinary society of scholars, teachers, and researchers, contains information on the society, a student page, a brief biography of Piaget, and Internet links.

National Center for Children in Poverty (NCCP): www.nccp.org

Site presented by the NCCP of the Mailman School of Public Health of Columbia University contains media resources and child poverty facts as well as information about childcare and early education, family support, and public welfare.

Zero to Three: www.zerotothree.org

Site presented by Zero to Three: National Center for Infants, Toddlers, and Families, a national nonprofit charitable organization with the aim to strengthen and support families, contains information about infant and toddler behavior and development, child maltreatment, childcare and education, and public policy.

Early Childhood

Debra J. Woody and David Woody III

Learning Objectives

4.1 Compare one's own emotional and cognitive reactions to three case studies.

4.2 Summarize typical physical, cognitive and language, moral, personality and emotional, and social development during early childhood.

4.3 Describe the role of play in early childhood development.

4.4 Analyze the roles of biology and the environment in creating development delays and disabilities.

4.5 Evaluate the possible benefits of early childhood education.

4.6 Identify special issues that face the multigenerational family with young children.

4.7 Give examples of risk factors and protective factors during early childhood.

4.8 Apply knowledge of early childhood to recommend guidelines for social work engagement, assessment, intervention, and evaluation.

CASE STUDY 4.1

TERRI'S TERRIBLE TEMPER

Terri's mother and father, Mr. and Mrs. Smith, an Anglo couple, really seem at a loss about what to do. They adopted Terri, age 3, when she was an infant. They describe to their social worker how happy they were to finally have a child. They had tried for many years, spent a lot of money on fertility procedures, and had almost given up on the adoption process when Terri seemed to be "sent from heaven." Their lives were going well until a year ago, when Terri turned 2. Mrs. Smith describes an overnight change in Terri's behavior. Terri has become a total terror at home and at preschool. In fact, the preschool has threatened to dismiss Terri if her behavior does not improve soon. Terri hits and takes toys from other children, she refuses to cooperate with the teacher, and she does "what she wants to do."

Mr. and Mrs. Smith admit that Terri runs their household. They spend most evenings after work coaxing Terri into eating her dinner, taking a bath, and going to bed. Any attempt at a routine is nonexistent. When the Smiths try to discipline Terri, she screams, hits them, and throws things. They have not been able to use time-outs to discipline her because Terri refuses to stay in the bathroom, the designated time-out place. She runs out of the bathroom

and hides. When they attempt to hold her in the bathroom, she screams until Mr. Smith gets too tired to continue to hold her or until she falls asleep. Mr. and Mrs. Smith admit that they frequently let Terri have her way because it is easier than saying no or trying to discipline her.

The "straw that broke the camel's back" came during a family vacation. Mrs. Smith's sister and family joined the Smiths at the beach. Mr. Smith describes the vacation as a total disaster. Terri refused to cooperate the entire vacation. They were unable to eat at restaurants because of her tantrums, and they were unable to participate in family activities because Terri would not let them get her ready to go. They tried allowing her to choose the activities for the day, which worked until other family members tired of doing only the things that Terri wanted to do. Terri would scream and throw objects if the family refused to eat when and where she wanted or go to the park or the beach when she wanted. Mrs. Smith's sister became so frustrated with the situation that she vowed never to vacation with them again. In fact, it was the sister who insisted that they get professional help for Terri.

CASE STUDY 4.2

JACK'S NAME CHANGE

Until last month, Jack Lewis, an African American 4-year-old boy, lived with his mother, Joyce Lewis, and father, Charles Jackson Lewis, in what Joyce describes

as a happy home. She was shocked when she discovered that her husband was having an affair with a woman at work. She immediately asked him to leave and has filed for divorce. Charles moved in with his girlfriend and has not contacted Joyce or Jack at this point. Joyce just can't believe that this is happening to her. Her mother had the same experience with Joyce's father but had kept the marriage going for the sake of Joyce and her siblings. Joyce, conversely, is determined to live a different life from the life her mother chose. She saw how depressed her mother was until her death at age 54. Joyce states that her mother died of a broken heart.

Although Joyce is determined to live without Charles, she is concerned about how she and Jack will live on her income alone. They had a comfortable life before the separation, but it took both incomes. Although she plans to seek child support, she knows she will need to move, because she cannot afford the mortgage on her own. Joyce would prefer for Jack not to have contact with his father. In fact, she is seriously considering changing Jack's name because he was named after his father. Joyce has tried to explain the situation to Jack as best she can. However, in the social worker's presence, she told Jack that she hopes he does not grow up to be like his father. She also told Jack that his father is the devil and is now living with a witch.

Joyce also shares that Jack has had difficulty sleeping and continues to ask when his father is coming home. Joyce simply responds to Jack by telling him that they probably will never see Charles again.

CASE STUDY 4.3
A NEW ROLE FOR RON AND ROSILAND'S GRANDMOTHER

Ron, age 3, and Rosiland, age 5, have lived with Ms. Johnson, their Anglo grandmother, for the last year. Their mother, Shirley, was sent to prison a year ago after conviction of drug trafficking. Shirley's boyfriend is a known drug dealer and had asked Shirley to make a "delivery" for him. Shirley was arrested as she stepped off the bus in another state where she had taken the drugs for delivery. Ron and Rosiland were with her when she was arrested, because she had taken them with her. Her boyfriend thought that a woman traveling with two young children would never be suspected of delivering drugs.

Ron and Rosiland were put into foster care by Child Protective Services until Ms. Johnson arrived to pick them up. It had taken her 2 weeks to save enough money to get to the children and fly them all home. Ms. Johnson shares with the social worker how angry she was that Shirley's boyfriend refused to help her get the children home. Shirley calls the children when she can, but because her crime was a federal offense, she has been sent to a prison far away from home. The children ask about her often and miss her terribly. Ms. Johnson has told the children that their mom is away but has not told them that she will be away for some time. She is also unsure how much they understand about what happened, even though they were present when their mom was arrested.

Ms. Johnson shares that she has no choice but to care for the children, although this is definitely not the life she had planned. She was looking forward to living alone; her husband died several years ago. With her small savings, she was planning to visit her sister in another state for an extended visit. But that money is gone now, because these funds were used to help get the children home. She seems to love both of the children but confides that the children "drive her crazy." She is not accustomed to all the noise, and they seem to need so much attention from her. Getting into the habit of having a scheduled day is also difficult for Ms. Johnson. Both children attend preschool, an arrangement Shirley made before her incarceration. Ms. Johnson describes the fact that the children attend preschool as a blessing, because it gives her some relief. Her social worker suspects that preschool is a blessing for the children as well.

TYPICAL DEVELOPMENT IN EARLY CHILDHOOD

As children like Terri Smith, Jack Lewis, and Ron and Rosiland Johnson emerge from toddlerhood, they turn their attention more and more to the external environment. Just as when in infancy and toddlerhood they worked at developing some regularity in their body rhythms, attachment relationships, and emotional states, they now work to discover some stability and regularity in the external world. That is not always an easy task, given their limitations in cognitive and language development. Some children emerge from toddlerhood with a sense of confidence in the availability of support and a beginning sense of confidence in themselves. Other children, unfortunately, leave toddlerhood more challenged than when they entered that stage (Sroufe, Egeland, Carlson, & Collins, 2005). Much happens in all interrelated dimensions of development from age 3 to 6, however, and most children emerge from early childhood with a much more sophisticated ability to understand the world and their relationships to it. They work out this understanding in an increasingly wider world, with major influences coming from family, school, peer groups, neighborhood, and the media (Mokrova, O'Brien, Calkins, Leerkes, & Marcovitch, 2012).

Some child development scholars still refer to the period from age 3 to 6 as the preschool age, but others have recently begun to refer to this period as early school age, reflecting the fact that a large number of children are enrolled in some form of group-based experience during this period. In 2011, 48% of 3- and 4-year-olds in the United States were enrolled in nursery school, at least part time, compared with 10% in 1965 (Davis & Bauman, 2013). In this chapter, we simply refer to this period from 3 to 6 years of age as early childhood. Remember as you read that the various types of development discussed in this chapter under separate headings actually are interdependent, and sometimes the distinctions between the dimensions blur.

International literature criticizes the notion of a universal early childhood. It suggests, instead, multiple and diverse early childhoods, based on class, race, gender, geography, and time (see Dahlberg, Moss, & Pence, 2007; Waller, 2009). Cultural psychologists report that 96% of participants in research studies about human behavior come from Western industrialized countries, countries whose populations make up only 12% of the world (Henrich, Heine, & Norenzayan, 2010). There are growing criticisms that all children of the world are evaluated against Western developmental psychology science, which is a mix of statistical averages and historically and culturally specific value judgments (Dahlberg et al., 2007; Nybell, Shook, & Finn, 2009). In this chapter, we have tried to broaden the view of early childhood, where the literature allows, but please keep this criticism in mind as you read. Also keep in mind the great inequity in the environments children are born into. Many children of the world are still reared in households without access to even basic necessities such as safe drinking water and sanitation (UNICEF, 2016).

Physical Development

Terri Smith, Jack Lewis, and Ron and Rosiland Johnson are at an age when they are likely to be running,

skipping, jumping, and using their fingers to create objects. They are also growing bigger and stronger. And early childhood is another period of rapid brain growth.

As Chapter 3 explained, infants and toddlers grow rapidly. From ages 3 to 6, physical growth slows. On average, height during this stage increases about 2 to 3 inches per year, and the young child adds about 5 pounds of weight per year. As a result, young children look leaner. From ages 2 to 6, young children's appetites tend to decline, and around age 3 many young children go through a fussy eating phase where foods once tolerated are no longer accepted and the introduction of new foods is resisted (Fildes et al., 2016). Picky eating appears to be a relatively stable individual trait, but in most cases, picky eating does not show significant effects on growth (Hafstad, Abebe, Torgersen, & von Soest, 2013; Mascola, Bryson, & Agras, 2010). Young children require a healthy diet of the same foods that adults need.

However, globally, many children suffer from malnutrition. There are three forms of malnutrition: *stunting*, which refers to children who are short for their age due to nutritional deficits, *overweight*, which refers to children who are too heavy for their height because of food intake high in calories, and *wasting*, which refers to children who are too thin for their height because of acute malnutrition (UNICEF, World Health Organization, & World Bank Group, 2017). In 2016, almost one quarter (22.9%) of the world's children younger than 5 years of age were stunted in growth due to malnutrition, with the highest prevalence in South Asia and Africa. More than half of all stunted children under 5 lived in Asia, and more than one third lived in Africa. At the same time, increasing rates of children have been found to be overweight in most regions of the world. Globally, 6% of children younger than 5 years of age were overweight in 2016, a 43% increase since 1990 (UNICEF, World Health Organization, & World Bank Group, 2017). Almost half of all overweight children under 5 lived in Asia, and one quarter lived in Africa. Also in 2016, the lives of 7.7% of the world's children under age 5 were threatened by wasting. More than two thirds of all wasted children under the age of 5 lived in Asia, and more than one quarter lived in Africa (UNICEF, World Health Organization, & World Bank Group, 2017). As suggested in the previous chapter, the importance of adequate nutrition cannot be overemphasized; poor nutrition is involved in at least half of the child deaths in the world each year. It magnifies the effect of every disease.

Great variation exists in the height and weight of young children, and racial and ethnic differences in height and weight are still evident in the early childhood years. For example, in the United States, African American children in early childhood on average are taller than White and Hispanic children of the same age, and there is some evidence that Hispanic American children weigh more on average than other young children (Dennison, Edmunds, & Stratton, 2006). Children of low economic status are more likely than other children to be overweight during early childhood, but severe food insecurity may lead to growth inhibition (Wang & Zhang, 2006). Even in the affluent United States, 12.4% of households were categorized as food insecure at some point during the year in 2016 (Coleman-Jensen, Rabbitt, Gregory, & Singh, 2017).

As noted in Chapter 3, the brain continues to be shaped by experience throughout early childhood and beyond. Brain growth continues at a rapid pace with an increase in synapses and connections among brain regions. By age 5, the brain is 90% of its adult size (Christen & Narvaez, 2012). Synaptic pruning and myelination continue, and motor and cognitive abilities increase by leaps and bounds because of increased interconnections between brain cells, which allow for more complex cognitive and motor capability (Davies, 2011; Dean et al., 2014). These abilities are perhaps even more accelerated with the availability of technology and media appropriate for young children that further stimulate brain development (Courage & Setliff, 2009). There is little research to date to clarify the benefits of and drawbacks to use of information and communication technology with young children, but what little research there is suggests that brain development may be enhanced with the use of interactive technologies that help children develop curiosity, problem solving, and independent thinking skills but hampered by passive engagement with technology (Mercer, 2013). Because of the great plasticity of the brain, each new wave of technological advancement, like earlier development of written language, results in new brain-mediated capabilities that had previously been unexpressed (Kneas & Perry, 2011).

Through a process called **lateralization**, the two hemispheres of the brain begin to operate slightly differently, allowing for a wider range of activity. Simply stated, brain functioning becomes more specialized. The left hemisphere is activated during tasks that require analytical skills, including speaking and reading. Tasks that involve emotional expression and spatial skills, such as visual imagery, require response from the right hemisphere. With the development of the right hemisphere and the social-emotional components there, young children develop the ability to reflect on the feelings and thoughts of others (James & Bose, 2011). In left-handed people, the right hemisphere is dominant and language often spans the two hemispheres. Brain lateralization was identified early in neuroscientific research, but current thinking is that we should avoid applying the right hemisphere/left hemisphere paradigm too rigidly. The hemispheres are in constant communication, and the tasks performed by each hemisphere are much more complex than once thought (Fogarty, 2009; Peng & Wang, 2011).

The brain is the most plastic during the first few years of life, and the immature brain is especially sensitive to injury. In recent years, neurodevelopmental researchers have been concerned about the impact of early lead (Pb) exposure on brain development. Neuropsychological studies have found that children exposed to lead and other heavy metals such as cadmium and mercury during early brain development are more vulnerable to behavioral and cognitive deficits that can last a lifetime (Barkur & Bairy, 2016). It is estimated that in the United States, more than 500,000 children ages 1 to 5 years old had Pb levels higher than the Centers for Disease Control and Prevention acceptable level in 2012, and some researchers suspect that neurodevelopment is negatively impacted at even lower levels (Senut et al., 2012). Children with low family income—who have other developmental risk factors as well—have been found to be particularly vulnerable to higher levels of lead in the blood. Attention was brought to this issue in 2016 due to the water crisis in Flint, Michigan (Gump et al., 2009; Lin, Rutter, & Park, 2016).

Because of other developments in the brain, children also obtain and refine some advanced motor skills during this time, such as running, jumping, and hopping, but less is known about motor development in early childhood compared with infancy and toddlerhood (Keenan & Evans, 2009). Early intervention specialists suggest the gross motor milestones presented in Exhibit 4.1. In addition to these **gross motor skills**—skills that require use of the large muscle groups—young children develop **fine motor skills**—skills that require use of small muscle groups such as hands, wrists, and fingers and involve eye-hand coordination. Suggested fine motor milestones are also presented in Exhibit 4.1. As you review these suggested milestones, remember that there is much variability in motor development in early childhood. For example, one child may be advanced in gross motor skills and lag in fine motor skills, or the opposite. In addition, different motor skills are valued in different developmental niches, and the expression of motor skills will depend on the tools available to the child. With these cautions, parents and other adults who spend time with young children will find the milestones presented in Exhibit 4.1 to be helpful to keep in mind as they interact with young children.

Increases in fine motor skills allow young children to become more self-sufficient. However, allowing the extra time needed for young children to perform self-care tasks can be frustrating to adults. Ms. Johnson, for example, has lived alone for some time now and may need to readjust to allowing extra time for the children to "do it themselves." Spills and messes, which are a

EXHIBIT 4.1 ● **Gross Motor and Fine Motor Skills in Early Childhood**

	Gross Motor Skills	Fine Motor Skills
Most 3-year-olds can	Run forward Jump in place Stand on one foot with support Walk on tiptoe Avoid obstacles in path Catch an 8-inch ball Climb and walk up stairs with alternating feet Kick a ball forward Ride a tricycle Climb a ladder	Turn single pages Snip with scissors Hold crayons with thumb and finger Use one hand consistently Imitate circular, vertical, and horizontal strokes Paint with some wrist action Make dots, lines, and circular strokes Roll, pound, squeeze, and pull clay Build a tower of up to nine cubes String ½-inch beads Cut along a line Use a fork Manage large buttons Dress self with supervision
Most 4-year-olds can	Run around obstacles Walk on a line Balance on one foot for 5–10 seconds Hop on one foot Push, pull, and steer wheeled toys Use a slide independently Jump over a 6-inch-high object and land on both feet Throw a ball overhead Catch a bouncing ball	Copy crosses and squares Print some letters Use table utensils Cut on a line Build a tower of nine small blocks
Most 5-year-olds can	Walk backward toe to heel Jump forward 10 times without falling Walk up and down stairs independently with alternating feet Turn a somersault Walk on tiptoes Walk on a balance beam Jump rope	Lace shoes but not tie Grasp pencil like an adult Color within lines Cut and paste simple shapes

part of this developmental process, are also often difficult for adults to tolerate.

Cognitive and Language Development

A few years ago, the first author of this chapter was at a doctor's office when a mother walked into the waiting area with her son, about age 3. The waiting area was very quiet, and the young child's voice seemed loud in the silence. The mother immediately began to "shh" her son. He responded by saying, "I don't want to shh, I want to talk." Of course, everyone laughed, which made the child talk even louder. The mother moved immediately to some chairs in the corner and attempted to get her son to sit. He refused, stating that he wanted to stand on one foot. The mother at once attempted to engage him with the toys she had with her. They played with an electronic game in which the child selects pieces to add to a face to make a complete face. This game kept the child's attention for a while until he became bored. The mother told him to "make the game stop." The child responded by yelling at the game, demanding that it stop making the face. The mother, understanding that her son had taken a literal interpretation of her comments, rephrased her directions and showed her son how to push the stop button on the game.

Next, the two decided to read *The Lion King*. The child became very confused, because in the book, different from his memory of the movie, the main character, Simba, was already an adult at the beginning. The child, looking at the pictures, argued that the adult lion was not Simba but instead was Simba's father. The mother attempted to explain that this book begins with Simba as an adult. She stated that just as her son will grow, Simba grew from a cub to an adult lion. The son looked at his mother bewildered, responding with, "I am not a cub; I am a little boy." The mother then tried to make the connection that just like the son's daddy was once a boy, Simba grew up to be a lion. The boy responded by saying that men and lions are not the same. Needless to say, the mother seemed relieved when her name was called to see the doctor.

This scene encapsulates many of the themes of cognitive and moral development in early childhood. As memory improves, and the store of information expands, young children begin to think much more in terms of categories, as the little boy in the doctor's office was doing (Davies, 2011; Newman & Newman, 2015). He was now thinking in terms of cubs, boys, lions, and men. They also begin to recognize some surprising connections between things. No doubt, in a short time, the little boy will recognize a connection between boys and

PHOTO 4.1 During early childhood, young children make advancements in the development of fine motor skills, including the ability to draw.

© iStockphoto.com

cubs, men and lions, boys and men, as well as cubs and lions. Young children are full of big questions such as where do babies come from, what happens to people when they die, where does the night come from, and so on. They can think about themselves and about other people. They engage in creative and imaginative thought and begin to develop humor, empathy, and altruism. They make great strides in language development and the ability to communicate. And they make gradual progress in the ability to judge right and wrong and to regulate behavior in relation to that reasoning.

Piaget's Stages of Cognitive Development

In early childhood, children fit into the second stage of cognitive development described by Piaget, the preoperational stage. This stage is in turn divided into two substages:

Substage 1: Preconceptual stage (ages 2 to 3). The most important aspect of the preoperational stage is the development of symbolic representation, which occurs in the preconceptual stage. Through play, children learn to use symbols and actively engage in what Piaget labeled deferred imitation. Deferred imitation refers to the child's ability to view an image and then, significantly later, recall and imitate the image. For example, 3-year-old Ella, who watches the *Dora the Explorer* cartoon on TV, fills her backpack with a pretend map and other items she might need, such as a blanket and a flashlight, puts it on, creates a pretend monkey companion named Boots, and sets off on an adventure, using the kitchen as a barn, the space under the dining table as the woods, and keeping her eyes open all the while for the "mean" Swiper the Fox. Ella's cousin, Zachery, who is enthralled with the *Bob the Builder* cartoon, often pretends that he is Bob the Builder when he is playing with his toy trucks and tractors. Whenever Zachery encounters a problem, he will sing Bob's theme song, which is "Bob the Builder, can we fix it, yes we can!!"

Substage 2: Intuitive stage (ages 4 to 7). During the second part of the preoperational stage, children use language to represent objects. During the preconceptual stage, any object with long ears may be called "bunny." However, during the intuitive stage, children begin to understand that the term *bunny* represents the entire animal, not just a property of it. However, although young children are able to classify objects, their classifications are based on only one attribute at a time. For example, given a set of stuffed animals with various sizes and colors, the young child will group the animals either by color or by size. In contrast, an older child who has reached the intuitive stage may sort them by both size and color.

In early childhood, children also engage in what Piaget termed **transductive reasoning**, or a way of thinking about two or more experiences without using abstract logic. This can be explained best with an illustration. Imagine that 5-year-old Sam immediately smells chicken when he enters his grandmother's home. He comments that she must be having a party and asks who is coming over for dinner. When the grandmother replies that no one is coming over and that a party is not planned, Sam shakes his head in disbelief and states that he will just wait to see when the guests arrive. Sam recalls that the last time his grandmother cooked chicken was for a party. Because grandmother is cooking chicken again, Sam thinks another party is going to occur. This type of reasoning is also evident in the example of the

mother and child in the doctor's office. Because the child saw Simba as a cub in the movie version of *The Lion King*, he reasons that the adult lion in the picture at the beginning of the book cannot possibly be Simba.

One last related preoperational concept described by Piaget is **egocentrism**. According to Piaget, in early childhood, children perceive reality only from their own experience and believe themselves to be at the center of existence. They are unable to recognize the possibility of other perspectives on a situation. For example, a 3-year-old girl who stands between her sister and the television to watch a program believes that her sister can see the television because she can. This aspect of cognitive reasoning could be problematic for most of the children described in the case examples. Jack may believe that it is his fault that his father left the family. Likewise, Ron and Rosiland may attribute their mother's absence to their behavior, especially given that they were present when she was arrested. More recent experimental research has found that the ability to see another's point of view begins to develop by age 2 and continues to develop throughout early childhood (Davies, 2011). Researchers are finding that young children have the capacity for nonegocentric thinking but do not consistently demonstrate that capacity (Engel, 2005).

Vygotsky's Sociocultural Perspective

According to Russian psychologist Lev Vygotsky (see Vygotsky, Hanfmann, Vakar, & Kozulin, 2012), we are all embedded in a social context that shapes how we think. Most of what children learn comes from collaborating with other people. In particular, children learn by interacting with more skilled partners who serve as models and provide instruction that children internalize over time. These partners may be parents or teachers, but they may also be peers and siblings. According to Vygotsky, it is through interaction that children learn to think. The more expert partner provides a *scaffolding* that allows the child to bridge the gap between the current level of knowledge and understanding and a cognitive task at hand. Research suggests that adults tend to provide children with learning scaffolds. For example, when reading a book to a child, adults tend to point to items, describe characters' emotional states, explain, ask questions, and respond sensitively to the child to help the child understand the material (Silva, Strasser, & Cain, 2014). Effective teachers assign children tasks they can accomplish with some assistance, provide just enough help so that the child can learn to complete the task independently, and provide the types of environments that stimulate children to complete more challenging tasks on their own (Wass & Golding, 2014).

Information Processing Theory

The information processing perspective proposes that in early childhood, children become better at attending to stimuli, encoding and retrieving memories, and problem solving (Bjorklund & Causey, 2018; Schwartz, 2018). (For a visual representation of information processing theory, refer to Exhibit 3.5 in Chapter 3.) Although the ability to sustain *attention* improves in early childhood, young children have trouble switching their attention from one stimulus to another (Hanania & Smith, 2010). Young children are also well known for their relatively poor selective attention abilities of focusing, particularly on aspects of a situation relevant to the task at hand. They are easily distracted and spend much time off task. Even 5-year-old children are easily distracted by stimuli in the environment (Bjorklund & Causey, 2018).

Recognition memory, the ability to recognize a stimulus that was encountered before, is nearly perfect in 4- and 5-year-old children. *Recall memory,* the ability to generate a memory of a stimulus that was encountered earlier without seeing it again, is much less developed in early childhood (Myers & Perlmutter, 2014). Young children are not very effective at using memory strategies, those cognitive activities that help us remember. Children do not start to consistently apply memory strategies until middle childhood (Schwartz, 2018). Most people have no memories prior to age 3, a situation known as *infantile amnesia,* and recent research indicates that we are unable to remember much of anything before the age of 3.5 or 4 years (Bjorklund & Causey, 2018). *Autobiographical memory,* the memory of personally meaningful events, develops steadily from 3 to 6 years (Schwartz, 2018). Young children are better at remembering things they did than things they watched.

An issue of concern to researchers is the accuracy of young children's memories and their suggestibility or inclination to accept and act on suggestions of others. Can their memories be trusted to make them good eye witnesses to events? In laboratory study, young children typically recall only a small portion of information from an event if asked for memory recall, but children's recall memory is influenced by a number of interacting factors. Research consistently shows that people of all ages report more inaccurate information when they are asked misleading questions. The research also indicates that children ages 3 to 6 are more vulnerable to suggestion than either school-age children or adults (Bjorklund & Causey, 2018). For this reason, the child protective and criminal justice systems have developed careful protocols for using young children as eyewitnesses.

Early childhood is also a period of rapid growth in cognitive flexibility, the ability to change *problem-solving* strategies when an initial strategy doesn't work. From around age 4 to 6, children show improvements in their ability to adjust responses and alternate back and forth between strategies. One research team found that mothers' provision of emotional support, but not cognitive support, during problem-solving activities contributes to the development of cognitive flexibility across early childhood (Zeytinoglu, Calkins, & Leerkes, 2018). Another research team found that shyness interferes with the development of social problem solving in early childhood (Walker, Degnan, Fox, & Henderson, 2013). This is a reminder of the interconnectedness of development in all dimensions.

Theory of Mind

Theory of mind refers to children's awareness of their own and other people's mental processes, and to the understanding that other people can have different states of awareness than our own (Bjorklund & Causey, 2018; Schwartz, 2018). Theory of mind is tested in early childhood using the false-belief test, which tests the understanding that you may know something that someone else doesn't know. Here is a classic false-belief test. Children ages 3, 4, and 5 were shown a bag of M&M's. While the child was watching, the M&M's were poured out of the bag and into a bag marked "crayons." Both boxes were then sealed up so that nobody could see what was inside. At this point, a research assistant who had not seen the transfer of M&M's comes into the room, and the child is asked where the research assistant thinks the M&M's are. All the 3-year-olds and some of the 4-year-olds incorrectly answered that the research assistant knew that the M&M's were in the crayon box. These children knew that the M&M's were now in the crayon box and they could not understand that the research assistant would be missing that knowledge. Most of the 5-year-olds realized that because the research assistant had not seen the switch, he or she would not know the actual location of the M&M's (Wimmer & Perner, 1983). Versions of the false-belief test have been conducted with nonhuman animals, and no experiment has shown that even chimpanzees can pass the false-belief test (Schwartz, 2018).

Children's performance on false-belief tests is closely associated with language development (Bernard & Deleau, 2007). When parents and other adults talk with children about mental states and emotions, connect them to specific situations, and discuss causes and consequences, children develop more complex understanding of other people's perspectives (Pavarini, Hollanda

Souza, & Hawk, 2012). Cross-cultural studies suggest, however, that compared with European American parents, Chinese parents engage in less talk about mental states when talking with children, and yet Chinese children perform just as well as Euro-American children on false-belief tasks. Chinese parents do often talk with their children about information concerning other people, however (Liu, Wellman, Tardif, & Sabbagh, 2008). Siblings also provide young children with opportunities to develop theory of mind, and young children with siblings have been found to perform better on false-belief tests than children without siblings (McAlister & Peterson, 2013).

Language Skills

Language development is included under cognitive development because it is the mechanism by which cognitive interpretations are communicated to others. For language to exist, children must be able to "organize" their experiences. At 2 years of age, the average child knows about 500 words, and the average 3-year-old child has a vocabulary of 900 to 1,000 words. By 6 years of age, children are often using about 2,600 words and can understand more than 20,000 words (Kuther, 2017). Children around the world develop language without formal instruction (Bjorklund & Causey, 2018). Young children ask "why" questions, persistently and often assertively, to learn about the world. Three-year-old speech is generally clear and easy to understand. At every point in development, however, children differ in the size of the vocabularies they command, the complexity of the language structure used, and the skill with which they communicate (Hoff, 2006).

By the fourth year of life, language development is remarkably sophisticated. The vocabulary is becoming more and more adequate for communicating ideas, and 4-year-olds are usually speaking in sentences of 8 to 10 words. They have mastered language well enough to tell a story mostly in words, rather than relying heavily on gestures, as toddlers must do. But perhaps the most remarkable aspect of language development in early childhood is the understanding of grammar rules. By age 4, young children in all cultures understand the basic grammar rules of their language (Gardiner, 2018). They accomplish this mostly by a figuring-out process. As they figure out new grammar rules, as with other aspects of their learning, they are overly regular in using those rules, a phenomenon known as **overregularization**, because they have not yet learned the exceptions. So we often hear young children make statements such as "she goed to the store," or perhaps "she wented to the store."

There are two different approaches to studying language development. One approach focuses on the mental processes by which language is acquired and conceptualizes language ability as primarily a function of genetics. Although somewhat influenced by the environment, children are thought to develop language skills as long as the appropriate genetic material is in place (Chomsky, 1968; Hoff, 2005). The other approach focuses on the way the social contexts in which children live shape language acquisition (Bronfenbrenner & Morris, 1998). Erika Hoff (2006) proposes a model that synthesizes these two approaches, a model that considers both "how the mind acquires language" and "how the social context shapes language development" (p. 56). She argues that children need both a language model and opportunities for communicative interaction to support language development. Language is not learned simply by overhearing it, as many of us have learned from our efforts to learn a new language in adolescence or adulthood. Language development is a social process; children learn language by listening to others speak and by asking questions. Past toddlerhood, children increasingly take charge of their own language acquisition by asking questions and initiating dialogues (Hoff, 2006). Parents can assist children by asking questions, eliciting details, and encouraging children to reflect on their experiences. As children grow older, they are often corrected by caregivers and preschool teachers in the misuse of words or phrases (Chapin & Altenhofen, 2010).

It appears that the developmental niche has an impact on the development of language skills. Children are talked to a great deal in some cultures and very little in other cultures (Hoff, 2006). North American parents tend to talk a lot about objects when speaking to their infants and toddlers, whereas Asian parents tend to use more verbs and fewer nouns. Considerable research indicates that infants and toddlers who are talked to a great deal acquire language skills earlier than infants and toddlers who are talked to less (Hoff, 2006). Across cultures, there is consistent evidence that parents with higher socioeconomic status, on average, speak more to their children, elicit more conversations with their children, use larger vocabularies in conversations with their children, and engage in fewer verbal behavioral prohibitions than parents with lower socioeconomic status (Hoff, 2006; Zhang, Jin, Shen, Zhang, & Hoff, 2008). This means that many low-income children enter elementary school with smaller vocabularies than their more privileged peers unless they are provided with support for language development. Some research indicates that both low-income and high-income mothers use more complex speech when reading books to their children, and book reading can attenuate the language disadvantage of low-income children (Hoff, 2003).

From observation of their environment—physical and social surroundings, child-rearing customs, and caregiver personality—children learn a set of regulations, or rules for communication, that shape their developing language skills. Children have an innate capacity for language, but the structuring of the environment through culture is what allows language development to occur. Two special types of language learners deserve greater attention: multilingual language learners and deaf and hard-of-hearing language learners.

Hoff (2006) reports that half of the children in the world live in multilingual situations. And yet research on language acquisition among multilingual children is very young. There is some evidence that children learning two languages tend to have smaller vocabularies in each language than monolingual children, but vocabulary size depends on the amount of exposure to each language and the opportunities to speak each language (Hoff, 2006). Recent research indicates, however, that learning two languages simultaneously in the first 3 years of life lays down the brain structures for later language learning (Klein, Mok, Chen, & Watkins, 2014).

Language development is a particularly important area of development for deaf and hard-of-hearing (DHH) children. Unless they have deaf parents, who will teach them sign language, these children require intervention to acquire language. Three common methods provide DHH children with access to language: sign language, simultaneous communication, and spoken language. Various sign languages, using manual signs, have developed in deaf communities around the world. Simultaneous communication uses signs from traditional sign languages plus newly created signs to correspond to spoken language. These new sign systems can theoretically be used simultaneously with speech, but in reality, this is very challenging because signs are longer in duration than words. Some children are exposed to spoken language only, and technological innovations, such as hearing aids and cochlear implants, are making that a more realistic choice for children with less severe hearing loss. The choice of method is influenced by attitudes about how important it is for children to fit into a mainstream hearing world. Of paramount importance is that hearing loss be detected at birth or shortly after, which is now possible, and that access to language begin in the early days and weeks. There is strong evidence that not having access to language in the early months has long-term negative consequences for language development. The method of language exposure should fit the sp... loss (Lederberg, Schick, & Sper...

Moral Development

Young children's improved cognitive development of theory of mind influence mo... ing. Young children begin to move from a mora... based on outside approval to a more internalized m... sense, with a rudimentary moral code. They engage in a process of taking society's values and standards as their own. They begin to integrate these values and standards into both their worldview and their self-concept. There are three components of moral development during early childhood (Newman & Newman, 2015):

1. *Knowledge* of the moral code of the community and how to use that knowledge to make moral judgments

2. *Emotions* that produce both the capacity to care about others and the capacity to feel guilt and remorse

3. *Actions* to inhibit negative impulses as well as to behave in a **prosocial** or helpful and empathic manner

Understanding Moral Development

Moral development has been explored from several theoretical perspectives found to have merit. Three of these approaches to moral development are explored here.

1. *Psychodynamic approach*. Sigmund Freud's psychoanalytic theory proposed three distinct structures of the personality: id, ego, and superego. According to Freud, the superego is the personality structure that guides moral development. There are two aspects to the superego: the *conscience*, which is the basis of a moral code, and the *ego ideal*, which is a set of ideals expected in a moral person. Freud (1927) thought the superego is formed from the ages of 4 to 7, but more recent psychodynamic formulations suggest that infancy is the critical time for the beginning of moral development (Kohut, 1971). Freud thought children would have more highly developed superegos when their parents used strict methods to inhibit the children's impulses. Contemporary research indicates the opposite, however, finding that moral behavior is associated with parental warmth, democratic decision making, and modeling of temptation resistance (Kochanska, Forman, Aksan, & Dunbar, 2005). New psychodynamic models emphasize a close, affectionate bond with the caregiver as the

is supported
ds these care-
development
breastfeeding,
d support (see
believed that
than females,

e perspective of
shaped by envi-
ments. Children
are likely to ~~rep~~ ~~_____~~ ~~_____~~ warded, and they
are likely to feel tension when they think about doing
something they have been punished for in the past.
From this perspective, parental consistency in response
to their children's behavior is important. Social learning theory also suggests that children learn moral conduct by observing models. Albert Bandura (1977) found
that children are likely to engage in behaviors for which
they see a model rewarded and to avoid behaviors that
they see punished. This can be problematic for children
who watch a lot of television, because they may come
to view violence as an acceptable way to solve interac-
tional conflict if they see violence go unpunished.

3. *Cognitive developmental approach.* Piaget's theory
of cognitive development has been the basis for stage
models of moral reasoning, which assume that children's
moral judgments change as their cognitive development
allows them to examine the logical and abstract aspects
of moral dilemmas. Moral development is assisted by
opportunities to encounter new situations and different
perspectives. The most frequently researched stage model
is that presented by Lawrence Kohlberg (1969, 1976) and
summarized in Exhibit 4.2. Kohlberg described three levels of moral reasoning, with two stages in each level. It
was expected that in early childhood, children will operate at the **preconventional level of moral reasoning**, with their reasoning about moral issues based, first,
on what gets them rewarded or punished. This type of
moral reasoning is thought to be common among toddlers. In the second stage, moral reasoning is based on
what benefits either the child or someone the child cares
about. This is consistent with the child's growing capacity
for attachments. There is some empirical evidence that
children ages 3 to 6 do, indeed, begin to use the type of
moral reasoning described in Stage 2 (Walker, 1989). The
idea of a hierarchical sequence of stages of moral development has been challenged as being based on a Western
cultural orientation, but longitudinal studies in a variety
of countries have produced support for the idea of evolution of moral reasoning (Gielen & Markoulis, 2001).

EXHIBIT 4.2 ●	Kohlberg's Stages of Moral Development
Level I	Preconventional
	Stage 1: Moral reasoning is based on whether behavior is rewarded or punished.
	Stage 2: Moral reasoning is based on what will benefit the self or loved others.
Level II	Conventional
	Stage 3: Moral reasoning is based on the approval of significant others.
	Stage 4: Moral reasoning is based on upholding societal standards.
Level III	Postconventional
	Stage 5: Moral reasoning is based on social contracts and cooperation.
	Stage 6: Moral reasoning is based on universal ethical principles.

Source: Based on Kohlberg, 1969, 1976.

All these approaches to moral development in early
childhood have been criticized for leaving out two
key ingredients for moral development: **empathy**, or
the ability to understand another person's emotional
condition, and **perspective taking**, or the ability
to see a situation from another person's point of view
(Eisenberg, 2000). Neuroscientific research currently
suggests that a special type of brain cell, called a *mirror neuron*, is key to the development of empathy. Have
you ever noticed how you instinctively smile when you
see someone else smiling? Mirror neurons allow us to
sense the move another person is about to make and
the emotions he or she is experiencing. Emotion is con-
tagious, because mirror neurons allow us to feel what
the other person feels through a brain-to-brain connection. Daniel Goleman (2006) calls this primal empathy;
it is based on feelings, not thoughts. He has coined
the phrase *social intelligence* to refer to this ability to be
attuned to another person. It appears that humans have
multiple systems of mirror neurons, and scientists are
in the early stages of learning about them. Studies have
found that people with autism have a dysfunctional
mirror neuron system (Goleman, 2006).

There is growing agreement that empathy and prosocial behavior begin in infancy and grow throughout
early childhood (Paulus, 2014). Toddlers as young as
18 months help adults with instrumental tasks or offer
assistance with simple activities. From 18 to 24 months

of age, toddlers respond to others' emotional and physical distress with expressions of concern and comfort (Hoffman, 2007). By age 3 or 4, children across cultures have been found to be able to recognize the type of emotional reaction that other children might have to different situations. Perspective taking, which is a thinking rather than feeling activity, grows in early childhood and is another important ingredient in moral development. One research team studied children at ages 3½ years and 5½ years and found that a sophisticated understanding of both emotional and mental states was associated with increased consideration of the emotional and mental states of others (Lane, Wellman, Olson, LaBounty, & Kerr, 2010). Longitudinal research has found that children who show empathy and perspective taking at 4 and 5 years of age are more likely to exhibit prosocial behavior and sympathy during adolescence and early adulthood (Eisenberg et al., 1999). Some researchers have suggested that the development of moral emotions can be studied by examining the development of sharing behaviors. Ongley and Malti's (2014) research indicates that fairness norms and aversions to inequality develop between early and middle childhood, and that is particularly the case for girls who show a preference for fairness in early childhood. There is compelling evidence of the capacity of children in early childhood to attend to the emotional and mental states of peers.

There has been considerable examination of the degree to which Kohlberg's model is responsive to gender and cultural experience, in view of the study population on which his theory is based—Harvard male undergraduates (Donleavy, 2008; Sherblom, 2008). Carol Gilligan (1982) notes that gender plays a significant role in how one experiences and acts on themes of ethical thinking, justice, and notions of individuality and connectedness. She suggests strong gender bias in Kohlberg's theory, and her research indicated that women's moral thought is guided by caring and maintaining the welfare of others whereas men use more abstract principles of justice. As you can see from Exhibit 4.2, caring for others and maintaining harmony in relationships would put women in Stage 3, at the highest. A similar criticism has been lodged about the poor fit of Kohlberg's theory with many non-European cultures that are more collectivist oriented than European and North American societies. Indeed, studies of Buddhist monks find that older monks barely reach Kohlberg's Stage 4, indicating that their moral reasoning is not as well developed as Western male adolescents, according to Kohlberg's model (Huebner & Garrod, 1993). The researchers suggest that the moral ideal in Western cultures is an autonomous individual with strong convictions who sticks up for those convictions. In contrast, the Buddhist moral ideal is guided by compassion and detachment from one's own individuality. How such themes are transmitted to young children can be strong guideposts for managing and participating in interpersonal relationships.

One aspect of moral reasoning is *distributive justice*, or the belief about what constitutes a fair distribution of goods and resources in a society. Cross-cultural studies suggest that cultures hold different views on what constitutes a "fair" distribution of resources. Some societies see fairness in terms of need whereas other societies see fairness in terms of merit. Reasoning about distributive justice starts in early childhood but is not well articulated until middle childhood (Gardiner, 2018).

Helping Young Children Develop Morally

Growing evidence indicates that some methods work better than others for helping children develop moral reasoning and conduct. Particularly helpful activities are those that help children control their own behavior, help them understand how their behavior affects others, show them models of positive behavior, and get them to discuss moral issues (Arsenio & Gold, 2006). It is important, however, to consider a child's temperament when undertaking disciplinary actions. Some children are more sensitive to messages of disapproval than others; sensitive children require a small dose of criticism, and less sensitive children usually require more focused and directive discipline (Kochanska, 1997). Brian Edmiston (2010) suggests that one important way for adults to assist young children to develop morally is to engage in dramatic play that helps children develop ethical identities.

Although religious beliefs play a central role in most societies in clarifying moral behavior, little research has been done to explore the role of religion in moral development in young children. Research (Roof, 1999) has indicated that adults often become affiliated with a religious organization when their children are in early childhood, even if the parents become "religious dropouts" after the children are out of the home. Religious rituals link young children to specific actions and images of the world as well as to a community that can support and facilitate their moral development. The major world religions also teach parents about how to be parents. Young children, with their comfortable embrace of magic, easily absorb religious stories on topics that may be difficult for adults to explain. Religion that emphasizes love, concern, and social justice can enrich the young child's moral development. Conversely, religion that is harsh and judgmental may produce guilt and a sense of worthlessness, which do not facilitate higher levels of moral reasoning.

CRITICAL THINKING QUESTIONS 4.1

What have you observed about the differences in gross and fine motor development among young children, as outlined in Exhibit 4.1? How do you think culture and social class affect gross and fine motor development during this period? What types of social policies might help to narrow the social class disparities in language development? What do you see as the benefits and drawbacks to being multilingual during early childhood? What special challenges might caregivers face in their attempts to assist Terri Smith, Jack Lewis, and Ron and Rosiland Johnson with moral development?

Personality and Emotional Development

The key concern for Jack Lewis and for Ms. Johnson's grandchildren—Ron and Rosiland—is their emotional development. Specifically, will they grow into happy, loving, well-adjusted people despite the disruptions in their lives? Writing about the early childhood years, Sroufe and colleagues (2005) suggest this as the period of life when a coherent personality emerges: "It is no exaggeration to say that the person emerges at this time" (p. 121). Based on a longitudinal study of 180 children born into poverty, they conclude that behavior and adaptation during early childhood predict later behavior and adaptation, something they did not find to be the case with the predictive power of behavior and adaptation in infancy and toddlerhood. They suggest that the important themes of development during this period are self-direction, agency, self-management, and self-regulation. Young children do face important developmental tasks in the emotional arena. This section addresses these tasks, drawing on Erikson's theory of psychosocial development.

Erikson's Theory of Psychosocial Development

Erikson labeled the stage of emotional development that takes place during the early childhood years as *initiative versus guilt* (ages 3 to 6). (Refer to Exhibit 3.8 for the complete list of Erikson's stages.) Children who pass successfully through this stage learn to get satisfaction from completing tasks. They develop imagination and fantasies and learn to handle guilt about their fantasies.

At the beginning of this stage, children's focus is on family relationships. They learn what roles are appropriate for various family members, and they learn to accept parental limits. In addition, they develop gender identity through identification with the parent of the same sex. Age and sex boundaries must be appropriately defined at this stage, and parents must be secure enough to set limits and resist the child's possessiveness.

By the end of this stage, the child's focus turns to friendships outside the family. Children engage in cooperative play and enjoy both sharing and competing with peers. Children must also have the opportunity to establish peer relationships outside the family. This is one of the functions the preschool program serves for Ms. Johnson's grandchildren.

Children who become stuck in this stage are plagued with guilt about their goals and fantasies. They become confused about family roles and issues of identity. These children are overly anxious and self-centered.

Emotions

Growing cognitive and language skills give young children the ability to understand and express their feelings and emotions. Children ages 3 to 5 can recognize and label simple emotions, and they learn about themselves when they talk about their anxieties and fears (Hansen & Zambo, 2007). Children in early childhood can also identify feelings expressed by others—as the earlier discussion of empathy illustrated—and use creative ways to comfort others when they are upset. A friend describes the response of her 5-year-old son Marcus when he saw her crying about the sudden death of her brother in a car accident. Marcus hugged his mom and told her not to cry, because, although she was sad about Uncle Johnny, she still had Marcus. Marcus promised his mother to never drive a car so she would not have to worry about the same thing happening to him. This attempt to reduce his mother's sadness is a typical response from a child of this age (Findlay, Girardi, & Coplan, 2006).

The ability to understand emotion continues to develop as young children have more opportunity to practice these skills. Children reared in homes in which emotions and feelings are openly discussed are better able to understand and express feelings (Bradley, 2000). Early childhood educators Cory Cooper Hansen and Debby Zambo (2007) recommend the use of children's literature to help children understand and manage emotions. Here are some of their recommendations for how to do that (p. 277):

- Respect all responses to talks about emotions.

- Ask children to describe the emotions of story characters.

- Talk about your own emotions about story characters.

- Encourage children to draw, write, or paint about the emotions of story characters as well as their own emotional reactions.

- Sing or chant about emotions and how to handle them.

- Brainstorm ways that story characters can handle their emotions.

- Practice reading emotions from pictures in books.

- Use stuffed animals to "listen" to children's stories.

Most child development scholars agree that all emotions, including those that have been labeled "negative" (anger, sadness, guilt, disgust), are adaptive, but more needs to be learned about how the negative emotions can become problematic for children (Cole, Luby, & Sullivan, 2008). We know that by the first grade, most children can regulate their emotions well enough to learn, obey classroom rules, and develop friendships (Calkins & Hill, 2007). But we also know that emotional receptivity makes young children vulnerable to environmental stress, and early exposure to adverse situations can have a negative effect on the brain, cardiovascular, and endocrine processes that support emotional development (Gunnar & Quevedo, 2007). It is important to recognize when emotional development is getting off course, and researchers are at work to develop understanding of that issue. For example, we know that most young children have tantrums. For most children, anger and distress are expressed in quick peaks in anger intensity that decline into whining and comfort-seeking behavior. Researchers are finding, however, that the tantrums of depressed young children are more violent, destructive, verbally aggressive, and self-injurious; they also have a longer recovery time (Belden, Thompson, & Luby, 2008). It is important to avoid both overreacting and underreacting to children's difficulties in regulating their emotions (Hane, Cheah, Rubin, & Fox, 2008).

Aggression

One behavior that increases during the early childhood years is aggression. Two types of aggression are observed in young children: **instrumental aggression**, which occurs while fighting over toys and space, and **hostile aggression**, which is an attack meant to hurt another individual. Instrumental aggression typically appears at about 1 year of age and increases from toddlerhood into early childhood as children begin

to play with other children (Hay, Hurst, Waters, & Chadwick, 2011). By age 4, most children have developed the ability to control their aggression at times and use words instead of physical action. Recently, researchers have studied another typology of aggression: physical aggression and relational aggression. **Physical aggression**, as the name suggests, involves using physical force against another person. **Relational aggression** involves behaviors that damage relationships without physical force, behaviors such as threatening to leave a relationship unless a friend complies with demands or using social exclusion or the silent treatment to get one's way. Researchers are finding that boys make greater use of physical aggression than girls, and girls make greater use of relational aggression (Ostrov, Crick, & Stauffacher, 2006).

Although some children continue high levels of aggression into middle childhood, usually physical aggression peaks early in the early childhood years (Alink et al., 2006). By the end of the early childhood years, children learn better negotiation skills and become better at asking for what they want and using words to express feelings. Terri Smith, in the first case study in this chapter, obviously has not developed these moderating skills.

Attachment

In early childhood, children still depend on their attachment relationships for feelings of security. In particularly stressful times, the attachment behavior of the young child may look very much like the clinging behavior of the 2-year-old. For the most part, however, securely attached children will handle their anxieties by verbalizing their needs. For example, at bedtime, the 4-year-old child may say, "I would like you to read one more story before you go." This increased ability to verbalize wants is a source of security. In addition, many young children continue to use transitional objects, such as blankets or a favorite teddy bear, to soothe themselves when they are anxious (Davies, 2011).

In their longitudinal study of 180 children born into poor families, Sroufe et al. (2005) examined, among other things, how attachment style in infancy and toddlerhood affected the developmental trajectory into early childhood. Here are some of the findings:

- Anxiously attached infants and toddlers were more dependent on their mothers and performed more poorly on teaching tasks at age 3½ than either securely or avoidant attached toddlers.

- Securely attached infants and toddlers rated higher on curiosity, agency, activity, self-esteem, and positive emotions at age 4½ than either anxiously or avoidant attached toddlers.

- Securely attached infants and toddlers had better emotion regulation in early childhood than anxiously attached toddlers.

Sroufe and colleagues also found that temperament was not a powerful predictor of early childhood behavior.

Social Development

In early childhood, children become more socially adept than they were as toddlers, but they are still learning how to be social and how to understand the perspectives of other people. The many young children who enter group care face increasing demands for social competence.

Peer Relations

In early childhood, children form friendships with other children of the same age and sex; boys gravitate toward male playmates and girls choose girls. Across cultures, young children's friendship groups are likely to be segregated by sex (Barbu, Le Maner-Idrissi, & Jouanjean, 2000; Maccoby, 2002a). When asked about the definition of a friend, most children in this age group think of someone with whom they play (Corsaro, 2018). For example, the neighbor children of the first author made their initial approach to her young son by saying, "Let's be friends; let's play" and "I'll be your friend if you will be mine." Young children do not view friendship as a trusting, lasting relationship, but even this limited view of friendship is important for this age group. As peer relationships become more important, around age 3, children are motivated to be accepted by peers. This motivation is the incentive for development of such skills as sharing, cooperating, negotiating, and perspective taking. Nevertheless, peer relations in early childhood are often marked by conflict and falling-outs (Davies, 2011).

Research indicates that young children are at a higher risk of being rejected by their peers if they are aggressive and comparatively more active, demonstrate a difficult temperament, are easily distracted, and demonstrate lower perseverance (Campbell, 2002). One would wonder, then, how young peers respond to Terri Smith. The rejection of some children is long lasting. It is important, therefore, to intervene early to help children like Terri Smith learn more prosocial behavior.

Peer relationships in early childhood are associated with early attachments. A child who has had secure relationships with parents in the first 3 years is likely to have good social skills and to expect peer relations to be positive. In contrast, peer interactions are often difficult for young children with insecure working models.

Self-Concept

Young children first understand themselves in concrete terms such as "I have black hair. I have bunk beds in my room." By about age 3.5, children include emotions and attitudes in their self-descriptions. The young child seems to vacillate between grandiose and realistic views of the self (Davies, 2011). Children are aware of their growing competence, but at the same time, they have normal doubts about the self, based on realistic comparisons of their competence with the competence of adults. In early childhood, children begin to develop a self-concept, which includes a perception of oneself as a person who has desires, attributes, preferences, and abilities.

Some investigators have suggested that during early childhood, the child's ever-increasing understanding of the self in relation to the world begins to become organized into a **self-theory** (Epstein, 1973, 1991, 1998). As children develop the cognitive ability to categorize, they use categorization to think about the self. By age 2 or 3, children can identify their gender and race (discussed in greater detail shortly) as factors in understanding who they are. As they develop theory of mind, from ages 4 to 6, young children become more aware that different people have different perspectives on situations. This helps them to begin to understand cultural expectations and sensitizes them to the expectations that others have for them.

This growing capacity to understand the self in relation to others leads to self-evaluation, or **self-esteem**. Very early interpersonal experiences provide information that becomes incorporated into self-esteem. Messages of love, admiration, and approval lead to a positive view of the self (Brown, Dutton, & Cook, 2001). Messages of rejection or scorn lead to a negative view of the self (Heimpel, Wood, Marshall, & Brown, 2002). In addition to these interpersonal messages, young children observe their own competencies and attributes and compare them with the competencies of other children as well as adults. And they are very aware of being evaluated by others, their peers as well as important adults (Newman & Newman, 2015).

Of course, a young child may develop a positive view of the self in one dimension, such as cognitive abilities, and a negative view of the self in another dimension, such as physical abilities. Children also learn that some abilities are more valued than others in the various environments in which they operate. For example, in individualistic-oriented societies, self-reliance, independence, autonomy, and distinctiveness are valued whereas interdependence and harmony are valued in most collectivistic-oriented societies. Self-esteem is based on different values in these different types of cultures (Brown, 2003). Every culture probably includes both individualistic and collectivistic beliefs (Turiel, 2004), but the balance of these two belief systems varies greatly from culture to culture. An example of the way these beliefs play out and influence self-development from an early age was described by Markus and Kitayama (2003), who noted that in U.S. coverage of the Olympics, athletes are typically asked about how they personally feel about their efforts and their success. In contrast, in Japanese coverage, athletes are typically asked "Who helped you achieve?" This idea of an interdependent self is consistent with cultural relational theory as well as feminist and Afro-centric perspectives on relationships.

Recently, cognitive neuroscientists have been exploring the ways the brain gives rise to development of a sense of self. They have found that a right fronto-parietal network, which overlaps with mirror neurons, is activated during tasks involving self-recognition and discrimination between the self and the other (Kaplan, Aziz-Zadeh, Uddin, & Iacoboni, 2008). Viewing one's own face leads to greater signal changes in the inferior frontal gyrus (IFG), the inferior occipital gyrus, and the inferior parietal lobe. In addition, there is greater signal change in the right IFG when hearing one's own voice compared with hearing a friend's voice (Kaplan et al., 2008). Beginning evidence also indicates that the cortical midline structures (CMS) of the brain are involved in self-evaluation and in understanding of others' emotional states. In addition, there is beginning evidence of at least one pathway that connects the mirror neurons and the CMS, allowing for integration of self and other understanding (Uddin, Iacoboni, Lange, & Keenan, 2007).

Gender Role Development

During early childhood, gender becomes an important dimension of how children understand themselves and others. Researchers have suggested four components to gender identity during early childhood:

1. *Making correct use of the gender label.* By age 2, children can usually accurately identify others as either male or female, based on appearance.

2. *Understanding gender as stable.* Later, children understand that gender is stable, that boys grow up to be men and girls to be women.

3. *Understanding gender constancy.* Even with this understanding of gender stability, young children, with their imaginative thinking, continue to think that girls can turn into boys and boys into girls by changing appearance. For example, a 3-year-old given a picture of a girl is able to identify the person as a girl. But if the same girl is shown in another picture dressed as a boy, the 3-year-old will label the girl a boy. It is not until sometime from ages 4 to 7 that children understand *gender constancy*, the understanding that one's gender does not change, that the girl dressed as a boy is still a girl.

4. *Understanding the genital basis of gender.* Gender constancy has been found to be associated with an understanding of the relationship between gender and genitals.

Before going further, it is important to differentiate among five concepts: sex, gender, gender identity, gender expression, and sexual orientation. *Sex* refers to biologically linked distinctions determined by chromosomal information. An infant's external genitalia are usually used as the determinant of sex. In most humans, chromosomes, hormones, and genitalia are consistent, and determining sex is considered unambiguous. However, this is not always the case. Chromosomal, genetic, anatomical, and hormonal aspects of sex are sometimes not aligned. *Gender* includes the cognitive, emotional, and social schemes associated with being female or male. *Gender identity* refers to one's sense of being male or female, a topic that receives more attention in the chapter on adolescence. *Gender expression* is the physical and behavioral display of one's gender identity. *Sexual orientation* refers to one's preference for sexually intimate partners. It appears that gender identity development begins with recognition of sex differences.

Reviews of thousands of research studies find few differences between boys and girls (Leaper, 2013; Martin & Ruble, 2010). The largest difference is in aggression. During early childhood, boys tend to exhibit more physical and verbal aggression than girls, and girls show more relational aggression than boys (Ostrove & Godleski, 2010). Young girls also show more empathy, compliance, and cooperation with adults than young boys. Although there are no gender differences in intelligence tests, young girls have better verbal, mathematical, and fine motor skills than young boys, and young boys tend to be better at tasks requiring spatial abilities (Ardila, Rosselli, Matute, & Inozemtseva, 2011; Miller

& Halpern, 2014). These differences appear as early as toddlerhood (Leaper, 2013). However, the gender differences are not large, and there is more variability within sex groups than between boys and girls.

In terms of the debate about the causes of gender differences, there are two competing perspectives: the biological determination perspective and the socially constructed perspective. There is some evidence to support each of these perspectives, suggesting, not surprisingly, that behavior is multiply determined. In terms of verbal ability, there is some evidence that females use both hemispheres of the brain for solving verbal problems whereas males use mostly the left hemisphere, but the findings in this regard are not consistent. Relatively strong evidence indicates that estrogen probably does contribute to women's verbal advantage. Men who take estrogen in their transsexual treatments to become female score higher on verbal learning than men who do not take estrogen as part of their transsexual transformation. Testosterone appears to play a role in spatial ability. Males who produce low levels of testosterone during the developmental years have less well-developed spatial ability; in addition, testosterone replacement therapy in older men improves their spatial functioning. Interestingly, there is only a small sex difference in aggression when behavior is studied in the laboratory but a very large difference outside the laboratory. That is not convincing evidence that biology is the only basis for the gender differences in aggression (Garrett, 2009).

In terms of the socially constructed perspective, we know that human societies use gender as an important category for organizing social life. There are some rather large cultural and subcultural variations in gender role definitions, however. Existing cultural standards about gender are pervasively built into adult interactions with young children and into the reward systems developed for shaping child behavior. Much research indicates that parents begin to use gender stereotypes to respond to their children from the time of birth (Gardiner, 2018). They cuddle more with infant girls and play more actively with infant boys. Later, they talk more with young girls and expect young boys to be more independent. Researchers have found that the nature of parental influence on children's gender role development is more complex than this. Parents may hold to stereotypical gender expectations in some domains but not in others. For example, parents may have similar expectations for boys and girls in terms of sharing or being polite (McHale, Crouter, & Whiteman, 2003). (Note: Unless otherwise specified by researchers, we have used the language of "gender difference" rather than "sex difference" because research indicates that these differences are both biologically and socially constructed.)

Evidence that gender differences in verbal, visual, and mathematical skills are at least partially socially constructed can be found in data that indicate that differences in all three areas have decreased over the same time period that gender roles have changed toward greater similarity. The dramatic difference in aggression across societies suggests a strong cultural influence on it (Garrett, 2009).

Once toddlers understand their gender, they begin to imitate and identify with the same-sex parent, if he or she is available. Once young children begin to understand gender role standards, they become quite rigid in their playing out of gender roles—only girls cook, only men drive trucks, only girls wear pink flowers, only boys wear shirts with footballs. This gender understanding also accounts for the preference of same-sex playmates and sex-typed toys (Davies, 2011). As they learn about sex and gender, young children tend to describe their own sex in positive terms and the other sex in less positive terms. Remember, though, that the exaggeration of gender stereotypes in early childhood is in keeping with the struggle during this period to discover stability and regularity in the environment—a type of overregularization that is a part of cognitive development in early childhood.

Even though the cognitive, emotional, behavioral, and social differences between young boys and girls are small—and the variation within sex groups is larger than the variation between boys and girls—stereotypes about appropriate gender roles pervade society, and young children are responsive to those stereotypes. Children learn **gender typing**—expectations about people's behavior based on their biological sex—in their interactions with adults, from the media, and with peers. Researchers have found high rigidity in gender-typed behaviors in early childhood across ethnic groups in the United States, with most gender-typed behaviors increasing from ages 3 to 4 (Halim, Ruble, Tamis-LeMonda, Lurye, & Greulich, 2014). In some countries, including the United States, gender norms are becoming less rigid, and some young children resist the gender binary they encounter as they grow. Researchers are studying how parents can help gender nonconforming young children negotiate that binary in a supportive way (see Rahilly, 2015). One research team found that young daughters of same-sex couples report more flexible gender attitudes than daughters of heterosexual couples, but no differences were found between the sons of same-sex couples and the sons of heterosexual couples. Lesbian mothers reported more flexible attitudes about gender roles than either gay fathers or heterosexual fathers. Parental division of childcare labor was a better predictor of children's gender typing than the parents' gender attitudes (Sumontha, Farr, & Patterson, 2017). Another research team found that gender typing in early childhood predicted sexual orientation at age 15, with gender nonconforming young children more likely to report a less exclusive heterosexual orientation in adolescence (Li, Kung, & Hines, 2017). Gender identity, gender expression, and sexual orientation are explored in subsequent chapters in this book. Social workers can be helpful to gender nonconforming children and their families as they negotiate societal gender and sexual orientation binaries.

As young children become more interested in issues of sex and gender, they become increasingly interested in their genitals. They are interested, in general, in how their bodies work, but the genitals seem to hold a special interest as the young child learns through experimentation that the genitals can be a source of pleasure. From ages 3 to 5, children may have some worries and questions about genital difference; little girls may think they once had a penis and wonder what happened to it. Little boys may fear that their penises will disappear, like their sister's did. During early childhood, masturbation is used both as a method of self-soothing and for pleasure. Young children also "play doctor" with each other and often want to see and touch their parents' genitals. Many parents and other caregivers are confused about how to handle this behavior, particularly in our era of heightened awareness of childhood sexual abuse. In general, parents should not worry about genital curiosity or about children experimenting with touching their own genitals. They should remember, however, that at this age children may be overstimulated by seeing their parents' genitals. And we should always be concerned when children want to engage in more explicit adultlike sexual play that involves stimulation of each other's genitals (Davies, 2011; Newman & Newman, 2015).

Racial and Ethnic Identity

Cognitive theory suggests that constructing a sense of self involves multiple identities. For young children of racial and ethnic minority groups, racial and ethnic identity is typically a particularly salient part of identity development (Hudley & Irving, 2012). Findings from research suggest that children first learn their own racial identity before they are able to identify the race of others (Kowalski, 2003). Elements of racial and ethnic identity awareness have been found to occur as early as age 3. Most children begin to self-identify as a member

PHOTO 4.2 Play is one of the few elements in the development of children that is universal—regardless of culture.

Getty/Robert Griffin

of a racial group by ages 3 to 4, but identification with an ethnic group does not usually occur until later in childhood, from 5 to 8 years of age (Blackmon & Vera, 2008). Early identification of others by race is limited to skin color, which is more easily recognized than ethnic origin. Young children may label a Latino/Latina individual, for example, as either non-White or White, depending on the individual's skin color. Young children also show a preference for members of their own race over another, but they do not reject others based on race (Brewer, 1999). Perhaps this choice is similar to the preference for same-sex playmates, a result of young children attempting to learn their own identity.

Social scientists concerned about the development of self-esteem in children of color have investigated racial bias and preference using children in early childhood as research participants. The most famous of these studies was conducted by Kenneth Clark and Mamie Clark in 1939. They presented African American children with Black dolls and White dolls and concluded that African American children responded more favorably to the White dolls and had more negative reactions to the Black dolls. A similar study 40 years later, observing young Black children in Trinidad and African American children in New York, reported similar results (Gopaul-McNicol, 1988). The young children from both New York and Trinidad preferred and identified with the White dolls. Interestingly, the same results have been reported more recently in studies of Taiwanese young children (Chang, 2001). Most of the Taiwanese children in the study indicated a preference for the White dolls and demonstrated a "pro-white attitude." Another more recent study found that African American children growing up in a mainly European American community tend to choose White images or dolls, but those growing up in a predominantly African American community tend to choose Black images or dolls (Cameron, Alvarez, Ruble, & Fuligni, 2001). Furthermore, when young children were not asked to make a preference between images, they showed interest in Asian, White, and Black images or dolls and did not make judgments based on race or ethnicity (Kowalski, 2003).

It is questionable, however, whether preferences and biases found in research are equated with self-concept and low self-esteem for children of color. Most argue that they are not. For example, racial bias and self-concept were not related among the young Taiwanese children (Chang, 2001). Likewise, findings from studies about young African American children indicate high levels of self-concept despite the children's bias in favor of the White culture and values (Crain, 1996; Spencer, 1984). Spencer concludes that young Black children compartmentalize personal identity (self-concept) from knowledge about racial stereotypes in the dominant culture.

CRITICAL THINKING QUESTIONS 4.2

What types of children's literature might be particularly useful to help Terri Smith, Jack Lewis, and Ron and Rosiland Johnson in their emotional development? What types of stories would you look for if you were to work with these children? How concerned should we be about Terri Smith's tantrums? Do you think her emotional development is getting off course? What challenges might each of these children face in developing self-esteem? How might a social worker help each of these children to develop a positive self-evaluation?

© Kelly Redinger/ Design Pics/ Corbis

PHOTO 4.3 During early childhood, children engage in cooperative play and enjoy sharing and competing with peers.

The Role of Play

The young child loves to play, and play is essential to all aspects of early child development. We think of the play of young children as fun-filled and lively. And yet it serves a serious purpose. Through play, children develop the motor skills essential for physical development, learn the problem-solving skills and communication skills fundamental to cognitive development, express the feelings and gain the self-confidence needed for emotional growth, and learn to cooperate and resolve social conflicts. Essentially, play is what young children are all about; it is their work.

As children develop in all areas during early childhood, their play activities and preferences for play materials change over time. Hughes (2010) makes the following recommendations about the preferred play materials at different ages during early childhood:

- *Three-year-olds:* props for imaginative play, such as dress-up clothes, doctor kits, and makeup; miniature toys that represent adult models, such as toy trucks, gas stations, dolls, doll houses, and airplanes; art materials, such as paint brushes, easels, marker pens, and crayons

- *Four-year-olds:* vehicles, such as tricycles and wagons; play materials to develop fine motor skills, such as materials for sewing, stringing beads, coloring, painting, and drawing; books that involve adventure

- *Five-year-olds:* play materials to develop precision in fine motor skills, such as coloring books, paints and brushes, crayons, marker pens, glue, scissors, stencils, sequins and glitter, clay, and Play-Doh; play materials that develop cognitive skills, such as workbenches, play cards, table games, and board games

In recent years, there has been a dramatic increase in the availability of computers and other instructional technology. These technologies have made their way into early childhood education programs, but there is controversy among early childhood educators about the positive and negative aspects of these technologies for early childhood development. There is evidence of benefits of instructional technologies in the preschool classroom. For example, 4- and 5-year-old children can use technology to develop language, art, mathematics, and science skills. Conversely, some early childhood educators are concerned that computers and other instructional technologies contribute to social isolation and limit children's creative play (Hughes, 2010). Adults must give serious consideration to how to balance the positive and negative aspects of these technologies.

Parental decision making about the early childhood use of electronic equipment—cell phones, gaming systems, and computers—is now a critical part of parenting. What equipment, at what age, involving what content, with what peers, and with how much supervision are some of the questions parents ponder. Other questions that challenge parents are where the equipment is stored and who is responsible for monitoring the amount of time a child spends with technology. A good deal of research has focused on the negative aspects of electronic use in early childhood, but Olson (2010) argues that the potential for positive learning exists in such areas as gender roles and managing aggressive impulses as well as in building relationships with parents and peers.

The predominant type of play in early childhood, beginning around the age of 2, is **symbolic play**, otherwise known as fantasy play, pretend play, or imaginary play (Hughes, 2010). Children continue to use vivid imaginations in their play, as they did as toddlers, but they also begin to put more structure into their play. Thus, their play is intermediate between the fantasy play of toddlers and the structured, rules-oriented play of middle childhood. Although toddler play is primarily nonverbal, the play of young children often involves highly sophisticated verbal productions. There is some indication that this preference for symbolic play during early childhood exists across cultures, but the themes of the play reflect the culture in which it is enacted (Roopnarine, Shin, Donovan, & Suppal, 2000).

Symbolic play during early childhood has six primary functions: providing an opportunity to explore reality, contributing to cognitive development, practicing for morality, allowing young children to gain control over their lives, serving as a shared experience and opportunity for development of peer culture, and as the route to attachment to fathers. These functions are now explained in more detail.

Play as an Opportunity to Explore Reality

Young children imitate adult behavior and try out social roles in their play (Davies, 2011; Hughes, 2010). They play house, school, doctor, police, firefighter, and so on. As they "dress up" in various guises of adult roles, or even as spiders and rabbits, they are using fantasy to explore what they might become. Their riding toys allow them to play with the experience of having greater mobility in the world.

Play's Contribution to Cognitive Development

The young child uses play to think about the world, to understand cause and effect (Roskos & Christie, 2000). Throughout early childhood, young children show increasing sophistication in using words in their dramatic play. Some researchers have asked this question: Does symbolic play facilitate cognitive development, or does symbolic play require mature cognitive abilities? The question is unresolved; the available evidence indicates only that cognitive development is connected with play in early childhood (Roopnarine et al., 2000). Childhood sociologists have found that children create sophisticated language games for group play that facilitate the development of language and logical thinking (Corsaro, 2018). A number of researchers have studied how young children build literacy skills through play, particularly play with books (Roskos & Christie, 2000). Play focused on language and thinking skills has been described as **learning play** (Meek, 2000).

Play as Practice for Morality

In their fantasy play, young children begin to think about "good" and "bad" behavior and to try out roles of superheroes and "bad guys." They can discharge aggressive impulses in the relative safety of pretend play (Davies, 2011). As they try to figure out good and bad, they can easily have their feelings hurt if they think another child is accusing them of being bad as they engage in play.

Play as an Opportunity to Gain Control

In his cross-cultural study of play, childhood sociologist William Corsaro (2018) demonstrates that young

PHOTO 4.4 Young children use play to think about the world and to understand cause and effect.

© Erna Vader/iStockphoto.com

children typically use dramatic play to cope with fears. They incorporate their fears into their group play and thus develop some mastery over stress and anxiety. This perspective on young children's play is the cornerstone of play therapy (Chethik, 2000). Anyone who has spent much time in a childcare center has probably seen a group of 4-year-olds engaged in superhero play, their flowing capes improvised with towels pinned on their shirts. Such play helps the child compensate for feelings of inadequacy and fear that come from recognizing that one is a small person in a big world (Davies, 2011). Corsaro (2018) suggests that the love for climbing toys that bring small children high over the heads of others serves the same purpose.

Children in preschool settings have also been observed trying to get control over their lives by subverting some of the control of adults. Corsaro (2018) describes a preschool where the children had been told they could not bring any play items from home. The preschool teachers were trying to avoid the kinds of conflicts that can occur over toys brought from home. The children in this preschool found a way to subvert this rule, however; they began to bring in very small toys, such as matchbox cars, that would fit in their pockets out of sight when teachers were nearby. Corsaro provides a number of other examples from his cross-cultural research of ways that young children use play to take some control of their lives away from adults.

Play as a Shared Experience

Increasing emphasis is placed on the way that play in early childhood contributes to the development of peer culture. Many researchers who study the play of young children suggest that **sociodramatic play**, or group fantasy play in which children coordinate their fantasy, is the most important form of play during this time. Young children are able to develop more elaborate fantasy play and sustain it by forming friendship groups, which in turn gives them experience with group conflict and group problem solving that carries over into the adult world (Corsaro, 2018). Group play also helps young children learn to understand and follow rules.

As young children play in groups, they attempt to protect the opportunity to keep the play going by restricting who may enter the play field (Corsaro, 2018). Young children can often be heard making such comments as, "We're friends; we're playing, right?" Or perhaps, "You're not our friend; you can't play with us." The other side of the coin is that young children must learn how to gain access to play in progress (Garvey, 1984). An important social skill is being able

to demonstrate that they can play without messing the game up. Young children learn a set of do's and don'ts to accomplish that goal (see Exhibit 4.3) and develop complex strategies for gaining access to play.

Conflict often occurs in young children's play groups, and researchers have found gender and cultural variations in how these conflicts get resolved. Young girls have been found to prefer dyadic (two-person) play interactions, and young boys enjoy larger groups (Benenson, 1993). These preferences may not hold across cultures, however. For example, White middle-class young girls in the United States are less direct and assertive in challenging each other in play situations than either African American girls in the United States or young girls in an Italian preschool (Corsaro, 2018). Greater assertiveness may allow for more comfortable play in larger groups.

Play as the Route to Attachment to Fathers

Most of the efforts to understand attachment focus on the link between mothers and children and the effect of the maternal relationship. More recently, though, there has been growing concern about and interest in the importance of fathers in the development of attachment for young children. Some suggest that father–child attachment may be promoted mainly through

EXHIBIT 4.3 ● Do's and Don'ts of Getting Access to Play in Progress
Do's
Watch what's going on
Figure out the play theme
Enter the area
Plug into the action
Hold off on making suggestions about how to change the action
Don'ts
Ask questions for information (if you can't tell what's going on, you'll mess it up)
Mention yourself or your reactions to what is going on
Disagree or criticize what is happening

Source: Based on Garvey, 1984.

play, much like the mother–child relationship may be the result of caregiving activities (Laflamme, Pomerleau, & Malcuit, 2002; Roggman, 2004). Differences in play style noted for mothers versus that seen in fathers is of particular interest. Investigators conclude that more physical play is seen between fathers and young children compared with more object play and conventional play interaction between mothers and children (Goldberg, Clarke-Stewart, Rice, & Dellis, 2002). Both forms of play can involve the display of affection by the parent. Thus, both forms of play contribute to the development of parent–child attachment. This research challenges the notion that only certain kinds of play have the potential to effect positive attachment and affirms the notion that there is developmental value for children in father–child physical play. In fact, physical play stimulates and arouses children and takes them out of their comfort zone. Roggman (2004) further notes that the style of play often ascribed to fathers provides opportunity for young children to overcome their limits and to experience taking chances in a context where there is some degree of confidence that they will be protected.

One research team studied the activities of African American, White, and Latino fathers with their sons and daughters in early childhood (Leavell, Tamis-LeMonda, Ruble, Zosuls, & Cabrera, 2012). They found that all three groups of fathers engaged in more physical play with their sons than with their daughters. They also engaged in more learning play with their daughters. The Black fathers reported the highest levels of play activities with their young children.

Developmental Delays and Disabilities

Children develop at different rates. Most developmental problems in infants and young children are more accurately described as developmental delays, offering the hope that early intervention, or even natural processes, will mitigate the long-term effects. Developmental delays may exist in cognitive skills, communication skills, social skills, emotion regulation, behavior, and fine and gross motor skills. Children with developmental disabilities have long-term physical, mental, intellectual, or sensory impairments that, in interaction with environmental barriers, may hinder their full and effective participation in society. Disability is neither purely biological nor social but "the interaction between health conditions and environmental and personal factors" (World Health Organization & UNICEF, 2012, p. 7). Available data indicate an increasing prevalence

of disability in early childhood. Although the exact reasons for this increase are not clear, it is thought to be related to improved survival of children with disabilities and improved identification of impairments in early childhood (Parish et al., 2016).

Global initiatives for disability-inclusive early childhood development programs recommend integrated and multidisciplinary interventions at three levels: *primary prevention* to reduce the incidence of developmental disabilities caused by diverse biological and environmental risk factors such as malnutrition and poverty; *secondary prevention* through early detection; and *tertiary prevention* through comprehensive community-based programs (Olusanya, Krishnamurthy, & Wertlieb, 2018). Many young children with developmental difficulties, including emotional and behavioral concerns, are inaccurately assessed and misdiagnosed. The American Academy of Pediatrics encourages rigorous screening for developmental delays and other developmental difficulties during well-child checkups, including the use of standardized assessment tools (see https://brightfutures.aap.org/Bright%20Futures%20Documents/MSRTable_ECVisits_BF4.pdf). Given the difficulty of accurate assessment, assessment in young children should include many disciplines to gain as broad an understanding as possible (Parish et al., 2016). Assessment and service delivery should also be culturally relevant. In other words, culture and other related issues—such as family interaction patterns and stress, the social environment, ethnicity, acculturation, social influences, and developmental expectations—should all be considered when evaluating a child's developmental abilities.

For those children who have been labeled developmentally delayed, the main remedy has been social skill development. In one such program, two types of preschool classrooms were evaluated (Roberts, Burchinal, & Bailey, 1994). In one classroom, young developmentally delayed children were matched with nondelayed children of the same age; in another classroom, some of the nondelayed children were the same age as the developmentally delayed children and some were older. Social exchange between the children with delays and those without delays was greater in the mixed-aged classroom. Another study evaluated the usefulness of providing social skills training to children with mild developmental disabilities (Lewis, 1994). In a preschool setting, developmentally delayed children were put in situations requiring social interaction and were praised for successful interaction. This method increased social interaction between the young children.

It is important to recognize the parental stress that often accompanies care of children with developmental disabilities. The time of diagnosis is often experienced as a crisis for the parents of children with disabilities and may be followed by a period of grief. Coming to terms with the diagnosis and associated grief can help parents to develop sensitive caregiving and healthy attachment and even transform their understanding of human variation (Bhopti, 2017; Pelchat, Levert, & Bourgeois-Guérin, 2009). Social workers who assist parents with this process must be familiar with the different types of stressors faced by these parents, most notably financial stress. The need to provide intensive care for young children with disabilities often means that at least one parent must reduce or curtail paid work roles. One research team found that 51% of U.S. caregivers of children with either autism spectrum disorder (ASD) or intellectual disability had to either cease working or reduce work hours (Saunders et al., 2015). In addition to the loss of occupational income, families of young children with disabilities often have expenses related to adaptations to the home environment, assistive devices, and different therapy and personal assistance services (Parish et al., 2016). Nonfamily provided childcare is more expensive than for young children without disability. In addition to financial stress, parents of young children with disabilities often face the stress of intensive around-the-clock caregiving and the social isolation that accompanies such intensive caregiving. Parents may have to be strong advocates for their children to be included in early childhood education programs.

In the 1980s, concern about the quality of education in the United States led to upgrades in the elementary school curriculum. Many skills previously introduced in the first grade became part of the kindergarten curriculum. This has led to increased concern about kindergarten readiness, the skills that the young child should have acquired before entering kindergarten, as well as how to provide for the needs of developmentally delayed children in the kindergarten classroom. It has also led to controversies about when to begin to think of developmental delays as disabilities. A growing concern is that children with developmental problems should not be placed in kindergarten classrooms that do not provide support for their particular developmental needs (Litty & Hatch, 2006). States vary in how much support they provide to children with developmental delays to allow them to participate in fully inclusive classrooms (classrooms where they are mainstreamed with children without developmental delays), but a growing group of children with developmental delays in the United States are participating as full citizens in inclusive classrooms

during preschool and kindergarten (Guralnick, Neville, Hammond, & Connor, 2008). Before leaving this discussion, we would like to emphasize one important point. When working with young children, we want to recognize and respect the variability of developmental trajectories. At the same time, however, we want to be attentive to any aspects of a child's development that may be lagging expected milestones so that we can provide extra support to young children in specific areas of development (Spinrad et al., 2007).

CRITICAL THINKING QUESTIONS 4.3

How can play be used to help Terri Smith, Jack Lewis, and Ron and Rosiland Johnson in their multidimensional development? What do you see as particular needs each of them has that could be at least partially addressed with play?

EARLY CHILDHOOD EDUCATION

It is a relatively new idea to provide formalized education for young children, but three strands of research indicate the importance of formal education to support social awareness, group interaction skills, and cognitive development during early childhood to prepare children to live in contemporary knowledge-driven economies. First, neuroscientific research indicates the critical importance of brain development in the early years. Second, social science research indicates that high-quality early childhood education programs improve readiness for primary school. And third, econometric research indicates that high-quality early childhood education programs save societies significant amounts of money over time (Economist Intelligence Unit, 2012). Early childhood education has been found to be especially important for children from low-income households in highly unequal societies who are likely to enter primary school far behind their peers and experience an achievement gap throughout their schooling years (Heckman, 2006, 2008). Despite mounting evidence that greater investment in early childhood education reduces costs at later stages of education, most societies continue to prioritize tertiary, secondary, and primary education over early childhood education (Economist Intelligence Unit, 2012).

Rates of enrollment in early childhood education vary across the world, and program quality varies as well. In 2011, 64% of U.S. 3- to 4-year-olds were involved in formal education compared to over 90% of the same-age children in France, Germany, Italy, and the United Kingdom (Stephens, Warren, Harner, & Owen, 2015). With increasing concern about the need for early childhood learning, the Lien Foundation of Singapore commissioned the Economist Intelligence Unit (EIU) to study "preschool education" (which we are calling early childhood education) on a global scale. The EIU (2012) developed the Starting Well Index to rank early childhood education in 45 countries on four indicators: social context, availability, affordability, and quality. The United States, tied with the United Arab Emirates for an overall rank of 24th among the 45 countries, was ranked 28th for social context, 31st for availability, 16th for affordability, and 22nd for quality. The countries with the top five overall rankings were Finland, Sweden, Norway, the United Kingdom, and Belgium, all countries that put high value on state-supported early childhood education.

Much evidence indicates that low-income and racial minority students in the United States have less access to quality early childhood education than their age peers (Ravitch, 2013). In the past few years, access, spending, and support for state-funded prekindergarten (pre-K) programs has been growing slowly in the United States, but the progress is mixed with some states moving boldly and others regressing. In 2015–2016, three states plus the District of Columbia served more than 70% of 4-year-olds in state-funded pre-K programs, and 18 states plus the District of Columbia served more than 30% of 4-year-olds. At the same time, seven states offered no pre-K programs (Barnett et al., 2017). President Donald Trump's fiscal year 2018 budget included an $85 million cut for Head Start, the federally funded program that provides early childhood education for impoverished children. This eliminated progress made in 2017 in supporting Head Start educators, pediatric nurses, learning specialists, and childcare workers and disrupted efforts to implement new performance standards (National Head Start Association, 2017). Wealthy families compete for slots for their young children in expensive preschool programs, called the "baby ivies," that provide highly enriched early learning environments, further advancing opportunities for children in privileged families (Kozol, 2005).

Longitudinal research consistently shows the long-term benefits of quality early childhood education programs for children from impoverished families. One longitudinal study followed a group of children who attended the High/Scope Perry Preschool Program in Ypsilanti, Michigan, until they reached age 40 (Schweinhart et al., 2005). From 1962 to 1967, the researchers identified a sample of 123 low-income African

American children who had been assessed to be at high risk of school failure. They randomly assigned 58 of these children to attend a high-quality 2-year preschool program for 2- and 3-year-olds, while the other 65 attended no preschool program. The program met for 2½ hours per day, 5 days a week, and teachers made home visits every 2 weeks. The teachers in the preschool program had bachelor's degrees and education certification. No more than eight children were assigned to a teacher, and the curriculum emphasized giving children the opportunity to plan and carry out their own activities. By age 40, the preschool participants, on average, were doing better than the nonparticipants in several important ways:

- They were more likely to have graduated from high school (65% vs. 45%).
- They were more likely to be employed (76% vs. 62%).
- They had higher median annual earnings ($20,800 vs. $15,300).
- They were more likely to own their own home (37% vs. 28%).
- They were more likely to have a savings account (76% vs. 50%).
- They had fewer lifetime arrests (36% vs. 55% arrested five or more times).
- They were less likely to have spent time in prison or jail (28% vs. 52% never sentenced).

The researchers report that the preschool program cost $15,166 per child and the public gained $12.90 for every dollar spent on the program by the time the participants were 40 years old. The savings came from reduced special education costs, increased taxes derived from higher earnings, reduced public assistance costs, and reduced costs to the criminal justice system. Nobel Prize–winning economist James Heckman and colleagues (Heckman et al., 2010) have reanalyzed the data to rule out alternative assumptions and concluded that the estimated rates of social return fall by 7% to 10%. More recently, economist Lynn Karoly (2016) estimated that because of the rarity of such preschool programs at the time of the intervention, the benefit was probably as high as $17 for every dollar invested, a net benefit that exceeds $300,000 per child. She estimates that in today's context, with a majority of children attending formal preschool, a more realistic return is in the range of $3 to $4 for every dollar spent, still a good return on a public expenditure.

 Another longitudinal study began in North Carolina in 1972, when 112 low-income infants were randomly assigned to either a quality preschool program or no program (Masse & Barnett, 2002). The group assigned to the preschool program was enrolled in the program for 5 years instead of the 2 years in the High/Scope Perry study. The participants in this study were followed to the age of 21. The children who participated in the preschool program were less likely to repeat grades, less likely to be placed in special education classes, and more likely to complete high school. It is important to note that the researchers in this study also investigated the impact of the preschool program on the mothers. They found that the preschool program mothers earned $3,750 more per year than the mothers whose children did not attend the program, for a total of $78,750 more over 21 years.

These two longitudinal studies investigated the impact of quality preschool education on low-income children, but there is also preliminary evidence of the benefit of early childhood education on all children. A study conducted at Georgetown University has examined the effect of pre-K programs in Tulsa, Oklahoma. These programs are considered high quality because teachers are required to have a bachelor's degree, there are no more than 10 children per teacher, and teachers are paid on the same scale as public school teachers. The researchers found that children who attended pre-K scored better on letter-word identification, spelling, and applied problems than children of the same age who had not attended pre-K. This was true regardless of race or socioeconomic status. Karoly (2016) estimates net benefits of the Tulsa pre-K program to be in the range of $10,000 to $16,000 per student. Results from other research indicate that public funding of early childhood education can help close the gap in preschool education between low-income and higher-income children (Greenberg, 2010).

Perhaps the most promising finding about the benefits of early childhood education programs for impoverished families comes from a recent reanalysis of the long-term benefits for the first participants of the Head Start program. Barr and Gibbs (2017) found that the benefits from Head Start participation did not accrue just to the participating generation but were also associated with improved long-term outcomes for the second generation—the children of the Head Start participants. The second generation had decreased teen parenthood and criminal engagement and increased educational attainment, and the effects were large in magnitude, as large as demonstrated by the participating generation.

These studies suggest that early childhood education programs are good for children, families, communities, and society. With such evidence in hand, social workers can join with other child advocates to build broad coalitions to educate the public about the multilevel benefits and to push for public policy that guarantees universal quality early childhood education.

EARLY CHILDHOOD IN THE MULTIGENERATIONAL FAMILY

Curiosity and experimentation are the hallmarks of early childhood. Young children are sponges, soaking up information about themselves, their worlds, and their relationships. They use their families as primary sources of information and as models for relationships. Where there are older siblings, they serve as important figures of identification and imitation. Aunts, uncles, cousins, and grandparents may also serve this role, but parents are, in most families, the most important sources of information, support, and modeling for young children.

Parents play two very important roles for their 3- to 6-year-old child: educator and advocate (Newman & Newman, 2015). As educators, they answer children's big and little questions, ask questions to stimulate thinking and growth in communication skills, provide explanations, and help children figure things out. They teach children about morality and human connectedness by modeling honest, kind, thoughtful behavior and by reading to their children about moral dilemmas and moral action. They help children develop emotional intelligence by modeling how to handle strong feelings and by talking with children about the children's strong feelings. They take young children on excursions in their physical worlds as well as in the fantasy worlds found in books. They give children opportunities to perform tasks that develop a sense of mastery.

Not all parents have the same resources for the educator role or the same beliefs about how children learn. And some parents take their role as educators too seriously, pushing their young children into more and more structured time with higher and higher expectations of performance. Many of these parents are pushing their own frustrated dreams onto their young children. The concern is that these children are deprived of time for exploration, experimentation, and fantasy.

In the contemporary era, children are moving into organized childcare settings at earlier ages. As they do so, parents become more important as advocates who understand their children's needs. The advocate role is particularly important for parents of young children with disabilities. These parents may need to advocate to ensure that all aspects of early childhood education programs are accessible to their children.

For some children, like Ron and Rosiland Johnson, it is the grandparent and not the parent who serves as the central figure. Estimates are that in 2011, 7.7 million children were living with a grandparent or other relative, with 3 million of these children being cared for primarily by that grandparent. These numbers rose rapidly after the recession of 2008. In 80% of the cases where children live with a grandparent, at least one of the child's parents is also living in the household. Many of the parents in these households need assistance: 44% had a baby as a teen, 12% have a disability, 21% are unemployed, and 29% have less than a high school education (Livingston, 2013). Some custodial grandparents describe an increased purpose for living, but others describe increased isolation, worry, physical and emotional exhaustion, and financial concerns (Clarke, 2008). These are some of the same concerns expressed by Ms. Johnson. In addition, grandparents caring for children with psychological and physical problems experience high levels of stress (Sands & Goldberg, 2000).

The literature indicates that young children often do better under the care of grandparents than in other types of homes. However, children like Ron and Rosiland, who are parented by their grandparents, must often overcome many difficult emotions. These children struggle with issues of grief and loss related to loss of their parent(s) and feelings of guilt, fear, embarrassment, and anger. These feelings may be especially strong for young children who feel they are somehow responsible for the loss of their parent(s). Although children in this age group are capable of labeling their feelings, their ability to discuss these feelings with any amount of depth is very limited. In addition, grandparents may feel unsure about how to talk about the situation with their young grandchildren. Professional intervention for the children is often recommended. Some mental health practitioners have had success providing group sessions that help grandparents gain control over their grandchildren's behavior, resolve clashes in values between themselves and their grandchildren, and help grandparents avoid overindulgence and set firm limits.

Grandparents are often important figures in the lives of young children even when they do not serve as primary caregivers; they provide practical, financial, and emotional support. They may offer different types of practical support, coming to the aid of the family when needs arise. Or they may serve as the childcare provider while parents work or provide babysitting services in the evening. They also provide financial support, depending on their financial circumstances. They may provide cash assistance or buy things such as clothes and toys for the children; it is distressing to some grandparents if they lack the financial resources to buy things

for their grandchildren. Grandparents may also provide emotional support and advice to parents of young children; this is something that can be done at a distance by a variety of electronic technologies when grandparents live at some distance from the children (Clarke, 2008). Research indicates that grandmother involvement during early childhood can be a protective factor for socioemotional development but does not protect children from the impact of low household income (Barnett, Scaramella, Neppi, Ontai, & Conger, 2010).

Noting that one quarter of young children in the United States and United Kingdom receive informal care from grandparents, one research team raised the question of agreements and disagreements between a sample of parents and grandparents about feeding and physical activity in young children (Eli, Howell, Fisher, & Nowicka, 2016). They found the following areas of agreement and disagreement:

- Parents and grandparents generally agreed on which foods were healthy, but grandparents were more likely to provide foods such as sugar, candy, soda, and fast food to children on a regular basis.

- Both parents and grandparents saw "indulgent" feeding as part of the grandparent role.

- Grandparents saw parents as the ultimate authority over the child's diet.

- Parents and grandparents agreed that physical activity is an important part of the young child's daily activities.

- Parents and grandparents rarely discussed the young child's physical activity, largely because they perceived no disagreements on this issue.

Both parents and grandparents appear to engage in practices to promote family harmony and stability.

CRITICAL THINKING QUESTIONS 4.4

Based on the research noted earlier, what types of social policies would you like to see enacted in early childhood education? The United States has less vigorous state support for early childhood education than many other wealthy nations. What factors do you think influence the policy decisions about early childhood education in the United States and other wealthy nations? How could a social worker help Ron and Rosiland Johnson and their grandmother to thrive while Ron and Rosiland's mother is incarcerated?

RISKS TO HEALTHY DEVELOPMENT IN EARLY CHILDHOOD

This section addresses a few risk factors that social workers are likely to encounter in work with young children and their families: poverty, homelessness, ineffective discipline, divorce, and violence (including child abuse). The next section outlines protective factors that ameliorate the risks.

Poverty

As reported in Chapter 3, 1 billion children around the world live in poverty. In the United States, 5.1 million (43%) children ages 3 to 5 lived in low-income families in 2016; 2.4 million (21%) lived in poverty, and 1.1 million (9%) lived in deep poverty (Koball & Jiang, 2018). Poverty—in the form of food insecurity, inadequate health care, and overcrowded living conditions—presents considerable risks to children's growth and development. In 2014, in the United States, 15% of young children in White households lived with food insecurity, compared to 34% of children in Black, non-Hispanic households and 29% of children in Hispanic households (Center for the Study of Social Policy, 2014). A study of the Northern Cheyenne Indian reservation in southeastern Montana found that 70% of all households were food insecure (Whiting & Ward, 2008). Inadequate nutrition is a serious threat to all aspects of early childhood development. Inadequate health care means that many acute conditions become chronic. Overcrowding is problematic to young children in that it restricts opportunities for play, the means through which most development occurs.

Research indicates that young children reared in poverty are significantly delayed in language and other cognitive skills (Locke, Ginsborg, & Peers, 2002). The effects of poverty on children in early childhood appear to be long lasting, and disadvantage accumulates over time. Children who experience poverty during their early years are less likely to complete school than children whose initial exposure to poverty occurred in the middle childhood years or during adolescence. Researchers have also found that children who live in poverty are at high risk for low self-esteem, peer conflict, depression, and childhood psychological disorders. Poverty is often associated with other risk factors such as overwhelmed parents, living in a violent setting or in deteriorated housing, and instability of frequent changes in residence and schools (Bartholomae & Fox, 2010). Evidence suggests that early poverty is associated with decreased adult earnings (Duncan, Magnuson, Kalil, & Ziol-Guest, 2012).

Not all young children who live in poverty fare poorly, however. In their longitudinal study of 180 children born into poverty, Sroufe et al. (2005) report that four groups emerged by early childhood: they grouped 70 children into a very competent cluster who were high in enthusiasm, persistence, compliance, and affection for the mother. They grouped another 25 children into a very incompetent cluster characterized by high negativity and low compliance and affection. The other almost half of the children were grouped into two clusters that fell between very competent and very incompetent.

Homelessness

Families with children make up one third of the homeless population, and it is estimated that 42% of homeless families have children younger than age 6 (Kilmer, Cook, Crusto, Strater, & Haber, 2012). Homeless children are sick more often, are exposed to more violence, and experience more emotional and behavioral problems and more delayed development than low-income housed children. Families experiencing homelessness have often faced a range of risks, adversities, and problems before becoming homeless. Becoming homeless also brings a host of stressors, and the service systems themselves often unintentionally present adversities (Kilmer et al., 2012). Residential instability can disrupt learning and routines that support school engagement as well as relationships with teachers and peers (Cutuli et al., 2013).

Kristen Paquette and Ellen Bassuk (2009) note that parents' identities are often closely tied to relationships they maintain, especially with their children, and that homelessness undermines their ability to protect those they have a responsibility to protect. Like all parents, homeless parents want to provide their children with basic necessities. Being homeless presents dramatic barriers and challenges for parents, who too often lose the ability to provide essentials for their children, including shelter, food, and access to education. They must look for jobs and housing while also adhering to shelter rules. Their parenting is public, easily observed, and monitored by others. Making available family-centered supportive services, including psychoeducation focused on increasing skills parents need to navigate constraints of temporary and transitional housing experiences, and the impact of such traumatic challenges on their children, is important (Kilmer et al., 2012). Homeless parents need be involved with a meaningful social support system that links them to organizations and professionals in the community who might offer resources and options that support them to engage in effective parenting. In families staying in family emergency shelters the summer before a young child's kindergarten or first-grade year, parental support of competence and resilience was associated with the child's positive peer relationships and school performance (Herbers, Cutuli, Supkoff, Narayan, & Masten, 2014).

Ineffective Discipline

Discipline is the methods a parent uses to teach and socialize children toward acceptable behavior. Parents often struggle with how forceful to be in response to undesired behavior. The Smiths are a good example of this struggle. And, indeed, the research on parental styles of discipline finds that the question of the appropriate style of parenting young children is quite complex.

A good place to begin this discussion is with the work of Diana Baumrind (1971), who, after extensive research, described three parenting styles—authoritarian, authoritative, and permissive—that use different combinations of two factors: warmth and control (see Exhibit 4.4). The **authoritarian parenting** style uses low warmth and high control. These parents favor punishment and negative reinforcement, and children are treated as submissive. Children reared under an authoritarian parenting style have been found to be withdrawn, anxious, hostile, and moody and to have difficulty managing stress (Baumrind, Larzelere, & Owens, 2010; Gagnon et al., 2013). Baumrind considered the **authoritative parenting** style, in which parents are warm and sensitive to the child's needs but remain firm in their expectations that children follow standards of behavior, to be the most desirable approach to discipline and behavior management. Authoritative parents explain and encourage discussion about rules, and when rules are violated they explain what the child did wrong and respond with actions that are closely connected to the misdeed. The authoritative parenting style has been found to be associated with academic achievement, self-esteem, and social competence (see Domenech Rodriguez, Donovick, & Crowley, 2009; Fay-Stammbach, Hawes, & Meredith, 2014). The **permissive parenting** style is warm and accepting: self-expression is emphasized and there are few rules and expectations for the children's behavior. Baumrind suggested that many children lack the self-regulation to limit their own behavior, and research indicates that permissive parenting is associated with socioemotional immaturity and poor self-regulatory capacity. Children reared from the permissive parenting orientation tend to be impulsive, rebellious, and bossy and show low persistence in pursuing tasks (Jewell, Krohn,

Scott, Carlton, & Meinz, 2008; Piotrowski, Lapierre, & Linebarger, 2013). The Smiths' style of parenting probably fits here. Certainly, Terri Smith's behavior mirrors behavior exhibited by children reared with the permissive style. In later work, Baumrind (1991) presented a fourth parenting style, **disengaged parenting**, also known an uninvolved parenting; these parents are focused on their own needs rather than the needs of the child, aloof, and unresponsive. Baumrind's typology of parenting styles has been the building block of much theorizing and research on parenting styles and child outcomes.

Stephen Greenspan (2006) questions Baumrind's suggestion that authoritative parenting is the best parenting. He suggests that Baumrind paid too little attention to the context in which parental discipline occurs, arguing that there are times to exercise control and

EXHIBIT 4.4 ● Baumrind's Four Parenting Styles		
Parenting Style	**Description**	**Type of Discipline**
Authoritarian	Parents who use this type of parenting are rigid and controlling. Rules are narrow and specific, with little room for negotiation, and children are expected to follow the rules without explanation.	Cold and harsh Physical force No explanation of rules provided
Authoritative	These parents are more flexible than authoritarian parents. Their rules are more reasonable, and they leave opportunities for compromises and negotiation.	Warm and nurturing Positive reinforcement Set firm limits and provide rationale behind rules and decisions
Permissive	The parents' rules are unclear, and children are left to make their own decisions.	Warm and friendly toward their children No direction given
Disengaged	The parents are focused on their own needs rather than the needs of the children.	Aloof Unresponsive

Source: Adapted from Baumrind, 1971, 1991.

times to tolerate a certain level of behavioral deviance and that a wise parent knows the difference between these types of situations. Greenspan proposes that another dimension of parenting should be added to Baumrind's two dimensions of warmth and control. He calls this dimension *tolerance* and recommends a style of parenting called *harmonious*. He suggests that harmonious parents are warm and set limits when they feel they are called for, overlooking some child behaviors in the interests of facilitating child autonomy and family harmony. It seems that many parents, like Terri Smith's parents, struggle with knowing which situations call for firm control and which call for tolerating some defiance.

Parenting styles are prescribed in part by the community and culture; therefore, it is not surprising that there is growing sentiment that Baumrind's parenting typology may be a good model for understanding parenting in White, middle-class families but may not work as well for understanding parenting in other cultural groups. We examine two streams of research that have explored racial and ethnic variations in parenting styles: research on Latino families and research on African American families.

Strong support has not been found for Baumrind's parenting typology in research on Latino parenting styles. Some researchers have described Latino parenting as permissive and others have described it as authoritarian. One research team (Domenech Rodriguez et al., 2009), like Greenspan, suggests that another dimension of parenting should be added to Baumrind's two-dimension model of warmth and control. They call this dimension "autonomy granting," which they describe as allowing children autonomy of individual expression in the family. This seems to be very close to what Greenspan meant by tolerance, because he writes of tolerance of emotional expression in the spirit of autonomy. Domenech Rodriguez and colleagues (2009) suggest that these three dimensions—warmth, control, and autonomy granting—can be configured in different ways to produce the eight parenting styles found in Exhibit 4.5.

In their preliminary research, which involved direct observation of 56 first-generation Latino American families, Domenech Rodriguez et al. (2009) found that the majority (61%) used a protective parenting style but had different expectations for male and female children. There seems to be merit in adding the dimension of autonomy granting, because it may help to capture the parenting styles of cultural groups that are less individualistic than European American culture.

A relatively long line of research has questioned the appropriateness of applying Baumrind's model to understand African American parenting, and the issues

EXHIBIT 4.5 ● Three-Dimensional Model of Parenting Styles

Parenting Style	Warmth	Control	Autonomy Granting
Authoritative	High	High	High
Authoritarian	Low	High	Low
Permissive	High	Low	High
Neglectful	Low	Low	Low
Protective	High	High	Low
Cold	Low	High	High
Affiliative	High	Low	Low
Neglectful II	Low	Low	High

Source: Based on Domenech Rodriguez et al., 2009.

are proving to be complex. Much of this research has looked at the use of physical discipline, with the finding that physical discipline causes disruptive behaviors in White families but not Black families (see Lau, Litrownik, Newton, Black, & Everson, 2006, for a review of this research). Researchers have suggested that Black children may regard physical discipline as a legitimate parenting behavior because there is a culture of using physical discipline out of concern for the child: high levels of firm control are used along with high levels of warmth and affection. Conversely, it is argued that White children may regard physical discipline as an act of aggression because it is often used when parents are angry and out of control (Lansford, Deater-Deckard, Dodge, Bates, & Pettit, 2004). The idea is that the context of the physical discipline and the meaning made of it will influence its impact. However, research by Lau et al. (2006) did not replicate earlier research that found that the effects of physical discipline differed by race. They found that for both Black and White children, physical discipline exacerbated impulsive, aggressive, and noncompliant behaviors for children who had exhibited behavioral problems at an early age. However, they also found that parental warmth protected against later problems in White children but seemed to exacerbate early problems in Black children. The researchers concluded that professionals must recognize that parenting may need to take different forms in different communities. Clearly, this issue needs further investigation.

Research also indicates differences in parenting style based on the socioeconomic environment in which parenting occurs (Slatcher & Trentacosta, 2012). Low-income parents have been noted to be more authoritarian than more economically advantaged parents. Using observation methods, one research team found that the socioeconomic differences in parenting styles is not that straightforward, however. They found that middle-class parents routinely use subtle forms of control while, at the same time, trying to instill autonomy in their children. Their children spend a large portion of their time under adult supervision, in one activity or another. The researchers also found that low-income parents tend to value conformity but allow their school-aged children to spend considerable leisure time in settings where they do not have adult supervision, consequently affording them considerable autonomy (Weininger & Lareau, 2009).

Findings from studies about punishment and young children indicate that punishment is often used in response to early childhood behavior that is age appropriate. So rather than encouraging the independence that is otherwise expected for a child, such age-appropriate behavior is discouraged (Culp, McDonald Culp, Dengler, & Maisano, 1999). In addition, evidence indicates that brain development can be affected by the stress created by punishment or physical discipline (Glaser, 2000). Harsh punishment and physical discipline interfere with the neural connection process that begins in infancy and continues throughout early childhood. But for many low-income parents, harsh punishment may be less an issue of control or "bad parenting" than an effort to cope with a desperate situation.

As you can see, there are many controversies about effective parenting for young children, and this is an issue about which parents and professionals often have strong feelings. Research is beginning to recognize that different parenting styles may work well in different developmental niches. To make the issue even more complicated, scholars such as Judith Rich Harris (1998) and Steven Pinker (2002) argue that behavioral traits have such a strong genetic component that we should avoid overemphasizing the role of parenting style in behavioral outcomes. In fact, they argue that we have overemphasized the role of families in shaping behavior, other than by providing genetic heritage. Harris also argues that the peer group and community have more impact on child identity and behavior than parents. No doubt, Harris and Pinker would argue that the inconsistent findings about the impact of parenting styles are evidence that parenting style is not a supremely important variable in child development. Of course, we are learning more about the genetic component of human behavior, but we are also learning about the plasticity of the brain to be affected by experience. Parents are a

very large part of that experience throughout life, but in early childhood, other people come to be a part of the context of ongoing brain development. Recent research on *epigenetics* is uncovering how environments affect gene expression and providing convincing evidence of the important role of the social environment for turning genes on or silencing them (Combs-Orme, 2013). In an era of great advancements in the biological sciences, epigenetic research is reminding us that "social workers can have their biggest influence through social policies that work hand in hand with nature to prevent the development of many of the problems that plague our nation and world (Combs-Orme, 2013, p. 28).

Divorce and Parental Relationship Dissolution

At age 4, Jack Lewis is one of many young children adjusting to parental divorce or relationship dissolution. Jack's parents were married, but nonmarital parental relationships are even more vulnerable to dissolution than marital relationships. There is much complexity in the analysis of divorce rates, but the divorce rate in the United States appears to have increased steadily from the late 19th century through the 1970s, with a sharp drop in the 1950s and a steep incline beginning in the 1960s. It peaked in 1981 and has been dropping slightly since then but is still one of the highest in the world; the marriage rate has also been dropping in the same period (Ciabattari, 2017; Greene, Anderson, Forgatch, Degarmo, & Hetherington, 2012). Recent estimates indicate that 40% of women married to men in the United States will divorce before their 15th anniversary (Copen, Daniels, Vespa, & Mosher, 2012). Same-sex marriage is too recent around the world to allow adequate analysis of the divorce rate among same-sex couples. Second and third marriages are more likely to end in divorce than first marriages. The average length of a marriage that ends in divorce is 8 years, and the average age of first divorce is 30. In the United States, divorce rates are highest among couples with lower income, less education, and early relationship formation.

Divorce and relationship dissolution is a process, not a single event. For the partners it is a process of uncoupling. The first step toward divorce is not usually mutual. It typically begins with one person who has a nagging feeling of dissatisfaction but a lot of ambivalence about moving toward divorce. In the United States and most European countries, two thirds to three quarters of divorces are initiated by women. Marital conflict often escalates as one party begins to disengage emotionally, and the divorce decision frequently ends up being mutual (Ahrons, 2016). In the case of the Lewis family, Jack's father began to disengage from the family as he developed another romantic relationship, but it was Jack's mother who started the process of legal divorce.

The divorce and relationship dissolution process must be negotiated in multiple dimensions, including legal divorce, physical divorce, financial divorce, emotional and social divorce, and parental divorce (Ciabattari, 2017). Where there was a legal partnership contract, *legal divorce* must be negotiated in the legal system. The legal divorce process is an adversarial one that often fuels animosity between the partners as it appears to be doing with Jack Lewis's parents. Alternative legal processes, such as mediation and collaborative divorce, have been developed to promote a less adversarial process, but these approaches are not accessible to all families.

Physical divorce must also occur; a couple or family who once resided under one roof must develop a plan for living in separate places. At least some member(s), and maybe all, of the family will have to relocate. The Jack Lewis family situation is not unusual; financial divorce often means that a family home is no longer affordable for either parent. Where there are children or other co-residing family members, decisions must be made about who resides with whom. Belongings of all types must be separated. Marriage is not just a legal relationship; it is also an economic one. *Financial divorce* is an important part of the divorce process. Partners must disentangle their financial interdependence and resolve issues about fairness in the distribution of financial resources. On average, women's family income declines about one third after divorce, and the economic consequences of relationship dissolution are also high for women in cohabiting relationships.

No matter who initiates the process of divorce or relationship dissolution, *emotional and social divorce* is stressful. Two people who have thought of themselves as a couple must develop independent identities. All involved family members experience a sense of loss, and many experience anger and blame (Ahrons, 2016). Jack Lewis misses his father, but for his mother, Joyce, the sense of loss is covered with anger and blame. Social networks must be renegotiated. Where does the divorced family fit with their former network of coupled friends? What happens to the patterns of interactions with shared friends? How much interaction will partners have with the former partner's kin? New friendships are often formed and social networks reorganized.

When the divorcing couple has children, a primary legal decision is how to care for them; this decision is central to the *parental divorce* process. Both *legal custody* (who has legal rights and responsibilities to make decisions about the children) and *physical custody* (where the children will reside) must be decided. In the past, legal custody and physical custody always went to the same parent, to the father in the 19th century and to the mother more recently. Today, both parents often share legal custody and the child resides primarily with one parent. When custody decisions are disputed, general practice recently has been that each parent's postdivorce parenting responsibilities should be based on their predivorce involvement with the child. Joint custody, both legal and physical, has become more common. Ongoing contact between Jack Lewis and his father is uncertain in the early days of the legal divorce process.

Family studies researchers have been particularly interested in how children are affected by divorce. A long line of research has found that children who experience a parental breakup have lower educational achievement, lower levels of psychological well-being, and more problems in their own marriages (see Amato, 2010). Recently, however, family researchers have taken a new look at this research and concluded that it fails to adequately represent the wide variety of outcomes for children in both married and divorced families (Ahrons, 2016; Ciabattari, 2017). They note that most of the research has focused on averages and not looked at the differences within each group. They further note that the average reported differences between children of divorced families and children of married families are quite small. One of the most commonly cited findings is that 20% of children whose parents are divorced experience behavioral or mental health problems, compared to 10% of children whose parents are married. Another way of looking at this is that four out of five children whose parents are divorced do not experience such negative outcomes. One research team who has studied the diversity of outcomes for children after divorce found that 18% declined on measures of well-being, 14% improved, and 68% had no change (Amato & Anthony, 2014). Longitudinal studies have also found that children whose parents divorce have often begun to have behavioral and academic problems before the divorce (Strohschein, 2005), similar to the problems found in children living in high-conflict married families (Amato, 2005). Another issue with the research is that it typically does not account for differences in relationship stability of both the residential and nonresidential parents following divorce.

Research clearly identifies three factors that contribute to healthy adjustment of children to divorce:

(1) having basic economic and psychological needs met; (2) ongoing interaction with important people in their lives; and (3) a generally supportive and cooperative relationship between their parents. There is consistent evidence, however, that the economic well-being of women and children declines after divorce. And shared parenting after divorce or other breakup is almost always challenging. Hetherington and Kelly (2002) found that divorced co-parents fell into three categories: conflicted (25%), cooperative (25%), and parallel (50%). Parallel co-parents avoid fighting, but they also avoid talking with each other; both parents interact positively with the children, but they do not coordinate with each other. It remains to be seen what type of co-parenting relationship, if any, will be worked out between Joyce and Charles Lewis if the early intense hostilities subside once the legal divorce is finalized.

Researchers are finding that fathers are more involved in their children's lives after a breakup than was the case in past eras. One research team studied father involvement 12 years after divorce or relationship dissolution, including both formerly married and never married fathers (Cheadle, Amato, & King, 2010). They found that the largest group of fathers (38%) had stable and frequent involvement with the children over the 12-year period, 32% had low involvement during the 12 years, 23% were highly involved in the years following the breakup with declining involvement over time, and 8% increased their involvement during the 12 years. Fathers who were active in child-rearing while in the home are likely to stay involved after divorce or relationship dissolution.

It seems clear that divorce is a crisis for most adults, typically lasting 1½ to 2 years, and Joyce Lewis provides a good example of the multiple dimensions of that crisis. Stress increases in the run-up to the divorce, during the divorce, and in the immediate aftermath. However, the stress level typically subsides within a year after divorce as families adjust relationships and routines (Demo & Fine, 2010). There is evidence that African American women get more social support than White women following divorce (Orbuch & Brown, 2006).

Violence

Many parents complain that keeping violence away from children requires tremendous work even in the best of circumstances. Children witness violence on television and through video and computer games and hear about it through many other sources. In the worst of circumstances, young children not only are exposed

to violence but become victims of it as well. This section discusses three types of violence experienced by many young children: community violence, domestic violence, and child maltreatment.

Community Violence

In Case Study 3.3 in Chapter 3 of this book, Irma Velasquez lost one child to community violence and has organized her life around trying to protect 14-month-old Henry from a similar incident. In some neighborhoods, acts of violence are so common that the communities are labeled "war zones." However, most residents prefer not to be combatants. Research indicates that about 38% of children and adolescents witness violence in their communities, and the number is much higher in some urban neighborhoods (Kennedy & Ceballo, 2014). Community violence can be a pervasive aspect of family and neighborhood life. One study of urban mothers of young children enrolled in Head Start found that three quarters of the mothers reported witnessing drug transactions and violence in their neighborhood, including incidences such as witnessing people being physically assaulted, robbed, or threatened with a weapon. In addition, two thirds of the mothers reported being personally either physically threatened or assaulted, having their home broken into, or being robbed on the street (Farver, Xu, Eppe, Fernandez, & Schwartz, 2005).

Feeling unsafe can interfere with a young child's natural curiosity about the world and with the development of trusting relationships. Living in terror has an impact on brain and nervous system development (Guerra & Dierkhising, 2012). Children exposed to chronic community violence show symptoms of anxiety and PTSD, including exaggerated startle response, difficulty eating and sleeping, and cognitive problems (Fowler, Tompsett, Braciszewski, Jacquies-Tiura, & Baltes, 2009; Kennedy & Caballo, 2014). They may have trouble regulating their emotions and are more prone than other children to be aggressive and disruptive (McMahon et al., 2013; Sharkey, Tirado-Strayer, Papachristos, & Rover, 2012). As we can see with Irma Velasquez from Chapter 3, a parental sense of helplessness about community violence can interfere with a caregiver's ability to promote healthy child development.

Some children are more resilient in the face of community violence than others. Three factors have been found to promote such resilience: (1) a supportive adult in the environment; (2) a protected space in the neighborhood that is a safe haven; and (3) personal protective factors such as easy temperament or intelligence

(Jain & Cohen, 2013). Community interventions can help to build such resources for children in endangered neighborhoods.

For many children living in violent neighborhoods, the death of a close friend or family member is commonplace. When the second author of this chapter (David) was employed at a community child guidance center, he found that appointments were often canceled so the parents could attend funerals. Living so intimately with death has grave effects on young children. In one study of young children whose older siblings had been victims of homicide, the surviving siblings showed symptoms of depression, anxiety, psychosocial impairment, and post-traumatic stress disorder (Freeman, Shaffer, & Smith, 1996). These symptoms are similar to those observed in young children in situations of political and military violence—for example, in Palestinian children in the occupied West Bank (Qouta, Punamaki, & El-Sarraj, 2003) and in children in Cape Town, South Africa (Shields, Nadasen, & Pierce, 2008). Perhaps the label *war zone* is an appropriate one for violent communities. However, positive, affectionate, caregiving relationships—whether by parents or other family members or individuals in the community—can play an important mediating role in how violence is managed by young children (Shields et al., 2008).

Domestic Violence

The family is the social group from whom we expect to receive our greatest love, support, nurturance, and acceptance. And yet family relationships are some of the most violent relationships in many societies. Research indicates that men are as likely as women to be victims of intimate violence, but women are more likely to miss work, report depression, be injured, receive death threats, and be killed by their partners (Jasinski, Blumenstein, & Morgan, 2014). Some suggest that physical violence between siblings may be the most common form of family violence (Gelles, 2010). Domestic violence may take the form of verbal, psychological, or physical abuse, although physical abuse is the form most often implied. It is difficult to produce accurate statistics about the amount of family violence because what happens in families is usually "behind closed doors," but the Childhood Domestic Violence Association (2014) estimates that 5 million children witness domestic violence each year in the United States. Almost three decades of international research indicate that young children experience serious negative physical, emotional, cognitive, and social impacts on development from involvement in domestic violence (see Australian Domestic & Family Violence

Clearinghouse, 2011). Children are particularly vulnerable to neurobiological and attachment disruptions from experiencing domestic violence from ages 3 to 6 (Carpenter & Stacks, 2009). Children often witness the violence between parents, but they may also be accidently hurt or they may attempt to intervene (Edelson, 1999; Humphreys & Stanley, 2015). Children who witness violence have the same negative developmental outcomes as children who are victims of physical abuse (Kitzmann, Gaylord, Holt, & Kenny, 2003). In a study of 60 children ages 1 to 6 who witnessed domestic violence, the majority of children showed clinical signs of both internalizing (depression and anxiety) and externalizing (aggressive actions toward others) behavior problems (Zerk, Mertin, & Proeve, 2009). They demonstrated high levels of distress, sleep disturbances, and poor concentration.

Domestic violence does not always affect children's long-term development, however. In one study, one third of the children seemed unaffected by the domestic violence they witnessed at home; these children were well adjusted and showed no signs of distress, anxiety, or behavior problems (Spilsbury et al., 2008). Two factors may buffer the effect domestic violence has on children:

1. *Amount of domestic violence witnessed by the child.* The more violent episodes children witness, the more likely they are to develop problematic behavior.

2. *Relationship between the child and the mother,* assuming the mother is the victim. If the mother–child relationship remains stable and secure, the probability of the child developing behavioral difficulties decreases significantly—even when the amount of violence witnessed by the child is relatively high.

Unstable family conditions and provocative behaviors within families serve to destabilize child functioning. Experiencing a lack of safety and low levels of nurturance serve to create an environment of risk for children (Turner et al., 2012).

Child Maltreatment

It is difficult to estimate the rate of **child maltreatment**, because many incidences are never reported, and much that is reported is not determined to be child maltreatment. Approximately 4 million referrals were made to Child Protective Services in the United States in 2015 involving 7.2 million children

(Child Welfare Information Gateway, 2017). About three fifths of the referrals were screened in for investigation, and approximately one fifth of the children investigated were found to be victims of abuse or neglect; an estimated 683,000 children were considered victims of abuse and neglect. An estimated 1,670 children died because of abuse and/or neglect, and most (72.9%) of these victims were younger than 3 years of age. The most prevalent forms of child maltreatment include neglect (75.3%), physical abuse (17.2%), sexual abuse (8.4%), and psychological maltreatment (6.2%). National incidence data indicate that the majority of child victims in 2015 were either White (43.2%), Hispanic (23.6%), or African American (21.4%). Risk factors for child maltreatment exist at all ecological levels: child, parent, community, and society (see Font & Berger, 2014; Widom, 2014). Exhibit 4.6 provides an overview of research findings about risk factors for child maltreatment at these four ecological levels.

Child maltreatment creates risks to all aspects of growth and development, as shown in Exhibit 4.7,

but children ages birth to 6 are at highest risk of having long-lasting damage (Pecora & Harrison-Jackson, 2011). In their longitudinal research of 180 children born into poverty, Sroufe et al. (2005) found that young children who had been physically abused as toddlers had higher levels of negativity, noncompliance, and distractibility than other children. Those whose mothers were psychologically unavailable demonstrated more avoidance of and anger toward the mother. Children with a history of all types of maltreatment had lower self-esteem and agency and demonstrated more behavior problems than other children. Children with a history of neglect were more passive than other children.

PROTECTIVE FACTORS IN EARLY CHILDHOOD

Many of the factors listed in Chapter 3 that promote resiliency during the infant and toddler years are equally relevant during the early childhood years. Other

---

EXHIBIT 4.6 ● Risk Factors for Child Maltreatment at the Child, Parent, Community, and Societal Level

Child	Parent	Community	Society
Premature birth	Poor conflict resolution skills	Low socioeconomic resources	High levels of economic inequality
Low birth weight	Poor communication skills	Lack of access to medical care, adequate childcare, and social services	Gender inequality
Birth anomalies	Lack of knowledge of child development		Lack of societal family support systems
Physical/cognitive/emotional disability	Negative attitudes toward child	High levels of unemployment	High valuing of individualism
Chronic or serious illness	Lack of social support	Inadequate schools	
Temperamentally difficult	Low self-esteem	Environmental toxins	
Inattentive or overactive	Poor impulse control	Community violence	
Aggressive	Poor coping skills		
	High stress level		
	Depression		
	Anxiety		
	Substance abuse		
	Psychopathology		
	Low family income		
	Unemployment		
	Homelessness		

EXHIBIT 4.7 ● Potential Effects of Child Abuse on Growth and Development

Physical Impairments	Cognitive Impairments	Emotional Impairments
Physical Abuse and Neglect		
Burns, scars, fractures, broken bones, damage to vital organs and limbs	Delayed cognitive skills	Negative self-concept
Malnourishment	Delayed language skills	Increased aggressiveness
Physical exposure	Intellectual disability	Poor peer relations
Poor skin hygiene	Delayed reality testing	Poor impulse control
Poor (if any) medical care	Overall disruption of thought processes	Anxiety
Poor (if any) dental care		Inattentiveness
Serious medical problems		Avoidant behavior
Serious dental problems		
Failure-to-thrive syndrome		
Death		
Sexual Abuse		
Trauma to mouth, anus, vaginal area	Hyperactivity	Overly adaptive behavior
Genital and rectal pain	Bizarre sexual behavior	Overly compliant behavior
Genital and rectal bleeding		Habit disorders (e.g., nail biting)
Genital and rectal tearing		Anxiety
Sexually transmitted disease		Depression
		Sleep disturbances
		Night terrors
		Self-mutilation
Psychological/Emotional Abuse		
	Pessimistic view of life	Alienation
	Anxiety and fear	Intimacy problems
	Distorted perception of world	Low self-esteem
	Deficits in moral development	Depression

protective factors also come into play (see Jenson & Fraser, 2016, for a summary of these factors).

Social support. Social support mediates many potential risks to the development of young children. Social support aids young children in several ways. Having a consistent and supportive aunt or uncle or preschool teacher who can set firm but loving limits, for example, may buffer the effects of a parent with ineffective skills. At the community level, preschools, religious programs, and the like may

help to enhance physical and cognitive skills, self-esteem, and social development.

Positive parent–child relationship. A positive relationship with at least one parent helps children to feel secure and nurtured. Remember from Chapter 3 that a sense of security is the foundation on which young children build initiative during the early childhood years. Even if Jack Lewis never has contact with his father, Charles, a positive relationship with Joyce, his mother, can mediate this loss.

Effective parenting. In early childhood, children need the opportunity to take initiative but also need firm limits, whether they are established by parents or grandparents or someone else who adopts the parent role. Terri Smith, for example, has not been able to establish self-control because her boundaries are not well defined. Effective parenting promotes self-efficacy and self-esteem and provides young children with a model of how they can take initiative within boundaries.

Self-esteem. A high level of self-worth may allow young children to persist in mastery of skills despite adverse conditions. Perhaps a high level of self-esteem can enhance Jack Lewis's and Ron and Rosiland Johnson's development despite the disruptions in their lives. In addition, research indicates that self-esteem is a protective factor against the effects of child abuse.

● *Good emotional self-regulation.* The ability to respond to ongoing demands with a range of emotions in a socially tolerable and sufficiently flexible manner is an essential life skill and one that protects against environmental stressors. Terri Smith needs assistance in developing this personal protective factor.

● *Intelligence.* Even in young children, a high IQ serves as a protective factor. For example, young children with high IQs were less likely to be affected by maternal psychopathology (Tiet et al., 2001). Others suggest that intelligence results in success, which leads to higher levels of self-esteem (Jenson & Fraser, 2016). For young children, then, intelligence may contribute to mastery of skills and independence, which may enhance self-esteem. Intelligence may also protect children through increased problem-solving skills, which allow for more effective responses to adverse situations.

● *Support for early learning.* Positive teacher expectations, effective classroom management, and relationships with positive and prosocial peers can serve as protection in the face of family and community stressors.

CRITICAL THINKING QUESTIONS 4.5

What type of parenting style do you think your parents used when you were a child? Did both parents use the same parenting style? Do you think the parenting style(s) used by your parents was effective? How do you think your parents' parenting style was affected by culture? Would you want to use the same parenting style that your parents used if you were a parent? Why or why not?

IMPLICATIONS FOR SOCIAL WORK PRACTICE

Knowledge about early childhood has several implications for social work practice with young children.

● Become well acquainted with theories and empirical research about growth and development among young children.

● Continue to promote the elimination of poverty and the advancement of social justice.

● Collaborate with other professionals in the creation of laws, interventions, and programs that assist in the elimination of violence.

● Create and support easy access to services for young children and their parents.

● Assess younger children in the context of their environment.

● Become familiar with the physical and emotional signs of child abuse.

● Directly engage younger children in an age-appropriate intervention process.

● Provide support to parents and help facilitate positive parent–child relationships.

● Encourage and engage both mothers and fathers in the intervention process.

● Provide opportunities for children to increase self-efficacy and self-esteem.

● Help parents understand the potential effects of negative environmental factors on their children.

Key Terms

authoritarian parenting 143
authoritative parenting 143
child maltreatment 148
discipline 143
disengaged parenting 143
egocentrism 122
empathy 126
fine motor skills 119
gender typing 132
gross motor skills 119
hostile aggression 129

instrumental aggression 129
lateralization 119
learning play 135
overregularization 124
permissive parenting 143
perspective taking 126
physical aggression 129
preconventional level
    of moral reasoning 126
prosocial 125
relational aggression 129

self-esteem 130
self-theory 130
sociodramatic play 136
symbolic play 135
transductive reasoning 122

Active Learning

1. Watch any child-oriented cartoon on television. Describe the apparent and implied messages (both positive and negative) available in the cartoon about race and ethnicity and gender differences. Consider how these messages might affect gender and ethnic development in young children.

2. Observe preschool-age children at play. Record the types of play that you observe. How well do your observations fit with what is described about play in this chapter?

3. You have been asked to present a psychoeducational workshop on early childhood cognitive development for the parents of a local Head Start program. Prepare an outline for the presentation. What advice would you give the parents on how they can assist their young children in their cognitive development?

Web Resources

American Academy of Child & Adolescent Psychiatry: www.aacap.org

Site presented by the American Academy of Child & Adolescent Psychiatry contains concise and up-to-date information on a variety of issues facing children and their families, including day care, discipline, children and divorce, child abuse, children and TV violence, and children and grief.

Children's Defense Fund: www.childrensdefense .org

Site presented by the Children's Defense Fund, a private nonprofit child advocacy organization, contains information on issues, the Black Community Crusade for Children, the Child Watch Visitation Program, and a parent resource network.

National Family Resiliency Center (NFRC): http://nfrchelp.org

Site presented by the NFRC contains information about support groups, resources for professionals, and frequently asked questions.

Play Therapy International: www.playtherapy.org

Site presented by Play Therapy International contains reading lists, articles and research, news, and information about training and careers in play therapy.

U.S. Department of Health & Human Services: www.hhs.gov

Site maintained by the U.S. Department of Health & Human Services contains news and information on health topics, prevention, and safety.

Middle Childhood

Leanne Wood Charlesworth

Learning Objectives

5.1 Compare one's own emotional and cognitive reactions to three case studies.

5.2 Describe how the social context of middle childhood has changed over time and place.

5.3 Identify examples of the ways the multigenerational family influences middle childhood development.

5.4 Summarize typical physical, cognitive, cultural identity, emotional, social, and spiritual development during middle childhood.

5.5 Analyze the role of formal schooling in middle childhood development.

5.6 Analyze special challenges to middle childhood development.

5.7 Give examples of important risk factors and protective factors in middle childhood.

5.8 Apply knowledge of middle childhood to recommend guidelines for social work engagement, assessment, intervention, and evaluation.

CASE STUDY 5.1

ANTHONY'S IMPENDING ASSESSMENT

Anthony is a 6-year-old African American boy living in an impoverished section of a large city in the United States. Anthony's mother Sephora was 14 when Anthony was born, and Anthony's father James was 15. James has always spent a great deal of time with Anthony. Although James now also has a 2-year-old daughter from another relationship, he has told Sephora that Anthony and Sephora are the most important people in his life. Once Anthony was out of diapers, James began spending even more time with him, taking Anthony along to visit friends and, occasionally, on overnight outings.

James's father was murdered when James was a toddler, and he rarely sees his mother, who struggles with substance addiction. James lived with his paternal grandparents until he was in his early teens, when he began to stay with a favorite uncle. Many members of James's large extended family have been incarcerated on charges related to their involvement in the local drug trade. James's favorite uncle is a well-known dealer. James has been arrested a few times and is currently on probation.

Sephora and Anthony live with her mother. Sephora obtained her general equivalency diploma after Anthony's birth, and she has held a variety of jobs at local fast-food chains. Sephora's mother, Cynthia, receives Supplemental Social Security Income/Disability because she has been unable to work for several years due to advanced rheumatoid arthritis, which was diagnosed when she was a teenager. Sephora remembers her father only as a loud man who often yelled at her when she made noise. He left Cynthia and Sephora when Sephora was 4 years old, and neither has seen

him since. Cynthia seemed pleased when Anthony was born, and she has been a second mother to him, caring for him while Sephora attends school and work and socializes with James and her other friends.

Anthony has always been very active and energetic, frequently breaking things and creating messes throughout the apartment. To punish Anthony, Cynthia spanks him with a belt or other object—and she sometimes resorts to locking him in his room until he falls asleep. Sephora and James are proud of Anthony's wiry physique and rough and tough play; they have encouraged him to be fearless and not to cry when he is hurt. Both Sephora and James use physical punishment as their main discipline strategy with Anthony, but he usually obeys them before it is needed.

Anthony entered kindergarten at a local public school last fall. When he started school, his teacher told Sephora that he seemed to be a very smart boy, one of the only boys in the class who already knew how to write his name and how to count to 20. It is now spring, however, and Sephora is tired of dealing with Anthony's teacher and other school staff. She has been called a number of times, and recently the school social worker requested a meeting with her. Anthony's teacher reports that Anthony will not listen and frequently starts fights with the other children in the classroom. Anthony's teacher also states that Anthony constantly violates school rules, like waiting in line and being quiet in the hallways, and doesn't seem bothered by threats of punishment. Most recently, Anthony's teacher has told Sephora that she would like Anthony assessed by the school psychologist.

CASE STUDY 5.2

JASMINE'S HEADACHES

Jasmine, a Caucasian 9-year-old girl, is the middle child in her family. She has a 5-year-old brother Jordan and a 13-year-old sister, Jenesis. For as long as Jasmine can remember, her mother has worked all the time. She works at a hospital now and used to work at a nursing

home. Jasmine has heard her mother say that she likes taking care of people when they are sick.

Jasmine misses her father. Her mother always tells Jenesis and Jasmine that they should never touch drugs or they will become just like their dad, who

Acknowledgments: The author would like to acknowledge the past contributions of Jim Wood and Pamela Viggiani to the development of this chapter.

used to smoke marijuana and then began using heroin. Jasmine remembers that in the last year her dad lived with them, he would often hit their mom. Jasmine knows her dad is in prison now, and her mom says she is glad he is gone. But Jasmine can remember fun times with her dad when she was little and hopes he will return soon.

Jasmine describes her family as poor, and she can't really remember a time when she wasn't poor. She lived in the city most of her life and lost track of how many different places she stayed. Even though she likes school, she was never able to stay in one school too long. Around the same time that Jasmine's dad went to jail, they moved in with Jasmine's grandma in the country, and weeks passed before Jasmine and her siblings started school nearby. During that time, Jasmine and Jenesis stayed home and took care of Jordan while their mom and grandma drove to their jobs in the city. When Jasmine's grandma died unexpectedly, her mom didn't have enough money to pay all the bills and they had to leave the house. They loaded the family's clothes into their grandma's car and began sleeping in the car,

frequently parking at a deserted campground near their grandma's old home.

Jasmine's grandma used to call her an old soul. She loves to read and pretends to be Jordan's teacher. Jasmine has always made sure Jordan is taken care of when her mom is working. She won't eat until Jordan has had enough, and she is proud that she taught Jordan how to brush his teeth and tie his shoes. She likes it when her mom says she is the only one who never worries her. Jenesis makes her mom angry, and the two argue a lot. A few weeks ago, Jenesis was caught drinking and smoking with friends, and Jasmine knows that Jenesis cuts herself. Jasmine thinks it is Jenesis's fault that the school called Child Protective Services.

Jasmine thinks she should not tell anyone how much her head hurts lately. Telling her mom or her teacher would just cause more trouble. Everyone tells Jasmine how smart she is, but lately when she has to take a test, her head hurts and her heart starts beating fast. Last week, she asked to go to the nurse's office during a test because she felt sick and her head hurt so much she thought she would cry.

CASE STUDY 5.3
GABRIELA'S NEW LIFE

Gabriela is an 11-year-old girl who moved from a small border city in northern Mexico to a midsize city in the western mountain region of the United States toward the end of her third-grade year. She lives with her mother, Teresa, and her father, Daniel, in a small apartment; her only sibling is an older half brother who still lives in Mexico. In the first months in her new school, Gabriela was involved in several conflicts with peers. Although Gabriela's teacher suspected that some of Gabriela's classmates were making fun of her weight, she also believed that Gabriela's difficulty with the English language was a contributing factor. Although Gabriela's school does not usually encourage English-learning students to repeat a grade, it was decided that she should repeat fourth grade because she was the youngest in the class and had formed a warm bond with her very nurturing teacher. She remained with the same teacher in her repeat year in fourth grade. She is now in fifth grade and is doing well with her schoolwork; her English-language skills are growing strong. However, she still struggles to make friends and appears to have low self-esteem. She recently began to participate in a girls' self-esteem group at school and seems to be gaining confidence.

Prior to moving to the United States, Gabriela's mother, Teresa, lived all her life in the same small Mexican border city. Her father, Daniel, was born in the United States to Mexican American parents living in a rural community in Arizona, near the border with Mexico. In his early twenties, he moved to the small city where Teresa lived to start a construction company with a cousin. That is where he met Teresa and where Gabriela was born. When Gabriela was 5, the construction company failed. Another cousin told Daniel about a new factory being developed in the U.S. city where the family now lives, a factory that would manufacture parts for the technology industry. Daniel was able to secure a position with the building and grounds department in this new factory.

The original plan was that Teresa and Gabriela would follow Daniel to the United States as soon as he obtained his new job. That did not happen for 4 years, but their move was finally precipitated by Teresa's growing health problems. Once she and Gabriela were in the United States, they were covered by Daniel's health insurance and Teresa was diagnosed with diabetes. She and her doctor have struggled to stabilize her condition.

(Continued)

(Continued)

The family reunification has not been smooth. Teresa and Gabriela have found that Daniel consumes large amounts of alcohol and is unpredictable and often aggressive when drunk. Teresa and Daniel fight a lot. The three of them were all sleeping in one bed in the small apartment, and a report was made to Child Protective Services when Gabriela told her teacher that her father had touched her inappropriately, through her clothing, one night when he was drunk. The child protection worker mandated that Daniel should not sleep in the same bed as Gabriela. Gabriela has confided to the school social worker and guidance counselor that she wants her mother to leave her father, but her mother would not be able to get health insurance if she left because of her citizenship status. She says that her mother tells her, "Gabriela, I am waiting for you to grow up, and I can live with you." Gabriela says that she feels a great pressure to take care of her mother.

HISTORICAL PERSPECTIVE ON MIDDLE CHILDHOOD

Conceptions of middle childhood are historically and socially constructed. Beliefs about children reflect the cultural contexts in which they develop; across time, cultural groups have held deeply distinct views of children as inherently good or evil, in need of protection and nurturing or discipline and correction (Fass & Mason, 2000; Mintz, 2004). The age range classified as middle childhood is subject to debate. Today in the United States, it is most often defined as the period beginning at approximately ages 5 or 6 and ending at approximately ages 10 to 12 (Marotz & Allen, 2013). It is common to think of middle childhood as consisting of an early (approximately ages 6 through 8) and late (approximately ages 9 through 12) phase. In many cultural groups, children progressing through middle childhood have been viewed as increasingly capable of working and contributing to the well-being of their families and communities. Beginning in the 20th century, a fairly universal shift occurred in the world's perceptions of children. Children passing through middle childhood became categorized as "school age," and their education became a societal priority. Child labor and compulsory education laws supported and reinforced this shift in societal values.

However, in many communities school-age children continue to play important economic roles for families. Many young children from financially impoverished families work, and in countries striving toward universal primary school education, children must balance their economic productivity with time spent in school (Karraker, 2013). Although this significant diversity exists among children, middle childhood is generally viewed in the United States as a time when education, play, and social activities should dominate daily life (Cole & Durham, 2008).

Images of middle childhood often include children who are physically active and intellectually curious, making new friends and learning new things. But as Anthony, Jasmine, and Gabriela demonstrate, middle childhood is filled with both opportunities and challenges. For some children, it is a period of particular vulnerability. When we think of school-age children, our thoughts may include images of child poverty and related school inequities, family and community violence, sexual victimization or **precociousness** (early development), learning challenges, and physical and emotional ailments such as anxiety, malnutrition, depression, asthma, and obesity. In some parts of the world, children in this developmental phase are vulnerable to war, forced enlistment as soldiers, slave-like labor, and being sold as sex workers in an international child trafficking economy (Human Rights Watch, 2018).

MIDDLE CHILDHOOD IN THE MULTIGENERATIONAL FAMILY

During middle childhood, the child's social world expands dramatically. Although the family is not the only relevant force in a child's life, it remains an extremely significant influence on development. Families are often in a constant state of change, and so the school-age child's relationships with family members and the environment the family inhabits are likely to be different from the child's first experiences as an infant and toddler. For example, consider the changes in Anthony, Jasmine, and Gabriela's families over time and the ways in which their relationships have been continually evolving.

Despite the geographical distances that often exist between family members today, nuclear families are still emotional subsystems of extended, multigenerational family systems. The child's nuclear family is significantly shaped by past, present, and anticipated future experiences, events, and relationships (Coll & Szalacha, 2004;

McGoldrick et al., 2016). Profoundly important factors such as historical events, culture, and social structure, as well as family members' experiences and characteristics, often influence children through their family systems. Relatives' experiences or characteristics may be biologically based and therefore fairly obvious, or they may include more nebulous qualities such as acquired emotional strengths or wounds. For example, consider Anthony's grandmother, an African American woman who grew up with the legacy of slavery under Jim Crow laws and legal segregation in the United States and as a child was repeatedly sexually victimized. Children become connected to events or phenomena such as a familial history of violence and trauma or a group history of discrimination and oppression (restrictions and exploitation), even in the absence of direct experiences in the present generation (see Gapp et al., 2014; Miller & Garran, 2008).

Thus, the developing school-age child is shaped not only by events and individuals explicitly evident in the present time and physical space but also indirectly by those events and individuals who more directly influenced the lives of their parents, grandparents, great-grandparents, and beyond. These influences—familial, cultural, and historical—shape all aspects of every child's development in an abstract and complex fashion.

CRITICAL THINKING QUESTIONS 5.1

When you think of middle childhood for Anthony, Jasmine, and Gabriela, do you think of it as a time of promise or a time of vulnerability? Explain. What do you see as the strengths in their multigenerational families? What do you see as the special challenges in their multigenerational families?

DEVELOPMENT IN MIDDLE CHILDHOOD

New developmental tasks are undertaken in middle childhood, and development occurs within multiple dimensions. Although each developmental domain is considered separately for our analytical purposes, changes in the developing child reflect the dynamic interaction continuously occurring across these dimensions.

Physical Development

During middle childhood, physical development typically continues steadily, but children of the same chronological age may vary greatly in stature, weight, and sexual development. For most children, height and weight begin to advance less rapidly than during prior developmental phases, but steady growth continues. The nature and pace of physical growth during this period are shaped by both genetic and environmental influences in interaction (Jurimae, 2013).

Most children progressing from kindergarten to early adolescence experience improvements in their fine and gross motor skills. Underscoring the profoundly diverse experiences of children in the United States, both overuse injuries and childhood obesity are viewed as contemporary threats to healthy physical development (Daniels & Hassink, 2015; DiFiori et al., 2014). Some children experience limited opportunities for physical activity whereas others encounter pressure to gain the skill mastery associated with a particular interest such as sports, dance, or music. Medical professionals caution that school-age children possess unique physical vulnerabilities related to the growth process and thus are particularly susceptible to the ailments associated with either an overly sedentary lifestyle or excessive physical training. The American Medical Society for Sports Medicine (DiFiori et al., 2014) urges adults to attend to the risk of psychological burnout and overuse injury among children and youth. Meanwhile, as the prevalence of childhood obesity in the United States increases, the American Academy of Pediatrics offers guidance on how to increase activity levels among sedentary school-age children (Daniels & Hassink, 2015).

Middle childhood is a developmental phase of entrenchment or eradication of many potent risk or protective factors manifesting in the physical developmental domain (Mah & Ford-Jones, 2012). Focusing on risk, for children residing in chronically impoverished countries and communities, issues such as malnutrition and chronic illness threaten physical health. Seemingly innocuous issues such as poor dental hygiene, an untreated ear infection, or mild visual impairment may become more serious as they begin to impact other areas of development such as cognitive, emotional, or social well-being. In the United States, health issues including childhood cancer and lead poisoning are of contemporary concern. Although susceptibility to risk varies across socioeconomic and ethnic groups, unintentional death and physical injury (for example, motor vehicle injuries, drowning, playground accidents, and sports-related injuries) represent a major threat to the well-being of all school-age children (Centers for Disease Control and Prevention, 2012). Moreover, as children move into middle childhood they gain other new risks: approximately one third of rapes occur before age 12, homicide risk increases, and among children ages 10 to 14, suicide is a leading cause of death (Smith et al., 2017). Some of the risks unique to middle childhood may be indirectly facilitated by declines in adult supervision and adult overestimation of children's safety-related knowledge and ability to implement safety practices. Children's continued physical and cognitive vulnerabilities (specifically, in judgment and decision-making processes) combine, potentially, with an increasing ability and propensity to engage in risk-taking behaviors (Berk, 2012).

Many children experience puberty during middle childhood. Focusing on racial differences, several studies have found that in the United States, non-Hispanic African American boys and girls begin puberty earlier than other children (Herman-Giddens et al., 2012; Herman-Giddens, 2013; Reynolds & Juvonen, 2012). Careful examination of puberty onset trends over a large span of time suggests that the trend toward earlier puberty has been leveling off in recent years. Specifically, the average age of menarche decreased from approximately 14.8 years in 1877 to about 12.8 years in the mid-1960s; today, approximately age 12 remains the mean age of menarche onset.

The movement in the 20th century toward earlier age of puberty onset brought much attention to the potential causes (Maron, 2015). A wide variety of multidisciplinary researchers across the globe are examining the complex nature of puberty timing in boys and girls (American Academy of Pediatrics, 2012), with the factors identified as relevant to onset including nutritional status, genetic predisposition (including those related to race/ethnicity), and endocrine-disrupting chemicals (EDCs) (Biro, Greenspan, & Galvez, 2012; Gamble, 2017; Wang, Needham, & Barr, 2005). Researchers studying central precocious puberty (defined as occurring before age 8 in girls and age 9 in boys) have confirmed the important role of EDCs and are intensively evaluating the effectiveness of a variety of interventions (Bulus et al., 2016). These researchers recognize that an important relationship, albeit complex, exists between puberty and social development for both boys and girls (Santrock, 2013). Although the challenges for boys should not be minimized, girls experiencing precocious or early onset puberty may be at particular risk (Mendle, 2014). Breast development and testicular enlargement typically begin at approximately age 10, and the need for earlier, effective health education for children is widely accepted among education and health professionals (Greenspan & Deardorff, 2015; Maron 2015).

PHOTO 5.1 New developmental tasks are undertaken in middle childhood, and development occurs within interacting developmental domains.

© Bonnie Jacobs/iStockphoto.com

Intervention focused on self-protection is a valuable prevention approach, and schools committed to the safety of their students must diligently educate staff and students about sexual development and health.

Because physical development is outwardly visible, it affects perceptions of self and the way a child is viewed and treated by peers and adults. Indeed, middle childhood is a developmental phase when children experience a rapid increase in public attention focused on various aspects of their physical growth and abilities. School-age children constantly compare themselves with others, and physical differences are often the topic of discussion. Self-awareness and perspective-taking ability expand, and many children worry about being "normal." Supportive family, school, and community environments serve as important protective factors; reassurance that physical development varies among people and that all development is "normal" is crucial.

Cognitive Development

For most children, the acquisition of new cognitive abilities early in middle childhood allows the communication of thoughts with increasing complexity. Education plays a major role in the cognitive development of children in the United States, if only because children spend most of their awake hours in school throughout these formative years. When Anthony, Jasmine, and Gabriela first entered school, their readiness to confront the challenges and opportunities school presents was shaped by prior experiences. Anthony, for example, entered school generally prepared for the academic skills emphasized in kindergarten. He was less prepared for the school's behavioral expectations.

Jean Piaget (1936/1952) played a significant role in our understanding of the cognitive development of children. In his terms, children start school during the second stage (preoperational thought) and finish school when they are completing the fourth and final stage of cognitive development (formal operations). In the third stage (concrete operations), children are able to solve concrete problems using logical problem-solving strategies. By the end of middle childhood, most enter the formal operations stage and become able to solve hypothetical problems using abstract concepts (refer to Exhibit 3.4 for an overview of Piaget's stages of cognitive development). Examples of expanding cognitive capacity include the ability to comprehend complex conceptual questions, advancing skill in categorizing and analyzing complicated systems of ideas or objects, and enhanced creative ability to generate ideas. As you observe children moving into and through middle childhood, you will often note these rapid gains in intellectual processes (Adler-Tapia, 2012). These brain-produced shifts in the child's understanding of self and the surrounding world are consistent with the ideas Piaget articulated regarding the concrete operational and formal operations stages of cognitive development.

Beyond Piaget's ideas, brain development and cognitive growth during middle childhood traditionally received less attention than research devoted to brain development and cognitive growth in prior developmental phases. As pointed out in Chapters 3 and 4, infancy, toddlerhood, and early childhood are viewed as "sensitive periods" in brain development. Researchers historically believed that by middle childhood, a child's brain development and functioning are profoundly shaped by the nature of earlier experiences. And yet we now also realize that remarkable brain plasticity continues, with brain structure and functioning capable of growth and refinement throughout the life course (Mah & Ford-Jones, 2012; National Research Council, 2012). The conceptual framework perhaps most useful to understanding this potential and the processes at play is nonlinear dynamic systems theory, also known as complexity or chaos theory (Applegate & Shapiro, 2005). Applied to this context, this theoretical perspective proposes that changes in one area or aspect of the neurological system may stimulate or interact with other neurological or broader physiological system components unpredictably, potentially leading to unanticipated outcomes. Brain development often follows a coherent developmental process, but brain plasticity in particular demonstrates the role of complex nonlinear neurological system dynamics and processes.

At least two aspects of middle childhood brain development are of particular contemporary interest. The first is that different brain regions appear to develop according to different timelines. In other words, middle childhood may be a sensitive period for certain aspects of brain development. Mah and Ford-Jones (2012) assert that during middle childhood, forebrain and midbrain feedback loops shift, facilitating changes in thoughts and behavior. The second important aspect of middle childhood brain development is the notion that brain synapses (connections between cells in the nervous system) that are initially present as children enter this developmental phase may be gradually eliminated if they are not used. As reported in Chapter 3, there seems to be a pattern of synaptogenesis or creation and fine-tuning of brain synapses, in the human cerebral cortex during early childhood, which is typically followed by a gradual pruning process that eventually reduces the overall number of synapses to their adult levels (National Research Council, 2012).

The **cerebral cortex** is the outer layer of gray matter in the human brain thought to be responsible for complex, high-level intellectual functions such as memory, language, and reasoning. Ongoing positive and diverse learning opportunities during middle childhood may help facilitate continued brain growth and optimal refinement. In other words, middle childhood is increasingly viewed as a rich phase of neuromaturation, resulting in recommendations to expose children to activities and experiences that capitalize on the language and other cognitive growth capacities present during these years (DelGiudice, 2018).

Variations in brain development and functioning play an important role in many aspects of learning, emotion, and behavior (Davidson & Begley, 2012; Kahneman, 2011). During middle childhood, identification and potential diagnosis of special learning needs typically peaks. There is interest in gender- or sex-based differences in brain functioning and learning styles and evidence that in the United States, boys are at higher risk than girls for poor literacy performance and special education placement (Weaver-Hightower, 2008). Although recent evidence suggests no statistically significant differences in male and female high school dropout rates (U.S. Department of Education, 2015a), the importance of sex or gender in shaping the human experience cannot be overstated. Sex and gender are profoundly influential organizing factors, and biological correlates may influence behavior and learning processes in ways we do not clearly understand. However, gender is but one of several personal and group characteristics relevant to understanding educational privilege specifically as well as risk and protection generally. Additional persistently influential factors impacting the likelihood of educational success in the United States are race or ethnicity and socioeconomic status.

A number of contemporary developmental theorists have focused on assessing the relevance and applicability of traditional developmental tasks to all children. Most agree that the central ideas of the theorists summarized in Exhibit 5.1 remain meaningful albeit at distinct levels of relevance. For example, Erikson's thoughts are widely recognized as important keys to understanding contemporary school-age children. In some areas, however, these developmental theories have been critiqued and subsequently expanded. This is particularly true in moral development.

The best-known theory of moral development is Lawrence Kohlberg's stage theory (for an overview of this theory, refer to Exhibit 4.2). Kohlberg's research on moral reasoning concluded that children do not enter the second level of *conventional moral reasoning*, or morality based on approval of authorities or upholding societal standards, until about age 9 or 10, sometime after they have the cognitive skills for such reasoning. However, Robert Coles (1987, 1997) emphasized the distinction between moral imagination—the gradually developed capacity to reflect on what is right and wrong—and moral conduct. He argued that *behavior* is shaped by daily experiences, reflecting the way the child is treated in his or her various environments such as home and school. The school-age child pays close attention to the consistency and the discrepancies between the moral "voices" and actions of the adults

EXHIBIT 5.1 ● Phases and Tasks of Middle Childhood		
Theorist	**Phase or Task**	**Description**
Freud (1938/1973)	Latency	Sexual instincts become less dominant; superego develops further.
Erikson (1950)	Industry versus inferiority	Capacity to cooperate and create develops; result is sense of either mastery or incompetence.
Piaget (1936/1952)	Concrete operational	Reasoning becomes more logical but remains at concrete level; principle of conservation is learned.
Piaget (1932/1965)	Moral realism and autonomous morality	Conception of morality changes from absolute and external to relative and internal.
Kohlberg (1969)	Preconventional and conventional morality	Reasoning based on punishment and reward is replaced by reasoning based on formal law and external opinion.
Selman (1980)	Self-reflective perspective taking	Ability develops to view one's own actions, thoughts, and emotions from another's perspective.

in his or her world, including parents, friends' parents, relatives, teachers, and coaches.

Carol Gilligan (1982) extensively criticized Kohlberg's theory of moral development as paying inadequate attention to girls' "ethic of care" and the keen emphasis girls often place on relationships and the emotions of others. Consistent with Gilligan's ideas, a number of developmental theorists have argued that girls possess heightened **interrelational intelligence**, which is based on emotional and social intelligence and is similar to Howard Gardner's concept of interpersonal intelligence (Borysenko, 1996). Such developmentalists, drawing on feminist scholarship, point out that both girls and boys advance rapidly in the cognitive and moral developmental domains during middle childhood but may be unique in their approaches to social relationships and interactions, and such differences may shape and reflect the distinct nature of development in all domains (Borysenko, 1996; Gilligan, 1982; Taylor, Gilligan, & Sullivan, 1995). It is also important to note that collectivist-oriented societies place a high value on connectedness, and research with groups from collectivist societies indicates that they do not score well on Kohlberg's model of moral development, leading to questions regarding the universal validity of this model. Moral development scholars today argue that moral development must be understood in a sociocultural context (Gardiner, 2018; Haidt, 2013).

A consistent research finding is that even among very young children, supportive caregiver relationships are associated with a child's capacity to understand or focus on the needs of others (Thompson, Meyer, & McGinley, 2006). Schwartz's value theory (2012) identifies self-enhancement (egocentric, focus on the self) versus self-transcendence (benevolence, focus on others) and conservation (conformity, security) versus openness to change (self-direction, independence) as persistent tensions in moral development research. Doring, Daniel, and Knafo-Noam (2016) point out that contrary to Kohlberg's model, self-transcendence (Thompson, 2012) and openness to change (Smetana, Jambon, & Ball, 2014) are evident in the thoughts and behavior of very young children. Contemporary research contradicts many of Kohlberg's beliefs and suggests moral development is far more complicated than early developmentalists believed (Lapsley & Carlo, 2014).

PHOTO 5.2 Middle childhood is a critical time for children to acquire a sense of self-confidence and develop conceptual thought.

© Josh Hodge/iStockphoto.com

Gabriela speaks English as a second language and in some ways is representative of many school-age children. In the United States, approximately 22% of all children ages 5 through 17 enrolled in school speak a language other than English at home (Annie E. Casey Foundation, 2015). Multi- and bilingual children in the United States were, at one point, thought to be at risk of developmental deficits. However, significant research demonstrates that bilingualism has positive impacts on cognitive development (Olsen et al., 2015). With growing understanding of the way environmental demands change brain structures, researchers have explored the relationship between bilingualism and the brain and have concluded that bilingualism enhances both cognitive and social development (Fan, Liberman, Keysar, & Kinzler, 2015; Javor, 2016). Grandchildren

Cultural Identity Development

Identity is an important aspect of social development, and by middle childhood, children are capable of thinking in a complex fashion about social group membership (Rogers, Zosuls, Halim, Ruble, & Hughes, 2012). During middle childhood, cognitive advances allow children to view themselves and others as capable of belonging to more than one "category" at once, as capable of possessing multiple heritages simultaneously (Butler-Sweet, 2011; Nuttgens, 2010). Contemporary developmentalists agree that children become much more aware of ethnic identities and other aspects of diversity such as socioeconomic status and gender identities during their middle childhood years. A child's cultural awareness and related beliefs are shaped by the nature of experiences such as exposure to diversity within the family and community, including school, contexts. Unlike the preschoolers' cognitive attraction to "black-and-white" classifications, children progressing through middle childhood are increasingly capable of understanding the complexities of group memberships; in other words, they are cognitively capable of rejecting oversimplistic stereotypes of individuals and groups (Davies, 2011).

For most children, gender is a critical and linked component of identity development during middle childhood. The integration of multiple aspects of identity, including but not limited to gender and ethnicity, may be a central part of the quest for a coherent identity that begins in middle childhood and continues well into adolescence and adulthood (Ghavami, Katsiaficas, & Rogers, 2016). Segregation based on gender, ethnicity or race, and social class is common in friendships at all ages, including middle childhood. Like adults, children are more likely to hold negative attitudes toward groups to which they do not belong (Haidt, 2013). However, successful cross-group childhood friendships are associated with positive social outcomes. A particular challenge for children such as Anthony or Gabriela may be blending contradictory values, standards, or traditions. Some children respond to cultural contradictions by identifying with the mainstream American culture (*assimilation*) in which they are immersed or by developing negative attitudes about their subcultural group memberships either consciously or subconsciously (*stereotype vulnerability*). Individual reactions, such as those of Gabriela, will be shaped by the child's unique experiences and social influences.

For all children, it is a major developmental task to integrate dual or multiple identities into a consistent personal identity (Vera et al., 2011). Many models of identity exist for children of mixed ethnicity, with new ideas and theories constantly emerging. Fluidity in multiracial identity appears to peak in early adolescence (Echols, Ivanich, & Graham, 2017). McAdoo (2001) asserts that, compared with children who identify with the majority group, children from nondominant groups are much more likely to possess awareness of their own group identity or identities as well as majority group characteristics. The terms *bicultural* and *multicultural competence* are used to refer to the skills children from nondominant groups must acquire to survive and thrive developmentally (Lum, 2011).

Identity development for children is extremely complex, and adults effectively support children by facilitating appreciation of heritage and development of an integrated identity along with positive self-regard (Chung, Bemak, & Grabosky, 2011). Children should be provided with opportunities to explore their dual or multiple heritages and to select their own terms for identifying and describing themselves (Nuttgens, 2010; Rollins & Hunter, 2013). The most positive outcomes seem to be associated with supportive family systems and involvement in social and recreational activities that expose children to their heritage and lead to self-affirmation (Hagelskamp, Suárez-Orozco, & Hughes, 2010; Lunkett, Behnke, Sands, & Choi, 2009). The family environment plays a critical role in shaping all aspects of development, and the family is the primary vehicle through which cultural identity is transmitted. Children typically learn, through their families, how to view their own ethnicity or race and that of others as well as coping strategies to respond to potential or direct exclusion, discrimination, or racism (Casas, Suzuki, Alexander, & Jackson, 2016).

Individuals and organizations within the child's social system can provide support for development of an integrated, positive sense of self by being sensitive to the complexities of ethnic/racial origin and ethnic/racial distinctions; they can also help by celebrating cultural diversity and increasing the cultural understanding of all children. Such interventions appear to encourage fewer negative stereotypes of peers belonging to non-dominant groups (Isenberg & Jolongo, 2003). Recent research suggests that race and ethnic background shape social behavior and status during the middle childhood years, and African American children may be disproportionately likely to be perceived by both within- and cross-ethnic group peers as "popular and cool" (Wilson, Rodkin, & Ryan, 2014, p. 1117). Intersectionality theory offers new insights into social relationships and identity development processes during childhood (see discussion of intersectionality theory in Chapter 1 of this book). Ghavami et al. (2016) point out the distinction between the study of multiple identities and the study of identity intersectionality (p. 35). The study of identity intersectionality focuses less on hierarchical group memberships and more on the ways in which various aspects of identity fuse together to create an individual's unique lens. They note that among children, although understanding of gender appears to emerge first, we understand relatively little about the timing of identity intersectionality.

In addition, new research on gender calls into question long-held beliefs about children and identity development. Developmentalists have widely agreed that gender constancy is a necessary prerequisite for understanding social group identification. However, research with transgender children suggests that some transgender children experience gender fluidity and others experience gender constancy, albeit not with the gender assigned at birth. As children experience sexual attraction, emerging sexuality contributes additional complexity to identity development. Also, the meaning assigned to different aspects of identity is influenced by the status of the relevant social group (for example, girls seem to report higher levels of gender centrality than boys; racial and ethnic minority children report higher levels of race and ethnicity centrality than racial majority children; immigrant children of color seem to view their ethnic identity as more salient than gender). In terms of social group stereotyping, children appear to become aware of gender stereotypes before they develop awareness of other group stereotypes, and children from lower-status social groups are more attuned to stereotypes at young ages (Ghavami et al., 2016; Rogers & Meltzoff, 2017). Intersectionality theory reveals the biased and reductionistic fashion through which identity has been studied in the past.

Emotional Development

As most children move from early childhood into and through middle childhood, they experience significant gains in their ability to identify and articulate their own emotions as well as the emotions of others. Typically, middle childhood is a period when thoughts become more expansive and emotions more controlled (Mah & Ford-Jones, 2012). Exhibit 5.2 summarizes several gains school-age children often make in emotional functioning. It is important to recognize that a variety of interconnected factors shape emotional development (Glowiak & Mayfield, 2016). These factors range from culture (Matsumoto & Hwang, 2011) to attachment history (Van de Walle, Bijttebier, Braet, & Bosmans, 2016). Most children in this age range develop adaptive coping skills that help them when encountering upsetting, stressful, or traumatic situations. As defined by Daniel Goleman (2006), **emotional intelligence** refers to the ability to "motivate oneself and persist in the face of frustrations, to control impulse and delay gratification, to regulate one's moods and keep distress from swamping the ability to think, to empathize and to hope" (p. 34). Emotional and social intelligence are inextricably linked, and as a result, interventions used with children experiencing social difficulties often focus on enhancing some aspect of emotional intelligence (see, for example, Birknerová, 2011). Goleman (2013) has more recently linked emotional intelligence with the ability to sustain focus, pointing out the relevance of practices such as mindfulness and meditation to behavior control.

EXHIBIT 5.2 ● Common Emotional Gains During Middle Childhood

- Ability to mentally organize and articulate emotional experiences
- Cognitive control of emotional arousal
- Ability to remain focused on goal-directed actions
- Ability to delay gratification based on cognitive evaluation
- Ability to understand and use the concept of planning
- Ability to view tasks incrementally
- Use of social comparison
- Influence of internalized feelings (e.g., self-pride, shame) on behavior
- Capacity to tolerate conflicting feelings
- Increasingly effective defense mechanisms

Source: Davies, 2011, pp. 360–363.

Goleman (2006, 2013) also asserts that social and emotional intelligence are key aspects of both moral reasoning and moral conduct. In other words, although often it may seem that advancing capacities in the moral domain occur naturally for children, positive conditions and interactions facilitate optimal emotional and social competencies (Duong & Bradshaw, 2017). Thus, a child like Anthony, with seemingly good academic promise, may not realize his potential without timely intervention targeting the development of critical emotional and social competencies. These competencies include, for example, self-awareness; impulse control; and the ability to identify, express, and manage feelings, including love, jealousy, anxiety, and anger. Healthy emotional development can be threatened by a number of issues, including challenges such as temperament, loss, and trauma. We increasingly recognize the vulnerability of school-age children to serious emotional and mental health issues. Assessment approaches that incorporate awareness of and attention to the possible existence of such issues are critical.

Fortunately, a substantial knowledge base regarding the promotion of positive emotional development exists. Judith Siegel (2013) summarizes the neuroscience research establishing emotional regulation as key to understanding the heritability of family violence. She describes trauma-informed interventions targeting family systems dynamics and emotional dysregulation as a step toward preventing the intergenerational transmission of violence. Similarly, Ross Thompson (2014) describes the promise of individual and multigenerational interventions focused on reversing the neurobiological changes that accompany chronic stress.

Richard Davidson and Sharon Begley (2012) have written extensively about the concept of "emotional style" and effective approaches to changing one's emotional style. Many emotion-focused intervention strategies appear effective with young children (see Colle & Del Giudice, 2011; Rapee, 2015). For example, Jasmine, like many children her age, is exhibiting signs of anxiety and could benefit from intervention focusing on the development of healthy coping strategies. A number of interacting, complex biopsychosocial-spiritual factors shape vulnerability to ailments such as anxiety and depression. Davidson and Begley assert that an individual's unique, brain-based emotional style reflects a combination of six concepts, or "substyles." These six (outlook, attention, sensitivity to context, social intuition, resilience, and self-awareness) interact to produce our emotional style, and although it is not easy, we are capable of changing our style.

Goleman (2006) argues that many cases of depression arise from deficits in two key areas of emotional competence: relationship skills and cognitive, or interpretive, style. In short, many children suffering from—or at risk of developing—depression likely possess a depression-promoting cognitive style (or "self-schema") including negative self-evaluation, pessimism, and hopelessness (Braet, Wante, Van Beveren, & Theuwis, 2015, p. 1261). Children with a potentially harmful outlook attribute setbacks in their lives to internal, personal flaws. Appropriate preventive intervention, based on a cognitive behavioral approach, teaches children that their emotions are linked to the way they think and facilitates productive, healthy ways of interpreting events and viewing themselves. For Jasmine, cognitive-behavioral-oriented intervention may be helpful. Gabriela is involved in a gender-specific intervention at school—a girls' self-esteem group. Jasmine might also benefit from a gender-specific intervention, perhaps with a particular focus on relational resilience. Gender-specific interventions are often most appropriate when the social problem is experienced primarily by one gender (Perry-Parrish & Zeman, 2011; Potter, 2004). Disordered eating and self-injurious behavior are examples of issues that impact all children but are disproportionately experienced by girls. Identifying the relevance of gender issues to a child's emotional state and considering a gender-specific intervention strategy are often appropriate.

The concept of "relational resilience" is built on relational-cultural theory's belief that "all psychological growth occurs in relationships": the building blocks of relational resilience are "mutual empathy, empowerment, and the development of courage" (Jordan, 2005, p. 79). For children experiencing adversity including **trauma** (severe physical or psychological injury), effective parenting can play a critical role in supporting resilience. Parent–child co-regulation refers to the idea of relationship responses that foster adaptive coping and emotional well-being (Herbers et al., 2014).

Many school-age girls and boys experience emotional distress because of significant loss. Jasmine has experienced much loss as she moved from home to home and school to school, the loss of her dad to addiction and prison, and the recent loss of her grandmother. The school counselor and social worker might want to explore with Gabriela what she experienced as loss in her move from Mexico to the United States. Children with close ties to extended family are particularly likely to experience loss of a close relative at a young age and therefore are more prone to this sort of depression. Loss,

health issues

trauma, and violence may present serious obstacles to healthy emotional development. Research demonstrates the remarkable potential resilience of children (see Goldstein & Brooks, 2013; Luthar, 2003; Werner & Brendtro, 2012), but both personal and environmental attributes play a critical role in processes of resilience. To support the healthy emotional development of children at risk, appropriate multilevel prevention and intervention efforts are crucial.

It can be challenging to tell when a troublesome behavior is just a part of child development or when it is something that should be discussed with a health professional. The U.S. National Institute of Mental Health suggests that parents and teachers should pay attention to signs and symptoms that interfere with the child's daily life in the last weeks or months, particularly if they are demonstrated in more than one setting. They suggest that the symptoms presented in Exhibit 5.3 might be warning signs that the child needs professional help. Anthony's constant motion may be one of the signs leading his teacher to want to have him assessed by the school psychologist. It seems important for Jasmine to receive professional assistance to consider whether her

---

EXHIBIT 5.3 ● Warning Signs That a Child May Need Help

Often feels anxious or worried

Has frequent tantrums or is intensely irritable much of the time

Is in constant motion, can't sit quietly for any length of time

Has trouble sleeping, including frequent nightmares

Loses interest in things he or she used to enjoy

Avoids spending time with friends

Has trouble doing well in school, or grades decline

Fears gaining weight; exercises, diets obsessively

Has low or no energy

Has spells of intense, inexhaustible activity

Harms herself or himself, such as cutting or burning skin

Engages in risky, destructive behavior

Harms others

Smokes, drinks, or uses drugs

Has thoughts of suicide

Thinks his or her mind is controlled or out of control, hears voices

Source: National Institute of Mental Health, 2018.

---

headaches and racing heart are signs of anxiety and, if so, how she can manage the anxiety. In Jasmine's family, Jenesis also needs professional evaluation and treatment regarding her cutting behavior and possibly for her use of alcohol and tobacco.

CRITICAL THINKING QUESTIONS 5.2

How would you describe the physical, cognitive, cultural identity, and emotional development of Anthony, Jasmine, and Gabriela? In what areas do they each show particular strengths? In what areas do they each show particular challenges? How could a social worker help each child to enhance development in areas where he or she is particularly challenged?

Social Development

Perhaps the most widely recognized developmental task of this period is acquiring feelings of *self-competence.* Traditional developmentalists have pointed out that the school-age child searches for opportunities to demonstrate personal skills, abilities, and achievements. This is what Erik Erikson (1963) was referring to when he described the developmental struggle of middle childhood as industry versus inferiority (refer to Exhibit 3.8 for a description of all eight of Erikson's psychosocial stages). *Industry* refers to a drive to acquire new skills and do meaningful "work." The experiences of middle childhood may foster or thwart the child's attempts to acquire an enhanced sense of *mastery* and self-efficacy. Family, peer, and community support enhance the child's growing sense of competence; lack of such support undermines this sense. The child's definitions of self and accomplishment vary greatly according to interpretations in the surrounding environment. External appraisal must be supportive and encouraging but also genuine for most children in this developmental phase to value such feedback. Some theorists argue that children must learn the value of perseverance and develop an internal drive to succeed (Seligman, Reivich, Jaycox, & Gillham, 2007; Snyder et al., 2013). Opportunities to excel and to fail are both valuable, along with sincere feedback and support. Ideally, the developing school-age child acquires the sense of personal competence and tenacity that will serve as a protective factor during adolescence and young adulthood.

Families play a critical role in supporting development of this sense of competence. For example, as the child learns to ride a bike or play a sport or musical

[handwritten note: Link between school shootings v. Bullying]

instrument, adults can provide specific feedback and praise. They can counter the child's frustration by identifying and complimenting specific improvements and emphasizing the role of practice and perseverance in producing improvements. Failures and setbacks can be labeled as temporary and surmountable rather than attributed to personal flaws or deficits. The presence of such social feedback loops is a key feature of supportive adult–child relationships, in the family, at school, and within other social contexts.

Middle childhood is a critical time for children to acquire a sense of competence, and yet children are not equally positioned to acquire feelings of self-competence as they enter this developmental phase, as Anthony's, Jasmine's, and Gabriela's stories suggest. Developmental pathways preceding entry into middle childhood are extremely diverse. Children experience this phase of life differently based not only on differences in the surrounding environment—such as family structure and socioeconomic status—but also on their personality differences. A particular personality and learning style may be valued or devalued, problematic or nonproblematic, in each of the child's expanding social settings (Berk, 2012). Thus, although Anthony, Jasmine, and Gabriela are moving through the same developmental period and facing many common tasks, they experience these tasks differently and will emerge into adolescence as unique individuals.

Each individual child's identity development highly depends on social networks of privilege and exclusion. A direct relationship exists between the level of control and power a child experiences and the degree of balance achieved between feelings of power (privilege) and powerlessness (exclusion) (Johnson, 2006; Tatum, 2007). As children move toward adolescence and adulthood, the amount of emotional, social, spiritual, and economic **capital**, or resources, acquired shapes self-efficacy and the likelihood of socioeconomic and educational success. Experiencing economically and socially just support systems is critical to optimum development (Dreyer, Chung, Szilagyi, & Wong, 2016).

Advancing language capability in middle childhood serves not only as a communication tool but also as a vehicle for more sophisticated introspection. Language is also a potential tool for positive assertion of self and more complex personal opinions as the child's social world expands (Beck, Kumschick, & Klann-Delius, 2012; Glowiak & Mayfield, 2016). In recent years, many elementary schools have added **character education** to their curricula. Such education often consists of direct teaching and curriculum inclusion of moral

and social values thought to be universal in a community (e.g., kindness, respect, honesty). Renewed focus on children's character education is in part related to waves of school violence, harassment, and bullying. Survey research with children suggests that bullying may peak in sixth grade, though children of all ages in school settings are at risk (National Center for Education Statistics, 2017a).

Legislative initiatives have encouraged school personnel to confront bullying and harassment in the school setting. Schools have been particularly responsive to these initiatives in the wake of well-publicized incidents of school violence. Today, most schools have character education programs in place along with policies designed to facilitate efficient and effective responses to aberrant behavior, including bullying and violence (Character.org, 2015; Diggs & Akos, 2016). The content and implementation details of such policies vary widely.

During the late 20th century, changes occurred in our views and understanding of bullying (Espelage & Swearer, 2011). In general, the public has become less tolerant of bullying, perhaps because of a fairly widespread belief that school shootings (such as the Chardon, Ohio, school shootings and the Columbine High School massacre) can be linked to bullying. Bullying is today recognized as a complex phenomenon, with both **direct bullying** (physical) and indirect bullying viewed as cause for concern. **Indirect bullying** refers to verbal, psychological, and social or "relational" bullying tactics and includes cyberbullying (Englander, 2013; Kyriacou, 2016; U.S. Department of Education, 2015b).

In recent years, interest has centered on the ways in which technology influences social relationships among children and youth as well as gender differences in relationships and bullying. Initially, attention was drawn to the previously underrecognized phenomenon of girls experiencing direct bullying, or physical aggression and violence, at the hands of other girls (Garbarino, 2007). Although both direct and indirect bullying cross genders, more recent attention has centered on the widespread existence of indirect, or relational, bullying among all children, but particularly among girls, and its potentially devastating consequences (Chesney-Lind & Jones, 2010; Cooley & Fite, 2016; Pepler, 2012; Simmons, 2011; U.S. Department of Education, 2015b). One positive outcome of recent attention to bullying is interest in establishing "best practices" in bullying prevention and intervention. The current knowledge base suggests that the most effective approach to reducing bullying within a school is implementation of a comprehensive, schoolwide prevention and intervention plan that addresses the contributing factors within all levels of the school and community environment (Klein, 2012; see stopbullying.gov).

Prevention research indicates communities possess great potential to provide important macro-level support and structure for children. Today, however, many communities provide as many challenges as opportunities for development. Communities in which challenges outweigh opportunities have been labeled "socially toxic," meaning they threaten positive development (Garbarino, 1995). In contrast, within a socially supportive environment, children have access to peers and adults who reinforce empathy, model *prosocial behavior*, and serve as protective factors to enhance the likelihood of healthy social development (Vanderbilt-Adriance et al., 2015). Cognitive and moral development of children is a social issue in the sense that mentoring takes place in the **zone of proximal development**—the theoretical space between the child's current developmental level and the child's potential level if given access to appropriate models and experiences in the social environment (Vygotsky et al., 2012). The child's competence is ideally impacted through social interactions in a dynamic and positive fashion, resulting in developmental progress.

The Peer Group

During middle childhood, peers play a powerful role in shaping school achievement as well as psychosocial well-being (van den Berg, Deutz, Smeekens, & Cillessen, 2017). Peer groups become nearly as influential as family members, and a desire for group belongingness is especially strong. Whereas individual friendships facilitate the development of critical capacities such as trust and intimacy, peer groups foster learning about conflict, cooperation, and leadership. Throughout middle childhood, the importance of *group norms* is highly evident (von Salisch, Haenel, & Freund, 2013). Children are sensitive, sometimes exceedingly so, to their peers' standards for behavior, appearance, and attitudes. Gabriela, for instance, may begin to devalue herself because she recognizes potential discrepancy between her appearance and group norms. Often it is not until adolescence that group norms may become more flexible, allowing for more individuality. This shift reflects the complex relationship among the developmental domains. In this case, the association between social and cognitive

development is illustrated by simultaneous changes in social relationships and cognitive capacities.

Gains in cognitive abilities promote more complex communication skills and greater social awareness. These developments, in turn, facilitate more complex peer interaction, which is a vital resource for the development of **social competence**. There is no uniform definition of social competence in part because the nature of this dynamic concept shifts with changing social contexts, but it generally refers to the ability to engage in sustained, positive, and mutually satisfactory social interactions and relationships. Prerequisites to social competence include skills such as communication ability, emotional regulation, problem solving, and a desire to obtain certain social outcomes such as having friends or being popular (Jackson & Cunningham, 2015). Supportive peer relationships reflect and support social competence, for they potentially discourage egocentrism, promote adaptive coping, and ultimately serve as a protective factor during the transition to adolescence (Spencer, Harpalani, Fegley, Dell'Angelo, & Seaton, 2003).

Gender and culture influence the quantity and nature of peer interactions observed among school-age children (Perry-Parrish & Zeman, 2011). Sociability, intimacy, social expectations and rules, and the value placed on various types of play and other social activities are all phenomena shaped by both gender and culture. Spencer et al. (2003) point out that children from nondominant groups are more likely to experience dissonance across school, family, and peer settings; for example, such children may experience language differences; misunderstandings of cultural traditions or expressions; and distinct norms, or rules, regarding dating behavior, peer intimacy, and cross-gender friendships. Although many youth experiencing dissonance across school, family, and peer systems may suffer from negative outcomes such as peer rejection or school failure, some demonstrate resilience and learn important coping skills that will serve them well later in life. In fact, Spencer et al. (2003) argue that given the clear trend toward increasing cultural diversity around the globe, "experiences of cultural dissonance and the coping skills they allow youth to develop should not be viewed as aberrant; instead, privilege should be explored as having a 'downside' that potentially compromises the development of coping and character" (p. 137).

However, a persistent finding is that, across gender and culture, peer acceptance is a powerful predictor of psychological adjustment. Recent research distinguishes between being perceived as popular versus being accepted and perceived with affection, identifying the role aggression may play in popularity achievement (Rodkin, Ryan, Jamison, & Wilson, 2013). Children may dislike a peer they view as popular and may like a peer they do not identify as popular. A study that remains influential in this area asked children to fit other children into particular categories. From the results, the researchers developed five general categories of social acceptance: popular, rejected, controversial, neglected, and average (Coie, Dodge, & Coppotelli, 1982). Rejected children are those actively disliked by their peers, and rejected status is strongly associated with poor academic and social outcomes (Lev-Wiesel, Sarid, & Sternberg, 2013). For this reason, we should be concerned about Gabriela's sense of peer rejection. Support for rejected children may include interventions to improve peer relations and psychological adjustment. Most of these interventions are based on social learning theory and involve modeling and reinforcing positive social behavior—for example, initiating interaction and responding to others positively. Such programs can help young children develop social competence and gain peer acceptance (Mikami et al., 2013; Mikami, Lerner, & Lun, 2010).

Friendship and Intimacy

Throughout middle childhood, children expand their ability to look at things from others' perspectives. In turn, their capacity to develop more intimate and complex friendships—based on awareness of others' thoughts, feelings, and needs—emerges (von Salisch et al., 2013; Zelazo, Chandler, & Crone, 2010). As a result, for many children, more complex and stable friendships begin to form for the first time in middle childhood. Although skills such as cooperation and problem solving are learned in the peer group, close friendships facilitate empathy while promoting trust and reciprocity. Ideally, children learn to maintain and nurture both close friendships and effective peer-group interactions. Gabriela may have had close friendships in Mexico but is struggling to develop friendships in her new school. Jasmine has moved from home to home and school to school, and this lack of housing and school stability has interfered with her ability to form close friendships. Intervention such as the girls' self-esteem group Gabriela is participating in may support the development of supportive peer relationships.

As children move through middle childhood, friendship begins to acquire a more intense emotional component (Jobe-Shields, Cohen, & Parra, 2011). In late middle childhood, children may gain close friendships based

on the emotional support provided for one another as much as, if not more than, common interests and activities. The concept of friend is transformed from the playmate of early childhood to confidant. The role of emotional support and intimacy in friendship becomes even more pronounced, and children increasingly value mutual understanding and loyalty in the face of conflict among peers (Woods, 2013). Indeed, friendship serves as a protective factor when facing social victimization and bullying (Fitzpatrick & Bussey, 2014).

Team Play

The overall incidence of physical aggression during peer activities decreases during middle childhood, and friendly rule-based play increases. This transition is due in part to the continuing development of perspective-taking ability, the ability to see a situation from another person's point of view. In addition, most school-age children are exposed to peers who differ in a variety of ways, including culture and personality.

Developmental changes result in shifts in group communication and interaction, reflecting an enhanced ability to understand the role of multiple participants in activities. These developments facilitate the transition to participation in more complex rule-based activities, such as team sports. When competition is minimized, involvement with team sports may provide great enjoyment and may have long-term benefits (Walters, Payne, Schluter, & Thomson, 2015). Research suggests linkages between physical activity in adulthood and participation in sports and other forms of regular exercise during childhood and adolescence (Mäkinen et al., 2010; Ortega et al., 2013). While participating in team sports and other similar group activities, other potential positive outcomes include the capacity for interdependence, cooperation, comprehension of division of labor, and healthy competition (American Alliance for Health, Physical Education, Recreation and Dance, 2013).

Gender Identity and Gender Roles

Although most children in middle childhood have a great deal in common based on their shared developmental phase, girls and boys differ significantly in areas ranging from their self-understanding and social relationships to school performance, interests, and life aspirations (Perry-Parrish & Zeman, 2011). Among most school-age children, gender identity, or an "internalized psychological experience of being male or female," is quite well-established (Diamond & Savin-Williams, 2003, p. 105). This is not, however, the case for all children. Many children experience a fluid sense of gender identity, particularly prior to the onset of puberty. Research indicates that the greater the **gender dysphoria** (feeling one's emotional and psychological identity as male or female to be different from one's assigned biological identity) experienced as a young child, the more likely it is that the child will continue to experience gender variance through adolescence (Wallien & Cohen-Kettenis, 2008). Puberty suspension or suppression through hormonal treatments is increasingly common among gender variant youth, to give them time to solidify their gender identity, but remains controversial (Lament, 2015). Lesbian, gay, bisexual, transgender, and questioning children and youth are particularly vulnerable to social isolation and other developmental challenges associated with negative social experiences in family and school settings (Burgess, 2009; Greytak & Kosciw, 2013).

Our understanding of the structure of gender roles is derived from various theoretical perspectives (Bromberg & O'Donohue, 2013). An anthropological or social constructionist orientation illuminates the ways in which gender shapes familial and societal systems and inevitably impacts individual development in an intangible yet profound fashion (Gardiner, 2018). Cognitive theory suggests that at the individual level, self-perceptions emerge. Gender, as one component of a psychological sense of self, joins related cognitions to guide children's gender-linked behaviors. A behavioral perspective suggests that gender-related behaviors precede self-perception in the development of gender role identity; in other words, at a very young age, girls start imitating feminine behavior and later begin thinking of themselves as distinctly female, and boys go through the same sequence in developing a masculine identity. Gender schema theory (see Bem, 1993, 1998), an information-processing approach to gender, combines behavioral and cognitive theories, suggesting that social influences and cognition work together to perpetuate gender-linked perceptions and behaviors.

Feminist psychodynamic theorists such as Nancy Chodorow (1991, 1999) have proposed that whereas boys typically begin to separate psychologically from their female caregivers in early childhood, most girls deepen their connection to and identification with their female caregivers throughout childhood. Such theorists propose, then, that as girls and boys transition into adolescence and face a new level of individuation, they confront this challenge from very different psychological places, and adolescent girls are more likely to find the task emotionally confusing if not deeply overwhelming. This feminist, psychoanalytic theoretical orientation represents one approach used to explain not only gender identity and role development but also

differences between boys and girls in their approaches to relationships and emotional expressiveness.

Women's studies experts have pointed out that school-age girls often seem to possess a "confident understanding of self," which too often disintegrates as they increasingly "discredit their feelings and understandings, experiencing increased self-doubt" during early adolescence and subsequently becoming susceptible to a host of internalizing and externalizing disorders linked to poor self-esteem (Potter, 2004, p. 60). A number of studies and theories attempt to explain this shift in girls' self-image and mental health as they transition to adolescence (Perry-Parrish & Zeman, 2011; Simmons, 2011), but Potter (2004) cautions against overgeneralization of the phenomena and in particular suggests that the trend may not apply widely across girls from differing ethnic groups, socioeconomic statuses, and sexual orientations.

During middle childhood, often boys' identification with "masculine" role attributes increases whereas girls' identification with "feminine" role attributes decreases (Potter, 2004). For instance, boys are more likely than girls to label a chore as a "girl's job" or a "boy's job." As adults, females are the more androgynous of the two genders, and this movement toward androgyny appears to begin in middle childhood (Diamond & Savin-Williams, 2003).

These differences have multiple causes, from social to cognitive forces. In the United States, during middle childhood and beyond, cross-gender behavior in girls is more socially acceptable than such behavior among boys (Pauletti, Cooper, & Perry, 2014). Diamond and Savin-Williams (2003) use the term *gender typicality*, or the "degree to which one's appearance, behavior, interests, and subjective self-concept conform to conventional gender norms" (p. 105). Research suggests that for both genders, a traditionally "masculine" identity is associated with a higher sense of overall competence and better academic performance (Boldizar, 1991; Newcomb & Dubas, 1992). Diamond and Savin-Williams (2003) also emphasize the role of culture in this relationship, pointing out that this is likely because the traits associated with male, or for girls, "tomboy," status are those most valued in many communities. These traits include qualities such as athleticism, confidence, and assertiveness. Indeed, communities with "more entrenched sexist ideologies" regarding male versus female traits are those in which boys exhibiting feminine behaviors are likely to suffer (p. 107).

In general, because of expanding cognitive capacities, as children leave early childhood and progress through middle childhood, their gender stereotypes gradually become more flexible, and most school-age children begin to accept that males and females can engage in the same activities (Kahraman & Başal, 2012). The relationships among gender identity, gender stereotyping, and individual gender role adoption are not clear-cut. Even children well aware of community gender norms and role expectations may not conform to gender role stereotypes in their actual behavior (Brinkman, Jedinak, Rosen, & Zimmerman, 2011; Gerouki, 2010). Our understanding of the complexities of gender and sexual identity development—and the relationships between the two during the life course—is in its infancy.

Technology and Social Development

In recent years, there has been intense interest in the ways in which technology impacts child development. In affluent nations, most children are technologically savvy by early childhood (Ernest et al., 2014). Technological advances in social media, gaming, television, and the music industry are just a few examples of the ways in which digital media impacts children, and in 2015 the National Academy of Sciences held a colloquium titled "Digital Media and Developing Minds" examining the extensive body of research suggesting both positive and negative implications for child development (Gentile et al., 2017).

Several researchers have pointed out potentially positive impacts of technology on children (Granic, Lobel, & Engels, 2014; Hsin, Li, & Tsai, 2014; Singer & Singer, 2011). Technology, whether directly or indirectly used for educational purposes, may enhance cognitive development. It presents children and the adults in their lives with opportunities for social connection that did not exist in the past. Children can maintain and develop relationships despite geographical or other separations. Social support positively influences children, and these relationships may promote the development of communication skills not supported through relationships initiated or maintained solely through in-person interaction. Some argue that technology presents children with positive opportunities for social interaction that do not "fit" in the busy weekly schedule of today's often overscheduled school-age child. In addition, some children report that use of technology allows them to explore aspects of their identity in a safe way not possible through in-person interactions. Indeed, personal identity development in areas such as sexuality and ethnicity can be informed in both positive and negative ways via media exposure. Some children also report that technology enables them to relax or escape from stressors associated with family, peer relationships, or other challenges.

Turkle (2011) explains the ways in which virtual creatures, enhanced by technology, promote prosocial behavior in young children. However, like the violent video game controversy, some question whether young children should be exposed to the complex ethical issues inherent in such toys or entertainment. In particular, is it appropriate to allow "tech creatures" to die when neglected, potentially harming children's developing capacity for empathy and understanding of the nature of human life? A related but distinct question to ponder is whether the attachments to "virtual" friends or creatures alter the nature of human attachment or attachment style among such children in some way.

Some children, like adults, report potentially unhealthy outcomes of technology use such as feeling more comfortable existing or interacting in a virtual rather than "real" environment and feeling more comfortable in a virtual identity (e.g., an avatar). Children are easily able to access an overwhelming quantity of media-based information, appropriate or inappropriate. Cyberbullying presents a significant threat to well-being among elementary school children (DePaolis & Williford, 2015), and use of entertainment and communication technologies before bed has been linked to sleep deprivation and associated poor health outcomes (Dube, Khan, Loehr, Chu, & Veugelers, 2017). Although access to online media may enhance cognitive development, there is ample evidence to support the harmful effects of such information access. Parents are increasingly distracted by media, finding it difficult to "turn off" from work and social connections, and research suggests a strong correlation between parent and children's use of technology (Terras & Ramsay, 2016). And yet information about effective parenting strategies is facilitated by access to media and new technologies. Similarly, parents can use technology to monitor or connect with their children more than ever before.

Focusing solely on the relationship between technology and social development, neuroscientists argue that both children and adults struggle to "unplug" because of the dopamine release associated with human connection, and received messages elicit this pleasure response to the point of addiction (Turkle, 2011; Zhou, Zhang, Liu, & Wang, 2017). Our knowledge of neurobiology suggests that the human relationship with technology is shaping the development of school-age children in a complex and profound fashion.

SPIRITUAL DEVELOPMENT

Spiritual development, historically neglected or subsumed within other developmental domains, is now widely recognized as a critical aspect of child development. Robert Coles (1990) is identified as one of the first Western developmentalists to draw connections between moral and spiritual development. Benson, Scales, Syvertsen, and Roehlkepartain (2012) define spiritual development as comprising awareness or awakening, interconnecting and belonging, and a way of life; or more specifically a synergistic process of "becoming aware of one's potential and possibility; becoming aware of the intersection of one's life with others, nature, and the universe; connecting and linking the self and one's potentials to ideals and narratives; and developing a life orientation that generates hope, purpose, and compassion" (p. 457). Richert and Granqvist (2014) distinguish between children's religious (anchored in an organized community) and spiritual (relationship with the sacred or transcendent) growth and review the cognitive basis of religious and spiritual development as children progress from early to middle childhood. They point out that for children, family plays a pivotal role in initially shaping religious and spiritual development both directly (modeling) and indirectly (contributing to attachment styles and coping strategies).

Richert and Granqvist (2014) examined spirituality as well as connections between spirituality and happiness within a sample of 8- to 12-year-old children. In their study, spirituality remained a significant happiness predictor even after removing the variance associated with individual temperament. Similar to scholars investigating adult spirituality and happiness, the researchers found that two particular aspects of spirituality—children's beliefs regarding the value of life and the quality of interpersonal relationships (also labeled the "personal" and "communal" domains of spirituality)—were particularly good predictors of happiness. Spirituality has long been established as supporting adaptive coping, and Clinton (2008) specifically found that among children suffering experiences of trauma in early childhood, higher levels of spiritual awareness are associated with more adaptive behavior, including more effective coping and resilience over time.

Lipscomb and Gersch (2012) have engaged in qualitative research employing a spiritual listening approach, which they describe as an attempt to elicit children's views "about the meanings they attach to their lives, their essential drives, motivation and desires . . . a method of tapping into children's individual spiritual journey at a particular point in their lives" (p. 8). With participants ages 10 and 11, Lipscomb and Gersch (2012) employed spiritual listening to inquire about the themes of identity, purpose, happiness, destiny, drive, and transition. Children shared views about identity, such as identity is "like an oyster" and "at first I was happy and I knew just what I was doing, but then people started bullying me just because of my skin colour

and then I started to think, who am I, what am I and why am I in this world" (p. 12). They also spoke about purpose, with such comments as "My purpose of life is having a mission. I don't really know what it is but I know it's a mission. I think my mission is to help other people, which is like my identity" (p. 13). The researchers noted that all children in their study were able to relate to these abstract and complex concepts. One of the strategies children used to connect philosophical ideas back to their concrete experiences was by referencing popular culture, including themes they had observed in media. The authors conclude that the technique of spiritual listening may support children's development as it facilitates children's ability to link the concrete nature of their lives to the metaphysical.

CRITICAL THINKING QUESTIONS 5.3

Why do you think peer acceptance is a powerful predictor of psychological adjustment in middle childhood? Why do you think cross-gender behavior is more socially acceptable for girls than for boys in the United States? How do you think Anthony, Jasmine, and Gabriela would respond to spiritual questioning?

MIDDLE CHILDHOOD AND FORMAL SCHOOLING

Before discussing the role of formal schooling in the life of the school-age child in the United States and other relatively affluent societies, it is important to note that there continue to be large global gaps in opportunities for education. Although educational participation is almost universal from ages 5 to 14 in affluent countries, many of the world's children do not receive even a primary education. In the current context of a knowledge-based global economy, the importance of formal schooling during middle childhood cannot be overstated, and yet a profound gap exists in average years of education between rich and poor countries (Winthrop & McGivney, 2015). In the United States, significant income inequality and the related income-based gap in schooling continues to widen (Duncan, Kalil, & Ziol-Guest, 2017).

Children entering school must learn to navigate a new environment that is often quite different from the family. In school, they are evaluated based on how well they perform tasks; people outside the family—teachers and other school staff as well as peers—begin shaping the child's personality, dreams, and aspirations. For children such as Gabriela, the environmental adjustment can be even more profound (Adelman & Taylor, 2015). At the same time, the school environment has the potential to serve as an important resource for the achievement of the physical, cognitive, emotional, social, and spiritual developmental tasks of middle childhood for all children.

Anthony, Jasmine, and Gabriela illustrate the potentially positive as well as painful aspects of schooling. Often, difficulties with peers create or compound academic challenges. If Gabriela's initial school experience in the United States had become socially threatening enough, she may have withdrawn from the environment, and her educational trajectory would have significantly shifted. Luckily, she had a nurturing teacher as well as a school counselor and school social worker to support her in the transition. Jasmine's and Anthony's school experiences will be pivotal in shaping their continued development in all domains. As children move through the middle years, they become increasingly aware that they are evaluated based on what they are able to do. In turn, they begin to evaluate themselves based on treatment by teachers and peers and on self-assessments of what they can and cannot do well (Garralda & Raynaud, 2010).

In the past few decades, school-age children have benefited from research and theory focusing on the concept of intelligence. Howard Gardner's work represented a paradigm shift in the field of education. He proposed that intelligence is neither unitary nor fixed and argued that intelligence is not adequately or fully measured by IQ tests. More broadly, in his theory of **multiple intelligences**, intelligence is "the ability to solve problems or fashion products that are of consequence in a particular cultural setting or community" (Gardner, 1993, p. 15). Challenging the idea that individuals can be described, or categorized, by a single, quantifiable measure of intelligence, Gardner proposed at least eight critical intelligences: verbal/linguistic, logical/mathematical, visual/spatial, musical/rhythmic, bodily/kinesthetic, naturalist, interpersonal, and intrapersonal (Campbell, Campbell, & Dickinson, 2004; Zeidner, Matthews, & Roberts, 2012). Recent educators, focusing on the practical application of multiple intelligence theory to work with school-age children in the educational context, have described this as the ability to be "smart" in the areas of words, numbers/logic, pictures, music, the body, nature, people, and self (Armstrong, 2017). In its practical application, multiple intelligence theory calls for the use of a wide range of instructional strategies that engage the range of strengths and intelligences of each student (Ghazi, Shahzada, Gilani, Shabbir, & Rashid, 2011). In addition to calling for innovative and diverse instructional strategies, multiple intelligence theory suggests achievement evaluation should consist of comprehensive assessments examining diverse areas of performance. Exhibit 5.4 provides definitions of the eight intelligences identified by Gardner.

EXHIBIT 5.4 ● Gardner's Eight Intelligences

Linguistic intelligence. The capacity to use language to express what is on your mind and to understand other people. Linguistic intelligence includes listening, speaking, reading, and writing skills.

Logical/mathematical intelligence. The capacity for mathematical calculation, logical thinking, problem solving, deductive and inductive reasoning, and the discernment of patterns and relationships. Gardner suggests that this type of intelligence is addressed by Piaget's model of cognitive development, but he does not think Piaget's model fits other types of intelligence.

Visual-spatial intelligence. The ability to represent the spatial world internally in your mind. Visual-spatial intelligence involves visual discrimination, recognition, projection, mental imagery, spatial reasoning, and image manipulation.

Bodily kinesthetic intelligence. The capacity to use your whole body or parts of your body to solve a problem, make something, or put on some kind of production. Gardner suggests that our tradition of separating body and mind is unfortunate because the mind can be trained to use the body properly and the body trained to respond to the expressive powers of the mind. He notes that some learners rely on tactile and kinesthetic processes, not just visual and auditory processes.

Musical intelligence. The capacity to think in musical images, to be able to hear patterns, recognize them, remember them, and perhaps manipulate them.

Intrapersonal intelligence. The capacity to understand yourself, to know who you are, what you can do, what you want to do, how you react to things, which things to avoid, which things to gravitate toward, and where to go if you need help. Gardner says we are drawn to people who have a good understanding of themselves because those people tend not to make mistakes. They are aware of their range of emotions and can find outlets for expressing feelings and thoughts. They are motivated to pursue goals and live by an ethical value system.

Interpersonal intelligence. The ability to understand and communicate with others, to note differences in moods, temperaments, motivations, and skills. Interpersonal intelligence includes the ability to form and maintain relationships and assume various roles within groups and the ability to adapt behavior to different environments. It also includes the ability to perceive diverse perspectives on social and political issues. Gardner suggests that individuals with this intelligence express an interest in interpersonally oriented careers, such as teaching, social work, and politics.

Naturalist intelligence. The ability to recognize and categorize objects and processes in nature. Naturalist intelligence leads to talent in caring for, taming, and interacting with the natural environment, including living creatures. Gardner suggests that naturalist intelligence can also be brought to bear to discriminate among artificial items such as sneakers, cars, and toys.

Source: Based on Gardner, 1999, 2006, 2008.

Many schools are ill-equipped to respond to the issues presented by children such as Gabriela, but when children are not supported and assisted by their school systems, the educational experience may assault healthy development. If the personal, familial, and educational support systems of a child at risk can be mobilized, they may counter the feelings of isolation in a new school environment. Carefully constructed and implemented interventions must be used to help children like Gabriela.

Today in the United States, Gabriela's situation is not rare. As noted earlier, about one in five U.S. students speak a language other than English at home (Annie E. Casey Foundation, 2015). Overall, the percentage of children living in the United States with at least one foreign-born parent rose from 15% in 1994 to 24% in 2012, remaining stable at approximately one in four children in 2016 (Federal Interagency Forum on Child and Family Statistics, 2017). In general, students in the United States are more diverse than ever before (Kent, 2015). Many challenges face children who have recently arrived in the United States, particularly those fleeing war-torn countries. Research suggests that immigrant and refugee children are at heightened risk of experiencing mental health challenges and school failure due to both pre- and postmigratory experiences (Adelman & Taylor, 2015).

There are a wide variety of risk factors for such children, such as potential post-traumatic stress and family disruption, the stress of a new language and culture, and potential discrimination and racism in the school and community environments. In addition, intergenerational language and cultural conflict can cause additional stress for children who have migrated to the United States. However, Adelman and Taylor (2015) caution against the tendency for professionals to overgeneralize or pathologize, pointing out that children can acquire resilience through the resettlement experience, and there is ample evidence of successful academic outcomes among immigrant and refugee students.

Children are best served when they are able to speak both their native language and the language of their host country (Kent, 2015). The need for specific strategies to also acknowledge and honor the "informal language register," while teaching the formal, has been identified by several literacy researchers (see Gee, 2012; Maier, Vitiello, & Greenfield, 2012). These researchers emphasize the importance of teaching children to recognize their internal, or natural, "speech" and the "register" they use in the school environment. Identifying and mediating these processes is best accomplished in the context of a caring relationship (Noddings, 2013).

PHOTO 5.3 As children get older, schools are the primary context for development in middle childhood.

By sensitively promoting an awareness of differences in the home and school, social workers and other adults can help children experience less confusion and alienation. Other aspects of the link between school and home are important as well because school and home are the two major spheres in which children exist during middle childhood. The more similar these two environments are, the more successful the child will be at school and at home. Students who experience vastly different cultures at home and at school may need support in accommodating the two worlds (Gregory, 2000). By the time Anthony, Jasmine, and Gabriela began school, they had acquired routines; habits; and cognitive, social, emotional, and physical styles and skills (Hayes, 2011). The transition to school is relatively easy for many students because the social environment in the school they attend matches the behavior modeled in the home environment; they transition with ease because, quite simply, they are familiar with the "rules" and the school is then accepting of them (Howard, 2010; Payne, 2013).

In contrast, children not fluent in expected language or speech patterns, not familiar with behavioral expectations, or not extensively exposed to school rules or materials such as scissors and books typically possess skills and curiosity but are often viewed as challenging or inferior in some way by school personnel (Murillo, 2010). When the school environment does not support the home environment and the home environment does not support the school environment, children face an increased risk of poor school outcomes. Schools that recognize the contribution of home to school success typically seek family involvement (Constable, 2006; Fan, Williams, & Wolters, 2012). Parental involvement in school is associated with better school performance (Duncan & Murnane, 2011). Schools serving diverse populations are becoming increasingly creative in their approaches to encouraging parent involvement, including the development of sophisticated interpretation and translation infrastructures (McNeal, 2012).

The U.S. educational system today struggles to correct its traditional structure, which both reflected and supported racial, ethnic, and class divisions (Darling-Hammond, 2010; Frankenberg & Debray, 2011; Kozol, 2005; Orfield, Kucsev, & Siegal-Harvey, 2012). For example, full-service schools attempt to provide school-based or school-linked health and social services for school children and their families (Dyson, 2011). This push for educational accountability and its impact on the lives of children is complex and highly controversial. The 2015 Every Student Succeeds Act (ESSA) replaced prior legislation (the No Child Left Behind Act) and reauthorized the 50-year-old Elementary and Secondary Education Act (ESEA) (U.S. Department of Education, 2017a). The U.S. Department of Education and private philanthropic organizations around the nation and globe today provide competitive grants targeting schools with a track record of improving student achievement and attainment (U.S. Department of Education Office of Innovation and Improvement, 2016). Many states have increased charter school options and shifted to merit-based teacher contracts tied, in part, to students' achievement on standardized assessments and tests. Such tests are a component of the national Common Core Curriculum, a testing regimen developed to assess student knowledge in a standardized fashion (Rich, 2013). Many believe such testing benefits all students, whereas others are convinced that the shift to a Common Core and its testing focus leaves struggling students further behind.

In recent years, funding from government and corporate sources is increasingly directed at poor, low-resourced school districts and students. The idea is to use such funding to increase business and community partnerships designed to serve historically excluded students and their families as well as expand educational options and build more instructional technology infrastructure. In addition, many schools have responded to calls for educational reform by implementing innovative practices designed to raise achievement of basic skills while attempting to meet the educational needs of all students (Center for Education Reform, 2017; Sherer, 2009). However, educational research has not had time to conclusively measure the long-range effects of such practices on a wide range of students, and there is evidence that districts with high percentages of Caucasian students and high family incomes underspend on poor and minority students (Shores & Ejdemyr, 2017).

As schools in the United States remain segregated by race and class, teaching students in the United States how to negotiate in a global society continues to be a challenge (Hannah-Jones, 2017). Schools comprised of high concentrations of Caucasian students from middle and high economic backgrounds will continue to struggle to develop in their students an understanding of diversity and a sense of the consequences of educational inequality. Schools with majority populations of color and financial disadvantage continue to lack the human and financial resources to meet the academic needs of all their students. The resulting unequal conditions compromise school achievement success for many students of color and lower chances for high school graduation. In a nation comprised of continuing school segregation, schools are increasingly expected to make their environments safe from harassment of all kinds, especially racial and sexual. The most effective schools develop students who are empowered partners in creating environments that build protective factors within the school environment. In this way, schools eliminate organizational and community cultures where intimidation and harassment have historically thrived.

CRITICAL THINKING QUESTIONS 5.4

Think about your own middle childhood years, ages 6 to 12. What are some examples of school experiences that helped you to feel competent and confident? What are some examples of school experiences that led you to feel incompetent and inferior? What biological, family, cultural, and other environmental factors led to success and failure in school?

SPECIAL CHALLENGES IN MIDDLE CHILDHOOD

In the last several decades in the United States, family structures have become more diverse than ever. The percentage of children living with both parents has steadily declined during the last 4 to 5 decades; approximately two thirds of children live with married parents, and one quarter live with one parent (Pew Research Center, 2015). Exhibit 5.5 illustrates recent trends in living arrangements of children in the United States.

Social and economic trends require parents of very young children to participate in the workforce to make ends meet. Legislation requires financially impoverished single parents who receive public assistance to remain engaged in or to reenter the workforce (Falk, 2017). Regardless of socioeconomic status, the school day and school vacations often do not coincide with parents' work schedules, and recent research suggests that because of parental employment, more than half of school-age children regularly need additional forms of supervision when school is not in session. Most of these children either participate in a before- or afterschool program (also known as wrap-around programs) or receive care from a relative; many low- and middle-income families struggle to find affordable childcare and often are forced to sacrifice quality childcare for economic reasons (Child Care Aware of America, 2016, 2017). About four in 10 parents of school-age children in the United States state that it is hard to find afterschool programs and activities that are both affordable and high quality (Pew Research Center, 2015).

This fact is particularly troubling because childcare quality has been linked to children's physical health as well as cognitive, emotional, and social development. These findings apply not only to early childhood programs but also to before- and afterschool programs for older children. Moreover, as children move from the early (ages 5 to 9) to later (10 to 12) middle childhood years, they are increasingly likely to take care of themselves during the before- and afterschool hours. Regular participation in a high-quality before- and afterschool program is positively associated with academic performance, and a significant body of research suggests that how school-age children spend their afterschool hours is strongly associated with the likelihood of engaging in risky behaviors (Afterschool Alliance, 2014). Inadequate and low-quality childcare is just one of the challenges facing school-age children—along with their families and communities—in the 21st century.

Poverty — Risk

Foremost among threats to children's healthy development is poverty, which potentially threatens positive development in all domains (see Johnson, Riis, & Noble, 2016; McCarty, 2016; Pascoe, Wood, Duffee, & Kuo, 2016). It is estimated that half of the world's children live in poverty, many in extreme poverty. That children should be protected from poverty is not disputed; in the United States, this societal value dates to the colonial period (Trattner, 1998). The nature of policies and programs targeted at ensuring the minimal daily needs of children are met, however, has shifted over time, as has success in meeting this goal (Bailey & Danzinger, 2013; Haveman, Blank, Moffitt, Smeeding, & Wallace, 2015).

| EXHIBIT 5.5 ● Trends in Living Arrangements of Children in the United States |

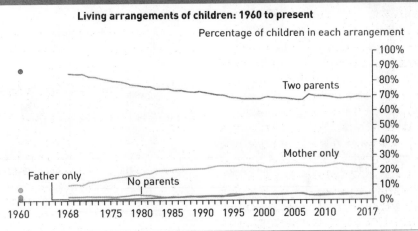

Living arrangements of children: 1960 to present

Source: U.S. Census Bureau, 2017a.

In the United States, the late 20th century brought a dramatic rise in the child poverty rate, which peaked in the early 1990s, declined for approximately a decade, and gradually increased during the 21st century; a relatively stable figure is that approximately one in five children in the United States lives in poverty (Child Trends, 2016a; McCarty, 2016). According to the National Center for Children in Poverty, of the approximately 24 million children in middle childhood (ages 6 through 11) in the United States in 2015, approximately 44%—10.7 million—lived in low-income families; and 21%—5.2 million—lived in poor families (Jiang, Granja, & Koball, 2017).

As illustrated in Exhibit 5.6, children in the middle childhood age range are less likely to live in low-income or poor families than their younger counterparts, and this trend continues as children grow toward adulthood. Caucasian children and children living in rural parts of the United States comprise the majority of poor children in the United States. Children from minority groups, however, are statistically overrepresented among the population of poor children (Child Trends, 2015, 2016a). (See Exhibit 5.7 for the percentage of children in low-income and poor families by race or ethnicity.) This is a persistent contemporary trend; in other words, although in absolute numbers Caucasian children consistently comprise the majority of poor children, children from Latino, African American, and American Indian families and children from families that have immigrated to the United States are consistently overrepresented among all children in poverty.

In general, the risk factors associated with child poverty are numerous, especially when poverty is sustained. A number of theoretical perspectives attempt to explain the ways in which poverty impacts child development (see McCarty, 2016). Limited income constrains a family's ability to obtain or invest in resources that promote positive development. Poverty negatively impacts caregivers' emotional health and parenting practices. Poverty is correlated with inadequate family, school, and neighborhood resources, and thus children experiencing family poverty are likely experiencing additional cumulative and systemic risk factors. For example, deep or extreme family poverty is correlated with homelessness, and poverty and homelessness combined increase a child's risk of abrupt family separation and experiencing or witnessing forms of trauma such as physical or sexual assault (Schneir, 2009). Poverty and associated housing instability is inversely associated with school attendance, a powerful predictor of academic achievement (Howland, Chen, Chen, & Min, 2017; Tobin, 2016). Jasmine and her siblings missed school when they moved in with their grandmother, and this disruption likely increased their academic risk. Available research suggests that homelessness may exacerbate rather than cause attendance and associated academic challenges; poverty is the primary causal variable (Canfield, Nolan, Harley, Hardy, & Elliott, 2016).

Poverty threatens optimal child development in a complex, synergistic fashion. Research suggests that children affected by three or more risk factors are significantly more likely to experience threats to healthy development and to employ maladaptive coping strategies as

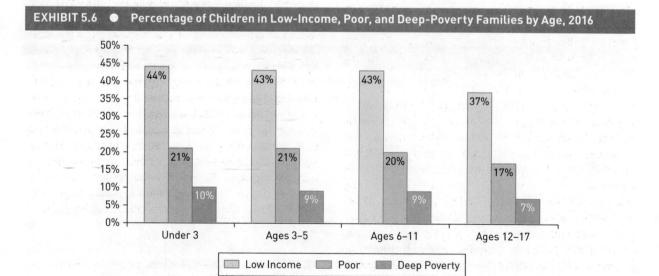

EXHIBIT 5.6 ● **Percentage of Children in Low-Income, Poor, and Deep-Poverty Families by Age, 2016**

Age	Low Income	Poor	Deep Poverty
Under 3	44%	21%	10%
Ages 3–5	43%	21%	9%
Ages 6–11	43%	20%	9%
Ages 12–17	37%	17%	7%

Source: Koball & Jiang, 2018, Figure 4.

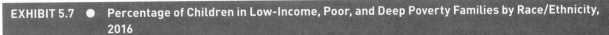

EXHIBIT 5.7 ● **Percentage of Children in Low-Income, Poor, and Deep Poverty Families by Race/Ethnicity, 2016**

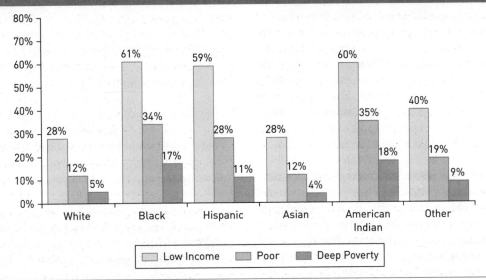

Source: Koball & Jiang, 2018, Figure 6.

they age (Robbins, Stagman, & Smith, 2012). Children who have spent any sustained part of their prenatal period, infancy, or early childhood in poverty have often already encountered several developmental challenges by the time middle childhood begins. In other words, duration and depth of childhood poverty matter. Children who enter, progress through, and leave middle childhood in poverty are at much greater risk of poor health and academic disengagement than those who briefly enter and then exit poverty during childhood (McCarty, 2016). Persistent or extreme poverty poses a significant threat to healthy child development around the world and within the United States (Alston, 2017; UNICEF & World Bank Group, 2016).

But what does it actually mean, to a child, to be poor? Being poor is a relative concept, the meaning of which is defined by perceptions of and real exclusion (DiNitto & Johnson, 2015; Kozol, 2005). In most communities, one must be *not* poor to be fully engaged and included. Lack of income and certain goods deprive poor people of what is expected among those who belong; thus, poverty results in perceived and real inabilities and inadequacies. For example, children often participate in extracurricular activities such as sports, music, or art. These programs typically involve registration, program, and equipment fees that are prohibitive to impoverished families. This is the essence of **relative poverty**, or the tendency to define one's poverty status

in relation to others within one's social environment. Fundamentally, then, poverty is as much a social as an economic phenomenon. Economic poverty is correlated with emotional, spiritual, and social support system impoverishment (Payne, 2013). Deficits accumulate and too often result in impediments to the development of critical capacities. James Garbarino (1995), a researcher who has studied causes of violent behavior among children, points to an innocent question once asked of him by a child: "When you were growing up, were you poor or regular?" (p. 137). As a child struggles with the developmental task of feeling included and acquiring a sense of belonging and competence, relative poverty sends a persistent message of social exclusion and incompetence. Many children living in poverty experience not only material deprivation but also a psychological sense of shame (Bessell, 2017). Jasmine has commented, "We were always poor." While getting to know her, it would be important to explore what this means to her, because a psychological sense of shame could be detrimental to her development. Although children are remarkably resilient, the complex and systemic nature of poverty presents formidable barriers to a child's coping skills.

Family and Community Violence

Many children regularly witness or are subject to violence in their homes, schools, and neighborhoods (Child Trends, 2016b; Mohammad, Shapiro, Wainwright, &

Carter, 2015). The atrocities witnessed or experienced by children residing within war-torn and low-income countries are often unimaginable to children and adults who have resided in the United States all their lives (Guedes, Bott, Garcia-Moreno, & Colombini, 2016). As Anthony's, Jasmine's, and Gabriela's stories reveal, experiencing violence deeply affects children (Fry et al., 2017). Many school-age children witness violence regularly, an experience that threatens their healthy development (Humphreys & Stanley, 2015). When compared to other common types of violence, exposure such as witnessing intimate partner violence and parent–child physical aggression appears to be associated with the most severe negative impacts on children's development (Maneta, White, & Mezzacappa, 2017).

Although child maltreatment, domestic violence, and community violence have always existed, they have been recognized as significant sources of child trauma only recently. Exposure to violence is a particular problem in areas where a lack of economic and social resources already produces significant challenges for children. Children are most likely to experience "polyvictimization" beginning in the middle childhood years (Finkelhor, Turner, Hamby, & Ormond, 2011; Molnar et al., 2016). Research indicates that for child survivors of violence and trauma, cognitive attributions and schema regarding the violence, particularly its causes, shape resilience (Collins et al., 2017). Social support and cultivation of hope are important factors in helping children successfully cope (Maneta et al., 2017).

In the United States, young children appear most susceptible to child maltreatment (Child Trends, 2016c). The number of children reported to Child Protective Services (CPS) agencies annually is staggering and generally stable. It is important to note that victims typically experience more than one type of abuse or neglect simultaneously and therefore are appropriately included in more than one maltreatment category (Child Welfare Information Gateway, 2017). Maltreatment subtype trends are also relatively stable over time; victims of child neglect consistently account for more than half of all child maltreatment victims. It is helpful for social workers in every setting to recognize the signs and symptoms of child maltreatment. Exhibit 5.8 provides an overview of the signs and symptoms of physical abuse, neglect, sexual abuse, and emotional maltreatment. In general, some type of child maltreatment should be suspected if the child

- shows sudden behavior changes or changes in school performance;
- has not received medical care for conditions brought to the parents' attention;
- has learning problems that cannot be attributed to specific physical or psychological causes;
- is always watchful, appearing to watch for something bad to happen;
- lacks adult supervision appropriate to the child's age;
- is overly compliant or withdrawn;
- comes to school (or other activities) early and stays late and does not want to go home;
- is reluctant to be around a particular person; or
- discloses maltreatment (Child Welfare Information Gateway, 2013).

African American and Native American children are consistently overrepresented among confirmed maltreatment victims. Careful examination of this issue, however, has concluded that although children of color are disproportionately represented within the child welfare population, studies that are cognizant of the relationship between culture and parenting practices, that control for the role of poverty, and that examine child maltreatment in the general population find no association between a child's race or ethnicity and likelihood of child maltreatment. Thus, it is likely that the disproportionate representation of children of color within the child welfare system is caused by the underlying relationship between poverty and race or ethnicity (Derezotes, Testa, & Poertner, 2005; Martinez, Gudiño, & Lau, 2013).

A variety of factors contribute to child maltreatment and family violence (World Health Organization, 2016b). These factors include parental, child, family, community, and cultural characteristics. Typically, the dynamic interplay of such characteristics leads to maltreatment, with the most relevant factors varying significantly depending on the type of maltreatment examined. For example, Anthony, Jasmine, and Gabriela could all be considered maltreatment victims, but each maltreatment situation is distinct from the others and the contributing factors vary significantly. Thus, multiple theoretical perspectives, particularly the life course, systems, and stress and coping perspectives, are helpful for understanding situations of child maltreatment.

The impact of maltreatment on the child victim varies based on a number of factors, including but certainly not limited to the type of maltreatment; the age of the child; and many other child, family, and community characteristics (Cicchetti, 2013). The Centers for Disease Control and Prevention (2016d) provides a helpful overview of child maltreatment consequences, pointing out that experiencing maltreatment as a child

EXHIBIT 5.8 ● Signs and Symptoms of Child Maltreatment	
Type of Maltreatment	**Signs and Symptoms**
Physical abuse	Unexplained burns, bites, bruises, broken bones, or black eyes on the child
	Fading bruises or other noticeable marks on the child after school absence
	Child seems frightened of parents
	Child shrinks at the approach of adults
	Child reports injury by a parent or other adult
	Child abuses animals or pets
	Parent or other caregiver offers conflicting or unconvincing explanation for child's injury
	Parent or other caregiver describes the child as evil
	Parent or other caregiver uses harsh physical discipline
	Parent or other caregiver has a history of abuse of a child
	Parent or other caregiver has a history of abusing animals or pets
Neglect	Child is frequently absent from school
	Child begs or steals food or money
	Child lacks needed medical or dental care
	Child is consistently dirty and has severe body odor
	Child lacks sufficient clothing for the weather
	Child abuses alcohol or other drugs
	Child states that there is no one at home to provide care
	Parent or other caregiver appears to be indifferent to the child
	Parent or other caregiver seems apathetic or depressed
	Parent or other caregiver behaves irrationally or in a bizarre manner
	Parent or other caregiver is abusing alcohol or other drugs
Sexual abuse	Child has difficulty walking or sitting
	Child suddenly refuses to change for gym or participate in physical activities
	Child reports nightmares or bedwetting
	Child experiences a sudden change in appetite
	Child demonstrates bizarre, sophisticated, or unusual sexual knowledge or behavior
	Child becomes pregnant or contracts a venereal disease
	Child reports sexual abuse by a parent or another adult caregiver
	Child attaches very quickly to strangers or new adults
	Parent or other caregiver is unduly protective of the child or limits the child's contact with other children
	Parent or other caregiver is secretive and isolated
	Parent or other caregiver is jealous or controlling with other family members

(Continued)

EXHIBIT 5.8 ● (Continued)	
Type of Maltreatment	**Signs and Symptoms**
Emotional maltreatment	Child shows extremes in behavior
	Child is either inappropriately adult or inappropriately infantile
	Child is delayed in physical or emotional development without a clear cause
	Child has attempted suicide
	Child reports a lack of attachment to the parent
	Parent or other caregiver constantly blames, belittles, or berates child
	Parent or other caregiver is unconcerned about the child and refuses to consider offers of help for the child's problems
	Parent or other caregiver overtly rejects the child

Source: Child Welfare Information Gateway, 2013.

is associated with an overwhelming number of negative health outcomes as an adult. As discussed in Chapter 4, these outcomes impact all developmental domains and include an increased likelihood of using or abusing alcohol and other substances, disordered eating, and susceptibility to mental and physical illnesses.

Children who experience trauma, induced by either indirect or direct exposure to violence, may experience *post-traumatic stress disorder* (PTSD)—a set of symptoms that includes feelings of fear and helplessness, reliving of the traumatic experience, and attempts to avoid reminders of the traumatic experience (American Psychological Association, 2017; International Society for Traumatic Stress Studies, 2016). Researchers have found changes in the brain chemistry of children exposed to chronic violence (Matto et al., 2014). Witnessing or experiencing violence adversely affects children in a number of areas, including the ability to function in school and the ability to establish stable, healthy relationships (Lang et al., 2008; Tomoda, Polcari, Anderson, & Teicher, 2012). Developmental trauma disorder developed as a concept due to the examination of processes and outcomes among young children who directly experience violence (Ogle, Rubin, & Siegler, 2013; van der Kolk, 2005). Secondary exposure to violence and trauma—such as when a child's parents suffer from PTSD—also may lead to negative outcomes for children (Wasserman & McReynolds, 2011).

The intergenerational nature of family violence has been established (Robboy & Anderson, 2011). Childhood exposure to violence significantly increases the likelihood of mental health difficulties and violence perpetration or revictimization. Currently, the focus is on understanding the specific pathways of intergenerational processes. It is clear that prolonged or chronic exposure to violence has multiple implications for child development. Children are forced to learn lessons about loss and death, often before they have acquired the cognitive ability to understand. They may therefore come to believe that the world is unpredictable and violent, a belief that threatens children's natural curiosity and desire to explore the social environment. Multiple experiences in which adults are unable to protect them often lead children to conclude that they must take on such responsibility for themselves, a prospect that can easily overwhelm the resources of a school-age child. Experiencing such helplessness may also lead to feelings of incompetence and hopelessness, to which children who experience chronic violence react in diverse ways. Responses may be passive, including withdrawal symptoms and signs of depression; or they may be active, including the use of aggression as a means of coping with and transforming the overwhelming feelings of vulnerability (Charlesworth, 2007).

The emotional availability of a parent or other caretaker who can support the child's need to make sense of or process traumatic events is critical. However, in situations of crisis stimulated by child maltreatment, domestic violence, and national or international violence, adults are often unable to support their children psychologically. Even with the best of parental resources, moreover, children developing in violent and chronically dangerous communities continue to experience numerous challenges to development. The child's need for autonomy and independence is directly confronted by the parent's need to protect the child's physical safety. For example, hours spent indoors to avoid danger do not promote the much-needed peer relationships and sense of accomplishment, purpose, and self-efficacy so critical during this phase of development (Hutchison, 2007).

Physical, Cognitive, Emotional, and Behavioral Challenges

Although the term *disability* is still widely used in academic discourse and government policy, many are actively seeking to change popular discourse to reflect the need to see all children as possessing a range of physical and mental abilities. In his book *The Power of Neurodiversity*, Thomas Armstrong (2010) points out that special education has historically been disease and deficit oriented. He provides examples supporting the argument that, across time, whether an individual is viewed as gifted or disabled has depended on the historical era, culture, and social context. Originally developed by Harvey Blume (1998) and Judy Singer (1999) in the context of autism discussions, the term *neurodiversity* draws attention to the strengths of all individuals. Armstrong points out the evolutionary functions and advantages of hyperactivity, autism, some mood disorders, and anxiety, arguing "diversity among brains is just as wonderfully enriching as biodiversity and the diversity among cultures" (p. 3). Today, the disability studies field has contributed to increasing recognition,

among professionals, of the socially constructed nature of both disability and diagnostic criteria (see, for example, Valle & Connor, 2010).

Although recognizing that disability and disabled labels are not helpful to realizing a vision of a just and equal society, information of relevance is shared here within the confines of this terminology. According to the Centers for Disease Control and Prevention (2017f), approximately 15% of children ages 3 through 17 have been diagnosed with one or more developmental disabilities, including attention deficit/hyperactivity disorder, autism spectrum disorder, cerebral palsy, hearing loss, intellectual disability, learning disability, vision impairment, and other less common developmental delays. The Individuals with Disabilities Education Act (IDEA) is the current law originally enacted in 1975 as the Education for All Handicapped Children Act. Most recently amended through the Every Student Succeeds Act, the IDEA mandates a free appropriate public education to children with disabilities and requires provision of special education services to eligible children.

According to the National Center for Education Statistics (2017b), in the 2014–2015 school year, approximately 13% of children ages 3 to 21 received special education services. As seen in Exhibit 5.9, among those

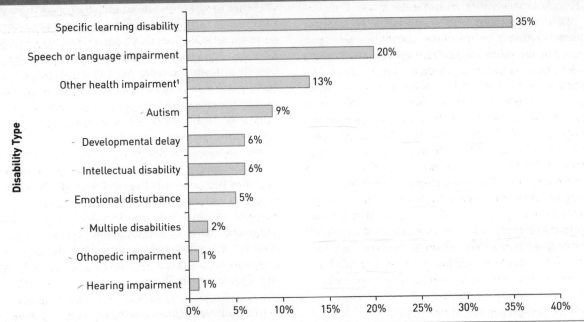

EXHIBIT 5.9 ● Percentage Distribution of Children and Youth Ages 3 to 21 Served Under the Individuals with Disabilities Education Act (IDEA), Part B, by Disability Type: School Year 2014–2015

Disability Type	Percentage
Specific learning disability	35%
Speech or language impairment	20%
Other health impairment[1]	13%
Autism	9%
Developmental delay	6%
Intellectual disability	6%
Emotional disturbance	5%
Multiple disabilities	2%
Othopedic impairment	1%
Hearing impairment	1%

Source: National Center for Education Statistics, 2017b, Figure 1.

[1]Other health impairments include having limited strength, vitality, or alertness due to chronic or acute health problems such as a heart condition, tuberculosis, rheumatic fever, nephritis, asthma, sickle cell anemia, hemophilia, epilepsy, lead poisoning

receiving special education services, approximately 35% had specific learning disabilities, 20% had speech or language impairments, and 13% had other health impairments. During the last several years in the United States, attention focused on particular developmental disabilities has increased (Centers for Disease Control and Prevention, 2017f), and students with diagnosed disabilities have been spending a larger percentage of their class time in general classes (National Center for Education Statistics, 2017b).

Attention Deficit/ Hyperactivity Disorder (ADHD)

ADHD is a commonly diagnosed childhood behavioral disorder. ADHD includes inattentive, impulsive-hyperactive, and combined inattentive-hyperactivity (American Psychiatric Association, 2013). It is possible that Anthony's teacher is pursuing assessment because she believes he is exhibiting signs of ADHD. Extensive diagnostic criteria for both ADD and ADHD are available through the *DSM-V*. The Centers for Disease Control and Prevention (2017f) report that in 2011 approximately 11% of children 4 to 17 years of age (6.4 million) had been diagnosed with ADHD; boys (13.2%) were more likely than girls (5.6%) to have been diagnosed with ADHD. The average age of ADHD diagnosis was 7, but children reported by their parents as having more severe ADHD symptomatology are typically diagnosed earlier. Prevalence of ADHD diagnosis varied substantially by state, from a low of 5.6% in Nevada to a high of 18.7% in Kentucky.

ADHD is associated with school failure or academic underachievement, but the relationship is complex in part because of the strong relationship between ADHD and a number of other factors also associated with school difficulties (Foley, 2011; Rietz, Hasselhorn, & Labuhn, 2012). The IDEA includes ADHD as a subcategory within "other health impairments," focusing on the heightened alertness to environmental stimuli component of health impairment (Turnbull, Turnbull, Wehmeyer, & Shogren, 2015). Approximately two thirds of the children identified in IDEA's category of "other health impairments" have been diagnosed with ADHD. And yet several studies suggest that the interpretation and evaluation of ADHD behaviors are significantly influenced by culturally linked beliefs (Rohde et al., 2005). In other words, the extent to which ADHD-linked behaviors are perceived as problematic varies according to individual and group values and norms.

Autism Spectrum Disorder (ASD)

Like ADHD, the *DSM-V* considers autism a neurodevelopmental disorder. The *DSM-V* considers essential features of autism spectrum disorder (ASD) impairment in reciprocal social communication and social interaction and restricted, repetitive patterns of behavior, interests, or activities. Symptoms typically limit functioning and are present from early childhood (American Psychological Association, 2013, p. 53). In recent years, controversy has surrounded autism spectrum disorder, including definitions, causes, and diagnostic criteria (Grandin & Panek, 2013; Shannon, 2011). According to the Centers for Disease Control and Prevention (2017f), autism spectrum disorder is typically diagnosed by age 3 in about 1 in 88 children, and boys are approximately 5 times more likely to be diagnosed (1 in 54) than girls (1 in 252). Although autism spectrum disorder typically manifests and is diagnosed before early childhood, some children may not receive formal assessment or diagnosis until their early or middle childhood years. Autism spectrum disorder often consists of impairment within reciprocal social interaction, verbal and nonverbal communication, and range of activities and interests (Insel, 2013), but all children are unique, and children diagnosed with autism spectrum disorder vary widely in terms of their intellectual and communicative abilities, the nature and severity of behavioral challenges, and appropriate interventions (Herbert & Weintraub, 2012).

Emotional/Behavioral Disorder

In many schools, the children presenting the greatest challenge to educators and administrators are those who consistently exhibit disruptive or alarming behavior yet do not clearly fit the criteria for a disability diagnosis. Although IDEA includes a definition for "seriously emotionally disturbed" children, not all school professionals and government education agencies consistently agree with or use this definition. According to the Center for Behavioral Health Statistics and Quality (2016), children with "emotional disturbance" are children and youth younger than 18 who have a diagnosable mental, behavioral, or emotional disorder that substantially interferes with or limits the child's role or functioning in family, school, or community activities (see also American Psychiatric Association, 2013). The "emotionally disturbed" label is typically applied to school-age children with emotional and behavioral challenges that appear to be the primary cause of academic difficulty. The IDEA criteria indicate that

> one or more of the following characteristics are exhibited over a long period of time and to a marked degree that adversely affects a child's educational performance: a. An inability to learn

that cannot be explained by intellectual, sensory, or health factors b. An inability to build or maintain satisfactory interpersonal relationships with peers and teachers c. Inappropriate types of behavior or feelings under normal circumstances d. A general pervasive mood of unhappiness or depression e. A tendency to develop physical symptoms or fears associated with personal or school problems. (Turnbull et al., 2015)

Approximately 75% of American high school students identified as having an emotional or behavioral disturbance are male, and 25% are African American (Turnbull et al., 2015). As a whole, students classified as emotionally disturbed represent about 5% of public school students receiving special education services, which is less than 1% of all public school students (National Center for Education Statistics, 2017b). However, this small population of students is viewed as relatively difficult to serve.

Disorders that may lead to the emotionally disturbed (ED) or emotionally and behaviorally disturbed (EBD) classification include anxiety disorder, mood disorder, oppositional defiant disorder, conduct disorder, and schizophrenia; behavioral patterns commonly identified are typically either predominantly externalizing (aggressive, acting out, noncompliant) or internalizing (withdrawal, depression, anxiety, obsession and compulsion). In recent years, steps have been taken toward eliminating the bias and discrimination too often present in the ED/EBD assessment process. In addition, after years of family blaming and a deficit orientation, professionals are striving to implement strengths-based and collaborative approaches to their work with this population of children and youth. Kaminski and Claussen (2017), in their review of effective psychosocial intervention for disruptive behavior in children under age 12, found that effective approaches fall into six main categories: parent behavior therapy, child behavior therapy, teacher training, parent-focused therapy, child-centered play therapy, and family problem solving. These interventions appear most impactful when combined with other effective services, such as treatment that addresses the effectiveness of prescribed medication, assessment of parental mental health needs, and supportive case management.

Early identification and intervention are key protective factors for a child with special needs. In addition, the social environment more generally may serve as either a risk or protective factor, depending on its response to the child. Although difference of any sort

is typically noticed by children and adults, students with special needs are at particular risk for being singled out by their peers, and middle childhood is a critical time in an individual's developmental trajectory. For children to acquire a positive sense of self, they need positive relationships with others. The healthy development of all children is facilitated by support in multiple contexts and at multiple levels to promote feelings of belonging. Educating all children and adults about special needs and encouraging the support of all students may help to minimize negative attitudes and incidents in the school and community (Gargiulo & Kilgo, 2011; Painter, 2012).

Students who feel misunderstood by their peers are particularly likely to feel alone or isolated in the school setting. Students who are socially excluded by their peers often develop a dislike of school. Some students who are teased, isolated, or harassed regularly may begin to withdraw or act out to cope with emotionally distressing experiences. Children with special needs face elevated risk of bullying (U.S. Department of Education, 2017b). Today, most states possess antibullying legislation, and bullying directed at a child because of a disability may be considered "disability harassment" when a hostile environment is created. In addition to potentially applicable state legislation, under Section 504 of the federal Rehabilitation Act of 1973 and Title II of the Americans with Disabilities Act of 1990, schools must address such harassment because the student is considered a member of a protected class in the eyes of civil rights legislation. In addition to local schools, the U.S. Department of Education and U.S. Department of Justice are responsible for responding to this type of harassment within school districts. Teachers, parents, and other school personnel who intervene early with students involved in bullying and harassment situations may prevent the escalation of such problems.

Children's adjustment to special needs highly depends on the adjustment of those around them. Families may respond in a number of ways to a diagnosis of a disability or serious illness. Often caregivers experience loss or grief stages; these stages may include the following: denial, withdrawal, rejection, fear, frustration, anger, sadness, adjustment, and acceptance (Ahmann, 2013; Richardson, Cobham, McDermott, & Murray, 2013). The loss and grief stages are not linear but can be experienced repeatedly as parents interface with educational, social, and medical institutions throughout their child's life. Awareness of and sensitivity to these reactions and stages and the ongoing nature of grief and loss is critical for those assessing the need for family intervention. Typically, parents are helped by advocacy and support groups and access to information and resources (McMillan, 2011). Families of children with special needs also typically desire independence and self-determination for their children. Family empowerment was an explicit focus of the Education for All Handicapped Children Act (Pub. L. No. 94-142) of 1975, which stressed parental participation in the development of an **individual education plan (IEP)** for each child. The IEP charts a course for ensuring that each child achieves as much support as possible in the academic realm. The need to include the family in decision making and planning is also embodied in today's IDEA. The IDEA requires that the IEP include specific educational goals for each student classified as in need of special educational services. In addition, the IDEA supports the placement of children with disabilities into integrated settings.

Prior to the IDEA, the education of children with disabilities was left to individual states. As a result, the population labeled "disabled" and the services provided varied greatly. Today, however, through various pieces of legislation and several court decisions, society has stated its clear desire to educate children with special needs in integrated settings (*least restrictive environment*) to the maximum extent possible. A recent examination of the nature of inclusion nationwide concluded that during the last few decades, students with special needs (including learning disabilities) were much more likely to be formally identified, but many states are not aggressively pursuing the ability to educate students with special needs in less restrictive settings, and often children with disabilities are placed in separate classrooms (DeLorenzo, 2015). Evaluations of the impact of inclusive settings on children's school success indicate positive academic gains for children with special needs and neutral impact on the academic performance for children without identified special needs (Gupta, Henninger, & Vinh, 2014). Many argue inclusion positively impacts the social and moral development of all children. However, others recommend caution regarding a "one size fits all" model of inclusion for all students with special needs, arguing that assessment of the optimal educational setting must be thorough and individualized (Goodfellow, 2012).

Family Disruption

Throughout history, most nuclear and extended families have succeeded in their endeavor to adequately protect and socialize their young. For many children, however, the family serves as both a protective and risk factor. Today, families are more diverse than ever in the United States. Among U.S. children, less than half (approximately 46%) live with two married parents who are both in their first marriage (Pew Research Center, 2015). Approximately 15% of children live with parents in a remarriage, and 7% live with parents who are cohabiting. The proportion of children living with one parent only has steadily increased in recent decades, from 9% in 1960 to 22% in 2000 and 26% in 2015, and approximately 5% of children in the United States live with neither parent.

Many married parents with children divorce and marry a second time, and thus approximately 15% of U.S. children live in blended family situations (Kumar, 2017). Many children experience the dissolution of their parents' nonmarital romantic relationships, and related attachments, without being counted in official "children of divorce" statistics or research. Although no reliable data on similar nonmarital relationship patterns exist, we can assume that similar trends exist among children's nonmarried parents and other caregivers. According to the Pew Research Center (2015), research suggests that over a 3-year period, about 31% of children younger than 6 experience a major change in their family or household structure, in the form of parental divorce, separation, marriage, cohabitation, or death. Based on surveys comparing attitudes toward cohabitation, premarital sex, and single parenting among adult members of younger versus older generations, ample evidence suggests that family composition in the United States will grow increasingly diverse in the future (Daugherty & Copen, 2016). Family structural arrangements vary by group membership. Asian American children are more likely than children from other racial and ethnic groups to be living with parents in their first marriage. Black children are more likely than children from other racial and ethnic groups to be living with a single mom (Pew Research Center, 2015).

Changes within families expose children to new people, new housing and income arrangements, and new family roles and responsibilities (Ahrons, 2016). Family disruption may immerse the child in poverty for the first time (Ducanto, 2010). As the body of relevant research grows in depth and breadth, it becomes apparent that divorce and other types of family disruption may detrimentally or positively impact children depending on the circumstances preceding and following the disruption (Stadelmann, Perren, Groeben, & von Klitzing, 2010). For example, if divorce brings an end to seriously dysfunctional family dynamics, tension, or violence and results in positive changes within the home environment, child outcomes may be positive. Alternatively, if the divorce disrupted a healthy, nurturing family system and led to declines in the emotional and financial health of the child's primary caregiver(s), child outcomes may be negative.

Historically, many children experienced family disruption because of the death of one or both parents (Amato, 2003). Although improvements in public health have significantly reduced the likelihood of parental death, a substantial number of children continue to experience the death of a primary caregiver. Compared with adults, children have fewer cognitive and other resources to cope with death and loss. For children coping with the death of a parent, the circumstances of the death and the adjustment of the remaining caregivers are critical variables impacting child outcomes. Children appear to be at highest risk of a variety of negative physiological and psychological outcomes when the parental death is sudden and social support is limited. All children experiencing grief associated with parental loss benefit from early and ongoing intervention including support groups, individual counseling, and family intervention (Pereira, Johnsen, Hauken, Kristensen, & Dyregrov, 2017).

In recent years, a number of studies have focused on children of suicide. This literature notes the potential long-term impacts of parental suicide on surviving children and identifies the ways in which outcomes may be carried through generations (Bisagni, 2012). These outcomes include not only the potential emotional devastation experienced by survivors but also the intergenerational transmission of suicide risk. Research indicates that suicidal behavior is elevated within some families, and this may be only in part due to the transmission of associated mental health challenges. In other words, the intergenerational transmission of suicide risk appears to be at least partially independent of other associated factors. There are a variety of theoretical frameworks relevant to understanding this relationship, with researchers recently speculating that elevated suicide risk among child survivors may be due to particular neurological risks including neural responses to loss (Tsypes, Owens, Hajcak, & Gibb, 2017). In the context of middle childhood, this is particularly concerning because suicide rates continue to rise in the general population but especially among children ages 10 to 14; suicide is now the third leading cause of death for children in this age range (Centers for Disease Control and Prevention, Division for Violence Prevention, 2015). Boys have historically been at higher risk of suicide completion than girls, but this appears to be shifting. In general, self-injurious and suicidal behavior increases as children transition to adolescence.

Many school-age children experience other types of disruption to their attachment relationships. According to the U.S. Department of Defense (2016), there are almost 2 million military children in the United States. This figure includes both active-duty military children (over 1 million) and reserve military children (approximately half a million), and approximately 350,000 children 6 to 11 years old are active-duty military children. Children in military families are at heightened risk of frequent moves, parental absence, and parental emotional distress (Murphey, 2013). The Department of Defense (2016) states that on average, children in military families move six to nine times during their school careers (3 times more frequently than most nonmilitary children).

Along with the stressors known to be associated with military service, military families often face social isolation. Some research suggests the risk of child maltreatment within military families may be highest during the months following a parent's return from deployment (Fifield, 2017). Although there are specialized resources available to children and parents in the military, there are also unique challenges. Due to the potential stigma associated with receiving individual or family services, military families may be particularly reluctant to seek help or engage with service providers.

Family disruption also occurs when children enter foster care. In 2015, the median age of children in foster care was 7.8 years, and there were approximately 400,000 children in foster care (U.S. Children's Bureau, 2017). Approximately one third were in relative homes, and about half were in nonrelative foster homes. Just over 40% were Caucasian, and boys and girls were fairly evenly represented. Family reunification was the goal for about one half of these children, adoption for approximately one quarter. Some children spend lengthy periods of time in a foster care setting, others enter and leave foster care rapidly and only once during their childhoods, and still other children cycle in and out of their home and foster care settings repeatedly. The median length of stay in foster care is 13 months, with just over one quarter of foster care children staying in care for more than 2 years. About half of the children leaving foster care in 2015 were reunited with parents or other primary caregivers, and 22% were adopted. Because over half of the children in foster care (approximately 270,000) are school-aged and research has clearly established that children in foster care face elevated odds of school disengagement, the Every Student Succeeds Act includes specific provisions focused on the educational success of children in foster care.

Foster care children have not only potentially experienced maltreatment as well as the trauma associated with being removed from their parent or primary caregiver, they also experience high levels of residential (and therefore school) mobility. For too many children residing in foster care, the result is poor academic achievement and grade retention. For this reason, the U.S. Department of Education and U.S. Administration for Children and Families are working together to facilitate more effective collaboration among local education and child welfare organizations.

Family disruption is stressful for all children. Great variation exists, however, in the circumstances preceding and following the family disruption, the nature of the changes involved, and how children respond to this type of stress. Critical factors in outcomes for children include social supports within the family and surrounding community, the child's characteristics, the emotional well-being of caregivers, and the quality of care received following the family disruption. Because children are diverse and middle childhood spans a wide age range, school-age children exhibit a variety of cognitive, emotional, and behavioral responses to family disruption. They may blame themselves and experience anxiety or other difficult emotions, or they may demonstrate a relatively mature understanding of the reasons behind the events and adaptive coping strategies.

Children experiencing family disruption without supports or those who have experienced difficulties preceding the disruption are most likely to experience long-term emotional and behavioral problems. Children placed in foster care or otherwise exposed to trauma or multiple losses are more likely to fall into this group (Webb & Dumpson, 2006). These children are likely to face additional stress associated with the cumulative losses of familiar places, belongings, and social networks (Mallon & Hess, 2014). However, with appropriate support and intervention as well as the presence of other protective factors, resilience is possible (see Guest, 2012).

RISK FACTORS AND PROTECTIVE FACTORS IN MIDDLE CHILDHOOD

School-age children face a variety of risks that undermine their struggles to develop a sense of purpose and self-worth. Risk factors are anything that increases the probability of a problem condition, its progression into a more severe state, or its maintenance (Luthar, 2003). Risk factors are moderated, however, by protective factors, either internal or external, that help children in the face

of risk (Werner & Brendtro, 2012). Risk and protective factors can be biological, psychological, social, and spiritual, and like all influences on development, they span the micro to macro continuum (Bronfenbrenner, 1996). Dynamic, always-evolving interaction occurs among risk and protective factors present in each dimension of the individual child and his or her environment.

Resilience—or "survival against the odds"—arises from an interplay of risk and protective factors and manifests as adaptive behavior producing positive outcomes (Jenson & Fraser, 2016). A variety of factors influence resilience during middle childhood. Whether a factor presents risk or protection often depends on its interaction with other factors influencing the individual child. For example, a highly structured classroom environment run by a "strict" teacher may function as a protective factor for one child while simultaneously functioning as a risk factor for another child.

The life course and systems perspectives provide tools for understanding positive development during middle childhood. These perspectives also facilitate assessment and intervention efforts. As social workers, we must recognize that resilience is rarely an innate characteristic. Rather, it is a process that may be facilitated by influences within the child's surrounding environment. Indeed, research suggests that high-risk behavior among children increases when they perceive declining family involvement and community support (Benson, Scales, & Roehlkepartain, 2011). A primary goal of the professions dedicated to child well-being must be facilitation of positive external supports for children and enhancement of the person–environment fit so as to maximize protective factors and minimize risk factors. Powerful risk factors include experiences of exclusion, violence, and persistent poverty. Protective factors include nurturing relationships and exposure to adaptive coping strategies. Children are most likely to thrive when they consistently have access to resources, both tangible (educational) and intangible (emotional).

CRITICAL THINKING QUESTIONS 5.5

There is general agreement that poverty and child maltreatment are among the most serious threats to healthy child development. How does poverty threaten physical, cognitive, emotional, social, and spiritual development during middle childhood? How does child maltreatment threaten physical, cognitive, emotional, social, and spiritual development during middle childhood?

IMPLICATIONS FOR SOCIAL WORK PRACTICE

This discussion of middle childhood suggests several practice principles for social workers and other professionals working with children.

- Development is multidimensional and dynamic; recognize the complex ways in which developmental influences interact and incorporate this understanding into your work with children.

- Support parents and other family members as critically important social, emotional, and spiritual resources for their children.

- Support family, school, and community attempts to stabilize environments for children.

- Incorporate identification of multilevel risk and protective factors into assessment and intervention efforts.

- Recognize and support resilience in children and families. Support the strengths of children and families and their efforts to cope with adversity.

- Recognize the critical influence of the school environment on growth and development and encourage attempts by school personnel to be responsive to all children and families.

- Understand the important role of peer groups in social and emotional growth and development; facilitate the development and maintenance of positive peer and other social relationships.

- Understand the ways in which the organization of schools reflects and supports the social injustice present in society. Support schools in their efforts to end practices and policies that sustain or reinforce inequalities.

- Facilitate meaningful teacher-family-child communication and school responsiveness to children experiencing difficulties in the school environment.

- Understand the effects of family, community, and societal violence on children and establish prosocial, nurturing, nonviolent environments whenever possible; provide opportunities for positive nurturing and mentoring of children in the school and community environments.

- Become familiar with and implement best practices in areas such as trauma, loss and grief, social skill development, and character education.

- Promote cultural competency and help children and other adults recognize and respect all forms of diversity and difference.

Key Terms

capital 166
cerebral cortex 160
character education 166
direct bullying 166
emotional intelligence 163
gender dysphoria 169

indirect bullying 166
individual education
  plan (IEP) 184
interrelational intelligence 161
multiple intelligences 172
precociousness 156

relative poverty 177
social competence 167
trauma 164
zone of proximal
  development 167

Active Learning

1. Working alone or in small groups, compare the risk and protective factors present for Anthony, Jasmine, and Gabriela. Brainstorm multilevel interventions you would consider if you were working with each child.

2. Working in pairs, consider the story of Anthony, Jasmine, or Gabriela (as assigned by the instructor). Each pair should identify the relevance of the various developmental theorists discussed in the chapter to the assigned child, focusing on the

theorist(s) whose idea(s) seem particularly relevant to the selected child. After approximately 20 minutes, form three small groups consisting of the pairs focusing on the same child. After comparing the similarities and differences in their assessments of the different theories, each group should report back to the full class.

3. As a class, create a list of debate topics raised directly or indirectly in the chapter (e.g., educational assessment/standardized testing, federal spending or programs to address child poverty, gun control to reduce violence against children, family structure and family disruption, inclusion for children with special needs). Debates can take place between teams or individuals. Each side will take 2 minutes to present their case, and each side will also have 1 minute for rebuttal.

4. Use task rotation for important chapter issues such as *family and community violence*: (1) How does child maltreatment or trauma impact childhood development? (2) How are child witnesses impacted by acts of violence? (3) What programs might schools employ to support students impacted by violence? (4) What interventions might a social worker pursue to help families impacted by violence? *Task rotation description*: Questions are posted on chart paper around the room. Each group starts at a question, discusses it, writes ideas in response on the chart paper, and then after a short time (less than 3 minutes) is stopped and rotated to the next chart. At the next chart, they are given a brief period to review the work of the previous group and add any ideas the first group missed. The groups are stopped and rotated until all groups have read and added to all issues listed on the charts. Whole-group review follows.

Web Resources

American Association of University Women: www.aauw.org

Site maintained by the American Association of University Women contains information on education and equity for women and girls, including a report card on Title IX, a law that banned sex discrimination in education.

Child Trauma Academy: www.childtraumaacademy.com

Site presented by the Child Trauma Academy contains information on the impact of child maltreatment on the brain and the physiological and psychological effects of trauma on children.

Child Welfare Information Gateway: www.childwelfare.gov

Site presented by the Administration for Children and Families contains information and resources to protect children and strengthen families, including statistics, prevention information, state statutes, family-centered practice, and publications.

Forum on Child and Family Statistics: www.childstats.gov

Official website of the Federal Interagency Forum on Child and Family Statistics offers easy access to federal and state statistics and reports on children and families, including international comparisons.

International Society for Traumatic Stress Studies (ISTSS): www.istss.org

Official website of ISTSS contains tools for assessing trauma, treatment guidelines, education and research, and public resources.

Military One Source: http://www.militaryonesource.mil/web/mos/family-relationships

Family relationships page of the Military One Source website contains information on parenting and children, special needs, and family life.

Search Institute: www.search-institute.org

Site presented by the Search Institute, an independent, nonprofit, nonsectarian organization with the goal of advancing the well-being of adolescents and children, contains information on 40 developmental assets and methods for building assets for child and youth development.

6

Adolescence

Susan Ainsley McCarter

Chapter Outline

Learning Objectives

Case Study 6.1: David's Coming-Out Process

Case Study 6.2: Carl's Struggle for Identity

Case Study 6.3: Monica's Quest for Mastery

The Social Construction of Adolescence Across Time and Space

The Transition From Childhood to Adulthood

Biological Aspects of Adolescence
- *Puberty*
- *The Adolescent Brain*
- *Nutrition, Exercise, and Sleep*

Psychological Aspects of Adolescence
- *Psychological Reactions to Biological Changes*
- *Changes in Cognition*
- *Identity Development*
  - Theories of Self and Identity
  - Gender Identity
  - Cultural Identity

Social Aspects of Adolescence
- *Relationships With Family*
- *Relationships With Peers*
- *Romantic Relationships*
- *Relationships With Organizations, Communities, and Institutions*

- School
- The Broader Community
- Work
- Technology

Adolescent Spirituality/Religiosity

Adolescent Sexuality
- *Sexual Decision Making*
- *Sexual Orientation*
- *Pregnancy and Childbearing*
- *Sexually Transmitted Infections*

Potential Challenges to Adolescent Development
- *Substance Use and Abuse*
- *Juvenile Delinquency*
- *Bullying*
- *School-to-Prison Pipeline*
- *Community Violence*
- *Dating Violence and Statutory Rape*
- *Poverty and Low Educational Attainment*
- *Obesity and Eating Disorders*
- *Depression and Suicide*

Social Work Grand Challenge: Ensure Healthy Development for All Youth

Risk Factors and Protective Factors in Adolescence

Implications for Social Work Practice

Key Terms

Active Learning

Web Resources

Learning Objectives

6.1 Compare one's own emotional and cognitive reactions to three case studies.

6.2 Analyze how the status of adolescence has varied across time and place.

6.3 Describe some of the transitions made in adolescence.

6.4 Summarize biological, psychological, social, and spiritual development during adolescence.

6.5 Analyze major themes in adolescent sexual development.

6.6 Describe some potential challenges to adolescent development.

6.7 Give examples of risk factors and protective factors for adolescent development.

6.8 Apply knowledge of adolescence to recommend guidelines for social work engagement, assessment, intervention, and evaluation.

CASE STUDY 6.1
DAVID'S COMING-OUT PROCESS

The social worker at Jefferson High School sees many facets of adolescent life. Nothing much surprises her—especially not the way some of the kids hem and haw when they're trying to share what's really on their mind. Take David Costa, for instance. When he shows up for his first appointment, he is simply asked to tell a bit about himself.

"Let's see, I'm 17," he begins. "I'm a center fielder on the varsity baseball team. What else do you want to know? My parents are from Bolivia and are as traditional as you can imagine. My dad, David Sr., teaches history and is the varsity soccer coach here at Jefferson. My mom is a geriatric nurse. I have a younger sister, Patti. Patti Perfect. She goes to the magnet school and is in the eighth grade."

"How are things at home?" his social worker asks.

"Whatever. Patti is perfect, and I'm a 'freak.' They think I'm 'different, arrogant, stubborn.' I don't know what they want me to be. But I don't think that's what I am. That may be because . . . because I'm gay. But I haven't come out to my parents. That's all I need!"

This is obviously a difficult confession for David to make to an adult, but with a little encouragement he continues: "There are a few other seniors at Jefferson who are out, but they aren't student athletes and so I don't really spend any time with them. Basically when the whole baseball team is together or when I'm with other kids from school, I just act straight. I talk about girls' bodies just like the other guys. I think that is the hardest, not being able to be yourself. It was really hard when I was about 13. I was so confused. I knew that men were supposed to be with women, not other men. What I was feeling was not 'normal,' and I thought I was the only one. I wanted to kill myself. That was a bad time."

David's tone changes. "Let's talk about something good. Let me tell you about Theo. I think Theo is hot! He's got a great body. I wonder if he'd like to hang out together—get to know me. He's a junior, and if we got together, I would hear about it. But I keep thinking about him and looking at him during school. I just need to say something to him. There's a club downtown that has over-18 night, maybe I could get him in."

CASE STUDY 6.2
CARL'S STRUGGLE FOR IDENTITY

Whereas David seeks out the social worker, Carl Fleischer, another 17-year-old, is sent to the social worker's office at the high school. He matter-of-factly shares that he is "an underachiever." He used to get an occasional B in his classes, but now it's mostly C's with an occasional D.

Is this what the Dr. said or an interpretation

When Carl is asked what he likes to do in his spare time, he replies, "I get high and play video games." Further probing elicits one-word answers until the social worker asks Carl about relationships. His face contorts as he slaps his ample belly: "I'm not exactly a sex symbol. According to my doctor, I'm a fatso. He says normal boys my age and height weigh at least 50 pounds less than I do. He also tells me to quit smoking and get some exercise. Whatever. My mom says I'm big-boned. She says my dad was the same way. I wouldn't know. I never met the scumbag. He left when my mom was pregnant. But you probably don't want to hear about that."

Carl won't say more on that topic, but with more prodding, he finally talks about his job, delivering pizzas two nights a week and on the weekends. "So if you need pizzas, call me at Antonio's. I always bring pies home for my mom on Tuesday and Friday nights. She works late those nights and so we usually eat pizza and catch the Tuesday and Friday night lineups on TV. She lets me smoke in the house—cigarettes, not weed. Although I have gotten high in the house a couple times. Anyway, I am not what you would call popular. I am just a fat, slow geek and a pizza guy. But there are some heads who come into Antonio's. I exchange pies for dope. Works out pretty well: They get the munchies, and the pies keep me in with the heads!"

CASE STUDY 6.3
MONICA'S QUEST FOR MASTERY

Monica Golden, a peer counselor at Jefferson High, hangs around to chat after a meeting of the peer counselors. Monica is the eldest and tallest daughter in a family of five kids. Monica's mother is the assistant principal at Grover Middle School, and her father works for the Internal Revenue Service. This year, in addition to being a Jefferson peer counselor, Monica is the vice president of the senior class, the treasurer for the Young Republicans, a starter on the track team, and a teacher at Sunday school.

When the social worker comments on the scope of these activities, Monica replies, "I really do stay busy. I worked at the mall last year, but it was hard to keep my grades up. I'm trying to get into college, so my family and I decided I shouldn't work this year. So I just babysit sometimes. A lot of my aunts and uncles have me watch their kids, but they don't pay me. They consider it a family favor. Anyway, I am waiting to hear back from colleges. They should be sending out the letters this week. You know, the fatter the envelope the better. It doesn't take many words to say, 'No. We reject you.' And I need

to either get into a state school or get a scholarship so that I can use my savings for tuition."

Next they talk a little about Monica's options, and she shares that her first choice is Howard University. "I want to surround myself with Black scholars and role models, and my dream is to be a pediatrician, you know. I love kids," Monica says. "I tried tons of jobs—that's where I got the savings. And, well, those with kids I enjoyed the most. Like I said, I've worked retail at the mall. I've worked at the supermarket as a cashier. And I've been babysitting since I was 12. That's what I like the most."

"I'd love to have kids someday. But I don't even have a boyfriend. I wear glasses. My parents say I don't need contacts; they think I'm being vain. Not that I don't have a boyfriend because I wear glasses. Guys think I'm an overachiever. They think I'm driven and demanding and incapable of having fun. That's what I've been told. I think I'm just ambitious and extroverted. But really, I just haven't had much time to date in high school. I've been so busy. Well, gotta run."

THE SOCIAL CONSTRUCTION OF ADOLESCENCE ACROSS TIME AND SPACE

If we were asked to describe David Costa, Carl Fleischer, and Monica Golden, attention would probably be drawn to their status as adolescents. Worldwide, the current generation of adolescents is the largest in history, and youth ages 10 to 24 comprise one quarter of the world's population. Nearly 90% of these youth live in low-income and middle-income countries, where they comprise a much larger proportion of the population than they do in high-income countries (Sawyer et al., 2012).

The adolescent status has changed across time and cultures. Adolescence was invented as a psychosocial concept in the late 19th and early 20th centuries as the United States made the transition from an agrarian to an urban-industrial society (Choudhury, 2010). Prior to this time, adolescents worked beside adults, doing what adults did for the most part. This is still the case for adolescents in many nonindustrial societies today, and in some cultures, adolescence is not recognized as a stage at all (Gardiner, 2018). As the United States and other societies became urbanized and industrialized, child labor legislation and compulsory education policies were passed, and adolescents were moved from the workplace to the school and became economically dependent on parents. The juvenile justice system was created in the United States in 1899 because youthful offenders had come to be regarded as different from adult offenders, with less culpability for their crimes because of their immaturity.

In 1904, G. Stanley Hall, an American psychologist, published *Adolescence: Its Psychology and Its Relations to Physiology, Anthropology, Sociology, Sex, Crime, Religion, and Education*. Hall proposed that adolescence is a period of "storm and stress," when hormones cause many psychological and social difficulties. Hall was later involved in the eugenics movement that intended to improve the human population by controlled selective breeding, and there seems to be racist and classist bias in his work on adolescence, which was not unusual in his time. His discussion suggests that poor youth are at risk of trouble because of their heredity whereas middle-class youth are at risk of being corrupted by the world around them (Finn, 2009). Janet Finn argues that the public, professional, and scholarly conversations about adolescence in the 20th and beginning of the 21st century have focused on adolescents as "trouble."

Jane Kroger (2007) suggests that many societies are clear about what they want their adolescents to avoid (alcohol and other drugs, delinquency, and pregnancy) but not as clear about what positive things they would like their youth to achieve. There is growing agreement that the societal context in which adolescence is experienced in the United States and other wealthy nations is becoming increasingly less supportive for adolescent development (Choudhury, 2010). This concern has led, in recent years, to the construction of a positive youth development movement, which has focused on youth "as resources to be developed, and not as problems to be managed" (Silbereisen & Lerner, 2007a, p. 7).

Perhaps no life course phase has been the subject of more recent empirical research than adolescence.

Most prominently, the National Longitudinal Study of Adolescent to Adult Health (Add Health) was initiated at the Carolina Population Center in 1994. It is a study of a representative sample of adolescents in Grades 7 through 12 during the 1994–1995 school year. This cohort has been followed through several waves of the study and is currently being reinterviewed from 2016 to 2018. The Add Health study includes measures of social, economic, psychological, and physical well-being as well as contextual information on the family, neighborhood, community, school, friendships, peer groups, and romantic relationships. Add Health data are now generating large numbers of research reports, a partial list of which can be retrieved at the website listed at the end of this chapter.

THE TRANSITION FROM CHILDHOOD TO ADULTHOOD

In many countries, adolescence is described as the transitional period between childhood and adulthood. It is more than that, of course. It is a very rich period of the life course in its own right. For many, it is a thrilling time of life full of new experiences. The word *adolescence* originates from the Latin verb *adolescere*, which means "to grow into maturity." It is a period of life filled with transitional themes in every dimension of the configuration of person and environment: biological, psychological, social, and spiritual. These themes do not occur independently or without affecting one another. For example, David Costa's experience may be complicated because he is gay and because his family relationships are strained, but it is also strengthened by his supportive friendships and his participation in sports. Carl Fleischer's transition is marked by several challenges—his weight, his substance use, his lack of a relationship with his father, his academic performance—but also by the promise of his developing computer expertise and entrepreneurial skills. Monica Golden's movement through adolescence may be eased by her academic, athletic, and social success, but it also could be taxed by her busy schedule and high expectations for herself.

Many cultures have specific **rites of passage**—ceremonies that demarcate the transition from childhood to adulthood. Often these rites include sexual themes, marriage themes, themes of becoming a man or a woman, themes of added responsibility, or themes of increased insight or understanding. Such rites of passage are found in most nonindustrialized societies where nearly 80% of girls and almost 70% of boys go through some form of initiation ritual (Gardiner, 2018). For example, in the Kaguru tribe of eastern Africa, 10- to 12-year-old boys are led into the bush, their clothes are removed, and they are ritually circumcised while also being taught the sexual practices of adulthood by male members of the community. When the Kaguru girl has her first menstruation, she is taught the "ways of womanhood" by her grandmother and older women of the tribe (Gardiner, 2018). For the most part, the transition from adolescence to adulthood is not marked by such clearly defined rituals in North America and many other Western countries. Some scholars who study adolescence have suggested that where there are no clearcut puberty rituals, adolescents will devise their own rituals, such as "hazing, tattooing, dieting, dress, and beautification rituals" (Kroger, 2007, p. 41).

Some groups in North America continue to practice rites of passage, however. In the United States, some Jews celebrate the bar mitzvah for boys and bat mitzvah for girls at the age of 13 to observe their transition to adulthood and to mark their assumption of religious responsibility. Many Latino families, especially of Mexican heritage, celebrate *quinceanera*, during which families

attend Mass with their 15-year-old daughter, who is dressed in white and then presented to the community as a young woman. Traditionally, she is accompanied by her *padrinos*, or godparents, who agree to support her parents in guiding her during this time. The ceremony is followed by a reception at which her father dances with her and presents her to the family's community of friends (Tatum, 2014). Among many First Nations/ Native American tribes in North America, boys participate in a vision quest at age 14 or 15. The boy is taken into a "sweat lodge," where his body and spirit are purified by the heat. He is assisted by a medicine man who advises him and assists with ritual prayers. Later he is taken to another place where he is left alone to fast for 4 days. Similarly, some First Nations/Native American girls take part in a ritual that involves morning running and baking a ceremonial cake (Gardiner, 2018).

Mainstream culture in the United States, however, has few such rites. Many young adolescents go through confirmation ceremonies in Protestant and Catholic churches. Otherwise, the closest thing to a rite of passage may be getting a driver's license, graduating from high school, registering to vote, graduating from college, or getting married. But these events all occur

PHOTO 6.1 Adolescence is a period filled with transitional themes in every dimension of life: biological, psychological, social, and spiritual.

© Don Hammond/Design Pics/Corbis

at different times and thus do not provide a discrete point of transition. Moreover, not all youth participate in these rites of passage. Even without a cultural rite of passage, all adolescents experience profound biological, psychological, social, and spiritual changes. In wealthy capitalist societies, these changes have been divided into three phases: early adolescence (ages 11 to 14), middle adolescence (ages 15 to 17), and late adolescence (ages 18 to 22). Exhibit 6.1 summarizes the typical biological, psychological, and social developments in these three phases. Of course, adolescent development varies from person to person and with time, culture, and other aspects of the environment. Yet deviations from the normative patterns of adolescent change may have psychological ramifications, because adolescents are so quick to compare their own development with that of their peers and because of the cultural messages they receive about acceptable appearance and behavior.

BIOLOGICAL ASPECTS OF ADOLESCENCE

Adolescence is a period of great physical change, marked by a rapid growth spurt in the early years, maturation of the reproductive system, redistribution of body weight, and continuing brain development. Adequate care of the body during this exciting time is of paramount importance.

Puberty

Puberty is the period of the life course in which the reproductive system matures. It is a process that begins before any biological changes are visible and occurs through interrelated neurological and endocrinological changes that affect brain development, sexual maturation, levels and cycles of hormones, and physical growth. The hypothalamus, pituitary gland, adrenal

---

EXHIBIT 6.1 ● Typical Adolescent Development

Stage of Adolescence	Biological Changes	Psychological Changes	Social Changes
Early (11–14)	Hormonal changes Beginning of puberty Physical appearance changes Possible experimentation with sex and substances	Reactions to physical changes, including early maturation Concrete/present-oriented thought Body modesty Moodiness	Changes in relationships with parents and peers Less school structure Distancing from culture/tradition Seeking sameness
Middle (15–17)	Completion of puberty and physical appearance changes Possible experimentation with sex and substances	Reactions to physical changes, including late maturation Increased autonomy Increased abstract thought Beginning of identity development Preparation for college or career	Heightened social situation decision making Continue to renegotiate family relationships More focus on peer group Beginning of one-to-one romantic relationships Moving toward greater community participation
Late (18–22)	Slowing of physical changes Possible experimentation with sex and substances	Formal operational thought Continuation of identity development Moral reasoning	Very little school/life structure Beginning of intimate relationships Renewed interest in culture/tradition

glands, and **gonads** (ovaries and testes) begin to interact and stimulate increased hormone production. It is the increase of these hormones that leads to the biological changes. Although androgens are typically referred to as male hormones and estrogens as female hormones, males and females in fact produce all three major **sex hormones**: androgens, progestins, and estrogens. Sex hormones affect the development and functioning of the gonads (including sperm production and ova maturation) and mating and childcaring behavior.

During puberty, increased levels of androgens in males stimulate the development and functioning of the male reproductive system; increased levels of progestins and estrogens in females stimulate the development and functioning of the female reproductive system. Specifically, the androgen testosterone, which is produced in males by the testes, affects the maturation and functioning of the penis, prostate gland, and other male genitals; the secondary sex characteristics; and the sex drive. The estrogen estradiol, which is produced in females by the ovaries, affects the maturation and functioning of the ovaries, uterus, and other female genitals; the secondary sex characteristics; and childcaring behaviors.

Primary sex characteristics are those directly related to the reproductive organs and external genitalia. For boys, these include growth of the penis and scrotum. During adolescence, the penis typically doubles or triples in length. Girls' primary sex characteristics are not so visible but include growth of the ovaries, uterus, vagina, clitoris, and labia.

Secondary sex characteristics are those not directly related to the reproductive organs and external genitalia. Secondary sex characteristics are enlarged breasts and hips for girls, facial hair and deeper voices for boys, and hair and sweat gland changes for both sexes. Female breast development is distinguished by growth of the mammary glands, nipples, and areolae. The tone of the male voice lowers as the larynx enlarges and the vocal cords lengthen. Both boys and girls begin to grow hair around their genitals and then under their arms. This hair begins with a fine texture and light color and then becomes curlier, coarser, and darker. During this period, the sweat glands also begin to produce noticeable odors.

Puberty is often described as beginning with the onset of menstruation in girls and production of sperm in boys, but these are not the first events in the puberty process. Menstruation is the periodic sloughing off of the lining of the uterus. This lining provides nutrients for the fertilized egg. If the egg is not fertilized, the lining sloughs off and is discharged through the vagina. However, for a girl to become capable of reproduction, she must not only menstruate but also ovulate. Ovulation, the release of an egg from an ovary, usually does not begin until several months after **menarche**, the onset of menstruation. For boys to reproduce, **spermarche**—the onset of the ability to ejaculate mobile sperm—must occur. Spermarche does not occur until after several ejaculations.

Girls typically first notice breast growth, then growth of pubic hair, and then body growth, especially hips. They then experience menarche; then growth of underarm hair; and finally, an increase in production of glandular oil and sweat, possibly with body odor and acne. Boys typically follow a similar pattern, first noticing growth of the testes; then growth of pubic hair; body growth; growth of penis; change in voice; growth of facial and underarm hair; and finally, an increase in the production of glandular oil and sweat, possibly with body odor and acne. Girls experience the growth spurt before they have the capacity for reproduction, but the opposite is the case for boys.

Pubertal timing varies greatly. Generally, girls begin puberty about 2 years earlier than boys. Girls most commonly begin menstruating from ages 10 to 14 and as late as 16.5 (Brooks-Gunn & Ruble, 2013), and boys begin producing sperm from ages 10 to 16, with an average age of about 13 (Tomova, Lalabonova, Robeva, & Kumanov, 2011). The age at which puberty begins has been declining in this century, but there is some controversy about the extent of this shift. In the United States, low socioeconomic status is associated with early puberty, but in parts of the world with high rates of extreme poverty, puberty is often delayed, and malnutrition and infectious disease are considered the cause (Kuther, 2017).

In addition to changes instigated by sex hormones, adolescents experience growth spurts. Bones are augmented by cartilage during adolescence, and the cartilage calcifies later, during the transition to adulthood. Typically, boys develop broader shoulders, straighter hips, and longer forearms and legs; girls typically develop narrower shoulders and broader hips. These skeletal differences are then enhanced by the development of additional upper-body musculature for boys and the development of additional fat deposits on thighs, hips, and buttocks for girls. These changes account for differences in male and female weight and strength.

The Adolescent Brain

As recently as 30 years ago, it was thought that human brain development was finalized by early childhood

(Choudhury, 2010). In the past 20 years, however, neuroimaging techniques have allowed researchers to study how the brain changes across the life course, and there is no doubt that the brain changes a great deal during adolescence (Colver & Longwell, 2013). Researchers are now able to study the adolescent brain using both magnetic resonance imaging (MRI), which provides an image of brain structure, and functional magnetic resonance imaging (fMRI), which provides a picture of metabolic function under specific circumstances (Blakemore, 2012; Sapolsky, 2017).

As discussed in earlier chapters, researchers have known for some time that the brain overproduces gray matter from development in the womb to about the age of 3 years, is highly plastic and thus shaped by experience, and goes through a pruning process. The neural connections or synapses that get exercised are retained during pruning, whereas the ones that are not exercised are eliminated. Brain research suggests that the adolescent brain undergoes another period of overproduction of gray matter just prior to puberty, peaking at about 11 years of age for girls and 12 years for boys, followed by another round of pruning. This process, like the infant's, is also affected by the individual's interactions with the outside world (Colver & Longwell, 2013).

The title of the chapter on adolescence in neuroscientist Robert Sapolsky's book *Behave* is "Adolescence; or Dude, Where's My Frontal Cortex?" Much interest surrounds recent findings about frontal lobe development during adolescence. The pruning process just described allows the brain to be more efficient to change in response to environmental demands and facilitates improved integration of brain activities. Recent research indicates that pruning occurs in some parts of the brain earlier than in others, in general progressing from the back to the front part of brain, with the frontal lobes among the latest to show the structural changes. The frontal lobes are key players in the "executive functions" of planning, working memory, and impulse control, and the latest research indicates that they are not fully developed until the mid-twenties (Blakemore & Robbins, 2012; Sapolsky, 2017). Sapolsky (2017) argues that nothing can be understood about adolescence without understanding the delayed development of the frontal cortex. As the synapses are pruned throughout adolescence, axons are myelinated (coated with a whitish fatty substance), a process that allows neurons to communicate in a more rapid and coordinated fashion. In addition, the adolescent brain is bombarded with gonadal hormones (Sapolsky, 2017). There is a lot going on in the adolescent brain. The frontal cortex is

the last brain region to mature; its development is less influenced by genes and more influenced by experience than other brain regions.

Because of the relatively late development of the frontal lobes, particularly the prefrontal cortex, different neuronal circuits are involved in the adolescent brain under different emotional conditions. The researchers make a distinction between "cold cognition" problem solving and "hot cognition" problem solving during adolescence. Cold-cognition problem solving occurs when the adolescent is alone and calm, as he or she typically would be in the laboratory. Conversely, hot-cognition problem solving occurs in situations where teens are with peers, emotions are running high, they are feeling sexual tension, and so on. The research indicates that in situations of cold cognition, adolescents as young as 12 or 13 can reason and problem solve as well as or better than adults. However, in situations of hot cognition, adolescent problem solving is much more impulsive (Blakemore & Robbins, 2012). Neuroimaging studies show that adolescents are dramatically sensitive to peer pressure and emotional contagion (Sapolsky, 2017).

Similar to all social mammals, human adolescents tend to demonstrate increased novelty seeking, increased risk taking, and greater affiliation with peers (Colver & Longwell, 2013; Sapolsky, 2017). Yet, for most individuals, these activities peak in adolescence and then taper off as newly formed identities set and youth mature out of these tendencies (Spear, 2010; Steinberg, 2009). Current research indicates that, overall, as compared with adults, three themes have emerged: (1) adolescents do not yet have adult levels of maturity, responsibility, impulse control, and self-regulation; (2) adolescents are less autonomous and more susceptible to outside pressures (such as those from their peers) than adults; and (3) adolescents are less capable than adults of weighing potential consequences and considering future implications of their behavior (McCarter & Bridges, 2011; Sapolsky, 2017; Spear, 2010). The emerging research on the adolescent brain is raising issues about social policy related to adolescents and is being used in ways that may be both helpful and hurtful to adolescent development (Steinberg, 2009). This is illustrated by two significant legal cases. In 2005, the U.S. Supreme Court heard the case of *Roper v. Simmons* (543 U.S. 551), involving 17-year-old Christopher Simmons, who had been convicted of murdering a woman during a robbery. He had been sentenced to death for his crime. His defense team argued that his still developing adolescent brain made him less culpable for his crime than an adult, and therefore he should not be subject to the death penalty. The neuroscience evidence may have tipped the scales in the Supreme Court's decision to overturn the death penalty for Simmons and all other juveniles (Haider, 2006). In another example, in 2006, the state of Kansas used an interpretation of neuroscience research to stipulate that "sexual acts with individuals under 16 years of age are illegal regardless of the age of the defendant." This would include any consensual touching by youth and classify such as criminal statutory rape except in instances where the individuals are married (Kansas Statutes, § 21-3502 and § 21-3504; Johnson, Blum, & Giedd, 2009).

The question being raised is, what is the extent of human agency, the capacity for decision making, among adolescents? The answer to that question will vary from adolescent to adolescent. There is great risk that neuroscience research will be overgeneralized to the detriment of adolescents. Johnson et al. (2009) caution that it is important to put the adolescent brain in context, remembering that there are complex interactions of the brain with other biological systems as well as with "multiple interactive influences including experience, parenting, socioeconomic status, individual agency and self-efficacy, nutrition, culture, psychological well-being, the physical and built environments, and social relationships and interactions" (p. 219). Johnson and colleagues also recommend that we avoid focusing on pathology and deficits in adolescent development and use neuroscience to examine the unique strengths and potentials of the adolescent brain. Colver and Longwell (2013) argue that though the adolescent brain leads to greater risk taking, it supports the challenges specific to adolescence and allows adolescents to "push ideas and boundaries to the limit" (p. 905). That perspective is in keeping with the increasing focus on positive psychology and the related positive youth development movement. Researchers at Duke University have created an interdisciplinary team whose mission is to educate society, especially young people, about the brain—how to use it effectively and how to keep it healthy. (A link to BRAINWORKS appears with the web resources at the end of this chapter.) Knowing more about the neurodevelopment of their own bodies may change the behaviors of some adolescents.

Nutrition, Exercise, and Sleep

At any stage along the life course, the right balance of nutrition, exercise, and sleep is important. As the transition from childhood to adulthood begins, early adolescent bodies undergo significant biological changes from their brains to the hair follicles on their legs and everywhere in between. Yet it appears that few adolescents maintain a healthy balance during their time in adolescent flux.

In many parts of the world, adolescents simply cannot get access to an adequate diet, resulting in high levels of anemia and youth who are underweight and overweight (Sawyer et al., 2012). In economically advanced nations, there is enough to eat, but adolescents often do not have a satisfactory diet to support the adolescent growth and development. In the United States, the Department of Health and Human Services (HHS) and the Department of Agriculture (USDA) work together to develop dietary guidelines for the United States, which are to be updated every 5 years. Their 2015–2020 guidelines recommend an intake of 2,200–3,200 calories a day, depending on activity level, for boys ages 14 to 18, with 10% to 30% from proteins, 45% to 65% from carbohydrates, and 25% to 35% from fats. For girls ages 14 to 18, they recommend an intake of 1,800 calories a day with the same nutritional distribution listed for boys (U.S. Department of Health and Human Services & U.S. Department of Agriculture [USDHHS/USDA], 2015a).

Additionally, adolescents should follow healthy eating patterns within an appropriate calorie level, including a variety of vegetables from all subgroups—dark green, red and orange, legumes (beans and peas), starchy, and other; fruits, especially whole fruits; grains, at least half of which are whole grains; fat-free or low-fat dairy, including milk, yogurt, cheese, and/or fortified soy beverages; a variety of protein foods, including seafood, lean meats and poultry, eggs, legumes (beans and peas), nuts, seeds, and soy products; and oils. They should limit saturated and trans fats, added sugars, and sodium (USDA/USDHHS, 2015a).

According to the Secretaries of Health and Human Services and Agriculture, "Half of all American adults have one or more preventable, chronic diseases, many of which are related to poor quality eating patterns and physical inactivity. Rates of these chronic, diet-related diseases continue to rise, and they come not only with increased health risks, but also at high cost" (USDA/USDHHS, 2015b, para. 1).

With these profound outcomes, food choices and activity levels are being evaluated more seriously in the United States than ever before, and social workers can certainly help with this. Consider all the factors that affect what you have for breakfast, lunch, and dinner.

What factors might affect David Costa, Carl Fleischer, and Monica Golden's food choices?

The National Youth Risk Behavior Surveillance System (YRBSS) monitors six types of health-risk behaviors that contribute to the leading causes of death and disability among youth and adults, including behaviors that contribute to unintentional injuries and violence; sexual behaviors that contribute to unintended pregnancy and sexually transmitted disease, including HIV infection; alcohol and other drug use; tobacco; unhealthy dietary behaviors; and inadequate physical activity. This chapter references data from the YRBSS 2015 (Kann et al., 2016) because this study presents the best available national data on adolescent risky health behaviors. Here is the first example. Data from YRBSS 2015 indicate that in the United States 31.5% of young people in Grades 9 to 12 had eaten fruit or drank 100% fruit juice two or more times per day during the past 7 days, 28% of students had eaten vegetables two or more times per day during the past 7 days, and 13.8% of students had not eaten breakfast during the past 7 days. This is a concern, given the need for well-balanced diets and increased caloric intake during a period of rapid neurobiological and physical growth. Many U.S. youth say they don't have time to eat breakfast or that they aren't hungry in the morning. Yet the research is convincing, indicating that adolescent students who eat breakfast report higher energy and less fatigue and perform better on cognitive tests than students who do not eat breakfast (Cooper, Bandelow, & Nevill, 2011).

The recommendation is also for most people of every age to engage in regular physical activity and reduce sedentary activities to promote health, psychological well-being, and a healthy body weight. Physical fitness should be achieved by including cardiovascular conditioning, stretching exercises for flexibility, and resistance exercises or calisthenics for muscle strength and endurance. The specific recommendation for children and adolescents (ages 6 to 17 years old) is to engage in at least 60 minutes of physical activity daily with a variety of exercises that are aerobic, muscle-strengthening, and bone-strengthening (Office of Disease Prevention and Health Promotion, 2008).

Again, the data are not promising. Nationwide, 48.6% of high school students reported being physically active for a total of at least 60 minutes a day on at least 5 of the 7 days preceding the survey. Conversely, 41.7% of students played video or computer games, or used the computer for something other than schoolwork, for 3 hours or more on an average school day, and 24.7% watched television for 3 hours or more on an average school day (Kann et al., 2016).

Along with other changes of puberty, there are marked changes in sleep patterns (Carskadon & Tarokh, 2014; Darchia & Cervena, 2014). Changes in circadian rhythms, triggered by hormonal changes, create a tendency to be more alert late at night and to wake later in the morning (Gamble et al., 2014). Given the mismatch of these sleep patterns with the timing of the school day, adolescents often doze off during school. Researchers have found that when adolescents are given unrestricted sleep opportunities, they average over 9 hours of sleep per night; consequently, it is suggested that adolescents need 8½ to 9¼ hours of sleep each night (Bartel, Gradisar, & Williamson, 2015). In light of research findings about the changes in circadian rhythms during adolescence, in 2014, the American Academy of Pediatrics urged middle schools and high schools to modify start times to better allow adolescents to get adequate sleep and improve their health and academic performance. They recommended a start time no earlier than 8:30 a.m. Data analyzed for the academic year 2011–2012 indicate that only 17.7% of public middle schools and high schools in the United States have a start time of 8:30 a.m. or later (Wheaton, Ferro, & Croft, 2015).

Researchers have found that millions of adolescents worldwide achieve less than 8 hours of sleep, especially on school nights. Survey data show that less than one third of U.S. high school students sleep at least 8 hours on school nights, and one quarter get less than 6 hours of sleep on school nights (Bartel et al., 2015; Wheaton et al., 2015). Researchers have recently noted the ways in which nighttime technology use contributes to insufficient sleep (Gamble et al., 2014).

Insufficient sleep is a debilitating problem for adolescents, resulting in sleepiness and fatigue; impaired academic performance; and increased risk for anxiety, depression, and substance abuse (Gamble et al., 2014; Pieters et al., 2015; Wong, Robertson, & Dyson, 2015). Sleep deprivation has also been linked to poor food choice. In one study, adolescents with sleep deprivation were less likely than well-slept adolescents to eat healthy food throughout the week and were more likely to eat fast food at least twice a week (Krueger, Reither, Peppard, Krueger, & Hale, 2013). Sleep deprivation can also lead to drowsiness or falling asleep at the wheel. It also heightens the effects of alcohol and can lead to increased use of caffeine and nicotine (Carskadon & Tarokh, 2014). As suggested, the risks of sleep deprivation are varied, and they can be serious.

CRITICAL THINKING QUESTIONS 6.1

What are the implications of recent research findings about the adolescent brain for social policy? This research is leading to a number of policy discussions about several issues, including the timing of the school day; regulations for adolescent driving, including the legal age of driving, whether evening driving should be allowed, whether other adolescents can be present in the car of an adolescent driver, and so on; the drinking age; and the age when a juvenile can be tried as an adult in a court of law. What opinions do you hold about these issues? How are those opinions shaped by recent brain research?

PSYCHOLOGICAL ASPECTS OF ADOLESCENCE

Psychological development in adolescence is multifaceted. Adolescents have psychological reactions, sometimes dramatic, to the biological, social, and cultural dimensions of their lives. They become capable of and interested in discovering and forming their psychological selves. They may show heightened creativity as well as interest in humanitarian issues; ethics; religion; and reflection and record keeping, as in a diary (Kuther, 2017). Adolescence is a time of increased emotional complexity and a growing capacity to understand and express a wider range of emotions and to gain insight into one's own emotions (Silvers et al., 2012). Three areas of psychological development are particularly noteworthy: psychological reactions to biological changes, changes in cognition, and identity development.

Psychological Reactions to Biological Changes

"Will my body ever start changing? Will my body ever stop changing? Is this normal? Am I normal? Why am I suddenly interested in girls? And why are the girls all taller (and stronger) than me? How can I ask Mom if I can shave my legs?" These are some of the questions mentioned when Jane Kroger (2007, pp. 33–34) asked a class of 12- and 13-year-old adolescents what type of questions they think most about. As you can see, themes of biological changes were pervasive. If you can remember your own puberty process, you probably are not surprised that researchers have found that pubertal adolescents are preoccupied with physical changes

and appearances (Price, 2009). Young adolescents are able to reflect on and give meaning to their biological transformations. Of course, responses to puberty are influenced by the way other people, including parents, siblings, teachers, and peers, respond to the adolescent's changing body. In addition, reactions to puberty are influenced by other events in the adolescent's life, such as school transition, family conflict, and peer relationships. Media images also play an important role (Ricciardelli, 2016).

It appears that puberty is usually viewed more positively by boys than by girls, with boys focused on increased muscle mass and physical strength and girls focused on increased body weight and fat deposits (Kenny, O'Malley-Keighran, Molcho, & Kelly, 2017). Adolescent females are consistently found to be more dissatisfied with their body shape than adolescent males (Edwards, Patrick, Skalicky, Huang, & Hobby, 2012). There is some evidence that body image is more positive among athletic girls than among nonathletic girls (Dorak, 2011). Earlier research indicated that African American adolescent girls are more satisfied with their body image and less inclined to eating disorders than Caucasian American girls, based on different cultural values for the ideal body (Franko & Striegel-Moore, 2002), but there is some evidence that this gap is closing (Edwards et al., 2012). Both adolescent males and females report pressure to conform to specific appearance ideals and rules, also suggesting that adolescents who fail to conform face such negative peer experiences as teasing, judging, and exclusion (Kenny et al., 2017). Recent research has focused on the role of social media in the development of negative body image perceptions (Craike et al., 2016; Tiggemann & Slater, 2017).

Reactions to menstruation are often mixed (Uskul, 2004). One study of Chinese American adolescent girls found 85% reported that they were annoyed and embarrassed by their first menstruation, but 66% also reported positive feelings (Tang, Yeung, & Lee, 2003). In a focus group of 53 women from 34 different countries, most of the participants had vivid memories of their first menstruation. They reported both positive and negative emotions, but negative reactions (such as embarrassment, shame, fear, shock, and confusion) were more often noted. Reactions to menarche were greatly affected by the type of information and level of support the young women received from their mothers (Golchin, Hamzehgardeshi, Fakhri, & Hamzehgardeshi, 2012). Research shows that pubescent girls talk with parents and friends about their first menstruation, but pubescent boys do not discuss with anyone their first ejaculation, an event sometimes seen as the closest male equivalent to first menstruation (Kroger, 2007). Pubescent boys may receive less information from adults about nocturnal ejaculations than their sisters receive about menarche.

Because the onset and experience of puberty vary greatly, adolescents need reassurance regarding their own growth patterns. Some adolescents will be considered early maturers, and some will be considered late maturers. Timing and tempo of puberty are influenced by genetics, social, and environmental factors, and there are ethnic differences, as well. On average, African American adolescents enter puberty earlier than Hispanic adolescents, who enter puberty earlier than Caucasian Americans (Ramnitz & Lodish, 2013). There are psychological and social consequences of early maturing for both male and female adolescents, but the research findings are not always consistent. A longitudinal study of Australian children found that those who experienced early puberty had more adjustment problems than their age peers; this was true for both boys and girls (Mensah et al., 2013). The researchers found, however, that the children who entered puberty early demonstrated more adjustment problems from early childhood through early adolescence. They concluded that the data support a "life course hypothesis that differences in pubertal timing and childhood adjustment may at least in part result from genetic and environmental factors early in life" (p. 122). Further longitudinal research is needed to provide better understanding of the early risk factors for a difficult transition to puberty. Although both early and late maturing have been found to present adjustment challenges for adolescents, with early maturing the most problematic, there is also evidence that adolescents' perceptions of their pubertal timing have a large influence on puberty-related outcomes (Mendle, 2014; Moore, Harden, & Mendle, 2014).

Changes in Cognition

Adolescence is a crucial phase in cognitive development, with development occurring in three main areas (Sanders, 2013):

1. *Improved reasoning skills*: the ability to consider a range of possibilities, to think hypothetically, and to engage in logical analysis

2. *Abstract thinking*: the ability to imagine things not seen or experienced

3. *Meta-cognition*: the ability to think about thinking

These abilities are components of Jean Piaget's fourth stage of cognitive development called formal operational thought (see Exhibit 3.4 for an overview of Piaget's stages of cognitive development). *Formal operational thought* suggests the capacity to apply hypothetical reasoning to various situations and the ability to use symbols to solve problems. David Costa, for example, demonstrated formal operational thought when he considered the possibility of getting to know Theo. He considered the reactions from his other friends if he were to get together with Theo, he examined his thoughts, and he formulated a strategy based on the possibilities and on his thoughts.

Whereas younger children focus on the here-and-now world in front of them, the adolescent brain is capable of retaining larger amounts of information. Thus, adolescents are capable of hypothesizing beyond present circumstances. This ability also allows adolescents to engage in decision making based on a cost-benefit analysis. As noted, brain research indicates that adolescent problem solving is as good as adult problem solving in cold-cognition situations but is not equally sound in hot-cognition situations. Furthermore, brain development alone does not result in formal operational thinking. The developing brain needs social environments that encourage hypothetical, abstract reasoning and opportunities to investigate the world (Cohen & Sandy, 2007; Gehlbach, 2006). Formal operational thinking is more imperative in some cultures than in others but is most imperative in many fields in the changing economic base of postindustrialized societies. One research team found that Taiwanese adolescents, who are reared in a collectivist culture, exercise formal operational thinking but rely on parents and other important people to validate their thoughts (Lee & Beckert, 2012). More research is needed to explore cultural variations in cognitive autonomy. It is also important to remember that although contemporary education is organized to facilitate formal operational thinking, students in the United States and around the world do not have equal access to sound curriculum and instruction.

Recent research suggests that adolescence is a period of profound advancements in social cognition, which is the processing, storing, and using of information about other people. Brain researchers are identifying the brain regions that are involved in *mentalizing*, or the ability to think about the mental states and intentions of others, and finding that these regions of the brain continue to develop throughout adolescence (Blakemore & Robbins, 2012). They argue that this helps to explain why adolescents are more sociable, form more complex peer relationships, and are more sensitive to peer acceptance and rejection than younger children (Blakemore, 2012). One research team has investigated another way of thinking about changes in social cognition during adolescence. They found that group identity becomes a dominant theme in early adolescence, and automatic evaluations develop based on in-group and out-group memberships, with a tendency for positive evaluation of in-group members and negative evaluation of out-group members. They found that although younger children are aware of group identities, they do not develop automatic evaluations based on them (Degner & Wentura, 2010). This would suggest that early adolescence is a good time to help young people think about their automatic evaluations related to group identity.

Identity Development

There is growing agreement that identity is a complex concept. **Identity** is a "person's self-definition as a separate and distinct individual, including behaviors, beliefs, and attitudes" (Gardiner, 2018, p. 89). **Social identity**, an important aspect of identity, is the part of the self-concept that comes from knowledge of one's membership in a social group and the emotional significance of that membership (Gardiner, 2018). Lene Arnett Jensen (2003) suggests that adolescents increasingly develop multicultural identities as they are exposed to diverse cultural beliefs, either through firsthand experience or through the media. She argues that the process of developing an identity presents new challenges to adolescents in a global society. Jensen gives the example of arranged marriage in India,

noting that on the one hand, Indian adolescents grow up with cultural values favoring arranged marriage, but on the other hand, they are increasingly exposed to values that emphasize freedom of choice. But identity is even more complex than that; it is increasingly examined from an *intersectional* perspective that recognizes the multiple social identities we must integrate, including gender identity, ethnic/racial identity, religious identity, social class identity, national identity, regional identity, and so on (see Shade, Kools, Weiss, & Pinderhughes, 2011).

Theories of Self and Identity

A number of prominent psychologists have put forward theories that address self or psychological identity development in adolescence. Exhibit 6.2 provides an overview of six theorists: Freud, Erikson, Kegan, Marcia, Piaget, and Kohlberg. All six help to explain how a concept of self or identity develops, and all six suggest that it cannot develop fully before adolescence. Piaget and Kohlberg suggest that some individuals may not reach these higher levels of identity development at all.

Sigmund Freud (1905/1953) thought of human development as a series of five psychosexual stages in the expression of libido (sensual pleasure). The fifth stage, the genital stage, occurs in adolescence, when reproduction and sexual intimacy become possible.

Building on Freud's work, Erik Erikson (1950, 1959, 1963, 1968) proposed eight stages of psychosocial development (refer to Exhibit 3.8 for a summary of Erikson's eight stages). He viewed psychosocial crisis as an opportunity and challenge. Each Eriksonian stage requires

EXHIBIT 6.2 ● Theories of Self or Identity in Adolescence		
Theorist	**Developmental Stage**	**Major Task or Processes**
Freud	Genital stage	To develop libido capable of reproduction and sexual intimacy
Erikson	Identity versus role diffusion	To find one's place in the world through self-certainty versus apathy, role experimentation versus negative identity, and anticipation of achievement versus work paralysis
Kegan	Affiliation versus abandonment (early adolescence)	To search for membership, acceptance, and group identity, versus a sense of being left behind, rejected, and abandoned
Marcia	Ego identity statuses	To develop one of these identity statuses: identity diffusion, foreclosure, moratorium, or identity achievement
Piaget	Formal operational thought	To develop the capacity for abstract problem formulation, hypothesis development, and solution testing
Kohlberg	Postconventional morality	To develop moral principles that transcend one's own society: individual ethics, societal rights, and universal principles of right and wrong

the mastery of a particular developmental task related to identity. Erikson's fifth stage, identity versus role diffusion, is relevant to adolescence. The developmental task is to establish a coherent sense of identity; failure to complete this task successfully leaves the adolescent without a solid sense of identity.

Robert Kegan (1982, 1994) asserts that there should be another stage between middle childhood and adolescence in Erikson's model. He suggests that before working on psychological identity, early adolescents face the psychosocial conflict of affiliation versus abandonment. The main concern is being accepted by a group, and the fear is being left behind or rejected. Successful accomplishment of group membership allows the young person to turn to the question of "Who am I?" in mid- and late adolescence.

James Marcia (1966, 1980) expanded on Erikson's notion that adolescents struggle with the issue of identity versus role diffusion, and his theory is the most researched of adolescent identity. Marcia proposed that adolescents vary in how easily they go about developing a personal identity, and he described four identity statuses based on two aspects of identity development—the amount of exploration being done toward identity development and the amount of commitment to a particular identity:

1. *Identity diffusion*: no commitment made to roles and values, with or without exploration

2. *Foreclosure*: commitment made to roles and values without exploration

3. *Moratorium*: exploration of roles and values without commitment

4. *Identity achievement*: exploration of roles and values followed by commitment

Jean Piaget proposed four major stages leading to adult thought (refer to Exhibit 3.5 for an overview of Piaget's stages). He expected the last stage, the stage of formal operations, to occur in adolescence, enabling the adolescent to engage in more abstract thinking about "who I am." Piaget (1972) also thought that adolescents begin to use formal operational skills to think in terms of what is best for society.

Lawrence Kohlberg (1976, 1984) expanded on Piaget's ideas about moral thinking to describe three major levels of moral development (refer to Exhibit 4.2 for an overview of Kohlberg's stage theory). Kohlberg thought that adolescents become capable of **postconventional moral reasoning**, or morality based

on moral principles that transcend social rules, but that many never go beyond conventional morality, or morality based on social rules.

These theories have been influential in conceptualizations of identity development. Morris Rosenberg (1986) provides another useful model of identity to keep in mind while working with adolescents—or perhaps to share with adolescents in the process of identity formation. His model includes both social identity and psychological identity but also incorporates physical traits, which taps into the important role that body image plays in adolescent development. Rosenberg suggests that identity comprises three major parts, outlined in Exhibit 6.3:

- *Social identity* is made up of several elements derived from interaction with other people and social systems, including social statuses, membership groups, and social types.

- *Dispositions* are self-ascribed aspects of identity.

- *Physical characteristics* are simply one's physical traits, which all contribute a great deal to sense of self.

Exhibit 6.4 uses Rosenberg's model to analyze the identities of David Costa, Carl Fleischer, and Monica Golden. Notice that disposition is an element of identity based on self-definition. In contrast, a label is determined by others, and physical characteristics are genetically influenced. David has an athletic body and thinks of himself as athletic, but his parents—and perhaps others—label him as a freak. He is working to incorporate the fact that he is different into his identity. Carl has been labeled as a fatso, an underachiever, and a smoker. He seems to have incorporated these negative labels into his identity. Monica has been labeled as an overachiever, but she does not absorb the negative label, reframing it instead as ambitious.

Scholars generally agree that identity formation is structured by the sociocultural context (see Gardiner, 2018; Kroger, 2007). Thus, the options offered to adolescents vary across cultures. North America and other Western societies that put a high value on autonomy offer more options for adolescents than more collectivist-oriented societies. Some writers suggest that having many options increases stress for adolescents (Gardiner, 2018). Think about the case studies of David Costa, Carl Fleischer, and Monica Golden. What is the sociocultural context of their identity struggles? What choices do they have, given their sociocultural contexts?

EXHIBIT 6.3 ● Rosenberg's Model of Identity

Social Identity	Disposition	Physical Characteristics
Social statuses: <u>basic</u> classifications or demographic characteristics, such as sex, age, and socioeconomic status	Attitudes (e.g., conservatism, liberalism)	Height
	Traits (e.g., generosity, bravery)	Weight
Membership groups: groups with which the individual shares an interest, belief, origin, or physical or regional continuity (e.g., groups based on religion, political party, or race)	Abilities (e.g., musical talent, athletic skill)	Body build
	Values (e.g., efficiency, equality)	Facial features
	Personality traits (e.g., introversion, extroversion)	
Labels: identifiers that result from social labeling (as when the boy who skips school becomes a delinquent)	Habits (e.g., making lists, getting up early)	
Derived statuses: identities based on the individual's role history (e.g., veteran, high school athlete, or Harvard alumnus)	Tendencies (e.g., to arrive late, to exaggerate)	
	Likes or preferences (e.g., romance novels, pizza)	
Social types: interests, attitudes, habits, or general characteristics (e.g., jock, geek, head, playboy, or go-getter)		
Personal identities: unique labels attached to individuals (e.g., first name, first and last names, social security number, fingerprints, or DNA)		

Source: **Based on Rosenberg, 1986.**

EXHIBIT 6.4 ● Examples of Adolescent Identity

Element of Identity	David	Carl	Monica
Social Identity			
Social statuses	Male, 17, middle class	Male, 17, working class	Female, 17, upper-middle class
Membership groups	Bolivian American, gay	European American, heads	African American, Christian, Young Republicans
Labels	Freak, athlete	Fatso, underachiever, smoker	Overachiever, brain
Derived statuses	Baseball player	Pizza deliverer	Senior class vice president, babysitter, track athlete
Social types	Jock	Geek, head (affiliate)	Brain, go-getter
Personal Identity	David Costa	Carl Fleischer	Monica Golden
Disposition	Athletic	Underachiever, not popular, fat, slow, likes to get high, likes to surf the Internet	Athletic, ambitious, extroverted, likes children
Physical Characteristics	Athletic build	Overweight	Tall

For those aspects of identity that we shape ourselves, individuals have four ways of trying on and developing a preference for certain identities.

1. *Future orientation.* By adolescence, youth have developed two important cognitive skills: They are able to consider the future, and they are able to construct abstract thoughts. These skills allow them to choose from a list of hypothetical behaviors based on the potential outcomes resulting from those behaviors. David Costa demonstrates future orientation in his contemplation regarding Theo. Adolescents also contemplate potential future selves.

2. *Role experimentation.* According to Erikson (1963), adolescence provides a psychosocial moratorium—a period during which youth have the latitude to experiment with social roles. Thus, adolescents typically sample membership in different cliques, build relationships with various mentors, take various academic electives, and join assorted groups and organizations—all in an attempt to further define themselves. Monica Golden, for instance, sampled various potential career paths before deciding on becoming a pediatrician.

3. *Exploration.* Whereas role experimentation is specific to trying new roles, exploration refers to the comfort an adolescent has with trying new things. The more comfortable the individual is with exploration, the easier identity formation will be.

4. *Self-evaluation.* During the quest for identity, adolescents are constantly sizing themselves up against their peers. Erikson (1968) suggested that the development of identity is a process of personal reflection and observation of oneself in relation to others. George Herbert Mead (1934) suggested that individuals create a **generalized other** to represent how others are likely to view and respond to them. The role of the generalized other in adolescents' identity formation is evident when adolescents act on the assumed reactions of their families or peers. For example, what Monica Golden wears to school may be based not on what she thinks would be most comfortable or look the best but rather on what she thinks her peers expect her to wear. Thus, she does not wear miniskirts to school because "everyone" (generalized other) will think she is "loose." Recent attention has been paid to identity as a life story that begins to be told in late adolescence, a story one tells oneself about one's past, present, and anticipated future (see McLean & Mansfield, 2012). This is called narrative identity.

Gender Identity

Adolescence, like early childhood, covered in Chapter 4, is a time of significant gender identification. **Gender identity** is how one perceives one's gender, and it begins in early childhood but is elaborated on and revised during adolescence (Steensma, Kreukels, de Vries, & Cohen-Kettenis, 2013). Efforts are often made at various developmental stages to integrate the biological, psychological, and social dimensions of sex and gender. *Gender expression* refers to how individuals express their gender and may include how they dress, their general appearance, the way they speak, or the way they carry themselves. *Gender roles* are societal expectations of how individuals should act, think, or feel based on their assigned gender or biological sex (note that gender roles are typically based on the binary male/female). Culture plays a large role in gender identity, gender expression, and gender roles. Gender roles can be a source of painful culture clash for some immigrant groups migrating to North America and Europe, harder for some ethnic groups than for others. But there is evidence that many immigrant families and individuals learn to be bicultural in terms of gender expectations, holding on to some traditional expectations while also innovating some new ways of doing gender roles (see Mann, Roberts, & Montgomery, 2017; Sue, Rasheed, & Rasheed, 2016).

In the majority of cases, gender identity develops in accordance with physical sex characteristics, but this does not always happen. Surprisingly little is known about the influences on adolescent gender identity development (Steensma et al., 2013). In recent years, the term *cisgender* has been used to describe situations in which people's gender identity matches their assigned gender or biological sex. In addition to cisgender men and women, additional genders include (but are not limited to) agender, without gender; genderfluid, a gender identity that is dynamic over time; intersex, an individual with male and female sex characteristics; and two-spirit, a Native American concept for those exhibiting both gender identities.

The American Psychiatric Association (2013) recognizes that often during adolescence, noncisgender youth may describe being uncomfortable with the gender roles expected of them based on their biological sex or being uncomfortable with their bodies (particularly during puberty). In the *Diagnostic and Statistical Manual 5*, gender identity disorder was replaced with *gender dysphoria*, which occurs when individuals experience significant distress about the incongruence between their assigned gender and their experienced gender (Cohen-Kettenis & Steensma, 2016). The distinction is that the diagnosis now is based on significant distress and not on the existence of incongruence.

Trans is an umbrella term used to include transgender, transsexual, and transvestite persons. *Transgender* describes youth who have been assigned a gender (based on their genitalia at birth) and identify as the "opposite" gender or uncomfortable with the gender binary. These individuals may or may not alter their bodies through surgery or hormones. *Transsexuals* are folks who wish to alter their physical bodies through surgery and/or hormones to have their bodies match their internalized gender identities. *Transvestite* refers to people who wear the clothing of the "opposite" gender and may also identify as cross-dressers or drag kings/queens. Current guidelines for hormonal treatment for adolescents who report gender incongruence is that they undergo treatment to suppress pubertal development at the time they first exhibit physical changes of puberty, using GnRH analogues to suppress pubertal hormones. This process is reversible at any time. When the adolescent is around the age of 16, or at an age when there is sufficient mental capacity to give informed consent, the guidelines recommend that the use of gender-affirming hormones be started with a gradual increase in the dosage of the sex hormones that match the gender identity. This process is partly irreversible. It is further recommended that sex hormone levels should be maintained in the normal range for the person's affirmed gender (Hembre et al., 2017).

Gender identity is not the same as sexual orientation. Gender identity is how I consider myself—male, female, somewhere in between, or neither—and sexual orientation refers to whether I am romantically/sexually attracted to members of the same sex, the opposite sex, both, or neither. As we work with adolescents and strive to understand and be responsive to their stories, we must allow youth to share their identities (if they are known or as they develop) with us and not assume that they are cisgender or heterosexual. Some adolescents will still be questioning and, thus, are unsure about their identity or orientation. Sexual orientation is discussed later under the Adolescent Sexuality section. The adolescents with whom you come in contact may find the visual depiction of identity, expression, attraction, and sex at the Genderbread Person website useful for thinking about their own gender identity and sexual attractions (It's Pronounced Metrosexual, 2017).

Cultural Identity

Research indicates that ethnic origin is not likely to be a key ingredient of identity for Caucasian North American adolescents, but it is often central to identity in adolescents of ethnic minority groups (Rivas-Drake et al., 2014). Considerable research indicates that adolescence is a time when young people evaluate their ethnic background and explore ethnic identity. The development of ethnic identity in adolescence has been the focus of research across Canada, the United States, and Europe in recent years as ethnic diversity increases in all these countries (see, e.g., Street, Harris-Britt, & Walker-Barnes, 2009). Ethnic minority youth are challenged to develop a sense of themselves as members of an ethnic minority group while also coming to terms with their national identity (Lam & Smith, 2009). Adolescents tend to have wider experience with multicultural groups than when they were younger and may be exposed to ethnic discrimination, which can complicate the development of cultural pride and belonging (Costigan, Su, & Hua, 2009).

Consider Monica Golden, who is an upper-middle-class African American teenager in a predominantly White high school. What are some of the potential added challenges of Monica's adolescent identity formation? Is it any wonder she is hoping to attend Howard University, an HBCU (historically Black college/university), where she could surround herself with African American role models and professional support networks, versus a TWI (traditionally White institution)?

The construction of an ethnic or racial identity is an important way for ethnic and racial minority adolescents to make a positive adjustment during the adolescent transition (Rivas-Drake et al., 2014). One meta-analysis of the research literature found that achieving a positive ethnic identity is associated with higher levels of self-esteem and lower levels of depression among ethnic minority individuals (Smith & Silva, 2011). Ethnic and racial identity has also been found to buffer the consequences of adverse life events and racial and ethnic discrimination (Galliher, Jones, & Dahl, 2011). In a comprehensive review of the research literature, Rivas-Drake and colleagues (Rivas-Drake et al., 2014) found that high levels of ethnic and racial identity are beneficial for African American adolescent psychosocial, academic, and health outcomes. The research evidence generally supports the psychosocial, academic, and health benefits of ethnic and racial identity for Latino, American Indian, and Asian American adolescents, but it is less consistent and sparser for these youth than for African American youth.

Researchers have found that ethnic minority adolescents tend to develop strong ethnic identity, but there is also variability within ethnic groups in terms of extent of ethnic identity. Costigan and colleagues

(2009) reviewed the literature on ethnic identity among Chinese Canadian youth and concluded that the evidence indicates a strong ethnic identity among these youth. Conversely, there was much variability in the extent to which these youth reported a Canadian national identity. Adolescents negotiated ethnic identity in diverse ways across different settings, with different approaches being used at home versus in public settings. Lam and Smith (2009) studied how African and Caribbean adolescents (ages 11 to 16) in Britain negotiate ethnic identity and national identity and had similar findings to those for Chinese Canadian youth. They found that both groups of adolescents, African and Caribbean, rated their ethnic identity higher than their national identity and reported more pride in their ethnic heritage than in being British. The researchers found, however, that girls reported stronger ethnic identity than boys.

The available research on cultural identity among ethnic minority youth indicates that most of these youth cope by becoming bicultural, developing skills to operate within at least two cultures. Research indicates that family conflict can arise when there are discrepancies in cultural identity between adolescents and their parents. One research team found that a sample of ethnic minority male and female adolescents had similar levels of disparity with their parents regarding ethnic identity. However, parent–adolescent discrepancies in ethnic identity were associated with elevated depression and social stress in female adolescents but not in male adolescents (Ansary, Scorpio, & Catanzariti, 2013). This research should alert social workers to tune in to the process of ethnic identity development when they work with ethnic minority youth. It appears that ethnic identity is a theme for both David Costa and Monica Golden. They both appear to be developing some comfort with being bicultural, but they are negotiating their bicultural status in different ways. Discussion about their ethnic identity might reveal more struggle than we expected. Some youth may be more likely to withdraw from the challenges of accessing mainstream culture rather than confronting these challenges and seeking workable solutions. We must be alert to this possibility.

CRITICAL THINKING QUESTIONS 6.2

What types of psychological reactions to their changing bodies do you see in the stories of David Costa, Carl Fleischer, and Monica Golden? What do you recall about your own psychological reactions to your changing body during puberty? What factors do you think influenced your reactions? With which groups did you identify during adolescence? What were your multiple social identities, and how did they intersect? Which identities/intersectionalities were most important to you during adolescence? Which identities/intersectionalities are important to you now?

SOCIAL ASPECTS OF ADOLESCENCE

The social environment—family, peers, organizations, communities, institutions, and so on—is a significant element of adolescent life. For one thing, as already noted, identity develops through social transactions. For another, as adolescents become more independent and move into the world, they develop their own relationships with more elements of their social environment.

Relationships With Family

Answering the question "Who am I?" includes a consideration of the question "How am I different from my brothers and sisters, my parents, and other family members?" For many adolescents, this question begins the process of **individuation**—the development of a self or identity that is unique and separate. David Costa seems to have started the process of individuation; he recognizes that he may not want to be what his parents want him to be. He does not yet seem comfortable with this idea, however. Carl Fleischer is not sure how he is similar to and different from his absent father. Monica Golden has begun to recognize some ways that she is different from her siblings, and she is involved in her own personal exploration of career options that fit her disposition. It would appear that she is the furthest along in the individuation process.

The concept of independence is largely influenced by culture, and mainstream culture in the United States places a high value on independence. However, as social workers, we need to recognize that the notion of the adolescent developing an identity separate from family is not acceptable to all cultural groups in the United States or other places around the world (Gardiner, 2018). One research team found that African American adolescents have less decision-making autonomy in middle adolescence than European American adolescents (Gutman & Eccles, 2007). Peter Nguyen (2008; Nguyen & Cheung, 2009) has studied the relationships between

Vietnamese American adolescents and their parents and found that a majority of the adolescents perceived their fathers as using a traditional authoritarian parenting style and see this as posing problems for the adolescents' mental health in the context of the multicultural society in the United States. Latino families in the United States have been found to keep very close boundaries around the family during adolescence (Garcia-Preto, 2016). Filial piety, respect for parents and ancestors, is a strong value in East Asian cultures (Schneider, Lee, & Alvarez-Valdivia, 2012). Our assessments of adolescent individuation should be culturally sensitive. Likewise, we must be realistic in our assessments of the ability of adolescents with cognitive, emotional, and physical impairments to function independently.

Overall, families tend to respond to the adolescent desire for greater independence by renegotiating family roles and opening family boundaries to allow for the adolescent's greater participation in relationships outside the family (Garcia-Preto, 2016). The research literature on the relationships between parents and their adolescents indicates that, in general, these relationships are "close, supportive, and warm" (Galambos & Kotylak, 2012). However, many families with adolescents have a high level of conflict. Conflict is particularly evident in families experiencing additional stressors, such as divorce and economic difficulties (Fine, Ganong, & Demo, 2010). Conflict also plays out differently at different points in adolescence. Research suggests that conflicts with parents increase around the time of puberty but begin to decrease after that (Galambos & Kotylak, 2012). Both parents and adolescents need some time to adjust to this new life stage.

Adolescent struggles for independence can be especially potent in multigenerational contexts (Garcia-Preto, 2016). These struggles typically come at a time when parents are in midlife and grandparents are entering late adulthood and both are facing stressors of their own. Adolescent demands for independence may reignite unresolved conflicts between parents and grandparents and stir the pot of family discord. Sibling relationships may also change in adolescence. Longitudinal research indicates that, compared with middle childhood, adolescents report lower levels of positive sibling relationships during early adolescence, followed by increased intimacy in midadolescence (Shanahan, Waite, & Boyd, 2012). The Society for Research on Adolescence prepared an international perspective on adolescence in the 21st century and reached three conclusions regarding adolescents and their relationships with their families:

- Families are and will remain a central source of support to adolescents in most parts of the world. Cultural traditions that support family cohesion, such as those in the Middle East, South Asia, and China, remain particularly strong, despite rapid change. A great majority of teenagers around the world experience close and functional relationships with their parents.

- Adolescents are living in a wider array of diverse and fluid family situations than was true a generation ago. These include divorced, single-parent, remarried, gay and lesbian, and multilocal families. More adolescents live in households without men. Because of AIDS, regional conflicts, and migratory labor, many adolescents do not live with their parents in some parts of the world.

- Many families are becoming better positioned to support their adolescents' preparation for adulthood. Smaller family sizes result in adults devoting more resources and attention to each child. Parents in many parts of the world are adopting a more responsive and communicative parenting style, which facilitates development of interpersonal skills and enhances mental health (Larson, Wilson, & Mortimer, 2002).

Relationships With Peers

In the quest for autonomy and identity, adolescents begin to differentiate themselves from their parents and associate with their peers. Peer influence is strongest in early adolescence (Hafen, Laursen, & DeLay, 2012). Early adolescents are likely to select friends that are similar to them in gender and interests, but by middle adolescence, the peer group often includes opposite-sex friends as well as same-sex friends (Seiffge-Krenge & Shulman, 2012). Most early adolescents have one close friend, but the stability of these friendships is not high. In early adolescence the peer group tends to be larger than in middle childhood; these larger peer groups are known as *cliques*. By midadolescence, the peer group is organized around common interests; these groups tend to be even larger than cliques and are generally known as *crowds* (Brown & Klute, 2003). David Costa hangs out with the athletic crowd but seeks support from gay peers. Carl Fleischer is making contact with the "heads" crowd. Monica Golden's crowds would include peer counselors and the Young Republicans. Peer relationships contribute to adolescents' identities, behaviors, and personal and social competence.

© Jack Hollingsworth/Digital Vision/ThinkStock

PHOTO 6.2 Peer relationships are a fertile testing ground for youth and their emerging identities.

Peer relationships are a fertile testing ground for youth and their emerging identities. Many adolescents seek out a peer group with compatible members, and inclusion or exclusion from certain groups can affect their identity and overall development. For some adolescents, participation in certain peer groups influences their behavior negatively. Peer influence may not be strong enough to undo protective factors, but if the youth is already at risk, the influence of peers becomes that much stronger. Sexual behaviors and pregnancy status are often the same for same-sex best friends. Substance use is also a behavior that most often occurs in groups of adolescents. The same is true for violent and delinquent behaviors. Researchers debate whether selection (choosing friends based on shared delinquent behaviors) or socialization (peer influence) plays a more important role here (Hafen et al., 2012).

Romantic Relationships

Until recently, adolescent romantic relationships received little or no attention from researchers. Since the beginning of the 21st century, theories of adolescent romantic relationships have been developed and a great number of studies have been conducted. Both the theories and the research have typically focused on heterosexual romantic relationships. The following discussion of heterosexual romantic relationships in adolescence is based on a recent review of the research on the topic by Seiffge-Krenge and Shulman (2012). Although same-sex romantic relationships are becoming more visible, there is very little research on same-sex romantic relationships in adolescence. What research there is has tended to focus on same-sex attractions in adolescence from a risk perspective. The following discussion of same-sex romantic relationships in adolescence is based on a review of research on the topic by Russell, Watson, and Muraco (2012).

With the hormonal changes of adolescence, youth begin to be interested in sexual gratification and emotional union with a partner. This typically begins with romantic fantasies in early adolescence, fantasies that are often shared in same-gender friendship groups. As they move into mixed-gender groups in midadolescence, heterosexual youth have an opportunity to meet potential romantic partners. Researchers in the United States have found that nearly all 13- and 14-year-old adolescents report romantic fantasies and a desire to date. By late adolescence, most youth in the United States have been involved in some kind of romantic relationship, and the rates are similar in other wealthy capitalist countries. The duration of romantic relationships is about 3 months in early adolescence and from 1 to 2 years in middle and late adolescence. Research indicates that most people have at least one romantic breakup during adolescence and that a breakup is a highly stressful event. (See Seiffge-Krenge & Shulman, 2012, for a fuller discussion of the research on adolescent heterosexual romantic relationships.) It is important to remember that in the United States and many other societies, romantic relationships develop through a dance of flirtation and dating, but in some cultures, the romantic relationship develops in the context of an arranged marriage.

In contrast to the burgeoning research on adolescent heterosexual romantic relationships, there is very little research on adolescent same-sex romantic relationships. There are a number of reasons why that research is hard to do, but an important reason is that, because of stigma and internalized homophobia, many youth with same-sex attractions do not "come out." Most of the research on this topic is based on small samples. Research indicates, however, that as society becomes more accepting, U.S. youth with same-sex attractions are becoming more likely to act on those attractions. One longitudinal study of a cohort born in the mid-1990s found that less than 10% of youth with same-sex attractions reported ever having a same-sex romantic relationship, and a majority of these youth reported ever having a heterosexual romantic relationship. Another study, conducted 10 years later, found that a majority of same-sex-attracted youth were currently or had recently been in a same-sex romantic relationship. Research finds that one issue for youth with same-sex attractions is the relatively small pool of potential romantic partners. One study found that gay male youth typically begin the romantic relationship with a sexual experience, and lesbian youth typically begin as close friends. Another study found that youth with same-sex attractions who reported heterosexual dating had higher levels of internalized homophobia than similar youth who did not engage in heterosexual dating. (See Russell et al., 2012, for a fuller discussion of the research on adolescent same-sex romantic relationships.)

PHOTO 6.3 Adolescents in many cultures become involved in romantic relationships during middle school and high school.

Relationships With Organizations, Communities, and Institutions

As adolescents loosen their ties to parents, they develop more direct relationships in other arenas such as school, the broader community, employment, and social media/technology.

School

In the United States, as well as in other wealthy nations, youth are required to stay in school through a large portion of adolescence. The situation is quite different in many poor nations, however, where children may not even receive a primary school education. In their time spent at school, adolescents gain skills and knowledge for their next step in life, either moving into the workforce or continuing their education. In school, they also have the opportunity to evolve socially and emotionally; school is a fertile ground for practicing future orientation, role experimentation, exploration, and self-evaluation.

Middle schools in the United States usually have a structured format and environment; high schools are less structured in both format and environment, allowing a gradual transition to greater autonomy. The school experience changes radically, however, at the college level. Many college students are away from home for the first time and are in very unstructured environments. David Costa, Carl Fleischer, and Monica Golden have had different experiences with structure in their environments to date. David's environment has required him to move flexibly between two cultures. That experience may help to prepare him for the unstructured college environment. Carl has had the least structured home life. It remains to be seen whether that has helped him to develop skills in structuring his own environment or left him with insufficient models for doing so. Monica is accustomed to juggling multiple commitments and expectations. Time management skills will help with the transition to college, but she may struggle with having freedom from pressing family and community expectations for the first time.

School is also an institutional context in the United States where cultures intersect, which may create difficulties for students whose appearance or behavior is different from the Eurocentric, female-centered education model. You may not realize how biased the educational model in the United States is until you view it through a different cultural lens. We can use a Native American lens as an example. Michael Walkingstick Garrett (1995) uses the experiences of the boy Wind-Wolf as an example of the incongruence between Native American culture and the typical education model:

> Wind-Wolf is required by law to attend public school. . . . He speaks softly, does not maintain eye contact with the teacher as a sign of respect, and rarely responds immediately to questions, knowing that it is good to reflect on what has been said. He may be looking out the window during class, as if daydreaming, because he has been taught to always be aware of changes in the natural world. These behaviors are interpreted by his teacher as either lack of interest or dumbness. (p. 204)

Children in the United States spend less time in school-related activities than do German, Korean, and Japanese children and have been noted to put less emphasis on scholastic achievement. Some researchers attribute oft-noted cross-cultural differences in mathematics achievement to these national differences in emphasis on scholastics (D. Newman, 2012). For adolescents, scholastic interest, expectations, and achievements may also vary, based not only on nationality but also on gender, race, ethnicity, economic status, and expectations for the future.

Participation in secondary education during adolescence has been increasing worldwide, but inequality persists. The United Nations Education, Scientific, and Cultural Organization (UNESCO, 2015) is concerned about the challenges faced by migrant students around the world, especially those forced to migrate because of deportation policies. In the United States, there has been concern about inequality across local school systems

and the experiences of ethnic, racial, religious, and sexual minorities, as well as students with disabilities in secondary education settings (see Balagna, Young, & Smith, 2013; Cianciotto, 2012; Seward & Khan, 2016; Wickrama & Vazsonyi, 2011). School experiences have been found to be entwined with both happiness and depressive symptoms during adolescence, with school experiences having a greater influence on happiness and depressive symptoms than happiness and depressive symptoms have on school experiences. (Stiglbauer, Gnambs, Gamsjäger, & Batinic, 2013; Wickrama & Vazsonyi, 2011). Of particular interest is the connection between negative school experiences and school disengagement, with school dropout the most severe form of school disengagement. National data indicate that the overall high school dropout rate in the United States decreased from 10.9% in 2000 to 5.9% in 2015 (National Center for Education Statistics, 2017c). In 2015, the dropout rate for males and females was similar, 6.3% for males and 5.4% for females. From 2000 to 2015, the school dropout rate narrowed between White and Black and Hispanic youth. For White youth, the dropout rate declined from 6.9% to 4.6%. The dropout rate for Black youth declined from 13.1% to 6.1%, and the dropout rate for Hispanic youth declined from 27.8% to 9.2% (National Center for Education Statistics, 2017c). These data seem to suggest a recent improvement in school engagement among Black and Hispanic youth.

The Broader Community

Recent studies have considered the ways adolescents attempt to contribute to society and found that they are increasingly using technology to engage in such activities as signing petitions and expressing opinions about societal issues (van Goethem et al., 2012). Adolescents and young adults were on the forefront of social unrest across North Africa and the Middle East in 2010 and 2011 and were able to use communication technologies to organize protest activities. Although they experienced success in their activism, they also faced serious threats to their lives (Sawyer et al., 2012). As this book goes to press, in the United States we are seeing growing activism among high schools around issues of gun violence, following a school shooting at the Marjory Stoneham Douglas High School in Parkland, Florida.

In the United States, the participation of high school students in volunteer work in the community is becoming common. Indeed, community service is required in many U.S. high schools. Flanagan (2004) argues that community volunteer service provides structured outlets for adolescents to meet a wider circle of community people and to experiment with new roles. The community youth development movement is based on the belief that such community service provides an opportunity to focus on the strengths and competencies of youth rather than on youth problems (see Villarruel, Perkins, Borden, & Keith, 2003). One research team found that participation in community service and volunteerism assisted in identity clarification and in the development of political and moral interests (McIntosh, Metz, & Youniss, 2005). Adolescent volunteering has also been found to reduce depression and increase positive emotions (Moreno, Furtner, & Rivara, 2013). Both parents and peers have been found to influence volunteering and other community engagement, with peers gaining in influence over the course of adolescence (van Goethem, van Hoof, van Aken, de Castro, & Raaijmakers, 2014).

Another way adolescents can have contact with the broader community is through a mentoring relationship with a community adult. The mentoring relationship may be either formal or informal. The mentor becomes a role model and trusted adviser. Mentors can be found in many places: in part-time work settings, in youth-serving organizations, in religious organizations, at school, in the neighborhood, and so on. There is unusually strong evidence for the positive value of mentoring for youth. Here are some examples of research in this area. Longitudinal research found that natural mentoring relationships with nonparental adults were associated with greater psychological well-being (DuBois & Silverhorn, 2005). Another study found that perceived mentoring from an unrelated adult in the work setting was associated with psychosocial competencies and adjustment in both U.S. and European samples (Vazsonyi & Snider, 2008). Longitudinal research with foster care youth has found that youth who had been mentored had better overall health, less suicidal ideation, fewer sexually transmitted infections (STIs), and less aggression in young adulthood than foster care youth who had not been mentored (Ahrens, DuBois, Richardson, Fan, & Lozano, 2008). Another study investigated the mentor relationship between an adolescent survivor of acquired brain injury and an adult mentor who was also a survivor of this injury. The researchers found that both the mentors and the adolescents derived benefit from the relationship, with the adolescents reporting gains in social and emotional well-being and identity development (Fraas & Bellerose, 2010). One last study of adolescents identified as "at risk" and involved in an 8-month mentoring program designed to prevent substance abuse found that the mentors helped the youth to improve relationships with family and at school and to increase their overall life skills (Zand et al., 2009). Social workers in a number of settings can be instrumental in encouraging mentoring relationships for adolescents.

Work

Like many adolescents, Carl Fleischer and Monica Golden also play the role of worker in the labor market. Limited employment can provide an opportunity for social interaction and greater financial independence. It may also lead to personal growth by promoting notions of contribution, responsibility, egalitarianism, and self-efficacy and by helping the adolescent to develop values and preferences for future jobs—answers to questions like "What kind of job would I like to have in the future?" and "What am I good at?" For example, Monica tried many jobs before deciding that she loves working with children and wants to become a pediatrician. In addition, employment may also offer the opportunity to develop job skills, time management skills, customer relation skills, money management skills, market knowledge, and other skills of value to future employers.

The U.S. Department of Labor has launched an initiative called YouthRules! that seeks to promote positive and safe work experiences for young workers (see www.youthrules.dol.gov). They have developed guidelines that are the social policy result of research that suggests that for youth, work, in spite of some positive benefits, may also detract from development by cutting into time needed for sleep, exercise, maintenance of overall health, school, family relations, and peer relations. Current guidelines for adolescent employment are overviewed in Exhibit 6.5.

Adolescent employment is often thought to promote positive psychosocial development. One research team has examined the positive and negative outcomes of adolescent employment among adolescents over age 16. The researchers found positive outcomes when adolescent workers are engaged in work that offers moderate levels of autonomy and skill use, moderate to high levels of learning, high levels of opportunities to be helpful, and supervisor and coworker support. Negative outcomes were found when youth workers reported moderate levels of work stress and work-school conflict (Rauscher, Wegman, Wooding, Davis, & Junkin, 2012). Another research team studied the relationships among adolescent work intensity, school performance,

EXHIBIT 6.5 ● Department of Labor Guidelines for Adolescent Paid Work

Age	Hours That Can Be Worked	Jobs That Can Be Done	Recommended Pay
Under 14	No guidelines	Limited to: *newspaper delivery *babysitting on casual basis *working as actor or performer *homeworker making evergreen wreaths *working for business owned by parents *other rules for agriculture workers	No guidelines
14 or 15	May not work: *more than 3 hours on school day *more than 18 hours per week during school year *more than 8 hours per day when school is not in session *more than 40 hours per week when school is not in session *before 7 a.m. or after 7 p.m. during the school year	Allowed jobs include: *retail occupations *intellectual or creative work such as computer programming, teaching, tutoring, singing, acting, or playing an instrument *errand or delivery work by foot, bicycle, and public transportation *clean-up and yard work that does not include using power-driven machinery *servicing cars and trucks, such as dispensing gasoline or oil and washing and hand polishing *food service, such as reheating food, washing dishes, cleaning equipment, and limited cooking *some food market services *loading or unloading objects for use at a worksite *certain tasks in sawmills and woodshops when certain criteria are met *lifeguard duties for 15-year-olds who meet certain requirements	In most circumstances, the federal minimum wage, $7.25 per hour, must be paid. As little as $4.25 may be paid for the first 90 consecutive calendar days of employment for any employer.
16 or 17	Unlimited hours	Any job that has not been declared hazardous by the secretary of labor is permissible for 16- and 17-year-olds.	In most circumstances, the federal minimum wage, $7.25 per hour, must be paid. As little as $4.25 may be paid for the first 90 consecutive calendar days of employment for any employer.
18	Unlimited hours	Any job	In most circumstances, the federal minimum wage, $7.25 per hour, must be paid. As little as $4.25 may be paid for the first 90 consecutive calendar days of employment for any employer.

Source: Based on YouthRules!, 2017.

and substance use in 10th- and 12th-grade students. They found that 12th graders were more likely to be employed than 10th graders and to spend longer hours on the job. White students were more likely to be employed than minority students, but among the students who were employed, African American and Hispanic students were more likely than White students to spend long hours on the job, and Asian American students were less likely than White students to work intensively. The researchers also found that intensive work was related, overall, to poor school performance and substance use, but the relationship between intensive work and problem behaviors was significantly weaker for Hispanic and African American students than for White and Asian American students—and significantly weaker for low-income students than for less economically disadvantaged students (Bachman, Staff, O'Malley, & Freedman-Doan, 2013). These findings suggest the need for further research about how different groups of adolescents benefit or are harmed by intensive work.

Technology

According to a 2018 report from the Pew Research Center, 95% of U.S. teens (ages 13 to 17) have a smartphone or access to one, and 88% report having access to a desktop or laptop computer at home (Anderson, 2018). Teens from households with an annual income of $75,000 or more are more likely than teens from households with an annual income of $30,000 or less to have access to a computer at home (96% vs. 75%). In addition, teens with parents with a bachelor's degree are more likely than teens with parents with a high school degree or less to have access to a computer at home (94% vs. 78%). With this high level of access to mobile Internet connections, teens engage in persistent online activities; 45% of teens report being online on a near-constant basis. In 2015, Facebook was the dominant online platform for teens, but in 2018 51% of teens reported using Facebook compared to 85% using YouTube, 72% using Instagram, and 69% using Snapchat. Girls are more likely than boys to say Snapchat

© iStockphoto.com

PHOTO 6.4 In wealthy nations, a sizable portion of an adolescent's life is spent in leisure pursuits.

is their most used site and boys are more likely than girls to identify YouTube as their most used site. Lower-income teens are more likely to use Facebook than higher-income teens, White teens are more likely than Hispanic and Black teens to use Snapchat, and Black teens are more likely than White teens to use Facebook. A majority of both boys and girls play video games, but gaming is almost universal among boys with 97% playing compared to 83% of girls. As new platforms are developed, teens are more likely than other age groups to try them out, and they are quite fluid in their usage. Some teens (31%) report that social media has a mostly positive effect on their lives, others (24%) report that it has a mostly negative effect, and the largest share (45%) report that social media has neither a positive nor negative effect on their lives.

Sherry Turkle (2011), professor of social studies of science and technology at the Massachusetts Institute of Technology, has been studying the impact of ICTs on human behavior since the 1990s. She acknowledges that the Internet fosters social connections, identity development, and access to information of almost any kind.

She also suggests that, like adults, today's adolescents are tethered to their technologies, living in a constant state of waiting for connection and endangering themselves by texting while walking or driving. Some adolescents complain that their technologies mean they are always "on call" to parents and friends alike. They work on identity development in an era when photos or messages can be sent to audiences they did not select. They are often physically present in one setting while mentally present in one or more other settings, and they interact with both parents and friends who are physically present while being mentally present elsewhere.

Common Sense Media explored technology addiction for adolescents and found that 69% of parents and 78% of teens check their mobile devices at least hourly, 48% of parents compared to 72% of teens feel the need to respond immediately to text/social media notifications on their devices, and 59% of parents believe their children are addicted to their mobile devices compared to 50% of the teens who feel they are addicted (Felt & Robb, 2016). Finally, parents, school officials, and legislators have become increasingly concerned about

© Izabela Habur/iStockphoto.com

PHOTO 6.5 Adolescents are prolific users of text messaging, bringing a high level of connectedness.

adolescents' exposure to sexually explicit material and pornography and direct contact, harassment, or exploitation via the Internet. Assessing prevalence rates of intentional pornography usage among adolescents is complicated by the method of data collection, sampling, and design. Peter and Valkenburg (2016) examined 20 years of research and found a great variation in the prevalence for lifetime pornography exposure, but boys were consistently found to make greater use of pornography than girls. They also found that pornography use among adolescents increased with advancing age and that pornography users were more likely than other adolescents to hold permissive sexual attitudes and gender-stereotypical sexual beliefs. Finally, the Crimes Against Children Research Center reports that Internet sex crimes are more often cases of statutory rape where adult offenders meet, develop relationships with, and openly seduce teenagers (Wolak, Finkelhor, Mitchell, & Ybarra, 2008).

CRITICAL THINKING QUESTIONS 6.3

Children and adolescents in the United States spend less time on school-related activities than students in most other high-income countries. Do you think children and adolescents in the United States should spend more time in school? How would you support your argument on this issue? How could high schools in the United States do a better job of supporting the cognitive development of adolescents? Should the high school be concerned about supporting emotional and social development of adolescents? Why or why not?

ADOLESCENT SPIRITUALITY/RELIGIOSITY

Psychologists and anthropologists have proposed that adolescence is a time of universal "spiritual awakening." Research has supported this idea, noting elements of service, inner spiritual growth, and a relationship with a higher power as a part of adolescent spirituality (Benson, Roehlkepartain, & Scales, 2012; Cobb, Kor, & Miller, 2015). Many cultures and religious traditions have coming-of-age rituals that have a spiritual component (Cobb et al., 2015). As adolescents develop greater capacity for abstract thinking, they often search for meaning in life experiences, and some researchers consider adolescence to be the most sensitive life stage for spiritual exploration (Kim & Esquivel, 2011; Magaldi-Dopman & Park-Taylor, 2010). In recent years, behavioral scientists and mental health professionals have developed an interest in spirituality/religiosity (S/R) as a source of resilience for adolescents (Kim & Esquivel, 2011). *Spirituality* is a personal search for meaning and relationship with the sacred, whether that is found in a deity or some other life force. *Religiosity* comprises beliefs and actions associated with an organized religious institution (Good, Willoughby, & Busseri, 2011). S/R includes both personal and institutional ways of connecting with the sacred.

Research on adolescent S/R is still in its infancy, and very little is known. To fill this gap, a Canadian research team undertook a longitudinal study to explore multiple dimensions of S/R. They studied 756 students in Grade 11 and the same students again in Grade 12 and found that at both time periods, the youth fell into a five-cluster typology of S/R:

1. Neither spiritual nor religious (14.2% of 11th graders and 13.4% of 12th graders)

2. Disconnected wonderers (35.9% of 11th graders and 44.6% of 12th graders)

3. High spirituality/high religiosity (16.7% of 11th graders and 8.3% of 12th graders)

4. Primarily spiritual (24.3% of 11th graders and 25.8% of 12th graders)

5. Meditators (9.0% of 11th graders and 7.9% of 12th graders)

The largest cluster at both time periods was the disconnected wonderers, a group that was not involved in any form of spiritual or religious practices but reported often wondering about spiritual issues. As you can see, this group grew from 11th to 12th grade, and the group with high spirituality/high religiosity declined. The meditators may or may not have been meditating as a spiritual practice; meditating may have been related to a physical fitness or other type of physical and/or mental health regimen.

Another research team studied spirituality and religion among a group of junior high and high school students in Israel. They found four patterns of spiritual life among their sample of adolescents. One group, consisting of 28% of the sample, had both strong religious practice and strong spiritual beliefs and experiences; this group was labeled Highest Overall Spirituality. Another group consisting of 28% of the sample had moderate to high levels of spiritual experience but generally no religious practice; this group was labeled the Spiritual Experience Group. A group labeled Religious Practice constituted the smallest group of the sample (11%); this group had moderate to high levels of religious practice and low levels of spiritual experience. The largest group in the sample (34%) reported low levels of spiritual experience and low levels of religious practice; this group was labeled the Lowest Overall Spirituality group (Cobb et al., 2015). This research did not examine how many in this low spirituality group might be the disconnected wonderers identified in the Canadian study.

The National Study of Youth and Religion (NSYR) is the most comprehensive longitudinal study of spirituality and religion among U.S. adolescents. Supported by the Lilly Endowment, this study began in August 2001 and was funded through December 2013. The NSYR's study found that the vast majority of U.S. teenagers (aged 13 to 17) identify themselves as Christian (56.4% Protestant [various denominations], 19.2% Catholic). Fifteen percent are not religious. In addition, 2.3% are Mormon/Latter-Day Saints, 1.5% are Jewish, and other minority faiths (Jehovah's Witness, Muslim, Eastern Orthodox, Buddhist, Pagan or Wiccan, Hindu, Christian Science, Native American, Unitarian Universalist, or two affiliations) each comprised less than 1% of the representative sample. Four out of 10 U.S. adolescents say they attend religious services once a week or more, pray daily or more, and are currently involved in a religious youth group. Eighty-four percent of the surveyed youth believe in God whereas 13% are unsure about belief in God, and 3% do not believe in God (Denton, Pearce, & Smith, 2008). The researchers found that the single most important social influence on the religious and spiritual lives of adolescents is their parents.

For many youth, spirituality may be closely connected to culture. Interventions with adolescents and their families should be consistent with their spirituality and religion, but knowing someone's cultural heritage will not always provide understanding of their religious or spiritual beliefs. For example, it is no longer safe to assume that all Latino Americans are Catholic. Today, there is much religious diversity among Latino Americans who increasingly have membership in Protestant denominations such as Methodist, Baptist, Presbyterian, and Lutheran, as well as in such religious groups as Mormons, Seventh-Day Adventists, and Jehovah's Witnesses. Moreover, the fastest growing religions among Latino Americans are the Pentecostal and evangelical denominations (Garcia, 2011). Many Latino Americans, particularly Puerto Ricans, combine traditional religious beliefs

with a belief in spiritualism, which is a belief that the visible world is surrounded by an invisible world made up of good and evil spirits who influence human behavior. Some Latino Americans practice Indigenous healing rituals, such as *Santeria* (Cuban American) and *curanderismo* (Mexican American). In these latter situations, it is important to know whether adolescents and their families are working with an Indigenous folk healer (Ho, Rasheed, & Rasheed, 2004). Although adolescents may not seem to be guided by their spirituality or religiosity, they may have underlying spiritual factors at work. As with any biological, psychological, or social dimensions of the individual, the spiritual dimensions of youth must be considered to gain the best understanding of the whole person.

ADOLESCENT SEXUALITY

With the changes of puberty, adolescents begin to have sexual fantasies, sexual feelings, and sexual attractions. They will come to understand what it means to be a sexual being and, similar to other facets of their identity, will explore their sexual identity. They will consider the kinds of people they find romantically and sexually attractive. Some will make decisions about engaging in various sexual behaviors. In this experimentation, some adolescents will contract sexually transmitted infections (STIs) and some will become pregnant. Unfortunately, some will also experience unwanted sexual attention and become victims of sexual aggression.

Sexual Decision Making

Transition into sexual behavior is partly a result of biological changes. The amount of the sex hormone DHEA in the blood peaks from ages 10 to 12, a time when both boys and girls become aware of sexual feelings. The way sexual feelings get expressed, however, can depend largely on sociocultural factors. Youth are influenced by the attitudes toward sexual activity that they encounter in their environment, at school; among peers, siblings, and family; in their clubs or organizations; in the media; and so on (Cox, Shreffler, Merten, Schwerdtfeger Gallus, & Dowdy, 2015). When and how they begin to engage in sexual activity are closely linked to what they perceive to be the activities of their peers (Hafen et al., 2012). Risk factors for early sexual activity include early puberty, poor parent–adolescent communication, weak parental monitoring, poor school performance, and sexually active peers (Negriff, Susman, & Trickett, 2011). Finally, beliefs and behaviors regarding sexuality are also shaped by one's culture, religion/spirituality, and value system. Adolescents report a variety of social motivations for engaging in sexual intercourse, including developing new levels of intimacy, pleasing a partner, impressing peers, and gaining sexual experience (Impett & Tolman, 2006).

As the pubertal hormones cause changes throughout the body, most adolescents spend time becoming familiar with those changes. For many, exploration includes **masturbation**, the self-stimulation of the genitals for sexual pleasure. In the most comprehensive U.S. sex study in decades, the National Survey of Sexual Health and Behavior conducted in 2009 included a nationally representative sample of 14- to 17-year-olds and questions about masturbation (Herbenick et al., 2010). Seventy-four percent of boys and 48% of girls reported ever masturbating. Masturbation has negative associations for some adolescents. Thus, masturbation may have psychological implications for adolescents, depending on the way they feel about it and how they think significant others feel about it. Female college students who are high in religiosity report more guilt about masturbation than female college students who are low in religiosity (J. Davidson, Moore, & Ullstrup, 2004).

The 2015 YRBSS suggests that in the United States the rate of engaging in sexual intercourse among high school students has decreased since the last survey. In 2015, approximately 41% of high school students reported having had sexual intercourse during their life, 3.9% had sexual intercourse for the first time before age 13, 11.5% have had sexual intercourse with four or more persons during their life, and 30.1% were sexually active during the last 3 months (Kann et al., 2016). Of the 30.1% of high school students who indicated that they are currently sexually active, 56.9% report that either they or their partner used a condom during last sexual intercourse, 20.6% had drunk alcohol or used drugs before their last sexual intercourse, and 13.8% reported not using any method to prevent pregnancy during their last sexual intercourse (Kann et al., 2016). Adolescents are about as likely to engage in oral sex as vaginal intercourse (Casey Copen, Chandra, & Martinez, 2012).

Adolescents need to develop skills for healthy management of sexual relationships. Early engagement in sexual intercourse has some negative consequences. One research team studied early adolescent sexual initiation in five countries, the United States, Finland, France, Poland, and Scotland, and found it to be a risk factor for substance abuse and poor school attachment (Madkour, Farhat, Halpern, Godeau, & Gabhainn,

2010). They also found that early sexual initiation was disruptive to the parent–adolescent relationship, particularly for female adolescents in the United States but not in the other countries.

Rates of sexual activity among teens in the United States are fairly comparable to those in western Europe, yet the incidence of adolescent pregnancy and childbearing in the United States exceeds that in other economically advanced countries (Martinez, Copen, & Abma, 2011). For instance, the teen birth rate in the United States in 2015 was more than twice the rate in Canada and more than 3 times the rate in Finland, Germany, Iceland, Italy, Libya, Luxembourg, Maldives, Norway, and Sweden (United Nations Population Division, 2017). This discrepancy is probably related to three factors: Teenagers in the United States make less use of contraception than teens in European countries, reproductive health services are more available in European countries, and sexuality education is more comprehensively integrated into all levels of education in most of Europe than in the United States.

Sexual Orientation

As they develop as sexual beings, adolescents begin to consider sexual attraction. **Sexual orientation** refers to erotic, romantic, and affectionate attraction to people of the same sex (gay or lesbian), the opposite sex (heterosexual), both sexes (bisexual), or none. There are also questioning adolescents who are less certain of their sexual orientation than those who label themselves as heterosexual, bisexual, or gay/lesbian, and increasingly we are aware that sexual orientation is more fluid and complex than we once thought (Poteat, Aragon, Espelage, & Koenig, 2009). Research indicates that the current generation of lesbian, gay, bisexual, and questioning youth uses the Internet to get information about sexual orientation and to begin the coming-out process. This provides a safe and anonymous venue for exploration and questioning as well as for initiating the coming-out process; it can lead to greater self-acceptance before coming out to family and friends (Bond, Hefner, & Drogos, 2009). Researchers are currently focusing on three indicators of same-sex sexual orientation: same-sex attractions; same-sex sexual behaviors; and self-labels as gay, lesbian, or bisexual (see Russell et al., 2012; Saewyc, 2011). Glover, Galliher, and Lamere (2009) suggest that sexual orientation should be conceptualized as a "complex configuration of identity, attractions, behaviors, disclosure, and interpersonal explorations" (pp. 92–93).

Theory and research about adolescent sexual orientation are not new, but there has been a very large increase in research on the topic in the past 15 years. The following discussion presents the major themes of Elizabeth Saewyc's (2011) comprehensive review of the research on adolescent sexual orientation published in the decade from 1998 to 2008. The research is still trying to untangle the multiple influences on sexual orientation, but there is general agreement that both genetic and environmental influences are involved. Researchers have struggled with how to define and measure sexual orientation, for example, whether to use measures of attraction, self-identity, or sexual behavior. Even though different measures are used across different studies, researchers consistently find that adolescents with a sexual orientation other than heterosexual report less supportive environments and less nurturing relationships with their parents than heterosexual youth. The research also consistently indicates that sexual minority youth have increased risk for developmental stressors and compromised health.

Research also suggests that sexual minority youth are coming out at earlier ages than in previous eras, but there is still much heterogeneity in the coming-out process. Those who come out earlier appear to be more comfortable with their sexual orientation status but also face increased rejection and harassment from family and peers. African American and Latino youth have a similar trajectory of sexual orientation development as White youth in most ways, but they are more delayed in making public disclosure, and they are less likely to be involved in gay-related social networks that tend to have mostly White membership.

Some evidence contends that most people remain consistent in their sexual attractions across the adolescent and young-adult periods, but youth with a sexual orientation other than heterosexual are much more likely than heterosexual youth to change their self-identification and sexual behavior over a 10-year period. Bisexuality has received much less research attention than homosexuality.

Research from a number of countries indicates that sexual minority youth have a higher prevalence of emotional distress, depression, self-harm, suicidal thinking, and suicidal attempts than heterosexual youth. They also have a higher prevalence of smoking and alcohol and other drug use, are likely to report an earlier sexual debut and to have more sexual partners, and have a higher prevalence of sexually transmitted infections. They are also more likely to be the targets of violence (Saewyc, 2011).

It is important to note that although sexual minority youth face increased risks to physical and mental health, most are successful in navigating the challenges they face and achieve similar levels of well-being as heterosexual youth. Several protective factors have been found to promote resilience in sexual minority youth, including supportive family relationships, supportive friends, supportive relationships with adults outside the family, positive connections with school, and spirituality/religiosity. These are the same protective factors that have been found to promote resilience in all youth, and, unfortunately, the research indicates that sexual minority youth, on average, receive less support in all these areas than heterosexual youth. Research indicates, however, that many sexual minority youth have protective factors specific to their sexual orientation, including involvement in gay-related organizations and attending schools with gay-straight alliances or schools where the staff is trained to make the school a safe zone for sexual minority youth. Consider David Costa's conflict over his sexual orientation. What do you see as the risk and protective factors he faces as he considers this aspect of identity?

There is hope that the changing legal status of same-sex relationships and the increased visibility of positive sexual minority role models will lead to decreased risk and increased protection for sexual minority youth. There is some evidence that growing numbers of the current generation of adolescents do not consider sexual orientation as central an identity concept as earlier generations and are less prone to make negative judgments about sexual orientations other than heterosexual.

Saewyc's (2011) research review indicates the important influence of school climate on the well-being of sexual minority youth. For decades, GLSEN (the Gay, Lesbian, and Straight Education Network) has conducted a National School Climate Survey (NSCS) to document the unique challenges that 6th- to 12th-grade LGBTQ students face and to identify interventions that can improve school climate. The 2015 NSCS (Kosciw, Greytak, Giga, Villenas, & Danischewski, 2016) found that 85.2% of LGBTQ (lesbian, gay, bisexual, transgender, and queer) students experienced verbal harassment at school and 56.2% reported hearing homophobic remarks from their teachers or other school staff. A third of LGBTQ students (31.8%) missed at least one entire day of school in the past month because they felt unsafe or uncomfortable. Moreover, several students noted discriminatory policies/procedures at their schools, including students being prevented from wearing clothes incongruent with their sex assigned at birth, attending a dance/function with someone of the same gender, or forming or promoting a GSA (gay/straight alliance) (Kosciw et al., 2016). Based on the 2015 NSCS findings, GLSEN makes five recommendations that have relevance for social workers working in school settings:

1. Increase student access to appropriate and accurate information regarding LGBTQ people, history, and events through inclusive curricula and library and Internet resources.

2. Support student clubs, such as GSAs, that provide support for LGBTQ students and address LGBTQ issues in education.

3. Provide professional development for school staff to improve rates of intervention and increase the number of supportive teachers and other staff available to students.

4. Ensure that school policies and practices, such as those related to dress codes and school dances, do not discriminate against LGBTQ students.

5. In individual schools and districts, adopt and implement comprehensive bullying/harassment policies that specifically include sexual orientation, gender identity, and gender expression, with clear and effective systems for reporting and addressing incidents that students experience. (Kosciw et al., 2016, p. xxv)

Pregnancy and Childbearing

In 2014, there were 249,078 babies born to adolescent girls aged 15 to 19 in the United States (Hamilton, Martin, Osterman, & Curtin, 2015). This is a birth rate of 24.2 per 1,000 15- to 19-year-old females. Of these births, approximately 89% occurred outside of marriage and 17% were to adolescents who already had a child. The teen pregnancy rate in the United States has declined relatively consistently since the early 1990s (the 1991 rate was 61.8/1,000), but it is still higher than the rate in many other economically advanced countries (Hamilton et al., 2015). Teenage pregnancy rates and birth rates vary considerably by race and ethnicity as well as by region of the country. In 2014, Hispanic/Latinx girls had the highest birth rate (38 per 1,000), and Black girls had the second highest rate (34.9 per 1,000), followed by their White counterparts (17.3 per 1,000) (Hamilton et al., 2015). The lowest teen birth rates were reported in the Northeast, Wisconsin, Minnesota, Indiana, Utah, and Washington, and the highest teen birth rates were from the southern region of the United States, from New Mexico east to West Virginia, plus Wyoming. (See how your state compares on pregnancy rates, birth rates, sexual activity, and contraceptive use at www.hhs.gov/ash/oah/resources-and-publications/facts.)

Adolescent pregnancies carry increased risks to the mother, including delayed prenatal care; higher rates of miscarriage, anemia, toxemia, and prolonged labor; and increased likelihood of being a victim of intimate partner violence (Pinzon & Jones, 2012). They also carry increased risks to the infant, including perinatal mortality, preterm birth, low birth weight, and developmental delays and disabilities (Pinzon & Jones, 2012). In many Asian, eastern Mediterranean, African, and Latin American countries, the physical risks of adolescent pregnancy are mitigated by social and economic support (Hao & Cherlin, 2004). In the United States, however, adolescent mothers are more likely than their counterparts elsewhere to drop out of school; be unemployed or underemployed; receive public assistance; have subsequent pregnancies; and have children with poorer educational, behavioral, and health outcomes. Teenage fathers may also experience lower educational and financial attainment (Pinzon & Jones, 2012).

The developmental tasks of adolescence are typically accomplished in this culture by going to school, socializing with peers, and exploring various roles. For the teenage mother, these avenues to development may be radically curtailed. The result may be long-lasting disadvantage. Consider Monica Golden's path. She obviously loves children and would like to have her own someday, but she would also like to become a pediatrician. If Monica were to become pregnant unexpectedly, an abortion would challenge her religious values and a baby could affect her health, challenge her future goals, and impact her educational and financial potential.

Sexually Transmitted Infections

Youth have always faced pregnancy as a possible consequence of their sexual activity, but other consequences include infertility and death as a result of **sexually transmitted infections (STIs)**, also known as sexually transmitted diseases (STDs). Adolescents aged 15 to 24 comprise half of the 20 million new cases of STIs each year in the United States, and one out of every four sexually active teenaged girls has an STD such as chlamydia or human papillomavirus (Centers for Disease Control and Prevention [CDC], 2017g).

Research has found several contextual and personal factors to be associated with STIs, including housing insecurity, exposure to crime, childhood sexual abuse, gang participation, frequent alcohol use, and depression (Buffardi, Thomas, Holmes, & Manhart, 2008). The CDC (2017g) adds that the "higher prevalence of STDs among adolescents also may reflect multiple barriers to accessing quality STD prevention and management services, including inability to pay, lack of transportation, long waiting times, conflict between clinic hours and work and school schedules, embarrassment attached to seeking STD services, method of specimen collection, and concerns about confidentiality" (para. 1).

Data collection on STIs is complicated for several reasons. State health departments have different requirements about which STIs must be reported. STIs are not always detected and reported. Some STIs, such as chlamydia and HPV (human papillomavirus) are often asymptomatic and go undetected. In addition, many surveys are not based on representative samples. So despite the fact that the best estimates available indicate that adolescents and young adults ages 15 to 24 constitute 25% of the sexually active population, they account for half of the STI diagnoses each year (CDC, 2017g).

Unfortunately, HIV/AIDS is also a risk to adolescent health around the world. In 2016, there were 30.8 to 42.9 million people living with HIV worldwide, according to the Joint United Nations Programme on HIV/AIDS (UNAIDS, 2017). The number of new HIV infections in 2016 is estimated from 1.6 to 2.1 million, and the number of AIDS-related deaths was from 830,000 to 1.2 million for the same year (UNAIDS, 2017). In the United States in 2015, young people aged 13 to 24 accounted for 22% of the new HIV diagnoses, and despite the fact that the rate for new HIV infections is declining for gay and bisexual men, they still made up most of the new cases in 2015 (CDC, 2017h). The Centers for Disease Control and Prevention cite five barriers to HIV prevention for youth: (1) Inadequate sex education: few high schools cover the 16 topics recommended by the CDC including information for gay and bisexual men, sex education does not begin early enough, and sex education has been declining over time (percentage of students required to receive HIV prevention information declined from 64% in 2000 to 41% in 2014); (2) youth risk behaviors, including rates of HIV testing, substance use, condom use, and multiple partners; (3) higher STD rates for youth; (4) HIV stigma, which means that youth may not feel comfortable disclosing their status; and (5) feelings of isolation. Gay and bisexual youth are more likely to experience bullying, violence, mental distress, substance use, and risky sexual behaviors. In the 2015 YRBSS, only 10.2% of students stated that they had been tested for HIV (Kann et al., 2016).

CRITICAL THINKING QUESTIONS 6.4

What sources of information did you use to learn about human sexuality when you were an adolescent? Which sources were the most useful and accurate? Do you believe that public schools should be involved in sexuality education? Why or why not? If so, what topics should be covered in such education?

POTENTIAL CHALLENGES TO ADOLESCENT DEVELOPMENT

Many adjustments must be made during adolescence in all areas of life. Adjustments to biological changes are a major developmental task of adolescence, family relationships are continuously renegotiated across the adolescent phase, and career planning begins in earnest for most youth in mid- to late adolescence. Most adolescents have the resources to meet these new challenges and adapt. But many adolescents engage in risky behaviors or experience other threats to physical and mental health. We have already looked at risky sexual behavior. Nine other threats to physical and mental health are discussed briefly here: substance use and abuse, juvenile delinquency, bullying, school-to-prison pipeline, community violence, dating violence and statutory rape, poverty and low educational attainment, obesity and eating disorders, and depression and suicide.

Substance Use and Abuse

In adolescence, many youth experiment with nicotine, alcohol, and other psychoactive substances with the motivation to be accepted by peers or to cope with life stresses (Weichold, 2007). For example, Carl Fleischer's use of tobacco and marijuana has several likely effects on his general behavior. Tobacco may make him feel tense, excitable, or anxious, and these feelings may amplify his concern about his weight, his grades, and his family relationships. Conversely, marijuana may make Carl feel relaxed, and he may use it to counteract or escape from his concerns.

The rate of illicit drug use declined among U.S. adolescents aged 12 to 17 from 11.6% in 2002 to 9.3% in 2008, then increased to 10.1% from 2009 to 2011, declined to 9.5% in 2012, and declined again to its lowest rate since 2002, 8.8%, in 2015, according to the Substance Abuse and Mental Health Services Administration's *National Survey on Drug Abuse and Health* (Substance Abuse and Mental Health Services Administration [SAMHSA], 2016). Earlier research suggested that high school students in the United States maintain a higher rate of illicit drug use than youth in other economically developed countries (Johnston, O'Malley, Bachman, & Schulenberg, 2004, 2005). More recent research indicates that rates of adolescent use of illicit substances are lower in Latin America than in the United States (Torres, Peña, Westhoff, & Zayas, 2008). Overall, in 2015, SAMHSA reports that for those aged 12 to 17 in the United States, 7% were currently using marijuana, 2% were misusing psychotherapeutic drugs, 1.1% were misusing pain relievers, 0.7% were misusing tranquilizers, 0.5% were misusing stimulants, and 0.1% were misusing sedatives (SAMHSA, 2016). SAMHSA also documented that 53,000 adolescents aged 12 to 17 reported currently using cocaine in 2015 (approximately 0.2% of the adolescent population), and less than 0.1% of youth were currently using heroin in 2015 (~5,000 adolescents). For that same age group and year, 0.5% were currently using hallucinogens, 0.5% were using inhalants, and 0.7% were using methamphetamines (SAMHSA, 2016). Alcohol continues to be the most widely used of all substances for adolescents. Approximately 20% of the 12-to-20 population reported drinking alcohol during the past month in 2015 (SAMHSA, 2016). Furthermore, 13.4% considered themselves binge drinkers (for boys, drinking 5 or more drinks on an occasion; for girls, drinking 4 or more drinks on an occasion), and 3.3% stated that they were heavy drinkers (those who engage in binge drinking on 5 or more days in the past 30 days) (SAMHSA, 2016). Tobacco use has steadily but only slightly declined over time. In 2015, 10.8% of 9th- to 12th-grade students had smoked cigarettes on at least one day in the previous month; 10.3% had smoked cigars, cigarillos, or little cigars; 7.3% had used smokeless tobacco; and 24.1% had used electronic vapor products including e-cigarettes, e-cigars, e-pipes, vape pipes, vaping pens, e-hookahs, and hookah pens on at least one day in the previous month (Kann et al. 2016).

When asked why youth choose to use alcohol and other drugs, adolescents cite the following reasons: to experiment, to have a good time with friends, to appear adult-like, to relieve tension and anxiety, to deal with romantic relationships, to get high, to cheer up, and to alleviate boredom (Palamar, Griffin-Tomas,

& Kamboukos, 2015; Patrick, Schulenberg, O'Malley, Johnston, & Bachman, 2011; Titus, Godley, & White, 2007). Adolescents also report the desire to gain insight as a reason for using marijuana (Palamar et al., 2015; Patrick et al., 2011). One research team studied the reasons for starting, continuing, and quitting use of alcohol and other drugs. The most common reasons for starting to use were to experiment and to be social. The most common reasons for continuing to use were liking the physiological effects and the assistance that alcohol and drugs provided for coping. The most common reasons for quitting were negative feedback and other problems associated with use (Titus et al., 2007).

Although many adolescents use alcohol and other substances, not all of them get into trouble with their usage, except for the potential legal trouble related to the illegality of their use of these substances. Some researchers have been interested in whether reasons for using during adolescence predict current and future problems with substance abuse. In longitudinal study, they have found that using alcohol and marijuana to experiment or to have fun with friends does not predict later problems. Reasons for using alcohol that did predict later substance abuse problems included using to get high, using because of boredom, using to relax, using to control emotions, and using to increase the effects of other drugs. The reasons for using marijuana during adolescence were not as predictive of future substance abuse problems, but using to get high and using to gain insight predicted more frequent long-term use (Patrick et al., 2011). Another research team found that using marijuana because of boredom, to gain insight, or to enhance the effect of other drugs increased the odds of using other illegal substances (Palamar et al., 2015). Problematic alcohol and drug use can have a negative influence on adolescents, their families, and their communities. Learning to regulate emotions is an important developmental task of adolescence, and using substances to regulate emotions can interfere with the learning process (Patrick et al., 2011). Because alcohol and illicit drugs alter neurotransmission, regular use can have harmful effects on the developing brain and nervous system (Wu, Woody, Yang, Pan, & Blazer, 2011). Early substance use increases the risk for later addiction and depression (Esposito-Smythers, Kahler, Spirito, Hunt, & Monti, 2011). Use of alcohol and other drugs can also affect the immune system and emotional and cognitive functioning, including sexual decision making (Weichold, 2007).

Some adolescents are clearly more at risk for substance abuse than others. National survey data indicate that Native American adolescents (47.5%) have the highest prevalence of past-year alcohol and other drug use of U.S. youth ages 12 to 17, followed by White adolescents (39.2%), Hispanic adolescents (36.7%), adolescents of multiple race or ethnicity (36.4%), African American adolescents (32.2%), and Asian or Pacific Islander adolescents (23.7%) (Wu et al., 2011). The same survey found racial and ethnic disparities in the prevalence of youth meeting the diagnostic criteria for substance-related disorders: Native American youth had the highest prevalence (15.0%), followed by adolescents of multiple race or ethnicity (9.2%), White adolescents (9.0%), Hispanic adolescents (7.7%), African American adolescents (5.0%), and Asian or Pacific Islander adolescents (3.5%).

Juvenile Delinquency

Almost every adolescent breaks the rules at some time—disobeying parents or teachers, lying, cheating, and perhaps even stealing or vandalizing. Many adolescents smoke cigarettes and drink alcohol and use other drugs; some skip school or stay out past curfew. For some adolescents, this behavior is a phase, passing as quickly as it appeared. Yet for others, it becomes a pattern and a probability game. Although most juvenile delinquency never meets up with law enforcement, the more times young people offend, the more likely they are to come into contact with the juvenile justice system.

In the United States, persons older than 5 but younger than 18 can be arrested for anything for which an adult can be arrested. (Children younger than 6 are said not to possess mens rea, which means "guilty mind," and thus are not considered capable of criminal intent.) In addition, they can be arrested for what are called **status offenses**, such as running away from home, skipping school, violating curfew, and possessing tobacco or alcohol—behaviors not considered crimes when engaged in by adults. When adolescents are found guilty of committing either a crime (by adult standards) or a status offense, we refer to their behavior as **juvenile delinquency**.

The Office of Juvenile Justice and Delinquency Prevention (OJJDP) reports that in 2014, approximately 975,000 delinquency cases were processed in the United States, a figure down 42% since 2005 (Hockenberry & Puzzanchera, 2017). The FBI reports that in 2014, 1,023,800 juveniles (persons younger than 18) were arrested, accounting for 9.1% of all arrests in the United States (Puzzanchera & Kang, 2017). The OJJDP and the vast majority of juvenile court jurisdictions categorize juveniles along a gender binary, female/male, based on biological primary sex characteristics. Although the

percentage of delinquency among those classified as girls increased from 19% in 1985 to 28% in 2005, it has plateaued since then with the 2014 rate also at 28%. In 2014, girls were involved in approximately 269,900 cases of delinquency, compared to 705,100 for boys (Hockenberry & Puzzanchera, 2017). It is important to note that for the total U.S. adolescent population in 2014, White/Caucasian youth comprised 54%, Hispanic/Latinx youth comprised 23%, Black/African American youth comprised 14%, Asian American youth comprised 5%, multiracial youth comprised 3%, American Indian/Alaska Native comprised 1%, and Native Hawaiian/Other Pacific Islanders comprised 0.5%. However, 43% of the delinquency cases handled in 2014 were for White/Caucasian youth, 36% were for Black/African American youth, 18% were for Hispanic/Latinx youth, 2% were for American Indian/Alaska Native youth, and 1% were for Asian American youth. Despite similar offending patterns and rates of self-reported crime, the delinquency case rate for Black youth (75.1 per 100,000) was triple the rate of White and Latinx youth (which were similar at 24.1 and 25.1 respectively) (Hockenberry & Puzzanchera, 2017) in a phenomenon called disproportionate minority contact (McCarter, 2011). This is an important issue for social work concern.

Bullying

Social workers are beginning to see the short- and long-term effects of bullying on children's physical and mental health. The U.S. Department of Education and other federal agencies have collaboratively developed an online bullying prevention website at stopbullying.gov. There, bullying is defined as "unwanted, aggressive behavior among school aged children that involves a real or perceived power imbalance," and three types of bullying are highlighted:

- *Verbal bullying*: saying or writing mean things (teasing, name calling, inappropriate sexual comments, taunting, threatening to cause harm)

- *Social/relational bullying*: hurting a person's reputation (leaving someone out on purpose, telling others not to be friends with someone, spreading rumors about someone, publicly embarrassing someone)

- *Physical bullying*: hurting a person's body or possessions (hitting/kicking/pinching, spitting, tripping/pushing, taking or breaking someone's things, making mean or rude hand gestures)

Most adolescents who bully may also have been victims of bullying, and both bullies and victims can have serious, lasting problems.

The 2015 YRBSS found that 20.2% of high school students had been bullied on school property in the 12 months preceding the survey (Kann et al., 2016). Prevalence rates were higher for girls (24.8%) than boys (15.8%); higher for White youth (23.5%) than Hispanic (16.5%) and Black youth (13.2%); and highest for younger youth, led by 9th graders (23.4%) and followed by 10th graders (20.8%), 11th graders (20.3%), and 12th graders (15.9%). Similarly, 15.5% of high school students had been cyberbullied or electronically bullied (via e-mail, chat rooms, instant messaging, websites, or texting) during the 12 months before the YRBSS, following the same prevalence trends as those bullied on school property with the exception of age.

School-to-Prison Pipeline

The "school-to-prison pipeline" refers to the pathway, most notably for vulnerable students, from the education system into the juvenile and criminal justice systems (American Civil Liberties Union, 2017). Eight factors typically affect youth in the school-to-prison pipeline: (1) "zero-tolerance" policies, (2) high-stakes testing, (3) exclusionary discipline, (4) race/ethnicity, (5) gender identity/sexual orientation, (6) socioeconomic status, (7) disability/mental health, and (8) school climate (which includes the presence of school resource officers [SROs], school social workers, guidance counselors, and nurses) (McCarter, 2017). Students of color, with disabilities, or with nonheterosexual orientation are overrepresented in school disciplinary actions. The U.S. Department of Education (2014) reports that, during the 2011–2012 school year, 3.5 million students were suspended in school, 3.45 million students were suspended out of school, and 130,000 students were expelled. Exhibit 6.6 lists the percentage of all school suspensions and expulsions by race/ethnicity during the 2011–2012 school year. For some time, the data have clearly shown that Black/African American students are suspended and expelled at 3 times the rate of White students, and students with disabilities are twice as likely as students without disabilities to receive out-of-school suspension (U.S. Department of Education, 2014). This is an important policy practice issue for social workers who work in school settings.

According to a Council of State Governments' study (Fabelo et al., 2011) of almost a million students in Texas, only 3% of the schools' disciplinary actions were for state-mandated suspensions and expulsions, demonstrating the role that local school discretion plays in suspensions and expulsions. In that study, approximately 83% of African American male students had at least one discretionary violation, meaning a violation of

EXHIBIT 6.6 ● Percentages of All School Suspensions and Expulsions by Race/Ethnicity, 2011–2012							
	White	Two or More	Hispanic/ Latino	Black/ African American	Native Hawaiian/ Pacific Islander	Asian	American Indian/ Alaska Native
Percentage of total enrollment	51%	2%	24%	16%	0.5%	5%	0.5%
Percentage of in-school suspensions	40%	3%	22%	32%	0.2%	1%	3%
Percentage of out-of-school suspensions	36%	3%	23%	33%	0.4%	2%	2%
Percentage of multiple out-of-school suspensions	31%	3%	21%	42%	0.3%	1%	2%
Percentage of expulsions	35%	3%	22%	34%	0.3%	1%	3%

Source: Based on U.S. Department of Education Office of Civil Rights, 2014.

the school's code of conduct rather than a violation of state law. When the state researchers used multivariate analyses to control for 83 different variables and isolate the effects of race on disciplinary action, they found that African American students had a 31% higher likelihood of school discretionary action when compared with identical White or Hispanic youth.

When students are suspended or expelled, the likelihood that they will repeat a grade, drop out, or have contact with the juvenile or criminal justice system increases significantly. Fabelo et al. (2011) report that students who have been suspended or expelled at least once have a more than 1-in-7 chance of subsequent contact with the juvenile justice system. Of David, Carl, and Monica, who do you think is most likely to face school disciplinary action and possible juvenile justice involvement? For what reasons?

Community Violence

The Bureau of Justice Statistics and the National Center for Education Statistics reported that in 2014 approximately 850,100 nonfatal victimizations occurred at school (includes 363,700 theft victimizations and 486,400 simple assault and serious violence victimizations) for students aged 12 to 18 (Zhang, Musu-Gillette, & Oudekerk, 2016). This equates to 33 nonfatal victimizations at school per 1,000 students; another 24 victimizations per 1,000 students occur away from school. From 1992 to 2014, the total victimization rate for students at school declined 82%. Notably, students in rural schools experienced higher rates of total victimization at school (53/1,000 students) as compared to students in suburban schools (28/1,000 students) (Zhang et al., 2016).

Data collected in 2015 as part of the YRBSS reveal that on at least 1 of the 30 days preceding the survey, 16.2% of high school students had carried a weapon and 5.3% had carried a gun. During the 12 months that preceded the survey, 2.9% had been in a physical fight for which they had to be treated by a doctor or nurse and 7.8% had been in a physical fight on school property one or more times in the last 12 months (Kann et al., 2016). Even if they are not perpetrators or direct victims of violence, many U.S. adolescents witness violence, and adolescents are at particular risk for exposure to violence. Exposure to community violence, either as victim or witness, has been linked to a variety of mental health outcomes, including involvement in antisocial behaviors, delinquency, and aggression, as well as depression, anger, anxiety, dissociation, post-traumatic stress, and trauma symptoms (Baskin & Sommers, 2015; Farrell, Mehari, Kramer-Kuhn, & Goncy, 2014). These outcomes have been found in samples of low-income families, inner-city youth, and suburban youth.

Homicide also disproportionately affects younger persons in the United States. In 2014, 4,300 youth aged 10 to 24 were the victims of homicide, representing 12 youth murders each day. Of those homicide victims, 86% were boys and 14% were girls. Homicide was the third leading cause of death for all juveniles ages 10 to 24, and 86% of the homicides in 2014 were committed with a firearm (CDC, 2016e).

School shootings have received considerable media attention since the 1990s, and many youth report feeling unsafe at school. Media attention to school shootings became more intensive as such shootings moved from urban to suburban and rural schools. Researchers report that school shootings are extraordinarily rare and schools remain one of the safest environments for children and youth. And yet when these tragedies occur, they devastate the school and community. Mongan (in press) distinguishes five types of school shootings: targeted school shootings, government school shootings, terroristic school shootings, mass school shootings, and rampage school shootings. In the *targeted school shooting,* the perpetrator targets one or more students or school staff and does not randomly shoot other people. This is by far the most frequent type of school shooting but not the one that gets the most media attention. *Government school shootings* are rare but typically involve law enforcement using force in instances of some type of disturbance. *Terroristic school shooting* is another rare type of school shooting. In these shootings, a school is attacked for political or ideological reasons. The specific school and victims are usually chosen at random. Terroristic school shootings have not occurred in the United States in recent times and are more likely to occur in places like Israel where there are active warring parties. *Mass school shootings* are done by perpetrators who have no current or past connection to the targeted school but choose a school setting because schools provide for a high number of causalities. *Rampage school shootings* are the type most people think of when they talk about school shootings. These shootings involve perpetrator(s) who are current or former members of the school and who shoot multiple victims, with at least some of the victims beings chosen at random. These school shootings are planned in advance and are not the result of impulsive behaviors. Mongan (in press) reports that there have been 35 rampage school shootings in primary and secondary schools in the United States since 1974, but I know of at least one that has occurred since his count.

After each rampage school shooting, people grapple with why it happened. A variety of explanations have been put forward, including perpetrator mental health, easy access to weapons, bullying of the perpetrator, violent video games, antidepressants, and neglectful or harsh parenting. Too many access doors was suggested as a factor in the recent rampage shooting in Santa Fe, Texas. Research suggests that none of these explanations is adequate to explain all rampage shootings. Mongan (in press) suggests that a process theoretical approach may be the most useful way to think about how perpetrators come to engage in rampage school shootings. He recommends Prochaska and DiClemente's (2005) transtheoretical stages of change model (TTM) to understand how a school shooter develops over an extended period. This model suggests that a behavior such as perpetrating a school shooting develops through stages of precontemplation, contemplation, preparation, and action. Most rampage school shootings end in the perpetrator either committing suicide or being killed, making it hard to develop an understanding of their motives for and processes of coming to be a school shooter.

Dating Violence and Statutory Rape

Dating violence is violence that occurs between two people in a close relationship; it includes physical violence, emotional violence, and sexual violence. **Acquaintance rape** can be defined as forced, manipulated, or coerced sexual contact by someone known to the victim. Women ages 16 to 24 are the primary victims of acquaintance rape, but junior high school girls are also at great risk (Lauritsen & Rezey, 2013). In the United States in 2015, 9.6% of high school students responded to the YRBSS that they had been hit, slapped, or physically hurt on purpose by their boyfriend or girlfriend at least once over the course of the 12 months that preceded the survey (Kann et al., 2016). The YRBSS data reveal that 6.7% of the students stated that they had been physically forced to have sexual intercourse against their will. This prevalence was higher for girls (10.3%) than boys (3.1%), and overall, the prevalence was higher among Black (10.5%) and Hispanic (8.8%) than White (7%) students. Because they are underreported, dating violence and acquaintance rape may be even more prevalent among adolescents than the data suggest.

Unfortunately, researchers have found that adolescent girls who report a history of experiencing dating violence are more likely to exhibit other serious health outcomes. Longitudinal research has found that female young adults who were victims of adolescent dating violence are more likely than other female young adults to report heavy episodic drinking, depressive symptoms, suicidal ideation, smoking, and further interpersonal violence victimization in young adulthood. Males victimized as adolescents are more likely to report antisocial behaviors, suicidal ideation, marijuana use, and interpersonal violence victimization in young adulthood (Exner-Cortens, Eckenrode, & Rothman, 2013). One researcher found that the majority of high school counselors report that their school does not have a protocol for responding to incidents of dating violence (Khubchandani et al., 2012). This is an area where school social workers can take the lead.

Statutory rape, a crime in every state in the United States, is having sex with someone younger than an age specified by law as being capable of making an informed, voluntary decision. Different states have established different ages of consent, usually from 16 to 18, and handle the offense in different ways. Throughout history, the age of consent has varied from 10 to 21 (Oudekerk, Farr, & Reppucci, 2013). The majority of victims of statutory rape are females ages 14 to 15, whereas 82% of the rape perpetrators of female victims are adults aged 18 and older (Snyder & Sickmund, 2006). About half of the male offenders of female victims in statutory rapes reported to law enforcement are at least 6 years older than their victims. For male victims of female perpetrators, the difference was even greater; in these incidents, half of the female offenders were at least 9 years older than their victims (Snyder & Sickmund, 2006). Adolescent romantic relationships with older partners have been found to increase the likelihood of early sexual activity, pregnancy, STIs, school problems, and delinquency (Oudekerk et al., 2013). On the other hand, there is also some concern that late-adolescent and young-adult perpetrators may face long-lasting negative consequences from legal problems that come from engaging in relationships they think of as consensual. One research team found that a sample of young adults thought that a sexual relationship between a 15-year-old and a partner who is 2, 4, or 6 years older should not be treated as a crime, but there was greater disagreement among the research participants as the gap in age got larger. There were no significant differences between men's and women's attitudes (Oudekerk et al., 2013).

Poverty and Low Educational Attainment

Additional threats to physical and mental health may stem from poverty and low educational attainment, both of which are rampant in the nonindustrialized world. Poverty is also a growing problem among U.S. adolescents aged 12 to 17. In 2014, 18% of U.S. adolescents lived in families with incomes below the poverty line (defined as a family of four making $23,850 or less) (U.S. Census Bureau, 2015). Black (36%), American Indian (34%), and Hispanic (31%) children and youth are more likely to live in poverty than Asian (13%) and White (12%) children and youth (Annie E. Casey Foundation, 2017). Living in poverty in adolescence increases the likelihood of low academic achievement, dropping out of school, teen pregnancy and childbearing, engaging in delinquent behavior, and unemployment during adolescence and young adulthood (Wight, 2011).

Low school attainment has a negative effect on adult opportunities and health across the adult life course. In the United States, high school graduation rates are a key measure of whether schools are making adequate yearly progress (AYP) under the provisions of the No Child Left Behind (NCLB) legislation. For a number of years, educational experts were confident that high school graduation rates in the United States had risen from about 50% in the mid-20th century to almost 90% by the end of the century (Pharris-Ciurej, Hirschman, & Willhoft, 2012). Around 2004, researchers began to suggest that a more accurate picture was that 65% to 70% of high school students actually earned a high school diploma. Controversies developed about how to measure high school graduation. A number of researchers noted that surveys were picking up high school equivalency certification (e.g., GED) as equivalent to high school graduation, leading to an overestimation of high school graduation and an underestimation of high school dropout rates. The percentage of high school credentials awarded through equivalency certificate has risen from 2% to 15% in recent years (Pharris-Ciurej et al., 2012). Unfortunately, the employment patterns and earnings of GED recipients are more similar to high school dropouts than to those who receive a high school diploma. Students from low-income families are 25% less likely than students from nonpoor families to graduate from high school. Recent research indicates that transition to 9th grade is a particularly vulnerable time for students who will later drop out of school (Pharris-Ciurej et al., 2012). The Annie E. Casey Foundation's (2017) Kids Count Data Center reports that one in six (17%) high school students do not graduate in 4 years.

Obesity and Eating Disorders

Weight concerns are so prevalent in adolescence that they are typically thought of as a normative part of this developmental period. Dissatisfaction with weight and attempts to control weight are widely reported by adolescents (Lam & McHale, 2012). As suggested earlier, the dietary practices of some adolescents put them at risk for overall health problems. These practices include skipping meals, usually breakfast or lunch; snacking, especially on high-calorie, high-fat, low-nutrition snacks; eating fast foods; and dieting. Poor nutrition can affect growth and development, sleep, weight, cognition, mental health, and overall physical health.

An increasing minority of adolescents in the United States is obese, and the risks and biopsychosocial consequences of this can be profound (Cromley, Neumark-Sztainer, Story, & Boutelle, 2010). The Centers for Disease Control and Prevention estimate that the percentage of adolescents aged 12 to 19 who are obese increased from 5% in 1980 to 20.5% in 2014 (obesity is defined as a BMI greater than or equal to the 95th percentile) (Ogden, Carroll, Fryar, & Flegal, 2015).

It is important to note that this is a worldwide trend. According to one report (James, 2006), almost half of the children in North and South America, about 38% of children in the European Union, and about 20% of children in China were expected to be overweight by 2010. Significant increases were also expected in the Middle East and Southeast Asia. Mexico, Brazil, Chile, and Egypt have rates comparable to fully industrialized countries. Although nationally representative data on obesity are rare, the available data indicate that child and adolescent obesity continues to increase around the world (Harvard School of Public Health, 2012).

This chapter has emphasized how tenuous self-esteem can be during adolescence, but the challenges are even greater for profoundly overweight or underweight youth. Overweight adolescents may suffer exclusion from peer groups and discrimination in education, employment, marriage, housing, and health care (Cromley et al., 2010). Carl Fleischer has already begun to face some of these challenges. He thinks of himself as a "fat, slow geek" and assumes females would not be interested in him because of his weight.

Adolescents' body dissatisfaction reflects the incongruence between the societal ideal of thinness and the beginning of normal fat deposits in pubescent young people. Body dissatisfaction is a significant factor in three feeding/eating disorders, **anorexia nervosa**, **bulimia nervosa**, and **binge eating disorder**, that often have their onset in adolescence. (See Exhibit 6.7 for a description of these disorders; American Psychiatric

| EXHIBIT 6.7 ● | Feeding and Eating Disorders That Often Begin in Adolescence |

Anorexia nervosa is characterized by a distorted body image and excessive dieting that results in severe weight loss. It involves a pathological fear of becoming fat.

Bulimia nervosa is characterized by episodes of binge eating followed by behaviors such as self-induced vomiting at least once a week to avoid weight gain.

Binge eating disorder is characterized by recurring episodes of eating significantly excessive amounts of food in a short period of time; the episodes are accompanied by feelings of lack of control.

Source: Based on American Psychiatric Association, 2013.

Association, 2013.) Epidemiological studies find that the overall incidence of anorexia nervosa has remained stable over the past decades, but there has been an increase among 15- to 19-year-old girls. It appears there might be a slight decrease of bulimia nervosa over the past 2 decades. Though anorexia and bulimia occur mainly in girls, binge eating, compared with these other disorders, is more common in boys (Smink et al., 2012). All three eating disorders have elevated mortality risk, but the risk is greatest in anorexia nervosa.

Depression and Suicide

Unipolar depression is common in adolescents worldwide. The probability of depression rises from 5% in early adolescence to as high as 20% by the end of adolescence (Thapar, Collishaw, Pine, & Thapar, 2012). Although there are no known gender differences in depression prior to adolescence, during adolescence, girls are about twice as likely as boys to have a major depressive disorder (Thapar et al., 2012).

Adolescent depression may also be underdiagnosed, among boys and girls alike, because it is difficult to detect. Many parents and professionals expect adolescence to be a time of ups and downs, moodiness, melodrama, anger, rebellion, and increased sensitivity. There are, however, some reliable outward signs of depression in adolescents: poor academic performance, truancy, social withdrawal, antisocial behavior, changes in eating or sleeping patterns, changes in physical appearance, excessive boredom or activity, low self-esteem, sexual promiscuity, substance use, propensity to run away from home, and excessive family conflict. Additional symptoms of depression not unique to adolescence include pervasive inability to experience pleasure, severe psychomotor retardation, delusions, and a

sense of hopelessness (Mayo Clinic, 2017a). Depressed adolescents often present with irritable rather than depressed mood (Thapar et al., 2012).

The many challenges of adolescence sometimes prove overwhelming. We have already discussed the risk of suicide among gay male and lesbian adolescents. In the United States during the 12 months preceding the 2015 YRBSS survey, 29.9% of high school students reported having felt so sad or hopeless almost every day for 2 weeks or more that they stopped doing some usual activities (Kann et al., 2016). Furthermore, 17.7% had seriously considered attempting suicide; 14.6% had made a suicide plan; 8.6% had actually attempted suicide; and 2.8% had made a suicide attempt that resulted in an injury, poisoning, or overdose that had to be treated by a doctor or nurse (Kann et al., 2016). Overall, suicide is the second leading cause of death for adolescents in the United States accounting for 17.4% of the deaths for those aged 10 to 24 in 2014 (Kochanek, Murphy, Xu, & Tejada-Vera, 2016). Cheryl King and Christopher Merchant (2008) have analyzed the research on factors associated with adolescent suicidal thinking and behavior and identified a number of risk factors: social isolation, low levels of perceived support, childhood abuse and neglect, and peer abuse.

SOCIAL WORK GRAND CHALLENGE: ENSURE HEALTHY DEVELOPMENT FOR ALL YOUTH

Recently, the American Academy of Social Work and Social Welfare identified 12 grand challenges for social work as a call to action (Padilla, & Fong, 2016). One of these 12 grand challenges is to "ensure healthy development for all youth," which focuses on behavioral and mental health problem prevention through primary health care. To this end, six recommendations are offered (American Academy of Social Work and Social Welfare, 2016):

1. Ensure that 10% of all public funds spent on young people support effective prevention programs.

2. Increase local and state capacity to support high-quality implementation of effective preventive interventions.

3. Develop community-level systems to monitor risk, protection, and behavioral-health outcomes.

4. Provide tested, effective, family-focused, preventive interventions without cost to

patients or families through primary health care providers.

5. Reduce the duration of untreated mental illness in young people.

6. Train and enable a workforce for effective prevention practice.

For more information, please visit the Grand Challenges website (http://aaswsw.org/grand-challenges-initiative) and read more about the ideas to ensure healthy development for all youth at https://csd.wustl.edu/Publications/Documents/PB1.pdf.

RISK FACTORS AND PROTECTIVE FACTORS IN ADOLESCENCE

There are many pathways through adolescence; both individual and group-based differences result in much variability. Some of the variability is related to the types of risk factors and protective factors that have accumulated prior to adolescence. In addition, as we have seen throughout this chapter, the journey through adolescence is impacted by the risk and protective factors encountered during this phase of life. Social disadvantage and negative experiences in infancy and early childhood put a child at risk of poor peer relationships and poor school performance during middle childhood, which increases the likelihood of risky behaviors in adolescence (Sawyer et al., 2012). Emmy Werner and associates (see Werner & Smith, 2001) have found, in their longitudinal research on risk and protection, that girls have a better balance of risk and protection in childhood, but the advantage goes to boys during adolescence. Their research indicates that the earlier risk factors that most predict poor adolescent adjustment are a childhood spent in chronic poverty, alcoholic and psychotic parents, moderate to severe physical disability, developmentally disabled siblings, school problems in middle childhood, conflicted relationships with peers, and family disruptions. The most important earlier protective factors are easy temperament, positive social orientation in early childhood, positive peer relationships in middle childhood, non-sex-typed extracurricular interests and hobbies in middle childhood, and nurturing from nonparental figures.

Much attention has also been paid to the increase in risk behaviors during adolescence (Silbereisen & Lerner, 2007b). Attention has been called to a set of factors that are risky to adolescent well-being and serve as risk factors for adjustment in adulthood as well. These factors include use and abuse of alcohol and other drugs; unsafe sex, teen pregnancy, and teen parenting; school underachievement, failure, and dropout; delinquency, crime, and violence; youth poverty and undernutrition; and marketing of unhealthy products and lifestyles (Sawyer et al., 2012). The risk and resilience research indicates, however, that many youth with several of these risk factors overcome the odds. Protective factors that have been found to contribute to resilience in adolescence include family creativity in coping with adversity, good family relationships, spirituality and religiosity, social support in the school setting, and school-based health services. Giving adolescents a voice in society has also been identified as a potential protective factor. As social workers, we will want to promote these protective factors while at the same time work to prevent or diminish risk factors.

CRITICAL THINKING QUESTIONS 6.5

Adolescence is a time of rapid transition in all dimensions of life—physical, emotional, cognitive, social, and spiritual. What personal, family, cultural, and other social factors help adolescents cope with all this change? What factors lead to dissatisfaction with body image and harmful or unhealthy behaviors? How well does contemporary society support adolescent development? What do you see as risk factors and protective factors for David Costa, Carl Fleischer, and Monica Golden?

IMPLICATIONS FOR SOCIAL WORK PRACTICE

Adolescence is a vulnerable period. Adolescents' bodies and psyches are changing rapidly in transition from childhood to adulthood. Youth are making some very profound decisions during this life course period. Thus, the implications for social work practice are wide ranging.

- When working with adolescents, meet clients where they are physically, psychologically, and socially—don't assume that you can tell where they are, and be aware that that place may change frequently.

- Be familiar with typical adolescent development and with the possible consequences of deviations from developmental timelines.

- Be aware of, and respond to, the adolescent's level of cognition and comprehension. Assess the individual adolescent's ability to contemplate the future, to comprehend the nature of human relationships, to consolidate specific knowledge into a coherent system, and to envision possible consequences from a hypothetical list of actions.

- Recognize that the adolescent may see you as an authority figure who is not an ally. Develop skills in building rapport with adolescents. Avoid slang terms until you have immersed yourself in adolescent culture long enough to be certain of the meaning of the terms you use.

- Assess the positive and negative effects of the school climate on the adolescent in relation to such issues as early or late maturation, popularity/sociability, culture, gender identity, and sexual orientation.

- Consider how to advocate for change in maladaptive school settings, such as those with Eurocentric models or homophobic environments.

- Seek appropriate resources to provide information, support, or other interventions to

assist adolescents in resolving questions of gender identity and sexual decision making.

- Link youth to existing suitable resources or programs, such as extracurricular activities, education on STIs, prenatal care, and LGBTQ (lesbian, gay, bisexual, transgender, queer) support groups.

- Provide information, support, or other interventions to assist adolescents in making decisions regarding use of alcohol, tobacco, or other drugs.

- Develop skills to assist adolescents with physical and mental health issues, such as nutritional problems, obesity, eating disorders, depression, and suicide.

- Participate in research, policy development, and advocacy on behalf of adolescents.

- Work at the community level to develop and sustain recreational and social programs and safe places for young people.

Key Terms

acquaintance rape 225
anorexia nervosa 226
binge eating disorder 226
bulimia nervosa 226
gender identity 204
generalized other 204
gonads 195
identity 201
individuation 206

juvenile delinquency 222
masturbation 217
menarche 195
postconventional moral reasoning 202
primary sex characteristics 195
puberty 194
rites of passage 192
secondary sex characteristics 195

sex hormones 195
sexual orientation 217
sexually transmitted infections (STIs) 219
social identity 201
spermarche 195
status offenses 222
statutory rape 225

Active Learning

1. Recalling your own high school experiences, which case study individual do you most identify with—David, Carl, or Monica? For what reasons? How can you keep your personal experiences with adolescence from biasing your social work practice? How could a social worker have affected your experiences?

2. Visit a public library and check out some preteen and teen popular fiction or magazines. Which topics from this chapter are discussed and how?

3. Have lunch at a local high school cafeteria. Be sure to go through the line, eat the food, and enjoy conversation with some students. What are their concerns? What are their notions about social work?

Web Resources

ABA's Juvenile Justice Committee: http://apps .americanbar.org/dch/committee .cfm?com=CR200000

Site presented by the American Bar Association's Juvenile Justice Committee contains links to juvenile justice–related sites.

Add Health: www.cpc.unc.edu/projects/ addhealth

Site presented by the Carolina Population Center contains a reference list of published reports of the National Longitudinal Study of Adolescent Health (Add Health), which includes measures of social, economic, psychological, and physical well-being.

Adolescent and School Health: www.cdc.gov/ healthyyouth

Site maintained by the Centers for Disease Control and Prevention contains links to a variety of health topics related to adolescents, including alcohol and drug use, sexual behavior, nutrition, youth suicide, and youth violence.

BRAINWORKS: https://sites.duke.edu/ brainworks/about-brainworks

Site presented by BRAINWORKS, an interdisciplinary team of neuroscientists, psychologists, physicians, and social scientists at Duke University, contains links to research and publications directed to public understanding of the brain.

Interagency Working Group on Youth Programs: https://youth.gov

Site maintained by the Interagency Working Group on Youth Program, created by representatives from 20 federal agencies, includes topics, funding sources, evidence and innovation, and federal resources for youth programs.

Social Work Grand Challenges: http://aaswsw .org/grand-challenges-initiative

Site maintained by the American Academy of Social Work and Social Welfare includes information on the Grand Challenges for Social Work, a groundbreaking initiative to champion social progress powered by science. It's a call to action for all of us to work together to tackle our nation's toughest social problems.

Understanding Sexual Health: www .ashasexualhealth.org/sexual-health

Site maintained by the American Sexual Health Association, which is dedicated to improving sexual health, contains information about sexual health, STDs, and publications.

Youth Risk Behavior Surveillance System (YRBSS): www.cdc.gov/healthyyouth/data/yrbs/ index.htm

Site presented by the Centers for Disease Control and Prevention contains the latest research on adolescent risk behavior.

7

Young Adulthood

Holly C. Matto

Chapter Outline

Learning Objectives

7.1 Compare one's own emotional and cognitive reactions to three case studies.

7.2 Define young adulthood.

7.3 Analyze the merits of three theoretical approaches to young adulthood (Erikson's psychosocial approach, Levinson's theory of

(Continued)

Acknowledgment: The author wants to thank Judy Chang, MSW student at George Mason University, for her research and written additions to this revised chapter.

(Continued)

life structure, and Arnett's theory of emerging adulthood).

7.4 Summarize the major themes in physical functioning in young adulthood.

7.5 Analyze how cognitive development, spiritual development, and identity development during young adulthood are related to the development of a psychological sense of self.

7.6 Identify major issues related to social development and social functioning in young adulthood.

7.7 Give examples of important risk factors and protective factors during young adulthood.

7.8 Apply knowledge of young adulthood to recommend guidelines for social work engagement, assessment, intervention, and evaluation.

CASE STUDY 7.1

CAROLINE SANDERS AS A TRANSGENDER YOUNG ADULT

Caroline Sanders states that she was always uncomfortable in her socially and physically designated male gender constraints for as far back as she can remember. In public schools in northern Virginia, she was often the focus of bullying for reasons she wasn't quite able to articulate at the time. In the past 2 years, Caroline accomplished milestones that heteronormative teenagers and young adults usually accomplish earlier, including getting a bank account, working outside the home, learning to drive, and living outside of her parents' home. She completed college but commuted from home and did not develop college friendships or participate in extracurricular activities. Although she lived 15 miles outside of Washington, DC, she had never been to DC except for class trips. Going to the DC Health Clinic to begin hormone therapy therefore was a significant challenge in many ways. Now 23 years old, Caroline identifies as female full-time with friends, at work, and with family. Three months ago she had gender confirmation surgery and is feeling more self-confident in her newly claimed full-time identity.

Caroline is the middle child of three in a middle-class Caucasian family with two heterosexual parents. She describes spending most of her time growing up at home alone in her own room playing video games and did not have a close relationship with either her older sister or younger brother even though they were each approximately 2 years apart. Her parents did not cultivate closeness, and because of work schedules and lack of structure, the family did not eat together or share time together in any regular way. Caroline did not confide in her siblings when she started the transition

process, and when she told her parents, in a letter, their response was quick and devastating. They blamed the therapist and wanted her to see another therapist/psychiatrist of their choosing who would, they believed, tell her she was not trans and set her straight. Her parents were extremely angry, her father volatile. Caroline was sharing an apartment with roommates at that time who were very supportive as they witnessed her transition, but the anger and threats of her parents continued to be very hurtful and difficult. Her mother maintains a limited but present relationship with Caroline, but her relationship with her father is now entirely absent. She currently has no contact with her siblings.

When Caroline determined it was the right time for her to transition in the workplace, she began by making an appointment with HR and management. Management was supportive and had an educational meeting on Friday with the other staff regarding being transgender in the workplace; Caroline came to work the following Monday as a woman. She had discussed her ongoing transition with two of her work colleagues prior to the meeting, which was helpful, but otherwise the process was very stressful for Caroline and seemingly for others as well. Caroline learned that several female coworkers lodged complaints focused on their discomfort in sharing the bathroom on their floor and in the company gym. She continues to go to work most days except when the stress becomes too large; at the same time, her relationships with several coworkers are blossoming because she is feeling more grounded and confident.

Caroline currently wonders if it would be wiser to move to another state where she could develop her identity without the memories of her male specter. In another state, she ponders, no one would stumble over her new name or, worse, misgender her from previous exposure to her as a male. She would be at work and with new friends as a woman with other women. She asks questions about rewriting her childhood story as a girl so that her story will be consistent if not true.

Although she never dated or had romantic interests, she is now wondering about her sexual orientation. Much is uncertain, but Caroline is thriving as a young woman with budding self-confidence and moments of joy.

—Vicki Kirsch

CASE STUDY 7.2
SHEILA HENDERSON'S LONG-AWAITED FAMILY REUNIFICATION

Sheila Henderson, 28 years old, her boyfriend, David, 30 years old, and her 8-year-old daughter, Johanna, from a previous relationship, all said goodbye at the Family Readiness Center at Fort Bragg, North Carolina, 18 months ago, as Sheila departed for her second tour to Afghanistan as a lieutenant in the infantry division of the United States Army. The family hasn't seen each other since, although they have participated in weekly family video calls. While Sheila was on tour, she sustained a closed-head injury when she was participating in a training exercise with her unit in Afghanistan. Her injury was deemed "minor" and not likely to cause significant or long-term impairment, but Sheila can't help but notice a change in her ability to handle emotions. She notices new limitations in her ability to concentrate and says she becomes easily agitated or "set off" over minor inconveniences, which is "not like her." And she cries more than she used to. She is opposed to calling her injury a disability and can't help but think that maybe it's just all in her mind anyway. She regularly experiences a variety of emotions, from frustration, anger, and resentment at her time spent away from family and friends, to loyalty and pride in serving her country. She occasionally feels guilty for taking so much time to "dwell" on her own challenges when she knows so many others have died or have been more seriously incapacitated while serving their country in Afghanistan and Iraq.

Now that she is returning from tour, Sheila knows she will struggle with transitioning back into life with her family but is giddy with excitement to be reunited with her daughter and to rejoin her boyfriend whom she says has had the most difficulty with her absence. Her boyfriend, though officially a civilian working as an accountant, considers the military community where they live to be family. There is an informal ethos in their community that military families care for each other's children when one or more parents are deployed, and David has benefited from this support while Sheila has been away. What concerns him most is Sheila's transition back into their family life. He can't help but wonder how she will respond to the year and a half of developmental changes Johanna has gone through and how she will jump back into the role of disciplining her behavior and facilitating the family routines and schedule that David has worked so hard to establish. In fact, of Johanna's 8 years, Sheila has really only been physically present for less than half of that time. David wonders how the routine will play itself out now and how the family will reunite together. There is also the lingering anticipation and unpredictability of the next possible deployment, and that keeps him up at night. He wonders why Sheila seems so at ease with the uncertainty, and he hopes he will be able to gain her strength in negotiating the ambiguity of their family's shared life space in the future. But for now, he's overjoyed that she's coming home. They have a lot of catching up to do.

Sheila joined the army after graduation from high school. Jobs were scarce in her rural West Virginia county, and she feels lucky to have found a place in the army. She comes from a Caucasian family with deep roots in rural West Virginia, but her family is struggling financially, and her community has been devastated by the downturn in the coal industry. She hears from her mother that a number of her high school friends have succumbed to the opioid epidemic. Sometimes when she thinks of folks back home, she feels helpless to make their lives better.

CASE STUDY 7.3

JONATHAN STUART AND KAI HALE AS OLDER PARENTS OF TWINS

Jonathan Stuart and Kai Hale have had a lot to celebrate in the past few years. In mid-December 2013, Jonathan, 37, and Kai, 39, got married. The couple will tell you they have been committed to each other since 1999, but on December 2, 2013, when Hawaii became the 15th state to recognize same-sex marriage, they rushed to officially ring in their love for each other in Honolulu—legally, at long last. And their love for each other will extend even further into a family of their own; they are going to be parents for the first time this summer. Their surrogate, Renee, is 2 months pregnant with twins. After an unsuccessful initial attempt at reproduction, the couple found a new surrogate and separate egg donor from whom two embryos, one from Jonathan and one from Kai, were successfully implanted.

By their own account Jonathan and Kai are comfortable financially—they wanted to wait to become parents until they were—but mixed in with their heightened excitement about the impending due date, they collectively experience anxiety about what the future might be like when the twins arrive. They know they are considered "older parents" by the medical industry's account—they are both older than 35—but they grapple more with the big questions of parenthood: Will they be good fathers? What will it be like to be responsible for two new vulnerable and totally dependent infants? What

kind of childcare arrangements do they want for their newborn babies? Should one of them take a leave from his job to care for the twins in that critical first year? The recent ultrasound that showed the twin heartbeats reined in these big questions and brought them back to the present moment. Their longtime dream of someday becoming parents is finally coming true. For now, that eases the anxiety, and they know in their hearts that with their love for each other they can weather through the challenges of parenting twins—even if they are "older" fathers.

Kai and Jonathan met at the University of Hawaii. Kai is a native Hawaiian who was originally from rural Waimea in Kauai County, Hawaii, and Jonathan, originally from Portland, Oregon, comes from a middle-class Caucasian family. Both came from families who valued education. Kai is a first-generation college student, and Jonathan's parents both have graduate degrees. They both talk about how influential their parents were in supporting their transition from high school to college. For Kai it was the extreme financial sacrifices his parents made on his behalf, and for Jonathan it was the emotional support he experienced for his studies from his mother. After they graduated from the university, Jonathan and Kai worked hard to build their careers in software development and the hospitality industry.

A DEFINITION OF YOUNG ADULTHOOD

Defining young adulthood and the transitional markers that distinguish this period from adolescence and middle adulthood has been the challenge and life's work of a number of developmental scholars. A broad challenge has been to determine a framework for identifying the developmental characteristics of young adulthood. For example, is a young adult one who has reached a certain biological or legal age? One who has achieved specific physiological and psychological milestones? Or perhaps one who performs certain social roles? Research, theory, and scholarly thinking about young adulthood present a variety of perspectives related to each of these dimensions. Current research suggests that the transitional markers that have traditionally defined adulthood in

decades past are no longer the most salient markers characterizing the young adult in today's society (e.g., see Arnett, 2015; Berlin, Furstenberg, & Waters, 2010; Furstenberg, 2015). Four common adulthood transition experiences are leaving home, finding a job, getting married, and becoming a parent. In 1960, 44% of men and 66% of women had completed these traditional adult benchmarks by age 25, and 73% of men and 75% of women had completed them by age 35. In 2010, only 8% of men and 16% of women had completed the benchmarks by age 25, and 42% of men and 55% of women had completed them by age 35. This means that young people were slightly more likely to have completed the benchmarks by age 25 in 1960 than they were to have completed them at age 35 in 2010 (Furstenberg, 2015). More recent data indicate that 24% of young adults between ages 25 to 34 reached a combination of these four transitional markers as compared to

45% of that age group in 1975 (Vespa, 2017). Historian Steven Mintz (2015) reports that the early timetable for making adult transitions was something of an anomaly in the mid-20th century, and current patterns of adult transitions are more similar to the long-term timetable of transitions than to the patterns during that period. There are international differences in home-leaving timing. For example, in Japan 64% of unmarried emerging adult men aged 25 to 29 reside with their parents, and 80% of unmarried emerging adult women reside with their parents (Newman, 2008).

Typical chronological ages associated with young adulthood are 23 to 39 (Ashford, LeCroy, & Williams, 2018) or 18 to 40 (Kuther, 2017). Some scholars assert that such broad ranges encompass too much variety of experience. In this book, however, we use a broad range of approximately 18 to 40. Although a wide age range can be useful in providing some chronological boundaries around this developmental period, from a life course perspective it is more useful to examine the social role transitions, important life events, and significant turning points associated with young adulthood. The major challenges facing young adults are taking responsibility for yourself, making independent decisions, and becoming financially independent, but attaining financial independence is becoming more delayed as advanced educational credentials are increasingly necessary to secure quality employment (Arnett, 2015). Young adults ages 18 to 25 agree that these—taking responsibility for yourself, making independent decisions, and becoming financially independent—are the markers of entry into young adulthood. Young persons who do not attend college are as likely as college students to say that making independent decisions based on their own values and belief systems is important for defining adult status.

Some scholars also define young adulthood as the point at which young persons become functioning members of the community, demonstrated by obtaining gainful employment, developing their own social networks, and establishing independent housing. Burstein (2013) notes that adulthood "sign posts" are changing, with more focus on the "social impact" young adults make in their communities as a marker of this transition. Young adults are increasingly seeking entrepreneurship opportunities with increased global social awareness and connection to issues that might lead to social action, all in a context of a "shared economy" (p. 107). In the national Clark poll of emerging adults, 86% of the sample agreed with the statement "It is important to me to have a career that does some good in the world" (Arnett & Schwab, 2012). From a psychosocial perspective, this period is seen as a time of progressive movement out of an individualized and egocentric sense of self and into greater connection with significant others.

From a cumulative advantage/disadvantage (CAD) perspective (Padgett & Remle, 2016; Pais, 2014), we need to be mindful of systematic creation of inequity in the distribution of opportunity and burden through such institutions as our labor market and educational system. Scholars suggest that advantages and disadvantages begin through inequities in early schooling, which are then replicated and immured throughout the life course (Crystal, Shea, & Reyes, 2016), but it is important to remember that advantages and disadvantages have already accrued before children enter school. Sheila Henderson grew up in an impoverished rural community where her peers felt "stuck" economically as the coal mining industry went bust, and now many of them are stuck in a process of addiction. CAD theory asks us to reflect on the ways in which our educational system replicates social stratification (binding one to a set socioeconomic location) or facilitates social and economic mobility. How do you think our educational system serves various communities? What about our labor market system? Which of our social institutions serve to preserve inequality and regulate opportunity, and which ones tend to facilitate social and economic mobility? What are some ways social workers can influence policies that preserve inequality and regulate opportunity?

Typical social role transitions in young adulthood are summarized in Exhibit 7.1. Timing of these transitions and psychological readiness for adopting adult roles are important factors in the individual's life course trajectory. The timing and sequencing of childbearing, entry into postsecondary educational institutions, and labor market attachment may have wide-ranging effects on economic viability and security over the long term. For example, very young single parents employed in full-time, low-wage work without adequate access to affordable quality childcare or health care will be faced with difficulty in affording and finding time for the additional higher education necessary to obtain employment with better wages, benefits, and work schedules (e.g., see Edin & Lein, 1997). Nonnormative early entry into family formation and parenthood is associated with lower self-reported health over the adult life course (Barban, 2013). However, it is important to consider that other macro-context variables may interact with individuals' planned sequences to influence

EXHIBIT 7.1 ● Social Role Transitions in Young Adulthood
• Leaving home
• Taking on work and/or education tasks
• Gaining financial independence
• Gaining independence in decision making
• Making a partnership commitment
• Becoming a parent
• Renegotiating relationships with parents
• Making time commitments to families of origin and to newly created families
• Starting a career
• Engaging with the community and the wider social world

PHOTO 7.1 Young adulthood is a challenging and exciting time in life, bringing new opportunities and new challenges.

life chances. Jonathan Stuart and Kai Hale waited to become parents until their late 30s when they were financially stable. Now as expectant parents they have little concern about how parenthood will affect their economic security but are more worried about how they will balance two careers and all the family obligations that will come with having twins. They have demanding work schedules but also a great deal of support from colleagues in their workplaces and have formed a strong social support network in Honolulu. For Caroline, other young-adult transition markers have needed to be coordinated with her gender transitioning process.

Nevertheless, young adulthood is a challenging and exciting time in life. Young people are confronted with new opportunities and the accompanying stressors associated with finances, occupational planning, educational pursuits, development of significant relationships, and new family roles (Kuther, 2017). Kenneth Keniston (1966), an eminent developmental scholar writing in the late 1960s, during an era of student activism and bold social expression, described young adulthood as a time of struggle and alienation between an individual and society. The nature of that struggle is different for different cohorts. Young adulthood remains a period of intrapersonal and interpersonal questing as well as a period of critiquing and questioning of social norms. Young persons grapple with decisions across several polarities: independence versus relatedness, family versus work, care for self versus care for others, and individual pursuits versus social obligations.

THEORETICAL APPROACHES TO YOUNG ADULTHOOD

Two prominent developmental theories, promulgated by Erik Erikson and Daniel Levinson, specifically address this life course phase. More recently, Jeffrey Jensen Arnett has proposed a theory of emerging adulthood.

Erikson's Psychosocial Theory

Erik Erikson's psychosocial theoretical framework is probably one of the most universally known approaches to understanding life course development. Young adulthood is one of Erikson's original eight stages of psychosocial development (refer to Exhibit 3.8). Erikson described it as the time when individuals move from the identity fragmentation, confusion, and exploration of adolescence into more intimate engagement with significant others (Erikson, 1968, 1978). Individuals who successfully resolve the crisis of **intimacy versus isolation** are able to achieve the virtue of love. An unsuccessful effort at this stage may lead the young adult to feel alienated, disconnected, and alone. We see Caroline struggling with relationship development from early in her middle childhood years, where bullying and distant family relationships were part of her interpersonal history. We might wonder, now, how that pattern of relational disengagement and social isolation

© JupiterImages/liquidlibrary/ThinkStock

might affect her ability for and interest in forming new adulthood partnerships. A fear at the core of this crisis is that giving of oneself through a significant, committed relationship will result in a loss of self and diminution of one's constructed identity. To pass through this stage successfully, young adults must try out new relationships and attempt to find a way to connect with others in new ways while preserving their individuality (Erikson, 1978; Fowler, 1981).

For example, we might wonder about the relational context of Sheila's family of origin and how it might be influencing her current relationships. What relationship templates were established in her years up to 5 years old? How are these relationships being replicated in her current family, particularly in her relationships with her daughter and her boyfriend? How are Sheila's own intimacy needs being addressed with so many geographic disruptions and work that is engaging but intense and at times unpredictable and physically and emotionally risky?

Levinson's Theory of Life Structure

Daniel Levinson (Levinson, Darrow, Klein, Levinson, & Mckee, 1978) describes adulthood as a period of undulating stability and stress, signified by transitions that occur at specific chronological times during the life course. He initially developed his theory based on interviews with men about their adult experiences; later he included women in the research (Levinson & Levinson, 1996). From his research he developed the concept of **life structure**, which he described as the outcome resulting from specific decisions and choices made along the life course in such areas as relationships, occupation, and childbearing. He considered the ages of 17 to 33 to be the **novice phase** of adulthood. In this approach, both Caroline Sanders and Sheila Henderson would be considered novice adults. It appears that that is a status Caroline would endorse. But what about Sheila, who has been a mother for 8 years and deployed to a war zone two times? According to Levinson, the transition into young adulthood, which occurs during the ages of 17 to 22, includes the tasks of leaving adolescence and making preliminary decisions about relationships, career, and belief systems; the transition out of this phase, which occurs about age 30, marks significant changes in life structure and life course trajectory.

During the novice phase, young persons' personalities continue to develop, and they prepare to differentiate (emotionally, geographically, financially) from their families of origin (Levinson et al., 1978). The transition to adulthood takes hold primarily in two domains: work and relationships. Levinson suggested that it may take up to 15 years for some individuals to resolve the transition to adulthood and to construct a stable adult life structure.

Building on Levinson's concepts, others have noted that cultural and societal factors affect life structure choices during young adulthood by constraining or facilitating opportunities (Schoon & Polek, 2011). For example, socioeconomic status, parental expectations, availability of and interactions with adult role models, neighborhood conditions, and community and peer group pressures may all contribute to a young person's decisions about whether to marry early, get a job or join the military before pursuing a college education or advanced training, or delay childbearing. Social and economic factors may directly or indirectly limit a young person's access to alternative choices, thereby rigidifying a young person's life structure. Along these lines, many researchers discuss the strong link between social capital and human capital, suggesting that a family's "wealth transfer" or extent of familial assets, such as the ability to pay for children's college education, is influential in opening or limiting young adults' opportunities for advanced education and viable employment (Friedline & West, 2016).

Jonathan Stuart and Kai Hale reflect on how these early familial expectations and support might have contributed to their decision to delay parenting until their late 30s. And as they have begun telling family and friends that they are soon-to-be parents of twins, they are curious about the varied responses they are getting to their pregnancy news—most have been congratulatory whereas some have expressed skepticism about how they will manage. Jonathan and Kai can't help but wonder whether such skepticism comes from the fact that they are perceived as older parents, because they are a dual-income family with two successful careers who will be trying to raise newborn twins, or if it is because they are a gay couple. Caroline Sanders had the economic support of her parents to attend college, but there could have been no such support if Sheila Henderson had desired to go to college after high school.

Especially in young adulthood, life structures are in constant motion, changing with time and evolving as new life circumstances unfold. Decisions made during the young-adulthood transition, such as joining the military, forgoing postsecondary education, or delaying childbearing, may not accurately or completely represent a young person's desired life structure or goals.

Social workers need to explore goal priorities and the resources and obstacles that will help or hinder the individual in achieving these goals. Social workers are also often called on to help young adults negotiate conflicting, incompatible, or competing life roles throughout this novice phase, such as renegotiating family and work responsibilities as parenthood approaches.

Arnett's Emerging Adulthood

A number of prominent developmental scholars who have written about the stages of adolescence and young adulthood in advanced industrial countries have described phenomena called "prolonged adolescence," "youthhood," or "psychosocial moratorium," which represent an experimentation phase of young adulthood (Arnett, 2000; Erikson, 1968; Settersten, Furstenberg, & Rumbaut, 2005; Sheehy, 1995). Jeffrey Jensen Arnett has gone one step further, defining a phase he terms **emerging adulthood** in some detail (Arnett, 2015). He describes emerging adulthood as a developmental phase distinct from both adolescence and young adulthood, occurring from ages 18 to 25 in industrialized societies, but he adds that for some people emerging adulthood spans the age period 18 to 29. There is considerable variation in personal journeys from emerging adulthood into young adulthood, but most individuals make the transition by age 30. Arnett conceptualized this new phase of life based on research showing that a majority of young persons ages 18 to 25 believe they have not yet reached adulthood and that a majority of people in their 30s do agree they have reached adulthood.

According to Arnett (2006, 2007), identity exploration has become the central focus of emerging adulthood, not of adolescence. Emerging adulthood is a period of prolonged exploration of social and economic roles where young people try out new experiences related to love, work, financial responsibilities, and educational interests without committing to any specific lasting plan. The social role experimentation of adolescence becomes further refined, more focused, and more intense, although commitment to adult roles is not yet solidified. Arnett explains this adulthood transition using an organizing framework that includes cognitive, emotional, behavioral, and role transition elements. After 20 years of research, Arnett (2015) proposes five features that make emerging adulthood distinct from both adolescence and young adulthood: identity exploration, instability, self-focus, feeling in-between, and possibilities/optimism (see Exhibit 7.2 for a description of these features).

EXHIBIT 7.2 ● Five Distinguishing Features of Young Adulthood

Identity exploration: Finding answers to the question "Who am I?" and trying out various choices, especially those related to love and work

Instability, in love, work, and residence

Self-focus, with limited focus on obligations to others

Feeling in-between, neither adolescent nor adult

Possibilities/optimism, a sense of hope and belief in opportunity to transform one's life

Source: Based on Arnett, 2015.

Most young persons in emerging adulthood are in education, training, or apprenticeship programs working toward an occupation; most individuals in their 30s have established a more solid career path and are moving through occupational transitions (e.g., promotion to leadership positions and recognition for significant accomplishments). From 1980 to 2010, the proportion of emerging adults attending college rose steeply in all the wealthy countries of the world including the United States (Arnett, 2015). In 2013, about 66% of high school graduates in the United States enrolled in 2- or 4-year colleges. About one third of students who enroll at a 2-year institution graduate within 3 years, and about two thirds of students who enroll in a 4-year institution graduate within 6 years (National Center for Education Statistics, 2014). Students who are the first in their families to attend college and those from racial and ethnic minority or low socioeconomic families tend to have the hardest time transitioning to college (Kuther, 2017). The likelihood of holding a bachelor's degree is higher for Asians and non-Hispanic Whites as compared to Hispanics or Blacks (Ryan & Bauman, 2016). Like many emerging adults, Caroline experienced a lack of attachment to her postsecondary institution because she lived at her parents' home and commuted to school, not allowing her to develop meaningful college friendships or participate in activities beyond her classes.

Experience with work results in many, if not most, emerging adults changing their occupational expectations. One longitudinal study examined young people's occupational expectations and accomplishments each year for the first 7 years after high school and again at age 30. The researchers found a great deal of instability during the late teens and early 20s, and by age 25, less than half of the emerging adults had careers that matched their expectations (Rindfuss, Cooksey, &

Sutterlin, 1999). It is not uncommon for someone to experience as many as seven job changes before the age of 29 (U.S. Bureau of Labor Statistics, 2016a).

Although marriage has traditionally been cited as a salient marker in the adulthood transition, current research shows that marriage has not retained its high status as the critical benchmark of adulthood. In 2015, the median age of marriage in the United States was 27 for women and 29 for men, an increase of 6 years since 1975 (Stritof, 2017). Exhibit 7.3 shows the trend in median age of marriage for both men and women from 1890 to 2015. Similar increases in the median age of marriage have occurred in Canada and some European countries. For example, in 2013, the median age of first marriage in Sweden was 36 for men and 33 for women, up 7 years since 1980 (Eurostat, 2015). There are variations in the age of first marriage with young people of low socioeconomic status marrying earlier.

Perhaps nothing demonstrates the instability and exploratory nature of emerging adulthood better than how often emerging adults move from one residence to another. Emerging adults in the 18-to-24 age group have the highest rate of residential mobility of any age group. Emerging adults either live with a partner, alone, with roommates, in their parents' home, or with other family members, with the majority living with their parents (Vespa, 2017). By race, data show that Hispanics and Blacks are more likely to live at home; Whites are equally likely to be living at home or with a spouse; and living with a spouse is the most common arrangement for Asian Americans (Copen, Daniels, Vespa, & Mosher, 2012). To demonstrate the high rate of residential mobility among emerging adults, Exhibit 7.4 shows the age-specific migration rates in the United States in the periods 2007–2009 and 2010–2012 (Benetsky, Burd, & Rapino, 2015). As you can see, the rate of migration peaks from ages 20 to 25 and declines steadily until about age 55. In our case example, Caroline Sanders, at age 23, is currently wondering if it would be wiser to move to another state where she could develop her gender identity without the memories of her male specter. Sheila Henderson, like other military personnel, experiences residential instability and considers the military a primary residence when deployed for months at a time.

Until recently, having children was, for biological and cultural reasons, an inevitable part of the period now called emerging adulthood. Effective methods of birth control and changing cultural views on parenthood and childlessness have made having children a choice (Mills, Rindfuss, McDonald, & te Velde, 2011). Women in the United States are less likely to give birth in their early 20s as earlier, a rate that dropped

EXHIBIT 7.3   ●   Estimated Median Age of First Marriage by Gender: 1890 to 2015

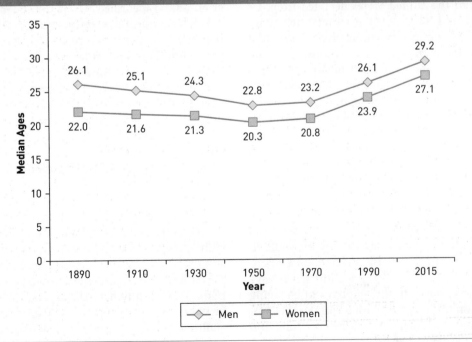

Source: Based on Stritof, 2017.

EXHIBIT 7.4 ● Age-Specific Migration Rates, 2007–2009 and 2010–2012

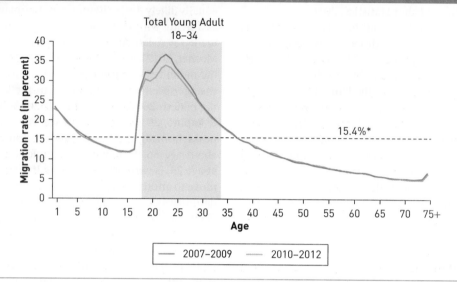

Source: Benetsky, Burd, & Rapino (U.S. Census Bureau), 2015, Figure 2.

*The average migration rate for the total population, 2007–2009 to 2010–2012.

from 31% to 24% from 1976 to 2016 (U.S. Census Bureau, 2016a). Close to three quarters (70%) of women ages 25 to 29 were mothers in 1976, which is now not seen until later at ages 30 to 34 (Vespa, 2017). Childbearing rates have declined in most industrialized countries. The average number of children born to a woman in the United States declined from 3.8 in the 1950s to 1.87 in 2017 (Central Intelligence Agency, 2017). The average number of children is even lower in many industrialized nations; for example, the average number born to a woman in Australia is 1.77; in Germany, 1.45; and in Japan, 1.41. This trend is not so pronounced in the nonindustrial and newly industrializing world, however. For example, the average number of children born to a woman in Malawi in 2017 is 5.49; in Afghanistan, 5.12; and in the Democratic Republic of Congo, 4.39 (Central Intelligence Agency, 2017).

Research with racial groups in the United States as well as research in other parts of the world finds agreement on three criteria that emerging adults see as signs of adulthood: taking responsibility for yourself, making independent decisions, and becoming financially independent (Arnett, 2015). Identity issues have a prominent role. Overall, the emphasis in emerging adulthood is on trying out new roles without the pressure of making a commitment. Schwartz, Cote, and Arnett (2005) examined the intersection of identity,

personal agency, and individualization during emerging adulthood. They proposed that with the diversity and changing nature of emerging adulthood, emerging adults must "individualize" their life courses. In the process of individualization, some emerging adults exercise more personal agency than others. Schwartz et al. (2005) identified two pathways in the individualization process: a **default individualization** pathway, in which adulthood transitions are defined by circumstance and situation rather than individual agency, and a **developmental individualization** pathway, in which adulthood transitions are defined by personal agency and deliberately charted growth opportunities in intellectual, occupational, and psychosocial domains. They found that across race and ethnicity, the difference between those who follow a developmental individualization pathway versus a default individualization pathway is a firmer commitment to goals, values, and beliefs (Schwartz et al., 2005). In addition, these researchers found that personal agency, across race and ethnicity, is associated with a more flexible and exploratory orientation to adulthood commitments and is less associated with premature closure and circumscribed commitment. A traditional definition of the separation-individuation process may not be appropriately applied to emerging adulthood, because true separation from the family of origin may appear only toward the end of young adulthood or, perhaps for some, during the transition to middle adulthood.

Cultural and Social Class Variations

One advantage of the theory of emerging adulthood is that it recognizes diversity. Individual routes of development (the timing and sequence of transitions) are contingent on socialization processes experienced within family, peer groups, school, and community. Specifically, environmental opportunities, expressed community attitudes, and family expectations may all influence the timing and sequencing of transitions during emerging adulthood. Socially constructed gauges of adulthood—such as stable and independent residence, completion of education, entry into a career path, and marriage or significant partnership—hold varying importance across families and cultures. It is important to remember, however, that after 20 years of research on the phenomenon, Arnett (2015) states that emerging adulthood is not a universal stage of the life course but "a life stage that exists under certain conditions that have occurred only quite recently and only in some cultures" (p. 24). Emerging adulthood exists mainly in wealthy societies of the West, along with the Asian countries of Japan and South Korea. And within any country, some cultures have an emerging adulthood phase and some do not. Arnett (2015) addresses this diversity by arguing that emerging adulthood exists as a life stage wherever there is a "gap of at least several years between the time young people finish secondary school and the time they enter adult roles in love and work" (p. 26).

For some young persons, decisions may be heavily weighted toward maintaining family equilibrium. For example, some may choose not to move out of the family home and establish their own residence in order to honor the family's expectation that children will continue to live with their parents, perhaps even into their 30s. For others, successful adult development may be defined through the lens of pragmatism; young persons may be expected to make decisions based on immediate, short-term, utilitarian outcomes. For example, they may be expected to enter the labor force and establish a career in order to care for a new family and release the family of origin from burden.

In wealthy nations, socioeconomic status and life circumstances impact the experience of emerging adulthood (Silva, 2013; Smith, 2011). For example, Caroline Sanders seems to be living out most of the traits of emerging adulthood at age 23, but at the same age Sheila Henderson was parenting from a war zone. One study examined the home-leaving behavior of poor and nonpoor emerging adults in the United States. Using a longitudinal data set and a family economic status measure that included a federal poverty line indicator and childhood public assistance receipt, the authors found significant home-leaving and returning differences between poor and nonpoor emerging adults (De Marco & Cosner Berzin, 2008). Specifically, having a family history of public welfare assistance, dropping out of high school, and becoming a teen parent were the characteristics most likely to predict leaving the family home before age 18. Repeated home leaving (leaving, returning, leaving again) was more frequent for nonpoor as compared with poor emerging adults. And when they left home, nonpoor emerging adults were more likely than poor emerging adults to transition to postsecondary educational opportunities (De Marco & Cosner Berzin, 2008).

International research that has focused specifically on foster youth aging out of care suggests that such youth face significant transitioning risks, such as homelessness, substance abuse, and involvement with the criminal justice system (Tweddle, 2007). More successful transitioning outcomes for former foster youth, such as finding stable housing and employment, are associated with having had a strong social support system and problem-solving skill development before leaving care (Stein, 2005; Tweddle, 2007).

Culture, race and ethnicity, and gender also have significant influence on young-adult roles and expectations. For example, as compared to Whites, African American and Mexican American emerging adults tend to leave the parental home later and more often return to the parental home. Such differences are explained by factors such as family relationships and emotional closeness, transitioning to school and work, and a family's economic resources (Lei & South, 2016).

Social norms may sanction the postponement of traditional adult roles (such as marriage) or may promote marriage and childbearing in adolescence. Arnett (2015) suggests that because of cultural beliefs that prohibit premarital sex and value large families, members of the Mormon Church tend to have a shortened emerging adulthood. There may be different family expectations about what it means to be a "good daughter" or "good son," and these expectations may be consistent or inconsistent with socially prescribed gender roles, potentially creating competing role demands. For example, a young woman may internalize her family's expectations of her going to college and having a career while at the same time being aware of her family's expectations that her brothers will go directly into a job to help support the family and her college expenses. In addition, this woman may internalize society's message that women can "do it all"—have a family and career—and yet see her friends putting priority on having a family and raising children. As a result, she may feel compelled to succeed in college and a career to make good on the privilege that her brothers did not have while at the same time feeling anxious about putting a career over creating a new family of her own. Over the last 4 decades, young women have made considerable economic gains, and young men have been falling behind (Vespa, 2017).

It is also important to remember the cohort effect when describing emerging adulthood. About one quarter of the Hispanic American population are young adults, with a median age of 28 in 2014. The Millennial generation of Hispanic Americans is less likely to be immigrants, more likely to be proficient in English, and more likely to originate from Mexico than older generations (Patten, 2016). Second-generation youth's cultural identity is influenced by parents who are the primary socialization agents to transmit cultural knowledge, language, and heritage. Strength of cultural identity is also influenced by birth order (Nesteruk, Helmstetter, Gramescu, Siyam, & Price, 2015). Nesteruk et al.'s (2015) study of emerging adults from ethnically diverse backgrounds found that ethnic identity formation was shaped by parental attitudes, knowledge of heritage and language, and the community.

Here are a couple of examples of cultural variations in the emerging-adult transition. One research team studied 450 college students in one southeastern U.S. state and found that African American, Latino, and Asian American students were more likely than White students to perceive themselves as adults, whereas the White students were more likely to perceive themselves as emerging adults. Likewise, low-income students were more likely than other students to perceive themselves as adults. The ethnic minority students were more likely than White students to put high value on family obligations. Students who perceived themselves as adults were less likely to binge drink, smoke cigarettes, and gamble than students who perceived themselves as emerging adults (Blinn-Pike, Worthy, Jonkman, & Smith, 2008). In another study examining the life course priorities of Appalachian emerging adults aged 19 to 24, the researchers found that high

family poverty, and particularly the combination of poverty and parental neglect, was associated with emerging adults' lower educational goals (Brown, Rehkopf, Copeland, Costello, and Worthman, 2009). In addition, the experience of traumatic stressors was associated with lowered economic attainment priorities among Appalachian emerging adults.

Some environments may offer limited education and occupational opportunities. Economic structures, environmental opportunities, family characteristics, and individual abilities also contribute to variations in transitioning during emerging adulthood. Young adults with developmental disabilities tend to remain in high school during the adulthood transitioning years of 18 to 21, as compared with their peers without such disabilities who are more likely to continue on to college or enter the workforce. Research suggests that more inclusive postsecondary environments that offer higher education opportunities for young adults with developmental disabilities, and the necessary accommodations for such adults to succeed, can increase their social and academic skills as well as facilitate productive interactions between young adults with and without disabilities (Casale-Giannola & Kamens, 2006). Some studies have shown that Latina mothers of young adults with developmental disabilities encourage family centered adulthood transitioning, with less emphasis on traditional markers of independence and more emphasis on the family's role in the young adults' ongoing decision making, with such mothers reporting that their young adults' social interactions were more important to them than traditional measures of productivity (Rueda, Monzo, Shapiro, Gomez, & Blacher, 2005).

Individuals who grow up in families with limited financial resources or who make important transitions during an economic downturn have less time for lengthy exploration than others do and may be encouraged to make occupational commitments as soon as possible. Although Kai Hale grew up in a rural area with limited financial means, his family's strong expectations and material sacrifices made to support his transition from high school to college, and then again from college to the work world, allowed him the opportunity for extended exploration of his career choices that others without such family support may not have. Indeed, research shows that childhood socioeconomic status is an important mediating factor in young-adult transitions (Smyer, Gatz, Simi, & Pedersen, 1998). For example, Astone, Schoen, Ensminger, and Rothert (2000) examined the differences between "condensed" (or time-restricted) and "diffuse" (or time-open) human capital development, with findings suggesting that a diffuse educational system offers opportunities for school reentry across the life course, which may be beneficial to young people who do not immediately enter higher education because of family or economic reasons, such as going into the military or entering the labor force. And, more specifically, they found that military service after high school increased the probability of returning to higher education for men but not for women. Sheila Henderson grew up in a family of limited financial resources in a community that had been economically devastated by the downturn in coal mining. When she graduated from high school, she saw joining the military as the best economic option.

A family's economic background and resources are strongly associated with the adult status of the family's children; high correlations exist between parents' income and occupational status and that of their children (Rank, 2005). Individuals with greater financial stability often have more paths to choose from and may have more resources to negotiate the stressors associated with this developmental period. In 2014, the Harvard University Graduate School of Education released the report *Creating Pathways to Prosperity* (Ferguson & Lamback, 2014). The report indicated that for affluent and academically skilled emerging adults, the academic pathway to prosperity is relatively smooth. However, students with fewer academic skills or who grow up in less affluent families and communities often face "narrow and poorly maintained pathways, full of potholes, detours, and missing road signs" (p. iv). The report recommended the expansion and upgrading of career and technical education.

Multigenerational Concerns

In today's society, young persons are increasingly becoming primary caregivers for elderly family members. Such responsibilities can dramatically affect a young adult's developing life structure. Family life, relationships, and career may all be affected (Dellmann-Jenkins & Blankemeyer, 2009). The demographic trend of delaying childbearing, with an increase of first births for women in their 30s and 40s and a decrease of first births to women in their 20s, suggests that young adults are also likely to face new and significant role challenges as primary caregivers for their own aging parents. This can result in young adults caring for the generation ahead of them as well as the generation behind them. An Associated Press article (Stobbe, 2009) cited a report from the U.S. Centers for Disease Control and Prevention on the link between premature births and infant mortality in the United States, with 1 in 8 premature births (defined as birth before 37 weeks' gestation) contributing to the United States' 30th ranking worldwide in infant death. Causes of premature birth are thought to be related to maternal risk factors, such as smoking, obesity, infection, and health care industry practices, such as early cesarean section delivery, induced labor, fertility treatments, and lack of access to prenatal care for some segments of the pregnant population (e.g., poor, low-income women). In addition to the special, intensive care premature babies need in the immediate year postbirth, such infants are also at risk for cognitive delays and vision, hearing, and learning disorders, which are often detected when children enter formal schooling. Therefore, for sandwich-generation families with children who have special physical, emotional, and/or learning needs, the challenge of providing the necessary care for their children while simultaneously providing care for their parents can be overwhelming.

The concern is that young adults will face a substantial caregiving burden, trying to help their aging parents with later-in-life struggles while nurturing their own children. We might see a shorter period of emerging adulthood for many people, which would mean that they have less opportunity to explore, to gain a sense of independence, and to form new families themselves. There may be less support for the notion of giving young people time to get on their feet and establish a satisfactory independent adulthood. In addition, young adults may increasingly experience the emotional responsibilities of supporting late-in-life divorcing parents or parents deciding to go back to school at the same time these young adults may be considering advanced educational opportunities themselves. Although currently Kai Hale and Jonathan Stuart's parents are in good health and seem to be aging well, there may be a time in the future when Kai and Jonathan will struggle with caregiving responsibilities for young twins and their aging parents, while also trying to manage two careers. Geographic distance may also pose a challenge given that Kai's parents remain in the rural area where he grew up and Jonathan's parents are on the mainland in Oregon. Being in the IT field, Jonathan knows quite a bit about the telehealth trends and technological advances being used in health care, and so his career expertise may one day be very important to his own family's well-being.

CRITICAL THINKING QUESTIONS 7.1

Which transitional markers do you see as the best indicators that one has become an adult? Why did you choose these particular markers? How do the stories of Caroline Sanders, Sheila Henderson, and Jonathan Stuart and Kai Hale fit with the developmental markers you have chosen?

PHYSICAL FUNCTIONING IN YOUNG ADULTHOOD

Physical functioning is typically at its height during early adulthood in all organs and body systems. But as young adults enter their 30s, an increased awareness of physical changes—in vision, endurance, metabolism, and muscle strength—is common (e.g., Bjorklund, 2015). With new role responsibilities in family, parenting, and career, young adults may also spend less time in exercise and sports activities than during adolescence and pay less attention to their physical health. And at the same time, young adults ages 19 to 25 have been the least insured when it comes to health care coverage as compared with any other age group. However, with the Affordable Care Act of 2010 young adults became eligible to stay on their parents' health insurance until age 26, and from 2010 to 2015, young adults age 19 to 25 gained health insurance coverage more than any other age group (Day, Vornovitsky, & Taylor, 2016). Caroline has been fortunate to be able to use the services at the DC Health Clinic to begin hormone therapy and SRS, which has provided a turning point in her identity and gender status.

Many young adults make an effort to maintain or improve their physical health, committing to exercise regimens and participating in wellness classes (such as yoga or meditation). They may choose to get more actively involved in community recreational leagues in such sports as hockey, soccer, racquetball, and Ultimate Frisbee. Sometimes physical activities are combined with participation in social causes, such as Race for the Cure runs, AIDS walks, or organized bike rides.

The number one threat to health and life during young adulthood is automobile accidents. In almost all high-income countries, automobile crashes are the leading cause of death in the 20s and 30s, but the rates are highest in the United States (Arnett, 2015). Automobile crashes, injuries, and fatalities peak in emerging adulthood (Insurance Institute for Highway Safety, 2017).

Behavioral risks to health in emerging and young adulthood may also include unprotected sex. The potential for sexually transmitted infections, including HIV, is related to frequent sexual experimentation and substance use, particularly binge drinking. One research team found that young adults who engaged in sexual behavior before age 16 were more likely than other young adults to have unprotected sex and to have more sexual partners (Vasilenko, Kugler, & Rice, 2016).

In North America, substance use, such as drug, alcohol, and tobacco use, typically begins in adolescence, peaks in the early 20s, and begins to decline in the 30s (Chen & Jacobson, 2012; Johnston, O'Malley, Bachman, Schulenberg, & Miech, 2014). According to the Substance Abuse and Mental Health Administration's most recent data from the National Survey on Drug Use and Health, one fourth of U.S. young adults aged 18 to 25 used illicit drugs in 2016, and 40% of this age group were binge alcohol users (Ahrnsbrak, Bose, Hedden, Lipari, & Park-Lee, 2017). There was an increase in marijuana users in the 26-and-older age group from 2008 to 2016, and a smaller increase among the 18-to-25 age group. Among the 18-to-25 age group, 10.7% were considered to have alcohol use disorder, 7.0% were considered to have illicit drug use disorder, and 1.1% were considered to have opioid use disorder. In addition, 22.1% were considered to have some form of mental illness. There were higher rates of mental illness and suicide thoughts among the 18-to-25 age group in 2016 than in 2008 and 2014. Sussman and Arnett (2014) suggest that emerging adulthood is the life stage most prone to development of one or more addictions.

Community and cultural affiliation may play a role in young adults' behavioral health decision making. Kei-ho Pih, Hirose, and Mao's (2012) study of low-wage Chinese immigrant communities found that families in these communities tended to rely on interpersonal relationships to provide important information and social connections to employment opportunities but that these intracommunity network connections were not as helpful for the dissemination of health care information. The authors identified limited English proficiency as a significant barrier that reduced the bridging social capital opportunities of key community members to be able to understand the majority community's health care system and its resources and, therefore, decreased the informational support they could provide to the community's residents. In addition, other studies have shown that socioeconomic (material) disadvantage and

© Tim Panell/Corbis

PHOTO 7.2 Young adults may choose to get more actively involved in community recreational leagues.

other environmental factors, such as neighborhood disorder, are significant risk factors for substance use in early adulthood (Kuipers, van Poppel, van den Brink, Wingen, & Kunst, 2012; Redonnet, Chollet, Fombonne, Bowes, & Melchior, 2012). Molina, Alegria, and Chen (2012) found that Latinos living in Latino immigrant-dense neighborhoods were at lower risk for an alcohol use disorder as compared with Whites, and foreign-born Latinos living in such Latino immigrant neighborhoods had less substance use risk compared with U.S.-born Latinos in the same neighborhoods. As acculturation increases, so does the risk for substance use and other physical and mental health problems. Asian Americans, a rapidly growing minority group in the United States, have seen an increase in substance use among young adults aged 18 to 29 (Grant et al., 2004), with significant physical and mental health consequences. Although African American youth and young adults tend to have lower substance use rates when in more racially homogeneous settings, substance use increases in frequency when Black youth reside in predominantly White

communities (Stock et al., 2013). Strong racial identity tends to have a protective effect in decreasing substance use risk for African American young adults, especially for youth living in predominantly Caucasian communities (Stock et al., 2013).

Online social networks are also important communities that shape the social norms in emerging adulthood and influence substance-use behavioral decision making. The social influence of network ties is not a new phenomenon, but the influence of social networking affiliations, and their influence on the development and maintenance of social norms that influence behavioral decision making, is a relatively new and important area to examine for an emerging-adulthood population for whom it is typical to engage in some form of social networking. Cook, Bauermeister, Gordon-Messer, and Zimmerman's (2013) data analysis from the Virtual Networks Study of emerging adults' (ages 18 to 24) online relationships found that drug use was associated with frequency of network discussion around drug use and network acceptance of drug use, which was stronger in effect for males as compared with females. In addition, alcohol use was associated with greater density and emotional closeness to network ties, and photos and discussions on such sites may create norms that encourage drinking within a network.

Other health concerns during young adulthood include type 1 diabetes ("juvenile diabetes"), typically diagnosed in childhood, adolescence, or young adulthood. Although this type of diabetes is less prevalent than type 2 (diagnosed in older adults), young adults do have a risk of getting type 1 diabetes in their 20s. Adults diagnosed with diabetes will have to adjust to lifestyle changes, such as more consistent exercise, modified diets, and monitoring of blood sugar levels. One longitudinal study found that young adults with type 1 diabetes who were more physically active were more likely to have good metabolic control than young adults who were not physically active (Schwandt et al., 2017).

Research has shown physical and psychosocial interactions. For example, obesity in adolescence is associated with depression and lower social attainment (i.e., educational, economic, work satisfaction) in young adulthood for females but not males (Merten, Wickrama, & Williams, 2008). Important associations exist between being overweight and having depression in adolescence and young adulthood for African American and White females (Franko, Streigel-Moore, Thompson, Schreiber, & Daniels, 2005). Geronimus, Hicken, Keene, and Bound's (2006) decades of research on the physical weathering hypothesis suggests that accelerated aging characterized by early onset of chronic disease may disproportionately affect African Americans as compared with Whites and may be linked to an environmental impact on the body, such as stress exposure, racial discrimination, and economic hardship. Newer research by Geronimus et al. (2015) examines biomarkers such as telomeres, indicators associated with the physical aging process, and their differential expression in different populations. These researchers used a community-based participatory research approach with a data set of 239 Black, White, and Mexican American adults in three depressed Detroit neighborhoods. They found that poor Whites had shorter telomeres than nonpoor Whites, poor and nonpoor Blacks had equivalent telomere lengths, and poor Mexican Americans had longer telomeres than nonpoor Mexican Americans. These findings are consistent with other research that finds limited health differences between poor and nonpoor Blacks and that poor Mexican Americans have better health than other poor people in the United States.

The changing economic environment, particularly the recent economic volatility experienced internationally, has also been found to affect physical health. According to the 2008 National Study of the Changing Workplace (Aumann & Galinsky, 2011), workers' overall health has declined from 2002 levels, with an increase in frequency of minor health problems (such as headaches), rising obesity rates, and rising stress levels (41% reported significant stress). Of those workers who experience chronic health problems, most report high blood pressure (21%), high cholesterol (14%), diabetes (7%), mental health disorder (4%), or heart condition (3%).

Research with teens and young adults has given rise to growing concern over post-concussive syndrome that may arise from repetitive concussions sustained from contact sports. Repetitive concussions may lead to increased risk of mild cognitive impairment and early dementia later in adulthood (Stern et al., 2011). Young adults who have played contact sports and sustained even mild repetitive concussions, and young adults like Sheila Henderson who have served in the military, particularly those who have been deployed in the last 2 decades of conflicts in Iraq and Afghanistan where there was heightened risk for traumatic brain injury, are particularly vulnerable to such long-term neurodegenerative concerns.

When working with young adults who have health challenges, social workers will want to assess the client's relationship to the health challenge and evaluate how the treatments are affecting the psychosocial developmental tasks of young adulthood. For example, an illness may increase a young person's dependence on others at a time when independence from parents is valued and individuals may have concerns about finding a mate. Societal stigma associated with the illness may be intense at a time when the individual is seeking more meaningful community engagements, and adjustment to the possibilities of career or parenthood delays may be difficult. Increasingly, social networking sites such as Patients Like Me (www.patientslikeme.com) are being used by young adults with chronic health conditions to create online communities to promote social interaction and information exchange. Users can create a shared health profile and find other users who have the same health condition to share treatment experiences. In February 2018, 607,153 members were tracking more than 2,800 medical conditions.

In addition, young-adult partners who struggle with infertility problems may have to confront disappointment from family members and adjust to feelings of unfulfilled social and family expectations. Costs of treatment may be prohibitive, and couples may experience a sense of alienation from peers who are moving rapidly into parenthood and child-rearing. See Chapter 2 in this book for further discussion of infertility.

CRITICAL THINKING QUESTIONS 7.2

Levinson talks about how culture and society affect young adults' life structure. How do you think our American society's changing marriage laws, to make them inclusive of marriage for same-sex couples, will affect family formation and family health and well-being for same-sex couple families like Jonathan Stuart and Kai Hale? How does socioeconomic status affect life structure for gay couples, particularly in areas of access to reproductive technological advances?

THE PSYCHOLOGICAL SELF

Young adulthood is a time when an individual continues to explore personal identity and his or her relationship to the world. Cognition, spirituality, and identity are intertwined aspects of this process.

Cognitive Development

Psychosocial development depends on cognitive and moral development, which are parallel processes (Fowler, 1981). Young adulthood is a time when individuals expand, refine, and challenge existing belief systems, and the college environment is especially fertile ground for such broadening experiences. Late adolescents and young adults are also entering Piaget's formal operations stage, during which they begin to develop the cognitive ability to apply abstract principles to enhance problem solving and to reflect on thought processes (refer to Exhibit 3.4 for an overview of Piaget's stages of cognitive development). These more complex cognitive capabilities, combined with a greater awareness of personal feelings, characterize cognitive development in young adulthood (Gardiner, 2018).

The abstract reasoning capabilities of adulthood and the awareness of subjective feelings can be applied to life experiences in ways that help individuals negotiate life transitions, new roles, stressors, and challenges (Labouvie-Vief, 2005). You might think of the development in cognitive processing from adolescence to young adulthood as a gradual switch from obtaining information to using that information in more applied ways. Young adults are better able to see things from multiple viewpoints and from various perspectives than adolescents are.

With increasing cognitive flexibility, young adults begin to solidify their own values and beliefs. They may opt to retain certain traditions and values from their family of origin while letting go of others to make room for new ones. During this sorting-out process, young adults are also defining what community means to them and what their place in the larger societal context might be like. Individuals begin establishing memberships in, and attachments to, selected social, service, recreational, and faith communities. Research indicates that religious beliefs, in particular, are reevaluated and critically examined in young adulthood, with individuals sorting out beliefs and values they desire to hold on to and those they choose to discard (Arnett, 2015). However, there is a danger that discarded family beliefs may not be replaced with new meaningful beliefs. Many emerging adults view the world as cold and disheartening and are somewhat cynical about the future. With this common pitfall in mind, we can take comfort from Arnett's finding that nearly all the 18- to 24-year-olds who participated in one of his studies believed they would ultimately achieve their goals at some point (Arnett, 2000).

In terms of moral development, Lawrence Kohlberg (1976) categorized individuals ages 16 and older as fitting into the postconventional stage, which has these characteristics (refer to Exhibit 4.2 for an overview of Kohlberg's stages of moral reasoning):

- Greater independence in moral decision making
- More complex contemplation of ethical principles
- Development of a "moral conscience"
- Move from seeking social approval through conformity to redefining and revising values and selecting behaviors that match those values
- Recognition of larger systems and appreciation for community
- Understanding that social rules are relativistic, rather than rigid and prescribed

Young adults begin to combine the principles of utility and production with the principle of equality, coming to the realization that individual or group gain should not be at the detriment of other individuals or social groups.

Kohlberg's research indicates that people do not progress in a straight line through the stages of moral development. Late adolescents and young adults may regress to conventional moral reasoning as they begin the process of critical reflection. In any case, successful resolution of the adolescent identity crisis, separation from home, and the willingness and ability to take responsibility for others are necessary, but not sufficient, conditions for postconventional moral development (Kohlberg, 1976).

Spiritual Development

As mentioned earlier, young adulthood is a time when individuals explore and refine their belief systems. Part of that process is development of **spirituality**, a focus on that which gives meaning, purpose, and direction to one's life. Spirituality manifests itself through one's ethical obligations and behavioral commitment to values and ideologies. It is a way of integrating values relating to self, other people, the community, and a "higher being" or "ultimate reality" (Hodge, 2001). Spirituality has been found to be associated with successful marriage (Kaslow & Robison, 1996), considerate and responsible interpersonal relations (Ellison, 1992), positive self-esteem (Ellison, 1993), more adaptive approaches to coping with stress (Tartaro, Luecken, & Gunn, 2005), and general well-being (George, Larson, Koenig, & McCullough, 2000). Other studies have found that searching for and finding meaning after experiencing traumatic experiences reduces the presence of depressive symptoms in emerging adults, but only for those who experienced a moderate to high frequency of traumatic events (Woo & Brown, 2013).

Spirituality develops in three dimensions related to one's connection with a higher power (George et al., 2000; Hodge, 2001):

1. *Cognition*: beliefs, values, perceptions, and meaning related to work, love, and life

2. *Affect*: sense of connection and support; attachment and bonding experiences; psychological attachment to work, love, and life

3. *Behavior*: practices, rituals, and behavioral experiences

Generally, consistency across all three dimensions is necessary for a vigorous spiritual life. Research has shown that religious behavioral practices are correlated with life course stages. One study found that religiosity

scores (reflecting beliefs, practices, and personal meaning) were higher for a group of emerging adults (ages 18 to 25) than for a group of adolescents (ages 14 to 17) (Glover, 1996), suggesting a growing spiritual belief system with age. Individuals making the transition from adolescence into young adulthood seem to place a particularly high value on spirituality. In addition, religious participation has been found to increase with age, even within the young-adulthood stage (Gallup & Lindsay, 1999; Stolzenberg, Blair-Loy, & Waite, 1995; Wink & Dillon, 2002). Most of the research on spirituality and religion across the life course has focused on late-life adults, and consequently less is known about spirituality and religion in the lives of young adults (Barry, Nelson, Davarya, & Urry, 2010).

Etengoff and Daiute (2013) examined the small and large system influences on the religious development and cultural construction of self in emerging adulthood for Sunni-Muslim Americans. Social, institutional, and community interactions offered emerging adults important opportunities to reflect on and practice their religious beliefs and, in many cases, initiated a new transition in understanding and religious orientation. Some study participants reported that such reflection led them to become more spiritual, whereas others reported that it was the conversations with new acquaintances who were spiritually curious and asked questions they could not answer about their own religion that prompted their greater involvement in Muslim study and practice. It was through these dynamic interactions within various sociocultural spaces that religious development occurred in these emerging adults, with the age of 18 being a particularly salient chronological marker for such pronounced deepening exploration.

In an attempt to understand the development of spirituality, James W. Fowler (1981) articulated a theory of six stages of faith development. Fowler's research suggested that two of these stages occur primarily in childhood and two others occur primarily during late adolescence and young adulthood. Fowler's stages are very closely linked with the cognitive and moral development paradigms of Piaget and Kohlberg. Adolescents are typically in a stage characterized by **synthetic-conventional faith**, during which faith is rooted in external authority. Individuals ages 17 to 22 usually begin the transition into **individuative-reflective faith**, a stage when the person begins to let go of the idea of external authority and looks for authority within the self (Fowler, 1981). During this time, young adults establish their own belief system and evaluate personal values, exploring how those values fit with the various social institutions, groups, and individuals with whom they interact.

The transition from synthetic-conventional faith to individuative-reflective faith usually occurs in the early to mid-20s, although it may occur in the 30s and 40s or never at all (Fowler, 1981). An individual's faith development is associated with his or her early attachments to other people, which serve as templates for understanding one's connection to more abstract relationships and help shape these relationships. Faith growth, therefore, is heavily related to cognitive, interpersonal, and identity development.

The process also depends on crises confronted in the 20s and 30s; challenges and conflict are critical for change and growth in faith. In one study, young-adult women who were HIV-positive were interviewed in order to explore coping strategies, women's experiences of living with the diagnosis, and life transformations or changes (Dunbar, Mueller, Medina, & Wolf, 1998). The majority of women discussed the spiritual dimensions activated by their illness, such as renewing relationships, developing a new understanding of the self, experiencing heightened connections with nature and higher powers, and finding new meaning in the mundane. The interviews revealed several themes related to spiritual growth, including "reckoning with death," which led to the will to continue living and renewed "life affirmation"; finding new meaning in life; developing a positive sense of self; and achieving a "redefinition of relationships." These young women found new meaning and purpose in their lives, which gave them renewed opportunities for social connection (Dunbar et al., 1998).

Identity Development

Identity development is generally associated with adolescence and is often seen as a discrete developmental marker, rather than as a process spanning all stages of the life course. However, identity development—how one thinks about and relates to oneself in the realms of love, work, and ideologies—continues well into adulthood. Ongoing identity development is necessary to make adult commitments possible, to allow individuals to abandon the insular self, and to embrace connection with important others. In addition, continuing identity development is an important part of young adults' efforts to define their life's direction (Kroger, 2007; Kroger, Martinussen, & Marcia, 2010).

We see this in the Latino community that is becoming increasingly diverse, and organizations are recognizing the need to respond to a changing Latino identity. For example, the National Council of La Raza is a well-known Latino activist organization. In August 2017, they changed their organization name to UnidosUS to attract younger Latinos who did not feel connected to la raza, a traditional Chicano term that translates to "race" but is colloquially known as "the people." Use of the term became popular in the 1960s and 1970s, but some in the organization were afraid the term pushed away some of the conservative members of the community. One misinterpretation of the term la raza is that it implies the racial superiority of the Hispanic and Latino population. The organization wanted to move away from the controversial term to attempt to unite the Latino population (Diaz-Hurtado, 2017).

The classic work of James Marcia (1966) defined stages of identity formation in terms of level of exploration and commitment to life values, beliefs, and goals (as discussed in Chapter 6) as follows:

- Diffused (no exploration, no commitment)
- Foreclosed (no exploration, commitment)
- Moratorium (exploration, no commitment)
- Achievement (exploration, commitment)

Marcia (1993) has stated that people revisit and redefine their commitments as they age. As a result, identity is not static but dynamic, open, and flexible. More recently, he has suggested that during times of great upheaval and transition in young adulthood, people are likely to regress to earlier identity modes (Marcia, 2002). One meta-analysis of research on identity development in adolescence and young adulthood found that the proportions of people in foreclosed and diffused stages decreased over time whereas the proportions in the achievement stage increased over time. The analysis indicated that a relatively large proportion of individuals had not attained identity achievement by young adulthood (Kroger et al., 2010).

Research exploring this notion of identity formation as a process that continues deep into adulthood shows several interesting outcomes. In one study researchers interviewed women and men ages 27 to 36 to explore the process of commitment in five domains of identity: religious beliefs, political ideology, occupational career, intimate relationships, and lifestyle (Pulkkinen & Kokko, 2000). Results showed that men and women differed in their overall commitment to an identity at age 27. Women were more likely to be classified in Marcia's foreclosed identity status, and men were more likely to be classified in the diffused identity status. However, these gender differences diminished with age, and by age 36, foreclosed and achieved identity statuses were more prevalent than diffused or moratorium statuses for both men and women. This trend of increasing commitment with age held constant across all domains except political ideology, which showed increased diffusion with age. Also, across ages, women were more likely than men to be classified in the achieved identity status for intimate relationships; for men, the diffused identity status for intimate relationships was more prevalent at age 27 as compared with age 36.

More recently, a research team examined the intersection of Marcia's model of identity development and Erikson's classification of identity in terms of *synthesis* (a sense of self-knowledge and a feeling that one knows where one is headed) and *confusion* (feelings of being "mixed up" and unclear of what one is doing in life) in a sample of college students (Schwartz et al., 2015). The researchers expected and found that synthesis and confusion can exist in the same person. Unlike the Pulkkinen and Kokko (2000) study, they found that the male students in their sample had more trouble than the female students with identity issues. They also found that research participants from immigrant families reported more confusion and fragmented sense of self than other students. They further found that college students with a synthesized profile scored highest on well-being scores, and those who fit Marcia's diffused criteria scored lowest on well-being.

The young adult who is exploring and expanding identity experiences tension between independence and self-sufficiency on one hand and a need for connection with others and reliance on a greater whole on the other. Young adults are often challenged to find comfort in connections that require a loosening of self-reliant tendencies. Some suggest that the transition into adulthood is signified by increased self-control while simultaneously submitting to the social conventions, structure, and order of the larger community. We can see that Jonathan Stuart and Kai Hale are circling back through this identity construction space where they are considering how they will take on the new parent role, moving from a care-for-self focus that defined the early years of their young-adult lives to an interdependent commitment to care for others.

Another study of the development of identity well into adulthood used a sample of women in their 20s (Elliott, 1996). Researchers found that the transition into young adulthood excites new definitions of identity and one's place in society, leading to potential changes in self-esteem and psychological self-evaluations. Although self-esteem tends to remain stable in young adulthood, several factors appeared to influence self-esteem in a positive or negative direction.

- Marriage may have a positive effect on self-esteem if it strengthens a young adult's economic stability and social connectedness.

- Parenthood is likely to have a negative effect if the role change associated with this life event significantly increases stresses and compromises financial stability.

- Receiving welfare is likely to decrease a young woman's self-esteem over time.

- Employment may mitigate the negative effects brought about by the transition into parenthood.

Employment tends to expand one's self-construct and identity and can offer a new parent additional social support as well as a supplemental source of validation. However, the extent to which employment will operate as a stress buffer is contingent on the occupational context and conditions. Certainly, good-quality jobs with benefits may enhance, and are unlikely to harm, a woman's psychological well-being (Elliott, 1996). However, dead-end, low-paying jobs do not help with the stresses of parenthood and have the potential to undermine a young woman's self-esteem. We see that Caroline Sanders's work environment has provided formal (education and training) supports to help create a positive place of employment for Caroline during her gender transition, but the informal day-to-day uncomfortable interactions with coworkers in the shared living space of the work environment have proven stressful. Social workers need to be aware of how people's work life impinges on their development of identity.

Some scholars suggest that identity development for African American emerging adults may be significantly influenced by "stereotype threat" whereby there is a collective internalization that society expects African American emerging adults to fail. Identity development, then, for some emerging adults may require confrontation with held stereotypes at a collective level that serve to inform how they are expected to perform as a group (Arnett & Brody, 2008).

Research shows that social networking media sites, such as Facebook, that allow the development of and participation in Internet communities, have significant impact on emerging adults' identity and social development (Pempek, Yermolayeva, & Calvert, 2009). Such social networking technology offers young adults the opportunity to create personal identity profiles that can be shared and responded to in a public forum.

CRITICAL THINKING QUESTIONS 7.3

Erik Erikson suggested that adolescence is the primary life stage for identity development, but recent theory and research suggest that identity is open and flexible and continues to develop across adulthood. What do you think about this recent suggestion that identity development is an ongoing process? What types of experiences in young adulthood might affect identity development? Do you think your identity has changed since late adolescence? If so, which aspects of your identity have changed? What role do you think new technologies, particularly smartphones and the Internet, have on young-adult identity development?

SOCIAL DEVELOPMENT AND SOCIAL FUNCTIONING

There are, of course, many paths to early adulthood, and not all arrive at this phase of the life course with equal resources for further social role development. This section looks at some of the special challenges faced by young adults as they negotiate new social roles and the impact on social functioning in young adulthood—particularly regarding interpersonal relationships and work attachment.

Katherine Newman (2012), in *The Accordion Family*, offers an international comparative analysis of the young-adulthood transition, demonstrating that countries with weak welfare states tend to put families in the role of safety net provider, with adult children relying on their parents for support for longer periods of time, more than countries with more generous welfare states. The research presents a demographic landscape that looks much different from a generation ago, where it takes longer to launch adult children due to extended educational requirements, credentials that often require unpaid internships, and the high cost of higher education and housing. Thus, currently more emerging adults depend on their families of origin and/or extended social networks, and for longer periods of time, than ever before. Given this situation, perhaps it is not surprising that one research team found that U.S. parents of emerging adults reported a higher desired age for marriage than was reported by the emerging adults themselves (Willoughby, Olson, Carroll, Nelson, & Miller, 2012).

Research has shown that problem behavior in young adults is linked to challenges experienced in negotiating new social roles (see Kroger, 2007). However, it is oftentimes difficult to definitively capture the direction of influence. For example, does prior "deviant" behavior create difficulties in committing to work, or does a failure in finding a good job lead to problematic behaviors?

A 2003 Child Trends study (Hair, Ling, & Cochran, 2003) of educationally disadvantaged youth identifies six categories of vulnerable youth making the transition to adulthood: out-of-school youth, youth with incarcerated parents, young welfare recipients, youth transitioning out of incarceration, runaway/homeless youth, and youth leaving foster care. The largest group was out-of-school youth, although there is considerable overlap among these vulnerable categories. Many of these educationally disadvantaged youth lack parental monitoring, supervision, and support that would help facilitate the transition into adulthood. A later study by the Urban Institute identified three groups of vulnerable youth making the transition to adulthood: youth from distressed neighborhoods, youth from low-income families, and youth with depression and/or anxiety (Macomber et al., 2009). Along these lines, poor social functioning in young adulthood appears to be linked to a variety of difficulties in making the transition to new roles.

- Problems in school and family in adolescence lead to social functioning problems in young adulthood.

- Unstable employment for males is associated with strained relationships, criminality, and substance abuse.

- Men who have many behavioral problems in young adulthood can be differentiated from young-adult males who do not exhibit behavioral problems by several childhood factors, such as aggressive history, problems in school and family, and lack of formal educational attainment.

The transition to young adulthood from the secondary school environment can be challenging, particularly for students with learning disabilities. These students drop out of high school at a higher rate than students without these challenges. Results from a qualitative study suggest some reasons why (Lichtenstein, 1993), one being that many students with learning disabilities worked while in high school, often because employment provided an environment where they could gain control over decision making, exercise authority, garner support, and increase self-esteem—outcomes that such students were not able to experience in the traditional educational system. In this study, working during the high school years was related to later employment but was also related to the risk of dropping out of high school altogether before graduation. These findings suggest a need for a well-tailored individual education plan (IEP) for each learning-disabled youth that outlines how that person can best make the transition out of high school and which postschool opportunities might be appropriate, as well as a need for better transitioning services and active follow-up. In addition, the parents of students with learning disabilities need to be educated on their rights, and parent advocacy efforts within the school need to be strengthened (Lichtenstein, 1993). Fay Ginsburg and Rayna Rapp (2013), two anthropologists who are also parents of children with learning disabilities, have found that many U.S. school systems are wildly out of compliance with federal legislation that mandates transition planning for young adults with disabilities as they prepare to leave high school. This is an advocacy issue for social workers who work in school systems.

The Child Trends study of educationally disadvantaged youth (Hair et al., 2003) cites 12 empirically evaluated programs that operate to facilitate adulthood transitioning for youth: Alcohol Skills Training Program; Job Corps; JOBSTART; Job Training Partnership Act; New Chance; Nurse Home Visitation Program; Ohio Learning, Earning and Parenting Program; School Attendance Demonstration Project; Youth Corps; AmeriCorps; Skill-Based Intervention on Condom Use; and Teenage Parent Demonstration. These programs primarily focus on educational and employment gains, and most showed solid gains in employment and improvement in school attendance and completion of a general equivalency or high school diploma, but not definitive gains in increased earnings or job retention. Specifically, the Youth Corps program showed the most significant outcomes for African American males, who earned higher incomes from their employment, had better employment relationships, and were more likely to have attained advanced education than those who did not participate in the program. Latino males who participated in the program also showed increased employment and work promotions as compared with

those who did not participate, whereas White males actually showed negative effects from participation in that they were less likely to be employed and received lower earnings from their work. African American, Latina, and White females all benefited from participation, showing increased work hours and higher educational aspirations (Hair et al., 2003).

A summary of empirically tested programs found to positively influence young-adulthood transitioning include the following: Alcohol Skills Training geared to college students; AmeriCorps for youth ages 17 and older; Job Corps; JOBSTART for 16- to 24-year-old disadvantaged youth; and the Job Training Partnership Act, aimed at increasing educational and occupational advancement of adults and out-of-school youth (Bronte-Tinkew, Brown, Carrano, & Shwalb, 2005).

Connecting to mentors, particularly for high-risk populations, is critical to success. Paid community service opportunities that facilitate meaningful connections among different youth populations (e.g., those living in high-risk communities and those volunteering within such communities) can provide opportunities for young adults to develop skills and enhance social capital. For example, AmeriCorps deploys members throughout the United States to work in nonprofit and other public and community organizations. Such experiences promote members' connection to civic society; expand critical thinking about social problems; instill a sense of purpose and meaning; and facilitate a critical "insider" understanding of the social, economic, and political environment (Benner, 2007). In their review of service-learning experiences, Lemieux and Allen (2007) discuss the value of involving emerging adults in working with vulnerable populations, such as children with disabilities and older adults, and identify the enhanced problem-solving abilities, civic understanding, and enduring commitment to service that come from such opportunities. Service learning experiences have been shown to change attitudes and perceptions toward vulnerable populations, such as substance-dependent mothers (Hogan & Bailey, 2010) and older adult populations (Singleton, 2009).

Another special population likely to face challenges in making the transition into young adulthood is young persons with more severe emotional difficulties. Approximately three quarters of adults with psychiatric diagnoses experienced symptoms before age 24, with symptom expression peaking in the early 20s (McGorry & Purcell, 2009). These young adults often have trouble forming meaningful interpersonal relationships, maintaining employment, managing physical health needs, and gaining financial independence. Research indicates that young adults living with mental illness are more likely than young adults not living with mental illness to use social networking sites to create a supportive community. They express an interest in using such sites to seek information about community integration, independent living, social skills, and overcoming isolation (Gowen, Deschaine, Gruttadara, & Markey, 2012).

Research shows that disability diagnosis and severity may influence social outcomes. For example, young adults with severe cognitive disability and coexisting impairments tend to show the most limited leisure involvement and date less frequently than those young adults with cerebral palsy, hearing loss, or epilepsy (Van Naarden Braun, Yeargin-Allsopp, & Lollar, 2006, 2009).

Many young adults with developmental and/or emotional disabilities may have tenuous experience with the labor market and weakened connections to work. Often their families do not have sufficient resources to help them make the transition from high school, potentially delaying the youth's opportunity to live independently. Many of these young persons do not have a stable support network, and as a result, they are at higher than usual risk for homelessness (Davis & Vander Stoep, 1997). In a 20-year longitudinal study following a cohort of individuals with developmental delays who were first diagnosed at age 3, both parents and their young-adult children expressed concern about the young adults' social isolation and inability to find gainful employment. Many of the young adults were concerned about not having enough peer involvement and too much parental involvement in their lives. Three types of parent–young adult relationships tended to emerge: (1) *dependent* relationships, which were comfortable to the young adults in that parents responded to needs in appropriate quality and quantity; (2) *independent* relationships, which were comfortable to the young adults in that parents responded to young adult needs only in times of crisis; and (3) *interdependent* relationships, which were the most conflictual of the three types and were characterized by young-adult resentment of parental involvement (Keogh, Bernheimer, & Guthrie, 2004).

Another group of youth at risk in the transition from late adolescence to early adulthood are those with poor relationships with their parents. Emotional maltreatment in childhood has been shown to increase depersonalization symptomology, such as emotional numbing and detachment, which is associated with poor psychological functioning in adulthood (O'Laoide, Egan, & Osborn, 2017). Emotional intimacy

in the parent–child relationship has been found to be important in the development of self-esteem, with the benefits lasting into adulthood. For example, Poon and Knight (2013) found in their longitudinal data analysis that parental emotional support in emerging adulthood served a buffering role in preserving health and well-being later in adulthood, contributing to enhanced midlife psychosocial outcomes. Specifically, maternal support was associated with emotional well-being, and paternal support was associated with improved health. However, engaging and satisfying employment seems to mediate a poor parent–child relationship, increasing the youth's well-being (Roberts & Bengston, 1993). We wonder how Caroline's current work environment, and the supports that may be formed there over time, might positively nourish her confidence and well-being, and mitigate the ill-effects of Caroline's own family's estrangement and lack of acceptance.

Youth with unstable attachments to adult caregivers, like many foster care youth transitioning out of the foster care system, have a great need for developmentally appropriate and culturally sensitive supportive services as they make the transition into young adulthood. Social workers should examine the ways in which formal services facilitate the transition to adulthood for youths who have no informal supports. Certainly, terminating services to these youths at the age of majority, without making arrangements for them to receive adult services, will undermine the efforts made during the youth's adolescence and put these individuals at a disadvantage as young adults (Davis & Vander Stoep, 1997). Particularly for individuals with developmental disabilities, there may be a strong need for services to continue into young adulthood (Keogh et al., 2004). Social workers can advocate for policies that recommend and fund such services.

Finally, the immigration experience for youth may pose a risk during the adulthood transition. Research shows that more than one third (38.2%) of young-adult Latinos do not have a high school degree, and immigration transition and associated stressors as well as socioeconomic barriers may be contributing factors (U.S. Census Bureau, 2012). As social workers, we must ask about the context of the immigration experience and examine how it influences young-adult development. For example, was immigration a choice? Were there family separations along the way, and what was the nature of such separations? What motivated the immigration experience? Was there a change in the family's socioeconomic and/or role statuses? What are the hardships encountered in the new country? Are these hardships experienced differently by different members of the same family? What is the level of the family's and individual members' acculturation? It is important to assess for the extent of intergenerational stress that may have developed from the immigration experience because studies show that both high and low levels of acculturation are associated with risk behaviors such as substance abuse and mental health problems.

Relationship Development in Young Adulthood

Erikson's concept of intimacy, which relies on connection with a significant partner, is at the core of relationship development during early adulthood. Typically, young adults develop sustained commitments to others and come to recognize a responsibility for others' well-being. This developmental process may manifest as thoughtful awareness in the early years, changing to more active behavioral commitment in later years—for example, caring for children or aging parents, getting involved in the community, and taking on social obligations.

Intimacy, which can be defined as a sense of warmth or closeness, has three components: interdependence with another person, self-disclosure, and affection (Perlman & Fehr, 1987). Intimacy may take the form of cognitive/intellectual intimacy, emotional intimacy, sexual intimacy, physical intimacy apart from a sexual relationship, and spiritual intimacy. When reflecting on intimate relations, some people talk about finding a "soul mate"; feeling intensely connected; sharing values, beliefs, and philosophical inquiries; and feeling as though the relationship has strong direction and purpose.

Establishing intimacy is a multifaceted process. Exhibit 7.5 lists some of the tasks involved in fostering an intimate relationship with someone. The ability to perform these tasks depends not only on personal abilities (see Busch & Hofer, 2012) but also on external factors, such as the individual's family background. Research has found two family factors in adolescence to be important in the ability to develop intimate relationships during young adulthood: (1) a positive relationship with the mother (e.g., effective, clear communication with her, as well as mutual respect and empathy) and (2) adaptability of the family unit (e.g., good habits of conflict resolution and appropriate discipline) (Robinson, 2000). The young adult's ability to develop intimate relationships also depends on favorable environmental conditions, such as having

adequate resources to accommodate stressors, handle life responsibilities, and deal effectively with the multiple life transitions of this developmental stage.

An individual's family relationships and attachment to the family unit as a whole are transformed during young adulthood. The family's life course stage and the psychosocial development of individual members will influence the nature of family relationships in young adulthood. Generally, though, young adults may see parents, siblings, and relatives less frequently as work, romantic attachments, and new family responsibilities take precedence. With greater independence, geographic distance may also preclude more visits. Thus, time spent together may center on holiday celebrations. As traditional family roles evolve, young adults may take more active responsibility for holiday preparations. They may find themselves wanting to spend less time with old friends and more time with family. As young adults have children, holiday activities and family interactions may increasingly focus on the new generation.

Romantic Relationships

Romantic relationships are a key element in the development of intimacy during early adulthood. **Romantic love** has been described as a relationship that is sexually oriented, is "spontaneous and voluntary," and occurs between equal partners (Solomon, 1988). Satisfaction in romantic partnerships depends on finding a delicate

EXHIBIT 7.5 ● **Tasks in Fostering Intimacy**
• Effectively negotiating expectations for the relationship
• Negotiating roles and responsibilities
• Making compromises
• Prioritizing and upholding values
• Deciding how much to share of oneself
• Identifying and meeting individual needs
• Identifying and meeting partnership needs
• Renegotiating identity
• Developing trust and security
• Allowing for reciprocal communication
• Making time commitments to partner
• Effectively resolving conflict and solving problems
• Demonstrating respect, support, and care

PHOTO 7.3 The transition from emerging adulthood to young adulthood is marked by solidifying role commitments, such as marriage.

balance between positive and negative interactions across time (Gottman, 1994).

Anthropologist Helen Fisher (2004) suggests that the choice of romantic partners is based on three distinct emotional systems: lust, attraction, and attachment. *Lust* is sexual attraction and is associated with androgen hormones. *Attraction* involves feeling great pleasure in the presence of the romantic interest and thinking of the other person all the time. Fisher suggests that attraction is associated with increased levels of dopamine and norepinephrine and decreased levels of serotonin, which are neurotransmitters in the brain. Fisher's description of *attachment* is similar to Bowlby's concept described in Chapter 3 of this book. It involves a sense of security when in the presence of the attachment figure, which is the romantic partner in this discussion. Attachment has been associated with the hormone oxytocin.

In the United States, heterosexual romantic love has traditionally been considered a precursor to marriage. However, a recent trend in romantic relationships is to have sex earlier but marry later. The practice of unmarried couples sharing a home has increased steadily over the past 3 decades, and about two thirds of U.S. couples live together before marriage (Manning, 2013). It is important to remember, however, that in many parts of the world and among many recent immigrant groups to the United States, marriage is arranged and not based on romantic courtship. Many other variations in relationship development exist as well, represented by single-parent families, childless couples, gay and lesbian partnerships, couples who marry and choose to live apart to establish individual career tracks, and couples where partners are in different life stages (e.g., early adulthood and middle adulthood).

In the past, increasing education decreased women's likelihood of marrying, but recent data suggest a reversal of that trend. The cohort of women who recently graduated from college, both Black and White, are likely to marry later than women of their cohort without a college education, but their rate of eventual marriage will be higher (Goldstein & Kenney, 2001). The researchers interpret this trend to indicate that marriage is increasingly becoming a choice only for the most educated members of society. Given the advantages of rner family, this trend may contribute toward idening economic gap in our society. Although rriages and partnerships typically expand a young ult's social support network, this might not be the case for all individuals, and social workers should be cautious about making such assumptions.

An increasing awareness of variation in relationships has prompted research into all sorts of romantic attachments. One focus is same-sex relationships. Young adults are more likely to identify as LGBTQ compared to other age groups (Brown, 2017). Family acceptance of an LGBTQ adolescent is a significant predictor of positive outcomes during the transition to young adulthood (Snapp, Watson, Russell, Diaz, & Ryan, 2015). The term *Latinx* or *Latin@* is being used by individuals of Latin American descent who identify on the spectrum from gender fluid, genderqueer, or gender nonconforming to non-binary or agender. Latinx is also often used in place of either Latino or Latina to embrace all in the Latinx community under a single term (Ramirez & Blay, 2017). An estimated 0.6% of the population, or 1.4 million adults, identify as transgender in the United States, and an estimated 0.7% (206,000) of young adults identify as transgender (Flores et al., 2016). These estimations have doubled since 2011. Researchers suggest that this increase is due to the increase in social acceptance and visibility of transgender people (Flores et al., 2016). Trans people may fall all along the heterosexual-homosexual continuum. Caroline Sanders is currently curious about her own sexual orientation and, although she does not have a history of experimenting in romantic relationships, she may be at a time in her life course where she is more open to exploring such possibilities.

One study that identified three "scripts" in lesbian relationships helps to differentiate romantic attachment from other kinds of intimacy (Rose & Zand, 2000):

1. The "romance" script combines emotional intimacy and sexual attraction. It is characterized by an attenuated dating period and quick commitment to a relationship.

2. "Friendship" is a script in which individuals fall in love and are emotionally committed, though sexual behaviors are not necessarily a part of the relationship. Research shows that this is the most common script among lesbians, emphasizing emotional intimacy over sexuality. Women have suggested that the ambiguity implicit in this script often makes defining the relationship difficult.

3. "Sexually explicit" focuses on sexual attraction and leaves emotional intimacy at the periphery. This script is void of any direct expression of future commitment.

Lesbian and gay partnering becomes more complex if the coming-out process begins in early adulthood. The individuals involved have to negotiate through their parents' emotional reactions and responses at the same time the new relationship is developing. One study found that lesbian and gay partners are less likely to identify family as a significant social support as compared with heterosexual couples (Kurdek, 2004). One possible reason is that siblings and other relatives may be forced to confront their own comfort, biases, and values associated with the young adult's relationship. If gay and lesbian couples decide to have children, their own parents will inevitably be forced to confront the homosexual identity in order to develop their grandparent role with the new child.

One research team (Suter, Daas, & Bergen, 2008) investigated how lesbian couples negotiate a family identity through the use of symbols and rituals. They interviewed mothers of 16 two-parent lesbian families who had conceived their children through donor insemination. They found that the great majority of the couples in their sample used two types of symbols to develop a family identity. Most of the couples chose to use a hyphenated last name for the mothers and the children, to signify to the world that they are family. One mother reported continuing with her unhyphenated last name to remind her parents who were unsupportive of her partner relationship that she was their daughter and therefore her children were their grandchildren—in hopes of encouraging them to behave like grandparents to her children. All but one of the couples reported choosing sperm donors who had physical characteristics similar to the nonbiological mother, explaining that "looking related" symbolized familyhood.

Even in families where "acceptance" has taken root, people in the family's social network may have limited understanding that is difficult to work through. Family members who thought they had come to terms with the young adult's sexual orientation may find themselves harboring anger, hurt, disappointment, or confusion about how the young person's life trajectory is affecting their own life trajectories. Other complicating factors related to gay and lesbian relationship development can be connections with the larger community and with the gay and lesbian community itself. Regardless of the sexuality of young-adult clients, social workers need to consider the client's partner when exploring intimacy issues. These partners may be a valuable resource in matters relating to the partnership itself as well as relations with the family of origin. Social workers also need to assess the adequacy of a young adult's support system across multiple dimensions and to identify and respond to any perceived gaps. A signature stride forward is the 2015 U.S. Supreme Court decision in *Obergefell v. Hodges* that made same-sex marriage legal in all 50 United States.

Although intimate relationships are typically a source of support, violence between intimate partners is a widespread public health issue. It is not limited by social class, culture, race, ethnicity, marital status, or sexual orientation. **Intimate violence** includes physical violence, sexual abuse, and psychological harm. Victims often experience several forms of violence. **Intimate terrorism** is a pattern of coercive control and repeated severe battering (Johnson, 2008). Victims of intimate terrorism report that fear is their main motivation for staying in relationships that include this abuse (Leone, Lape, & Xu, 2013). Males and females are equally likely to be the perpetrators of intimate violence and intimate terrorism, but women are more likely to miss work, report depression, be injured, receive death threats, and be killed by their partners (Jasinski, Blumenstein, & Morgan, 2014). Partners who abuse are more likely than nonabusive partners to have depression, anxiety, and low self-esteem, and to be possessive, jealous, and controlling toward their partners (Johnson, Giordano, Longmore, & Manning, 2014). Sometimes intimate violence is mutual, with some couples lacking other methods to manage conflict. Some victims use violence while resisting intimate attacks. Intimate terrorism is usually one-way and escalates over time. The goal of intervention in intimate terrorism is to protect the safety of the victim, but for the couple who engages in mutual violence to resolve conflict, conflict resolution training can be helpful (Johnson, 2008).

Parenthood

Regardless of when parenthood happens, the transition is an exciting and challenging one. Parenting is an interactive process, with reciprocal parent–child and child–parent influences (Maccoby, 2002b). New parents are faced with new responsibilities: caregiving responsibilities, added housework, financial demands, loss of sleep, and less leisure time (Nelson, Kushlev, & Lyubomirsky, 2014). Often when partners begin thinking about becoming parents, their own memories of being parented and those experiences of their own parent–child attachment prompt emotional and even physical reactions. For example, research shows that childhood stressors impact hypothalamic-pituitary-adrenal (HPA) functioning and disrupt the stress response system during pregnancy, implicating additional risk for preterm birth, even after controlling for experienced adulthood stressors (Gillspie, Christian, Alston, & Salsberry, 2017). The multiple role transitions that mark entry into parenthood during young adulthood can be both exciting and challenging, as new familial interdependencies evolve. New social obligations and responsibilities associated with caregiving affect the relationship between the young-adult partners and between the young adults and their parents.

Often, the nature of the partners' relationship before parenthood will determine how partners manage the demands of these changing roles (Durkin, 1995). Adjustment to parenthood, and successful role reorganization, depends on five dimensions (Cowan, 1991):

1. Individual factors, such as how role changes affect one's sense of self

2. Quality of the partners' relationship (e.g., how the couple negotiates responsibilities and their decision-making capabilities)

3. Quality of the relationship between the young adults and their children

4. Quality of each partner's relationships with his or her family of origin

5. Quality of external relationships (e.g., school, work, community)

How partners negotiate the division of labor along gender lines also influences parenting and marital satisfaction. Much of the parenting literature has focused on the role strain mothers face in maintaining work commitments alongside new parenting responsibilities. More recent literature has focused on the more positive aspects of mothers' participation in the workforce (Gürsory & Bicakci, 2007; Losoncz & Bortolotto, 2009). However, fatherhood and the positive impact of paternal parenting on both child well-being and the father's own successful male adult development need further exploration.

There has been interest in recent years in the role of fathers in the lives of children, and father involvement has been shown to have a positive effect on children in such areas as academic success and reducing likelihood of delinquency and substance abuse (cited in Jones &

Mosher, 2013). A National Survey of Family Growth examined U.S. fathers' (ages 15 to 44) involvement with their children from 2006 to 2010 (Jones & Mosher, 2013). This study included both biological and nonbiological fathers and co-residential fathers as well as nonresidential fathers. A larger percentage of non-Hispanic White fathers had co-residential children than either non-Hispanic Black or Hispanic fathers. As might be expected, a higher percentage of co-residential fathers (90%) were involved in bathing, diapering, or dressing their children than nonresidential fathers (31%). Among co-residential fathers, Black fathers (70%) were more likely than White (60%) or Hispanic (45%) fathers to bathe, dress, diaper, or help their children use the toilet. Likewise, Black nonresidential fathers (66%) were more likely than White nonresidential fathers (61%) and Hispanic nonresidential fathers (34%) to be involved in these activities with children in the past 4 weeks. On the other hand, co-residential Hispanic fathers (71%) were more likely than co-residential White fathers (64%) to eat daily meals with their children. Fathers who lived with their children were twice as likely as fathers who did not live with their children to perceive themselves as doing a very good job as a father. Other research has shown that very young fathers have significant mental health needs (Weinman, Buzi, & Smith, 2005).

Kathryn Edin and Timothy Nelson (2013) contributed an in-depth examination of fatherhood and the meaning it plays in low-income men's lives. Over 7 years, Edin and Nelson documented the lived experiences of unmarried low-income fathers and their perceptions of parenting children in the urban environments of Philadelphia and Camden, New Jersey. When asked, "What would your life be like without your children?" fathers explained that they did not see their children "as millstones but as life preservers, saviors, redeemers" (p. 58). Children, the interviews showed, facilitated a connection to life and love, helped men stay out of institutions (jails, drug rehabs), and motivated in men a commitment to doing well by and for their children. The child was often at the core of the connection between the father and the child's mother. Babies often represent the symbolic opportunity to transition to a "fresh start" or a new life trajectory, regardless of the tenuous relationship a man might have with the baby's mother. When fathers have children as a result of many different relationships, they may selectively focus on one child with whom to devote time and resources, rather than trying to desperately make limited time and resources distribute equally across all children. Fathers discussed the increased difficulty they experienced in keeping up relationships with their sons and daughters as their children aged. Relational fathering, or the importance of spending quality time with their children, was emphasized over the financial role. "Why muster the effort to avoid pregnancy when being appropriately 'situated' is viewed as a contingency that may never occur?" (Edin & Nelson, 2013, p. 227). Think for a moment about how you think we do as a society in *valuing* and *supporting* the fathering role of men across socioeconomic strata.

Research on tasks associated with responsible fathering identify the provision of economic and emotional support to children, basic caregiving, offering guidance and control, and "being there" (or being present) as most important to the fathering role as defined by young fathers and linked to successful fathering (Peart, Pungello, Campbell, & Richey, 2006). Fathers who are highly involved with their children often describe their peers' parents as being influential in their own development as a father (Masciadrelli, Pleck, & Stueve, 2006). Further research needs to account for the presence of male **fictive kin** (nonrelatives that are considered family) and their role in helping young adults develop as fathers, and to document the strengths of special populations of fathers, such as young African American fathers (see Connor & White, 2006).

As for mothers, the evidence suggests that maternal employment may have a positive influence on her sense of self, leading to better outcomes for her children. However, Pamela Stone's (2007) book *Opting Out?* reminds us that the decision to opt out of careers, even after intensive postsecondary advanced education and career success, may be related to institutional barriers experienced in the employment sector rather than an indicator of personal choice or family preference. For example, workplace environments that require long work hours or that may have inflexible family policies that compete with family demands may pose barriers to choosing full-time work for some families.

With these findings in mind, it becomes necessary to identify groups for whom employment opportunities may be limited. Parents of children with disabilities fall into this category. Research shows that 12% of children in the United States have at least one developmentally related functional limitation that requires special attention and care (Hogan & Msall, 2002). Parenting a child with a functional disability demands extra care, which may decrease a parent's opportunity to enter or continue participation in the labor market. One study suggested that two thirds of families with a child who has a functional limitation will experience significant changes in labor force participation (Hogan & Msall, 2002).

Low-income mothers are another group for whom maternal employment is significantly related to child well-being (Zaslow & Emig, 1997). Employment often creates childcare difficulties. However, characteristics associated with positive parenting (e.g., the mother's ability to express warmth to the child, her lack of depressive symptoms, and the quality of her verbal interaction with the child) have been found to mediate the ill effects on child well-being that may arise in welfare-to-work programs, which sometimes leave low-income mothers with poor childcare options (McGroder, Zaslow, Moore, Hair, & Ahluwalia, 2002). Other studies have found that parents who have more social support are better at parenting (Marshall, Noonan, McCartney, Marx, & Keefe, 2001).

Given that the vast majority of women with children younger than age 6 are employed in the workforce, it is important to understand how workplace policies and conditions support or undermine parenting, particularly for low-income workers for whom employment is often characterized by unpredictable schedules and who often have little control or input into their day-to-day work routine (Gassman-Pines, 2013). Research has found that, indeed, mothers who were in emerging adulthood and working in low-wage jobs experienced significant distress in mother–child interactions related to both high and low workload stressors, as compared with mothers in other socioeconomic classes and as compared with older mothers.

Helping young adults to develop parenting efficacy may assist them to overcome environmental conditions and improve their children's well-being. Unfortunately, research shows that one of the biggest gaps in independent living services for young adults transitioning out of foster care is in parenting skills development (the other was housing preparation) (Georgiades, 2005). Another study compared the effects of increasing the mother's parenting efficacy in White and Black families characterized by a weak marriage and living in economically disadvantaged neighborhoods (Ardelt & Eccles, 2001). The Black families showed greater benefits in the form of increased academic success for their children. Parenting efficacy also contributed more to positive child outcomes in Black families with a compromised marriage than in Black families where the marriage was strong and secure. Parenting-related protective factors in Latino families include respect, familism, and biculturalism (Chapman & Perreira, 2005).

Mentoring and Volunteering

Although young adults seek out older adult mentors in work as they begin establishing themselves in new careers, young persons also often serve as mentors themselves. Serving as a mentor can help young adults move through the adulthood transition by facilitating new experiences and helping them to develop new roles that require "taking care of others" as opposed to "being taken care of" themselves. As young adults refine their ideologies, beliefs, and values, they form group affiliations consistent with their emerging identity, career, relationships, community, and religious and political views.

With the Edward M. Kennedy Serve America Act (signed April 21, 2009), President Obama reauthorized and expanded the service opportunities funded by the Corporation for National and Community Service, such as initiating the Summer of Service programs aimed at engaging youth in tutoring, recreation, and service opportunities.

Some examples of current groups and mentoring programs young adults might get involved in include 20 Something, a gay/lesbian young-adult social group; Young Democrats/Young Republicans political groups; YMCA/YWCA; and Big Brothers/Big Sisters youth mentoring programs. Service-related groups young adults may choose to become involved with include Junior Achievement, a nonprofit organization that brings young adults together with elementary school students to teach children economic principles, and Streetwise Partners, where young adults help low-income and unemployed persons with job skills training. College students may also get actively involved in Habitat for Humanity projects or student associations such as the College Hispanic American Society, Campus Crusaders for Christ, and Association of Black Students, which spearhead philanthropic and community integration activities.

CRITICAL THINKING QUESTIONS 7.4

What social roles are Caroline Sanders, Sheila Henderson, and Jonathan Stuart and Kai Hale playing? What special challenges have each faced in social development during emerging and young adulthood? Community engagement and commitment to larger community roles is often heralded as a marker of adulthood. What are the specific ways in which each of the people in our case examples have engaged in meaningful ways in their communities?

Young Adults and Technology

Writer and educator Marc Prensky (2010) describes the current cohort of young adults as the first generation of "digital natives," in contrast to their elders who are "digital immigrants" who have had to learn new information and communication technologies in their adulthood. He notes that digital immigrants will never have the same fluidity and ease with the language of communication technology as the generations that have grown up with it. It is important to remember that this can be said about the current cohort of young adults but not about the life stage of young adulthood itself. It is a cohort, not a developmental issue. During this cohort's early years in the 1990s, the use of personal computers was rapidly expanding, DVDs and MP3 players were introduced, and Google, Amazon, and eBay first appeared. As this cohort passed through adolescence, Facebook, YouTube, Wikipedia, and Twitter joined the scene, and iPhones and tablet computers were introduced. By the time they reached emerging adulthood, smartphones were an instrument in their pocket that could perform many functions (Arnett, 2015).

In the United States, 90% of young adults with Internet access use social media (Villanti et al., 2017); 87% report having a smartphone with Internet access, and 75% have a personal computer with Internet access. It is estimated that the typical U.S. emerging adult is engaged with media of some kind for about 12 hours a day; they are electronically connected much of their waking hours (Arnett, 2015). Non-Hispanic, Black young adults report lower rates of access to such technologies compared to other groups. Black young adults and those with less than a college education used LinkedIn more than other demographic groups, and Tumblr and Snapchat have higher rates of use among female young adults (Villanti et al., 2017). In a survey of 19- to 32-year-olds, frequent social media use was associated with greater perception of social isolation (Primack et al., 2017). However, it is unclear whether individuals who already feel socially isolated are more likely to use social media, or if individuals with mental health challenges more frequently report using social media to connect with other people (Primack et al., 2017).

Certainly, this experience of being always connected electronically is changing social relationships, and scholars are raising questions about the nature of that change. Sherry Turkle (2015), an enthusiast for the promise of digital technology, is also one of the most vocal critics of what that technology is doing to social relationships. She proposes that "face-to-face conversation is the most human—and humanizing—thing we do" (p. 3). It is in face-to-face interactions, she argues, that we develop the human capacity for empathy. She fears that chronic online connection is interfering with our face-to-face connections and the development of empathy. Many young adults seem to share Turkle's concerns. One national poll, the Clark poll, of emerging adults found that 50% of 18- to 29-year-olds agreed that "sometimes I feel like I spend too much time on social networking websites" (Arnett & Schwab, 2012). A 2013 report by the Pew Research Center found that 18- to 29-year-olds had decreased the time they spent on Facebook in the past year (Rainie, Smith, & Duggan, 2013). The Clark poll of emerging adults found that 36% of 18- to 29-year-olds agreed that "I feel anxious if I have to go more than a couple of hours without checking for electronic messages" (Arnett & Schwab, 2012).

Nitzburg and Farber (2013) found that emerging adults with anxious and disorganized, as compared with secure, adult attachment styles tended to use Facebook as a way of avoiding intimate face-to-face human interaction and to gain emotional connection in a safe way. A study in Indonesia also found that young adults with anxious attachment style were more active in using Facebook than other young adults, but young adults with avoidant attachment style were reluctant to use Facebook (Andangsari, Gumilar, & Godwin, 2013).

Work and the Labor Market

Caroline Sanders is employed and has found the workplace to be both supportive and a source of stress during her gender transition. It appears that Sheila Henderson's military career is important to her, and she is well aware of the bleak employment situation for young adults back in the rural community where she grew up. Jonathan Stuart and Kai Hale have stable and lucrative careers in the software development and hospitality industries. In the national Clark poll of emerging adults, 79% of 18- to 29-year-olds agreed with this statement: "It is more important to enjoy my job than to make a lot of money," and 86% agreed that "it is important to me to have a career that does some good in the world" (Arnett & Schwab, 2012).

For many young adults, however, work is a "dream deferred," the theme of a hearing of the U.S. Senate Committee on Banking, Housing, and Urban Affairs in June 2014. Testifying at the hearing, Heidi Shierholz, economist at the Economic Policy Institute, reported that the job prospects for young workers remain dim.

She stated that 17.7% of high school graduates and 11.2% of college graduates were neither employed nor enrolled in school. She further reported that many college graduates were working in jobs that do not require a college degree and that the wages of young-adult workers with a college degree had declined since 2007. At the same hearing, Keith Hall, senior research fellow at the Mercatus Center at George Mason University, testified that the employment rate for young adults ages 18 to 29 was 63.9%, lower than it was at the end of the recession that started in 2007.

U.S. economists have referred to the decade of 2000–2010 as the "lost decade." After 2 decades of about 20 million new jobs gained per decade, wage and salary jobs decreased in the decade 2000–2010. During this decade, the employment rates of working-age Americans declined for all age groups under the age of 57, and the employment rates of the 57-and-older group increased because people could not afford to retire. The greatest declines in employment rates occurred in the 16-to-19 age group, followed by young adults ages 20 to 24. There was a 10.7% decline in employment rates for the age group 20–24, with the decline for males (12.8%) steeper than for females (8.7%). There was a similar pattern of decline for all but five wealthy countries in the Organisation for Economic Co-operation and Development (OECD), but the United States saw more decline than some other countries, falling from 5th in overall employment rate in 2000 to 13th in 2012 (Sum, Khatiwada, & McHugh, 2014).

Danziger and Ratner (2010) note that "one key marker of the transition to adulthood is achieving success in the labor market" (p. 134). Failure to meet that marker interferes with the ability to meet other adult transition markers such as living independently, marriage, and parenthood. They call attention to the decline in labor market involvement of emerging and young adults noted in the previous paragraph and suggest several trends in the economic institution that are driving this decline: increased use of labor-saving technologies, increased globalization, declining unionization, failure of the minimum wage to keep up with inflation, increased use of casual (e.g., part-time, short-term) versus permanent employment, and an increasing portion of workers working in low-wage jobs as the bulk of economic gains go to the wealthiest families and highest earners. Over the past 3 decades, young males with a high school education have taken longer to reach economic self-sufficiency than in earlier eras, and young women are more likely to attain economic self-sufficiency than in earlier eras. During this period, median earnings increased for women but were largely unchanged for men.

Danziger and Ratner (2010) analyzed declines in the employment rate of high school graduates ages 25 to 34 from 1979 to 2007 and found racial/ethnic differences. Among men, the employment rate fell 23% for non-Hispanic Blacks, 7.3% for non-Hispanic Whites, and 4.4% for Hispanics. Danziger and Ratner report that the dramatic rise in incarceration of young Black men during this period, and the negative effect of criminal record on future employment opportunities, was a large factor in the greater decline in employment among young Black men. Employer racial discrimination is another important factor. Sociological studies have shown that White men with a prison record are more likely to be hired than Black men without a prison record (Lui, Robles, Leondar-Wright, Brewer, & Adamson, 2006). Among women, employment rates increased during this period for all three groups of women, Non-Hispanic White, non-Hispanic Black, and Hispanic.

Inflation-adjusted median annual earnings of employed high school male graduates ages 25 to 34 declined from 1973 to 2007. The rates of earnings declines were 25% for Black non-Hispanic males, 26% for White non-Hispanic males, and 29% for Hispanic males. During the same period, inflation-adjusted median annual earnings of employed high school female graduates increased by 7% for both Black and Hispanic women and by 37% for White women. For college educated men ages 25 to 34, the inflation-adjusted median earnings remained about the same from 1973 to 2007, and the earnings for college educated women improved at about the same rate as for high school educated women (Danziger & Ratner, 2010).

The decline in employment opportunities has enormous ramifications for the trajectory of young adults in the labor market. The situation has been exacerbated by changes in tertiary (college-level) education, where tuitions have been increasing and financial aid has been declining. Many college graduates, particularly those who come from low-income families who are not able to subsidize their higher education, graduate with enormous student loan debt, only to struggle to find a foothold in the labor market. Several groups of young adults have been found to be particularly vulnerable in the tight labor market:

- Young adults with criminal records (Danziger & Ratner, 2010)

- Youth aging out of foster care (Hook & Courtney, 2011)

- Young adults with physical and mental disabilities (Verhoof, Maurice-Stam, Heymans, & Grootenhuis, 2012)

- Young adults who experienced a variety of types of childhood adversity (Lund, Andersen, Winding, Biering, & Labriola, 2013)

- Young adults who were early onset persistent problem drinkers (Paljärvi, Martikainen, Pensola, Leinonen, & Herttua, 2015)

Graduating from high school or college during an economic downturn can have long-term impact on the work life trajectory. Lost economic opportunities in young adulthood can reduce the cumulative labor experience necessary for middle-adulthood career trajectories. Recommendations include offering more paid internships to teens and young adults, work-based learning activities, and strengthening programs that help young adults transition from high school to work or college. One example is the New Collar Jobs Act of 2017 (H.R. 3393) that uses tax code modifications to encourage employee training and certification in cybersecurity and to promote job growth and skill development, with loan repayment for employees who choose to do such cybersecurity work in economically distressed geographic areas. Funding is also increased for advanced technology education programs and for federal Cybercorps scholarships.

The transition into the world of work is an important element of social development during early adulthood. A young adult's opportunity for successful adulthood transitioning into the labor market depends on a variety of dimensions, including **human capital** (talents, skills, intellectual capacity, social development, emotional regulatory capacity) as well as **community assets** such as public infrastructure (e.g., adequate transportation to get to work), community networks, and educational opportunities. In addition, family capital is important. "Transformative assets," or those family contributions that aid in deferring the immediate economic costs of long-term investments such as a college education or the down payment for a house, are differentially spread across race, with half of White families giving young adults this investment edge, whereas data show that only 20% of Black families are able to do so (Lui et al., 2006). Resource transfers from parents to adult children can facilitate adulthood transitions. Inequality in intergenerational resource transfer can, then, magnify differences in young-adulthood transitional outcomes. Black and Hispanic young adults

live with parents at higher rates than Whites; not surprisingly, a family's resources are associated with the amount of support the family can provide their young-adult children (Hardie & Seltzer, 2016).

This human capital situation coupled with the fact that, in some states, children of undocumented immigrants do not receive in-state tuition for higher education, makes the prospects of getting into and affording a college education out of reach for many young adults and erodes their longer-term access to asset growth and economic stability. For example, one study found that societal integration is compromised for young persons without Deferred Action for Childhood Arrivals (DACA) status, leading to decreased well-being and a felt sense of isolation. Increased control, enhanced sense of belonging, and hope for self-sufficiency were experienced with DACA status. However, self-sufficiency came with more pressure to support one's family and the stressors associated with the uncertainty that accompanies DACA status (Siemons, Raymond-Flesh, Auerswald, & Brindis, 2017).

One report (Draut & Silva, 2004) indicates that young adults face daunting economic challenges characterized by underemployment, the high cost of purchasing a first home, and rising debt from student loans and credit cards. According to another report, in 2004 adults aged 18 to 24 spent close to 2 times the amount on debt expenditures as they did in 1992, with approximately 30% of income going to paying off their debt (Mintel Report, 2004). There are intergenerational Black-White racial disparities in young-adult student debt, with Blacks holding disproportionately greater debt as compared to White young adults. Parental wealth has been found to be influential in buffering student debt accumulation for White young adults but not for Black young adults. Differential debt risk may also confer differential risk by race in other adulthood transitions, such as home ownership and/or marriage and childbearing, because debt may delay entry into these adulthood transitions (Addo, Houle, & Simon, 2016).

Given that our educational institution operates as society's gatekeeper to economic opportunities, we need to examine how it prepares our youth for future employment as well as how and to whom such opportunities are afforded. For example, of the estimated 400,000 homeless households in the United States, about 32,000 are unaccompanied young adults (U.S. Department of Housing and Urban Development, 2017). LGBTQ youth make up about 20% of youth involved in the juvenile justice system and almost 50% of youth who are homeless (Remlin, Cook, Erney, Cherepon, & Gentile, 2017).

Transitional living programs for homeless youth ages 16 to 22 offer housing and services that help youth develop financial stability through connecting to educational and vocational opportunities, while providing mental health and support services (Curry & Petering, 2017). These services and supports are important in helping such youth attain entry into the labor market.

A Child Trends report summarized specific empirically validated competencies shown to increase high school students' success in the labor market: second language competency; ability to interact with others to problem-solve and work through conflict; critical thinking skills; planfulness; good judgment; strong work ethic such as reliability and professionalism in the work environment; having had internship experience; and general self-management skills such as responsibility, initiative, and time management skills (Lippman & Keith, 2009). Policies and programs such as the Foster Care Independence Act (Pub. L. No. 106-169) and the John H. Chafee Foster Care Independence Program of 1999 provide additional support for postsecondary education, vocational training, housing, health care, and counseling until age 21 and are a good start in responding to these specific needs (U.S. Children's Bureau, 2012).

Alejandro Portes and Ruben G. Rumbaut (2001), in their book *Legacies: The Story of the Immigrant Second Generation*, based on results from the Children of Immigrants Longitudinal Study (CILS), noted that the structural labor market change of the past few decades disproportionately affects immigrants, particularly youth in late adolescence who will be emerging into this new occupational landscape. "Increasing labor market inequality implies that to succeed socially and economically, children of immigrants today must cross, in the span of a few years, the educational gap that took descendants of Europeans several generations to bridge," the authors note (p. 58). An important finding

PHOTO 7.4 A major challenge facing young adults is attaining independent financial stability and establishing autonomy and decision making.

© Patricia Nelson/iStockphoto.com

from the CILS is the contrast in job selection between older and younger generations of immigrants. Today's young people are more likely to turn down "traditional immigrant jobs" that are seen as unfulfilling, in contrast to older immigrants who often felt compelled to take any job available in their youth without such questioning (Portes & Rumbaut, 2001).

The dilemma facing disadvantaged youth entering adulthood is vexing. Labor market attachment is not only the surest route to material well-being, but labor market attachment also has been found to be significantly related to mental health and psychosocial well-being. One study looked at factors associated with well-being and adjustment from ages 16 to 21. The study found that experiences of unemployment were significantly associated with thoughts of suicide, substance abuse, and crime (Fergusson, Horwood, & Woodward, 2001). Benefits of work include increased self-esteem, increased social interaction, and external validation through social recognition. Increasingly, therefore, youths' life trajectories will be determined by access to advanced education and then good jobs.

RISK FACTORS AND PROTECTIVE FACTORS IN YOUNG ADULTHOOD

A longitudinal study that followed a cohort of individuals born in 1955 from infancy to age 40 identified clusters of protective factors at significant points across the life course (see Exhibit 7.6) that are associated with successfully making the transition to adulthood (Werner & Smith, 2001). The researchers identified high-risk individuals and then determined the specific factors that influenced their positive adaptation to adulthood at age 32. The protective factors included successful early social, language, and physical development; good problem-solving skills in middle childhood; educational and work expectations and plans by age 18; and social maturity and a sense of mastery and control in late adolescence. Family factors included stable maternal employment when the child was 2 to 10 years old, access to a variety of social support sources, and the child's sense of belonging within the family unit at age 18. Community factors included having access to nurturing, caring adults in one's community, including the presence of adult mentors, and having access to "enabling," as opposed to "entrapping," community niches (see Saleebey, 2012).

Other researchers have identified similar protective factors associated with successful developmental transitions into emerging adulthood and young adulthood, including childhood IQ, parenting quality, and socioeconomic status. Adaptation in emerging adulthood, specifically, is associated with an individual's planning capacity, future motivation, autonomy, social support, and coping skills (Masten et al., 2004).

Risk factors that researchers found to be associated with the transition to adulthood included low family income during infancy, poor reading achievement by age 10, problematic school behavior during adolescence, and adolescent health problems (Werner & Smith, 2001). For men, an excessive number of stressful events, living with an alcoholic or mentally ill father, and substance abuse contributed to problematic coping in early adulthood. Other studies have found that adolescent fatherhood can be a risk factor for delinquency, which, in turn, can lead to problematic entry into adulthood (Stouthamer-Loeber & Wei, 1998). For women, a sibling death in early childhood, living with an alcoholic or mentally ill father, and a conflicted relationship with the mother were significant risk factors for successful coping at age 32 (Werner & Smith, 2001).

One study (Ringeisen, Casaneuva, Urato, & Stambaugh, 2009) found that although about half (48%) of young adults with a maltreatment history had mental health problems, only 25% of these young adults received treatment services for their problems. In particular, there was a significant decline in those receiving services in adolescence (47.6%) compared to those continuing to receive such services in adulthood (14.3%). Data suggest that there is a significant risk of losing continuity of mental health services when making the move out of adolescence and into young adulthood, with data showing particularly high risk for non-Whites and those without Medicaid assistance (Ringeisen et al., 2009). Other studies of youth aging out of the foster care system have found similar declining trends in mental health service use during the adolescent-adult transition. A study by McMillan and Raghavan (2009) found that 60% of 19-year-old foster youth dropped out of services during the transition from the pediatric system of care to the adult service system. This is significant given that 24,000 youth age out of foster care each year (National Association of Counties, 2008) and that former foster youth (ages 19 to 30) have twice the rate of post-traumatic stress disorder as U.S. war veterans (Pecora et al., 2005) and more severe mental health and behavioral problems than the general population and youth who have a maltreatment history but not foster care placement (Lawrence, Carlson, & Egeland, 2006).

EXHIBIT 7.6 ● **Common Core Protective Factors Predicting Adult Adaptation**

	Individual Characteristics	Caregiving Context
Infancy	Autonomy; social competence Health status	Maternal competence Emotional support Number of stressful events
Middle childhood	Academic proficiency Health status	Emotional support to child (extended family; mentor) Number of stressful events
Adolescence	Self-efficacy Health status	Emotional support to child (peer relations; feelings about family) Number of stressful events
Young adulthood	Temperament Health status	Emotional support (quality of partner, work, and community relationships) Number of stressful events

Source: Adapted from Werner & Smith, 2001, pp. 161–163.

One longitudinal study (Jones et al., 2016) showed that the nature of the family environment in childhood (ages 10–12) was related to more positive adolescent functioning at 13 to 14 years of age and healthy functioning in young adulthood (ages 30–33) (p. 729). In addition, depression in one's family of origin is directly related to depression and anxiety in emerging adulthood (age 21), depression diagnosis in the early 30s, and a greater chance of electing to be part of a substance-involved peer group. A family's substance use when a child was ages 10 to 12 is associated with adolescent (ages 15–18) selection of peers who are substance-involved, and peer substance use at this middle-late adolescent stage is associated with a substance use diagnosis in emerging adulthood (age 21) (Jones et al., 2016). Other researchers have examined mental health profiles of emerging adults with a history of Child Protective Services involvement. Results show that ADHD and trauma symptoms are unique features specific to this population; antisocial and avoidant personality characteristics are also prevalent (Lee, Festinger, Jaccard, & Munson, 2017).

A study of the effects of war on adult mental health reveals other risk factors social workers should be aware of. Although some researchers have found that military service often provides youth a positive opportunity in transitioning into adulthood (Werner & Smith, 2001) and frequently leads to facilitating a young adult's return to higher education (Astone et al., 2000), the

ravages of war experienced during military service can pose significant mental health risk. For example, Hoge, Auchterlonie, and Milliken (2006) examined the prevalence of mental health problems and service use among military personnel who returned from service in Iraq and found that one fifth (19.1%) of those returning from Iraq had at least one mental health problem, with about one third (35%) of those adults accessing mental health services during their first year back home. In addition, those personnel assessed as having a mental health condition were more likely to subsequently leave the military as compared with those personnel who returned home without a mental health condition. Therefore, it appears that although military service can be a positive path for many transitioning youth, the nature and quality of a youth's military experience may influence later physical and mental health outcomes as well as work trajectory decisions (e.g., to leave the military early). It appears that military service in a time of war may be a risk factor rather than protective factor. In addition, the availability of, access to, and quality of mental health care for military personnel upon their return home may also contribute to the severity of wartime service as a risk factor. We see Sheila Henderson's struggle with her own military deployments—the time away from family, physical risks, and reliance on the community to provide family support in her absence. Sheila's story helps us to see that it may be difficult to disentangle the emotional and physical sequelae related to a traumatic brain injury and illustrates the challenges in family reintegration.

Entering the military is a career choice for many young adults, but for others with limited formal education, it may be the only employment opportunity that comes with comprehensive benefits. This seems to have been the case for Sheila Henderson. Choosing military employment requires contracting into a work environment that can be unpredictable, dangerous, and relatively inflexible (i.e., high demand, low control, and variable deployments), which can all exacerbate work-family stress and impact family well-being (Wadsworth & Southwell, 2013). Studies have found that parental stress is the most important factor that affects children's behavioral and emotional functioning when a military parent is deployed. Family support programming that focuses on helping nondeployed parents strengthen their ability to provide care for their children during a military spouse's deployment is important for military families. Gewirtz, Erbes, Polusny, Forgatch, and DeGarmo (2011) offer specific strategy recommendations to support parenting in military families, including working from the family's strengths and recognizing the resilience that exists in military families, focusing on stressors affecting the family during deployment, and helping parents develop emotional regulation strategies as part of their parenting skills. Other strategies include helping parents set appropriate limits, keeping rituals and routines as usual during the time of deployment, and enhancing the problem-solving capacity of the family unit (Gewirtz et al., 2011).

Knowledge of risk and protective factors related to the adulthood transition can help social workers assess young-adult clients' current challenges, vulnerabilities, strengths, and potentials. Gaining an accurate understanding of the client's developmental history provides guidance to the social worker in formulating appropriate goals and intervention strategies. It is important to remember your own assumptions of "risk" with clients in order to clarify the unique impact such experiences have on individual clients.

CRITICAL THINKING QUESTIONS 7.5

How do you think cumulative advantage and cumulative disadvantage affect human behavior during young adulthood? What personal, family, cultural, and other social factors during childhood and adolescence have an impact on the transition into young adulthood? What do you see as the risk and protective factors in the stories of Caroline Sanders, Sheila Henderson, and Jonathan Stuart and Kai Hale?

IMPLICATIONS FOR SOCIAL WORK PRACTICE

This discussion of young adulthood suggests several practice principles for social workers.

- Recognize that social roles during emerging adulthood may be different from those later in young adulthood.

- Explore cultural values, family expectations, attitudes toward gender roles, and environmental constraints and resources that may influence life structure decisions and opportunities when working with young-adult clients.

- Assess specific work, family, and community conditions as they pertain to young-adult clients' psychological and social well-being; be aware of any caregiving roles young adults may be playing.

- Where appropriate, help young adults to master the tasks involved in developing intimate relationships.

- Where appropriate, assist young adults with concerns about differentiating from family of origin and do so in a culturally sensitive manner.

- Work with other professionals to advocate for policies that promote transitional planning and connect youth to the labor market, particularly for youth aging out of foster care placements, correction facilities, group home environments, or other formal residential mental health settings.

- Take the initiative to develop mentoring programs that build relations between young adults and younger or older generations.

- Take the initiative to develop parenting classes for first-time parents and recognize and develop the unique strengths of fathers, especially in mentoring teen fathers to increase parenting skills.

- Understand the ways that social systems promote or deter people from maintaining or achieving health and well-being.

- Discover, appraise, and attend to changing locales, populations, scientific and technological developments, and emerging societal trends.

Key Terms

community assets 262
default individualization 240
developmental
   individualization 240
emerging adulthood 238
fictive kin 258

human capital 262
individuative-reflective faith 248
intimacy 254
intimacy versus isolation 236
intimate terrorism 257
intimate violence 257

life structure 237
novice phase 237
romantic love 254
spirituality 248
synthetic-conventional faith 248

Active Learning

1. Identify one current social issue as portrayed in the media (e.g., housing, immigration policies, health care access or coverage or affordability, living wage) and explore how this social issue uniquely affects young adults.

2. Create your own theory of young adulthood. What are some of the important characteristics? What makes someone a young adult? What differentiates this stage from adolescence and middle adulthood? Start the process by answering the following question: "Do you consider yourself to be an adult?"

3. Choose one of the case studies at the beginning of the chapter (Caroline Sanders, Sheila Henderson, or Jonathan Stuart and Kai Hale). Change the gender for that case without changing any other major demographic variable. Explore how your assumptions change about the individual's problems, challenges, and potential. Now choose a different case. Change the race or ethnicity for that case and again explore your assumptions. Finally, using the remaining case, change the socioeconomic status and again explore how your assumptions change.

Web Resources

AmeriCorps NCCC (Corporation for National & Community Services): www.nationalservice .gov/programs/americorps

Site details AmeriCorps' programs for young adults ages 18 to 24, offering full-time residential community service opportunities. Target goals include developing

youths' leadership capacity through intensive and directed community service.

Child Trends: www.childtrends.org

Site of Child Trends, a nonprofit research organization located in Washington, DC, provides data and reports focused on child well-being and marriage and family, to include fatherhood and parenting.

National Fatherhood Initiative: www .fatherhood.org

Site of the National Fatherhood Initiative provides numerous resources and links to other fatherhood sites and discusses educational and outreach campaigns under way to promote involved fathering and family well-being.

National Guard Youth Challenge: www .jointservicesupport.org/ngycp

Site reports on success stories of a multistate program that targets youth who have dropped out of high school to provide them with a 5-month residential program and ongoing mentoring services to facilitate their entry into employment, higher education/training, or the military.

National LGBTQ Task Force: www.thetaskforce .org

Site presented by the National LGBTQ Task Force contains information about the task force, news and views, special issues, state and local organizations, and special events.

National Survey of Family Growth: www.cdc .gov/nchs/nsfg.htm

Site of the National Center for Health Statistics offers reports, other publications, and data from their CDC-sponsored survey documenting family formation issues in adulthood, such as fertility and family planning, sexual behavior, and health.

Work and Family Researchers Network: http://workfamily.sas.upenn.edu

Site of the international membership organization of interdisciplinary work on the family and work (formerly the Sloan Work and Family Research Network) contains news, frequently asked questions, an online repository of research on work and the family, a literature database, a research newsletter, resources for teaching, research profiles, and work and family links. Part of the network's mission is to inform policymakers on key family-work issues.

Middle Adulthood

Elizabeth D. Hutchison

Learning Objectives

8.1 Compare one's own cognitive and emotional reactions to three case studies.

8.2 Summarize the changing construction of middle adulthood.

8.3 Critique three theories of middle adulthood: Erikson's theory of generativity, Jung's and Levinson's theories of finding balance, and life span theory of the gain-loss balance.

(Continued)

(Continued)

8.4 Give examples of biological changes, changes in health status, and intellectual changes during middle adulthood.

8.5 Critique three approaches to considering personality changes in middle adulthood: trait approach, human agency approach, and life narrative approach.

8.6 Summarize research on spiritual development during middle adulthood.

8.7 Describe major themes of relationships in middle adulthood.

8.8 Analyze major challenges related to work in middle adulthood.

8.9 Give examples of risk factors and protective factors for middle adulthood.

8.10 Apply knowledge of middle adulthood to recommend guidelines for social work engagement, assessment, intervention, and evaluation.

CASE STUDY 8.1

MARK RASLIN, FINDING STABILITY AT 42

Mark Raslin was born in Seattle, Washington, and raised as an only child in a White, lower-middle-class family who moved into a small two-bedroom apartment in the suburbs of Washington, DC, when he was 4 years old. He describes an extremely traumatic upbringing, characterized by abuse, abandonment, and parental mental illness and alcoholism. His parents often left him for several days at a time when he was as young as 5 years old. He reports that his mother abused alcohol and drugs and was hospitalized "a lot" for a severe mental health disorder. One frightening night when he was 9 years old, his father was arrested for check forgery. His mother was drunk and threatened to kill him and then commit suicide. His father left the family soon after that night, leaving Mark alone with his very unstable mother. He recalls feeling abandoned, scared, and angry in a chaotic home.

Mark says that he experienced "crazy anger . . . uncontrolled rage" throughout his entire childhood, often throwing, hitting, and breaking things. He also reports that he was teased a lot as a kid and had a very difficult time keeping friends. His rage and destructive behavior led to his admission to a local youth shelter when he was 11 years old. He recalls attempting to choke himself by wrapping a phone cord around his neck and telling others he wanted to die. The shelter did not want to keep him after the suicide attempt and sent him home to his mother.

Back home, Mark called the sheriff because of his mother's ongoing physical abuse and then moved in with his dad. His dad resisted this arrangement and had to be pressured by the sheriff's office to take Mark in. He remembers moving a lot with his dad, being left alone a lot, and his dad buying him cigarettes and alcohol when he was only 12 years old. Mark's experimentation with other drugs as a teenager quickly escalated to addiction, leading to treatment for polysubstance dependency at the age of 16. He stayed with his father until he was emancipated when he turned 17.

Mark dropped out of high school and has been intermittently homeless since. After leaving his father's home, he sometimes "couch surfed" with friends or his mother. Other times, he slept outdoors or at different shelters in the Virginia/Washington, DC, area. He says he had a couple of close friends and enjoyed playing guitar in a band, but his mental health issues and drug use often resulted in volatile behavior that alienated him from others. He was arrested for public drunkenness and trespassing and was involuntarily admitted to a state hospital where he was diagnosed with bipolar I disorder, manic with psychotic features.

This has been a pervasively disabling condition for him. Throughout most of young adulthood, he had periods of stability where he would find work and begin to form relationships, but this never lasted much longer than 6 months. He would periodically engage with mental health services, but he had a hard time committing to services because of trust issues. He abused a variety of drugs in efforts to numb the negative emotions and painful memories. He struggled to support himself with part-time jobs, but angry outbursts led to problems with employers.

A significant turning point occurred when Mark was in his mid-30s, when he met Rachel. They began dating and were in a committed relationship within a couple years. This time was marked by occasional mood disturbances, but this relationship seemed to have a stabilizing influence on Mark. He tried to cut down on drinking and stopped using drugs. He also started working full time at Office Depot and was more consistent with his mental health and substance abuse treatment. He proposed to Rachel, and they had a daughter together when he was 37 years old. Mark remembers the 5 years with Rachel as the first period of relative stability he had experienced. He suggests that Rachel was largely responsible for this stability because she managed most of the household affairs, took care of all the bills, and reminded him to take his medications.

His 4 years of employment at Office Depot reflected a significant achievement for Mark until a traumatic incident derailed his progress. Mark reports that he was a victim of armed robbery while working a night shift, and it appears that this experience triggered a relapse. He became very paranoid, anxious, and depressed. He started experiencing mood swings again and began to self-medicate with alcohol and marijuana and to withdraw from his family. He lost his job; he was hospitalized a couple of times; and Rachel and his daughter left, a devastating loss that contributed to a prolonged period of decompensation.

Mark then entered a 3-year period of chronic homelessness and unemployment, sometimes living outdoors, other times sleeping at gas stations and shelters. He was also incarcerated several times. One day, a social worker with a homeless outreach team struck up a conversation with him at the local drop-in center. At that point, Mark was living in the woods, coping with a manic episode, and facing an upcoming hearing for failure to pay child support. Beginning to recognize the significant role his mental health issues were playing in his problematic functioning, Mark agreed to work with the social worker on applying for social security disability benefits.

Approval for benefits was another significant turning point for Mark. He was able to secure stable housing and begin making consistent child support payments. He moved into a sober living house that provided him with the stability to establish healthy routines and consistent compliance with mental health and substance abuse treatment. He also found a sponsor and developed a stronger support network, all of which were vital to his recovery efforts. After a year of working with the homeless outreach team and a substance abuse therapist, Mark was able to achieve a prolonged period of stability.

Mark is now 42 years old and reports that he feels like he is starting "to find myself" again. His personal warmth and sense of humor have been more evident as he experiences stability in life. He is trying a return to part-time employment as a dishwasher, and this provides a sense of purpose and a self-esteem boost. Mark has also experienced a renewed motivation to return to music and has joined a church band where he plays guitar. He is encouraged by these positive developments but still acknowledges an underlying sadness and desire to reconnect with his daughter. Mark's therapist continues to work with him on issues related to his earlier trauma and sense of abandonment while also holding him accountable for his recovery process. Mark is working through his anger issues and trying to see if he can reestablish a relationship with his elderly parents who are experiencing their own health issues. He is skeptical that he can overcome his strong feelings of resentment toward them but would like to see if he can come to a place of greater acceptance of who they are.

—Derek Morch

CASE STUDY 8.2

LISA BALINSKI, TRYING TO BALANCE IT ALL AT 50

Lisa Balinski grew up in a lower-middle-class neighborhood in a midsize city in Minnesota. Her parents were both brought to the United States from Poland as small children, during World War II. They grew up in a neighborhood where social life revolved around the Polish-speaking Catholic church, where they met and married. Lisa was an only child, and her parents worked hard in the small Polish restaurant they opened soon after marrying. She started helping out in the restaurant at an early age, with increasing responsibilities over time. Her parents were proud when she graduated from college and got a job teaching at the neighborhood high school.

The day after her college graduation, Lisa married Adam, her high school sweetheart. Adam had been working in the neighborhood hardware store since he graduated from high school and had been patiently waiting for Lisa to finish college. During their first year of marriage, Lisa was overwhelmed, trying to adapt to

(Continued)

(Continued)

two new roles—wife and teacher—at the same time, and she and Adam were both thrilled when she learned that she was pregnant in the early spring of that year. Their plan was for Lisa to return to teaching in a few years, after getting a family started.

Adam's and Lisa's parents were thrilled about the baby girl, Rachel, but Lisa found the transition to motherhood more challenging than she had expected. Adam, on the other hand, seemed to be a natural and was an enormous help with the baby. They found, however, that they had underestimated the costs of a baby, and when Rachel was 6 months old, they decided to move in with Lisa's parents. The house was a bit crowded, but Lisa was happy to have her mother's help in the mornings before she went to the restaurant, and her mother loved having a chance to spend more time with Rachel.

When Rachel was 18 months old, Adam got a promotion at work, and with what they had saved over the past year, Lisa and Adam were able to move into an apartment of their own. When Rachel was 2½ years old, Lisa gave birth to another baby girl, Kristi. She was pleasantly surprised to find that she was more relaxed than she had been with Rachel, and for the first time since college, Lisa began to feel competent.

Finances were still tight, and when Kristi was 2 years old, Lisa began to do some substitute teaching. She hired her neighbor to watch the girls on the days that she was called in to teach. She really enjoyed being back in the classroom and took a full-time teaching position after a couple of years of subbing. After 2 years of full-time teaching, she began to take evening courses toward a master's degree. Adam supported her in this decision and stepped up to provide more help with household chores. He enjoyed the chance to grow even closer to his daughters.

With Adam and Lisa both working, they were able to buy a small house of their own in a more middle-class neighborhood. This was a good time in their lives. They were both enjoying their work, Lisa was becoming a respected teacher, and they enjoyed fixing up the house and participating in their daughters' varied activities. With two sets of grandparents close by, Rachel and Kristi reveled in having a loving multigenerational family.

When Lisa and Adam were 40 years old, Adam was seriously injured in an automobile accident. He was hospitalized for several weeks and spent 6 more weeks in a rehabilitation center. This was a very difficult time for the family. Lisa and her daughters realized how much they had depended on Adam to keep the family functioning, and Lisa worried that she was giving too much responsibility to Rachel and Kristi. She was happy to have an opportunity to talk with the rehabilitation social worker about these issues. And now, 10 years later, Lisa reports that although this was a stressful time for the family, good things came from it. Her family became much closer emotionally and she learned that she was stronger than she thought.

Adam recovered well from his accident and returned to work to find that Lisa and his daughters were not the only ones to develop new respect for him during his absence. His time away from work had also shown his boss what a valuable employee he was. He received another good promotion, which was welcomed at a time when the daughters were beginning college. Lisa was offered a vice principal position at school, but she turned it down, because she enjoyed being in the classroom—and she wanted to be free to challenge school district policies. She had become known as one of the best supervising teachers for education students from the local university.

Now, at age 50, Lisa says she has an overfull life. Last year, her father died suddenly of a heart attack, and her bereft mother has moved in with Lisa and Adam. They helped her to close the restaurant and sell the house. Lisa is growing increasingly concerned that her mother is immobilized with depression. Most afternoons when she arrives home from work, she finds that her mom is still in bed and has not eaten all day. Rachel recently became engaged and wants help with planning the wedding, and Kristi is struggling to find direction since leaving college. Adam continues to be a major support to Lisa, but he has needed to work longer hours in recent months. Lisa thinks she needs to talk with a mental health worker about her mother and how to be helpful to Kristi. Currently, she and Adam are helping Kristi pay her rent, but they are wondering if they should recommend that Kristi come home to live with them, instead.

CASE STUDY 8.3

MAHA AHMED, STRUGGLING TO FIND MEANING AND PURPOSE AT 57

Maha Ahmed, age 57, is an Arab American woman seeking psychotherapy for depression. Maha reports this is her first major episode of depression and that it started a year and a half ago, soon after her mother died. Maha feels sad most days of the week, has interrupted sleep and poor appetite, and hasn't been as interested in activities she previously enjoyed doing.

Maha was born in Palestine to a middle-class family. When she was 6 years old her family fled Palestine to Jordan when their home was demolished in the 1967 Six-Day War. Maha, her parents, grandmother, and three siblings reestablished themselves in a suburban town in Jordan where her father quickly found work as a carpenter. Maha and her siblings went to a local school and had little trouble integrating into their new environment, but they greatly missed their previous home and friends from Palestine.

Maha's parents were not as resilient. Maha's mother developed a deep depression and spent most of her time in her room in bed. Maha's grandmother tried her best to keep the household going in her daughter's emotional absence. Maha's father also struggled with significant depression and PTSD but recovered within a few years.

Despite her mother's depression, Maha felt very connected to her and made sure to always take care of her. Immediately after school Maha would greet her mother and stay in her mother's room for hours talking and doing her homework. Maha felt that she could make her mother proud by being a good student and spending time with her. When Maha's father criticized her mother for not helping out with household chores, Maha would always step in and defend her. Similarly, if Maha's siblings fought, although the youngest, Maha would be the first to intervene.

Maha was a good student and eventually went to high school and then college where she met a young man who was studying medicine. They got married and moved into a nearby home in the same neighborhood as her parents. By that time Maha's grandmother had passed away and all her siblings had moved out except her older sister who never married. Maha frequently visited her parents and spent a great deal of time there.

When Maha found out that her husband was offered a job in a prestigious hospital in New York, she was both happy for him and devastated that she would have to leave her mother. After relocating to New York, Maha had three children and became a stay-at-home mother.

Maha assimilated into American culture by learning the language and being heavily involved in her children's schools. She made several friends at her local mosque, who just like her moved to the United States during adulthood. Maha and her friends liked to exchange stories about raising children in a different culture than their native culture, political issues, and how they missed their countries of origin.

Maha took very good care of her children, her marriage, and her home and still managed to make time to spend hours on the phone with her mother every week, speaking with her and directing her sister on how to take care of her. Maha felt proud that she could juggle taking care of multiple generations of family at the same time.

Maha's depression began to develop after her second eldest daughter got married and moved away. Her eldest daughter, who is also married and has children, was always fiercely independent and distant, but Maha did not expect that her second child would decrease communication with her after she got married. As the year progressed, Maha's third child, her only son, decided to move out after finishing college and getting a job, a situation that was strange to Maha. She didn't understand why her son would move out of the house if he didn't need to. Maha thought she would be happy to see her children successful, but when she realized that they all left her to live independently she felt abandoned.

Maha's children call her once or twice a week and visit every few weeks, which she finds inadequate and very hurtful. Maha is unsure if it is her fault her children do not respect their elders (by spending time with them), if she is not understanding something about American family culture, or if her children don't love her. Maha thought that after her children got older her family would expand, but instead her children went off and created their own families.

Maha is seeking help for her depression and guidance in her family life. She doesn't know if she did something to her children for them to leave her or if this is how later adulthood is supposed to be. She is wondering if she should go back to school to focus on herself, for she has always been taking care of others. On the one hand Maha feels like she may be too old, but on the other hand she feels there is nobody left to take care of but herself.

—Najwa Awad

THE CHANGING SOCIAL CONSTRUCTION OF MIDDLE ADULTHOOD

Although their life paths have been very different, Mark Raslin, Lisa Balinski, and Maha Ahmed are all in the life course phase of middle adulthood. Not so long ago, middle adulthood was nearly an unstudied terrain. Recently, however, because of a confluence of demographic trends and research accomplishments, there has been intense interest in the middle-adult years in affluent societies. Although we still have only a hazy picture of middle adulthood, that picture is coming into better focus.

Changing Age Demographics

At the time of the 2010 national census, those in the middle-adult years constituted over one quarter of the U.S. population (Lachman, Teshale, & Agrigoroaei, 2015), and so it is not surprising that researchers have been taking a serious interest in the middle-adult phase of the life course for the past 2 decades. Beginning in the 1990s, an interdisciplinary group of researchers in North America and Europe launched several large research projects to move our understanding of middle adulthood from mythology to science (see Brim, Ryff, & Kessler, 2004; Willis & Martin, 2005). These researchers span the fields of anthropology, biology, demography, epidemiology, genetics, health care policy, medicine, neuroscience, psychology, and sociology. From a life course perspective, it is important to note that most of what we "know" about middle adulthood is based on research on the cohort known as the baby boom generation, a group born from 1946 to 1964 and spanning the ages of 54 to 72 in 2018. Therefore, it is important to remember that this cohort is the result of a large surge of births that occurred after World War II.

The current large cohort of midlife adults, the largest middle-aged cohort ever alive (Cohen, 2012), was created by 15 years of high fertility, but increasing life expectancy is another contributing factor. In 1900, the median age of the U.S. population was 22.9 and the average life expectancy at birth was 47.3 years. By 1950, the median age was 30.2 years and average life expectancy was 68.2 years, and by 2000, the median age was 35.3 and the average life expectancy was 76.8 (Arias, 2012; Hobbs & Stoops, 2002). In 2015, the estimated median age was 37.8 years (The Statistics Portal, 2017) and the estimated average life expectancy at birth was 78.8 years (Centers for Disease Control and Prevention, 2016f). These changing demographics are presented in Exhibit 8.1. These data do not mean that no one lived past what we now consider middle age in 1900. The average life expectancy in 1900 was deflated by high rates of infant mortality. Indeed, in 1900, 18% of the population of the United States was 45 years old or older. This compares with 28% in 1950 and 34% in 2000. Living past age 45 is not new, but more people are doing it. This trend has an enormous impact on our understanding of the adult life course (Wahl & Kruse, 2005).

Longevity and birth rates vary across global populations. Mass longevity and declining birth rates hold true in wealthy postindustrial societies, but in poor and newly industrializing societies, the trends are radically different. International data show a high life expectancy of 89.5 years in Monaco and a low of 50.2 years in Chad in 2016 estimates (Central Intelligence Agency, 2017). In that same year, the average life expectancy was less than 55 years in 12 countries. Social workers who work in the international arena or with immigrant families will need to develop appropriate understanding of how the life course varies across world populations.

EXHIBIT 8.1 ● Changing Life Expectancy and Median Age in the United States

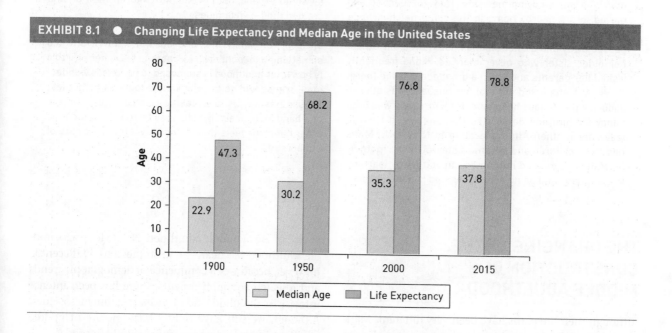

A Definition of Middle Adulthood

Before we go further, we need to pause and consider *who* is included in middle adulthood. In the most general sense, we are talking about people who are in midlife, or the central part of the life course. Beyond that, we do not have generally agreed-on ages to include in middle adulthood. The most frequently used definition of middle adulthood includes those persons ages 40 to 64, and that is the definition I use in this chapter, but some scholars use a lower limit as young as age 30 and an upper limit as late as age 70. The U.S. Census Bureau uses the ages of 45 to 64, and the Pew Research Center uses 50 to 64 (Cohen, 2012; Taylor, Morin, Parker, Cohn, & Wang, 2010). In 2009, most respondents to a Pew Research Center poll said that midlife ended at 71, but older respondents and those with more schooling reported later ages than other respondents, and men reported earlier ages than women (Taylor et al., 2010). Dittmann-Kohli (2005) suggests that middle adulthood is "a friendly expression for not being young anymore but not really very old yet" (p. 323).

Some authors argue that middle adulthood should not be thought of in terms of chronological age but instead in terms of achieving certain developmental tasks. Generally, midlife adults have established a family; settled into and peaked in a career; and taken responsibility for their children, parents, and community. Psychologist Margie Lachman (2015) suggests that midlife is best thought of in terms of roles, timing of life events, and life experiences. The life course perspective would suggest that any definition of middle adulthood must include biological aging processes, subjective perceptions, and social roles as well as historical and generational contexts.

Some authors have been critical of any approach to defining middle adulthood that includes an age range as wide as 40 to 64. They suggest that the beginning of midlife is very different from the latter part of midlife and that lumping these parts of the life course together may lead to contradictory findings. They call for a division of middle adulthood into early midlife and late midlife (Kohli & Künemund, 2005; Lachman, 2004). You may recall a similar concern about the boundaries of young adulthood noted in Chapter 7. Late adulthood, which is divided into late adulthood and very late adulthood in this book, encompasses an even larger age span, potentially from 65 to 100-plus. As longevity increases, the adult portion of life is likely to be divided into finer and finer phases.

Culture and the Construction of Middle Adulthood

With the identification of a middlehood, societies must construct roles for, and make meaning of, middle adulthood. Wahl and Kruse (2005) argue that middle adulthood was created by the increase of life expectancy in modern society. Evidence indicates, however, that middle adulthood has been incorporated into views of the life course since at least the early Middle Ages (Dittmann-Kohli, 2005). In his book *Welcome to Middle Age! (And Other Cultural Fictions)*, Richard Shweder (1998) suggests that middle age is a "cultural fiction," and the fiction does not play out the same way in all cultures. He does not use *fiction* to mean false but to mean, instead, that ideas about middle age are culturally created.

In some parts of the world today, middle adulthood is not defined as a separate stage of life, but to the extent it is recognized, it is thought of as "maturity" and seen in relation to transitions in family roles. In other cultures, aging is associated with power and creativity, and middle adulthood is seen as the "prime of life," a time of fullness, activity, and spiritual growth. In the United States, since middle adulthood was first identified as a separate life stage in the latter part of the 19th century, two cultural views of this life stage have competed. One view sees middle adulthood as a positive time of having accumulated resources for coping; the other view sees middle adulthood as a negative time of decline and loss (see Cohen, 2012; Hagerty, 2016). This latter view of decline and loss (of being "over the hill") often seems to permeate popular culture. However, much of the recent research on middle adulthood reveals an attempt to recast midlife as the "prime of life." What images come to mind when you think of middle adulthood? Do you think first of sagging chins, wrinkles, reading glasses, thinning or graying hair, hot flashes, loss of sex drive, and so on, or do you think first of emotional and spiritual maturity that gives power, creativity, and influence? What images do you think Mark Raslin, Lisa Balinski, and Maha Ahmed have of middle adulthood?

THEORIES OF MIDDLE ADULTHOOD

Few theories focus directly on middle adulthood, but a number of theories address middle adulthood as a part of a larger developmental framework. Themes from three of those theories are presented here.

Erikson's Theory of Generativity

According to Erik Erikson's (1950) life span theory, the psychosocial struggle of middle adulthood is *generativity versus stagnation* (refer to Exhibit 3.8 for an overview of Erikson's psychosocial stage theory). **Generativity** is the ability to transcend personal interests to provide care and concern for younger and older generations; it encompasses "procreation, productivity, and creativity, and thus the generation of new beings, as well as of new products and new ideas, including a kind of self-generation concerned with further identity development" (Erikson, 1982, p. 67). Generative adults provide "care, guidance, inspiration, instruction, and leadership" (McAdams, 2001, p. 395) for future generations. Failure to find a way to contribute to future generations, or to contribute to the general well-being, results in self-absorption and a sense of stagnation. Erikson saw generativity as an instinct that works to perpetuate society. As he enters middle adulthood, Mark Raslin strives to become generative. He would like to reconnect with his daughter and see if he can reestablish a relationship with his elderly parents. Lisa Balinski expresses generativity in her teaching, mentoring of student teachers, and care of her mother and adult children. Throughout middle adulthood, Maha Ahmed provided care and support to her children and her husband and long-distance emotional care of her mother. Now, as she approaches late adulthood, she has a strong desire to be an active part of her adult children's lives and is not sure how to create purpose and meaning without an active caregiving role. As a social worker, you will most likely encounter people like Maha who struggle with a sense of stagnation in middle adulthood.

Dan McAdams and Ed de St. Aubin (de St. Aubin, McAdams, & Kim, 2004; McAdams, 2006; McAdams & de St. Aubin, 1992, 1998) have expanded on the work of Erikson and presented a model of generativity that includes the seven components found in Exhibit 8.2. McAdams and de St. Aubin (1992, 1998) see generativity coming from both the person (personal desire) and the social and cultural environment (social roles and cultural demand).

Even though Erikson outlined midlife generativity in 1950, generativity was not a subject of empirical investigation until the 1980s (Peterson & Duncan, 2007). There is limited longitudinal research to answer the question of whether midlife adults are more generative than people in other life course phases. Most of the cross-sectional research on generativity reports greater generativity during middle adulthood than in young adulthood or late adulthood (An & Cooney,

EXHIBIT 8.2 ● **McAdams and de St. Aubin's Seven Components of Generativity**
1. Inner desire for immortality and to be needed
2. Cultural demand for productivity
3. Concern for the next generation
4. Belief in the species
5. Commitment
6. Action: creating, maintaining, or offering
7. Development of a generative life story

Source: Adapted from McAdams, Hart, & Maruna, 1998.

2006; McAdams, 2001; Zucker, Ostrove, & Stewart, 2002), but other researchers have found that generativity continues to grow past middle adulthood, and there is growing interest in generativity in older adults (Bates & Goodsell, 2013; Ehlman & Ligon, 2012). Researchers have also found some evidence of generative concern and motivation in late adolescence and young adulthood, while also finding that middle-aged adults have a greater sense of capacity for generativity than these younger groups (Hastings, Griesen, Hoover, Creswell, & Dlugosh, 2015; Matsuba et al., 2012).

Research also finds that generativity is associated with gender, class, and race. Several researchers (Marks, Bumpass, & Jun, 2004; McAdams & de St. Aubin, 1992; McKeering & Pakenham, 2000) have found that men who had never been fathers scored particularly low on measures of generativity, but not being a mother did not have the same effect for women. However, An and Cooney (2006) did not find parenting to be more associated with generativity for men than women but did find that midlife women are more involved in both private and public caring than midlife men. Another research project found that as generativity increases for adults ages 35 to 74, so does psychological well-being, and this association between generativity and well-being is equally strong for childless adults as for parents (Rothrauff & Cooney, 2008). Generativity has been found to increase with educational (Keyes & Ryff, 1998) and income levels (Jones & McAdams, 2013). A number of researchers have found Black adults to score higher on measures of generativity than White adults. Jones and McAdams (2013) found that African American late midlife adults reported higher levels of generativity, political and civic engagement, public service motivation, and religious engagement than White late midlife adults.

Researchers have investigated how generativity is developed and found that individuals who score high on measures of generativity in midlife report positive earlier relationships with parents, teachers, and mentors (Jones & McAdams, 2013). One research team (Hastings et al., 2015) found that serving in the mentor role increases generative concern, generative action, and generative commitment among college students. Another research team found that participating in intergenerational activities increased generativity among adults aged 60 and over (Gruenewald et al., 2016). There has been little attempt to study how high levels of generativity during midlife are related to development during late adulthood, but one recent study found that adults with high levels of generativity in midlife, even when controlling for adolescent intelligence and level of education, had stronger cognitive performance and less depression 3 to 4 decades later (Malone, Liu, Vaillant, Rentz, & Waldinger, 2016).

There are many ways to express generativity, from active parenting to political activism. Researchers have recently made a distinction between *individual, agentic, or familial generativity* that is oriented only to those with biological kinship versus *social or communal generativity* that is oriented to the community and wider world (Morselli & Passini, 2015; Rubinstein, Girling, de Medeiros, Brazda, & Hannum, 2015). The latter type of generativity is based on social inclusion and extension of social care to those groups that have been oppressed and marginalized by society (Morselli & Passini, 2015). Some researchers have been particularly interested in the links between midlife generativity and pro-environment behaviors (Wells, Taheri, Gregory-Smith, & Manika, 2016). Lisa Balinski is engaging in both family and communal generativity and sometimes feels overwhelmed with the demands of both types of generativity. Maha Ahmed engaged in high levels of family generativity throughout middle adulthood. Perhaps expanding her generative activities beyond the family could reenergize her in late midlife.

Jung's and Levinson's Theories of Finding Balance

Both Carl Jung and Daniel Levinson suggest that middle adulthood is a time when individuals attempt to find balance in their lives in several ways. Jung (1971) sees middle adulthood as a time when we discover and reclaim parts of the self that were repressed in the search for conformity in the first half of life. He emphasizes the importance of gender identity in middle adulthood. Adults are thought to begin to move from the stereotyped gender role behavior of young adulthood to a more androgynous behavioral repertoire at this age. There is some evidence to support this idea. One research team found that scales measuring femininity and masculinity were among those that revealed the most change from the ages of 43 to 52 (Helson & Wink, 1992). A study that followed a sample of third-grade Finnish children for 30 years found that boys and girls adopted traditional gender behaviors in adolescence, but by age 40, the men had become less aggressive and the women had become more assertive (Pulkkinen, Feldt, & Kokko, 2005). Longitudinal research that followed adults from their 30s to their 80s had a similar finding. Although there was great variation within gender groups in measures of masculinity and femininity at every age, the average man became significantly higher in femininity over time, and the average woman became significantly lower in femininity over time (Jones, Peskin, & Livson, 2011). A great deal of research demonstrates that androgyny (having both female and male characteristics) is associated with high self-esteem and life satisfaction in middle adulthood (Matud, Bethencourt, & Ibáñez, 2014). It is important to remember that longitudinal research, that followed the same people over a number of years, was started decades ago and may not adequately reflect the more expansive gender expectations that now exist in many places.

Jung also suggested that **extroversion**, or orientation to the external world, and **introversion**, or orientation to the internal world, come into greater balance in middle adulthood. He suggested that the challenges of establishing family and work roles demand extroversion in young adulthood, but in middle adulthood individuals tend to turn inward and explore their own subjective experience. We will see later, in the discussion of the Big Five personality traits, that research supports this idea. With the help of his social worker, Mark Raslin is beginning to show a more reflective side and to make sense of the trauma and abandonment he experienced with his parents. Lisa Balinski seems to have been tuned in to her own subjective experience when she turned down the vice principal position. Maha Ahmed is exploring her inner life of depression and its connection to both earlier life experiences and current disappointments about her family life.

Daniel Levinson (Levinson, 1986, 1990; Levinson & Levinson, 1996; Levinson et al., 1978) conceptualized the life course as a sequence of eras, each with its own biopsychosocial character (Levinson & Levinson, 1996) with major changes from one era to the next. Changes do occur within eras, but these changes are small and do not involve major revision of the life structure. Adult life is composed of alternating periods of relative stability and periods of transition. As mentioned in Chapter 7, a key concept of Levinson's theory is *life structure*, by which he means "the underlying pattern or design of a person's life at a given time" (Levinson & Levinson, 1996, p. 22). In most cases, family and occupation are the central components in the life structure, but people vary widely in how much weight they assign to each. During the transition to middle adulthood, individuals often try to give greater attention to previously neglected components. Levinson sees this transition in terms of balancing four opposing aspects of identity: young versus old, creation versus destruction, feminine versus masculine, and attachment versus separation (Levinson, 1977). Recent research has focused on how midlife adults attempt to balance the multiple roles of paid worker, parent, spouse, and caregiver of older adults (see Fischer, Zvonkovic, Juergens, Engler, & Frederick, 2015; Frisvold, Lindquist, & McAlpine, 2012; Gareis, Barnett, Ertel, & Berkman, 2009).

Life Span Theory and the Gain-Loss Balance

Life span theory has much in common with the life course perspective introduced in Chapter 1 of this book. It is more firmly rooted in psychology, however, whereas the life course perspective has more multidisciplinary roots and emphasizes the historical and cultural context of life course development. Life span theory is based in ongoing transactions between persons and environments and begins with the premise that development is lifelong. Six central propositions of life span theory as they relate to middle adulthood are summarized in Exhibit 8.3.

We focus here particularly on the proposition that midlife development is based on both gains and losses. Life span researchers have raised this question: What is the balance of gains and losses in midlife (Baltes, Lindenberger, & Staudinger, 1998)? Much attention has been paid in recent years to midlife happiness, life satisfaction, and well-being, with conflicted findings. Several economist researchers have presented data that indicate a *u-bend* in average psychological well-being over the life course (starting high, dipping over time, and then beginning an upward slope), with the low point occurring in middle adulthood (see Blanchflower & Oswald, 2008; Cheng, Powdthavee, & Oswald, 2017). They found this pattern in 92 "developed and developing nations." These studies have measured well-being by asking one question: "How satisfied are you with your life overall?" (Cheng et al., 2017, p. 130). Other researchers have found that individuals show some loss of happiness, on average, in their 40s, but in their 50s show an increase in positive emotions over a 10-year period (Lachman et al., 2015). Several life span researchers have suggested that well-being is multidimensional and not adequately measured by a one-item question. They have proposed these six dimensions of well-being: self-acceptance, positive relations with others, autonomy, environmental mastery, purpose in life, and personal growth (see Ryff & Singer, 2006). Using this broader definition of well-being, a Swiss research team found that midlife adults reported higher levels of self-acceptance, autonomy, mastery over the environment, purpose in life, and positive relations with others than

---

EXHIBIT 8.3 ● **Central Propositions of Life Span Theory as They Relate to Middle Adulthood**

- Human development is lifelong, and no age period is supreme in the developmental trajectory. Midlife cannot be studied in isolation; it must be studied in terms of both its antecedents and its consequences.

- Development involves both gains and losses.

- Biological influences on development become more negative, and cultural support becomes more important, with increasing age in adulthood. A distinction can be made between early and late midlife.

- With increasing age in adulthood, there is an overall reduction in resources. At midlife, adults must put a major effort into managing resources.

- Even though challenges increase and biological resources decrease in midlife, there is still possibility for change.

- The experience of midlife adults may depend on cultural and historical contexts.

Source: Adapted from Staudinger & Bluck, 2001, pp. 17–18.

young adults (Demiray & Bluck, 2014). And, yet, when asked what age they would most like to be, on average, midlife adults wished to be younger than their age (Lachman et al., 2015).

Psychologist Margie Lachman (2015) suggests that midlife is pivotal in the life course because it is a period at the intersection of growth and decline. It is neither the lowest point nor the highest point of life trajectories. Many physical and cognitive functions are on a downward path and the multiple roles of middle adulthood may create stress, but midlife is also a peak time for many in terms of occupational status, family leadership, sense of mastery, and self-esteem. It is important to note that gains or losses in midlife are defined and given meaning in cultural contexts and are influenced by both group-based and individual-based attributes. Patricia Cohen (2012) argues that although there are many psychological and spiritual gains in middle adulthood, in our current cultural focus on the physiological aspects of middle adulthood "a successful midlife has become equated with an imitation of youth" (p. 13).

One might wonder how Mark Raslin, Lisa Balinski, and Maha Ahmed see the gain-loss balance in their phase of middle adulthood. With professional help, Mark Raslin seems to be making gains in emotion regulation, relationships, economic security, and self-esteem. He reports that he is starting to "find myself." For Lisa Balinski, midlife so far has been a time of professional competence, economic security, and deepening relationship with her husband but also a time of the loss of her father and incapacitation of her mother. For Maha Ahmed, the early years of middle adulthood were a satisfying time of busy family relationships and long-distance parental caregiving, but she is struggling in late midlife to find a replacement for the active caregiving role that gave her such pleasure, purpose, and meaning. She appears to see more loss than gain in this life phase, but in therapy she is beginning to think about new possibilities for meaning and purpose.

As we review the research on changes in middle adulthood in the remaining sections of this chapter, it is important to note that it is hard to know whether what we are learning about midlife is tied to a specific cohort, the baby boomers. Research on middle adulthood is quite new, and there are no long-term longitudinal studies available of earlier cohorts of midlife adults. Among the factors to keep in mind as you read research results is that the baby boomers represent a very large cohort and have, throughout their adulthood, faced more competition for jobs and other resources than earlier cohorts. Also keep in mind that there are many

individual variations on the journey to midlife and beyond, and both advantage and disadvantage accumulate over time. Averages are usually reported, but those averages mask great differences related to factors such as social class; race and ethnicity; gender, gender identity, and gender expression; sexual orientation; abilities and disabilities; and life experiences.

CRITICAL THINKING QUESTIONS 8.1

What do you think is the balance of gains and losses in Mark Raslin's early phase of middle adulthood compared with his experience with young adulthood? What are the gains, and what are the losses? What about Lisa Balinski; what was the balance of gains and losses for her in the early phase of middle adulthood compared with young adulthood? What were the gains, and what were the losses? What do you see as the potential gains and losses as she enters the later phase of middle adulthood? And what about Maha Ahmed in the late phase of middle adulthood; what is the balance of gains and losses for her in this phase of life compared with earlier phases? What are the gains, and what are the losses?

BIOLOGICAL CHANGES AND PHYSICAL AND MENTAL HEALTH IN MIDDLE ADULTHOOD

There have been dramatic changes in the last few decades in the number of adults who enjoy healthy and active lives in the years from 45 to 65 and beyond. However, some physical and mental decline does begin to occur. Most biological systems reach their peak performance in the mid-20s. Age-related changes over the next 20 to 30 years are usually gradual, accumulating at different rates in different body systems. The changes are the result of interactions of biology with psychological, sociocultural, and spiritual factors, and individuals play a very active role in the aging process throughout adulthood, as we can see in the life trajectories of Mark Raslin, Lisa Balinski, and Maha Ahmed. However, by age 50, the accumulation of biological change becomes physically noticeable in most people. Amy Lodge and Debra Umberson (2013) suggest that because Western culture worships youthful bodies, we have developed an "ideology of midlife decline" (p. 225). In the chapter on adolescence, we emphasized the importance of psychological reactions to biological changes, and recent research indicates that late midlife is another period of the life course when this issue becomes important (see Lodge & Umberson, 2012; Perz & Ussher, 2008).

The biggest stories in biological functioning and physical and mental health in middle adulthood are in physical appearance, mobility, and the reproductive system; and in changes in health, more specifically the beginnings of chronic disease. There are enormous individual differences in the timing and intensity of these changes, but some changes affect almost everyone, such as *presbyopia* (inability to focus sharply for near vision) for both men and women and menopause for women. Typical changes in physical appearance and mobility during middle adulthood are summarized in Exhibit 8.4.

Changes in the Reproductive System and Sexuality

Perhaps the most often noted biological change in middle adulthood is the lost or diminished reproductive capacity. Although both men and women experience reproductive changes during adulthood, changes in women have received much more attention from researchers and the popular media than changes in men. For this reason, the following discussion begins with what is known about women's reproductive changes during middle adulthood.

In middle adulthood, women's capacity to conceive and bear children gradually declines until menopause, when the capacity for conceiving children ends (although reproductive technology to extend a woman's reproductive life may eventually become more generally available). **Menopause** is the permanent cessation of menstruation and for research purposes is usually defined as 12 consecutive months with absence of menstruation (Woods & Mitchell, 2016). The average age of women having their last period is 51 years, but it can occur in the 40s or late 50s.

Although female menopause is often described as a less gradual process than occurs in men, it is a more gradual process than often recognized. The menopause process begins when the woman is in her 30s and begins to have occasional menstrual cycles without ovulation, or the production of eggs. By the mid- to late 40s, the supply of egg cells is depleted, ovarian production of hormones slows, and more and more menstrual cycles occur without ovulation. The menstrual cycle becomes irregular, some menstrual periods are skipped, and the production of estrogen drops. In this period, known as *perimenopause*, changes in the reproductive system begin to be noticed. **Perimenopause** is defined as the period of time that begins immediately prior to menopause, when there are biological and clinical indicators that reproductive capacity is reaching exhaustion, and continues through the first year after the last menstrual period (Mayo Clinic, 2017b). Symptoms often proposed to be associated with perimenopause include hot flashes, night sweats, vaginal dryness, headaches, insomnia, fatigue, anxiety, depression, irritability, memory loss, difficulty concentrating, and weight gain.

Although perimenopause, and purported associated symptoms and discomforts, has received much

EXHIBIT 8.4 ● Changes in Physical Appearance and Mobility in Middle Adulthood		
Changes in Physical Appearance	**Changes in Mobility**	**Changes in Reproductive System & Sexuality**
Skin begins to sag and wrinkle. Brown pigmentation appears in spots exposed to sunlight. Skin becomes drier. Hair on head becomes thinner and grayer. Hair may appear in unwanted places (ears, chin). Body build changes, with height loss and weight gain (increased body fat).	Progressive loss of muscles leads to loss of strength. Progressive loss of bone mineral leads to less strong, more brittle bones. Cartilage that protects joints begins to degenerate, interfering with ease of movement.	Women: Supply of egg cells is depleted, and ovarian production of hormones slows; women gradually lose capacity to conceive children, which ends with menopause (cessation of menstruation); vaginal dryness results. Men: Testes shrink gradually; volume of seminal fluid declines; testosterone level declines; frequency and intensity of orgasm decreases; erection becomes more difficult to achieve.

attention in the popular media in recent years, intensive scientific study of the phenomenon is just beginning. This increased interest seems to come from a confluence of factors. Chief among those factors is that the current baby boom generation of women, who are now in midlife or beyond, have, as a cohort, asserted their control over their reproductive lives and challenged taboos about sexuality. Two other influential factors include epidemiological studies that identified estrogen decline in menopause as a risk factor for osteoporosis and cardiovascular disease and the development of medications for the "treatment" of menopause. To date, however, research on the connection between menopause and many of the symptoms believed to be a consequence is far from conclusive.

Decreased estrogen results in genital atrophy, including a decrease in uterus size. The blood supply to the vagina and surrounding nerves and glands is reduced. The tissues become thinner and drier and cannot produce sufficient lubrication for comfortable intercourse, and there is also increased risk of infection unless estrogen replacement or an artificial lubricant is used. The breast nipples have reduced sensitivity (Woods & Mitchell, 2016).

Menopause is big business in the United States, but perhaps not as big as it once was. Starting in the 1940s, menopause was constructed as a deficiency disease, a disease that could be treated pharmaceutically with hormone replacement therapy (HRT). The purpose of the treatment was not to prolong reproductive capacity but rather to treat the symptoms thought to be associated with menopause. The popularity of HRT has waxed and waned since the 1970s as new research, often with contradictory findings, has indicated both benefits and risks associated with its use. At the time this chapter is being written, the current state of evidence suggests that a combination of estrogen and progestin therapy has beneficial effects on osteoporosis and on such menopausal symptoms as hot flashes and vaginal dryness. It may reduce the risk of colon cancer. Unfortunately, the research also indicates that a combination of estrogen and progestin increases the risk for breast cancer, heart attack, stroke, deep vein thrombosis, and gallbladder disease. The use of estrogen without progestin increases the risk of uterine cancer (American College of Obstetricians and Gynecologists [ACOG], 2015). The current recommendation is that each woman has to weigh the benefits and risks for her individual situation. The concerns about the risks of HRT, now commonly known as menopausal hormone therapy, have led to recent efforts to find alternative, plant-derived

treatments for menopausal symptoms that will not carry the risks of HRT; this research is in the early stages (Wuttke et al., 2014).

Unlike women, men do not experience a major rapid change in fertility as they age. Changes in the male reproductive system occur mostly in the testes, with testicular tissue decreasing. There is some disagreement about how much decline occurs in the hormone testosterone in aging men, but there is agreement that the decline is gradual, no greater than 1% per year. Problems with erectile function and reduced sexual desire may develop. The tubes that carry sperm may harden and become less elastic. The quantity of viable sperm begins to decrease in the late 40s and 50s, but fairly old men have been known to father children. Although the findings are inconsistent, research has begun to show that advanced paternal age may be associated with pregnancy complications and miscarriage as well as increased incidence of disorders like autism, schizophrenia, and bipolar disorders in the offspring (Sharma et al., 2015). Although little research has been done on the topic, there has been some speculation that, in some men, the decline in testosterone is associated with low energy, muscle and bone loss, sleep disturbance, and decreases in motivation and self-confidence (Mayo Clinic Staff, 2017). This condition is called male menopause, climacteric, or *andropause*.

Just as hormone replacement for women became a lucrative business for pharmaceutical companies in the last decades of the 20th century, testosterone replacement has been an expanding business for them in the past 3 decades. David Handelsman (2015) reported a 10-fold increase in the United States and a 40-fold increase in Canada of testosterone use over 3 decades. Most of the prescribing of testosterone is done by doctors who are not complying with prevailing prescribing guidelines. You probably have noticed that a number of the suggested symptoms of testosterone deficiency are very similar to the symptoms often proposed for female menopause. The evidence for the association between these symptoms and testosterone deficiency is even sparser than the evidence for symptoms of female menopause, however. Given the still unfolding history of the benefits and risks of HRT for women, it seems wise to proceed with caution with testosterone therapy (Handelsman, 2015).

Researchers have begun to take interest in the sexual lives of midlife and older adults, but most of that research has focused on heterosexual couples. Much less is known about the sexual lives of midlife gay males and lesbians. The research indicates that age is a major predictor of diminished sexual desire, decreased sexual frequency, and decreased intensity of the sexual response, particularly after age 45 (Avis et al., 2017; Karraker, DeLamater, & Schwartz, 2011; Lodge & Umberson, 2016). Midlife men and women with partners in midlife have been found to be equally likely to be sexually active, but the frequency of sexual activity declines for women more than men over middle and late adulthood (Lindau & Gavrilova, 2010). Researchers have found, however, that the increasing proportion of women who are widowed is the major explanation for this sex difference in the research findings (Karraker et al., 2011). Both menopause in women and chronic health problems in men have been found to contribute to the decline in sexual activity in midlife. One large community-based study of middle-aged women who were sexually active tracked their sexual functioning over a 14.5-year period (Avis et al., 2017). The researchers found that the women who experienced natural menopause reported a decline in sexual functioning that began approximately 20 months before the last menstrual period. The decline had slowed somewhat but had not ceased 1 year after the last menstruation. Women who had menopause induced by hysterectomy reported a decline in sexual functioning immediately after surgery, and the decline persisted in the postsurgical period. In both women with natural menopause and women with hysterectomy-induced menopause, increased pain with intercourse and decreased sexual desire were the most often reported symptoms of the decline in sexual functioning. Important racial/ethnic differences in the experience of sexuality during the transition to menopause were noted. African American women experienced a smaller decline in sexual functioning than White women, and Japanese women experienced a larger decline. Research also indicates that both men and women report men's physical health problems as a common reason for sexual inactivity (Lindau & Gavrilova, 2010).

Midlife couples have been found to be distressed when they experience physical changes that affect their sex lives (Lodge & Umberson, 2012). One research team interviewed heterosexual men about their reactions to their female partners' menopause and found that most of the research participants talked about a trajectory of loss associated with their wives' menopause. The research participants also reported that the topic of menopause symptoms was taboo and their relationships could have benefited from better knowledge of menopause (Liao, Lunn, & Baker, 2015). In another study, in-depth interviews were conducted with both gay and heterosexual midlife men (Lodge & Umberson, 2013). These researchers found that gay midlife men were more likely than heterosexual midlife men to report concerns about how the attractiveness of their bodies would affect their sexual relationships. Both gay and heterosexual males reported concerns about whether their bodies could still perform sexual functions such as achieving and maintaining an erection.

Changes in the Brain

Currently, intense research efforts are exploring what is happening in the middle-aged brain, but information is limited as to what healthy brain functioning looks like in middle age (see Park & Festini, 2016, for a review of the available research). Some brains age better than others, resulting in much variability in middle-aged brains. The current thinking is that individual differences in the midlife brain may be predictive of brain health in old age, and it may become possible to predict brain diseases such as Alzheimer's disease (AD) many years before the disease becomes evident. There is strong evidence that gray and white matter volume declines with age and that cortical thinning occurs by middle age (see Guo et al., 2016; Shaw, Abhayaratna, Sachdev, Anstey, & Cherbuin, 2016). The biggest reductions in cortical gray matter have been found in the prefrontal cortex and hippocampus. Shrinkage has also been found in the association cortices, cerebellum, caudate, and inferior temporal cortex (Park & Festini, 2016). There is considerable variation in gray matter reduction in middle adulthood, and some individuals may not experience it at all. There is also evidence that amyloid and neurofibrillary tangles, both associated with AD, begin to accumulate in many brains in midlife (Park & Festini, 2016). Gender differences in brain structural changes have been found. Overall, women exhibit greater brain reduction than men. They also exhibit greater reduction of the outer surfaces of the brain than men whereas men exhibit greater reduction of the inner, midline surfaces of the brain than women (Guo et al., 2016).

Researchers are also finding a change in patterns of neural activity during middle age. Most notably, people in middle age begin to use both sides of their brains to solve problems for which only one side was used in the past, a process called *bilateralization* (Park & Festini, 2016). The two hemispheres of the brain become better integrated. For example, when young adults are presented with verbal material, they tend to show activation in the left hemisphere, but midlife adults presented with the same verbal material tend to show activation in both hemispheres. This type of bilateral activation occurs across many types of tasks. It is thought that the midlife brain recruits the additional hemisphere to compensate for brain shrinkage and to maintain cognitive functioning.

The available evidence indicates that both genetics and environment play a role in structural and functional changes in the midlife brain. Both the apolipoprotein E type 4 allele and the cholinergic receptor gene CHRNA have been implicated in genetic predisposition to deterioration in brain structure and function during midlife (Park & Festini, 2016). Poor vascular health, diabetes, and obesity in midlife have also been found to be factors in brain volume depletion (Haley, 2014; Ronan et al., 2016). On the other hand, greater midlife exercise has been found to predict larger total brain volume and increased gray matter in midlife, particularly in the frontal lobes (Rovio et al., 2010). Using longitudinal data of identical twins, one research team found that approximately 70% of the variance in brain volume and 45% of variance in cortical thickness was related to genetic influences (Kremen et al., 2010).

In summarizing the situation of the midlife brain, Barbara Strauch (2010) notes that "this middle-aged brain, which just as it's forgetting what it had for breakfast can still go to work and run a multinational bank or school or city . . . then return home to deal with . . . teenagers, neighbors, parents" (pp. xvi–xvii). Research indicates that starting in middle age, the brain's ability to tune out irrelevant material wanes, leading to more time in daydream mode but also greater capacity to capture "the big picture." Midlife adults can minimize the hazards of brain changes by staying engaged with the world: having a life purpose, maintaining strong relationships, engaging in physical activity, and getting adequate sleep and nutrition. Brain researchers are at work on brain training exercises to improve memory in midlife and are reporting some success (Hagerty, 2016).

Changes in Health Status

Health during middle adulthood is highly variable, but overall midlife is characterized by good health. In general, there are some positive changes: The frequency of unintentional injury decreases, as does susceptibility to colds and allergies. Conversely, although many people live through middle adulthood with little disease or disability, the frequency of chronic illness, persistent symptoms, and functional disability begins to rise in midlife. And the death rate increases continuously over the adult years. However, there has been a long-term decline in mortality rates (death rates) in the United States, and from 1970 to 2013, mortality rates for midlife adults ages 45 to 54 decreased by 44%. Similar improvements in midlife mortality were found in all rich countries but not in less affluent countries (Case & Deaton, 2015). In the United States, cancer is the leading cause of death in middle adulthood, followed by heart disease (Centers for Disease Control and Prevention [CDC], 2017i).

The National Center for Health Statistics (2017a) indicates that in 2015 there were significant gender and race/ethnicity differences in the death rates in middle adulthood, with men having higher death rates than women in Black, Asian or Pacific Islander, and White populations, and Blacks of both genders having alarmingly higher death rates than their White and Asian counterparts. Asians and Pacific Islanders had much lower death rates across middle adulthood than Whites. These racial health disparities have existed in the United States for a long time, but a much-reported analysis of morbidity and mortality in midlife indicates some recent shift in some of this pattern. Case and Deaton (2015) report an increase in the morbidity (disease) and mortality (death) rates of middle-aged White-non-Hispanic men and women in the United States from 1999 to 2013. During the same period, the mortality rate of Black non-Hispanics and Hispanics continued the earlier pattern of decline as did the morbidity and mortality rates among other age groups. The increased death rates for middle-aged non-Hispanic Whites have been attributed to drug and alcohol poisoning, suicide, and chronic liver disease. This is reflected in CDC (2017i) data (found in Exhibit 8.5) indicating that, overall in 2015, liver disease was the fourth highest cause of death among the U.S. population aged 45 to 54, and suicide was the fifth highest cause of death in this age group. Midlife Whites with the least education had the most marked increases, and, in fact, mortality rates for Whites with a college education continued to fall during the designated period. Interestingly, unlike their White contemporaries, the mortality rates for Blacks and Hispanics with low educational achievement continued to fall during this period. This pattern of increased morbidity and mortality among Whites with low educational achievement was not found in other rich countries where the mortality rates fell more rapidly for midlife adults with low education than for those with higher educations during the same period. Social analysts are currently exploring explanations for this unexpected trend, and a life course perspective would alert us to give thought to the circumstances this

EXHIBIT 8.5 ● Five Leading Causes of Death in Select Age Groups in the United States, 2015	
15–24 years	Unintentional injury
	Suicide
	Homicide
	Cancer
	Heart disease
25–34 years	Unintentional injury
	Suicide
	Homicide
	Cancer
	Heart disease
35–44 years	Unintentional Injury
	Cancer
	Heart disease
	Suicide
	Homicide
45–54 years	Cancer
	Heart disease
	Unintentional injury
	Liver disease
	Suicide
55–64 years	Cancer
	Heart disease
	Unintentional injury
	COPD
	Diabetes mellitus
65+	Heart disease
	Cancer
	COPD
	Cerebrovascular disease
	Alzheimer's disease

Source: **Based on Centers for Disease Control and Prevention, 2017i.**

COPD: chronic obstructive pulmonary disease (includes chronic bronchitis and emphysema)

The most common forms of cerebrovascular disease are cerebral thrombosis, cerebral embolism, and cerebral hemorrhage.

cohort of White midlife adults with low education have experienced at earlier phases of their life journey.

In the past century, there has been a change in the types of diseases likely to affect health across the life course in affluent countries. In the early 1900s, when life expectancy was in the mid-40s, most deaths were caused by infectious diseases, such as pneumonia, tuberculosis, and influenza (Sapolsky, 2004). With the increase in life expectancy, chronic disease plays a more important role in the great stretch of middle adulthood and beyond. People are now living long enough to experience a chronic illness: "We are now living well enough and long enough to slowly fall apart. . . . The diseases that plague us now are ones of slow accumulation of damage—heart disease, cancer, cerebrovascular disorders" (Sapolsky, 2004, p. 3).

The prevalence of chronic conditions increases with each decade from middle adulthood on. (Note: *Prevalence* measures the proportion of a population that has a disease at a point in time. *Incidence* measures the number of new cases of a disease or condition over a period of time, such as 1 year.) There is an increase in potentially fatal chronic conditions as well as nonfatal chronic conditions. The important role of chronic illness as cause of death is demonstrated in Exhibit 8.5, which reports the five leading causes of death for select age groups in the United States. Except for unintentional injury, suicide, and homicide, all the leading causes of death are chronic diseases: heart disease, cancer, liver disease, chronic obstructive pulmonary disease (COPD; includes chronic bronchitis and emphysema), cerebrovascular disease, and diabetes. With advancing age, chronic conditions replace unintentional injury, suicide, and homicide as primary causes of death.

As you can see from Exhibit 8.5, unintentional injury is the leading cause of death in the 35-to-44 age group. Lisa Balinski's husband, Adam, was lucky to recover from the serious injuries he sustained in an automobile accident at age 40. The period of his recovery and rehabilitation were a very stressful time for the family. If Adam had not had good health insurance, the costs of his rehabilitation program could have meant financial ruin for the family, and their life trajectories over the next decade might have been very different from what we read about.

It is important to note that there are some global differences in causes of death. The World Health Organization (WHO, 2017c) reports on the leading causes of death in low-income, lower-middle-income, upper-middle-income, and high-income countries. In high-income, upper-middle-income countries, and lower-middle-income countries, heart disease is the number one cause of death and stroke is number two. In low-income countries, however, lower respiratory infection (pneumonia) is the number one cause and diarrheal disease is number two. These data indicate that chronic illness is the major cause of death in high-income and middle-income countries, but infectious diseases continue to be a major challenge in less affluent nations.

Death is not the only outcome of chronic illness. As Sapolsky (2004) suggests, chronic disease often has a slow course and involves some level of disability over a number of years. WHO uses the concept of disability adjusted life year (DALY) to measure the sum of the years lost because of premature death *plus* the number of years spent in states of poor health or disability. There is much international evidence that socioeconomic position is a powerful predictor of both mortality and poor health. WHO has calculated the worldwide causes of DALYs for low-income countries, lower-middle-income countries, upper-middle-income countries, and high-income countries. The leading worldwide causes are presented in Exhibit 8.6, which also shows how these causes are distributed across countries of different income levels. It is important to note that WHO data include mental and behavioral health as well as physical health conditions, whereas health statistics in the United States do not. Therefore, WHO data are useful because they give a better picture of the impact of mental and behavioral health conditions on global health. As you can see in Exhibit 8.6, mental and behavioral disorders are listed as the sixth greatest cause of global disease burden. One group of researchers (Vigo, Thornicroft, & Atun, 2016) argues that the global burden of mental illness has been underestimated for several reasons, including the overlap between psychiatric and neurological disorders, exclusion of personality disorders, and failure to consider the contribution of severe mental illness to mortality. They estimate that the global burden of mental illness accounts for 32.4% of years lived with a disability and 13.0% of DALYs instead of the 7.2% found in Exhibit 8.6. They note that this more inclusive understanding of mental illness brings the contribution of mental illness to global disability burden about to the level of cardiovascular disease and well ahead of cancer.

EXHIBIT 8.6 ● Leading Causes of Disease Burden (DALYs) Worldwide and for Low-Income Countries, Lower-Middle-Income Countries, Upper-Middle-Income Countries, and High-Income Countries, 2011

Cause	World (%)	Low-Income Countries (% Total)	Lower-Middle-Income Countries (% Total)	Upper-Middle-Income Countries (% Total)	High-Income Countries (% Total)
Infectious and parasitic diseases	16.5	30.9	19.3	7.5	2.3
Cardiovascular disease	13.8	5.7	11.6	21.2	18.4
Injuries	10.8	9.1	10.7	12.6	10.0
Cancers	8.1	3.3	4.7	12.8	18.3
Neonatal conditions	8.4	12.9	11.3	3.8	1.1
Mental and behavioral disorders	7.2	4.2	5.8	9.6	12.1
Respiratory infections	6.3	10.0	7.8	2.0	1.8
Respiratory disease (COPD)	4.9	3.1	5.4	5.1	5.7
Musculoskeletal disease	4.0	1.9	2.7	5.4	8.6

Source: Based on Murray et al., 2012.

Mark Raslin's story demonstrates the important impact that mental health conditions can have on life trajectories, and Lisa Balinski is concerned about whether mental health issues will jeopardize the quality of her mother's late adulthood. Maha Ahmed saw both her mother and father struggle with depression after their resettlement in Jordan, but she had not struggled with depression until recently as she grieved her mother's death while also feeling that she was losing her children. It is important to note, however, that the data in Exhibit 8.6 are for all age groups and not just for middle adulthood. There is evidence that baby boomers in the United States and Europe have higher rates of depression and substance abuse than previous generations (Piazza & Charles, 2006), and this finding is supported by Case and Deaton's (2015) finding of increasing morbidity and mortality among White midlife adults with low education, due in part to increases in drug overdoses, suicide, and alcoholic-related liver mortality. A longitudinal study in the Netherlands found that mental health tends to improve across the life course, but a minority of midlife adults shows persistently high levels of depressive symptoms and loneliness across the middle-adult years (Deeg, 2005). Longitudinal research of women in the United States also found that persistent or recurrent depression is common among midlife women (Bromberger, Kravitz, Youk, Schott, & Joffe, 2016). Maha Ahmed has sought psychotherapy for her symptoms of depression in hopes that her depression will not be as persistent as her mother's. Many researchers of middle adulthood emphasize that reporting average results can mask the great variability in middle-adult trajectories. Researchers have found that "midlife is a particularly high-risk period for either delayed onset or reactivated PTSD" (Solomon & Mikulincer, 2006, p. 664). A longitudinal investigation of PTSD symptoms among combat veterans found that the symptoms decreased in the early years following combat trauma but had been reactivated in many veterans in the 20-year follow-up (Horesh, Solomon, Keinan, & Ein-Dor, 2013). It is important for social workers to recognize the possibility of delayed and reactivated PTSD in their midlife clients. This will be particularly important in the years ahead as veterans of the Iraq and Afghanistan wars become clients in every social service sector.

It appears that the multiple losses and demands involved in displacement from their Palestinian homeland played a large role in depression experienced by Maha Ahmed's parents. This is not an unusual experience for immigrants who had no control over the decision to resettle. Given Maha's current depression,

it is possible that her parents had a predisposition to depression, but certainly the traumatic resettlement would have exacerbated their mental health problems. Immigrants who endured violence and other trauma in their country of origin or during the migration process are particularly vulnerable to depression, anxiety, and PTSD (Saraga, Gholam-Rezaee, & Preisig, 2013). As Karen Aroian and Anne E. Norris (2003) note, "Depression significantly impairs immigrants' ability to adapt to the new country and has serious emotional and economic consequences for immigrants and their families" (p. 420). Aroian and Norris found high levels of depression in a sample of immigrants from the former Soviet Union; they also found that the severity and longevity of depressive symptoms were correlated with the level of immigration-related stressors. They concluded that mental health interventions with depressed immigrants should focus on relieving these stressors by focusing on such practical issues as learning English and obtaining employment as well as on emotional issues such as loss, trauma, and feeling at home in the new country.

Before we leave this discussion about changes in health in midlife, it is important to revisit the idea of cumulative disadvantage as it relates to midlife health and to go back to the earlier notation of racial health disparities in middle adulthood. Life course scholars have theorized that inequalities in midlife health status are a result of developmental opportunities and vulnerabilities at each stage of the life course (Johnson, Schoeni, & Rogowski, 2012; Shonkoff et al., 2012). They suggest two primary pathways for the effect of earlier life experiences on midlife health: (1) early adverse circumstances may fundamentally alter the body's basic physiology, with health consequences showing up later; and (2) social disadvantage at one stage leads to social disadvantage at a later stage, resulting in a cumulative physiological toll. Life course researchers have been investigating the developmental factors that contribute to racial health disparities across adulthood and have found that disparities in health between Blacks and Whites exist at all life stages and grow across the adult life course (Pais, 2014). One research team found that, on average, Black adults reach a level of health deterioration about 30 years earlier than their White counterparts (Johnson et al., 2012). They further found that three quarters of the racial differences in health over the age of 55 are explained by childhood socioeconomic conditions and young-adult family and neighborhood factors. Living in a neighborhood of concentrated poverty prior to middle adulthood significantly increases the likelihood of midlife health problems, whether or not the individual comes from an impoverished family. Another research team (Turiano, Chapman, Agrigoroaei, Infurna, & Lachman, 2014) found that perceived control over one's life reduced mortality risk among adults with low education, indicating that perception of control buffers the mortality risk associated with educational disadvantage. These kinds of research findings have great implications for social policy, not only because of equity issues but also because poor health of its population carries enormous economic costs for a society. The Turiano et al. (2014) research on perceived control may be useful to social analysts trying to understand the increasing morbidity and mortality among White midlife adults with low education in the United States (Case & Deaton, 2015).

● **CRITICAL THINKING QUESTIONS 8.2**

How does culture influence the reactions of midlife adults to the biological changes that occur in this life phase? How are the reactions to these changes affected by socioeconomic status? What images of these changes are presented in the popular media in the United States? How have your ideas about middle adulthood been influenced by the popular media?

INTELLECTUAL CHANGES IN MIDDLE ADULTHOOD

Perhaps no domain of human behavior in middle adulthood arouses more concern about the balance of gains and losses than intellectual functioning. You may have taken note of the variety of supplements and herbal remedies marketed to midlife adults with promises of maintaining mental alertness and mental acuity. Reading the earlier discussion of brain shrinkage can heighten the concern about what happens to our cognitive functioning in midlife. And yet middle-aged adults are often at the peak of their careers and filling leadership roles in several domains. Most of the recent presidents of the United States were men older than 50. Most multinational corporations are run by midlife adults.

Research on cognitive changes in middle adulthood is recent, but there is growing and clear evidence that cognitive performance remains relatively stable for the majority of midlife adults (Schaie, 2013). However, a significant subset of midlife adults shows important gains in cognitive functioning, and another significant subset shows important decline. The amount of gain and decline varies across different types of cognitive functioning. For example, one study found that depending on the specific cognitive skill, the proportion of midlife adults who were stable in performance ranged from 53% to 69%, the proportion who gained ranged from 6% to 16%, and the proportion who declined ranged from 15% to 31% (Willis & Schaie, 2005).

Researchers are finding that individual differences in intellectual performance increase throughout middle adulthood (Martin & Zimprich, 2005). These increasing variations are related to both biological and environmental factors. Several biological risk factors have been identified for cognitive decline in midlife—including hypertension, diabetes, high cholesterol, and the APOE gene (a gene that has been associated with one type of Alzheimer's disease). Adverse circumstances early in life, including low socioeconomic position during childhood, have also been found to be a risk for midlife cognitive decline (Osler, Avlund, & Mortensen, 2012). Several protective factors have also been identified, including education; work or other environments that demand complex cognitive work; control beliefs; social support; cognitive exercise, including computer use; and physical exercise (Agrigoroaei & Lachman, 2011; Lachman et al., 2010; Tun & Lachman, 2010). These findings are consistent with the increasing evidence of brain plasticity throughout the life course and suggest that cognitive decline can be slowed by engaging in activities that train the brain. The news on this front keeps getting better. Lachman and colleagues (2010) found that frequent cognitive activity, such as writing, reading, attending lectures, or playing word games, can compensate for lower education.

The Seattle Longitudinal Study (SLS) has studied intellectual changes from the early 20s to very old age by following the same individuals over time as well as drawing new samples at each test cycle. Schaie (2013) summarized the findings about changes for selected mental abilities across the life course, paying attention to gender differences. By incorporating data on new participants as the survey progressed, the researchers were also able to study generational (cohort) differences, addressing the question of whether the current baby boom midlife cohort is functioning at a higher intellectual level than their parents' generation. Schaie (2013) summarizes the findings for six mental abilities defined in Exhibit 8.7: word fluency, verbal memory, numeric facility, spatial orientation, inductive reasoning, and perceptual speed.

EXHIBIT 8.7 ● Six Mental Abilities Studied in the Seattle Longitudinal Study (SLS)

Word fluency: ability to engage in verbal recall to write and speak easily; focuses on the speed and ease with which words are used rather than on understanding of verbal concepts

Verbal memory: ability to memorize and recall language units, such as word lists

Numeric facility: ability to understand numerical relationships, to work with figures, and to solve simple quantitative problems rapidly and accurately

Spatial orientation: ability to visualize and mentally manipulate spatial configurations in two- and three-dimensional space

Inductive reasoning: ability to recognize and understand novel concepts or relationships; involves the ability to solve logical problems

Perceptual speed: ability to find figures, make comparisons, and carry out simple tasks involving visual perception with speed and accuracy

Source: Schaie, 2013.

Research from the SLS (Schaie, 2013) shows that these six intellectual abilities peak at different points in the average human life course. On average, perceptual ability peaks in the 20s; numeric facility peaks in the late 30s; inductive reasoning and spatial orientation peak in the 50s; and word fluency and verbal memory peak in the 60s. Even by the late 80s, word fluency and inductive reasoning show only modest declines. In the United States, speed is highly valued, and quick thinking is typically seen as an indication of high intelligence. In many non-Western countries, perceptual speed is not so highly valued (Gardiner, 2018). On the other hand, word fluency and inductive reasoning are highly valued in the wealthy information societies.

Willis and Schaie (2005, 2006) found gender differences in the changes in intellectual abilities during middle adulthood. On average, men were found to reach peak performance somewhat earlier than women, except for perceptual speed for which, on average, women begin to decline somewhat earlier than men.

Schaie (2013) also reports cohort differences in selected intellectual abilities. The trend is for recent cohorts to score higher in midlife than previous cohorts scored during midlife on three of the abilities: verbal memory, spatial orientation, and inductive reasoning. The peak performance on numeric facility occurred in the cohort born in 1924 and declined thereafter.

The SLS found that some individuals begin to decline intellectually in their 40s, whereas other individuals maintain high levels of intellectual functioning into very advanced age (Schaie, 2013). The researchers also found that virtually no person declines on all six abilities even after age 88. The research suggests several factors that influence the rate of intellectual decline across adulthood, including genetics; chronic diseases such as cardiovascular disease, diabetes, cancer, and arthritis; the quality of health care across the life course; engagement in high-risk behaviors; socioeconomic status; educational level; working in occupations that provide complex and intellectually stimulating environments; family functioning; and personality style.

Longitudinal research in Germany explored cognitive change during middle adulthood but used a different classification of dimensions of cognition than used in the SLS. Zimprich and Mascherek (2010) studied four dimensions of cognition: fluid intelligence (the ability to think quickly and think abstractly), crystallized intelligence (the ability to use knowledge from accumulated learning), processing speed, and memory. They found that over a 12-year period in middle adulthood, research participants showed significant declines in fluid intelligence, processing speed, and memory. In contrast, they showed gains in crystallized intelligence. Life span theorists suggest that the gains in crystallized intelligence coupled with a brain that adapts to midlife changes by using both hemispheres to perform intellectual tasks makes midlife the best phase of life for intellectual functioning (Lachman et al., 2015).

PERSONALITY CHANGES IN MIDDLE ADULTHOOD

Does it appear to you that Mark Raslin, Lisa Balinski, and Maha Ahmed have grown "more like themselves" over their life course trajectories, or do you see changes in their personalities as they travel the life course? Little attention has been paid to the issue of personality in middle adulthood until quite recently. The literature that does exist on the topic consists largely of an argument about whether personality is stable or dynamic during middle adulthood. Dan McAdams and Bradley Olson (2010) suggest that the theoretical attempts to address that question can be divided into three main categories, which I am calling the trait approach, the human agency approach, and the life narrative approach. The confluence of research based on these approaches indicates that middle adulthood is a time of both continuity and change.

Trait Approach

According to the **trait approach**, personality traits are enduring characteristics rooted in early temperament and influenced by genetic and organic factors. (An opposing view is the *state approach* that assumes that personality changes over time.) A large and growing international research literature focuses on the degree to which individuals exhibit five broad personality traits, often referred to as the Big Five personality traits: neuroticism, extroversion, conscientiousness, agreeableness, and openness to experience (Hampson & Goldberg, 2006; Lucas & Donnellan, 2011; Pulkkinen, Kokko, & Rantanen, 2012). See Exhibit 8.8 for descriptions of these traits.

Research on the Big Five personality traits suggests long-term stability in terms of the ranking of the traits for a given individual. For example, a person who is high in agreeableness at one point in adulthood will continue to be high in agreeableness across the life course (Lucas & Donnellan, 2011). However, recent research suggests that there may be some gender differences in the stability of trait ranking, with men showing more consistency than women (Pulkkinen et al., 2012) and some traits (extroversion and conscientiousness) showing more consistency than others (Hampson & Goldberg, 2006). Studies of identical and fraternal twins suggest that adult personality traits have a large genetic base, with about a 50% heritability quotient (McAdams & Olson, 2010). That, of course, leaves a great deal of room for environmental influences, but scholars who favor the idea that personality is stable across adulthood argue that people with particular personality traits choose environments that reinforce those traits.

Another way to look at the question of stability or change in personality traits in adulthood is to look at mean levels of particular traits at different points in the adult life course. A number of both cross-sectional and longitudinal studies have done this and found that mean levels of extroversion (activity and thrill seeking) and openness to experience decline with age starting in middle adulthood. Conversely, the mean level of agreeableness has been found to increase with age, and mean levels of conscientiousness and emotional stability have been found to peak in middle adulthood (see Lucas & Donnellan, 2011). What's more, these patterns of age-related changes in personality have been found in cross-cultural research that included samples from Croatia, Germany, Italy, Portugal, South Korea, and the United States (Gardiner, 2018). These findings suggest that some personality change does occur in middle adulthood, but McAdams and Olson (2010) note that studies of mean changes are unable to tell the more complex story of middle-adult personality. Some people change more than others and sometimes in ways that are not consistent with overall trends. Social workers should be aware of overall trends but pay close attention to the specific story lines of unique individuals.

Some researchers have found gender differences in personality traits to be greater than age-related differences (Lachman & Bertrand, 2001). Women score higher than men in agreeableness, conscientiousness, extroversion, and neuroticism. Men, conversely, score higher than women on openness to experience (Lehmann, Denissen, Allemand, & Parke, 2013). These gender differences in personality have been found in 26 cultures, but the magnitude of differences varied across cultures. The researchers were surprised to find that the biggest gender differences occurred in European and North American cultures, where traditional gender roles are less pronounced than in many other countries (Costa, Terracciano, & McCrae, 2001).

Human Agency Approach

Other personality psychologists, consistent with life course scholars, have recently placed human agency at the center of adult personality development, focusing on how human agency facilitates change in midlife personality (McAdams & Pals, 2006). They are interested in motives, goals, plans, strategies, values, schemas, and choices and see these as important forces in adult personality. They recognize the ways that culture influences motives, goals, and the like (McAdams & Olson, 2010). Researchers in this vein of thought have found that middle-aged adults, on average, focus their goals on the future of their children and on prosocial societal engagement (Freund & Riediger, 2006). This appears to be true for both Lisa Balinski and Maha Ahmed. You

---

EXHIBIT 8.8 ● The Big Five Personality Traits

- *Neuroticism*: tendency to be moody, anxious, hostile, self-conscious, and vulnerable

- *Extroversion*: tendency to be energetic, outgoing, friendly, lively, talkative, and active

- *Conscientiousness*: tendency to be organized, reliable, responsible, hardworking, persistent, and careful

- *Agreeableness*: tendency to be cooperative, generous, cheerful, warm, caring, trusting, and gentle

- *Openness to experience*: tendency to be curious, imaginative, creative, intelligent, adventurous, and nonconforming

probably recognize that this is the essence of generativity as presented by Erikson (1950). Researchers have also found that whereas young adults set goals to expand the self and change the environment to fit their goals, midlife adults are more likely to set goals that involve changing the self to adjust to the environment (Wrosch, Heckhausen, & Lachman, 2006).

The concept of human agency is consistent with humanistic models of personality that see middle adulthood as an opportunity for continued growth. It is also consistent with the work of neo-Freudians like Carl Jung, Erik Erikson, and George Vaillant who propose that middle adulthood is a time when the personality ripens and matures. Jung conceptualizes middle adulthood as a time of balance in the personality. Although Erikson sees early life as important, he suggests that societal and cultural influences call for different personal adaptations over the life course. Vaillant (1977, 2002, 2012) suggests that with age and experience, **coping mechanisms**, or the strategies we use to master the demands of life, mature. He divides coping mechanisms into *immature mechanisms* (denial, projection, passive aggression, dissociation, acting out, and fantasy) and *mature mechanisms* (sublimation, humor, altruism, and suppression). He proposes that as we age across adulthood, we make more use of mature coping mechanisms such as altruism, sublimation, and humor and less use of immature coping mechanisms such as denial and projection. Definitions for both the immature and mature coping mechanisms are found in Exhibit 8.9. One research team found evidence of personality growth throughout middle adulthood, with slow and steady favorable resolution of earlier life tasks (suggested by Erikson) of industry, identity, and intimacy, suggesting that work on these tasks continues into middle adulthood (Whitbourne, Sneed, & Sayer, 2009). They also found that midlife change regarding these life tasks was influenced by life history, a finding consistent with the life narrative approach.

Life Narrative Approach

Beginning in the 1980s, personality psychologists began to develop new theories of personality development that conceptualize the developing person as a storyteller who puts together characters, plots, and themes to develop an evolving story of the self, a **life narrative approach** (McAdams, 1985, 2006; McLean, Pasupathi, & Pals, 2007). These stories may include high points, low points, turning points, and intersecting plot lines.

EXHIBIT 8.9 ● Coping Mechanisms

Immature Coping Mechanisms

Acting out. Ideas and feelings are acted on impulsively rather than reflectively.

Denial. Awareness of painful aspects of reality are avoided by negating sensory information about them.

Dissociation. Painful emotions are handled by compartmentalizing perceptions and memories and detaching from the full impact.

Fantasy. Real human relationships are replaced with imaginary friends.

Passive-aggression. Anger toward others is turned inward against the self through passivity, failure, procrastination, or masochism.

Projection. Unacknowledged feelings are attributed to others.

Mature Coping Mechanisms

Altruism. Pleasure is attained by giving pleasure to others.

Mature humor. An emotion or thought is expressed through comedy, allowing a painful situation to be faced without individual pain or social discomfort.

Sublimation. An unacceptable impulse or unattainable aim is transformed into a more acceptable or attainable aim.

Suppression. Attention to a desire or impulse is postponed.

Source: Vaillant, 1977, 2002, 2012.

McAdams and Olson (2010) suggest that in modern societies, people begin to put together their life narratives, which can be thought of as narrative identities, in adolescence or young adulthood. They suggest that in the construction of the life narrative, adults draw on stories from childhood, stories rooted in culture. Maha Ahmed's story of midlife family relationships is strongly rooted in her Arab culture. Mark Raslin is coming to terms with early neglect and trauma as he composes a life story in the transition to middle adulthood.

In contrast to the trait approach, which has received considerable longitudinal research attention, there has been little longitudinal research to explore the changes in life narratives across adulthood. Cross-sectional research has suggested that midlife adults construct more complex and coherent life narratives than adolescents and young adults (Baddeley & Singer, 2007), with increased tendency to draw summary conclusions about the self from the narrative (McLean et al., 2007). One research team found that the life narratives of midlife adults older than age 50 used more positive and fewer negative emotional words than the life narratives of college students (Singer, Rexhaj, & Baddeley, 2007). McAdams and Olson (2010) note that culture provides the menu of stories from which individuals choose to develop their own life narratives. They further note that identity choices are shaped by the confluence of social locations—gender, race, ethnicity, social class, geographical location, and so on—in which a person exists.

Although there is evidence that midlife adults often engage in review and reappraisal, there is general agreement that midlife crisis is not common. Data from the Midlife in the United States (MIDUS) longitudinal study indicate that 10% to 20% of adults do have a crisis in midlife (Lachman et al., 2015). A study in the United Kingdom found that 40% to 60% of adults reported a life appraisal crisis during adulthood, but about the same number said they experienced such crises in young adulthood as reported experiencing them in midlife (Robinson & Wright, 2013). One research team found that turning points are most likely to occur in young adulthood (Wethington, Kessler, & Pixley, 2004), but another research team found that when older adults were asked to identify turning points in their lives, there was some clustering of situations in middle adulthood (Cappeliez et al., 2008).

Erikson suggested that the life task to be resolved in middle adulthood is generativity versus stagnation. Research on life narratives shows much diversity in midlife narrative identities. For many midlife adults, life narratives are full of themes of agency, relationships, generativity, and personal growth, of forgiveness and overcoming obstacles. For others, depression, depletion, stagnation, and life gone bad are the content of the life narrative (McAdams & Olson, 2010). One research team examined the effect of major stressful life events on personality development in middle adulthood (Sustin, Costa, Wethington, & Eaton, 2010). They found that sometimes, major stressful events are viewed as lessons learned, and other times they are viewed as negative turning points. The interpretation of the event is what determines the impact on personality traits, if any. When the person sees the stressful event as a point when life changed direction for the worse, neuroticism increases. If, however, the person sees the stressful event as a life lesson, there is an increase in both extroversion and conscientiousness. Positive turning points, on the other hand, are not associated with change in personality traits.

Let's consider the situations of Mark Raslin, Lisa Balinski, and Maha Ahmed. Mark reports that he had a significant turning point when he met Rachel. This was a positive turning point that had a stabilizing impact on his life for 5 years. Unfortunately, being a victim of robbery was a negative turning point that interrupted the period of stability. Mark's work with a social worker to get approval for social security disability benefits has been another positive turning point that provided him with much-needed economic security. With the help of mental health professionals and psychotropic medications, Mark appears to be developing more positive themes for his life narrative, and he has shown less neuroticism and growth in conscientiousness in recent years. Lisa Balinski talks of Adam's automobile accident as a time of great family stress, but, 10 years later, she speaks about it as a positive turning point in family cohesion and a time of personal growth when she recognized some of her own strengths. Maha Ahmed had high levels of conscientiousness even as a child and seems to have a life narrative of being a sensitive caregiver. Her mother's death intersecting with her young-adult children leaving home has left her adrift, and she appears to be beginning to develop a new life narrative that embraces a fuller set of assets and skills. The therapist can play a role in helping her to expand her narrative in such a way so as to embrace the next phase of life.

SPIRITUAL DEVELOPMENT IN MIDDLE ADULTHOOD

Institutional religion has been a source of social belonging and support for Maha Ahmed. Mark Raslin has

PHOTO 8.1 Religion and spiritual connectedness often play a major role in the lives of midlife adults.

© Lynn Johnson/National Geographic Society/Corbis

joined a church band as he expands his social network and is motivated to pick up an old love of music. The major world religions associate spiritual growth with advancing age (see McCullough, Enders, Brion, & Jain, 2005; Wink & Dillon, 2002). And yet the burgeoning literature on middle adulthood pays little attention to the issue of spiritual development. The primary effort has been with models of spiritual development proposing that humans have the potential for continuous spiritual growth across the life course.

For example, James Fowler's theory of faith development (1981) proposes six stages of faith. The first two stages occur primarily in childhood. These are the four stages that can occur in adulthood:

1. *Synthetic-conventional faith.* The basic worldview of this faith stage is that spiritual authority is found outside the individual. In this faith stage, the individual relies on a pastor or rabbi or other spiritual leader to define morality. Many people remain in this faith stage throughout their lives and never progress to the other stages.

2. *Individuative-reflective faith.* The adult no longer relies on outside authority and begins to look for authority within the self, based on moral reasoning. The individual also takes responsibility for examining the assumptions of his or her faith.

3. *Conjunctive faith.* In this stage, the individual looks for balance in such polarities as independence and connection, recognizes that there are many truths, and opens out beyond the self in service to others. Fowler proposes that many people never reach the stage of **conjunctive faith**, and if they do, they almost never reach it before middle adulthood.

4. *Universalizing faith.* In Fowler's final stage, **universalizing faith**, individuals lead selfless lives based on principles of absolute love and justice. Fowler notes that only rare individuals reach this stage.

Fowler's theory has received support in cross-sectional research but has not been put to the test in longitudinal research. Therefore, it should be applied with caution, recognizing that it may reflect the influences of culture and historical time on faith development.

Fowler's description of conjunctive faith overlaps with theories of middle adulthood previously discussed in this chapter. For example, the reference to balance calls to mind the theories of Jung and Levinson, who saw middle adulthood as a time of bringing balance to personality and life structure. In addition, the idea of opening oneself in service to others is consistent with Erikson's idea of generativity as the psychosocial struggle of middle adulthood. The emphasis is on spirituality as a state of "being connected." Using data from a national survey of midlife adults in the United States, one researcher has found a strong correlation between regular participation in religious activities and community volunteer service, particularly in terms of making financial contributions to community organizations and charities (Rossi, 2004).

Actually, there are two models of spiritual development in adulthood (Wink & Dillon, 2002). Fowler's theory can be called a growth model, an approach that sees spiritual growth as a positive outcome of a maturation process. The other model sees increased spirituality across the adult life course as an outcome of adversity (Wink and Dillon call it an adversity model) rather than as a natural maturation process; in this view spirituality becomes a way to cope with losses, disappointments, and difficulties. One rare longitudinal study of spiritual development across the adult life course found evidence for both models (Wink & Dillon, 2002). The researchers found a strong tendency for increased spirituality beginning in late middle adulthood, something that occurred among all research participants but was more pronounced among women than men. They also found that experiencing negative life events in early adulthood was associated with higher levels of spirituality in middle and late adulthood. Maha Ahmed's therapist might want to explore with Maha what she sees as the trajectory of her spiritual development, particularly as it relates to the current symptoms of depression.

Although Fowler's conceptualization of faith included both religious faith as well as the more personal, non-religiously based search for purpose and meaning, commonly referred to as spirituality, most of the research on faith development across the life course has focused on the concept of religiousness or religiosity. This research suggests that for most people, religiousness is quite stable across the life course, meaning that people who are highly religious relative to their peers at any given point in time are likely to be more highly religious than their peers at any other point in time (McCullough et al., 2005; Roberts & Yamane, 2016). Much of the existing longitudinal research indicates that, on average, adults in the United States become more religious over time, but for most people religiosity is not a straight line but is punctuated by temporary increases or reductions related to life events and transitions (McCullough et al., 2005; Roberts & Yamane, 2016).

Some research suggests that it may be even more complex than this. Using longitudinal data over a 60-year time span for two cohorts, one born in the early 1920s and the other born in the late 1920s, Dillon and Wink (2007) found a U-curve of religiousness over the life course. Religiousness was high in adolescence and late adulthood but, on average, lower in middle adulthood. Another research team used longitudinal data from the Terman study, begun in 1921, of highly intelligent children and adolescents (McCullough et al., 2005). These researchers found three distinct trajectories of religious development during adulthood. A first group, making up 40% of the sample, entered adulthood as slightly religious but became more religious throughout midlife and declined in religiousness after that. A second group, 41% of the sample, had low levels of religiousness in young adulthood and became less religious over time. A third group, 19% of the sample, entered adulthood with relatively high levels of religiousness that increased throughout adulthood. The researchers note that their sample was less religious than the U.S. general population, and representative samples look more like the third group.

The two longitudinal studies noted in the previous paragraph indicate both cohort and other group-based differences in religiousness in middle adulthood. In the report of their findings, McCullough and colleagues (2005) note that the trend toward increasing religiousness across the life course is more pronounced in Japan than in the United States but does not show up at all in research on adults in the Netherlands. The Dillon and Wink (2007) study found that although both cohorts in their study showed a U-curve pattern in religiousness, the decline in religiousness began in the younger cohort while they were in their 30s, but the decline in the older cohort did not begin until the late 40s. They suggest that the different ages of these two cohorts during the Great Depression and World War II may have been an influential factor in this difference.

Wade Clark Roof (1993) has been interested in the question of cohort effects on spiritual journeys. His book *A Generation of Seekers* reported on the "spiritual journeys of the baby boom generation" in the United States. Drawing on survey data and interview responses, Roof suggested that the baby boom generation was "changing America's spiritual landscape" (p. 50). He reported that most baby boomers grew up in religious households, but 58% of his sample dropped their relationship with religious institutions for at least 2 years during their adolescence or young adulthood. Roof acknowledged that earlier generations had also dropped out of religion during early adulthood, but not in the numbers found in his sample of baby boomers. He suggests that the turmoil of the 1960s and 1970s, with a youth culture that questioned authority, was probably largely responsible for the high rate of dropout among baby boomers. Roof found that about one fourth of his sample that had dropped out had returned to religious activities by the end of the 1980s. For many of them, their return seemed to be related to having children at home. Roof found that religious affiliation and activity did not tell the whole story about the spiritual lives of baby boomers, however. Regardless of religious affiliation, baby boomers were involved in an intense search for personal meaning (Roof, 1993). But for many of Roof's sample, the current spiritual journey was a very personal, introspective quest—one that embraced a wide range of nontraditional as well as traditional beliefs.

In a follow-up study with the same sample from 1995 to 1997, Roof (1999) found that many boomers had shifted in their religious affiliation again. More than half of the earlier dropouts who had returned to religious activities by the late 1980s had dropped out again. But, conversely, one half of those who had dropped out in the 1980s had returned to religious activities by the mid-1990s. Presence of children in the home again seemed to be the factor that motivated a return to religion.

Roof suggested that the baby boomers are leading a shift in U.S. religious life away from an unquestioning belief to a questioning approach and toward a belief that no single religious institution has a monopoly on truth. That shift is certainly not total, however. Roof identifies five types of contemporary believers from his sample: 33% are born-again or evangelical Christians, 25% are old-line mainstream believers, 15% are dogmatists who see one truth in the doctrine and form of their religious tradition, 15% are metaphysical seekers, and 12% are nonreligious secularists. Thus, almost three quarters of his sample could be classified as more or less unquestioning adherents of a particular system of beliefs but with an increasing trend toward recognition of the legitimacy of multiple spiritual paths. It is important to note that religion plays a much more central role in the lives of adults in the United States than it does in European countries. Just over half (53%) of the U.S. population report that religion is very important in their life, almost double the percentage reporting the same in Poland, the country showing the highest score for religiosity in the European Union. In general, wealthier countries report lower religiosity than poorer countries, but the United States is the exception to this pattern (Wike, 2016).

Unfortunately, Roof does not analyze racial and ethnic differences in religious and spiritual expression for his baby boom sample. Others have found evidence, however, that Black and Hispanic midlife adults have higher levels of religiousness than White midlife adults (Fitchett et al., 2007). Black and Hispanic baby boomers have been much more constant in their religious beliefs and participation than White baby boomers and are far more likely to consider religion very important in their lives.

CRITICAL THINKING QUESTIONS 8.3

What were your reactions to reading the research about intellectual changes in middle adulthood? What, if anything, surprised you about the findings? Do you think of personality as more stable or more dynamic in middle adulthood? What factors contribute to personality stability in midlife? What factors contribute to personality change in midlife? Do you agree with Roof's research conclusions that baby boom midlife adults have led a shift in U.S. religious life away from an unquestioning belief to a questioning approach? Explain your answer.

RELATIONSHIPS IN MIDDLE ADULTHOOD

Social relationships play a major role in life satisfaction and physical well-being across the life course. In contemporary life, both women and men fulfill multiple social roles in midlife. The most central roles are related to family and paid work. Relationships with family, friends, and coworkers are an important part of life in middle adulthood, and some scholars argue that the current generation of midlife adults are experiencing unprecedented complexity in their configurations of relationships (Blieszner & Roberto, 2006). The life course perspective reminds us that relationships in middle adulthood have been shaped by relationships in earlier life phases, in the attachment process in infancy as well as in family and peer relationships in childhood, adolescence, and young adulthood. Although current relationships are shaped by our experiences with earlier relationships, longitudinal research indicates that it is never too late to develop new relationships that can become turning points in the life course (Vaillant, 2012; Werner & Smith, 2001).

Numerous studies have examined how social networks change over the life course. Researchers have been interested in different types of social networks and have used the term **global network** to indicate all existing social relationships that a person has with such people as family members, spouses and romantic partners, friends, coworkers, neighbors, religious congregations, and so forth. The **personal network** is a subnetwork of the closest relationships. Most of us are involved in other subnetworks, such as friendship networks, family networks, and work-related networks. Researchers have been interested in the changing size of social networks and the changing nature of specific subnetworks (Wrzus, Hänel, Wagner, & Neyer, 2013).

Two main theories have been used to think about how social networks change over the life course: socioemotional selectivity theory and social convoy theory. **Socioemotional selectivity theory** (SST) proposes that social goals change over the life course based on shifts in perspectives about how much time one has left to live, and changes in social goals result in changes in social networks (Carstensen, 1995). More specifically, this theory suggests that during adolescence and young adulthood, when life left to live seems unlimited, people focus on gathering information and resources from a large network of diverse relationships. Beginning with midlife, when life ahead begins to seem increasingly limited, people focus more on the emotional aspects of relationships and the social network decreases in size as peripheral relationships decrease but close relationships do not. **Social convoy theory** suggests that we each travel through life with a *convoy*, or a network of social relationships that protect, defend, aid, and socialize us (Antonucci, Ajrouch, & Birditt, 2014; Antonucci & Akiyama, 1987, 1997; Antonucci, Akiyama, & Takahashi, 2004). Relationships in the convoy differ in level of closeness and are affected in different ways across the life course. The closest relationships are expected to be stable over time, but the more peripheral relationships are assumed to be less stable and prone to drop away over time with changing circumstances. Social convoy theory acknowledges that the convoy can have damaging effects on individuals, contributing more stress than support and creating problems rather than solving them.

Cornelia Wrzus and colleagues (2013) suggest that, even though they propose different reasons for the changes, both socioemotional selectivity theory and social convoy theory indicate that the global network becomes smaller across adulthood, with a continuous decrease in peripheral relationships while close relationships with family and close friends remain. They conducted a meta-analysis of 277 studies, which included both Western and non-Western samples, of age-related changes in social networks to test these ideas. Both cross-sectional and longitudinal studies found that the global network size increased during adolescence and emerging adulthood, plateaued in the mid-20s and early 30s, and continuously decreased after that. The size of personal and friendship networks decreased across adulthood. The size of family networks was highly consistent across adulthood, however. In middle adulthood, new relationships are often added to the family network, with adult children marrying and having children of their own, but there are also losses of parents and other older relatives. The meta-analysis also revealed that personal and friendship networks were significantly smaller in more recent studies. It also indicated that there were no significant differences in family network size between countries with collectivist values and those with more individualistic values. The global and personal networks were larger, however, in more individualistically oriented countries. It is important to note that studies from non-Western countries were scarce in the database used for the meta-analysis.

Some research has found racial and ethnic differences as well as social class differences in reported convoys in the United States. Whites have been found to have larger convoys than African Americans, and the convoys of African American adults as well as adults with low incomes have a higher proportion of kin in them than the convoys of higher-income White adults (Ajrouch, Antonucci, & Janevic, 2001; Antonucci, Akiyama, & Merline, 2001; Montague, Magai, Consedine, & Gillespie, 2003). A study conducted in Taiwan suggests that in our very mobile times, when younger generations leave home to follow jobs in global cities, some people may have only one or two circles in their convoys, instead of the three proposed by social convoy theory (Chen, 2006). Certainly, it is important to understand the very dynamic nature of convoys in the lives of many people in a globalized world.

Most of the other research on midlife adult relationships is based on the premise that the marital or partner relationship is the focal relationship in middle adulthood. Consequently, too little is known about other familial and nonfamilial relationships. Recently, however, gerontologists have suggested that a variety of relationships are important to adults in late adulthood, and this hypothesis has led to preliminary investigations of a variety of relationships in middle adulthood. In the following sections, we look first at multigenerational family relationships and then review the limited research on friendship.

Middle Adulthood in the Context of the Multigenerational Family

The life circumstances of midlife adults are very much influenced by the number of living generations in the family. In 1990, Bengtson, Rosenthal, and Burton proposed that increased longevity was leading to an increase in the number of generations in the family, with fewer people in each generation, leading to what has been described as a beanpole-shaped family, tall and thin (Putney & Bengtson, 2003). Four- and even 5-generation families were expected to become the norm. This raised concern about the possibility that midlife adults would become stressed by the need to simultaneously provide care to both the oldest and the youngest family generations, a situation sometimes called "both-end carers" (Lundholm & Malmberg, 2009).

Other researchers argue that the trend toward greater longevity must be placed alongside two other trends, low fertility and delayed childbearing, when considering the generational structure of contemporary families. They suggest that these latter two trends may cancel out the effect of increased longevity. Matthews and Sun (2006) used data from two waves of the National Survey of

Families and Household to investigate what percentage of U.S. families included 4 or more generations. They found that in the early 1990s the majority of their adult respondents, who were age 22 or older, reported 3-generation families, with 32% reporting at least 4-generation families. Adults ages 51 to 61 were slightly more likely than other adults to report at least 4-generation families (37%). They also found social class and racial differences in the likelihood of living in 4-generation families. As socioeconomic status increased, the likelihood of a 4-generation family decreased, and Blacks were more likely than Whites to live in 4-generation families. Matthews and Sun conclude that the timing of childbearing is playing a bigger role than longevity in the generational structure of families. Adults with higher levels of education and income begin childbearing at a later age than their peers with less education and income.

Lundholm and Malmberg (2009) used data from the Swedish registry to investigate what percentage

PHOTO 8.2 Research finds a lot of intergenerational solidarity in contemporary families.

of 55-year-old Swedish residents lived in families of 4 generations in 1990 and in 2005. They found a large decrease from 1990 to 2005 in 55-year-olds who had grandchildren, from 70% to 35%. They also found that the percentage of 55-year-olds who had living parents increased from 37% to 47% from 1990 to 2005, an increase not nearly as dramatic as the decrease in the percentage having grandchildren. They further found that after the year 2000, the percentage of 55-year-olds who became grandparents while their own parents were still alive decreased from 28% to 18%. Lundholm and Malmberg (2009) conclude that in Sweden demographic trends are not resulting in more midlife adults becoming both-end carers. They found, however, that after 1996, 4-generation families became more common for adults with less education, similar to Matthews and Sun's findings with a U.S. sample. Other researchers have noted, however, that many midlife adults are still providing simultaneous care to aging parents and their emerging adult offspring who are making a slow transition to adulthood because of the dual challenges of economic downturns and increasing demand for prolonged education. This is the situation for Lisa Balinski and was recently the situation for Maha Ahmed.

There is much popular speculation that family ties are weakening as geographic mobility increases. Research suggests, however, more intergenerational solidarity than we may think (Kohli & Künemund, 2005; Wrzus et al., 2013). Certainly, we see much intergenerational solidarity in the families of Lisa Balinski, and Maha Ahmed. Using a national representative sample in the United States, Putney and Bengtson (2003) identified five types of extended family relationships. About one quarter (25.5%) of the families were classified as *tightly knit*, and another quarter (25.5%) were classified as *sociable*, meaning that family members are engaged with each other but do not provide for, and receive concrete assistance from, each other. The remaining families were about evenly split among the *intimate-but-distant* (16%); *obligatory*, or those who have contact but no emotional closeness or shared belief system (16%); and *detached* (17%) classifications. It is important to note that no one type of extended family relationship was found to be dominant, suggesting much diversity in intergenerational relationships in the United States. Ethnicity is one source of that variation. For example, Black and Hispanic families report stronger maternal attachments than are reported in White families, and they are also more likely to reside in multigenerational households. One researcher has also found much diversity in intergenerational relationships in Taiwan (Chen, 2006).

Despite the evidence that intergenerational family relationships are alive and well, there is also evidence that many family relationships include some degree of conflict. One longitudinal study concluded that about 1 in 8 adult intergenerational relationships can be described as "long-term lousy relationships" (Bengtson, 1996). Although Mark Raslin would like to improve his relationships with his daughter and his parents, he probably would agree that his relationships with his parents are "long-term lousy relationships."

Whether or not midlife adults become both-end carers, several researchers (see, e.g., Sotirin & Ellingson, 2006) have found that they are the kinkeepers in multigenerational families and that this holds true across cultures. **Kinkeepers** are family members who work at keeping family members across the generations in touch with one another and who make sure that both emotional and practical needs of family members are met. Historically, when nuclear families were larger, kinkeepers played an important role in working to maintain ties among large sibling groups. With increased longevity and multiple generations of families, kinkeepers play an important role in the multigenerational family, working to maintain ties across the generations, ties among grandparents, parents, children, grandchildren, siblings, aunts, uncles, nieces, nephews, and cousins.

Researchers have found that most kinkeepers are middle-aged women (Sotirin & Ellingson, 2006). Women help larger numbers of kin than men and spend 3 times as many hours helping kin. Because of this kinkeeping role, midlife women have been described as the "sandwich generation." This term was originally used to suggest that midlife women are simultaneously caring for their own children as well as their parents. Research suggests that with demographic changes, few women still have children at home when they begin to care for parents, but midlife women continue to be "sandwiched" with competing demands of paid work roles and intergenerational kinkeeping (Kohli & Künemund, 2005).

It appears that Lisa Balinski is playing an important kinkeeping role in her 3-generation family. Since her father's death, she has provided assistance of various kinds to her mother. She also continues to be very involved in providing emotional support and guidance to her young-adult daughters. She seems to be indicating that she feels like she is engaged in both-end caring and trying to balance her family caring roles with her employee role. She describes her current life as overfull. Although Maha Ahmed was not employed, she was a major kinkeeper in her 3-generation family throughout her middle adulthood. She is not sure what to do with herself now that her caregiving responsibilities are sharply curtailed.

Relationships With Spouse or Partner

In recent decades, there has been an increased diversity of marital statuses at midlife. Some men and women have been married for some time, some are getting married for the first time, some are not yet married, some will never marry, some were once married but now are divorced, some are in a second or third marriage, and some are not married but are living in a long-term committed relationship with someone of the same or opposite sex. In recent years, many long-term same-sex couples have finally been able to form a legal marriage in middle adulthood in an increasing number of countries, including the United States. Adults such as Mark Raslin who have struggled with mental health issues are more likely than other adults to be single.

The number of couples cohabiting rather than marrying has been increasing for almost 3 decades. The 2000 U.S. census reported that 5.5 million couples were living together but not married, up from 3.2 million in 1990 (Simmons & O'Connell, 2003). The majority of these couples were opposite-sex partners, but 1 in 9 was a same-sex couple. In 2016, the U.S Census Bureau found that 18 million adults were living in cohabiting relationships (Stepler, 2017). About half of the cohabiting couples were younger than 35, but the number of cohabiting adults ages 50 and older increased by 75% from 2007 to 2016, the biggest rate of increase of any age group. Most cohabiters age 50 or older have been previously married. One research team found that midlife African American men with higher education and income were more likely to be married than cohabiting, whereas the opposite was true of midlife African American men with lower education and income. This finding is consistent with research that finds that African Americans place greater emphasis than European Americans on security and upward mobility as requirements for marriage (Cutrona, Russell, Burzette, Wesner, & Bryant, 2011). Of course, many cohabiting couples will marry each other at some point.

We know very little about the different midlife experiences of partners of different marital statuses, but there is evidence that each person brings prior relationship experiences to partner relationships of all types. Möller and Stattin (2001) reviewed the empirical literature on these relationships and identified a number of characteristics of prior relationships that have been found to influence partner relationships in adulthood. For example, affection and warmth in the household during the preschool years has been associated with long and happy partnerships in adulthood. Interactions with peers during adolescence help to build the social skills necessary to sustain partner relationships. Based on these findings, Möller and Stattin (2001) engaged in longitudinal research with a Swedish sample to investigate the links between early relationships and later partner relationships. They found that warm relationships with parents during adolescence are associated with later satisfaction in the partner relationship. Relationships with fathers were more strongly related to partner satisfaction for males than for females. Contrary to previous research, Möller and Stattin found that the quality of parents' marital relationship was not associated with the quality of later partner relationships. The parent–child relationship was a better predictor of later partner relationships than the quality of the parents' marital relationships. Research suggests that secure attachment in childhood is associated with better conflict resolution in adult spouse and partner relationships (Mitchell, 2016).

For heterosexual marriages, a long line of research indicates a U-shaped curve in marital happiness, with high marital satisfaction in the preparental years of marriage, a decline in the middle parental years, and a rise in the later postparental years (Mitchell, 2016). It is important to remember, however, that many adults are marrying for the first time in midlife and others are marrying for a second or more times, and it is unclear how the above-mentioned research applies to such couples. Midlife adults are balancing a variety of roles: family roles, work roles, and community roles, and this requires partners to coordinate their role enactments. In one study of African American midlife baby boomers, couples described how they share responsibilities; stay engaged with work, family, and faith; and make time for each other to keep their relationship alive (Carolan & Allen, 1999). One researcher (Mitchell, 2010) found that couples from familistic/collectivist cultural orientations tended to perceive competing midlife caregiving responsibilities as less damaging to their marriages compared to couples from more individualistic cultural backgrounds.

Researchers have found individual, microcontextual, and macrocontextual factors to be associated with marital satisfaction (see Mitchell, 2016, for a review of this research). At the individual level, marital satisfaction is enhanced by the ability to successfully resolve conflict. At the microcontextual level, perceived fairness in family work is associated with high marital satisfaction,

and chronic economic adversity is associated with low marital satisfaction. At the macrocontextual level, public policy that supports family life (such as income supports, paid family leave, accessible health care) can play a role in reducing stress on the couple relationship.

The 2010 U.S. census found 594,000 same-sex couple households in the United States, about 1% of all couple households (U.S. Census Bureau, 2011). Of these same-sex couple households, 115,000, or about 19%, reported having children in the household. There is general agreement, however, that U.S. census data on same-sex relationships is incomplete, and the Census Bureau is currently at work trying to improve their methods for collecting these data (Kreider, Bates, & Mayol-Garcia, 2017). Midlife gay and lesbian partnerships have been found to be more egalitarian than married heterosexual couples and to divide household labor more evenly (Zdaniuk & Smith, 2016). Kurdek (2004) compared gay, lesbian, and married heterosexual couples in long-term relationships. In this study, the gay and lesbian couples lived without children and the married heterosexual couples lived with children. For 50% of the comparisons, gay and lesbian couples did not differ from married heterosexual couples with children. Three major differences between gay and lesbian couples and married heterosexual couples were found: (1) gay and lesbian couples reported more autonomy and more equality; (2) gay and lesbian couples were better at conflict resolution; and (3) heterosexual married couples had more support from their families. In a later project, Kurdek (2008) followed four groups of couples—gay couples without children, lesbian couples without children, heterosexual married couples without children, and heterosexual married couples with children—for the first 10 years they cohabited. Lesbian partners reported the highest relationship quality at all points of assessment and showed no change in relationship quality over time. Gay partners reported the second highest relationship quality and also showed no change over time. Both groups of heterosexual couples reported lower levels of relationship quality than both gay and lesbian partners, and both groups also reported change over time. Heterosexual couples without children reported a steep decline in relationship quality in the early years followed by stability. In contrast, heterosexual couples with children reported a steep decline in the early years, followed by a gradual decline until year 8 when another period of steep decline began. This research begins to clarify some different experiences in partner relationships of various types but only covers relationships through the young-adult period. One hopes further longitudinal research will continue into middle adulthood and will also investigate relationships of gay and lesbian couples with children.

There is even less research about bisexual and transgender relationships than about gay and lesbian relationships. Weinberg, Williams, and Pryor (2001) followed 56 people who identify as bisexual from young adulthood to middle adulthood. They found that the participants continue to report a bisexual identity and attraction to members of both sexes in middle adulthood. However, they also report less involvement in the bisexual community and more investment in work or a partner and a move toward activity with just one sex. In other words, there was no change in bisexual attraction but a growing commitment to work and partnerships. Given the historical stigma about bisexuality among both straight and gay adults, disclosing a bisexual identity to romantic partners is sometimes fraught with problems (see Hartman-Linck, 2014), but one UK research team found that the younger cohort in their study reported disclosing their sexual identity earlier in the relationship than the older cohort (Anderson, Scoats, & McCormack, 2015). The younger cohort also reported greater acceptance of their bisexual identity than the older cohort, but the majority of men in both the younger and older cohort desired monogamous relationships. Disclosing transgender status in the context of romantic relationships is also a challenge for transgender adults, and many report fear of rejection (Iantaffi & Bockting, 2011). The participants in one study of transgender relationships reported, however, that they do disclose their transgender status to romantic partners. In this same study, two thirds of the transgender research participants reported that they were in monogamous relationships (Iantaffi & Bockting, 2011).

The current generation of midlife adults has more complex marital biographies than earlier generations. The baby boomers were the first cohort to divorce and remarry in large numbers during young adulthood, and remarriages are 2.5 times as likely to end in divorce as first marriages. From 1980 to 2010, the percentage of midlife remarriages rose from 18% to 32%. One in four persons who divorced in 2010 was 50 years old or older, compared with 1 in 10 in 1990 (Brown & Lin, 2012). The overall divorce rate is higher for women than men, higher for Blacks than for Whites or Hispanics, and higher for those with a high school education compared with those with a college education. Men report more marital satisfaction than women in the United States and Chinese Malaysia (Mickelson, Claffey, & Williams,

2006; Ny, Loy, Gudmunson, & Cheong, 2009), and most divorces are initiated by women (Ahrons, 2016).

Although there is a period of adjustment to divorce, midlife adults cope better with divorce than young adults (Greene et al., 2012). Some individuals actually report improved well-being after divorce. Women have been found to be more adversely affected by a distressed marriage and men more adversely affected by being divorced (Hetherington & Kelly, 2002). However, the financial consequences of divorce for women are negative. After divorce, men are more likely to remarry than women, and Whites are more likely to remarry than African Americans.

Relationships With Children

Although a growing number of midlife adults are parenting young or school-age children, most midlife adults are parents of adolescents or young adults. Delayed childbearing increases the likelihood that midlife adults will be stretched to provide care to their aging parents while also engaged in intense parenting to young children (Fingerman, Pillemer, Silverstein, & Suitor, 2012). Parenting adolescents can be a challenge if parent–child conflict escalates. Croatian mothers with high levels of conflict with their adolescent children have been found to feel a greater sense of isolation (Keresteš, Brković, & Jagodić, 2012). Launching young-adult offspring from the nest is a happy experience for many families, particularly in the United States and the industrialized European countries, but it is a family transition that has been undergoing changes in the past 20 years, coming at a later age for parents and becoming more fluid in its timing and progress (Newman, 2008). Research in Vancouver, Canada, with British, Chinese, southern European, and South Asian participants found strong cultural influences on the expectations of young-adult launching, with South Asian midlife parents more likely than other parents to report extreme emotional difficulty in launching their young-adult offspring (Mitchell & Wister, 2015). Indeed, there are many cultural variations in beliefs about when and whether young adults leave the family home, and multigenerational living is what is expected in many families, for both economic and cultural reasons. Cultural influences seem to play a large role in Maha Ahmed's emotional difficulties in launching her young-adult offspring.

In the United States and the industrialized European countries, it became common for young adults to live outside the family prior to marriage in the 1960s. Then, in the United States, in the 1980s, two trends became evident: increased age at first leaving home and increased incidence of returning home. Data from 2016 indicate that 15% of U.S. young adults ages 25 to 35 lived in their parents' home, a 5% increase over the share of Generation Xers living in their parents' home at the same age in 2000 (10%) and an even larger increase over the share of the Silent Generation who lived at home in 1964 (8%). Living at home with parents in young adulthood is more common among young adults with less education and more common among young-adult males than among young-adult females (DeSilver, 2016; Fry, 2017). A similar trend is occurring in many European countries, and most European countries have higher rates of young adults living with parents than in the United States (DeSilver, 2016). Recent research indicates that a broad array of factors shape the young-adult decision to leave and/or return to the parental home (South & Lei, 2015; Stone, Berrington, & Falkingham, 2014). Those factors include leaving home to attend college, leaving home to form a romantic union, moving home after completing college, moving home after dissolution of a romantic relationship, staying home or returning home because of emotional closeness with mother, staying home or returning home because of parental health problems, leaving home with instrumental support of parents, and staying home because of lack of economic resources.

Blieszner and Roberto (2006) argue that "lifestyles of midlife baby-boom parents revolve around their children" (p. 270). Recent research supports that idea. In a summary of findings of three studies, Fingerman, Pillemer, and colleagues (2012) report that the current generation of midlife adults is much more involved in the lives of their adult children than their parents were with them, a trend that began when their offspring were young children. Contemporary young adults report more frequent contact with and more similar values to their parents than occurred in earlier decades; they also report receiving more support. Middle-aged parents report offering each adult child a listening ear and emotional support more than once per week, giving advice once a month, and providing practical and financial assistance at least several times per year. Providing support to children is associated with better psychological well-being in midlife adults, and receiving various kinds of support from their midlife parents is associated with better adjustment and well-being of young adults. In general, mothers have closer relationships with their young-adult children than fathers, and divorced fathers have been found to have weaker emotional attachments with their adult children than either married fathers or divorced mothers. Midlife

parents help their young-adult children in different ways, depending on the resources they have to share. Relationships with young-adult children are important to both Lisa Balinski and Maha Ahmed, but both have questions about the best way to support their young-adult offspring.

It is important to note the exchange of material resources between generations. Mark Raslin would like to find a way to be supportive to both his daughter and his aging parents while also continuing to work on his own recovery. He has limited financial resources but takes pride in his recent ability to provide child support for his daughter. Lisa and Adam Balinski moved in with Lisa's parents after their baby was born, until they could afford a place of their own, and now they are providing a home for Lisa's mother and wondering if they should do the same for their young-adult daughter, Kristi. Maha Ahmed was a major source of emotional support to her mother after the family resettled in Jordan, even after Maha and her husband moved to the United States. She has been a nurturing wife and mother who was proud of her ability to juggle the care of multiple generations of the family for so many years. She and her husband were in a position to pay for higher education for their children and to offer financial assistance as they made the transition to adult roles. With the help of her therapist, Maha is now considering what she can expect to receive from her children. Research in Europe suggests that intergenerational financial transfers are common and often sizable, with midlife and late-life adults serving as an important source of financial and practical support for younger adults, often helping with household chores and paperwork (Brandt, 2013). Padgett and Remle (2016) found similar patterns of financial assistance from midlife parents to adult children in the United States and note that this pattern of intergenerational transfer is one source of cumulative advantage or cumulative disadvantage.

Research also indicates that midlife adults can be negatively affected by their relationships with their adult children. Greenfield and Marks (2006) found that midlife adults whose adult children have problems such as chronic disease or disability, emotional problems, problems with alcohol or other substances, financial problems, work-related problems, partner relationship problems, and so on report lower levels of well-being than midlife adults who do not report such problems in their adult children. Ha, Hong, Seltzer, and Greenberg (2008) found that midlife parents of adult children with developmental disabilities or mental health problems were more likely than parents of nondisabled children to report higher levels of negative emotions, decreased psychological well-being, and somatic symptoms. Seltzer et al. (2009) found that midlife adults had more negative emotions, more disruption in cortisol, and more physical symptoms on the days they spent more time with their disabled children. Fingerman, Cheng, Birditt, and Zarit (2012) found that midlife parents are only as happy as their least happy young-adult child. These findings suggest a need for social service support for midlife parents whose adult children are facing ongoing challenges.

Relationships With Parents

Most research shows that middle-aged adults are deeply involved with their aging parents (Fingerman, Pillemer et al., 2012). As suggested in the stories of Mark Raslin, Lisa Balinski, and Maha Ahmed, the nature of the relationship with aging parents changes over time. A cross-national study of adults in Norway, England, Germany, Spain, and Israel found that across countries, support was bidirectional, with aging parents providing emotional and financial support to their midlife adult children and also receiving support from them (Lowenstein & Daatland, 2006). As the parents' health begins to deteriorate, they turn more to their midlife children for help, as is the case for Lisa Balinski and was earlier the case for Maha Ahmed. The Pew Research Center (Parker & Patten, 2013) found that when adults were asked if their parent over the age of 65 needed help to handle their affairs or take care of themselves, 69% reported that their parents needed no assistance. About 60% of the adults who reported that their parents needed some help were midlife adults in their 40s and 50s. About 17% of adults in their 40s who had a parent over the age of 65 reported providing some day-to-day assistance to a parent, and 29% of adults in their 50s reported providing such care. About 10% of adults in their 40s and 50s reported being a primary caregiver for a parent. About 13% of adults in their 40s and 50s with aging parents had provided all of three types of support to their parents: caregiving support, financial support, and emotional support. Black and Hispanic midlife adults were much more likely to be providing financial aid to their parents than White midlife adults, and adults with lower incomes were more likely than those with higher incomes to provide some financial support to their parents.

Traditionally, and typically still, caregivers to aging parents are daughters or daughters-in-law (Fingerman, VanderDrift, Dotterer, Birditt, & Zarit, 2011). This continues to be the case, even though a great majority of midlife women are employed full-time. This does not tell the whole story, however. The baby boom cohort has more siblings than earlier and later cohorts, and there is some evidence that caregiving is often shared among siblings, with sisters serving as coordinators of the care (Hequembourg & Brallier, 2005). Pillemer and Suitor (2014) found that in situations where there are siblings, the choice of who will provide care to an elder parent usually comes down to a daughter who lives in greatest proximity to the caregiver and shares the caregiver's values. They also found that prior to the need for caregiving, the care recipient correctly predicted which child would do the primary caregiving. In spite of competing demands from spouses and children, providing limited care to aging parents seems to cause little psychological distress. Extended caregiving, conversely, has been found to have some negative effects as midlife adults try to balance a complex mix of roles (Savia, Almeida, Davey, & Zant, 2008), but there is also some evidence of rewards of caregiving (Robertson, Zarit, Duncan, Rovine, & Femia, 2007).

Most of the research on caregiving focuses on *caregiver burden*, or the negative effects on mental and physical health caused by caregiver stress. Compared with matched comparison groups who do not have caregiving responsibilities, caregivers of elderly parents report more depressive symptoms, taking more antidepressant and antianxiety medication; poorer physical health; and lower marital satisfaction (Sherwood, Given, Given, & Von Eye, 2005). Savia et al. (2008) found that psychological distress was greater on days that adult children provided assistance to aging parents, but they also found more distressed mood among caregivers with higher caregiving demands and lower resources. Another research team studying caregiver burden in caregivers of individuals with dementia found that the number of hours devoted to caregiving was a significant predictor of caregiver burden. They also found that having multiple helpers did not relieve caregiver burden and that caregivers who lived with the care recipient had higher levels of caregiver burden (Kim, Chang, Rose, & Kim, 2012).

Although this research is not as prevalent, some researchers have been interested in a phenomenon they call *caregiver gain* or *caregiver reward*. One early proponent of this line of inquiry found that the majority of caregivers have something positive to say about their caregiving experiences (Kramer, 1997). One group of researchers was interested in the balance of positive and negative emotions in family caregivers of older adults with dementia (Robertson et al., 2007). They found considerable variation in the responses of caregivers in terms of the balance of stressful and positive experiences of caregiving. The stressful experiences included behavior problems of the care receiver; need to provide personal assistance with activities such as eating, dressing, grooming, bathing, toileting, and transferring into bed; role overload; and role captivity (feeling trapped in caregiver role). The positive experiences of caregiving included caregiving rewards such as growing personally, repaying care receiver, fulfilling duty, and getting perspective on what is important in life; sense of competence; and positive behaviors in care receiver. The researchers identified groups of caregivers according to their levels of distress. The most well-adjusted group had more resources in terms of health, education, and so on and reported fewer behavior problems and fewer needs for personal assistance of the care recipients. Another research team studied feelings of rewards among family caregivers during ongoing palliative care (Henriksson, Carlander, & Arestedt, 2015). The family caregivers reported generally high levels of reward. The largest source of reward was a feeling of being helpful to a loved one, and personal growth of the caregiver was also mentioned as a less important source of reward.

Culture appears to play a role in whether providing care to aging parents is experienced as burden or gain. For example, Lowenstein and Daatland (2006) found a strong expectation of providing care for parents in Spain and Israel but a more negotiable obligation in northern Europe. In countries where caregiving is normalized, caregiving is often provided out of affection, not obligation; may be shared among family members; and may be less likely to be experienced as burden. This seems to be the way that Maha Ahmed thinks about family caregiving. Evans and colleagues (Evans et al., 2009) report that Hispanic caregivers have been found to have slightly less caregiver burden than Anglos. Fingerman et al. (2011) found that middle-aged Blacks, on average, give more support of all kinds to aging parents and are more likely to report an expectation that one support one's parents and that personal rewards are found in providing such support. Very individualistic families value individual independence and may find elder care particularly troublesome to both caregiver and care recipient. However, there is evidence that both individualistically oriented families and collectivist-oriented families experience negative effects of long-term, intensive caregiving, especially those families with few economic and social resources (Robertson et al., 2007).

Although there is clear evidence of the importance of intergenerational ties across the life course, few researchers have explored the intergenerational relationships between midlife gay men and lesbian women and their parents and parents-in-law. Reczek (2014) engaged in such a study and found that a large majority (86%) of the respondents described their relationship with at least one of their own or their partner's parents as being supportive. A smaller majority (78%) also described their relationship with at least one of their own or their partner's parents as being conflictual. In their descriptions of supportive relationships with parents, they described parents who integrated them and their partners into everyday and special family events, parents who referred to their partners in family terms such as son- or daughter-in-law, parents who allowed them and their partners to provide social support to the parents, and parents who spoke affirmatively of their gay or lesbian identity. In their descriptions of conflictual relationships with parents, they described parents who limited interactions or engaged in negative interactions with them, parents who made traumatizing statements about them or created traumatizing situations for them, or parents whom they believed would usurp their right to be involved in health decisions about their partner. When thinking about these findings, it is important to remember that the respondents were midlife adults who came of age before widespread gay activism, and their intergenerational experiences might be very different from the next generation of midlife gay and lesbian adults.

Other Family Relationships

Midlife is typically a time of launching children and a time when parents die. It is also a time when new family members get added by marriage and grandchildren are born. However, family relationships other than marital relationships and parent–child relationships have received little research attention. The grandparent–grandchild relationship has received the greatest amount of research attention, followed by a small body of research on sibling relationships.

Not all midlife adults are involved in the grandparenting role, but data from the United States and Europe indicate that, for those who do become grandparents, the average age for making the transition to grandparenthood is 51 for women and 54 for men (Leopold & Skopek, 2015). The data also indicate large variations in the timing of grandparenthood across countries. The average age for becoming a grandmother varies from 46 in Ukraine to 57 in Switzerland, and the pattern is similar for becoming a grandfather (age 49 in Ukraine and 58 in Switzerland). The average age of becoming a grandparent is about 10 years earlier in eastern Europe than in western Europe, and the United States falls between these two, age 49 for grandmothers and 52 for grandfathers. Of course, average age masks the great variation within a given country, and the transition to grandparenthood can occur in the early 30s or in late adulthood. Neither Lisa Balinski nor Maha Ahmed have become grandmothers at age 50 and 57. It appears that this is a role that both would embrace.

Leopold and Skopek (2015) also studied how grandparenthood is juxtaposed with other adult roles during midlife and found this period to be a time of competing roles. In all countries they studied, active parenting ended before grandparenthood, but grandparenting began before the empty nest in all countries except for West Germany and Norway. This latter finding about the sequencing of grandparenting and empty nest is affected by the trend of young adults staying longer in the parental home, as discussed earlier. In eastern Europe, people become grandparents many years before experiencing the empty nest, but in western Europe these transitions are spaced more closely. Again, the United States falls between these two regions. The data also indicate that, overall, grandparenthood tends to coincide closely with the death of the last surviving parent; however, for grandmothers (but not grandfathers), grandparenthood precedes the death of the last surviving parent in most countries. This may result in midlife grandmothers assuming caregiving responsibilities for both young grandchildren and aging parents. This period of multiple family roles usually occurs from the mid-40s to the mid-50s for women and from the late 40s to the late 50s for men. In addition to the multiple family roles, many grandparents are still engaged in paid work activity, with grandparenthood preceding retirement by at least 5 years, and many more in most countries.

There are many styles of grandparenting and many cultures of grandparenting. In cultures with large extended families and reverence for elders—such as in China, Mexico, and many Asian and African countries—grandparents often live with the family. In the United States, Asian American, African American, Hispanic American, and Italian American grandparents are more likely to play an active role in the lives of grandchildren than other ethnic groups (Gardiner, 2018). In a study of European grandparents, Neuberger & Haberkern (2014) found that different European countries have different family cultures and expectations about the role of grandparents. For example, in the Netherlands and Denmark, grandparents are not considered to be obliged to play large support roles in their grandchildren's lives, but grandparents in the Mediterranean countries are expected to play large support roles with their children and grandchildren. Neuberger & Haberkern (2014) also found that the overall quality of life of grandparents in countries with high expectations for grandparenting is associated with whether they comply with these expectations. In a qualitative study of grandparenting in New Zealand, grandparents talked about the importance of "being there" for their grandchildren while also avoiding "interfering" by overstepping the parents' authority or offering uninvited advice (Breheny, Stephens, & Spilsbury, 2013).

Research has indicated gender differences in enactment of the grandparent role as well, with most research suggesting that grandmothers, particularly maternal grandmothers, play more intimate roles in their grandchildren's lives than grandfathers. However, Bates and Goodsell (2013) argue that grandfathers have been underrepresented in research on grandparenting and recommend a more focused research effort to examine these relationships. In their own exploratory research, they found wide variation in grandfather–grandson relationships, but grandsons saw grandfathers involved in seven domains of grandfathering work: lineage work, mentoring work, spiritual work, character work, recreation work, family identity work, and investment work. They concluded that "generative grandfathers provided grandsons with meaningful interactive experiences that built developmental competencies, including those that potentially might lead to strong generativity" (p. 46). In a study of gay grandfathers, the majority of grandfathers reported close or extremely close relationships with their grandchildren (Tornello & Patterson, 2016). As found with other grandparenting studies, the gay grandfathers reported closer relationships with grandchildren who live in closer proximity to them. Almost all of these gay grandfathers had disclosed their sexual orientation to their adult children, and those whose offspring disapproved of their sexual orientation reported poorer mental health. A study of lesbian and bisexual grandmothers, conducted 10 years earlier than this study of gay grandfathers, found that disclosure of sexual orientation to adult children and grandchildren was a primary issue for these grandmothers (Orel & Fruhauf, 2006). In this study as well as the study of gay grandfathers, being open about the grandparent sexual orientation was associated with closer relationships with grandchildren.

Researchers have noted two potential problems for grandparents. First, if adult children divorce, custody agreements may fail to attend to the rights of grandparents for visitation (Blieszner & Roberto, 2006). And baby boom adults are often serving as stepgrandparents, a role that can be quite ambiguous. Second, if adult children become incapacitated by substance abuse, illness, disability, or incarceration, grandparents may be recruited to step in to raise the grandchildren. The number of children cared for by grandparents in the United States has risen dramatically in the past 30 years. In 2011, 7.7 million children in the United States lived with a grandparent, and 3 million of them were being cared for primarily by the grandparent (Livingston, 2013). Black children were twice as likely to be cared for by a grandparent as Hispanic and White children. Unfortunately, grandparents with the fewest resources are often the ones called on to become primary caregivers to their grandchildren.

Baby boomers have more siblings than earlier and later cohorts, and most midlife adults today have at least one sibling. Sibling relationships have been found to be important for the well-being of both men and women in midlife. Siblings often drift apart in young adulthood, but contact between siblings increases in late midlife (McGoldrick & Watson, 2016). Midlife adults are often brought together around the care and death of aging parents, and research indicates that sibling contact decreases again after the death of the last parent (Khodyakov & Carr, 2009). Sibling collaboration in the care of aging parents may bring them closer together or may stir new as well as unresolved resentments. Pillemer and colleagues (Pillemer, Suitor, Pardo, & Henderson, 2010) found that midlife adults who recall their mothers playing favorites when they were children often have problematic relationships in midlife. Although step- and half siblings tend to stay connected to each other, their contact is less frequent than the contact between full siblings.

Research in the Netherlands found that brothers provide more practical support to siblings, and sisters provide more emotional support (Voorpostel & van der Lippe, 2007). In Taiwan, however, brother–brother dyads were found to provide the most companionship and emotional support of any dyad type (Lu, 2007). In the Netherlands, siblings seemed to overcome geographic distance to provide emotional support more easily than friends, but relationship quality was an important predictor of which sibling groups would offer emotional support (Voorpostel & van der Lippe, 2007).

Maha Ahmed was an important lifeline for her sister who was caring for their parents back in Jordan. Their mutual concern about their parents' health drew them closer over time.

Relationships With Friends

Midlife adults have fewer friends in their social convoys than do adolescents and young adults, but they also continue to report at least a few important friendships (Wrzus et al., 2013). It has been suggested that midlife adults have less time than other adult age groups for friendships. Baby boom midlife adults are good friends with about seven people on average; these friends are usually of the same age, sex, race or ethnicity, social class, education, and employment status (Blieszner & Roberto, 2006). One research team (Chang, Choi, Bazarova, & Löckenhoff, 2015) extended socioemotional selectivity theory to the study of online networking and found that compared to younger adults, middle-aged adults had fewer friends on Facebook, but a higher proportion of the Facebook friends of midlife adults were actual friends than was true for younger adults.

Friendships appear to have an impact on midlife well-being for both men and women, although they do not seem to be as important as close familial relationships. For instance, the adequacy of social support, particularly from friends, at age 50 predicts physical health for men at age 70 (Vaillant, 2012). In a German sample that included both men and women, activities with friends increased positive mood and life satisfaction of midlife adults (Huxhold, Miche, & Schüz, 2013).

Given this research, we might want to know more about Lisa Balinksi's friendship network. Mark Raslin's recent participation in social events is providing him an opportunity to expand his social convoy and appears to be adding an important dimension to his life circumstances. Maha Ahmed developed close women friendships after moving to the United States, friendships that helped her cope with issues of child-rearing and cross-cultural living. Her therapist can help her explore the current adequacy of her social support system and to consider whether either old friends or new friends could bring more joy to her life.

It appears that the importance of friends in the social convoy varies by sexual orientation, race, and marital status. Friends are important sources of support in the social convoys of gay and lesbian midlife adults, often serving as an accepting "chosen family" for those who have traveled the life course in a homophobic society (Croghan, Moone, & Olson, 2014). These chosen families provide much care and support to each other, as evidenced by the primary caregiving they have provided in times of serious illness such as AIDS and breast cancer (Muraco & Fredriksen-Goldsen, 2011). Taking care of friends is often seen as a responsibility in some LGBTQ friend networks, and one research team found that midlife individuals reported that helping friends in their LGBTQ network raises their esteem. On average, they also reported tenuous ties to family networks (Muraco & Fredriksen-Goldsen, 2011). Friends also become family in many African American families. The literature on African American families often calls attention to the "non-blood" family members as a strength for these families (Boyd-Franklin & Karger, 2012). Friendships also serve an important role in the social convoys of single midlife adults, serving as a chosen family rather than a "poor substitute" for family (Berliner, Jacob, & Schwartzberg, 2016).

CRITICAL THINKING QUESTIONS 8.4

The research indicates that family ties remain strong in societies around the world. What do you think about this? Do you think the family ties are strong in your multigenerational family? Are there kinkeepers in your multigenerational family? If so, who are they, and why do you think they play this role? What have you observed about your own friendship networks over time?

WORK IN MIDDLE ADULTHOOD

Like Lisa Balinski, the majority of midlife adults engage in paid labor, but the first decade of the 21st century was a precarious time for middle-aged workers, and Mark Raslin is an example of the precariousness. In the deep economic recession of 2008, workers age 45 and older had a lower unemployment rate than younger workers, but they were disproportionately represented among the long-term unemployed (Luo, 2009). In 2011, the median duration of unemployment for job seekers age 55 and older was 35 weeks, compared with 26 weeks for younger job seekers (U.S. Government Accountability Office, 2012). These midlife baby boomers are too young to draw a pension or social security (before the age of 62) or to have medical coverage through Medicare. Therefore, it is no surprise that in the first 3 months of the enrollment period for the Affordable Care Act's federal and state marketplaces, 55% of enrollees were ages 45 to 64 (Shear & Pear, 2014).

Work and retirement have different meanings for different people. Among the meanings work can have are the following (Friedmann & Havighurst, 1954):

- A source of income
- A life routine and way of structuring time
- A source of status and identity
- A context for social interaction
- A meaningful experience that provides a sense of accomplishment

Given these meanings, employment is an important role for midlife adults in many parts of the world, for men and women alike. Involuntary unemployment can be a source of great stress.

In affluent societies, the last decades of the 20th century saw a continuing decline in the average age of retirement, particularly for men (Moen, 2003). This trend existed alongside trends of longer midlife and late-adulthood periods and the fact that many adults are entering midlife healthier and better educated than in previous eras. Improved pension plans were at least partially responsible for the trend of declining age of retirement. But with the demise of defined-benefit pension plans, and particularly after the recession of 2008, retirement patterns have been changing again, with older adults remaining engaged in the workforce later in life (Boveda & Metz, 2016; Carr & Kail, 2012).

Overall, the work patterns of middle-aged workers in the United States have changed considerably in the past 3 decades. Four trends stand out.

1. *Greater job mobility among middle-aged workers.* Changes in the global economy have produced job instability for middle-aged workers. In the late 20th century, corporate restructuring, mergers, and downsizing revolutionized the previous lockstep career trajectories and produced much instability in midcareer employment (Leon-Guerrero, 2014). Midlife white-collar workers who had attained midlevel management positions in organizations have been vulnerable to downsizing and reorganization efforts aimed at flattening organizational hierarchies. Midlife blue-collar workers have been vulnerable to changes in job skill requirements as the global economy shifts from an industrial base to a service base. Within these broad trends, gender, class, and race have all made a difference in the work patterns of midlife adults (Leon-Guerrero, 2014). Women are more likely than men to have job disruption throughout the

adult life course, although those with higher education and higher income are less vulnerable to job disruption. In the most recent recession, however, men were more vulnerable to job loss than women. Race is a factor in the midlife employment disruption for men but not for women. Although Black men have more job disruptions than White men, there are no race differences for women when other variables are controlled. Research indicates that loss of work in middle adulthood is a very critical life event that has negative consequences for physical and emotional well-being (Kang & Kim, 2014).

2. *Greater variability in the timing of retirement.* Some midlife workers retire in their late 50s. Today, many other midlife adults anticipate working into their late 60s or early 70s. The decision to retire is driven by both health and financial status (more particularly, the availability of pension benefits). Longitudinal research indicates that earlier retirement is associated with poor self-rated health and chronic disease (Stafford et al., 2017). Although availability of a pension serves as inducement for retirement, men and women who work in physically demanding jobs often seek early

retirement whether or not they have access to a pension. Some leave the workforce because of disability and become eligible for social security disability benefits.

3. *Blurring of the lines between working and retirement.* Many people now phase into retirement (Carr & Kail, 2012). Some middle-aged retirees return to work in different occupational fields than those from which they retired, a phenomenon known as encore career. Some large organizations are supporting late middle-aged adults to pursue encore careers in teaching, health care, and social services (Alboher, 2014; Schulaka, 2016). Encore careers are usually thought of as something that can be done only by financially wealthy adults, but Marc Feedman (cited in Schulaka, 2016) reports that in 2014, 57% of U.S. adults in encore careers had household incomes of less than $45,000. Other workers leave a career at some point in middle adulthood for a part-time or temporary job. Increasing numbers of middle-aged workers leave a career position because of downsizing and reorganization and find reemployment in a job with less financial reward, a "bridge job" that carries them into retirement (Stafford et al., 2017).

© Bonnie Jacobs/iStockphoto.com

PHOTO 8.3 Changes in the global economy have produced job instability for middle-aged workers, and job retraining often becomes essential.

PHOTO 8.4 Research indicates that middle-aged workers often have greater work satisfaction, organizational commitment, and self-esteem than younger workers.

4. *Increasing educational reentry of midlife workers.* This trend has received little research attention. However, workers with high levels of educational attainment prior to middle adulthood are more likely than their less-educated peers to retrain in middle adulthood (Luo, 2009). This difference is consistent with the theory of cumulative advantage; those who have accumulated resources over the life course are more likely to have the resources for retraining in middle adulthood. But in this era of high job obsolescence, relatively few middle-aged adults will have the luxury of choosing to do one thing at a time; to remain marketable, many middle-aged adults will have to combine work and school. Community colleges in the United States have become increasingly active in developing relatively inexpensive programs for midlife career switchers (Freedman & Goggin, 2008 Schulaka, 2016).

These trends aside, there is both good news and bad news for the middle-aged worker in the beginning of the 21st century. Research indicates that middle-aged workers have greater work satisfaction, organizational commitment, and self-esteem than younger workers, but this is truer for white-collar workers than for blue-collar workers (Hu, Kaplan, & Dalal, 2010; Ng & Feldman, 2010). Blue-collar workers tend to have fewer opportunities to control their work activities than white-collar workers, and control over work is associated with job satisfaction. Even though women face barriers to career achievement in many work sectors, they tend to show higher or similar job satisfaction to men (Zou, 2015). Lisa Balinski appears to be a good example of this finding. However, with the current changes in the labor market, employers are ambivalent about middle-aged employees. Employers may see middle-aged workers as hardworking and experienced, but they also often cut higher-wage older workers from the payroll as a short-range solution for reducing operating costs and staying competitive.

For some midlife adults, such as Mark Raslin, the issue is not how they will cope with loss of a good job but rather how they can become established in the labor market. In the previous industrial phase, poverty was caused by unemployment. In the current era, the major issue is the growing proportion of low-wage, no-benefit jobs. Black men with a high school education or less have been particularly disadvantaged in the current phase of industrialization, largely because of the declining numbers of routine production jobs. Adults with disabilities have an even harder time finding work that can support them. In 2015, the unemployment rate for persons with a disability was higher than for persons without a disability in all age groups and among all educational attainment groups. The unemployment rate for persons with a disability was 10.7%, about twice that of persons with no disability (5.1%) (U.S. Bureau of Labor Statistics, 2016b). Even with legislation of the past few decades, much remains to be done to open educational and work opportunities to persons with disabilities.

Middle-aged workers, like younger workers, are deeply affected by a changing labor market. Like younger workers, they must understand the changing patterns in work life and be proactive in maintaining and updating their skills. However, that task is easier for middle-aged workers who arrive in middle adulthood with accumulated resources. Marginalization in the labor market in adulthood is the result of cumulative disadvantage over the life course. Unfortunately, adults such as Mark Raslin who have employment disruptions early in the adult life course tend to have more job disruption in middle adulthood as well.

RISK FACTORS AND PROTECTIVE FACTORS IN MIDDLE ADULTHOOD

From a life course perspective, midlife behavior has both antecedents and consequences. Earlier life experiences can serve either as risk factors or as protective factors for health and well-being during middle adulthood. And midlife behaviors can serve either as risk factors or as protective factors for future health and well-being. The rapidly growing body of literature on risk, protection, and resilience based on longitudinal research has recently begun to add to our understanding of the antecedents of midlife behavior (see Exhibit 8.10 for a summary of the antecedent risk and protective factors in middle adulthood).

One of the best-known programs of research is a study begun by Emmy Werner and associates with a cohort born in 1955 on the island of Kauai, Hawaii. The research participants turned 40 in 1995, and Werner and Ruth Smith (2001) captured their risk factors, protective factors, and resilience in *Journeys from Childhood to Midlife*. They summarize their findings by suggesting that they "taught us a great deal of respect for the self-righting tendencies in human nature and for the capacity of *most* individuals who grew up in adverse circumstances to make a successful adaptation in adulthood" (p. 166). At age 40, compared with previous decades, the overwhelming majority of the participants

EXHIBIT 8.10 ● Antecedent Risk Factors and Protective Factors for Well-Being in Middle Adulthood

Risk Factors	Protective Factors
Severe perinatal trauma	Nurturing caregiver in infancy
Small-for-gestational-age birth weight	Loving relationship with at least one adult in childhood and adolescence
Early childhood poverty	
Childhood abuse and neglect	Good peer relationships in childhood and adolescence
Out-of-home care in childhood	Emotional and instrumental support in childhood and adolescence
Chronic or traumatic stress	Continuing education during adulthood
Serious health problems in early childhood	Military service
Problems in early schooling	Being engaged with the world
Parental alcoholism and/or serious mental illness	Have a sense of purpose
Health problems in adolescence	Reading, writing, and word games
Health problems in the 30s	Physical exercise
Early marriage	Positive beliefs
Never marrying (for men)	Sense of control
Smoking	Healthy emotion regulation
Poor diet	Altruism
Obesity	Community support
Loneliness	Use of "shift-and-persist" strategies

reported "significant improvements" in work accomplishments, interpersonal relationships, contributions to community, and life satisfaction. Most adults who had a troubled adolescence had recovered by midlife. Many of these adults who had been troubled as youth reported that the "opening of opportunities" (p. 168) in their 20s and 30s had led to major *turning points*. Such turning points included continuing education at community college, military service, marriage to a stable partner, religious conversion, and survival despite a life-threatening illness or accident. At midlife, participants were still benefiting from the presence of a competent, nurturing caregiver in infancy, as well as from the emotional support along the way of extended family, peers, and caring adults outside the family.

Although this research is hopeful, Werner and Smith (2001) also found that 1 out of 6 of the study cohort was doing poorly at work and in relationships. The earlier risk factors associated with poor midlife adjustment include severe perinatal trauma, small-for-gestational-age birth weight, early childhood poverty, serious health problems in early childhood, problems in early schooling, parental alcoholism and/or serious mental illness, health problems in adolescence, and health problems in the 30s. Mark Raslin's early life produced several of these risk factors: early childhood poverty, parental substance abuse and mental health problems, problems in early schooling, and health problems in the 30s. In addition, he continues to struggle with the aftermath of early trauma and family instability. For men, the most powerful risk factor was parental alcoholism from birth to age 18. Women were especially negatively affected by paternal alcoholism during their adolescence. It is interesting to note that the long-term negative effects of serious health problems in early childhood and adolescence were just beginning to show up at age 40. We are also learning that some negative effects of childhood and adolescent trauma may not present until early midlife.

Other longitudinal research has found that childhood adversity continues to be a risk factor for health and well-being in middle adulthood. Low socioeconomic status in childhood has been found by a number of researchers to be a risk factor for poor midlife health (see Chen, Miller, Lachman, Gruenewald, & Seeman, 2012). Some researchers are finding that one pathway from early adversity to compromised health in midlife is increased inflammation in the body caused by chronic or traumatic stress. They also find that early adversity is associated with adverse life events throughout adolescence and young adulthood, further adding to the accumulation of inflammation (see Hostinar, Lachman, Mroczek, Seeman, & Miller, 2015). This line of research suggests that early life adversity puts down biological markers that accelerate the aging process. A Swedish research team found that out-of-home care (OHC) in childhood was associated with a twofold risk of disadvantage in middle adulthood, with disadvantage defined as economic hardship, unemployment, and mental health problems (Brännström, Vinnerljung, Forsman, & Almquist, 2017). Despite this increased risk of midlife disadvantage related to childhood OHC, 56% of the males and 47% of the females who had received OHC did not have disadvantaged outcomes in midlife. This reminds us that risk factors increase the likelihood of disadvantage but do not ensure it. Other risk factors for poor health and well-being in middle adulthood found in the research include early marriage (Keenan, Ploubidis, Silverwood, & Grundy, 2017); men who never married or cohabited (Ploubidis, Silverwood, DeStavola, & Grundy, 2015); and smoking, poor diet, obesity, and loneliness (Lachman, Teshale, & Agrigoroaei, 2015).

One of the best trends in life course research is an increased interest in the protective factors that alleviate the risk of adversity. The most common finding is that emotional and instrumental support in the face of adversity protects against midlife health problems (see Slopen, Chen, Priest, Albert, & Williams, 2016). Other protective factors identified in longitudinal research include a nurturing mother; being engaged with the world; having a sense of purpose; reading, writing, and word games; physical exercise; positive beliefs; sense of control; healthy emotion regulation; altruism; and community support (Lachman et al., 2015; Ryff et al., 2012). One interesting finding is that even in the face of inequalities and discrimination, midlife racial minority adults in the United States report higher psychological well-being than midlife Whites (Ryff et al., 2012). It has been suggested that members of racial minorities may make greater use than Whites of "shift-and-persist" strategies. Shift-and-persist involves an approach to life that includes positively reappraising stress and regulating negative emotions related to stress (shift) in combination with maintaining a focus on goals (persist) (Chen et al., 2012; Ryff et al., 2012).

Studies have also examined the effects of midlife behavior, specifically the effects on subsequent health (see Dioussé, Driver, & Gaziano, 2009). They have found a number of health behaviors that are risk factors for more severe and prolonged health and disability problems in late adulthood. These include smoking, heavy alcohol use, diet high in fats, overeating, and sedentary lifestyle. Economic deprivation and high levels of stress have also been found to be risk factors throughout the life course. Behaviors that are receiving much research attention as protective factors for health and well-being in late adulthood are a healthy diet; a physical fitness program that includes stretching exercises, weight training, and aerobic exercise; meditation; and giving and receiving social support (Cohen, 2012; Davidson & Begley, 2012).

CRITICAL THINKING QUESTIONS 8.5

What have you observed about the work life of the midlife adults in your family? How has the work life of the midlife adults in your family been affected by growing insecurity in the labor market, if at all? How are the midlife adults in your family working to balance family and work? How well are their efforts working? What evidence do you see of antecedent risk factors and protective factors that are affecting the midlife experiences of Mark Raslin, Lisa Balinski, and Maha Ahmed? What evidence do you see of current behaviors that might have consequences, either positive or negative, for their experiences with late adulthood?

IMPLICATIONS FOR SOCIAL WORK PRACTICE

This discussion has several implications for social work practice with midlife adults.

- Be familiar with the unique pathways your clients have traveled to reach middle adulthood.

- Recognize the role that culture plays in constructing beliefs about appropriate midlife roles and assist clients in exploring their beliefs.

- Help clients to think about their own involvement in generative activity and the meaning this involvement has for their lives.

- Become familiar with biological changes and special health issues in middle adulthood. Engage midlife clients in assessing their own health behaviors.

- Be aware of your own beliefs about intellectual changes in middle adulthood and evaluate those against the available research.

- Be aware of both stability and the capacity for change in personality in middle adulthood.

- Help clients assess the role that spirituality plays in their adjustments in middle adulthood and, where appropriate, to make use of their spiritual resources to solve current problems.

- Engage midlife clients in a mutual assessment of their involvement in a variety of relationships, including romantic relationships, relationships with parents, relationships with children, other family relationships, and relationships with friends.

- Collaborate with social workers and other disciplines to advocate for governmental and corporate solutions to work and family life conflicts.

KEY TERMS

conjunctive faith 292
coping mechanism 290
extroversion 277
generativity 276
global network 294
human agency approach 289

introversion 277
kinkeepers 297
life narrative approach 290
life span theory 278
menopause 280
perimenopause 280

personal network 294
social convoy theory 295
socioemotional selectivity theory 294
trait approach 289
universalizing faith 292

ACTIVE LEARNING

1. Think about how you understand the balance of gains and losses in middle adulthood. Interview three midlife adults ranging in age from 40 to 65 and ask them whether they see the current phase of their lives as having more gains or more losses over the previous phase.

2. Draw your social convoy as it currently exists with three concentric circles:

   Inner circle of people who are so close and important to you that you could not do without them

   Middle circle of people who are not quite that close but are still very close and important to you

   Outer circle of people who are not as close and important as those in the two inner circles but still close enough to be considered part of your support system

   What did you learn from engaging in this exercise? Do you see any changes you would like to make in your social convoy?

3. Working alone or in groups of three or four, talk about the meanings of work for you and make a list of all the meanings mentioned. How does your list compare with the list proposed by Friedmann and Havighurst (1954)? Talk about your expectations about how your work life trajectory will go over the next 10 years. What do you expect to be the special challenges of your work life, and what do you expect to be the special rewards?

WEB RESOURCES

Boomers International: http://boomersint.com/bindex.htm

Site presented by Boomers International: World Wide Community for the Baby Boomer Generation contains information from the trivial to the serious on the popular culture of the baby boomer generation.

Encore.org: www.encore.org

Site presented by the Encore.org organization that is spearheading efforts to engage later-life adults in second careers to benefit society contains resources for employers as well as workers interested in encore careers.

Families and Work Institute: www.familiesandwork.org

Site presented by the Families and Work Institute contains information on work life research, community mobilization forums, information on the Fatherhood Project, and frequently asked questions.

Max Planck Institute for Human Development: www.mpib-berlin.mpg.de/en

Site presented by the Max Planck Institute for Human Development, Berlin, Germany, contains news and research about life course development.

Midlife in the United States: www.midus.wisc.edu

Site presented by Midlife Development in the U.S. (MIDUS) contains an overview of recent research on midlife development, multimedia presentations, featured publications, and links to other human development research projects.

Late Adulthood

Matthias J. Naleppa and Kristina M. Hash

Learning Objectives

9.1   Compare one's own emotional and cognitive reactions to three case studies.

9.2   Summarize major themes of the demographic characteristics of people in late adulthood.

9.3   Give examples of diversity in the late-adult population.

9.4   Describe how age is culturally constructed.

9.5   Critique psychosocial theoretical perspectives on social gerontology: disengagement theory,

(Continued)

activity theory, continuity theory, social con-struction theory, feminist theories, social exchange theory, life course perspective, age stratification, productive aging, and environ-mental gerontology.

9.6 Summarize the major biological, psychologi-cal, personality, and intellectual changes in late adulthood.

9.7 Give examples of social role changes and family relationships in late adulthood.

9.8 Describe the search for personal meaning in late adulthood.

9.9 Compare formal and informal resources for meeting the needs of elderly persons.

9.10 Give examples of risk factors and protective fac-tors of late adulthood.

9.11 Apply knowledge of late adulthood to recom-mend guidelines for social work engagement, assessment, intervention, and evaluation.

CASE STUDY 9.1
THE SMITHS IN EARLY RETIREMENT

The Smiths are a Caucasian couple in their early retire-ment years who have sought out couples counseling. Lois Smith is 66 and Gene Smith is 68 years of age. They have lived in the same quiet suburban neighborhood since they married 20 years ago. When they met, Gene was a widower and Lois had been divorced for 3 years. They have no children from this marriage but three chil-dren from Lois's first marriage. The Smiths are grand-parents to the three children of their married daughter, who lives 4 hours away. Their two sons are both single and live in a different city. The Smiths visit their children frequently, but family and holiday gatherings usually take place at the Smiths' house.

The Smiths live in a comfortable home, but their neighborhood has changed over the years. When they bought the house, many other families were in the same life stage, raising adolescent children and seeing them move out as young adults. Many of the neighbors from that time have since moved, and the neighborhood has undergone a change to young families with children. Although the Smiths feel connected to the community, they do not have much interaction with the people in their immediate neighborhood. Only one other neigh-bor, a woman in her mid-80s, is an older adult. This neighbor has difficulty walking and no longer drives a car. The Smiths help her with chores around the house and often take her shopping.

Until her divorce, Lois had focused primarily on raising her children. After the divorce at age 43, she needed to enter the job market. Without formal education beyond high school, she had difficulty finding employment. She worked in a number of low-paying short-term jobs before finding a permanent posi-tion as a secretary at a small local company. She has only a small retirement benefit from her 12 years on that job. Gene had worked as a bookkeeper and later assistant manager with a local hardware store for more than 30 years. Although their combined retire-ment benefits enable them to lead a comfortable retirement, Gene continues to work at the hardware store part-time.

The transition into retirement has not been easy for the Smiths. Both Gene and Lois retired last year, which required them to adjust all at once to a decrease in income. Much more difficult, however, has been the loss of status and feeling of void that they are expe-riencing. Both were accustomed to the structure provided by work. Gene gladly assists in his former company part-time, but he worries that his employer will think he's getting too old. Lois has no plans to reenter the workforce. She would like her daughter to live closer so she could spend more time with the grandchildren. Although the infrequency of the vis-its with the grandchildren has placed some strain on Lois's relationship with her daughter, especially in the period following her retirement, Lois has now begun to enjoy the trips to visit with her daughter as a wel-come change in her daily routine. But those visits are relatively infrequent, and Lois often wishes she had more to do.

Acknowledgment: The authors wish to thank Dr. Peter Maramaldi, Dr. Michael Melendez, and Rosa Schnitzenbaumer for contributions to this chapter.

CASE STUDY 9.2

MS. RUBY JOHNSON, CARETAKER FOR 3 GENERATIONS

Ms. Ruby Johnson is a handsome woman who describes herself as a "hard-boiled, 71-year-old African American" who spent the first 30 years of her life in Harlem, until she settled in the Bronx, New York. She married at 19 and lived with her husband until her 30th birthday. During her initial assessment for case management services, she explained her divorce with what appeared to be great pride. On her 29th birthday, Ruby told her husband that he had one more year to choose between "me and the bottle." She tolerated his daily drinking for another year, but when he came home drunk on her 30th birthday, she took their 6-year-old daughter and left him and, she explained, "never looked back."

Ruby immediately got a relatively high-paying—albeit tedious—job working for the postal service. At the same time, she found the Bronx apartment, in which she has resided for the past 41 years. Ruby lived there with her daughter, Darlene, for 18 years until she "put that girl out" on what she describes as the saddest day of her life.

Darlene was 21 when she made Ruby the grandmother of Tiffany, a vivacious little girl in good health. A year later, Darlene began using drugs when Tiffany's father abandoned them. By the time Darlene was 24, she had a series of warnings and arrests for drug possession and prostitution. Ruby explained that it "broke my heart that my little girl was out there sellin' herself for drug money." Continuing the story in an unusually angry tone, she explained that "I wasn't gonna have no 'ho' live in my house."

During her initial interview, Ruby's anger was betrayed by a flicker of pride when she explained that Darlene, now 46, has been drug-free for more than 20 years. Tiffany is 25 and lives with her husband and two children. They have taken Darlene into their home to help Ruby. Ruby flashed a big smile when she shared that "Tiffany and Carl [her husband] made me a great-grandma twice, and they are taking care of Darlene for me now." Darlene also has a younger daughter—Rebecca—from what Ruby describes as another "bad" relationship with a "no-good man."

Rebecca, age 16, has been living with Ruby for the past 2 years since she started having difficulty in school and needed more supervision than Darlene was able to provide.

In addition, about a year ago, Ruby became the care provider for her father, George. He is 89 and moved into Ruby's apartment because he was no longer able to live independently after his brother's death. On most week-nights, Ruby cooks for her father, her granddaughter, and everyone at Tiffany's house as well. Ruby says she loves having her family around, but she just doesn't have half the energy she used to have.

Ruby retired 5 years ago from the postal service, where she worked for 36 years. In addition to her pension and social security, she now earns a small amount for working part-time providing childcare for a former coworker's daughter. Ruby explains that she has to take the extra work in order to cover her father's prescription expenses not covered by his Medicare benefits and to help pay medical/prescription bills for Tiffany's household. Tiffany and Carl receive no medical benefits from their employers and have been considering lowering their income to qualify for Medicaid benefits. As this is being written in 2017, they are confused about the future of the Affordable Care Act. Ruby wants them to keep working, so she has been trying to use her connections to get them jobs with the postal service. Ruby reports this to be her greatest frustration, because her best postal service contacts are "either retired or dead." Although Ruby's health is currently stable, she is particularly concerned that it may worsen. She is diabetic and insulin dependent and worries about all the family members for whom she feels responsible. During the initial interview, Ruby confided that she thinks her physical demise has begun. Her greatest fear is death; not for herself, she says, but for the effect it would have on her family. She then asked her social worker to help her find a way to ensure their well-being after her death.

—Peter Maramaldi

CASE STUDY 9.3

JOSEPH AND ELIZABETH MENZEL, A GERMAN COUPLE

Christine, the 51-year-old daughter of Joseph and Elizabeth Menzel, came to the geriatric counseling center in a small town in Bavaria, Germany. She indicated that she could no longer provide adequate care to her parents and requested assistance from the geriatric social work team. Christine described the family situation as follows.

Her parents, Joseph and Elizabeth, live in a small house about 4 miles away from her apartment. Her brother Thomas also lives close by, but he can only provide help on the weekends because of his employment situation. The 79-year-old mother has been diagnosed with dementia of the Alzheimer's type. Her increasing forgetfulness is beginning to interfere with her mastery of the household and some other activities of daily living. Her 84-year-old father's behavior is also adding to the mother's difficulties. Joseph Menzel is described as an authoritarian and a very dominant person. For example, Christine says that he does not allow his wife to select which television shows she can watch or what music she can to listen to, even though she would like to make such choices by herself. According to the daughter, his behavior seems to add to Elizabeth Menzel's confusion and lack of personal confidence. At the same time, however, Joseph Menzel spends a lot of his time in bed. Sometimes he does not get up all day and neglects his own personal care. It is not clear how much his staying in bed is related to his general health condition; he has silicosis and congestive heart failure.

The couple lives a fairly isolated life and has no friends. Family members, the son Thomas, the daughter Christine and her partner, four grandchildren, and a brother of Elizabeth Menzel are the only occasional visitors. Christine's primary concern is with her mother's well-being. The mother needs assistance with the instrumental activities of daily living as well as with her health care. Having full-time employment, Christine indicates that she has a hard time providing the assistance and care she thinks is needed. Chores such as doctors' visits, shopping, cleaning, and regular checking in with the parents can be done by her and her brother. However, additional care responsibilities seem to be beyond Christine's capacity at this time. During the initial contact with Christine, the following services were discussed:

- An application for additional funding through the long-term care insurance (German Pflegeversicherung) will be completed. Because Elizabeth Menzel suffers from dementia, she would be eligible for higher levels of support.

- A local care provider will be hired to help with managing medications. It is expected that this may help the parents get used to receiving outside assistance, in case they require higher levels of support with physical care and hygiene down the road. Having someone stop by daily will also provide an added measure of security and social contact.

- The Menzels will apply for daily lunch delivery through the local Meals on Wheels service.

- A volunteer will be found through the local volunteer network. This person should stop by one to two times per week to engage the mother in activities such as music, walks, playing games, or memory training.

- Elizabeth Menzel will be asked whether she would like to attend the weekly Erzählcafé meetings, a local group for persons with dementia.

- Joseph Menzel will receive information from the geriatric counseling center regarding how to attend to his wife's dementia. Furthermore, an assessment will be completed to establish whether he has depression, and, if needed, he will be connected to relevant medical services.

- In addition to receiving assistance from the geriatric counseling center, Christine will be invited to participate in a support group for relatives and caregivers of persons with dementia.

All the described services and programs were secured within a short succession. After three initial visits, Elizabeth Menzel has established a good relationship with the volunteer helper and indicates that she likes attending the Erzählcafé meetings. After the assistance for his wife started, Joseph Menzel opened up to having a conversation with the geriatric social worker. He indicated that he was thinking a lot lately about his own personal biography. He and his wife were displaced after the war. They grew up as neighbors in Silesia (today part of Poland). Both of their families had to leave everything behind and flee overnight in October 1946. After staying in various refugee camps, their families finally ended up in Bavaria. This is where they started dating and finally married. Having lost everything, they had to start all over again. They had to work hard for everything they have today. Joseph Menzel worked his entire life as a miner, supplementing his income through a second job painting houses. His wife was employed as a seamstress. Respected for their hard work and engagement, they were soon accepted as members of their new community. However, Joseph Menzel says that he has never come to terms with his postwar displacement and the loss of his homeland. He started a community group and organized regular meetings for displaced persons. Together with his daughter, he also wrote a book about his homeland. Now he feels too weak and ill to do anything. He just wants to stay at home and sit in his recliner all day. After talking with the geriatric social worker, Joseph Menzel overcame his initial reluctance and agreed to have additional contacts with the geriatric counseling center.

—Rosa Schnitzenbaumer

DEMOGRAPHICS OF THE OLDER POPULATION

As you can see from the stories of Gene and Lois Smith, Ruby Johnson, and Joseph and Elizabeth Menzel, older adults do not live primarily in the past. Like all other individuals, their day-to-day life incorporates past, present, and future orientations. In terms of their life span, they have more time past them and less time ahead, but research regularly shows that the overemphasis on the past is a myth (Mayer et al., 1999). Research from the longitudinal Berlin Aging Study has been able to dispel some of the commonly held beliefs about older adults. According to their research as well as findings from other studies, older adults

- are not preoccupied with death and dying,

- are able and willing to learn new things,

- still feel that they can and want to be in control of their life,

- still have life goals,

- do not live primarily in the past, and

- still live an active life, their health permitting.

Data collection for the Berlin Aging Study II began in 2009 and will provide new information about the aging process in the years to come.

The term *late adulthood* covers about one quarter to one third of a person's life and includes active and less active, healthy and less healthy, working and nonworking persons. Late adulthood encompasses a wide range of age-related life experiences. Someone reaching late adulthood today and having lived in the United States has experienced school segregation and busing for the purposes of school integration, Martin Luther King's "I have a dream" speech, the election of the first African American president, and the appointment of the first Latina Supreme Court justice. He or she may have experienced the Dust Bowl and two world wars and would have grown up listening to radio shows before TV existed. The person may have been at Woodstock and could be in the age cohort of Mick Jagger and Bob Dylan. Every client in the opening case studies could be considered old, and yet, they are functioning in different ways and at different levels. In the context of U.S. society, the term *old* can have many meanings. These meanings reflect attitudes, assumptions, biases, and cultural interpretations of what it means to grow older. In discussing life course trajectories, we commonly use the terms *older population* or *elderly persons* to refer to those over 65 years of age. But an Olympic gymnast is "old" at age 25, a president of the United States is "young" at age 50, and a 70-year-old may not consider herself "old" at all.

Late adulthood is perhaps a more precise term than *old*, but it can still be confusing because of the almost 50-year range of ages it may include. Late adulthood is considered to start at 65 and continue through the 85-and-older range. Considering age 65 as the starting point for late adulthood is somewhat arbitrary, because there is no sudden change to our physiology, biology, or personality. Rather, it can be traced back to Bismarck's social insurance schemes in Germany more than 100 years ago and the introduction of the Social Security Act in the United States in 1935. In both cases, 65 years was selected for retirement based on population statistics and expected survival rates. Many people today reach the life stage of late adulthood. In 2017, there were approximately 655 million people 65 years or older in the world, and by 2050 this number is expected to increase to 1.6 billion (World Bank, 2017). In 2012, the World Health Organization estimated that, worldwide, adults aged 65 and older will outnumber children younger than age 5 within 5 years, and by 2050, older adults will outnumber children younger than age 14. Globally, the United States is fairly young compared to other wealthy nations, with 46 million people or 15% of its population consisting of people 65 and older in 2014 (Federal Interagency Forum on Aging-Related Statistics, 2016). Most European countries average 20% or more of their population at 65 or older. Japan's and Italy's older populations stood at 27% of the total population in 2016, and for Germany, Italy, Greece, and Finland it was above 20% (Federal Interagency Forum on Aging-Related Statistics, 2016).

According to U.S. census data, the 85-and-older population is the fastest growing segment of the aging population. As baby boomers enter this age group, the pace will only pick up with a projected increase from 6.3 million people in 2015 to 14.6 million in 2040 and 20 million by 2060 (Administration on Aging, 2016; Federal Interagency Forum on Aging-Related Statistics, 2016). From 1980 to 2015, the centenarian population (people age 100 and older) had a larger percentage increase than the population as a whole, and there were 76,974 centenarians in 2015 (Administration on Aging, 2016). In 2015, persons reaching age 65 had an average life expectancy of an additional 19.4 years (20.6 years for females and 18 for males). A child born in 2015 could expect to live 78.8 years, more than 30 years longer than a child born in 1900. Life expectancy at age 65 increased by 2.5 years from 1900 to 1960 but by 4.2 years from 1960 to 2007 (Administration on Aging, 2016).

Increased life expectancy is a product of a number of factors: decreased mortality of children and young adults, decreased mortality among the aging, improved health technology, and other factors. The enormous increase in life expectancy is not unique to the United States. Indeed, recent research found that the United States has the lowest average life expectancy of 17 high-income countries, including European countries, Canada, Australia, and Japan. The researchers speculated that these differences in life expectancy are related to differences in access to health care, health behaviors, income inequality, and physical environments (dependence on automobiles) (Woolf & Aron, 2013). But increasing life expectancy is not just happening in high-income countries. About 60% of the population older than 65 lives in low- and middle-income countries, and this may increase to 75% by 2020 (Hooyman, Kawamoto, & Kiyak, 2018). However, the average life expectancy at birth is 55 in the least economically advanced countries, compared with an average of 77 in the most economically advanced countries (Hooyman et al., 2018).

Life expectancy in the United States varies by race, sex, and socioeconomic status. In 2010, the overall life expectancy at birth in the United States was 78.7 years (Hoyert & Xu, 2012). It was 86.5 for Asian Americans, 82.8 for Latinos, 78.9 for Whites, 76.9 for Native Americans, and 74.6 for African Americans (Henry J. Kaiser Family Foundation, 2013). Life expectancy increased more for the Black population than for the White population from 1975 to 2015, narrowing the life expectancy gap from 6.6 years to 3.5 years (National Center for Health Statistics, 2017b). In 2015, females had an average life expectancy at birth of 81.2 years compared with an average of 76.3 years for males (National Center for Health Statistics, 2017b). Life expectancy increases with socioeconomic advantage, and recent research indicates that as income inequality grows, life expectancy is actually falling in some segments of the U.S. working class. In 2008, U.S. men and women with less than 12 years of education had life expectancies at the level experienced in the 1950s and 1960s (Olshansky et al., 2012).

Age structure, the segmentation of society by age, will affect the economic and social condition of the nation, especially as it regards dependence. An interesting side effect of the growing elderly population is a shifting **dependency ratio**—a demographic indicator that expresses the degree of demand placed on society by the young and the aged combined, the ratio of dependent age groups to the working-age population. There are three dependency ratios: the old-age dependency ratio, the number of elders 65 and older per 100 people ages 20 to 64; the youth dependency ratio, the number of children younger than 20 per 100 persons ages 20 to 64; and the total dependency ratio, the combination of both categories (U.S. Census Bureau, 2010). The nature of the U.S. dependency ratio has changed gradually over the past century, as the percentage of children and adolescents in the population has decreased and the percentage of dependent older adults has increased. As Exhibit 9.1 demonstrates, the old-age dependency ratio is predicted to continue to increase at a fairly rapid pace in the near future. The overall dependency ratio is expected to stabilize to about 85 youth and older adults per 100 persons ages 20 to 64 from 2030 to 2050 (U.S. Census Bureau, 2010). The social and economic implications of this increase in the dependency ratio are the focus and concern of many scholars and policymakers.

The older population encompasses a broad age range and is often categorized into subgroups: the young-old (ages 65 to 74), the middle-old (ages 75 to 84), and the oldest-old (over 85). The Smiths and Ruby Johnson exemplify the young-old, the Menzels the middle-old. In this chapter, we discuss those persons in the young-old and middle-old categories, ages approximately 65 to 84. Very late adulthood is discussed in Chapter 10, covering ages 85 and older.

The poverty rate among older adults has decreased significantly over the past decades. Whereas 29% of Americans over age 65 lived in poverty in 1966, it was 8.8% in 2015 (Administration on Aging, 2016; Federal Interagency Forum on Aging-Related Statistics, 2016). Another 5% of older adults were classified as near-poor in 2015. Yet it is important to note that 36% of those over age 65 are in the highest income group, the largest percentage for any age group (Federal Interagency Forum on Aging-Related Statistics, 2016). Older persons living alone are much more likely to be poor (15.4%) than those living with families (5.7%) (Administration on Aging, 2016).

The geographic distribution of the elderly population varies considerably across the United States. In 2015, more than half (51%) of persons 65 and older lived in 10 states: California, Florida, Texas, New York, Pennsylvania, Ohio, Illinois, Michigan, North Carolina, and New Jersey (Administration on Aging, 2016). Older adults are less likely than other age groups to change

EXHIBIT 9.1 ● Youth and Elderly Dependency Ratios in the United States, 1900, 1995, 2010, and 2030

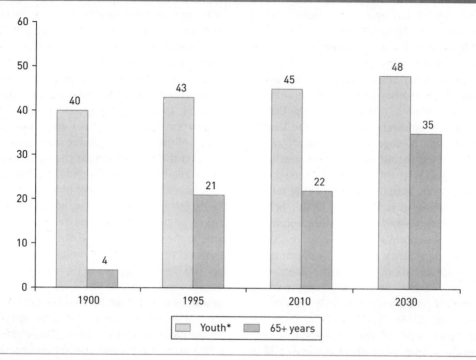

Source: U.S. Census Bureau, 2010.

*1900 and 1995 youth dependency based on newborns to 17-year-olds; 2010 and 2030 dependency based on newborns to 19-year-olds.

residence; from 2015 to 2016, 3% of older adults moved compared with 13% of the younger-than-65 population. Residential mobility can lead to changing age structures within neighborhoods and thus affect the elderly person's life. One study noted that the role of neighborhood structural context, as measured by poverty, residential stability, and aged-based demographic concentration, was predictive of the health and well-being of elders (Subramanian, Kubzansky, Berman, Fay, & Kawachi, 2006). For example, the Smiths used to be a "typical" family in their neighborhood. Now, as one of only two households with elderly occupants, they are the exception.

DIVERSITY OF THE LATE-ADULT POPULATION

Considering the changing demographics of and the cultural factors that define this population, the increasing diversity of older adults in the United States should be illuminated. The United States is one of the most racially and ethnically diverse societies in the world, and the aging population reflects the shifting racial and ethnic trends in the general population. In 2015, 9% of the population over age 65 was African American, 8% was Hispanic, 4% was Asian or Pacific Islander, and less than 1% was Native American and Native Hawaiian/Pacific Islander. Less than 1% also identify as being of two or more races (Administration on Aging, 2016). From 2005 to 2015, the percentage of the older-adult population that was ethnic minority increased from 18% to 22% and is expected to be 28% in 2030. It is even more striking to consider that from 2015 to 2030 the White (not Hispanic) population over 65 is expected to increase by 43% whereas the ethnic minority population in this age group will grow by 99%. Hispanics are the fastest growing segment of the older-adult population, with an expected increase of 123% from 2015 to 2030; during this same period, other older-adult ethnic groups are projected to increase by 80% to 90%.

Though increasing in number, ethnic minorities experience unique challenges in older adulthood. Adequate income is a greater problem for minority elders, with 18.4% of older African Americans, 17.5% of older Hispanic Americans, and 11.8% of older Asian Americans living in poverty, compared with 6.6% of older Whites (Administration on Aging, 2016). The term *health disparity* is commonly used to describe the differences in health outcomes faced by diverse populations, where one or more populations are identified to be at a disadvantage (U.S. Department of Health and Human Services, Office of Disease Prevention and Health Promotion, 2010). Ethnic minorities of all ages experience health disparities for they typically experience higher rates of chronic health conditions, receive poorer care, and have less access to care (U.S. Department of Health and Human Services, 2014). Income, language, cultural norms, and access to health care barriers are contributors to these disparities for ethnic minority elders (Centers for Disease Control and Prevention, 2013). As a major protective factor against these risks, however, ethnic minorities may have the benefit of close support networks that they depend on throughout their life courses. These networks may include family of origin, extended family, neighbors, and members of religious organizations. Cultural values and a sense of filial responsibility among some ethnic minorities may strengthen this network and allow for greater care from members of the family of origin (Chow, Auh, Scharlach, Lehning, & Goldstein, 2010; Miyawaki, 2016; Taylor, Chatters, Woodward, & Brown, 2013).

Although the majority in terms of number, women 65 years of age and older are considered a minority in terms of status and challenges in aging. Women presently do and will continue to outnumber men in the age-65-and-older population. Currently, the ratio is 127 women for every 100 men, and in the 85+ segment it is even higher, 190 women for every 100 men. The median income of older persons in 2015 was $31,372 for males and $18,250 for females. Older women are more likely than older men to be poor (10% versus 7%) and are more likely to live alone (35% compared to 20%). When considering women over 75, almost half live alone. Additionally, older women are more than 3 times as likely to be widowed as men (Administration on Aging, 2016). In terms of health, women 65+ have greater functional limitations and disabilities than men. Women also have higher rates of depression (Federal Interagency Forum on Aging-Related Statistics, 2016). Furthermore, midlife and older women take on the primary responsibilities as caregivers and providers of assistance to spouses and parents; women account for 60% of family caregivers for persons over 50 (National Alliance for Caregiving and AARP, 2015).

Women provide a great deal of care and support to family members and others throughout the life course. As a result, their support relationships and networks are often stronger and more emotionally robust than their male counterparts (Hooyman et al., 2018; Stevens & Van Tilburg, 2011).

Lesbian, gay, bisexual, transgender, and queer (LGBTQ) people are another social minority that faces unique challenges as they age. Older LGBTQ individuals exhibit higher rates of health conditions such as obesity, disability, and HIV and are at greater risk for depression, loneliness, and substance abuse. In addition, they are at an increased risk for suicide and for being the victims of violence throughout their lives (Fredriksen-Goldsen et al., 2011; Hash & Rogers, 2017). Lifelong oppression and discrimination compromises both mental and physical health outcomes for this group of older adults. This population has also experienced unsupportive policies and professionals, which has likely caused them to be more apprehensive about seeking such health and social services as in-home services, support groups, case management, mental health services, and care in assisted living and skilled nursing facilities (Gugliucci et al. 2013; Hash, 2006; Hash & Rogers, 2017; Stein, Beckerman, & Sherman, 2010).

Although LGBTQ elders have primarily lived through a period in which their identities and relationships were not supported and were even pathologized or criminalized, recent events have improved the landscape for LGBTQ people of all ages (Hash & Rogers, 2017). In 2013, 81-year-old Edie Windsor won the Supreme Court case (*United Sates v. Windsor*) that paved the way for marriage equality in the United States by repealing the Defense of Marriage Act (DOMA) (Gabbett, 2013). Two years after DOMA was ruled unconstitutional, 65-year-old former Olympic gold medal athlete Bruce Jenner came out as transgender, became known as Kaitlyn, and granted visibility to the lives of older transgender individuals (Bissinger, 2015). Living through unfriendly societal times and dealing with unsupportive family, professionals, and policies may have helped LGBTQ elders build resilience throughout their lifetimes and make them uniquely prepared to cope with the challenges of older adulthood (Fredriksen-Goldsen et al., 2011; Hash & Rogers, 2013). Many older LGBTQ individuals have also built alternative support networks in the face of adversity, which include friends, current and former partners, and accepting family-of-origin members—networks that can provide assistance in later years (Masini & Barrett, 2008; Metlife Mature Market Institute, 2010).

PHOTOS 9.1A & B The ethnic and racial diversity of the older population in the United States underscores the importance of taking cultural differences in perceptions of aging into account.

Like ethnic and social minorities, older adults residing in small towns and rural areas also face many special challenges (Hash, Wells, & Spencer, 2015). Rural communities typically have older populations than urban areas, with a mean age of 42.5 as compared to 37.6 for the United States as a whole (U.S. Census Bureau, 2011–2015a). Nineteen percent of people in rural areas are age 65 or older, compared to 14% in urban areas and in the United States as a whole (U.S. Census Bureau, 2011–2015b). Rural residents of all ages suffer from higher rates of individual and community-level poverty than their urban counterparts. Rural elders also have the added disadvantages of poorer health, more chronic health conditions, and greater mobility limitations (Bennett, Olatosi, & Probst, 2008; Laditka, Laditka, Olatosi, & Elder, 2007). Rural residents also do not have access to the wide range of health and human services available in most urban areas (U.S. Department of Health and Human Services, 2008). This includes a shortage of medical specialists and difficulty accessing public transportation (Hartman & Weierbach, 2013; H. Li, 2006; Park et al., 2010). Despite the challenges, the rural context is often praised for being tight-knit and providing access to a strong informal support network. For those who age in small towns and rural areas, this means that they might seek assistance from friends, neighbors, members of religious groups, as well as nuclear and extended family in the absence of formal care services (Hash, Wells, & Spencer, 2015).

CULTURAL CONSTRUCTION OF LATE ADULTHOOD

The ethnic and racial diversity of the older population in the United States underscores the complexity and importance of taking cultural differences in perceptions of aging into account. A salient example of cultural differences in approaches to aging is the contrasts between traditional Chinese and mainstream U.S. beliefs and values. China has been described in anthropological literature as a "gerontocracy," wherein older people are venerated, given deference, and valued in nearly every task. Benefiting from the Confucian value of filial piety, older people hold a revered position in the family and society.

By contrast, consider the traditional cultural influences in the United States, where individualism, independence, and self-reliance are core values that inherently conflict with the aging process. In the United States, older people have traditionally been collectively regarded as dependent, and cultural values dictate that older people living independently are given higher regard than those requiring assistance. As people age, they strive to maintain the independence and avoid—at all costs—becoming a burden to their family. Older people in the United States typically resort to intervention from private or social programs to maintain their independence rather than turning to family. By contrast, Chinese elders traditionally looked forward to the day when they would become part of their children's household, to live out their days being venerated by their families (Gardiner, 2018).

No discussion of comparisons between cultures would be complete without mention of differences that occur within groups. An individual Chinese person might value independence. And an individual in the United States might be closer to the Confucian value of filial piety than traditional U.S. values. Additionally, processes such as acculturation, assimilation, and bicultural socialization further influence the norms, values, expectations, and beliefs of all cultural groups, including that which is considered the dominant cultural norm. Globalization of economic and information exchange also impacts and changes the cultural norms of all countries so that culture must be construed as something that is dynamic, fluid, emergent, improvisational, and enacted (Gardiner, 2018). In fact, U.S. values of aging appear to be shifting, influenced in part by political and market forces. In the United States, we are now bombarded with contradictory information about aging—media presentations of long-lived, vibrant older adults are juxtaposed with media presentations of nursing home horror stories.

In his book *Aging Well*, George Vaillant (2002) raises the question "Will the longevity granted to us by modern medicine be a curse or a blessing?" (p. 3). The answer, he suggests, is influenced by individual, societal, and cultural values, but his research makes him optimistic. Vaillant (2002, 2012) reports on the most long-term longitudinal research available, the Study of Adult Development. The study includes three separate cohorts totaling 824 persons, all of whom have been studied since adolescence, covering almost 75 years:

1. *268 socially advantaged graduates of Harvard University born about 1920.* These research participants were selected for their physical and psychological health as they began college.

2. *456 socially disadvantaged inner-city men born in 1930.* These research participants were selected because they were nondelinquent at age 14. Half of their families were known to five or more social agencies, and more than two thirds of their families had been recent public welfare recipients.

3. *90 middle-class intellectually gifted women born about 1910.* These participants were selected for their high IQs when they were in California elementary schools.

A significant limitation of the study is the lack of racial and ethnic diversity among the participants, who are almost exclusively White. The great strength of the study is its ability to control cohort effects by following the same participants over such a long period of time.

Much of the news from the Study of Adult Development is good. Vaillant reminds us that Immanuel Kant wrote his first book of philosophy at 57, Titian created many artworks after 76, Ben Franklin invented bifocals at 78, and Will Durant won a Pulitzer Prize for history at 83. Unless they develop a brain disease, the majority of older adults maintain a "modest sense of well-being" (2002, p. 5) until a few months before they die. Older adults are also less depressed than the general population and tend to remember pleasant more than unpleasant events (Vaillant, 2012). Many older adults acknowledge hardships of aging but also see a reason to continue to live. Vaillant (2002) concludes that "positive aging means to love, to work, to learn something we did not know yesterday, and to enjoy the remaining precious moments with loved ones" (p. 16). Although he found many paths to successful aging, Vaillant identifies six traits for "growing old with grace," found in Exhibit 9.2.

Another recent study using longitudinal data from the Americans' Changing Lives (ACL) study continues to examine the question of the impact of life expectancy and quality of life as a person ages. This is a nationally representative sample of adults age 25 and older, first interviewed in 1986 and reinterviewed in 1989, 1994, and 2001/2002 (House, Lantz, & Herd, 2005). A fifth wave of data collection was completed in May 2012, and data analysis is in the early stages as this chapter is being written (Americans' Changing Lives, 2017). The sample for this study has more racial diversity than the

---

EXHIBIT 9.2 ● Six Traits for Growing Old With Grace

1. Caring about others and remaining open to new ideas
2. Showing cheerful tolerance of the indignities of old age
3. Maintaining hope
4. Maintaining a sense of humor and capacity for play
5. Taking sustenance from past accomplishments while remaining curious and continuing to learn from the next generation
6. Maintaining contact and intimacy with old friends

Source: Based on Vaillant, 2002, pp. 310–311.

Study of Adult Development. The ACL was designed to address one central dilemma of research on aging and health: whether increased life expectancy in the United States and other economically advanced nations foreshadowed a scenario of longer life but worsening health with the result of increasing numbers of chronically ill and functionally limited and disabled people requiring expensive medical and long-term care—or whether, through increased understanding of psychosocial as well as biomedical risk factors, the onset of serious morbidity and attendant functional limitation and disability could be potentially postponed or "compressed."

These authors focused on socioeconomic disparities in health changes through the middle and later years. They represent a set of scholars examining the theoretical concept of *cumulative advantage and disadvantage* and its role in understanding differential aging among various populations (Schöllgen, Huxhold, & Tesch-Römer, 2010). (See Chapter 1 for a discussion of these concepts.) They argue that multiple interacting factors throughout the life course impact the quality of the health of older individuals. For example, early poverty, lifetime of poverty, poor environmental conditions, poor education, race, and gender have a direct impact on how a person will age. It is not a simple linear causal track but instead reflects the complexity of interacting risk and protective factors.

Reviewing research findings from the ACL study, House et al. (2005) examined the impact of two factors related

to socioeconomic status (SES), education and income, on poor health. They found that overall socioeconomic disparities do impact health outcomes rather than the reverse. Additionally, they found that education has a greater impact than income on the onset of functional limitations or disabilities. Income, however, has a greater impact on the progression of functional limitations. Finally, the impact of educational disparities on the onset of functional limitations increased strikingly in later-middle and early old age, with more highly educated individuals postponing limitations and thus compressing the number of years spent with limitations (House et al., 2005).

PSYCHOSOCIAL THEORETICAL PERSPECTIVES ON SOCIAL GERONTOLOGY

How social workers see and interpret aging will inspire our interventions with older adults. **Social gerontology**—the social science that studies human aging—offers several theoretical perspectives that can explain the process of growing old. Ten predominant theories of social gerontology are introduced here. An overview of the primary concepts of each theory is presented in Exhibit 9.3.

1. *Disengagement theory.* **Disengagement theory** suggests that as elderly individuals grow older, they

EXHIBIT 9.3 ● Psychosocial Theoretical Perspectives on Social Gerontology

Theory	Primary Theme
Disengagement theory	Elderly persons gradually disengage from society.
Activity theory	Level of life satisfaction is related to level of activity.
Continuity theory	Elderly persons continue to adapt and continue their interaction patterns.
Social construction theory	Self-concepts arise through interaction with the environment.
Feminist theories	Gender is an important organizing factor in the aging experience.
Social exchange theory	Resource exchanges in interpersonal interactions change with age.
Life course perspective/life course capital perspective	Aging is a dynamic, lifelong process characterized by many transitions. People accumulate human capital during the life course to address their needs.
Age stratification perspective	Society is stratified by age, which determines people's roles and rights.
Productive aging theory	A new generation of older adults is more physically active, mobile, healthy, and economically secure.
Environmental gerontology	Place and environment impact social role, status, and activities of older adults.

gradually decrease their social interactions and ties and become increasingly self-preoccupied (Cumming & Henry, 1961). This is sometimes seen as a coping mechanism in the face of ongoing deterioration and loss (Tobin, 1988). In addition, society disengages itself from older adults. Although disengagement is seen as a normative and functional process of transferring power within society, the theory does not explain, for example, the fact that a growing number of older persons, such as Gene and Lois Smith and Ruby Johnson, continue to assume active roles in society (Hendricks & Hatch, 2006). Although it was the first comprehensive theory trying to explain the aging process (Achenbaum & Bengston, 1994), disengagement theory has received much criticism and little research support. To the contrary, research conducted through the National Social Life Health and Aging Project shows that older Americans are generally well-connected and engaged in community life according to their abilities (Cornwell, Laumann, & Schumm, 2008). Disengagement theory is now widely discounted by gerontologists (Hooyman et al., 2018).

2. *Activity theory.* **Activity theory** states that higher levels of activity and involvement are directly related to higher levels of life satisfaction in elderly people (Havighurst, 1968). If they can, individuals stay active and involved and carry on as many activities of middle adulthood as possible. There is growing evidence that physical activity is associated with postponing functional limitation and disability (Benjamin, Edwards, & Bharti, 2005). Activity theory has received some criticism for not addressing relatively high levels of satisfaction for individuals such as Ms. Johnson, whose level of activity is declining. It also does not address the choice made by many older individuals to adopt a more relaxed lifestyle. Some argue that the theory does not adequately address factors such as ethnicity, lifestyle, gender, and socioeconomic status (Eliopoulus, 2010; Moody & Sasser, 2015). Activity theory also does not sufficiently take into account individual life circumstances and loses sight of personhood in order to satisfy society's view of how people should age (Moody & Sasser, 2015).

3. *Continuity theory.* **Continuity theory** was developed in response to critiques of the disengagement and activity theories. According to continuity theory, individuals adapt to changes by using the same coping styles they have used throughout the life course, and they adopt new roles that substitute for roles lost because of age (Neugarten, Havighurst, & Tobin, 1968). Individual personality differences are seen as a major influence in adaptation to old age. Those individuals who were active earlier in life stay active in later life, whereas those who adopted a more passive lifestyle continue to do so in old age. Older adults also typically retain the same stance concerning religion and sex as they always did. Current scholarship considers the interaction between personal and contextual factors that promote or impede the accomplishment of desired goals and new roles, recognizing that individuals have control over some contextual factors but not others (Brandtstadter, 2006). Continuity theory might help counsel someone such as Lois Smith. Just as she adapted actively to her divorce by reentering the job market later in life, she might actively seek new roles in retirement. She might find great satisfaction in volunteering in her church and in being a grandmother. Continuity theory is difficult to empirically test (Hooyman et al., 2018). There is also criticism regarding the definition of "normal aging." The theory distinguishes normal aging from pathological aging and does not sufficiently address older persons with chronic health conditions (Quadagno, 2007).

4. *Social construction theory.* **Social construction theory** aims to understand and explain the influence of social definitions, social interactions, and social structures on the individual elderly person. This theoretical framework suggests that ways of understanding are shaped by the cultural, social, historical, political, and economic conditions in which knowledge is developed; thus, values are associated with various ways of understanding (Dean, 1993). Conceptions about aging arise through interactions of an individual with the social environment (Dannefer & Perlmutter, 1990). The recent conceptualization of "gerotranscendence" is an example of the application of social constructionist theory to aging. The idea of gerotranscendence holds that human development extends into old age and does not simply end or diminish with aging (Hooyman et al., 2018; Tornstam, 2005). According to this theory, aging persons evaluate their lives in terms of the time they have ahead and try to derive a sense of identity, self, and place in the world (Degges-White, 2005; Tornstam, 2005). Using focus group methodology, Wadensten (2005) found that participants identified the concept of gerotranscendence as salient and beneficial to them because it gave them a more positive view of aging, allowing them to affirm themselves as they are.

5. *Feminist theories.* Proponents of **feminist theories** of aging suggest that gender is a key factor in understanding a person's aging experience. They contend

that because gender is a critical social stratification factor with attendant power, privilege, and status that produces inequalities and disparities throughout the life course, we can only understand aging by taking gender into account (Arber & Ginn, 1995). Gender is viewed as influencing the life course trajectory by impacting access and opportunity, health disparities, and disparities in socioeconomic opportunities and by creating a lifelong condition of "constrained choice" (Rieker & Bird, 2005). Gabriela Spector-Mersel (2006) argues that in Western societies, older persons have been portrayed as "ungendered." Older men are in a paradoxical position because the metaphors for old age are the opposite of the metaphors for masculinity in these societies. Think, for example, about Joseph Menzel's experience as a caregiver to his wife and how some of his role obligations differ from his lifelong role expectations as a man. Also, consider Ms. Johnson's experience as a single older woman. How might her personal situation differ if she were a man?

6. *Social exchange theory.* **Social exchange theory** is built on the notion that an exchange of resources takes place in all interpersonal interactions (Blau, 1964; Homans, 1961). This theory is rooted in an analysis of values developed from a market-driven capitalist society. Individuals will only engage in an exchange if they perceive a favorable cost/benefit ratio or if they see no better alternatives (Hendricks, 1987). As individuals become older, the resources they can bring to the exchange begin to shift. Social exchange theory bases its explanation of the realignment of roles, values, and contributions of older adults on this assumption. For example, many older persons get involved in volunteer activities; this seemingly altruistic activity may also be seen as fulfilling an emotional need that provides a personal gain. Thus, they are able to adjust and adapt to the altered exchange equation. Older individuals who withdraw from social activities may perceive their personal resources as diminished to the point where they have little left to bring to an exchange, thus leading to their increasing seclusion from social interactions. As social workers, then, it is important to explore how older couples such as Joseph and Elizabeth Menzel are dealing with the shift in resources within their relationship. Several studies indicate that maintaining reciprocity is important for older individuals (Fiori, Consedine, & Magai, 2008). For example, one study of reciprocity among residents of assisted living looked at the positive contributions of aging care recipients to their social relationships, including their interactions with caregivers (Beel-Bates, Ingersoll-Dayton, & Nelson, 2007).

7. *Life course perspective.* From the life course perspective, the conceptual framework for this book, aging is a dynamic, lifelong process. Human development is characterized by multidirectionality, multifunctionality, plasticity, and continuity in the person's experiences of gains and losses over the life course (Greve & Staudinger, 2006). Individuals go through many transitions in the course of their life span. Human development continues through aging and involves the interaction of person-specific factors, social structures, and personal agency (Hendricks & Hatch, 2006). The era they live in, the cohort they belong to, and personal and environmental factors influence individuals during these transitions. "Life course capital" is a contemporary addition to the life course perspective. The theory states that people, over the course of their life, accumulate human capital (resources) they can use to address their needs. This capital can take on various forms; it may be social, biological, psychological, or developmental human capital (Hooyman et al., 2018). This accumulation of life course capital has an impact on a person's aging, for example, on his or her health (e.g., morbidity, mortality) or wealth (e.g., standard of living in retirement).

8. *Age stratification perspective.* The **age stratification perspective** falls into the tradition of the life course perspective (Foner, 1995; Riley, 1971). Stratification is a sociological concept that describes a hierarchy in a given society. Social stratification is both multidimensional and interactive for individuals occupy multiple social locations with varying amounts of power, privilege, and status. The age stratification perspective suggests that, similar to the way society is structured by socioeconomic class, it is also stratified by age. Roles and rights of individuals are assigned based on their membership in an age group or cohort. Individuals proceed through their life course as part of that cohort. The experience of aging differs across cohorts because cohorts differ in size, composition, and experience with an ever-changing society. Current scholarship argues that social stratifications of gender, race or ethnicity, and socioeconomic status are pertinent stratifications to consider in aging, given the cumulative effect of disparities that are the result of such stratification (George, 2005).

9. *Productive aging.* **Productive aging theory** focuses on the positive changes that have occurred to the older-adult population. A new generation of older adults is more independent and better off than previous cohorts in many areas, including health, economic status, mobility, and education (Kaye, 2005). Productive

aging is not necessarily the continuation of an older person as contributor to the workforce but includes other behavior that is satisfying and meaningful to the older person. This approach maintains that the focus of aging theories has been too much on the losses, crises, and problems of aging, while neglecting the positive side of becoming older. Proponents of this perspective distinguish between three dimensions of productive aging: inner affective, inner utilitarian, and outer utilitarian (Kaye, 2005). The internal affective dimension focuses on personal growth and factors improving quality of life. The internal utilitarian dimension emphasizes functional growth, and the focus of the external utilitarian dimension is on societal contributions made by older adults to their communities, families, and friends (Kaye, 2005). Exhibit 9.4 provides an overview of these dimensions.

10. *Environmental gerontology*. Central to **environmental gerontology** is the concept of place (Gubrium, 1978) and the ecological model of aging first presented by Lawton (Lawton, 1986; Lawton & Nahemow, 1973). As much a perspective as a theory, environmental gerontology focuses on the interplay among system, person, place, and time throughout the life course (Moore, 2014). Differing from the life course perspective's focus on life capital, place and environment play a key role in environmental gerontology. Although older adults may want to continue assuming certain roles or carrying out certain actions, their physical or cognitive losses in combination with environmental factors may hinder their possibilities to do so. This in turn may impact the person's social roles and statuses (Moore, 2014). For example, when older adults live in environments that present them with opportunities for more physical activity and social interaction, they tend to stay more mobile and engaged. Efforts to create age-friendly communities and the movement toward aging in place have been influenced by environmental gerontology.

EXHIBIT 9.4 ● Dimensions of Productive Aging			
Dimension	**Inner (Affective)**	**Inner (Utilitarian)**	**Outer (Utilitarian)**
Focus and activity	Wellness promotion Life review Self-help Self-improvement Social interaction	Retirement planning Travel Recreation Physical exercise Education	Job training Employment Volunteer service Family support
Primary impact	Self	Self	Self and others
Specific outcomes	Increased personal growth Self-discovery Self-actualization Improved mental health Reduced isolation	Increased financial security Heightened intellectual stimulation Increased fitness and health Increased life security Increased knowledge and skills	Increased financial well-being Continued socialization Maintained identity and purpose Enhanced community well-being Heightened philanthropic expression
General outcomes (all three dimensions)	Enhanced self-esteem Heightened morale Higher quality of life Increased life satisfaction Heightened emotional and physical well-being	Enhanced self-esteem Heightened morale Higher quality of life Increased life satisfaction Heightened emotional and physical well-being	Enhanced self-esteem Heightened morale Higher quality of life Increased life satisfaction Heightened emotional and physical well-being

Source: Adapted from Kaye, 2005, p. 13.

PHOTO 9.2 Variables that often predict healthy aging include practicing healthy habits such as exercising, eating well, maintaining a healthy weight, and not smoking or abusing alcohol.

CRITICAL THINKING QUESTIONS 9.1

At what age will you consider yourself "old"? What do you think your favorite activity will be when you are old? What do you think your biggest challenge will be when you are old? What do you think will be important to you when you are old? Where do you get your ideas about old age?

BIOLOGICAL CHANGES IN LATE ADULTHOOD

Every day, our bodies are changing. In a sense, then, our bodies are constantly aging. As social workers, however, we need not be concerned with the body's aging until it begins to affect the person's ability to function in her or his world, which typically begins to occur in late adulthood. There are more than 300 biological theories of why our bodies age, but no single theory fully explains biological aging (Lipsky & King, 2015). In this discussion, we follow Kunlin Jin's (2010) lead and consider two categories of theories: programmed aging theories and damage or error theories. The following discussion of these theories is taken from a review article by Jin. We also discuss developmental biocultural co-constructivism, a newer theoretical approach to aging in the human environment.

Programmed aging theories suggest that aging follows an internal biological clock that regulates development, growth, and aging (Lipsky & King, 2015). Jin (2010) identifies three subcategories of programmed

aging theories. *Programmed longevity theory* proposes that biological aging occurs due to gene activity, but the genetic mechanisms of biological aging are not yet known. *Endocrine theory* proposes that biological clocks act through hormones to influence the pace of aging. Recent research indicates that hormones play an active role in regulating biological aging. *Immunological theory* proposes that the immune system is programmed to decline over time. There is strong evidence that the immune system peaks at puberty and gradually declines throughout adulthood.

Damage or error theories of aging emphasize the role of environmental assaults that cause cumulative damage to various biological systems and the failure of the body to fix the damage (Lipsky & King, 2015). Jin (2010) identifies five subcategories of damage or error theories. *Wear and tear theory* proposes that parts of the body wear out from repeated use. *Rate of living theory* proposes that the rate of basal metabolism impacts the length of the life span. *Cross-linking theory* proposes that an accumulation of cross-linked proteins damages cells and tissues. *Free radicals theory* proposes that superoxide and other free radicals cause damage to cells, eventually resulting in cell and organ death. *Somatic DNA damage theory* proposes that aging results from accumulated damage to the genetic integrity of the body's cells. Jin (2010) reports some evidence for each of the damage or error theories, but no one theory is sufficient to explain biological aging.

Developmental biocultural co-constructivism is a recent theoretical orientation to human development (Li, 2009). Although not a theory of aging per se, it adds important concepts for understanding the process of human aging. Theorists following this perspective claim that "brain and culture are in a continuous, interdependent, co-productive transaction and reciprocal determination" (Baltes, Rösler, & Reuter-Lorenz, 2006, p. 3). With this definition, they go beyond the nature and nurture debate, which focuses on whether nature or nurture makes the greater contribution to human behavior. In their view, this does not sufficiently address the *active* and *multidirectional* nature of this process. Developmental biocultural co-constructivism "gives equal standing to both the brain and the environment" (Baltes et al., 2006, p. 8). The perspective presumes dynamic reciprocal interactions of culture and human environment with the biology of a person. The brain is considered a dependent variable, that is, being coshaped by experiences and culture, and human behavior is "inherently the outcome of a 'dialogue' among and 'co-production' of genes, brain,

© iStockphoto.com

PHOTO 9.3 Social workers need to be concerned with aging if and when it affects a person's ability to function in his or her world.

and culture" (Baltes et al., 2006, p. 6). This is not a passive process. Rather, it can be described as a "shared and *collaborative production*, including *reciprocal modifications* and which under some conditions involves qualitatively new states whose emergence cannot be fully predicted from either of the two sources alone" (Baltes et al., 2006, p. 8, italics in original). Longitudinal research seems to provide support to this theory. For example, Schooler and Mulatu (2004) found reciprocal effects between the intellectual functioning and the complexity of tasks older adults had to fulfill during their employment years.

Health and Longevity

The **mortality rate**—the frequency at which death occurs within a population—has declined significantly for all segments of the population in the United States during the last century. From 1990 to 2014, the overall age-adjusted death rates for all causes of death for individuals 65 years and older declined by 20%. In this age bracket, death rates from heart disease and stroke declined by more than 50%. However, the death rates for some diseases increased; death rates from chronic lower respiratory diseases increased by 57%, and death rates from diabetes mellitus were higher in 2014 than in 1981 but lower than in 2001. In 2014, the leading causes of death for people 65 and older were, in descending order, heart disease, cancer, chronic lower respiratory diseases, stroke, Alzheimer's disease, and influenza/pneumonia. Diabetes was the sixth leading cause of death among non-Hispanic Whites but the fourth leading cause of death among non-Hispanic Blacks and Hispanics. Overall death rates in 2014 were higher for older men than for older women (Federal Interagency Forum on Aging-Related Statistics, 2016).

As mortality has decreased, **morbidity**—the incidence of disease—has increased. In other words, the proportion of the population suffering from age-related chronic conditions has increased in tandem with the population of elderly persons. In 2009–2010, for people 65 years or older, the most prevalent and debilitating chronic conditions in descending order were hypertension (54% of men, 57% of women), arthritis (45% of men, 56% of women), heart disease (37% of men, 26% of women), cancer (28% of men, 21% of women), and diabetes (24% of men, 18% of women). Chronic illnesses are long-term, rarely cured, and costly.

The prevalence of chronic conditions varies significantly by gender, race, and ethnicity. Older women report higher levels of asthma, arthritis, and hypertension than do older men, who are more likely to report heart disease, cancer, and diabetes (Federal Interagency Forum on Aging Related Statistics, 2016). Racial and ethnic differences also exist. Non-Hispanic Blacks report higher levels of hypertension (69% compared with 54%) and diabetes (32% compared with 18%) than non-Hispanic Whites. Hispanics report higher levels of diabetes than Whites (33% compared with 18%). Physical decline is also associated with SES, but it is difficult to separate SES from race and ethnicity because minority groups tend to be overrepresented in lower SES groups (Wilmoth & Longino, 2006).

A chronic condition can have considerable impact on a family system. In Ms. Johnson's case, the seven people for whom she cares—including two toddlers, an adolescent, an adult daughter who is functionally impaired, a granddaughter and her husband who both are at risk of leaving the workforce, and an aging father—are all affected by her chronic diabetes. This case illustrates the untold impact of chronic conditions in aging populations that are rarely described by national trend reports.

For many people, illness and death can be postponed through lifestyle changes. In recent years, the importance of preventing illness by promoting good health has received considerable attention. The goals of health promotion for older adults include preventing or delaying the onset of chronic disease and disability; reducing the severity of chronic diseases; and maintaining mental health, physical health, and physical functioning as long as possible. Ways to promote health in old age include improving dietary habits, increasing activity levels and physical exercise, stopping smoking, and obtaining regular health screenings (blood sampling, blood pressure measurement, cancer screening, glaucoma screening) (Centers for Disease Control and Prevention, 2013; Erickson, Gildengers, & Butters, 2013). An important finding has been the roles of self-efficacy, sense of mastery, positive attitude, and social supports in improving the quality of life and delaying functional limitation and disability (Meisner, 2012).

Age-Related Changes in Physiology

All systems of the body appear to be affected during the aging process. Consider the nervous system. In the brain, neurons and synapses are the transmitters of information throughout the nervous system. Brain volume shrinks, with a slow decrease starting after age 30, and there is a decrease in synapses and a loss of glial cells (Schuff et al., 2012). Many neural fibers lose their coating of myelin, causing communication among neurons to slow. Declines are especially large in the prefrontal cortex, responsible for executive function (Lu et al., 2013). Because we are born with many more neurons and synapses than we need to function, problems usually do not arise. If the older adult develops brain deficits in one area of the brain, he or she may make up for these deficits by increasing activity in other brain regions (Barulli & Stern, 2013). However, a neurological injury or disease may result in more permanent and serious consequences for an older person. This is just one of the changes that may affect the brain, spinal cord, nerves, and mechanisms controlling other organs in the body. We look more closely at changes in the brain and neurodegenerative diseases in the next section. A recent exciting find is that *neurogenesis*—the process of developing new neurons—continues throughout the life course. New neurons are created in the hippocampus and striatum throughout life but at a slower rate than prenatally (Ernst et al., 2014). Although many of these new neurons die off, some survive when exposed to experiences that require new learning. It is estimated that about 2% of neurons are renewed each year (Spalding et al., 2013).

Our cardiovascular system also changes in several ways as we become older. With age, the heart experiences cell loss and becomes more rigid. The cardiac output—the amount of blood pumped per minute—decreases throughout adult life, and the pulse slows with age. The arteries become less elastic and harden, which can result in arteriosclerosis. Fatty lipids accumulate in the walls of the blood vessels and make them narrower, which can cause atherosclerosis. As a result of these changes, less oxygen is available for muscular activities. With advancing age, it takes longer for the blood pressure and heart rate to return to normal resting levels after stressful events (Science Buddies, 2014).

The respiratory system too changes with age. Beginning at about 20 to 25 years of age, a person's lung capacity decreases throughout the life span. Breathing becomes a bit more labored. Respiratory muscle strength decreases with age and can interfere with effective coughing (Sharma & Goodwin, 2006). There is great variation in the effect of lung function, however; in healthy older adults who do not smoke, respiratory function is quite good enough for daily activities (Bjorklund, 2015; Sharma & Goodwin, 2006).

The most important age-related change in our skeletal system occurs after age 30, when the destruction of bones begins to outpace the reformation of bones. The gradual decrease in bone mass and bone density can cause osteoporosis, a condition in which the bones become brittle and fragile. Osteoporosis occurs in 20% of women older than 50 and half of women older than 80 (Bjorklund, 2015). It is estimated that bone mineral content decreases by 5% to 12% per decade from the 20s through the 90s. One result is that we get shorter as we age. As the cartilage between the joints wears thin, arthritis, a chronic inflammation of the joints, begins to develop. Although many individuals suffer from some form of arthritis in their 40s, the symptoms are often not painful until late adulthood. Some of these changes can be ameliorated by diet and exercise and by avoiding smoking and alcohol.

With increasing age, the muscular system declines in mass, strength, and endurance. As a consequence, an elderly person may become fatigued more easily. In addition, muscle contractions begin to slow down, which contributes to deteriorating reflexes and incontinence. However, the muscular system of older individuals can be successfully strengthened through weight training and changes in diet and lifestyle (Bjorklund, 2015).

Changes in the neurological, muscular, and skeletal systems have an impact on the sensory system and the sense of balance, which contributes to the increase in accidental falls and bone fractures in late adulthood. Vision decreases with age, and older persons need more light to reach the retina in order to see. The eye's adaptation to the dark slows with age, as does visual acuity, the ability to detect details. Age-related decreases in hearing are caused by degenerative changes in the spiral organ of the ear and the associated nerve cells. Many older adults have a reduced ability to hear high-pitched sounds. By age 65, about one third of adults have significant hearing loss, with men being more likely than women to suffer hearing loss (Bjorklund, 2015). Age-related changes in taste appear to be minimal. Differences may reflect individual factors, such as exposure to environmental conditions like smoking, periodontal disease, or use of medications, rather than general processes of aging. The smell receptors in the nose can decrease with age, however, and become less sensitive (Hooyman et al., 2018).

The integumentary system includes the skin, hair, and nails. The skin comprises an outer layer (epidermis) and an inner layer (dermis). With age, the epidermis becomes thinner and pigment cells grow and cluster, creating age spots on the skin (Bjorklund, 2015). The sweat and oil-secreting glands decrease, leaving the skin drier and more vulnerable to injury. Much of the fat stored in the hypodermis, the tissue beneath the skin, is lost in age, causing wrinkles. The skin of an older person often feels cool because the blood flow to the skin is reduced (Bjorklund, 2015).

Sexual potency begins to decline at age 20, but without disease, sexual desire and capacity continue in late adulthood. Vaillant (2002) reports that *frequency* of sexual activity decreases, however. He found that partners in good health at 75 to 80 often continue to have sexual relations but that the average frequency is approximately once in every 10 weeks. Some illnesses and some medications can affect the ability of older adults to have and enjoy sex, as can problems in the relationship.

Contemporary views on the physiology of aging focus on longevity. For the past 2 decades, an anti-aging medicine movement has focused on developing biomedical interventions that will delay or reverse the biological changes of aging. There are more than 26,000 members of the American Academy of Anti-Aging Medicine (ABMS), but A4M is not recognized by established medical organizations. Science and technology are creating possibilities that show promise for the future, but there is no evidence that these gains have increased the maximum life span of humans. Some of the more promising possibilities in this area include calorie-restricted diets (Ikeno et al., 2013); supernutrition using properly dosed dietary supplements of multivitamins and multiminerals along with the use of fresh, whole, unprocessed foods (Minor, Allard, Younts, Ward, & de Cabo, 2010); hormone therapy, including growth hormone (Reed, Merriam, & Kargi, 2013); gene manipulation (Zhang et al., 2012); and organ and tissue cloning (Nazarenko, 2015). Anti-aging medicine is a big business (Flatt, Settersen, Ponsaran, & Fishman, 2013), but the scientific evidence is sparse. We can expect, however, that humans will continue to seek ways to extend longevity.

The Aging Brain and Neurodegenerative Diseases

Before discussing the most common neurodegenerative diseases, dementia, Alzheimer's disease, and Parkinson's disease, we would like to provide a brief overview of the brain and how it functions. The brain is probably the most complex and least well-understood part of the human body. It weighs about 3 pounds, or about 2%

of a person's weight, and is made up of various types of cells. The most essential brain cells are the neurons. They are the "communicators," responsible for most of the information processing in our brain. Between the neurons are synaptic gaps. Our brain has more than 100 trillion of these so-called synapses (Alzheimer's Association, 2013). Information flows from a neuron through the synapses to neuroreceptors, which are the receiver of the next neuron. More than 50 types of such neurotransmitters exist, including dopamine, serotonin, acetylcholine, and norepinephrine. Glial cells are the second major type of brain cells. They are the "housekeepers," providing neurons with nutrition, insulating them, and helping transport damaged cells and debris (Alzheimer's Association, 2013). Capillaries are tiny blood vessels that provide the brain with oxygen, energy, nutrition, and hormones and transport waste. The brain has 400 billion such capillaries. Twenty percent of a person's blood flows through these capillaries to the brain (Alzheimer's Association, 2013).

The brain consists of two cerebral hemispheres. Current science believes that the difference is less in what information the two hemispheres process than in how they process it (Alzheimer's Association, 2013). It seems that the left hemisphere works on the details, whereas the right hemisphere processes the broader picture. Each brain hemisphere consists of four lobes.

The frontal lobe is the "organizer." This is where thinking, planning, memory, problem solving, and movement are processed. The parietal lobe deals with perceptions and inputs from our senses. It sits right behind the frontal lobe. The occipital lobe processes vision and sits at the back of the cerebral hemisphere. Finally, the temporal lobe focuses on taste, smell, sound, and memory storage. It sits at the side of the brain and below the frontal lobe. At the back bottom of the brain is the cerebellum. This is where balance, coordination, and motor coordination occur. Located below it is the brain stem, connecting the brain with the spinal cord. It manages the body functions that are immediately responsible for our survival such as breathing, heart rate, and blood pressure (Alzheimer's Association, 2013).

Several changes occur to the brain as we age. From ages 20 to 90, the brain loses 5% to 10% of its weight (Palmer & Francis, 2006). The areas most affected by this decrease are the frontal lobe and the hippocampus. A general loss of neurons also occurs. At the same time, the normal aging brain does not appear to lose synapses (Palmer & Francis, 2006). The transmission of information between neurons through the neurotransmitters can also decrease in some brain regions as we

age. Furthermore, there is less growth of new capillaries and a reduced blood flow caused by narrowing arteries in the brain. Plaques and tangles develop in and around the neurons (see discussion of Alzheimer's disease shortly) and inflammation and damage by free radicals increase (Alzheimer's Association, 2013). At the same time, the effects of these changes on performing tasks and memory are generally fairly small. Scores for task performance, for example, are similar for younger and older adults, when the older group is provided with additional time. Older adults can compensate and adapt well to many age-related brain changes. Part of this adaptation occurs through changes in the brain. Neuroimaging shows that some brain functions seem to get reorganized as the brain ages. Imaging results point to a process in which the aging brain starts using areas of the two hemispheres that were previously not focusing on performing those tasks to compensate for age-related loss (Stern, Hines, & Travis, 2014). Negative changes can also be offset by age-related overall improvements in some cognitive areas such as verbal knowledge or vocabulary (Alzheimer's Association, 2013). Other brain changes, however, can become more challenging. We now turn to some of these neurodegenerative diseases.

Dementia

Dementia is the term for brain disease in which memory and cognitive abilities deteriorate over time. It may be significantly unrecognized and undiagnosed in many older adults. Dementia is considered a syndrome—a group of symptoms—with a number of causes. The most common symptoms are difficulties with memory, language, and problem solving (Alzheimer's Association, 2017). An estimated 46.8 million people worldwide were living with dementia in 2017, and someone in the world develops dementia every 3 seconds. It is expected that the number of people living with dementia will almost double every 20 years. A majority, 58%, of people with dementia live in low- and middle-income countries (Alzheimer's Disease International, 2017). The first nationally representative population-based study of the prevalence of dementia in the United States, conducted in 2007, found the prevalence among persons aged 71 and older to be 13.9%. The prevalence increased with age; it was 5.0% for older adults aged 71 to 79 and 37.4% for those aged 90 or older (Plassman et al., 2007). A more recent study found that the prevalence of dementia among people in the United States age 65 years or older decreased from 11.6% in 2000 to 8.8% in 2012.

More years of education was associated with a lower risk of dementia, and during the 2000–2012 period in which the prevalence of dementia was declining, the average education level in the United States rose from 11.8 years to 12.7 years (Langa et al., 2017). The rate of dementia for those with a bachelor's or higher degree is around 5%, and it is about 21% for those with less than a high school degree (Federal Interagency Forum on Aging Related Statistics, 2016). One review of medical records of a geriatric clinic in Thailand found that 7% of patients with dementia-like symptoms had reversible causes (Muangpaisan, Petcharat, & Srinonprasert, 2012), and another review of medical records in one Brazilian outpatient dementia clinic, conducted over a 10-year period, found that 19% of patients with dementia-like symptoms had reversible causes (Bello & Schultz, 2011). The Alzheimer's Association (2017) estimates that 9% of people with dementia-like symptoms do not have dementia. Common reversible causes of dementia-like symptoms include social isolation, poor nutrition, vitamin B12 deficiency, dehydration, prescription and nonprescription drugs, a brain tumor, subdural hematomas, meningiomas, hypothyroid, syphilis or AIDS, anxiety, or severe depression, and the cognitive decline is reversible if identified and treated early enough (Alzheimer's Association, 2017; Joshi & Morley, 2006; Yousuf et al., 2010). Dementia is not curable. In the advanced stages, the person may repeat the same words over and over again, may have problems using appropriate words, and may not recognize a spouse or other family members. At the same time, the person may still be able to recall and vividly describe events that happened many years ago. Epidemiological studies indicate that Alzheimer's disease is the most common form of dementia, responsible for about 60% to 80% of cases (Alzheimer's Association, 2017).

The initial stage of cognitive dysfunction is called *age-associated memory impairment* (AAMI). Exhibit 9.5 summarizes the difference between dementia and typical age-related changes in memory and cognition. AAMI is sometimes followed by even greater memory loss and diagnosed as *mild cognitive impairment* (MCI), which may progress to dementia. AAMI and MCI involve primarily memory loss, whereas dementia results in disruption of daily living and difficulty or inability to function normally. It is estimated that approximately 15% to 20% of people over age 65 have MCI, and 32% of people with MICI develop Alzheimer's disease within 5 years (Alzheimer's Association, 2017). MCI does not always lead to dementia.

EXHIBIT 9.5 ● **Signs of Dementia Compared With Typical Age-Related Changes in Memory and Cognition**	
Signs of Dementia	**Typical Age-Related Changes**
Memory loss that disrupts daily life	Sometimes forgetting names or appointments but remembering them later
Challenges in planning or solving problems	Making occasional errors when balancing a checkbook
Difficulty completing familiar tasks	Occasionally needing help using technology
Confusion with time or place	Getting confused about the day of the week but figuring it out
Trouble understanding visual images and spatial relationships	Vision changes related to cataracts, glaucoma, or macular degeneration
Problems with words in speaking and writing	Sometimes having trouble finding the right word
Misplacing things and losing the ability to retrace steps	Misplacing things from time to time and retracing steps to find them
Decreased or poor judgment	Making a bad decision once in a while
Withdrawal from work or social activities	Sometimes feeling weary of work, family, and social obligations
Changes in mood and personality	Developing very specific ways of doing things and becoming irritable when a routine is disrupted

Source: Based on Alzheimer's Association, 2017, Table 2, p. 9.

Risk factors for cognitive decline and dementia include age, family history, Down syndrome, heavy alcohol use, high blood pressure, obesity, depression, diabetes, smoking, and sleep apnea (Mayo Clinic, 2017c). No positive answer has yet been found for how to prevent dementia. However, several studies suggest that social engagement as well as physical and intellectual activity may slow cognitive decline and the progression of dementia (Anderson & Grossberg, 2014; Renaud, Bherer, & Maquestiaux, 2010; Savica & Petersen, 2011).

Alzheimer's Disease

As noted, **Alzheimer's disease** (AD) is the most common type of dementia. Dementia is one of the costliest conditions to society; in 2017 care for people with AD in the United States was estimated to cost $259 billion (Alzheimer's Association, 2017). From 2000 to 2014, deaths from heart disease—the leading cause of death—declined, but deaths from AD nearly doubled during this same period. As populations around the world age, this trend can be seen on a global level as well. AD is characterized by a progression of stages. A general distinction is made between mild, moderate, and severe stages of AD, although the description of the symptoms shows that the stages are not completely distinct. Exhibit 9.6 provides an overview of the three stages of Alzheimer's disease and the related symptoms.

Early detection and diagnosis of Alzheimer's disease is still difficult. The period from the diagnosis of Alzheimer's disease to death ranges from 3 to 4 years to up to 10 years, depending on the person's age. However, it is believed that the changes in the brain that cause Alzheimer's disease begin 10 or even 20 years before its onset. Consequently, there is a strong focus on trying to find biomarkers in cerebrospinal fluids, blood, or urine that may help to detect the presence of developing Alzheimer's disease (Alzheimer's Association, 2017).

In the mild or early stage, the first signs of the disease, such as forgetfulness, confusion, and mood and personality changes, appear. This stage may be the most stressful for many persons afflicted with Alzheimer's disease, because they often are very aware of the changes happening to their mind. Fluctuations in the severity of symptoms are common, both within a day and between days. Oftentimes the person will start to experience significant anxiety related to these changes.

Moderate-stage Alzheimer's disease is characterized by increased memory loss, problems organizing thoughts and language, difficulty recognizing friends and family members, and restlessness. As the disease progresses the person may exhibit reduced impulse control, repetitive behavior and speech, hallucinations, delusion, and suspiciousness.

In late-stage Alzheimer's disease, a person is often bedridden and has increasing health difficulties. The most common reason for death in the late stage is aspiration pneumonia, when the person can no longer swallow properly and fluids and food end up in the lungs (Alzheimer's Association, 2017). Mrs. Menzel would fall into the earlier phases of the disease and would be considered to have mild- to moderate-stage dementia.

Despite significant progress in researching the disease and trying to find cures, much is still unknown. Current thinking is that multiple factors, not one single cause, are involved in the development of AD. Research shows that brains of persons with Alzheimer's disease have an unusual accumulation of two substances: neurofibrillary tangles and beta-amyloidal plaques. Amyloidal plaques are a substance building up *outside* the neuron cells. The plaques develop when amyloidal peptides, proteins associated with the cell membrane of neurons, divide improperly and turn into beta amyloid, which in turn is toxic to neurons. The neurons die and together with the proteins create these lumps (Alzheimer's Association, 2017). Neurofibrillary tangles form inside the neurons. These tangles are caused by a protein (tau) breaking down and sticking together with other tau proteins to create tangled clumps *inside* the neuron cells. When these tangles develop, they reduce the neurons' ability to communicate with other neurons. The neuron cells eventually die, which over time leads to brain atrophy (Alzheimer's Association, 2017). The role of the plaques and tangles is still not well understood, but scans show that the brains of people with advanced AD show inflammation, dramatic shrinkage from cell loss, and widespread debris from dead and dying neurons (Alzheimer's Association, 2017).

Six drugs have been approved by the U.S. Food and Drug Administration for the treatment of Alzheimer's (Alzheimer's Association, 2017). They temporarily improve symptoms by increasing the amount of neurotransmitters in the brain. The effectiveness of these drugs varies from person to person and is limited in duration. Data from the Cardiovascular Risk Factors, Aging and Dementia (CAIDE) study suggest that caffeine intake in midlife may reduce the risk of dementia. The authors of the study looked at a subset of study participants who were followed over a 21-year period and found that, adjusted for factors such as lifestyle and various health factors, drinking 3 to 5 cups of coffee daily reduced the risk of AD and other dementias by 65% (Eskelinen, Ngandu, Tuomilehto, Soininen, &

EXHIBIT 9.6 ● Stages and Symptoms of Alzheimer's Disease	
Stage of Alzheimer's Disease	**Typical Symptoms**
Mild stage	Memory loss for recent events
	Poor judgment leading to bad decisions
	Loss of spontaneity and initiative
	Taking longer to complete normal daily tasks
	Repeating questions
	Trouble handling money and paying bills
	Wandering and getting lost
	Losing things or misplacing them in odd places
	Mood and personality changes
	Increased anxiety and/or aggression
Moderate stage	Increased memory loss and confusion
	Inability to learn new things
	Difficulty with language, reading, writing, and numbers
	Difficulty organizing thoughts and thinking logically
	Shortened attention span
	Problems coping with new situations
	Difficulty carrying out multistep tasks, such as getting dressed
	Problems recognizing family and friends
	Hallucinations, delusions, and paranoia
	Impulsive behaviors
	Inappropriate outbursts of anger
	Restlessness, agitation, anxiety, tearfulness, wandering
	Repetitive statements or movement
Severe or late stage	Inability to communicate
	Loss of physical abilities, including walking, sitting, and swallowing
	Weight loss
	Seizures
	Skin infections
	Groaning, moaning, or grunting
	Increased sleeping
	Loss of bowel and bladder control

Source: **Based on National Institute on Aging, 2017.**

Kivipelto, 2009). However, currently no cure for the disease is on the horizon.

Parkinson's Disease

Parkinson's disease (PD) is a *chronic* (persisting over a long time) and *progressive* (symptoms get worse over time) movement disorder that primarily affects older adults over the age of 70. However, as in the case of movie star Michael J. Fox, it can afflict persons earlier in life as well. It is thought that PD is the second most common neurodegenerative disease, following Alzheimer's disease. Data on the incidence and prevalence of PD are scarce and contradictory, but one research team found that, in 2010, 630,000 people in the United States had diagnosed PD, about 1.2% of the population over age 65. The researchers note that this prevalence rate, no doubt, underestimates the total prevalence because it is based on cases that have become severe enough to be diagnosed (Kowal, Dall, Chakrabarti, Storm, & Jain, 2013). A similar prevalence rate has been reported in Taiwan, from 1% to 2% of the population over age 65 (Liu, Li, Lee, & Sun, 2016).

The four primary symptoms of PD include tremors (arms, legs, head), rigidity (stiffness of limbs), bradykinesia (trouble with and slowness of movement), and postural instability (insecure gait and balance). It can also cause language problems and cognitive difficulties and in extreme cases lead to a complete loss of movement. The disease is difficult to accurately diagnose, because some features of the normal aging process can be mistaken for PD (National Institute of Neurological Disorders and Stroke, 2014). Tremors, slower movements, or insecure walking all may be part of normal aging, symptoms of depression, or medication-induced side effects. Even though PD is a neurodegenerative movement disorder, it often has mental health consequences. For example, cognitive impairment, dementia, depression, and sleep disorders may be associated with or co-occur with PD (National Institute of Neurological Disorders and Stroke, 2014).

PD is caused by a gradual loss of cells that produce dopamine in a part of the brain called the *substantia nigra*, which is located at the base of the frontal brain area and is involved in coordinating a body's movements. The chemical dopamine is a neurotransmitter that transmits information about movement in the brain. A decrease in neurons that transmit information with the help of dopamine alters the processing of information related to physical movement (National Institute of Neurological Disorders and Stroke, 2014). Losing neurons in the substantia nigra, which is a part of the basal ganglia, is part of normal aging. We are born with 400,000 neurons in this part of the brain; at age 60 we have about 250,000 neurons left. However, research indicates that persons afflicted with Parkinson's disease may have as little as 60,000 to 120,000 neurons present in this part of the brain (Palmer & Francis, 2006). Research has also found a decrease in the nerve endings that produce norepinephrine, a neurotransmitter responsible for some of the body's automatic functions like blood pressure and pulse (National Institute of Neurological Disorders and Stroke, 2014). The brain cells of a person with PD also include abnormal clumps of a protein (synuclein) called Lewy bodies. It is not clear whether this contributes to the disease by preventing the cells from working correctly or whether it is an attempt of the body to bind these harmful proteins to keep other cells working (National Institute of Neurological Disorders and Stroke, 2014).

Several drugs are available to address PD. A combination of these drugs with physical rehabilitation has shown great success in reducing the symptoms of the disease. There are three categories of drugs currently used to treat the symptoms of PD. The first group of medications works on increasing the dopamine levels in the brain. Levodopa is an example of such a drug. It is the most common medication for treating Parkinson's disease and has been used with success for more than 40 years. A second type of drug affects other neurotransmitters such as acetylcholine; these drugs can sometimes help with tremors. The third category of drugs used for PD are drugs such as antidepressants, which are used to ease the nonmovement symptoms of PD (National Institute of Neurological Disorders and Stroke, 2014). A more recent approach to treating the effects of PD is deep brain stimulation. Using this method, a tiny electrode is surgically implanted into the brain. Through a pulse generator this implant then stimulates the brain and stops tremors and other symptoms. This treatment does not usually help with speech problems, balance, anxiety, depression, and dementia that accompany PD (National Institute of Neurological Disorders and Stroke, 2014).

CRITICAL THINKING QUESTIONS 9.2

Would you like to know that your aging process could be reversed with anti-aging medicine? What are the reasons for your answer? How would society be affected if more of us could live to be well past 100 years of age? What social justice issues might arise about access to anti-aging medicine?

PSYCHOLOGICAL CHANGES IN LATE ADULTHOOD

Without good longitudinal research, it has been difficult to understand psychological changes in late adulthood. Because cross-sectional research cannot control for cohort effects, we need to exercise great caution in interpreting findings of age differences in cross-sectional research. Three areas that have received a lot of attention are changes in personality, changes in intellectual functioning, and mental health and mental disorders in late adulthood. The Berlin Aging Study, one of the largest studies of older adults, included numerous measures of psychological aging. Findings suggest that one should not think about a uniform process of psychological aging (Baltes & Mayer, 1999). Rather, changes in areas such as cognition, social relationships, self, and personality occur to a large extent independent of each other.

Personality Changes

A couple of theorists have addressed the issue of how personality changes as individuals age. As noted in Chapter 8, Erik Erikson's (1950) life span theory proposes that the struggle of middle adulthood is generativity versus stagnation (refer to Exhibit 3.8 for an overview of Erikson's stages of psychosocial development). You may recall that generativity is the ability to transcend personal interests to guide the next generation. The struggle of late adulthood, according to Erikson, is **ego integrity versus ego despair**. *Integrity* involves the ability to make peace with one's "one and only life cycle" and to find unity with the world. Erikson (1950) also noted that from middle adulthood on, adults participate in a "wider social radius," with an increasing sense of social responsibility and interconnectedness. Vaillant (2002, 2012) has considered the personality changes of late adulthood. He found that for all three of the cohorts in the Study of Adult Development, mastery of generativity tripled the likelihood that men and women would find their 70s to be a time of joy instead of despair. He also proposed that another life task, guardianship, comes between generativity and integrity. **Guardianship** involves taking on the task of passing on the traditions of the past to the next generation, and guardians extend their concern to concern for the culture as a whole. In addition, Vaillant (2002) suggests that humans have "elegant unconscious coping mechanisms that make lemonade out of lemons" (p. 91).

Vaillant (2002, 2012) finds support for the proposition that coping mechanisms mature with age. He found that over a 25-year period, the Harvard men made significant increases in their use of altruism and humor and significant decreases in their use of projection and passive aggression. Overall, he found that 19 of 67 Harvard men made significant gains in the use of mature coping mechanisms from ages 50 to 75, 28 men were already making strong use of mature mechanisms at age 50, use of mature mechanisms stayed the same for 17 men, and only 4 out of the 67 men used fewer mature coping mechanisms with advancing age. Vaillant (1993) in part attributed this maturation in coping to the presence of positive social support and the quality of marriages. These findings are consistent with findings from another longitudinal study of aging that found that in late adulthood, participants became more forgiving, more able to meet adversity cheerfully, less prone to take offense, and less prone to venting frustrations on others (McCrae & Costa, 1990). Langle and Probst (2004) suggest that this might be the result of older adults being required to face fundamental questions of existence because coping with the vicissitudes of life looms ever larger during aging.

Despite a commonly held belief, one area of personality that seems to change little or even improve with becoming older is the level of happiness experienced by a person. Lacey, Smith, and Ubel (2006) found that on average, people's perceptions of their happiness increase with age. They manage stress better, have a more positive outlook, and set more achievable and realistic goals for themselves. Other research shows similar levels of happiness in older adults as in the general population (Pew Center for Social and Demographic Trends, 2009). Health status has been found to be one of the most influential predictors of happiness in late life (Angner, Ghandhi, Purvis, Amante, & Allison, 2013).

In Chapter 8, we read that there are controversies about whether personality changes or remains stable in middle adulthood. There are similar controversies in the literature on late adulthood. Findings from the large-scale Berlin Aging Study indicate that, on the whole, self and personality change only little with age (Staudinger, Freund, Linden, & Maas, 1999). Vaillant (2002, 2012), conversely, found evidence for both change and continuity. He suggests that personality has two components: temperament and character. Temperament, he concludes, does not change, and adaptation in adolescence is one of the best predictors of adaptation in late adulthood. Studies on depression, anxiety, and suicidal ideation in late adulthood support this idea that coping and adaptation in adolescence are a good predictor of later life temperament. Conversely, character, or adaptive style, does change, influenced by both experiences with the environment and the maturation process. Vaillant (2002) attributes this change in adaptive style over time to the fact that many genes are "programmed to promote plasticity," or the capacity to be shaped by experience. One personality change noted in Chapter 8 to occur in middle age is gender role reversal, with women becoming more dominant and men becoming more passive. This pattern has also been noted in late adulthood (Vaillant, 2012). Another longitudinal study found that cognitive abilities and changes in late life predict personality change (Wettstein, Tauber, Kuźma, & Wahl, 2017). Cognitive decline and low cognitive abilities in late life were found to be associated with some changes in the Big Five personality traits (for an overview of the Big Five personality traits, review Exhibit 8.8 in Chapter 8 of this book). More specifically, cognitive decline and low cognitive abilities in late life were found to predict increases in neuroticism and decreases in extraversion and openness. On the other hand, personality traits were not found to influence changes in cognitive abilities.

Intellectual Changes, Learning, and Memory

Answering the question about how our intellectual capabilities change in late adulthood is a complex and difficult task. One often-cited study on age-related intellectual changes found that fluid intelligence declines with age, but crystallized intelligence increases (Horn, 1982). **Fluid intelligence** is the capacity for abstract reasoning and involves such things as the ability to "respond quickly, to memorize quickly, to compute quickly with no error, and to draw rapid inferences from visual relationships" (Vaillant, 2002, p. 238). **Crystallized intelligence** is based on accumulated learning and includes the ability to reflect and recognize (e.g., similarities and differences, vocabulary) rather than to recall and remember. This theory has received much criticism, however, because it was based on a cross-sectional comparison of two different age groups. Researchers who followed a single cohort over time found no general decline of intellectual abilities in late adulthood (Schaie, 1984). Rather, they found considerable individual variation. Other longitudinal research has found that fluid intelligence declines earlier than crystallized intelligence, which has been found to remain the same at 80 as at 30 in most healthy older adults (Vaillant, 2002). Aspects of crystallized intelligence, such as world knowledge, continue to grow into the 60s and show only gradual declines in the 70s (Ornstein & Light, 2010).

Learning and memory are closely related; we must first learn before we can retain and recall. Memory performance, like the impact of aging on intelligence, demonstrates a wide degree of variability. One study suggests that the effects of aging on the underlying brain processes related to retention and recall are dependent on individual memory performance, and the researchers

call for further investigation of performance variability in normal aging (Duarte, Ranganath, Trujillo, & Knight, 2006). When we process information, it moves through several stages of memory (Bjorklund, 2015; Hooyman et al., 2018):

- *Sensory memory.* New information is initially recorded in sensory memory. Unless the person deliberately pays attention to the information, it is lost within less than a second. There seems to be little age-related change in this type of memory.

- *Primary memory.* If the information is retained in sensory memory, it is passed on to the primary memory, also called recent or short-term memory. Primary memory has only limited capacity; it is used to organize and temporarily hold information.

- *Working memory.* This refers to the process of actively reorganizing and manipulating information that is still in primary memory. Although there are some age-related declines in working memory, there seems to be little age-related decline in primary memory.

- *Secondary memory.* Information is permanently stored in secondary memory. This is the memory we use daily when we remember an event or memorize facts for an exam. The ability to recall seems to decline with age, but recognition capabilities stay consistent.

- *Tertiary memory.* Information is stored for extended periods, several weeks or months, in tertiary memory, also called remote memory. This type of memory experiences little age-related change.

Another way to distinguish memory is between intentional and incidental memory. **Intentional memory** relates to events you plan to remember. **Incidental memory** relates to facts you have learned without the intention to retain and recall. Research suggests that incidental memory declines with old age, but intentional memory does not (Direnfeld & Roberts, 2006).

Another element of intellectual functioning studied in relation to aging is *brain plasticity,* the ability of the brain to change in response to stimuli. Research indicates that even older people's brains can rewire themselves to compensate for lost functioning in particular regions and, in some instances, may even be able to generate new cells. As a result, people are capable of life-long learning, despite myths to the contrary. Typically, researchers have used years of education as the proxy and predictor of decline in cognitive ability, memory, and executive function. Manly, Schupf, Tang, and Stern (2005) found that literacy was a better predictor of learning, memory, retention, and cognitive decline than educational years. This is especially salient for minority ethnic groups whose access to formal education may be limited. However, adult education and intellectual stimulation in later life may actually help maintain cognitive health. Not only are humans capable of lifelong learning, but the stimulation associated with learning new things may reduce the risk of impairments (Willis, Schaie, & Martin, 2009).

Mental Health and Mental Disorders

A number of longitudinal studies indicate that, without brain disease, mental health improves with age (Vaillant, 2012). Older adults have a lower prevalence of mental disorders than young and middle-age adults. This finding is supported by virtually all epidemiological studies ever conducted (Bengtson, Gans, Putney, & Silverstein, 2009; Kessler et al., 2005). Although older adults are at greater risk to certain brain diseases such as dementia, these disorders are not a part of the normal aging process. It is estimated that 15% to 25% of older adults living in the community have some type of mental health disorder, but higher rates are found among older adults living in long-term care facilities, where an estimated 10% to 40% have mild to moderate impairment and 5% to 10% have serious impairment (Hooyman et al., 2018). About 20% of first admissions to psychiatric hospitals are adults aged 65 and older. It is estimated that only about 25% of older adults who need mental health services ever receive them. However, many of the more common mental disorders associated with older age can be diagnosed and treated in elderly persons much as they would be in earlier adulthood (Rodda, Walker, & Carter, 2011). Given the aging of the population, the need for geropsychiatric research and clinical practice is likely to increase.

Some of the more commonly diagnosed mental disorders in late adulthood include the following.

- *Depression.* The most common mental health problem in older adults is depression (Hooyman et al., 2018). Symptoms of depression include sadness and depressed mood, loss of interest, weight loss, insomnia, and fatigue. To be

diagnosed, the depressive episode has to persist for at least 2 weeks. Many depressive episodes in older adults are associated with problems in coping with difficult life events, such as death of a loved person or physical illness. Research also indicates that when major depression occurs for the first time in late life, it is often related to Alzheimer's disease (van Reekum et al., 2005) or cardiovascular disease (Kala et al., 2016). Treatment with antidepressive medication, especially in combination with psychotherapy, significantly improves depressive symptoms in most older adults (Rodda et al., 2011). Comparison of White and Black older persons found that lower education and functional disability were common risk factors for severe depressive symptoms for both groups, and sense of mastery and satisfaction with support were common protective factors. Advanced age was a risk factor for Caucasians, but not for African Americans, and being female and being less religious were risk factors for African Americans but not for Caucasians (Jang, Borenstein, Chiriboga, & Mortimer, 2005). This is yet another reminder of the important role of religious coping among many African Americans. A study of depression in older adults in Beijing found that economic hardship and poor physical health were the strongest risk factors. The researchers also found a risk factor that had not been identified in studies in other countries: lack of the expected filial piety in the older adults' offspring (Ning et al., 2011). It should be noted that depression is not a normal part of aging. Moreover, longitudinal research has found no increase in clinical levels of depression with age (Helmchen et al., 1999).

Depression is the leading cause of suicide in late adulthood. In the past, the highest rates of suicide were among older adults, but in recent years, suicide rates have been increasing among adults ages 45 to 64. In 2015, the highest rate of suicide in the United States was among middle-age adults ages 45 to 64, a rate of 19.6 per 100,000 population. The second highest rate occurred in older adults age 85 and older, 19.4 per 100,000 population (American Foundation for Suicide Prevention, 2017). Among the most prevalent risk factors are depression, prior suicide attempts, pain and medical conditions that limit life expectancy, social isolation and declining role functioning, feeling hopeless, and abuse of medications and illicit substances (Conwell, Van Orden, & Caine, 2011).

- *Anxiety.* Anxiety in older adults is similar to that in the younger population, but anxiety has not received the same attention in geriatric practice and research as some of the other mental health problems such as depression. Diagnosis and treatment, however, are often more complex and difficult, because anxiety in older adults is often masked with physical health complaints but also may be an indication of an underlying mental or physical disorder (Grenier et al., 2012; Kasckow et al., 2013). Symptoms of anxiety include tension, worry, apprehension, and physiological symptoms such as dizziness, gastrointestinal distress, palpitations, urinary disturbance, sweating, and tremors. About 9% of the general older-adult population experiences considerable anxiety levels (Bengtson et al., 2009). For older adults, anxiety is frequently connected with chronic conditions and co-occurs with neurodegenerative diseases such as Alzheimer's and Parkinson's diseases. One study found that 5.2% of community-dwelling older adults with cardiovascular disease met the criteria for anxiety disorder, and 14.8% had anxiety symptoms that did not meet the threshold to be diagnosed as an anxiety disorder (Grenier et al., 2012). Anxiety symptoms often coexist with depressive symptoms in older adults, as they do with other adults, and the combination of the two, even when they do not meet the threshold for diagnosis for major depression or anxiety disorder, increases the risk for dementia and hospitalization for cardiovascular disease (Kasckow et al., 2013). Situational stressors that may trigger anxiety in older adults include financial concerns, physical stressors, and loss and loneliness. One study found that non-Hispanic Whites had twice the rate of anxiety symptoms as either non-Hispanic Blacks or Hispanics (Ostir & Goodwin, 2006). There is evidence that cognitive behavioral therapy is as effective with older adults as with younger adults, and one feasibility trial found that older adults with anxiety disorder showed significant improvement in symptoms after completion of an 8-week online cognitive behavioral treatment program. The participants reported a high level of satisfaction with the program, but their gains were not maintained at a 3-month follow-up (Zou et al., 2012).

- *Delirium.* One of the two most prevalent cognitive disorders in the elderly population, **delirium** is an acute delusional state characterized by disturbance in attention and awareness (Marcantonio, 2017). Delirium has a sudden onset (a few hours or days), after which follows a brief and fluctuating course that includes impairment of consciousness, drowsiness, disorientation to time and place, inability to remember events before delirium began, problems concentrating, and incoherent thinking and speech. It has the potential for improvement when the causes are treated. Prevalent causative factors include alcohol or sedative drug withdrawal, drug abuse, body chemical disturbances, poisons, central nervous system disturbances, factors such as toxicity from medications, low oxygen states, infections, retention of urine and feces, undernutrition and dehydration, surgery, and metabolic conditions (Joshi & Morley, 2006; MedlinePlus, 2016). The prevalence of delirium increases with age and is very common in acute care hospitals, particularly among postoperative patients and intensive care patients. About 50% of older patients have delirium after such high-risk procedures as hip-fracture repair and cardiac surgery (Marcantonio, 2017). Many older adults with delirium have an underlying dementia (Anand & MacLullich, 2013).

- *Dementia.* The other most prevalent cognitive disorder among older adults is dementia, which was discussed earlier in the context of neurodegenerative disease. Dementia has a slower onset than delirium and is not characterized by an impairment of consciousness. Rather, dementia is characterized by multiple impairments of the person's cognitive functioning.

- *Substance abuse.* Although it is hard to get good data, there is increasing evidence that a growing number of older adults are misusing and abusing alcohol and psychoactive prescription medications (Blow & Barry, 2012). Community surveys have reported prevalence rates from 1% to 16% of problem drinking for older adults. In 2002, 0.5% of adults 65 and older reported alcohol dependence. Although light to moderate drinking typically causes no health concerns for younger adults, these amounts may cause a number of negative health effects in older adults. In addition, older adults take more prescription medications than young adults, and research suggests that two types of prescription drug medications are abused by a small but significant group of older adults: opioid medications used for treatment of pain and benzodiazepines used for treatment of anxiety and insomnia. Benzodiazepines have been associated with cognitive losses, confusion, and depressed mood. The current generation of older adults rarely uses illicit drugs, but it is expected that the abuse of these substances will increase in older adults as the baby boomers reach late adulthood (Blow & Barry, 2012). When working with older adults, it is important to assess for levels of use of alcohol as well as psychoactive prescription medications.

CRITICAL THINKING QUESTIONS 9.3

George Vaillant suggests that his longitudinal research indicates that humans have "elegant unconscious coping mechanisms that make lemonade out of lemons." Think of a late-life adult you know who has made or is making lemonade out of lemons. What challenges has this person faced in earlier life or in late adulthood? What is it about this late-life adult that makes you think of her or him as making lemonade out of lemons? What types of coping mechanisms do you think this person uses to deal with adversities?

SOCIAL ROLE TRANSITIONS AND LIFE EVENTS OF LATE ADULTHOOD

Transitions are at the center of the life course perspective, and people experience many transitions, some of them very abrupt, in late adulthood. Retirement, death of a spouse or partner, institutionalization, and one's own impending death are among the most stressful events in human existence, and they are clustered in late adulthood. Several other events are more benign but may still enter into the social worker's analysis of the changing configuration of person and environment represented by each of the case studies at the beginning of the

chapter. Despite the concern of the impact of the loss of social roles, studies have demonstrated that older adults generally adapt to late-life role transitions and maintain emotional well-being (Hinrichsen & Clougherty, 2006).

Families in Later Life

As you saw with the Smiths, the Menzels, and Ms. Johnson, families continue to play an important role in the life of an older person. With increased longevity, however, the post–empty nest and postretirement period lengthens (Walsh, 2016a). Thus, the significance of the marital or partner relationship increases in late adulthood. As older individuals are released from their responsibilities as parents and members of the workforce, they are able to spend more time together. Some studies have suggested a U-shaped curve of marital satisfaction, with the highest levels during the first period of the marital relationship and in late adulthood and lower levels during the childbearing years (Bjorklund, 2015). Moreover, overall satisfaction with the quality of life seems to be higher for married elderly individuals than for the widowed or never married. For married couples, the spouse is the most important source of emotional, social, and personal support in times of illness and need of care.

About 29% of noninstitutionalized U.S. older adults live alone. The most common living arrangement for men older than 65 is with their wife; in 2016, 73% of men older than 65 lived with their spouse (Administration on Aging, 2016). The picture is different for older women; only 47% of women age 65 and older live with a spouse, and by age 75, almost half (46%) of women live alone.

Living arrangements for older adults vary by race and ethnicity. In 2008, the proportion of White (41%) and Black (42%) women living alone was similar. Fewer older Hispanic women lived alone (27%), and even fewer Asian women lived alone (22%) (Jacobsen, Mather, Lee, & Kent, 2011). Older Black women (25%) are less likely than Asian (45%), White (44%), and Hispanic (41%) women to live with a spouse (Jacobsen et al., 2011). White women (13%) are less likely than Black (32%), Asian (32%), or Hispanic (31%) women to live with relatives other than a spouse. Black men (30%) are more likely to live alone than White (18%), Hispanic (13%), or Asian (11%) men. Black men (54%) are also less likely than Asian (77%), White (74%), and Hispanic (67%) men to live with a spouse. Men of every race and ethnicity are less likely than women of the same race and ethnicity to live with a relative other than their spouse:

PHOTO 9.4 As older couples are released from responsibilities as parents and members of the workforce, they are able to spend more time together.

15% of Hispanic men, 11% of Black men, 10% of Asian men, and 6% of White men (Jacobsen et al., 2011). A complex relationship among culture, socioeconomic status, and individual personality has to be considered in accounting for the ethnic and racial differences in living arrangements. Drawing inferences based solely on cultural differences is overly simplistic given the use of ethnic and racial categories devised by the U.S. Census Bureau as proxies for cultural identity.

Family relationships have been found to be closer and more central for older women than for older men. Mother–daughter relationships have been found to be particularly strong (Silverstein & Bengtson, 2001). Additionally, friendship appears to be a more important protective factor for older women than for older men. Friendships have been associated with lower levels of cognitive impairment and increased quality-of-life satisfaction (Beland, Zunzunegui, Alvardo, Otero, & del Ser, 2005).

Never married older adults constitute a very small group of the current elderly population. It will further decrease for some time as the cohort of baby boomers, with its unusually high rate of marriage, enters late adulthood (Bjorklund, 2015). However, the proportion

of elderly singles and never marrieds will probably increase toward the middle of the next century, because the cohort that follows the baby boomers has had an increase in the number of individuals remaining single.

Singlehood caused by divorce in late adulthood is increasing, however, as divorce is becoming more socially accepted in all population groups. As in all stages of life, divorce in later life may entail financial problems, especially for older women, and it may be especially difficult to recuperate financially in postretirement. Divorce also results in a change of kinship ties and social networks, which are important sources of support in later life. The incidence of remarriage after divorce or widowhood is significantly higher for older men than for older women. The fact that there are more elderly women than men contributes to this trend. Even if older adults are not themselves divorced, they may need to adjust to the enlarged and complicated family networks that come from the divorces and remarriages of their children and grandchildren (Walsh, 2016a).

Sibling relationships play a special role in the life of older adults. Siblings share childhood experiences and are often the personal tie with the longest duration. Siblings are typically not the primary source of personal care, but they often play a role in providing emotional support. Sibling relationships often change over the life course, with closer ties in pre-adulthood and later life and less involvement in early and middle adulthood. Women's ties with siblings have been found to be more involved than those of men (Bjorklund, 2015).

Co-residence of multiple generations of the family has been gradually decreasing in Western societies since the 19th century, but the multigenerational family household has been making a comeback in Europe and the United States in recent years (Albuquerque, 2011). Although the percentage of persons living in multigenerational family households decreased in the United States from 24.7% in 1950 to 12.1% in 1980, it has since increased back up to 16.1% in 2010. This can be attributed to several factors, including demographic changes, the burst of the housing market and increase of foreclosures, high unemployment rates during the last recession, and a high rate of immigration from Latin America and Asia (Pew Center for Social and Demographic Trends, 2010). The resurgence of multigenerational households has resulted in more interactions and exchanges across generations. Contrary to common belief, intergenerational exchanges between adult children and elderly parents are not one-directional. Children often take care of their elderly parents, but healthy elderly persons also provide significant assistance to their adult children, as is the case with Ms. Johnson. Research with multigenerational households in Portugal found that resources flowed both ways, particularly when the older generation was still young-old. Some contributions the older generation provided to the household include income from employment, childcare, and household chores (Albuquerque, 2011).

Grandparenthood

Gene and Lois Smith, Ruby Johnson, and Joseph and Elizabeth Menzel are grandparents, and Ruby Johnson is a great-grandmother. As people live longer, increasing numbers are becoming grandparents and great-grandparents. In addition, the current cohort of older adults is spending more years as grandparents than earlier cohorts did (Bjorklund, 2015). The transition to grandparenthood typically occurs in middle adulthood, and grandparents may be in their 30s or over 100 or anywhere in between (Hooyman et al., 2018). The grandchildren of older adults are more likely to be adolescents and young adults than to be young children. Great-grandchildren, however, are likely to be young.

In some cases, older people such as Ms. Johnson are assuming full responsibility for parenting their grandchildren. Beginning in the early 1990s, the U.S. Census Bureau began to note an increasing number of children younger than 18 living with grandparents, rising from 3% in 1970 to 5.5% in 1997 (Bryson & Casper, 1999). Today, approximately 2.7 million grandparents in the United States assume primary caregiving responsibilities for their grandchildren (Manns, Atler, & Fruhauf, 2017). This has been viewed by some as a negative trend, but there is no inherent reason why grandchildren receiving care from grandparents is problematic, and, indeed, across time and place, grandparents have sometimes been seen as appropriate caregivers. Many cultural groups often have multigenerational households that are not predicated on dysfunction within the family. Recall that large percentages of Asian, Hispanic, and Black elders live with family members not their spouse. It does appear, however, that the current trend is influenced by recent economic conditions as well as parental teen pregnancy, drug addiction, mental and physical health problems, incarceration, and death (Livingston, 2013; Taylor, Marquis, Batten, & Coall, 2016). As a result, new physical, emotional, and financial demands are placed on grandparents with already limited resources. Sometimes custodial grandparents are also caring for their own impaired adult child. Compared with their noncustodial counterparts, custodial grandparents have a higher rate of physical and mental health problems (Hayslip, Blumenthal, & Garner, 2014). However, many custodial grandparents and their grandchildren benefit or even thrive from the circumstance, and the parenting outcomes are often very positive. Parsons and Peluso (2013) compiled a list of famous custodial grandchildren that includes the likes of George Washington, Barack Obama, Bill Clinton, Clarence Thomas, Eric Clapton, Oprah Winfrey, Pierce Brosnan, Tammy Wynette, and Tipper Gore. They all have in common the fact that they were raised by their grandparents.

Grandparenthood is a normative part of the family life cycle, but the majority of grandparents do not co-reside with their grandchildren. In general, being a grandparent is a welcome and gratifying role for most individuals, but it may increase in significance and meaning for an older person. The Smiths, for example, both enjoy being grandparents, and Lois Smith especially gains pleasure and satisfaction from her role as grandmother to her daughter's children. Many grandparents today are maintaining relationships with grandchildren by means of various technologies, including texting, social networking sites, and webcam interactions.

Even when they do not co-reside with their grand-children, grandparents can play an important role in their grandchildren's lives. Here are some examples from research. Candace Kemp (2005) found that both adult grandchildren and their grandparents see their relationship as a safety net that can be tapped when needed. Another research team found that emerging adults who had lived with a single parent or in a step-parent home had fewer depressive symptoms if they had a strong relationship with a grandparent (Ruiz & Silverstein, 2007). Another study found that the quality of the relationship with the maternal grandmother pre-dicted the psychological adjustment of emerging adults after parental divorce (Henderson, Hayslip, Sanders, & Louden, 2009). And another study found that adoles-cents in single-parent homes had fewer difficulties with school conduct and peer relations if they had high lev-els of involvement with grandparents (Attar-Schwartz, Tan, Buchanan, Flouri, & Griggs, 2009). One last study found that grandparents play a critical role when a grandchild has a disability, and the grandparent derives much joy and satisfaction from the grandparent–grand-child relationship (Woodbridge, Buys, & Miller, 2011).

Family researchers have begun to take a strong inter-est in the grandparenting role, but little is known about grandparent–grandchild relationships. A classic study of middle-class grandparents in the early 1960s identified several styles of grandparents: formal grandparents, fun seekers, distant figures, surrogate parents, and mentors (Neugarten & Weinstein, 1964). A more recent study by Margaret Mueller and her associates focused particu-larly on the relationships between grandparents and adolescent grandchildren; the average age of grandpar-ents in this study was 69 years old (Mueller, Wilhelm, & Elder, 2002). This study identified five dimensions of the grandparenting role in 451 families: face-to-face contact, activities done together, intimacy, assistance, and authority/discipline. Each of these grandparenting dimensions is defined in Exhibit 9.7. Using a statistical clustering method, the researchers identified five styles of grandparenting:

1. *Influential grandparents* are highly involved in all aspects of grandparenting, scoring high on all five dimensions. These grandparents constituted 17% of the sample. Ms. Johnson is grandparenting Rebecca in this manner.

2. *Supportive grandparents* are highly involved in the lives of their grandchildren but do not see themselves in a role of disciplinarian or authority figure. About a quarter of the sample fit this pattern.

3. *Passive grandparents* are moderately involved in their grandchildren's lives, but they do not provide instrumental assistance and do not see themselves as discipline/authority figures. About 19% of the sample fit this pattern. Lois and Gene Smith seem to be following this pattern of grandparenting.

4. *Authority-oriented grandparents* see their role as authority figures as the central component in their grandparenting, and they are relatively inactive in their grandchildren's lives compared with both influential and supportive grandparents. These grandparents constitute about 13% of the sample.

5. *Detached grandparents* are the least involved, scoring lowest on all the dimensions of grandparenting. This was the largest group, comprising about 28% of the sample.

This research is helpful because it demonstrates that the grandparent role may be played in many ways. Several factors may influence the style of grandparenting, including geographic proximity, ages of grandparents

EXHIBIT 9.7 ● Dimensions of Grandparenting Role	
Dimension	**Definition**
Face-to-face contact	How often grandparents see their grandchildren
Activities done together	Participation in shared activities, such as shopping, working on projects together, attending grandchildren's events, teaching the grandchild a skill
Intimacy	Serving as confidant, companion, or friend; discussing grandparent's childhood
Assistance	Providing instrumental assistance, such as financial aid and/or interpersonal support
Discipline and authority	Disciplining the grandchild or otherwise serving as an authority figure

Source: Based on Mueller et al., 2002.

and grandchildren, number of grandchildren, and family rituals. There is a major drawback to the sample, however; it is entirely White and midwestern. It does not, therefore, address the possibility of cultural variations in grandparenting roles. For example, one research team investigated Chinese American grandmothering and found that these grandmothers spent significant amounts of time with their grandchildren and considered their grandparenting style to be based on a sense of responsibility to teach their grandchildren to have good character and to honor filial piety. Their high involvement with their grandchildren was formal and hierarchical, unlike the friendly companionate style characterized by many European American grandparents (Nagata, Cheng, & Tsai, 2010). The researchers caution not to assume that formal and detached relationships necessarily result in low involvement. They also note language and acculturation issues that can interfere with grandparent–grandchild relationships in immigrant families.

A smaller-scale study of grandparenting in 17 Native American families, including Sioux, Creek, Seminole, Choctaw, and Chickasaw, also addresses the issue of cultural variation (Weibel-Orlando, 2001). Like the research of Mueller and her associates, this study identified five styles of grandparenting:

1. *The distanced grandparent* lives at considerable geographic distance from grandchildren but also has psychological and cultural distance. This type of grandparenting is not common among Native Americans. It is most likely to occur if the family has migrated to an urban area and the grandparents return to their ancestral homeland after retirement.

2. *The ceremonial grandparent* also lives at considerable geographic distance from grandchildren but visits regularly. Intergenerational visits are times for ethnic ceremonial gatherings, and grandparents model appropriate ceremonial behavior.

3. *The fictive grandparent* assumes the elder role with children who are not biologically related. These grandparents may have no grandchildren of their own or may live at a great distance from their biological grandchildren.

4. *The custodial grandparent* lives with the grandchildren and is responsible for their care. This style of grandparenting is usually the result of parental death, incapacitation, or abandonment and is based on necessity rather than choice.

5. *The cultural conservator grandparent* actively pursues the opportunity to have grandchildren live with her (all such grandparents were women in this study) so that she might teach them the Native American way of life.

Think about your relationships with your grandparents. How would you characterize their grandparenting styles? Did you have different types of relationships with different grandparents? Did your grandparents have different types of relationships with different grandchildren? What might explain any differences?

Work and Retirement

Until the 20th century, the average worker retired about 3 years before death. Increased worker productivity, mass longevity, and social security legislation changed that situation, however. The labor force participation of men aged 65 or older declined steadily from 1900, when it was about 66%, to 1985, when it was 15.8%. From 1986 to 2002, it stabilized at 16% to 18% but began to increase after 2002. The labor force participation of women aged 65 and older rose slightly from 1900 to 1956, from about 8% to 10.8%. It fell to 7.3% in 1985, remained at 7% to 9% from 1986 to 2002, and then began to rise. In 2015, 18.9% of adults aged 65 and older were in the labor force, including 23.4% of men and 15.3% of women (Administration on Aging, 2016). It is thought that this recent upward shift in the labor force participation of older adults is related to both financial considerations and improved health. Changes to social security policy allowed older adults to continue working and still receive partial social security benefits, but two other changes have increased the financial necessity for older adults to stay in the labor force: a reduction in pension plans and the scheduled increase in age for receiving full social security benefits. In addition, many older adults faced losses in savings, investments, and home equity during the economic recession that started in 2007 (Bjorklund, 2015).

Retirement patterns vary with social class. Vaillant found that only 20% of his sample of surviving inner-city men were still in the workforce at age 65, but half of the sample of Harvard men were still working full-time at 65. The inner-city men retired, on average, 5 years earlier than the Harvard men. Poor health often leads to earlier retirement among less advantaged adults

(Hooyman et al., 2018). In addition, higher levels of education make workers eligible for more sedentary jobs, which are a better fit with the declining energy levels in late adulthood (Vaillant, 2002).

The "appropriate" age for retirement in the United States is currently understood to be 65. This cultural understanding has been shaped by social security legislation enacted in 1935. However, the 1983 Social Security Amendments included a provision for a gradual increase in the age at which a retired person could begin receiving social security retirement benefits. Exhibit 9.8 shows the schedule for increasing the age for receiving full benefits. In arguing for this legislative change, members of Congress noted increased longevity and improved health among older adults.

Older adults who continue to work fall into two groups: those who could afford to retire but choose to continue working and those who continue to work because of financial need. Older adults of the first group usually receive great satisfaction in sharing their knowledge and expertise and gain a feeling of purpose from being productive. Members of the second group continue to work out of necessity. Because economic status in old age is influenced by past employment patterns and the resultant retirement benefits, this second group consists of individuals who had lower-paying employment throughout their lives. This group also includes elderly divorced or widowed women who depended on their husband's retirement income and are now faced with poverty or near poverty. Lifelong gender inequality in wages contributes to inequality in pension and retirement funds (Hooyman et al., 2018). Gene Smith falls into the first category, because he continued working even though he and his wife had sufficient combined benefits to retire. However, Lois Smith's own benefits would not have enabled her to lead a financially comfortable retirement if she were not married, and she would probably face some financial hardship if she were to become a widow. Ruby Johnson continues to be employed part-time out of financial necessity.

When we think about retirement, we often picture individuals cleaning up their desks to stop working completely and sit in a rocking chair on the front porch. Yet there are many ways of retiring from the workforce. Some individuals do cease work completely, but others continue with part-time or part-year employment. Others may retire for a period and then reenter the labor market, as Gene Smith did when his former employer offered him a part-time position. Retirement is a socially accepted way to end an active role in the workforce, but the transition to retirement is becoming much more blurred than we typically think (Hooyman et al., 2018). Most persons retire because of advancing age, health problems, a desire to pursue other interests, or simply a wish to relax and lead the life of a retiree.

Individuals vary in whether they view retirement as something to dread or something to look forward to. Most often, however, retirement is a positive experience. Vaillant (2002) found no evidence in his longitudinal research that retirement is bad for physical health. For every person who indicated that retirement was bad for her or his health, four retirees indicated that retirement had improved their health. Vaillant noted four conditions under which retirement is perceived as stressful (p. 221):

1. Retirement was involuntary or unplanned.

2. There are no other means of financial support besides salary.

3. Work provided an escape from an unhappy home life.

4. Retirement was precipitated by preexisting bad health.

EXHIBIT 9.8 ● Amended Age to Receive Full Social Security Benefits (1983)	
Year of Birth	**Full Retirement Age**
1937 and earlier	65
1938	65 and 2 months
1939	65 and 4 months
1940	65 and 6 months
1941	65 and 8 months
1942	65 and 10 months
1943–1954	66
1955	66 and 2 months
1956	66 and 4 months
1957	66 and 6 months
1958	66 and 8 months
1959	66 and 10 months
1960 and later	67

Source: Social Security Administration, 2017a.

These conditions are present among only a fraction of retirees, but social workers may come in contact with some of those retirees.

Vaillant found that retirement has generally been rewarding for many of the participants of his study. Four basic activities appear to make retirement rewarding:

1. Replacing workmates with another social network

2. Rediscovering how to play

3. Engaging in creative endeavors

4. Continuing lifelong learning

Caregiving and Care Receiving

As retirement unfolds, declining health may usher in a period of intensive need for care. It is estimated that 35% of people age 65 and older have some type of disability (Administration on Aging, 2016). The majority of older adults with disabilities live in the community and receive predominately informal care from spouses, children, and extended family. Among older adults who need care and live in the community, about 9% rely exclusively on formal care, and about 70% rely exclusively on informal care. It is estimated that if informal care was unavailable, long-term care costs would double (Hooyman et al., 2018). Women are the primary source of caregiving in old age. Daughters are more likely than sons to take care of elderly parents. Moreover, elderly men tend to be married and thus are more likely to have a wife available as caregiver (Walsh, 2016a).

Caregiving can be an around-the-clock task and often leaves caregivers overwhelmed and exhausted (see Chan, Malhotra, Malhotra, Rush, & Ostbye, 2013). Mr. Menzel is a good example of the burden that can be experienced by an elderly spouse. Programs that can assist caregivers such as him in reducing their exceptional levels of stress have received much attention. Many programs combine educational components—for example, information about and training in adaptive coping skills—with ongoing support through the opportunity to share personal feelings and experiences. In recent years, social workers have been using telephone and computer-mediated support groups to assist family caregivers and have found many benefits of these virtual groups (Jones & Meier, 2011; Toseland & Larkin, 2010). Respite programs for caregivers are also available. In-home respite programs provide assistance through a home health aide or a visiting nurse (Petrovic, 2013). Community-based respite is often provided through adult day care and similar programs.

Although there is much evidence that caregiving can be stressful, it is important to remember that not all caregivers have the same reactions to their caregiving responsibilities, and there are gains as well as losses associated with the caregiver role. Gains include pride and greater closeness with the care recipient. Some research indicates that African American caregivers provide a higher level of care than White caregivers but typically report less stress, anxiety, and feelings of burden related to caregiving. They are more likely than White caregivers to see caregiving as a spiritual experience (Dilworth-Andersen et al., 2005).

Based on their research on the topic, Rhonda Montgomery and Karl Kosloski (2000, 2009) developed a caregiver identity theory. Their framework consists of seven "career markers," stages individuals typically move through in their career as caregivers. The first marker signifies the time when the dependency situation begins. One person needs assistance with routine activities and another person starts performing caregiving tasks. The second marker is reached when the self-definition as a caregiver begins; that is, the person incorporates the role of caregiver into his or her personal and social identity. Marker 3 is characterized by the performance of personal care tasks. At this time, caregiving family members begin to evaluate whether to continue as caregivers or seek alternatives. Although spousal caregivers may already see themselves as such after reaching Marker 2, they now begin to unambiguously identify with their new role. The next marker is reached when outside assistance is sought and formal service use is considered. Whether outside help is requested depends on factors such as seeing one's personal situation as deficient, recognizing the potential service as addressing that deficiency, and the psychological and monetary cost-benefit of using the service (Montgomery & Kosloski, 1994). Considering nursing home placement is the fifth marker. Although the institutional placement is considered at earlier phases, the decision now is more imminent. Nursing home placement is the sixth marker. When caregiving becomes too overwhelming, a nursing home placement may be pursued. Caregiving often continues after a family member enters a nursing home. Although caregivers are relieved from direct care, they continue to be involved in the emotional and social aspects of care in the nursing home (Naleppa, 1996). Although many individuals will spend some time in a nursing home, others never enter such an institution and die at home. The final marker in Montgomery and Kosloski's caregiver identity theory is the termination of the caregiver role. This may occur because of recovery or death of the care recipient or through "quitting" as a caregiver.

Stress and burden are not experienced only by the caregiver. Although there has been very little research on the topic, it is suggested that the care recipient also experiences significant strain. Requiring care is a double loss: The person has lost the capability to perform the tasks for which he or she needs assistance and the person has also lost independence. Having to rely on others for activities that one has carried out independently throughout one's adult life can be the source of tremendous emotional and psychological stress. Some individuals respond by emotional withdrawal, whereas others become agitated and start blaming others for their situation. Still others make the best of the situation and even find benefits, such as being able to reside in the community, reducing the economic costs of care, and becoming closer to caregivers (Bjorklund, 2015).

Think of Joseph Menzel. His stress as a care receiver was probably amplified by culturally defined norms promoting independence, individuality, and pride. Helping someone like him to overcome his uneasiness about receiving assistance may include asking him to verbalize his worries, listening to him express his feelings, and looking together at ways that he could overcome his uneasiness in small steps.

Widowhood

A spouse's or partner's death may be the most stressful event in a person's life, but the existing research literature focuses on death of a heterosexual spouse. Widowhood within the context of a heterosexual spousal relationship is more common among women than men. In 2016, 34% of U.S. women aged 65 or older were widowed, compared with 12% of men (Administration on Aging, 2016). A similar pattern can be found in other economically advanced societies (see Fang et al., 2012; Schaan, 2013). Two factors drive this gender difference: women have tended to marry men who are a few years older than themselves, and women live longer than men. On average, women also have a longer duration of widowhood, and men are more likely than women to remarry after spousal death.

Considerable research across cultures has found that spousal death is associated with deteriorating health, increased depression, and even death, but there are some inconsistencies in the research. Although this research has focused on heterosexual married couples, the findings are likely to be applicable to other long-term partnered couples. Some studies have found that depressive symptoms are more pronounced for widowed men than for widowed women (Carr, 2004), others have found that widowed women suffer more from depressive symptoms (Lee & DeMaris, 2007), and still others have found no gender differences in the impact of spousal death on mental health (Schaan, 2013). A consistent finding in the research is that the negative effects of widowhood are particularly strong during the first years after spousal loss and then diminish over time.

One recent longitudinal study investigated depressive symptoms of widowed men and women older than age 50 in 11 European countries. Widowed persons were found to have more depressive symptoms than married persons; although women had more depressive symptoms than men, no gender differences in the effect of widowhood on depressive symptoms were found (Schaan, 2013). Consistent with earlier studies, this study found that loss of a spouse has more negative impact on mental health for widowed females and males who rated their marriage as positive and less negative impact on widowed females and males who had provided care to their spouses before their death. The study also found some cross-national differences in the negative impact of widowhood on mental health, and the researcher suggested that future research should investigate whether social welfare policies play a role in mitigating the negative effects of spousal death on mental health, noting a consistent finding of financial hardship as a risk factor for depression.

Researchers have also found that spousal death is not only linked to deteriorating health and increased depression but is also associated with risk of death of the surviving partner, a phenomenon known as the "widowhood effect" (Brenn & Ytterstad, 2016). One research project examined data from a nationally representative sample of persons older than 60 in Taiwan, followed across five periods from 1989 to 2003, to study the impact of widowhood on mortality (Fang et al., 2012). The researchers found that spousal death was associated with a twofold risk of death in both men and women. They also found that the likelihood of death among widowed males was strongest for men who had been in poorer health prior to widowhood, but the same pattern was not found among widowed females. The researchers suggested that this finding might reflect the gender role division of labor that had been used by the couples. Another recent research project found that the highest widowhood effect occurred among the youngest men (Brenn & Yttterstad, 2016). Loss, grief, and bereavement are discussed in greater detail in Chapter 10.

Adjustment to widowhood is facilitated by a person's own inner strength, family support, a strong network of friends and neighbors, and membership in a religious organization or an active community. The family is the most important source of emotional, social, and financial support during this time (Walsh, 2016b).

Institutionalization

Another myth of aging is that older individuals are being abandoned and neglected by their families and being pushed into nursing homes to get them out of the way. Fewer elderly persons are institutionalized than we generally assume, but the risk for entering a nursing home or similar institutional setting increases significantly with age. In 2015, 3.1% of the population 65 years and older lived in institutional settings (Administration on Aging, 2016). However, the risk of entering an institutional setting increases with age. Only 1% of older adults aged 65 to 74, compared with 9% of those 85 and older, lived in institutional settings. Additionally, 2.7% of older adults live in self-described senior housing with at least one supportive service. It is important to note that these data reflect the number of older adults living in institutional settings at a given point in time. The data do not reflect the movement in and out of such facilities, and it is estimated that 39% of people aged 65 and older will spend some time in a nursing home at some point; the percentage rises to 49% at age 85 (Hooyman et al., 2018). About three quarters of the residents of nursing homes are women, and about 86% are White (Hooyman et al., 2018). It remains to be seen whether Gene Smith, Lois Smith, Ms. Johnson, or Mr. or Mrs. Menzel will spend some time before death in a nursing home.

Most children and spouses do not use nursing homes as a dumping ground for their elderly relatives. They turn to nursing homes only after they have exhausted all other alternatives. Nor is institutionalization a single, sudden event. It is a process that starts with the need to make a decision, continues through the placement itself, and ends in the adjustment to the placement (Naleppa, 1996).

Researchers have taken a close look at the factors that predict a person's entry into a nursing home. Among the most important are the condition and needs of the elderly individual. Functional and behavioral deficits, declining health, previous institutionalization, and advanced age all contribute to the decision to enter a nursing home. Family characteristics that are good predictors of institutionalization include the need for 24-hour caregiving, caregiver feelings of distress, caregiver health and mental status, and caregiving environment (Naleppa, 1996). The placement decision itself is emotionally stressful for all involved and can be viewed as a family crisis (Chang & Schneider, 2010). Yet it can be considered a normative part of the family life cycle. The process of making a placement decision itself unfolds in stages. A grounded theory study of the nursing home placement decision among Chinese family caregivers in Taiwan identified four stages: initiating the placement decision, assessing and weighing the decision, finalizing the decision, and evaluating the decision (Chang & Schneider, 2010). Because many nursing home placements are arranged from the hospital for an elderly individual who entered the hospital expecting to return home, many older adults and their families may not have time to progress well through these stages. For those who unexpectedly enter a nursing home from the hospital, it may be advisable to arrange a brief visit home to say farewell to their familiar environment. Although society has developed rituals for many occasions, unfortunately no rituals exist for this difficult life transition.

Entering a nursing home means losing control and adjusting to a new environment, but the culture of nursing homes is changing. Increasingly, nursing homes focus on resident-centered care that offers more choices in such matters as waking and eating times. The new culture emphasizes a more home-like atmosphere, including companion animals; breaking large facilities into smaller communities; and humanizing staff–care recipient relationships. Evaluation of the impact of these changes on residents and staff indicate lower levels of boredom and helplessness among residents and less job turnover among staff (Hooyman et al., 2018). How well a person adjusts to moving to a nursing home depends on many factors. If the elderly individual sees entering the nursing home in a favorable light and feels in control, adjustment may proceed well. Frequent visits by relatives and friends also help in the adaptation to the new living arrangement.

CRITICAL THINKING QUESTIONS 9.4

Retirement has occurred in different ways for Gene and Lois Smith, Ruby Johnson, and Joseph and Elizabeth Menzel. What factors influenced the decision to retire and the adjustment to retirement for each one of them? At what age do you expect to retire? If you were promised a full pension that would allow you to stop working now, would you want to continue to work? Why or why not? What does work mean to you? Do you work to live or live to work? What factors do you think a person should consider when making decisions about retirement?

THE SEARCH FOR PERSONAL MEANING

As adults become older, they spend more time reviewing their life achievements and searching for personal meaning. In gerontology, the concept of **life review** as a developmental task of late adulthood was introduced by Robert Butler (1963). He theorized that this self-reflective review of one's life is not a sign of losing short-term memory, as had been assumed. Rather, life review is a process of evaluating and making sense of one's life. It includes a reinterpretation of past experiences and unresolved conflicts. Newer forms of clinical interventions rooted in narrative theory underscore the importance of providing structure, coherence, and opportunity for meaning making of one's experience that "storying" provides (Goodcase & Love, 2017). Social workers can influence a more positive outcome of a life review through relationship, empathic listening and reflection, witness to the story, and providing alternative reframes and interpretations of past events. For example, promoting a story of resiliency as a lifelong process helps to reframe stories that support successful mastery of challenges and compensatory recovery in the face of adversity.

The life review can lead to diverse outcomes, including depression, acceptance, or satisfaction (Butler, 1987). If the life review is successful, it leads the individual to personal wisdom and inner peace. But the reassessment of one's life may also lead to despair and depression. This idea that the process of life review may lead to either acceptance or depression is similar to the eighth stage of Erikson's theory of adult development; through the life review, the individual tries to work through the conflict between ego integrity (accepting oneself and seeing one's life as meaningful) and despair (rejecting oneself and one's life) (Goodcase & Love, 2017).

The ways in which individuals review their lives differ considerably. Some undertake a very conscious effort of assessing and reevaluating their achievements; for others, the effort may be subtle and not very conscious. Life review is believed to be a common activity for older adults, regardless of how they pursue it across cultures and time.

The concept of **reminiscence** is closely related to life review. Most older persons have a remarkable ability to recall past events. They reminisce about the past and tell their stories to anyone who is willing to listen, but they also reminisce when they are on their own. This reminiscing can serve several functions (Sherman, 1991):

- Reminiscing may be an enjoyable activity that can lift the spirits of the listener and of the person telling the story.

- Some forms of reminiscing are directed at enhancing a person's image of self, as when individuals focus on their accomplishments.

- Reminiscing may help the person cope with current or future problems, letting her or him retreat to the safe place of a comfortable memory or recall ways of coping with past stressors.

- Reminiscing can assist in the life review, as a way to achieve ego integrity.

Reminiscing combines past, present, and future orientations (Sherman, 1991). It includes the past, which is when the reviewed events occurred. However, the construction of personal meaning is an activity also oriented to the present and future, providing purpose and meaning to life. One study examined the association between reminiscence frequency, reminiscence enjoyment or regret, and psychological health outcomes. The study found that high frequency of reminiscence and having regret was associated with poor psychological health. Reminiscence enjoyment, conversely, was positively associated with psychological health outcomes (Mckee et al., 2005). The Erzählcafé that Elizabeth Menzel visits tries to incorporate this by regularly including group activities that foster reminiscing in a safe, positive, and fun environment.

Another factor in the search for personal meaning is religious or spiritual activity. Cross-sectional research has consistently found that humans become more religious or spiritual in late adulthood (Moody & Sasser, 2015). There seems to be consensus in the cross-sectional research from the United States that religiosity increases in late adulthood, with a short period of health-related drop-off in attendance at religious services at the end of life. Older adults are also more likely than other age groups to participate in private religious behaviors such as prayer, reading of sacred texts, or meditation (Bjorklund, 2015). One longitudinal study that followed a sample of men and women from age 31 to 78 found that women and men tend to increase in spirituality between the mid-50s and mid-70s (Wink & Dillon, 2002). Vaillant's (2012) longitudinal research did not find support for this idea among his sample of Harvard men, and he suggests that the nature of the sample may be an important factor in this finding.

RESOURCES FOR MEETING THE NEEDS OF ELDERLY PERSONS

The persons in the case studies at the beginning of this chapter needed several kinds of assistance. Lois and Gene Smith, for example, needed some counseling to help them settle comfortably into retirement together. Gene went back to work to fill some of his leisure hours, but Lois needed some suggestions about the volunteer opportunities that could give meaning to her life. Ms. Johnson requires a level of assistance most practically provided by effective and comprehensive case management. The Menzels' needs were quite different. Elizabeth Menzel is confronted with Alzheimer's-related care and assistance needs. Much of this assistance has been provided by her daughter Christine and her husband Joseph. Joseph Menzel, in turn, needs some respite services to prevent him from being overwhelmed by the demands of giving care. This respite is being provided by his wife's weekly attendance in an Alzheimer's social group meeting.

The types of support and assistance that elderly persons receive can be categorized as either formal or informal resources. Formal resources are those provided by formal service providers. They typically have eligibility requirements that a person must meet to qualify. Some formal resources are free, but others are provided on a fee-for-service basis, meaning that anyone who is able to pay can request the service. Informal resources are those provided through families, friends, neighbors, churches, and so forth. Elderly persons receive a considerable amount of support through these informal support networks. As the society ages, more attention will need to be paid to the interaction between the informal and formal support systems (Wacker & Roberto, 2014).

Informal Resources

The family is the most important provider of informal resources for many older individuals. Usually family members can provide better emotional and social support than other providers of services. Family members know the person better and are more available for around-the-clock support. Different family members tend to provide different types of assistance. Daughters tend to provide most of the caregiving and are more involved in housekeeping and household chores. Sons are more likely to aid with household repairs and financial matters (Hooyman et al., 2018).

However, the family should not be considered a uniformly available resource or support. Not all family networks are functional and able to provide needed support. As Ms. Johnson's story illustrates, even when family members are involved in the elderly person's life, they may place additional demands on the older person instead of relieving the burden. The increased presence of women in the labor market places them in a particularly difficult position—trying to balance the demands of raising children, taking care of their parents or partner, and being part of the workforce. Furthermore, the size of the family network available to support elderly persons is decreasing due to the decreasing average number of children in a family (Walsh, 2016a).

A second source of informal resources is friends and neighbors, who often provide a significant amount of care and assistance. Although they may be less inclined than family members would be to provide personal care, friends and neighbors like Gene and Lois Smith often offer other forms of assistance, such as running errands or performing household chores. Sometimes a system of informal exchanges evolves—for example, an elderly woman invites her elderly neighbor over for meals while he mows her lawn and drives her to medical appointments.

Finally, informal resources are also provided by religious and community groups. Religious-related resources include social and emotional support through group activities and community events. It is this form of support that an active retired person such as Lois Smith finds most helpful. In addition, some religious groups are involved in providing more formal resources, such as transportation or meal services.

Formal Resources

The second type of support for older adults is the formal service delivery system, which offers a wide range of services. Four different social security trust funds are the backbone of formal resources to older people in the United States.

1. *Old-Age and Survivors Insurance (OASI).* The retirement and survivors' component of the U.S. Social Security system is a federally administered program that covers almost all workers. To qualify, a person must have worked at least 10 years in employment covered by the program. The benefit is based on the individual's earnings and is subject to a maximum benefit amount. Through cost-of-living adjustments, the amount is adjusted annually for inflation. Many older individuals are able to supplement this benefit with private pension benefits (Social Security Administration, 2017b).

2. *Hospital Insurance Trust Fund (Medicare Part A).* This fund covers a major part of the cost of hospitalization as well as a significant part of the costs of skilled nursing facility care, approved home health care, and under certain conditions, hospice care. Depending on the type of service needed, beneficiaries pay a one-time copayment or a percentage of the actual costs. Most beneficiaries do not need to pay a monthly premium (Medicare.gov, 2017a).

3. *Supplementary Medical Insurance. Medicare Part B* covers medical costs such as physicians' services, inpatient and outpatient surgery, and ambulance services, as well as laboratory services, medical equipment, outpatient mental health services, second opinions for surgery, and preventive services such as flu vaccinations. Under the Affordable Care Act, Part B also covers screening mammograms, colorectal cancer screenings, and an annual wellness visit without a copayment charge (Medicare.gov, 2017b). Beneficiaries pay a monthly premium. Some services require a copayment or a deductible. *Medicare Part D,* a result of the Medication Prescription Drug Improvement and Modernization Act of 2003, became effective on January 1, 2006. It was designed to provide older adults and people with disabilities access to prescription drug coverage. Rather than being administered by the federal government, as in the case of Part A and Part B, Part D is administered by private insurance plans that are then reimbursed by the Centers for Medicare and Medicaid Services (CMS) (Medicare.gov, 2017c). Participants can choose from a number of private insurance plans, but the choices are not straightforward. Plans with the lowest premiums may not cover the drugs needed by a particular participant. In addition, plans may change their drug prices frequently. The initial coverage was limited to drug costs of $2,400, and catastrophic coverage did not pick up until drug costs reached $3,850, placing considerable financial burden on many older beneficiaries. This problem with Medicare Part D was termed the "doughnut hole." The health reform bill passed in March 2010 attempts to close the doughnut hole over time (National Committee to Preserve Social Security & Medicare, 2016).

4. *Disability insurance.* This component provides benefits for workers younger than 62 with a severe long-term disability. There is a 5-month waiting period, but the benefits continue as long as the disability exists.

In addition, Supplemental Social Security Income (SSI) is a financial need-based program that provides cash benefits to low-income, aged, blind, and disabled persons. It is not part of the social security trust funds but is a federal welfare program.

Other formal services are available regionally. Here is an overview of some of the most important ones (see Wacker & Roberto, 2014, for a fuller discussion of community resources for older adults).

*   *Adult day care.* Some elderly individuals have conditions that prevent them from staying at home while their caregiver is at work, or the caregiver may benefit from respite. Two forms of adult day care exist for such situations. *The social adult day care model* provides meals, medication, and socialization but no personal care. *The medical adult day care model* is for individuals who need medical care, nursing services, physical or occupational therapy, and more intensive personal care.

*   *Senior centers.* Community forums for social activities, educational programs, and resource

information are available even in small communities.

- *Home health care services.* Several types of home health care are available, varying greatly in level of assistance and cost. They range from homemakers who assist with household chores, cleaning, and errands to registered nurses who provide skilled nursing service, use medical equipment, and provide intravenous therapy.

- *Hospice programs.* The purpose of a hospice program is to provide care to the terminally ill. Through inpatient or outpatient hospice, patients typically receive treatment by a team of doctors, nurses, social workers, and care staff.

- *Senior housing.* An elderly person may require a change in his or her living arrangement for a number of reasons, and several alternative living arrangements are available. Senior apartments and retirement communities are for persons who can live independently. They typically offer meals and housekeeping services but no direct care. Many offer transportation, community rooms, and senior programs.

- *Adult homes.* For seniors in need of more assistance, adult homes usually have rooms, rather than apartments, and provide meals, medication management, and supervision.

- *Health-related senior facilities.* For those in need of nursing care and intensive assistance with activities of daily living, residents live in private or semiprivate rooms and share living and dining rooms. Medications, meals, personal care, and some therapeutic services are provided. Included in this category is the growing number of *assisted living facilities*, which may provide small apartments as well as single rooms. The skilled nursing facility provides the highest level of care, including nursing and personal care and an array of therapeutic services. Several noninstitutional alternatives to the nursing home exist, including *adult foster care* programs that operate in a similar way to foster care programs for children and adolescents.

- *Nutrition programs.* Deficits in nutrition can affect a person's health and the aging process. Nutritional services are provided through a number of programs, the best known being Meals on Wheels.

- *Transportation services.* Public and private providers offer transportation for elderly persons with mobility problems.

- *Power of attorney.* Some elderly persons have difficulty managing their legal and financial affairs. A **power of attorney (POA)** is a legal arrangement by which a person appoints another individual to manage his or her financial and legal affairs. The person given the POA should be a person the client knows and trusts. Standard POA forms can usually be found at office supply stores or on websites for state bar associations, but legal advice is highly recommended for specific situations. The POA must be witnessed and notarized. A POA can be limited (in scope or for a certain time period), general (no restrictions), or durable (begins after the client reaches a specified level of disability).

With so many types of services available, the social worker's most daunting task is often assessing the elderly person's needs. It may also be a challenge, however, to find quality services that are affordable. Thus, advocacy on behalf of older adults remains a concern of the social work profession.

Naturally, the ways formal and informal resources are offered differ among countries and even regions of a country. As can be deduced from our discussion of the problems older adults face, many are neither unique to an individual nor country specific. Rather, they are occurring as part of the aging process for older adults around the globe. The United States often uses an incremental approach to policy changes. In Germany, where the Menzels live, policy change usually takes a longer time, but when it occurs, the new policies are often very comprehensive and far-reaching in their application. These types of difference in policy development are related to other differences in the political cultures of countries.

Technology and the Late-Adult Population

Many types of technology can be important resources for late-life adults. It is exciting to think that the current cohort of late-life adults has seen some of the innovations in technology noted in Exhibit 9.9, and much more.

EXHIBIT 9.9 ● Innovations in Technology in the Last 100 Years	
Television	Cellular telephones
Air conditioning and refrigeration	Smartphones
Space rockets	Personal computers
Jet airliners	Portable computers
Microwave ovens	The World Wide Web and Internet
Behind-the-ear hearing aids	Wireless Internet
Stereos	Electronic books
Clock radios	Computer tablets
Handheld video cameras	Robots
VHS and DVR video players and recorders	Touchscreens
Digital photography	Smart homes
Compact disk and MP3 players	Home monitoring systems
Gaming devices and players	3-D printers

Not only has the past century witnessed many technological developments, but it has also experienced an increasing pace of these advances. Consider the shrinking number of years it has taken new technology to reach market saturation, with a majority of households using the technology (Strategy and Transformation, 2015):

- Electricity: 46 years
- Telephone: 35 years
- Black and white TV: 26 years
- Computer: 16 years
- Mobile phone: 13 years
- Internet: 7 years
- Smartphone: 2.5 years

Given the rapid progress and everyday use of technology, concern has arisen about the challenges this presents to older adults because it is thought that adoption of new technology is usually more difficult for older adults than for younger generations. A major challenge is that many elders do not feel confident in their ability to use and master technology and state that they must ask others to show them how to use a new device or technology. Physical challenges and disabilities may also prevent them from being able to access new technologies (Pew Research Center, 2017b). Although the latest communication technology can allow older adults to stay in touch with friends, children, and grandchildren, a lack of confidence in using new technology can be a challenge for grandparents who are raising their grandchildren. Some older adults may not understand social media (and its risks) and other technology being used by children in their care.

Despite challenges, almost 70% of those over age 70 use some form of technology for communication, such as e-mail, text messaging, and social networking, to stay connected. Older, as opposed to younger, adults primarily use smartphones to talk on the phone instead of heavily using their other features (American Association of Retired Persons, 2016). The rate of smartphone ownership among older adults has been growing, and 42% of older adults in the United States own the technology, up from 18% in 2013. Ownership is much higher among older adults who are younger, better educated, and higher earners. Use of the Internet has also grown significantly among this population, from 14% in 2000 to 67% today. Older adults are also using tablets, with

32% reporting owning a computer tablet and 19% having an e-reader. Over a third of older adults also use some form of social media (e.g., Facebook, Instagram, Twitter) (Pew Research Center, 2017b).

With a growing number using it, communication technology holds great promise for improving the lives of older adults. As mentioned earlier, social media and other communication technology can keep elders connected with their friends and families. Telemedicine is growing in popularity and access and can provide doctor visits for older adults who cannot easily leave their homes or community. Apps can help people manage medications, prepare for medical procedures, and so much more. For those who have difficulty accessing transportation, driverless cars may be a future solution. And finally, home monitoring technology may become more widespread to alert family and medical personnel when an older adult is in crisis (Brenoff, 2015).

Another very important type of technology that can be a valuable resource for late-life adults is **assistive technology**, technology developed and used to assist individuals with physical impairments to perform functions that might otherwise be difficult or impossible. Assistive technology can be as low-tech as colorful Post-it notes to serve as visual reminders for late-life adults experiencing minor memory changes or as high-tech as assistive robots for people with mobility impairments. Examples include manual wheelchairs, motorized wheelchairs, motorized scooters, and other aids that enhance mobility; hearing aids, telephone communication devices, listening devices, visual and audible signal systems, and other products that enhance the ability to hear; and voice-synthesized computer modules, optic scanners, talking software, and other communication devices (Gilson, 2019; Hutchison, 2019).

RISK FACTORS AND PROTECTIVE FACTORS IN LATE ADULTHOOD

Chapter 8 suggests that midlife behavior has both antecedents and consequences. The same can be said for late adulthood. Early life experiences can serve either as risk factors or as protective factors for health and well-being during late adulthood. And late-adult behaviors can serve either as risk factors or as protective factors for future health and well-being.

As the longest-term longitudinal research available on late-adult behavior, Vaillant's Study of Adult Development (2002, 2012) provides the clearest understanding of the antecedents of late-adult well-being. Like Emmy Werner, who has studied a cohort until midlife (see Chapter 8), Vaillant is impressed with the self-righting tendencies in human nature. He suggests that what goes right in childhood is more important for life in late adulthood than what goes wrong. A warm relationship with their mothers was a strong protective factor at age 80 for his sample of Harvard men (Vaillant, 2012). He also suggests that unhappy childhoods become less important over the stages of adulthood. Consequently, Vaillant suggests that it is more important to count the protective factors than to count the risk factors. Although he found childhood experiences to diminish in importance over time, Vaillant also found that much of the resilience, or lack thereof, in late adulthood is predicted by factors that were established by age 50. He suggests that risk factors and protective factors change over the life course. He emphasizes that longitudinal research demonstrates that "everything affects everything else" (2012, p. 258) and that the "etiology of successful aging is multifactorial" (2012, p. 259).

Exhibit 9.10 lists six variables that Vaillant (2002, 2012) was surprised to find did not predict healthy aging and seven factors that he did find to predict healthy aging. Some of the factors that did not predict healthy aging did predict good adjustment at earlier adult stages. In terms of stress, Vaillant found that if we wait a few decades, many people recover from psychosomatic illness. In terms of parental characteristics, he found that they are still important for predicting adaptation at age 40 but not by age 70. In terms of both childhood temperament and general ease in social relationships, he found that they are strong predictors of adjustment in young adulthood but no longer important at age 70.

Conversely, Vaillant found that the seven factors on the right side of Exhibit 9.10, collectively, are strong predictors of health 30 years in the future. He also found that each variable, individually, predicted healthy aging, even when the other six variables were statistically controlled. Vaillant has chosen to frame each of these predictive factors in terms of protection; he sees risk as the flip side of protection. He notes the danger of such a list of protective factors: that it is used to "blame the victim" rather than provide guidance for aging well. He sees the list of predictors as "good news," however, because they all represent something that can be controlled to some extent.

EXHIBIT 9.10 ● Variables That Affect Healthy Aging	
Variables That Do Not Predict Healthy Aging	**Variables That Do Predict Healthy Aging**
Ancestral longevity	Not smoking, or stopping young
Cholesterol	Using mature coping mechanisms
Stress	Not abusing alcohol
Parental characteristics	Healthy weight
Childhood temperament	Stable marriage
General ease in social relationships	Some exercise
	Years of education

Source: Vaillant, 2002.

By following cohorts across the period of young-old and middle-old, Vaillant (2002) also has some suggestions about the consequences of late-adult behavior. We have already looked at his prescription for growing old gracefully. In addition, he notes the following personal qualities in late adulthood to bode well for continued well-being:

- Good self-care
- Future orientation; ability to anticipate, plan, and hope
- Capacity for gratitude and forgiveness
- Capacity for empathy, to imagine the world as the other sees it
- Desire to do things with people rather than to them

CRITICAL THINKING QUESTIONS 9.5

Think back to the case studies at the beginning of this chapter, the stories of Gene and Lois Smith, Ruby Johnson, and Joseph and Elizabeth Menzel. Of these five older adults, which one would you particularly like to engage in life review? What are your reasons for this choice? What do you consider the risk factors and protective factors that have influenced the period of late adulthood for each one of them?

IMPLICATIONS FOR SOCIAL WORK PRACTICE

Several practice principles for social work with older adults can be recommended.

- When working with an older adult, consider the person's life history.
- Develop self-awareness of your views on aging and how different theoretical perspectives may influence your practice.
- Be conscious that age-related social roles change over time and vary for different cohorts.
- Identify areas in which you can assist an elderly client in preventing future problems, such as health-related difficulties.
- Develop an understanding of and skills to assess the difference between the physical, biological, psychological, and socioemotional changes that are part of normal aging and those that are indicative of a problematic process. Develop an understanding of how such factors may affect the intervention process.
- Develop an understanding of the different types of families in later life. Because older adults continue to be part of their families, it may be beneficial to work with the entire family system.
- Develop an understanding of the retirement process and how individuals adjust differently to this new life stage.
- Carefully assess an elderly person's caregiving network. Be conscious of the difficulties that the caregiving situation poses for both the caregiver and the care recipient. Be conscious of the potential for caregiver burnout and familiarize yourself with local caregiver support options.
- Develop an understanding of the process of institutionalizing an older adult. Be careful not to label it as an act of abandonment. Rather, be aware that institutionalization is stressful for all involved and is typically done only as a last resort. Develop an understanding of the process of adaptation to nursing home placement and skills to

assist an older adult and his or her family with that adaptation.

- When assessing the need for service, be conscious of the availability of formal and informal support systems. Develop an understanding and knowledge of the formal service delivery system.

- Avoid treating older persons as if they were incapable of making decisions simply because they may not be able to carry out the decision. Rather, involve them to the maximum extent possible in any decisions relating to their personal life and care, even if they are not able to carry out the related actions.

KEY TERMS

activity theory (of aging) 323
age stratification perspective 324
Alzheimer's disease 332
assistive technology 353
continuity theory
    (of aging) 323
crystallized intelligence 336
damage or error theories
    of aging 326
delirium 338
dementia 330
dependency ratio 317

developmental biocultural
    co-constructivism 326
disengagement theory (of
    aging) 322
ego integrity versus ego
    despair 335
environmental gerontology 325
feminist theories (of aging) 323
fluid intelligence 336
guardianship 335
incidental memory 336
intentional memory 336

life review 348
morbidity 327
mortality rate 327
power of attorney (POA) 351
productive aging theory 324
programmed aging theories 326
reminiscence 348
social construction theory
    (of aging) 323
social exchange theory
    (of aging) 324
social gerontology 322

ACTIVE LEARNING

1. Think about the three case studies presented at the outset of this chapter (Smith, Johnson, and Menzel). Which theory or theories of social gerontology seem to be the best fit with each of these individuals?

2. Think of examples of how older adults are presented in the media (TV, movies, advertisements). How are they typically characterized? What does this say about our society's views on aging? Think of examples of how older adults could be presented in an

age-appropriate way in the media. Develop a short script for an advertisement that features older adults.

3. Think about your own extended family. What roles do the members of the oldest generation play in the family? How do the different generations interact, exchange resources, and influence each other? How do the different generations deal with their role changes and life transitions as they age? In what ways do the different generations support and hinder each other in life transitions?

WEB RESOURCES

Administration for Community Living: www.acl.gov
Site of the federal agency responsible for increasing access to community support and resources for older

Americans and people with disabilities, includes programs, grants, and news.

Agency for Healthcare Research and Quality: www.ahrq.gov

Site provides consumer, patient, and clinical practice information focused on specific populations: aging, women, and rural.

American Association of Retired Persons: www .aarp.org

Organizational site provides a wide range of resources for health, technology, travel, law, and policy and advocacy.

Federal Interagency Forum on Aging-Related Statistics: www.agingstats.gov

Site covers 31 key indicators of the lives of older people in the United States and their families.

National Caucus and Center on Black Aging: www.ncba-aged.org

Site contains aging news for policymakers, legislators, advocacy groups, minority

professionals, and consumers addressing finances, caregiving, intergenerational issues, and governmental programs.

National Council on Aging: www.ncoa.org

Site presented by the National Council on Aging (NCOA) contains information on advocacy, programs, publications, and a number of good links to other aging resources.

National Institute on Aging: www.nia.nih.gov

Site presented by the National Institute on Aging (NIA) contains information about the NIA, news and events, health information, research programs, funding and training, and the National Advisory Council on Aging.

Social Security Administration: www.ssa.gov

Site maintained by the U.S. Social Security Administration contains benefits information and online direct services.

Very Late Adulthood

Pamela J. Kovacs and Annemarie Conlon

Chapter Outline

Learning Objectives

10.1 Compare one's own emotional and cognitive reactions to three case studies.

10.2 Summarize major themes in the historical and cultural contexts of people in very late adulthood, including centenarians.

10.3 Describe approaches for evaluating functional capacity in very late adulthood.

10.4 Summarize the major issues in relationships in very late adulthood.

10.5 Describe the housing continuum experienced by people in very late adulthood.

10.6 Analyze the importance of spirituality in very late adulthood.

10.7 Summarize what social workers need to know about the dying process.

10.8 Summarize what social workers need to know about loss, grief, and bereavement.

10.9 Apply knowledge of very late adulthood, dying, and bereavement to recommend guidelines for social work engagement, assessment, intervention, and evaluation.

CASE STUDY 10.1

MARGARET DAVIS STAYS AT HOME

Margaret Davis has lived in her small, rural community in southern West Virginia for all of her 85 years. It is in this Appalachian mountain town that she married her grade-school sweetheart, packed his pail for long shifts in the mine, and raised their four children. It has been more than 30 years since she answered the door to receive the news that her husband had perished in an accident at the mine. She remains in that same house by herself, with her daughter living in a trailer on the same property and one of her sons living just down the road. Her other son recently moved to Cleveland to find work, and her other daughter lives in the same town but has been estranged from the family for several years.

Mrs. Davis has hypertension and was recently diagnosed with type 2 diabetes. The nurse from the home health agency is assisting her and her daughter with learning to give insulin injections. It is the nurse who asks for a social work consult for Mrs. Davis. The nurse and Mrs. Davis's daughter are concerned that she is becoming increasingly forgetful with her medications and often neglects her insulin regime. They also suspect that she is experiencing some incontinence, because her living room couch and carpet smell of urine. Mrs. Davis and her daughter Judy greet the social worker at her home. They have been baking this morning and offer a slice of peanut butter pie. Judy excuses herself to go to her trailer to make a phone call. The social worker asks Mrs. Davis about how her insulin regime has been going and if she feels that she could keep up with the injections. She responds that she has learned to give herself the shots and "feels pretty fair." The social worker conveys the concern that she may be missing some of the injections and other medications as well. To this she replies, "Oh, don't worry about me, I'm fine." The social worker proceeds to ask the sensitive question as to whether she has been having trouble with her bladder or getting to the bathroom. This causes Mrs. Davis to become very quiet. Looking up at the social worker she shares that witches have been visiting her house late at night and have been urinating in her living room. The witches are very "devious," but because she is a very religious person, she does not feel that they will harm her.

Judy returns to the home and joins her mother and the social worker. Judy voices her concern about her mother's safety, noting the problems with medications and with general forgetfulness. Judy is able to prepare meals, dispense the medications, and give insulin injections in the morning because she works evenings at a factory. Judy's daughter, Tiffany, has been staying overnight in the home but complains of her grandmother's wandering and confusion late at night. As a result, she is often exhausted during her day shifts at a nursing home in the next county and in caring for her small children. When asked about Mrs. Davis's son's involvement in her care, Judy responds, "He works and is in the Guard some weekends. He handles Mom's money mostly, and his wife, well, she has her own problems." Judy also reported that her mother has Medicare, but she was not sure if that would be sufficient to pay for all her mother's care long-term. Judy is also worried because her old car has been giving her problems lately, and the repairs are becoming expensive. She concludes by stating, "We promised Mom that she would never go to a home . . . we take care of our own."

—Kristina M. Hash
—Meenakshi Venkataraman

CASE STUDY 10.2

PETE MULLIN LOSES HIS SISTER'S SUPPORT

Pete Mullin and Lucy Rauso, brother and sister, ages 96 and 92, have lived together since the death of Lucy's husband, Tony, 25 years ago. Pete and Lucy are second-generation Irish Catholic Americans, and Tony Rauso was Italian American. Pete was married in his 30s but had lived alone since his divorce at age 55. Pete and Lucy were both in their early 70s when they decided to pool their limited savings and retirement income to buy a small home in a rural retirement community in central Florida. The promise of a lower cost of living and milder winters, and the fact that many of their friends had moved or died, made it easier for Lucy and Pete to leave the community in Massachusetts where they had spent their entire lives.

Pete has been estranged from his one daughter since his divorce but is in touch with a granddaughter who "found" him when she moved to Florida a few years ago. Lucy has one surviving son in New Jersey and several grandchildren who provide limited financial support and some social support via phone calls and an occasional visit. Pete has enjoyed his life and, despite some difficulty with his vision and hearing, manages to get around well in his familiar surroundings. He is especially fond of tending his orchids in the back porch.

Lucy has just been hospitalized with chronic heart failure and is not expected to make it through the night. A neighbor has brought Pete to the intensive care unit to be with Lucy. Pete states that together he and Lucy managed to provide for each other and served as each other's durable power of attorney and health care surrogate and in general made it possible for each of them to remain in their home. He wonders what will happen to him after Lucy's death. He knows that many people his age live in nursing homes, but he prefers to stay in his own home. He wonders if the Meals on Wheels will still come to the home, because their eligibility was based on Lucy's diagnosis of chronic heart failure. He hopes he will die soon and quickly like Lucy.

The social worker employed for the Meals on Wheels program has been asked to make a home visit within the week following Lucy's death to reassess Pete's eligibility for services. The social worker had not realized how much her job would involve working with people who have experienced a major loss, whether death of a loved one as in Pete's case or the accompanying losses that come with illness, disability, and aging.

CASE STUDY 10.3

MARIE CIPRIANI IS LOSING HER LIFE PARTNER

Marie Cipriani was born in a small apartment house on the Lower East Side of Manhattan 86 years ago. Just one year before her birth, Marie's mother passed through Ellis Island with Marie's three older sisters. Her father and two brothers, already established in the States, eagerly awaited their arrival. Years later, when Marie was an adolescent, the family moved to Long Island. Today, Marie lives in a modest two-bedroom home that she shares with Irene Wright, her partner of 42 years. Irene, a petite 79-year-old African American woman, has recently been diagnosed with stage IV lung cancer. The disease has progressed rapidly, hastening Irene's decision to transition to hospice service.

Jessica, the hospice social worker, met with Irene and Marie at their home this past Friday afternoon. Marie was making soup while Irene reclined in the warmth of the backyard sun. Marie immediately put the soup on simmer and accompanied Jessica out back to meet Irene. Marie was apprehensive because she was not sure how this stranger felt about two women sharing their lives together. However, when Jessica asked them how long they had lived in their home and complimented them on the length of their relationship, Marie began to feel at ease. Jessica worked from a family systems perspective and considered both Irene and Marie her clients. She discovered that Marie's siblings died years earlier. And, although Marie had one son from a previous marriage, he had died of congestive heart failure last June at age 64. Marie has no other close relatives. Irene, however, has two younger sisters who never understood Irene's relationship with Marie. "They generally do not visit when I am around," Marie said, hinting to Jessica that the relationship with Irene's family is rocky. "I don't know what they will do now because I am not leaving Irene's side."

Jessica was concerned about what would happen to Marie after Irene died. Although Marie appeared to be in good physical shape, going through the grieving process might impact Marie's mental and physical health. Should Marie's health decline, who will she rely on for help? Moreover, even though the United States has marriage equality, Marie and Irene are not legally married. If they do not have all the proper paperwork in place, Marie could find herself at risk for eviction.

VERY LATE ADULTHOOD: CHARTING NEW TERRITORY

At 85, 86, 92, and 96, respectively, Margaret Davis, Marie Cipriani, Lucy Rauso, and Pete Mullin are charting new territory. They are a part of the rapidly growing population older than age 85, many of whom are surprised they are living so long.

In the first edition of this book (1999), the chapter on late adulthood covered all persons 65 and older. The fact that subsequent editions present this content in two chapters (Late Adulthood and Very Late Adulthood) indicates the scope and rapidity of the demographic changes taking place in the United States and other late-industrial societies. Within the past 20 to 25 years, some researchers have begun to more methodically consider age distinctions after age 65 or 75, given the population growth in this age group.

This chapter summarizes some of the emerging literature on very late adulthood, including those who reach 100—our **centenarians**. (Much of what appears in the previous chapter on late adulthood applies as well.) The current knowledge about very late adulthood is growing as the population and related interest increase each year. However, given the scarcity of longitudinal studies that have followed a cohort from early adulthood deep into very late adulthood, it is difficult to tease out the cohort effects in the available cross-sectional research.

One issue that comes up at all adult stages is the ages included in the stage. As you have seen throughout this book, chronological markers of age are arbitrary at best and influenced by biological age, psychological age, social age, and spiritual age. But it is fairly standard to think of 85 and older as old old, oldest old, or very late adulthood. The category of the very old, those older than 80, is also referred to by some as the "fourth age" (Hazan, 2011, p. 11). This is more about circumstances in one's life than about age; for example, the "third age" refers to being older and still remaining independent, and the "fourth age" refers to a time when people are more dependent and in need of care (Lloyd, 2015). This is less a chronological distinction than a reflection of changes in life circumstances that often happen as one approaches age 80. For the most part, we use "very-late-life adults" to describe people in this life course phase, but we also use "old old" and "oldest old" when citing work where those terms are used. However, keep in mind that chronological age may not be the best marker for categorizing very-late-life adults (Agronin, 2011). Loss of health might be a better criterion for categorization

as very late adulthood or old old. Nevertheless, in keeping with the other chapters in the book, this chapter uses a chronological distinction.

The drawback to using a chronological marker for entry into very late adulthood is that the path through very late adulthood is quite diverse, and for many people older than 85, ill health is not a central theme of their lives. In his book *Aging Well*, George Vaillant (2002) reminds us that

- Frank Lloyd Wright designed the Guggenheim Museum at age 90,
- Dr. Michael DeBakey obtained a patent for a surgical innovation when he was 90, and
- Grandma Moses was still painting at 100.

In addition, we add the following:

- Sarah and Elizabeth Delany (1993) published their book *Having Our Say: Our First 100 Years* when Sarah "Sadie" was 103 and Elizabeth "Bessie" was 101.
- Sadie Delany (1997) later published *On My Own at 107: Reflections on Life Without Bessie*.
- Daniel Schorr was heard weekly on National Public Radio as the senior news analyst until the age of 93, having served as a news journalist for more than 60 years.
- Anna Halprin, a pioneer in the experimental postmodern dance world and expressive arts healing movement, continues to write and teach about dance/movement as an expressive therapy at age 96, even after a cancer diagnosis in 1972.
- Business owner Samuel Myers actively worked at his dry-cleaning business until 3 months before he died at age 97.
- Golfer Pauline Whitacre continues to golf into her 80s, shooting better than her age.
- Since turning 85, actress Betty White has won a Grammy, an Emmy, and three SAG awards. Now, at 96, she continues to act in various TV roles.
- At 98, Angie MacLean, from Bridgeport, Connecticut, had been bartending for 81 years.
- Leila Alice Denmark was a practicing pediatrician until her retirement at age 103.

So, there is much variation in the age at which health issues take on great importance. Margaret Davis has reached this stage in her mid-80s. Marie Cipriani remains healthy at 86 while she cares for a younger life partner who is on hospice service at age 79. Lucy Rauso reached it in her early 90s, and it does not yet seem to have overtaken Pete Mullin in his mid-90s. But sooner or later in very late adulthood, health issues and impending death become paramount.

With our current ways of living, often with busy and pressured work schedules and families geographically scattered, late-industrial societies pose challenges as one ages. That portion of the physical environment attributable solely to human efforts was designed, in the main, by and for those in young and middle adulthood, not for children, persons with various types of physical disabilities, or older adults. However, increasingly, the current cohort of very-late-life adults is charting new territory, and some aspects of society are preparing for the growth in this age group. What can we learn from people who reach 85 and beyond, and what do social work practitioners need to know to provide meaningful and relevant interventions?

As Erik Erikson suggested, we have one and only one life cycle (at least in this incarnation). For some of us, death will come quickly, but for others, death will come after a protracted period of disease and disability. One of the life tasks we face in late adulthood is to come to terms with our one and only life cycle, and the evidence suggests that most very-late-life adults do that remarkably well. We began this book with a discussion of conception, pregnancy, and childbirth, the starting line of the life course, and in this chapter we end the book with a discussion of death and dying, the finish line of the life course. Although this might sound linear, Erikson noted in relation to his life cycle chart that it "becomes really meaningful only when you have observed it as a weaving or, even better, have undertaken to weave it yourself" (Erikson & Erikson, 1997, p. 2). Our challenge as social workers is to be open to the uniqueness of each person's tapestry.

VERY LATE ADULTHOOD IN HISTORICAL AND CULTURAL PERSPECTIVE

There have always been those who outlive their cohort group, but greater numbers of people are surpassing the average life expectancy. Overall, the 85-and-older population is the fastest-growing segment both in the United States and worldwide. This age group is projected to grow from 6.1 million in 2015 to more than 19 million by 2050 in the United States and from 54.1 million to 204.7 million worldwide (United Nations, 2017; U.S. Census Bureau, 2017b).

The phenomenon of the baby boom generation helps explain the current growth in the midlife age groups as well as these projections for future growth in the older-than-85 population. But what else accounts for the fact that persons 85 and older are the fastest-growing segment of the older-adult population? Contributing factors may include access to better health care in early and middle years; earlier diagnosis and improved technology for treatment and overall health care; increased education on prevention leading to less smoking, less consumption of alcohol and saturated fats; and increased exercise (Hooyman et al., 2018). Additionally, a shift from infectious disease and catastrophic events to chronic illnesses has led to increased longevity (Hansen, Oren, Dennis, & Brown, 2016).

Due to the heterogeneity of pathways to healthy aging (Lowsky, Olshansky, Bhattacharya, & Goldman, 2014), one is cautioned against stereotyping very-late-life adults to describe them. For instance, the *intersectionality* of one's socioeconomic status, gender, race, ethnicity, sexual orientation, and experiences is embedded within these overall statistics (see Chapter 1 for a discussion of intersectionality theory). Life expectancy at birth in the United States in 2015 was 84.1 years for Hispanic women, 82.5 for women who are Native Hawaiian and other Pacific Islander, 82 years for Asian and non-Hispanic White women, 80.3 for American Indian/Alaskan Native (Census Bureau language) women, and 78.9 years for Black women. For men, life expectancy for the same period was projected at 79.6 years for Hispanic males, 77.7 for men who are Native Hawaiian and other Pacific Islander, 77.5 years for Asian and non-Hispanic White men, 74.7 years for American Indian/Alaska Native men, and 72.9 years for Black men (National Center for Health Statistics, 2017b). Among very-late-life adults, women outnumber men 2 to 1, and 4 out of 5 centenarians are women (U.S. Census Bureau, 2017b). As the data show, very late adulthood is largely a woman's territory. Pete Mullin is an exception to this trend. Culturally, the most significant fact is that very-late-life adults, like other age groups, are becoming more diverse. It is projected that from 2012 to 2050, the racial and ethnic breakdown of the U.S. population of adults age 85 and older will change in the following way: the percentage of this population that is non-Hispanic White will decline from 84.5% to 69.1%;

the percentage that is non-Hispanic Black will grow from 6.8% to 10.3%; the percentage that is Hispanic will grow from 5.8% to 13.1%; the percentage that is Asian will grow from 2.1% to 5.7%; and the percentage of all other racial and ethnic groups, including mixed race, will grow from 0.5% to 1.2% (U.S. Census Bureau, 2017b). These trends indicate an increased diversity among the old old.

Census data such as these are of interest to researchers studying *ethnogerontology*, the study of the causes, processes, and consequences of race, national origin, and culture on individual and population aging (Hooyman et al., 2018). Calasannti and King (2015) refer to the intersectionality of age, gender, race, and sexuality on aging. Poverty is another indicator of interest with the older population, given decreased earning power and increased health-related expenses. Older women (13%) were almost twice as likely to be poor as older men (7%) in 2010. Overall, the poverty rate increases with age, with 8.0% of people aged 65 to 74, 9.1% of people aged 75 to 84, and 12.4% of those 85 and older living in poverty. Race and ethnicity are also related to poverty among older adults, with 20.7% of older African Americans, 19% of older Hispanic Americans, 16.7% of older Asian Americans, and 7.9% of older non-Hispanic White Americans living in poverty (U.S. Census Bureau, 2016b).

Chapter 1 suggests that one of the themes of the life course perspective is that individual and family development must be understood in historical context. It is particularly important when we interact with very-late-life adults to be aware of the historical worlds in which their life journeys have taken place. Inquiring about this will help social workers better understand a person's resilience, responses to life challenges, and personal goals. For example, one's experience with the Holocaust, the Depression, war, or other personal trauma may help contextualize current stressors, resilience, and other responses to life.

Chapter 1 also discusses the concept of *cohort effects*, which suggests that a historical event affects one cohort differently than it affects subsequent cohorts because of the life phase in which it occurred. Let's look, for example, at the wide use of the World Wide Web (the Internet). It was experienced by

- the current cohort of 85-year-olds when they were in their 60s,

- the current cohort of 65-year-olds when they were in their 40s, and

- the current cohort of 45-year-olds when they were in their 20s.

PHOTO 10.1 French supercentenarian Jeanne Calment lived to the age of 122 years and 164 days (February 1875–August 1997), the longest confirmed human life span. In the United States, the number of centenarians totaled more than 70,000 in 2014.

Eric Fougere/Getty Images

For the current cohort of 25-year-olds and those younger, it may be hard to remember when social media and other aspects of the Internet were not part of their lives.

Individuals' cultural backgrounds also play a role in their perceptions of very late adulthood. Margaret Davis has spent her entire life in an impoverished small Appalachian town where families are expected to "take care of their own." In contrast, Pete Mullin and Lucy Rauso relocated from Massachusetts to Florida in their 70s, moving away from family and friends. Marie Cipriani grew up in New York in an Italian immigrant family. For the past 42 years, she has lived on Long Island with her female partner. Social workers need to try to understand clients' years in their previous homes and any important historical markers in those settings. They also need to know something about migration experiences.

WHAT WE CAN LEARN FROM CENTENARIANS

"Forget about Generation X and Generation Y. Today, the nation's most intriguing demographic is Generation

Roman numeral C—folks age 100 and over" (Harvard Health Letter, 2002, p. 1). Beyond age 100 seems to be a time of both resilience and ongoing development and vulnerability (Poon & Cohen-Mansfield, 2011).

Although very few 100-year-old people were known to exist in the United States in 1900, there were 70,344 of them in 2014. The majority of these centenarians were women (81.3%) (U.S. Census Bureau, 2017b). By 2050, it is estimated that more than 386,000 people in the United States and 3.2 million worldwide will reach the century mark (United Nations, 2017; U.S. Census Bureau, 2017b).

A small number of these centenarians, those aged 110 and older, are considered supercentenarians. As of January 2013, there were 63 validated supercentenarians throughout the United States, 58 women and 5 men (Coles, 2013). However, more than counting numbers, researchers want to know the answers to fundamental questions about human health and longevity, such as the following:

- What does it take to live a long life?

- How much do diet, exercise, and other lifestyle factors matter compared with "good" genes and other genetic factors?

- What is the quality of life among very-late-life adults?

- What role do individual characteristics such as gender, race or ethnicity, personality, and socioeconomic status play in longevity?

- What is the role of social support, religion and spirituality, and social environment in longevity?

Much of what is known about centenarians in the United States comes from the work of Leonard Poon and his colleagues (Baek, Martin, Siegler, Davey, & Poon, 2016; Cho, Martin, & Poon, 2014; Poon et al., 2007) in the Georgia Centenarian Study and from the New England Centenarian Study (Sebastiani & Perls, 2012; Sebastiani et al., 2013). These and other centenarian studies try to understand the interrelationship between multiple variables such as family longevity, gender, personality, environmental support, adaptation skills, individual traits, life satisfaction, and health.

These studies reveal that because frailer individuals die sooner, those remaining are a relatively robust group. Although these "extra" years are for the most part healthy years, several studies report high levels of disease with respect to the nervous system and senses (women 63%, men 49%), musculoskeletal and connective tissue diseases (women 59%, men 44%), disorders related to joints (women 44%, men 35%), digestive diseases (women 42%, men 37%), and dementia (18%–44%, not differentiated by gender) (Hazra, Dregan, Jackson, & Gulliford, 2015). What is more notable, however, is that the period of serious illness and disability for those who make it to 100 tends to be brief. Some factors thought to contribute to centenarians' robustness in U.S. studies are physical activity, such as walking, biking, golfing, and swimming, and mental exercise such as reading, painting, and playing a musical instrument. The Okinawa Centenarian Study notes the importance of the traditional lifestyle that includes high physical activity, social integration at all ages, a deep spirituality, adaptability, and optimistic attitudes (cited in Hooyman et al., 2018). A cluster of personality traits—low neuroticism (reflecting emotional stability), high competence, and high extroversion—were found among centenarians in the Georgia study (Martin, da Rosa, & Poon, 2011).

However, 100 is still old, and life expectancy is short at 100, with most only living 1 to 2 more years. In the New England study, 75% of the people were still living at home and taking care of themselves at 95. By age 102, this number had dropped to 30%—which is still quite remarkable (Terry, Sebastiani, Andersen, & Perls, 2008).

The gender gap in very late adulthood widens further past age 100, with female centenarians outnumbering males 4 to 1. However, men who reach their 100th birthday are, on the whole, healthier than their female counterparts, reporting lower incidence of dementia and other serious medical problems. What do we know about the causes of this gender gap? Estrogen may give women an edge in longevity. Another possibility is that there may be some protective genes in the X chromosome, of which women have two but men only one. Others theorize that menstruation and systems related to childbirth better equip women to eliminate toxins from the body. Another hypothesis is that genetics are relatively neutral, but women tend to be more social, and these connections are thought to be critical in weathering old age (Margrett et al., 2011).

In general, findings point to a life course of healthy lifestyles among centenarians: They have a sense of purpose, a method for lessening stress, eat smaller meals at the end of the day, rely primarily on a plant-based diet, drink one or two glasses of wine per day, belong to a faith-based community, have a strong sense of family, and live in a close-knit community (Buettner & Skemp, 2016). Future cross-cultural studies in which differences in diet, physical activity, and other lifestyle factors can be compared will be important in helping researchers better understand the influence of these multiple contributing variables. Overall, Poon and Cohen-Mansfield (2011) remind us it is important to focus on emotional as well as physical health and not to assume that physical decline necessarily means a decline in emotional well-being.

CRITICAL THINKING QUESTIONS 10.1

Imagine that you are having lunch with Leila Alice Denmark (noted earlier in the chapter) on the day she retires as a practicing pediatrician at the age of 103. How do you imagine the conversation going? What questions would you like to ask her? How do you think life will be different for centenarians in 2050?

FUNCTIONAL CAPACITY IN VERY LATE ADULTHOOD

Although people who reach 85 years of age and older demonstrate resilience in the simple fact of their longevity, they continue to face an increased incidence of chronic illness and debilitation with age. Chapter 9 provides a good overview of changes in physiology and mental functioning that begin to occur in late adulthood and only become more prevalent with advancing age. Unfortunately, much of the available information does not distinguish the 85-and-older cohort group from the larger 65-and-older group. We do know that the likelihood of living in a nursing home increases with age. Among nursing home residents, about 16.5% are 65 to 74 years old, 26.4% are 75 to 84, and 42.9% are 85 and older (Centers for Medicare & Medicaid Services, 2015). U.S. Census Bureau (2012) data show that 35.2% of female centenarians and 18.2% of male centenarians were living in a nursing or group residence compared with 19.2% of females and 10.9% of males ages 90 to 99. Many late-life adults enter a nursing home for a period of convalescence after hospitalization and then return to home or another setting.

The prevalence of older adults with a disability and those needing assistance with **instrumental activities of daily living (IADLs)**, activities that are not necessary for fundamental functioning but do allow an individual to live independently, increases steadily with age. Of those ages 65 to 69, 35% report a disability with 6.9% needing assistance; of those ages 70 to 74, 42.6% report a disability with 10.8% needing assistance; of those 75 to 79, 53.6% report a disability with 15.4% needing assistance; and of those age 80 and older, 70.5% report a disability with 30.2% needing assistance (Brault, 2012). Limitations in **activities of daily living (ADLs)**, basic care activities, also increase with age; 1.6% of those ages 65 to 74, 3.5% of those ages 75 to 84, and 9.7% of those age 85 and older need assistance with three or more activities (National Center for Health Statistics, 2009). (Exhibit 10.1 lists common ADLs and IADLs.)

In general, all persons experience **primary aging**, or changes that are a normal part of the aging process. There is a recognized slowing with age—slowing of motor responses, sensory responses, and intellectual functioning. For example, the percentage of older adults in the United States with significant visual loss increases during late and very late adulthood: 12.2% among the 65- to 75-year-olds and 15.5% among those older than 75 (American Foundation for the Blind, 2013). Similarly, 37% of 61- to 70-year-olds, 60% of 71- to 80-year-olds, and 80% of persons 85 and older experience hearing loss of 25 dB (Walling & Dickson, 2012).

EXHIBIT 10.1   ● Common Activities of Daily Living (ADLs) and Instrumental Activities of Daily Living (IADLs)
Activities of Daily Living
Bathing and toileting
Dressing
Walking a short distance
Shifting from a bed to a chair
Eating
Instrumental Activities of Daily Living
Doing light housework
Doing the laundry
Using transportation
Handling finances
Using the telephone
Taking medications

In addition, many experience **secondary aging** caused by disease; effects of the environment; and/or engagement in health-compromising behaviors such as smoking, alcohol, and drug use (Bjorklund, 2015). Access to health care, ample and nutritious food, safe and affordable housing, safe working conditions, and other factors that influence the quality of life also affect longevity.

Although late adulthood is a time of loss of efficiency in body systems and functioning, the body is an organism that repairs and restores itself as damage occurs. Those persons who live to be 85 and older may be fortunate enough to have a favorable genetic makeup. But they may also have found ways to compensate, to prevent, to restore, and to maintain other health-promoting behaviors. Most very-late-life adults come to think of themselves in ways that fit their circumstances. They narrow the scope of their activities to those that are most cherished, and they carefully schedule their activities to make the best use of their energy and talents.

Sooner or later, however, most very-late-life adults come to need some assistance with ADLs and IADLs. As a society, we must grapple with the question of who will provide that assistance. Currently, most of the assistance is provided by family members. But as families grow smaller, fewer adult children exist to provide such care. A number of family theorists have begun to wonder how multigenerational families might adjust their relationships and better meet long-distance caregiving needs (Horowitz & Boerner, 2017).

Chapter 9 provides an overview of dementia and more specifically Alzheimer's disease (AD). To better understand the progression of AD in the oldest old and compare it with the progression among younger older adults, functional ADLs and cognitive mini mental status evaluations, or MMSEs, were studied in a cohort of adults who were older than 85 and a cohort of adults who were younger than 85, all living in a community in France (Nourhashemi et al., 2009). The progression of cognitive impairment was the same across groups; however, after adjusting for age and dependency (help with ADLs), the progression of dependence occurred more quickly for the older group. In sum, even among the oldest old, dementia shortened life, especially among women. Studies such as this have important public health consequences, helping us better prepare for the type of care some of our oldest citizens, and our most rapidly growing age group, may need.

Ginesi, Jenkins, and Keenan (2016) suggest that improved understanding of brain disorders involved in different types of dementia is likely to become a major focus of biomedical research in the 21st century. They report that current evidence clearly indicates that dementia is caused by an interplay of "genes, lifestyle, and environmental factors" (p. 18). There is evidence that the medical community is beginning to recognize the dignity and worth of people with dementia, with growing understanding that all health care staff should be educated about dementia (Prahl, Krook, & Fagerberg, 2016). Webb (2017) promotes using a person-centered, relational approach when interacting with people with dementia. He and other researchers are using conversation analysis to learn the most effective ways to converse with people with dementia to empower people with dementia to interact more equally in conversations. Others are developing methods to increase empathy in the caregivers of those with dementia. Here is one example. One Dutch research team tested a virtual reality simulation movie and e-course intervention to allow caregivers of people with dementia to experience what it is like to have dementia (Wijma, Veerbeek, Prins, Pot, & Willemse, 2017). Using a pretest-posttest design, the researchers found that this intervention was associated with improved understanding of dementia and empathy for people with dementia.

RELATIONSHIPS IN VERY LATE ADULTHOOD

Much of what is presented in Chapter 9 under the Families in Later Life section applies also to very late adulthood. Research that looks specifically at relationship patterns among very-late-life adults notes the following themes (Barusch, 2012; Litwin & Levinson, 2017):

1. Individuals continue to desire and need connections to other people throughout life.

2. In very late adulthood, people interact with others less frequently, and old-old adults make thoughtful selections about the persons with whom they interact.

3. Age per se doesn't account for diminishing social networks; rather, it is the combination of older age and limitations related to increased disability.

Relationships With Family and Friends

Social isolation is a powerful risk factor not only for the development of cognitive and intellectual decline in very late adulthood but also for physical illness (Hoogendijk et al., 2016; Steptoe, Shankar, Demakakos, & Wardle, 2013). A sense of connectedness with family and friends can be achieved in person; on the phone; and more recently via e-mail, Facebook, chat rooms, blogs, Skype, and other social networking technology. This section focuses on relationships with people; however, remember that pets, plants, and other connections with nature bring comfort to any age group, including older adults.

Pertinent to very-late-life adults is the increased likelihood that one will have lost a spouse or partner, friends, an adult child, or other family members to death, illness, debilitation, or relocation. Loss is more prevalent during this stage than at other times of life, but there is also greater opportunity for intergenerational family contact as 4-, 5-, and 6-generation families become more common.

Siblings often provide companionship and caregiving for each other, as Pete Mullin and Lucy Rauso did in the case study. Siblings are comforting because they are part of one's cohort and have experienced many of the same family events. In addition, siblings tend to be the most long-standing relationships in a person's life (Hooyman et al., 2018). However, as we see with Marie Cipriani and Irene Wright, this is not always the case. Irene's relationship with her siblings is strained due to their nonacceptance of her life partner. Marie's siblings, who might have been able to provide support, have all died.

Obviously, sibling relationships may range from loving and close to ambivalent, distant, or even hostile. Sharing responsibility for aging parents may create greater closeness between siblings or increase tension. There is some evidence that sibling relationships are especially important sources of support among members of lower socioeconomic groups. Close relationships especially with sisters in very late adulthood have been found to be positively related to positive mental health (McGoldrick & Watson, 2016).

Relationships with adult children are another important part of the social networks of very-late-life adults, as is the case with Margaret Davis. Very-late-life adults in the United States are in fact institutionalized more often for social reasons than for medical reasons (Hooyman et al., 2018). One reason for this is that approximately 1 in 5 women 80 and older has been childless throughout her life or, like Marie Cipriani, has outlived her children. In addition, baby boomers and their children tended to have more divorces and fewer children, decreasing the caregiving options for their parents and grandparents

(Hooyman et al., 2018). Racial and ethnic variations exist, however. The proportion of multigenerational relationships that involve parents living with adult children tends to be higher among some families of color, especially African Americans (Hooyman et al., 2018). Approximately 2.7 million grandparents are responsible for their grandchildren; more than 1.5% of these grandparents are age 80 and above (Ellis & Simmons, 2014). Also, families with a collectivist heritage prefer to have elderly parents reside with their grown children. It is important to understand and honor historical and cultural expectations of each family when addressing the caregiving and health care needs of aging members. Geographic separation, most often because of the adult child's mobility, tends to interfere with intergenerational interaction among family members, although many manage "intimacy at a distance" (Hooyman et al., 2018, p. 281) or strong emotional ties despite the separation.

Agencies serving older adults and children often seek opportunities for contact across generations. Whether referred to as inter-, multi-, or cross-generational, many programs recognize the benefits of activities that bring older adults, young parents, teens, and/or children and infants together. Each has something to offer and something to receive. Some examples include elders providing tutoring, telephone support, or assistance in day care and school settings or serving as surrogate grandparents; adolescents providing assistance around the yards and homes of older adults, helping to write life reviews, or being pen or computer pals; and children and elders interacting around crafts, music, gardening, storytelling, or other activities that create ways of being together (Hooyman et al., 2018).

Relationships with friends remain important in very late adulthood. In general, women have fewer economic resources but more social resources and richer, more intimate relationships than do older men (Hooyman et al., 2018). But over time, women tend to outlive partners, friends, and other key members of their social support system, often being left to deal with end-of-life decisions at an advanced age, without the social and perhaps financial support of earlier life.

Relationships with a domestic partner become much less likely in very late adulthood than in earlier phases of life. Very-late-life adults have the potential to have shared 60 to 70 years with a spouse or partner. Such long-term relationships, where they do exist, present the risk of tremendous loss when one member of the relationship dies. (Widowhood is presented in more detail in Chapter 9.) Because women outnumber men

PHOTO 10.2 Loss is more prevalent during this stage than at other times of life, but there is also greater opportunity for intergenerational family contact as 4-, 5-, and 6-generation families become more common.

© Rich Legg/iStockphoto.com

2 to 1 after the age of 85, heterosexual men stand a greater chance of starting a new relationship than heterosexual women. With women living longer than men, lesbian domestic partnerships may have the greatest opportunity for continued long-term relationships in very late adulthood. However, this is not the case for Marie Cipriani and Irene Wright.

Intimacy and Sexuality in Very Late Adulthood

Given the scarcity of men and the fact that many partners and friends have died, many persons 85 and older, especially women, are more alone in this life stage than at other times in their lives. The implications for intimacy and sexuality for heterosexual women are significant. Although limited research has been conducted specifically about intimacy and sexuality with this age group, some tentative conclusions can be drawn from literature on aging. In particular, a summer 2001 issue of *Generations* focused on "Intimacy and Aging," including the expressions of intimacy in a variety of relationships, challenges related to physical and mental illness, gay and lesbian relationships, and separation of couples because of institutionalization.

A greater understanding of intimacy may help people "navigate between current binary discourses of asexual old age and 'sexy seniors'" (Sandberg, 2013, p. 261). Intimacy is much broader than sexuality, which has been identified as only one of five major components of intimacy (Moss & Schwebel, cited in Blieszner & deVries, 2001). The five major components of intimacy in this view are the following:

1. *Commitment.* Feeling of cohesion and connection

2. *Affective intimacy.* A deep sense of caring, compassion, and positive regard and the opportunities to express the same

3. *Cognitive intimacy.* Thinking about and awareness of another, sharing values and goals

4. *Physical intimacy.* Sharing physical encounters ranging from proximity to sexuality

5. *Mutuality.* A process of exchange or interdependence

Closeness is inherent in cognitive, affective, and physical intimacy. Communication, or self-disclosure, facilitates intimacy. In sum, intimacy is about connection, closeness, and trust, whether it is physical, sexual, emotional, or spiritual intimacy (Barusch, 2012). Guided by culturally informed practice and a belief that older adults are continuing to grow and develop, how might social workers work to help older adults minimize barriers to intimacy in their lives?

Although sexuality is only one aspect of intimacy, it deserves additional attention; it should not be neglected, as it often is in our interaction with older adults. A study aimed at preparing health care professionals to engage with older adults about emotional and physical intimacy concluded that "regular sexual activity is a normal finding in advanced age" (Lochlainn & Kenny, 2013). However, there may be barriers to meeting one's sexual desires. The lack of a sexual partner because of divorce, death, or illness is one of the most common reasons for an older adult reporting low interest in sex and little sexual activity. However, there are other physical and psychosocial conditions that impact the level of sexual interest, satisfaction, and performance of older adults, and social workers need to be comfortable addressing this important aspect of quality of life. Medical conditions such as heart disease, diabetes, arthritis, chronic pain, depression, and medications prescribed to address these and other conditions may reduce or restrict movement or sexual function as well as impact pleasure (Hooyman et al., 2018). Some of the more common psychosocial factors associated with reduced sexual desire or sexual dysfunction include restrictive beliefs about sexuality and aging, role changes because of illness or disability in one or both partners, anxiety about sexual function, and psychological disorders (Lochlainn & Kenny, 2013). Depression and substance abuse are more prevalent in older adults with sexual dysfunction. Also, cultural ideals about body image, perceived sexual attractiveness, and expression of emotions that may influence capacity for intimacy make it more difficult for some older adults to embrace age-related changes (Mayo Foundation for Medical Education and Research, 2007).

Relationships With Organizations and Community

Relationships with the wider world peak in young and middle adulthood. They grow more constricted as access to social, occupational, recreational, and religious activities becomes more difficult due to decreased mobility and independence and as the physical and cognitive impairments associated with age increase. As mobility declines, community-based programs such as Meals on Wheels can become important resources to people like Pete Mullin and Lucy Rauso, not only providing them with essential resources such as food but serving also as a connection to the community.

One organizational relationship becomes more likely with advancing age, however. As people live longer and need greater assistance, many move into some form of institutional care. When reading the upcoming discussion about the housing continuum, consider the benefits and the challenges each option presents.

The Use of Technology

The use of computer technology and the Internet has steadily increased over the past 20 years. However, although adults age 85 and older access the Internet, the percentage of those who do is small (Anderson & Perrin, 2017). Those more likely to use the Internet generally have a higher socioeconomic status, are more educated, are actively involved in the community, and have a social network that encourages Internet usage (Anderson & Perrin, 2017; Choi & DiNitto, 2013a, 2013b). Conversely, those less likely to use the Internet are less likely to have the resources to obtain computers or other devices for accessing the Internet and/or are more likely to have cognitive, perceptual, or motor skill deficits; vision impairment; or difficulty with ADLs and IADLs (Choi & DiNitto, 2013a).

Like any other age group, older adults use the Internet for online banking and to pay bills, for shopping, to refill prescriptions, to contact medical providers, to participate in online forums and support groups, to communicate with family and friends, and to search for health-related and nonhealth-related information. However, those 85 and older most often use the Internet for e-mail or text messages (Choi & DiNitto, 2013b).

Internet usage does have its benefits for those age 85 and older. Although the findings are mixed, it has been suggested that Internet usage increases communication within social groups, allows the maintenance of long-distance relationships, increases access to health information and resources, allows those who are mobility challenged to participate in online health self-management programs and support groups, and enables access to community, religious groups, and organization websites (Choi & DiNitto, 2013b).

In addition to the Internet, robots are being developed for improving the sociophysical environment for older adults (Rogers & Mitzner, 2017). Currently, robots can be used to assist with everyday tasks and activities as well as to increase social interactions for those who are mobility or cognitively challenged. The development of robotics is still in the early stages, but robots have been used in elder care in Japan (where robots are typically thought of as human) for a number of years (Turkle, 2011). Maintenance of the robots may require a team approach to turn the machine on and off and to keep it clean. Additionally, because this is a new field, ethical issues must be considered.

CRITICAL THINKING QUESTIONS 10.2

What have you observed about the functional capacity of the very old adults that you know? How much assistance have they needed with ADLs and IADLs? How did they react to needing assistance? Who provided the assistance? How have you seen very old adults cope with the reality that many of their relatives and friends die while they still live? How have you seen very old adults make use of technology to create and maintain relationships?

THE HOUSING CONTINUUM

As people live longer, the likelihood of illness and disability increases; spouses, partners, adult children, and friends die, and the chance of needing more support than is available to the very-late-life adults in their own home increases. Review the section on informal and formal resources in Chapter 9 for a description of the variety of options along the continuum as need for assistance increases.

Other than skilled nursing care reimbursed by Medicare and other health insurance, the majority of assistance people need must be paid for privately. Financing is a major problem for low-income and even many middle-income people. Women, especially women of color, are overrepresented in lower socio-economic categories, and in very late adulthood, safe, affordable housing options are a serious concern. But even Pete Mullin and Lucy Rauso found housing a problem until they moved in together and pooled their resources. Margaret Davis's daughter, Judy, is determined that Margaret won't go "to a home," but she is also worried about how costly Margaret's care will become in the future. What if Marie Cipriani needs to leave her home? Will she find living arrangements that welcome a lesbian woman?

Current trends indicate that in the future, the following housing options will be in greater demand and hopefully more readily available (The Equal Rights Center, 2014; Fox et al., 2017):

- Shared housing, shared expenses, and support by family members and friends

- Housing designs that are adaptable to the needs of the inhabitants over time

- Options for care and assistance in the home with education and support available to family and other informal caregivers, home health skilled services, reverse mortgages, home equity loans

- Independent living facilities, including retirement villages and naturally occurring retirement communities such as inner-city high-rise retirement communities close to medical, cultural, and recreational activities

- Assisted-living facilities that provide 24-hour assistance, continuing-care retirement communities that offer a range of services

- Nursing homes providing custodial care only (the number of skilled nursing facilities that also provide custodial care is likely to decrease, with their role taken over by assisted-living facilities)

- Housing options that are welcoming to people who are lesbian, gay, bisexual, transgender, and queer (LGBTQ)

Access and receptivity to this continuum of options are influenced by several factors: geographic location, including urban and rural location; socioeconomic status; race; ethnicity; gender; sexual orientation; family support; and health care status. Specifically, a substantial disparity in nursing home admissions of non-Hispanic White and minority late-life adults continues

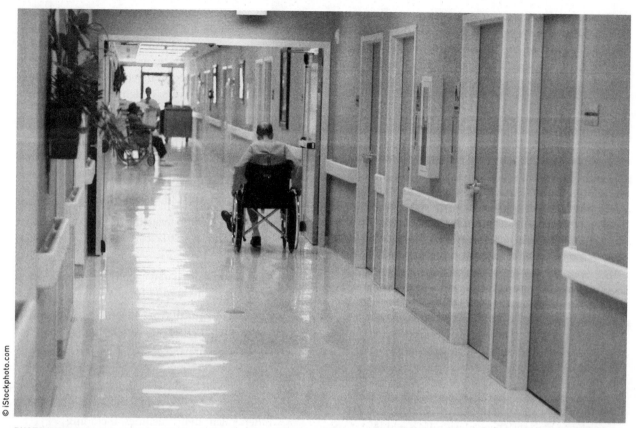

© iStockphoto.com

PHOTO 10.3 Although those who reach 85 and older demonstrate resilience by surviving, they continue to face increased incidence of chronic illness and debilitation with increased age.

to exist, particularly among women (Thomeer, Mudrazija, & Angel, 2015). African American men and women more often report a need for help with their ADLs and are less likely to receive the appropriate level of care than White men and women (Hooyman et al., 2018). Obtaining assistance with ADLs and IADLs can be expensive. Moreover, LGBTQ elders indicate trepidation about mainstream senior housing options and possible discrimination (The Equal Rights Center, 2014). Some of the current cohort of very-late-life adults have arrived at that stage without any expectation that they would live so long or any preparation for such a prolonged life. And some arrive there after a full life course of limited resources, as is the situation with Margaret Davis.

SPIRITUALITY IN VERY LATE ADULTHOOD

When the first author, Pam, called her 85-year-old aunt to wish her a happy birthday, Pam's uncle said, "She has been thinking a lot more about the hereafter." Curious about what sounded like a connection to aging and spirituality, Pam asked her aunt to tell her more. Her aunt added with a chuckle, "Yes, I go into a room and I wonder *What am I here after?*" On one hand, Pam's aunt was trying to make light of some short-term memory loss. But Pam also knew that increasingly her aunt had been questioning the meaning of life and wondering about her own death, following the recent death of her 58-year-old son to cancer.

There is often a conceptual division when describing religion and spirituality, with religion connected to an institution and spirituality being a more personal experience. Bishop (2011) cautions against this binary conceptualization, suggesting that the two are more often related than independent of each other, and some longitudinal research indicates that the two are highly correlated in late-life adults (Vaillant, 2012). More simply, spirituality is the search for meaning, purpose, and morality and develops through relationships with self, others, and one's understanding of the universe (Nelson-Becker, Canda, & Nakashima, 2016; Sheridan, 2019). Social workers seek to understand what role, if any, religion and spirituality play in the unique lives of their clients. Given barriers related to mobility, vision, hearing, and other access issues, older adults may feel disenfranchised and less connected to religious institutions that had once been a meaningful source of social support (Bishop & Martin, 2011).

The following discussion about spirituality refers to aging in general, not specifically to very-late-life adults, but is included in this chapter because of the connection among aging, loss, spirituality, and meaning making. Often when faced with crises—particularly those of life-limiting illness, disability, and/or loss—one tends to reexamine the meaning of life. And although illness, disability, and loss occur throughout life, these challenges tend to accumulate and come at a faster pace during very late adulthood. Dalby (2006) notes that some aspects of spirituality pertain across the life course; however, the following themes become more relevant with aging: integrity, humanistic concern, changing relationships with others and greater concern for younger generations, relationship with a transcendent being or power, self-transcendence, and coming to terms with death.

With age, losses accumulate in the following areas:

- *Relationships:* to children, spouses and partners, friends, and others
- *Status and role:* in family, work, and society
- *Health:* in stamina, mobility, hearing, vision, and other physical and cognitive functions
- *Control and independence:* in finances, housing, health care, and other decision-making arenas

Whether incremental or sudden, these losses can be difficult for members of a society where personal autonomy, independence, and sense of control are highly valued. Ironically, a focus on spirituality often coincides with decreased mobility and independence and diminishing social contact, limiting access to religious services and other opportunities for spiritual fulfillment and social support.

The search for meaning is a central element of Erik Erikson's (1963) eighth developmental task, referred to as maturity. It involves the challenge of *ego integrity versus ego despair* and centers on one's ability to process what has happened in life and accept these experiences as integral to the meaning of life. As Erik and Joan Erikson (1997) moved into their 8th decade, they began writing about a ninth stage. Joan published this previously unfinished work in 1997 following Erik's death in 1994

at the age of 92. She revisits the meaning of wisdom and integrity in light of the losses that occur with time and, despite the challenges, declares that "to grow is a great privilege" (p. 128). When describing this ninth stage, she refers to "gerotranscendence" and the work of Lars Torstam of Sweden, who coined the word as a possible path toward wisdom as we age. Joan Erikson, a dancer, played with the concept, calling it "gerotranscen*dance*" to note the room for creativity as we move though the "process towards maturation and wisdom" (p. 123).

Other important spiritual challenges facing elders include transcendence beyond oneself and a sense of connectedness to others (McInnis-Dittrich, 2014). An elderly person's struggle to maintain independence and the ability to make choices in the face of multiple challenges, versus becoming dependent on others, is both psychosocial and spiritual, calling for a social work response addressing both. It is important to remember that culture, race, religious upbringing, and other life experiences may influence each person's spiritual journey.

Very late adulthood is often a time for slowing down, looking back, and reaching out—steps that make sense developmentally as one nears the end of life. Over time, people tend to review their lives, some informally and others more formally. Social workers, family members, volunteers, or friends help facilitate this process of reflection and meaning making (Hooyman et al., 2018). This may involve helping people shape their memories and experiences to share with others, whether they are shared orally or in writing. Guided discussions with questions about emotions (happy memory, proud feeling), events (first job, wedding day, first move), or relationships (important people) are helpful for older adults addressing Erikson's developmental task integrity or wholeness versus despair (McCoyd & Walter, 2016).

The subject of spirituality is separated in this chapter from the subject of dying to emphasize the point that spirituality is not just about preparing for death. Rather, it is about making meaning of one's life (Bishop, 2011; Gordon, 2013; Nelson-Becker et al., 2016), transcending oneself, and remaining connected to others (McInnis-Dittrich, 2014).

CRITICAL THINKING QUESTIONS 10.3

Why do you think it is important to people like Margaret Davis, Pete Mullin, and Marie Cipriani to stay in their own homes? The majority of very old adults today are women. What are the implications of this for housing policy and programs for this age group? How have you observed the very old adults in your family cope with the accumulation of loss? What role did religion and spirituality play in their coping?

THE DYING PROCESS

The topic of death and dying is almost always in the last chapter of a human behavior textbook, reflecting the hope that death will come as late as possible in life. Obviously, people die in all stages of life, but very late adulthood is the time when dying is considered "on time." This does not mean it is easy, especially for those left behind who have never known life without this beloved family member; it is, however, usually less of a shock and perhaps anticipated.

Despite our strong cultural predisposition toward denial of the topic, and perhaps in response to this, there have been important efforts to talk about death, starting most notably with Elisabeth Kübler-Ross's book *On Death and Dying* in 1969. In the late 1990s, initiatives such as the Project on Death in America (PDIA) funded by the Soros Foundation and end-of-life initiatives funded by the Robert Wood Johnson Foundation set out to change mainstream attitudes about death and dying. The mission of PDIA was to understand and transform the culture and experience of dying and bereavement. It promoted initiatives in research, scholarship, the humanities, and the arts and fostered innovations in the provision of care, education, and policy. Television programs such as the Public Broadcasting Service's *On Our Own Terms: Moyers on Dying* facilitated public education and community dialogue (Moyers, Mannes, Pellet, O'Neill, & Moyers, 2000). TV series, such as *Desperate Housewives*, integrated death and dying into a beloved character's storyline (Cherry, 2012).

Death cafés have sprung up in communities around the world offering a place for strangers to gather to talk about death. Since 2011 when Jon Underwood held the first Death Café in his basement in England, more than 5,000 have been held in 51 countries. The objective is "to increase awareness of death with a view to helping people make the most of their (finite) lives" (Death Café, 2017). The majority of attendees at the first death cafés held in the United States (nine events held in Columbus, Ohio) were predominantly women ages 45 to 64, with one quarter under 35 and 22% over 65 (Span, 2013). Although our oldest elders may not be attending, the movement can benefit their personal

and professional caregivers. The increase in the number of death doulas, end-of-life coaches, and others outside the formal medical professions assisting people before, during, and after a death occurs reflects growing interest of some to participate more fully in this part of life's journey (Raymond, 2017).

The following adjectives used to describe death are found in both the professional and popular literature: *good*, *meaningful*, *respectful*, *appropriate*, *timely*, *peaceful*, *sudden*, *tragic*, *prolonged*, and *natural*. One can be said to die well, on time, before one's time, and in a variety of ways and places. This terminology reflects an attempt to embrace, acknowledge, tame, and integrate death into one's life. Other language is more indirect, using euphemisms, metaphors, medical terms, and slang, reflecting a need to avoid directly talking about death—suggesting that the person is "lost," has "passed away," or has "expired" (DeSpelder & Strickland, 2015). It is important for social workers to be attentive to words that individuals and families choose because they often reflect culture and/or religious background and comfort level (Bullock, 2011).

As with life, the richness and complexity of death are best understood from a multidimensional framework with biological, psychological, social, and spiritual dimensions (Bern-Klug, 2004; McCoyd & Walter, 2016). The following conceptualizations of the dying process acknowledge that dying and other losses, and the accompanying bereavement, are processes that differ for each unique situation yet share some common characteristics.

In *On Death and Dying*, Kübler-Ross (1969) described stages that people tend to go through in accepting their own inevitable death or that of others, summarized in Exhibit 10.2. Although these stages were written with death in mind, they have application to other loss-related experiences, including the aging process. Given time, most individuals experience these five reactions, although not necessarily in this order. People often shift back and forth between the reactions rather than experience them in a linear way, get stuck in a stage, and/or skip over others. Kübler-Ross suggests that, on some level, hope of survival persists through all stages.

Although these reactions may fit people in general, very-late-life adults appear to experience far less denial about the reality of death than other age groups (McInnis-Dittrich, 2014). As they confront their limitations of physical health and become socialized to death with each passing friend and family member, most very-late-life adults become less fearful of death. Unfortunately, some professionals and family members

EXHIBIT 10.2 ● Stages of Accepting Impending Death

Denial. The person denies that death will occur: "This is not true. It can't be me." This denial is succeeded by temporary isolation from social interactions.

Anger. The individual asks, "Why me?" The person projects his or her resentment and envy onto others and often directs the anger toward a supreme being, medical caregivers, family members, and friends. (Older adults may be less apt to raise this question and instead reflect on how fortunate they have been to live so long.)

Bargaining. The individual starts bargaining in an attempt to postpone death, proposing a series of deals with God, self, or others: "Yes, me, but I will do . . . in exchange for a few more months."

Depression. A sense of loss follows. Individuals grieve about their own end of life and about the ones that will be left behind. A frequent reaction is withdrawal from close and loved persons: "I just want to be left alone."

Acceptance. The person accepts that the end is near and the struggle is over: "It's okay. My life has been . . ."

Source: Based on Kübler-Ross, 1969.

may not be as comfortable expressing their feelings related to death and dying, which may leave the elder feeling isolated.

A fear of prolonged physical pain or discomfort, as well as fear of losing a sense of control and mastery, trouble very-late-life adults most. Some have suggested that older adults who are dying need a safe and accepting relationship in which to express the fear, sadness, anger, resentment, or other feelings related to the losses that come at the end of life (Agronin, 2011; Bowlby, 1980).

Advance Directives

On a more concrete level, social workers can help patients and families discuss, prepare, and enact health care **advance directives**, or documents that give instructions about desired health care if, in the future, individuals cannot speak for themselves. Such discussions can provide an opportunity to clarify values and wishes regarding end-of-life treatment. Ideally, this conversation has been started prior to very late adulthood (see Chapter 9 regarding a power of attorney and other health care decision-making processes). If not, helping people to communicate their wishes regarding life-sustaining measures, who they want to act on their behalf when they are no longer competent to make these

decisions, and other end-of-life concerns helps some people feel empowered.

Since the passage of the Patient Self-Determination Act in 1990, hospitals and other health care institutions receiving Medicare or Medical Assistance funds are required to inform patients that should their condition become life-threatening, they have a right to make decisions about their medical care (McInnis-Dittrich, 2014). In some settings, social workers are assigned this task. The two primary forms of advance directives are the living will and the durable power of attorney for health care.

A **living will** describes the medical procedures, drugs, and types of treatment that one would choose for oneself if able to do so in certain situations. It also describes the situations for which the patient would want treatment withheld. For example, one may instruct medical personnel not to use any artificial means or heroic measures to keep one alive if the condition is such that there is no hope for recovery. Although a living will allows an individual to speak for oneself in advance, a durable power of attorney designates someone else to speak for the individual.

The promotion of patient rights has helped many patients feel empowered and has comforted some family members, but this topic is not without controversy. Because the laws vary from state to state, laypersons and professionals must inquire about the process if they relocate from one state to another. Also, rather than feeling comforted by knowing a dying person's wishes, some family members experience the burden of difficult decision making that once was handled by the physician.

Some health care professionals grapple with the increasing availability of life-extending options that have complicated the process of dying. In his book *Modern Death: How Medicine Changed the End of Life*, Dr. Haider Warraich (2017) reflects on his experience as a physician both in Pakistan and the United States. He suggests that "we have delayed death and have also made getting there more difficult" (p. 59). Living longer with chronic diseases leads to people outliving the "vigor of their bodies and the wisdom of their brains" (p. 33). Whether one dies at home or in a nursing home depends on the availability of social support, which often declines with age. In *Being Mortal: Medicine and What Matters in the End*, Dr. Atul Gawande (2014) questions whether the commitment to extend life has extended suffering with procedures whose goals run counter to the human spirit. He promotes the use of medicine not only to improve life but also

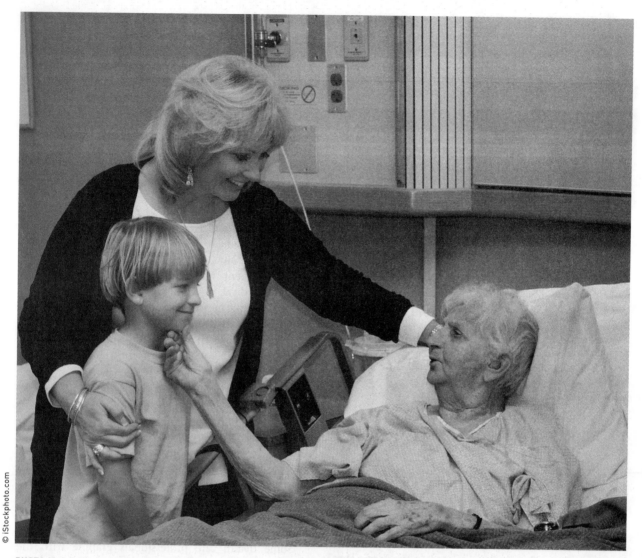

© iStockphoto.com

PHOTO 10.4 Palliative care focuses on providing pain and symptom management when cure of disease is no longer an option. The patient and the family together are the unit of care.

to enhance the quality of its ending. Jessica Nutik Zitter (2017), an ICU and palliative care physician, writes in *Extreme Measures: Finding a Better Path to the End of Life* that "in our zeal to save life, we often worsen death" (p. 47). These physicians/authors note the importance of engaging patients and their loved ones in conversations about ongoing medical treatment and the benefits and costs of them. Gawande (2014) emphasizes that both patients and their families deserve to know the trade-offs in any medical treatments. Social workers can play an important role in these challenging family discussions.

Several advocacy groups have developed in response to the complexity of these decisions. The Campaign to End Unwanted Medical Treatment (2017) argues that patients with advanced illness, and especially those at the end of life, want and need access to a "full range of well-coordinated medical care and treatment, including curative care, palliative care and hospice care" (para. 4). They advocate for improved discussion between patients and health care professionals so patients have the information they need to make informed choices and then to have those choices honored. The right-to-die organization Compassion & Choices (2017) has been integral in the legalization of aid in dying, or physician-assisted suicide, in at least seven states and strongly advocates for quality palliative care and symptom management.

Some ethnic, racial, and religious groups may be skeptical of advance directives. Because of historical distrust of the White medical establishment, some African American and Hispanic families have preferred life-sustaining treatment over the refusal of treatment inherent in advance directives (Volker, 2005). However, this may be changing gradually with time, greater representation of persons of color as health care providers, and culturally relevant educational outreach. Among some religious groups, the personal control represented in advance directives is seen to interfere with a divine plan and is considered a form of passive suicide. For some Asian Americans who value a more collectivist perspective, the Western health care emphasis on autonomy and individualist decision making, pillars of the Patient Self-Determination Act, may be a barrier, requiring culturally sensitive discussion about hospice and palliative care services (Min & Moon, 2016). Social workers must approach each patient and family with an openness to learn about their values and wishes.

Care of People Who Are Dying

Although some associate hospice and palliative care with "giving up" and there being "nothing left to do," in fact hospices provide **palliative care**—a form of care focusing on pain and symptom management as opposed to curing disease. The focus is on "caring, not curing" (National Hospice and Palliative Care Organization [NHPCO], 2015), when curative focused treatment is no longer available or desired. Palliative care attends to psychological, social, and spiritual issues in addition to physical needs. The goal of palliative care is to achieve the best possible quality of life for patients and their families.

Hospice is one model of palliative care, borrowed from the British, that began in the United States in the mid-1970s to address the needs of dying persons and their loved ones. It is more a philosophy of care than a place, with most people receiving hospice services where they reside at the end of life, whether that is their private residence (35.7%), an inpatient hospice facility (31.8%), a nursing or residential facility (23.2%), or an acute care hospital (9.3%) (NHPCO, 2015). Marie Cipriani's partner, Irene Wright, receives hospice services in their home. Hospice services are typically available to persons who have received a prognosis of 6 months or less and who are no longer receiving care directed toward a cure. Exhibit 10.3 summarizes the key ideas that distinguish hospice care from more traditional care of the dying.

EXHIBIT 10.3 ● Key Ideas of Hospice Care
The patient and the family (as defined by the patient) are the unit of care.
Care is provided by an interdisciplinary team composed of physician, nurse, nurse's aide, social worker, clergy, volunteer, and other support staff who attend to the spectrum of biopsychosocial and spiritual needs of the patient and family.
The patient and family have chosen hospice services and are no longer pursuing aggressive, curative care but selecting palliative care for symptom management.
Bereavement follow-up is part of the continuum of care available to family members after the patient's death.

Sources: McInnis-Dittrich, 2014; NHPCO, 2015.

The National Hospice and Palliative Care Organization (2015) estimates that the United States had 6,100 hospice programs in 2015 serving most rural, suburban, and urban communities in all 50 states and territories that were involved in just under one half of all deaths. In 2014 approximately 84% of hospice patients were 65 years of age or older, and of those, 41.1% were 85 and older. When hospice care was first established in the United States in the 1970s, cancer patients accounted for most hospice admissions. Over time, hospice responded to the needs of others with end-stage disease, with cancer more recently representing 36.6% of admissions. Other primary diagnoses include dementia (14.8%), heart disease (14.7%), lung disease (9.3%), and other (e.g., liver disease, kidney disease, stroke, and HIV/AIDS) (NHPCO, 2015).

Social inequalities and racial disparities lead to persons of color historically being underrepresented in hospice care and health care in general. Initiatives through NHPCO, the Soros Foundation's Faculty Scholar program, and the Robert Wood Johnson Foundation's Promoting Excellence in End-of-Life Care have focused on program development specific to the needs of patients and families in African American, Hispanic/Latino, Native American, and other communities underserved by more traditional hospice programs (Crawley et al., 2000; NHPCO, 2015).

Palliative care programs are emerging in hospital settings to address pain and symptom management in patients who might not fit the hospice criteria. Some hospitals have palliative care units specializing in management of short-term, acute symptoms; others have palliative care consultative services that bring their expertise to medical, oncology, pediatric, and other units throughout the hospital (McCoyd & Walter, 2016; Reith & Payne, 2009).

End-of-Life Signs and Symptoms

Family members and others caring for a dying person often experience anxiety when they do not have adequate information about the dying process. Most families appreciate knowing what to expect, and honest information can help allay their fears of the unknown (Cagle & Kovacs, 2009; Proot et al., 2004). Pete Mullin, for instance, might benefit by knowing what to expect as his sister is dying. Likewise for Marie Cipriani, who is caring for her dying partner. Many hospice services provide written information about symptoms of death for those families anticipating the death of a loved one at home. Exploring how best to provide information, when, and to whom is an important part of the social worker's assessment.

Obviously, each individual situation will differ, but the following general information about symptoms of impending death, summarized in Exhibit 10.4, helps people prepare (Lamers, 2013; Reith & Payne, 2009).

- *Temperature and circulation changes.* The patient's arms and legs may become cool to the touch, and the underside of the body may darken in color as peripheral circulation slows down. Despite feeling cool to touch, the patient is usually not aware of feeling cold, and light bed coverings usually provide sufficient warmth.

- *Sleeping.* The dying patient will gradually spend more time sleeping and at times may be difficult to arouse as metabolism decreases. The patient will gradually retreat from the surroundings. It is best to spend more time with the patient during the most alert times.

- *Vision and hearing.* Clarity of vision and hearing may decrease. The patient may want the lights on as vision decreases. Hearing is the last of the five senses to be lost, so it should not be assumed that an unresponsive patient cannot hear. Speech should be soft and clear but not louder than necessary. Many patients talk until minutes before death and are reassured by the exchange of words between loved ones.

- *Secretions in the mouth and congestion.* Oral secretions may become more profuse and collect in the back of the throat. Most people are familiar with the term *death rattle*, a result

of a decrease in the body's intake of fluids and inability to cough up normal saliva. Tilting the head to the side and elevating the head of the bed will ease breathing. Swabbing the mouth and lips also provides comfort.

- *Incontinence.* Loss of bowel and bladder function may occur around the time of death or as death is imminent, as the muscles begin to relax. The urine will become very dark in color. If needed, pads should be used to keep skin clean and dry.

- *Restlessness and confusion.* The patient may become restless or have visions of people or things that do not exist. These symptoms may be a result of a decrease in the oxygen circulation to the brain and a change in the body's metabolism. Someone should stay with the patient, reassuring the person in a calm voice, telling the person it is okay to let go, and using oxygen as instructed. Soft music, back rubs, and gentle touch may help soothe the patient. The patient should not be interfered with or restrained yet should be prevented from falling.

- *Eating, drinking, and swallowing.* Patients will have decreased need for food and drink. It may be helpful to explain that feeding will not improve the condition and in fact may exacerbate symptoms. Slight dehydration may be beneficial in reducing pulmonary secretions and easing breathing. Dehydration also generally results in mild renal insufficiency that is mildly sedating. To withhold food and water feels counterintuitive, however, because food and water are usually equated with comfort and sustaining life. Ice chips, small sips of water, and small amounts of food that have meaning to the patient and family are more helpful than forcing food or liquids.

- *Breathing changes.* Breathing may become irregular, with periods of 10 to 30 seconds of no breathing. This symptom is very common and indicates a decrease in circulation and buildup of body waste products. Elevating the head of the bed and turning the patient on his or her side often helps relieve irregular breathing patterns.

- *Pain.* Frequent observation will help determine if the patient is experiencing pain. Signs of discomfort include moaning, restlessness, and a furrowed brow. Medication should be given as instructed, or the nurse or physician should be contacted if pain persists.

EXHIBIT 10.4 ● Signs and Symptoms of Impending Death

Lowered temperature and slowed circulation

Deeper and longer periods of sleep

Decreased acuity of vision and hearing

Increased secretions in the mouth and congestion

Incontinence

Restlessness and confusion

Reduced need for eating and drinking and difficulty swallowing

Irregular and interrupted breathing

Increased signs of pain

Sources: Lamers, 2013; Reith & Payne, 2009.

Dying may take hours or days; no one can predict the time of death even when the person is exhibiting signs and symptoms of dying. The following are signs that death has occurred:

- Breathing stops
- Heart stops beating
- Bowel or bladder control is lost
- No response to verbal commands or shaking
- Eyelids may be slightly open with eyes fixed on a certain spot
- Mouth may fall open slightly as the jaw relaxes

Such explicit discussion of death with those attending a dying family member or close friend may seem upsetting, but this knowledge is also comforting and can help ease the anxiety related to the fear of the unknown. Dying persons are often comforted knowing that their family members have the informational, medical, and social support they need to help them in their caregiving role. It is also helpful to have funeral plans in place so that one phone call to the mortuary facilitates the process, rather than facing difficult and emotional decisions at the time of death.

LOSS, GRIEF, AND BEREAVEMENT

Loss is a common human experience. There is a great deal of evidence that people of all cultures have strong, painful reactions to the death of the people to whom

PHOTO 10.5 Many factors influence the way in which a person adjusts to death and dying, including one's religion and philosophy of life, personality, and other traits.

they are emotionally attached (Doka & Tucci, 2009; Thieleman, 2015). Sadness, loneliness, disbelief, and anxiety are only a few of the feelings a person may experience in times of bereavement. The challenge is to refrain from making grief the problem, thereby pathologizing someone's experience, and to understand the complexities related to death in a society that has grown increasingly old-age and death avoidant (Jenkinson, 2012). Without understanding the importance of mourning customs, grief expressions, and cultural traditions, one runs the risk of pathologizing grief reactions (Thieleman, 2015). So we offer the following, cautioning against turning someone's grief into a problem and encouraging readers to help others understand grief as a normal part of life, perhaps even a skill that we need to learn (Jenkinson, 2012).

Grief, bereavement, and *mourning* are words that are often used interchangeably, perhaps because no one word "reflects the fullness of what a death introduces into the life of an individual, family or community"

© iStockphoto.com/PeopleImages

(Silverman, 2004, p. 226). The following definitions help distinguish the various aspects of this process:

- **Loss**. The severing of an attachment an individual has with a loved one, a loved object (such as a home or country), or an aspect of one's self or identity (such as a body part or function; physical or mental capacity; or role or position in family, society, or other context) (Stroebe, Stroebe, & Hansson, 1993). Silverman (2004) suggests that loss doesn't happen to us; rather, it is "something we must make sense out of, give meaning to, and respond to" (p. 226).

- **Bereavement**. The state of having suffered a loss.

- **Grief**. The normal internal reaction of an individual experiencing a loss. Grief is a complex coping process, is highly individualized (Stroebe et al., 1993), and is an expected period of transition (Silverman, 2004).

- **Mourning**. The external expression of grief (Stroebe et al., 1993); a "social process including the cultural traditions and rituals that guide behavior after a death" (Silverman, 2004, p. 226).

The rituals associated with death vary in historical and cross-cultural context (Bullock, 2011; Doka & Tucci, 2009; Thieleman, 2015). In some cultures, the dead are buried; in other cultures, the dead are burned and the ashes are spread. In some places and times, a surviving wife might have been burned together with her husband. In the United States, death rituals can be as different as a traditional New Orleans funeral, with street music and mourners dressed in white, or a somber and serene funeral with hushed mourners dressed in black. Some cultures prescribe more emotional expression than others. Some cultures build ritual for the expression of anger, and some do not.

Throughout life, we are faced with many losses, some that occur by death but many that occur in other ways as well. For example, Margaret Davis lost her husband to death, but she has also lost a daughter through estrangement and faced much loss of independence and privacy as she increasingly needed assistance from her children and grandchildren. Pete Mullin lived through the losses related to divorce and retirement. Marie Cipriani has experienced similar losses, as well as the loss of her siblings and her adult child. Recently, the burgeoning literature on loss, grief, and bereavement

has recognized that there may be similar processes for grieving all losses, including those that occur for reasons other than death. Loss is one of the most important themes in our work as social workers. For example, we encounter loss caused by foster care placement, divorce, disease and disability, migration and immigration, forced retirement, and so on. Disenfranchised grief occurs when a loss is not honored or recognized by individuals and/or society because of the nature of one's relationship, such as often occurs with same-sex couples, like Marie Cipriani and Irene Wright; a prisoner; or a mistress or ex-spouse/partner. *Ambiguous* loss complicates grief because the loss is often unclear, without resolution or closure. The loss can be physical with a psychological presence, such as suicide, incarceration, infertility, immigration, adoption, and when people are missing in war or natural disasters. The loss can be more psychological with a physical presence, such as dementia, coma, chronic mental illness, addiction, and autism (Boss & Yeats, 2014). Often multiple dynamics complicate a person's grief process. The oldest old have lived longer and have typically experienced many losses. Depending on social and psychological supports, many also have developed remarkable resilience and found a way to integrate these experiences.

CRITICAL THINKING QUESTIONS 10.4

What does death mean to you? Is it the final process of life, the beginning of life after death, a joining of the spirit with a cosmic consciousness, rest and peace, a continuation of the spirit, or something else? How has culture influenced your understanding of the meaning of death? How has religion influenced your understanding of the meaning of death? How might your understanding of the meaning of death affect your work with someone who is dying? What does it mean to live a good life?

Theories and Models of Loss

A variety of theorists have sought to make sense of the complex experience of loss. Much of the literature on grief and bereavement for the past century has been influenced by Sigmund Freud's (1917/1957) classic article "Mourning and Melancholia." Freud described the "work of mourning" as a process of severing a relationship with a lost person, object, or ideal. He suggested that this happens over time as the bereaved person is repeatedly faced with situations that remind him or her that the loved person (object or ideal) has, indeed, been lost. From this classic work came the idea of a necessary period of **grief work** to sever the attachment bond, an idea that has been the cornerstone of a number of stage models of the grief process.

In the United States, Erich Lindemann (1944) was a pioneer in grief research. Through his classic study of survivors of a fire at the Cocoanut Grove Lounge in Boston, he conceptualized grief work as both a biological and a psychological necessity. The common reactions to loss that he identified included the following:

- Somatic distress, occurring in waves lasting from 20 minutes to an hour, including tightness in throat, choking and shortness of breath, need for sighing, empty feeling in abdomen, lack of muscular power, and intense subjective distress

- Preoccupation with image of deceased, yearning for the lost one to return, wanting to see pictures of the deceased or touch items associated with the deceased

- Guilt

- Hostile reactions, toward the deceased as well as toward others

- Loss of patterns of conduct, where the ability to carry out routine behaviors is lost

Lindemann proposed that grief work occurs in stages, an idea that has been popular with other theorists and researchers since the 1960s. A number of stage models of grief have been proposed, and four are presented in Exhibit 10.5. As you can see, although the number and names of stages vary somewhat among theorists and researchers, in general the stage models all agree that grief work progresses from disbelief and feelings of unreality, to painful and disorganizing reactions, to a kind of "coming to terms" with the loss. Stages or phases run the risk of being misused when taken too literally; however, they have served to remind us that grief is a process with different parts that people experience in their own time (Harris & Winokuer, 2015).

J. William Worden (2009) took a somewhat different approach, writing about the "tasks of mourning" rather than stages of mourning. He considered *task* to be more consistent with Freud's concept of grief work given that the mourner needs to take action and do something rather than passively move through grief. Worden suggests that the following four tasks of mourning are important when a person is adapting to a loss:

Task I: to accept the reality of the loss. Working through denial takes time, because this involves both an intellectual and an emotional acceptance. Some people have traditional rituals that help with this process.

Task II: to work through the pain of grief. Because people are often uncomfortable with the outward displays of grief, our society often interferes with this task. People often seek a geographic cure or quickly replace the lost person with a new relationship but often still have this task to complete.

Task III: to adjust to an environment in which the deceased is missing. This includes filling roles previously filled by the deceased and making appropriate adjustments in daily activities. In terms of roles, many widows report being thrown the first

Typical Stages	Erich Lindemann (1944)	Elisabeth Kübler-Ross (1969)	John Bowlby (1980)	Therese Rando (1993)
Disbelief and feelings of unreality	Shock and disbelief	Denial and isolation	Numbness	Avoidance
Painful and disorganizing reactions	Acute mourning	Anger Bargaining Depression	Yearning Disorganization Despair	Confrontation
A kind of "getting over" the loss	Resolution	Acceptance	Reorganization	Accommodation

EXHIBIT 10.5 ● Four Stage Models of Grief

time they have to cope with a major home repair. Regarding adjustments in daily activities, many bereaved persons report that they find themselves automatically putting the favorite foods of the deceased in their grocery carts.

Task IV: to emotionally relocate the deceased and move on with life. This task was best described by Sadie Delany after the loss of her beloved sister, Bessie: "I don't want to get over you. I just want to find a way to live without you" (Delany, 1997).

In the past few decades, there has been a critique of the idea of grief work. A highly influential article, "The Myths of Coping with Loss" (Wortman & Silver, 1989), disputed two major themes of the traditional view of grief work: distress is an inevitable response to loss, and the failure to experience distress is a sign of improper grieving. In fact, a number of researchers have found that those who show the highest levels of distress immediately following a loss are more likely than those who show little distress to be depressed several years later. In another vein, Silverman (2004) challenges the notion of "tasks," which suggests something can be completed, recommending that we focus instead on "issues and processes" (p. 237).

Given the tremendous diversity among individuals based on gender, culture, personality style, and life experience, as well as the various circumstances surrounding a loss, the grieving process is not easily defined, but theorists and practitioners continue to try to provide some framework for understanding the process. Camille Wortman and Roxanne Silver (1990) proposed that at least four patterns of grieving are possible: normal, chronic, delayed, and absent. Worden (2009) elaborated on these patterns:

1. *Normal or uncomplicated grief.* Relatively high level of distress soon after the loss encompassing a broad range of feelings and behaviors, followed by a relatively rapid recovery.

2. *Chronic or prolonged grief.* High level of distress continuing over a number of years without coming to a satisfactory conclusion.

3. *Delayed grief (or inhibited, suppressed, or postponed grief).* Little distress in the first few months after the loss, but high levels of distress later.

4. *Absent grief.* No notable level of distress either soon after the loss or later. Some question this notion and wonder if it is not absent but masked or delayed; observation over time is important.

Given these critiques of traditional models of grief, theorists and researchers have looked for other ways to understand the complex reactions to loss. The study of bereavement has been influenced by developments in the study of stress and trauma reactions. Research on loss and grief has produced the following findings (Bonanno & Kaltman, 1999):

- It is the evaluation of the nature of the loss by the bereaved survivor that determines how stressful the loss is.

- How well a coping strategy works for dealing with loss depends on the context and the nature of the person–environment encounter.

- Maintaining some type of continued bond with the deceased, a strong sense of the continued presence of the deceased, may be adaptive.

- The capacity to minimize negative emotions after a loss allows the bereaved to continue to function in areas of personal importance.

- Humor can aid in the grief process by allowing the bereaved to approach the enormity of the loss without maximizing psychic pain or alienating social support.

- In situations of traumatic loss, there is a need to talk about the loss, but not all interpersonal relationships can tolerate such talk.

Martin and Doka (2000) propose an approach to adult bereavement that explores the role of gender, culture, and other characteristics that influence a person's grieving style. This approach includes two aspects of adaptive grieving: the internal experience of loss and the outward expression relating to the loss. Martin and Doka (2000) suggest that adaptive grieving styles exist on a continuum with intuitive grievers at one end and instrumental grievers at the other end. Intuitive grievers experience and express their grief primarily through emotion, and instrumental grievers experience and express their grief primarily through a cognitive, behavioral, problem-solving approach. They suggest that few people tend to be at either extreme of the continuum, but rather most tend to have a blended style of grieving, using both intuitive and instrumental strategies (Doughty, 2009). They assert that the difficulty may arise when an individual for whatever reason uses a grieving style that conflicts with their more natural adaptive style. Doughty (2009) sought more empirical feedback about this model, in addition to the strong anecdotal evidence from practitioners. She surveyed 20 experts in the field of thanatology to examine their opinions about this model. Consensus was found on the following items: the uniqueness of the griever; recognition of multiple factors influencing the grief process; the use of both cognitive and affective strategies in adapting to bereavement; and both internal and external pressures to grieve in certain ways.

Grief is a multidimensional process—a normal life experience—that theorists and practitioners continue to try to understand. There seems to be general agreement that culture, experience, gender, age, and other personal characteristics influence how one copes with loss.

Culture and Bereavement

Some suggest that all people feel the same pain with grief but that cultural differences shape our mourning rituals, traditions, and behavioral expressions of grief (Walsh, 2012). Although there are good sources for exploring ethnic variations related to death and grief (see Cacciatore & DeFrain, 2015; Irish, Lundquist, & Nelson, 1993), we hesitate to provide overviews of various cultural groups, because of the diversity within groups, as well an increasing cultural diversity in most communities. So instead we suggest you come to each encounter with an openness and curiosity, acknowledging people as the experts about what has been helpful in the past and inquiring about what you need to know to best work with them. Hooyman and Kramer (2006) provide detailed suggestions for conducting a good cross-cultural assessment and communication (see pp. 174–178), some of which include the following:

- Do your homework before talking to members of the group.

- Begin by listening to their story using open-ended questions.

- Approach them with humility and caution, recognizing them as "insiders" who have the more immediate and critical knowledge of their experience.

- Never judge or have predetermined ideas of what they should feel or do.

- Recognize potential cultural conflicts and respect their decisions and choices.

- Use and train qualified interpreters, understanding the benefits and limitations of doing so.

Important components of an assessment include reactions to loss; mourning style; level of acculturation; cultural history; the role and presence of religion and/or spirituality; grieving rituals; family dynamics, including intergenerational relationships; and other components of any good multidimensional assessment such as social support, financial resources, strengths, and personality. Inquire more specifically about the following:

- Their interpretation of the illness and/or death (asking what they call it, think caused it, think will help, fear most)

- Questions relevant to the care of the body after the death and related beliefs and rituals

- How people in their family and culture commonly express grief (i.e., who, when, how long)

Knowledge about beliefs, values, and customs puts certain behaviors in a context that will help guide your work.

Regarding cultural norms, consider the following:

- In the United States, the dominant culture tends to psychologize grief, understanding it in terms of sadness, depression, anger, and other emotions.

- In China and other Eastern societies, grief is often somatized, or expressed in terms of physical pain, weakness, and other physical discomfort (Walsh, 2012). Gender differences exist in many cultures, including the dominant U.S. culture, where men have learned to be less demonstrative with emotions of grief and sadness than women (Walsh, 2012).

- Explore and try to locate where an individual's cultural approach to death is on the continuum of death-denying and death-accepting orientations (Thieleman, 2015).

Mourning and funeral customs also differ a great deal even within groups. For example, among African Americans, customs vary depending on whether the family is Southern Baptist, Catholic, Unitarian Universalist, Muslim, or Pentecostal; in fact, "religion may be a stronger determining factor than race alone" (Barrett, 2009, p. 85). Perhaps because of some vestiges of traditional African culture and slavery and a strong desire to celebrate the person's life and build up a sense of community, funerals are important external expressions of mourning in many Black communities.

Tremendous diversity exists within the Latino cultures in the United States, depending on country of origin and degree of acculturation; however, for the most part these subgroups share Latino values, language, religion, and traditional family structure. Some Latino cultural themes that can influence care at the end of life include *familismo* (emphasis of family over individual), *personalismo* (trust building over time based on mutual respect), *jerarquismo* (respect for authority and hierarchy), *presentismo* (focus on present more than past or future), *espiritismo* (belief that good and evil spirits can impact health), and *fatalism* (fate determines life outcomes) (Sandoval-Cros, 2009).

Given approximately 350 distinct Native American tribes in the United States and more than 596 bands among the First Nations in Canada, and because of the differing degrees of acculturation and religious practices from one group to another, it is difficult to provide useful generalizations about this cultural group (Brokenleg & Middleton, 1993). Most understand death as a natural end of life, not fearing it, and although it may be a painful separation for the living who are left behind, rituals exist to help with the transition (Cox, 2009).

A good source of more specific information about rituals and practices is websites on particular cultural/ethnic groups such as "Hmong Americans: Dying and Death Ritual" (http://sfsuyellowjournal.wordpress.com/2011/11/17/hmong-americans-dying-and-death-ritual). Sites such as these are often written by members of the respective community, and they too remind you of the great diversity among their members. The complex and at times impersonal health care system in the United States can be inadvertently insensitive to important cultural traditions. For example, in some cultures, proper handling of the body, time to sit with the deceased, and other traditions are valued. For one specific example, the Hmong believe that proper burial and worship of ancestors directly influence the safety and health of the surviving family members. They believe that the spiritual world coexists with the physical world and that each person has several souls that must be appropriately sent back to the spiritual world.

These are only a few examples of the rich diversity and complexity you will face in working in our increasingly multiethnic society. You cannot possibly know all the specific traditions, so start by knowing that you do not know, and do your homework about the worlds of the different groups you serve, including being open to their story and teachings. There is much to learn about how others make sense of these mysterious times of life—enjoy!

CRITICAL THINKING QUESTIONS 10.5

Think of your first experience of a human loss due to death. What do you remember observing the adults in your life do? How did the adults explain what was happening to you? What do you recall thinking and feeling at the time? What death rituals were used to acknowledge the loss? How do you think your current attitudes and beliefs about loss and grief are influenced by this early experience?

THE LIFE COURSE COMPLETED

In this book, we have explored the seasons of the life course. These seasons have been and will continue to be altered by changing demographics. As a society, we have a challenge ahead of us to see that newborns begin the life course on a positive foot and that everyone reaches the end of life with the opportunity to see his or her life course as a meaningful whole. As social workers, we have a responsibility to take a look at our social institutions and evaluate how well they guarantee the opportunity for each individual to meet basic needs during each season of life, as well as whether they guarantee the opportunity for interdependence and connectedness appropriate to the season of life. We close this book with a quote by Socrates about how we would do well to learn from our elders (Agronin, 2011, p. 279): "I enjoy talking with very old people. They have gone before us on a road by which we, too, may have to travel, and I think we do well to learn from them what it is like."

IMPLICATIONS FOR SOCIAL WORK PRACTICE

All the implications for practice listed in Chapter 9 on late adulthood apply in very late adulthood as well. See the following resources for additional information about social work practice and end-of-life-related patient and family care: Callahan, (2017); Csikai and Jones (2007); Hooyman and Kramer (2006); Kashushin and Egan (2008); Kovacs, Bellin, and Fauri (2006); and Walsh (2012). In addition, the following practice principles focus on the topics of spirituality; relationships; the dying process; and loss, grief, and bereavement.

- Given the links among aging, disability, loss, and spirituality, consider doing a spiritual assessment to find ways to help very-late-life adults address increasing spiritual concerns.

- Assess the impact of loss in the lives of your very-late-life clients—loss of partners, friends, children, and other relationships but also loss of role, status, and physical and mental capacities.

- Recognize and be delighted when very-late-life adults are grateful for their "extra time."

- Assess the loneliness and isolation that may result from cumulative loss.

- Be informed about available formal and informal resources to help minimize isolation for older adults.

- Be aware of your own feelings about death and dying so that you may become more comfortable being physically and emotionally present with clients and their loved ones.

- Identify literature, websites, cultural experiences, key informants, and other vehicles for ongoing education about your clients' cultural, ethnic, and religious and spiritual practices that are different from your own. Remember, the client may be your best teacher.

- Assume that the very-late-life adult continues to have needs for intimacy. Stretch your conceptualization of intimacy to include any relationship the person might have, wish for, or grieve, including a spouse or partner, friends, children, self, and community.

Key Terms

activities of daily living (ADLs) 364	grief work 379	loss 378
advance directives 373	hospice 375	mourning 378
bereavement 378	instrumental activities	palliative care 375
centenarian 360	of daily living (IADLs) 364	primary aging 364
grief 378	living will 373	secondary aging 365

Active Learning

1. Take an inventory of your assumptions about what it is like to be 85 and older. What are your biggest fears? What do you think would be the best part of reaching that age? Think about how these assumptions might influence your feelings about working with clients in very late adulthood.

2. You have recently been hired as the social worker at an assisted-living facility, and Margaret Davis, Pete Mullin, and Marie Cipriani have all recently moved in. All three are unhappy to be there, preferring their prior living arrangements. Pete's sister and Marie's partner recently died. You want to help them share some of their recent experiences related to loss but want to be sensitive to the diversity in life experience they bring with them. What barriers might you face in accomplishing your goal? What are some ways you might begin to help them?

3. Think about relationships among poverty, gender, sexual orientation, and race as one ages in the United States today. Identify ways that social workers can influence policies that affect housing, health care, and other essential services directly related to quality of life in very-late-life adulthood.

Web Resources

Administration for Community Living: www.acl.gov

Site of U.S. Department of Health and Human Services Administration for Community Living contains help and resources, information about programs and activities, a newsroom, and funding opportunities.

American Society on Aging: www.asaging.org

Site provides general information about aging-related services, including a link to LGBT Aging Issues Network (LAIN) and LGBT Aging Resources Clearinghouse (LARC) and information on older adults, alcohol, medication, and other drugs.

Compassion & Choices: Care and Choice at the End of Live: www.compassionandchoices.org

Site maintained by Compassion & Choices, the nation's oldest, largest, and most active nonprofit organization committed to improving care and expanding options for the end of life.

Generations United: www.gu.org

Site maintained by Generations United (GU), the national membership organization focused solely on improving the lives of children, youth, and older people through intergenerational strategies, programs, and public policies. See site for links to resources, bibliographies, and so on.

Hospice Foundation of America: www.hospice foundation.org

Site contains information for locating hospice programs, a newsletter, and links to resources.

National Association of Social Workers: www.socialworkers.org

Site provides access to resources related to aging and social work practice, including some online courses.

National Center for Gerontological Social Work Education: www.cswe.org/Centers-Initiatives/Centers/Gero-Ed-Center

Site maintained by the Council on Social Work Education Gero-Ed Center (National Center for Gerontological Social Work Education) provides resources for aging and end-of-life care.

National Hospice and Palliative Care Organization: www.nhpco.org

Site maintained by the National Hospice and Palliative Care Organization contains information on the history and current development of hospice and palliative care programs, advance directives, grief and bereavement, caregiving, and other related topics.

National Resource Center on LGBT Aging: www.lgbtagingcenter.org

Site of the National Resource Center on LGBT Aging formed in 2010 provides education, training, and critical resources to providers, organizations, and consumers.

Office on Aging: www.apa.org/pi/aging

Site presented by the Office on Aging of the American Psychological Association contains news briefs, publications, and links to aging organizations.

The Retirement Research Foundation Aging-Related Resources: www.rrf.org/resources/aging-related-websites

Site provides links to many age-related websites.

U.S. Department of Health and Human Services: www.hhs.gov/aging/index.html

Site provides links to governmental programs and information on healthy aging, caregiving, elder justice, retirement, and local resources.

• References •

Abajobir, A., Kisely, S., Williams, G., Strathearn, L., & Najman, J. (2017). Height deficit in early adulthood following substantiated childhood maltreatment: A birth cohort study. *Child Abuse & Neglect, 64*, 71–78.

Abajobir, A., Maravilla, J., Alati, R., & Najman, J. (2016). A systematic review and meta-analysis of the association between unintended pregnancy and perinatal depression. *Journal of Affective Disorders, 192*, 56–63.

Abendroth, A., Huffman, M., & Treas, J. (2014). The parity penalty in life course perspective: Motherhood and occupational status in 13 European countries. *American Sociological Review, 79*(5), 993–1014.

Abrams, K., Rifkin, A., & Hesse, E. (2006). Examining the role of parental frightened/frightening subtypes in predicting a disorganized attachment within a brief observational procedure. *Development and Psychopathology, 18*(2), 345–361.

Achenbaum, W. A., & Bengtson, V. C. (1994). Re-engaging the disengagement theory of aging: Or the history and assessment of theory development in gerontology. *The Gerontologist, 34*(6), 756–763.

Addo, F. R., Houle, J. N., & Simon, D. (2016). Young, black, and (still) in the red: Parental wealth, race, and student loan debt. *Race and Social Problems, 8*(1), 64–76.

Adelman, H. S., & Taylor, L. (2015). Immigrant children and youth in the USA: Facilitating equity of opportunity at school. *Education Science, 5*(4), 323–344.

Adler-Tapia, R. (2012). *Child psychotherapy: Integrating developmental theory into clinical practice.* New York: Springer.

Administration on Aging. (2016). *A profile of older Americans: 2016.* Retrieved from www.giaging.org/documents/A_Profile_of_Older_Americans__2016.pdf.

Advanced Fertility Center of Chicago. (2014). *Single cycle IVF cost details—Advanced Fertility Center of Chicago.* Retrieved from www.advancedfertility.com/ivfprice.htm.

Afterschool Alliance. (2014). *Keeping kids safe and supported in the hours after school. Issue Brief No. 65.* MetLife Foundation Afterschool Alert. Retrieved from http://afterschoolalliance.org/documents/issue_briefs/issue_KeepingKidsSafe_65.pdf.

Agrigoroaei, S., & Lachman, M. (2011). Cognitive functioning in midlife and old age: Combined effects of psychosocial and behavioral factors. *The Journals of Gerontology, Series B: Psychological Sciences and Social Sciences, 66B*(Suppl. 1), i130–i140.

Agronin, M. E. (2011). *How we age: A doctor's journey into the heart of growing old.* Philadelphia: Da Capo Press.

Ahmann, E. (2013). Making meaning when a child has mental illness: Four mothers share their experiences. *Pediatric Nursing, 39*(4), 202–205.

Ahrens, K., DuBois, D., Richardson, L., Fan, M., & Lozano, P. (2008). Youth in foster care with adult mentors during adolescence have improved adult outcomes. *Pediatrics, 121*(2), 246–252.

Ahrnsbrak, R., Bose, J., Hedden, S., Lipari, R., & Park-Lee, E. (2017). *Key substance use and mental health indicators in the United States. Results from the 2016 National Survey on Drug Use and Health.* Publication No. SMA 17-5044, NSDUH Series H-52). Rockville, MD: Center for Behavioral Health Statistics and Quality, Substance Abuse and Mental Health Services Administration. Retrieved from www.samhsa.gov/data/sites/default/files/NSDUH-FFR1-2016/NSDUH-FFR1-2016.pdf.

Ahrons, C. R. (2016). Divorce: An unscheduled family transition. In M. McGoldrick, B. Carter, & N. Garcia-Preto (Eds.), *The expanded family life cycle: Individual, family, and social perspectives* (5th ed., pp. 376–393). Boston: Allyn & Bacon.

Ainsworth, M., Blehar, M., Waters, E., & Wall, S. (1978). *Patterns of attachment: A psychological study of the strange situation.* Hillsdale, NJ: Lawrence Erlbaum.

Ajrouch, K., Antonucci, T., & Janevic, M. (2001). Social networks among blacks and whites: The interaction between race and age. *Journal of Gerontology: Social Sciences, 56*(2), S112–S118.

Alboher, M. (2014). Encore careers: Unprecedented opportunities. *People & Strategy, 37*(2), 59–60.

Albuquerque, P. (2011). Grandparents in multigenerational households: The case of Portugal. *European Journal of Ageing, 8*(3), 189–198.

Alink, L., Mesmon, J., & van Zeijl, J. (2006). The early childhood aggression curve: Development of physical aggression in 10- to 50-month-old children. *Child Development, 77*(4), 954–966.

Alio, A. P., Lewis, C. A., Scarborough, K., Harris, K., & Fiscella, K. (2013). A community perspective on the role of fathers during pregnancy: A qualitative study. *British Medical Journal: Pregnancy and Childbirth, 12*(1), 1–11.

Al Maghaireh, D., Abdullah, K. L., Chan, C. M., Piaw, C. Y., & Al Kawafha, M. M. (2016). Systematic review of qualitative studies exploring parental experiences in the neonatal intensive care unit. *Journal of Clinical Nursing, 25*(19/20), 2745–2756.

Al-Memar, M., Kirk, E., & Bourne, T. (2015). The role of ultrasonography in the diagnosis and management of early pregnancy complications. *Obstetrician and Gynaecologist, 17*(3), 173–181.

Alston, P. (2017). *Statement on visit to the USA, by Professor Philip Alston, United Nations Special Rapporteur on extreme poverty and human rights*. Washington, DC: United Nations Human Rights Office of the High Commissioner. Retrieved from www.ohchr.org/EN/NewsEvents/Pages/DisplayNews.aspx?NewsID=22533&LangID=E.

Alwin, D. (2012). Integrating varieties of life course concepts. *The Journals of Gerontology, Series B: Psychological Sciences and Social Sciences, 67*(2), 206–220.

Alwin, D., McCammon, R., & Hofer, S. (2006). Studying baby boom cohorts within a demographic and developmental context: Conceptual and methodological issues. In S. Whitbourne & S. Willis (Eds.), *The baby boomers grow up: Contemporary perspectives on midlife* (pp. 45–71). Mahwah, NJ: Lawrence Erlbaum.

Aly, H., Hammad, T., Nada, A., Mohamed, M., Bathgate, S., & El-Mohandes, A. (2010). Maternal obesity, associated complications and risk of prematurity. *Journal of Perinatology, 30*(7), 447–451.

Alzheimer's Association. (2013). *2013 Alzheimer's disease facts and figures*. Chicago: Author.

Alzheimer's Association. (2017). 2017 Alzheimer's disease facts and figures. *Alzheimer's & Dementia, 13*(4), 325–373.

Alzheimer's Disease International. (2017). *Dementia statistics*. Retrieved from www.alz.co.uk/research/statistics.

Amato, P. (2003). Family functioning and child development: The case of divorce. In R. M. Lerner, F. Jacobs, & D. Wertlieb (Eds.), *Handbook of applied developmental science* (Vol. 1, pp. 319–333). Thousand Oaks, CA: Sage.

Amato, P. (2005). The impact of family formation change on the cognitive, social, and emotional well-being of the next generation. *The Future of Children, 15*(2), 75–96.

Amato, P. (2010). Research on divorce: Continuing trends and new developments. *Journal of Marriage and Family, 72*(3), 650–666.

Amato, P., & Anthony, C. (2014). Estimating the effects of parental divorce and death with fixed effects models. *Journal of Marriage and Family, 76*(2), 370–386.

American Academy of Pediatrics. (2012). *American Academy of Pediatrics study documents early puberty onset in boys*. Retrieved from www.aap.org/en-us/about-the-aap/aap press-room/pages/AAP-Study-Documents-Early-Puberty-Onset-In-Boys.aspx.

American Academy of Social Work & Social Welfare. (2016). *Policy recommendation for meeting the grand challenge to ensure healthy development for all youth*. Retrieved from https://csd.wustl.edu/Publications/Documents/PB1.pdf.

American Alliance for Health, Physical Education, Recreation and Dance. (2013). Maximizing the benefits of youth sport. *Journal of Physical Education, Recreation and Dance, 84*(7), 8–13.

American Association of Retired Persons. (2016). *2016 technology trends among mid-life and older Americans*. Washington, DC: Author.

American Civil Liberties Union. (2017). *What is the school-to-prison pipeline?* Retrieved from www.aclu.org/issues/juvenile-justice/school-prison-pipeline.

American College of Medical Genetics. (2016). *ACMG releases policy statement on noninvasive prenatal screen (NIPS) for detection of fetal aneuploidy*. Retrieved from www.acmg.net/docs/NIPS_Final.pdf.

American College of Nurse-Midwives. (2012). *Position statement on transgender/transsexual/gender variant health care*. Retrieved from www.midwife.org/ACNM/files/ACNMLibraryData/UPLOADFILENAME/000000000278/Transgender%20Gender%20Variant%20Position%20Statement%20December%202012.pdf.

American College of Nurse-Midwives. (2013). Miscarriage. *Journal of Midwifery & Women's Health, 58*(4), 479–480.

American College of Nurse-Midwives. (2015). *Midwives & birth in the United States.* Retrieved from www.midwife.org/acnm/files/ccLibraryFiles/Filename/000000005948/EssentialFactsAboutMidwives-021116FINAL.pdf.

American College of Obstetricians and Gynecologists. (2012a). ACOG Committee opinion no. 536: Human immunodeficiency virus and acquired immunodeficiency syndrome and women of color. *Obstetrics and Gynecology, 120*(3), 735–739.

American College of Obstetricians and Gynecologists. (2012b). Committee opinion no. 512: Health care for transgender individuals. *Obstetrics and Gynecology, 118*(6), 1454–1458.

American College of Obstetricians and Gynecologists. (2013). *Genetic disorders.* Retrieved from www.acog.org/~/media/For%20Patients/faq094.pdf?dmc=1&ts=201312 28T1710532555.

American College of Obstetricians and Gynecologists. (2015). *Hormone therapy.* Retrieved from www.acog.org/Patients/FAQs/Hormone-Therapy.

American College of Obstetricians and Gynecologists. (2017a). *Ectopic pregnancy.* Retrieved from www.acog.org/Patients/FAQs/Ectopic-Pregnancy.

American College of Obstetricians and Gynecologists. (2017b). *Tobacco, alcohol, drugs, and pregnancy.* Retrieved from www.acog.org/Patients/FAQs/Tobacco-Alcohol-Drugs-and-Pregnancy.

American College of Obstetricians and Gynecologists. (2017c, October). *Marijuana use during pregnancy and lactation.* Retrieved from www.acog.org/Resources-And-Publications/Committee-Opinions/Committee-on-Obstetric-Practice/Marijuana-Use-During-Pregnancy-and-Lactation.

American Foundation for the Blind. (2013). *Special report on aging and vision loss.* Retrieved from www.afb.org/info/blindness-statistics/adults/special-report-on-aging-and-vision-loss/235.

American Foundation for Suicide Prevention. (2017). *Suicide statistics.* Retrieved from https://afsp.org/about-suicide/suicide-statistics/.

American Pregnancy Association. (2017a). *Preimplantation genetic diagnosis benefits and concerns.* Retrieved from http://americanpregnancy.org/infertility/preimplantation-genetic-diagnosis/.

American Pregnancy Association. (2017b). *Miscarriage.* Retrieved from http://americanpregnancy.org/pregnancy-complications/miscarriage/.

American Pregancy Association. (2017c). *Pregnancy and eating disorders.* Retrieved from http://americanpregnancy.org/pregnancy-health/pregnancy-and-eating-disorders/.

American Psychiatric Association. (2013). *Diagnostic and statistical manual of mental disorders: DSM-5.* Washington, DC: Author.

American Psychological Association. (2017). *Post-traumatic stress disorder.* Retrieved from www.apa.org/topics/ptsd/index.aspx.

American Society for Reproductive Medicine. (2013). Consideration of the gestational carrier: A committee opinion. *Fertility and Sterility, 99*(7), 1838–1841.

Americans' Changing Lives. (2017). *Understanding social disparities in health and aging: The Americans' changing lives study.* Retrieved from www.isr.umich.edu/acl.

amfAR The Foundation for AIDS Research. (2017). *Statistics: Women and HIV/AIDS.* Retrieved from www.amfar.org/about-hiv-and-aids/facts-and-stats/statistics--women-and-hiv-aids/.

Amudha, M., Rani, S., Kannan, K., & Manavalan, R. (2013). An updated overview of causes, diagnosis, and management of infertility. *International Journal of Pharmaceutical Sciences Review & Research, 18*(1), 155–164.

An, J., & Cooney, T. (2006). Psychological well-being in mid to late life: The roles of generativity development and parent-child relationships across the lifespan. *International Journal of Behavioral Development, 30*(5), 410–421.

Anand, A., & MacLullich, A. (2013). Delirium in hospitalized older adults. *Medicine, 41*(1), 39–42.

Andangsari, E., Gumilar, I., & Godwin, R. (2013). Social networking sites use and psychological attachment need among Indonesian young adults population. *International Journal of Social Science Studies, 1*(2), 133–138.

Anderson, E., Scoats, R., & McCormack, M. (2015). Metropolitan bisexual men's relationships: Evidence of a cohort effect. *Journal of Bisexuality, 15*, 21–39.

Anderson, K., & Grossberg, G. (2014). Brain games to slow cognitive decline in Alzheimer's Disease. *JAMDA, 15*, 536–537.

Anderson, M. (2018, May 31). *Teens social media and technology 2018.* Retrieved from www.pewinternet.org/2018/05/31/teens-social-media-technology-2018/.

Anderson, M., & Perrin, A. (2017). *Tech adoption climbs among older adults.* Washington, DC: Pew Internet & American Life Project. Retrieved from www.pewinternet.org/2017/05/17/tech-adoption-climbs-among-older-adults/.

Andriani, H., & Hsien, W. (2014). Adverse effects of parental smoking during pregnancy in urban and rural areas. *BMC Pregnancy and Childbirth, 14*(1), 1–26.

Angioni, S., Cofelice, V., Pontise, A., Tinnelli, R., & Socolov, R. (2014). New trends of progestins treatment of endometriosis. *Gynecological Endocrinology, 30*(11), 769–773.

Angioni, S., Cofelice, V., Sedda, F., Stochino, L., Mltinu, F., Pontis, A., & Melis, G.(2015). Progestins for symptomatic endometriosis: Results of clinical studies. *Current Drug Therapy, 10*(2), 91–104.

Angner, E., Ghandhi, J., Purvis, K., Amante, D., & Allison, J. (2013). Daily functioning, health status, and happiness in older adults. *Journal of Happiness Studies, 14*, 1563–1574.

Anguita, M. (2014). The future of contraception: The male contraceptive pill. *Nurse Prescribing, 12*(1), 6–8.

Annie E. Casey Foundation. (2015). *One in five American kids speak a language other than English at home.* Retrieved from www.aecf.org/blog/one-in-five-american-kids-speak-a-language-other-than-english-at-home/.

Annie E. Casey Foundation. (2017). *2017 kids count data book.* Retrieved from www.aecf.org/m/resourcedoc/aecf-2017kidscountdatabook.pdf.

Ansary, N., Scorpio, E., & Catanzariti, D. (2013). Parent-adolescent ethnic identity discrepancies and adolescent psychosocial maladjustment: A study of gender differences. *Child and Adolescent Social Work Journal, 30*, 275–291.

Antonucci, T., Ajrouch, K., & Birditt, K. (2014). The convoy model: Explaining social relations from a multidisciplinary perspective. *The Gerontologist, 54*(1), 82–92.

Antonucci, T., & Akiyama, H. (1987). Social networks in adult life and a preliminary examination of the convoy model. *Journal of Gerontology: Social Sciences, 42*, S519–S527.

Antonucci, T., & Akiyama, H. (1997). Concern with others at midlife: Care, comfort, or compromise? In M. Lachman & J. James (Eds.), *Multiple paths of midlife development* (pp. 145–169). Chicago: University of Chicago Press.

Antonucci, T., Akiyama, H., & Merline, A. (2001). Dynamics of social relationships in midlife. In M. Lachman (Ed.), *Handbook of midlife development* (pp. 571–598). New York: Wiley.

Antonucci, T., Akiyama, H., & Takahashi, K. (2004). Attachment and close relationships across the life span. *Attachment & Human Development, 6*(4), 353–370.

Applegate, J., & Shapiro, J. (2005). *Neurobiology for clinical social work: Theory and practice.* New York: W. W. Norton.

Arber, S., & Ginn, J. (1995). *Connecting gender and aging: A sociological approach.* Philadelphia: Open University Press.

Ardelt, M., & Eccles, J. S. (2001). Effects of mothers' parental efficacy beliefs and promotive parenting strategies on inner-city youth. *Journal of Family Issues, 22*(8), 944.

Ardila, A., Rosselli, M., Matute, E., & Inozemtseva, O. (2011). Gender differences in cognitive development. *Developmental Psychology, 47*(4), 984–990.

Arias, E. (2012). United States life tables, 2008. *National Vital Statistics Report, 61*(3), 1–64.

Armstrong, T. (2010). *The power of neurodiversity: Unleashing the advantages of your differently wired brain.* Cambridge, MA: DaCapo Press.

Armstrong, T. (2017). *Multiple intelligences in the classroom* (4th ed.). Alexandria, VA: ASCD.

Arnett, J. J. (2000). Emerging adulthood: A theory of development from the late teens through the twenties. *American Psychologist, 55*(5), 469–480.

Arnett, J. J. (2006). G. Stanley Hall's adolescence: Brilliance and nonsense. *History of Psychology, 9*, 186–197.

Arnett, J. J. (2007). Suffering, selfish, slackers? Myths and reality about emerging adults. *Journal of Youth and Adolescence, 36*, 23–29.

Arnett, J. J. (2015). *Emerging adulthood: The winding road from the late teens through the twenties* (2nd ed.). New York: Oxford University Press.

Arnett, J. J., & Brody, G. H. (2008). A fraught passage: The identity challenges of African-American emerging adults. *Human Development, 51*, 291–293.

Arnett, J. J., & Schwab, J. (2012). *The Clark University Poll of Emerging Adults: Thriving, struggling, and hopeful.* Worcester, MA: Clark University. Retrieved from www2.clarku.edu/clark-poll-emerging-adults/pdfs/2015-clark-poll-report.pdf

Aroian, K., & Norris, A. (2003). Depression trajectories in relatively recent immigrants. *Comprehensive Psychiatry, 44*(5), 420–427.

Arsenio, W., & Gold, J. (2006). The effects of social injustice and inequality on children's moral judgments and behavior: Towards a theoretical model. *Cognitive Development, 21*, 388–400.

Asgharpour, M., Virrarreal, S., Schummers, L., Hutcheon, J., Shaw, D., & Norman, W. V. (2017). Inter-pregnancy interval and pregnancy outcomes among women with delayed childbearing: Protocol for a systematic review. *Systematic Reviews, 6*, 1–4.

Ashford, J., LeCroy, C., & Williams, L. (2018). *Human behavior in the social environment: A multidimensional perspective* (6th ed.). Belmont, CA: Cengage Learning.

Ashton, D. (2011). Lesbian, gay, bisexual, and transgender individuals and the family life cycle. In M. McGoldrick, B. Carter, & N. Garcia-Preto (Eds.), *The expanded family life cycle: Individual, family, and social perspectives* (4th ed., pp. 115–132). Boston: Allyn & Bacon.

Astone, N. M., Schoen, R., Ensminger, M., & Rothert, K. (2000). School reentry in early adulthood: The case of inner-city African Americans. *Sociology of Education, 73*, 133–154.

Attar-Schwartz, S., Tan, J., Buchanan, A., Flouri, E., & Griggs, J. (2009). Grandparenting and adolescent adjustment in two-parent biological, lone parent, and step-families. *Journal of Family Psychology, 23*, 67–75.

Aumann, K., & Galinsky, E. (2011). *The state of health in the American workforce: Does having an effective workplace matter?* New York: Families and Work Institute. Retrieved from http://familiesandwork.org/site/research/reports/HealthReport_9_11.pdf.

Australian Domestic & Family Violence Clearinghouse. (2011). *The impact of domestic violence on children: A literature review.* Retrieved from www.earlytraumagrief.anu.edu.au/files/ImpactofDVonChildren.pdf.

Avis, N., Colvin, A., Karlamangal, A., Crawford, S., Hess, R., Waetjen, L. E., . . . Greendale G. A. (2017). Change in sexual functioning over the menopausal transition: Results from the Study of Women's Health Across the Nation. *Menopause: The Journal of the North American Menopause Society, 24*(4), 379–390.

Avison, W. (2010). Incorporating children's lives into a life course perspective on stress and mental health. *Journal of Health and Social Behavior, 51*(4), 361–375.

Axia, V., & Weisner, T. (2002). Infant stress reactivity and home cultural ecology of Italian infants and families. *Infant Behavior & Development, 25*(3), 255–268.

Azrin, N., & Foxx, R. (1989). *Toilet training in less than a day.* New York: Simon & Schuster.

Azzi, A. E. (2011). *Identity and participation in culturally diverse societies: A multidisciplinary perspective.* Malden, MA: Wiley-Blackwell.

Bachman, J., Staff, J., O'Malley, P., & Freedman-Doan, P. (2013). Adolescent work intensity, school performance, and substance use: Links vary by race/ethnicity and socioeconomic status. *Developmental Psychology, 49*(11), 2125–2134.

Bäckström, C., & Hertfelt Wahn, E. (2011). Support during labour: First-time fathers' descriptions of requested and received support during the birth of their child. *Midwifery, 27*, 67–73.

Baddeley, J., & Singer, J. (2007). Charting the life story's path: Narrative identity across the life span. In J. Clandinin (Ed.), *Handbook of narrative research methods* (pp. 177–202). Thousand Oaks, CA: Sage.

Baek, Y., Martin, P., Siegler, I. C., Davey, A., & Poon, L. W. (2016). Personality traits and successful aging: Findings from the Georgia centenarian study. *The International Journal of Aging and Human Development, 83*(3), 207–227.

Bahrick, L., Lickliter, R., & Flom, R. (2006). Up versus down: The role of intersensory redundancy in the development of infants' sensitivity to the orientation of moving objects. *Infancy, 9*, 73–96.

Bailey, M., & Danziger, S. (Eds.). (2013). *Legacies of the war on poverty.* New York: Russell Sage.

Baillargeon, R. (2004). Infants' physical world. *Current Directions in Psychological Science, 13*(3), 89–94.

Bakhru, A., & Stanwood, N. (2006). Performance of contraceptive patch compared with oral contraceptive pill in a high-risk population. *Obstetrics and Gynecology, 108*(2), 378–386.

Balagna, R., Young, E., & Smith, T. (2013). School experiences of early adolescent Latinos/as at risk for emotional and behavioral disorders. *School Psychology Quarterly, 28*(2), 101–121.

Balasch, J., & Gratacos, E. (2011). Delayed childbearing: Effects on fertility and the outcome of pregnancy. *Current Opinion in Obstetric Gynecology, 24*(3), 187–193.

Baldacchino, D. (2011). Myocardial infarction: A turning point in meaning in life over time. *Cardiovascular Nursing, 20*(2), 107–114.

Baldur-Felskov, B., Kjaer, S., Albieri, V., Steding-Jessen, M., Kjaer, T., Johansen, C., . . . Jensen, A. (2013). Psychiatric disorder in women with fertility problems: Results from a large Danish register-based cohort study. *Human Reproduction, 28*(3), 683–690.

Baltes, P. B., Lindenberger, U., & Staudinger, U. (1998). Lifespan theory in developmental psychology. In R. Lerner (Ed.), *Handbook of child psychology* (5th ed., pp. 1029–1143). New York: Wiley.

Baltes, P. B., & Mayer, K. U. (Eds.). (1999). *The Berlin Aging Study: Aging from 70 to 100.* Cambridge, UK: Cambridge University Press.

Baltes, P. B., Rösler, F., & Reuter-Lorenz, P. A. (2006). Prologue: Biocultural co-constructivism as a theoretical metascript. In P. B. Baltes, P. A. Reuter-Lorenz, & F. Rössler, (Eds.), *Life span development and the brain: The perspective of biocultural co-constructivism* (pp. 3–39). Cambridge, UK: Cambridge University Press.

Bandura, A. (1977). *Social learning theory.* Englewood Cliffs, NJ: Prentice Hall.

Bandura, A. (2002). Social cognitive theory in cultural context. *Applied Psychology: An International Review, 51*(2), 269–290.

Bandura, A. (2006). Toward a psychology of human agency. *Perspectives on Psychological Science, 1*(2), 164–180.

Barajas, R., Philipsen, N., & Brooks-Gunn, J. (2008). Cognitive and emotional outcomes for children in poverty. In D. Crane & T. Heaton (Eds.), *Handbook of families & poverty* (pp. 311–333). Thousand Oaks, CA: Sage.

Barban, N. (2013). Family trajectories and health: A life course perspective. *European Journal of Population, 29*(4), 357–385.

Barbaro, J., & Dissanayake, C. (2012). Early markers of autism spectrum disorders in infants and toddlers prospectively identified in the Social Attention and Communication Study. *Autism, 17*(1), 64–86.

Barbu, S., Le Maner-Idrissi, G., & Jouanjean, A. (2000). The emergence of gender segregation: Towards an integrative perspective. *Current Psychology of Letters: Behavior, Brain, and Cognition, 3*, 7–18.

Barclay, L. (2009). ACOG issues guidelines for stillbirth management. *Obstetrics & Gynecology, 113*, 748–761.

Barker, D., & Thornburg, K. (2013). The obstetric origins of health for a lifetime. *Clinical Obstetrics and Gynecology, 56*(3), 511–519.

Barker, K. K. (1998). "A ship upon a stormy sea": The medicalization of pregnancy. *Social Science & Medicine, 47*(8), 1067–1076.

Barkur, R., & Bairy, L. (2016). Histological study on hippocampus, amygdala and cerebellum following low lead exposure during prenatal and postnatal brain development in rats. *Toxicology and Industrial Health, 32*(6), 1052–1063.

Barnett, M., Scaramella, L., Neppi, T., Ontai, L., & Conger, R. (2010). Grandmother involvement as a protective factor for early childhood social adjustment. *Journal of Family Psychology, 24*(5), 635–645.

Barnett, W. S. Friedman-Krauss, A., Weisenfeld, E., Horowitz, M., Kasmin, R., & Squires, J. (2017). *The state of preschool 2016.* Brunswick, NJ: National Institute for Early Education Research. Retrieved from http://nieer.org/wp-content/uploads/2017/08/FullYB_8.21.17_compressed.pdf.

Barr, A., & Gibbs, C. (2017). *Breaking the cycle? Intergenerational effects of an anti-poverty program in early childhood.* Retrieved from https://static1.squarespace.com/static/563b95a2e4b0c51a8b87767c/t/59b2e1d259cc681cdd587b22/1504895485410/Barr+%26+Gibbs_Intergenerational_2017.pdf.

Barr, P. (2015). Guilt, shame, and fear of death predict neonatal intensive care unit-related parental stress. *Journal of Reproductive and Infant Psychology, 33*(4), 402–413.

Barrett, R. (2009). Sociocultural considerations: African Americans, grief, and loss. In D. J. Doka & A. S. Tucci (Eds.), *Living with grief: Diversity and end-of-life care* (pp. 79–91). Washington, DC: Hospice Foundation of America.

Barros, A., Matijasevich, A., Santos, I., & Halpern, R. (2010). Child development in a birth cohort: Effect of child stimulation is stronger in less educated mothers. *International Journal of Epidemiology, 39*, 285–294.

Barry, C., Nelson, L., Davarya, S., & Urry, S. (2010). Religiosity and spirituality during the transition to adulthood. *International Journal of Behavioral Development, 34*(4), 311–324.

Bartel, K., Gradisar, M., & Williamson, P. (2015). Protective and risk factors for adolescent sleep: A meta-analytic review. *Sleep Medicine Reviews, 21*, 72–85.

Bartholomae, S., & Fox, J. (2010). Economic stress and families. In S. Price, C. Price, & P. McKenry (Eds.), *Families & change: Coping with stressful events and transitions* (pp. 185–209). Thousand Oaks, CA: Sage.

Barulli, D., & Stern, Y. (2013). Efficiency, capacity, compensation, maintenance, plasticity: Emerging concepts in cognitive reserve. *Trends in Cognitive Sciences, 17*(10), 502–509.

Barusch, A. (2012). Intimacy in later life: Reflections on love and care. *Journal of Aging Life Care, Spring.* Retrieved from www.aginglifecarejournal.org/intimacy-in-later-life-reflections-on-love-and-care/.

Baskin, D., & Sommers, I. (2015). Trajectories of exposure to community violence and mental health symptoms among serious adolescent offenders. *Criminal Justice and Behavior, 42*(6), 587–609.

Bates, J., & Goodsell, T. (2013). Male kin relationships: Grandfathers, grandsons, and generativity. *Marriage & Family Review, 49*, 26–50.

Bauldry, S., Shanahan, M., Boardman, J., Miech, R., & Macmillan, R. (2012). A life course model of self-rated health through adolescence and young adulthood. *Social Science & Medicine, 75*, 1311–1320.

Baumrind, D. (1971). Current patterns of parental authority. *Developmental Psychology Monographs, 41*(1 Pt. 2), 1–103.

Baumrind, D. (1991). The influence of parenting style on adolescent competence and substance use. *Journal of Early Adolescence, 11*(1), 56–95.

Baumrind, D., Larzelere, R., & Owens, E. (2010). Effects of preschool parents' power assertive patterns and practices on adolescent development. *Parenting: Science & Practice, 10*(3), 157–201.

Bayer, J., Ukoumunne, O., Lucas, N., Wake, M., Scalzo, K., & Nicholson, J. (2011). Risk factors for childhood mental health symptoms: National Longitudinal Study of Australian Children. *Pediatrics, 128*(4), 1–15.

Beck, L., Kumschick, I. R., Eid, M., & Klann-Delius, G. (2012). Relationship between language competence and emotional competence in middle childhood. *Emotion, 12*(3), 503–514.

Beel-Bates, C. A., Ingersoll-Dayton, B., & Nelson, E. (2007). Deference as a form of reciprocity on aging. *Research on Aging, 29*, 626–643.

Behrens, K., Hesse, E., & Main, M. (2007). Mothers' attachment status as determined by the Adult Attachment Interview predicts their 6-year-olds' reunion responses: A study conducted in Japan. *Developmental Psychology, 43*(6), 1553–1567.

Beksinska, M., Smit, J., Greener, R., Piaggio, G., & Joanis, C. (2015). The female condom learning curve: Patterns of female condom failure over 20 years. *Contraception, 91*(1), 85–90.

Beland, F., Zunzunegui, M., Alvarado, B., Otero, A., & del Ser, T. (2005). Trajectories of cognitive decline and social relations. *The Journals of Gerontology, Series B: Psychological Sciences and Social Sciences, 60*(6), 320–330.

Belden, A., Thompson, N., & Luby, J. (2008). Temper tantrums in healthy versus DSM-IV depressed and disruptive preschoolers: Defining tantrum behaviors associated with clinical problems. *Journal of Pediatrics, 152*(1), 117–122.

Bellieni, C. (2016). The best age for pregnancy and undue pressures. *Journal of Family and Reproductive Health, 10*(3), 40–42.

Bellinger, D. (2017). Childhood lead exposure and adult outcomes. *Journal of the American Medical Association, 317*(12), 1219–1220.

Bello, V., & Schultz, R. (2011). Prevalence of treatable and reversible dementias. A study in a dementia outpatient clinc. *Dementia & Neuropsychologia, 5*(1), 44–47.

Belsky, J. (1987). Infant day care and socioemotional development: The United States. *Journal of Child Psychology and Psychiatry, 29*, 397–406.

Belsky, J., & Braungart, J. M. (1991). Are insecure-avoidant infants with extensive day care experience less stressed by and more independent in the strange situation? *Child Development, 62*, 567–571.

Belsky, J., Campbell, S., Cohn, J., & Moore, G. (1996). Instability of infant-parent attachment security. *Developmental Psychology, 32*, 921–924.

Bem, S. L. (1993). *The lenses of gender: Transforming the debate on sexual inequality.* New Haven, CT: Yale University Press.

Bem, S. L. (1998). Gender schema theory and its implications for child development: Raising gender-aschematic children in a gender-schematic society. In D. L. Anselmi & A. L. Law (Eds.), *Questions of gender: Perspectives and paradoxes.* Boston: McGraw Hill.

Benasich, A., & Leevers, H. (2003). Processing of rapidly presented auditory cues in infancy: Implications for later language development. In H. Hayne & J. Fagen (Eds.), *Progress in infancy research* (Vol. 3, pp. 245–288). Mahwah, NJ: Lawrence Erlbaum.

Benenson, J. (1993). Greater preference among females than males for dyadic interaction in early childhood. *Child Development, 64*, 544–555.

Benetsky, M., Burd, C., & Rapino, M. (2015, March). *Young adult migration: 2007–2009 to 2010–2012.* Washington, DC: U.S. Census Bureau. Retrieved from www.census.gov/content/dam/Census/library/publications/2015/acs/acs-31.pdf.

Bengtson, V. L. (1996). Continuities and discontinuities in intergenerational relationships over time. In V. Bengtson & K. Schaie (Eds.), *Adulthood and aging* (pp. 246–268). New York: Springer.

Bengtson, V. L., Gans, D., Putney, N. M., & Silverstein, M. (2009). *Handbook of theories of aging* (2nd ed.). New York: Springer.

Bengtson, V. L., Rosenthal, C., & Burton, L. (1990). Families and aging: Diversity and heterogeneity. In R. Binstock & L. George (Eds.), *Handbook of aging and the social sciences* (3rd ed., pp. 263–287). New York: Academic Press.

Benjamin, K., Edwards, N. C., & Bharti, V. K. (2005). Attitudinal, perceptual, and normative beliefs influencing the exercise decisions of community-dwelling physically frail seniors. *Journal of Aging and Physical Activity, 13*(3), 276–293.

Benner, A. (2011). The transition to high school: Current knowledge, future directions. *Educational Psychology Review, 23*, 299–328.

Benner, M. A. (2007). AmeriCorps: Idaho community HealthCorps. *Journal of Rural Mental Health, 31*(3), 29–34.

Bennett, K. J., Olatosi, B., & Probst, J. C. (2008). *Health disparities: A rural-urban chartbook*. Retrieved from www.rural healthresearch.org/publications/676.

Benson, P., Roehlkepartain, E., & Scales, P. (2012). Spirituality and positive youth development. In L. Miller (Ed.), *The Oxford handbook of psychology and spirituality* (pp. 468–488). Oxford, UK: Oxford University Press.

Benson, P. L., Scales, P. C., & Roehlkepartain, E. C. (2011). *A fragile foundation: The state of developmental assets among American youth* (2nd ed.). Minneapolis, MN: Search Institute.

Benson, P. L., Scales, P. C., Syvertsen, A. K., & Roehlkepartain, E. C. (2012). Is youth spiritual development a universal developmental process? An international exploration. *Journal of Positive Psychology, 7*(6), 453–470.

Bergen, D., & Davis, D. (2011). Influences of technology-related playful activity and thought on moral development. *American Journal of Play, 4*(1), 80–99.

Berk, L. E. (2012). *Infants, children, and adolescents* (7th ed.). Boston: Pearson/Allyn & Bacon.

Berlin, G., Furstenberg, F., & Waters, M. (2010). Introducing the issue: Transition to adulthood. *The future of Children, 20*(1), 3–18.

Berliner, K., Jacob, D., & Schwartzberg, N. (2016). Single adults and the life cycle. In M. McGoldrick, N. Garcia-Preto, & B. Carter (Eds.), *The expanded family life cycle: Individual, family, and social perspectives* (5th ed., pp. 190–204). Boston: Pearson.

Bernard, S., & Deleau, M. (2007). Conversational perspective-taking and false belief attribution: A longitudinal study. *British Journal of Developmental Psychology, 25*(3), 443–460.

Bernier, A., Calkins, S., & Bell, M. (2016). Longitudinal associations between the quality of mother-infant interactions and brain development across infancy. *Child Development, 87*(4), 1159–1174.

Bern-Klug, M. (2004). The ambiguous dying syndrome. *Health and Social Work, 29*(1), 55–65.

Berry-Bibee, E. N., Tepper, N. K., Jatlaoui, T. C., Whiteman, M. K., Mamieson, D. J., & Curtis, K. M. (2016). The safety of intrauterine devices in breastfeeding women: A systematic review. *Contraception, 94*(6), 725–738.

Bessell, S. (2017). Money matters . . . but so do people: Children's views and experiences of living in a "disadvantaged" community. *Children and Youth Services Review.* doi:10.1016/j.childyouth.2017.06.010

Bhopti, A. (2017). Promoting the occupations of parents of children with disability in early childhood intervention services – Building stronger families and communities. *Australian Occupational Therapy Journal, 64,* 419–422.

Billingsley, A. (1999). *Mighty like a river: The black church and social reform.* New York: Oxford University Press.

Birknerová, Z. (2011). Social and emotional intelligence in school environment. *Asian Social Science, 7*(10), 241–248.

Biro, F. M., Greenspan, L. C., & Galvez. M. P. (2012). Puberty in girls of the 21st century. *Journal of Pediatric and Adolescent Gynecology, 25*(5), 298–294.

Bisagni, F. (2012). Shrapnel: Latency, mourning and the suicide of a parent. *Journal of Child Psychotherapy, 38*(1), 22–31.

Bishop, A. J. (2011). Spirituality and religiosity connections to mental and physical health among the oldest old. In L. W. Poon & J. Cohen-Mansfield (Eds.), *Understanding well-being in the oldest old* (pp. 227–239). New York: Cambridge University Press.

Bishop, A. J., & Martin, P. (2011). The measurement of life satisfaction and happiness in old-old age. In L. W. Poon & J. Cohen-Mansfield (Eds.), *Understanding well-being in the oldest old* (pp. 290–331). New York: Cambridge University Press.

Bissinger, B. (2015, June 30). Caitlyn Jenner: The full story. *Vanity Fair.* Retrieved from www.vanityfair.com/hollywood/2015/06/caitlyn-jenner-bruce-cover-annie-leibovitz.

Bjorklund, B. (2015). *The journey of adulthood* (8th ed.). Boston: Pearson.

Bjorklund, D., & Causey, K. (2018). *Children's thinking: Cognitive development and individual differences* (6th ed.). Thousand Oaks, CA: Sage.

Blackmon, S., & Vera, E. (2008). Ethnic and racial identity development in children of color. In J. Asamen, M. Ellis, & G. Berry (Eds.), *The Sage handbook of child development, multiculturalism, and the media* (pp. 47–61). Thousand Oaks, CA: Sage.

Blakemore, S. (2012). Imaging brain development: The adolescent brain. *Neuroimaging, 61,* 397–406.

Blakemore, S., & Robbins, T. (2012). Decision-making in the adolescent brain. *Nature Neuroscience, 15*(9), 1184–1191.

Blanchflower, D., & Oswald, A. (2008). Is well-being U-shaped over the life cycle? *Social Science & Medicine, 66,* 1733–1749.

Blasco-Fontecilla, H., Delgado-Gomez, D., Legido-Gil, T., Leon, J., Perez-Rodriguez, M., & Baca-Garcia, E. (2012).

Can the Holmes-Rahe Social Readjustment Rating Scale (SRRS) be used as a suicide risk scale? An exploratory study. *Archives of Suicide Research, 16,* 13–28.

Blass, E., Ganchrow, J., & Stiner, J. (1984). Classical conditioning in newborn humans 2-48 hours of age. *Infant Behavior and Development, 7,* 223–235.

Blau, P. M. (1964). *Exchange and power in social life.* New York: Wiley.

Blieszner, R., & deVries, B. (2001). Perspectives on intimacy. *Generations, 25*(2), 7–8.

Blieszner, R., & Roberto, K. (2006). Perspectives on close relationships among the baby boomers. In S. Whitbourne & S. Willis (Eds.), *The baby boomers grow up: Contemporary perspectives on midlife* (pp. 261–281). Mahwah, NJ: Lawrence Erlbaum.

Blinn-Pike, L., Worthy, S., Jonkman, J., & Smith, G. R. (2008). Emerging adult versus adult status among college students: Examination of explanatory variables. *Adolescence, 43*(171), 577–591.

Blow, F., & Barry, K. (2012). Alcohol and substance misuse in older adults. *Current Psychiatry Reports, 14,* 310–319.

Blume, H. (1998, September). Neurodiversity. *The Atlantic.* Retrieved from www.theatlantic.com/magazine/archive/1998/09/neurodiversity/305909/.

Blunden, S., Thompson, K., & Dawson, D. (2011). Behavioural sleep treatments and night time crying in infants: Challenging the status quo. *Sleep Medicine Reviews, 15,* 327–334.

Boat, A. C., Sadhasivam, S., Loepke, A. W., & Kurth, C. D. (2011). Outcome for the extremely premature neonate: How far do we push the edge? *Pediatric Anesthesia, 21*(7), 765–770.

Bobo, W., & Yawn, B. (2014). Concise review for physicians and other clinicians: Postpartum depression. *Mayo Clinic Proceedings, 89*(6), 835–844.

Boivin, A., Zhong-Cheng, L., Audibert, F., Masse, B., Lefebreve, F., Tessier, R., & Nuyt, A. M. (2012). Pregnancy complications among women born preterm. *Canadian Medical Association Journal, 184*(16), 1777–1784.

Boldizar, J. (1991). Assessing sex typing and androgyny in children: The children's sex role inventory. *Developmental Psychology, 27,* 505–515.

Bolin, M., Akerud, H., Cnattingius, S., Stephansson, O., & Wikstrom, A. K. (2013). Hyperemesis gravidarum and risks of placental dysfunction disorders: A population-based cohort study. *BJOG: An International Journal of Obstetrics and Gynaecology, 120*(5), 541–547.

Bonanno, G., & Kaltman, S. (1999). Toward an integrative perspective on bereavement. *Psychological Bulletin, 125*(6), 760–776.

Bond, B., Hefner, V., & Drogos, K. (2009). Information-seeking practices during the sexual development of lesbian, gay, and bisexual individuals: The influence and effects of coming out in a mediated environment. *Sexuality & Culture, 13,* 32–50.

Borges-Costa, J., Matos, C., & Pereira, F. (2012). Sexually transmitted infections in pregnant adolescents: Prevalence and association with maternal and foetal morbidity. *Journal of the European Academy of Dermatology & Venereology, 26*(8), 972–975.

Borysenko, J. (1996). *A woman's book of life: The biology, psychology, and spirituality of the feminine life cycle.* New York: Riverhead Books.

Boss, P., & Yeats, J. R. (2014). Ambiguous loss: A complicated type of grief when loved ones disappear. *Bereavement Care, 33*(2), 63–69.

Boulet, S., Schieve, L., & Boyle, C. (2011). Birth weight and health and developmental outcomes in US children, 1997–2005. *Maternal and Child Health Journal, 15*(7), 836–844.

Boveda, I., & Metz, A. (2016). Predicting end-of-career transitions for baby boomers nearing retirement age. *The Career Development Quarterly, 64,* 153–168.

Bowlby, J. (1969). *Attachment and loss.* New York: Basic Books.

Bowlby, J. (1980). *Attachment and loss: Loss, sadness, and depression* (Vol. 3). New York: Basic Books.

Bowlby, J. (1982). *Attachment and loss* (Vol. 1). New York: Basic Books.

Boyd-Franklin, B., & Karger, M. (2012). Intersections of race, class, and poverty: Challenges and resilience. In F. Walsh (Ed.), *Normal family processes* (4th ed., pp. 273–296). New York: Guilford Press.

Boyle, M. H., Miskovic, V., Van Lieshout, R., Duncan, L., Schmidt, L. A., Hoult, L., . . . Saigal, S. (2011). Psychopathology in young adults born at extremely low birth weight. *Psychological Medicine, 41*(8), 1763–1774.

Boyle, M. H., Racine, Y., Georgiades, K., Snelling, D., Hong, S., Omariba, W., ... Rao-Melacini, P. (2006). The influence of economic development level, household wealth and maternal education on child health in the developing world. *Social Science & Medicine, 63*(8), 2242–2254.

Brache, V., Payan, L. J., & Faundes, A. (2013). Current status of contraceptive vaginal rings. *Contraception, 87*(3), 264–272.

Bradley, S. E. K. (2000). *Affect regulation and the development of psychopathology*. New York: Guilford Press.

Braet, C., Wante, L., Van Beveren, M., & Theuwis, L. (2015). Is the cognitive triad a clear marker of depressive symptoms in youngsters? *European Child & Adolescent Psychiatry, 24*(10), 1261–1268.

Brandt, M. (2013). Intergenerational transfers to adult children in Europe: Do social policies matter? *Journal of Marriage and Family, 75*(1), 235–251.

Brandtstadter, J. (2006). Adaptive resources in later life: Tenacious goal pursuits and flexible role adjustment. In M. Csikszentmihalyi & I. Csikszentmihalyi (Eds.), *A life worth living: Contributions to positive psychology* (pp. 143–164). New York: Oxford Press.

Brännström, L., Vinnerljung, B., Forsman, B., & Almquist, Y. (2017). Children placed in out-of-home care as midlife adults: Are they still disadvantage or have they caught up with their peers? *Child Maltreatment, 22*(3), 205–124.

Branum, A. M., & Jones, J. (2015). *Trends in long-acting reversible contraception use among U.S. women aged 15–44.* NCHS data brief, no 188. Hyattsville, MD: National Center for Health Statistics.

Brault, M. W. (2012). *Americans with disabilities: 2010.* Washington, DC: United States Census Bureau. Retrieved from www.census.gov/library/publications/2012/demo/p70-131.html.

Breheny, M., Stephens, C., & Spilsbury, L. (2013). Involvement without interference: How grandparents negotiate intergenerational expectations in relationships with grandchildren. *Journal of Family Studies, 19*(2), 174–184.

Brenn, T., & Ytterstad, E. (2016). Increased risk of death immediately after losing a spouse: Cause-specific mortality following widowhood in Norway. *Preventive Medicine, 89*, 251–256.

Brennan, D., & Spencer, A. (2009). Life events and oral-health-related quality of life among young adults. *Quality of Life Research, 18*(5), 557–565.

Brenoff, A. (2015, May 4). 10 ways technology could change aging in the next 10 years. *The Huffington Post.* Retrieved from www.huffingtonpost.com/2015/05/04/10-ways-technology-could-change-aging_n_7155100.html.

Brewer, M. (1999). The psychology of prejudice: Ingroup love or outgroup hate? *Journal of Social Issues, 55*(3), 429–444.

Brezina, P. R., & Zhao, Y. (2012). The ethical, legal, and social issues impacted by modern assisted reproductive technology. *Obstetrics and Gynecology International.* Article ID 686253. doi:10:1155/2012/686253

Bridgett, D., Gartstein, M., Putnam, S., McKay, T., Iddins, E., Robertson, C., . . . Rittmueller, A. (2009). Maternal and contextual influences and the effect of temperament development during infancy on parenting in toddlerhood. *Infant Behavior & Development, 32*, 103–116.

Brim, O., Ryff, C., & Kessler, R. (Eds.). (2004). *How healthy are we? A national study of well-being at midlife.* Chicago: University of Chicago Press.

Brinkman, B. G., Jedinak, A., Rosen, L. A., & Zimmerman, T. S. (2011). Teaching children fairness: Decreasing gender prejudice among children. *Analyses of Social Issues & Public Policy, 11*(1), 61–81.

Brokenleg, M., & Middleton, D. (1993). Native Americans: Adapting, yet retaining. In D. Irish, K. Lundquist, & V. Nelsen (Eds.), *Ethnic variations in dying, death, and grief: Diversity in universality* (pp. 101–112). Washington, DC: Taylor & Francis.

Bromberg, D. S., & O'Donohue, W. T. (2013). *Handbook of child and adolescent sexuality: Developmental and forensic psychology.* Boston: Elsevier Science.

Bromberger, J., Kravitz, H., Youk, A., Schott, L., & Joffe, H. (2016). Patterns of depressive disorders across 13 years and their determinants among midlife women: SWAN Mental Health Study. *Journal of Affective Disorders, 206*, 31–40.

Bronfenbrenner, U. (1993). The ecology of cognitive development: Research models and fugitive findings. In R. Wozniak & K. Fischer (Eds.), *Development in context: Acting and thinking in specific environments* (pp. 3–44). Hillsdale, NJ: Lawrence Erlbaum.

Bronfenbrenner, U. (1996). *The ecology of human development: Experiments by nature and design.* Cambridge, MA: Harvard University Press.

Bronfenbrenner, U., & Morris, P. (1998). The ecology of developmental processes. In W. Damon (Series Ed.) & R. M. Lerner (Vol. Ed.), *Handbook of child psychology: Vol 1. Theoretical models of human development* (5th ed., pp. 993–1028). New York: Wiley.

Bronte-Tinkew, J., Brown, B., Carrano, J., & Shwalb, R. (2005). *Logic models and outcomes for youth in the transition to adulthood.* Washington, DC: Child Trends. Retrieved from www.childtrends.org/wp-content/uploads/2014/05/2005-13LogicModelsTransitiontoAdulthood.pdf.

Brooker, R., Buss, K., Semery-Chalifant, K., Aksan, M., Davidson, R., & Goldsmith, H. (2013). The development of stranger fear in infancy and toddlerhood: Normative development, individual differences, antecedents, and outcomes. *Developmental Science, 16*(6), 864–878.

Brooks-Gunn, J., & Ruble, D. (2013). Developmental processes in the experience of menarche. In A. Baum & J. Singer (Eds.), *Issues in child health and adolescent health: handbook of psychology and health* (pp. 117–148). New York: Psychology Press.

Broussard, B. (2012). Psychological and behavioral traits associated with eating disorders and pregnancy: A pilot study. *Journal of Midwifery & Women's Health, 57*(1), 61–66.

Brown, A. (2017, June 13). *5 key findings about LGBT Americans*. Washington, DC: Pew Research Center. Retrieved from www.pewresearch.org/fact-tank/2017/06/13/5-key-findings-about-lgbt-americans/.

Brown, B., & Klute, C. (2003). Friendships, cliques, and crowds. In G. Adams & M. Berzonsky (Eds.), *Blackwell handbook of adolescence* (pp. 330–345). Oxford, UK: Blackwell.

Brown, J. (2003). The self-enhancement motive in collectivistic cultures: The rumors of my death have been greatly exaggerated. *Journal of Cross-Cultural Psychology, 34,* 603–605.

Brown, J., Dutton, K., & Cook, K. (2001). From the top down: Self-esteem and self-evaluation. *Cognition and Emotion, 15,* 615–631.

Brown, R. A., Rehkopf, D. H., Copeland, W. E., Costello, E. J., & Worthman, C. M. (2009). Lifecourse priorities among Appalachian emerging adults: Revisiting Wallace's organization of diversity. *ETHOS, 37*(2), 225–242.

Brown, S., & Lin, I.-F. (2012). The gray divorce revolution: Rising divorce among middle-aged and older adults, 1990–2010. *The Journals of Gerontology, Series B: Psychological Sciences and Social Sciences, 67*(6), 731–741.

Brown, T. (2014, October 3). World's first baby born after uterine transfer. *Medscape Medical News.* Retrieved from www.medscape.com/viewarticle/832827.

Bruce, S., & Muhammad, Z. (2009). The development of object permanence in children with intellectual disability, physical disability, autism, and blindness. *International Journal of Disability, Development & Education, 56*(3), 229–246.

Bruce, S., & Vargas, C. (2013). Teaching object permanence: An action research study. *Journal of Impairment & Blindness, 107*(1), 60–64.

Brückner, H., & Mayer, K. (2005). De-standardization of the life course: What it might mean? And if it means anything, whether it actually took place? In R. MacMillan (Ed.), *The structure of the life course: Standardized? Individualized? Differentiated?* (pp. 27–53). New York: Elsevier.

Bryson, K., & Casper, L. (1999). *Coresident grandparents and grandchildren.* Washington, DC: U.S. Census Bureau.

Brzeski, N. (2013, May 5). Birthing shelters. *HuffPost.* Retrieved from www.huffingtonpost.com/nicole-field-brzeski/birthing-shelters_1_b_2812798.html.

Buettner, D., & Skemp, S. (2016). Blue zones: Lessons from the world's longest lived. *American Journal of Lifestyle Medicine, 10*(5), 318–321.

Buffardi, A., Thomas, K., Holmes, K., & Manhart, L. (2008). Moving upstream: Ecosocial and psychosocial correlates of sexually transmitted infections among young adults in the United States. *American Journal of Public Health, 98*(6), 1128–1136.

Bullock, K. (2011). The influence of culture on end-of-life decision making. *Journal of Social Work in End-of-Life & Palliative Care, 7,* 83–98.

Bulus, A., Asci, A., Erkekough, P., Balci, A., Andiran, N., & Kocer-Gümüsel, B. (2016). The evaluation of possible role of endocrine disruptors in central and peripheral precocious puberty. *Toxicology Mechanisms and Methods, 26*(7), 493–500.

Burgess, W. C. (2009). Internal and external stress factors associated with the identity development of transgender and gender variant youth. In G. P. Mallon (Ed.), *Social work practice with transgender and gender variant youth* (pp. 53–62). London: Routledge.

Burns, L., Mattick, R. P., & Wallace, C. (2007). Smoking patterns and outcomes in a population of pregnant women and other substance use disorders. *Tobacco Research, 10*(6), 969–974.

Burstein, D. (2013). *Fast future: How the millennial generation is shaping our world.* Boston: Beacon Press.

Busch, H., & Hofer, J. (2012). Self-regulation and milestones of adult development: Intimacy and generativity. *Developmental Psychology, 48*(1), 282–293.

Butler, R. N. (1963). The life review: An interpretation of reminiscence in the aged. *Psychiatry, 26*(1), 65–70.

Butler, R. N. (1987). Life review. In G. L. Maddox (Ed.), *The encyclopedia of aging: A comprehensive resource in gerontology and geriatrics* (2nd ed., pp. 397–398). New York: Springer.

Butler-Sweet, C. (2011). "Race isn't what defines me": Exploring identity choices in transracial, biracial, and monoracial families. *Social Identities: Journal for the Study of Race, Nation and Culture, 17*(6), 747–769.

Cabrera, N., Fitzgerald, H., Bradley, R., & Roggman, L. (2014). The ecology of father-child relationships: An expanded model. *Journal of Family Theory & Review, 6*(4), 336–354.

Cácamo, R., Vermeer, H., van der Veer, R., & van Ijzendoorn, M. (2016). Early full-time day care, mother-child attachment, and quality of the home environment in Chile: Preliminary findings. *Early Education and Development, 27*(4), 457–477.

Cacciatore, J., & DeFrain, J. (Eds.). (2015). *The world of bereavement: Cultural perspectives on death in families*. Basel, Switzerland: Springer International.

Cagle, J. G., & Kovacs, P. J. (2009). Education: A complex and empowering social work intervention at the end of life. *Health & Social Work, 34*(1), 17–27.

Calasannti, T., & King, N. (2015). Intersectionality and age. In J. Twigg & W. Martin (Eds.), *Routledge handbook of cultural gerontology* (pp. 193–200). Philadelphia: Routledge.

Calkins, S., & Hill, A. (2007). Caregiver influences on emerging emotion regulation: Biological and environmental transactions in early development. In J. Gross (Ed.), *Handbook of emotion regulation* (pp. 229–248). New York: Guilford Press.

Callahan, A. M. (2017). *Spirituality and hospice social work*. New York: Columbia University Press.

Cameron, J., Alvarez, J., Ruble, D., & Fuligni, A. (2001). Children's lay theories about ingroups and outgroups: Reconceptualizing research on prejudice. *Personality and Social Psychology Review, 5*, 118–128.

Cameron, S. T., Glasier, A., & Johnstone, A. (2012). Pilot study of home self administration of depo-medroxyprogesterone acetate for contraception. *Contraception, 85*(5), 458–464.

Campaign to End Unwanted Medical Treatment. (2017). *About us*. Retrieved from http://endumt.org/about-us/.

Campbell, L., Campbell, B., & Dickinson, D. (2004). *Teaching & learning through multiple intelligences*. Boston: Allyn & Bacon.

Campbell, S. (2002). *Behavioral problems in preschool children* (2nd ed.). New York: Guilford Press.

Canfield, J., Nolan, J., Harley, D., Hardy, A., & Elliott, W. (2016). Using a person-centered approach to examine the impact of homelessness on school absences. *Child & Adolescent Social Work, 33*(3), 199–205.

Cao, C., & O'Brien, K. O. (2013). Pregnancy and iron homeostasis: An update. *Nutrition Reviews, 71*(1), 35–51.

Cappeliez, P., Beaupré, M., & Robitaille, A. (2008). Characteristics and impact of life turning points for older adults. *Ageing International, 32*, 54–64.

Carlson, E. (2009). 20th-century U.S. generations. *Population Bulletin, 64*, 1–17.

Carolan, M., & Allen, K. (1999). Commitments and constraints to intimacy for African American couples at midlife. *Journal of Family Issues, 20*(1), 3–4.

Carpenter, G., & Stacks, A. (2009). Developmental effects of exposure to intimate partner violence in early childhood: A review of the literature. *Children and Youth Services Review, 31*(8), 831–839.

Carpentier, N., Bernard, P., Grenier, A., & Guberman, N. (2010). Using the life course perspective to study the entry into the illness trajectory: The perspective of caregivers of people with Alzheimer's disease. *Social Science & Medicine, 70*(10), 1501–1508.

Carr, D. (2004). Gender, preloss marital dependence, and older adults' adjustment to widowhood. *Journal of Marriage and the Family, 66*(1), 220–235.

Carr, D., & Kail, B. (2012). The influence of unpaid work on the transition out of full-time paid work. *The Gerontologist, 53*(1), 92–101.

Carskadon, M., & Tarokh, L. (2014). Developmental changes in sleep biology and potential effects on adolescent behavior and caffeine use. *Nutrition Reviews, 72*(Suppl. 1), 60–64.

Carstensen, L. (1995). Evidence for a life-span theory of socioemotional selectivity. *Current Directions in Psychological Science, 4*, 151–156.

Casale-Giannola, D., & Kamens, M. W. (2006). Inclusion at a university: Experiences of a young woman with Down syndrome. *Mental Retardation, 44*(5), 344–352.

Casas, J., Suzuki, L., Alexander, C., & Jackson, M. (2016). *Handbook of multicultural counseling*. Thousand Oaks, CA: Sage.

Case, A., & Deaton, A. (2015). Rising morbidity and mortality in midlife among white non-Hispanic Americans in the 21st century. *PNAS, 112*(49). Retrieved from www.pnas.org/cgi/doi/10.1073/pnas.1518393112.

Casey Copen, E., Chandra, Q., & Martinez, G. (2012). Prevalence and timing of oral sex with opposite-sex partners among females and males aged 15–24 years: United States, 2007–2010. *National Health Statistics Reports, 56*. Retrieved from https://permanent.access.gpo.gov/gpo53303/nhsr056.pdf.

Catanos, R., Rogers, W., & Lotz, M. (2013). The ethics of uterine transplantation. *Bioethics, 27*(2), 65–73.

Center for Behavioral Health Statistics and Quality. (2016). *2014 National Survey on Drug Use and Health: DSM-5 changes: Implications for child serious emotional disturbance* (unpublished internal documentation). Rockville, MD: US Substance Abuse and Mental Health Services

Administration. Retrieved from www.samhsa.gov/data/sites/default/files/NSDUH-DSM5ImpactChildSED-2016.pdf.

Center for Economic and Policy Research. (2009). *Parental leave policies in 21 countries.* Washington, DC: Author.

Center for Education Reform. (2017). *Charting a new course: The case for freedom, flexibility and opportunity through charter schools.* Washington, DC: Author.Retrieved from www.edreform.com/issues/choice-charter-schools/achievement/.

Center for Research on Women With Disabilities (CROWD). (2017). *Sexuality and reproductive health—Pregnancy and delivery.* Retrieved from www.bcm.edu/research/centers/research-on-women-with-disabilities/?pmid=1448.

Center for the Study of Social Policy. (2014). *Food insecurity in early childhood.* Retrieved from www.cssp.org/publications/general/document/Food-Insecurity-Early-Childhood.pdf.

Centers for Disease Control and Prevention. (2012). *Child injury.* Retrieved from www.cdc.gov/vitalsigns/childinjury/index.html.

Centers for Disease Control and Prevention. (2013). *The state of aging and health in America 2013.* Atlanta, GA: Centers for Disease Control and Prevention, U.S. Department of Health and Human Services.

Centers for Disease Control and Prevention. (2014a). *Breastfeeding report card: United States/2014.* Retrieved from www.cdc.gov/breastfeeding/pdf/2014breastfeeding reportcard.pdf.

Centers for Disease Control and Prevention. (2014b). *Women with disabilities.* Retrieved from www.cdc.gov/ncbddd/disabilityandhealth/women.html.

Centers for Disease Control and Prevention. (2015a). *Key statistics for the National Survey of Family Growth (2011–2013).* Retrieved from www.cdc.gov/nchs/nsfg/key_statistics/c.htm#currentuse.

Centers for Disease Control and Prevention. (2015b). *Contraception: How effective are birth control methods?* Retrieved from www.cdc.gov/reproductivehealth/contraception/index.htm.

Centers for Disease Control and Prevention. (2016a). *Infertility.* Retrieved from www.cdc.gov/nchs/fastats/infertility.htm.

Centers for Disease Control and Prevention. (2016b). *Diagnosis during pregnancy: Prenatal testing.* Retrieved from www.cdc.gov/ncbddd/birthdefects/diagnosis.html.

Centers for Disease Control and Prevention. (2016c). *The opioid epidemic: By the numbers.* Retrieved from www.hhs.gov/sites/default/files/Factsheet-opioids-061516.pdf.

Centers for Disease Control and Prevention. (2016d). *Child abuse and neglect: Consequences.* Atlanta: GA: Author. Retrieved from www.cdc.gov/violenceprevention/child abuseandneglect/consequences.html.

Centers for Disease Control and Prevention. (2016e). *Youth violence.* Retrieved from www.cdc.gov/violenceprevention/pdf/yv-datasheet.pdf.

Centers for Disease Control and Prevention. (2016f). *Health, United States, 2015.* Retrieved from www.cdc.gov/nchs/data/hus/hus15.pdf#015.

Centers for Disease Control and Prevention. (2017a). Evaluating *Genomic tests.* Retrieved from www.cdc.gov/genomics/gtesting/index.htm.

Centers for Disease Control and Prevention. (2017b). *Infertility FAQs.* Retrieved from www.cdc.gov/reproductive health/infertility/index.htm.

Centers for Disease Control and Prevention. (2017c). *Facts about stillbirth.* Retrieved from www.cdc.gov/ncbddd/still birth/facts.html.

Centers for Disease Control and Prevention. (2017d). *Preterm birth.* Retrieved from www.cdc.gov/reproductive health/maternalinfanthealth/pretermbirth.htm.

Centers for Disease Control and Prevention. (2017e). *HIV among women.* Retrieved from www.cdc.gov/hiv/group/gender/women/index.html.

Centers for Disease Control and Prevention. (2017f). *Facts about developmental disabilities.* Atlanta, GA: Author. Retrieved from www.cdc.gov/ncbddd/developmental disabilities/facts.html.

Centers for Disease Control and Prevention. (2017g). *2016 sexually transmitted disease surveillance: STDs in adolescents and young adults.* Retrieved from www.cdc.gov/std/stats16/adolescents.htm.

Centers for Disease Control and Prevention. (2017h). *HIV among youth.* Retrieved from www.cdc.gov/hiv/group/age/youth/index.html.

Centers for Disease Control and Prevention. (2017i). *10 leading causes of death by age group, United States – 2015.* Retrieved from www.cdc.gov/injury/wisqars/pdf/leading_causes_of_death_by_age_group_2015-a.pdf.

Centers for Disease Control and Prevention. (2018a). *2016 sexually transmitted diseases surveillance.* Retrieved from www.cdc.gov/std/stats16/default.htm.

Centers for Disease Control and Prevention. (2018b). *Developmental monitoring and screening.* Retrieved from www.cdc.gov/ncbddd/childdevelopment/screening.html.

Centers for Disease Control and Prevention. (2018c). *Infant mortality.* Retrieved from www.cdc.gov/reproductive health/maternalinfanthealth/infantmortality.htm.

Centers for Disease Control and Prevention Division for Violence Prevention. (2015). *Suicide: Facts at a glance.* Retrieved from www.cdc.gov/violenceprevention/pdf/suicide-datasheet-a.pdf.

Centers for Medicare and Medicaid Services. (2012). *Strong start for mothers and newborns.* Retrieved from http://innovations.cms.gov/initiatives/strong-start/index.html.

Centers for Medicare and Medicaid Services. (2015). *Nursing home data compendium, 2013.* Baltimore: Author. Retrieved from www.cms.gov/Medicare/Provider-Enrollment-and-Certification/Certificationand Complianc/downloads/nursinghomedatacompendium_508.pdf.

Central Intelligence Agency. (2017). *The world factbook.* Retrieved from www.cia.gov/library/publications/resources/the-world-factbook/index.html.

Cerniglia, L., & Cimino, S. (2015). Maternal and paternal psychopathological risk in children with non-organic failure to thrive. *Peer J PrePrints.* Retrieved from https://peerj.com/preprints/1162.pdf.

Chan, A., Malhotra, C., Malhotra, R., Rush, A., & Ostbye, T. (2013). Health impacts of caregiving for older adults with functional limitations: Results from Singapore Survey on Informal Caregiving. *Journal of Aging and Health, 25*(6), 998–1012.

Chang, L. (2001). The development of racial attitudes and self concepts of Taiwanese preschoolers (China). *Dissertation Abstracts International: Section A: Humanities & Social Sciences, 61*(8-A), 3045.

Chang, P., Choi, C., Bazarova, N., & Löckenhoff, C. (2015). Age differences in online social networking: Extending socioemotional selectivity theory to social network sites. *Journal of Broadcasting & Electronic Media, 59*(2), 221–239.

Chang, Y., & Schneider, J. (2010). Decision-making process of nursing home placement among Chinese family caregivers. *Perspectives in Psychiatric Care, 46*(2), 108–118.

Chapin, L., & Altenhofen, S. (2010). Neurocognitive perspectives in language outcomes of Early Head Start: Language and cognitive stimulation and maternal depression. *Infant Mental Health Journal, 31*(5), 486–498.

Chapman, M. V., & Perreira, K. M. (2005). The well-being of immigrant Latino youth: A framework to inform practice. *Families in Society, 86*, 104–111.

Character.org. (2015). *Character education: What states are doing.* Retrieved from www.character.org/wp-content/uploads/What-States-Are-Doing.pdf.

Charlesworth, L. (2007). Child maltreatment. In E. Hutchison, H. Matto, M. Harrigan, L. Charlesworth, & P. Viggiani (Eds.), *Challenges of living: A multidimensional working model for social workers* (pp. 105–139). Thousand Oaks, CA: Sage.

Cheadle, J., Amato, P., & King, V. (2010). Patterns of non-resident father contact. *Demography, 47*(1), 205–225.

Chen, C. (2006). A household-based convoy and the reciprocity of support exchange between adult children and noncoresiding parents. *Journal of Family Issues, 27*(8), 1100–1136.

Chen, E., Miller, G., Lachman, M., Gruenewald, T., & Seeman, T. (2012). Protective factors for adults from low-childhood socioeconomic circumstances: The benefits of shift-and-persist for allostatic load. *Psychosomatic Medicine, 74*, 178–186.

Chen, P., & Jacobson, K. (2012). Developmental trajectories of substance use from early adolescence to young adulthood: Gender and racial/ethnic differences. *Journal of Adolescent Health, 50*(2), 154–163.

Chen, X. (2009). The linkage between deviant lifestyles and victimization: An examination from a life course perspective. *Journal of Interpersonal Violence, 24*(7), 1083–1110.

Cheng, T., Powdthavee, N., & Oswald, A. (2017). Longitudinal evidence for a midlife nadir in human well-being: Results from four data sets. *The Economic Journal, 127*, 126–142.

Cherry, M. (Writer), & Grossman, D. (Director). (2012). Finishing the hat [Television series episode]. In M. Berry et al. (Producers), *Desperate Housewives*. Burbank, CA: NBC Studios.

Chervenak, F., McCullough, L., Brent, R., Levene, M., & Arabin, B. (2013). Planned home birth: The professional responsibility response. *American Journal of Obstetrics and Gynecology, 208*(1), 31–38.

Chesney-Lind, M., & Jones, N. (2010). *Fighting for girls: New perspectives on gender and violence.* Albany: State University of New York Press.

Chethik, M. (2000). *Techniques of child therapy: Psychodynamic approaches* (2nd ed.). New York: Guilford Press.

Chetu, C. (2017). The impact of miscarriage on subsequent pregnancy: Thematic analysis. *Journal of Experiential Psychotherapy, 20*(2), 16–23.

Child Care Aware of America. (2016). *Child care in America: 2016 state fact sheets.* Retrieved from https://usa.child careaware.org/advocacy-public-policy/resources/research/statefactsheets2016/.

Child Care Aware of America. (2017). *Parents and the high cost of child care.* Retrieved from https://usa.childcareaware .org/wp-content/uploads/2017/12/2017_CCA_High_Cost_ Report_FINAL.pdf.

Child Trends Data Bank. (2016). *Low and very low birth weight infants: Indicators on children and youth.* Retrieved from www.childtrends.org/wp-content/uploads/2016/12/57_ Low_Birth_Weight.pdf.

Child Trends. (2014). *Immunization.* Bethesda, MD: Author.

Child Trends. (2015). *It matters: Child poverty.* Retrieved from www.childtrends.org/multimedia/it-matters-poverty/.

Child Trends. (2016a). *Children in poverty: Indicators of child and youth well-being.* Child Trends Data Bank. Retrieved from www.childtrends.org/wp-content/uploads/2016/12/04_ Poverty.pdf.

Child Trends. (2016b). *Children's exposure to violence: Indicators of child and youth well-being.* Retrieved from www.childtrends.org/wp-content/uploads/2016/05/118_ Exposure_to_Violence-1.pdf.

Child Trends. (2016c). *Child maltreatment: Indicators of child and youth well-being.* Retrieved from www.childtrends.org/ wp-content/uploads/2016/09/40_Child_Maltreatment .pdf.

Child Welfare Information Gateway. (2013). *What is child abuse and neglect? Recognizing the signs and symptoms.* Retrieved from www.childwelfare.gov/pubpdfs/whatiscan .pdf.

Child Welfare Information Gateway. (2017). *Child maltreatment 2015: Summary of key findings.* Washington, DC: U.S. Department of Health and Human Services, Children's Bureau.

Childhood Domestic Violence Association. (2014). *10 startling statistics about children of domestic violence.* Retrieved from https://cdv.org/2014/02/10-startling-domestic-violence-statistics-for-children/.

Cho, J., Martin, P., & Poon, L. (2014). Successful aging and subjective well-being among oldest-old adults. *The Gerontological Special Issue: Successful Aging, 55*(1), 132–143.

Chodorow, N. (1991). *Feminism and psychoanalytic theory.* New Haven, CT: Yale University Press.

Chodorow, N. (1999). *The reproduction of mothering: Psychoanalysis and the sociology of gender.* Berkeley: University of California Press.

Choi, N. G., & DiNitto, D. M. (2013a). The digital divide among low-income homebound older adults: Internet use patterns, eHealth literacy, and attitudes toward computer/Internet use. *Journal of Medical Internet Research, 15*(5), e97.

Choi, N. G., & DiNitto, D. M. (2013b). Internet use among older adults: Association with health needs, psychological capital, and social capital. *Journal of Medical Internet Research, 15*(5), e93.

Chomsky, N. (1968). *Language and mind.* New York: Harcourt Brace Jovanovich.

Choudhury, S. (2010). Culturing the adolescent brain: What can neuroscience learn from anthropology? *SCAN, 5,* 159–167.

Chow, J. C.-C., Auh, E. Y., Scharlach, A. E., Lehning, A. J., & Goldstein, C. (2010). Types and sources of support received by family caregivers of older adults from diverse racial/ethnic groups. *Journal of Ethnic and Cultural Diversity in Social Work, 19,* 175–194.

Christen, M., & Narvaez, D. (2012). Moral development in early childhood is key for moral enhancement. *AJOB Neuroscience, 3*(4), 25–26.

Chung, R., Bemak, F., & Grabosky, T. (2011). Multicultural-social justice leadership strategies: Counseling and advocacy with immigrants. *Journal for Social Action in Counseling & Psychology, 3*(1), 86–102.

Ciabattari, T. (2017). *Sociology of families: Change, continuity, and diversity.* Thousand Oaks, CA: Sage.

Cianciotto, J. (2012). *LGBT youth in America's schools.* Ann Arbor: University of Michigan Press.

Cicchetti, D. (2013). Annual research review: Resilient functioning in maltreated children—past, present, and future perspectives. *Journal of Child Psychology & Psychiatry, 54*(4), 402–422.

Claas, M. J., de Vries, L. S., & Bruinse, H. W. (2011). Maternal characteristics of a cohort of preterm infants with a birth weight <750 g without major structural anomalies and chromosomal abnormalities. *American Journal of Perinatology, 28*(5), 367–375.

Clark, K., & Clark, M. (1939). The development of consciousness of self and the emergence of racial identification in Negro preschool children. *Journal of Social Psychology, 10,* 591–599.

Clark, P. A. (2009). Embryo donation/adoption: Medical, legal, and ethical perspectives. *The Internet Journal of Law, Healthcare, and Ethics, 5*(2), 1–12.

Clark, R., Glick, J., & Bures, R. (2009). Immigrant families over the life course. *Journal of Family Issues, 30*(6), 852–872.

Clarke, L. (2008). Grandparents: A family resource? In D. R. Crane & T. Heaton (Eds.), *Handbook of families & poverty* (pp. 365–380). Thousand Oaks, CA: Sage.

Clearfield, M., & Nelson, N. (2006). Sex differences in mothers' speech and play behavior with 6-, 9-, and 14-month-old infants. *Sex Roles, 54*(1/2), 127–137.

Cleland, K., Raymond, E. G., Westley, E., & Trussell, J. (2014). Emergency contraception review: Evidence-based recommendations for clinicians. *Clinical Obstetrics & Gynecology, 57*(4), 741–750.

Clinton, J. (2008). Resilience and recovery. *International Journal of Children's Spirituality, 13*(3), 213–222.

Cobb, E., Kor, A., & Miller, L. (2015). Support for adolescent spirituality: Contributions of religious practice and trait mindfulness. *Journal of Religion and Health, 54*, 862–870.

Cohen, A. A., McEvoy, C., & Castile, R. C. (2010). Respiratory morbidity and lung function in preterm infants of 32 to 36 weeks' gestational age. *Pediatrics, 126*(1), 115–128.

Cohen, J., & Sandy, S. (2007). The social, emotional and academic education of children: Theories, goals, methods and assessments. In R. Bar-On, J. Maree, & M. Elias (Eds.), *Educating people to be emotionally intelligent* (pp. 63–77). Westport, CT: Praeger.

Cohen, P. (2012). *In our prime: The invention of middle age.* New York: Scribner.

Cohen-Kettenis, P., & Steensma, T. (2016). Gender dysphoria. In J. Norcross, G. VandenBos, D. Feeheim, & N. Pole (Eds.), *APA handbook of clinical psychology: Psychopathology and health* (pp. 395–406). Washington, DC: American Psychological Association.

Coie, J. D., Dodge, K. A., & Coppotelli, H. (1982). Dimensions and types of social status: A cross age perspective. *Developmental Psychology, 18*, 557–570.

Cole, J., & Durham, D. L. (2008). *Figuring the future: Globalization and the temporalities of children and youth.* Santa Fe, NM: School for Advanced Research Press.

Cole, P., Luby, J., & Sullivan, M. (2008). Emotions and the development of childhood depression: Bridging the gap. *Child Development Perspectives, 2*(3), 141–148.

Coleman-Jensen, A., Rabbitt, M., Gregory, C., & Singh, A. (2017). *Household food insecurity in the United States in 2016.* Washington, DC: U.S. Department of Agriculture. Retrieved from www.ers.usda.gov/publications/pub-details/?pubid=84972.

Coles, L. S. (2013). Validated worldwide supercentenarians, living and recently deceased. *Rejuvenation Research, 16*(1), 82–84.

Coles, R. (1987). *The moral life of children.* Boston: Houghton Mifflin.

Coles, R. (1990). *The spiritual life of children.* Boston: Houghton Mifflin.

Coles, R. (1997). *The moral intelligence of children.* New York: Random House.

Coll, C. G., & Szalacha, L. A. (2004). The multiple contexts of middle childhood. *Future of Children, 14*(2), 80–97.

Colle, L., & Del Giudice, M. (2011). Patterns of attachment and emotional competence in middle childhood. *Social Development, 20*(1), 51–72.

Collins, K. S., Clarkson Freeman, P. A., Unick, G. J., Bellin, M. H., Reinicker, P., & Strieder, F. H. (2017). Child attributions mediate relationships between violence exposure and trauma symptomology. *Advances in Social Work, 18*(1), 284–299.

Collins, P. H. (2012). Looking back, moving ahead: Scholarship in service to social justice. *Gender & Society, 26*, 14–22.

Colver, A., & Longwell, S. (2013). New understanding of adolescent brain development: Relevance to transitional healthcare for young people with long term conditions. *Archives of Disease in Childhood, 98*, 902–907.

Combs-Orme, T. (2013). Epigenetics and the social work imperative. *Social Work, 58*(1), 23–30.

Combs-Orme, T., & Renkert, L. (2009). Fathers and their infants: Caregiving and affection in the modern family. *Journal of Human Behavior in the Social Environment, 19*(4), 394–418.

Compassion & Choices. (2017). *About Compassions & Choices.* Retrieved from www.compassionandchoices.org/who-we-are/.

Condon, J. (2006). What about dad? Psychosocial and mental health issues for new fathers. *Australian Family Physician, 35*(9), 690–692.

Conger, R., & Conger, K. (2008). Understanding the processes through which economic hardship influences families and children. In D. Crane & T. Heaton (Eds.), *Handbook of families & poverty* (pp. 64–81). Thousand Oaks, CA: Sage.

Connor, M. E., & White, J. L. (2006). *Black fathers: An invisible presence in America.* Mahwah, NJ: Lawrence Erlbaum.

Constable, R. T. (2006). *School social work: Practice, policy, and research.* Chicago: Lyceum Books.

Conwell, Y., Van Orden, K., & Caine, E. D. (2011). Suicide in older adults. *The Psychiatric Clinics of North America, 34*(2), 451–468.

Cook, R., Bird, G., Catmur, C., Press, C., & Heyes, C. (2014). Mirror neurons: From origin to function. *The Behavioral and Brain Sciences*, *37*(2), 177–192.

Cook, S. H., Bauermeister, J. A., Gordon-Messer, D., & Zimmerman, M. A. (2013). Online network influences on emerging adults' alcohol and drug use. *Journal of Youth and Adolescence*, *42*, 1674–1686.

Cooley, J. L., & Fite, P. J. (2016). Peer victimization and forms of aggression during middle childhood: The role of emotion regulation. *Journal of Abnormal Child Psychology*, *44*(3), 535–546.

Cooper, S., Bandelow, S., & Nevill, M. (2011). Breakfast consumption and cognitive function in adolescent school children. *Physiology and Behavior*, *103*(5), 431–439.

Copen, C. (2012). *Prevalence of timing of oral sex with opposite-sex partners among females and males aged 15-24 years: United States, 2007–2010*. Hyattsville, MD: U.S. Department of Health and Human Services.

Copen, C. E., Daniels, K., Vespa, J., & Mosher, W. D. (2012). First marriages in the United States: Data from the 2006–2010 National Survey of Family Growth. *National Health Statistics Reports*, (49), 1–21.

Cornwell, B., Laumann, E. O., & Schumm, L. P. (2008). The social connectedness of older adults: A national profile. *American Sociological Review*, *73*(2), 185–203.

Corsaro, W. (2018). *The sociology of childhood* (5th ed.). Thousand Oaks, CA: Sage.

Costa, P., Terracciano, A., & McCrae, R. (2001). Gender differences in personality traits across cultures: Robust and surprising findings. *Journal of Personality and Social Psychology*, *81*(2), 322.

Costigan, C., Su, T., & Hua, J. (2009). Ethnic identity among Chinese Canadian youth: A review of the Canadian literature. *Canadian Psychology*, *50*(4), 261–272.

Council on Social Work Education. (2015). *Educational policy and accreditation standards*. Alexandria, VA: Author.

Courage, M., & Howe, M. (2010). To watch or not to watch: Infants and toddlers in a brave new electronic world. *Developmental Review*, *30*, 101–115.

Courage, M., & Setliff, A. (2009). Debating the impact of television and video material on very young children: Attention, learning, and the developing brain. *Child Development Perspectives*, *3*(1), 72–78.

Cowan, P. A. (1991). Individual and family life transitions: A proposal for a new definition. In P. A. Cowan & M. Hetherington (Eds.), *Family transitions* (pp. 3–30). Hillsdale, NJ: Lawrence Erlbaum.

Cox, G. R. (2009). Death, dying, and end of life in American-Indian communities. In D. J. Doka & A. S. Tucci (Eds.), *Living with grief: Diversity and end-of-life care* (pp. 107–115). Washington, DC: Hospice Foundation of America.

Cox, R., Shreffler, K., Merten, M., Schwerdtfeger Gallus, K., & Dowdy, J. (2015). Parenting, peers, and perceived norms: What predicts attitudes toward sex among early adolescents? *Journal of Early Adolescence*, *35*(1), 30–53.

Cozolino, L. (2014). *The neuroscience of human relationships* (2nd ed.). New York: W. W. Norton.

Craike, M., Young, J., Symons, C., Pain, M., Harvey, T., Eime, R., & Payne, W. R. (2016). Trends in body image of adolescent females in metropolitan and non-metropolitan regions: A longitudinal study. *BMC Public Health*, *16*(1), 1143. doi:10:1186/s2889-016-3815-1

Crain, R. (1996). The influences of age, race, and gender on child and adolescent multidimensional self-concept. In B. Bracken (Ed.), *Handbook of self-concept* (pp. 395–420). New York: Wiley.

Crawley, L., Payne, R., Bolden, J., Payne, T., Washington, P., & Williams, S. (2000). Palliative and end-of-life care in the African American community. *Journal of the American Medical Association*, *284*(19), 2518–2521.

Creanga, A. A., Shapiro-Mendoza, C. K., Bish, C. L., Zane, S., Berg, C. J., & Callaghan, W. M. (2011). Trends in ectopic pregnancy mortality in the United States 1980–2007. *Obstetrics and Gynecology*, *117*(4), 837–843.

Croghan, C., Moone, R., & Olson, A. (2014). Friends, family, and caregiving among midlife and older lesbian, gay, bisexual, and transgender adults. *Journal of Homosexuality*, *61*(1), 79–102.

Cromley, T., Neumark-Sztainer, D., Story, M., & Boutelle, K. (2010). Parent and family associations with weight-related behaviors and cognitions among overweight adolescents. *Journal of Adolescent Health*, *47*(3), 263–269.

Crystal, S., Shea, D., & Reyes, A. (2016). Cumulative advantage, cumulative disadvantage, and evolving patterns of late-life inequality. *The Gerontologist*, *57*(5), 910–920. doi:10.1093/geront/gnw056

Csikai, E. L., & Jones, B. (2007). *Teaching resources for end of life and palliative care courses*. Chicago: Lyceum Books.

Culp, R., McDonald Culp, A., Dengler, B., & Maisano, P. (1999). First-time young mothers living in rural communities use of corporal punishment with their toddlers. *Journal of Community Psychology*, *27*(4), 503–509.

Cumming, E., & Henry, W. (1961). *Growing old*. New York: Basic Books.

Curry, S. R., & Petering, R. (2017). Resident perspectives on life in a transitional living program for homeless young adults. *Child & Adolescent Social Work Journal, 34*, 507–515.

Cutrona, C., Russell, D., Burzette, R., Wesner, K., & Bryant, C. (2011). Predicting relationship stability among midlife African American couples. *Journal of Consulting and Clinical Psychology, 79*(6), 814–825.

Cutuli, J. J., Desjardins, C. D., Herbers, J. E., Long, J. D., Heistad, D., Chan, C. K., . . . Masten, A. S. (2013). Academic achievement trajectories of homeless and highly mobile students: Resilience in the context of chronic and acute risk. *Child Development, 84*(3), 841–857.

Dahlberg, G., Moss, P., & Pence, A. (2007). *Beyond quality in early childhood education and care: Postmodern perspectives* (2nd ed.). New York: Routledge Falmer.

Dalby, P. (2006). Is there a process of spiritual change or development associated with ageing? A critical review of research. *Aging and Mental Health, 10*(1), 4–12.

Daniels, K., Daugherty, J., & Jones, J. (2014). Current contraceptive status among women aged 15-44: United States, 2011-2013. *NCHS Data Brief, 173*. Retrieved from www.cdc.gov/nchs/data/databriefs/db173.pdf.

Daniels, S. R., & Hassink, S. G. (2015). The role of the pediatrician in primary prevention of obesity. *Pediatrics, 136*(1), 275–294.

Danks, M., Cherry, K., Burns, Y., & Gray, P. (2017). Are behavior problems in extremely low-birthweight children related to their motor ability? *Acta Paediatrica, 106*, 568–572.

Dannefer, D. (2003a). Whose life course is it, anyway? Diversity and "linked lives" in global perspective. In R. Settersten Jr. (Ed.), *Invitation to the life course: Toward new understandings of later life* (pp. 259–268). Amityville, NY: Baywood.

Dannefer, D. (2003b). Toward a global geography of the life course: Challenges of late modernity for life course theory. In J. Mortimer & M. Shanahan (Eds.), *Handbook of the life course* (pp. 647–659). New York: Kluwer Academic/Plenum.

Dannefer, D., & Perlmutter, M. (1990). Development as a multidimensional process: Individuals and social constituents. *Human Development, 33*, 108–137.

Danziger, S., & Ratner, D. (2010). Labor market outcomes and the transition to adulthood. *The Future of Children, 20*(1), 133–158.

Darchia, N., & Cervena, K. (2014). The journey through the world of adolescent sleep. *Reviews in the Neuroscience, 25*(4), 585–604.

Darling-Hammond, L. (2010). *The flat world and education: How America's commitment to equity will determine our future.* New York: Teachers College Press.

Daugherty, J., & Copen, C. (2016). Trends in attitudes about marriage, childbearing, and sexual behavior: United States, 2002, 2006–2010, and 2011–2013. *Division of Vital Statistics National Health Statistics Reports, 92*, 1–10. Retrieved from www.cdc.gov/nchs/data/nhsr/nhsr092.pdf.

Davidson, J., Moore, N., & Ullstrup, L. (2004). Religiosity and sexual responsibilities: Relationships of choice. *Journal of Health Behavior, 28*(4), 335–346.

Davidson, R. J., & Begley, S. (2012). *The emotional life of your brain: How its unique patterns affect the way you think, feel, and live—and how you can change them.* New York: Penguin Books.

Davies, D. (2011). *Child development: A practitioner's guide* (3rd ed.). New York: Guilford Press.

Davis, J., & Bauman, K. (2013). *School enrollment in the United States: 2011.* Washington, DC: U.S. Census Bureau. Retrieved from www.census.gov/prod/2013pubs/p20-571.pdf.

Davis, M., & Vander Stoep, A. (1997). The transition to adulthood for youth who have serious emotional disturbance: Developmental transition and young adult outcomes. *Journal of Mental Health Administration, 24*(4), 400–427.

Day, J., Vornovitsky, M., & Taylor, D. (2016). *Another look at health insurance coverage rates for young adults.* Washington, DC: U.S. Census Bureau. Retrieved from www.census.gov/newsroom/blogs/random-samplings/2016/09/another-look-at-health-insurance-coverage-rates-for-young-adults.html.

Dean, D., O'Muircheartaigh, J., Dirks, H., Waskiewicz, N., Walker, L., Doernberg, E., . . . Deoni, S. C. (2014). Characterizing longitudinal white matter development during early childhood. *Brain Structure & Function, 220*(4), 1921–1933.

Dean, R. G. (1993). Teaching a constructivist approach to clinical practice. In J. Laird (Ed.), *Revisioning social work education: A social constructionist approach* (pp. 55–75). New York: Haworth Press.

Deardorf, M. (2016). *Pregnancy discrimination and the American worker.* New York: Palgrave Macmillan.

Death Café. (2017). *What is Death Café?* Retrieved from http://deathcafe.com/what/.

DeBellis, M. D., & Zisk, A. (2014). The biological effects of childhood trauma. *Child and Adolescent Psychiatry Clinical North America, 23*(2), 185–222.

De Brucker, M., Halentjens, P., Evensepoel, J., Devroey, P., Collins, J., & Tournaye, H. (2009). Cumulative delivery rates in different age groups after artificial insemination with donor sperm. *Human Reproduction, 24*(8), 1891–1899.

Declercq, E. (2012). Trends in midwife attended births in the United States, 1989–2009. *Journal of Midwifery and Women's Health, 57*(4), 321–326.

Declercq, E., Sakala, C., Corry, M., Applebaum, S., & Herrlich, A. (2014). Major survey findings of listening to mothers (SM) III: Pregnancy and birth: Report of the Third National U.S. Survey of Women's Childbearing Experiences. *Journal of Perinatal Education, 23*(1), 9–16.

Deeg, D. (2005). The development of physical and mental health from late midlife to early old age. In S. Willis & M. Martin (Eds.), *Middle adulthood: A lifespan perspective* (pp. 209–241). Thousand Oaks, CA: Sage.

DeFranco, E., Chen, A., Zu, F., Hall, E., Hossain, M., Haynes, E., . . . Muglia, L. (2014). Air pollution and risk of prematurity: Exposure to airborn particulate matter during pregnancy is associated with preterm birth risk. *American Journal of Obstetrics and Gynecology, 201*(1 Suppl.), S346.

Degges-White, S. (2005). Understanding gerotranscendence in older adults: A new perspective for counselors. *Adultspan Journal, 4*(1), 36–48.

Degner, J., & Wentura, D. (2010). Automatic prejudice in childhood and early adolescence. *Journal of Personality and Social Psychology, 98*(3), 356–374.

Delany, S., & Delany, E., with Hearth, A. (1993). *Having our say: The Delany sisters' first 100 years*. New York: Kodansha International.

Delany, S., & Hearth, A. (1997). *On my own at 107: Reflections on life without Bessie*. New York: HarperCollins.

Delaunay-El Allam, M., Marlier, L., & Schaal, B. (2006). Learning at the breast: Preference formation for the artificial scent and its attraction against the odor of maternal milk. *Infant Behavior and Development, 29*(3), 308–321.

DelGiudice M. (2018). Middle childhood: An evolutionary-developmental synthesis. In N. Halfon, C. Forrest, R. Lerner, & E. Faustman (Eds.), *Handbook of life course health development* (pp. 95–108). New York: Springer.

Della Porta, D., & Diani, M. (2006). *Social movements: An introduction* (2nd ed.). Malden, MA: Blackwell.

Dellmann-Jenkins, M., & Blankemeyer, M. (2009). Emerging and young adulthood and caregiving. In K. Shifren (Ed.), *How caregiving affects development: Psychological implications for child, adolescent, and adult caregivers* (pp. 93–117). Washington, DC: American Psychological Association.

DeLorenzo, J. P. (2015). *School districts' responsibilities to provide students with disabilities with specially designed instruction and related services in the least restrictive environment*. Retrieved from www.p12.nysed.gov/specialed/publications/2015-memos/least-restrictive-environment-distric-responsibilities.html.

De Marco, A. C., & Cosner Berzin, S. (2008). The influence of family economic status on home-leaving patterns during emerging adulthood. *Families in Society, 89*(2), 208–218.

Demiray, B., & Bluck, S. (2014). Time since birth and time left to live: Opposing forces in constructing psychological wellbeing. *Ageing Society, 34*(7), 1193–1218.

Demo, D., & Fine, M. (2010). *Beyond the average divorce*. Thousand Oaks, CA: Sage.

Deng, J., Lian, Y., Shen, C., Zhang, M., Wang, Y., & Zhou, H. (2012). Adverse life event and risk of cognitive impairment: A 5-year prospective longitudinal study in Chongquing, China. *European Journal of Neurology, 19*(4), 631–637.

Dennis, C., & Chung-Lee, L. (2006). Postpartum depression help-seeking barriers and maternal treatment preferences: A qualitative systematic review. *Birth, 33*(4), 323–331.

Dennison, B., Edmunds, J., & Stratton, H. (2006). Rapid infant weight gain predicts childhood overweight. *Obesity, 14*(3), 491–499.

Denton, M. L., Pearce, L. D., & Smith, C. (2008). *Religion and spirituality on the path through adolescence* (Research report No. 8). National Study of Youth and Religion, University of North Carolina at Chapel Hill. Retrieved from https://youthandreligion.nd.edu/assets/102568/religion_and_spirituality_on_the_path_through_adolescence.pdf.

Derauf, C., LaGasse, L., Smith, L., Newman, E., Shah, R., Arria, A., . . . Lester, B. (2011). Infant temperament and high-risk environment relate to behavior problems and language in toddlers. *Journal of Developmental & Behavioral Pediatrics, 32*(2), 125–135.

DePaolis, K., & Williford, A. (2015). The nature and prevalence of cyber victimization among elementary school children. *Child & Youth Care Forum, 44*(3), 377–393.

Derezotes, D., Testa, M., & Poertner, J. (2005). *Race matters in child welfare: The overrepresentation of African American children in the system*. Washington, DC: CWLA Press.

De Schipper, J., Tavecchio, L., & Van IJzendoorn, M. (2008). Children's attachment relationship with day care caregivers: Associations with positive caregiving and the child's temperament. *Social Development, 17*(3), 454–470.

DeSilver, D. (2016). *In the U.S. and abroad, more young adults are living with their parents*. Washington, DC: Pew

Research Center. Retrieved from www.pewresearch.org/fact-tank/2016/05/24/in-the-u-s-and-abroad-more-young-adults-are-living-with-their-parents/.

DeSpelder, L. A., & Strickland, A. L. (2015). *The last dance: Encountering death and dying* (10th ed.). Boston: McGraw-Hill.

de St. Aubin, E., McAdams, D., & Kim, T. (2004). *The generative society: Caring for future generations*. Washington, DC: American Psychological Association.

DeVries, C., & De Vries, R. (2007). Childbirth education in the 21st century: An immodest proposal. *Journal of Perinatal Education, 16*(4), 38–48.

Dewey, D., Creighton, D., Heath, J. A., Wilson, B. N., Anseeuw-Deks, D., Crawford, S. G., & Sauve, R. (2011). Assessment of developmental coordination in children born with extremely low birth weights. *Developmental Neuropsychology, 36*(1), 42–56.

Diamond, L. M., & Savin-Williams, R. C. (2003). Gender and sexual identity. In R. M. Lerner, F. Jacobs, & D. Wertlieb (Eds.), *Handbook of applied developmental science* (Vol. 1, pp. 101–121). Thousand Oaks, CA: Sage.

Diaz-Hurtado, J. (2017, July 21). The largest U.S. Latino advocacy group changes its name, sparking debate. *NPR*. Retrieved from www.npr.org/sections/codeswitch/2017/07/21/538381366/the-largest-latino-advocacy-group-changes-their-name-sparking-debate.

Dick-Read, G. (1944). *Childbirth without fear: Principles and practices of natural childbirth*. New York: Harper & Row.

DiFiori, J. P., Benjamin, H. J., Brenner, J. S., Gregory, A., Jayanthi, N., & Landry, G. L., . . . Luke, A. (2014). Overuse injuries and burnout in youth sports: A position statement from the American Society for Sports Medicine. *British Journal of Sports Medicine, 48*(4), 287–288.

Diggs, C. R., & Akos, P. (2016). The promise of character education in middle school: A meta-analysis. *Middle Grades Review, 2*(2), Article 4. Retrieved from http://scholarworks.uvm.edu/mgreview/vol2/iss2/4.

Dignam, B., & Adashi, E. (2014). Health rights in the balance: The case against perinatal shackling of women behind bars. *Health and Human Rights, 16*(2), E13–E23.

Dillon, M., & Wink, P. (2007). *In the course of a lifetime: Tracing religious belief, practice, and change*. Berkeley: University of California Press.

Dilworth-Andersen, P., Brummett, B., Goowdwin, P., Williams, S., Williams, R., & Siegler, I. (2005). Effects of race on cultural justification for caregiving. *Journal of Gerontology: Social Sciences, 60B*(5), S257–S262.

DiNitto, D., & Johnson, D. (2015). *Social welfare: Politics and public policy* (8th ed.). Boston: Allyn & Bacon.

Dioussé, L., Driver, J., & Gaziano, J. (2009). Relation between modifiable lifestyle factors and lifetime risk of heart failure. *Journal of American Medical Association, 302*(4), 394–400.

Direnfeld, D., & Roberts, J. (2006). Mood congruent memory in dysphoria: The roles of state affect and cognitive style. *Behavior Research and Therapy, 44*(9), 1275–1285.

Dittmann-Kohli, F. (2005). Middle age and identity in a cultural and lifespan perspective. In S. Willis & M. Martin (Eds.), *Middle adulthood: A lifespan perspective* (pp. 319–353). Thousand Oaks, CA: Sage.

Djundeva, M. (2015). Linked lives. In J. D. Wright (Ed.), *International encyclopedia of the social & behavioral sciences* (2nd ed., Vol. 14, pp. 230–235). Oxford, UK: Elsevier.

Doka, K. J., & Tucci, A. S. (2009). *Living with grief: Diversity and end-of-life care*. Washington, DC: Hospice Foundation of America.

Domenech Rodriguez, M., Donovick, M., & Crowley, S. (2009). Parenting styles in a cultural context: Observations of "protective parenting" in first-generation Latinos. *Family Process, 48*(2), 195–210.

Donleavy, G. (2008). No man's land: Exploring the space between Gilligan and Kohlberg. *Journal of Business Ethics, 80*(4), 807–822.

Doody, K. J., Boome, E. J., & Doody, K. M. (2016). Comparing blastocyst quality and live birth rates of intravaginal culture using INVOcell to traditional in vitro incubation in a randomized open-label prospective controlled trial. *Journal of Assisted Reproduction and Genetics, 33*(4), 495–500.

Dooley, M., Dineen, T., Sarma, K., & Nolan, A. (2014). The psychological impact on infertility and fertility treatment on the male partner. *Human Fertility, 17*(3), 203–209.

Dorak, F. (2011). Self-esteem and body image of Turkish adolescent girls. *Social Behavior and Personality, 39*(4), 553–562.

Doring, A. K., Daniel, E., & Knafo-Noam, A. (2016). Introduction to the special section value development from middle childhood to early adulthood—New insights from longitudinal and genetically informed research. *Social Development, 25*(3), 471–481.

Doughty, E. A. (2009). Investigating adaptive grieving styles: A Delphi Study. *Death Studies, 33*(5), 462–480.

Dragoman, M. V. (2014). The combined oral contraceptive pill—recent developments, risks, and benefits. *Best Practice and Research Clinical Obstetrics and Gynaecology, 28*(6), 825–834.

Drake, B. (2014). *6 new findings about millennials*. Pew Research Center. Retrieved from www.pewresearch.org/fact-tank/2014/03/07/6-new-findings-about-millennials.

Draut, T., & Silva, J. (2004). *Generation broke: The growth of debt among young Americans. Borrowing to make ends meet series*. Retrieved from www.demos.org/sites/default/files/publications/Generation_Broke.pdf.

Drehmer, M., Duncan, B. B., Kac, G., & Schmidt, A. I. (2013). Association of second and third trimester weight gain in pregnancy with maternal and fetal outcomes [Special section]. *PLoS One, 8*(1), 1–8.

Dreyer, B., Chung, P. J., Szilagyi, P., & Wong, S. (2016). Child poverty in the United States today: Introduction and executive summary. *Academic Pediatrics, 16*(3), S1–S5.

Duarte, A., Ranganath, C., Trujillo, C., & Knight, R. T. (2006). Intact recollection memory in high-performing older-adults: RP and behavioral evidence. *Journal of Cognitive Neuroscience, 18*(1), 33–47.

Dube, N., Khan, K., Loehr, S., Chu, Y., & Veugelers, P. (2017). The use of entertainment and communication technologies before sleep could affect sleep and weight status: A population-based study among children. *The International Journal of Behavioral Nutrition and Physical Activity, 14*(1), 97. doi:10.1186/s12966-017-0547-2

DuBois, D., & Silverthorn, N. (2005). Characteristics of natural mentoring relationships and adolescent adjustment: Evidence from a national study. *Journal of Primary Prevention, 26*(2), 69–92.

Ducanto, J. N. (2010). Divorce and poverty are often synonymous. *American Journal of Family Law, 24*(2), 87–94.

Duch, H., Fisher, E., Ensari, I., & Harrington, A. (2013). Screen time use in children under 3 years old: A systematic review of correlates. *International Journal of Behavioral Nutrition and Physical Activity, 10*, 102. Retrieved from www.ijbnpa.org/content/10/1/102.

Dunbar, H. T., Mueller, C. W., Medina, C., & Wolf, T. (1998). Psychological and spiritual growth in women living with HIV. *Social Work, 43*, 144–154.

Duncan, G., Kalil, A., & Ziol-Guest, K. (2017). Increasing inequality in parent income and children's schooling. *Demography, 54*(5), 1603–1626.

Duncan, G., Magnuson, K., Kalil, A., & Ziol-Guest, K. (2012). The importance of early childhood poverty. *Social Indicators Research, 108*(1), 87–98.

Duncan, G. J., & Murnane, R. J. (2011). *Whither opportunity? Rising inequality, schools, and children's life chances*. New York: Russell Sage Foundation.

Dunne, C., & Roberts, J. (2016). Social egg freezing: A viable option for fertility preservation. *British Columbia Medical Journal, 58*(10), 573–577.

Duong, J., & Bradshaw, C. P. (2017). Links between contexts and middle to late childhood social-emotional development. *American Journal of Community Psychology, 60*(3–4), 538–554.

Dupre, M. (2008). Educational differences in health risks and illness over the life course: A test of cumulative disadvantage theory. *Social Science Research, 37*(4), 1253–1266.

Durkin, K. (1995). *Developmental social psychology*. Malden, MA: Blackwell.

Dyson, A. (2011). Full service and extended schools, disadvantage, and social justice. *Cambridge Journal of Education, 41*(2), 177–193.

Easton, S., Coohey, C., Rhodes, A., & Moorthy, M. (2013). Posttraumatic growth among men with histories of child sexual abuse. *Child Maltreatment, 18*(4), 211–220.

Echols, L., Ivanich, J., & Graham, S. (2017). Multiracial in middle school: The influence of classmates and friends on changes in racial self-identification. *Child Development*. doi:10.1111/cdev.13000

Eckman, J. (2014, March 8). An ethical dilemma: Genetic and reproductive technologies and the human embryo. *Issues in Perspective*. Retrieved from http://graceuniversity.edu/iip/2014/03/14-03-08-1/.

Economist Intelligence Unit. (2012). *Starting well: Benchmarking early education across the world*. Retrieved from http://graphics.eiu.com/upload/eb/Lienstartingwell.pdf.

Edelson, J. (1999). Children's witnessing of adult domestic violence. *Journal of Interpersonal Violence, 14*(8), 839–970.

Edin, K., & Lein, L. (1997). *Making ends meet*. New York: Russell Sage Foundation.

Edin, K., & Nelson, T. J. (2013). *Doing the best I can: Fatherhood in the inner city*. Berkeley: University of California Press.

Edmiston, B. (2010). Playing with children, answering with our lives: A Bakhtinian approach to coauthoring ethical identities in early childhood. *British Journal of Educational Studies, 58*(2), 197–211.

Edwards, C. (1992). Normal development in the preschool years. In E. V. Nuttall, I. Romero, & J. Kalesnik (Eds.), *Assessing and screening preschoolers* (pp. 9–22). Boston: Allyn & Bacon.

Edwards, E., Eiden, R., & Leonard, K. (2006). Behavior problems in 18–36-month-old children of alcoholic fathers: Secure mother-father attachment as a protective factor. *Developmental and Psychopathology, 18*(2), 395–407.

Edwards, T., Patrick, D., Skalicky, A., Huang, Y., & Hobby, A. (2012). Perceived body shape, standardized body-mass index, and weight-specific quality of life of African-American, Caucasian, and Mexican-American adolescents. *Quality of Life Research, 21*(6), 1101–1107.

Egley, A., Jr., & Howell, J. C. (2013, September). *Highlights of the 2011 National Youth Gang Survey.* Washington, DC: U.S. Department of Justice, Office of Justice Programs, Office of Juvenile Justice and Delinquency Prevention. Retrieved from www.ojjdp.gov/pubs/242884.pdf.

Ehlman, K., & Ligon, M. (2012). The application of a generativity model for older adults. *International Journal of Aging and Human Development, 74*(4), 331–344.

Eidelman, A., & Schanler, R. (2012). Breastfeeding and the use of human milk. *Pediatrics, 129*(5), 827–841.

Eisenberg, N. (2000). Emotion, regulation, and moral development. *Annual Review of Psychology, 51,* 665–697.

Eisenberg, N., Guthrie, I., Murphy, B., Shepard, S., Cumberland, A., & Carlo, G. (1999). Consistency and development of prosocial dispositions: A longitudinal study. *Child Development, 70*(6), 1360–1372.

Eisenhauer, E., Uddin, D., Albert, P., Paton, S., & Stoughton, R. (2011). Establishment of a low birth weight registry and initial outcomes. *Maternal and Child Health Journal, 15*(7), 921–930.

Ekamper, P., van Poppel, F., Stein, A. D., Bijwaard, G. E., & Lumey, L. H. (2015). Prenatal famine exposure and adult mortality from cancer, cardiovascular disease and other causes through age 63 years. *American Journal of Epidemiology, 181*(4), 271–279.

Eke, A. C., Saccone, G., & Berghella, V. (2016). Selective serotonin reuptake inhibitor (SSRI) use during pregnancy and the risk of preterm birth: A systematic review and meta-analysis. *BJOG: An International Journal of Obstetrics & Gynaecology, 123*(12), 1900–1907.

Elder, G., Jr. (1974). *Children of the Great Depression.* Chicago: University of Chicago Press.

Elder, G., Jr. (1994). Time, human agency, and social change: Perspectives on the life course. *Social Psychology Quarterly, 57*(1), 4–15.

Elder, G., Jr. (1998). The life course as developmental theory. *Child Development, 69*(1), 1–12.

Eli, K., Howell, K., Fisher, P., & Nowicka, P. (2016). A question of balance: Explaining differences between parental and grandparental perspectives on preschoolers' feeding and physical activity. *Social Science & Medicine, 154,* 28–35.

Eliopoulus, C. (2010). *Gerontological nursing* (7th ed.). Philadelphia: Lippincott, Williams & Wilkins.

Elliott, M. (1996). Impact of work, family, and welfare receipt on women's self-esteem in young adulthood. *Social Psychology Quarterly, 59*(1), 80–95.

Ellis, R. R., & Simmons, T. (2014). Coresident grandparents and their grandchildren: 2012. Current Population Reports (pp. 20–576). Washington, DC: U.S. Census Bureau.

Ellis, S. A., Wojnar D. M., & Pettinato M. (2014). Conception, pregnancy, and birth experiences of male and gender variant gestational parents: It's how we could have a family. *Journal of Midwifery and Women's Health, 60*(1), 62–69.

Ellison, C. G. (1992). Are religious people nice? Evidence from a national survey of Black Americans. *Social Forces, 71*(2), 411–430.

Ellison, C. G. (1993). Religious involvement and self-perception among Black Americans. *Social Forces, 71*(4), 1027–1055.

Emmett, T., & Alant, E. (2006). Women and disability: Exploring the interface of multiple disadvantage. *Development of Southern Africa, 23*(4), 455–460.

Engel, S. (2005). *Real kids: Creating meaning in everyday life.* Cambridge, MA: Harvard University Press.

Englander, E. K. (2013). *Bullying and cyberbullying: What every educator needs to know.* Cambridge, MA: Harvard University Press.

Enke, C., Hausmann, A. O., Miedaner, F., Roth, B., & Woopen, C. (2017). Communicating with parents in the neonatal intensive care units: The impact on parental stress. *Patient Education and Counseling, 100*(4), 710–719.

Epstein, S. (1973). The self-concept revisited: Or, a theory of a theory. *American Psychologist, 28,* 404–416.

Epstein, S. (1991). Cognitive-experiential self-theory: An integrative theory of personality. In R. Cutis (Ed.), *The self with others: Convergences in psychoanalytic, social, and personality psychology* (pp. 111–137). New York: Guilford Press.

Epstein, S. (1998). Cognitive-experiential self-theory. In D. Barone & M. Hersen (Eds.), *Advanced personality* (pp. 211–238). New York: Plenum Press.

The Equal Rights Center. (2014). *Opening doors: An investigation of barriers to senior housing for same-sex couples.* Washington, DC: Author.

Erickson, K., Gildengers, A., & Butters, M. (2013). Physical activity and brain plasticity in late adulthood. *Dialogues in Clinical Neuroscience, 15*(1), 99–108.

Erikson, E. H. (1950). *Childhood and society.* New York: Norton.

Erikson, E. H. (1959). The problem of ego identity. *Psychological Issues, 1,* 101–164.

Erikson, E. H. (1963). *Childhood and society* (2nd ed.). New York: Norton.

Erikson, E. H. (1968). *Identity: Youth and crisis*. New York: Norton.

Erikson, E. H. (Ed.). (1978). *Adulthood*. New York: Norton.

Erikson, E. H. (1982). *The life cycle completed*. New York: Norton.

Erikson, E. H., & Erikson, J. M. (1997). *The life cycle completed: Extended version with new chapters on the ninth stage of development*. New York: W. W. Norton.

Ernest, J. M., Causey, C., Newton, A. B., Sharkins, K., Summerlin, J., & Albaiz, N. (2014). Extending the global dialogue about media, technology, screen time, and young children. *Childhood Education, 90*(3), 182–191.

Ernst, A., Alkass, K., Bernard, S., Salehpour, M., Perl, S., Tisdale, J., . . . Frisén, J. (2014). Neurogenesis in the striatum of the adult human brain. *Cell, 156*(5), 1072–1083.

Eskelinen, M., Ngandu, T., Tuomilehto, J., Soininen, H., & Kivipelto, M. (2009). Midlife coffee and tea drinking and the risk of late-life dementia: A population-based CAIDE study. *Journal of Alzheimer's Disease, 16*(1), 85–91.

Espelage, D. L., & Swearer, S. M. (2011). *Bullying in North American schools*. New York: Routledge.

Esposito-Smythers, C., Kahler, C., Spirito, A., Hunt, J., & Monti, P. (2011). Treatment of co-occuring substance abuse and suicidality among adolescents: A randomized trial. *Journal of Consulting and Clinical Psychology, 79*(6), 728–739.

Etengoff, C., & Daiute, C. (2013). Sunni-Muslim American religious development during emerging adulthood. *Journal of Adolescent Research, 28*(6), 690–714.

Eurostat. (2015). *Marriages and births in Sweden*. Retrieved from http://ec.europa.eu/eurostat/statistics-explained/index.php/Marriages_and_births_in_Sweden.

Evans, B., Crogan, N., Belyea, M., & Coon, D. (2009). Utility of the life course perspective in research with Mexican American caregivers of older adults. *Journal of Transcultural Nursing, 20*(1), 5–14.

Exner-Cortens, D., Eckenrode, J., & Rothman, E. (2013). Longitudinal associations between teen dating violence victimization and adverse health outcomes. *Pediatrics, 131*(1), 71–78.

Ezkurdia, I., Juan, D., Rodriguez, J., Frankish, A., Diekhans, M., Harrow, J., . . . Tress, M. L. (2014). Multiple evidence strands suggest that there may be as few as 19,000 human protein-coding genes. *Human Molecular Genetics, 23*(22), 5866–5878.

Fabelo, T., Thompson, M. D., Plotkin, M., Carmichael, D., Marchbanks, M. P., & Booth, E. A. (2011). *Breaking schools' rules: A statewide study of how school discipline relates to students' success and juvenile justice involvement*. New York: Council of State Governments Justice Center. Retrieved from https://csgjusticecenter.org/wp-content/uploads/2012/08/Breaking_Schools_Rules_Report_Final.pdf.

Falicov, C. (2016). Migration and the life cycle. In M. McGoldrick, N. Garcia Preto, & B. Carter (Eds.), *The expanding family life cycle: Individual, family, and social perspectives* (5th ed., pp. 222–239). Boston: Pearson.

Falk, G. (2017). *Temporary Assistance for Needy Families (TANF): The work participation standard and engagement in welfare-to-work activities*. Retrieved from www.everycrsreport.com/reports/R44751.html.

Fan, F., Zou, Y., Ma, A., Yue, Y., Mao, W., & Ma, X. (2009). Hormonal changes and somatopsychologic manifestations in the first trimester of pregnancy and post partum. *International Journal of Gynecology and Obstetrics, 105*(1), 46–49.

Fan, S., Liberman, Z., Keysar, B., & Kinzler, K. D. (2015). The exposure advantage: Early exposure to a multilingual environment promotes effective communication. *Psychological Science, 26*(7), 1090–1097.

Fan, W., Williams, C. M., & Wolters, C. A. (2012). Parental involvement in predicting school motivation: Similar and differential effects across ethnic groups. *Journal of Educational Research, 105*(1), 21–35.

Fang, S., Huang, N., Chen, K., Yeh, H., Lin, K., & Chen, C. (2012). Gender differences in widowhood effects among community-dwelling elders by causes of death in Taiwan. *Annals of Epidemiology, 22*(7), 457–465.

Farmer, R. (2009). *Neuroscience and social work practice: The missing link*. Thousand Oaks, CA: Sage.

Farrell, A., Mehari, K., Kramer-Kuhn, A., & Goncy, E. (2014). The impact of victimization and witnessing violence on physical aggression among high-risk adolescents. *Child Development, 85*(4), 1694–1710.

Farroni, T., Menon, E., Rigato, S., & Johnson, M. H. (2007). The perception of facial expressions in newborns. *European Journal of Developmental Psychology, 4*(1), 2–13.

Farver, J., Xu, Y., Eppe, S., Fernandez, A., & Schwartz, D. (2005). Community violence, family conflict and preschoolers' socioemotional functioning. *Developmental Psychology, 41*(1), 160–170.

Fass, P., & Mason, M. (Eds.). (2000). *Childhood in America*. New York: New York University Press.

Fawley-King, K., & Merz, E. (2014). Effects of child maltreatment on brain development. In H. Matto, J. Strolin-Goltzman, & M. Ballan (Eds.), *Neuroscience for social work: Current research and practice* (pp. 111–139). New York: Springer.

Fawzy, M., Saravelos, S., Li, T., & Metwally, M. (2016). Do women with recurrent miscarriage constitute a high-risk obstetric population? *Human Fertility, 19*(1), 9–15.

Fayed, L. (2018, March 21). Uterine transplants: Hope for women with uterine factor infertility UFI). *Very Well Family*. Retrieved from www.verywellfamily.com/uterine-transplants-513976.

Fay-Stammbach, T., Hawes, D., & Meredith, P. (2014). Parenting influences on executive function in early childhood: A review. *Child Development Perspectives, 8*(4), 258–264.

Federal Interagency Forum on Aging-Related Statistics. (2016). *Older Americans 2016: Key indicators of well-being*. Washington, DC: U.S. Government Printing Office. Retrieved from https://agingstats.gov/docs/LatestReport/Older-Americans-2016-Key-Indicators-of-WellBeing.pdf.

Federal Interagency Forum on Child and Family Statistics. (2017). *America's children: Key national indicators of well-being*. Retrieved from www.childstats.gov/pdf/ac2017/ac_17.pdf.

Feeney, J., Dooley, C., Finucane, C., & Kenny, R. (2015). Stressful life events and orthostatic blood pressure recovery in older adults. *Health Psychology, 34*(7), 765–774.

Feldman, R. (2003). Infant-mother and infant-father synchrony: The coregulation of positive arousal. *Infant Mental Health Journal, 24*(1), 1–23.

Feldman, R. (2004). Mother infant skin-to-skin contact and the development of emotion regulation. In S. Shohov (Ed.), *Advances in psychology research* (Vol. 27, pp. 113–131). Hauppauge, NY: Nova Science.

Feldman, R., & Masalha, S. (2007). The role of culture in moderating the links between early ecological risk and young children's adaptation. *Development & Psychopathology, 19*(1), 1–21.

Felitti, V., Anda, R., Nordenburg, D., Williamson, D., Spitz, A., Edwards, V., . . . Marks, J. S. (1998). Relationship of childhood abuse and household dysfunction to many of the leading causes of death in adults: The Adverse Childhood Experiences (ACE) Study. *American Journal of Preventive Medicine, 14*(4), 245–258.

Felt, L. J., & Robb, M. B. (2016, May). *Technology addiction: Concern, controversy, and finding balance*. San Francisco: Common Sense Media.

Ferguson, R., & Lamback, S. (2014, June). *Creating pathways to prosperity: A blueprint for action*. Report issued by the Pathways to Prosperity Project at the Harvard Graduate School of Education and the Achievement Gap Initiative at Harvard University. Retrieved from www.agi.harvard.edu/pathways/CreatingPathwaystoProsperityReport2014.pdf.

Fergusson, D. M., Horwood, L. J., & Boden, J. (2009). Reactions to abortion and subsequent mental health. *The British Journal of Psychiatry, 195*, 420–426.

Fergusson, D. M., Horwood, L. J., & Woodward, L. J. (2001). Unemployment and psychosocial adjustment in young adults: Causation or selection? *Social Science & Medicine, 53*(3), 305.

Ferraro, K., & Shippee, T. (2009). Aging and cumulative inequality: How does inequality get under the skin? *The Gerontologist, 49*(3), 333–343.

Fifield, J. (2017). *Why child abuse in military families may be going unreported*. Pew Charitable Trusts. Retrieved from www.pewtrusts.org/en/research-and-analysis/blogs/stateline/2017/06/07/why-child-abuse-in-military-families-may-be-going-unreported.

Figueiredo, B., & Conde, A. (2011). Anxiety and depression in women and men from early pregnancy to 3-months postpartum. *Archives of Women's Mental Health, 14*(3), 247–255.

Figueiredo, B., Pacheco, A., Costa, R., Conde, A., & Teixeira, C. (2010). Mother's anxiety and depression during the third pregnancy trimester and neonate's mother versus stranger's face/voice visual preference. *Early Human Development, 86*(8), 479–485.

Fildes, A., Llewellyn, C., Van Jaarsveld, C., Fisher, M., Cooke, L., & Wardle, J. (2016). Common genetic architecture underlying food fussiness in children, and preference for fruits and vegetables. *The American Journal of Clinical Nutrition, 103*(4), 1099–1104.

Findlay, L., Girardi, A., & Coplan, R. (2006). Links between empathy, social behavior, and social understanding in early childhood. *Early Childhood Research Quarterly, 21*(3), 347–359.

Fine, M., Ganong, L., & Demo, D. (2010). Divorce: A risk and resilience perspective. In S. Price, C. Price, & P. McKenry (Eds.), *Families & change: Coping with stressful events and transitions* (4th ed., pp. 211–233). Thousand Oaks, CA: Sage.

Finer, L., & Zolna, M. (2016). Declines in unintended pregnancy in the United States, 2008–2011. *New England Journal of Medicine, 374*, 843–852.

Fingerman, K., Cheng, Y. P., Birditt, K., & Zarit, S. (2012). Only as happy as the least happy child: Multiple grown children's problems and successes and middle-aged parents' well-being. *The Journals of Gerontology, Series B: Psychological Sciences and Social Sciences, 67*(2), 184–193.

Fingerman, K., Cheng, Y. P., Wesselmann, E., Zarit, S., Furstenberg, F., & Birditt, K. (2013). Helicopter parents and landing pad kids: Intense parental support of grown children. *Journal of Marriage and Family, 74*, 880–896.

Fingerman, K., Pillemer, K., Silverstein, M., & Suitor, J. (2012). The baby boomers' intergenerational relationships. *The Gerontologist, 52*(2), 199–209.

Fingerman, K., VanderDrift, L., Dotterer, A., Birditt, D., & Zarit, S. (2011). Support to aging parents and grown children in Black and White families. *The Gerontologist, 51*(4), 441–452.

Finkelhor, D., Turner, H., Hamby, S., & Ormrod, R. (2011, October). Polyvictimization: Children's exposure to multiple types of violence, crime and abuse. *Juvenile Justice Bulletin*. Washington, DC: U.S. Department of Justice.

Finn, J. (2009). Making trouble. In L. Nybell, J. Shook, & J. Finn (Eds.), *Childhood, youth, & social work in transformation: Implications for policy & practice* (pp. 37–66). New York: Columbia University Press.

Fiori, J. L., Consedine, N. S., & Magai, C. (2008). Ethnic differences in patterns of social exchange among older adults: The role of resource context. *Ageing & Society, 28*(4), 495–524.

Fischer, J., Zvonkovic, A., Juergens, C., Engler, R., & Frederick, H. (2015). Work, family, and well-being at midlife: A person-centered approach. *Journal of Family Issue, 36*(1), 56–86.

Fisher, C., Hauck, Y., Bayes, S., & Byme, J. (2012). Participants experience of mindfulness-based childbirth education: A qualitative study. *British Medical Journal, 12*(1), 126–135.

Fisher, H. (2004). *Why we love: The nature and chemistry of romantic love*. New York: Holt.

Fitchett, G., Murphy, P., Kravitz, H., Everson-Rose, S., Krause, N., & Powell, L. (2007). Racial/ethnic differences in religious involvement in a multi-ethnic cohort of midlife women. *Journal for the Scientific Study of Religion, 46*(1), 119–132.

Fitzpatrick, S., & Bussey, K. (2014). The role of perceived friendship self-efficacy as a protective factor against the negative effects of social victimization. *Social Development, 23*(1), 41–60.

Flanagan, C. (2004). Institutional support for morality: Community-based and neighborhood organizations. In T. A. Thorkildsen & H. Walberg (Eds.), *Nurturing morality* (pp. 173–183). New York: Kluwer Academic/Plenum.

Flatt, M., Settersten, R., Ponsaran, R., & Fishman, J. (2013). Are "anti-aging medicine" and "successful aging" two sides of the same coin? Views of anti-aging practitioners. *The Journals of Gerontology, Series B: Psychological Sciences and Social Sciences, 68*(6), 944–955.

Floccia, C., Christophe, A., & Bertononcini, J. (1997). High-amplitude sucking and newborns: The quest for underlying mechanisms. *Journal of Experimental Child Psychology, 64*, 175–198.

Flores, A., Herman, J., Gates, G., & Brown, T. (2016). *How many adults identify as transgender in the United States?* Los Angeles: The Williams Institute. Retrieved from http://williamsinstitute.law.ucla.edu/wp-content/uploads/How-Many-Adults-Identify-as-Transgender-in-the-United-States.pdf.

Flores, P., & Porges, S. (2017). Group psychotherapy as a neural exercise: Bridging polyvagal theory and attachment theory. *Psychotherapy, 67*(2), 202–222.

Fogarty, R. (2009). *Brain compatible classrooms* (3rd ed.). Thousand Oaks, CA: Corwin.

Fogtmann, M., Seshamani, S., Kroenke, C., Xi, C., Chapman, T., Wilm, J., . . . Studholme, C. (2014). A unified approach to diffusion direction sensitive slice registration and 3-D DTI reconstruction from moving fetal brain anatomy. *IEEE Transactions on Medical Imaging, 33*(2), 272–289.

Foley, M. (2011). A comparison of family adversity and family dysfunction in families of children with attention deficit hyperactivity disorder (ADHD) and families of children without ADHD. *Journal for Specialists in Pediatric Nursing, 16*(1), 39–49. doi:10.1111/j.1744-6155.2010.00269.x

Foner, A. (1995). Social stratification. In G. L. Maddox (Ed.), *The encyclopedia of aging: A comprehensive resource in gerontology and geriatrics* (2nd ed., pp. 887–890). New York: Springer.

Font, S., & Berger, L. (2014). Child maltreatment and children's developmental trajectories in early to middle childhood. *Child Development, 86*(2), 227–259.

Fowler, J. (1981). *Stages of faith: The psychology of human development and the quest for meaning*. San Francisco: Harper.

Fowler, P., Tompsett, C., Braciszewski, J., Jacques-Tiura, A., & Baltes, B. (2009). Community violence: A meta-analysis on the effect of exposure and mental health outcomes of children and adolescents. *Development and Psychopathology, 21*(1), 227–259.

Fox, S., Kenny, L., Day, M. R., O'Connell, C., Finnerty, J., & Timmons, S. (2017). Exploring the housing needs of older people in standard and sheltered social housing. *Gerontology and Geriatric Medicine, 3.* doi:10.1177/2333721417702349

Fraas, M., & Bellerose, A. (2010). Mentoring programme for adolescent survivors of acquired brain injury. *Brain Injury, 24*(1), 50–61.

Frankenberg, E., & Debray, E. H. (2011). *Integrating schools in a changing society: New policies and legal options for a multiracial generation.* Chapel Hill: University of North Carolina Press.

Franko, D. L., & Striegel-Moore, R. H. (2002). The role of body dissatisfaction as a risk factor for depression in adolescent girls: Are the differences Black and White? *Journal of Psychosomatic Research, 53*(5), 975–983.

Franko, D. L., Striegel-Moore, R. H., Thompson, D., Schreiber, G. B., & Daniels, S. R. (2005). Does adolescent depression predict obesity in black and white young adult women? *Psychological Medicine, 35*(10), 1505–1513.

Fredriksen-Goldsen, K. I., Kim, H. J., Emlet, C. A., Muraco, A., Erosheva, E. A., Hoy-Ellis, C. P., & Petry, H. (2011). *The aging and health report: Disparities and resilience among lesbian, gay, bisexual, and transgender older adults.* Seattle, WA: Institute for Multigenerational Health.

Freedman, M., & Goggin, J. (2008). Fifty plus: Encore careers provide success, fulfilment in second half of life. *Community College Journal, 78*(6), 34–36.

Freeman, L., Shaffer, D., & Smith, H. (1996). Neglected victims of homicide: The needs of young siblings of murder victims. *American Journal of Orthopsychiatry, 66*(3), 337–345.

Freud, S. (1905/1953). Three essays on the theory of sexuality. In J. Strachey (Ed. & Trans.), *The standard edition of the complete works of Sigmund Freud* (Vol. 7, pp. 135–245). London: Hogarth.

Freud, S. (1917/1957). Mourning and melancholia. In J. Strachey (Ed. & Trans.), *The standard edition of the complete psychological works of Sigmund Freud* (Vol. 14, pp. 237–258). London: Hogarth.

Freud, S. (1927). Some psychological consequences of the anatomical distinction between the sexes. *International Journal of Psychoanalysis, 8,* 133–142.

Freud, S. (1938/1973). *An outline of psychoanalysis.* London: Hogarth Press.

Freund, A. M., & Riediger, M. (2006). Goals as building blocks of personality and development in adulthood. In D. K. Mroczek & T. Little (Eds.), *Handbook of personality development* (pp. 353–372). Mahwah, NJ: Lawrence Erlbaum.

Friedline, T., & West, S. (2016). Young adults' race, wealth, and entrepreneurship. *Race and Social Problems, 8*(1), 42–63.

Friedman, S. H., & Boyle, D. E. (2008). Attachment in US children experiencing nonmaternal care in the early 1990s. *Attachment & Human Development, 10*(3), 225–261.

Friedmann, E., & Havighurst, R. (1954). *The meaning of work and retirement.* Chicago: University of Chicago Press.

Frisvold, M., Lindquist, R., & McAlpine, C. (2012). Living life in the balance at midlife: Lessons learned from mindfulness. *Western Journal of Nursing Research, 34*(2), 265–278.

Frith, L., & Blyth, E. (2013). They can't have my embryo: The ethics of conditional embryo donation. *Bioethics, 27*(6), 317–324.

Fry, D., Fang, X., Elliott, S., Casey, T., Zheng, X., Li, J., . . . McCluskey, G. (2017). The relationships between violence in childhood and educational outcomes: A global systematic review and meta-analysis. *Child Abuse & Neglect, 75,* 6–28.

Fry, R. (2017). *It's becoming more common for young adults to live at home – and for longer stretches.* Washington, DC: Pew Research Center. Retrieved from www.pewresearch.org/fact-tank/2017/05/05/its-becoming-more-common-for-young-adults-to-live-at-home-and-for-longer-stretches/.

Fry, R., Igielnik, R., & Patten, E. (2018). *How millennials today compare with their grandparents 50 years ago.* Washington, DC: Pew Research Center. Retrieved from www.pewresearch.org/fact-tank/2018/03/16/how-millennials-compare-with-their-grandparents/.

Furstenberg, F. (2015). Becoming adults: Challenges in the transition to adult roles. *American Journal of Orthopsychiatry, 85*(5 Suppl.), S14–S21.

Gabbett, A. (2013, June 26). Edith Windsor and Thea Spyer: "A love affair that just kept on and on and on." *The Guardian.* Retrieved from www.theguardian.com/world/2013/jun/26/edith-windsor-thea-spyer-doma.

Gable, I., Gostin, L., & Hodge, J. (2008). HIV/AIDS, reproductive and sexual health, and the law. *American Journal of Public Health, 98*(10), 1779–1786.

Gagnon, S., Huelsman, T., Reichard, A., Kidder-Ashley, P., Griggs, M., Stuby, J., & Bollinger, J. (2013). Help me play! Parental behaviors, child temperament, and preschool peer play. *Journal of Child and Family Studies, 23*(5), 872–884.

Galambos, N., & Kotylak, L. (2012). Transformations in parent-child relationships from adolescence to adulthood. In B. Laursen & W. A. Collins (Eds.), *Relationship pathways from adolescence to young adulthood* (pp. 23–42). Thousand Oaks, CA: Sage.

Galliher, R., Jones, M., & Dahl, A. (2011). Concurrent and longitudinal effects of ethnic identity and experiences of discrimination on psychosocial adjustment of Navajo adolescents. *Developmental Psychology, 47,* 509–526.

Gallup, G., Jr., & Lindsay, D. M. (1999). *Surveying the religious landscape: Trends in U.S. beliefs*. Harrisburg, PA: Morehouse.

Gamble, A., D'Rozario, A., Bartlett, D., Williams, S., Bin, Y. S., Grunstein, R., & Marshall, N. S. (2014). Adolescent sleep patterns and night-time technology use: Results of the Australian Broadcasting Corporation's Big Sleep Survey. *PLoS One, 9*(11), e111700. doi:10.1371/journal.pone.0111700

Gamble, J. (2017). Puberty: Early starters. *Nature, 550,* 510–511.

Gapp, K., Jawaid, A., Sarkies, P., Bohacek, J., Pelczar, P., & Prados, J., . . . Mansuy, I. M. (2014). Implication of sperm RNAs in transgenerational inheritance of the effects of early trauma in mice. *Nature Neuroscience, 17*(5), 667–669.

Garad, R., McNamee, K., Bateson, D., & Harvey, C. (2012). Update on contraception. *Australian Nursing Journal, 20*(4), 34–37.

Garbarino, J. (1995). *Raising children in a socially toxic environment*. San Francisco: Jossey-Bass.

Garbarino, J. (2007). *See Jane hit: Why girls are growing more violent and what we can do about it*. New York: Penguin Books.

Garcia, B. (2011). Cultural competence with Latino Americans. In D. Lum (Ed.), *Culturally competent practice* (4th ed., pp. 302–332). Belmont, CA: Brooks/Cole.

Garcia, D., & Siddiqui, A. (2009). Adolescents' psychological well-being and memory for life events: Influences on life satisfaction with respect of temperamental dispositions. *Journal of Happiness Studies, 10*(4), 407–419.

Garcia-Preto, N. (2016). The transformation of the family system during adolescence. In M. McGoldrick, N. Garcia-Preto, & B. Carter (Eds.), *The expanded family life cycle: Individual, family, and social perspectives* (5th ed., pp. 305–320). Boston: Pearson.

Gardiner, H. (2018). *Lives across cultures: Cross-cultural human development* (6th ed.). Boston: Pearson.

Gardner, H. (1993). *Multiple intelligences: The theory in practice*. New York: Basic Books.

Gardner, H. (1999). *Intelligence reframed: Multiple intelligences for the 21st century*. New York: Basic Books.

Gardner, H. (2006). *Multiple intelligences: New horizons*. New York: Basic Books.

Gardner, H. (2008). *Multiple intelligences: New horizons*. New York: Basic Books

Gareis, K., Barnett, R., Ertel, K., & Berkman, L. (2009). Work-family enrichment and conflict: Additive effects, buffering, or balance? *Journal of Marriage and the Family, 71,* 696–707.

Gargiulo, R. M., & Kilgo, J. L. (2011). *An introduction to young children with special needs: Birth through age 8*. Belmont, CA: Wadsworth/Cengage Learning.

Gariepy, A. M., Creinin, M. D., Smith, K. J., & Xiao, X. (2014). Probability of pregnancy after sterilization: A comparison of hysteroscopic versus laparoscopic sterilization. *Contraception, 90*(2), 174–181.

Garralda, M. E., & Raynaud, J.-P. (2010). *Increasing awareness of child and adolescent mental health*. Lanham, MD: Jason Aronson.

Garrett, B. (2009). *Brain & behavior: An introduction to biological psychology* (2nd ed.). Thousand Oaks, CA: Sage.

Garrett, M. W. (1995). Between two worlds: Cultural discontinuity in the dropout of Native American youth. *The School Counselor, 10,* 199–208.

Gartstein, M., Gonzales, C., Carranza, J., Adaho, S., Rothbart, M., & Yang, S. (2006). Studying cross-cultural differences in the development of infant temperament: People's Republic of China, the United States of America, and Spain. *Child Psychiatry and Human Development, 37*(2), 145–161.

Gartstein, M., Knyazev, G., & Slobodskaya, H. (2005). Cross-cultural differences in the structure of temperament: United States of America (U.S.) and Russia. *Infant Behavior and Development, 28,* 54–61.

Gartstein, M., Peleg, Y., Young, B., & Slobodskaya, H. (2009). Infant temperament in Russia, United States of America, and Israel: Differences and similarities between Russian-speaking families. *Child Psychiatry and Human Development, 40,* 241–256.

Garvey, C. (1984). *Children's talk*. Cambridge, MA: Harvard University Press.

Gassman-Pines, A. (2013). Daily spillover of low-income mothers' perceived workload to mood and mother-child interactions. *Journal of Marriage and Family, 75,* 1304–1318.

Gawande, A. (2014). *Being mortal: Medicine and what matters in the end*. New York: Henry Holt & Co.

Gawande, S., Vaidya, M., Tadke, R., Kirpekar, V., & Bhave, S. (2011). Progressive muscle relations in hyperemesis gravidarum. *Journal of South Asia Federation of Obstetrics and Gynecology, 3*(1), 28–32.

Gee, J. P. (2012). *Social linguistics and literacies: Ideology in discourse* (4th ed.). New York: Routledge.

Gehlbach, H. (2006). How changes in students' goal orientations relate to outcomes in social studies. *Journal of Education Research, 99,* 358–370.

Geiger, B. (1996). *Fathers as primary caregivers*. Westport, CT: Greenwood.

Gelles, R. (2010). Violence, abuse, and neglect in families and intimate relationships. In S. Price, C. Price, & P. McKenry (Eds.), *Families & change: Coping with stressful events and transitions* (4th ed., pp. 119–139). Thousand Oaks, CA: Sage.

Generations. (2001, Summer). Intimacy and aging. *25*(2).

Genetics Home Reference. (2013). *Genetic disorders A to Z.* Retrieved from http://ghr.nlm.nih.gov.

Gentile, D., Bailey, K., Bavelier, D., Brockmeyer, J., Cash, H., Coyne, S.,. . . . Young, K. (2017). Internet gaming disorder in children and adolescents. *Pediatrics, 140*(2), 81–85.

George, L. K. (2005). Socioeconomic status and health across the life course: Progress and prospects. *The Journals of Gerontology, Series B: Psychological Sciences and Social Sciences, 60B,* S135–S139.

George, L. K. (2009). Conceptualizing and measuring trajectories. In G. Elder Jr. & J. Giele (Eds.), *The craft of life course resource* (pp. 163–186). New York: Guilford Press.

George, L. K., Larson, D. B., Koenig, H. G., & McCullough, M. E. (2000). Spirituality and health: What we know, what we need to know. *Journal of Social & Clinical Psychology, 19*(1), 102–116.

Georgiades, S. D. (2005). Emancipated young adults' perspectives on independent living programs. *Families in Society, 86*(4), 503–510.

Georgsdottir, I., Erlingsdottir, G., Hrafnkelsson, B., Haraldsson, A., & Dagbjartsson, A. (2012). Disabilities and health of extremely low-birthweight teenagers: A population-based study. *Acta Paediatrica, 101,* 518–523.

Gerhardt, S. (2004). *Why love matters: How affection shapes a baby's brain.* New York: Brunner-Routledge.

Geronimus, A. T., Hicken, M., Keene, D., & Bound, J. (2006). "Weathering" and age patterns of allostatic load scores among blacks and whites in the United States. *American Journal of Public Health, 96,* 826–833.

Geronimus, A., Pearson, J., Linnenbringer, E., Schulz, A., Reyes, A., Espel, E. . . . Blackburn, E. (2015). Race-ethnicity, poverty, urban stressors, and telomere length in a detroit community-based sample. *Journal of Health and Social Behavior, 56*(2), 199–224.

Gerouki, M. (2010). The boy who was drawing princesses: Primary teachers' accounts of children's non-conforming behaviours. *Sex Education, 10*(4), 335–348.

Gewirtz, A. H., Erbes, C. R., Polusny, M. A., Forgatch, M. S., & DeGarmo, D. S. (2011). Helping military families through the deployment process: Strategies to support parenting. *Professional Psychology: Research and Practice, 42,* 56–62.

Ghavami, N., Katsiaficas, D., & Rogers, L. O. (2016). Toward an intersectional approach in developmental science: The role of race, gender, sexual orientation and immigration status. *Advances in Child Development and Behavior, 50*(1), 31–73.

Ghazi, S., Shahzada, G., Gilani, U., Shabbir, M., & Rashid, M. (2011). Relationship between students' self perceived multiple intelligences and their academic achievement. *International Journal of Academic Research, 3*(2), 619–623.

Gielen, U., & Markoulis, D. (2001). Preference for principled moral reasoning: A developmental and cross-cultural perspective. In L. Adler & U. Gielen (Eds.), *Cross-cultural topics in psychology* (2nd ed., pp. 81–101). Westport, CT: Praeger/Greenwood.

Gilligan, C. (1982). *In a different voice: Psychological theory and women's development.* Cambridge, MA: Harvard University Press.

Gillspie, S. L., Christian, L. M., Alston, A. D., & Salsberry, P. J. (2017). Childhood stress and birth timing among African American women: Cortisol as biological mediator. *Psychoneuroendocrinology, 84,* 32–41.

Gilman, S. (2012). The successes and challenges of life course epidemiology: A commentary on Gibb, Fergusson and Horwood. *Social Science & Medicine, 75*(12), 2124–2128.

Gilson, S. (2019). The biological person. In E. Hutchison (Ed.), *Dimensions of human behavior: Person and environment* (6th ed.). Thousand Oaks, CA: Sage.

Ginesi, L., Jenkins, C., & Keenan, B. (2016). New approaches to understanding dementia. *Nursing Times, 112*(25), 16–19.

Ginsburg, F., & Rapp, R. (2013). Entangled ethnography: Imagining a future for young adults with learning disabilities. *Social Science & Medicine, 99,* 187–193.

Glaser, D. (2000). Child abuse and neglect and the brain— A review. *Journal of Child Psychology and Psychiatry, 41*(1), 97–116.

Global Issues. (2013). *Poverty facts and stats.* Retrieved from www.globalissues.org/article/26/poverty-facts-and-stats.

Glover, J., Galliher, R., & Lamere, T. (2009). Identity development and exploration among sexual minority adolescents: Examination of a multidimensional model. *Journal of Homosexuality, 56*(1), 77–101.

Glover, R. (1996). Religiosity in adolescence and young adulthood: Implications for identity formation. *Psychological Reports, 78,* 427–431.

Glowiak, M., & Mayfield, M. A. (2016). Middle childhood: Emotional and social development. In D. Capuzzi, M. D. Stauffer, D. Capuzzi, M. D. Stauffer (Eds.), *Human growth and development across the lifespan: Applications for counselors* (pp. 277–306). Hoboken, NJ: John Wiley.

Godfrey, J., & Lawrence, R. (2010). Toward optimal health: The maternal benefits of breastfeeding. *Journal of Women's Health, 19*(9), 1597–1602.

Golchin, N., Hamzehgardeshi, Z., Fakhri, M., & Hamzehgardeshi, L. (2012). The experience of puberty in Iranian adolescent girls: A qualitative content analysis. *BMC Public Health, 12*, 698. doi:10.186/1471-2458-12-698

Goldberg, W., Clarke-Stewart, K., Rice, J., & Dellis, E. (2002). Emotional energy as an explanatory construct for fathers' engagement with their infants. *Parenting: Science & Practice, 2*(4), 379–408.

Goldstein, J., & Kenney, C. (2001). Marriage delayed or marriage forgone? New cohort forecasts of first marriage for U.S. women. *American Sociological Review, 66*(4), 506–519.

Goldstein, S., & Brooks, R. B. (2013). *Handbook of resilience in children.* New York: Springer.

Goleman, D. (2006). *Social intelligence: The new science of human relationships.* New York: Bantam.

Goleman, D. (2013). *Focus: The hidden driver of excellence.* New York: Harper Collins.

Gong, F., Xu, J., Fujishiro, K., & Takeuchi, D. (2011). A life course perspective on migration and mental health among Asian immigrants: The role of human agency. *Social Science & Medicine, 73*, 1618–1626.

Good, M., Willoughby, T., & Busseri, M. (2011). Stability and change in adolescent spirituality/religiosity: A person-centered approach. *Developmental Psychology, 47*(2), 538–550.

Goodcase, E., & Love, H. (2017). From despair to integrity: Using narrative therapy for older individuals in Erikson's last stage of identity development. *Clinical Social Work, 45*, 354–363.

Goodfellow, A. (2012). Looking through the learning disability lens: Inclusive education and the learning disability embodiment. *Children's Geographies, 10*(1), 67–81.

Goodman, S., & Brand, S. (2009). Infants of depressed mothers: Vulnerabilities, risk factors, and protective factors for the later development of psychopathology. In C. H. Zeanah, Jr. (Ed.), *Handbook of infant mental health* (3rd ed., pp. 153–170). New York: Guilford Press.

Goodwin, R., Thompson, R., & Winer, A. (2015). The individual child: Temperament, emotion, self, and personality. In M. H. Bornstein & M. E. Lamb, *Developmental science: An advanced textbook* (7th ed., pp. 491–534.) New York: Psychology Press.

Gopaul-McNicol, S. (1988). Racial identification and racial preference of Black preschool children in New York and Trinidad. *Journal of Black Psychology, 14*(2), 65–68.

Gordon, J., DiMattina, M., Reh, A., Botes, A., Celia, G., & Payson, M. (2013). Utilization and success rates of unstimulated in vitro fertilization in the United States: An analysis of the Society for Reproductive Technology Database. *Fertility and Sterility, 100*(2), 392–395.

Gordon, T. A. (2013). Good grief: Exploring the dimensionality of grief experiences and social work support. *Journal of Social Work in End-of-Life & Palliative Care, 9*(1), 27–42.

Goshin, L., Arditti, J., Dallaire, D., Shlafer, R., & Hollihan, A. (2016). An international rights perspective on maternal criminal justice involvement in the United States. *Psychology, Public Policy, and Law, 23*(1), 53–67.

Gottman, J. M. (1994, May/June). Why marriages fail. *Family Therapy Networker,* 41–48.

Govande, V. P., Brase, K. J., Das, U. G., Koop, J. I., Lagatta, J., & Basir, M. A. (2013). Prenatal counseling beyond the threshold of viability. *Journal of Perinatology, 33*(5), 358–362.

Govtrack. (2013). *S.252. PREEMIE Reauthorization Act.* Retrieved from www.govtrack.us/congress/bills/113/s252.

Gowen, K., Deschaine, M., Gruttadara, D., & Markey, D. (2012). Young adults with mental health conditions and social networking websites: Seeking tools to build community. *Psychiatric Rehabilitation Journal, 35*(3), 245–250.

Grandin, T., & Panek, R. (2013). *The autistic brain: Thinking across the spectrum.* Boston: Houghton Mifflin Harcourt.

Granic, I., Lobel, A., & Engels, R. (2014). The benefits of playing video games. *American Psychologist, 69*(1), 66–78.

Grant, B. F., Dawson, D. A., Stinson, F. S., Chou, S. P., Dufour, M. C., & Pickering, R. P. (2004). The 12-month prevalence and trends in DSM-IV alcohol abuse and dependence: United States, 1991–1992 and 2001–2002. *Drug and Alcohol Dependence, 74*, 223–234.

Greenberg, J. (2010). Assessing policy effects on enrollment in early childhood education and care. *Social Service Review, 84*(3), 461–490.

Greene, S., Anderson, E., Forgatch, M., DeGarmo, D., & Hetherington, E. M. (2012). Risk and resilience after divorce. In F. Walsh (Ed.), *Normal family processes* (4th ed., pp. 102–127). New York: Guilford Press.

Greenfield, E., & Marks, N. (2006). Linked lives: Adult children's problems and their parents' psychological and relational well-being. *Journal of Marriage and Family, 68*, 442–454.

Greenspan, L., & Deardorff, J. (2015). *The new puberty: How to navigate early development in today's girls.* New York: Rodale Books.

Greenspan, S. (2006). Rethinking "harmonious parenting" using a three-factor discipline model. *Child Care in Practice, 12*(1), 5–12.

Gregory, S. T. (2000). *The academic achievement of minority students: Perspectives, practices, and prescriptions.* Lanham, MD: University Press of America.

Greil, A. L., McQuillan, J., Lowry, M., & Shreffler, K. M. (2011). Infertility treatment and fertility-specific distress: A longitudinal analysis of a population-based sample of U.S. women. *Social Science and Medicine, 73*(1), 87–94.

Greil, A. L., McQuillan, J., Shreffler, K. M., Johnson, K. M., & Slauson-Blevins, K. S. (2011). Race-ethnicity and medical services for infertility: Stratified reproduction in a population-based sample of U.S. women. *Journal of Health and Social Behavior, 52*(4), 493–509.

Grenier, S., Potvin, O., Hudon, C., Boyer, R., Préville, M., & Desjardins, L. (2012). Twelve-month prevalence and correlates of subthreshold and threshold anxiety in community-dwelling older adults with cardiovascular diseases. *Journal of Affective Disorders, 136*(3), 724–732.

Greve, W., & Staudinger, U. M. (2006). Resilience in later adulthood and old age: Resources and potentials for successful aging. In D. Cicchetti & D. J. Cohen (Eds.), *Developmental psychopathology: Risk, disorder and adaptation* (Vol. 3, pp. 796–840). Hoboken, NJ: John Wiley & Sons.

Greytak, E. A., & Kosciw, J. G. (2013). Responsive classroom curriculum for lesbian, gay, bisexual, transgender, and questioning students. In E. S. Fisher, K. Komosa-Hawkins (Eds.), *Creating safe and supportive learning environments: A guide for working with lesbian, gay, bisexual, transgender, and questioning youth and families* (pp. 156–174). New York: Routledge/Taylor & Francis Group.

Grogan-Kaylor, A., & Otis, M. (2007). Predictors of parental use of corporal punishment. *Family Relations, 56*, 80–91.

Grose, J. (2015, May 12). To battle the scourge of "double dipping," Australia will cut paid family leave. *Slate.* Retrieved from www.slate.com/blogs/xx_factor/2015/05/12/australia_paid_family_leave_as_the_u_s_makes_snail_s_pace_progress_they.html/.

Gruenewald, T., Tanner, E., Fried, L., Carlson, M., Xue, Q., Parisi, J., . . . Seeman, T. E. (2016). The Baltimore experience corps trial: Enhancing generativity via intergenerational activity engagement in late life. *The Journals of Gerontology, Series B: Psychological Sciences and Social Sciences, 71*(4), 661–670.

Grünebaum, A., McCullough, L., Sapra, K., Arabin, B., & Chervenak, F. (2017). Planned home births: The need for additional contraindications. *American Journal of Obstetrics and Gynecology, 216*(4), 401.e1–401.e8.

Gubrium, J. (1978). Notes on the social organization of senility. *Urban Life, 7*, 23–44.

Guedes, A., Bott, S., Garcia-Moreno, C., & Colombini, M. (2016). Bridging the gaps: A global review of intersections of violence against women and violence against children. *Global Health Action, 9*(1). doi:10.3402/gha.v9.31516

Guerra, N., & Dierkhising, C. (2012). The effects of community violence on child development. *Encyclopedia of early childhood development.* Retrieved from www.child-encyclopedia.com/sites/default/files/textes-experts/en/907/the-effects-of-community-violence-on-child-development.pdf.

Guest, Y. (2012). Reflections on resilience: A psycho-social exploration of the life long impact of having been in care during childhood. *Journal of Social Work Practice, 26*(1), 109–124.

Gugliucci, M. R., Weaver, S. A., Kimmel, D. C, Littlefield, M., Hollander, L., & Hennessy, J. (2013). *Gay, lesbian, bisexual, and transgender (GLBT) aging in Maine: Community needs assessment.* Portland, ME: AARP. Retrieved from www.maine4a.org/image_upload/AARP-SAGE-GLBT-Report-2013-pdf.pdf.

Guittar, S., & Guittar, N. (2015). Intersectionality. In J. D. Wright (Ed.), *International encyclopedia of the social and behavioral sciences* (2nd ed., Vol. 12, pp. 657–662). Oxford, UK: Elsevier.

Gump, B., Reihman, J., Stewart, P., Lonky, E., Granger, D., & Matthews, K. (2009). Blood lead (pb) levels: Further evidence for an environmental mechanism explaining the association between socioeconomic status and psychophysiological dysregulation in children. *Health Psychology, 28*(5), 614–620.

Gunnar, M., & Quevedo, K. (2007). The neurobiology of stress and development. *Annual Review of Psychology, 58*, 145–173.

Guo, J., Isohanni, M., Miettunen, J., Jääskeläinen, E., Kiviniemi, V., Nikkinen, J., . . . Murray, G. K. (2016). Brain structural changes in women and men during midlife. *Neuroscience Letters, 615*, 107–112.

Gupta, S. S., Henninger, W. R., & Vinh, M. E. (2014). *First steps to preschool inclusion: How to jumpstart your program-wide plan.* Baltimore: Brookes.

Guralnick, M., Neville, B., Hammond, M., & Connor, R. (2008). Continuity and change from full-inclusion early childhood programs through the early elementary period. *Journal of Early Intervention, 30*(3), 237–250.

Gürsory, F., & Bicakci, M. (2007). A comparison of parental attitude perceptions in children of working and nonworking mothers. *Social Behavior & Personality: An International Journal, 35*(5), 693–706.

Guterman, K. (2015). Unintended pregnancy as a predictor of child maltreatment. *Child Abuse & Neglect, 48*, 160–169.

Guterman, N., & Embry, R. (2004). Prevention and treatment strategies targeting physical child abuse and neglect. In P. Allen-Meares & M. Fraser (Eds.), *Intervention with children and adolescents: An interdisciplinary perspective* (pp. 130–158). Boston: Allyn & Bacon.

Gutman, H. (1976). *The Black family in slavery and freedom, 1750–1925*. New York: Pantheon.

Gutman, L., & Eccles, J. (2007). Stage-environment fit during adolescence: Trajectories of family relations and adolescent outcomes. *Developmental Psychology, 43*, 522–537.

Guttmacher Institute. (2015). *Fact sheet: Contraception in the United States*. Retrieved from www.guttmacher.org/pubs/fb_contr_use.html.

Guttmacher Institute. (2016). *Unintended pregnancy in the United States*. Retrieved from www.guttmacher.org/sites/default/files/factsheet/fb-unintended-pregnancy-us_0.pdf.

Guttmacher Institute. (2018). *Induced abortion in the United States*. Retrieved from www.guttmacher.org/sites/default/files/factsheet/fb_induced_abortion.pdf.

Ha, J., Hong, J., Seltzer, M., & Greenberg, J. (2008). Age and gender differences in the well-being of midlife and aging parents with children with mental health or developmental problems: Report of a national study. *Journal of Health and Social Behavior, 49*(3), 3010–3016.

Hafen, C., Laursen, B., & DeLay, B. (2012). Transformations in friends' relationships across the transition into adolescence. In B. Laursen & W. A. Collins (Eds.), *Relationship pathways from adolescence to young adulthood* (pp. 69–89). Thousand Oaks, CA: Sage.

Hafstad, G., Abebe, D., Torgersen, L., & von Soest, T. (2013). Picky eating in preschool children: The predictive role of the child's temperament and mother's negative affectivity. *Eating Behaviors, 14*(3), 274–275.

Hagelskamp, C., Suárez-Orozco, C., & Hughes, D. (2010). Migrating to opportunities: How family migration motivations shape academic trajectories among newcomer immigrant youth. *Journal of Social Issues, 66*(4), 717–739. doi:10.1111/j.1540-4560.2010.01672.x

Hagerty, B. (2016). *Life reimagined: The science, art, and opportunity of midlife*. New York: Riverhead Books.

Haider, A. (2006). Roper v. Simmons: The role of the science brief. *Ohio State Journal of Criminal Law, 375*, 369–377.

Haidt, J. (2013). Moral psychology for the twenty-first century. *Journal of Moral Education, 42*(3), 281–297.

Hair, E., Ling, T., & Cochran, S. W. (2003). *Youth development programs and educationally disadvantaged older youths: A synthesis*. Washington, DC: Child Trends.

Hale, B., & Worden, T. (2009). *World's oldest mother dies of cancer just three years after giving birth to twin boys, sparking new ethical debate*. Retrieved from www.dailymail.co.uk/femail/article-1199866/Worlds-oldest-mother-dies-cancer-just-years-giving-birth-twin-boys.html.

Haley, A. (2014). Vascular functions and brain integrity in midlife: Effects of obesity and metabolic syndrome. *Advances in Vascular Medicine*. Retrieved from doi:10.1155/2014/653482.

Halim, M., & Ruble, D., Tamis-LeMonda, C., Lurye, L., & Greulich, F. (2014). Pink frilly dresses and the avoidance of all things "girly": Children's appearance rigidity and cognitive theories of gender development. *Developmental Psychology, 50*(4), 1091–1101.

Hall, G. (1904). *Adolescence: Its psychology and its relations to physiology, anthropology, sociology, sex, crime, religion, and education*. New York: Appleton.

Hall, J., Jaekel, J., & Wolke, D. (2012). Gender distinctive impacts on prematurity and small for gestational age (SGA) on age-6 attention problems. *Child and Adolescent Mental Health, 17*(4), 238–245.

Hall, W. J. (2008). Centenarians: Metaphor becomes reality. *Archives of Internal Medicine, 168*(3), 262–263.

Hamada, A., Esteves, S. C., & Agarwai, A. (2011). The role of contemporary andrology in unraveling the mystery of unexplained male infertility. *Oral Reproductive Science Journal, 3*, 27–41.

Hamilton, B. E., Martin, J. A., Osterman, M. J. K., & Curtin, S. C. (2015). *Births: Final data for 2014*. Hyattsville, MD: National Center for Health Statistics.

Hamilton, R., Innella, N., & Bounds, D. (2016). Living with genetic vulnerability: A life course perspective. *Journal of Genetic Counseling, 25*, 49–61.

Hampson, S., & Goldberg, L. (2006). A first large cohort study of personality trait stability over the 40 years between elementary school and midlife. *Journal of Personality and Social Psychology, 91*(4), 763–779.

Hanania, R., & Smith, L. (2010). Selective attention and attention switching: Towards a unified developmental approach. *Developmental Science, 13*(4), 622–635.

Handelsman, D. (2015). Irrational exuberance in testoster-one prescribing: When will the bubble burst? *Medical Care, 53*(9), 743–745.

Hane, A., Cheah, C., Rubin, K., & Fox, N. (2008). The role of maternal behavior in the relation between shyness and social reticence in early childhood and social withdrawal in middle childhood. *Social Development, 17*(4), 795–811.

Hankivsky, O. (2012). Women's health, men's health, and gender and health: Implications of intersectionality. *Social Science & Medicine, 74*(11), 1712–1720.

Hannah-Jones, N. (2017, September 6). The resegregation of Jefferson County. *New York Times*. Retrieved from www.nytimes.com/2017/09/06/magazine/the-resegregation-of-jefferson-county.html.

Hansen, C., & Zambo, D. (2007). Loving and learning with Wemberly and David: Fostering emotional development in early childhood education. *Early Childhood Education Journal, 34*(4), 273–278.

Hansen, V., Oren, E., Dennis, L. K., & Brown, H. E. (2016). Infectious disease mortality trends in the United States, 1980–2014. *Journal of the American Medical Association, 316*(20), 2149–2151.

Hao, L., & Cherlin, A. J. (2004). Welfare reform and teen-age pregnancy, childbirth, and school dropout. *Journal of Marriage and Family, 66*, 179–184.

Hardie, J. H., & Seltzer, J. A. (2016). Parent-child relation-ships at the transition to adulthood: A comparison of Black, Hispanic, and White immigrant and native-born youth. *Social Forces, 95*(1), 321–354.

Hareven, T. (Ed.). (1978). *Transitions: The family and the life course in historical perspective*. New York: Academic Press.

Hareven, T. (1982a). *Family time and industrial time: The rela-tionship between the family and work in a New England indus-trial community*. New York: Cambridge University Press.

Hareven, T. (1982b). American families in transition: Historical perspectives on change. In F. Walsh (Ed.), *Normal family processes* (pp. 446–466). New York: Guilford Press.

Hareven, T. (Ed.). (1996). *Aging and generation relations over the life course: A historical and cross-cultural perspective*. New York: Walter de Gruyter.

Hareven, T. (2000). *Families, history, and social change*. Boulder, CO: Westview.

Harkness, S., & Super, C. (2003). Culture and parenting. In M. Bornstein (Ed.), *Handbook of parenting* (2nd ed., Vol. 2, pp. 253–280). Mahwah, NJ: Lawrence Erlbaum.

Harkness, S., & Super, C. (2006). Themes and variations: Parental ethnotheories in Western cultures. In K. Rubin (Ed.), *Parental beliefs, parenting, and child development in cross-cultural perspectives* (pp. 61–80). New York: Psychology Press.

Harris, D. L., & Winokuer, H. R. (2015). *Principles and prac-tice of grief counseling* (2nd ed.). New York: Springer.

Harris, J. (1998). *The nurture assumption: Why children turn out the way they do*. New York: Touchstone.

Hartman, R. M., & Weierbach, F. M. (2013, February). *Elder health in rural America*. National Rural Health Association Policy brief. Retrieved from www.ruralhealthweb.org/getattachment/Advocate/Policy-Documents/ElderHealthinRuralAmericaFeb2013.pdf.aspx?lang=en-US.

Hartman-Linck, J. E. (2014). Keeping bisexuality alive: Maintaining bisexual visibility in monogamous relation-ships. *Journal of Bisexuality, 14*(2), 177–193.

Harvard Health Letter. (2002). Aging—living to 100: What's the secret? *Harvard Health Letter, 27*(3), 1–3.

Harvard School of Public Health. (2012). *Child* obesity. Retrieved from www.hsph.harvard.edu/obesity-prevention-source/obesity-trends/global-obesity-trends-in-children/.

Harwood, R. (1992). The influence of culturally derived values on Anglo and Puerto Rican mothers' perceptions of attachment behavior. *Child Development, 63*(4), 822–839.

Hash, K. M. (2006). Caregiving and post-caregiving experi-ences of midlife and older gay men and lesbians. *Journal of Gerontological Social Work, 47*(3/4), 121–138.

Hash, K. M., & Rogers, A. (2013). Clinical practice with older LGBT clients: Overcoming lifelong stigma through strength and resilience. *Clinical Social Work Journal, 41*(3), 249–257.

Hash, K. M., & Rogers, A. (2017). Introduction to LGBT aging. Contemporary issues and future directions in les-bian, gay, bisexual, and transgender (LGBT) aging. *Annual Review of Gerontology and Geriatrics, 37*(1), 1–12. New York: Springer.

Hash, K. M., Wells, R., & Spencer, S. M. (2015). Who are rural elders? In K. M. Hash, E. T. Jurkowski, & J. A. Krout (Eds.), *Aging in rural places: Programs, policies, and profes-sional practice* (pp. 23–41). New York: Springer.

Hastings, L., Griesen, J., Hoover, R., Cresell, J., & Dlugosh, L. (2015). Generativity in college students: Comparing and explaining the impact of mentoring. *Journal of College Student Development, 56*(7), 651–669.

Hattier, M., Matson, J., Sipes, M., & Turygin, N. (2011). Communication deficits in infants and toddlers with devel-opment disabilities. *Research in Developmental Disabilities, 32*(6), 2108–2113.

Hauck, Y., Fenwick, J., Dhaliwal, S., & Butt, J. (2011). A Western Australian survey of breastfeeding initiation, prevalence and early cessation patterns. *Maternal and Child Health Journal, 15*(2), 260–268.

Haumont, D. (2016). *Environment and early developmental care of newborns.* Switzerland: Springer International.

Haveman, R., Blank, R., Moffitt, R., Smeeding, T., & Wallace, G. (2015). The war on poverty: Measurement, trends, and policy. *Journal of Policy Analysis and Management, 34*(3), 593–638.

Havighurst, R. J. (1968). Personality and patterns of aging. *The Gerontologist, 8*(1), 20–23.

Haviland, W., Prins, H., Walrath, D., & McBride, B. (2017). *Anthropology: The human challenge* (15th ed.). Boston: Cengage Learning.

Hay, D., Hurst, S., Waters, C., & Chadwick, A. (2011). Infants' use of force to defend toys: The origins of instrumental aggression. *Infancy, 16*(5), 471–489.

Hayes, D. (2011). Predicting parental home and school involvement in high school African American adolescents. *High School Journal, 94*(4), 154–166.

Hayslip, B., Blumenthal, H., & Garner, A. (2014). Social support and grandparent caregiver health: One-year longitudinal findings for grandparents raising their grandchildren. *Journal of Gerontology B: Psychological Sciences and Social Services, 70*, 804–812.

Hazan, H. (2011). From ageless self to selfless age: Toward a theoretical turn in gerontological understanding. In L. W. Poon & J. Cohen-Mansfield (Eds.), *Understanding well-being in the oldest old* (pp. 11–26). New York: Cambridge University Press.

Hazra, N. C., Dregan, A., Jackson, S., & Gulliford, M. C. (2015). Differences in health at age 100 according to sex: Population-based cohort study of centenarians using electronic health records. *Journal of the American Geriatrics Society, 63*(7), 1331–1337.

Health Encyclopedia. (2018). *Newborn reflexes.* Rochester, NY: University of Rochester Medical Center. Retrieved from www.urmc.rochester.edu/encyclopedia/content.aspx?ContentTypeID=90&ContentID=P02630.

Health Resources and Services Administration. (2012). *Affordable care act maternal, infant, and early childhood home visiting program.* Retrieved from www.ok.gov/health2/documents/MIECHV-Needs%20Assessment%20Guidance.pdf.

Health Resources and Services Administration. (2016, November). *Recommended uniform screening panel.* Retrieved from www.hrsa.gov/advisorycommittees/mchbadvisory/heritabledisorders/recommendedpanel/index.html.

Healthline. (2018). *Ectopic pregnancy.* Retrieved from www.healthline.com/health/pregnancy/ectopic-pregnancy#outlook.

Healthy People. (2016). *Access to health services.* Retrieved from www.healthypeople.gov/2020/topics-objectives/topic/Access-to-Health-Services.

Heckman, J. (2006). Skill formation and the economics of investing in disadvantaged children. *Science, 312*(5782), 1900–1902.

Heckman, J. (2008). *Schools, skills, and synapses.* National Bureau of Economic Research. Retrieved from www.nber.org/papers/w14064.pdf?new_windows=1.

Heckman, J., Moon, S., Pinto, R., Savelyev, P., & Yavitz, A. (2010). The rate of return to the HighScope Perry Preschool Program. *Journal of Public Economics, 94*(1–2), 114–128.

Heimpel, S., Wood, J., Marshall, J., & Brown, J. (2002). Do people with low self-esteem really feel better? Self-esteem differences in motivation to repair negative moods. *Journal of Personality and Social Psychology, 82*(1), 128–147.

Heisler, E. J. (2012). *The U.S. infant mortality rate: International comparisons, underlying factors, and federal programs.* Congressional Research Service. Retrieved from www.fas.org/sgp/crs/misc/R41378.pdf.

Helbig, A., Kaasen, A., Mait, U. F., & Haugen, G. (2013). Does antenatal maternal psychological distress affect placental circulation in the third trimester? *PLoS One, 8*(2), 1–7.

Helmchen, H., Baltes, M., Geiselmann, S., Kanowski, S., Linden, M., Reischies, F., . . . Wilms, H.-U. (1999). Psychiatric illness in old age. In P. Baltes & K. Mayer (Eds.), *The Berlin Aging Study: Aging from 70 to 100* (pp. 167–196). Cambridge, UK: Cambridge University Press.

Helson, R., & Wink, P. (1992). Personality change in women from the early 40s to the early 50s. *Psychology and Aging, 7*, 46–55.

Hembre, W., Cohen-Kettenis, P., Gooren, L., Hannema, S., Meyer, W., Murad, H., . . . T'Sjoen, G. (2017). Endocrine treatment of gender-dysphoric/gender-incongruent persons: An Endocrine Society Clinical Practice Guideline. *The Journal of Clinical Endocrinology Metabolism, 102*(11), 3869–3903.

Henderson, C., Hayslip, B., Sanders, L., & Louden, L. (2009). Grandmother-grandchild relationship quality predicts psychological adjustment among youth from divorced families. *Journal of Family Issues, 30*(9), 1245–1264.

Hendricks, J. (1987). Exchange theory in aging. In G. L. Maddox (Ed.), *The encyclopedia of aging* (pp. 238–239). New York: Springer.

Hendricks, J., & Hatch, L. R. (2006). Lifestyle and aging. In R. H. Binstock & L. K. George (Eds.), *Handbook of aging and the social sciences* (pp. 301–319). Amsterdam, The Netherlands: Elsevier.

Henrich, J., Heine, S., & Norenzayan, A. (2010). The weirdest people in the world? *Behavioral and Brain Sciences, 33*(2–3), 61–83.

Henriksson, A., Carlander, I., & Arestedt, K. (2015). Feelings of rewards among family caregivers during ongoing palliative care. *Palliative and Supportive Care, 13*(6), 1509–1517.

Henry J. Kaiser Family Foundation. (2013). *Life expectancy at birth (in years) by race/ethnicity.* Retrieved from kff.org/other/state-indicator/life-expectancy-by-re.

Hepper, P. (2015). Behavior during the prenatal period: Adaptive for development and survival. *Child Development Perspectives, 9*(1), 38–43.

Hequembourg, A., & Brallier, S. (2005). Gendered stories of parental caregiving among siblings. *Journal of Aging Studies, 19*(1), 53–71.

Herbenick, D., Reece, M., Schick, V., Sanders, S., Dodge, B., & Fortenberry, J. D. (2010). Sexual behavior in the United States: Results from a national probability sample of men and women ages 14–94. *Journal of Sexual Medicine, 7*(Suppl. 5), 255–265.

Herbers, J. E., Cutuli, J. J., Supkoff, L. M., Narayan, A. J., & Masten, A. S. (2014). Parenting and coregulation: Adaptive systems for competence in children experiencing homelessness. *American Journal of Orthopsychiatry, 84*(4), 420–430.

Herbert, J., Eckerman, C., Goldstein, R., & Stanton, M. (2004). Contrasts in classical eyeblink conditioning as a function of premature birth. *Infancy, 5*(3), 367–383.

Herbert, M. R., & Weintraub, K. (2012). *The autism revolution: Whole-body strategies for making life all it can be.* New York: Ballantine Books.

Herberth, G., Weber, A., Röder, S., Elvers, H. E., Krämer, U., Schins, R., . . . LISAplus Study Group. (2008). Relation between stressful life events, neuropeptides and cytokines: Results from the LISA birth cohort study. *Pediatric Allergy & Immunology, 19*(8), 722–729.

Herman-Giddens, M. E. (2013). The enigmatic pursuit of puberty in girls. *Pediatric, 132*(6), 1125–1126.

Herman-Giddens, M. E., Steffes, J., Harris, D., Slora, E., Hussey, M., Doweshen, S. A., & Reiter, E. O. (2012). Secondary sexual characteristics in boys: Data from the pediatric research in office settings network. *Pediatrics, 132*(5), 1058–1070.

Herrel, L. A., Goodman, M., Goldstein, M., Goldstein, M., & Hsiao, W. (2015). Outcomes of microsurgical vasovasostomy for vasectomy reversal: A meta-analysis and systematic review. *Urology, 85*(4), 819–825.

Herron, J. (2013, January 31). Bundle of joy: The costs of adoption vs. surrogacy. *Yahoo Finance.* Retrieved from https://finance.yahoo.com/news/bundle-joy-costs-adoption-vs-100000304.html.

Hetherington, E. M., & Kelly, J. (2002). *For better or for worse: Divorce reconsidered.* New York: W. W. Norton.

Hetherington, T., & Boddy, J. (2013). Ecosocial work with marginalized populations: Time for action on climate change. In M. Gray, J. Coates, & T. Hetherington (Eds.), *Environmental social work* (pp. 46–61). New York: Routledge.

Hetzner, N., Razza, R., Malone, L., & Brooks-Gunn, J. (2009). Associations among feeding behaviors during infancy and child illness at two years. *Maternal and Child Health Journal, 13*(6), 795–805.

Heymann, J., & McNeill, K. (2013). *Changing children's chances: New findings on child policy worldwide.* UCLA World Policy Analysis Centre. Retrieved from https://bettercarenetwork.org/sites/default/files/attachments/Changing%20Children%27s%20Chances.pdf.

Hinrichsen, G. A., & Clougherty, K. F. (2006). Role transitions. In G. Henrichsen & K. Clougherty (Eds.), *Interpersonal psychotherapy for depressed older adults* (pp. 133–152). Washington, DC: American Psychological Association.

Hitlin, S., & Elder, G., Jr. (2007). Time, self, and the curiously abstract concept of agency. *Sociological Theory, 25*(2), 170–191.

Ho, M., Rasheed, J., & Rasheed, M. (2004). *Family therapy with ethnic minorities* (2nd ed.). Thousand Oaks, CA: Sage.

Hobbs, F., & Stoops, N. (2002). *Demographic trends in the 20th century.* Census 2000 Special Reports, Series CENSR-4. Washington, DC: U.S. Government Printing Office.

Hockenberry, S., & Puzzanchera, C. (2017). *Juvenile court statistics 2014.* Pittsburgh, PA: National Center for Juvenile Justice. Retrieved from www.ojjdp.gov/ojstatbb/njcda/pdf/jcs2014.pdf.

Hodge, D. R. (2001). Spiritual assessment: A review of major qualitative methods and a new framework for assessing spirituality. *Social Work, 46*(3), 203–214.

Hodnett, E., Downe, S., & Walsh, D. (2012). Alternative versus conventional institutional settings for birth. *Cochrane Database System Review.* doi:10.1002/14651858.CD000012.pub4

Hodnett, E., Gates, S., Hofmeyr, J., Sakala, C., & Weston, J. (2012). Continuous support for women during childbirth. *Cochrane Database System Review.* doi:10:CD003766. Retrieved from www.ncbi.nlm.nih.gov/pubmed/21328263.

Hoff, E. (2003). The specificity of environmental influence: Socioeconomic status affects early vocabulary development via maternal speech. *Child Development, 74*(5), 1368–1378.

Hoff, E. (2005). *Language development.* Belmont, CA: Wadsworth/Thomson Learning.

Hoff, E. (2006). How social contexts support and shape language development. *Developmental Review, 26,* 55–88.

Hoff, E. (2009). *Language development* (4th ed.). Pacific Grove, CA: Cengage.

Hoffkling, A., Obedin-Maliver, J., & Sevelius, J. (2017). From erasure to opportunity: A qualitative study of the experiences of transgender men around pregnancy and recommendations for providers. *BMC Pregnancy and Childbirth, 17*(Suppl. 2), 332. Retrieved from https://bmcpregnancy childbirth.biomedcentral.com/articles/10.1186/s12884-017-1491-5.

Hoffman, A., Rüttler, V., & Nieder, A. (2011). Ontogeny of object permanence and object tracking in the carrion crow. *Animal Behavior, 82*(2), 359–367.

Hoffman, M. (2007). The origins of empathic morality in toddlerhood. In C. Brownell & C. Kopp (Eds.), *Socioemotional development in the toddler years: Transitions and transformations* (pp. 132–145). New York: Guilford Press.

Hogan, D. P., & Msall, M. E. (2002). Family structure and resources and the parenting of children with disabilities and functional limitations. In J. G. Borkowski, S. Landesman Ramey, & M. Bristol-Power (Eds.), *Parenting and the child's world* (pp. 311–344). Mahwah, NJ: Lawrence Erlbaum.

Hogan, S. R., & Bailey, C. E. (2010). Service learning as a mechanism for change in attitudes and perceptions of human services students toward substance-dependent mothers. *Journal of Teaching in Social Work, 30*(4), 420–434.

Hoge, C. W., Auchterlonie, J. L., & Milliken, C. S. (2006). Mental health problems, use of mental health services, and attrition from military service after returning from deployment to Iraq or Afghanistan. *Journal of the American Medical Association, 295*(9), 1023–1032.

Hoge, E., Bui, E., Luana, M., Metcalf, C., Morris, L., Robinaugh, D., . . . Simon, N. M. (2013). Randomized controlled trial of mindfulness meditation for generalized anxiety disorder: Effects on anxiety and stress reactivity. *Journal of Clinical Psychiatry, 74*(8), 786–792.

Holmes, T. (1978). Life situations, emotions, and disease. *Psychosomatic Medicine, 19,* 747–754.

Holmes, T., & Rahe, R. (1967). The social readjustment rating scale. *Journal of Psychosomatic Research, 11*(2), 213–218.

Homans, G. C. (1961). *Social behavior: Its elementary forms.* New York: Harcourt Brace Jovanovich.

Hoogendijk, E. O., Deeg, D. J., Poppelaars, J., van der Horst, M., van Groenou, M. I. B., Comijs, H. C., . . . Huisman, M. (2016). The Longitudinal Aging Study Amsterdam: Cohort update 2016 and major findings. *European Journal of Epidemiology, 31*(9), 927–945.

Hook, J., & Courtney, M. (2011). Employment outcomes of former foster youth as young adults: The importance of human, personal, and social capital. *Children and Youth Services Review, 33*(10), 1855–1865.

Hooyman, N., Kawamoto, K., & Kiyak, H. A. (2018). *Social gerontology: A multidisciplinary perspective* (10th ed.). New York: Pearson.

Hooyman, N. R., & Kramer, B. J. (2006). *Living through loss: Interventions across the life span.* New York: Columbia University Press.

Horesh, D., Solomon, Z., Keinan, G., & Ein-Dor, T. (2013). The clinical picture of late-onset PTSD: A 20-year-longitudinal study of Israeli war veterans. *Psychiatry Research, 208*(3), 265–273.

Horn, J. L. (1982). The theory of fluid and crystallized intelligence in relation to concepts of cognitive psychology and aging in adulthood. In F. I. M. Craik & S. Trehub (Eds.), *Aging and cognitive processes* (pp. 237–278). New York: Plenum.

Horowitz, A., & Boerner, K. (2017). Long-distance caregiving unique challenges and service needs. In J. M. Wilmoth & M. D. Silverstein (Eds.), *Later-life social support and service provision in diverse and vulnerable populations: Understanding networks of care* (pp. 136–154). New York: Routledge.

Hostinar, C., Lachman, M., Mroczek, D., Seeman, T., & Miller, G. (2015). Additive contributions of childhood adversity and recent stressors to inflammation at midlife: Findings from the MIDUS Study. *Developmental Psychology, 51*(11), 1630–1644.

House, J. S., Lantz, P. M., & Herd, P. (2005). Continuity and change in the social stratification of aging and health over the life course: Evidence from a nationally representative longitudinal study from 1986 to 2001/2002 (Americans' Changing Lives Study). *The Journals of Gerontology, Series B: Psychological Sciences and Social Sciences, 60B,* 15–26.

Howard, T. C. (2010). *Why race and culture matter in schools: Closing the achievement gap in America's classrooms.* New York: Teachers College Press.

Howell, D., Wysocki, K., & Steiner, M. (2010). Toilet training. *Pediatrics in Review, 31*(6), 262–263.

Howland, A., Chen, L., Chen, M., & Min, M. (2017). Exploring socio-demographics, mobility, and living arrangement as risk factors for academic performance among children experiencing homelessness. *Preventing School Failure: Alternative Education for Children and Youth, 61*(4), 268–279.

Hoyert, D., & Xu, J. (2012). Deaths: Preliminary data for 2011. *National Vital Statistics Reports, 61*(6), 1–51.

Hser, Y., Longshore, D., & Anglin, M. (2007). The life course perspective on drug use. *Evaluation Review, 31*(6), 515–547.

Hsin, C., Li, M., & Tsai, C. (2014). The influence of young children's use of technology on their learning: A review. *Journal of Educational Technology & Society, 17*(4), 85–99.

Hu, X., Kaplan, S., & Dalal, R. (2010). An examination of blue- versus white-collar workers' conceptualizations of job satisfaction facets. *Journal of Vocational Behavior, 76*(2), 317–325.

Hubley, A., & Arim, R. (2012). Subjective age in early adolescence: Relationships with chronological age, pubertal timing, desired age, and problem behaviors. *Journal of Adolescence, 35*(2), 357–366.

Hudley, C., & Irving, M. (2012). Ethnic and racial identity in childhood and adolescence. In K. Harris, S. Grahman, T. Urdan, S. Grahma, J. Royer, & M. Zeidner (Eds.), *APA Educational Psychology Handbook. Vol. 2: Individual differences and cultural and contextual factors* (pp. 267–292). Washington, DC: American Psychological Association.

Huebner, A., & Garrod, A. (1993). Moral reasoning among Tibetan monks: A study of Buddhist adolescents and young adults in Nepal. *Journal of Cross-Cultural Psychology, 24*, 167–185.

Hug, L., Sharrow, D., & You, D. (2017). *Levels and trends in child mortality. Report 2017.* UNICEF. Retrieved from www.unicef.org/publications/files/Child_Mortality_Report_2017.pdf.

Hughes, F. (2010). *Children, play, and development* (4th ed.). Thousand Oaks, CA: Sage.

Huinink, J., & Feldhaus, M. (2009). Family research from the life course perspective. *International Sociology, 24*(3), 299–324.

Human Rights Watch. (2018). *Child labor.* Retrieved from www.hrw.org/topic/childrens-rights/child-labor.

Humphreys, C., & Stanley, N. (2015). *Domestic violence and protecting children: New thinking and approaches.* London: Jessica Kingsley.

Hutchison, E. (2007). Community violence. In E. Hutchison, H. Matto, M. Harrigan, L. Charlesworth, & P. Viggiani (Eds.), *Challenges of living: A multidimensional working model for social workers* (pp. 71–104). Thousand Oaks, CA: Sage.

Hutchison, E. (2019). The physical environment. In E. Hutchison (Ed.), *Dimensions of human behavior: Person and environment* (6th ed.). Thousand Oaks, CA: Sage.

Hutchison, E., Matto, H., Harrigan, M., Charlesworth, L., & Viggiani, P. (2007). *Challenges of living: A multidimensional working model for social workers.* Thousand Oaks, CA: Sage.

Huxhold, O., Miche, M., & Schüz, B. (2013). Benefits of having friends in older ages: Differential effects of informal social activities on well-being in middle-aged and older adults. *Journals of Gerontology, Series B: Psychological Sciences and Social Sciences, 69*(3), 366–375.

Hygen, B., Belsky, J., Stenseng, F., Lydersen, S., Guzey, I., & Wichstrom, L. (2015). Child exposure to serious life events, COMT, and aggression: Testing differential susceptibility theory. *Developmental Psychology, 51*(8), 1098–1104.

Iantaffi, A., & Bockting, W. (2011). Views from both sides of the bridge? Gender, sexual legitimacy and transgender people's experiences of relationships. *Culture, Health & Sexuality, 13*(3), 355–370.

Idring, S., Magnusson, C., Lundberg, M., Ek, M., Rai, D., Svensson, A., . . . Lee, B. K. (2014). Parental age and the risk of autism spectrum disorders: Findings from a Swedish population-based cohort. *International Journal of Epidemiology, 43*(1), 107–115.

Ikeno, Y., Hubbard, G., Lee, S., Dube, S., Flores, L., Roman, M., . . . Bartke, A. (2013). Do Ames Dwarf and calorie-restricted mice share common effects on age-related pathology? *Pathobiology of Aging & Age-Related Disease, 3*, 1–4.

Impett, E., & Tolman, D. (2006). Late adolescent girls' sexual experiences and sexual satisfaction. *Journal of Adolescent Research, 21*(6), 628–646.

Inderbitzin, M. (2009). Reentry of emerging adults: Adolescent inmates' transition back into the community. *Journal of Adolescent Research, 24*(4), 453–476.

Insel, T. (2013). *Director's blog: The four kingdoms of autism.* National Institute of Mental Health. Retrieved from www.nimh.nih.gov/about/directors/thomas-insel/blog/2013/the-four-kingdoms-of-autism.shtml.

Institute of Medicine. (2006). *Preterm birth: Causes, consequences and prevention.* Washington, DC: National Academies Press.

Insurance Institute for Highway Safety. (2017). *General statistics.* Retrieved from www.iihs.org/iihs/topics/t/general-statistics/fatalityfacts/overview-of-fatality-facts.

International Federation of Persons With Physical Disability. (2017). *Violence against women: Forced sterilization of women with disabilities is a reality in Europe.* Retrieved from www.fimitic.org/content/violence-against-women-forced-sterilization-women-disabilities-reality-europe.

International Society for Traumatic Stress Studies. (2016). *Trauma victim: Information for adult victims of trauma.* Oakbrook Terrace, IL: Author.

Iono, C., Colombo, C., Brazzoduro, V., Mascheroni, E., Confalonieri, E., Castoldi, F., & Lista, G. (2016). Mothers and fathers in the NICU: The impact of preterm birth on parental distress. *Europe's Journal of Psychology, 12*(4), 604–621.

Irish, D., Lundquist, K., & Nelsen, V. (1993). *Ethnic variations in dying, death, and grief: Diversity in universality.* Washington, DC: Taylor & Francis.

Isenberg, J. P., & Jolongo, M. (2003). *Major trends and issues in early childhood education: Challenges, controversies, and insights* (2nd ed.). New York: Teachers College Press.

It's Pronounced Metrosexual. (2017). *The genderbread person v 3.* Retrieved from http://itspronouncedmetrosexual.com/2015/03/the-genderbread-person-v3/#sthash.wv1Gj3zG.FJdXe3Q9.dpbs.

Iwata, S., Iwata, O., & Matsuishi, T. (2013). Sleep patterns of Japanese preschool children and their parents: Implications of co-sleeping. *Acta Paediatrica, 102*(6), 257–262.

Jackson, A., & Mott, P. (2007). Reproductive health care for women with spina bifida. *Scientific World Journal, 7,* 1875–1883.

Jackson, S. L., & Cunningham, S. A. (2015). Social competence and obesity in elementary school. *American Journal of Public Health, 105*(1), 153–158.

Jacobsen, L., Mather, M., Lee, M., & Kent, M. (2011). America's aging population. *Population Bulletin, 66*(1), 1–18.

Jacobstein, R., & Polis, C. B. (2014). Progestin-only contraception: Injectables and implants. *Best Practice and Research: Clinical Obstetrics & Gynaecology, 28*(6), 795–806.

Jahromi, L., Putnam, S., & Stifter, C. (2004). Maternal regulation of infant reactivity from 2 to 6 months. *Developmental Psychology, 40*(4), 477–487.

Jain, S., & Cohen, A. (2013). Behavioral adaptation among youth exposed to community violence: A longitudinal multidisciplinary study of family, peer and neighborhood-level protective factors. *Prevention Science: The Official Journal of the Society for Prevention Research, 14*(6), 606–617.

James, K., & Bose, P. (2011). Self-generated actions during learning objects and sounds create sensori-motor systems in the developing brain. *Cognition, Brain, Behavior, 15*(4), 485–503.

James, S., Chilvers, R., Havermann, D., & Phelps, J. Y. (2010). Avoiding legal pitfalls in surrogacy arrangements. *Reproductive BioMedicine Online, 21*(7), 862–867.

James, W. P. T. (2006). The challenge of childhood obesity. *The International Journal of Pediatric Obesity, 1*(1), 7–10.

Jang, Y., Borenstein, A. R., Chiriboga, D. A., & Mortimer, J. A. (2005). Depressive symptoms among African American and white older adults. *The Journals of Gerontology, Series B: Psychological Sciences and Social Sciences, 6*(6), 313–319.

Jansen, P., Raat, H., Mackenbach, J., Jaddoe, V., Hofman, A., Verhulst, F., & Tiemeier, H. (2009). Socioeconomic inequalities in infant temperament. *Social Psychiatry and Psychiatric Epidemiology, 44*(2), 87–95.

Jasinski, J., Blumenstein, L., & Morgan, R. (2014). Testing Johnson's typology: Is there gender symmetry in intimate terrorism? *Violence and Victims, 29*(1), 73–88.

Jatlaoui, T., & Curtis, K. M. (2016). Safety and effectiveness data for emergency contraceptive pills among women with obesity: A systematic review. *Contraception, 94*(6), 605–611.

Jatlaoui, T., Shah, J., Mandel, M., Krashin, J., Suchdev, D., Jamieson, D., & Pazol, K. (2017). Abortion surveillance – United States, 2014. *MMWR Surveillance Summaries, 66*(2), 1–48.

Javor, R. (2016). Bilingualism, theory of mind and perspective-taking: The effect of early bilingual exposure. *Psychology and Behavioral Sciences, 5*(6), 143–148.

Jean, A., & Stack, D. (2012). Full-term and very-low-birth-weight preterm infants' self-regulating behaviors during a still-face interaction: Influences of maternal touch. *Infant Behavior and Development, 35*(4), 779–791.

Jee, H., & Park, J. (2017). Selection of an optimal set of biomarkers and comparative analyses of biological age estimation models in Korean females. *Archives of Gerontology and Geriatrics, 70,* 84–91.

Jenkins, J., & Foster, E. (2014). The effects of breastfeeding exclusivity on early childhood outcomes. *American Journal of Public Health, 104*(Suppl.), S128–S135.

Jenkinson, S. (2012). *The skill of brokenheartedness: Euthanasia, palliative care and power.* Retrieved from www.youtube.com/watch?v=6dbmXWLCaRg.

Jennings, K., Sandberg, I., Kelley, S., Valdes, L., Yaggi, K., Abrew, A., & Macey-Kalcevic, M. (2008). Understanding of self and maternal warmth predict later self-regulation in toddlers. *International Journal of Behavioral Development, 32*(2), 108–188.

Jensen, J. (2013). Vaginal ring delivery of selected progesterone receptor modulators for contraception. *Contraception, 87*(3), 314–318.

Jensen, L. A. (2003). Coming of age in a multicultural world: Globalization and adolescent cultural identity formation. *Applied Developmental Science, 7*(3), 188–195.

Jenson, J., & Fraser, M. (2016). *Social policy and children and families: A risk and resilience perspective* (3rd ed.). Thousand Oaks, CA: Sage.

Jewell, J., Krohn, E., Scott, V., Carolton, M., & Meinz, E. (2008). The differential impact of mothers' and fathers' discipline on preschool children's home and classroom behavior. *North American Journal of Psychology, 10*(1), 173–188.

Jiang, Y., Granja, M. R., & Koball, H. (2017). *Basic facts about low-income children: Children 6 through 11 years, 2015.* National Center for Children in Poverty. Retrieved from www.nccp.org/publications/pdf/text_1173.pdf.

Jin, K. (2010). Modern biological theories of aging. *Aging and Disease, 1*(2), 72–74.

Jobe-Shields, L., Cohen, R., & Parra, G. R. (2011). Patterns of change in children's loneliness: Trajectories from third through fifth grades. *Merrill-Palmer Quarterly, 57*(1), 25–47.

Johnson, A. G. (2006). *Privilege, power, and difference.* Boston: McGraw-Hill.

Johnson, M. (2008). *A typology of domestic violence: Intimate terrorism, violent resistance, and situational couple violence.* Boston: Northeastern University Press.

Johnson, M., Crosnoe, R., & Elder, G. (2011). Insights on adolescence from a life course perspective. *Journal of Research on Adolescence, 21*(1), 273–280.

Johnson, R., Browne, K., & Hamilton-Giachritsis, C. (2006). Young children in institutional care at risk of harm. *Trauma, Violence & Abuse, 7*(1), 34–60.

Johnson, R., Schoeni, R., & Rogowski, J. (2012). Health disparities in mid-to-late life: The role of earlier life family and neighborhood socioeconomic conditions. *Social Science & Medicine, 74*, 625–636.

Johnson, S., Blum, R., & Giedd, J. (2009). Adolescent maturity and the brain: The promise and pitfalls of neuroscience research in adolescent health policy. *Journal of Adolescent Health, 45*(3), 216–221.

Johnson, S. B., Riis, J. L., & Noble, K. G. (2016). Start of the art review: Poverty and the developing brain. *Pediatrics, 137*(4), 1–16.

Johnson, W., Giordano, P., Longmore, M., & Manning, W. (2014). Intimate partner violence and depressive symptoms during adolescence and young adulthood. *Journal of Health and Social Behavior, 55*(1), 39–55.

Johnston, L., O'Malley, P., Bachman, J., & Schulenberg, J. (2004). *Monitoring the future national results on adolescent drug use: Overview of key findings, 2003* (NIH Publication No. 04-5506). Bethesda, MD: National Institute of Drug Abuse.

Johnston, L., O'Malley, P., Bachman, J., & Schulenberg, J. (2005). *Monitoring the future national results on adolescent drug use: Overview of key findings, 2004* (NIH Publication No. 06-5882). Bethesda, MD: National Institute of Drug Abuse.

Johnston, L., O'Malley, P., Bachman, J., Schulenberg, J., & Miech, R. (2014). *Monitoring the Future: National survey results on drug use, 1975–2013: College students and adult ages 19–55* (Vol. 2). Ann Arbor: Institute for Social Research, the University of Michigan. Retrieved from www.monitoringthefuture.org/pubs/monographs/mtf-vol2_2014.pdf.

Jones, A., & Meier, A. (2011). Growing www.parentsof suicide: A case study of an online support community. *Social Work with Groups, 34*(2), 101–120.

Jones, B., & McAdams, D. (2013). Becoming generative: Socializing influences recalled in late stories in late midlife. *Journal of Adult Development, 20*(3), 158–172.

Jones, C., Peskin, H., & Livson, N. (2011). Men's and women's change and individual differences in change in femininity from age 33 to 85: Results from the intergenerational studies. *Journal of Adult Development, 18*(4), 155–163.

Jones, J., & Mosher, W. (2013). *Fathers' involvement with their children: United States, 2006–2010. National Health Statistics Reports No. 71.* Hyattsville, MD: National Center for Health Statistics.

Jones, J., Mosher, W., & Daniels, K. (2012, May 18). Current contraceptive use in the United States, 2006–2010 and changes in patterns of use since 1995. *National Health Statistics Report, 60.* Retrieved from www.cdc.gov/nchs/data/nhsr/nhsr060.pdf.

Jones, R. K., Lindberg, L. D., & Higgins, J. A. (2014). Pull and pray or extra protection? Contraceptive strategies involving withdrawal among US adult women. *Contraception, 90*(4), 416–421.

Jones, T. M, Hill, K. G., Epstein, M., Lee, J. O., Hawkins, J. D., & Catalano, R. F. (2016). Understanding the interplay of individual and social-developmental factors in the progression of substance use and mental health from childhood to adulthood. *Development and Psychopathology, 28*(3), 721–741.

Jordan, J. (2005). Relational resilience in girls. In S. Goldstein & R. Brooks (Eds.), *Handbook of resilience in children* (pp. 79–90). New York: Kluwer Academic/Plenum.

Joshi, S., & Morley, J. (2006). Cognitive impairment. *Medical Clinics of North America, 90*(5), 769–787.

Joss-Moore, L., & Lane, R. (2009). The developmental origins of adult diseases. *Current Opinions in Pediatrics, 21*(2), 230–234.

Jung, C. (1971). *The portable Jung.* New York: Viking Press.

Jurimae, J. (2013). *Growth, physical activity, and motor development in prepubertal children.* Ipswich, MA: Ebsco.

Kahneman, D. (2011). *Thinking fast and slow.* New York: Farrar, Straus and Giroux.

Kahraman, P., & Başal, H. (2012). Sex stereotypes of seven-eight year old girls and boys living in urban and rural areas. *International Journal of Human Sciences, 9*(1), 46–60.

Kala, P., Hudakova, N., Jurajda, M., Kasparek, T., Ustohal, L., Parenica, J., . . . Kanovsky, J. (2016). Depression and anxiety after acute myocardial infarction treated by primary PCI. *PLoS One, 11*(4). doi:10.137/journal.pone.0152367

Kamerman, S. (1996). Child and family policies: An international overview. In E. Zigler, S. Kagan, & N. Hall (Eds.), *Children, families, and government: Preparing for the twenty-first century* (pp. 31–48). New York: Cambridge University Press.

Kaminski, J. W., & Claussen, A. H. (2017). Evidence base update for psychosocial treatments for disruptive behaviors in children. *Journal of Clinical Child & Adolescent Psychology, 46*(4), 477–499.

Kang, M. Y., & Kim, H. R. (2014). Association between voluntary/involuntary job loss and the development of stroke or cardiovascular disease: A prospective study of middle-aged to older workers in a rapidly developing Asian country. *PLoS One, 9*(11), e. 113495.

Kann, L., McManus, T., Harris, W. A., Shanklin, S., Flint, K., Hawkins, J., . . . Zaza, S. (2016). Youth risk behavior surveillance — United States, 2015. *Morbidity and Mortality Weekly Report (MMWR) Surveillance Summary 2016, 65*(6), 1–180.

Kaplan, J., Aziz-Zadeh, L., Uddin, L., & Iacoboni, M. (2008). The self across the senses: An fMRI study of self-face and self-voice recognition. *Social Cognitive & Affective Neuroscience, 3*(3), 218–223.

Karoly, L. (2016). The economic returns to early childhood education. *The Future of Children, 26*(2), 37–55.

Karraker, A., DeLamater, J., & Schwartz, C. (2011). Sexual frequency decline from midlife to later life. *The Journals*

of Gerontology, Series B: Psychological Sciences and Social Sciences, 66(4), 502–512.

Karraker, M. W. (2013). *Global families.* Thousand Oaks, CA: Sage.

Kasckow, J., Karp, J., Whyte, E., Butters, M., Brown, C., Begley, A., . . . Reynolds, C. F. (2013). Subsyndromal depression and anxiety in older adults: Health related, function, cognitive and diagnostic implications. *Journal of Psychiatric Research, 47*(5), 599–603.

Kashushin, G., & Egan, M. (2008). *Gerontological home health care: A guide for the social work practitioner.* New York: Columbia University Press.

Kaslow, F., & Robison, J. A. (1996). Long-term satisfying marriages: Perceptions of contributing factors. *The American Journal of Family Therapy, 24*(2), 153–170.

Kaur, P., Shorey, L., Ho, E., Dashwood, R., & Williams D. E. (2013). The epigenome as a potential of cancer and disease prevention in prenatal development. *Nutritional Reviews, 71*(7), 441–457.

Kaye, L. W. (2005). The emergence of the new aged and the productive aging perspective. In L. W. Kaye (Ed.), *Perspectives on productive aging: Social work with the new aged* (pp. 3–18). Washington, DC: NASW.

Keenan, K., Ploubidis, G., Silverwood, R., & Grundy, E. (2017). Life-course partnership history and midlife health behaviors in a population-based birth cohort. *J. Epidemiol Community Health, 71*, 232–238.

Keenan, T., & Evans, S. (2009). *An introduction to child development* (2nd ed.). Thousand Oaks, CA: Sage.

Kegan, R. (1982). *The evolving self: Problem and process in human development.* Cambridge, MA: Harvard University Press.

Kegan, R. (1994). *In over our heads: The mental demands of modern life.* Cambridge, MA: Harvard University Press.

Kei-ho Pih, K., Hirose, A., & Mao, K. R. (2012). The invisible unattended: Low-wage Chinese immigrant workers, health care, and social capital in Southern California's San Gabriel Valley. *Sociological Inquiry, 82*(2), 236–256.

Kelly, Y., Sacker, A., Schoon, I., & Nazroo, J. (2006). Ethnic differences in achievement of developmental milestones by 9 months of age: The Millenium Cohort Study. *Developmental Medicine & Child Neurology, 48*(10), 825–830.

Kemp, C. (2005). Dimensions of grandparent-adult grandchild relationships: From family ties to intergenerational friends. *Canadian Journal on Aging, 24*(2), 161–177.

Keniston, K. (1966). *The uncommitted: Alienated youth in American society.* New York: Harcourt, Brace, & World.

Kennedy, T., & Ceballo, R. (2014). Who, what, when, and where? Toward a dimensional conceptualization of community violence exposure. *Review of General Psychology, 18*(2), 69–81.

Kenny, U., O'Malley-Keighran, M., Molcho, M., & Kelly, C. (2017). Peer influences on adolescent body image: Friends or foes? *Journal of Adolescent Research, 32*(6), 768–799.

Kent, L. (2015). *Five facts about America's students.* Washington, DC: Pew Research Center. Retrieved from www.pewresearch.org/fact-tank/2015/08/10/5-facts-about-americas-students/.

Keogh, B. K., Bernheimer, L. P., & Guthrie, D. (2004). Children with developmental delays twenty years later: Where are they? How are they? *American Journal on Mental Retardation, 109*(3), 219–230.

Keresteš, G., Broković, I., & Jagodić, G. (2012). Predictors of psychological well-being of adolescents' parents. *Journal of Happiness Studies, 13*(6), 1073–1089.

Kessler, R., Berglund, P., Demler, O., Jin, R., Merikangas, K., & Walters, E. (2005). Life-time prevalence and age-of-onset distributions of DSM-IV disorders in the National Comorbidity Survey Replication. *Archives of General Psychiatry, 62*(6), 593–602.

Keyes, C., & Ryff, C. (1998). Generativity in adult lives: Social structural contours and quality of life consequences. In D. McAdams & E. de St. Aubin (Eds.), *Generativity and adult development: How and why we care for the next generation* (pp. 227–263). Washington, DC: American Psychological Association.

Khandaker, G. M., Dibben, C. R. M., & Jones, P. B. (2012). Does maternal body mass index during pregnancy influence risk of schizophrenia in the adult offspring? *Obesity Reviews, 13*(6), 518–527.

Khaw, L., & Hardesty, J. (2007). Theorizing the process of leaving: Turning points and trajectories in the stages of change. *Family Relations, 56*(4), 413–425.

Khodyakov, D., & Carr, D. (2009). The impact of late-life parental death on adult sibling relationships. *Research on Aging, 31*(5), 495–519.

Khubchandani, J., Price, J., Thompson, A., Dake, J., Wiblishauser, M., & Telljohann, S. (2012). Adolescent dating violence: A national assessment of school counselors' perceptions and practices. *Pediatrics, 130*(2), 202–210.

Kilmer, R., Cook, J., Crusto, C., Strater, K., & Haber, M. (2012). Understanding the ecology and development of children and families experiencing homelessness: Implications for practice, supportive services, and policy. *American Journal of Orthopsychiatry, 82*(3), 389–401.

Kim, H., Chang, M., Rose, K., & Kim, S. (2012). Predictors of caregiver burden in caregivers of individuals with dementia. *Journal of Advanced Nursing, 68*(4), 846–855.

Kim, S., & Esquivel, G. (2011). Adolescent spirituality and resilience: Theory, research, and educational practices. *Psychology in the Schools, 48*(7), 755–765.

King, C., & Merchant, C. (2008). Social and interpersonal factors relating to adolescent suicidality: A review of the literature. *Archives of Suicide Research, 12*(3), 181–196.

King, W. (2009). Toward a life-course perspective of police organizations. *Journal of Research in Crime and Delinquency, 46*(2), 213–244.

Kirk, D. (2012). Residential change as a turning point in the life course of crime: Desistance or temporary cessation? *Criminology, 50*(2), 329–357.

Kitayama, S., Karasawa, M., & Mesquita, B. (2004). Collective and personal processes in regulating emotions: Emotion and self in Japan and the United States. In P. Philippot & R. Feldman (Eds.), *The regulation of emotion* (pp. 251–276). Mahwah, NJ: Lawrence Erlbaum.

Kitzmann, K., Gaylor, N., Holt, A., & Kenny, E. (2003). Child witnesses to domestic violence: A meta-analytic review. *Journal of Consulting and Clinical Psychology, 71*(2), 339–352.

Klein, D., Mok, D., Chen, J., & Watkins, K. (2014). Age of language learning shapes brain structure: A cortical thickness study of bilingual and monolingual individuals. *Brain & Language, 131,* 20–24.

Klein, J. (2012). *The bully society: School shootings and the crisis of bullying in America's schools.* New York: New York University Press.

Kliman, H., & Milano, K. (2013). The majority of miscarriages are caused by genetic abnormalities. *Fertility and Sterility, 100*(3), S306–S306.

Kneas, D., & Perry, B. (2011). *Using technology in the early childhood classroom.* Retrieved from http://teacher.scholastic.com/professional/bruceperry/using_technology.htm.

Knitzer, J. (2007). Putting knowledge into policy: Toward an infant-toddler policy agenda. *Infant Mental Health Journal, 28*(2), 237–245.

Ko, J., Farr, S., Dietz, P., & Robbins, C. (2012). Depression and treatment among U.S. pregnant and nonpregnant women of reproductive age, 2005–2009. *Journal of Women's Health, 21*(8), 830–836.

Koball, H., & Jiang, Y. (2018). *Basic facts about low-income children: Children under 18 years, 2016.* National Center for Children in Poverty. Retrieved from http://nccp.org/publications/pub_1194.html.

Kochanek, K. D., Murphy, S. L., Xu, J., & Tejada-Vera, B. (2016, June). Deaths: Final data for 2014. *National Vital Statistics Reports, 65*(4), 1–122.

Kochanska, G. (1997). Multiple pathways to conscience for children with different temperaments: From toddlerhood to age 5. *Developmental Psychology, 33*(2), 228–240.

Kochanska, G., Aksan, N., & Joy, M. (2007). Children's fearfulness as a moderator of parenting in early socialization: Two longitudinal studies. *Developmental Psychology, 43*(1), 222–237.

Kochanska, G., Forman, D., Aksan, N., & Dunbar, S. (2005). Pathways to conscience: Early mother-child mutually responsive orientation and children's moral emotion, conduct, and cognition. *Journal of Child Psychology and Psychiatry, 46*(1), 19–34.

Koehn, M. (2008). Contemporary women's perceptions of childbirth education. *Journal of Perinatal Education, 17*(1), 11–18.

Koert, E., & Daniluk, J. C. (2017). When time runs out: reconciling permanent childlessness after delayed childbearing. *Journal of Reproductive and Infant Psychology, 35*(4), 342–352.

Kohlberg, L. (1969). Stage and sequence: The cognitive developmental approach to socialization. In D. A. Goslin (Ed.), *Handbook of socialization theory and research* (pp. 347–480). Chicago: Rand McNally.

Kohlberg, L. (1976). Moral stages and moralization: The cognitive-developmental approach. In T. Lickona (Ed.), *Moral development and behavior: Theory, research, and social issues* (pp. 31–53). New York: Holt.

Kohlberg, L. (1984). *Essays on moral development: Vol. 2. The psychology of moral development.* San Francisco: Harper & Row.

Kohli, M., & Künemund, H. (2005). The midlife generation in the family: Patterns of exchange and support. In S. Willis & M. Martin (Eds.), *Middle adulthood: A lifespan perspective* (pp. 35–61). Thousand Oaks, CA: Sage.

Kohut, H. (1971). *The analysis of the self.* New York: International Universities Press.

Kolman, K. B., Hadley, S. K., & Jordahllafrato, M. A. (2015). Long-acting reversible contraception: Who, what, when, and how. *Journal of Family Medicine, 64*(8), 479–484.

Kondrat, M. E. (2008). Person-in-environment. In T. Mizrahi & L. Davis (Eds.), *Encyclopedia of social work* (20th ed., Vol. 3, pp. 349–354). New York: NASW Press/Oxford Press.

Koraly, L. (2016). The economic returns to early childhood education. *The Future of Children, 26*(2), 37–55.

Kosciw, J. G., Greytak, E. A., Giga, N. M., Villenas, C., & Danischewski, D. J. (2016). *The 2015 national school climate survey: The experiences of lesbian, gay, bisexual, transgender, and queer youth in our nation's schools.* New York: GLSEN. Retrieved from www.glsen.org/research.

Kovács, Á., & Mehler, J. (2009). Flexible learning of multiple speech structures in bilingual infants. *Science, 325*(5940), 611–612.

Kovacs, P. J., Bellin, M. H., & Fauri, D. F. (2006). Family-centered care: A resource for social work in end-of-life and palliative care. *Journal of Social Work in End-of-Life & Palliative Care, 2*(1), 13–27.

Kowal, S., Dall, T., Chakrabarti, R., Storm, M., & Jain, A. (2013). The current and projected economic burden of Parkinson's disease in the United States. *Movement Disorders, 28*(3), 311–318.

Kowalski, K. (2003). The emergence of ethnic and racial attitudes in preschool-aged children. *Journal of Social Psychology, 143*(6), 677–690.

Kozhimannil, K. B., Hardeman, R., Attanasio, L., Blauer-Peterson, C., & O'Brien, M. (2013). Doula care, birth outcomes, and costs among Medicaid beneficiaries. *American Journal of Public Health, 103*(4), 113–121.

Kozol, J. (2005). *The shame of the nation: The restoration of apartheid schooling in America.* New York: Crown.

Kramer, B. (1997). Gain in the caregiving experience: Where are we? What next? *The Gerontologist, 37*, 218–232.

Kreider, R., Bates, N., & Mayol-Garcia, Y. (2017). *Improving measurement of same-sex couple households in Census Bureau surveys: Results from recent tests.* Washington, DC: U.S. Census Bureau. Retrieved from www.census.gov/content/dam/Census/library/working-papers/2017/demo/SEHSD-WP2017-28.pdf.

Kremer, H., Ironson, G., & Kaplan, L. (2009). The fork in the road: HIV as a potential positive turning point and the role of spirituality. *AIDS Care, 21*(3), 368–377.

Kremen, W., Prom-Wormley, E., Panizzon, M., Eyler, L., Fischl, B., Neale, M., . . . Fennema-Notestine, C. (2010). Genetic and environmental influences on the size of specific brain regions in midlife: The VETSA MRI study. *NeuroImage, 49*(2), 1213–1223.

Kristof, N., & WuDunn, S. (2009). *Half the sky: Turning oppression into opportunity for women worldwide.* New York: Vintage.

Kroger, J. (2007). *Identity development: Adolescence through adulthood* (2nd ed.). Thousand Oaks, CA: Sage.

Kroger, J., Martinussen, M., & Marcia, J. (2010). Identity status change during adolescence and young adulthood: A meta-analysis. *Journal of Adolescence, 33*(5), 683–698.

Krueger, A. K., Reither, E., Peppard, P. E., Krueger, P. M., & Hale, L. (2013). Do sleep-deprived adolescents make less healthy food choices? *Proceedings of the Annual SLEEP Conference*, Baltimore.

Kübler-Ross, E. (1969). *On death and dying.* New York: Macmillan.

Kubota, T., & Hata, L. (2013). Epigenomics comes of age with expanding roles in biological understanding and clinical application. *Journal of Human Genetics, 59*, 395.

Kuipers, M. A. G., van Poppel, M. N. M., van den Brink, W., Wingen, M., & Kunst, A. E. (2012). The association between neighborhood disorder, social cohesion and hazardous alcohol use: A national multilevel study. *Drug and Alcohol Dependence, 126*(1–2), 27–34.

Kumar, K. (2017). The blended family life cycle. *Journal of Divorce & Remarriage, 58*(2), 110–125.

Kunze, F., Raes, A., & Bruch, H. (2015). It matters how old you feel: Antecedents and performance consequences of average relative subjective age in organizations. *Journal of Applied Psychology, 100*(5), 1511–1526.

Kurcinka, M. S. (2006). *Sleepless in America: Practical strategies to help your family get the sleep it deserves.* New York: HarperCollins.

Kurdek, L. (2004). Are gay and lesbian cohabiting couples *really* different from heterosexual married couples? *Journal of Marriage and the Family, 66*(4), 880–900.

Kurdek, L. (2008). Change in relationship quality for partners from lesbian, gay male, and heterosexual couples. *Journal of Family Psychology, 22*(5), 701–711.

Kurtz, L. (2016). *Gods in the global village: The world's religions in sociological perspective* (4th ed.). Thousand Oaks, CA: Sage.

Kuther, T. (2017). *Lifespan development: Lives in context.* Thousand Oaks, CA: Sage.

Kwon, M.-K., Luck, S., & Oakes, L. (2014). Visual short-term memory for complex objects in 6- 8-month-old infants. *Child Development, 85*(2), 564–577.

Kyriacou, C. (2016). A psychological typology of cyberbullies in schools. *Psychology of Education Review, 40*(2), 24–27.

Labouvie-Vief, G. (2005). Self-with-other representations and the organization of the self. *Journal of Research in Personality, 39*(1), 185–205.

Lacey, H. P., Smith, D. M., & Ubel, P. A. (2006). I hope I die before I get old: Mispredicting happiness across the adult life span. *Journal of Happiness Studies, 7*(2), 162–182.

Lachman, M. (2004). Development in midlife. *Annual Review of Psychology, 55*, 305–331.

Lachman, M. (2015). Mind the gap in the middle: A call to study midlife. *Research in Human Development, 12*(3–4), 327–334.

Lachman, M., Agrigoroaei, S., Murphy, C., & Tun, P. (2010). Frequent cognitive activity compensates for education differences in episodic memory. *American Journal of Geriatric Psychiatry, 18*(1), 4–10.

Lachman, M., & Bertrand, R. (2001). Personality and the self in midlife. In M. Lachman (Ed.), *Handbook of midlife development* (pp. 279–309). New York: Wiley.

Lachman, M., Teshale, S., & Agrigoroaei, S. (2015). Midlife as pivotal period in the life course: Balancing growth and decline at the crossroads of youth and old age. *International Journal of Behavioral Development, 39*(1), 20–31.

Laditka, J. N., Laditka, S. B., Olatosi, B., & Elder, K. T. (2007). The health trade-off of rural residence for impaired older adults: Longer life, more impairment. *The Journal of Rural Health, 23*(2), 124–132.

Laflamme, D., Pomerleau, A., & Malcuit, G. (2002). A comparison of fathers' and mothers' involvement in childcare and stimulation behaviors during free play with their infants at 9 and 15 months. *Sex Roles, 47*(11–12), 507–518.

Lagan, B., Sinclair, M., & Kernohan, W. (2010). Internet use in pregnancy informs women's decision-making: A web-based survey. *Birth, 37*(2), 106–115.

Lam, C., & McHale, S. (2012). Developmental patterns and family predictors of adolescent weight concerns: A replication and extension. *International Journal of Eating Disorders, 45*(4), 524–530.

Lam, V., & Smith, G. (2009). African and Caribbean adolescents in Britain: Ethnic identity and Britishness. *Ethnic and Racial Studies, 32*(7), 1248–1270.

Lamaze, F. (1958). *Painless childbirth: Psychoprophylactic method* (L. R. Celestin, Trans.). London: Burke.

Lament, C. (2015). Transgender children: Conundrums and controversies—An introduction to the section. *The Psychoanalytic Study of The Child, 68*(1), 13–27.

Lamers, W. (2013). *Signs of approaching death.* Washington, DC: Hospice Foundation of America. Retrieved from https://hospicefoundation.org/End-of-Life-Support-and-Resources/Coping-with-Terminal-Illness/Signs-of-Approaching-Death.

Lancet, The. (2013). *Maternal and child nutrition*. Retrieved from www.thelancet.com/pdfs/journals/lancet/PIIS0140-6736(13)60988-5.pdf.

Lancet, The. (2016, January). *Ending preventable stillbirths: An executive summary for the Lancet Series*. Retrieved from www.thelancet.com/pb/assets/raw/Lancet/stories/series/stillbirths2016-exec-summ.pdf.

Landes, S., Wilder, J., & Williams, D. (2017). The effect of race and birth cohort on the veteran mortality differential. *Social Science & Medicine, 179*, 37–44.

Lane, J., Wellman, H., Olson, S., LaBounty, J., & Kerr, D. (2010). Theory of mind and emotion understanding predict moral development in early childhood. *British Journal of Development Psychology, 28*(Pt. 4), 871–889.

Lang, A. J., Aarons, G. A., Gearity, J., Laffaye, C., Satz, L., Dresselhaus, T. R., & Stein, M. B. (2008). Direct and indirect links between childhood maltreatment, posttraumatic stress disorder, and women's health. *Behavioral Medicine, 33*(4), 125–135.

Langa, K., Larson, E., Crimmins, E., Faul, J., Levine, D., Kabeto, M., & Weir, D. (2017). A comparison of the prevalence of dementia in the United States in 2000 and 2017. *JAMA Internal Medicine, 177*(1), 51–58.

Langle, A., & Probst, C. (2004). Existential questions of the elderly. *Archives of Psychiatry and Psychotherapy, 6*(2), 15–20.

Lansford, J., Deater-Deckard, K., Dodge, K., Bates, J., & Pettit, G. (2004). Ethnic differences in the link between physical discipline and later adolescent externalizing behaviors. *Journal of Child Psychology and Psychiatry, 45*(4), 801–812.

Lapsley, D., & Carlo, G. (2014). Moral development at the crossroad: New trends and possible futures. *Developmental Psychology, 50*(1), 1–7.

Larson, R. W., Wilson, S., & Mortimer, J. T. (2002). Adolescence in the 21st century: An international perspective—Adolescents' preparation for the future. *Journal of Research on Adolescence, 12*(1), 159–166.

Laskov, I., Birnbaum, R., Maslovitz, S., Kupferminc, M., Lessing, J., & Mony, A. (2012). Outcome of singleton pregnancy in women ≥ 45 years old: A retrospective cohort study. *Journal of Maternal-Fetal & Neonatal Medicine, 25*(11), 2190–2193.

Latva, R., Lehtonen, L., Salmelin, R. K., & Tamminen, T. (2007). Visits by the family to the neonatal intensive care unit. *Acta Paediatricia, 96*(2), 215–200.

Lau, A., Litrownik, A., Newton, R., Black, M., & Everson, M. (2006). Factors affecting the link between physical discipline and child externalizing problems in Black and White families. *Journal of Community Psychology, 34*(1), 89–103.

Laughlin, L. (2013). *Who's minding the kids? Child care arrangements: Spring 2011*. Washington, DC: U.S. Census Bureau. Retrieved from www.census.gov/prod/2013pubs/p70-135.pdf.

Lauritsen, J., & Rezey, M. (2013). *Measuring the prevalence of crime with the National Crime Victimization Survey*. Washington, DC: U.S. Department of Justice, Office of Justice Programs, Bureau of Justice Statistics. Retrieved from www.bjs.gov/content/pub/pdf/mpcncvs.pdf.

Lawrence, C. R., Carlson, E. A., & Egeland, B. (2006). The impact of foster care on development. *Development and Psychopathology, 18*(1), 57–76.

Lawton, M. P. (1983). Environment and other determinants of well-being in older people. *The Gerontologist, 23*(4), 349–357.

Lawton, M. P. (1986). *Environment and aging*. Albany, NY: Center for the Study of Aging.

Lawton, M. P., & Nahemow, L. (1973). Ecology and the aging process. In C. Eisdorfer & M. P. Lawton (Eds.), *The psychology of adult development and aging* (pp. 619–674). Washington DC: American Psychological Association.

Leaper, C. (2013). Gender development during childhood. In P. Zelaz (Ed.), *The Oxford handbook of developmental psychology: Vol. 2. Self and other* (pp. 326–377). New York: Oxford University Press.

Leavell, A., Tamis-LeMonda, C., Ruble, D., Zosuls, K., & Cabrera, N. (2012). African American, White, and Latino fathers' activities with their sons and daughters in early childhood. *Sex Role, 66*, 53–65.

Lederberg, A., Schick, B., & Spencer, P. (2013). Language and literacy development of deaf and hard-of-hearing children: Successes and challenges. *Developmental Psychology, 49*(1), 15–30.

Lee, C., & Beckert, T. (2012). Taiwanese adolescent cognitive autonomy and identity development: The relationship of situational and agential factors. *International Journal of Psychology, 47*(1), 39–50.

Lee, G., & DeMaris, A. (2007). Widowhood, gender, and depression: A longitudinal analysis. *Research on Aging, 29*(1), 56–72.

Lee, T., Festinger, T., Jaccard, J., & Munson, M. R. (2017). Mental health subgroups among vulnerable emerging adults, and their functioning. *Journal of the Society for Social Work and Research, 8*(2), 161–188.

Leeder, E. (2004). *The family in global perspective: A gendered journey.* Thousand Oaks, CA: Sage.

Leek, C. (2015). Mechanisms of cumulative advantage among NGOs engaging men in violence prevention. *Journal of Men's Studies, 23*(2), 177–193.

Lehmann, R., Denissen, J., Allemand, M., & Parke, L. (2013). Age and gender differences in motivational manifestations of the Big Five from age 16 to 60. *Developmental Psychology, 49*(2), 365–383.

Lei, L., & South, S. J. (2016). Racial and ethnic differences in leaving and returning to the parental home: The role of life course transitions, socioeconomic resources, and family connectivity. *Demographic Research, 34*(4), 109–142.

Leisering, L. (2003). Government and the life course. In J. Mortimer & M. Shanahan (Eds.), *Handbook of the life course* (pp. 205–225). New York: Kluwer Academic/Plenum.

Lemieux, C. M., & Allen, P. D. (2007). Service learning in social work education: The state of knowledge, pedagogical practicalities, and practice conundrums. *Journal of Social Work Education, 43*(2), 309–325.

Leone, J., Lape, M., & Xu, Y. (2013). Women's decisions to not seek formal help for partner violence: A comparison of intimate terrorism and situational couple violence. *Journal of Interpersonal Violence, 29*(10), 1850–1876.

Leong, F., Eggerth, D., & Flynn, M. (2014). A life course perspective on immigrant occupation health and well-being. *Contemporary Occupational Health Psychology: Global Perspectives on Research and Practice, 3*(1), 97–113.

Leon-Guerrero, A. (2014). *Social problems: Community, policy, and social action* (4th ed.). Thousand Oaks, CA: Sage.

Leopold, L. (2016). Cumulative advantage in an egalitarian country? Socioeconomic health disparities over the life course in Sweden. *Journal of Health and Social Behavior, 57*(2), 257–273.

Leopold, T., & Skopek, J. (2015). The demography of grandparenthood: An international profile. *Social Forces, 94*(2), 801–832.

Leventon, J., & Bauer, P. (2013). The sustained effect of emotional signals on neural processing in 12-month-olds. *Developmental Science, 16*(4), 485–409.

Levinson, D. (1977). The mid-life transition. *Psychiatry, 40*(2), 99–112.

Levinson, D. (1986). A conception of adult development. *American Psychologist, 41*(1), 3–13.

Levinson, D. (1990). A theory of life structure development in adulthood. In C. N. Alexander & E. J. Langer (Eds.), *Higher stages of human development* (pp. 35–54). New York: Oxford University Press.

Levinson, D., Darrow, C., Klein, E., Levinson, M., & McKee, B. (1978). *The seasons of a man's life.* New York: Knopf.

Levinson, D., & Levinson, J. (1996). *The seasons of a woman's life.* New York: Ballantine Books.

Lev-Wiesel, R., Sarid, M., & Sternberg, R. (2013). Measuring social peer rejection during childhood: Development and validation. *Journal of Aggression, Maltreatment & Trauma, 22*(5), 482–492.

Lewis, M. (2005). The child and its family: The social network model. *Human Development, 48*(1), 8–27.

Lewis, T. (1994). A comparative analysis of the effects of social skills training and teacher directed contingencies on social behavior of preschool children with disabilities. *Journal of Behavioral Education, 4*, 267–281.

Li, C. I., Beaber, E. F., Tang, M. C., Porter, P., Daling, J. R., & Malone, K. E. (2012). The effects of depo medroxyprogesterone acetate on breast cancer risk among women 20–44 years of age. *Cancer Research, 72*(8), 2028–2035.

Li, G., Kung, K., & Hines, M. (2017). Childhood gender-typed behavior and adolescent sexual orientation: A longitudinal population-based study. *Developmental Psychology, 53*(4), 764–777.

Li, H. (2006). Rural older adults' access barriers to in-home and community-based services. *Social Work Research, 30*(2), 109–118.

Li, S.-C. (2006). Biocultural co-construction of life span development. In P. B. Baltes, P. A. Reuter-Lorenz, & F. Rössler (Eds.), *Life span development and the brain: The perspective of biocultural co-constructivism* (pp. 40–60). Cambridge, UK: Cambridge University Press.

Li, S.-C. (2009). Brain in macro experiential context: Biocultural co-construction of life span neurocognitive development. *Progress in Brain Research, 178*, 17–29.

Liang, K. (2014). The cross-domain correlates of subjective age in Chinese oldest-old. *Aging & Mental Health, 18*(2), 217–224.

Liao, L., Lunn, S., & Baker, M. (2015). Midlife menopause: Male partners talking. *Sexual and Relationship Therapy, 30*(1), 167–180.

Lichtenstein, S. (1993). Transition from school to adulthood: Case studies of adults with learning disabilities who dropped out of school. *Exceptional Children, 59*(4), 336–347.

Lie, K. K., Groholt, E. K., & Eskild, A. (2011). Association of cerebral palsy with apgar score in low and normal birthweight infants: Population based cohort study. *Obstetric Anesthesia Digest, 31*(3), 154–155.

Light, A. D., Obedin-Maliver, J., Sevelius, J. M., & Kerns, J. L. (2014). Transgender men who experienced pregnancy after female-to-male gender transitioning. *Obstetrics and Gynecology, 124*(6), 1120–1127.

Lightstone, A., Bailey, S. K., & Voros, P. (2015). Collabortive music therapy via remote video technology to reduce a veteran's symptoms of severe, chronic PTSD. *Arts & Health, 7*(2), 123–136.

Lima-Pereira, P., Bermudez-Tamayo, C., & Jasienska, G. (2012). Use of the internet as a source of health information amongst participants of antenatal classes. *Journal of Clinical Nursing, 21*(3/4), 322–330.

Lin, J., Rutter, J., & Park, H. (2016, January 21). Events that led to Flint's water crisis. *New York Times.* Retrieved from www.nytimes.com/interactive/2016/01/21/us/flint-lead-water-timeline.html.

Lindau, S. T., & Gavrilova, N. (2010). Sex, health, and years of sexually active life gained due to good health: Evidence from two US population based cross sectional surveys of ageing. *British Medical Journal. 340*:c810. doi:10.1136/bmj.c810

Lindemann, E. (1944). Symptomatology and management of acute grief. *American Journal of Psychiatry, 101*(2), 141–148.

Lindström, M., Modén, B., & Rosvall, M. (2013). A life-course perspective on economic stress and tobacco smoking: A population-based study. *Addiction, 108*(7), 1305–1314.

Linn, J., Wilson, D., & Fako, T. (2015). Historical role of the father: Implications for childbirth education. *International Journal of Childbirth Education, 30*(1), 12–18.

Lippman, L., & Keith, J. (2009). *A developmental perspective on workplace readiness: Preparing high school students for success.* Washington, DC: Child Trends. Retrieved from www.childtrends.org/wp-content/uploads/2009/04/Child_Trends-2009_04_28_RB_WorkReady.pdf.

Lipscomb, A., & Gersch, I. (2012). Using "spiritual listening tools" to investigate how children describe spiritual and philosophical meaning in their lives. *International Journal of Children's Spirituality, 17*(1), 5–23.

Lipsky, M., & King, M. (2015). Biological theories of aging. *Disease-a-Month, 61*(11), 460–466.

Liptak, A. (2013, June 13). Justices, 9-0, bar patenting genes. *New York Times.* Retrieved from www.nytimes.com/2013/06/14/us/supreme-court-rules-human-genes-may-not-be-patented.html.

Litty, C., & Hatch, J. A. (2006). Hurry up and wait: Rethinking special education identification in kindergarten. *Early Childhood Education Journal, 33*(4), 203–208.

Litwin, H. (2011). Social relationships and well-being in very late life. In L. W. Poon & J. Cohen-Mansfield (Eds.), *Understanding well-being in the oldest old* (pp. 213–226). New York: Cambridge University Press.

Litwin, H., & Levinson, M. (2017). The association of mobility limitation and social networks in relation to late-life activity. *Ageing & Society,* 1–20.

Liu, C., Li, C., Lee, P., & Sun, Y. (2016). Variations in incidence and prevalence of Parkinson's Disease in Taiwan: A population-based nationwide study. *Parkinson's Disease.* 8756359. doi:10.1155/2016/8756359

Liu, C., & Tronick, E. (2013). Re-conceptualizing prenatal life stresses in predicting post-partum depression: Cumulative-, specific-, and domain-specific approaches to calculating risk. *Pediatric and Perinatal Epidemiology, 27*(5), 481–490.

Liu, D., Wellman, H., Tardif, T., & Sabbagh, M. (2008). Theory of mind development in Chinese children: A meta-analysis of false-belief understanding across cultures and languages. *Developmental Psychology, 44*(2), 523–531.

Livingston, G. (2013). *At grandmother's house we stay.* Washington, DC: Pew Research Center. Retrieved from www.pewsocialtrends.org/2013/09/04/at-grandmothers-house-we-stay/.

Livingston, G. (2016). *Among 41 nations, U.S. is the outlier when it comes to paid parental leave.* Washington, DC: Pew Research Center. Retrieved from www.pewresearch.org/fact-tank/2016/09/26/u-s-lacks-mandated-paid-parental-leave/.

Lloyd, L. (2015). The fourth age. In J. Twigg & W. Martin (Eds.), *Routledge handbook of cultural gerontology* (pp. 261–268). New York: Routledge.

Lochlainn, M., & Kenny, R. (2013). Sexual activity and aging. *Journal of the American Medical Directors Association, 14*(8), 565–572.

Locke, A., Ginsborg, J., & Peers, I. (2002). Development and disadvantage: Implications for the early years and beyond. *International Journal of Language & Communication Disorders, 37*(1), 3–15.

Lodge, A., & Umberson, D. (2012). All shook up: Sexuality of mid- to later life married couples. *Journal of Marriage and Family, 74*(3), 428–443.

Lodge, A., & Umberson, D. (2013). Age and embodied masculinities: Midlife gay and heterosexual men talk about their bodies. *Journal of Aging Studies, 27*(3), 225–232.

Lodge, A., & Umberson, D. (2016). Sexual intimacy in mid- and late-life couples. In B. Mitchell (Ed.), *Couple relationships in the middle and later years: Their name, complexity, and role in health and illness* (pp. 115–134). Washington, DC: American Psychological Association.

Loftin, R. W., Habli, M., & DeFranco, E. A. (2010). Late preterm births. *Review in Obstetrics and Gynecology, 3*(1), 10–19.

Lombardi, J. (2012). The federal policy environment. In Institute of Medicine and National Research Council, *From neurons to neighborhoods: An update: Workshop summary* (pp. 26–30). Paper presented at Committee on From Neurons to Neighborhoods: Anniversary Workshop, Washington, DC. Washington, DC: The National Academies Press.

Long, D. (2015). Precocious puberty. *Pediatrics in Review, 36*(7), 319–321.

Losoncz, I., & Bortolotto, N. (2009). Work-life balance: The experience of Australian working mothers. *Journal of Family Studies, 15*(2), 122–138.

Lothian, J. A. (2008). Choice, autonomy, and childbirth education. *Journal of Perinatal Education, 17*(1), 35–38.

Lowe, J., Erickson, S., MacLean, P., & Duvall, S. (2009). Early working memory and maternal communication in toddlers born very low birth weight. *Acta Paediatrica, 98*(4), 660–663.

Lowe, J., MacLean, P., Duncan, A., Aragón, C., Schrader, R., Caprihan, A., . . . Phillips, J. P. (2012). Association of maternal interaction with emotional regulation in 4- and 9-month infants during the Still Face Paradigm. *Infant Behavior and Development, 35*(2), 295–302.

Lowenstein, A., & Daatland, S. (2006). Filial norms and family support in a comparative cross-national context: Evidence from the OASIS study. *Ageing and Society, 26*(2), 203–223.

Lowsky, D. J., Olshansky, S. J., Bhattacharya, J., & Goldman, D. P. (2014). Heterogeneity in healthy aging. *Journals of Gerontology Series A: Biomedical Sciences and Medical Sciences, 69*(6), 640–649.

Lu, P. (2007). Sibling relationships in adulthood and old age: A case study in Taiwan. *Current Sociology, 55*(4), 621–637.

Lu, P., Lee, G., Tishler, T., Meghpara, M., Thompson, P., & Bartzokis, G. (2013). Myelin breakdown mediates age-related slowing in cognitive processing speed in health elder men. *Brain and Cognition, 81*(1), 131–138.

Luby, J., Belden, A., Whalen, D., Harms, M., & Barch, D. (2016). Breastfeeding and childhood IQ: The mediating role of gray matter. *Journal of the American Academy of Child and Adolescent Psychiatry, 55*(5), 367–375.

Lucas, R., & Donnellan, M. B. (2011). Personality development across the life span: Longitudinal analyses with a national sample from Germany. *Journal of Personality and Social Psychology, 101*(4), 847–861.

Luchowski, A.T., Anderson, B. L., Power, M. L., Raglan, G. B., Espey, E., & Schulkin, J. (2014). Obstetrician-gynecologists and contraception: Long-acting reversible contraception practices and education. *Contraception, 89*(6), 578–583.

Lui, M., Robles, B., Leondar-Wright, B., Brewer, R., & Adamson, R. (2006). *The color of wealth*. New York: The New Press.

Lum, D. (2011). *Culturally competent practice: A framework for understanding diverse groups and justice issues* (4th ed.). Belmont, CA: Brooks/Cole, Cengage Learning.

Lund, L. K., Vik, T., Skranes, J., Brubakk, A. M., & Indredavik, M. S. (2011). Psychiatric morbidity in two low birth weight groups assessed by diagnostic interview in young adulthood. *Acta Paediatricia, 100*(4), 598–604.

Lund, T., Anderson, J., Winding, T., Biering, K., & Labriola, M. (2013). Negative life events in childhood as risk indicators of labour market participation in young adulthood: A prospective birth cohort study. *PLoS One, 8*(9), 1–7.

Lundholm, D., & Malmberg, G. (2009). Between elderly parents and grandchildren—Geographic proximity and trends in four-generation families. *Population Ageing, 2*(3–4), 121–137.

Lunkett, S., Behnke, A., Sands, T., & Choi, B. (2009). Adolescents' reports of parental engagement and academic achievement in immigrant families. *Journal of Youth & Adolescence, 38*(2), 257–268. doi:10.1007/s10964-008-9325-4

Luo, M. (2009, April 12). Longer unemployment for those 45 and older. *New York Times*. Retrieved from www.nytimes.com/2009/04/13/us/13age.html?pagewanted=all&_r=0.

Luthar, S. (Ed.). (2003). *Resilience and vulnerability: Adaptation in the context of childhood adversities*. New York: Cambridge University Press.

Luz, R., George, A., Vieux, R., & Spitz, E. (2017). Antenatal determinants of parental attachment and parenting alliance: How do mothers and fathers differ? *Infant Mental Health Journal, 38*(2), 183–197.

Lyons-Ruth, K., & Jacobvitz, D. (2008). Attachment disorganization: Genetic factors, parenting contents, and developmental transformation from infancy to adulthood. In J. Cassidy & P. R. Shaver (Eds.), *Handbook of attachment: Theory, research, and clinical applications* (2nd ed., pp. 666–697). New York: Guilford Press.

Maccoby, E. E. (2002a). Gender and group processes: A developmental perspective. *Current Directions in Psychological Science, 11,* 55–58.

Maccoby, E. E. (2002b). Parenting effects: Issues and controversies. In J. G. Borkowski, S. Landesman Ramey, & M. Bristol-Power (Eds.), *Parenting and the child's world* (pp. 35–45). Mahwah, NJ: Lawrence Erlbaum.

MacDonald, T., Noel-Weiss, J., West D., Walks, M., Biener, M., Kibbe, A., & Myler, E. (2016, May 16). Transmasculine individuals' experiences with lactation, chestfeeding, and gender identity: A qualitative study. *BMC Pregnancy and Childbirth, 16,* 106. Retrieved from https://bmcpregnancychildbirth.biomedcentral.com/articles/10.1186/s12884-016-0907-y.

MacDorman, M., Mathews, M., & Declercq, E. (2012). Home births in the United States, 1990–2009. *NCHS Data Brief,* No. 84. Hyattsville, MD: National Center for Health Statistics. Retrieved from www.cdc.gov/nchs/data/databriefs/db84.pdf.

Macomber, J., Pergamit, M., Vericker, T., Kuehn, D., McDaniel, M., Zielewski, E., . . . Johnson, H. (2009). *Vulnerable youth and the transition to adulthood.* Retrieved from www.urban.org/sites/default/files/publication/30601/411948-Vulnerable-Youth-and-the-Transition-to-Adulthood.pdf.

Madkour, A., Farhat, T., Halpern, C., Godeau, E., & Gabhainn, S. (2010). Early adolescent sexual initiation as a problem behavior: A comparative study of five nations. *Journal of Adolescent Health, 47*(4), 389–398.

Magaldi-Dopman, D., & Park-Taylor, J. (2010). Sacred adolescence: Practical suggestions for psychologists working with adolescents' religious and spiritual identity. *Professional Psychology: Research and Practice, 41*(5), 382–390.

Mah, V., & Ford-Jones, E. (2012). Spotlight on middle childhood: Rejuvenating the "forgotten years." *Paediatrics & Child Health, 17*(2), 81–83.

Maier, M. F., Vitiello, V. E., & Greenfield, D. B. (2012). A multilevel model of child- and classroom-level psychosocial factors that support language and literacy resilience of children in Head Start. *Early Childhood Research Quarterly, 27*(1), 104–114.

Main, M., & Hesse, E. (1990). Parents' unresolved traumatic experiences are related to infant disorganized attachment status: Is frightened and/or frightening parental behavior the linking mechanism? In M. Greenberg, D. Cicchetti, & E. M. Cumming (Eds.), *Attachment in the preschool years: Theory, research and intervention* (pp. 161–182). Chicago: University of Chicago Press.

Mäkinen, T. E., Borodulin, K., Tammelin, T., Rahkonen, O., Laatikainen, T., & Prättälä, R. (2010). The effects of adolescence sports and exercise on adulthood leisure-time physical activity in educational groups. *International Journal of Behavioral Nutrition & Physical Activity, 7*(1), 27. doi:10.1186/1479-5868-7-27

Malacova, E., Casey, A., Bremner, A., Hart, R., Stewart, L. M., & Preen, D. B. (2015). Live delivery outcome after tubal sterilization reversal: A population-based study. *Fertility and Sterility, 104*(4), 921–926.

Mallon, G. P., & Hess, P. M. C. (2014). *Child welfare for the twenty-first century: A handbook of practices, policies, and programs.* New York: Columbia University Press.

Malone, J., Liu, S., Vaillant, G., Rentz, D., & Waldinger, R. (2016). Midlife Eriksonian psychosocial development: Setting the stage for late-life cognitive and emotional health. *Developmental Psychology, 52*(3), 496–508.

Maneta, E., White, M., & Mezzacappa, E. (2017). Parent-child aggression, adult-partner violence, and child outcomes: A prospective, population-based study. *Child Abuse & Neglect, 68,* 1–10.

Manly, J. J., Schupf, N., Tang, M., & Stern, Y. (2005). Cognitive decline and literacy among ethnically diverse elders. *Journal of Geriatric Psychiatry and Neurology, 18*(4), 213–217.

Mann, S., Roberts, L., & Montgomery, S. (2017). Conflicting cultural values, gender role attitudes, and acculturation: Exploring the context of reproductive and mental health of Asian-Indian immigrant women in the U.S. *Issues in Mental Health Nursing, 38*(4), 301–309.

Manning, W. (2013). *Trends in cohabitation: Over twenty years of change, 1987–2010.* Retrieved from www.bgsu.edu/content/dam/BGSU/college-of-arts-and-sciences/NCFMR/documents/FP/FP-13-12.pdf.

Manns, A., Atler, K., & Furhauf, C. (2017). Daily activities and experiences of custodial grandparents: An exploratory study. *Physical and Occupational Therapy in Geriatrics, 35*(1), 34–48.

Marcantonio, E. (2017). Delirium in hospitalized older adults. *New England Journal of Medicine, 377*(15), 1456–1466.

March of Dimes. (2015, October). *The impact of premature birth on society.* Retrieved from www.marchofdimes.org/mission/the-economic-and-societal-costs.aspx.

March of Dimes. (2017). *Fighting premature birth: The Prematurity Campaign.* Retrieved from www.marchofdimes.org/mission/prematurity-campaign.aspx.

Marcia, J. E. (1966). Development and validation of ego-identity status. *Journal of Personality and Social Psychology, 3*(5), 551–558.

Marcia, J. E. (1980). Identity in adolescence. In J. Adelson (Ed.), *Handbook of adolescent psychology* (pp. 159–187). New York: Wiley.

Marcia, J. E. (1993). The ego identity status approach to ego identity. In J. E. Marcia, A. S. Waterman, D. R. Mattesson, S. L. Arcjer, & J. L. Orlofksy (Eds.), *Ego identity: A handbook for psychosocial research* (pp. 3–21). New York: Springer.

Marcia, J. E. (2002). Identity and psychosocial development in adulthood. *Identity: An International Journal of Theory and Research, 2*(1), 7–28.

Margrett, J. A., Daugherty, K., Martin, P., MacDonald, M., Davey, A., Woodard, J. L., . . . Poon, L. W. (2011). Affect and loneliness among centenarians and the oldest old: The role of individual and social resources. *Aging & Mental Health, 15*(3), 385–396.

Marks, N., Bumpass, L., & Jun, H. (2004). Family roles and well-being during the middle life course. In O. Brim, C. Ryff, & R. Kessler (Eds.), *How healthy are we? A national study of well-being at midlife* (pp. 514–549). Chicago: University of Chicago Press.

Markus, H., & Kitayama, S. (2003). Models of agency: Sociocultural diversity in the construction of action. In G. Berman & J. Berman (Eds.), *Cross-cultural differences in perspectives on the self* (pp. 2–57). Lincoln: University of Nebraska Press.

Markus, H., & Nurius, P. (1986). Possible selves. *American Psychologist, 41*(9), 954–969.

Maron, D. F. (2015). Early puberty: Causes and effects. *Scientific American, 312*(5), 28–30.

Marotz, L. R., & Allen, K. E. (2013). *Developmental profiles: Pre-birth through adolescence*. Belmont, CA: Wadsworth/ Cengage Learning.

Marra, J., McCarthy, E., Lin, H. J., Ford, J., Rodis, E., & Frisman, L. (2009). Effects of social support and conflict on parenting among homeless mothers. *American Journal of Orthopsychiatry, 79*(3), 348–356.

Marsh, H., & Kleitman, S. (2005). Consequences of employment during high school: Character building, subversion of academic goals, or a threshold? *American Educational Research Journal, 42*(2), 331–370.

Marshall, N. L., Noonan, A. E., McCartney, K., Marx, F., & Keefe, N. (2001). It takes an urban village: Parenting networks of urban families. *Journal of Family Issues, 22*(2), 163–168.

Marshall, V., & Mueller, M. (2003). Theoretical roots of the life-course perspective. In W. Heinz & V. Marshall (Eds.), *Social dynamics of the life course: Transitions, institutions, and interrelations* (pp. 3–32). New York: Aldine de Gruyter.

Martin, C., & Ruble, D. (2010). Patterns of gender development: *Annual Review of Psychology, 61*, 353–381.

Martin, J. A., Hamilton, B. E., Osterman, M. J. K., Curtin, S., & Mathews, T. J. (2013). Births: Final data for 2012. *National Vital Statistics Reports, 62*(9). Retrieved from www.cdc.gov/nchs/data/nvsr/nvsr62/nvsr62_09.pdf.

Martin, J. A., Hamilton, B. E., Osterman, M. J. K., Driscoll, A. K., & Matthews, T. J. (2017). Births: Final data for 2015. *National Vital Statistics Reports, 66*(1). Retrieved from www.cdc.gov/nchs/data/nvsr/nvsr66/nvsr66_01.pdf.

Martin, J. W., Kitchen, D. F., & Wheeler, G. R. (2016). Labor and employment law. *Mercer Law Review, 67*(4), 955–974.

Martin, M., & Zimprich, D. (2005). Cognitive development in midlife. In S. Willis & M. Martin (Eds.), *Middle adulthood: A lifespan perspective* (pp. 179–206). Thousand Oaks, CA: Sage.

Martin, P., da Rosa, G., & Poon, L. W. (2011). The impact of life events on the oldest old. In L. W. Poon & J. Cohen-Mansfield (Eds.), *Understanding well-being in the oldest old* (pp. 96–110). New York: Cambridge University Press.

Martin, T. L., & Doka, K. J. (2000). *Men don't cry . . . women do: Transcending gender stereotypes of grief*. Philadelphia: Brunner/Mazel.

Martinez, G., Copen, C., & Abma, J. (2011). Teenagers in the United States: Sexual activity, contraceptive use, and childbearing, 2006–2010 National Survey of Family Growth. National Center for Health Statistics. *Vital Health Statistics, 23*(31). Retrieved from www.cdc.gov/nchs/data/series/sr_23/sr23_031.pdf.

Martinez, J. I., Gudiño, O. G., & Lau, A. S. (2013). Problem-specific racial/ethnic disparities in pathways from maltreatment exposure to specialty mental health service use for youth in child welfare. *Child Maltreatment, 18*(2), 98–107.

Martinez-Torteya, C., Bogat, G. A., von Eye, A., & Levendosky, A. (2009). Resilience among children exposed to domestic violence: The role of risk and protective factors. *Child Development, 80*(2), 562–577.

Martins, M. V., Peterson, B. D., Costa, P., Costa, M. E., Lund, R., & Schmidt, L. (2013). Interactive effects of social support and disclosure on fertility-related stress. *Journal of Social and Personal Relationships, 30*(4), 371–388.

Mascarenhas, M. N., Flaxman, S. R., Boerma, T., Vanderpoel, S., & Stevens, G. A. (2012). National, regional, and global trends in infertility prevalence since 1990: A systematic analysis of 277 health surveys. *PLOS Medicine, 9*(12). Retrieved from http://journals.plos.org/plosmedicine/article?id=10.1371/journal.pmed.1001356.

Masciadrelli, B. P., Pleck, J. H., & Stueve, J. L. (2006). Fathers' role model perceptions: Themes and linkages with involvement. *Men and Masculinities, 9*(1), 23–34.

Mascola, A., Bryson, S., & Agras, W. (2010). Picky eating during childhood: A longitudinal study to age 11 years. *Eating Behaviors, 11*(4), 253–257.

Masini, B. E., & Barrett, H. A. (2008). Social support as a predictor of psychological and physical well-being and lifestyle in lesbian, gay, and bisexual adults aged 50 and over. *Journal of Gay and Lesbian Social Services, 20*(1–2), 91–110.

Masse, L., & Barnett, W. S. (2002). *A benefit cost analysis of the Abecedarian Early Childhood Intervention.* Retrieved from http://nieer.org/wp-content/uploads/2002/11/Abecedarian Study.pdf.

Masten, A. S., Burt, K. B., Roisman, G. I., Obradovic, J., Long, J. D., & Tellegen, A. (2004). Resources and resilience in the transition to adulthood: Continuity and change. *Development and Psychopathology, 16*, 1071–1094.

Matson, J., Fodstad, J., & Dempsey, T. (2009). What symptoms predict the diagnosis of autism or PDD-NOS in infants and toddlers with developmental delays using the baby and infant screen for autism traits. *Developmental Neurorehabilitation, 12*(6), 381–388.

Matsuba, M. K., Pratt, M., Norris, J., Mohle, E., Alisat, S., & McAdams, D. (2012). Environmentalism as a context for expressing identity and generativity: Patterns among activists and uninvolved youth and midlife adults. *Journal of Personality, 80*(4), 1091–1115.

Matsumoto, D., & Hwang, H. S. (2011). Culture, emotion, and expression. In M. J. Gelfand, C. Chiu, Y. Hong, M. J. Gelfand, C. Chiu, & Y. Hong (Eds.), *Advances in culture and psychology,* (Vol. 1, pp. 53–98). New York: Oxford University Press.

Mathews, T. J., & MacDorman, M. F. (2013). Infant mortality statistics from the 2009 period linked birth/infant death data set. *National Vital Statistics Reports, 61*(8). Retrieved from www.cdc.gov/nchs/data/nvsr/nvsr61/nvsr61_08.pdf.

Matijila, M., Hoffman, A., & van der Spuy, Z. M. (2017). Medical conditions associated with recurrent miscarriage—is BMI the tip of the iceberg? *European Journal of Obstetrics and Gynecology and Reproductive Biology, 214*, 91–96.

Matthews, S., & Sun, R. (2006). Incidence of four-generation family lineages: Is timing of fertility or mortality a better explanation? *The Journals of Gerontology, Series B: Psychological Sciences and Social Sciences, 61B*(2), S99–S106.

Matto, H., Strolin-Goltzman, J., & Ballan, M. (Eds.). (2014). *Neuroscience for social work: Current research and practice.* New York: Springer.

Matud, M. P., Bethencourt, J., & Ibáñez, I. (2014). Relevance of gender raoles in life satisfaction in adult people. *Personality and Individual Differences, 70*, 206–211.

Mayer, K. U., Baltes, P. B., Baltes, M., Borchelt, M., Delius, J., Helmchen, H., . . . Wagner, M. (1999). What do we know about old age and aging? Conclusions from the Berlin Aging Study. In P. B. Baltes & K. U. Mayer (Eds.), *The Berlin Aging Study: Aging from 70 to 100* (pp. 475–519). Cambridge, UK: Cambridge University Press.

Mayo Clinic. (2015). *Withdrawal method.* Retrieved from www.mayoclinic.org/tests-procedures/withdrawal-method/about/pac-20395283.

Mayo Clinic. (2017a). *Teen depression.* Retrieved from www.mayoclinic.org/diseases-conditions/teen-depression/symptoms-causes/syc-20350985.

Mayo Clinic. (2017b). *Perimenopause.* Retrieved from www.mayoclinic.org/diseases-conditions/perimenopause/home/ove-20253772.

Mayo Clinic. (2017c). *Dementia.* Retrieved from www.mayoclinic.org/diseases-conditions/dementia/symptoms-causes/syc-20352013?p=1.

Mayo Clinic. (2018). *Infertility.* Retrieved from www.mayoclinic.org/diseases-conditions/infertility/diagnosis-treatment/drc-20354322.

Mayo Clinic Staff. (2017). *Male menopause: Myth or reality.* Retrieved from www.mayoclinic.org/healthy-lifestyle/mens-health/in-depth/male-menopause/art-20048056?pg=1.

McAdams, D. (1985). *Power, intimacy, and the life story: Personological inquiries into identity.* New York: Guilford Press.

McAdams, D. (2001). Generativity in midlife. In M. Lachman (Ed.), *Handbook of midlife development* (pp. 395–443). New York: Wiley.

McAdams, D. (2006). *The redemptive self: Stories Americans live by.* New York: Oxford University Press.

McAdams, D., & de St. Aubin, E. (1992). A theory of generativity and its assessment through self-report, behavioral acts, and narrative themes in autobiography. *Journal of Personality and Social Psychology, 62*(6), 1003–1015.

McAdams, D., & de St. Aubin, E. (Eds.). (1998). *Generativity and adult development: How and why we care for the next generation.* Washington, DC: American Psychological Association.

McAdams, D., Hart, H., & Maruna, S. (1998). The anatomy of generativity. In D. McAdams & E. de St. Aubin (Eds.), *Generativity and adult development: How and why we care for the next generation* (pp. 7–43). Washington, DC: American Psychological Association.

McAdams, D., & Olson, B. (2010). Personality development: Continuity and change over the life course. *Annual Review of Psychology, 61*, 517–542.

McAdams, D., & Pals, J. (2006). A new big five: Fundamental principles for an integrative science of personality. *American Psychologist, 61*(3), 204–217.

McAdoo, H. P. (2001). Parent and child relationships in African American families. In N. B. Webb (Ed.), *Culturally diverse parent-child and family relationships: A guide for social workers and other practitioners* (pp. 89–106). New York: Columbia University Press.

McAlister, A., & Peterson, C. (2013). Siblings, theory of mind, and executive functioning in children aged 2–6 years: New longitudinal evidence. *Child Development, 84*(4), 1442–1458.

McCarter, M. M. (2016, May 14). Why the affordable care act should cover infertility. *The Blog*. Retrieved from www.huffingtonpost.com/melissa-miles-mccarter/why-the-affordable-care-a_1_b_7268978.html.

McCarter, S. A. (2011). Disproportionate minority contact in the American juvenile justice system: Where are we after 20 years, a philosophy shift, and three amendments? *Journal of Forensic Social Work, 1*(1), 96–107.

McCarter, S. A. (2017). The school-to-prison pipeline: A primer for social workers. *Social Work, 62*(1), 53–61.

McCarter, S. A., & Bridges, J. B. (2011). Determining the age of jurisdiction for adolescents: The policy debate. *Journal of Policy Practice, 10*(3), 168–184.

McCarty, A. T. (2016). Child poverty in the United States: A tale of devastation and the promise of hope. *Sociological Compass, 10*(7), 623–639.

McClure, E. (2000). A meta-analytic review of sex differences in facial expression processing and their development in infants, children and adolescents. *Psychological Bulletin, 126*(3), 424–453.

McCormick, M. S., Litt, J. S., Smith, V. C., & Zupancic, A. F. (2011). Prematurity: An overview and public health implications. *Annual Review of Public Health, 32*, 367–379.

McCoyd, J. L. M., & Walter, C. A. (2016). *Grief and loss across the lifespan: A biopsychosocial perspective* (2nd ed.). New York: Springer.

McCrae, R., & Costa, P., Jr. (1990). *Personality in adulthood*. New York: Guilford Press.

McCullough, M., Enders, C., Brion, S., & Jain, A. (2005). The varieties of religious development in adulthood: A longitudinal investigation of religion and rational choice. *Journal of Personality and Social Psychology, 89*(1), 78–89.

McDonald, T., Noel-Weiss, J., West, D., Walks, M., Biener, M., Kibbe, A., & Myler, E. (2016). Transmasculine individuals' experiences with lactation, chestfeeding, and gender identity: A qualitative study. *BMC Pregnancy and Childbirth, 16*. doi:10.1186/s12884-016-0907-y

McFarland, M., Pudrovska, T., Schieman, S., Ellison, C., & Bierman, A. (2013). Does a cancer diagnosis influence religiosity? Integrating a life course perspective. *Social Science Research, 42*(2), 311–320.

McGoldrick, M., Petkov, B., & Carter, B. (2016). Becoming parents: The family with children. In M. McGoldrick, N. Garcia Preto, & B. Carter (Eds.), *The expanding family life cycle: Individual, family, and social perspectives* (5th ed., pp. 280–303). Boston: Pearson.

McGoldrick, M., & Watson, M. (2016). Siblings and the life cycle. In M. McGoldrick, N. Preto, & B. Carater (Eds.), *The expanded family life cycle: Individual, family, and social perspectives* (5th ed., pp. 172–189). Boston: Pearson.

McGorry, P., & Purcell, R. (2009). Youth mental health reform and early intervention: Encouraging early signs. *Early Intervention in Psychiatry, 3*(3), 161–162.

McGroder, S. M., Zaslow, M. J., Moore, K. A., Hair, E. C., & Ahluwalia, S. K. (2002). The role of parenting in shaping the impacts of welfare-to-work programs on children. In J. G. Borkowski, S. Landesman Ramey, & M. Bristol-Power (Eds.), *Parenting and the child's world* (pp. 383–410). Mahwah, NJ: Lawrence Erlbaum.

McHale, S., Crouter, A., & Whiteman, S. (2003). The family contexts of gender development in childhood and adolescence. *Social Development, 12*(1), 125–148.

McInnis-Dittrich, K. (2014). *Social work with elders: A biopsychosocial approach to assessment and intervention* (4th ed.). Boston: Pearson.

McIntosh, H., Metz, E., & Youniss, J. (2005). Community service and identity formation in adolescence. In J. Mahoney, R. Larson, & J. Eccles (Eds.), *Organized activities as contexts of development: Extracurricular activities, after-school and community programs* (pp. 331–351). Mahwah, NJ: Lawrence Erlbaum.

McIntosh, P. (1988). *White privilege: Unpacking the invisible knapsack*. (Available from Peggy McIntosh, Wellesley College Center for Research on Women, Wellesley, MA 02181.)

Mckee, K. J., Wilson, F., Chung, C. M., Hinchliff, S., Goudie, F., Elford, H., . . . Mitchell, C. (2005). Reminiscence, regrets and activity in older people in residential care: Associations with psychological health. *British Journal of Clinical Psychology, 44*(Pt. 4), 543–561.

McKeering, H., & Pakenham, K. (2000). Gender and generativity issues in parenting: Do fathers benefit more than mothers from involvement in child care activities? *Sex Roles, 43*(7–8), 459–480.

McKenna, J. (2002). Breastfeeding and bedsharing: Still useful (and important) after all these years. *Mothering, 114,* 28–37.

McLean, K., & Mansfield, C. (2012). The co-construction of adolescent narrative identity: Narrative processing as a function of adolescent age, gender, and maternal scaffolding. *Developmental Psychology, 48*(2), 436–447.

McLean, K., Pasupathi, M., & Pals, J. (2007). Selves creating stories creating selves: A process model of self-development. *Personality and Social Psychology Review, 11*(3), 262–278.

McMahon, S. (2013). Enhancing motor development in infants and toddlers: A multidisciplinary process for creating parent education materials. *Newborn & Infant Nursing Reviews, 13,* 35–41.

McMahon, S., Todd, N., Martinez, A., Coker, C., Sheu, C., Washburn, J., & Shah, S. (2013). Aggressive and prosocial behavior: Community violence, cognitive, and behavioral predictors among urban African American youth. *American Journal of Community Psychology, 51*(3–4), 407–421.

McMichael, P. (2017). *Development and social change: A global perspective* (6th ed.). Thousand Oaks, CA: Sage.

McMillan, D. (2011). *Challenge and resiliency: The stories of primary caregivers of people with Asperger's syndrome.* Auckland, New Zealand: University of Auckland.

McMillan, J. C., & Raghavan, R. (2009). Pediatric to adult mental health service use of young people leaving the foster care system. *Journal of Adolescent Health, 44*(1), 7–13.

McNeal, R. B. (2012). Checking in or checking out? Investigating the parent involvement reactive hypothesis. *Journal of Educational Research, 105*(2), 79–89.

Mead, G. H. (1934). *Mind, self and society.* Chicago: University of Chicago Press.

Medicare.gov. (2017a). *What Part A covers.* Retrieved from www.medicare.gov/what-medicare-covers/part-a/what-part-a-covers.html.

Medicare.gov. (2017b). *What Part B covers.* Retrieved from www.medicare.gov/what-medicare-covers/part-b/what-medicare-part-b-covers.html.

Medicare.gov. (2017c). *Drug coverage (Part D).* Retrieved from www.medicare.gov/part-d/.

MedlinePlus. (2015). *Male infertility.* Retrieved from https://medlineplus.gov/maleinfertility.html.

MedlinePlus. (2016). Delirium. *U.S. National Library of Medicine/National Institutes of Health.* Retrieved from https://medlineplus.gov/ency/article/000740.htm.

Meek, M. (2000). Foreword. In K. Roskos & J. Christie (Eds.), *Play and literacy in early childhood: Research from multiple perspectives* (pp. vii–xiii). Mahwah, NJ: Lawrence Erlbaum.

Mehall, K., Spinrad, T., Eisenberg, N., & Gaertner, B. (2009). Examining the relations of infant temperament and couples' marital satisfaction to mother and father involvement: A longitudinal study. *Fathering, 7*(1), 23–48.

Meisner, B. (2012). A meta-analysis of positive and negative age stereotype priming effects on behavior among older adults. *The Journals of Gerontology, Series B: Psychological Sciences and Social Sciences, 67*(1), 13–17.

Mendelson, T., Cluxton-Keller, F., Vullo, G. C., Tandon, D., & Noazin, S. (2017). NICU-based interventions to reduce maternal depressive and anxiety symptoms: A meta-analysis. *Pediatrics, 139*(3), 1–12.

Mendle, J. (2014). Beyond pubertal timing: New directions for studying individual differences in development. *Current Directions in Psychological Science, 23*(3), 215–219.

Mensah, F., Bayer, J., Wake, M., Carlin, J., Allen, N., & Patton, G. (2013). Early puberty and childhood social and behavioral adjustment. *Journal of Adolescent Health, 53*(1), 118–124.

Merce, L. T., Barco, M. J., Alcazar, J. L., Sabatel, R., & Trojano, J. (2009). Intervillous and uteroplacental circulation in normal early pregnancy and early pregnancy loss assessed by 3-dimensional power doppler angiography. *American Journal of Obstetrics and Gynecology, 200*(3), 315.e1–315.e8.

Mercer, J. (2013). *Child development: Myths and misunderstandings* (2nd ed.). Thousand Oaks, CA: Sage.

Mercuri, E., Baranello, G., Romeo, D., Cesarini, L., & Ricci, D. (2007). The development of vision. *Early Human Development, 83*(12), 795–800.

Merten, J., Wickrama, K. A. S., & Williams, A. L. (2008). Adolescent obesity and young adult psychosocial outcomes: Gender and racial differences. *Journal of Youth & Adolescence, 37*(9), 1111–1122.

Merton, R. (1968). The Matthew Effect in science: The reward and communications systems of science. *Science, 159,* 56–63.

Metlife Mature Market Institute. (2010). *Still out, still aging: The Metlife study of lesbian gay, bisexual, and transgendered baby boomers.* Westport, CT: Author.

Meyer, D., Wood, S., & Stanley, B. (2013). Nurture is nature: Integrating brain development, systems theory, and attachment theory. *The Family Journal: Counseling and Therapy for Couples and Families, 21*(2), 162–169.

Michalsen, V. (2011). Mothering as a life course transition: Do women go straight for their children? *Journal of Offender Rehabilitation, 50*(6), 349–366.

Mickelson, K., Claffey, S., & Williams, S. (2006). The moderating role of gender and gender role attitudes on the link between spousal support and marital quality. *Sex Roles, 55*(1–2), 73–82.

Mikami, A., Griggs, M., Lerner, M. D., Emeh, C. C., Reuland, M. M., Jack, A., & Anthony, M. R. (2013). A randomized trial of a classroom intervention to increase peers' social inclusion of children with attention-deficit/hyperactivity disorder. *Journal of Consulting & Clinical Psychology, 81*(1), 100–112.

Mikami, A., Lerner, M. D., & Lun, J. (2010). Social context influences on children's rejection by their peers. *Child Development Perspectives, 4*(2), 123–130.

Miklowitz, D., & Johnson, B. (2009). Social and familial factors in the course of bipolar disorder: Basic processes and relevant interventions. *Clinical Psychology: Science & Practice, 16*(2), 281–296.

Miller, D., & Halpern, D. (2014). The new science of cognitive sex differences. *Trends in Cognitive Sciences, 18*(1), 37–45.

Miller, J., & Garran, A. M. (2008). *Racism in the United States: Implications for the helping professions.* Belmont, CA: Thomson Brooks/Cole.

Mills, M., Rindfuss, R., McDonald, P., & te Velder, E. (2011). Why do people postpone parenthood? Reasons and social policy incentives. *Human Reproduction Update, 17*(6), 848–860.

Min, J., Silverstein, M., & Lendon, J. (2012). Intergenerational transmission of values over the family life course. *Advances in Life Course Research, 17*(3), 112–120.

Min, J. W., & Moon, A. (2016). Older Asian Americans. In D. B. Kaplan & B. Berkman (Eds.), *The Oxford handbook of social work in health and aging* (2nd ed., pp. 515–525). New York: Oxford University Press.

Minor, R., Allard, J., Younts, C., Ward, T., & de Cabo, R. (2010). Dietary interventions to extend life span and health span based on calorie restriction. *The Journals of Gerontology: Biological Sciences, 65*(7), 695–703.

Mintel Report. (2004). *Lifestyles of young adults.* Chicago: Mintel International Group.

Mintz, S. (2004). *Huck's raft: A history of American childhood.* Boston: Harvard University Press.

Mintz, S. (2015). *The prime of life: A history of modern adulthood.* Cambridge, MA: Harvard University Press.

Mirucka, B., Bielecka, U., & Kisielewska, M. (2016). Positive orientation, self-esteem, and satisfaction with life in the context of subjective age in older adults. *Personality and Individual Differences, 99*, 206–210.

Mishra, G., Cooper, R., & Kuh, D. (2010). A life course approach to reproductive health: Theory and methods. *Maturita, 65*(2), 92–97.

Mitchell, B. (2010). Midlife marital happiness and ethnic culture: A life course perspective. *Journal of Comparative Family Studies, 41*(1), 167–183.

Mitchell, B. (2016). Happily ever after? Marital satisfaction during the middle adulthood years. In J. Bookwala (Ed.), *Couple relationships in the middle and later years: Their nature, complexity, and role in health and illness* (pp. 17–36). Washington, DC: American Psychological Association.

Mitchell, B., & Wister, A. (2015). Midlife challenge or welcome departure? Cultural and family-related expectations of empty nest transitions. *The International Journal of Aging and Human Development, 8*(4), 260–280.

Mitchell, K., Dick, A., DiMartino, D., Smith, B., Niles, B., Koenen, K., & Street, A. (2014). A pilot study of randomized controlled trial of yoga as an intervention to PTSD symptoms in women. *Journal of Traumatic Stress, 27*(2), 121–128.

Miyamoto, T., Tsujimura, A., Miyagawa, Y., Koh, E., Namiki, M., & Sengoku, K. (2012). Male infertility and its causes in humans. *Advances in Urology.* doi:10.1155/2012/38420. Retrieved from www.hindawi.com/journals/au/2012/384520/.

Miyawaki, C. (2016). Caregiving practice patterns of Asian, Hispanic, and non-Hispanic white American family caregivers of older adults across generations. *Journal of Cross-Cultural Gerontology, 31*(1), 35–55.

Moen, P. (2003). Midcourse: Navigating retirement and a new life stage. In J. Mortimer & M. Shanahan (Eds.), *Handbook of the life course* (pp. 269–291). New York: Kluwer Academic/Plenum.

Mohammad, E., Shapiro, E., Wainwright, L., & Carter, A. (2015). Impacts of family and community violence exposure on child coping and mental health. *Journal of Abnormal Child Psychology, 43*(2), 203–215.

Mokrova, I., O'Brien, M., Calkins, S., Leerkes, E., & Marcovitch, S. (2012). Maternal expressive style and children's emotional development. *Infant and Child Development, 21*(3), 617–633.

Molina, K. M., Alegria, M., & Chen, C.-N. (2012). Neighborhood context and substance use disorders: A comparative analysis of racial and ethnic groups in the United States. *Drug and Alcohol Dependence, 125*(Suppl. 1), S35–S43.

Möller, K., & Stattin, H. (2001). Are close relationships in adolescence linked with partner relationships in midlife? A longitudinal prospective study. *International Journal of Behavioral Development, 25*(1), 69–77.

Molnar, B. E., Goerge, R. M., Gilsanz, P., Hill, A., Subramanian, J. K., Duncan, D. T., . . . Beardslee, W. R. (2016). Neighborhood-level social processes and substantiated child maltreatment. *Child Abuse & Neglect, 51*, 41–53.

Mongan, P. (in press). *Rampage school shootings: Understanding why they occur and how to prevent them.* Sand Diego, CA: Cognella.

Mongillo, E., Briggs-Gowan, M., Ford, J., & Carter, A. (2009). Impact of traumatic life events in a community sample of toddlers. *Journal of Abnormal Child Psychology, 37*(4), 455–468.

Montague, D., Magai, C., Consedine, N., & Gillespie, M. (2003). Attachment in African American and European American older adults: The roles of early life socialization and religiosity. *Attachment and Human Development, 5*(2), 188–214.

Montgomery, R. J. V., & Kosloski, K. D. (1994). A longitudinal analysis of nursing home placement for dependent elders cared for by spouses vs. adult children. *The Journals of Gerontology: Social Sciences, 49*(2), S62–S74.

Montgomery, R. J. V., & Kosloski, K. D. (2000). Family caregiving: Change, continuity and diversity. In P. Lawton & R. Rubenstein (Eds.), *Alzheimer's disease and related dementias: Strategies in care and research.* New York: Springer.

Montgomery, R. J. V., & Kosloski, K. D. (2009). Caregiving as a process of changing identity: Implications for caregiver support. *Generations, 33*, 47–52.

Montirosso, R., Fedeli, C., Murray, L., Morandi, F., Brusati, R., Perego, G., & Borgatti, R. (2012). The role of negative maternal affective states and infant temperament in early interactions between infants with cleft lip and their mothers. *Journal of Pediatric Psychology, 37*(2), 241–250.

Moody, H. R., & Sasser, J. (2015). *Aging: Concepts and controversies* (8th ed.). Los Angeles: Sage.

Moore, J., & Abetz, J. (2016). Uh oh. Cue the [new] mommy wars: The ideology of combative mothering in popular U.S. newspaper articles about attachment parenting. *Southern Communication Journal, 81*(1), 49–62.

Moore, K. D. (2014). An ecological framework of place: Situating environmental gerontology within a life course perspective. *The International Journal of Aging and Human Development, 79*(3), 183–209.

Moore, K. L., Persaud, T. V. N., & Torchia, M. G. (2013). *Before we are born: Essentials of embryology and birth defects* (8th ed.). Philadelphia: Saunders/Elsevier.

Moore, S., Harden, K. P., & Mendle, J. (2014). Pubertal timing and adolescent sexual behavior in girls. *Developmental Psychology, 50*(6), 1734–1745.

Moraru, L., Sameni, R., Schneider, U., Haueisen, J., Schleußner, E., & Hoyer, D. (2011). Validation of fetal auditory evoked cortical responses to enhance the assessment of early brain development using fetal MEG measurements. *Physiological Measurement, 32*(11), 1847–1868.

Moreno, M., Furtner, F., & Rivara, F. (2013). Adolescent volunteering. *JAMA Pediatrics, 167*(4), 400. doi:10.1001/jamapediatrics.2013.2118

Morris, T., & McInerney, K. (2010). Media representations of pregnancy and childbirth: An analysis of reality television programs in the United States. *Birth, 37*(2), 134–140.

Morselli, D., & Passini, S. (2015). Measuring prosocial attitudes for future generations: The Social Generativity Scale. *Journal of Adult Development, 22*(3), 173–182.

Morton, C., & Hsu, C. (2007). Contemporary dilemmas in American childbirth education: Findings from a comparative ethnographic study. *Journal of Perinatal Education, 16*(4), 25–37.

Mosher, W., Jones, J., & Abma, J. (2012). *Intended and unintended births in the United States: 1982-2010.* Retrieved from www.cdc.gov/nchs/data/nhsr/nhsr055.pdf.

Moyers, B. D., Mannes, E., Pellet, G., O'Neill, J. D., & Moyers, J. D. (2000). *On our own terms: Moyers on dying.* New York: Films for the Humanities & Sciences.

Muangpaison, W., Petcharat, C., & Srinonprasert, V. (2012). Prevalence of potentially reversible conditions in dementia and mild cognitive impairment in geriatric care. *Geriatrics & Gerontology International, 12*(1), 59–64.

Mueller, M., Wilhelm, B., & Elder, G. (2002). Variations in grandparenting. *Research on Aging, 24*(3), 360–388.

Muir, D., & Lee, K. (2003). The still face effect: Methodological issues and new applications. *Infancy, 4*(4), 483–491.

Munakata, Y., McClelland, J., Johnson, M., & Siegler, R. (1997). Rethinking infant knowledge: Toward an adaptive process account of successes and failures in object permanence tasks. *Psychological Review, 104*(4), 618–713.

Muraco, A., & Fredriksen-Goldsen, K. (2011). "That's what friends do": Informal caregiving for chronically ill midlife and older lesbian, gay, and bisexual adults. *Journal of Social and Personal Relationships, 28*(8), 1073–1092.

Murano, T., & Cocuzza, T. (2009). Ectopic pregnancy. *Emergency Medicine Reports: The Practical Journal for Emergency Physicians, 30*(23), 281–287.

Murillo, E. G. (2010). *Handbook of Latinos and education: Theory, research and practice.* New York: Routledge.

Murphey, D. (2013). Home front alert: The risks facing young children in military families. *Child Trends Research Brief.* Retrieved from www.childtrends.org/wp-content/uploads/2013/07/2013-31MilitaryFamilies.pdf.

Murray, C., Thos, T., Lozano, R., Naghavi, M., Flaxman, A., Michaud, C., . . . Memish, Z. A. (2012). Disability-adjusted life years (DALYs) for 291 diseases and injuries in 21 regions, 1990–2010: A systematic analysis for the Global Burden of Disease Study 2010. *The Lancet, 380*(9859), 21976–2223.

Muscat, T., Obst, P., Cockshaw, W., & Thorpe, K. (2014). Beliefs about infant regulation, early infant behaviors, and maternal postnatal depressive symptoms. *Birth, 42*(2), 206–213.

Myers, N., & Perlmutter, M. (2014). Memory in the years from two to five. In P. Ornstein (Ed.), *Memory development in children* (pp. 191–218). New York: Psychology Press.

Nagata, D., Cheng, W., & Tsai, A. (2010). Chinese-American grandmothering: A qualitative exploration. *Asian American Journal of Psychology, 1*(2), 151–161.

Naleppa, M. J. (1996). Families and the institutionalized elderly: A review. *Journal of Gerontological Social Work, 27*(1–2), 87–111.

Nappi, R. E. (2013). Counseling on vaginal delivery of contraceptive hormones: Implications for women's body knowledge and sexual health. *Gynecological Endocrinology, 29*(13), 1015–1021.

National Alliance for Caregiving and AARP. (2015). *Caregiving in the U.S. 2015.* Washington, DC: Authors. Retrieved from www.aarp.org/content/dam/aarp/ppi/2015/caregiving-in-the-united-states-2015-report-revised.pdf.

National Association of Counties. (2008). *Youth aging out of foster care.* Retrieved from www.naco.org/sites/default/files/documents/Youth%20Aging%20Out%20of%20Foster%20Care.pdf.

National Association of Perinatal Social Workers. (2017). *About NAPSW.* Retrieved from www.napsw.org/vision-and-history.

National Association of Social Workers. (2003). *NASW standards for integrating genetics into social work practice* (Item # S03). Washington, DC: Author.

National Association of Social Workers. (2017). *Code of ethics of the National Association of Social Workers.* Washington, DC: Author.

National Center for Chronic Disease Prevention and Health Promotion. (2014). *Assisted reproductive technology: National summary report.* Retrieved from www.cdc.gov/art/pdf/2014-report/art-2014-national-summary-report.pdf#page=24.

National Center For Education Statistics. (2014). *The condition of education - 2014.* Washington, DC: Author. Retrieved from https://nces.ed.gov/pubs2014/2014083.pdf.

National Center for Education Statistics. (2017a). *Indicators of school crime and safety: 2016.* Retrieved from https://nces.ed.gov/pubs2017/2017064.pdf.

National Center for Education Statistics. (2017b). *Children and youth with disabilities.* Retrieved from https://nces.ed.gov/programs/coe/indicator_cgg.asp.

National Center for Education Statistics. (2017c). *The condition of education 2017.* NCES 2017-144. Retrieved from https://nces.ed.gov/pubs2017144.pdf.

National Center for Health Statistics. (2009). *Limitations in activities of daily living and instrumental activities of daily living, 2003–2007.* Retrieved from www.cdc.gov/nchs/data/health_policy/adl_iadl_tables.pdf.

National Center for Health Statistics. (2017a). *LCWK1. Deaths, percent of total deaths, and death rates for the leading causes of death in 5-year age groups, by race and Hispanic origin, and sex: United States, 2015.* Retrieved from www.cdc.gov/nchs/nvss/mortality_tables.htm.

National Center for Health Statistics. (2017b). *Health, United States, 2016 with chartbook on long-term trends in health.* Hyattsville, MD: U.S. Department of Health and Human Services, Centers for Disease Control and Prevention. Retrieved from www.cdc.gov/nchs/data/hus/hus16.pdf.

National Committee to Preserve Social Security & Medicare. (2016). *Closing the Medicare Part D donut hole.* Retrieved from www.ncpssm.org/documents/general-archives-2016/closing-the-medicare-part-d-donut-hole/.

National Down Syndrome Society (NDSS). (2018). *Down syndrome facts.* Retrieved from www.ndss.org/about-down-syndrome/down-syndrome-facts/.

National Eating Disorders Association. (2016). *Pregnancy and eating disorders.* Retrieved from www.nationaleatingdisorders.org/pregnancy-and-eating-disorders.

National Head Start Association. (2017, May 23). *NHSA statement on FY 2018 president's budget.* Retrieved from www.nhsa.org/pr-update/nhsa-statement-fy-2018-president%E2%80%99s-budget.

National Hospice and Palliative Care Organization. (2015). *NHPCO's facts and figures on hospice care in America 2015.* Alexandria, VA: Author.

National Human Genome Research Institute. (2010). *The human genome project completion: Frequently asked questions.* Retrieved from www.genome.gov/11006943/.

National Human Genome Research Institute. (2017). *Specific genetic disorders.* Retrieved from www.genome.gov/10001204/.

National Institute of Mental Health. (2018). *Child and adolescent mental health.* Retrieved from www.nimh.nih.gov/health/topics/child-and-adolescent-mental-health/index.shtml.

National Institute of Neurological Disorders and Stroke. (2014). *Parkinson's disease: Hope through research.* Retrieved from www.ninds.nih.gov/Disorders/Patient-Caregiver-Education/Hope-Through-Research/Parkinsons-Disease-Hope-Through-Research#What is Parkinsons.

National Institute on Aging. (2017). *What are the signs of Alzheimer's disease?* Retrieved from www.nia.nih.gov/health/what-are-signs-alzheimers-disease?utm_campaign=top_promo_box&utm_content=%20symptoms&utm_medium=web&utm_source=%20ad_fact_sheet#very.

National Institutes of Health. (2017). *Preconception counselling and care for women of childbearing age living with HIV.* Retrieved from https://aidsinfo.nih.gov/guidelines/html/3/perinatal/153/reproductive-options-for-hiv-concordant-and-serodiscordant-couples.

National Library of Medicine. (2017, April). *Emergency contraceptive agents: Levonorgestrel and ulipristal.* Retrieved from https://livertox.nih.gov/EmergencyContraceptiveAgents.htm.

National Newborn Screening and Global Resource Center (NNSGRC). (2014). *Newborn screening.* Retrieved from http://genes-r-us.uthscsa.edu/sites/genes-r-us/files/nbsdisorders.pdf.

National Partnership for Women & Families. (2012). *Why the Affordable Care Act matters for women: Better care for pregnant women and mothers.* Retrieved from http://go.nationalpartnership.org/site/DocServer/PREGNANT_WOMEN.pdf?docID=10006.

National Research Council. (2012). *From neurons to neighborhoods: An update: Workshop summary.* Washington, DC: National Academies Press.

National Women's Law Center. (2011). *Mothers behind bars: States are failing.* Retrieved from https://nwlc.org/resources/mothers-behind-bars-states-are-failing/.

Natsuaki, M., Ge, X., Leve, L., Neiderhiser, J., Shaw, D., Conger, R. D., . . . Reiss, D. (2010). Genetic liability, environment, and the development of fussiness in toddlers: The roles of maternal depression and parental responsiveness. *Developmental Psychology, 46*(5), 1147–1158.

Navidian, A., Saravani, Z., & Shakiba, M. (2017). Impact of psychological grief counseling on the severity of post-traumatic stress symptoms in mothers after stillbirth. *Issues in Mental Health Nursing, 38*(8), 650–654.

Nazarenko, N. (2015). Beyond human: Engineering our future evolution. *Foresight, 17*(3), 298–301.

Nazzi, T., & Gopnik, A. (2001). Linguistic cognitive abilities in infancy: When does language become a tool for categorization? *Cognition, 80*(3), B11–B20.

Needham, A. (2001). Object recognition and object segregation in 4-5-month-old infants. *Journal of Experimental Child Psychology, 78*(1), 3–24.

Negriff, S., Susman, E., & Trickett, P. (2011). The developmental pathway from pubertal timing to delinquency and sexual activity from early to late adolescence. *Journal of Youth and Adolescence, 40*(10), 1343–1356.

Nelson, C. (2001). The development and neural bases of face recognition. *Infant and Child Development, 10*, 3–18.

Nelson, C., & Luciana, M. (2008). *Handbook of developmental cognitive neuroscience* (2nd ed.). Cambridge, MA: MIT Press.

Nelson, S., Kushlev, K., & Lyubomirsky, S. (2014). The pains and pleasures of parenting: When, why, and how is parenthood associated with more or less well-being? *Psychological Bulletin, 140*(3), 846–895.

Nelson-Becker, H., Canda, E. R., & Nakashima, M. (2016). Spirituality in professional practice with older adults. In D. B. Kaplan & B. Berkman (Eds.), *The Oxford handbook of social work in health and aging* (2nd ed., pp. 73–84). New York: Oxford University Press.

Neri, E., Agostini, F., Baldoni, F., Facondi, E., Biasini, A., & Monti, F. (2017). Preterm infant development, maternal distress and sensitivity: The influence of severity of birth weight. *Early Human Development, 106*, 19–24.

Nesteruk, O., Helmstetter, N.-M., Gramescu, A., Siyam, M. H., & Price, C. A. (2015). Development of ethnic identity in young adults from immigrant families: "I want to hold onto my roots, but I also want to experience new routes." *Marriage & Family Review, 51*(5), 466–487.

Neuberger, F., & Haberkern, K. (2014). Structured ambivalence in grandchild care and the quality of life among European grandparents. *European Journal of Ageing, 11*(2), 171–181.

Neugarten, B. L., Havighurst, R. J., & Tobin, S. S. (1968). Personality and patterns of aging. In B. L. Neugarten (Ed.), *Middle age and aging*. Chicago: University of Chicago Press.

Neugarten, B. L., & Weinstein, K. K. (1964). The changing American grandparent. *Journal of Marriage and the Family, 26*(2), 199–204.

Newcomb, N., & Dubas, J. (1992). A longitudinal study of predictors of spatial ability in adolescent females. *Child Development, 63*(1), 37–46.

Newman, B., & Newman, P. (2015). *Development through life: A psychosocial approach* (12th ed.). Stamford, CT: Cengage Learning.

Newman, D. (2012). *Sociology: Exploring the architecture of everyday life* (9th ed.). Thousand Oaks, CA: Sage.

Newman, K. S. (2008). Ties that bind: Cultural interpretations of delayed adulthood in Western Europe and Japan. *Sociological Forum, 23*(4), 645–669.

Newman, K. S. (2012). *The accordion family: Boomerang kids, anxious parents and the private toll of global competition*. Boston: Beacon Press.

Newman, L., Sivaratnam, C., & Komiti, A. (2015). Attachment and early brain development – neuroprotective interventions in infant-caregiver therapy. *Translational Developmental Psychiatry, 3*(1), 28647. doi:10.3402/tdp.ve.28647

Ng, T., & Feldman, D. (2010). The relationships of age with job attitudes: A meta-analysis. *Personnel Psychology, 63*(3), 677–718.

Nguyen, P. (2008). Perceptions of Vietnamese fathers' acculturation levels, parenting styles, and mental health outcome in Vietnamese American adolescent immigrants. *Social Work, 53*(4), 337–346.

Nguyen, P., & Cheung, M. (2009). Parenting styles as perceived by Vietnamese American adolescents. *Child and Adolescent Social Work Journal, 26*, 505–581.

Ning, L., Pang, L., Chen, G., Song, X., Zhang, J., & Zheng, X. (2011). Risk factors for depression in older adults in Beijing. *The Canadian Journal of Psychiatry, 56*(8), 466–473.

Nishitani, S., Miyamura, T., Tagawa, M., Sumi, M., Takase, R., Doi, H., . . . Shinohara, K. (2009). The calming effect of a maternal breast milk odor on the human newborn infant. *Neuroscience Research, 63*(1), 66–71.

Nitzburg, G. C., & Farber, B. A. (2013). Putting up emotional (Facebook) walls? Attachment status and emerging adults' experiences of social networking sites. *Journal of Clinical Psychology: In Session, 69*(11), 1183–1190.

Noddings, N. (2013). *Caring: A relational approach to ethics and moral education*. Berkeley: University of California Press.

Noergaard, B., Johannessen, H., Fenger-Gron, J., Kofoed, P., & Ammentorp, J. (2016). Participatory action research in the field of neonatal intensive care: Developing an intervention to meet the fathers' needs: A case study. *Journal of Public Health Research, 5*(3), 122–129.

Nourhashemi, F., Gilletee-Guyonnet, S., Rolland, Y., Cante, C., Hein, C., & Vellas, B. (2009). Alzheimer's disease progression in the oldest old compared to younger elderly patients: Data from the REAL, FR study. *International Journal of Geriatric Psychiatry, 24*(2), 149–155.

Nuttgens, S. (2010). Biracial identity theory and research juxtaposed with narrative accounts of a biracial individual. *Child & Adolescent Social Work Journal, 27*(5), 355–364.

Ny, K., Loy, J., Gudmunson, C., & Cheong, W. (2009). Gender differences in marital and life satisfaction among Chinese Malaysians. *Sex Roles, 60*, 33–43.

Nybell, L., Shook, J., & Finn, J. (Eds.). (2009). *Childhood, youth, and social work in transformation: Implications for policy and practice*. New York: Columbia University Press.

Oaklander, M. (2015, December 11). Women now have as many miscarriages as abortions. *Time*. Retrieved from http://time.com/4144897/birth-rate-abortion-miscarriage/.

Obedin-Maliver, J., & Makadon, H. J. (2016). Transgender men and pregnancy. *Obstetric Medicine, 9*(1), 4–8.

Office of Disease Prevention and Health Promotion. (2008). *Physical activity guidelines: Chapter 3: Active children and adolescents*. Retrieved from https://health.gov/paguidelines/guidelines/chapter3.aspx.

Ogden, C. L., Carroll, M. D., Fryar, C. D., & Flegal, K. M. (2015, November). *Prevalence of obesity among adults and youth: United States, 2011–2014*. NCHS Data Brief 219. Retrieved from www.cdc.gov/nchs/data/databriefs/db219.pdf.

Ogden, J., Stavrinaki, M., & Stubbs, J. (2009). Understanding the role of life events in weight loss and weight gain. *Psychology, Health, & Medicine, 14*(2), 239–249.

Ogle, C. M., Rubin, D. C., & Siegler, I. C. (2013). The impact of the developmental timing of trauma exposure on PTSD symptoms and psychosocial functioning among older adults. *Developmental Psychology, 49*(11), 2191–2200.

O'Hara, M., & McCabe, J. (2013). Postpartum depression: Current status and future directions. *Annual Review of Clinical Psychology, 9*, 397–407.

O'Laoide, A., Egan, J., & Osborn, K. (2017). What was once essential, may become detrimental: The mediating role of depersonalization in the relationship between childhood emotional maltreatment and psychological distress in adults. *Journal of Trauma & Dissociation*, 1–21. doi:10.1080/15299732.2017.1402398

Olsen, R. K., Pagelinan, M. M., Bogulski, C., Chakravarty, M. M., Luk, G., Grady, C. L., & Bialystok, E. (2015). The effect of lifelong bilingualism on regional grey and white matter volume. *Brain Research, 1612*, 128–139.

Olshansky, S. J., Antonucci, T., Berkman, L., Binstock, R., Boersch-Supan, A., Cacioppo, J., . . . Rowe, J. (2012). Differences in life expectancy due to race and educational differences are widening, and many may not catch up. *Health Affairs, 31*(8), 1803–1810.

Olson, C. (2010). Children's motivations for video game play in the context of normal development. *Review of General Psychology, 14*(2), 180–187.

Olsson, H., Strand, S., & Kristiansen, L. (2014). Reaching a turning point – how patients in forensic care describe trajectories of recovery. *Scandinavian Journal of Caring Sciences, 28*(3), 505–514.

Olusanya, B. (2010). Is undernutrition a risk factor for sensorineural hearing loss in early infancy? *British Journal of Nutrition, 103*, 1296–1301.

Olusanya, B., Krishnamurthy, V., & Wertlieb, D. (2018). Global initiatives for early childhood development should be disability inclusive. *Pediatrics, 141*(3). doi:10.1542/peds.2017-4055

Ongley, S., & Malti, T. (2014). The role of moral emotions in the development of children's sharing behavior. *Developmental Psychology, 50*(4), 1148–1159.

Oppenheimer, D., & Kelso, E. (2015). Information processing as a paradigm for decision making. *Annual Review of Psychology, 66*, 277–294.

O'Rand, A. (2009). Cumulative processes in the life course. In G. Elder & J. Giele (Eds.), *The craft of life course research* (pp. 121–140). New York: Guilford Press.

Orbuch, T., & Brown, E. (2006). Divorce in the context of being African American. In M. Fine & J. Harvey (Eds.), *Handbook of divorce and relationship dissolution* (pp. 481–498). Mahwah, NJ: Erlbaum.

Orel, N., & Fruhauf, C. (2006). Lesbian and bisexual grandmothers' perceptions of the grandparent-grandchild relationship. *Journal of GLBT Family Studies, 2*(1), 43–70.

Orfield, G., Kucsev, J., & Siegal-Harvey, G. (2012). *E Pluribus . . . separation: Deepening double segregation for more students.* Los Angeles: The Civil Rights Project. Retrieved from https://civilrightsproject.ucla.edu/research/k-12-education/integration-and-diversity/mlk-national/e-pluribus. . .separation-deepening-double-segregation-for-more-students.

Ornoy, A., & Yacobi, S. (2012). Alcohol and drugs of abuse in pregnant women: Effects on the fetus and newborn, mode of action and maternal treatment. In B. Johnson (Ed.), *Addiction medicine: Science and practice* (pp. 1413–1433). New York: Springer + Business Media.

Ornstein, P., & Light, L. (2010). Memory development across the life span. In R. Lerner (Series Ed.) & W. Overton (Vol. Ed.), *Handbook of life-span development: Vol. 1. Biology, cognition, and methods across the life span.* Hoboken, NJ: Wiley.

Ortega, F. B., Konstabel, K., Pasquali, E., Ruiz, J. R., Hurtig-Wennlöf, A., Mäestu, J., . . . Sjöström, M. (2013). Objectively measured physical activity and sedentary time during childhood, adolescence and young adulthood: A cohort study. *PLoS One, 8*(4), 1–8.

Orth, U., & Luciano, E. (2015). Self-esteem, narcissism, and stressful life events: Testing for selection and socialization. *Journal of Personality and Social Psychology, 109*(4), 707–721.

Osler, M., Avlund, K., & Mortensen, E. (2012). Socioeconomic position early in life, cognitive development and cognitive change from young adulthood to middle age. *European Journal of Public Health, 23*(6), 974–980.

Osofsky, J., Stepka, P., & King, L. (2017). The impact of early trauma on development. In J. Osofsky, P. Stepka, & L. King (Eds.), *Treating infants and young children impacted by trauma: Interventions that promote healthy development* (pp. 15–39). Washington, DC: American Psychological.

Ostir, G., & Goodwin, J. (2006). High anxiety is associated with an increased risk of death in an older tri-ethnic population. *Journal of Clinical Epidemiology, 59*(5), 534–540.

Ostrov, J., Crick, N., & Stauffacher, K. (2006). Relational aggression in sibling and peer relationships during early childhood. *Journal of Developmental Psychology, 27*(3), 241–253.

Ostrov, J., & Godleski, S. (2010). Toward an integrated gender-linked model of aggression subtypes in early and middle childhood. *Psychological Review, 117*(1), 233–242.

Oudekerk, B., Farr, R., & Reppucci, N. D. (2013). Is it love or sexual abuse? Young adults' perceptions of statutory rape. *Journal of Child Sexual Abuse, 22*(7), 858–877.

Owens, J. (2005). Introduction: Culture and sleep in children. *Pediatrics, 115*(1), 201–203.

Ozgoli, G., Goli, M., & Simbar, M. (2009). Effects of ginger capsules on pregnancy, nausea, and vomiting. *Journal of Alternative and Complementary Medicine, 15*(3), 243–246.

Padgett, C., & Remle, R. C. (2016). Financial assistance patterns from midlife parents to adult children: A test of the cumulative advantage hypothesis. *Journal of Family Economic Issues, 37*(3), 435–449.

Padilla, Y. C., & Fong, R. (2016). Identifying grand challenges facing social work in the next decade: Maximizing social policy engagement. *Journal of Policy Practice, 15*(3), 133–144.

Page, A., Milner, A., Morrell, S., & Taylor, R. (2013). The role of under-employment and unemployment in recent birth cohort effects in Australian suicide. *Social Science & Medicine, 93*, 155–162.

Painter, K. (2012). Outcomes for youth with severe emotional disturbance: A repeated measures longitudinal study of a wraparound approach of service delivery in systems of care. *Child & Youth Care Forum, 41*(4), 407–425.

Pais, J. (2014). Cumulative structural disadvantage and racial health disparities: The pathways of childhood socioeconomic influence. *Demography, 51*, 1729–1753.

Palamar, J., Griffin-Tomas, M., & Kamboukos, D. (2015). Reasons for recent marijuana use in relation to use of other illicit drugs among high school seniors in the United States. *The American Journal of Drug and Alcohol Abuse, 41*(4), 323–331.

Paljärvi, T., Martikainen, P., Pensola, T., Leinonen, T., & Herttua, K. (2015). Life course trajectories of labour market participation among young adults who experienced severe alcohol-related health outcomes: A retrospective cohort study. *PLoS One, 10*(5), 1–14.

Palmer, A. M., & Francis, P. T. (2006). Neurochemistry of aging. In J. Pathy, A. J. Sinclair, & E. J. Morley (Eds.), *Principles and practice of geriatric medicine* (4th ed., pp. 59–67). Chichester, UK: John Wiley & Sons.

Palomba, S., Falbo, A., Dicelio, A., Materozzo, C., & Zullo, F. (2012). Nexplanon: A new implant for long-term contraception: A comprehensive descriptive review. *Gynecological Endocrinology, 28*(9), 710–721.

Papavasileiou, E., & Lyons, S. (2015). A comparative analysis of the work values of Greece's "Millennial" generation. *The International Journal of Human Resource Management, 26*(17), 2166–2186.

Paquette, K., & Bassuk, E. (2009). Parenting and homelessness: Overview and introduction to the special edition. *American Journal of Orthopsychiatry, 79*(3), 292–298.

Parish, S., Saville, A., Swaine, J., & Igdalsky, L. (2016). Policies and programs for children and youth with disabilities. In J. Jenson & M. Fraser (Eds.), *Social policy for children and families: A risk and resilience perspective* (3rd ed., pp. 201–226). Thousand Oaks, CA: Sage.

Park, D., & Festini, S. (2016). The middle-aged brain: A cognitive neuroscience perspective. In R. Cabeze, L. Nyberg, & D. Park (Eds.), *Cognitive neuroscience of aging: Linking cognitive and cerebral aging.* Oxford Scholarship Online. doi:10.1093/acprof:oso/9780199372935:003.0015. Retrieved from www.oxfordscholarship.com.

Park, N. S., Roff, L. L., Sun, F., Parker, M. W., Klemmack, D. L., Sawyer, P., . . . Allman, R. M. (2010). Transportation difficulty of Black and White rural older adults. *Journal of Applied Gerontology, 29*(1), 70–88.

Parker, K., & Patten, E. (2013). *The sandwich generation: Rising financial burdens for middle-aged Americans.* Washington, DC: Pew Research Center. Retrieved from www.pewsocialtrends.org/2013/01/30/the-sandwich-generation/.

Parra-Cordeno, M., Rodrigo, R., Barja, P., Bosco, C., Rencoret, G., & Sepulveda Martinez, A. (2013). Prediction of early and late pre-eclampsia from maternal characteristics, uterine artery Doppler and markers of vasculogenesis during first trimester of pregnancy. *Ultrasound in Obstetrics and Gynecology, 41*(5), 538–544.

Parsell, C., Eggins, E., & Marston, G. (2017). Human agency and social work research: A systematic search and synthesis of social work literature. *British Journal of Social Work, 47*, 238–255.

Parsons, M., & Peluso, P. R. (2013). Grandfamilies and their grand challenges. In P. R. Peluso, R. E. Watts, & M. Parsons (Eds.), *Changing aging, changing family therapy* (pp. 45–61). New York: Routledge.

Pascoe, J. M., Wood, D. L., Duffee, J. H., & Kuo, A. (2016). Mediators and adverse effects of child poverty in the United States. *Pediatrics, 137*(4), 1–17.

Passel, J., & Cohn, D. (2008). *U.S. population projections: 2005–2050.* Retrieved from www.pewhispanic.org/2008/02/11/us-population-projections-2005-2050/.

Patil, C. L., Abrams, E. T., Steinmetz, A., & Young, S. L. (2012). Appetite sensations and nausea and vomiting in pregnancy: An overview of explanations. *Ecology of Food and Nutrition, 51*(5), 394–417.

Patrick, M., Schulenberg, J., O'Malley, P., Johnston, L., & Bachman, J. (2011). Adolescents' reported reasons for alcohol and marijuana use as predictors of substance use and problems in adulthood. *Journal of Studies on Alcohol and Drugs, 72*(1), 106–116.

Patrick, S. W., Schumacher, R. E., Benneyworth, B. D., Krans, E. E., McAllister, J. M., & Davis, M. M. (2012). Neonatal abstinence syndrome and associated health care expenditures: United States, 2000–2009. *Journal of the American Medical Association, 307*, 1934–1940.

Patten, E. (2016). *The nation's Latino population is defined by its youth.* Washington, DC: Pew Research Center. Retrieved from www.pewhispanic.org/2016/04/20/the-nations-latino-population-is-defined-by-its-youth/.

Pauletti, R. E., Cooper, P. J., & Perry, D. G. (2014). Influences of gender identity on children's maltreatment of gender-nonconforming peers: A person x target analysis of aggression. *Journal of Personality and Social Psychology, 106*(5), 843–866.

Paulus, M. (2014). The emergence of prosocial behavior: Why do infants and toddlers help, comfort, and share? *Child Development Perspectives, 8*(2), 77–81.

Pavarini, G., Hollanda Souza, D., & Hawk, C. (2012). Parental practice and theory of mind development. *Journal of Child and Family Studies, 22*(6), 844–853.

Payne, R. K. (2013). *A framework for understanding poverty: A cognitive approach* (5th ed.). Highlands, TX: Aha! Process.

Pearlin, L., & Skaff, M. (1996). Stress and the life course: A paradigmatic alliance. *The Gerontologist, 36*(2), 239–247.

Pearlstein, T., Howard, M., Salisbury, A., & Zlotnick, C. (2009). Pospartum depression. *American Journal of Obstetrics & Gynecology, 200*(4), 357–364.

Peart, N. A., Pungello, E. P., Campbell, F. A., & Richey, T. G. (2006). Faces of fatherhood: African-American young adults view the paternal role. *Families in Society, 87*(1), 71–83.

Pecora, P. J., & Harrison-Jackson, M. (2011). Child welfare policies and programs. In J. Jenson & M. Fraser (Eds.), *Social policy for children and families: A risk and resilience perspective* (2nd ed., pp. 57–112). Thousand Oaks, CA: Sage.

Pecora, P. J., Kessler, R. C., Williams, J., O'Brien, K., Downs, A. C., English, D., . . . Holmes, K. (2005). *Improving family foster care: Findings from the Northwest Foster Care Alumni Study.* Seattle, WA: Casey Family Programs.

Pelchat, D., Levert, M.-J., & Bourgeois-Guérin, V. (2009). How do mothers and fathers who have a child with a disability describe their adaptation/transformation process? *Journal of Child Health Care, 13*(3), 239–259.

Pempek, T. A., Yermolayeva, Y. A., & Calvert, S. L. (2009). College students' social networking experiences on Facebook. *Journal of Applied Developmental Psychology, 30*(3), 227–238.

Peng, G., & Wang, W. (2011). Hemisphere lateralization is influenced by bilingual status and composition of words. *Neuropsychologia, 49*(7), 1981–1986.

Pepino, M. Y., & Mennella, J. A. (2006). Children's liking of sweet tastes: A reflection of our basic biology. In W. Spillane (Ed.), *Optimising sweet taste in foods* (pp. 54–65). Cambridge, UK: Woodhead.

Pepler, D. J. (2012). *The development and treatment of girlhood aggression.* New York: Psychology Press.

Pereira, M., Johnsen, I., Hauken, M. A., Kristensen, P., & Dyregrov, A. (2017). Early interventions following the death of a parent: Protocol of a mixed methods systematic review. *JMIR Research Protocols, 6*(6), 127. doi:10.2196/resprot.7931

Perlman, D., & Fehr, B. (1987). The development of intimate relationships. In D. Perlman & S. Duck (Eds.), *Intimate relationships: Development, dynamics, & deterioration* (pp. 13–42). Newbury Park, CA: Sage.

Perrig-Chiello, P., & Perren, S. (2005). Impact of past transitions on well-being in middle age. In S. Willis & M. Martin (Eds.), *Middle adulthood: A lifespan perspective* (pp. 143–178). Thousand Oaks, CA: Sage.

Perry, B. (2002). Childhood experience and the expression of genetic potential: What childhood neglect tells us about nature and nurture. *Brain & Mind, 3*(1), 79–100.

Perry, M. (2015). Contraception: Choices and contraindications. *Nurse Prescribing, 13*(5), 236–240.

Perry-Parrish, C., & Zeman, J. (2011). Relations among sadness regulation, peer acceptance, and social functioning in early adolescence: The role of gender. *Social Development, 20*(1), 135–153.

Perz, J., & Ussher, J. (2008). "The horror of this living decay": Women's negotiation and resistance of medical discourses around menopause and midlife. *Women's Studies International Forum, 31*(4), 293–299.

Peter, J., & Valkenburg, P. M. (2016). Adolescents and pornography: A review of 20 years of research. *The Journal of Sex Research, 53*(4–5), 509–531.

Peters, E., Lusher, J., Banbury, S., & Chandler, C. (2016). Relationships between breast-feeding, co-sleeping, and somatic complaints in early childhood. *Infant Mental Health Journal, 37*(5), 574–583.

Peterson, B., & Duncan, L. (2007). Midlife women's generativity and authoritarianism: Marriage, motherhood, and 10 years of aging. *Psychology and Aging, 22*(3), 411–419.

Petrovic, K. (2013). Respite and the internet: Accessing care for older adults in the 21st century. *Computers in Human Behavior, 29*(6), 2448–2452.

Pew Center for Social and Demographic Trends. (2009). *Growing old in America: Expectations vs. reality.* Retrieved from www.pewsocialtrends.org/2009/06/29/growing-old-in-america-expectations-vs-reality.

Pew Center for Social and Demographic Trends. (2010). *The return of the multi-generational family household.* Retrieved from www.pewsocialtrends.org/files/2010/10/752-multi-generational-families.pdf.

Pew Research Center. (2015). *Parenting in America: The American Family.* Retrieved from www.pewsocialtrends.org/2015/12/17/1-the-american-family-today/.

Pew Research Center. (2017a). *On abortion, persistant divides between - and within - the two parties.* Retrieved from www.pewresearch.org/fact-tank/2017/07/07/on-abortion-persistent-divides-between-and-within-the-two-parties-2/.

Pew Research Center. (2017b). *Tech adoption climbs among older adults.* Retrieved from http://assets.pewresearch.org/wp-content/uploads/sites/14/2017/05/16170850/PI_2017.05.17_Older-Americans-Tech_FINAL.pdf.

Pharris-Ciurej, N., Hirschman, C., & Willhoft, J. (2012). The 9th grade shock and the high school dropout crisis. *Social Science Research, 41*(3), 709–730.

Piaget, J. (1932/1965). *The moral judgment of the child.* New York: Free Press.

Piaget, J. (1936/1952). *The origins of intelligence in children.* New York: International Universities Press.

Piaget, J. (1972). Intellectual evolution from adolescence to adulthood. *Human Development, 15*(1), 1–12.

Piazza, J., & Charles, S. (2006). Mental health among baby boomers. In S. Whitbourne & S. Willis (Eds.), *The baby boomers grow up: Contemporary perspectives on midlife* (pp. 111–146). Mahwah, NJ: Lawrence Erlbaum.

Pierce, B. (2017). *Genetics: A conceptual approach* (6th ed.). New York: W. H. Freeman.

Pierce, K. (2011). Early functional brain development in autism and the promise of sleep fMRI. *Brain Research, 1380,* 162–174.

Pieters, S., Burk, W., Van der Vorst, H., Dahl, R., Wiers, R., & Engels, R. (2015). Prospective relationships between sleep problems and substance use, internalizing and externalizing problems. *Journal of Youth and Adolescence, 44*(2), 379–388.

Pillemer, K., & Suitor, J. J. (2014). Who provides care? A prospective study of caregiving among adult siblings. *The Gerontologist, 54*(4), 589–598.

Pillemer, K., Suitor, J. J., Pardo, S., & Henderson, C. (2010). Mothers' differentiation and depressive symptoms among adult children. *Journal of Marriage and the Family, 72*(2), 333–345.

Pinker, S. (2002). *The blank slate: The modern denial of human nature.* New York: Penguin.

Pinzon, J., & Jones, V. (2012). Care of adolescent parents and their children. *Pediatrics, 130*(6), 1743–1756.

Piotrowski, J., Lapierre, M., & Linebarger, D. (2013). Investigating correlates of self-regulation in early childhood with a representative sample of English-speaking American families. *Journal of Child and Family Studies, 22*(3), 423–436.

Plassman, B., Langa, K., Fisher, G., Heeringa, S., Weir, D., Ofstedal, M., . . . Wallace, R. B. (2007). Prevalence of dementia in the United States: The aging, demographics, and memory study. *Neuroepidemiology, 29*(1–2), 125–132.

Ploubidis, G., Silverwood, R., DeStavola, B., & Grundy, E. (2015). Life-course partnership status and biomarkers in midlife: Evidence from the 1958 British Birth Cohort. *American Journal of Public Health, 105*(8), 1596–1603.

Pollak, L. (2013). *Millennials at work: The global generation.* Retrieved from www.lindseypollak.com/millennials-at-work-the-global-generation/.

Poon, C. Y. M., & Knight, B. G. (2013). Parental emotional support during emerging adulthood and baby boomers' well-being in midlife. *International Journal of Behavioral Development, 37*(6), 498–504.

Poon, L. W., & Cohen-Mansfield, J. (2011). *Understanding well-being in the oldest old.* New York: Cambridge University Press.

Poon, L. W., Jazwinski, M., Green, R. C., Woodard, J. L., Martin, P., Rodgers, W. L., . . . Dai, J. (2007). Methodological considerations in studying centenarians: Lessons learned from the Georgia Centenarian Studies. *Annual Review of Gerontology & Geriatrics, 27*(1), 231–264.

Portes, A., & Rumbaut, R. G. (2001). *Legacies.* Berkeley: University of California Press.

Poteat, V. P., Aragon, S., Espelage, D., & Koenig, B. (2009). Psychosocial concerns of sexual minority youth: Complexity and caution in group differences. *Journal of Consulting and Clinical Psychology, 77*(1), 196–201.

Potter, C. (2004). Gender differences in childhood and adolescence. In P. Allen-Meares & M. Fraser (Eds.), *Intervention with children and adolescents: An interdisciplinary perspective* (pp. 54–79). Boston: Allyn & Bacon.

Practice Committees of American Society for Reproductive Medicine—Society for Assisted Reproductive Technology.

(2013). Mature oocyte cryopreservation: A guideline. *Fertility and Sterility, 99*(1), 37–43.

Prahl, C., Krook, C., & Fagerberg, I. (2016). Understanding the role of an educational model in developing knowledge of caring for older persons with dementia. *Nurse Education in Practice, 17*, 97–101.

Premberg, A. (2006). Fathers' experience of childbirth education. *Journal of Perinatal Education, 15*(2), 21–28.

Premberg, A., Carlsson, G., Hellström, A., & Berg, M. (2011). First-time fathers' experiences of childbirth: A phenomenological study. *Midwifery, 27*(6), 848–853.

Premberg, A., Hellström, A.-L., & Berg, M. (2008). Experiences of the first year as father. *Scandinavian Journal of Caring Sciences, 22*(1), 56–63.

Prensky, M. (2010). *Teaching digital natives: Partnering for real learning.* New York: Corwin.

Price, B. (2009). Body image in adolescents: Insights and implications. *Paediatric Nursing, 21*(5), 38–43.

Price, C., Bush, K., & Price, S. (2017). *Families and change: Coping with stressful events and transitions* (5th ed.). Thousand Oaks, CA: Sage.

Price, S. K. (2008a). Stepping back to gain perspective: Pregnancy loss history, depression, and parenting capacity in the Early Childhood Longitudinal Study, Birth Cohort (ECLS-B). *Death Studies, 32*(2), 97–122.

Price, S. K. (2008b). Women and reproductive loss: Client-worker dialogues designed to break the silence. *Social Work, 53*(4), 367–376.

Primack, B. A., Shensa, A., Sidani, J. E., Whaite, E. O., Lin, L. Y., Rosen, D., . . . Miller, E. (2017). Social media use and perceived social isolation among young adults in the U.S. *American Journal of Preventive Medicine, 53*(1), 1–8.

Prior, N. (2013). *Juvenile justice and alternative education: A life course assessment of best practices.* El Paso, TX: LFB Scholarly.

Prochaska, J., & DiClemente, C. (2005). The transtheoretical approach. In J. Norcross & M. Godfried (Eds.), *Handbook of psychotherapy integration* (2nd ed., pp. 147–176). New York: Oxford University Press.

Proot, I. M., Abu-Saad, H. H., ter Meulen, R. H. J., Goldsteen, M., Spreeuwenberg, C., & Widdershoven, G. A. M. (2004). The needs of terminally ill patients at home: Directing one's life, health and things related to beloved others. *Palliative Medicine, 18*(1), 53–61.

Pulkkinen, L., Feldet, T., & Kokko, K. (2005). Personality in young adulthood and functioning in middle age. In S. L. Willis & M. Martin (Eds.), *Middle adulthood: A lifespan perspective* (pp. 99–141). Thousand Oaks, CA: Sage.

Pulkkinen, L., & Kokko, K. (2000). Identity development in adulthood: A longitudinal study. *Journal of Research in Personality, 34*(4), 445–470.

Pulkkinen, L., Kokko, K., & Rantanen, J. (2012). Paths from socioemotional behavior in middle childhood to personality in middle adulthood. *Developmental Psychology, 48*(5), 1283–1291.

Putney, N., & Bengtson, V. (2003). Intergenerational relations in changing times. In J. Mortimer & M. Shanahan (Eds.), *Handbook of the life course* (pp. 149–164). New York: Kluwer Academic/Plenum.

Puzzanchera, C., & Kang, W. (2017). *Easy access to FBI arrest Statistics 1994–2014.* Pittsburgh, PA: National Center for Juvenile Justice. Retrieved from www.ojjdp.gov/ojstatbb/ezaucr/.

Qouta, S., Punamaki, R., & El-Sarraj, E. (2003). Prevalence and determinants of PTSD among Palestinian children exposed to military violence. *European Psychiatry and Adolescent Psychiatry, 12*(6), 265–272.

Quadagno, J. (2007). *Aging and the life course: An introduction to social gerontology* (4th ed.). Hightstown, NJ: McGraw-Hill.

Quevedo, L., Silva, R., Godoy, R., Jansen, K., Matos, M., Tavares Pinheiro, K., Pinheiro, R. T. (2012). The impact of maternal post-partum depression on the language development of children at 12 months. *Child: Care, Health and Development, 38*(3), 420–424.

Rabkin, J., Balassone, M., & Bell, M. (1995). The role of social workers in providing comprehensive health care to pregnant women. *Social Work in Health Care, 20*(3), 83–97.

Racine, E., Frick, K., Guthrie, J., & Strobino, D. (2009). Individual net-benefit maximization: A model for understanding breastfeeding cessation among low-income women. *Maternal and Child Health Journal, 13*(2), 241–249.

Rahilly, E. (2015). The gender binary meets the gender-variant child: Parents' negotiations with childhood gender variance. *Gender & Society, 29*(3), 338–361.

Rainie, L., Smith, A., & Duggan, M. (2013). *Coming and going on Facebook.* Washington, DC: Pew Research Center. Retrieved from www.pewinternet.org/2013/02/05/coming-and-going-on-facebook/.

Rakison, D., & Poulin-Dubois, D. (2001). Developmental origin of the animate-inanimate distinction. *Psychological Bulletin, 127*, 209–228.

Ramirez, T., & Blay, Z. (2017, October 17). Why people are using the term "Latinx." *HuffPost.* Retrieved from www.huffingtonpost.com/entry/why-people-are-using-the-term-latinx_us_57753328e4b0cc0fa136a159.

Ramm, K., Mannix, T., Parry, Y., & Gaffney, M. (2017). A comparison of sound levels in open plan versus pods in a neonatal intensive care unit. *Health Environments Research and Design Journal, 10*(3), 30–39.

Ramnitz, M., & Lodish, M. (2013). *Racial disparities in pubertal development. Seminars in Reproductive Med, 31*, 333–339.

Ramsey, J., Langlois, J., Hoss, R., Rubenstein, A., & Griffin, A. (2004). Origins of a stereotype: Categorization of facial attractiveness by 6-month-old infants. *Developmental Science, 7*(2), 201–211.

Rando, T. (1993). *Treatment of complicated mourning.* Champaign, IL: Research Press.

Randolph, A. L., Hruby, B. T., & Sharif, S. (2015). Counseling women who have experienced pregnancy loss: A review of the literature. *Adultspan Journal, 14*(1), 2–10.

Rank, M. R. (2005). *One nation, underprivileged: Why American poverty affects us all.* New York: Oxford University Press.

Rapee, R. M. (2015). Nature and psychological management of anxiety disorders in youth. *Journal of Pediatrics and Child Health, 51*(3), 280–284.

Raphael, D., & Bryant, T. (2015). Power, intersectionality and the life-course: Identifying the political and economic structures of welfare states that support or threaten health. *Social Theory & Health, 13*(3/4), 245–266.

Rauscher, K., Wegman, D., Wooding, J., Davis, L., & Junkin, R. (2012). Adolescent work quality: A view from today's youth. *Journal of Adolescent Research, 28*(5), 557–590.

Ravitch, D. (2013). *Reign of error: The hoax of the privatization movement and the danger to America's public schools.* New York: Alfred A. Knopf.

Raymond, C. (2017, August 4). *Services a death doula provides?* Retrieved from www.verywell.com/what-is-a-death-doula-1132512?print.

Reczek, C. (2014). The intergenerational relationships of gay men and lesbian women. *Journals of Gerontology, Series B: Psychological Sciences and Social Sciences, 69*(6), 909–919.

Redfern, J. S., & Sinclair, B. (2014). Improving health care encounters and communication with transgender patients. *Journal of Communication in Healthcare, 7*(1), 25–40.

Redonnet, B., Chollet, A., Fombonne, E., Bowes, L., & Melchior, M. (2012). Tobacco, alcohol, cannabis and other illegal drug use among young adults: The socioeconomic context. *Drug and Alcohol Dependence, 121*(3), 231–239.

Reed, M., Merriam, G., & Kargi, A. (2013). Adult growth hormone deficiency: Benefits, side effects, and risks of growth hormone. *Frontiers of Epidemiology, 4*, 64. doi:10.3389/fendo.2013.00064. Retrieved from www.frontiersin.org/articles/10.3389/fendo.2013.00064/full.

Reichard, R. (2015, August 29). *Why we say Latinx: Trans and gender non-conforming people explain.* Retrieved from http://projectqueer.org/post/149193115009/why-we-say-latinx-trans-gender-nonconforming.

Reith, M., & Payne, M. (2009). *Social work in end-of-life and palliative care.* Chicago: Lyceum Books.

Remlin, C. W., Cook, M. C., Erney, R., Cherepon, H., & Gentile, K. (2017). *Safe havens: Closing the gap between recommended practice and reality for transgender and gender-expansive youth in out-of-home care.* New York: Lambda Legal. Retrieved from www.lambdalegal.org/sites/default/files/tgnc-policy-report_2017_final-web_05-02-17.pdf.

Renaud, M., Bherer, L., & Maquestiaux, F. (2010). A high level of physical fitness is associated with more efficient response preparation in older adults. *The Journals of Gerontology: Psychological Sciences, 65B*(3), 756–766.

Repetti, R., Taylor, S., & Seeman, T. (2002). Risky families: Family social environments and the mental and physical health of offspring. *Psychological Bulletin, 128*(2), 330–366.

Reproductive Health Access Project. (2014). *Your birth control choices.* Retrieved from www.reproductiveaccess.org/resource/birth-control-choices-fact-sheet/?gclid=COHmuuTWhsgCFQwYHwodonABaA.

Reuben, A., Caspi, A., Belsky, D., Broadbent, J., Harrington, H., Sugden, K., . . . Moffitt, T. E. (2017). Association of childhood blood lead levels with cognitive function and socioeconomic status at age 38 years and with IQ change and socioeconomic mobility between childhood and adulthood. *Journal of the American Medical Association, 317*(12), 1244–1251.

Reynolds, B., & Juvonen, J. (2012). Pubertal timing fluctuations across middle school: Implications for girls' psychological health. *Journal of Youth & Adolescence, 41*(6), 677–690.

Reznick, J., Morrow, J., Goldman, B., & Snyder, J. (2004). The onset of working memory in infants. *Infancy, 6*(1), 145–154.

Ricciardelli, L. (2016). *Adolescence and body image: From development to preventing dissatisfaction.* New York: Routledge.

Rich, M. (2013, August 15). School standards' debut is rocky, and critics pounce. *New York Times.* Retrieved from www.nytimes.com/2013/08/16/education/new-education-standards-face-growing-opposition.html.

Richardson, M., Cobham, V., McDermott, B., & Murray, J. (2013). Youth mental illness and the family: Parents' loss and grief. *Journal of Child & Family Studies, 22*(5), 719–736.

Richert, R. A., & Granqvist, P. (2014). Religious and spiritual development in childhood. In R. F. Paloutzian & C. L. Park (Eds.), *Handbook of the psychology of religion and spirituality* (2nd ed., pp. 165–182). New York: Guilford Press.

Richmond, M. (1917). *Social diagnosis.* New York: Russell Sage.

Ridenour, A., Yorgason, J., & Peterson, B. (2009). The infertility resilience model: Assessing individual, couple, and external predictive factors. *Contemporary Family Therapy: An International Journal, 31*(1), 34–51.

Rieker, P. R., & Bird, C. E. (2005). Rethinking gender differences in health: Why we need to integrate social and biological perspectives. *The Journals of Gerontology, Series B: Psychological Sciences and Social Sciences, 60B,* 40–47.

Rieser-Danner, L. (2003). Individual differences in infant fearfulness and cognitive performance: A testing, performance, or competence effect? *Genetic, Social, and General Psychology Monographs, 129*(1), 41–71.

Rietz, C., Hasselhorn, M., & Labuhn, A. (2012). Are externalizing and internalizing difficulties of young children with spelling impairment related to their ADHD symptoms? *Dyslexia (10769242), 18*(3), 174–185.

Riley, M. W. (1971). Social gerontology and the age stratification of society. *The Gerontologist, 11,* 79–87.

Rindfuss, R. R., Cooksey, E. C., & Sutterlin, R. L. (1999). Young adult occupational achievement: Early expectations versus behavioral reality. *Work & Occupations, 26*(2), 220–263.

Ringeisen, H., Casanueva, C. E., Urato, M., & Stambaugh, L. F. (2009). Mental health service use during the transition to adulthood for adolescents reported to the child welfare system. *Psychiatric Services, 60*(8), 1084–1091.

Riordan, J., & Auerbach, K. (1999). *Breastfeeding and human lactation* (2nd ed.). Sudbury, MA: Jones & Bartlett.

Rivas-Drake, D., Seaton, E., Markstrom, C., Quintana, S., Syed, M., Lee, R., . . . Ethnic and Racial Identity in the 21st Century Study Group. (2014). Ethnic and racial identity in adolescence: Implications for psychosocial, academia, and health outcomes. *Child Development, 85*(1), 40–57.

Robbins, T., Stagman, S., & Smith, S. (2012). *Young children at risk: National and state prevalence of risk factors.* New York: Columbia University National Center on Children in Poverty.

Robboy, J., & Anderson, K. G. (2011). Intergenerational child abuse and coping. *Journal of Interpersonal Violence, 26*(17), 3526–3541.

Roberts, E., Burchinal, M., & Bailey, D. (1994). Communication among preschoolers with and without disabilities in same-age and mixed-age classes. *American Journal on Mental Retardation, 99,* 231–249.

Roberts, K., & Yamane, D. (2016). *Religion in sociological perspective* (6th ed.). Thousand Oaks, CA: Sage.

Roberts, R. E. L., & Bengston, V. L. (1993). Relationship with parents, self-esteem, and psychological well-being in young adulthood. *Social Psychology Quarterly, 56*(4), 263–278.

Robertson, S., Zarit, S., Duncan, L., Rovine, M., & Femia, E. (2007). Family caregivers' patterns of positive and negative affect. *Family Relations, 56,* 12–23.

Robinson, L. C. (2000). Interpersonal relationship quality in young adulthood: A gender analysis. *Adolescence, 35*(140), 775–785.

Robinson, O., & Wright, G. (2013). The prevalence, types and perceived outcomes of crisis episodes in early adulthood and midlife: A structured retrospective-auto-biographical study. *International Journal of Behavioral Development, 37*(5), 407–416.

Rockwood, N. M., & Pendergast, A. (2016). The association between female-factor infertility and depression and anxiety. *UBC Medical Journal, 8*(1), 14–16.

Rodda, J., Walker, Z., & Carter, J. (2011). Depression in older adults. *British Medical Journal, 343,* 683–687.

Rodkin, P. C., Ryan, A. M., Jamison, R., & Wilson, T. (2013). Social goals, social behavior, and social status in middle childhood. *Developmental Psychology, 49*(6), 1139–1150.

Rogers, L., & Meltzoff, A. (2017). Is gender more important and meaningful than race? An analysis of racial and gender identity among Black, White, and mixed-race children. *Cultural Diversity and Ethnic Minority Psychology, 23*(3), 323–334.

Rogers, L. O., Zosuls, K. M., Halim, M. L., Ruble, D., & Hughes, D. (2012). Meaning making in middle childhood: An exploration of the meaning of ethnic identity. *Cultural Diversity and Ethnic Minority Psychology, 18*(2), 99–108.

Rogers, W. A., & Mitzner, T. L. (2017). Envisioning the future for older adults: Autonomy, health, well-being, and social connectedness with technology support. *Futures, 87,* 133–139.

Roggman, L. (2004). Do fathers just want to have fun? *Human Development, 47,* 228–236.

Roggman, L., Boyce, L., Cook, G., Christiansen, K., & Jones, D. (2004). Playing with daddy: social toy play, early head start, and developmental outcomes. *Fathering, 2,* 83–108.

Rogoff, B., & Chavajay, P. (1995). What's become of research on the cultural basis of cognitive development? *American Psychologist, 50*(10), 859–873.

Rohde, L., Szobot, C., Polanczyk, G., Schmitz, M., Martins, S., & Tramontina, S. (2005). Attention-deficit/hyperactivity disorder in a diverse culture: Do research and clinical findings support the notion of a cultural construct for the disorder? *Biological Psychiatry*, *57*(11), 1436–1441.

Rollins, A., & Hunter, A. G. (2013). Racial socialization of biracial youth: Maternal messages and approaches to address discrimination. *Family Relations*, *62*(1), 140–153.

Romeu, J., Cotrina. L., Perapoch, J., & Lines, M. (2016). Assessment of environmental noise and its effect on neonates in a neonatal intensive care unit. *Applied Acoustics*, *111*, 161–169.

Ronan, L., Flexander-Bloch, A., Wagstyle, K., Farooqi, S., Brayne, C., Tyler, L., . . . Fletcher, P. C. (2016). Obesity associated with increased brain age from midlife. *Neurobiology of Aging*, *47*, 63–70.

Rönkä, A., Oravala, S., & Pulkkinen, L. (2003). Turning points in adults' lives: The effects of gender and amount of choice. *Journal of Adult Development*, *10*(3), 203–215.

Roof, W. (1993). *A generation of seekers: The spiritual journeys of the baby boom generation*. San Francisco: HarperCollins.

Roof, W. (1999). *Spiritual marketplace: Baby boomers and the remaking of American religion*. Princeton, NJ: Princeton University Press.

Rooij, S., Wouters, H., Yonker, J., Painter, R., & Roseboom, T. (2010). Prenatal undernutrition and cognitive function in late adulthood. *Proceedings of the National Academy of Sciences*, *107*(9), 16681–16886.

Roopnarine, J., Shin, M., Donovan, B., & Suppal, P. (2000). Sociocultural contexts of dramatic play: Implications for early education. In K. Roskos & J. Christie (Eds.), *Play and literacy in early childhood: Research from multiple perspectives* (pp. 205–220). Mahwah, NJ: Lawrence Erlbaum.

Roper v. Simmons, 543 U.S. 551 (2005).

Rose, S., & Zand, D. (2000). Lesbian dating and courtship from young adulthood to midlife. *Journal of Gay & Lesbian Social Services*, *11*(2/3), 77–104.

Roseboom, T., Painter, R. C., van Abeelen, A. F. M., Veenendall, M. V. E., & de Rooij, S. R. (2011). Hungry in the womb: What are the consequences? Lessons from the Dutch famine. *Maturitas*, *70*(2), 141–145.

Rosenberg, M. (1986). *Conceiving the self*. Malabar, FL: Robert E. Krieger.

Rosenberg, S., Ellison, M., Fast, B., Robinson, C., & Lazar, R. (2013). Computing theoretical rates of Part C eligibility based on developmental delays. *Maternal and Child Health Journal*, *17*, 384–390.

Roskos, K., & Christie, J. (2000). *Play and literacy in early childhood: Research from multiple perspectives*. Mahwah, NJ: Lawrence Erlbaum.

Rossi, A. (2004). Social responsibility to family and community. In O. Brim, C. Ryff, & R. Kessler (Eds.), *How healthy are we? A national study of well-being at midlife* (pp. 550–585). Chicago: University of Chicago Press.

Roth, M. Y., Page, S. T., & Bremner, W. J. (2016). Male hormonal contraception: Looking back and moving forward. *Andrology*, *4*(1), 4–12.

Rothrauff, T., & Cooney, T. (2008). The role of generativity in psychological well-being: Does it differ for childless adults and parents? *Journal of Adult Development*, *15*(3/4), 148–159.

Rovio, S., Spulber, G., Nieminen, L., Niskanen, E., Winblad, B., Tuomilehto, J., . . . Kivipelto, M. (2010). The effect of midlife physical activity on structural brain changes in the elderly. *Neurobiology of Aging*, *31*(11), 1927–1936.

Rowley, S., Helaire, L., & Banerjee, M. (2010). Reflecting on racism: School involvement and perceived teacher discrimination in African American mothers. *Journal of Applied Developmental Psychology*, *31*(1), 83–92.

Ruark, A., Kennedy, C., Mazibuko, N., Dlamini, L., Nunn, A., Green, E., & Surkan, P. J. (2016). From first love to marriage and maturity: A life-course perspective on HIV risk among young Swazi adults. *Culture, Health & Sexuality*, *18*(7), 812–825.

Rubinstein, R., Girling, L., deMedeiros, K., Brazda, M., & Hannum, S. (2015). Extending the framework of generativity theory through research: A qualitative study. *The Gerontologist*, *55*(4), 548–599.

Rueda, R., Monzo, L., Shapiro, J., Gomez, J., & Blacher, J. (2005). Cultural models of transition: Latina mothers of young adults with developmental disabilities. *Exceptional Children*, *71*(4), 401–414.

Ruffman, T., Slade, L., & Redman, J. (2005). Young infants' expectations about hidden objects. *Cognitive*, *97*(2), B35–B43.

Ruhstaller, K. E., Bastek, J. A., Thomas, A., Mcelrath, T. E., Perry, S. I., & Durnwald, C. (2016). The effect of early excessive weight gain on the development of hypertension in pregnancy. *American Journal of Perinatology*, *33*(12), 1205–1210.

Ruiz, S., & Silverstein, M. (2007). Relationships with grandparents and the emotional well-being of late adolescent and young adult grandchildren. *Journal of Social Issues*, *63*(4), 793–808.

Rush, M., & Seward, R. (2016). *Working paper series – WP 44. Comparative family policies and the politics of parental leave in the USA*. University College Dublin School of Social

Policy, Social Work and Social Justice. Retrieved from https://www.ucd.ie/t4cms/Working%20Paper%2044%20on%20Parental%20Leave%20in%20the%20USA.pdf.

Russell, S., Watson, R., & Muraco, J. (2012). The development of same-sex intimate relationships during adolescence. In B. Laursen & W. A. Collins (Eds.), *Relationship pathways from adolescence to young adulthood* (pp. 215–233). Thousand Oaks, CA: Sage.

Rutter, M. (1996). Transitions and turning points in developmental psychopathology: As applied to the age span between childhood and mid-adulthood. *International Journal of Behavioral Development, 19*(3), 603–636.

Ryan, C. L., & Bauman, K. (2016). *Educational attainment in the United States: 2015.* Washington, DC: U.S. Census Bureau. Retrieved from www.census.gov/content/dam/Census/library/publications/2016/demo/p20-578.pdf.

Rybak, A. (2015). Organic and nonorganic feeding disorders. *Annals of Nutrition & Metabolism, 66*(Suppl. 5), 16–22.

Ryff, C., Friedman, E., Fuller-Rowell, T., Love, G., Miyamoto, Y., Morozink, J., . . . Tsenkova, V. (2012). Varieties of resilience in MIDUS. *Social and Personality Psychology Compass, 6*(11), 792–806.

Ryff, C., & Singer, B. (2006). Best news yet on the six-factor model of well-being. *Social Science Research, 335*(4), 1103–1119.

Sabbagh, M., & Baldwin, D. (2001). Learning words from knowledgeable versus ignorant speakers: Links between preschoolers' theory of mind and semantic development. *Child Development, 72,* 1054–1070.

Saewyc, E. (2011). Research on adolescent sexual orientation: Development, health disparities, stigma, and resilience. *Journal of Research on Adolescence, 21*(1), 256–272.

Sagi, A., Koren-Karie, N., Gini, M., Ziv, Y., & Joels, T. (2002). Shedding further light on the effects of various types and quality of early child care on infant-mother attachment relationships: The Haifa study of early child care. *Child Development, 73,* 1166–1186.

Saleebey, D. (2012). *The strengths perspective in social work practice* (6th ed.). Upper Saddle River, NJ: Pearson.

Salihu, H. M., Myers, J., & August, E. M. (2012). Pregnancy in the workplace. *Occupational Medicine, 62*(2), 88–97.

Salvatore, J., Meyers, J., Yan, J., Alieve, F., Lansford, J., Pettit, G., . . . Dick, D. M. (2015). Intergenerational continuity in parents' and adolescents' externalizing problems: The role of life events and their interaction with GABRA2. *Journal of Abnormal Psychology, 124*(3), 709–728.

Sandberg, L. (2013). Just feeling a naked body close to you: Men, sexuality and intimacy in later life. *Sexualities, 16*(3–4), 261–282.

Sanders, R. (2013). Adolescent psychosocial, social, and cognitive development. *Pediatrics in Review, 34*(8), 354–359.

Sandoval-Cros, C. (2009). Hispanic cultural issues in end-of-life care. In D. J. Doka & A. S. Tucci (Eds.), *Living with grief: Diversity and end-of-life care* (pp. 117–126). Washington, DC: Hospice Foundation of America.

Sands, R., & Goldberg, G. (2000). Factors associated with stress among grandparents raising their grandchildren. *Family Relations, 49*(1), 97–105.

Santrock, J. W. (2013). *Child development* (14th ed.). Boston: McGraw Hill.

Sapolsky, R. (2004). *Why zebras don't get ulcers* (3rd ed.). New York: Henry Holt.

Sapolsky, R. (2017). *Behave: The biology of humans at our best and worst.* New York: Penguin.

Saraga, M., Gholam-Rezaee, M., & Preisig, M. (2013). Symptoms, comorbidity, and clinical course of depression in immigrants: Putting psychopathology in context. *Journal of Affective Disorders, 252,* 795–799.

Saunders, B., Tilford, J., Fussell, J., Schulz, E., Casey, P., & Kuo, D. (2015). Financial and employment impact of intellectual disability on families with autism. *Families, Systems, & Health, 33*(1), 1–9.

Savia, J., Almeida, D., Davey, A., & Zant, S. (2008). Routine assistance to parents: Effects on daily mood and other stressors. *The Journals of Gerontology, Series B: Psychological Sciences & Social Sciences, 36B*(3), S154–S161.

Savica, R., & Petersen, L. C. (2011). Prevention of dementia. *Psychiatric Clinics of North America, 34*(1), 127–145.

Sawin, K. S. (1998). Health care concerns for women with physical disability and chronic illness. In E. Q. Youngkin & M. S. Davis (Eds.), *Women's health: A primary care clinical guide* (2nd ed., pp. 905–941). Stamford, CT: Appleton & Lange.

Sawyer, S., Afifi, R., Bearinger, L., Blakermore, S., Dick, B., Ezeh, A., & Patton, G. (2012). Adolescence: A foundation for future health. *The Lancet, 379*(9826), 1630–1641.

Scarlett, A. G., Naudeau, S., Salonius-Pasternak, D., & Ponte, I. (2005). *Children's play.* Thousand Oaks, CA: Sage.

Schaan, B. (2013). Widowhood and depression among older Europeans: The role of gender, caregiving, marital quality, and regional context. *The Journals of Gerontology, Series B: Psychological Science and Social Sciences, 68*(3), 431–442.

Schady, N. (2011). Parents' education, mothers' vocabulary, and cognitive development in early childhood: Longitudinal evidence from Ecuador. *American Journal of Public Health, 101*(12), 2299–2307.

Schaie, K. W. (1984). The Seattle Longitudinal Study: A 21-year exploration of psychometric intelligence in adulthood. In K. W. Schaie (Ed.), *Longitudinal studies of adult psychological development* (pp. 64–135). New York: Guilford Press.

Schaie, K. W. (2013). *Developmental influences on adult intelligence: The Seattle Longitudinal Study* (2nd ed.). New York: Oxford.

Scherger, S. (2009). Social change and the timing of family transitions in West Germany: Evidence from cohort comparisons. *Time & Society, 18*(1), 106–129.

Schneider, B., Lee, M., & Alvarez-Valdivia, I. (2012). Adolescent friendship bonds in cultures of connectedness. In B. Laursen & W. A. Collins (Eds.), *Relationship pathways from adolescence to young adulthood* (pp. 113–134). Thousand Oaks, CA: Sage.

Schneir, A. (2009). *Psychological first aid for youth experiencing homelessness.* The National Child Traumatic Stress Network. Retrieved from www.nctsn.org/sites/default/files/assets/pdfs/pfa_homeless_youth.pdf.

Schöllgen, I., Huxhold, O., & Tesch-Römer, C. (2010). Socioeconomic status and health in the second half of life: Findings from the German Ageing Survey. *European Journal of Ageing, 7*(1), 17–28.

Schooler, C., & Mulatu, M. S. (2004). Occupational self-direction, intellectual functioning, and self-directed orientation in older workers: Findings and implications for individuals and societies. *American Journal of Sociology, 110*(1), 161–197.

Schoon, I., & Polek, E. (2011). Teenage career aspirations and adult career attainment: The role of gender, social background, and general cognitive ability. *International Journal of Behavioral Development, 35*(3), 210–217.

Schore, A. N. (2002). Dysregulation of the right brain: A fundamental mechanism of traumatic attachment and the psychopathogenesis of post-traumatic stress disorder. *Australian and New Zealand Journal of Psychiatry, 36*(1), 9–30.

Schroeder, R., Giordano, P., & Cernkovitch, S. (2010). Adult child-parent bonds and life course criminality. *Journal of Criminal Justice, 38*(4), 562–571.

Schuff, N., Tosun, D., Insel, P., Chiang, G., Truran, D., Aisen, P., . . . Alzheimer's Disease Neuroimaging Initiative. (2012). Nonlinear time course of brain volume loss in cognitively normal and impaired elders. *Neurobiology of Aging, 33*(5), 845–855.

Schulaka, C. (2016). Marc Freedman on encore careers and embracing a new stage of life. *Journal of Financial Planning, April*, 14–19.

Schulze, P., & Carlisle, S. (2010). What research does and doesn't say about breastfeeding: A critical review. *Early Child Development & Care, 180*(6), 703–718.

Schwandt, A., Hermann, J., Rosenbauer, J., Boettcher, C., Dunstheimer, D., Grulich-Henn, J., . . . Holl, R. W; DPV Initiative. (2017). Longitudinal trajectories of metabolic control from childhood to young adulthood in type 1 diabetes from a large German/Austrian registry: A group-based modelling approach. *Diabetes Care, 40*(3), 309–316.

Schwartz, B. (2018). *Memory: Foundations and applications* (3rd ed.). Los Angeles: Sage.

Schwartz, S., Cote, J., & Arnett, J. (2005). Identity and agency in emerging adulthood: Two developmental routes in the individualization process. *Youth and Society, 37*(2), 201–229.

Schwartz, S., Hardy, S., Zamboanga, B., Meca, A., Waterman, S., & Picariello, S. (2015). Identity in young adulthood: Links with mental health and risky behavior. *Journal of Applied Developmental Psychology, 36*, 39–52.

Schwartz, S. H. (2012). An overview of the Schwartz theory of basic values. *Online Readings in Psychology and Culture, 2*(1). doi:10.9707/2307-0919.1116

Schweinhart, L., Montie, J., Xiang, Z., Barnett, W., Belfield, C., & Nores, M. (2005). *Lifetime effects: The High/Scope Perry preschool study through age 40.* Ypsilanti, MI: High/Scope Educational Research Foundation.

Science Buddies. (2014). Cardiovascular system science: Investigate heart-rate recovery. *Scientific American.* Retrieved from www.scientificamerican.com/article/cardiovascular-system-science-investigate-heart-rate-recovery-time1/.

Seabrook, J., & Avison, W. (2012). Socioeconomic status and cumulative disadvantage processes across the life course: Implications for health outcomes. *Canadian Review of Sociology, 49*(1), 50–68.

Sebastiani, P., & Perls, T. T. (2012). The genetics of extreme longevity: Lessons from the New England Centenarian Study. *Frontiers in Genetics, 3*, 277. doi:10.3389/fgene.2012.00277

Sebastiani, P., Sun, F. X., Andersen, S. L., Lee, J. H., Wojczynski, M. K., Sanders, J. L., . . . Perls, T. T. (2013). Families enriched for exceptional longevity also have increased health-span: Findings from the long life family study. *Frontiers in Public Health, 1*, 38. doi:10.3389/fpubh.2013.00038

Sedgh, G., Bearak, J., Singh, S., Bankole, A., Popinchalk, A., Ganatra, B., . . . Alkema, L. (2016). Abortion incidence between 1990 and 2014: Global, regional, and subregional levels and trends. *The Lancet, 388*(10041), 258–267.

Sedgh, G., Singh, S., & Hussain, R. (2014). Intended and unintended pregnancies worldwide in 2012 and recent trends. *Studies in Family Planning, 45*(3), 301–314.

Sedgh, G., Singh, S., Shah, I. H., Ahman, E., Henshaw, S. K., & Bankote, A. (2012). Induced abortion: Incidence and trends worldwide from 1995 to 2008. *The Lancet, 379*(9816), 625–632.

Segall, M., Dasen, P., Berry, J., & Poortinga, Y. (1999). *Human behavior in global perspective* (2nd ed.). Boston: Allyn & Bacon.

Seiffge-Krenge, I., & Shulman, S. (2012). Transformations in heterosexual romantic relationships across the transition into adolescence. In B. Laursen & W. A. Collins (Eds.), *Relationship pathways from adolescence to young adulthood* (pp. 157–189). Thousand Oaks, CA: Sage.

Seligman, M. E. P., Reivich, K., Jaycox, L., & Gillham, J. (2007). *The optimistic child: A proven program to safeguard children against depression and build lifelong resilience.* Boston: Houghton Mifflin.

Selman, R. (1980). *The growth of interpersonal understanding.* New York: Acadmic Press.

Seltzer, M., Almeida, D., Greenberg, J., Savla, J., Stawski, R., Hong, J., & Taylor, J. L. (2009). Psychosocial and biological markers of daily lives of midlife parents of children with disabilities. *Journal of Health and Social Behavior, 50*(1), 1–15.

Seng, J., Lopez, W., Sperlich, M., Hamam, L., & Meldrum, C. (2012). Marginalized identities, discrimination, burden, and mental health: Empirical exploration of an interpersonal-level approach to modeling intersectionality. *Social Science & Medicine, 75*(12), 2437–2445.

Sengane, M. (2009). The experience of Black fathers concerning support for their wives/partners during labour. *Curationis, 32*(1), 67–73.

Sengsavang, S., Willemsen, K., & Krettenauer, T. (2015). Why be moral? Children's explicit motives for prosocial-moral action. *Frontiers in Psychology, 6,* 552. doi:10.3389/fpsyg.2015.00552

Senturk, M. B., Yildiz, G., Yildiz, P., Yorguner, N., & Cakmak, Y. (2017). The relationship between hyperemesis gravidarum and maternal psychiatric well-being during and after pregnancy: Controlled study. *Journal of Maternal-Fetal & Neonatal Medicine, 30*(11), 1314–1319.

Senut, M.-C., Cingolani, P., Sen, A., Kruger, A., Shaik, A., Hirsch, H., . . . Ruden, D. (2012). Epigenetics of early-life lead exposure and effects on brain development. *Epigenomics, 4*(6), 665–674.

Serati, M., Barkin, J., Orsenigo, G., Altamure, A., & Buoli, M. (2017). Research review: The role of obstetric and neonatal complications in childhood attention deficit and hyperactivity disorder – a systematic review. *The Journal of Child Psychology and Psychiatry, 58*(12), 1290–1300.

Settersten, R. A., Furstenberg, F. F., & Rumbaut, R. G. (2005). *On the frontier of adulthood: Theory, research, and public policy.* Chicago: University of Chicago Press.

Settersten, R. A., & Mayer, L. U. (1997). The measurement of age, age structuring, and the life course. *Annual Review of Sociology, 23,* 233–261.

Seward, D., & Khan, S. (2016). Towards an understanding of Muslim American adolescent high school experiences. *International Journal for the Advancement of Counselling, 38*(1), 1–11.

Seward, R., & Rush, M. (2016). Changing fatherhood and fathering across cultures towards convergence in work-life balance: Divergent progress or stalemate? In I. Crepi & E. Ruspini (Eds.), *Balancing work and family in changing society: The father's perspective* (pp. 13–32). New York: Palgrave Macmillan.

Shade, K., Kools, S., Weiss, S., & Pinderhughes, H. (2011). A conceptual model of incarcerated adolescent fatherhood: Adolescent identity development and the concept of intersectionality. *Journal of Child and Adolescent Psychiatric Nursing, 24*(2), 98–104.

Shanahan, L., Waite, E., & Boyd, T. (2012). Transformations in sibling relationships from adolescence to adulthood. In B. Laursen & W. A. Collins (Eds.), *Relationship pathways from adolescence to young adulthood* (pp. 43–66). Thousand Oaks, CA: Sage.

Shanahan, M. (2000). Pathways to adulthood in changing societies: Variability and mechanisms in life course perspective. *Annual Review of Sociology, 262*(1), 667–692.

Shannon, J. B. (2011). *Autism and pervasive developmental disorders sourcebook.* Detroit, MI: Omnigraphics.

Sharkey, P., Tirado-Strayer, N., Popachristos, A., & Rover, C. (2012). The effect of local violence on children's attention and impulse control. *Amercian Journal of Public Health, 102*(12), 2287–2293.

Sharma, G., & Goodwin, J. (2006). Effect of aging on respiratory system physiology and immunology. *Clinical Interventions in Aging, 1*(3), 253–260.

Sharma, R., Agarwal, A., Rohra, V., Assidi, M., Abu-Elmagd, M., & Turki, R. (2015). Effects of increased paternal age on sperm quality, reproductive outcome and associated epigenetic risks to offspring. *Reproductive Biology and Endocrinology, 13*(35). doi:10.1186/s12958-015-0028-x

Shaw, M., Abhayaratna, W., Sachdev, P., Anstey, K., & Cherbuin, N. (2016). Cortical thinning at midlife: The PATH Through Life Study. *Brain Topography, 29*(6), 875–884.

Shear, M., & Pear, R. (2014, January 13). Older pool of health care enrollees stirs fears on costs. *New York Times*. Retrieved from www.nytimes.com/2014/01/14/us/health-care-plans-attracting-more-older-less-healthy-people.html.

Sheehan, M., & Sheehan, M. (2013). Management of the pregnant substance abusing woman. *Clinical Obstetrics and Gynecology, 56*(1), 97–106.

Sheehy, G. (1995). *New passages*. New York: Random House.

Sherblom, S. (2008). The legacy of the "care challenge": Re-envisioning the outcome of the justice-care debate. *Journal of Moral Education, 37*(1), 81–98.

Sherer, M. (2009). *Challenging the whole child: Reflections on best practices in learning, teaching and leadership*. Alexandria, VA: Association for Supervision & Curriculum Development.

Sheridan, M. J. (2019). The spiritual person. In E. Hutchison (Ed.), *Dimensions of human behavior: Person and environment* (6th ed.). Thousand Oaks, CA: Sage.

Sherman, E. (1991). *Reminiscence and the self in old age*. New York: Springer.

Sherwood, P., Given, C., Given, B., & von Eye, A. (2005). Caregiver burden and depressive symptoms: Analysis of common outcomes in caregivers of elderly patients. *Journal of Aging Health, 17*(2), 125–147.

Shields, N., Nadasen, K., & Pierce, L. (2008). The effects of community violence on children in Cape Town South Africa. *Child Abuse & Neglect, 32*(5), 589–601.

Shlafer, R., Stang, J., Dallaire, D., Forestell, C., & Hellerstedt, W. (2017). Best practices of nutrition care of pregnant women in prison. *Journal of Correctional Health Care, 23*(3), 297–304.

Shonkoff, J., Garner, A., & The Committee on Psychosocial Aspects of Child and Family Health. (2012). The life-long effects of early childhood adversity and toxic stress. *American Academy of Pediatrics, 129*(1), e232–e246.

Shonkoff, J., & Phillips, D. (Eds.). (2000). *From neurons to neighborhoods: The science of early childhood development*. Washington, DC: National Academy Press.

Shores, K., & Ejdemyr, S. (2017). *Do school districts spend less money on poor and minority students?* Washington, DC: Brown Center Chalkboard, Brookings Institution. Retrieved from www.brookings.edu/blog/brown-center-chalkboard/2017/05/25/do-school-districts-spend-less-money-on-poor-and-minority-students/.

Shreffler, K. M., Greil, A. L., & McQuillan, J. (2011). Pregnancy loss and distress among U.S. women. *Family Relations, 60*(3), 343–355.

Shweder, R. (Ed.). (1998). *Welcome to middle age! (and other cultural fictions)*. Chicago: University of Chicago Press.

Siegel, J. P. (2013). Breaking the links in intergenerational violence: An emotional regulation perspective. *Family Processes, 52*(2), 163–178.

Siemons, R., Raymond-Flesh, M., Auerswald, C. L., & Brindis, C. D. (2017). Coming of age on the margins: Mental health and wellbeing among Latino immigrant young adults eligible for Deferred Action for Childhood Arrivals (DACA). *Journal of Immigrant Minority Health, 19*, 543–551.

Silbereisen, R., & Lerner, R. (2007a). *Approaches to positive youth development*. Thousand Oaks, CA: Sage.

Silbereisen, R., & Lerner, R. (2007b). Approaches to positive youth development: A view of the issues. In R. Silbereisen & R. Lerner (Eds.), *Approaches to positive youth development* (pp. 3–30). Thousand Oaks, CA: Sage.

Silva, J. (2013). *Coming up short: Working class adulthood in an age of uncertainty*. New York: Oxford University Press.

Silva, M., Strasser, K., & Cain, K. (2014). Early narrative skills in Chilean preschool: Questions scaffold the production of coherent narratives. *Early Childhood Research Quarterly, 29*(2), 205–213.

Silverman, P. R. (2004). Bereavement: A time of transition and changing relationships. In J. Berzoff & P. R. Silverman (Eds.), *Living with dying: A handbook for end-of-life healthcare practitioners* (pp. 226–241). New York: Columbia University Press.

Silvers, J., Gabrieli, J., McRae, K., Gross, J., Remy, K., & Ochsner, D. (2012). Age-related differences in emotional reactivity, regulation, and rejection sensitivity in adolescence. *Emotion, 12*(6), 1235–1247.

Silverstein, M., & Bengtson, V. (2001). Intergenerational solidarity and the structure of adult child-parent relationships in American families. In A. Walker, M. Manoogian-O'Dell, L. McGraw, & D. L. White (Eds.), *Families in later life: Connections and transitions* (pp. 53–61). Thousand Oaks, CA: Pine Forge Press.

Simeoni, U., Ligi, I., Buffat, C., & Boubred, F. (2011). Adverse consequences of accelerated neonatal growth: Cardiovascular and renal issues. *Pediatric Nephrology, 26*(4), 493–508.

Simoni, M. K., Lin, M., Collins, S. C., & Mu, L. (2017). Women's career priority is associated with attitudes towards family planning and ethical acceptance of reproductive technologies. *Human Reproduction, 32*(10), 2069–2075.

Simmons, R. (2011). *Odd girl out: The hidden culture of aggression in girls*. Boston: Mariner Books/Houghton Mifflin Harcourt.

Simmons, T., & O'Connell, M. (2003). *Married-couple and unmarried-partner households: 2000*. Washington, DC: U.S. Census Bureau.

Singer, D., & Singer, J. (2011). *Handbook of children and the media* (2nd ed.). Thousand Oaks, CA: Sage.

Singer, J. (1999) "Why can't you be normal for once in your life?": From a "problem with no name" to a new category of difference. In M. Corker & S. French (Eds.), *Disability discourse* (pp. 59–67). Buckingham, UK: Open University Press.

Singer, J., Rexhaj, B., & Baddeley, J. (2007). Older, wiser, and happier? Comparing older adults' and college students' self-defining memories. *Memory, 15*(8), 886–898.

Singh, L., Morgan, J., & Best, C. (2002). Infants' listening preferences: Baby talk or happy talk? *Infancy, 3*(3), 365–394.

Singleton, J. L. (2009). Service learning: The effect on BSW student interest in aging. *The Journal of Baccalaureate Social Work, 14*(1), 31–43.

Sipotz, K. (2015). From failing to thriving: Infant mental health intervention for a nonorganic failure to thrive diagnosis. *Zero to Three, 35*(6), 38–42.

Sisson, G. (2012). Finding a way to offer something more: Reframing teen pregnancy prevention. *Sexuality Research and Social Policy, 9*(1), 57–69.

Slade, A. (2005). Parental reflective functioning: An introduction. *Attachment and Human Development, 7*(3), 269–281.

Slatcher, R., & Trentacosta, C. (2012). Influences of parent and child negative emotionality on young children's everyday behaviors. *Emotion, 12*(5), 932–942.

Sleep Center. (2016). Baby *sleep training: The basics*. Retrieved from www.babycenter.com/0_baby-sleep-training-the-basics_1505715.bc.

Slopen, N., Chen, Y., Priest, N., Albert, M., & Williams, D. (2016). Emotional and instrumental support during childhood and biological dysregulation in midlife. *Preventive Medicine, 84*, 90–96.

Smetana, J., Jambon, M., & Ball, C., (2014). The social domain approach to children's moral and social judgments. In M. Killeen & J. Smetana (Eds.), *Handbook of moral development* (2nd ed., pp. 23–45). New York: Taylor & Francis.

Smink, E., van Hoeken, D., & Hoek, H. (2012). Epidemiology of eating disorders: Incidence, prevalence and mortality. *Current Psychiatry Reports, 14*(4), 406–414.

Smith, C. (2011). *Lost in translation: The dark side of emerging adulthood*. New York: Oxford University Press.

Smith, K., & Lipari, R. (2017, January 27). *Women of childbearing age and opioids*. Substance Abuse and Mental Health Administration (SAMHA). Retrieved from www.samhsa.gov/data/sites/default/files/report_2724/ShortReport-2724.html.

Smith, S., Chen, J., Basile, K., Gilbert, L., Merrick, M., Patel, N., . . . Jain, A. (2017). *The National Intimate Partner and Sexual Violence Survey (NISVS): 2010-2012 state report*. Atlanta, GA: National Center for Injury Prevention and Control, Centers for Disease Control and Prevention. Retrieved from www.cdc.gov/violenceprevention/pdf/NISVS-StateReportBook.pdf.

Smith, T., & Silva, L. (2011). Ethnic identity and personal well-being of people of color: A meta-analysis. *Journal of Counseling Psychology, 58*(1), 42–60.

Smoley, B., & Robinson, C. (2012). Natural family planning. *American Family Physician, 86*(10), 924–928.

Smyer, M. A., Gatz, M., Simi, N. L., & Pedersen, N. L. (1998). Childhood adoption: Long-term effects in adulthood. *Psychiatry: Interpersonal and Biological Processes, 61*(3), 191.

Snapp, S. D., Watson, R. J., Russell, S. T., Diaz, R. M., & Ryan, C. (2015). Social support networks for LGBT young adults: Low cost strategies for positive adjustment. *Family Relations, 64*, 420–430.

Snyder, F. J., Acock, A. C., Vuchinich, S., Beets, M. W., Washburn, I. I., & Flay, B. R. (2013). Preventing negative behaviors among elementary-school students through enhancing students' social-emotional and character development. *American Journal of Health Promotion, 28*(1), 50–58.

Snyder, H., & Sickmund, M. (2006). *Juvenile offenders and victims: 2006 national report*. Washington, DC: U.S. Department of Justice, Office of Justice Programs, Office of Juvenile Justice and Delinquency Prevention.

Social Security Administration. (2017a). *Retirement planner: Full retirement age*. Retrieved from www.ssa.gov/planners/retire/retirechart.html.

Social Security Administration. (2017b). *Old-age and survivors insurance*. Retrieved from www.ssa.gov/OP_Home/rulings/oasi-toc.html.

Social Welfare History Archives. (1952). *Who should teach what in human growth and behavior*. Workshop at 1952 AASSW Annual Meeting. Box 31. Folder 2.

Society for Maternal and Fetal Medicine. (2015, February 2). Impact of fetal gender on risk of preterm birth. *Science Daily*. Retrieved from www.sciencedaily.com/releases/2015/02/150202123708.htm.

Solmeyer, A., & Feinberg, M. (2011). Mother and father adjustment during early parenthood: The roles of infant temperament and coparenting relationship quality. *Infant Behavior and Development, 34*(4), 504–514.

Solomon, R. C. (1988). *About love: Reinventing romance for modern times.* New York: Simon & Schuster.

Solomon, Z., Helvitz, H., & Zerach, G. (2009). Subjective age, PTSD and physical health among war veterans. *Aging & Mental Health, 13*(3), 405–413.

Solomon, Z., & Mikulincer, M. (2006). Trajectories of PTSD: A 20-year longitudinal study. *American Journal of Psychiatry, 163*(4), 659–666.

Sonfield, A. (2010). The potential of health care reform to improve pregnancy-related services and outcomes. *Guttmacher Policy Review, 13*(3), 13–17.

Sotirin, P., & Ellingson, L. (2006). The "other" women in family life. In K. Floyd & M. Morman (Eds.), *Widening the family circle: New research on family communication* (pp. 81–99). Thousand Oaks, CA: Sage.

South, S., & Lei, L., (2015). Failures-to-launch and boomerang kids: Contemporary determinants of leaving and returning to the parental home. *Social Forces, 94*(2), 863–890.

Spalding, K., Bergmann, O., Alkass, K., Bernard, S., Salehpour, M., Huttner, H., . . . Frisén, J. (2013). Dynamics of hippocampal neurogenesis in adult humans. *Cell, 153*(6), 1219–1227.

Span, P. (2013, June 16). Death be not decaffeinated: Over cup, groups face taboo. *New York Times.* Retrieved from https://newoldage.blogs.nytimes.com/2013/06/16/death-be-not-decaffeinated-over-cup-groups-face-taboo/?_php=true&_type=blogs&_r=0.

Spear, L. P. (2010). *The behavioral neuroscience of adolescence.* New York: W. W. Norton.

Spector-Mersel, G. (2006). Never-aging stories: Western hegemonic masculinity scripts. *Journal of Gender Studies, 15*(1), 67–82.

Spence, K., Henderson-Smart, D., New, K., Evans, C., Whitelaw, J., Woolnough, R., & Australian and New Zealand Neonatal Network. (2010). Evidence-based clinical practice guideline for management of newborn pain. *Journal of Paediatrics and Child Health, 46*(4), 184–192.

Spencer, M. (1984). Black children's race awareness, racial attitudes and self concept: A reinterpretation. *Journal of Child Psychology and Psychiatry, 25*(3), 433–441.

Spencer, M. B., Harpalani, V., Fegley, S., Dell'Angelo, T., & Seaton, G. (2003). Identity, self, and peers in context: A culturally sensitive, developmental framework for analysis. In R. M. Lerner, E. Jacobs, & D. Wertlieb (Eds.), *Handbook of applied developmental science* (Vol. 1, pp. 123–142). Thousand Oaks, CA: Sage.

Spieker, S., Nelson, D., & Petras, A. (2003). Joint influence of child care and infant attachment security for cognitive and language outcomes of low-income toddlers. *Infant Behavior & Development, 26*(3), 326–344.

Spilsbury, J., Kahana, S., Drotar, D., Creeden, R., Flannery, D., & Friedman, S. (2008). Profiles of behavioral problems in children who witness domestic violence. *Violence and Victims, 23*(1), 3–17.

Spinrad, T., Eisenberg, N., Gaertner, B., Popp, T., Smith, C., Kupfer, A., . . . Hofer, C. (2007). Relations of maternal socialization and toddlers' effortful control to children's adjustment and social competence. *Developmental Psychology, 43*(5), 1170–1186.

Spracklen, C., Ryckman, K., Triche, E., & Saftlas, A. (2016). Physical activity during pregnancy and subsequent risk of preeclampsia and gestational hypertension: A case control study. *Maternal and Child Health Journal, 20*(6), 1193–1202.

Sroufe, L. A., Egeland, B., Carlson, E., & Collins, W. A. (2005). The development of the person: The Minnesota study of risk and adaptation from birth to adulthood. New York: Guilford Press.

Stadelmann, S., Perren, S., Groeben, M., & von Klitzing, K. (2010). Parental separation and children's behavioral/emotional problems: The impact of parental representations and family conflict. *Family Process, 49*(1), 92–108.

Stafford, M., Cooper, R., Cadar, D., Carr, E., Murray, E., Richards, M., . . . Kuh, D. (2017). Physical and cognitive capability in mid-adulthood as determinants of retirement and extended working life in a British cohort study. *Scandinavian Journal of Work, Environment & Health, 43*(1), 15–23.

Stanford Children's Health. (2018). *Nutrition during pregnancy.* Retrieved from www.stanfordchildrens.org/en/topic/default?id=nutrition-during-pregnancy-85-P01227.

Stapleton, S. R., Osborne, C., & Illuzzi, J. (2013). Outcomes of care in birth centers: Demonstration of a durable model. *Journal of Midwifery and Women's Health, 58*(1), 3–14.

Stark, M. D., Keathley, R. S., & Nelson, J. A. (2011). A developmental model for counseling infertile couples. *Family Journal, 19*(2), 225–230.

Statistic Brain. (2017). Adoption statistics. Retrieved from www.statisticbrain.com/adoption-statistics/.

The Statistics Portal. (2017). *Median age of the resident population of the United States from 1960 to 2015.* Retrieved from www.statista.com/statistics/241494/median-age-of-the-us-population/.

Staudinger, U. M., & Bluck, S. (2001). A view on midlife development from life-span theory. In M. Lachman (Ed.), *Handbook of midlife development* (pp. 3–39). New York: Wiley.

Staudinger, U. M., Freund, A. M., Linden, M., & Maas, I. (1999). Self, personality, and life regulation: Facets of psychological resilience in old age. In P. B. Baltes & K. U. Mayer (Eds.), *The Berlin Aging Study: Aging from 70 to 100* (pp. 302–328). Cambridge, UK: Cambridge University Press.

Steele, J. L., Slater, R. O., Zamarro, G., Miller, T., Li, J., Burkhauser, S., & Bacon, M. (2017). Effects of dual-language immersion programs on student achievement: Evidence from lottery data. *American Educational Research Journal, 54*(1 Suppl.), 282S–306S.

Steen, M., Downe, S., Bamford, N., & Edozien, L. (2012). Not-patient and not-visitor: A metasynthesis fathers' encounters with pregnancy, birth and maternity care. *Midwifery, 28*(4), 422–431.

Steensma, T., Kreukels, B., de Vries, A., & Cohen-Kettenis, P. (2013). Gender identity development in adolescence. *Hormones and Behavior, 64*(2), 288–297.

Stein, G., Beckerman, N., & Sherman, P. (2010). Lesbian and gay elders and long-term care: Identifying the unique psychosocial perspectives and challenges. *Journal of Gerontological Social Work, 53*(5), 421–435.

Stein, M. (2005). Resilience and young people leaving care: Implications for child welfare policy and practice in the UK. In R. J. Flynn, P. M. Dudding, & J. G. Barber (Eds.), *Promoting resilience in child welfare* (pp. 264–278). Ottawa: University of Ottawa Press.

Steinberg, J., & Finer, L. (2011). Examining the association of abortion history and current mental health: A reanalysis of the National Comorbidity Survey using a common-risk-factors model. *Social Science & Medicine, 72*(1), 72–82.

Steinberg, L. (2009). Should the science of adolescent brain development inform public policy? *American Psychologist, 64*(8), 739–750.

Stephan, Y., Chalabaev, A., Kotter-Grühn, D., & Jaconelli, A. (2013). "Feeling younger, being stronger": An experimental study of subjective age and physical functioning among older adults. *The Journals of Gerontology, Series B: Psychological Sciences and Social Sciences, 68*(1), 1–7.

Stephan, Y., Demulier, V., & Terracciano, A. (2012). Personality, self-rated health, and subjective age in a life-span sample: The moderating role of chronological age. *Psychology and Aging, 27*(4), 875–880.

Stephan, Y., Sutin, A., Caudroit, J., & Terracciano, A. (2016). Sujective age and changes in memory in older adults. *Journal of Gerontology B Psychological Sciences, 71*(4), 675–683.

Stephens, M., Warren, L., Harner, A., & Owen E. (2015). *Comparative indicators of education in the United States and other G-20 countries: 2015.* Washington, DC: National Center for Education Statistics. Retrieved from https://nces.ed.gov/pubs2016/2016100.pdf.

Stepler, R. (2017). *Number of U.S. adults cohabiting with a partner continues to rise, especially among those 50 and older.* Washington, DC: Pew Research Center. Retrieved from www.pewresearch.org/fact-tank/2017/04/06/number-of-u-s-adults-cohabiting-with-a-partner-continues-to-rise-especially-among-those-50-and-older/.

Steptoe, A., Shankar, A., Demakakos, P., & Wardle, J. (2013). Social isolation, loneliness, and all-cause mortality in older men and women. *Proceedings of the National Academy of Sciences, 110*(15), 5797–5801.

Stern, P., Hines, P., & Travis, J. (2014). The aging brain. *Science, 346*(6209), 566–567.

Stern, R. A., Riley, D. O., Daneshvar, D. H., Nowinski, C. J., Cantu, R. C., & McKee, A. C. (2011). Long-term consequences of repetitive brain trauma: Chronic traumatic encephalopathy. *PM&R, 3*(10 Suppl. 2), S460–S467.

Stevens, N., & Van Tilburg, T. (2011). Cohort differences in having and retaining friends in personal networks in later life. *Journal of Social and Personal Relationships, 28*(1), 24–43.

Stiglbauer, B., Gnambs, T., Gamsjääger, M., & Batinic, B. (2013). The upward spiral of adolescents' positive school experiences and happiness: Investigating reciprocal effects over time. *Journal of School Psychology, 51*(2), 231–242.

Stiles, J., & Jernigan, T. (2010). The basics of brain development. *Neuropsychology Review, 20*(4), 327–348.

Stobbe, M. (2009, November 3). *Premature births worsen U.S. infant death rates.* Associated Press. Retrieved from www.nevadaappeal.com/news/premature-births-worsen-u-s-infant-death-rate/.

Stock, M. L., Gibbons, F. X., Gerrard, M., Houlihan, A. E., Weng, C.-Y., Lorenz, F. O., & Simons, R. L. (2013). Racial identification, racial composition, and substance use vulnerability among African American adolescents and young adults. *Health Psychology, 32*(3), 237–247.

Stockard, J., & O'Brien, R. (2002). Cohort effects on suicide rates: International variation. *American Sociological Review, 67*(6), 854–872.

Stokke, G., Gjlsvik, B. L., Flaatten, K. T., Birkeland, E., Flaatten, H., & Trovik, J. (2015). Hyperemesis gravidarum, nutritional treatment by nasogastric tube feeding: A 10 year retrospective cohort study. *Acta Obstetricia et Gynecologicica Scandinavica, 94*(4), 359–367.

Stolzenberg, R. M., Blair-Loy, M., & Waite, L. J. (1995). Religious participation in early adulthood: Age and family life cycle effects on church membership. *American Sociological Review, 60*(1), 84–104.

Stone, J., Berrington, A., & Falkingham, J. (2014). Gender, turning points, and boomerangs: Returning home in young adulthood in Great Britain. *Demography, 51*(1), 257–276.

Stone, P. (2007). *Opting out? Why women really quit careers and head home.* Berkeley: University of California Press.

Stouthamer-Loeber, M., & Wei, E. H. (1998). The precursors of young fatherhood and its effect on delinquency of teenage males. *Journal of Adolescent Health, 22*(1), 56–65.

Stovall, K., & Dozier, M. (1998). Infants in foster care: An attachment theory perspective. *Adoption Quarterly, 2*(1), 55–88.

Strategy and Transformation Consulting. (2015). *Digitale transformation: Warum sie so wichtig für unternehen ist!* Retrieved from www.strategy-transformation.com/digitale-transformation/.

Strauch, B. (2010). *The secret life of the grown-up brain: The surprising talents of the middle-aged mind.* London: Viking.

Street, J., Harris-Britt, A., & Walker-Barnes, C. (2009). Examining relationships between ethnic identity, family environment, and psychological outcomes for African American adolescents. *Journal of Child and Family Studies, 18*(4), 412–420.

Street, K., Whitlingum, G., Gibson, P., Cairns, P., & Ellis, M. (2008). Is adequate parenting compatible with maternal drug use? A 5-year follow-up. *Child: Care, Health, and Development, 34*(2), 204–206.

Streri, A. (2005). Touching for knowing in infancy: The development of manual abilities in very young infants. *European Journal of Developmental Psychology, 2*(4), 325–343.

Stritof, S. (2017). Estimated median age of first marriage by gender: 1890 to 2016. *The Spruce.* Retrieved from www.thespruce.com/estimated-median-age-marriage-2303878.

Stroebe, M., Stroebe, W., & Hansson, R. (1993). *Handbook on bereavement: Theory, research and intervention.* New York: Cambridge University Press.

Strohschein, L. (2005). Parental divorce and child mental health trajectories. *Journal of Marriage and Family, 67*(5), 1286–1300.

Struge-Apple, M., Davies, P., & Cummings, E. (2006). Impact of hostility and withdrawal in interparental conflict on parental emotional unavailability and children's adjustment difficulties. *Child Development, 77*(6), 1623–1641.

Sublett, J. (2013). Neonatal abstinence syndrome: Therapeutic intervention. *The American Journal of Maternal/Child Nursing, 18*(2), 102–107.

Subramanian, S. (2014). Extremely low birth weigh infant. *Medscape.* Retrieved from https://emedicine.medscape.com/article/979717-overview.

Subramanian, S. V., Kubzansky, L., Berman, L., Fay, M., & Kawachi, I. (2006). Neighborhood effects on the self-rated health of elders: Uncovering the relative importance of structural and service-related neighborhood environments. *The Journals of Gerontology, Series B: Psychological Sciences and Social Sciences, 61B*(3), 153–161.

Substance Abuse and Mental Health Services Administration (SAMHSA). (2016, September). *National survey on drug abuse and health.* Retrieved from www.samhsa.gov/data/sites/default/files/NSDUH-FFR1-2015/NSDUH-FFR1-2015/NSDUH-FFR1-2015.pdf.

Sue, D., Rasheed, M., & Rasheed, J. (2016). *Multicultural social work practice: A competency-based approach to diversity and social justice* (2nd ed.). Hoboken, NJ: Wiley.

Sullivan, M. C., Msall, M. E., & Miller, R. J. (2012). 17-year outcome of preterm infants with diverse neonatal morbidities: Part I. Impact on physical, neurological, and psychological health. *Journal for Specialists in Pediatric Nursing, 17*(3), 226–241.

Sum, A., Khatiwada, I., McHugh, W., & Kent, W. (2014). Deteriorating labor market fortunes for young adults. *Challenge, 57*(3), 60–83.

Sumontha, J., Farr, R., & Patterson, C. (2017). Children's gender development: Associations with parental sexual orientation, division of labor, and gender ideology. *Psychology of Sexual Orientation and Gender Diversity, 4*(4), 438–450.

Sussman, S., & Arnett, J. J. (2014). Emerging adulthood: Developmental period facilitative of the addictions. *Evaluation & the Health Professions, 37*(2), 147–155.

Sustin, A., Costa, P., Wethington, E., & Eaton, W. (2010). Turning points and lessons learned: Stressful life events and personality trait development across middle adulthood. *Psychology and Aging, 25*(3), 524–533.

Suter, E., Daas, K., & Bergen, K. (2008). Negotiating lesbian family identity via symbols and rituals. *Journal of Family Issues, 29*(1), 26–47.

Suto, M., Takehara, K., Yamane, Y., & Ota, E. (2017). Effects of prenatal childbirth education for partners of pregnant women on paternal postanatal mental health and couple relationship: A systematic review. *Journal of Affective Disorders, 210*, 115–121.

Szydlik, M. (2012). Generations: Connections across the life course. *Advances in Life Course Research, 17*(3), 100–111.

Taddio, A., Shah, V., Gilbert-Macleod, C., & Katz, J. (2002). Conditioning and hyperalgesia in newborns exposed to repeated heel lances. *Journal of American Medical Association, 288*(7), 857–861.

Takahashi, K. (1990). Are the key assumptions of the "strange situation" procedure universal? A view from Japanese research. *Human Development, 33*(1), 23–30.

Tam, E., Rosenbluth, G., Rogers, E., Ferriero, D., Glidden, D., Goldstein, R., . . . Barkovich, A. J. (2011). Cerebellar hemorrhage on magnetic resonance imaging in preterm newborns associated with abnormal neurologic outcome. *The Journal of Pediatrics, 158*(2), 245–250.

Tamaru, S., Kikuchi, A., Takagi, K., Wakamatsu, M., Ono, K., Horikoshi, T., . . . Nakamura, T. (2011). Neurodevelopmental outcomes of very low birth weight and extremely low birth weight infants at 18 months corrected age associated with prenatal factors. *Early Human Development, 87*(1), 55–59.

Tamis-LeMonda, C., Kahana-Kalman, R., & Yoshikawa, H. (2009). Father involvement in immigrant and ethnically diverse families from the prenatal period to the second year: Prediction and mediating mechanisms. *Sex roles, 60*(7), 496–509.

Tang, C., Yeung, D., & Lee, A. (2003). Psychosocial correlates of emotional responses to menarche among Chinese adolescent girls. *Journal of Adolescent Health, 33*(3), 193–201.

Tartaro, J., Luecken, L., & Gunn, H. (2005). Exploring heart and soul: Effects of religiosity/spirituality and gender on blood pressure and cortisol stress response. *Journal of Health Psychology, 10*(6), 753–766.

Tate, A., Dezateux, C., Cole, T., & The Millennium Cohort Study Child Health Group. (2006). Is infant growth changing? *International Journal of Obesity, 30*(7), 1094–1096.

Tatum, B. D. (2007). *Can we talk about race? And other conversations in an era of school resegregation.* Boston: Beacon Press.

Tatum, C. (2014). *Encyclopedia of Latino culture: From Calaveras to quinceaneras.* Santa Barbara, CA: ABC-CLIO, LLC.

Tavernise, S. (2015, January). High rates of opioid prescriptions among women raise birth defect fears. *New York Times.* Retrieved from www.nytimes.com/2015/01/23/health/high-rates-of-opioid-prescriptions-among-women-raise-alarm.html.

Taylor, C., Golding, J., & Emond, A. (2016). Blood mercury levels and fish consumption in pregnancy: Risks and benefits for birth outcomes in prospective observational birth cohort. *International Journal of Hygiene and Environmental Health, 219*(6), 513–520.

Taylor, J. M., Gilligan, C., & Sullivan, A. M. (1995). *Between voice and silence: Women and girls, race and relationship.* Cambridge, MA: Harvard University Press.

Taylor, L., Swerdfeger, A., & Eslick, G. (2014). Vaccines are not associated with autism: An evidence-based meta-analysis of case-control and cohort studies. *Vaccine, 32*(29), 3623–3629.

Taylor, M., Marquis, R., Batten, R., & Coall, D. (2016). Understanding mental health travails of custodial grandparents. *Occupational Therapy in Mental Health, 32*(3), 259–280.

Taylor, P., Morin, R., Parker, K., Cohn, E., & Wang, W. (2010). *Growing old in America: Expectations vs. reality.* Retrieved from www.pewsocialtrends.org/files/2010/10/Getting-Old-in-America.pdf.

Taylor, R., Chatters, L., Woodward, A., & Brown, E. (2013). Racial and ethnic differences in extended family, friendship, fictive kin, and congregational informal support networks. *Family Relations, 62*(4), 609–624.

Terras, M., & Ramsay, J. (2016). Family digital literacy practices and children's mobile phone use. *Frontiers in Psychology, 7,* 1957. doi:10.3389/fpsyg.2016.01957

Terry, D. F., Sebastiani, P., Andersen, S. L., & Perls, T. T. (2008). Disentangling the roles of disability and morbidity in survival to exceptional old age. *Archives of Internal Medicine, 168*(3), 277–283.

Thapar, A., Collishaw, S., Pine, D., & Thapar, A. (2012). Depression in adolescence. *The Lancet, 379*(9820), 1056–1067.

Thieleman, K. (2015). Epilogue: Grief, bereavement, and ritual across cultures. In J. Cacciatore & F. DeFrain (Eds.), *The world of bereavement: Cultural perspectives on death in families* (pp. 287–298). Basel, Switzerland: Springer International.

Thoman, E., & Ingersoll, E. (1993). Learning in premature infants. *Developmental Psychology, 28*(4), 692–700.

Thomas, A., Chess, S., & Birch, H. G. (1968). *Temperament and behavior disorders in children.* New York: New York University Press.

Thomas, A., Chess, S., & Birch, H. G. (1970). The origin of personality. *Scientific American, 223*(2), 102–109.

Thomeer, M., Mudrazija, S., & Angel, J. (2015). How do race and ethnicity affect nursing home admission? *The Journal of Gerontology: Series B, 70*(4), 628–638.

Thompson, A. E. (2015). Childhood obesity. *Journal of the American Medical Association, 314*(8), 850. doi:10.1001/jama.2015.6674

Thompson R. A. (2012). Whither the preconventional child? Toward a life-span moral development theory. *Child Development Perspectives*, 6(4), 423–429.

Thompson, R. A. (2014). Stress and child development. *The Future of Children*, 24(1), 41–59.

Thompson R. A., Meyer S., & McGinley M. (2006). Understanding values in relationships: The development of conscience. In M. Killen & J. Smetana (Eds.), *Handbook of moral development* (pp. 267–297). Mahwah, NJ: Erlbaum.

Tian, R., MacGibbon, K., Martin, B., Mulin, P., & Fejzo, M. (2017). Analysis of pre- and post-pregnancy issues in women with hyperemesis gravidarum. *Autonomic Neuroscience; Basic and Clinical*, 202, 73–78.

Tiet, A., Bird, H., Hoven, C., Wu, P., Moore, R., & Davies, M. (2001). Resilience in the face of maternal psychopathology and adverse life events. *Journal of Child and Family Studies*, 10(3), 347–365.

Tiggemann, M., & Slater, A. (2017). Facebook and body image concern in adolescent girls: A prospective study. *International Journal of Eating Disorders*, 50(1), 80–83.

Tisi, G., Franzini, A., Messina, G., Savino, M., & Gambini, O. (2014). Vagus nerve stimulation therapy in treatment-resistant depression: A series report. *Psychiatry and Clinical Neurosciences*, 68(8), 606–611.

Titus, J., Godley, S., & White, M. (2007). A post-treatment examination of adolescents' reasons for starting, quitting, and continuing the use of drugs and alcohol. *Journal of Child & Adolescent Substance Abuse*, 16(2), 31–49.

Tobin, K. J. (2016). Homeless students and academic achievement: Evidence from a large urban area. *Urban Education*, 51(2), 197–220.

Tobin, S. (1988). Preservation of the self in old age. *Social Casework: The Journal of Contemporary Social Work*, 66(9), 550–555.

Tomoda, A., Polcari, A., Anderson, C. M., & Teicher, M. H. (2012). Reduced visual cortex gray matter volume and thickness in young adults who witnessed domestic violence during childhood. *Plos ONE*, 7(12), 1–11.

Tomova, A., Lalabonova, R., Robeva, R., & Kumanov, P. (2011). Timing of pubertal maturation according to the age at first conscious ejaculation. *Andrologia*, 43(3), 163–166.

Tornello, S., & Patterson. C. (2016). Gay grandfathers: Intergenerational relationships and mental health. *Journal of Family Psychology*, 30(5), 543–551.

Tornstam, L. (2005). *Gerotranscendence: A developmental theory of positive aging*. New York: Springer.

Torres, J., & Young, M. (2016). A life-course perspective on legal status stratification and health. *SSM – Population Health*, 2, 141–148.

Torres, L., Peña, J., Westhoff, W., & Zayas, L. (2008). A cross-national comparison of adolescent alcohol and drug use behaviors: U.S. Hispanics and youth in the Dominican Republic. *Journal of Drug Issues*, 38(1), 149–170.

Toseland, R., & Larkin, H. (2010). Developing and leading telephone groups. *Social Work With Groups*, 34(1), 21–34.

Trattner, W. (1998). *From poor law to welfare state: A history of social welfare in America* (6th ed.). New York: Free Press.

Treyvaud, K., Doyle, L. W., Lee, K. J., Roberts, G., Cheong, J. L. Y., Inder, T. E., & Anderson, P. J. (2011). Family functioning, burden, and parenting stress 2 years after very preterm birth. *Early Human Development*, 87(60), 427–431.

Trojner-Bregar, A., Blickstein, I., Lucovnik, M., Steblovnik, L., Verdenik, I., & Tul, N. (2018). The relationship between cesarean section rate in term singleton pregnancies, maternal weight, and weight gain during pregnancy. *Journal of Perinatal Medicine*, 44(4), 393–396.

Tsypes, A., Owens, M., Hajcak, G., & Gibb, B. E. (2017). Neural responses to gains and losses in children of suicide attempters. *Journal of Abnormal Psychology*, 126(2), 237–243.

Tucker, D., & MacKenzie, M. (2012). Attachment theory and change processes in foster care. *Children and Youth Services Review*, 34(11), 2208–2219.

Tun, P., & Lachman, M. (2010). The association between computer use and cognition across adulthood: Use it so you won't lose it? *Psychology and Aging*, 25(3), 560–568.

Turati, C., Montirosso, R., Brenna, V., Ferrara, V., & Borgatti, R. (2011). A smile enhances 3-month-olds' recognition of an individual face. *International Society on Infant Studies*, 16(3), 306–317.

Turiano, N., Chapman, B., Agrigoroaei, S., Infurna, F., & Lachman, M. (2014). Perceived control reduces mortality risk at low, not high, education levels. *Health Psychology*, 33(8), 883–890.

Turiel, E. (2004). Commentary: Beyond individualism and collectivism: A problem or progress? *New Directions in Child and Adolescent Development*, 104, 91–100.

Turkle, S. (2011). *Alone together: Why we expect more from technology and less from each other*. New York: Basic Books.

Turkle, S. (2015). *Reclaiming conversation: The power of talk in a digital age*. New York: Penguin.

Turnbull, A. P., Turnbull, H. R., Wehmeyer, M. L., & Shogren, K. A. (2015). *Special education in today's schools* (8th ed.). New York: Pearson.

Turner, H., Finkelhor, D., Ormrod, R., Hamby, S., Leeb, R., Mercy, J., & Holt, M. (2012). Family context, victimization, and child trauma symptoms: Variations in safe, stable, and nurturing relationships during early and middle childhood. *American Journal of Orthopsychiatry, 82*(2), 209–219.

Tweddle, A. (2007). Youth leaving care: How do they fare? *New Directions for Youth Development, 113,* 15–31.

Tyagi, A., & Cohen, M. (2016). Yoga and heart rate variability: A comprehensive review of the literature. *International Journal of Yoga, 9*(2), 97–113.

Uddin, L., Iacoboni, M., Lange, C., & Keenan, J. (2007). The self and social cognition: The role of cortical midline structures and mirror neurons. *Trends in Cognitive Sciences, 11*(4), 153–157.

Uhlenberg, P. (1996). Mutual attraction: Demography and life-course analysis. *The Gerontologist, 36*(2), 226–229.

Umberson, D., Pudrovska, T., & Reczek, C. (2010). Parenthood, childlessness, and well-being: A life course perspective. *Journal of Marriage and Family, 72,* 612–629.

UNAIDS. (2017). *UNAIDS data 2017.* Retrieved from www.unaids.org/sites/default/files/media_asset/20170720_Data_book_2017_en.pdf.

UNICEF. (2012). *Report Card 10: Measuring child poverty: New league tables of child poverty in the world's rich countries.* Florence, Italy: UNICEF Innocenti Research.

UNICEF. (2016). *The state of the world's children 2016: A fair chance for every child.* New York: Author. Retrieved from www.unicef.org/publications/files/UNICEF_SOWC_2016.pdf.

UNICEF & World Bank Group. (2016). *Ending extreme poverty: A focus on children.* Retrieved from www.unicef.org/publications/files/Ending_Extreme_Poverty_A_Focus_on_Children_Oct_2016.pdf.

UNICEF, World Health Organization, & World Bank Group. (2017). *Levels and trends in child maltnutrition.* Retrieved from www.who.int/nutgrowthdb/jme_brochoure2017.pdf.

United Nations. (2017). *World population prospects: The 2017 revision.* Washington, DC: Department of Economic and Social Affairs, Population Division.

United Nations, Department of Economic and Social Affairs, Population Division. (2016). *Population pyramids of the world from 1950 to 2100 – United States and Uganda 2016.* Retrieved from www.populationpyramid.net/world/2016/.

United Nations Educational, Scientific and Cultural Organization, Institute for Statistics. (2015). *Education for all 2000–2015: Achievements and challenges.* Retrieved from http://unesdoc.unesco.org/images/0023/002322/232205e.pdf.

United Nations Population Division. (2017). *World population prospects.: Adolescent fertility rate (births per 1,000 women ages 15-19).* Retrieved from https://data.worldbank.org/indicator/SP.ADO.TFRT.

Urban Child Institute. (2018). *Baby's brain begins now: Conception to age 3.* Retrieved from www.urbanchildinstitute.org/why-0-3/baby-and-brain.

Ursache, A., Blair, C., Stifter, C., & Voegtline, K. (2013). Emotional reactivity and regulation in infancy interact to predict executive functioning in early childhood. *Developmental Psychology, 49*(1), 127–137.

U.S. Bureau of Labor Statistics. (2016a). *Americans at age 31: Labor market activity, education and partner status summary: Results from a longitudinal survey.* Retrieved from www.bls.gov/news.release/nlsyth.nr0.htm.

U.S. Bureau of Labor Statistics. (2016b). *Persons with a disability: Labor force characteristics summary.* Retrieved from www.bls.gov/news.release/disabl.nr0.htm.

U.S. Bureau of Labor Statistics. (2017). *Table 6. Employment status of mothers with own children under 3 years old by single year of age of youngest child and marital status, 2016–2017 annual averages.* Retrieved from www.bls.gov/news.release/famee.t06.htm.

U.S. Census Bureau. (2010). *The next four decades: The older population in the United States: 2010 to 2050: Population estimates and projections.* Washington, DC: U.S. Department of Commerce, Economics and Statistics Administration, U.S. Census Bureau.

U.S. Census Bureau. (2011). *Same-sex couple households.* Retrieved from www.census.gov/prod/2011pubs/acsbr10-03.pdf.

U.S. Census Bureau. (2011–2015a). *GCT0101 median age of the total population. American Community Survey 5-Year estimates.* Retrieved from http://factfinder2.census.gov.

U.S. Census Bureau. (2011–2015b). *GCT0103 percent of the total population who are 65 years and over. American Community Survey 5-Year estimates.* Retrieved from http://factfinder2.census.gov.

U.S. Census Bureau. (2012). *Statistical abstracts of the United States: 2012.* Washington, DC: Author.

U.S. Census Bureau. (2015). *Current population survey, 2014 annual social and economic supplement.* Retrieved from www2.census.gov/programs-surveys/cps/techdocs/cpsmar14R.pdf.

U.S. Census Bureau. (2016a). *Historical table 1: Percent childless and births per 1,000 women in the last 12 months.* Washington, DC: Author. Retrieved from www.census.gov/data/tables/time-series/demo/fertility/his-cps.html.

U.S. Census Bureau. (2016b). *Annual social and economic (ASEC) supplement. POV-34 2015.* Washington, DC: Author. Retrieved from www.census.gov/data/tables/time-series/demo/income-poverty/cps-pov/pov-34.html.

U.S. Census Bureau. (2017a). *Figure CH-1: Living arrangements of children: 1960 to present.* Retrieved from https://census.gov/content/dam/Census/library/visualizations/time-series/demo/families-and-households/ch-1.pdf.

U.S. Census Bureau. (2017b). *Projected population by age, sex, race, and Hispanic origin for the United States: 2014 to 2060, Table 1.* Washington, DC: Author. Retrieved from www.census.gov/data/datasets/2014/demo/popproj/2014-popproj.html.

U.S. Children's Bureau. (2012). *John H. Chafee Foster Care Independence Program.* Retrieved from www.acf.hhs.gov/cb/resource/chafee-foster-care-program.

U.S. Children's Bureau. (2017). *Foster care statistics 2016.* Retrieved from www.childwelfare.gov/pubs/factsheets/foster/.

U.S. Department of Agriculture. (2015, September 29). *USDA National Nutrient Database for Standard Reference.* Retrieved from https://ndb.nal.usda.gov/ndb/.

U.S. Department of Defense. (2016). *Month of the military child.* Retrieved from www.defense.gov/News/Special-Reports/0416_militarychild/.

U.S. Department of Education. (2014). *School climate and discipline: Know the data.* Retrieved from www2.ed.gov/policy/gen/guid/school-discipline/data.html.

U.S. Department of Education. (2015a). *Early high school dropouts: What are their characteristics?* Retrieved from https://nces.ed.gov/pubs2015/2015066.pdf.

U.S. Department of Education. (2015b). *New data show a decline in school-based bullying.* Retrieved from www.ed.gov/news/press-releases/new-data-show-decline-school-based-bullying.

U.S. Department of Education. (2017a). *Every student succeeds act.* Retreived from www.ed.gov/essa?src=rn.

U.S. Department of Education. (2017b). *Bullying and youth with disabilities and special health needs.* Retrieved from www.stopbullying.gov/at-risk/groups/special-needs/index.html.

U.S. Department of Education Office for Civil Rights. (2014). *Data snapshot: School discipline.* Retrieved from https://ocrdata.ed.gov/downloads/crdc-school-discipline-snapshot.pdf.

U.S. Department of Education Office of Innovation and Improvement. (2016). *U.S. Department of Education announces inaugural education innovation and research competition.* Retrieved from www.ed.gov/news/press-releases/us-department-education-announces-inaugural-education-innovation-and-research-competition.

U.S. Department of Health and Human Services (USDHHS). (2014). *National healthcare disparities report: 2011.* Agency for Healthcare Research and Quality, Rockville, MD. Retrieved from https://archive.ahrq.gov/research/findings/nhqrdr/nhdr11/index.html.

U.S. Department of Health and Human Services. (2016). *Trends in U.S. adoptions: 2008–2012.* Retrieved from www.childwelfare.gov/pubPDFs/adopted0812.pdf.

U.S. Department of Health and Human Services & U.S. Department of Agriculture. (2015a). *2015–2020 dietary guidelines for Americans* (8th ed.). Retrieved from https://health.gov/dietaryguidelines/2015/resources/2015-2020_Dietary_Guidelines.pdf.

U.S. Department of Health and Human Services & U.S. Department of Agriculture. (2015b). *Message from the Secretaries.* Retrieved from https://health.gov/dietaryguidelines/2015/guidelines/message/.

U.S. Department of Health & Human Services. National Advisory Committee on Rural Health and Human Services. (2008). *The 2008 Report to the Secretary: Rural Health and Human Services Issues.* Retrieved from www.hrsa.gov/advisorycommittees/rural/2008secreport.pdf.

U.S. Department of Health and Human Services (USDHHS). Office of Disease Prevention and Health Promotion. (2010). *Healthy people 2020.* Washington, DC. Retrieved from www.hhs.gov/opa/title-x-family-planning/preventive-services/healthy-people-2020/index.html.

U.S. Department of Housing and Urban Development. (2017). *HUD 2016 continuum of care homeless assistance programs homeless populations and subpopulations.* Washington, DC: Author. Retrieved from www.hudexchange.info/resource/reportmanagement/published/CoC_PopSub_NatlTerrDC_2016.pdf.

U.S. Equal Employment Opportunity Commission. (2008). *Genetic Information Nondiscrimination Act (GINA) of 2008.* Retrieved from www.eeoc.gov/laws/statutes/gina.cfm.

U.S. Equal Employment Opportunity Commission. (2015, June 25). *Enforcement guidance: Pregnancy discrimination and related issues.* EEOC Notice No. 915.003. Retrieved from www.eeoc.gov/laws/guidance/pregnancy_guidance.cfm.

U.S. Government Accountability Office. (2012). *Unemployed older workers: Many experience challenges regaining employment and face reduced retirement security.* Washington, DC: Author. Retrieved from www.gao.gov/assets/600/590408.pdf.

U.S. Senate Committee on Banking, Housing, and Urban Affairs. (2014, June 25). *Dreams deferred: Young workers and recent graduates in the U.S. economy.* Retrieved from www.gpo.gov/fdsys/pkg/CHRG-113shrg91270/pdf/CHRG-113shrg91270.pdf.

Uskul, A. (2004). Women's menarche stories from a multicultural sample. *Social Science & Medicine, 59*(4), 667–679.

Vaillant, G. (1977). *Adaptation to life.* Boston: Little, Brown.

Vaillant, G. (1993). *The wisdom of the ego.* Cambridge, MA: Harvard University Press.

Vaillant, G. (2002). *Aging well: Surprising guideposts to a happier life from the Landmark Harvard Study of Adult Development.* Boston: Little, Brown.

Vaillant, G. (2012). *Triumphs of experience: The men of the Harvard Grant Study.* Cambridge, MA: Belknap Press.

Valle, J., & Connor, D. (2010). *Rethinking disability: A disability studies approach to inclusive practices (a practical guide).* New York: McGraw Hill-Education.

Van de Walle, M., Bijttebier, P., Braet, C., & Bosmans, G. (2016). Attachment anxiety and depressive symptoms in middle childhood: The role of repetitive thinking about negative affect and about mother. *Journal of Psychopathology and Behavioral Assessment, 38*(4), 615–630.

van den Berg, Y. M., Deutz, M. F., Smeekens, S., & Cillessen, A. N. (2017). Developmental pathways to preference and popularity in middle childhood. *Child Development, 88*(5), 1629–1641.

van der Kolk, B. A. (2005). Developmental trauma disorder: Toward a rational diagnosis for children with complex trauma histories. *Psychiatric Annals, 35*(5), 401–408.

van der Kolk, B. (2014). *The body keeps the score: Brain, mind, and body in the healing of trauma.* New York: Viking.

van der Kolk, B., Hodgdon, H., Gapen, M., Musicaro, R., Suvak, M., Hamlin, E., & Spinazzola, J. (2016). A randomized controlled study of neurofeedback for chronic PTSD. *PLoS One, 11*(12), e0166752.

van der Kolk, B., Stone, L., West, J., Rhodes, A., Emerson, D., Suvak, M., & Spinazzola, J. (2014). Yoga as an adjunctive treatment for posttraumatic stress disorder: A randomized controlled trial. *Journal of Clinical Psychiatry, 75*(6), e559–e565.

van Goethem, A., van Hoof, A., van Aken, M., de Castro, B., & Raaijmakers, Q. (2014). Socialising adolescent volunteering: How important are parents and friends? Age dependent effects of parents and friends on adolescents' volunteering behaviors. *Journal of Applied Developmental Psychology, 35*(2), 94–101.

van Goethem, A., van Hoof, A., van Aken, M., Raajmakers, Q., Boom, J., & de Castro, B. (2012). The role of adolescents' morality and identity in volunteering: Age and gender differences in a process model. *Journal of Adolescence, 35*(3), 509–520.

Van Naarden Braun, K., Yeargin-Allsopp, M., & Lollar, D. (2006). Factors associated with leisure activity among young adults with developmental disabilities. *Research in Developmental Disabilities, 27*(5), 567–583.

Van Naarden Braun, K., Yeargin-Allsopp, M., & Lollar, D. (2009). Activity limitations among young adults with developmental disabilities: A population-based follow-up study. *Research in Developmental Disabilities, 30*(1), 179–191.

van Reekum, R., Binns, M., Clarke, D., Chayer, C., Conn, D., Hermann, N., . . . Stuss, D. T. (2005). Is late life depression a predictor of Alzheimer's disease: Results from a historical cohort study. *International Journal of Psychiatry, 20*(1), 80–82.

van Seeter, J. A. H., Chua, S. J., Mol, B. W. J., & Koks, C. A. M. (2017). Tubal anastomosis after previous sterilization: A systematic review. *Human Reproduction Update, 23*(3), 358–370.

Vanderbilt-Adriance, E., Shaw, D. S., Brennan, L. M., Dishion, T. J., Gardner, F., & Wilson, M. N. (2015). Child, family, and community protective factors in the development of children's early conduct problems. *Family Relations, 64*(1), 64–79.

Vasilenko, S., Kugler, K., & Rice, C. (2016). Timing of first sexual intercourse and young adult health. *Journal of Adolescent Health, 59*(3), 291–297.

Vaughan, D. A., Cleary, B. J., & Murphy, D. J. (2014). Delivery outcomes for nulliparous women at the extremes of maternal age: A cohort study. *BJOG: An International Journal of Obstetrics and Gynaecology, 121*(3), 261–268.

Vazsonyi, S., & Snider, J. B. (2008). Mentoring, competencies, and adjustment in adolescents: American part-time employment and European apprenticeships. *International Journal of Behavioral Development, 32*(1), 46–55.

Vennemann, M., Hense, H., Bajanowski, T., Blair, P., Complojer, C., Moone, R., & Kiechl-Kohlendorfer, U. (2012). Bed sharing and the risk of sudden infant death syndrome: Can we resolve the debate? *The Journal of Pediatrics, 160*(1), 44–50.

Vera, E. M., Vacek, K., Coyle, L. D., Stinson, J., Mull, M., Doud, K., . . . Langrehr, K. J. (2011). An examination of culturally relevant stressors, coping, ethnic identity, and subjective well-being in urban, ethnic minority adolescents. *Professional School Counseling, 15*(2), 55–66.

Verhoof, E., Maurice-Stam, H., Heymans, H., & Grootenhuis, M. (2012). Growing into disability benefits? Psychosocial course of life of young adults with a chronic somatic disease of disability. *ACTA Paediatrica, 101*(1), 19–26.

Vespa, J. (2017). *The changing economics and demographics of young adulthood: 1975–2016.* Washington, DC: US Census Bureau. Retrieved from www.census.gov/content/dam/Census/library/publications/2017/demo/p20-579.pdf.

Vigo, D., Thornicroft, G., & Atun, R. (2016). Estimating the true global gurden of mental illness. *Lancet Psychiatry, 3,* 171–178.

Vikat, A., Speder, Z., Beets, G., Billari, F., & Buhler, C. (2007). Generations and Gender Survey (GGS): Towards a better understanding of relationships and processes in the life course. *Demographic Research Online, 17*(14), 389–440.

Villanti, A. C., Johnson, A. L., Ilakkuvan, V., Jacobs, M. A., Graham, A. L., & Rath, J. M. (2017). Social media use and access to digital technology in US young adults in 2016. *Journal of Medical Internet Research, 19*(6), e196. doi:10.2196/jmir.7303

Villarruel, F., Perkins, D., Borden, L., & Keith, J. (2003). *Community youth development: Programs, policies, and practice.* Thousand Oaks, CA: Sage.

Volker, D. L. (2005). Control and end-of-life care: Does ethnicity matter? *American Journal of Hospice & Palliative Care, 22*(6), 442–446.

Volling, B., Blandon, A., & Kolak, A. (2006). Marriage, parenting, and the emergence of early self-regulation in the family system. *Journal of Child and Family Studies, 15*(4), 493–506.

von Salisch, M., Haenel, M., & Freund, P. (2013). Emotion understanding and cognitive abilities in young children. *Learning & Individual Differences, 26,* 15–19.

Voorpostel, M., & van der Lippe, T. (2007). Support between siblings and between friends: Two worlds apart? *Journal of Marriage and Family, 69*(5), 1271–1282.

Vygotsky, L. S., Hanfmann, E., Vakar, G., & Kozulin, A. (2012). *Thought and language.* Cambridge, MA: MIT Press.

Wacker, R., & Roberto, K. (2014). *Community resources for older adults: Programs and services in an era of change* (4th ed.). Thousand Oaks, CA: Sage.

Wadensten, B. (2005). Introducing older people to the theory of gerotranscendence. *Journal of Advanced Nursing, 52*(4), 381–388.

Wadsworth, S. M., & Southwell, K. (2013). Military families: Extreme work and extreme "work-family." *The ANNALS of the American Academy of Political and Social Science, 638,* 163–183.

Wahl, H., & Kruse, A. (2005). Historical perspectives of middle age within the life span. In S. Willis & M. Martin (Eds.), *Middle adulthood: A lifespan perspective* (pp. 3–34). Thousand Oaks, CA: Sage.

Walker, D., & Worrell, R. (2008). Promoting healthy pregnancies through perinatal groups: A comparison of Centering Pregnancy group prenatal care and childbirth education classes. *Journal of Perinatal Education, 17*(1), 27–34.

Walker, L. (1989). A longitudinal study of moral reasoning. *Child Development, 5,* 33–78.

Walker, O., Degnan, K., Fox, N., & Henderson, H. (2013). Social problem solving in early childhood: Developmental change and the influence of shyness. *Journal of Applied Developmental Psychology, 34*(4), 185–193.

Waller, T. (2009). Modern childhood: Contemporary theories and children's lives. In T. Waller (Ed.), *An introduction to early childhood* (2nd ed., pp. 2–15). Thousand Oaks, CA: Sage.

Wallerstein, I. (1974). *The modern world system: Capitalist agriculture and the origins of the European world economy in the 16th century.* New York: Academic Press.

Wallerstein, I. (1979). *The capitalist world economy.* London: Cambridge University Press.

Wallien, M. S., & Cohen-Kettenis, P. T. (2008). Psychosocial outcome of gender dysphoric children. *Journal of the American Academy of Child and Adolescent Psychiatry, 47*(12), 1413–1423.

Walling, A. D., & Dickson, G. M. (2012). Hearing loss in older adults. *American Family Physician, 85*(12), 1150.

Walsh, F. (2016a). Families in later life: Challenges, opportunities, and resilience. In M. McGoldrick, N. Garcia-Preto, & B. Carter (Eds.), *The expanded family life cycle: Individual, family, and social perspectives* (5th ed., pp. 261–277). Boston: Pearson.

Walsh, F. (2016b). *Strengthening family resilience* (3rd ed.). New York: Guilford Press.

Walsh, J. (2019). The psychological person: Cognition and emotion. In E. Hutchison (Ed.), *Dimensions of human behavior: Person and environment* (6th ed.). Thousand Oaks, CA: Sage.

Walsh, K. (2012). *Grief and loss: Theories and skills for the helping professions* (2nd ed.). New York: Pearson.

Walter, C. A., & McCoyd, J. L. M. (2016). *Grief and loss across the lifespan: A biopsychosocial perspective* (2nd ed.). New York: Springer.

Walters, S. R., Payne, D., Schluter, P. J., & Thomson, R. W. (2015). "It just makes you feel invincible": A Foucauldian analysis of children's experiences of organized team sports. *Sport, Education and Society, 20*(2), 241–257.

Waltes, R., Duketis, E., Knapp, M., Anney, R., Huguet, G., Schlitt, S., . . . Chiocchetti, A. G. (2014). Common variants in genes of the postsynaptic FMRP signaling pathway are risk factors for autism spectrum disorders. *Human Genetics, 133*(6), 781–792.

Wang, L., Wang, S., & Huang, C. (2008). Preterm infants of educated mothers have better outcome. *Acta Paediatrica, 97*, 568–573.

Wang, R., Needham, L., & Barr, D. (2005). Effects of environmental agents on attainment of puberty: Considerations when assessing exposure to environmental chemicals in the National Children's Study. *Environmental Health Perspectives, 113*(8), 1100–1107.

Wang, Y., & Zhang, Q. (2006). Are American children and adolescents of low socioeconomic status at increased risk of obesity? Changes in the association between overweight and family income between 1971 and 2002. *American Journal of Clinical Nutrition, 84*(4), 707–716.

Warboys, R. (2015). Breastfeeding as birth control. *Midwives, 18*, 72–73.

Warner, D., & Brown, T. (2011). Understanding how race/ethnicity and gender define age-trajectories of disability: An intersectionality approach. *Social Science & Medicine, 72*(8), 1236–1248.

Warraich, H. (2017). *Modern death: How medicine changed the end of life.* New York: St. Martin's Press.

Wass, R., & Golding, C. (2014). Sharpening a tool for teaching: The zone of proximal development. *Teaching in Higher Education, 19*(6), 671–684.

Wasserman, G. A., & McReynolds, L. S. (2011). Contributors to traumatic exposure and posttraumatic stress disorder in juvenile justice youths. *Journal of Traumatic Stress, 24*(4), 422–429.

Watson, J., & Crick, F. (1953). Molecular structure of nucleic acids. *Nature, 171*, 737–738.

Weaver-Hightower, M. B. (2008). *The politics of policy in boys' education: Getting boys "right."* New York: Palgrave Macmillan.

Webb, J. (2017). Conversation takes two: Understanding interactions with people with dementia. *Disability & Society, 32*(7), 1102–1106.

Webb, N., & Dumpson, J. (2006). *Working with traumatized youth in child welfare.* New York: Guilford Press.

Weibel-Orlando, J. (2001). Grandparenting styles: Native American perspectives. In A. Walker, M. Manoogian-O'Dell, L. McGraw, & D. White (Eds.), *Families in later life: Connections and transitions* (pp. 139–145). Thousand Oaks, CA: Pine Forge Press.

Weichold, K. (2007). Prevention against substance misuse: Life skills and positive youth development. In R. Silbereisen & R. Lerner (Eds.), *Approaches to positive youth development* (pp. 293–310). Thousand Oaks, CA: Sage.

Weinberg, M., Williams, C., & Pryor, D. (2001). Bisexuals at midlife. *Journal of Contemporary Ethnography, 30*(2), 180–208.

Weingartner, N. (2008). *Ohio woman, 56, gives birth to her own granddaughters.* Retrieved from www.digitaljournal.com/article/261656.

Weininger, E., & Lareau, A. (2009). Paradoxical pathways: An ethnographic extension of Kohn's findings on class and childrearing. *Journal of Marriage and Family, 71*(3), 680–695.

Weinman, M. L., Buzi, R. S., & Smith, P. B. (2005). Addressing risk behaviors, service needs, and mental health issues in programs for young fathers. *Families in Society, 86*(2), 261–266.

Weisner, T. (2005). Attachment as cultural and ecological problem with pluralistic solutions. *Human Development, 48*, 89–94.

Wells, V., Taheri, B., Gregory-Smith, D., & Manika, D. (2016). The role of generativity and attitudes on employees home and workplace water and energy saving behaviours. *Tourism Management, 56*, 63–74.

Wendell, A. (2013). Overview and epidemiology of substance abuse in pregnancy. *Clinical Obstetrics and Gynecology, 56*(1), 5–14.

Werner, E., & Brendtro, L. (2012). Risk, resilience, and recovery. *Reclaiming Children and Youth, 21*(1), 18–23.

Werner, E. E., & Smith, R. S. (2001). *Journeys from childhood to midlife.* Ithaca, NY: Cornell University Press.

Wethington, E., Kessler, R., & Pixley, J. (2004). Turning points in adulthood. In O. Brim, C. Ryff, & R. Kessler (Eds.), *How healthy are we? A national study of well-being at midlife* (pp. 586–613). Chicago: University of Chicago Press.

Wettstein, M., Tauber, B., Kuźma, E., & Wahl, H. (2017). The interplay between personality and cognitive ability across 12 years in middle and late adulthood: Evidence for reciprocal associations. *Psychology and Aging, 32*(3), 259–277.

Wheaton, A., Ferro, G., & Croft, J. (2015). School start times for middle school and high school students – United

States, 2011–12 school year. *Morbidity and Mortality Weekly Report, 64*(30), 809–813.

Whitbourne, S., Sneed, J., & Sayer, A. (2009). Psychosocial development from college through midlife: A 34-year sequential study. *Developmental Psychology, 45*(5), 1328–1340.

Whiting, E., & Ward, C. (2008). Food insecurity and provisioning. In D. R. Crane & T. Heaton (Eds.), *Handbook of families and poverty* (pp. 198–219). Thousand Oaks, CA: Sage.

Wickrama, T., & Vazsonyi, A. (2011). School contextual experiences and longitudinal changes in depressive symptoms from adolescence to young adulthood. *Journal of Community Psychology, 39*(5), 566–575.

Widom, C. (2014). Longterm consequences of child maltreatment. In J. Korbin & R. Krugman (Eds.), *Handbook of child maltreatment* (Vol. 2, pp. 225–447). Dordrecht, The Netherlands: Springer.

Wierckx, K., Van Caenegem, E., Pennings, G., Elaut, E., Dedecker, D., Vande Peer, F., . . . T'Sjoen, G. (2012). Reproductive wish in transsexual men. *Human Reproduction, 27*(2), 483–487.

Wight, V. (2011). Adolescents and poverty. *The Prevention Researcher, 18*(4), 3–6.

Wijma, E. M., Veerbeek, M. A., Prins, M., Pot, A. M., & Willemse, B. M. (2017). A virtual reality intervention to improve the understanding and empathy for people with dementia in informal caregivers: Results of a pilot study. *Aging & Mental Health*, 1–9. doi:10.1080/13607863.2017.13 48470

Wike, R. (2016). *5 ways Americans and Europeans are different*. Washington, DC: Pew Research Center. Retrieved from www.pewresearch.org/fact-tank/2016/04/19/5-ways-americans-and-europeans-are-different/.

Wilber, K. (2000). *Integral psychology: Consciousness, spirit, psychology, therapy*. Boston: Shambhala.

Wilber, K. (2001). *A theory of everything: An integral vision for business, politics, science, and spirituality*. Boston: Shambhala.

Willinger, M., Ko, C., Hoffman, H., Kessler, R., & Corwin, M. (2003). Trends in infant bed sharing in the United States. 1993–2000. *Archives of Pediatrics and Adolescent Medicine, 157*(1), 43–49.

Willis, S., & Martin, M. (Eds.). (2005). *Middle adulthood: A lifespan perspective*. Thousand Oaks, CA: Sage.

Willis, S., & Schaie, K. W. (2005). Cognitive trajectories in midlife and cognitive functioning in old age. In S. Willis & M. Martin (Eds.), *Middle adulthood: A lifespan perspective* (pp. 243–275). Thousand Oaks, CA: Sage.

Willis, S., & Schaie, K. W. (2006). Cognitive functioning in the baby boomers: Longitudinal and cohort effects. In S. Whitbourne & S. Willis (Eds.), *The baby boomers grow up: Contemporary perspectives on midlife* (pp. 205–234). Mahwah, NJ: Lawrence Erlbaum.

Willis, S., Schaie, K., & Martin, M. (2009). Cognitive plasticity. In V. Bengtson, D. Gans, N. Putney, & M. Silverstein (Eds.), *Handbook of theories of aging* (2nd ed.). New York: Springer.

Willoughby, B., Olson, C., Carroll, J., Nelson, L., & Miller, R. (2012). Sooner or later? The marital horizons of parents and their emerging adult children. *Journal of Social and Personal Relationships, 29*(7), 967–981.

Wilmoth, J. M., & Longino, C. F. (2006). Demographic trends that will shape U.S. policy in the twenty-first century. *Research on Aging, 28*(3), 269–288.

Wilson, T. M., Rodkin, P. C., & Ryan, A. M. (2014). The company they keep and avoid: Social goal orientation as a predictor of children's ethnic segregation. *Developmental Psychology, 50*(4), 1116–1124.

Wimmer, H., & Perner, J. (1983). Beliefs about beliefs: Representation and constraining function of wrong beliefs in young children's understanding of deception. *Cognition, 13*(1), 103–108.

Windsor, R., Clark, J., Davis, A., Wedeles, J., & Abroms, L. (2017). A process evaluation of the WV smoking cessation and reduction of pregnancy treatment (SCRIPT) dissemination initiative: Assessing the fidelity and delivery for state-wide, home-based healthy start services. *Maternal and Child Healthy Journal, 21*(1), 96–107.

Wink, P., & Dillon, M. (2002). Spiritual development across the adult life course: Findings from a longitudinal study. *Journal of Adult Development, 9*(1), 79–94.

Winthrop, R., & McGivney, E. (2015). *Why wait 100 years? Bridging the gap in global education*. Washington DC: Brookings Institution.

Wisner, K., Chambers, C., & Sit, D. (2006). Postpartum depression: A major public health problem. *Journal of American Medical Association, 296*(21), 2616–2618.

Witt, W., Wisk, L., Cheng, E., Hampton, J., & Hagen, E. (2012). Preconception mental health predicts pregnancy complications and adverse birth outcomes: A national population-based study. *Maternal and Child Health Journal, 16*(7), 1525–1541.

Wolak, J., Finkelhor, D., Mitchell, K., & Ybarra, M. (2008). Online "predators" and their victims: Myths, realities and implications for prevention and treatment. *American Psychologist, 63*(2), 111–128.

Wolke, D., Eryigit-Madzwamuse, S., & Gutbrod, T. (2014). Very preterm/very low birthweight infants' attachment: Infant and maternal characteristics. *Archives of Disease in Childhood. Fetal and Neonatal Edition, 99*(1), F70–F75.

Wong, M., Robertson, G., & Dyson, R. (2015). Prospective relationship between poor sleep and substance-related problems in a national sample of adolescents. *Alcoholism: Clinical and Experimental Research, 39*(2), 355–362.

Woo, C. R. S., & Brown, E. J. (2013). Role of meaning in the prediction of depressive symptoms among trauma-exposed and nontrauma-exposed emerging adults. *Journal of Clinical Psychology, 69*(12), 1269–1283.

Woodbridge, S., Buys, L., & Miller, E. (2011). "My grandchild has a disability": Impact on grandparenting identity, roles and relationships. *Journal of Aging Studies, 25*(4), 355–363.

Woods, N., & Mitchell, E. (2016). *The Seattle Midlife Women's Health Study: A longitudinal prospective study of women during the menopausal transition and early postmenopause.* Retrieved from https://womensmidlifehealthjournal.biomedcentral.com/articles/10.1186/s40695-016-0019-x.

Woods, R. (2013). *Children's moral lives: An ethnographic and psychological approach.* Hoboken, NJ: Wiley.

Woolf, S., & Aron, L. (Eds.). (2013). *U.S. health in international perspective: Shorter lives, poorer health.* Washington, DC: Institute of Medicine.

Woolridge, M., & Shapka, J. (2012). Playing with technology: Mother-toddler interaction scores lower during play with electronic toys. *Journal of Applied Developmental Psychology, 33*(5), 211–218.

Worden, J. W. (2009). *Grief counseling and grief therapy: A handbook for the mental health practitioner* (4th ed.). New York: Springer.

World Bank. (2017). *Population ages 65 and above, total.* Retrieved from https://data.worldbank.org/indicator/SP.POP.65UP.TO.

World Health Organization. (2012). *Are you ready? What you need to know about ageing.* Retrieved from www.who.int/world-health-day/2012/toolkit/background/en/.

World Health Organization. (2016a). *The neglected tragedy of stillbirths.* Retrieved from www.who.int/reproductivehealth/topics/maternal_perinatal/stillbirth/en/.

World Health Organization. (2016b). *Child maltreatment.* Retrieved from www.who.int/mediacentre/factsheets/fs150/en/.

World Health Organization. (2017a). *Family planning/contraception.* Retrieved from www.who.int/mediacentre/factsheets/fs351/en/.

World Health Organization. (2017b). *Preterm birth.* Retrieved from www.who.int/mediacentre/factsheets/fs363/en/.

World Health Organization. (2017c). *The top 10 causes of death.* Retrieved from www.who.int/mediacentre/factsheets/fs310/en/.

World Health Organization & UNICEF. (2012). *Early childhood development and disability: A discussion paper.* Retrieved from http://apps.who.int/iris/bitstream/10665/75355/1/9789241504065_eng.pdf?ua=1.

World Health Organization Multicentre Growth Reference Study Group. (2006a). Assessment of differences in linear growth among populations in the WHO Multicentre Growth Reference Study. *Acta Paediatrica* (Suppl.), *450,* 56–65.

World Health Organization Multicentre Growth Reference Study Group. (2006b). WHO motor development study: Windows of achievement for six gross motor developmental milestones. *Acta Paediatrica (Suppl.), 450,* 86–95.

World Health Organization Multicentre Growth Reference Study Group. (2006c). Assessment of sex differences and heterogeneity in motor milestone attainment among populations in the WHO Multicentre Growth Reference Study. *Acta Paediatrica* (Suppl.), *450,* 66–75.

Wortman, C., & Silver, R. (1989). The myths of coping with loss. *Journal of Consulting and Clinical Psychology, 57*(3), 349–357.

Wortman, C., & Silver, R. (1990). Successful mastery of bereavement and widowhood: A life course perspective. In P. Baltes & M. Baltes (Eds.), *Successful aging: Perspectives from the behavioral sciences* (pp. 225–264). Cambridge, UK: Cambridge University Press.

Wright, C., Cox, K., & Couteur, A. (2011). Symposium II. Infant and childhood nutrition and disease: How does infant behavior relate to weight gain and adiposity? *Proceedings of the Nutrition Society, 70,* 485–493.

Wright, P. M. (2011). Barriers to a comprehensive understanding of pregnancy loss. *Journal of Loss and Trauma, 16*(1), 1–12.

Wrigley, E. (1966). Family limitation in pre-industrial England. *Economic History Review, 19*(1), 82–109.

Wrosch, C., Heckhausen, J., & Lachman, M. (2006). Goal management across adulthood and old age: The adaptive value of primary and secondary control. In D. K. Mroczek & T. Little (Eds.), *Handbook of personality development* (pp. 399–421). Mahwah, NJ: Lawrence Erlbaum.

Wrzus, C., Hänel, M., Wagner, J., & Neyer, F. (2013). Social network changes and life events across the life span: A meta-analysis. *Psychological Bulletin, 139*(1), 53–80.

Wu, L., Woody, G., Yang, C., Pan, J., & Blazer, D. (2011). Racial/ethnic variations in substance-related disorders among adolescents in the United States. *Archives of General Psychiatry*, 68(11), 1176–1185.

Wuttke, W., Jarry, H., Haunschild, J., Stecher, G., Schuh, M., & Seidlova-Wuttke, D. (2014). The non-estrogenic alternative for the treatment of climacteric complaints: Black cohosh (Cimicifuga or Actae racemosa). *Journal of Steroid Biochemistry and Molecular Biology*, 139, 302–310.

Wyckoff, A. (2013). AAP: Babies born at home must receive same standard of care as in medical facility. *American Academy of Pediatrics News*, 34(5), 29.

Xiong, F., & Zhang, L. (2013). Role of hypothalamic pituitary-adrenal axis in developmental programming of health and disease. *Frontiers in Neuroendocrinology*, 34(1), 27–46.

Xu, H., Eisenberg, L., Maddden, T., Secura, G., & Peiper, J. (2014). Medical contraindications in women seeking combined hormonal contraceptions. *American Journal of Obstetrics and Gynecology*, 210(3), 210.e1–210.e5.

Yaman, S., & Altay, N. (2015). Posttraumatic stress and experiences of parents with a newborn in the neonatal intensive care unit. *Journal of Reproductive and Infant Psychology*, 33(2), 140–152.

Yi, S.-H., Joung, Y.-S., Choe, Y., Kim, E.-H., & Kwon, J.-Y. (2015). Sensory processing difficulties in toddlers with nonorganic failure-to-thrive and feeding problems. *Journal of Pediatric Gastroenterology and Nutrition*, 60(6), 819–824.

Yoshikawa, H. (2011). *Immigrants raising citizens: Undocumented parents and their young children.* New York: Russell Sage Foundation.

Yousuf, R., Fauzi, A., Wai, K., Amran, M., Akter, S., & Ramli, M. (2010). Potentially reversible causes of dementia. *International Journal of Collaborative Research on Internal Medicine & Public Health*, 2(8), 258–265.

YouthRules!. (2017). *Know the rules.* Retrieved from www.youthrules.gov/know-the-limits/index.htm.

Zajicek-Farber, M. (2009). Postnatal depression and infant health practices among high-risk women. *Journal of Child & Family Studies*, 18(2), 236–245.

Zand, D., Thomson, N., Cervantes, R., Espiritu, R., Klagholz, D., Lablanc, L., & . . . Taylor, A. (2009). The mentor-youth alliance: The role of mentoring relationships in promoting youth competence. *Journal of Adolescence*, 32(1), 1–17.

Zangaglia, R., Pacchetti, C., Pasotti, C., Mancini, F., Servello, D., Sinforiani, E., . . . Nappi G. (2009). Deep brain stimulation and cognitive functions in Parkinson's disease: A three year controlled study. *Movement Disorder*, 24(11), 1621–1628.

Zaslow, M. J., & Emig, C. A. (1997). When low-income mothers go to work: Implications for children. *Future of Children*, 7(1), 110–115.

Zdaniuk, B., & Smith, C. (2016). Same-sex relationships in middle and late adulthood. In J. Bookwala (Ed.), *Couple relationships in the middle and later years: Their nature, complexity, and role in health and illness* (pp. 95–114). Washington, DC: American Psychological Association.

Zeidner, M., Matthews, G., & Roberts, R. D. (2012). *What we know about emotional intelligence: How it affects learning, work, relationships, and our mental health.* Cambridge, MA: MIT Press.

Zelazo, P. D., Chandler, M. J., & Crone, E. (2010). *Developmental social cognitive neuroscience.* New York: Psychology Press.

Zerfu, T. A., & Ayele, H. T. (2013). Micronutrients and pregnancy: Effects of supplementation on pregnancy and pregnancy outcomes: A systematic review. *Nutrition Journal*, 12(1), 1–5.

Zerk, D., Mertin, P., & Proeve, M. (2009). Domestic violence and maternal reports of young children's functioning. *Journal of Family Violence*, 24(7), 423–432.

Zethraeus, N., Dreber, A., Ranehill, E., Blomberg, L., Labrie, F., von Schoultz, B., . . . Hirschberg, A. L. (2017). A first-choice combined oral contraceptive influences general well-being in healthy women: A double-blind randomized, placebo-controlled trial. *Fertility and Sterility*, 107(5), 1238–1245.

Zeytinoglu, S., Calkins, S., & Leerkes, E. (2018). Maternal emotional support but not cognitive support during problem-solving predicts increases in cognitive flexibility in early childhood. *International Journal of Behavioral Development*, 1–12. doi:10.1177/0165025418757706

Zhan, J., Dinov, I. D., Li, J., Zhang, Z., Hobel, S., Shi, Y., . . . Liu, S. (2013). Spatial-temporal atlas of human fetal brain development during the early second trimester. *NeuroImage*, 82, 115–126.

Zhang, A., Musu-Gillette, L., & Oudekerk, B. A. (2016, May). *Indicators of school crime and safety: 2015.* The Bureau of Justice Statistics and the National Center for Education Statistics, NCJ 249758. Retrieved from www.bjs.gov/index.cfm?ty=pbdetail&iid=5599.

Zhang, J., Zhao, J., Jiang, W., Shan, X., Yang, X., & Gao, J. (2012). Conditional gene manipulation: Creating a new biological era. *Journal of Zhejiang University Science B*, 13(7), 511–524.

Zhang, Y., Jin, X., Shen, X., Zhang, J., & Hoff, E. (2008). Correlates of early language development in Chinese children. *International Journal of Behavioral Development, 32*(2), 145–151.

Zheng, W., Suzuki, K., Tanaka, T., Kohama, M., & Yamagata, Z. (2016). Association between maternal smoking during pregnancy and low birthweight: Effects by maternal age. *PLoS One, 11*(1), 1–9.

Zhou, P., Zhang, C., Liu, J., & Wang, Z. (2017). The relationship between resilience and internet addiction: A multiple mediation model through peer relationship and addiction. *Cyber Psychology, Behavior & Social Networking, 20*(10), 634–639.

Zimprich, D., & Mascherek, A. (2010). Five views of a secret: Does cognition change during middle adulthood? *European Journal of Ageing, 7*(3), 135–146.

Zitter, J. N. (2017). *Extreme measures: Finding a better path to the end of life.* New York: Penguin Random House.

Zou, J., Dear, B., Titov, N., Lorian, C., Johnston, L., Spence, J., . . . Sachdev, P. (2012). Brief internet-delivered cognitive behavioral therapy for anxiety in older adults: A feasibility trial. *Journal of Anxiety Disorder, 26*(6), 650–655.

Zou, M. (2015). Gender, work orientations and job satisfaction. *Work, Employment & Society, 29*(1), 3–22.

Zucker, A., Ostrove, J., & Stewart, A. (2002). College-educated women's personality development in adulthood: Perceptions and age differences. *Psychology and Aging, 17*(2), 236–244.

• Glossary •

Acquaintance rape: Forced, manipulated, or coerced sexual contact by someone you know.

Activities of daily living (ADLs): Basic self-care activities, such as bathing, dressing, walking a short distance, shifting from a bed to a chair, using the toilet, and eating.

Activity theory (of aging): A theory of aging that proposes that higher levels of activity and involvement are directly related to higher levels of satisfaction in older adults.

Advance directives: Documents that give instructions about desired health care if, in the future, an individual cannot speak for herself or himself.

Age norm: The behaviors expected of people of a specific age in a given society at a particular time.

Age stratification perspective: Theory of social gerontology proposed by Riley (1971) and Foner (1995). Similar to the way society is structured by socioeconomic class, it is also stratified by age. Roles and rights of individuals are assigned based on their membership in an age group or cohort. Individuals proceed through their life course as part of that cohort. Theory falls into the tradition of the life course perspective.

Age structuring: The standardizing of the ages at which social role transitions occur, by developing policies and laws that regulate the timing of these transitions.

Alzheimer's disease: The most common type of dementia, a progressive and incurable deterioration of key areas of the brain.

Anorexia nervosa: An eating disorder characterized by a dysfunctional body image and voluntary starvation in the pursuit of weight loss.

Assisted reproductive technologies (ART): A range of techniques to help women who are infertile to conceive and give birth.

Assistive technology: Technology developed and used to assist individuals with physical impairments to perform functions that might otherwise be difficult or impossible.

Attachment: An enduring emotional bond between two people who are important to each other. Provides affection and a sense of security.

Authoritarian parenting: A parenting style, identified by Baumrind, that involves unresponsive, inflexible, harsh, and controlling interactions with the child.

Authoritative parenting: A parenting style, identified by Baumrind, that involves responsive and supportive interactions with the child while also setting firm limits. Thought to be the most effective parenting style.

Bereavement: The state of having suffered a loss.

Binge eating disorder: Characterized by recurring episodes of eating significantly excessive amounts of food in a short period of time, accompanied by feelings of lack of control.

Biological age: A person's level of biological development and physical health, as measured by the functioning of the various organ systems.

Brain plasticity: The ability of the brain to change in response to stimuli.

Bulimia nervosa: An eating disorder characterized by a cycle of binge eating; feelings of guilt, depression, or self-disgust; and purging.

Capital: A term used in different ways by different disciplines but generally refers to having the potential, capacity, and resources to function, produce, or succeed; in the social sciences, refers to possession of attributes associated with civic engagement and economic success.

Centenarian: A person who is 100 years old or older.

Cerebral cortex: The outer layer of gray matter in the human brain thought to be responsible for complex, high-level intellectual functions such as memory, language, and reasoning.

Character education: The direct teaching and curriculum inclusions of mainstream values thought to be universal by a community (e.g., kindness, respect, tolerance, and honesty).

Child maltreatment: Physical, emotional, and sexual abuse and neglect of children, most often by adult caregivers. Definitions vary by culture and professional discipline but typically entail harm, or threatened harm, to the child.

Chromosomes: Threadlike structures composed of DNA and proteins that carry genes and are found within each body cell nucleus.

Cognition: Ability to process and store information and solve problems. Commonly called thinking.

Cohort: Group of persons who are born in the same time period and who are of the same age group at the time of specific historical events and social changes.

Cohort effects: The effects of social change on a specific cohort.

Community assets: Community resources such as public infrastructure (e.g., adequate transportation to get to work), community networks, and educational opportunities.

Concrete operations stage: The third stage in Piaget's theory of cognitive development. School-age children (ages 7 to 11) begin to use logical reasoning, but their thinking is not yet abstract.

Conjunctive faith: The fifth faith stage in James Fowler's theory of faith development, a stage when individuals look for balance among competing moral systems, recognize that there are many truths, and open themselves in service to others.

Continuity theory (of aging): Theory of social gerontology initially proposed by Neugarten, Havighurst, and Tobin (1968) in response to critiques of the disengagement and activity theories. Individuals adapt to changes by using the same coping styles they have used throughout the life course, with new roles serving as substitutes for roles lost because of age.

Coping mechanism: Strategy used to master the demands of life.

Crystallized intelligence: The ability to use knowledge from accumulated learning.

Cumulative advantage: The accumulation of increasing advantage as early advantage positions an individual for later advantage.

Cumulative disadvantage: The accumulation of increasing disadvantage as early disadvantage positions an individual for later disadvantage.

Damage or error theories of aging: Theories of biological aging that emphasize the role of environmental assaults that cause cumulative damage to various biological systems.

Default individualization: A pathway in young adulthood that involves making transitions defined by circumstance and situation.

Delirium: An acute delusional state characterized by disturbance in attention and awareness.

Dementia: Impairment or loss of cognitive functioning caused by damage in the brain tissue. Dementia is not part of the brain's normal aging process, but its prevalence increases with age.

Dependency ratio: A demographic indicator expressing the degree of demand placed on society by the dependent young and the dependent elderly combined.

Developmental biocultural co-constructivism: A theory of human development that postulates dynamic reciprocal interactions between the human environment and the biology of the person.

Developmental delay: Delay in developing skills and abilities in infants and preschoolers.

Developmental disability: Name given when a child has a lifelong impairment that results in functional limitations in some dimension or dimensions, such as mobility, self-care, communication, or learning.

Developmental individualization: A pathway in young adulthood that involves making transitions defined by personal agency and deliberately charted growth opportunities in intellectual, occupational, and psychosocial domains.

Developmental niche: The cultural context into which a particular child is born that guides every aspect of the developmental process.

Direct bullying: Intentionally inflicting emotional or physical harm on another person through fairly explicit physical or verbal harassment, assault, or injury.

Discipline: The methods a parent uses to teach and socialize children toward acceptable behavior.

Disengaged parenting: Aloof, withdrawn, and unresponsive parenting.

Disengagement theory (of aging): Theory of social gerontology that suggests that as elderly individuals grow older, they gradually decrease their social interactions and ties and become increasingly self-preoccupied.

Dominant genes: Genes that express themselves if present on one or both chromosomes in a pair.

Ego integrity versus ego despair: The psychosocial crisis of Erik Erikson's eighth stage of development that centers on one's ability to process what has happened in life and accept these experiences as integral to the meaning of life.

Egocentrism: The assumption by children in the preoperational stage of cognitive development that others perceive, think, and feel just the way they do. Inability to recognize the possibility of other perspectives.

Embryo: The stage of prenatal development beginning in the 2nd week and lasting through the 8th week.

Emerging adulthood: A developmental phase distinct from both adolescence and young adulthood, occurring from ages 18 to 25 in industrialized societies.

Emotional intelligence: The ability to motivate oneself to persist in the face of frustration, to control impulses, to delay gratification, to regulate one's moods, and to empathize with others; theory proposed by Daniel Goleman.

Empathy: Ability to understand another person's emotional condition.

Environmental gerontology: A perspective on aging that focuses on the interplay between system, person, place, and time, with particular emphasis on the place and environment in which aging occurs.

Event history: The sequence of significant events, experiences, and transitions in a person's life from birth to death.

Extremely low birth weight (ELBW): A newborn weight of less than 1,000 grams (2.2 pounds).

Extroversion: Orientation to the external world, in contrast to introversion, which is orientation to the internal world.

Feminist theories (of aging): Theory of social gerontology suggesting that, because gender is a central organizing principle in our society, we can only understand aging by taking gender into account.

Fertilization: The penetration of an ovum by a spermatozoon, usually occurring in the fallopian tube.

Fertilization age: The number of completed weeks of pregnancy counting from 14 days after the beginning of the last menstrual period to the birth of the neonate.

Fetal viability: The capability to survive outside the womb, typically requiring at least 25 weeks.

Fetus: The developing organism from the 9th week of pregnancy to birth.

Fictive kin: Friends who are neither biologically nor romantically related to the family but are adopted as family and given the same rights and responsibilities as family members.

Fine motor skills: Skills based on small muscle movements, particularly in the hands, as well as eye-hand coordination.

Fluid intelligence: Abstract reasoning skills.

Formal operations stage: The fourth and final stage in Piaget's theory of cognitive development, generally experienced in adolescence. Involves the capacity to apply hypothetical reasoning and to use symbols to solve problems.

Gender dysphoria: Feeling one's emotional and psychological identity as male or female to be different from one's assigned biological identity.

Gender identity: Understanding of oneself as a male or female.

Gender typing: Expectations about people's behavior based on their biological sex.

Generalized other: A construction that represents how others might view and respond to our behavior.

Generativity: The ability to transcend personal interests to provide care and concern for generations to come.

Genes: Basic units of heredity, made of DNA and found on chromosomes.

Genetic liability: The state of being prone to hereditary disorders.

Genotype: The totality of the hereditary information present in an organism.

Germ cell: The ova and spermatozoa whose function is to reproduce the organism.

Gestation: The length of maturation time from conception to birth. In humans it averages 280 days, with a range of 259 to 287 days.

Gestational age: The number of completed weeks of pregnancy counting from the first day of the last normal menstrual cycle to the birth of the neonate.

Global network: The social network made up of all social relationships a person has.

Gonads: Sex glands—ovaries in females and testes in males.

Grief: The normal internal reaction of an individual experiencing a loss, a complex process that is highly individualized.

Grief work: A necessary period of working to sever the attachment bond to a lost person or object.

Gross motor skills: Skills based on large muscle group movements and most easily observed during whole-body movements, such as hopping, skipping, and running.

Guardianship: A stage of psychosocial development proposed by George Vaillant to come between Erik Erikson's stages of generativity and integrity, a stage when older adults take on the task of passing on the traditions of the past to the next generation and extend their concerns to concern for the culture as a whole.

Hospice: Program that provides care to the terminally ill. Patients typically receive treatment by a team of doctors, nurses, social workers, and care staff through inpatient or outpatient care.

Hostile aggression: Aggression that is an attack meant to hurt another individual.

Human agency: The use of personal power to achieve one's goals.

Human agency approach: An approach to personality in middle adulthood interested in the way motives, goals, plans, strategies, values, schemas, and choices lead to stability and change in personality in middle adulthood.

Human capital: Individual assets such as talents, skills, intellectual capacity, social development, and emotional regulatory capacity.

Identity: A person's self-definition as a separate and distinct individual.

Incidental memory: Memory that relates to facts a person has learned without the intention to retain and recall.

Indirect bullying: Less explicit and less detectable than direct bullying, including subtler verbal, psychological, and social or "relational" bullying tactics.

Individual education plan (IEP): An individualized, collaboratively developed plan that focuses on facilitating achievement and is designed to respond to the unique needs of a child with a disability in the school setting. Such plans are mandated by the Individuals with Disabilities Education Act of 1990.

Individuation: The development of a self and identity that are unique and separate.

Individuative-reflective faith: The fourth stage of James Fowler's six-stage model of faith development, a stage when adults no longer rely on outside authority and look for authority within the self.

Infant: A young child in the first year of life.

Infant mortality: The death of a child before his or her first birthday.

Infertility: The inability to create a viable embryo.

Information processing theory: A theory of cognition interested in the mechanisms through which learning occurs; focuses specifically on memory encoding and retrieval.

Instrumental activities of daily living (IADLs): Activities that are not necessary for fundamental functioning but that do allow an individual to live alone, activities such as doing light housework, doing the laundry, using transportation, handling finances, using the telephone, and taking medications.

Instrumental aggression: Aggression that occurs while fighting over toys and space.

Intentional memory: Memory that relates to events that a person plans to remember.

Interactive genes: Corresponding genes that give separate yet controlling messages.

Interrelational intelligence: Based on emotional and social intelligence and similar to Howard Gardner's concept of interpersonal intelligence.

Intersectionality theory: A pluralist theory of social identity that recognizes that all of us are simultaneously members of a number of socially constructed identity groups.

Intimacy: Characteristic of close interpersonal relationships, includes interdependence, self-disclosure, and affection.

Intimacy versus isolation: Erik Erikson's description of the developmental task of young adulthood, a time when individuals move from the identity fragmentation, confusion, and exploration of adolescence into more intimate engagement with significant others or become isolated.

Intimate terrorism: A pattern of coercive control and repeated severe battering.

Intimate violence: Violence between romantic partners that includes physical violence, sexual abuse, and psychological harm.

Introversion: Orientation to the internal world, in contrast to extroversion, which is orientation to the external world.

Juvenile delinquency: Acts that, if committed by an adult, would be considered crimes, plus status offenses such as running away from home, skipping school, violating curfew, and possession of tobacco or alcohol.

Kinkeepers: Family members who work at keeping family members across the generations in touch with one another and make sure that both emotional and practical needs of family members are met.

Late preterm birth: Birth that occurs at 34 to 36 weeks' gestation.

Lateralization: Process in which the two hemispheres of the brain begin to operate slightly differently during early childhood.

Learning play: Play focused on language and thinking skills.

Life course perspective: An approach to human behavior that looks at how biological, psychological, and social factors act independently, cumulatively, and interactively to shape people's lives from conception to death and across generations.

Life event: Incident or event that is brief in scope but is influential on human behavior.

Life narrative approach: An approach to personality in middle adulthood that conceptualizes the developing person as a storyteller who puts together characters, plots, and themes to develop an evolving story of the self.

Life review: A process of evaluating and making sense of one's life. It includes a reinterpretation of past experiences and unresolved conflicts. The process of life review relates to the eighth stage of Erikson's theory of adult development (ego integrity versus ego despair).

Life span theory: A theory that begins with the premise that development is lifelong and is based in ongoing transactions between persons and environments; based in psychology, whereas the life course perspective has more multidisciplinary roots.

Life structure: In Levinson's seasons of adulthood theory, the patterns and central components of a person's life at a particular point in time.

Living will: A document that describes the medical procedures, drugs, and types of treatment an individual would choose for himself or herself if able to do so in certain situations. It also describes the situations for which this individual would want treatment withheld.

Loss: The severing of an attachment an individual has with a loved one, a love object, or an aspect of one's self or identity.

Low birth weight (LBW): A newborn weight of less than 2,500 grams (5 pounds, 8 ounces).

Masturbation: Self-stimulation of the genitals for sexual pleasure.

Menarche: The onset of menstruation.

Menopause: Permanent cessation of menstruation, usually defined as 12 consecutive months with absence of menstruation.

Miscarriage: Naturally occurring loss of a fetus prior to 20 weeks' gestation; also known as spontaneous abortion.

Morbidity: The incidence of disease and illness in a population group.

Mortality rate: The incidence of death in a population group.

Motor skills: Control over movements of body parts.

Mourning: The external expression of grief, also a process, influenced by the customs of one's culture.

Multifactorial inheritance: Genetic traits that are controlled by multiple genes.

Multigravida: A pregnant woman who has previously experienced pregnancy.

Multipara: A mother who has previously given birth.

Multiple intelligences: Howard Gardner's theory that humans have at least eight critical intelligences: verbal/linguistic, logical/mathematical, visual/spatial, musical/rhythmic, bodily kinesthetic, naturalist, interpersonal, and intrapersonal.

Myelination: A process by which axons and neurons are coated with a fatty substance called myelin, leading to more rapid neural communications.

Neonate: Infant up to 1 month of age.

Neurogenesis: The creation of new neurons.

Neurons: Specialized nerve cells that store and transmit information.

Novice phase: According to Daniel Levinson, the ages of 17 to 22, in which the transition into young adulthood occurs, including the tasks of leaving adolescence and making preliminary decisions about relationships, career, and belief systems.

Object permanence: The ability to understand that objects exist even when they cannot be seen.

Oppression: The intentional or unintentional act or process of placing restrictions on an individual, group, or institution; may include observable actions but more typically refers to complex, covert, interconnected processes and practices (such as discriminating, devaluing, and exploiting a group of individuals) reflected in and perpetuating exclusion and inequalities over time.

Overregularization: Grammatical errors made during language development where language rules are applied generally without attention to exceptions.

Palliative care: Active care of patients who have received a diagnosis of a serious, life-threatening illness; a form of care focusing on pain and symptom management as opposed to curing disease.

Perimenopause: A period of time that begins immediately prior to menopause in women, when there are biological and clinical indicators that a woman's reproductive capacity is reaching exhaustion, and continues through the first year after the last period.

Permissive parenting: A parenting style, identified by Baumrind, that involves no limit setting on the part of the parent.

Personal network: A subnetwork of the global network that includes the closest social relationships.

Perspective taking: The ability to see a situation from another person's point of view.

Phenotype: The expression of genetic traits in an individual.

Physical aggression: Aggression against another person using physical force.

Population pyramid: A chart that depicts the proportion of the population in each age group.

Postconventional moral reasoning: Third and final level of Lawrence Kohlberg's stage theory of moral development; morality based on moral principles that transcend societal rules.

Power of attorney (POA): A person appointed by an individual to manage his or her financial and legal affairs. A POA can be limited (in time or scope), general (no restrictions), or durable (begins after reaching a specified level of disability).

Precociousness: Early development; most often refers to a rare level of intelligence at an early age but may refer to "premature" ability or development in a number of areas.

Preconventional level of moral reasoning: First level of moral reasoning in Lawrence Kohlberg's stage theory of moral reasoning; morality based on what gets rewarded or punished or what benefits either the child or someone the child cares about.

Preoperational stage: The second stage in Piaget's theory of cognitive development. Young children (ages 2 to 7) use symbols to represent their earlier sensorimotor experiences. Thinking is not yet logical.

Primary aging: Changes that are a normal part of the aging process.

Primary sex characteristics: Physical characteristics directly related to maturation of the reproductive organs and external genitalia.

Primipara: A woman who is giving birth for the first time.

Privilege: Unearned advantage that comes from one's position in the social structure.

Productive aging theory: A theory that focuses on the positive changes that have occurred in the older adult population over time, including improved health and economic status; focuses on the positive side of aging rather than on the losses of aging.

Programmed aging theories: Theories of biological aging that start from the assumption that aging follows a biological timetable.

Prosocial: Behaving in a helpful or empathic manner.

Protective factors: Personal and societal factors (resources) that decrease the probability of developing and maintaining problem conditions later in life.

Psychological age: The capacities that people have and the skills they use to adapt to changing biological and environmental demands, including skills in memory, learning, intelligence, motivation, and emotions; also the age people feel.

Puberty: Stage during which individuals become capable of reproduction.

Recessive genes: Genes that express themselves only if present on both chromosomes in a pair.

Reflex: An involuntary response to a simple stimulus.

Relational aggression: Aggression that involves behaviors that damage relationships without physical force, such as threatening to leave a relationship unless a friend complies with demands or using social exclusion or the silent treatment to get one's way.

Relative poverty: A conceptualization of poverty that emphasizes the tendency to define one's poverty status in relation to others within one's social environment.

Reminiscence: Recalling and recounting past events. Reminiscing serves several functions: it may be an enjoyable activity, it may be directed at enhancing a person's self-image, it may serve as a way to cope with current or future problems, and it may assist in the life review as a way to achieve ego integrity.

Resilience: Healthy development in the face of risk factors. Thought to be the result of protective factors that shield the individual from the consequences of potential hazards.

Risk factors: Personal or social factors at one stage of development that increase the probability of developing and maintaining problem conditions at later stages.

Rites of passage: Ceremonies that demarcate transition from one role or status to another.

Romantic love: An intimate relationship that is sexually oriented.

Secondary aging: Changes caused by health-compromising behaviors such as smoking or environmental factors such as pollution.

Secondary sex characteristics: Physical characteristics associated with sexual maturation that are not directly related to the reproductive organs and external genitalia.

Self-esteem: The way one evaluates the self in relation to others.

Self-theory: An organized understanding of the self in relation to others; begins to develop in early childhood.

Sensitive period: A time in fetal development that is particularly sensitive to exposure to teratogens. Different organs have different sensitive periods. Also called critical period.

Sensorimotor stage: The first stage in Piaget's theory of cognitive development. Infants (newborn to 2 years) learn through sensory awareness and motor activities.

Sensory system: The system of senses: hearing, sight, taste, smell, touch; responsiveness to the body's position and sensitivity to pain.

Separation anxiety: When an infant becomes anxious at the signs of an impending separation from parents, at about 9 months of age.

Sex chromosomes: Chromosome pair number 23, which determines the sex of the individual.

Sex hormones: Hormones that affect the development of the gonads, functioning of the gonads, and mating and childcaring behavior; includes androgens, progestins, and estrogens.

Sex-linked trait: A trait controlled by a gene located on one of the sex chromosomes.

Sex ratio: The number of males per 100 females in a population.

Sexual orientation: Erotic, romantic, and affectionate attraction to people of the same sex, the opposite sex, or both sexes.

Sexually transmitted infections (STIs): Infectious diseases that are most often contracted through oral, anal, or vaginal sexual contact. Also called sexually transmitted diseases.

Small for gestational age (SGA): Lower than normal birth weight, given the number of weeks of gestation.

Social age: Age measured in terms of age-graded roles and behaviors expected by society—the socially constructed meanings of various ages.

Social competence: The ability to engage in sustained, positive, and mutually satisfactory peer interactions.

Social construction theory (of aging): A theory that attempts to understand and explain the influence of social definitions, social interactions, and social structures on the aging process.

Social convoy theory: A theory that suggests that we each travel through life with a *convoy*, or a network of social relationships that protect, defend, aid, and socialize us, with the closest relationships remaining stable over time and peripheral relationships being less stable.

Social exchange theory (of aging): A theory that attempts to understand the realignments of roles and values in late adulthood in light of the shifting resources that older adults bring to social exchanges.

Social gerontology: The social science that studies human aging.

Social identity: The part of the self-concept that comes from knowledge of one's membership in a social group and the emotional significance of that membership.

Social support: Help rendered by others that benefits an individual.

Sociodramatic play: Fantasy play in a group, with the group coordinating fantasies; important type of play in early childhood.

Socioemotional selectivity theory: A theory that proposes that social goals change over the adult life course based on shifts in perspectives about how much time one has left to live, and changes in social goals result in changes in one's social network.

Spermarche: Onset of the ability to ejaculate mobile sperm.

Spiritual age: The position of a person in the ongoing search for meaning and fulfilling relationships.

Spirituality: That which gives meaning, purpose, and direction to one's life.

Spontaneous abortion: Naturally occurring loss of a fetus prior to 20 weeks' gestation; also known as miscarriage.

Status offenses: Behaviors that would not be considered criminal if committed by an adult but are considered delinquent if committed by an adolescent—for example, running away from home, skipping school, violating curfew, and possessing tobacco or alcohol.

Statutory rape: A criminal offense that involves an adult engaging in sexual activities with a minor or a mentally incapacitated person.

Stranger anxiety: When an infant reacts with fear and withdrawal to unfamiliar persons, at about 9 months of age.

Symbolic functioning: The ability to think using symbols to represent what is not present.

Symbolic play: Fantasy play, begins around the age of 2.

Synapses: Neural connections.

Synaptic blooming: A period of overproduction of brain synapses during infancy, followed by a period of synapse pruning.

Synaptic pruning: Reduction of brain synapses to improve the efficiency of brain functioning; follows a period of blooming of synapses.

Synaptogenesis: The creation of synapses (neural connections).

Synthetic-conventional faith: The third stage of James Fowler's six-stage model of faith development; faith rooted in external authority.

Temperament: The characteristic way in which individuals approach and react to people and situations.

Teratogens: Substances present during prenatal life that adversely affect normal cellular development in form or function in the embryo or fetus.

Toddler: A young child from about 12 to 36 months of age.

Trait approach: A theoretical approach that proposes that personality traits are enduring characteristics rooted in early temperament and influenced by genetic and organic factors.

Trajectories: Relatively stable long-term processes and patterns of events, involving multiple transitions.

Transductive reasoning: Reasoning from one particular event to another particular event rather than in a logical causal manner.

Transitional object: Comfort object, such as a favorite blanket or stuffed animal, that toddlers often use to help them cope with separations from parents.

Transitions: Changes in roles and statuses that represent a distinct departure from prior roles and statuses.

Trauma: A physical or mental injury generally associated with violence, shock, or an unanticipated situation.

Turning point: A special event that produces a lasting shift in the life course trajectory.

Universalizing faith: The final stage of James Fowler's theory of faith development; a stage in which individuals lead selfless lives based on principles of absolute love and justice.

Very low birth weight (VLBW): A newborn weight of less than 1,500 grams (3 pounds, 3 ounces).

Working model: Model for relationships developed in the earliest attachment relationship.

Zone of proximal development: According to Vygotsky, the theoretical space between the child's current developmental level (or performance) and the child's potential level (or performance) if given access to appropriate models and developmental experiences in the social environment.

Zygote: A fertilized ovum cell.

• Index •

• About the Author •

Elizabeth D. Hutchison, MSW, PhD, received her MSW from the George Warren Brown School of Social Work at Washington University in St. Louis and her PhD from the University at Albany, State University of New York. She was on the faculty in the Social Work Department at Elms College from 1980 to 1987 and served as chair of the department from 1982 to 1987. She was on the faculty in the School of Social Work at Virginia Commonwealth University from 1987 to 2009, where she taught courses in human behavior and the social environment, social work practice, social work and social justice, and child and family policy; she also served as field practicum liaison. She has been a social worker in health, mental health, aging, and child and family welfare settings. She is committed to providing social workers with comprehensive, current, and useful frameworks for thinking about human behavior. Her other research interests focus on child and family welfare. She lives in Reno, Nevada, where she is a hands-on grandmother and an activist on local justice issues.

• About the Contributors •

Suzanne M. Baldwin, PhD, LCSW, MSW, BSN, RN, received her PhD in social work from the School of Social Work at Virginia Commonwealth University. She owns her own clinical social work practice, primarily focusing on working with families involved in the court systems and military family issues. She spent almost 2 decades working as a clinical nurse specialist in newborn intensive care units. She has taught human behavior, practice, communications, and research courses and supervised internships at Old Dominion University and at the School of Social Work at Virginia Commonwealth University. She is the mother of three adult children. Her oldest daughter was a patient in the neonatal intensive care unit (NICU), and her daughter's son spent a month in the NICU after his birth in 2009.

Leanne Wood Charlesworth, LMSW, PhD, is a professor and the BSW program director in the Department of Social Work at Nazareth College of Rochester, New York. She has practiced within child welfare systems, and her current areas of service and research are poverty and homelessness. She teaches human behavior and research methods at the undergraduate and graduate levels. She is also a registered yoga teacher and cofounder of the Rochester Yoga Service Network.

Annemarie Conlon, PhD, MBA, LICSW, teaches Perspectives on Aging to undergraduate students at Plymouth State University in New Hampshire. Her experience includes individual, family, and group practice with older adults in oncology and community settings. Her major areas of interest are ageism in health care and end of life.

Marcia P. Harrigan, MSW, PhD, is associate professor emeritus and former associate dean of Student and Academic Affairs in the School of Social Work at Virginia Commonwealth University. She has practiced in child welfare, juvenile justice, and mental health. Her major areas of interest are nontraditional family structures, family assessment, multigenerational households, and long-distance family caregiving. She has taught human behavior and practice courses. Her retirement allows

more time for her grandchildren, master gardener activities, and tutoring in a program for aging out foster care young adults enrolled in higher education.

Kristina M. Hash, LICSW, PhD, is a professor in the School of Social Work and director of the Gerontology Certificate Program at West Virginia University. Her research interests include geriatric education, rural gerontology, LGBTQ issues, and the use of technology in teaching and research. She is the recipient of national-, state-, and university-level teaching awards. Her book *Aging in Rural Places* was published in 2015, and her edited volume *Annual Review of Geriatrics and Gerontology: Contemporary Issues and Future Directions in Lesbian, Gay, Bisexual, and Transgender (LGBT) Aging* was published in 2017.

Pamela J. Kovacs, MSW, PhD, is associate professor emerita with the School of Social Work at Virginia Commonwealth University, where for 17 years she taught clinical practice, social work practice and health care, and qualitative research and served as a field liaison. Her earlier clinical practice that influenced her teaching and research included work with individuals, families, and groups in oncology, hospice, and mental health settings. Her major areas of interest were HIV/AIDS, hospice and palliative care, volunteerism, caregiving, and preparing social workers and other health care professionals to work with older adults and their families.

Holly C. Matto, MSW, PhD, is associate professor in the College of Health and Human Services Department of Social Work at George Mason University in Fairfax, Virginia. Prior to that, Dr. Matto was at Virginia Commonwealth University School of Social Work for 10 years, where she taught theories of human behavior, direct practice, and research methods in the master's and doctoral programs. She has more than 15 years of research and practice experience in the field of addiction science and has conducted treatment intervention studies with diverse substance abuse populations. Recently she conducted a clinical trial with Inova

Fairfax Hospital and Georgetown University's Center for Functional and Molecular Imaging that used neuroimaging technology to examine functional and structural brain change associated with behavioral health interventions for substance-dependent adults. She is currently engaged in research that examines the effects of an integrated music, imagery, and movement intervention to improve mood and promote cognitive functioning in older adult residents living in a long-term care facility.

Susan Ainsley McCarter, MS, MSW, PhD, is associate professor in the Department of Social Work at the University of North Carolina at Charlotte. She has worked as a juvenile probation officer; mental health counselor for children, adolescents, and families; social policy advocate; and mother. Her major area of interest is risk and protective factors for adolescents—specifically the disproportionate minority contact in the juvenile justice system. She currently teaches research methods and the MSW capstone course and has taught human behavior, social justice and diversity, social policy, and forensic social work courses at both the undergraduate and graduate levels.

Matthias J. Naleppa, MSW, PhD, is a faculty member at the School of Social Work at the Radford University Waldron College of Health and Human Services. Previously he held positions as professor of social work at the State University of Baden-Wuerttemberg in Stuttgart, Germany; the University of Applied Sciences in Bern, Switzerland; and Virginia Commonwealth University. He is a Hartford Geriatric Faculty Scholar. His research focuses on geriatric social work, short-term treatment, and international social work. Naleppa regularly conducts workshops on task-centered practice and geriatric social work in the United States, Europe, and Asia. He holds an MSW from the Catholic School of Social Work in Munich and a PhD from the University at Albany.

David Woody III, PhD, LCSW, is president and CEO of The Bridge—Homeless Recovery Center, in Dallas, Texas. After several years in academia at Texas Christian University, the University of Texas at Arlington, and Baylor University, Dr. Woody returned to work in the Dallas–Fort Worth metroplex, focusing on homelessness, mental health and substance abuse treatment, and affordable and permanent supportive housing. In addition to issues related to poverty, Dr. Woody's major areas of interest include research exploring strengths of African American single mothers and initiatives

enhancing the significance of fatherhood in the African American community.

Debra J. Woody, PhD, LCSW, is the senior associate dean in the School of Social Work at the University of Texas at Arlington. She is the director of the Center for Additions and Recovery Studies that provides recovery and parenting services to mothers and their children and school-based substance abuse prevention services to students and their families.

About the Case Study Contributors

Najwa Awad, MSW, LCSW-C, is a graduate from the School of Social Work at Virginia Commonwealth University. She is a psychotherapist in private practice with a focus on providing culturally sensitive counseling to women and minorities. She has a special interest in helping underserved Muslim communities and speaking in public forums about reducing stigma toward seeking mental health treatment. Beyond the outpatient setting, she provides services to individuals and families in group homes, schools, and the foster care system.

Nicole Footen Bromfield is an associate professor and associate dean at the Graduate College of Social Work at the University of Houston. She earned her PhD in public policy from Virginia Commonwealth University with a focus in health policy, and an MSW and BA in anthropology from West Virginia University. Her research interests are on women and children's health and social well-being, particularly in the Global South. Projects are framed with a social justice lens and driven by community needs with the desired outcome being social policy change. She has studied human trafficking and sex trafficking, surrogacy arrangements in the United States and India, and divorce from arranged marriages in the United Arab Emirates, among other inquiries. Most research projects have been qualitative, honoring and emphasizing the voices of participants.

Vicki Kirsch, PhD, LCSW, is the MSW program director and associate professor of social work at George Mason University. Her interests and practice focus on trauma and recovery, gender and sexualities, and issues of spirituality and religion. She has expertise in eye movement desensitization and reprocessing (EMDR) and dialectical behavior therapy (DBT) in addition to psychodynamic and relational psychotherapy. Prior to employment at GMU, she was associate director and director of training at the Wheelock College Counseling

Center and teaching associate in psychiatry at the Harvard Medical School. Dr. Kirsch has an active private practice in Fairfax, Virginia, where she primarily works with adult trauma survivors and transgender individuals and their families and facilitates a dialectical behavior program for adult women.

Peter Maramaldi, PhD, MPH, LCSW, is professor and director of the PhD program at the Simmons College School of Social Work, adjunct professor at the Harvard University T. H. Chan School of Public Health, and instructor at the Harvard School of Dental Medicine in Oral Health Policy and Epidemiology. His work on national research teams, as a social and behavioral scientist, has had consistent NIH and foundation funding for research in evidenced-based health promotion, patient safety, geriatrics, and interprofessional collaboration. Dr. Maramaldi is a leader in social work, serving on national boards, committees, and special work groups. He has received awards for mentoring and promoting the careers of new faculty. Prior to his academic career he was a clinical social worker in community-based public health and nonprofit management in New York City providing services to culturally and economically diverse populations. He received MSSW, MPH, MPhil, and PhD degrees from Columbia University, taking his first academic position at the University of Utah College of Social Work, with joint appointments in the College of Nursing, and the Huntsman Cancer Institute.

Derek Morch, LCSW, is a graduate of the School of Social Work at Virginia Commonwealth University. He has worked in a variety of settings providing mental health services, including outpatient psychotherapy, residential counseling, homeless outreach, and supporting families with children at risk for out-of-home placement. His areas of interest include ongoing practice with multicultural populations, co-occurring treatment, and housing issues for those with serious mental illness.

Rosa Schnitzenbaumer is a graduate of the Catholic School of Social Work, Munich, Germany, working as a geriatric social worker and licensed practical nurse for the Caritas Welfare Organization in Miesbach, Germany. She teaches as an adjunct faculty member for the School for Care Management at the University of Applied Sciences Innsbruck, Austria, and is a board member of the Adelheid Stein Institute for Therapeutic Roleplay. Throughout her career, she has been involved in developing and managing programs for older adults, including a regional outpatient geropsychiatric counseling center, individualized service systems for older adults, a senior volunteer network, and caregiver training programs. She has also initiated Erzählcafés, volunteer-led groups for persons with dementia.

Meenakshi Venkataraman, PhD, is a lecturer in the Department of Social Work at Metropolitan State University of Denver. She has taught human behavior at the graduate and undergraduate levels. Her research interests include psychological, social, and spiritual aspects of adult severe mental illness. She is also interested in international social work.